9781405196949-4
D1693428

The Wiley Blackwell Encyclopedia of Gender and Sexuality Studies

Wiley Blackwell Encyclopedias in Social Science
Consulting Editor: George Ritzer

Published

The Wiley Blackwell Encyclopedia of Globalization
Edited by George Ritzer

The Wiley Blackwell Encyclopedia of Social and Political Movements
Edited by David A. Snow, Donatella della Porta, Bert Klandermans, and Doug McAdam

The Wiley Blackwell Encyclopedia of Health, Illness, Behavior, and Society
Edited by William C. Cockerham, Robert Dingwall, and Stella Quah

The Wiley Blackwell Encyclopedia of Consumption and Consumer Studies
Edited by Daniel Thomas Cook and J. Michael Ryan

The Wiley Blackwell Encyclopedia of Family Studies
Edited by Constance L. Shehan

The Wiley Blackwell Encyclopedia of Race, Ethnicity, and Nationalism
Edited by John Stone, Rutledge M. Dennis, Polly S. Rizova, Anthony D. Smith, and Xiaoshuo Hou

The Wiley Blackwell Encyclopedia of Gender and Sexuality Studies
Editor-in-Chief: Nancy A. Naples, Associate Editors: renée c. hoogland, Maithree Wickramasinghe, and Wai Ching Angela Wong

Forthcoming

The Wiley Blackwell Encyclopedia of Social Theory
Edited by Bryan S. Turner, Chang Kyung-Sup, Cynthia Epstein, Peter Kivisto, William Outhwaite, and J. Michael Ryan

The Wiley Blackwell Encyclopedia of Urban and Regional Studies
Edited by Anthony M. Orum, Marisol Garcia, Dennis Judd, Bryan Roberts, and Pow Choon-Piew

The Wiley Blackwell Encyclopedia of Environment and Society
Edited by Dorceta E. Taylor, Kozo Mayumi, Jun Bi, Paul Burton, and Tor A. Benjaminsen

Related titles

The Blackwell Encyclopedia of Sociology
Edited by George Ritzer

The Concise Encyclopedia of Sociology
Edited by George Ritzer and J. Michael Ryan

The Wiley Blackwell Encyclopedia of Gender and Sexuality Studies

Editor-in-Chief

Nancy A. Naples

Associate Editors

renée c. hoogland

Maithree Wickramasinghe

Wai Ching Angela Wong

Volume IV

J–R

WILEY Blackwell

This edition first published 2016
© 2016 John Wiley & Sons, Ltd.

Registered Office
John Wiley & Sons Ltd, The Atrium, Southern Gate, Chichester, West Sussex, PO19 8SQ, UK

Editorial Offices
350 Main Street, Malden, MA 02148-5020, USA
9600 Garsington Road, Oxford, OX4 2DQ, UK
The Atrium, Southern Gate, Chichester, West Sussex, PO19 8SQ, UK

For details of our global editorial offices, for customer services, and for information about how to apply for permission to reuse the copyright material in this book please see our website at www.wiley.com/wiley-blackwell.

The right of Nancy A. Naples to be identified as the author of the editorial material in this work has been asserted in accordance with the UK Copyright, Designs and Patents Act 1988.

All rights reserved. No part of this publication may be reproduced, stored in a retrieval system, or transmitted, in any form or by any means, electronic, mechanical, photocopying, recording or otherwise, except as permitted by the UK Copyright, Designs and Patents Act 1988, without the prior permission of the publisher.

Wiley also publishes its books in a variety of electronic formats. Some content that appears in print may not be available in electronic books.

Designations used by companies to distinguish their products are often claimed as trademarks. All brand names and product names used in this book are trade names, service marks, trademarks or registered trademarks of their respective owners. The publisher is not associated with any product or vendor mentioned in this book.

Limit of Liability/Disclaimer of Warranty: While the publisher and author have used their best efforts in preparing this book, they make no representations or warranties with respect to the accuracy or completeness of the contents of this book and specifically disclaim any implied warranties of merchantability or fitness for a particular purpose. It is sold on the understanding that the publisher is not engaged in rendering professional services and neither the publisher nor the author shall be liable for damages arising herefrom. If professional advice or other expert assistance is required, the services of a competent professional should be sought.

Library of Congress Cataloging-in-Publication data is available for this book.

ISBN 9781405196949 (hardback)

Cover image: Clockwise from top left: Artists of street theater group ASSA (Ankara Cinema and Art Atelier) during a demonstration on International Women's Day © Piero Castellano/Pacific Press/LightRocket via Getty Images; Banyana beat Mali, Women's Championship match, South Africa, 2010 © Gallo Images/Alamy; Young girl from Oaxaca © Jennifer Bickham Mendez; Demonstration over same-sex marriages, Taipei, Taiwan, 2015 © Sam Yeh/AFP/Getty Images

Set in 10/12pt Minion by SPi Global, Chennai, India
Printed and bound in Singapore by Markono Print Media Pte Ltd

1   2016

Contents

Volume I

Editors   vii
Contributors   ix
Lexicon   xxxvii
Introduction and Acknowledgments   xlix

Gender and Sexuality Studies A–D   1

Volume II

Gender and Sexuality Studies E–F   497

Volume III

Gender and Sexuality Studies G–I   931

Volume IV

Gender and Sexuality Studies J–R   1471

Volume V

Gender and Sexuality Studies S–Y   2051

Index of Names   2619
Index of Subjects   2633

J

Judaism and Gender

JUDITH R. BASKIN
University of Oregon, USA

Prior to the last quarter of the twentieth century, few studies of Judaism and the Jewish experience addressed differences in men's and women's lives and status. More recently, scholars in all areas of Jewish studies have employed gender as a category of analysis to highlight both the profound differentiations in gender roles that have characterized Judaism as a lived religious and cultural tradition historically, a topic discussed below, as well as the significant and ongoing transformations in Jewish gender roles over the past 100 years. These changes in contemporary Jewish life, many of which result from the impact of feminism on Western democracies in the twentieth century, have expanded educational and vocational opportunities for women. These include intellectual, spiritual, and communal leadership roles in Jewish institutions, such as synagogues, seminaries, and organizations that were previously reserved for men. Increased attention to education for girls and women is evident in all forms of contemporary Judaism. Enhanced opportunities for women have also had demographic consequences for the Jewish community. Individuals who spend a significant portion of their twenties in study and in establishing a career are more likely to marry in their thirties or forties, later than typical ages of marriage in previous generations. Moreover, twenty-first century marriages of two Jewish individuals exhibit a fertility rate that is below replacement levels; this is both by choice and due to infertility problems that may be more common among older individuals. These patterns are not as typical in the traditional wings of the Jewish community, where early marriages and large families are encouraged. Jewish religious authorities across the denominational spectrum are strongly supportive of medical interventions and technologies that enable fertility.

Contemporary Judaism exists in diverse movements; in recent years, liberal approaches, including Reform, Progressive, Reconstructionist, and Conservative Judaisms, have affirmed the equal status of women and men in all aspects of Jewish life, leadership, and ritual practice. Among striking innovations in these forms of Judaism is egalitarian communal worship, in which women share the same space and assume the same responsibilities for participation and leadership as men, and even more significant, the professional training of women to receive rabbinic and cantorial ordination. In liberal Judaisms, traditional prayer language has been altered to include women explicitly as equal participants in communal congregational worship; liturgical changes include references to the matriarchs of ancient Israel, as well as the traditional invocations of the patriarchs, and substitutions of gender-neutral language about God in place of male designations of the deity. A parallel phenomenon is the development of new lifecycle rituals that address central moments of transformation in women's lives for which ceremonies did not previously exist. On the whole, however, the movement toward egalitarian communal prayer and religious leadership has discouraged gender-based performance of religious rituals. In Orthodox forms of Judaism, conversely, separate communal, worship, ritual, and social roles for women remain the norm. In some Orthodox settings, women's worship spaces, and leadership and vocational options, reflecting increased levels of female educational achievement, are emerging.

These multiple changes in traditional gender roles have also affected Jewish men. In more liberal forms of Judaism, some observers have expressed concern that the "feminization" of Jewish leadership roles, as more women become rabbis, cantors, educators, and lay leaders, may drive men away from synagogue participation. In some forms of Orthodox Judaism, reactions to such dramatic shifts in gender roles in the larger Jewish world have encouraged increased rigidity and resistance to expanding religious opportunities for women within these communities.

The greater visibility of lesbian, gay, bisexual, and transgendered Jews, linked with a growing acceptance of alternative lifestyles in the larger societies in which Jews live, has presented challenges to Jewish understandings of gender and gender roles. While Jewish families have traditionally consisted of a male and a female parent and their children, an increasing openness regarding diverse sexual orientations in Western countries has altered the makeup of families who participate in many progressive non-Orthodox Jewish communities. The most liberal Judaisms endorse the full participation of gay, lesbian, bisexual, and transgendered Jews in every area of Jewish life, while more conservative movements continue to struggle with the legacy of negative attitudes toward homosexuality in traditional rabbinic Judaism.

RABBINIC CONSTRUCTIONS OF GENDER ROLES

Rabbinic Judaism, which emerged in the early centuries of the Common Era from the Israelite religious traditions of the Hebrew Bible, constituted its worldview in binary terms. Such dualities distinguished the Creator from the created; human beings from all other creatures; the people of Israel from the nations of the world; the free man from the slave; and ritually permitted behaviors, animals, foods, and mixtures of materials from the ritually impure. Central among these dichotomies was the separation between men and women, which encompassed clearly stated distinctions between male and female intellectual and moral qualities, legal and religious obligations, and roles in the spheres of family, community, and education.

This essentialized view of gender, which evolved from men's responses to the physical differences between males and females and their biological processes, attributed specific intellectual and spiritual capacities to men and to women; the more culturally honored qualities were generally assigned to males. Women's perceived otherness and inferiority to men was often explained and justified by their secondary status in creation (rabbinic interpretations of the biblical creation narratives in Genesis 1–2:3 and Genesis 2:4–25 overwhelmingly privileged the latter account, which establishes male primacy). Thus, it is not surprising that women occupied a subordinate place in rabbinic Judaism's idealized view of a world in which only free unblemished Jewish men participated fully in the covenant that constituted the central relationship between God and the descendants of Jacob/Israel (Genesis 17). Entry into this covenant (*b'rit*), whose primary human obligation is obedience to the legal code revealed to Moses and the Israelites at Mount Sinai, was marked on the male body on the eighth day of life through the ritual of circumcision (*b'rit milah*). Rabbinic Judaism was convinced that men alone were fully created in the divine image, with all of the implications of potency, dominance, and generativity that follow from this analogy. Belief in the active agency of men and the passivity of women in reproduction was, therefore, an important component of rabbinic constructions of female difference, since this discourse argued that men were most like God in their ability to generate new life. Such a preeminent emphasis on male generativity devalued and minimized women's roles in reproduction and in Jewish communal life in general and also diminished their connection to the divine. While Jewish men participated in the public realms of synagogue worship, the house of study, and in the governance of their communities, women were exempted, in most instances, from the obligation to participate in communal prayer. While women did sometimes attend synagogue, by the Middle Ages they sat apart and at a distance from the central worship space, which was reserved for men. In fact, the public separation of female and male outside the domestic realm in virtually all arenas was a feature of life in Jewish communities until quite recent times.

In the rabbinic system, men perceived and portrayed women as problematic because their biological processes, particularly menstruation and post-partum blood, were believed to be threatening to male ritual purity. In a religious system that compared ritual impurity to a state of spiritual death, periodic female flows of blood embodied male anxieties about women as sources of potential pollution and as portents of physical extinction. Such fears, deeply rooted in the cultures of the ancient Near East, are voiced in various rulings found in Leviticus 11–15, where the *niddah*, the menstruating or postpartum woman, is listed among a number of sources of potential danger to male ritual purity. The seriousness with which separation from a *niddah* was taken in biblical times is evident in the fact that sexual contact with a *niddah* is punished by removal from the community (Leviticus 18:29). These biblical strictures were extended in rabbinic Judaism to include marital separation not only during the wife's menses but for a further week thereafter. Women were considered trustworthy in accurately reporting their status and marital relations resumed only after the wife's immersion in a ritual bath. This rabbinic extension by seven days, without biblical justification, of the length of time a wife and husband were to abstain from all physical contact, not only sexual activity, indicates how seriously the formulators of rabbinic literature and Jewish social practice took the prospect of even accidental contact with a *niddah*. Such attitudes also played a significant role in the separation of women from the central spaces of public worship and from acquiring the skills and knowledge that would have allowed them to participate in textual study, itself a form of worship activity. This is one of the major impacts of gender on limiting women's possibilities in rabbinic culture.

There can be little dispute that the formulators of rabbinic literature believed that to be female was significantly less desirable than to be male. However, women were also acknowledged and honored as essential to men, since they constituted the vital social mortar sustaining rabbinic society. As wives, mothers, and economic partners, women were indispensable and eminently worthy of recognition and appreciation. Women's roles included domestic nurturing, providing for the daily needs of husbands and children, and overseeing the early educations of their offspring. Women also participated in domestic religious rituals; some of these practices, such as kindling Sabbath and holiday lights, have traditionally been gendered. Both women and men contributed to the economic support of their households, working separately or together in crafts and trades or in business activities. Positive portrayals of women's economic involvement in the daily life of the family are already evident in biblical texts such as Proverbs 31:10–31. From rabbinic times forward, some wives wholly supported their families through entrepreneurial endeavors so that husbands could devote themselves to learning. As the Talmud put it, a woman who enabled her husband and sons to study was considered particularly meritorious (BT *Berakhot* 17a).

SEXUALITY IN JEWISH TRADITION

Sexuality is affirmed in the Hebrew Bible as a powerful human force with both positive and negative potentialities. Wives and minor daughters are consigned to male control (Leviticus 20:10; Deuteronomy 22:13–28) and several biblical narratives demonstrate the strength of sexual attraction, as in the account of Jacob's love for Rachel (Genesis 29:16–20); others record its potentially destructive consequences, as in the various events recounted in 2 Samuel 11–19. The Song of Songs preserves an idyllic vision of female–male erotic love, while Proverbs, on the other hand, warns young men to shun seductive women (Proverbs 5; 7; 31:2–5). Heterosexual love and its potential betrayal also underlie the powerful biblical metaphor of God and Israel as husband and wife (e.g., Hosea). Male homosexual relations are forbidden in Leviticus 18:22 and 20:13 and this prohibition continued in rabbinic Judaism. There are no allusions to lesbian sexual activity in biblical legislative or narrative texts.

Consciousness of the strength of human sexuality and its capacity to cause social disorder permeates rabbinic literature. Significant strands of rabbinic legislation are directed at keeping women under the control of a male relative or spouse and carefully orchestrating the transfer of women from one man to another through marriage. Rabbinic Judaism understands matrimony as the desirable state for all adults since it is within the marital union that procreation, a legal obligation for men, could take place and the lineage of children, could best be assured. Marriage not only served as a channel for sexual energies for both women and men, but also provided the sustaining societal mortar and gender-based division of labor on which rabbinic society depended. Sexuality outside of marriage was a constant threat to the social contract. Rabbinic writings constructed legal fences to limit contact between men and women outside the marital dyad in order to prevent the possibility of sexual desire or contact between inappropriate partners. These mandates are intended to avert adulterous or incestuous relationships and to prevent the conception and birth of illegitimate children (*mamzerim*), a significant concern in rabbinic culture.

Pleasurable sexual activity was seen as an essential component of a harmonious union and rabbinic Judaism taught that fulfilling his wife's sexual needs was among a husband's obligations within marriage. In fact, the Mishnah, the foundational rabbinic legal text, which teaches that a husband must provide his wife with regular conjugal visits, in addition to providing her with food and clothing, provides detailed guidelines for fulfillment of this matrimonial duty, based on the husband's occupation and the amount of time he spends at home (Mishnah *Ketubbot* 5:6). Such favorable attitudes about the value of marital sexual expression for its own sake are evident in the willingness of rabbinic authorities to allow married couples to use a contraceptive *mokh*, a cervical sponge or cap, and also in the willingness of rabbinic courts to enable a woman to be divorced from a man she finds sexually repellant.

In the area of conjugal relations, the married woman is treated as a person with rights as well as obligations. Thus, the husband's legal duty to have intercourse with his wife is matched by her corresponding obligation to consent. Each spouse incurs daily financial penalties for non-compliance, but the wife's penalty is more than twice as heavy as her husband's, an indication that the tradition values the woman's rights below those of the man. In either case, failure by the wife or the husband to be sexually available to the other is a cause for divorce.

In medieval Jewish mysticism marital sexuality took on a specifically redemptive function. Mystical writers maintained that each religiously inspired act of marital intercourse, particularly on the eve of Sabbath, secured among the Jewish people the indwelling presence of the *shekhinah*, the nurturing aspect of God most accessible to human experience. The *Iggeret ha-Kodesh* (The Holy Letter), a thirteenth-century mystical text on matrimonial relations, was among the earliest Jewish medieval works to constitute connubial sexuality as a salvific activity. Its advice on how men may please their wives was also directed to a higher mystical purpose through which marital intercourse was transformed into communion with the divine.

SEE ALSO: Creation Stories; Menstrual Rituals; Mysticism; Religion and Homophobia

FURTHER READING

Baskin, Judith R. 2002. *Midrashic Women: Formations of the Feminine in Rabbinic Literature*. Hanover, NH: University Press of New England for Brandeis University Press.

Baskin, Judith R. 2012. "Women and Gender Relations." In *Oxford Bibliographies in Jewish Studies*, edited by David Biale. Oxford: Oxford University Press.

Biale, David. 1992. *Eros and the Jews: From Biblical Israel to Contemporary America*, 153–158. New York: Basic Books.

Boyarin, Daniel. 1993. *Carnal Israel: Reading Sex in Talmudic Culture*. Berkeley: University of California Press.

Cohen, Shaye J. D. 2005. *Why Aren't Jewish Women Circumcised? Gender and Covenant in Judaism*. Berkeley: University of California Press.

Dzmura, Noach, ed. 2010. *Balancing on the Mechitza: Transgender in Jewish Community*. Berkeley: North Atlantic Books.

Greenberg, Steven. 2004. *Wrestling with God and Men: Homosexuality in the Jewish Tradition*. Madison: University of Wisconsin Press.

Hyman, Paula E. 1995. *Gender and Assimilation in Modern Jewish History: The Roles and Representation of Women*, 25–30. Seattle: University of Washington Press.

Kaplan, Marion, and Deborah Dash Moore, eds. 2011. *Gender and Jewish History*. Bloomington: Indiana University Press.

Judaism and Sexuality

GREGG DRINKWATER
University of Colorado, USA

Judaism is a highly decentralized religion, thus there is no single or unified Jewish perspective on lesbian, gay, bisexual, and transgender issues. The Jewish world can be divided into a diverse range of movements and branches of Judaism, and no central Jewish body has universally recognized authority over Jewish beliefs, practices, or structures. Some Jewish communities ordain openly LGBT rabbis and celebrate sexual and gender diversity, while in other communities, Jewish leaders denounce homosexuality and demand clear boundaries and distinctive roles for women and men. The majority of the Jewish world lies somewhere in between.

The branches of Judaism can most simply be divided into two main groups: those labeled Orthodox or traditional, who understand themselves as strictly following traditional Jewish law, or *halacha*, and those labeled progressive or liberal, who maintain a more flexible or adaptive relationship to Jewish law and religious traditions. These "progressive" branches of Judaism include the Reform Movement, Progressive Judaism (as Reform is generally called outside North America), Liberal Judaism (in the United Kingdom), the Reconstructionist Movement, Renewal Judaism, and Secular Humanism. The Orthodox and traditional branches include the Modern Orthodox, the so-called "Ultra-Orthodox," Hasidic Jews, and most Sephardic Jewish communities (descended from the Jews of medieval Spain, or more broadly, Jews who trace their ancestry to North Africa or the Middle East). Additionally, small historic Jewish communities with roots in India, Ethiopia, China, and elsewhere may also be understood as traditional in practice and belief. The Conservative Movement (called Masorti Judaism outside the United States) straddles this Orthodox/Progressive divide.

While Orthodox Jews tend toward condemnation (or quiet tolerance) of homosexuality and gender diversity, the progressive branches are more open to affirming LGBT people. Within this very general division, because of its decentralized structure, Jewish communal attitudes toward LGBT people reflect national, regional, and local norms among non-Jews in their home communities. Thus Jewish communities in cities or regions known for large LGBT populations or strong support for LGBT civil rights tend to be more liberal on LGBT issues than their counterparts, regardless of denomination, in places with weaker support for LGBT civil rights.

HOMOSEXUALITY AND GENDER DIVERSITY IN JEWISH TEXTS

In the Jewish tradition, "homosexuality" is not prohibited. Jewish law focuses on specific sexual acts, not a person's sexual orientation, identity, or desires. Sex between men has generally been understood as prohibited by two verses in Leviticus (Lev. 18:22 and 20:13) that both reference a man lying with another man "as with a woman" as "*toevah*," commonly translated as "abomination." Most Orthodox leaders consider these Levitical verses to ban unambiguously all sexual activity between men. Academic scholars of Jewish texts and many non-Orthodox rabbis offer alternative interpretations. Some see these verses as referencing only anal sex between men, and not other sexual acts, while others suggest that the ancient context of the Bible implies that the verses reference male–male rape and therefore should not be understood as a ban on consensual sex. For these scholars, the broadening of the ban to other male–male sexual acts was a later rabbinic innovation (see Brodsky 2009 for a detailed overview).

Sex between women is not prohibited in the Torah. However, it is seen as a violation of Jewish law based on rabbinic interpretations of passages in the Torah that are seen as indirectly referencing female–female sexual intimacy. Given the lack of a direct Torah ban, and that Orthodox authorities are almost universally male and thus less aware of female sexuality, lesbianism has been the subject of less discussion and debate within traditional Jewish communities.

Some Progressive leaders suggest that debating the "original" meaning of these texts is a distraction, because social and cultural norms around sexuality and gender have changed dramatically in the modern world. Just as most modern Jews reject biblically sanctioned slavery and polygyny, these leaders argue it is time to reject prohibitions on same-sex intimacy.

On transgender issues, Jewish tradition contains biblical verses prohibiting cross dressing and bodily mutilation, with specific references to castration, thus seeming to ban male-to-female sex reassignment surgery (SRS) and body modifications more generally. But as with the sexual prohibitions noted above, the exact meaning or applicability of these Jewish legal limits to modern contexts is debated. Scholars offer variant interpretations of the meaning and intent of the ban on cross dressing, noting loopholes contained within traditional texts. Likewise, Jewish law contains mechanisms for creating exceptions to legal parameters when human life is at stake. Psychiatrists and advocates for transgender inclusion note that cross dressing or SRS may be essential for the health and well-being of transgender individuals and thus these legal exceptions must therefore be invoked.

Within the biblical canon, some see the stories of David and Jonathan and of Ruth and Naomi as offering models for same-sex love that can help lesbian and gay people see reflections of themselves in biblical texts. Advocates of these interpretations vary on whether the biblical stories imply a sexual component, while such interpretations are generally rejected by Orthodox and traditional Jews (for details, see Greenberg 2005).

ORTHODOX/TRADITIONAL JUDAISM

There is tremendous variation within Orthodox Jewish communities on LGBT issues. Orthodox rabbis and communal leaders have spoken publicly in support of civil rights for LGBT people and for treating LGBT Jews with dignity and respect. Other Orthodox leaders reject such calls for inclusion, arguing that because Jewish law prohibits same-sex sexual activity and strictly regulates male and female gender roles, the affirmation of LGBT people threatens traditional Jewish practice.

The conversation on LGBT issues in the Orthodox world is almost entirely focused on lesbian and gay identities and same-sex intimacy, with gender identity and the inclusion of transgender Jews rarely surfacing in public debates. Bisexuals are perceived as having the ability to choose opposite-sex partners (whereas gays and lesbians are not), thus most Orthodox leaders who argue for gay and lesbian inclusion still encourage bisexual Jews to marry opposite-sex partners.

In 2010, Nathaniel Helfgot, a Modern Orthodox rabbi based in the United States, published a 12-point "Statement of Principles on the Place of Jews with a Homosexual Orientation in Our Community." Signed by over 200 primarily Modern Orthodox rabbis and communal leaders (most based in the US), the statement calls for treating all people with dignity and notes that "embarrassing, harassing, or demeaning someone with a homosexual orientation or same-sex attraction is a violation of Torah prohibitions that embody the deepest values of Judaism" (Helfgot 2010). The statement notes that Jewish law prohibits same-sex sexual acts and sees heterosexual marriages as the "sole legitimate outlet for human sexual expression," while encouraging sensitivity and understanding for individuals "with same-sex attractions and orientations." The statement specifically calls for welcoming gay and lesbian Jews into Jewish communal institutions, and for "acceptance and full embrace" of the children of gay and lesbian Jews. A small number of Orthodox rabbis and communal leaders have encouraged their communities to go even further, suggesting that the statement is too restrictive, and that a total ban on all forms of same-sex intimacy is counterproductive and emotionally damaging to gay and lesbian Jews.

In response to the "Statement of Principles" and the increasing visibility of LGBT Orthodox Jews, in 2011, a group of over 200 primarily ultra-Orthodox rabbis and leaders issued their own stricter statement, called the "Declaration on the Torah Approach to Homosexuality," which encourages therapy to change same-sex attractions, a hotly contested topic within Orthodox circles.

Rabbi Steven Greenberg became the first openly gay Orthodox rabbi after coming out in 1999, and in 2005 published *Wrestling with God and Men: Homosexuality in the Jewish Tradition*, exploring the textual basis for Orthodox Judaism's relationship to gay and lesbian people. In 2001, filmmaker Sandi Simcha DuBowski released the documentary *Trembling Before G-d*, which featured the stories of nine gay and lesbian Orthodox Jews, including Rabbi Greenberg, along with interviews with key Orthodox rabbis and communal leaders. The film sparked widespread dialogue on homosexuality within Orthodox communities worldwide and contributed to shifting the perspectives of many Orthodox leaders toward more compassion for the difficulties Orthodox gay and lesbian Jews face when trying to maintain their commitment to Judaism.

On the inclusion of transgender Jews, most Orthodox communities focus on a case-by-case basis. Orthodox leaders generally prohibit SRS before such surgery has taken place, but in cases where it has already taken place, Orthodox leaders sometimes allow for transgender Jews who have had SRS to participate in communal life, with some referencing a minority legal opinion from the 1970s by Rabbi Eliezer Waldenberg (1915–2006), a widely respected Israeli authority on medical issues and Jewish law, in which he wrote: "the external genitalia that are visible are the ones that determine gender for [Jewish law]" (Rabinowitz 2003, 8). When transgender Jews participate in Orthodox communities with the support of rabbinic leaders, it is generally understood that they should do so discreetly, conforming to communal norms for gendered dress and behavior.

CONSERVATIVE JUDAISM

The Conservative Movement, known as Masorti Judaism outside of the United States, developed in response to the growth in nineteenth-century Germany of Reform Judaism. Conservative/Masorti Judaism integrates traditional observance of Jewish law with modern ethical and moral sensibilities, scientific inquiry, and engagement with critical scholarship of sacred texts. Conservative Jews make up the second largest group of affiliated Jews in the United States, after the Reform Movement. Masorti-affiliated congregations can be found throughout the Jewish world.

The movement's leadership in the United States has encouraged Conservative synagogues to welcome LGBT Jews as members since the early 1990s. But on the question of religious practice and Jewish law, Conservative communities long maintained a more restrictive stance on same-sex sexual acts, ordination of LGBT rabbis, and same-sex unions. Official statements on LGBT issues have come from the Committee on Jewish Law and Standards (CJLS) of the movement's Rabbinical Assembly. In 1992, the consensus within the CJLS was to prohibit the ordination of LGBT people as rabbis and cantors, and to prohibit Conservative clergy from officiating at same-sex unions. In 2006, the CJLS affirmed two separate legal papers. One urged the movement to maintain the 1992 status quo. The other reversed the 1992 positions while maintaining a narrower ban only on anal sex between men (but noting that individuals would not be questioned on their private sexual practices) and paved the way for Conservative rabbinical schools to ordain openly gay rabbis, and allowing clergy to officiate at same-sex unions. Because both papers received a simple majority vote within the CJLS, both were offered as valid legal opinions, allowing individual Conservative/Masorti institutions to choose between them. The movement's two US rabbinical seminaries changed their policies to allow gay and lesbian rabbinical students (admission for openly bisexual and transgender students came a number of years later). The seminary in Israel shifted its policy on rabbinical students six years later in 2012.

In 2003, the CJLS approved a paper on the status of transsexuals concluding that individuals who have undergone SRS, and whose sex reassignment has been recognized by civil authorities, are considered to have changed their sex status according to Jewish law.

REFORM JUDAISM

Judaism's Reform Movement was founded in Germany during the early 1800s. Since the 1990s, the movement has been the largest in the United States and is characterized by a strong emphasis on social justice, individual autonomy in the interpretation of Torah, and gender equality in all facets of Jewish communal life. Most Reform institutions in the United States embrace LGBT people.

In 1977, the Central Conference of American Rabbis (or CCAR, the movement's North American rabbinical organization) passed a resolution calling for the decriminalization of homosexual acts between consenting adults and an end to discrimination against gays and lesbians. Since then, the US arm of the movement has continually supported the rights of LGBT people, both in civil and Jewish society. Public support for LGBT people among Reform/Progressive leaders in other countries is also strong, although more tepid in socially conservative countries. Leaders with Liberal Judaism in the United Kingdom have been very vocal in favor of LGBT inclusion.

In 1990, the CCAR endorsed admitting gay and lesbian Jews into Hebrew Union College (HUC, the movement's seminary) and the rabbinate, although a number of gay and lesbian rabbis received ordination prior to this 1990 decision, or came out as gay after ordination. Leo Baeck College, the Progressive seminary in the United Kingdom, saw its first openly gay students in 1984. Germany's Abraham Geiger College also admits gay and lesbian students. In 2003, HUC accepted its first openly transgender rabbinical student.

In 2000, the CCAR passed a resolution allowing Reform rabbis to officiate at same-sex commitment ceremonies. However, the resolution left the decision of whether or not to officiate up to each individual rabbi, out of recognition of the diverse opinions on the issue. Today, most, but not all, Reform clergy in the United States officiate at same-sex unions (although support for officiation is lower in other countries). The Reform Movement in the United States, the United Kingdom, and some other Western countries supports civil marriage equality for same-sex couples.

RECONSTRUCTIONIST JUDAISM

Reconstructionist Judaism is a uniquely American Jewish denomination, founded in the United States and almost entirely based in the United States (with a handful of congregations in other countries). Reconstructionism encourages traditional Jewish practices, but considers Judaism to be an evolving religious civilization and holds that modern Western secular morality can take precedence over Jewish law. Reconstructionism is the smallest of the Jewish movements.

Reconstructionist Judaism has been a long-time supporter of both LGBT civil rights and the inclusion of LGBT people in Jewish life. In 1985, the movement's national body adopted a resolution welcoming congregations serving primarily LGBT Jews. The movement began allowing its rabbis to perform marriages for same-sex couples in 1993. In 1984, the movement's rabbinical school adopted an admissions policy that prohibited discrimination based on sexual orientation and admitted its first openly gay student in 1984.

Although the movement did not officially pass a resolution in support of civil marriage for same-sex couples until 2004, the policies and practices of the movement have reflected this position since the early 1990s.

RENEWAL JUDAISM

Renewal Judaism, with roots in the counterculture of late 1960s and early 1970s, is not officially a separate Jewish movement, but rather a loosely organized coalition of like-minded Jews centered around ALEPH: The Alliance for Jewish Renewal and several affiliated institutions. Jewish Renewal attempts to reinvigorate Judaism through the use of mystical, Hasidic, musical, and meditative practices drawn from various spiritual backgrounds.

The ALEPH Statement of Principles, which acts as the basic unifying document of the Renewal movement, includes a section that specifically welcomes LGBT people. ALEPH also fully encourages LGBT people to become part of ALEPH's rabbinate. Although ALEPH has not published any official resolutions regarding the inclusion of transgender people in Jewish Renewal communities, the ALEPH Statement of Principles does include a reference to welcoming all people "regardless of ... gender identity."

REGIONAL DIFFERENCES

The United States and Israel are both home to roughly 6 million Jews each, representing approximately 80 percent of world Jewry. The next largest Jewish population, at just under 500,000, is in France, followed, in order of decreasing population, by Canada, the United Kingdom, Russia, Argentina, Germany, Brazil, and Australia. All other countries have fewer than 100,000 Jews.

Support for LGBT inclusion within the Jewish world is generally strongest and most developed in those countries where Orthodox Judaism accounts for a relatively small percentage of the national Jewish population (in the US it is roughly 10 percent). In those countries where Orthodox Judaism represents a larger share of the Jewish populations – often the majority – LGBT inclusion is more controversial. Inclusion is likewise more controversial in those countries and communities that are more culturally conservative on LGBT civil rights in general, as in the Jewish communities of Eastern Europe and Russia.

Israel accounts for roughly 40 percent of the world's Jews, but has a very mixed record on LGBT inclusion. Civil protections for LGBT people under Israeli law are very advanced, placing Israel among the most supportive legal environments for LGBT people globally. But support for religious inclusion of LGBT people in Judaism is relatively low, compared with the United States and some other Western countries. The vast majority of Israeli Jews identify either as secular or as Orthodox/traditional – the presence of the progressive Jewish movements in Israel is small, but growing. The Orthodox in Israel, like their counterparts globally, are generally negatively inclined toward LGBT inclusion in Jewish religious life. Secular Israelis may support Israel's pro-LGBT civil laws, but often have little interest in debates over LGBT inclusion in Judaism. This split is reflected in Israel's LGBT advocacy organizations, which are either focused primarily on secular civil rights (the Agudah, Israeli Gay Youth, Choshen, and other organizations), or are dedicated to expanding space for LGBT Jews within Orthodox Judaism (Hevruta, Bat Kol, Hod).

LGBT JEWISH INSTITUTIONS

Since the founding of the first Jewish LGBT organizations in 1972, such institutions have proliferated around the world, with nearly every sizable Jewish community having at least one LGBT organization. The first LGBT synagogue, Beth Chayim Chadashim, was founded in Los Angeles in 1972 (at first defining itself as a "gay and lesbian synagogue" and only later shifting to "LGBT") and quickly affiliated with Reform Judaism. That same year saw the founding of Chutzpah, a social group for gay Jews in San Francisco, and the Jewish Gay and Lesbian Group (JGLG) in London. Gay and lesbian synagogues quickly spread throughout the United States and Canada. However, some began closing or merging with other synagogues in the late 1990s/2000s as Judaism became more inclusive of LGBT Jews and as synagogues began experiencing declining membership generally.

In 1975, the Conference of Gay Jewish Organizations brought together representatives from Jewish gay groups in Washington, DC. This umbrella group eventually became the World Congress of GLBT Jews, acting as an information and resource-sharing network for Jewish LGBT organizations worldwide. Jewish organizations that focus on education, advocacy, and organizing toward the inclusion of LGBT Jews in Jewish life can be found throughout the Jewish world, with the largest concentration in the United States. The largest such organization, Keshet, was founded in Boston in 1996 and works throughout the United States.

SEE ALSO: Judaism and Gender; Lesbian and Gay Movements; Religion and Homophobia; Same-Sex Marriage; Sex Reassignment Surgery; Sexual Identity and Orientation

REFERENCES

Brodsky, David. 2009. "Sex in the Talmud: How to Understand Leviticus 18 and 20: Parashat Kedoshim (Leviticus 19:1–20:27)." In *Torah Queeries: Weekly Commentaries on the Hebrew Bible*, edited by Gregg Drinkwater, Joshua Lesser and David Shneer, 157–169. New York: New York University Press.

Greenberg, Steven. 2005. *Wrestling with God and Men: Homosexuality in the Jewish Tradition*. Madison: University of Wisconsin Press.

Helfgot, Nathaniel. 2010. Statement of Principles on the Place of Jews with a Homosexual Orientation in Our Community. Accessed November 1, 2014, at http://statementofprinciplesnya.blogspot.com/

Rabinowitz, Mayer E., and Committee on Jewish Law and Standards of the Rabbinical Assembly. 2003. Status of Transsexuals. YD 336.2003. Accessed September 10, 2015, at www.rabbinicalassembly.org/sites/default/files/public/halakhah/teshuvot/20012004/rabinowitz_transsexuals.pdf

FURTHER READING

Alpert, Rebecca. 1998. *Like Bread on the Seder Plate: Jewish Lesbians and the Transformation of Tradition*. New York: Columbia University Press.

Drinkwater, Gregg, Joshua Lesser, and David Shneer, eds. 2009. *Torah Queeries: Weekly Commentaries on the Hebrew Bible*. New York: New York University Press.

Dzmura, Noach, ed. 2010. *Balancing on the Mechitza: Transgender in Jewish Community*. Berkeley: North Atlantic Books.

Kabakov, Miryam, ed. 2010. *Keep Your Wives Away from Them: Orthodox Women, Unorthodox Desires*. Berkeley: North Atlantic Books.

Rapoport, Rabbi Chaim. 2004. *Judaism and Homosexuality: An Authentic Orthodox View*. London: Valentine Mitchell.

Shneer, David, and Caryn Aviv, eds. 2002. *Queer Jews*. New York: Routledge.

Kathoey

VARUNEE FAII SANGGANJANAVANICH
The University of Akron, USA

Kathoey is a Thai word believed to have its origin in the Khmer language of Cambodia. Kathoey is widely used by Thais and Western people when referring to Thai male-to-female (MtF) transgender and/or transsexual individuals. The Royal Institute Dictionary (2011) defines kathoey as a "person whose mind and manners are opposite to their sex" or "with both male and female sexual organs." In the context of Thai culture, kathoey is used to refer to men who wear women's costumes (cross-dressers), adopt female gender roles, stereotypes, and expectations (MtF transgender people), live full-time as a woman in a feminized body (MtF transsexual people), or have both female and male sexual organs (intersex people). Despite the fact that kathoeys are highly visible in Thai society, they are considered a sexual minority who have long been fighting for their human and legal rights.

Similar to other societies, Thai society embraces the concept of gender binary – a belief system indicating the existence of two genders, female and male. Thai culture has a strict gender boundary that clearly differentiates gender roles, stereotypes, and expectations. *Phu chai* or *bu rut* refers to male, men, and a representation of masculinity, whereas *phu ying* or *satri* refers to female, women, and a representation of femininity. Kathoey is a representation of neither gender nor sex. Rather, it represents a condition where men adopt female gender roles, stereotypes, and expectations. Thus, in an effort to construct a new gender, kathoey is termed *phet tee sam*, which means third sex.

Western scholars have noted that kathoeys are more readily accepted in Thai society compared to many transgender communities around the world (Jackson 1998), speculating that Buddhism may be accountable for such tolerance toward kathoeys in Thai culture. Through a Buddhist lens, kathoey can be viewed as a human condition resulting from negative *karma* acquired in one's previous life. There is hence nothing one can do but accept it as a given. Kathoey is viewed as an assigned condition that becomes a person's destiny, not something a person chooses. This belief leads to sympathy and compassion toward kathoeys rather than hatred and anger.

The social acceptance of kathoeys to some extent accounts for the prominent presence of kathoeys in popular media. However, popular representations of kathoeys tend to be stereotypical and often linked to other negatively depicted groups (e.g., sex workers, showgirls) (Ocha and Earth 2012). Kathoeys play an important role in the beauty, fashion, and entertainment industries, in which their physical beauty and attractiveness are highlighted.

Although there is a general acceptance of kathoeys among Thais, they are commonly discriminated against in the context of education and employment. While kathoeys dominate certain occupations such as cabaret workers, beauticians, and fashion designers, their presence in these occupations also continues to shape the public perception of their career potential. In recent years, kathoeys have been increasingly more represented in other industries such as sports, education, airlines, and politics (Saniotis 2006), which helps expand representations of kathoeys in more diverse careers and not limit them to stereotypical occupations.

In 2006, the Transgender Woman Group of Thailand (later named the TransFemales Association of Thailand) made a significant political effort to push the Thai government to grant human and legal rights to transsexual individuals. The aim was to amend the anti-discrimination article in the Thai Constitution to allow MtF transsexual individuals who undergo sex reassignment surgery to possess female gender identity on different types of identification (e.g., citizen card, driver's license, passport) as well as overturn the Thai army's definition of kathoey as mentally ill. Despite such efforts, kathoeys remain without legal rights as women in Thailand.

While the term kathoey is widely used and known, many transgender and transsexual people in Thailand consider it derogatory because of its negative associations with gender deviancy. An alternative and more respectful term is *Sao praphet song* – "a second type of woman." Many kathoeys do not consider this term representative of who they are, or of their gender identity, since it stamps them as second-class citizens (Chonwilai 2012). As a result, the TransFemales Association of Thailand has advocated the use of *kohn kham phet*, which is an exact translation of transgender in English. *Kham* means cross over or trans- and *phet* means sex or gender. *Kohn kham phet*, therefore, accurately describes those whose gender identity is incongruent with the sex assigned at birth and conveys political correctness when referring to kathoeys in Thai. The TransFemales Association suggests using *phu ying kham phet* or *satri kham phet* when referring to MtF transsexual individuals in Thailand.

SEE ALSO: Ladyboys; Third Genders; Trans Identities, Psychological Perspectives

REFERENCES

Chonwilai, Sulaiporn. 2012. "Kathoey: Male-to-Female Transgenders or Transsexuals." In *Thai Sex Talk: The Language of Sex and Sexuality in Thailand*, edited by Pimpawun Boonmongkon and Peter A. Jackson, 100–117. Chiang Mai, Thailand: Mekong Press.

Jackson, Peter A. 1998. "Male Homosexuality and Transgenderism in the Thai Buddhist Tradition." In *Queer Dharma: Voices of Gay Buddhists*, edited by Winston Leyland. San Francisco: Gay Sunshine Press.

Ocha, Witchayanee, and Barbara Earth. 2012. "Identity Diversification Among Transgender Sex Workers in Thailand's Sex Tourism Industry." *Sexualities*, 16: 195–216. DOI: 10.1177/1363460712471117.

Royal Institute of Thailand. 2011. "Royal Institute Dictionary." Accessed August 12, 2015, at http://rirs3.royin.go.th/dictionary.asp.

Saniotis, Arthur. 2006. "Gendered Ambivalence: Representations of Kathoey in Thailand." *Popular Culture Review*, 17: 31–43.

FURTHER READING

Jackson, Peter A. 2011. *Queer Bangkok: Twenty-First-Century Markets, Media and Rights*. Hong Kong: Hong Kong University Press.

Totman, Richard. 2003. *The Third Sex – Kathoey: Thailand's Ladyboys*. London: Souvenir Press.

Kibbutz/Kibbutzim

MICHAL PALGI
University of Haifa, Israel

The kibbutz way of life is an all-inclusive system in which members live, work, raise children, grow old, and pass away. The first kibbutz, Degania, was founded in 1910; today there are 267 kibbutzim (plural of "kibbutz"). The majority were formed by local and international groups of young people who had joined Zionist youth movements. Their goals were to cultivate the wilderness, create a just society, and rebuild a Jewish national entity in Israel, which would be a refuge from European anti-Semitism. Today, their size varies between 30 and 1,500 inhabitants, with an average of about 400. The total kibbutz population (approximately 150,000) constitutes 1.8 percent of Israel's population, yet its contribution to the national economy amounts to 45 percent of agricultural production and 8.4 percent of industrial output.

The main values that the kibbutz attempted to realize were:

1. Equality among members as well as among kibbutz communities: That meant that all members had the same standard of living, regardless of their gender, education, marital status, or job. Additionally, the kibbutz federation decided that there would not be differences in the standard of living in the different kibbutz communities.
2. Direct democracy, participation, and rotation of office holders: That meant that all members could participate in decision-making processes of the community and its economic enterprises. The general assembly (consisting of all members) elected individuals to suitable leadership positions for a limited amount of time (usually three or four years). This time limitation was to avoid stratification and long-term concentration of power within the community.
3. Equal value for all work: That meant that all types of work had the same social and economic value, whether they were manual or mental, whether they needed extensive training or not. Less popular jobs (like dishwashing in the dining hall) were performed, in rotation, by all members able to do the work.
4. Mutual guarantees and help within the kibbutz and between kibbutz communities: That meant supporting individuals with temporary or chronic problems – medical, economic, educational, or social. (Palgi and Reinharz 2013)

These values, as well as the organizational structures established by the kibbutzim, enabled (but did not ensure) gender equality. Almost all household tasks were carried out by the community: meals were cooked and served in the communal kitchen/dining hall; washing and mending of clothes were done in the communal laundry. Women and men were economically independent of each other: all women and men belonged to the workforce and received equal rewards for their work; single parents received the same allowance for children as couples did; and both women and men could participate in the governing bodies of the kibbutz. The economic emancipation of women was furthered by a system of collective education, which cared for the children almost 24 hours a day.

The expected gender equality envisioned and enabled by the socialist kibbutz ideology and structure did not materialize. In reality, there was a sharp gender division of labor: women worked mainly in "women's occupations" (education and services). Most of these jobs did not prepare women for managerial positions and caused them to be underrepresented in the administration of the kibbutz society and economy. Nevertheless, women had the same standard of living as men and there was no poverty among women or children (Palgi 2003).

Gender roles in the kibbutz were also affected by changes in the 1980s and the 1990s, mainly instigated by women. They included the transfer of many tasks from the responsibility of the kibbutz to that of the family. Two key examples were: the change from children sleeping in communal children's houses to sleeping in their parents' apartments and the shift in preparing and eating most (or all) meals from the communal kitchen/dining hall to the families' apartments.

During the last two decades, different forms of economic practices have been introduced into kibbutz communities, the vast majority swaying toward liberalism. The main reasons for this process have been ideological change among the new kibbutz generations and newcomers; an economic crisis questioning the sustainability of the kibbutz's collective way of life; and a negative sociopolitical environment that has developed nationally since the right-wing electoral victory of 1977. These new economic practices opened the outside job market to kibbutz members, who were no longer obliged to work mainly in the kibbutz. Thus, they expanded the variety of occupations women could choose from (Palgi 2003; Fogiel-Bijaoui 2007).

Many women improved their socioeconomic status because of this greater accessibility to professional and economic fields. At the same time, these women enjoyed the kibbutz practice of mutual aid, which helped ameliorate the vicissitudes of capitalism outside the kibbutz. Nevertheless, the economic changes presented hazards to many women, exposing them to social discrimination in the surrounding society. When the kibbutz lost some of its unique characteristics, women lost the advantages that the old kibbutz bestowed upon them: economic equality, equivalent social security, and legal equality. As a result, the status of women in the kibbutz is approaching the status of women in Israeli society in general, with its advantages and its drawbacks.

Seen in the larger contexts of gender studies and sociology, the history of gender in the kibbutz exemplifies the persistence of inequalities despite expressed goals of justice and egalitarianism, and despite building social structures to achieve those goals. It also exemplifies the long-term pervasiveness of general societal norms and trends on small, counter-culture organizations.

SEE ALSO: Gender Equality

REFERENCES

Fogiel-Bijaoui, Sylvie. 2007. "Women in the Kibbutz: The 'Mixed Blessing of Neo-Liberalism'." *Nashim: A Journal of Jewish Women's Studies and Gender Issues*, 13: 102–122. DOI: 10.1353/nsh.2007.0006.

Palgi, Michal. 2003. "Gender Equality in the Kibbutz: From Ideology to Reality." In *Jewish Feminism in Israel*, edited by Kalpana Misra and Melanie Rich, 106–132. Waltham: Brandeis University Press.

Palgi, Michal, and Shulamit Reinharz, eds. 2013. *The Kibbutz at One Hundred: A Century of Crises and Reinvention*. Piscataway Township: Transaction Publishers.

FURTHER READING

Russell, Raymond, Robert Hanneman, and Shlomo Getz. 2013. *The Renewal of the Kibbutz: From Reform to Transformation*. New Brunswick: Rutgers University Press.

Kinsey Scale

CHRISTINE L. QUINAN
Utrecht University, The Netherlands

The Kinsey Scale of Sexual Behavior was first developed in 1948 by Alfred Kinsey, Wardell Pomeroy, and Clyde Martin to show how sexuality cannot be framed as purely heterosexual or homosexual but is instead a continuum based on a number of factors, including behavior, desire, and fantasy. Also known as the Heterosexual-Homosexual Rating Scale, Kinsey and his colleagues created the seven-point spectrum to account for research findings based on more than 11,000 in-depth interviews. Although the majority of participants identified as heterosexual, results showed that sexual orientation was much more variable and diverse, as many spoke of experiences and thoughts that would place them somewhere in between "heterosexual" and "homosexual."

The seven points on the Kinsey Scale are as follows:

0   Exclusively heterosexual with no homosexual;
1   Predominantly heterosexual, only incidentally homosexual;
2   Predominantly heterosexual, but more than incidentally homosexual;
3   Equally heterosexual and homosexual;
4   Predominantly homosexual, but more than incidentally heterosexual;
5   Predominantly homosexual, only incidentally heterosexual;
6   Exclusively homosexual.

Kinsey also included an X for "no socio-sexual contacts or reactions," which would correspond to modern understandings of asexuality. When determining scores, Kinsey took into account both "overt sexual experience" and "psychosexual reactions." These two dimensions were, though, collapsed in assigning a single score (leading to eventual critique).

The Kinsey Scale was first published in *Sexual Behavior in the Human Male* (Kinsey, Pomeroy, and Martin 1998/1948) and was later elaborated on in *Sexual Behavior in the Human Female* (Kinsey et al. 1998/1953). The two texts are collectively known as the Kinsey Reports. The first volume was quite revolutionary in that it spoke candidly of a taboo topic and uncovered a diversity of human sexualities. Based on data gathered through a structured questionnaire memorized by the interviewers, the authors posited that approximately 10 percent of American males surveyed between the ages of 16 and 55 were "more or less exclusively homosexual for at least three years" (in the 5 to 6 range). This finding remains the source of the common assertion that 10 percent of the general public is homosexual.

Sexual Behavior in the Human Female further discusses the Kinsey Scale and compares data on male and female participants. Although women were found to be less sexual than men, one key finding was that women were more sexual than most believed them to be at that time period. The most oft-cited statistics are that 7 percent of single females (ages 20–35) and 4 percent of previously married females (ages 20–35) were a 3 on the Kinsey Scale. Additionally, 2–6 percent of females (ages 20–35) were more or less exclusively homosexual, and 1–3 percent of unmarried females (ages 20–35) were exclusively homosexual.

Kinsey's research was radical for its time in that it opened doors to new perspectives on sexuality. It formally acknowledged the range and variability of sexual orientation, showing that it is not fixed or static. It recognized bisexuality (a term Kinsey did not care for), while showing that most individuals are in fact in between heterosexual and homosexual (i.e., between 1 and 5 on the scale). In this way, it can be seen to have played a role in the "sexual revolution" of the 1960s.

The data sample upon which Kinsey's results were based was not, however, immune from criticism. Most notably, psychologist Abraham Maslow stated that the sample was inaccurate because it did not take into account volunteer bias, specifically that interviewees willing to speak about topics considered taboo skewed the potential of applying it to the general population. The sample was also critiqued for overrepresenting prison inmates and male prostitutes (although subsequent studies have shown that removing these subjects has little effect on the findings).

Despite the importance of the Kinsey Scale to sexology research and eventual gay rights movements, it has its limitations. The Kinsey Scale takes biological sex – rather than gender identity – as its point of departure when discussing attraction, which itself is conceived of in terms of sexual attraction. Research has since shown how other forms of attraction factor into sexual orientation, including romantic attraction and emotional attraction. The scale has also been critiqued for reducing sexual orientation to a linear continuum (rather than it being multidimensional) and for not taking into consideration a number of other variables, some of which were not yet known to sexologists. For example, the Kinsey Scale is not comprehensive enough to consider factors such as interaction between gender identity and sexual attraction/behavior, attraction to certain gender expressions, including transgender or transsexual partners, or changes in sexual orientation after transitioning to another sex/gender.

In the past decades, additional scales and charts have been created to factor in such dimensions. For example, the Klein Sexual Orientation Grid, developed by Fritz Klein in 1978, examined how sexuality changes over time (past, present, ideal). The Klein Grid also takes into account several other variables, including sexual attraction, sexual behavior, sexual fantasies, emotional preference, social preference, heterosexual/homosexual lifestyle, and self-identification. Michael Storms later proposed a two-dimensional chart with two axes that factor in degree of attraction and hetero- and homo-eroticism. A number of other graphs and images – including the viral "Genderbread Person" – have since been created to account for the multidimensional nature of sexuality and its intersection with gender identity, gender expression, and biological sex.

SEE ALSO: Bisexuality; The Hite Report on Female Sexuality; Lesbian Continuum; Sexual Identity and Orientation; Sexualities

REFERENCES

Kinsey, Alfred C., Wardell B. Pomeroy, and Clyde E. Martin. 1998. *Sexual Behavior in the Human Male*. Bloomington: Indiana University Press. Originally published in 1948.

Kinsey, Alfred C., Wardell B. Pomeroy, Clyde E. Martin, Paul H. Gebhard, and Institute of Sex Research. 1998. *Sexual Behavior in the Human Female*. Bloomington: Indiana University Press. Originally published in 1953.

FURTHER READING

Berkey, Braden Robert, Terri Perelman-Hall, and Lawrence A. Kurdek. 1990. "The Multidimensional Scale of Sexuality." *Journal of Homosexuality*, 19(4): 67–88. DOI: 10.1300/J082v19n04_05.

Diamond, Lisa M. 2003. "What Does Sexual Orientation Orient? A Biobehavioral Model Distinguishing Romantic Love and Sexual Desire." *Psychological Review*, 110(1): 173–192. DOI: 10.1037/0033-295X.110.1.173.

Diamond, Milton. 1993. "Homosexuality and Bisexuality in Different Populations." *Archives of Sexual Behavior*, 22(4): 291–310. DOI: 10.1007/BF01542119.

The Kinsey Institute. 2014. "Kinsey's Heterosexual-Homosexual Rating Scale." Accessed August

5, 2014, at http://www.kinseyinstitute.org/research/ak-hhscale.html.

Sell, Randall L. 1997. "Defining and Measuring Sexual Orientation: A Review." *Archives of Sexual Behavior*, 26(6): 643–658. DOI: 10.1023/A:1024528427013.

Kinship

KEVIN HENDERSON
University of Massachusetts Amherst, USA

Kinship may signify any number of social arrangements that organize the reproduction of material and cultural life. Kinship frequently denotes the network of social and political relationships that are formed out of familial ties through rules governing marriage, reproduction, and descent. Historically, kinship has referred to the social organization of sexual relationships through sanction and taboo. However, new scholarship on kinship has attempted to think explicitly about political and social belonging and the reproduction of material life outside the circuits of sexuality and biological reproduction, or, at least, outside the networks of heterosexual sexuality and the nuclear family. Kinship now often refers to the social, communal, or intimate bonds that are formed out of the metaphors of family and friendship. Scholarship on kinship covers a wide terrain and variously examines how the organization of kinship ties produces wide-ranging meanings about culture, community, citizenship, race, sex, gender, legitimacy, the control and inheritance of property, honor and shame, and dependency.

The study of kinship has its roots in social anthropology. Early studies of kinship tended to treat kinship as the main characteristic of "primitive," pre-state, or pre-industrial societies. In these societies, kin relations were seen as the primary organizing feature of economic, political, and ceremonial life. Kinship studies were used to explain the origins of incest taboos, cross-cousin marriages, clans and sections, and differential modes of patrilineal or matrilineal descent. Although kin relations were seen to vary widely from culture to culture and are not a mere list of biological or genetic relatives for the very reason that they are cultural/social relations, kinship studies came under criticism for its overemphasis on "natural" relations. Kinship fell out of use in many anthropological schools in the second half of the twentieth century due to critiques that kinship was not a universal category that could be studied cross-culturally but was rather particular to Western culture. David Schneider (1984) critiqued the study of kinship for its basis in European epistemologies that rely heavily on the metaphor of *blood* and explain human behavior primarily through "natural" or "biological" facts.

Anthropologists of gender have expanded this critique for the ways in which many studies of kinship were rooted in assumptions about the natural characteristics of men and women and their supposed natural roles in sexual procreation. Feminist theorists both critiqued and deployed aspects of kinship studies to give an account of sexual oppression and compulsory heterosexuality.

Gayle Rubin (2011), in her landmark 1975 essay "The Traffic in Women," employs Lévi-Strauss's *The Elementary Structures of Kinship* (1969) to give an account of what she coined "sex/gender systems." Lévi-Strauss argues that kinship systems rest in the exchange of women between men in the form of gift exchange in marriages. Men give the gift of a daughter or a sister to another man in matrimony for the purposes of establishing kinship ties and the transfer of "sexual access, genealogical statuses, lineage names and ancestors, rights, and people." For Rubin, the subordination of women can be seen as a product of these relations of exchange through which sex and gender are produced and organized.

Rubin then turns to an examination of Freudian and Lacanian psychoanalysis for its explanation of the Oedipal drama, the moment when a child learns the sexual rules embedded in one's kinship system. Before the Oedipal phase, the sexuality of a child is relatively unstructured. The Oedipal crisis sets in when a child begins to comprehend the kinship system and his or her place within it. The crisis is resolved when the child accepts that place and accedes to it, with the child's libido and gender identity organized in conformity with the kinship rules of the culture. Culturally based kinship rules thus accounts for the gendering of individuals. Consequently, there is nothing natural or biological about gender or the division of sexes. For Rubin, "feminism must call for a revolution in kinship" to dismantle the sex/gender system.

Contemporary conceptions of kinship have largely been separated from the institution of marriage. For example, Carol Stack's study of urban African American kinship, *All Our Kin* (1974), examines how kinship functions through networks of women, some of whom are biological relatives, but many who are not. Studies of gay and lesbian kinship, typified by Kath Weston's *Families We Choose* (1991), have produced vast accounts of the informal kinship structures generated by non-married same-sex parents and the children they raise. Queer kinship studies, conversely, have examined queer communities that use metaphors of kinship outside of childrearing relations, such as communities of drag queens that pass on "family" names and practice mutual care, networks of former lovers in lesbian communities, and leather-kink communities that use the language of family. Tim Dean (2009) argues that gay men in "bareback" subcultures that do not use condoms understand the viral transmission of HIV in terms of kinship, albeit as an alternative to normative heterosexual kinship.

Although modern kinship has been thought as outside of marriage and the nuclear family, feminist legal scholars warn of the ways in which biologized kinship categories remain at the heart of the modern liberal nation state. Jacqueline Stevens (1999) has pointed to the ways in which bloodlines are still used to define citizenship by Western states. Martha Fineman (1995) contends that family law in the United States continues to be defined by the "sexual family," that is, the dyadic sexual affiliation between a man and a woman. Nontraditional unions or non-heterosexual relationships must, by analogy, be equated with the paradigmatic kinship structure of the dyadic heterosexual couple for state recognition.

Given that biological notions are still read into the concept of kinship, future directions in kinship studies will have to grapple with rapid changes in reproductive technologies and new issues surrounding transnational adoptions and surrogacy. Increases in transnational migrations along with new ways of reproducing human life are sure to change the meaning and structures of kinship and, thus, restructure the meanings and practices of family, community, and nation.

SEE ALSO: Community Other Mothers; Extended Families; Fictive Kin; Same-Sex Families

REFERENCES

Dean, Tim. 2009. *Unlimited Intimacy*. Chicago: University of Chicago Press.
Fineman, Martha. 1995. *The Neutered Mother, the Sexual Family, and Other Twentieth Century Tragedies*. New York: Routledge.
Lévi-Strauss, Claude. 1969. *The Elementary Structures of Kinship*, trans. James Herle Bell, John Richard von Sturmer, and Rodney Needham. Boston: Beacon Press.

Rubin, Gayle. 2011. "The Traffic in Women: Notes on the 'Political Economy' of Sex." In *Deviations: A Gayle Rubin Reader*. Durham, NC: Duke University Press.

Schneider, David. 1984. *A Critique of the Study of Kinship*. Ann Arbor: University of Michigan Press.

Stack, Carol. 1974. *All Our Kin: Strategies for Survival in a Black Community*. New York: Harper and Row.

Stevens, Jacqueline. 1999. *Reproducing the State*. Princeton: Princeton University Press.

Weston, Kath. 1991. *Families We Choose*. New York: Columbia University Press.

FURTHER READING

Butler, Judith. 2004. "Is Kinship Always Already Heterosexual?" In *Undoing Gender*. New York: Routledge.

Franklin, Sarah and Susan McKinnon, eds. 1997. *Relative Values: Reconfiguring Kinship Studies*. Durham, NC: Duke University Press.

Kothi

HARJANT GILL

Towson University, Maryland, USA

Kothi (also spelled *koti* and *khoti*) is an identity that in contemporary India and Bangladesh is used by many effeminate men to signal their preference for being receptive (bottom) partners during sexual intercourse among men who have sex with men (MSM). While kothi-identified men often term their penetrative (top) partner "panthi," unlike kothi, panthi is a classification that the penetrative partners rarely use as an identity. Recognized within sexual rights discourse in India as a distinct identity within the broader umbrella of MSM, kothi is often cited as the "indigenous" or "localized" counterpart to Western categories of gay and bisexual which have become more popular over the last two decades. Kothi-identified men are often not fluent in English and belong to poor or working class backgrounds. Poor and working class men can rarely afford to participate in the mainstream gay culture in India, much of which largely exists online (on English language websites) or is concentrated in urban bars and exclusive nightclubs. Several members of the kothi communities, as well as activists organizing for sexual rights, regard the importance of kothi identity as resisting the increasingly homogenizing influence of the "global gay" culture enabled by late twentieth and early twenty-first-century globalization (Altman 2001).

Being a kothi typically implies embodying feminine mannerisms and demeanor. However, unlike hijra-identified individuals, most of whom permanently embody the third gendered identity and many of whom undergo castration, kothi-identified men largely engage in stereotypical performances of femininity such as exaggerated limp wrist, hip-swaying, and sexual bantering. Kothis often deploy the feminine pronoun when referring to other kothis. Like many MSMs in India, many kothi-identified men are also married, have children, and live heteronormative lives when not embodying the kothi identity. Some hijras also refer to themselves as kothi (in addition to being hijra) by the virtue of desiring to be penetrated during sexual intercourse. However, they have regional distinction to distinguish themselves from kothi-identified men such as *kada-catla koti* (in Hyderabad), which refers to kothis who dress in masculine attire and do not undergo any sex-change operation (Reddy 2005, 219).

The origins of the term are ambiguous, but scholars have rooted it in South India where the term has several regional meanings (Cohen 2005; Reddy 2005). Kothi continues to be used as an epithet to demarcate effeminate male-bodied individuals, similar to terms like "fag" and "sissy." However, in the mid-1990s, kothi was co-opted as sexual identity within the institutional discourse of the NAZ Foundation, a non-governmental organization (NGO) which works on issues related to sexual health and HIV/AIDS prevention among MSMs in India. Popularization of kothi classification within the HIV/AIDS prevention models created a "rift" over resources and political ideologies between organizations working with MSMs (Cohen 2005; Gupta 2005; Boyce 2007).

In the late 1990s, as communities of kothis started claiming more visible space within the burgeoning sexual rights movement in India, playing active roles as outreach workers and peer educators in various HIV/AIDS prevention campaigns, many kothis also experienced prejudice and discrimination by members of mostly gay male social groups and organizations, some of whom refused to include kothi-identified men into their social space. Several men in Mumbai's gay male social groups stopped attending meetings and threatened to boycott nightclubs if kothis were allowed to participate (Gupta 2005). This divide between the members of mostly English-speaking middle-class gay communities and non-English speaking working-class kothi communities has exposed the fissures within the sexual rights activism in India, where class, caste, and gender differences continue to pervade, revealing a fractured movement with varying social and political agendas. Since the HIV/AIDS crisis, communities of kothis and hijras have organized around their chosen identities, demanding recognition within what is often called the "LGBTKQH movement," the later three letters of the acronym representing kothi, queer, and hijra (Gupta 2005).

Frequently singled out for for their gendered presentation, many kothi-identified men experience greater instances of homophobia and violence, adding to their sense of marginalization (Shah and Bondyopadhyay 2007). Issues such as low self-esteem often contribute to greater willingness to have unprotected sex, which places them at a higher risk of contracting HIV/AIDS (Seabrook 1999). Kothi-identified men have also reported experiencing greater discrimination in the workplace or when looking for employment. Many of the men who identify as kothi engage in sex work. Kothi sex workers are often harassed, robbed, and sexually assaulted by the police.

Learning from hijras, many kothi-identified men have started banding together to form communities of "neighborhood gangs" where members of a particular gang look out for each other's safety and well-being (Reddy 2005, 48). Since the Delhi High Court struck down colonial-era sodomy laws in 2009, decriminalizing homosexuality pending the Indian Supreme Court's review of the judgment, there has been a greater visibility of sexual and gender minorities overall. However, many kothi-identified men continue to face stigma and discrimination.

SEE ALSO: *Hijra/Hejira*; LGBT Activism in South Asia; Same-Sex Sexuality in India

REFERENCES

Altman, Dennis. 2001. *Global Sex*. Chicago: University of Chicago Press.

Boyce, Paul. 2007. "'Conceiving *Kothis*': Men Who Have Sex with Men in India and the Cultural Subject of HIV Prevention." *Medical Anthropology*, 26: 175–203. DOI: 10.1080/01459740701285582.

Cohen, Lawrence. 2005. "The Kothi Wars: AIDS Cosmopolitanism and the Morality of Classification." In *Sex in Development: Science, Sexuality and Morality in Global Perspective*, edited by Vincanne Adams and Stacy L. Piggs, 269–303. Durham, NC: Duke University Press.

Gupta, Alok. 2005. "*Englishpur ki* Kothi: Class Dynamics in the Queer Movement in India." In *Because I Have a Voice: Queer Politics in India*, edited by Arvind Narrain, and Gautam Bhan, 123–142. New Delhi: Yoda.

Reddy, Gayatri. 2005. *With Respect to Sex: Negotiating Hijra Identity in South India*. Chicago: University of Chicago Press.

Seabrook, Jeremy. 1999. *Love in a Different: Men Who Have Sex with Men in India*. New York: Verso.

Shah, Vidya, Aditya Bondyopadhyay, and Parthiv Shah. 2007. *My Body is Not Mine: Stories of Violence and Tales of Hope, Voices from Kothi Community in India*. New Delhi: Naz Foundation International.

Ladyboys

DREDGE BYUNG'CHU KÄNG
Emory University, USA

Ladyboy refers to transgender women (male to female), usually in Thailand, but the term is also used in the Philippines, and to a lesser extent in other parts of Southeast Asia such as Singapore, Malaysia, Vietnam, Cambodia, and Laos. The term is rarely employed outside Asia, though it is also used to refer to transgender Asian women in Western countries. It is a construction combining the English "lady" with "boy." Such use of English to express terms referring to gender and sexuality is common in Thai uses of English (Enteen 2010). Ladyboy is used as shorthand to simply render a diverse range of local gender variations such as Thai *kathoey* or Filipina *bakla*. The term evolved from the context of tourism and contact with foreigners.

Ladyboy is generally not a gender identity but a label applied in settings involving contact with foreigners. In Thailand, the term is thus used synonymously with kathoey, the common term for a transgender woman. However, this encompasses a wide range of gender presentations and identities (Käng 2012). Other common terms that are more likely to constitute an identity include *sao-praphet-sorng* (second-category woman) and *phu-ying-kham-phet* (transsexual woman). Many ladyboys just as well refer to themselves as women. One difference in the categorization of "ladyboy" in the Philippines and in Thailand is that in the Philippines, a ladyboy can also be referred to as a "gay," since "gay" can encompass transgender people, whereas this is not the case in Thailand.

The term ladyboy is mostly applied to cabaret shows, sex tourism, and pornography (like "shemale" or "tranny"). While some transgender women, especially those in relationships with foreigners, will refer to themselves as a ladyboy, the term is considered stereotypical and offensive by some transgender women because of its associations with sex work (Käng 2012). Ladyboy is a neutral descriptor in workplaces such as cabarets and bars, where use of the term is commonplace. Ladyboy has its most positive appraisal in beauty pageants, the largest and most famous of which are tied to cabarets such as Tiffany. Their annual international beauty pageant is broadcast nationally in Thailand with wide viewership. Ladyboy beauty pageants are a common fixture of life in both urban and rural areas in Thailand and the Philippines. These pageants can also be integrated with local religious activities, such as Filipino Santacruzan festivals or Thai temple fairs.

Ladyboy cabarets such as Alcazar, Calypso, and Simon are among the most popular

The Wiley Blackwell Encyclopedia of Gender and Sexuality Studies, First Edition. Edited by Nancy A. Naples.
© 2016 John Wiley & Sons, Ltd. Published 2016 by John Wiley & Sons, Ltd.

attractions for tourists in Thailand and promote the "amazing" character and distinctiveness of Thailand. All major tourist destinations in Thailand (e.g., Bangkok, Pattaya, Chiang Mai, Phuket, and Samui) will have at least one ladyboy cabaret show. Ladyboy cabarets are also popular in the Philippines. While highlighting their beauty, the hook that ladyboys were born male also presents them like a freak show. Their popularity in Thailand has spread on the mainland Southeast Asian tourist circuit to neighboring Cambodia, where Phnom Penh and Siem Reap now both have ladyboy cabarets. Thai ladyboy cabarets also travel to play at venues throughout Europe and Asia, while Filipino ladyboys perform as contract entertainers in Japan.

The representations of ladyboys in Thailand are complex. They are often stereotyped as criminals in news reports. Their primary role in films is comic or tragic. At the same time, Thais often express great admiration and awe for ladyboys' "*wer*" (exceptional) beauty, claiming that cabaret performers, beauty contestants, and stars possess extreme physical characteristics unattainable for "real" women. In Thailand, cosmetic surgery and other processes of self-transformation are often valorized rather than stigmatized. Therefore, feminization for ladyboys can be positively viewed. The various transformations of the body including use of cosmetics and women's clothing, growing long hair, removal of facial and body hair, use of hormone pills or injections, breast implants, other injections and surgeries to modify the shape of various facial and body features (e.g., shaving the Adam's apple, lifting the eyebrows, enlarging the hips), and vaginoplasty all come at a high cost, which is associated with class status (Aizura 2009). Unfortunately, ladyboys often are unaware of or ignore the health risks and disfigurement associated with excessive use of hormones, home injection of silicone and oils, and surgeries provided without proper medical supervision or post-care instructions (e.g., use of antibiotics to prevent infection, bandaging, or dilation of the neo-vagina).

Southeast Asia is generally considered to be more tolerant of transgender people than other regions of the world (Peletz 2009). This is considered especially true in Thailand and the Philippines. Thus, there is a tautological explanation for the high numbers of ladyboys in these areas. There are many ladyboys because they are accepted. Ladyboys are accepted because there are many of them. However, high tolerance does not mean that ladyboys are free from discrimination, stigma, or violence. There are also different perceptions of acceptance from outsiders and insiders. While internationally circulating Thai films such as *Beautiful Boxer* and *Iron Ladies* suggest to foreigners that Thailand is very tolerant of transgender people, Western viewers who have seen popular Thai films such as *Sassy Players* or *Haunting Me* that never get exported would be offended at the portrayals (Käng 2011).

Ladyboys are generally limited to a number of professions in beauty salons, food service, entertainment, and sex work. Contrary to some popular Western accounts, ladyboys do not become transgender in order to gain lucrative employment. In Thailand, ladyboys are often stereotyped as sex workers and stigmatized in tourist areas. A ladyboy can be arrested simply for being with a Caucasian man, on the presumption that she is a sex worker. Ladyboys are often not admitted to hotels and some dance clubs frequented by tourists. The rationale is that ladyboys are either sex workers or thieves, thus in the latter case, foreigners must be protected from them. By Thai law, a transgender person does not have the ability to change their sex, even after sex reassignment surgery. Thus ladyboy national identification cards state they are male and they can be denied entry because their gender does not match their sex.

Ladyboys generally consider sexual relationships with other ladyboys to be repulsive. As they typically identify with heterosexual femininity (even if they are not gender normative), they seek masculine male partners. For the most part, partners of ladyboys, both local and foreign, consider themselves to be heterosexual men. Though they should not be stereotyped as such nor devalued for their occupation, a large proportion of ladyboys are sex workers. Ladyboy sex workers, both in Thailand and the Philippines, often state a preference for foreigners as both clients and boyfriends. Ladyboys can earn more money from foreigners as clients. Additionally, there are different expectations among local and foreign boyfriends. A local boyfriend would expect to be supported financially by the ladyboy, while she can expect to be supported by a foreigner. This can also lead to tiered relationships, in which a ladyboy has a foreign partner (typically older) who supports her, and she, in turn, supports her local lover (typically younger). Local partners of ladyboys are generally considered low class or lazy because of the support they receive.

Foreign partners tend to fetishize ladyboys. Many are explicitly looking for "a woman with a penis." Thus, in Thai ladyboy bars, sex workers are required to be pre-operative. However, both pre-operative and post-operative ladyboys can work in girl bars with other women or as independent freelancers on the street. This creates a great deal of anxiety among male sex tourists who are repulsed by the idea of having sex with another "man." Such men will often pass on tips to other foreigners for signs of someone being a ladyboy. This includes excessively beautiful and voluptuous women, being too feminine or too masculine, tall height, looking for Adam's apples and low-pitched voices, big feet or large hands, comparing finger lengths, checking the shape of elbows, making sure she is wearing a bra, and, as a last resort, groping her genitals (assuming one only cares if a ladyboy is pre-operative). Their anxieties prove their masculinity. On the other hand, there are many foreign men who think of the situation as local spice, something to try out in a situation where it is available.

SEE ALSO: Kathoey; Sex Tourism

REFERENCES

Aizura, Aren Z. 2009. "Where Health and Beauty Meet: Femininity and Racialisation in Thai Cosmetic Surgery Clinics." *Asian Studies Review*, 33: 303–317. DOI: 10.1080/10357820903153707.

Enteen, Jillana B. 2010. *Virtual English: Queer Internets and Digital Creolization*. New York: Routledge.

Käng, Dredge Byung'chu. 2011. "Queer Media Loci in Bangkok: Paradise Lost and Found in Translation." *GLQ: A Journal of Lesbian and Gay Studies*, 17(1): 169–191. DOI 10.1215/10642684-2010-027.

Käng, Dredge Byung'chu. 2012. "*Kathoey* 'In Trend': Emergent Genderscapes, National Anxieties and the Re-Signification of Male-Bodied Effeminacy in Thailand." Theme issue, "Queer Asian Subjects," *Asian Studies Review*, 36(4): 475–494. DOI: 10.1080/10357823.2012.741043.

Peletz, Michael. 2009. *Gender Pluralism: Southeast Asia since Early Modern Times*. New York: Routledge.

FURTHER READING

Jackson, Peter A., and Gerard Sullivan, eds. 1999. *Lady Boys, Tom Boys, Rent Boys: Male and Female Homosexualities in Contemporary Thailand*. New York: Harrington Park Press.

Language and Gender

ANN WEATHERALL
Victoria University of Wellington, New Zealand

This topic is about the connections between gender as a social category and language.

The relationships are complex and the topic has attracted considerable debate. A feminist perspective is pervasive in gender and language studies and importantly highlights the ideological or political nature of language. Robyn Lakoff's landmark publication *Language and Woman's Place* (1975) noted women's secondary position in society is reflected both in the ways they speak and the ways they are spoken of. Since then, significant shifts have occurred within the field. There have been fundamental changes in the way gender is theorized – from being understood as a biological categorization to one that is socially and culturally produced. Now, constructionism is a widely accepted way of conceptualizing gender identity. It posits language and discourse produce rather than reflect gendered meanings. The theoretical shift has brought with it a greater focus on diversity and pluralism. Research now tends to examine gender and language in particular linguistic contexts. Studies now examine identities within gender categories (e.g., women leaders, new men) and non-normative or queer sexual identities. With an increasingly globalized world, a much broader range of linguistic and cultural contexts has come under examination. Furthermore, new media such as online environments are also providing fruitful areas for innovative research.

Despite theoretical shifts in the field, Lakoff's (1975) work set an agenda for gender and language research. One topic is sexism in language. Early work documented how structural elements of language – for instance, grammar and vocabulary – ignored or negatively stereotyped women. Since then research has broadened to examine different languages and linguistic representations in different contexts including educational texts, self-help books, and advertising materials. A second theme is gendered patterns of speech. Claims of gender differences abound in academic and popular literature. However, there is neither consensus on what differentiates women's speech from men's, nor is there agreement on possible causes. One proposal has been to stop asking about differences, because such questions rest on flawed assumptions about the nature of gender identity and its relationships to language. Gender difference remains an important albeit controversial area in feminist language studies.

GENDER DIFFERENCES IN SPEECH

The topic of gender differences in language has a long history. Anthropological investigations in the nineteenth century described the existence of women's languages in "exotic" cultures. In the early twentieth century, linguistic experts suggested women's language abilities were fitted to their secondary role in society. At around the same time psychological investigations suggested sex differences in brain structure could be mapped to differences in language abilities. Much of the earliest work assumed gender differences in language arose out of natural or biological differences between the sexes.

The naturalness of gender differences and their interpretation as deficiencies in women were called into question with the feminist movement of the 1970s. Claims about men's natural superiority were dismissed as sexist and unscientific. Power – specifically male dominance in society – as well as sex-specific socialization processes were emphasized as better explanations for differences in language use than biological causes. There is now a general consensus that gendered patterns of language use have sociocultural origins rather than biological ones. Nevertheless, biological explanations persist in some academic and popular accounts. For example, evolutionary explanations have become widespread as a way of accounting for sex differences in verbal ability – even while the exact nature and extent of that difference remains controversial.

Assertions of a clear distinction between the language of women and that of men are now generally accepted as exaggerated. So-called women's languages only gave that impression because of the particular ways gender can be marked in the structures of language, such as in the pronoun and kinship systems. Furthermore, it is generally accepted that no definitive characteristics distinguish men's speech from women's speech. Candidate features of difference including the use of intensifiers, hedges, and particular lexical items have all been found to be multifunctional and used in the speech of both women and men. Even voice pitch has been questioned as a clear marker of gender of the speaker. The pitch range individual speakers are generally capable of means that both women and men can talk with high and deep voices. Transgender individuals easily adjust their voices to be consistent with their gender identity.

Although there are no direct and exclusive indexes of gender in speech, the idea of gendered patterns of speech is still widely accepted. The term "genderlect" has been coined to refer to a cluster of linguistic features that typically, although not exclusively, are associated with the speech of women and men. Quantitative research on language attitudes experimentally manipulates speech to get clear examples of masculine and feminine genderlects. Those studies find genderlects are differently evaluated on measures of power and likeability. The influence of gendered language use on impression formation shows the persistence of gender stereotyping.

Debates about the reality of actual gender differences in speech aside, there have been two competing theoretical explanations for gender differences in speech. They are known as the dominance and cultural approaches, respectively (Weatherall 2002). The dominance approach primarily uses power to explain differences. For example, men's dominance on the conversational floor can be understood as reflecting their pervasive social advantage in both public and private spheres. Women's deferential speaking style can be cast both as powerless and as evidence of their skillfulness at building interpersonal rapport. The cultural approach proposes the existence of gendered subcultures where boys and girls learn gender-typical speech behaviors. The cultural approach became a popular way of understanding supposed miscommunication between women and men (Tannen 1991).

Women's supposed powerless speech style importantly fueled a communication training industry designed to teach assertiveness. Feminists noted that communication training programs were more often targeted at women rather than men, implying their language was deficient and not men's. Furthermore, it has been shown that the idea of cross-gender miscommunication has emerged as a possible defense in cases of rape allegations.

An important additional way of understanding gender difference in language is a communities of practice approach. According to this view gender-differentiated ways of speaking are not generalizable because they are particular to local and social organizations (Eckert and McConnell-Ginet 2003). For example, different communities vary in the ways activities such as work and sport are stratified by gender, which influences social contact and the emergence of gender-differentiated linguistic variation. The spread of particular linguistic variants across language communities has been shown to be linked to patterns of social interaction, which are also influenced by particular and local social identifications such as "jocks" and "burnouts" (Eckert 1990). Research drawing on the communities of practice approach doesn't ask about gender difference; rather, it examines the difference gender makes.

SEXISM AND LANGUAGE

A second topic in gender and language studies that also has a long history is language and sexism. Great women throughout history have challenged the ways in which women are represented in language. Perhaps the earliest example is from the twelfth century when a Benedictine abbess, St. Hildegard of Bingen, purportedly attempted to construct a non-sexist language. Well-known feminist philosopher Simone de Beauvoir noted that in male-dominated cultures language tends to define women narrowly and negatively. Lakoff (1975) documented specific examples of male bias in English. For instance, male-specific terms (e.g., chairman and man) are also used generically to refer to women. Another example is that for equivalent reference terms, words for women tend to have negative or sexual connotations – compare bachelor with spinster and master with mistress. Other languages such as French, German, and Spanish mark gender and reflect a male bias in different ways.

A central theoretical issue underpinning discussions of sexism and language is the relationships between language, thought, and reality. According to a theory of linguistic relativity, sexist language can lead to biased thinking and result in discrimination against women. Linguistic relativity supports calls for non-sexist language policies in written publications such as newspapers and educational materials because language can shape thought. A different perspective argues that language simply reflects thought, in which case social change would precede language change and not the reverse. Either way, linguistic activism highlights and challenges language practices that encode social bias. Feminist language planners have documented sexism and agitate for the establishment of non-sexist language policies. More recently, a different but related concern has emerged, which is the way language can be understood as being homophobic and carrying implicit assumptions that people are heterosexual.

FROM ESSENTIALISM TO CONSTRUCTIONISM

The founding concerns of gender and language studies were underpinned by a set of ideas that can be glossed as essentialism. Questions of gender differences in language assume identity is some kind of essence within a person that expresses itself in speech. The idea that language reflects the nature of things is also part of concerns about sexist language. Assuming language is simply representational is associated with an essentialist theoretical perspective. One of its assumptions is a relatively straightforward referential relationship between words and the world, as it exists. A different but related aspect of essentialist thinking in gender and language studies is the biologically based classification of sex that underpins the gender categorizations used in research – men are male bodied and women are female bodied.

An alternative view to essentialism is constructionism. The concept of language is expanded by a constructionism perspective. Constructionist theory conceptualizes language as discourse – a nexus of power and knowledge that *produces* meaning and makes actions intelligible. For example, "corrective" genital surgery on intersex infants only makes sense within a cultural world where a gender-differentiated society rests on a binary, biologically based categorization system.

From a constructionist perspective, research that asks about gender differences in speech is posing the wrong questions. Investigating differences assumes stable gender categories underpin speech behavior patterns. However, according to a constructionist view speech doesn't reveal identity; rather, discourses produce the notion of gendered speech. If beliefs about women's and men's speech are conceptualized as different but related to how people actually do speak, then it explains why the exact nature of gendered speech styles has remained elusive. Ideas about women's language as different from men's language are produced by gender discourses, not directly related to how women and men actually speak.

The distinction between sexist language and gendered speech made in the foundational questions asked in gender and language studies collapses with a constructionist view. Language about women and men and the ways women and men speak are both aspects of discourses that produce gender as a social construction. The rise of constructionist ideas revitalized research into gender and language. One new strand of research asks about the overarching discourses that people use to make sense of the world and legitimate it. For example, a "discourse of gender difference" is pervasive. Advertisements for children's toys are one example of the ways a discourse of difference can manifest. Toys for boys, such as Action Man, are described in terms of adventure and action. In contrast, girls' toys such as Barbie dolls are described in more passive terms (Baker 2008) for explaining gender roles in society.

An important aspect of a constructionist view is the insight that gender discourses have a regulatory function. For example, gender discourses produce binary thinking about biological sex – that there are two and only two gender categories (women and men). One result is a practice where infants who are born with genital "anomalies" are surgically "corrected" so they are more clearly and unambiguously "male" or "female." The social marginalization of people who do not neatly fit into normative gender categories (e.g., feminine men, women leaders) is evidence of the power of normative gender discourses. As a result there has been an increasing interest in sexuality in gender and language research (Livia and Hall 1997).

The rise of constructionism also poses a challenge for gender and language studies. It is a theoretical approach that challenges and undermines the very categories that are its focus of interest. One response to the challenge is to reiterate that gender as a social categorization still works to disadvantage women, so understanding how that disadvantage is managed linguistically remains a vital area of research. Baxter's (2010) research is a good example of the continued importance of examining women's language. She importantly documents the kinds of language challenges and linguistic strategies women leaders in masculine occupations face in their day-to-day work.

FUTURE DIRECTIONS

The development of new information and communication technologies provides exciting new areas for gender and language research. Studies of new social media are drawing upon constructionist ideas to examine how text and images call into play established ideas about gender but are also productive in generating new gendered social categories. Gender and media studies document the emergence of new femininities and masculinities such as "ladettes" and "metrosexuals." Feminism remains an important critical approach that can trace how old patterns of social inequality continue or how new ones emerge.

Law of the Father

MARY MURRAY
Massey University, New Zealand

The "law of the father" is a term usually associated with the work of Jacques Lacan in his psychoanalytic account of the way in which children enter into patriarchal culture. Lacan identified three phases of psychosocial development involved in this process: the "imaginary order," the "mirror stage," and the "symbolic order." The imaginary order is a pre-linguistic, pre-Oedipal state of being. Babies experience a pleasurable and satisfying merging with the maternal body, experiencing no sense of separation and making no distinction between self and m/other. According to Lacan, at the age of about 6–8 months old the baby enters the "mirror stage." In the "mirror stage" the baby develops a unitary body image and unified, (though not yet separate) sense of selfhood. This occurs via a "mirror" which may be experienced/perceived on or via the mother's body. The "symbolic order" coincides with the Freudian Oedipal crisis. At this point unity between child and mother is split by entry of the father, and can involve repression of desire for the mother on the part of female and male children. Acquisition of language may coincide with the "symbolic order" (though some children may develop language a little later) and is fundamental to the development of conscious and unconscious realms of the psyche. Whereas Freud emphasized sexual prohibition within the family, Lacan emphasized the role of the father in enforcing the cultural law of the father, including the social taboo on incest, and the domain of received social meanings, logic, and gendered differentiation. The imaginary unity of the infant and mother is torn apart due to the intrusive impact of wider cultural and social processes.

Despite significant theoretical shifts in gender and language research, the foundational concerns retain relevance for languages other than English and in communities and cultures where some or all women have not benefited from some of the changes wrought by feminist movements. It is likely that feminist language research will lose its global significance only when all traces of gender as a category that organizes society are gone.

SEE ALSO: Androcentrism; Discourse and Gender; Essentialism; Gender Difference Research; Genderlect; Non-Sexist Language Use; Sexism in Language

REFERENCES

Baker, Paul. 2008. *Sexed Texts: Language, Gender and Sexuality*. London: Equinox.
Baxter, Judith. 2010. *Language of Female Leadership*. New York: Palgrave Macmillan.
Eckert, Penelope. 1990. *Linguistic Variation as Social Practice*. Oxford: Blackwell.
Eckert, Penelope, and Sally McConnell-Ginet. 2003. *Language and Gender*. New York: Cambridge University Press.
Lakoff, Robin. 1975. *Language and Woman's Place*. New York: Harper and Row.
Livia, Anna, and Kira Hall. 1997. *Queerly Phrased: Language, Gender and Sexuality*. New York: Oxford University Press.
Tannen, Deborah. 1991. *You Just Don't Understand: Women and Men in Conversation*. London: Virago.
Weatherall, Ann. 2002. *Gender, Language and Discourse*. London: Routledge.

FURTHER READING

Bucholtz, Mary. 2004. *Language and Woman's Place: Text and Commentaries*. Oxford: Oxford University Press.
Cameron, Deborah. 1998. "Gender, Language and Discourse: A Review Essay." *Signs*, 23(4): 945–967.
Crawford, Mary. 1995. *Talking Difference*. London: Sage.
Holmes, Janet, and Miriam Meyerhoff, eds. 2003. *Blackwell Handbook for Language and Gender*. Oxford: Blackwell.

According to Lacan, the law of the father is symbolized by his phallus. Due to their relationship to the phallus – women "lack" a penis – females make a negative entry into the symbolic order, which for Lacan is patriarchal.

Lacan's work has been contested to the extent that it has been interpreted as a justification for patriarchal social relationships, as well as being developed and utilized by feminists, particularly French feminists such as Irigaray, Cixous, and Kristeva. For example, whilst utilizing aspects of his conceptual framework, Julia Kristeva suggests adjustments or modifications to Lacan's position. Kristeva refers to an early "semiotic" pre-Oedipal phase of psychosocial development as an "anarchic" feminine phase (though not feminine in the sense of a fixed gendered identity) dominated by the mother's body. Kristeva sees the Oedipal "symbolic" law of the father as ordered, regulated, and rule governed; based on the repression of the anarchic/chaotic semiotic phase, the symbolic ensures a cohesive, unified speaking subject. However, for Kristeva, repression of the semiotic cannot be completely, if at all, guaranteed as semiotic pressures can rupture into the symbolic order. Kristeva perceives that desire for the archaic mother may not be fully repressed by the symbolic law of the father and can be interrupted by the semiotic. In this respect she cites, for example, music, writing (such as that by James Joyce in his stream-of-consciousness work *Ulysses*), poetry, madness, and revolutionary politics as semiotic irruptions and transgressive breaches of the apparent coherence of the symbolic law of the father. According to this perspective the law of the father, in the sense of patriarchal social structures and gender roles and relations, may never be as complete as it may seem in the analysis of the law of the father offered by Lacan.

Marxist feminists have also utilized the work of Lacan. In *Psychoanalysis and Feminism* (1974), for example, Juliet Mitchell suggests that Lacan was not advocating patriarchal relationships in his argument about the law of the father. Rather, Mitchell interprets Lacan's argument as an analysis of how patriarchal social structures and gendered relations occur in the process of psychosocial development of children. Later, in 1995, in a book entitled *The Law of The Father?* which focused on gender relations in the transition from feudalism to capitalism in England, Mary Murray looked at the unequal gender relations enshrined in law, especially property relations. Murray sees such relations as upholding both the material interests of class as well as those of patriarchy, even though the primary motivation for laws such as primogeniture (inheritance from the father by the eldest son) may have been to maintain property within the descent group rather than to explicitly disadvantage women. Murray also notes subsequent challenges to property laws that were both classed and gendered, which could of course be interpreted as challenges to aspects of the law of the father.

SEE ALSO: Gender Development, Feminist Psychoanalytic Perspectives on; Oedipal Conflict

REFERENCES

Mitchell, Juliet. 1974. *Psychoanalysis and Feminism*. New York: Vintage Books.
Murray, Mary. 1995. *The Law of the Father?* London: Routledge.

FURTHER READING

Grosz, Elizabeth. 1990. *Jacques Lacan: A Feminist Introduction*. London: Routledge.
Kristeva, Julia. 1990. *Julia Kristeva*. London: Routledge.

Leadership and Gender

RANGITA DE SILVA DE ALWIS
Global Women's Leadership Initiative, USA

Ann Friedman's "Why Female Politicians Aren't Always Pro-Women" challenges the notion that gender parity in politics is important because women lead differently from men. Friedman (2013, 4) writes that "Personally, I'm uncomfortable with the idea that a woman is biologically predisposed to govern or is discernibly different from a man of the same political persuasion." It is true that biological difference has not been scientifically proven. However, there is some research indicating that women do in fact lead differently. It has been argued that women leaders are seen as more accommodating (Chapman 1975) and more invested in interpersonal dynamics (Gardiner and Tiggemann 1999). These differences can be traced in concrete policies, treaties, constitutions, and laws.

A review of the 24 peace processes taking place between 1992 and 2010 shows that female representation was as low as 2.5 percent of signatories to peace treaties and 7.6 percent of negotiating parties.

On justice and reparation, women's statements seek accountability for gender-based violence and an end to impunity for crimes of sexual violence in war.

Women's recommendations have included an explicit demand that national governments recognize the impact of conflict on women and girls. In El Salvador in the 1990s, because the reinsertion Commission was constituted of six women and one man, women made up one third of the beneficiaries of land distribution and reintegration packages. There is a correlation between the participation of women and greater gender responsiveness in peace treaties (United Nations Entity for Gender Equality and the Empowerment of Women 2012).

On a global scale, there is also a correlation between the participation of women and gender responsive laws and policies. In India, the percentage of women elected leaders at the local government level has increased from less than 5 percent in 1992 to over 40 percent in 2000. Evidence shows that women in elected office in India are more likely to invest in public infrastructure – particularly safe drinking water – and are less likely to feed into corruption than their male counterparts. In their book *Energising Rural Development Through "Panchayats,"* scholars Bibek Debroy and Pitambar Datta Kaushik (2005, 170) outline the ways that women are changing local government in India:

> Some of the ways in which women are changing governance are evident in the issues they choose to tackle like water, alcohol abuse, education, health, and domestic violence. Women also express different values. Women value proximity whether it be a drinking water source, a fuel source, a crèche, a health center, a court of justice, or a court of administration.

The correlation between women's leadership and development outcomes is made clear by Raghabendra Chattopadhyay and Esther Duflo's (2004) research which shows that there was less corruption and more access to public goods in India's villages where council head positions were reserved for women.

Ellen Johnson Sirleaf, president of Liberia and Nobel Prize winner, is an example of a woman in leadership who has made a big impact. On day one of her first term as President, she discussed the taboo issue of rape in her inauguration speech, placing women and the issue of violence against women at the forefront of her presidency and thus creating a new discourse on leadership.

Because women were present at the process of negotiating the new Constitution in South Africa, the preamble of the Constitution contains a clause explaining gender oppression and its impact on society, in addition to an equality clause and a provision to protect women from cultural practices that discriminated against them, and a recognition of reproductive rights.

Having women in positions of leadership also changes the culture of justice. When there are women at the table, legislatures enact policies and measures that advance the development of women, their families, and their countries. Rwanda boasts the highest proportion of women parliamentarians in the world. Working across party lines, Rwanda's Forum of Women Parliamentarians (FFRP) helped to pass a law combating violence against women. When the number of women in the Costa Rican parliament reached a critical mass of over 30 percent, a General Law on the Protection of Adolescent Mothers was promulgated to provide free health services and education to young women. In Tanzania, a gender quota was enacted to ensure that women held no less than 20 percent of the seats in parliament. Because of women's presence, an amendment to the Land Act grants women equal access to land, loans, and credit. In the United States, women leaders have helped to pass bills that make women and families more secure including the Violence Against Women Act of 1994 and the Family and Medical Leave Act of 1993.

Other measures have enhanced assistance for survivors of domestic violence, increased penalties for batterers, supported federal rape-shield laws to protect rape victims, and furthered policies on payments of child support by non-custodial parents. In many cases, it was only after women took their place in Congress that critical issues such as healthcare, childcare and support, sexual harassment, domestic violence, and gender-based wage differentials were given priority.

Women's leadership makes a difference in the higher echelons of business. McKinsey's long-standing global research shows that companies with a higher ratio of women in top management positions tend to exhibit better organization and financial performance (Desvaux et al. 2008).

In the public sector, diversity of thought, experience and perspective are important to respond to some of the most complex issues from the economy to climate change, to job creation. Diversity at leadership levels in our parliaments and in government departments will increase the chances of finding solutions.

Although only 3 percent of Fortune 500 CEOs are women, McKinsey studies show that because of women's work in the marketplace America's GDP is approximately 25 percent higher than it would have been without women. Goldman Sachs argues that eliminating the remaining gap between male and female employment rates could boost GDP in America by a total of 9 percent, in the Eurozone by 13 percent, and in Japan by as much as 16 percent. Recent studies also show that higher numbers of women in executive positions can result in a higher rate of return on equity for corporations (Catalyst 2007; Catalyst "Why Diversity Matters" 2013). A Catalyst ("First Step" 2013) study stated that over time, a 10% increase in female board membership is associated with a 21% increase in female executive presence in companies.

When women lead, Kim Campbell, the former prime minister of Canada, argues that it enables men to be more of the things they want to be. She maintains that many men are not at their best in male-dominated organizations, and points out that when more women began to be elected to the House of Commons, the House stopped night sittings, and most men relished the opportunity to spend more time with their families. She writes, "It was the presence of women that began to push against the way the institution was created. Institutions are created by the people who inhabit them and have a voice in creating the institution's structure" (Campbell 2003, 125).

SEE ALSO: Convention on the Elimination of All Forms of Discrimination against Women; Customary Laws; Economic Globalization and Gender; Employment Discrimination; Governance and Gender; Gender, Politics, and the State: Overview; Glass Ceiling and Glass Elevator

REFERENCES

Campbell, Kim. 2003. "Different Rulers – Different Rules." In *The Difference "Difference" Makes: Women and Leadership*, edited by Deborah L. Rhode, 121–126. Stanford: Stanford University Press.

Catalyst. 2007. "The Bottom Line: Corporate Performance and Women's Representation on Boards." Accessed September 4, 2015, at http://catalyst.org/system/files/The_Bottom_Line_Corporate_Performance_and_Womens_Representation_on_Boards.pdf.

Catalyst. 2013a. "First Step: Gender Diversity at the Top Pays Off." Accessed September 4, 2015, at http://www.catalyst.org/system/files/first_step_gender_diversity_at_the_top.pdf.

Catalyst. 2013b. "Why Diversity Matters." Accessed September 4, 2015, at http://www.catalyst.org/system/files/why_diversity_matters_catalyst_0.pdf.

Chapman, J. Brad. 1975. "Comparison of Male and Female Leadership Styles." *Academy of Management Journal*, 18(3): 645–650.

Chattopadhyay, Raghabendra and Esther Duflo. 2004. "Women as Policy Makers: Evidence from a Randomized, Policy Experiment in India." *Econometrica*, 72(5): 1409–1443.

Debroy, Bibek, and Pitambar Datta Kaushik. 2005. *Energising Rural Development through "Panchayats."* New Delhi: Academic Foundation.

Desvaux, Georges, Sandrine Devillard-Hoellinger, and Mary C. Meaney. 2008. "A Business Case for Women." McKinsey & Company. Accessed September 4, 2015, at http://www.talentnaardetop.nl/uploaded_files/document/2008_A_business_case_for_women.pdf.

Friedman, Ann. 2013. "Why Female Politicians Aren't Always Pro-Women." *The Cut, New York Magazine*, April 9. Accessed September 4, 2015, at http://nymag.com/thecut/2013/04/why-female-politicians-arent-always-pro-women.html.

Gardiner, Maria and Marika Tiggemann. 1999. "Gender Differences in Leadership Style, Job Stress and Mental Health in Male- and Female-Dominated Industries." *Journal of Occupational and Organizational Psychology*, 72(3): 301–315.

Haraway, Donna J. 1994. "A Game of Cat's Cradle: Science Studies, Feminist Theory, Cultural Studies." *Configurations*, 2(1): 59–71.

United Nations Entity for Gender Equality and the Empowerment of Women. 2012. "Women's Participation in Peace Negotiations: Connections between Presence and Influence." Accessed September 4, 2015, at http://www.unwomen.org/~/media/headquarters/attachments/sections/library/publications/2012/10/wps sourcebook-03a-womenpeacenegotiations-en.pdf.

FURTHER READING

de Silva de Alwis, Rangita. 2013. "Why Women's Leadership Is the Cause of Our Time." *UCLA Journal of International Lay and Foreign Affairs*, 18(1): 87–124.

Kellerman, Barbara, and Deborah L. Rhode, eds. 2007. *Women and Leadership: The State of Play and Strategies for Change*, 1st ed. San Francisco: Jossey-Bass.

Rhode, Deborah, ed. 2003. *The Difference "Difference" Makes: Women and Leadership*, 1st ed. Stanford: Stanford Law and Politics.

The World Bank. 2011. *World Development Report 2012: Gender Equality and Development*. Washington, DC: The World Bank.

Leftist Armed Struggle, Women in

KATHARINA KARCHER
University of Cambridge, UK

The active involvement of women constitutes a distinctive feature of revolutionary leftist movements. Although women have played a part in armed conflicts and radical political movements throughout history, they tended to be outnumbered by men and have rarely played leading roles in armed political struggles. Revolutionary leftist groups in many parts of the world have broken with this tradition. Since the late nineteenth century, women have not only constituted a significant part of their membership (in some cases even the majority), they have also taken central positions in these organizations. The testimonies of female militants indicate that these revolutionary leftist movements were by no means free from sexist behavior and patriarchal structures, but they offered women possibilities and opportunities that states and other social institutions denied them because of their sex.

Although research on female involvement in armed political struggles still accounts for a relatively small part of the literature on political violence, it makes a critical contribution to this field of study. In the post-9/11 period, much attention has been paid to the activities of Islamist terrorist groups, which include rape, torture, killings, and other horrific attacks against women. There can be no doubt that it remains important to document and combat such crimes. Yet, it is equally important to acknowledge that women are not just passive victims of political violence. Women from a range of countries have expressed support for al-Qaeda, Islamic State of Iraq and the Levant (ISIL), and other Islamist terrorist groups. Although no more than a few women have participated in armed actions by these groups, they constitute up to 35% of the Kurdish militants, who have been fighting in the armed wing of the left-wing Kurdish Democratic Union Party against ISIL in Syria and Iraq (Dirik 2014). Since there is a tendency in the Western media to sexualize and exoticize female militants in the Women's Defense Units in Syria and in other armed struggles, critical research in this area has a double role to play: on the one hand, it seeks to contribute to a better understanding of the personal and political background, objectives, and experiences of female militants and of their roles in particular political conflicts; on the other, it has to challenge the gendered stereotypes about political violence that are reinforced by many journalists.

Like their male counterparts, women have participated in armed political struggles for a range of reasons, and they have identified with different theoretical and ideological positions. This brief overview could hardly reflect the vast range of leftist ideologies and armed leftist struggles, and it is not intended to be exhaustive. It focuses on socialist and anarchist movements in Europe. All of the groups discussed here have in common that they considered the use of revolutionary violence legitimate and necessary to fight for a more egalitarian society, but not all of them identified as part of the political "left." It should also be mentioned that women have played an active role in anti-colonial struggles and in guerrilla movements in Africa, Latin America, Asia, and the Middle East. Once regarded as public enemies, female members of the military wing of the African National Congress in South Africa and other African liberation movements are now celebrated as "flowers of the revolution" (Dlodlo 2011). In the second half of the twentieth century, thousands of women in Chile, Uruguay, Nicaragua, Cuba, El Salvador, Mexico, Peru, and other Latin American countries took up arms to fight for leftist guerrillas. Owing to its geographic focus, this entry can only touch upon movements outside Europe, but the references section includes suggestions for further reading.

One of the first political struggles in Europe in which women played a prominent role was the French Revolution from 1789 to 1799. In revolutionary France, female militants made their presence felt not only in literary salons and political clubs but also in armed rebellions (e.g., the march on Versailles on October 5, 1789). Inspired by feminist ideas and the egalitarian spirit of the *Declaration of the Rights of Man* from 1789, Olympe de Gouges (1748–1793) and other prominent members of the revolutionary movement demanded equal rights for female citizens, but their calls for gender equality were brutally suppressed. The new republic reinforced traditional gender norms: women were confined to a subordinate domestic role. The French case shows that the active participation of women in revolutionary movements does not necessarily improve their social status in post-revolutionary societies.

Coined in post-revolutionary France, the notion of the political "left" became an umbrella term for a range of progressive movements and ideologies. All had in common that they wanted to build a society that was more egalitarian and democratic than the *Ancien Régime*, Tsarist Russia, and other autocratic regimes. In the nineteenth century, these ideologies and movements gained prominence across Europe and became known as socialism. The year 1848 saw a wave of social upheavals. Drawing on socialist, nationalist, and liberal ideas, revolutionaries in France, Italy, Germany, Scandinavia, and Central Europe took up arms to fight for a share in the political decision process and for national self-determination. Across Europe, women formed groups and associations to support revolutionary (and counter-revolutionary) movements, and a number of female revolutionary militants participated in street fighting. Research has shown that women took part in conspiratorial activities in Poland, fought side-by-side with their husbands in German battlefields, and were on the barricades in Paris. The defeat of the revolutionary forces a few months later led to a wave of political repression. Once again, women were excluded from the public sphere.

The questions of how a more just society could be achieved and how it should be governed have been at the center of controversial debates among leftist theorists and activists. In the late nineteenth century, the socialist movement split into a Marxist and an anarchist wing. Karl Marx (1818–1883) and his followers argued that the creation of a communist party and a dictatorship of the proletariat were necessary conditions for a more egalitarian society. Mikhail Bakunin (1814–1876) and others, by contrast, opposed all forms of domination and hierarchy and insisted that a more just society had to be based on individual freedom and free association. While this political stance can be traced back much further in history, it has been known as "anarchism" since the mid-nineteenth century. Bakunin and Joseph Déjacque (1821–1864) were among the first anarchist thinkers who insisted that the liberation of women was essential to the liberation of all humans. Louise Michel (1830–1905) and other members of the Paris Commune of 1871, the Russian-born writer and activist Emma Goldman (1869–1940), and the labor activist and communist anarchist Lucy Eldine Gonzalez Parsons (c.1853–1942) were some of the most prominent women in the international anarchist movement.

Women played active roles in anarchist political violence between 1870 and the 1920s, which David C. Rapoport (2004) defined as the "first wave of modern terrorism." On January 24, 1878, the 28-year-old Vera Ivanovna Zasulich tried to kill the governor-general of St. Petersburg. Zasulich's attack against Fyodor Trepov met with wide public support and was considered exemplary of the anarchist "propaganda of the deed." She and other leftist rebels in Tsarist Russia believed that acts of "individual terror" against representatives of the autocratic regime were necessary to bring about a more egalitarian society (at the time the term "terrorism" did not have the same negative connotations as today). Women were involved in planning the assassination of Tsar Alexander II in 1881, and played a prominent role in the terrorist wing of the Party of Socialist Revolutionaries (SR) in the early twentieth century. According to party statistics, 15 percent of the SR terrorists were women (Boniece 2003, 582). Inspired by anarchist terrorists in Russia, militants in a range of other countries used the recently invented dynamite and other weapons to carry acts of political violence.

Whereas anarchism has remained a small movement in Russia, it became a major political force in Spain. In the late nineteenth and early twentieth centuries, the country saw a wave of protests and armed uprisings. Influenced by anarchist ideas, peasants and workers across Spain formed collectives and organized large-scale strikes. It was the poorest areas of the country in particular where political activists resorted to the anarchist propaganda of the deed. In 1882–1886 alone, Spanish anarchists assassinated more than 20 members of the political and economic elite (Chaliand and Blin 2007, 119). Unlike in other countries, the anarchist movement in Spain remained a strong political force well into the twentieth century. The 1930s saw the formation of the first women's groups in the anarchist movement in Spain. In preparation for the revolution, they formed the organization *Mujeres Libres* (Free Women). According to some sources, the Free Women had up to 30,000 members (see, e.g., Hogan 1999). While focusing on the education, support, and mobilization of women and girls, the organization distanced itself from the (bourgeois) women's movement. It took the stance that the liberation of women had to be part of a broader struggle against social hierarchies. After the military coup in 1936, leftist activists across the country took up arms to fight against General Francisco Franco and his troops. During the Spanish Civil War from 1936 to 1939, women supported the anti-fascist struggle by running hospitals and other facilities for male soldiers, by serving in various levels of political office and – at least temporarily – by engaging in front-line combat (Lannon 1991). The transition from a guerrilla force to a traditional army and the victory of Franco's troops in 1939 led to a demobilization of female forces.

The rise of fascism in Spain and other European countries led to a wave of repression against members of left-wing parties and other political dissidents. In the 1930s and 1940s, leftist groups in Italy, France, Spain, Greece, Poland, and a number of other countries formed armed resistance movements to fight against political repression and the rise of the political right. Glorified by the political left and demonized by the political right, women constituted a significant part of the fighting forces in these movements. As the Greek case illustrates, they took up arms for a range of reasons. According to Margaret Poulos Anagnostopoulou, women constituted up to 30 percent of combatants in the Greek Democratic Army (GDA). Many joined the GDA in self-defense, while others were driven by patriotic sentiment or communist idealism or were forcibly recruited (Anagnostopoulou 2001, 485). Although leftist partisan groups and communist armies in Europe and in the USSR emphasized their ideological commitment to gender equality, there can be little doubt that there were also pragmatic reasons for their active recruitment of women in the 1940s: they needed more fighters, but a great part of the adult male population was at the front or had been captured or killed. In many countries, the 1950s were characterized by a return to traditional gender norms, and a demobilization of female forces.

Rapoport (2004) identifies three successive, overlapping waves of modern terrorism that followed the anarchist wave of political violence in the late nineteenth and early twentieth century: a wave of anti-colonial struggles which began in the 1920s and ended in the 1960s, a "New Left" wave of terrorism which gathered momentum in the 1960s and ebbed in the wake of the Cold War, and a wave of religiously motivated violence which formed in 1979 and lasts to this day. While it should be noted that all of these political struggles involved women, female participation in political violence reached a new visibility and quality in the New Left wave of modern terrorism. In the 1960s, Marxism, anarchism, and other strands of leftist political thought experienced a revival in many Western countries, and young people protested against the Vietnam War, political repression, and imperialism and for more participatory forms of democracy. Although most activists in the New Left drew on nonviolent forms of protest, some turned to violence when they felt that peaceful means of protest had failed to achieve social change.

The 1970s saw the formation of armed leftist movements in several democratic states. Examples include the Red Brigades in Italy, Action Direct in France, the Red Army in Japan, the Weather Underground in the United States, and several groups in West Germany. Many of these groups formed strategic alliances with armed leftist groups in other parts of the world, e.g., the Popular Front for the Liberation of Palestine (PFLP) and other organizations in the Middle East.

Although there were significant tactical and political differences between these movements, they had two things in common. First, women constituted a significant part of their membership. Second, female group members played a number of roles ranging from carrying messages to taking leading positions. PFLP member Leila Khaled (1944–) participated in two hijackings and became an icon of Palestinian liberation. Fusako Shigenobu (1944–) played a leading role in the Japanese Red Army. Previous research suggests that women constituted 30 percent of the members of the Italian Red Brigades and more than one-third of the leadership of the Marxist–Leninist group (De Cataldo Neuburger and Valentini 1996, 7–8). In West Germany, the percentage of female militants in armed leftist groups was even higher. Beyond doubt, the best-known militant leftist group in the Federal Republic of Germany was the Red Army Faction (RAF), which existed for 28 years and killed 34 people. According to a recent study, almost half of the RAF members were female (Diewald-Kerkmann 2009, 275). Moreover, almost all of the group's leading ideologists were women. They included Ulrike Meinhof (1934–1976), Gudrun Ensslin (1940–1977), and Brigitte Mohnhaupt (1949–).

Although the active participation of women in the RAF was sometimes described as an "excess of women's liberation," the group did not have a feminist background or agenda. Like many other women who joined armed leftist struggles, the female militants of the RAF wanted to be equal to their male comrades, but rejected the women's movement as bourgeois. Drawing on the work of Karl Marx and Mao Zedong, the RAF considered the woman question to be a "side contradiction," which would be resolved if the class system could be overcome. This position was not shared by all women in the militant left in West Germany.

The militant feminist group Red Zora, for instance, held that patriarchy was older than capitalism, and the liberation of women was a prerequisite for liberation from all forms of oppression. Unlike the RAF and other militant leftist groups in West Germany, the Red Zora was an exclusively female group and took up central themes in German women's movements, including sexual objectification, trafficking in women, and transnational solidarity. Between 1977 and 1988, the group claimed responsibility for 45 arson attacks and bombings, most of which took place in the 1980s. The German case shows that while believing in gender equality, the majority of female militants did not identify as feminists.

There are no easy answers to the questions of what motivates women to join armed leftist struggles and to what effect (if any) their conduct has on the prevailing gender norms. Whether they succeeded in bringing about radical social change or not, it seems that revolutionary leftist movements since the nineteenth century have rarely effected more gender equality in post-revolutionary societies. Many of the women who took up arms to support these movements did not identify as feminists, and those who did could not necessarily count on the support of their comrades. Further research on historical and contemporary struggles needs to be conducted to develop a better understanding of the range of motives for and social consequences of female participation in revolutionary leftist movements.

SEE ALSO: Amazons; Anarchism and Gender; Feminism, Anarchist; Feminisms, Marxist and Socialist; Military Masculinity; Women Suicide Bombers (LTTE, Sri Lanka)

REFERENCES

Anagnostopoulou, Margaret Poulos. 2001. "From Heroines to Hyenas: Women Partisans During the Greek Civil War." *Contemporary European History*, 10: 481–501. DOI: 10.1017/S0960777301003083.

Boniece, Sally A. 2003. "The Spiridonova Case, 1906: Terror, Myth, and Martyrdom." *Kritika: Explorations in Russian and Eurasian History*, 4(3): 571–606. DOI: 10.1353/kri.2003.0034.

Chaliand, Gérard, and Arnaud Blin, eds. 2007. *The History of Terrorism. From Antiquity to al Qaeda*. Berkeley: University of California Press.

De Cataldo Neuburger, Luisella, and Tiziana Valentini. 1996. *Women and Terrorism*. Basingstoke: Palgrave Macmillan.

Diewald-Kerkmann, Gisela. 2009. *Frauen, Terrorismus und Justiz: Prozesse Gegen Weibliche Mitglieder der RAF und der Bewegung 2. Juni*. Düsseldorf: Droste.

Dirik, Dilar. 2014. "Western Fascination with 'Badass' Kurdish Women." *Aljazeera*, October 29, 2014. Accessed March 18, 2015, at http://www.aljazeera.com/indepth/opinion/2014/10/western-fascination-with-badas-2014102112410527736.html.

Dlodlo, Ayanda. 2011. "Flowers of the Revolution." *News24*, August 8, 2011. Accessed March 25, 2015, at http://www.citypress.co.za/columnists/flowers-of-the-revolution-20110808/.

Hogan, Deirdre. 1999. "Mujeres Libres – Free Women of Spain". *Workers Solidarity Movement*, July 8, 1999. Accessed March 1, 2015, at http://www.wsm.ie/c/mujeres-libres-anarchist-women-spain.

Lannon, Frances. 1991. "Women and Images of Women in the Spanish Civil War." *Transactions of the Royal Historical Society (Sixth Series)*, 1: 213–228. DOI: 10.2307/3679037.

Rapoport, David C. 2004. "The Four Waves of Terrorism". In *Attacking Terrorism: Elements of a Grand Strategy*, edited by Audrey Kurth Cronin and James M. Ludes, 46–73. Washington, DC: Georgetown University Press.

FURTHER READING

Rowbotham, Sheila. 1972. *Women, Resistance and Revolution*. Harmondsworth: Penguin.

Gonzalez-Perez, Margaret. 2006. "Guerrilleras in Latin America: Domestic and International Roles." *Journal of Peace Research*, 43: 313–329. DOI: 10.1177/0022343306063934.

Kampwirth, Karen. 2002. *Women and Guerrilla Movements. Nicaragua, El Salvador, Chiapas, Cuba*. University Park: Penn State University.

Melzer, Patricia. 2015. *Death in the Shape of a Young Girl. Women's Political Violence in the Red Army Faction*. New York: New York University Press.

Lesbian Continuum

RITA BÉRES-DEÁK
Central European University, Hungary

A concept developed by Adrienne Rich in her essay "Compulsory Heterosexuality and Lesbian Existence," the lesbian continuum expands the category of "lesbian" to include not only sexuality, but also a woman-identified experience including "the sharing of a rich inner life [with women], the bonding against male tyranny, the giving and receiving of practical and political support" (1993/1981, 239). The concept triggered fierce debates within lesbian feminism for several reasons, including the concept's political usefulness and its underlying definition of lesbianism.

The lesbian continuum model is categorized by Sedgwick under universalizing constructions of homosexuality; unlike the minoritizing models assuming homo- and heterosexuality as distinct categories, the lesbian continuum suggests that every woman has a lesbian potential (Sedgwick 1990). Rich claims that for women, heterosexuality needs to be "imposed, managed, organized, propagandized, and maintained by force" (1993/1981, 238–239). In response to a critique that she blurs female friendship and lesbianism (Snitow, Stansell, and Thompson 1983), she emphasizes the difference between lesbian continuum and lesbian existence, but still suggests that one ideally leads to the other (Rich 1993/1981).

The notion of the lesbian continuum is a product of lesbian feminism, which perceives lesbianism as a form of political resistance against patriarchy, emphasizing its political and social aspects (the "woman-identified woman") over sexuality. It also suits the purposes of lesbian feminism insofar as it posits lesbianism as ontologically different from male homosexuality (Rich 1993/1981; Bersani 1995). At the same time, it reflects a wider need in the emerging gay/lesbian movement to find its own history (Boswell 1989); while Rich understood this project not as finding lesbian relationships in the past but as unearthing traces of *"nascent feminist political content"* (Rich 1993/1981, 245), Rupp (2012) used the notion of lesbian continuum to detect sexual relationships between women in different cultures and times in history.

The concept of the lesbian continuum received various critiques within feminist circles. The question of whether it is justified to put the label "lesbian" on women who would not have identified as such (Ferguson, Zita, and Addelson 1981) resonates with similar concerns in gay male history (Boswell 1989); Rich is accused of universalizing a historically specific identity category (Ferguson, Zita, and Addelson 1981). Other critics point out that Rich denies non-lesbian feminine agency (Snitow, Stansell, and Thompson 1983; Ferguson, Zita, and Addelson 1981) and thus excludes many women from the scope of resistance to patriarchy (Ferguson, Zita, and Addelson 1981; Thompson 1981). Several authors are troubled by the fact that Rich does not give criteria for successful resistance, and thus fails to distinguish resistance from mere victimization (Ferguson, Zita, and Addelson 1981).

In spite of these criticisms, some lesbian feminist theorists welcomed the notion of lesbian continuum as a good strategic term, as it establishes historical continuity and erases the false binary between lesbians and straight women (Ferguson, Zita, and Addelson 1981). Another merit of the concept was said to be that in contrast with medical models of homosexuality, it treats lesbianism not as a form of deviance but as a positive value (Ferguson, Zita, and Addelson 1981).

The most fiercely debated element of the concept of lesbian continuum is its definition of lesbianism. Though Rupp (2012) has demonstrated that sexual activities between women have existed in various cultures and historical times, Rich does not consider sexuality as a criterion for lesbianism, and has been accused of desexualizing lesbians and ignoring the way genital sexuality between women has expanded their possibilities to resist patriarchy (Ferguson, Zita, and Addelson 1981). As she locates lesbianism in individual acts of resistance (Thompson 1981), Rich has also been criticized for downplaying the collective and social nature of lesbian identity (Ferguson, Zita, and Addelson 1981), which has been considered important both by lesbian feminists and by gay/lesbian identity politics.

Rich's more fluid approach to sexual orientation resurfaces in the 1990s, with new analyses of lesbianism as choice (Whisman 1996). Queer theory has extended this notion of fluidity to gender, and similar to Rich's lesbian continuum, a transgender continuum has been suggested to encompass forms of resistance to gender regimes (Cole and Cate 2008).

The concept of lesbian continuum has been used in various ways in cultural studies, from exploring resistance to patriarchy in novels (Ferguson, Zita, and Addelson 1981) to analyzing films where heroines show a fluid sexual orientation (Holmlund 2002). These approaches show different understandings of Rich's concept, but agree in rejecting rigid identity categories.

SEE ALSO: Compulsory Heterosexuality; Feminism, Lesbian; Feminism, Radical; Sexual Identity and Orientation

REFERENCES

Bersani, Leo. 1995. *Homos*. Cambridge, MA: Harvard University Press.

Boswell, John. 1989. "Revolutions, Universals, and Sexual Categories." In *Hidden from History: Reclaiming the Gay and Lesbian Past*, edited by Martin Duberman, Martha Vicinus, and George Chauncey, Jr., 17–36. New York: New American Library.

Cole, L. C., and Shannon L. C. Cate. 2008. "Compulsory Gender and Transgender Existence: Adrienne Rich's Queer Possibility." *Women's Studies Quarterly*, 36(3–4): 279–287.

Ferguson, Ann, Jacquelyn N. Zita, and Kathryn Pyne Addelson. 1981. "On 'Compulsory Heterosexuality and Lesbian Existence': Defining the Issues." In *Feminist Theory: A Critique of Ideology*, edited by Nannerl O. Keohane, Michelle Z. Rosaldo, and Barbara C. Gelpi, 147–188. Chicago: University of Chicago Press.

Holmlund, Chris. 2002. *Impossible Bodies: Femininity and Masculinity in the Movies*. New York: Routledge.

Rich, Adrienne. 1993. "Compulsory Heterosexuality and Lesbian Existence." In *The Lesbian and Gay Studies Reader*, edited by Henry Abelove, Michèle Aina Barale, and David M. Halperin, 227–254. New York: Routledge. First published 1981.

Rupp, Leila. 2012. "Sexual Fluidity 'Before Sex'." *Signs*, 37(4): 849–856.

Sedgwick, Eve Kosofsky. 1990. *Epistemology of the Closet*. Berkeley: University of California Press.

Snitow, Ann, Christine Stansell, and Sharon Thompson, eds. 1983. *Powers of Desire: The Politics of Sexuality*. New York: Monthly Review Press.

Thompson, Martha E. 1981. "Comment on Rich's 'Compulsory Heterosexuality and Lesbian Existence'." *Signs*, 6(4): 790–794.

Whisman, Vera. 1996. *Queer by Choice: Lesbians, Gay Men, and the Politics of Identity*. New York: Routledge.

Lesbian Cultural Criticism

LYNNE STAHL
Cornell University, USA

Lesbian cultural criticism is part of the broader field of lesbian studies, which emerged in the 1960s from various grassroots intellectual and activist movements within and alongside second-wave feminism. During the 1960s through 1980s, lesbian feminists in the United States (and abroad, though this entry focuses on US contexts), exasperated with the systemic misogyny, homophobia, and conservatism of mainstream culture, formed radical, sometimes separatist, collectives. Their goals included the denaturalization of heterosexuality and exposure of its complicity with patriarchal and capitalist structures that had traditionally oppressed females. The Washington, DC-based Furies Collective, for example, circulated anti-patriarchal writings through a newspaper; many other groups published magazines and manifestos to disseminate their views. Some, such as the Combahee River Collective, expressed frustrations with the anglocentrism of "mainstream" feminist and lesbian movements, highlighting the need to recognize intersections of racial, sexual, and economic oppressions.

In the 1970s, lesbian studies began to gain traction as an academic field. Lesbian and gay caucuses formed within several prominent scholarly organizations, including the Modern Language Association, the American Anthropological Association, and the American Sociological Association; they continue to thrive today (Zimmerman 2000). With its roots in community activism, the field of lesbian cultural criticism has been particularly open to perspectives from outside academic milieux, insisting on the need to recognize the institutionalized power relations subtending the university system and academia generally. Hence, while lesbian cultural criticism may take the form of traditional scholarly essays and monographs, it also frequently appears in alternative media, including film, comic strips, theater, performance art, and music.

Much lesbian cultural criticism focuses on identifying, exposing, and repudiating patriarchal and heteronormative power structures and ideologies; it is equally invested in exploring the specificities of the category "lesbian" and questions of lesbian aesthetics. Critics have debated, for instance, what might constitute a lesbian gaze (part of larger contentions in feminist film theory about how film shapes our "looks" at different bodies), lesbian voice (written, spoken, sung), or lesbian narrative, along with potential merits and perils of such definitions. Some lesbian critics maintain that conventional linear narrative is inherently heteronormative and that it necessarily reproduces oppressive ideologies even if a given narrative contains "positive" lesbian characters and themes. Others underscore the importance of lesbian visibility and the representation of lesbianism in dominant cultural forms.

Debates over what constitutes lesbianism as such have caused considerable discord over the years. While some see it as a spectrum or continuum encompassing female interrelations that need not be sexual – a view set forth in an influential essay by Adrienne Rich (1986) – others believe that, whether by biological imperative or personal choice, lesbianism necessarily entails sexual relations between women. Wolfe and Penelope (1993) note that "Lesbian theory … and Lesbian literary criticism … had the task of positing a Lesbian subject, experienced through a collective history and culture we have had to construct before we can begin to *de*construct Lesbian identity." Scholars in film, performance, and literary studies explore how lesbianism is signified in artistic and popular texts. However, even among such scholars, the usefulness of "lesbian" as a category of critical analysis remains contested.

The emergence of "queer" as a fluid term adopted by individuals who refuse to identify within the terms of normative sexuality has not put questions of definition to rest. Contemporary critics who designate their work as lesbian may do so in defiance of queer theory's often anti-identitarian inclinations (for example, Gayle Rubin's advocacy for a more pluralistic view of sexuality rooted in a broader "concept of benign sexual variation" than exists).

Although lesbian cultural criticism largely embraces the foundational feminist slogan that the personal is political, many critics are wary of what they see as the privatization of experience and the potential failure to recognize issues beyond the purview of one's own demographic situation. Gloria Anzaldúa's *Borderlands/La Frontera* (1987), for instance, combines prose and poetry in interrogating relations between geopolitical and sexual borders. Some lesbian writers eliminate the personal voice; others use it provisionally while noting their own complicity in ideological systems and practices (Munt 1992). Figures such as Anzaldúa, Audre Lorde, Cheryl Clarke, Dorothy Allison, and Cherríe Moraga have called, too, for critical attention to race, class, ethnicity, (dis)ability, and gender vis-à-vis sexuality; Anzaldúa and Moraga's anthology, *This Bridge Called My Back* (1981), in many ways laid the foundation for third-wave feminism with its focus on global perspectives and universal accessibility.

Lesbian artists and activists frequently launch critiques by satirizing or parodying oppressive social norms. For example, underground comics such as Diane DiMassa's *Hothead Paisan* and Alison Bechdel's *Dykes to Watch Out For* play humorously on cultural stereotypes of and paranoia about lesbians. Cheryl Dunye's documentary-style film *The Watermelon Woman* (1996) offers satirical insight into the historical erasure of black lesbianism and the glorification of masculinist cinematic practices while constructing its own hypothetical lesbian archive. Lesbian theater constitutes a prominent venue for performance-as-criticism; a lively New York theater scene has fostered such groups as the Five Lesbian Brothers, a troupe whose farcical, darkly funny plays offer acerbic feminist perspectives.

Today, lesbian cultural criticism does not typically constitute an official academic field or department. However, many educational institutions offer undergraduate and graduate degrees, minors, or certificates in lesbian, gay, bisexual, and transgender (LGBT) studies, women's studies, or gender and sexuality studies, interdisciplinary programs that draw faculty and students from a broad range of disciplines, including anthropology, history, literature, performance studies, political science, sociology, and others.

SEE ALSO: Feminist Film Theory; Lesbian Continuum; Lesbian Performance; Lesbian and Womyn's Separatism; Politics of Representation; Queer Theory

REFERENCES

Munt, Sally, ed. 1992. *New Lesbian Criticism: Literary and Cultural Readings*. New York: Columbia University Press.

Rich, Adrienne. 1986. "Compulsory Heterosexuality and Lesbian Existence." In *Blood, Bread, and Poetry: Selected Prose, 1979–1985*. New York: Norton.

Wolfe, Susan J., and Julia Penelope, eds. 1993. *Sexual Practice/Textual Theory: Lesbian Cultural Criticism*. Oxford: Blackwell.

Zimmerman, Bonnie, ed. 2000. *Lesbian Histories and Cultures: An Encyclopedia*. New York: Garland.

FURTHER READING

Butler, Judith. 1993. "Imitation and Gender Insubordination." In *The Lesbian and Gay Studies Reader*. London: Routledge.

Lesbian and Gay Movements

MANON TREMBLAY
University of Ottawa, Canada

The 1960s was a golden age of protest politics. By the end of this cycle of contentious events, many lesbians and gays were politically socialized and had acquired training in activism – skills that they used to highlight gender and sexuality issues once they applied them to the lesbian and gay (LG) movement. Indeed, 1960s protest politics offered lesbians and gays a cultural and political window of opportunity for contesting the hegemony of heteronormative social relations by demanding loud and strong that everyone's true bisexual nature be liberated. As the movement matured, however, this message, which was a poor fit with the gradually strengthening strategy of integration with heteronormative society and the claiming of rights, was ultimately drowned out.

This entry draws a general portrait of the LG movement after the late 1960s. The American movement is the main focus, both because it initiated the contemporary LG movement and because today it is the largest in the world in terms of resources and influence. The main thrust is that the LG movement evolved from a revolutionary (or liberationist) project in the early 1970s to relatively assimilationist and respectability-oriented homonormative activism today.

PREMISES OF THE LG MOVEMENT: GAY LIBERATION

The spontaneous uprisings that took place at the Stonewall Inn in June 1969 are commonly described as the founding moment of the LG movement in the West (Duberman 1994). However, this reading is increasingly being challenged because a vibrant gay subculture, instituted thanks to the activism of a network of homophile groups (notably the Mattachine Society and the Daughters of Bilitis), existed in the decades preceding Stonewall (D'Emilio 1998). In other words, proto-movement activities that occurred from the 1940s through the 1960s made the LG movement possible (see Stein 2012, 41–78).

The gay liberation movement (GLM), which existed from 1969 to 1972, was the first manifestation of LG activism. It drew its ideological parentage and activist style from 1960s counterculture and New Left politics, including the African American-led civil rights movement and the black power movement, the youth and student movements, the anti-war movement, and the women's movement – even though, as Stein (2012, 63) notes, these movements were homophobic and heterosexist. The women's movement, in particular, influenced the gay liberationists' methods (such as consciousness-raising groups) and ideas. Like the women's movement, the GLM was critical of the sexism propagated by oppressive gender roles (Weeks 1990, 196–197), which it saw as responsible for the subjugation of lesbian and gay people. However, the GLM adopted an ideological position distinct from the women's movement by challenging the restrictive categories of heterosexuality and homosexuality that inhibited expression of the bisexuality inherent to all human beings (Wittman 1992; Altman 2012, 80–116). Another way in which gay liberationists stood apart from feminists concerned the slogan "The Personal is Political": although the women's movement stated it, the GLM put it into practice with "coming out." From a personal point of view, this was an eminently political act marking lesbians' and gays' rejection of internalized self-hate. From a collective point of view, the strategy of "coming out" was instrumental in constructing a gay and lesbian identity and communities, either by manufacturing a collective consciousness based on new subjectivities and identities or by encouraging political activism (as evidenced by the slogan "Out of the Closets, into the Streets"). Thus, the GLM saw "coming out" as a personal and collective cultural and political empowering process: it meant rejecting the stigma previously attached to homosexuality and publicly affirming a new identity articulated around the pride of belonging to a lesbian or gay community.

On the organizational level, the GLM was splintered – composed of a myriad of short-lived, small, grassroots groups with sociocultural and political mandates, but not necessarily with any ties to each other and certainly no unity regarding their repertoire of actions. Following Stonewall, a multitude of gay liberationist groups were formed in the United States: the Gay Liberation Front (GLF) in New York, as well as autonomous gay liberation groups in Ann Arbor, Chicago, Detroit, Los Angeles, Philadelphia, and San Francisco. Above all, the GLF inspired the creation of similar groups elsewhere in the world: Argentina and Mexico (for instance, the Frente de Liberación Homosexual), Canada (the Front de libération homosexuel in Montreal and the University of Toronto Homophile Association), France (the Front homosexuel d'action révolutionnaire), Italy (Frente Unitario Omosessuale Rivoluzionario Italiano), and the United Kingdom (the London Gay Liberation Front), among others (see Adam 1995, 89–96).

At the beginning of the 1970s, LG activism was divided into two general trends in terms of goals and tactics. The first, more radical and revolutionary, embodied by the GLF and radical lesbian feminism, favored more confrontational and theatrical tactics (such as boycotting, picketing, "radical drag" and gender bending, street demonstrating, "zapping"), and what Bernstein (1997) calls "identity for critique" – deploying identities to challenge the "values, practices, and categories" of mainstream culture. An example of this is the battle waged by the GLF in 1971 to have the American Psychiatric Association remove homosexuality from the *Diagnostic and Statistical Manual of Mental Disorders* (DSM). Despite the existence of women's caucuses in a number of gay liberation groups, lesbians quickly became dissatisfied with GLF policy based on the needs and demands of men, who also controlled the movement's leadership and membership. Thus the stage was set for the emergence of radical feminist lesbian groups in parallel to gay liberationist groups. The second trend, liberal and reformist, drew on an equal rights agenda oriented toward decriminalization of homosexuality and acquisition of rights protecting lesbians and gays from discrimination in the workplace, education, health, housing, and so on (see, for example, Marotta 1981, 196–226). This trend postulated that the seeking and acquisition of rights was a (respectable) way to live and express one's lesbian or gay identity, and tactics included lobbying politicians and going to court. An example is the Gay Activists Alliance of New York, which was founded in December 1969 in a split from GLF-New York, which was considered too radical. In fact, during the 1970s the radical and revolutionary trend faded as the liberal and reformist trend gradually came to embody the LG movement.

In the early years, other cleavages undermined LG activism in terms of a wide range of identities, subjectivities, experiences, ideas, and practices. For example, although transgender (and transvestite) people had been in the forefront of early LG activism battles, they were gradually pushed to the margins of the movement, either because their presence – and especially their appearance – was seen as undermining the movement's credibility and therefore the possibility of success, or because they were the butt of criticism by lesbian feminists who saw them as a concrete manifestation of gender roles that they disparaged. Queens (later renamed the Queens Liberation Front) was created in New York in 1969. Bisexuals also distanced themselves from a movement that, over time, had silenced its critical approach based on transgression and subversion of the heterosexual order of regulation of desires and sexualities and advocacy for expression of everyone's true bisexual essence, to favor, instead, melting into the hegemonic model of heteronormativity, or even homonormativity (Duggan 2002). The National Bisexual Liberation Group was founded in New York in 1972. This critique of the regime of regulation of desires and sexualities between two poles posed as mutually exclusive – heterosexuality and homosexuality – was to be returned to the agenda by groups such as ACT UP, Outrage! (in Great Britain), Queer Nations, and SexPanic! in the late 1980s and 1990s, and today it is made by the bisexual movement.

During the second half of the 1970s, the LG movement was the theater of debates and struggles to define LG identities and communities. The reformist trend, for which LG issues had to be framed so that they could be viewed as respectable by mainstream society, engaged the LG movement in a process of institutionalization that included a new and professionalized style of organizing, as seen in organizations such as the National Gay Task Force (founded in 1973), the Gay Rights National Lobby (1976), the Lesbian Rights Project (1977), and the Human Rights Campaign Fund (1980) in the United States and, in the 1980s, EGALE in Canada and Stonewall in Great Britain. For that matter, the challenges faced by the LG movement in the 1980s accentuated its mainstreaming.

THE 1980S: AIDS AND THE SOCIAL CONSERVATIVE MOVEMENT

The HIV/AIDS crisis was a turning point in LG activism. The first cases were reported in the United States in 1981, and others soon followed elsewhere in the world. In general, governments were slow to respond to the pandemic, and the LG movement was forced to act. The HIV/AIDS crisis had two major effects on the LG movement: it contributed to its reactivation and led to its institutionalization, or even mainstreaming.

The LG movement, which had lost momentum in the second half of the 1970s, now had an opportunity to review its objectives, strategic and tactical repertoire, and allies. Since governments were paying lip service to HIV/AIDS, the crisis situation mobilized a new generation of lesbian and gay militants who had not lived through the liberationist years, and whose energies had been channeled into a myriad of grassroots organizations and localized collective protest demonstrations. For example, the radical street-based tactics of the AIDS Coalition to Unleash Power (ACT UP), founded in 1987, were reminiscent of those of the GLF from 1969 to 1972. Queer Nation and the Lesbian Avengers took up the torch in the 1990s, when ACT UP ran out of energy and lost its radical edge.

Although the HIV/AIDS pandemic stimulated grassroots activism, it also led, in parallel, to an AIDS movement that was largely institutionalized and in tune with mainstream politics. Whereas the GLF had looked upon the state with suspicion, the pandemic forced lesbians and gays to set up institutions to communicate and negotiate with it. As a consequence, the LG movement had to accept, at least in part, the rules of the political game and win the support of straight allies (including the media and the medical community), thus contributing to its mainstreaming. In order to deal with the HIV/AIDS crisis, the LG movement thus made some strategic choices, notably reframing and "degaying" the pandemic. HIV/AIDS was no longer a problem concerning gays and sex, but a question of public health and equality. On the one hand, such a sexual citizenship rationale helped to strengthen the LG movement's equal rights agenda; on the other hand, it played some part in deradicalizing an aspect of LG politics, and even led to a rise in strength of a homonormalized LG activism based on valorization of the heterosexual lifestyle and its adoption by lesbians and gays.

Although the equal rights discourse mobilized by LG activists with regard to the struggle against HIV/AIDS provided an opportunity to shed full light on the second-class citizenship status of LG people, it did not enable them to escape deep-seated social ostracism due to being associated with the disease (even though homosexuality had been taken out of the DSM not long before), or even death. Paradoxically, lesbian and gay communities gained visibility because a record number of gay people were dying (Vaid 1995, 81). What is more, discrimination against lesbians and gays, though common, became unsupportable, because it involved questions of life (such as access to treatment) and death (end-of-life care, funerals, inheritances). Homophobic discrimination helped to provoke the demands through which same-sex unions were to be recognized (see below), thus questioning the hegemony of heterosexuality, its postulated normativity, and the privileges that it entailed. All of this inevitably led to the unleashing of a social conservative movement.

Although the HIV/AIDS crisis did not give rise to social conservatism, it undoubtedly stimulated its mobilization on the political scene. In fact, the LG and social conservative movements were linked by a dynamic of movement and countermovement: the former questioned the monopoly of heteronormative social relations and advocated a broadening of the spectrum of legitimate sexualities, whereas the latter promoted the perpetuation of traditional sexual morality and patriarchal family structure. Social conservatism arose in a number of Western countries in recent decades (including Australia, Canada, France, Germany, and Great Britain), but it has proven to be a particularly powerful adversary to the LG movement in the United States (see Fetner 2008). However, even in that country social conservatism has not been able to completely dominate the LG movement, which has won significant victories, notably with regard to the recognition of same-sex unions.

THE 1990S AND BEYOND: BATTLES FOR RECOGNITION OF SAME-SEX UNIONS

During the 1990s and ensuing decades, the institutionalization of the LG movement continued, the objective being to make lesbians and gays into citizens on an equal footing with others. In fact, the argument that LG people's right to equality is a human right was more clearly heard, as part of a global human rights discourse that was particularly influential in Europe. As mentioned above, the HIV/AIDS pandemic brought to light the second-class citizen status of LG people and the discrimination that was part of their daily life. The acquisition of rights was thus necessary to address this inequality, and LG activism focused on the state for this purpose (notably through legislative lobbying, electoral politics, and court litigation).

In Waaldijk's (2000) view, three themes have been the cornerstone of the evolution of laws adopted with regard to homosexuality in major European countries since the eighteenth century: decriminalization, anti-discrimination, and partnership legislation. As a general rule, the wave of decriminalization of homosexuality (usually understood as sex between men) in the Western world lasted from post-revolutionary France (1791) to the US Supreme Court's *Lawrence v. Texas* decision (2003), which invalidated sodomy laws still on the books in a handful of states. In 2013, homosexual acts were illegal in 75 countries, a handful of which punished such acts with the death penalty (Itaborahy and Zhu 2013). A series of laws were adopted in Western countries to counter discrimination against lesbians and gays in terms of employment, health and social services, hate crimes, housing, family and parenting rights, and other areas. Yet, the protections extended were limited to individuals and did not take their intimate relations into account – hence demands for recognition of same-sex unions, a battle that clearly monopolized the LG movement's agenda starting in the mid-1990s.

In 2015, around 40 countries had national laws recognizing same-sex unions and registered partnerships, in more than 20 of which lesbian and gay couples could enter civil marriage (including Argentina, Brazil, South Africa, and Uruguay, as well as the United States where the Supreme Court legalized same-sex marriage in June 2015). Although HIV/AIDS had brought to light the importance of having same-sex unions recognized, the pandemic was not behind these demands; in fact, since the 1970s courts in the United States (notably the Supreme Court's *Baker v. Nelson* decision in 1971), Europe (starting with the Netherlands in 1990), and elsewhere in the world (for example, Canada, Israel, New Zealand, and South Africa) were led to pronounce on cases challenging the ban on civil marriages for same-sex couples. This litigation activism in no way signifies that recognition of same-sex unions was the object of consensus within the LG movement; on the contrary, a number of lesbians and gays criticized access to an institution seen as not egalitarian, bourgeois, and eminently heterosexist. In fact, the demand for state-sanctioned same-sex relationships was a reminder that the LG movement had always been torn between a liberationist tendency generally hostile to the state and a reformist tendency advocating assimilation into normative society and sameness with heterosexual people through an equal rights-based agenda. LG activists highlighted the equal rights discourse in the legislative arena and among the holders of executive power, as well as in the courts and human rights arenas at the national and supranational scales (such as the European Court of Human Rights and the United Nations Human Rights Committee): marriage was the consequence of a right to equality posed in terms of non-discrimination. Indeed, the idea was to show that intimate unions entered into by lesbians and gays were equal to (that is, of the same value as) those of straight people, making the heterosexual unions the gold standard or ideal to attain. Thus formulated, the demand for marriage equality not only strengthened the hegemonic status of heteronormative social relations, but homonormalized lesbians and gays up to then legitimated by a depoliticized and desexualized lifestyle by focusing on privacy, monogamy, respectability, domesticity, and consumption. The "regime of normal" thus broadened to include in mainstream society certain manifestations of LG life, but the basic middle-class model (monogamous couple, living together, consumers, united by a lifelong project, and so on) remained integral. Whereas the gay liberationists of the late 1960s had wanted each person to be free to express her or his innate bisexuality, same-sex marriage squarely imposed a single model of regulation of intimate relationships – that of the respectable, normal sexual citizen.

CONCLUSION

More than four decades after Stonewall, how can LG activism be summed up? Along with the women's movement, LG activism is among the movements from the 1960s cycle of protest that has had the greatest number of successes, at least in the West. As polls show, and although there have been great variations across time, place, and sociodemographics, public opinion has evolved with regard to homosexuality, indicating that LG activism has opened up a breach in the hegemony of heteronormativity by forcing the values, categories, and practices of mainstream culture to be revised. Nevertheless, one view is that this hegemony was simply reconfigured via homonormalization of LG people. In any case, the tension between the liberal and liberationist fringes of LG activism has been a source of strength rather than weakness: on the one hand, the LG movement has gained some rights to equality and non-discrimination; on the other hand, it has built LG identities and communities. From this point of view, although LG activism could be called a cultural movement, it is mainly political, because culture is eminently political. The LG movement is even more political because its resources, strategies and tactics, successes and failures, and allies and adversaries are greatly influenced by the political regime within which it exists (Engel 2001; Smith 2008). However, the LG movement is not simply dough that the state can easily mold; it has its share of influence on the state, the state's legislative, executive, and judicial actors, and the public decision-making process (Paternotte, Tremblay, and Johnson 2011). Since the late 1960s, no state has been able to ignore LG people, whose activism has not only helped to shape civil societies around the world, but is now taking place on the international scale via a transnational lesbian, gay, bisexual, and transgender (LGBT) rights network. However, the internationalization of the LG movement also bears the risk of "homo-Westernism," in which the Western (in fact, American) conception of LGBT citizenship becomes a cultural vehicle for planetary conquest. Perhaps not much has changed since Stonewall.

SEE ALSO: Anti-Racist and Civil Rights Movements; Coming Out; Consciousness-Raising; Gay and Lesbian Pride Day; Heteronormativity and Homonormativity; Women's Movements: Modern International Movements

REFERENCES

Adam, Barry D. 1995. *The Rise of a Gay and Lesbian Movement*. New York: Twayne.

Altman, Dennis. 2012. *Homosexual: Oppression and Liberation*. St. Lucia: University of Queensland Press. First published 1971.

Bernstein, Mary. 1997. "Celebration and Suppression: The Strategic Uses of Identity by the Lesbian and Gay Movement." *American Journal of Sociology*, 103: 531–565.

D'Emilio, John. 1998. *Sexual Politics, Sexual Communities,* 2nd ed. Chicago: University of Chicago Press. First published 1983.

Duberman, Martin B. 1994. *Stonewall*. New York: Plume.

Duggan, Lisa. 2002. "The New Homonormativity: The Sexual Politics of Neoliberalism." In *Materializing Democracy*, edited by Russ Castronovo and Dana D. Nelson, 175–194. Durham, NC: Duke University Press.

Engel, Stephen M. 2001. *The Unfinished Revolution*. Cambridge: Cambridge University Press.

Fetner, Tina. 2008. *How the Religious Right Shaped Lesbian and Gay Activism*. Minneapolis: University of Minnesota Press.

Itaborahy, L., and J. Zhu. 2013. *State-Sponsored Homophobia*. Brussels: International Lesbian, Gay, Sexual, Trans and Intersex Association. Accessed July 10, 2013, at http://www.old.ilga.org/Statehomophobia/ILGA_State_Sponsored_Homophobia_2013.pdf.

Marotta, Toby. 1981. *The Politics of Homosexuality*. Boston: Houghton Mifflin.

Paternotte, David, Manon Tremblay, and Carol Johnson. 2011. "Conclusion." In *The Lesbian and Gay Movement and the State*, edited by Manon Tremblay, David Paternotte, and Carol Johnson, 213–227. Farnham: Ashgate.

Smith, Miriam. 2008. *Political Institutions and Lesbian and Gay Rights in the United States and Canada*. New York: Routledge.

Stein, Marc. 2012. *Rethinking the Gay and Lesbian Movement*. New York: Routledge.

Vaid, Urvashi. 1995. *Virtual Equality*. New York: Anchor Books.

Waaldijk, Kees. 2000. "Civil Developments: Patterns of Reform in the Legal Position of Same-Sex Partners in Europe." *Canadian Journal of Family Law/Revue Canadienne de Droit Familial*, 17: 62–88.

Weeks, Jeffrey. 1990. *Coming Out: Homosexual Politics in Britain from the Nineteenth Century to the Present*. London: Quartet Books. First published 1977.

Wittman, Carl. 1992. "A Gay Manifesto." In *Out of the Closets: Voices of Gay Liberation*, edited by Karla Jay and Allen Young, 330–341. New York: NYU Press. First published 1970.

Lesbian, Gay, Bisexual, and Transgender Psychologies

ELIZABETH PEEL
University of Worcester, UK

DAMIEN W. RIGGS
Flinders University, Australia

Lesbian, gay, bisexual, and transgender (LGBT) psychology is the current term used to refer to what was previously known as the affirmative field of lesbian and gay psychology, which developed from the late 1960s onwards. This field of psychology is closely aligned to the psychology of sexualities, but with a specific focus on non-heterosexual and/or non-gender normative people. The term LGBT psychology signals a more unitary field than LGBT psychologies, the latter highlighting a multiplicity of psychological perspectives and also discrete bodies of psychological knowledge that focus on either lesbian, gay, bisexual, or transgender identities and topics (Clarke and Peel 2007). The epistemological frameworks and research methods utilized within the field of LGBT psychology differ between countries. In North America (and particularly the United States), positivist empiricism informed by liberal humanism is the dominant framework in this field (as with psychological research more generally). In Europe and in Australasia, by contrast, LGBT psychological research is commonly more aligned with post-positivist and critical psychological traditions such as social constructionism. While recognizing these epistemic differences, the field may be epitomized as:

> a branch of psychology that is affirmative of LGBTQ people. It seeks to challenge prejudice and discrimination against LGBTQ people and the privileging of heterosexuality in psychology and in the broader society. It seeks to promote LGBTQ concerns as legitimate foci for psychological research and promote non-heterosexist, non-genderist and inclusive approaches to psychological research and practice. It provides a range of psychological perspectives on the lives and experiences of LGBTQ people and on LGBTQ sexualities and genders. (Clarke et al. 2010, 6)

Of note in this definition is the emphasis upon norms related to both sexual orientation and gender. LGBT psychology has increasingly paid attention to the differential effects of gender norms amongst individuals within the LGBT acronym. For example, attention has increasingly been paid to acknowledging the significant differences between lesbian women and gay men, or the differences between transgender people and cisgender people (i.e., people whose gender identity accords with that expected of their natally assigned sex). Increased recognition has also been paid within the field of LGBT psychology to the overlaps and differences between sexual orientation and gender identity, for example, research on gay transgender men, or research on gender differences within lesbian couples. As such, LGBT psychology as a field has increasingly moved toward an intersectional approach to identity, whereby attention is paid not simply to sexual orientation or gender identity, but rather to the intersections of a range of identities such as gender, class, race, sexual orientation, ability, and religion (see Clarke et al. 2010 for an overview and synthesis of the field).

HISTORICAL OVERVIEW

A desire for positive social change, primarily on behalf of gay men and lesbian women, was the key driver in the establishment of what was first known as lesbian and gay psychology. Until the development of the field, psychology (and allied sexological and psychiatric disciplines) had a long history of pathologizing, dehumanizing, and subjecting non-heterosexual and/or non-gender normative individuals to degrading and inappropriate treatment, such as aversion therapy. Before the 1970s, most psychological research focused on the question of whether or not homosexuals and transsexuals were sick, and how they could be cured. Early pioneers in "gay affirmative" psychology, such as Evelyn Hooker (1957), challenged the assumption of homosexual pathology that predominated within psychology, using positivist-empiricist scientific methods. Academic activists from the 1970s and 1980s on fought to establish lesbian and gay psychology as a legitimate branch of the discipline of psychology.

Within the field that is now known as LGBT psychology itself, there have been ongoing debates over the most productive or appropriate modes of research. Kitzinger and Coyle (2002) argued that the field has been divided on the basis of what are seen as critical approaches, and what are seen as more mainstream approaches to psychological research. The former, it is suggested, seek to examine social norms including within psychology, whilst the latter accept the argument that psychological research is an exercise in discovering truths about the world. As the field has developed it has been increasingly recognized that both approaches have much to offer in terms of identifying and challenging social norms. This is perhaps nowhere more evident than in comparative research, which has dominated much of the field. While critiques have been made of comparative approaches (in that they assume that the experiences of LGBT people can only be understood when placed next to heterosexual and/or cisgender people), it can also be argued that comparative research highlights the effects of social norms that privilege heterosexual and cisgender people at the expense of LGBT people.

COMPARATIVE APPROACHES

A comparative approach with regard to transgender people can assist in highlighting the health disparities arising from social norms relating to gender identity. Quantitative research on HIV prevalence, for example, suggests that transgender women who engage in sex work are more likely to contract HIV than are transgender women who do not engage in sex work, and both cisgender men and cisgender women who engage in sex work (Operario, Soma, and Underhill

2008). The reasons for this, it is suggested, are because of the high levels of vulnerability that transgender women are subjected to in terms of poverty and unemployment arising from transphobia. For instance, transgender women who engage in sex work may be more likely to engage in unprotected anal intercourse if clients offer additional payment for sex without protection.

Importantly, qualitative research with transgender women who engage in sex work highlights the complexities and intersectionalities that surround sex work for transgender women. Findings from a study of transgender women of color in the United States who engage in sex work (Sausa, Keatley, and Operario 2007) suggest two competing factors at play: (1) sex work as a "rite of passage" for many transgender women (who may see sex work as a norm within transgender communities); and (2) sex work as a route to further marginalization (such as through clients encouraging drug use or unprotected intercourse). This research suggests that racism further compounds the latter factor, with transgender women of color's ability to "pass" as cisgender women (which, the authors suggest, may occur less readily than for white transgender women) impacting upon their ability to secure employment outside of sex work.

When considering gay (in this instance cisgender) men, comparative research focusing on parenting has usefully highlighted the specific experiences of gay fathers as they diverge from (and converge with) those of heterosexual fathers. For example, early US research by Bigner and Jacobsen (1989) compared 33 men who had their children in the context of a heterosexual relationship (but who at the time of the research identified as gay and continued to be involved in parenting their children), with 33 men who identified as heterosexual and who were fathers. Their research found that both groups reported similar levels of involvement and intimacy with their children. In terms of differences between the groups, the gay fathers tended to be more strict with their children, more responsive to their needs, and more consistent in their parenting style. A further notable point of difference was that the gay men suggested that having children enhanced their masculinity (in a context where identifying as gay was often read as denoting femininity), and that being a father facilitated entrance and acceptance in the general (nominally heterosexual) community.

More recently, Farr, Forssell, and Patterson (2010) have investigated similarities and differences between lesbian, gay, and heterosexual coupled adoptive parents in the United States. In terms of similarities, the research found no significant differences between each group of adoptive parents on measures of child adjustment, parenting behaviors, or couple adjustment. In terms of differences, their research found small but significant differences wherein the children of lesbian or gay parents were described as having fewer behavioral problems than were the children of heterosexual parents. Looking at 230 US gay adoptive parents alone, Tornello, Farr, and Patterson (2011) found that unique to gay men as adoptive parents appears to be the role of sensitivity to stigma. Those men in their study who reported higher levels of sensitivity to gay-related stigma reported higher levels of parenting stress. These findings echo Bigner and Jacobsen's (1989) early research where gay men were concerned about effects of stigmatization.

A small body of comparative research has importantly highlighted the experiences of bisexual people in terms of mental health. In most LGBT psychology research, bisexual people are unfortunately too often grouped together with lesbians or gay men (Barker 2007). Such an approach fails to recognize the specific experiences of bisexual people as a population, and contributes to the widespread assumption that bisexuality is not a valid or true sexual identity. Such stigmatization and marginalization are examined in the work of Ross, Dobinson, and Eady (2010), whose qualitative study of bisexual Canadians found that the sample felt marginalized at multiple levels: by a society in general that discounts bisexual people; in interactions with friends and (non-bisexual) partners who demanded that they refuse a bisexual identity and instead identify as lesbian or gay; and within themselves, where they felt that the previous two forms of marginalization led them to question their own identity.

Quantitative research by Jorm and colleagues (2002) has found that the discrimination identified by Ross, Dobinson, and Eady (2010) potentially leads to higher rates of poor mental health amongst bisexual people, as compared to lesbians, gay men, and heterosexual people. Jorm and colleagues found that bisexual participants reported the lowest levels of mental health of all of the groups, and that bisexual people reported the highest levels of current adverse life events, and the least amount of support from family.

Comparative research on lesbian women has frequently been undertaken with respect to division of household labor and parenting. In regards to the former, empirical research from both the United States and United Kingdom has consistently found that lesbian couples more equally distribute household labor, as compared with both gay couples and heterosexual couples. Lesbian couples are more likely to either share household duties on an entirely equal basis, or to allocate tasks on the basis of interests or skills. Either way, research suggests that this is not necessarily differentiated by income (as is the case with gay and heterosexual couples, where the higher income earner typically does less of the household work). When it comes to parenting, again research has consistently found that, when compared with gay parents or heterosexual parents, lesbian mothers take relatively equal shares in providing care to children (Tasker and Golombok 1997). Importantly, however, and as Oerton (1998) suggests, these findings of equal distribution of labor within lesbian households should not be taken as representing something essential about lesbian women that results in their sharing of household duties and parenting tasks. Rather, what is most important to note is the obvious, namely that lesbian couples are composed of two women, both of whom will likely have been raised in a society where women are expected to be responsible for household work. That women in lesbian relationships are aware of this expectation, and are willing to negotiate with their partner to achieve positive and supportive outcomes for the relationship and family, is thus a product of lesbian women's negotiations of gender norms.

Taken together, it is clear that there is much mileage to be gained from the use of comparative approaches within the field of LGBT psychology, both between each of the groups subsumed by the acronym and between these groups (who are located outside the norm) and the general (i.e., heterosexual cisgender) population (constituted as the norm).

INTERSECTIONALITY

Research and theorizing in the field of LGBT psychology have increasingly paid attention to the issue of intersectionality. Such an approach argues that rather than focusing solely on one form of identity, it is important to examine how a range of differing identities intersect with one another to produce both privileges and disadvantages. Taking the examples of comparative research from above, we can see that transgender women are disadvantaged more than cisgender women, but that all women are disadvantaged compared to men. Unpacking this further, we can see that transgender women of color constitute some of the most vulnerable women in Western societies.

Turning to look at lesbian mothers, whilst the findings of shared household duties and parenting responsibilities represent a hallmark of research on lesbian mothering, there are exceptions to this rule that are evident if we adopt an intersectional approach. For example, Sullivan's (1996) research on lesbian mothers suggests that class plays a significant role in determining the distribution of parental responsibilities, with working-class lesbian couples more likely to adhere to a more traditional model, with one of the women working and undertaking less of the household work, and one of the women being a stay-at-home mother taking the primary responsibility for the household. Australian research by Kentlyn (2006) suggests that although some lesbian couples may explicitly and publicly conform to such a traditional approach, gay couples are much more likely to engage in complex identity work to mask the non-gender normative tasks undertaken by gay men. For example, Kentlyn suggests that gay men who take primary responsibility for cooking and cleaning (tasks traditionally allocated to women) may be represented publicly by their partner as hypermasculine (in order to combat the negative stigma attached to men who undertake such tasks).

Importantly, then, an intersectional approach highlights Oerton's (1998) claim that same-sex relationships are not gender-free. Rather, all people living in Western societies, regardless of their sexual orientation, exist in a relationship to social norms and expectations about what it means to be a man or a woman, and indeed who is *allowed* to be a man or a woman. LGBT psychology has been at the forefront in terms of examining and identifying the mental health correlates of these expectations. As such, LGBT psychology has played an important role in identifying the negative impacts of social norms upon LGBT people, and in so doing continues to demonstrate that the issue at stake is not the level of pathology "inherent" to LGBT people (which, absent from discrimination, is no higher than the general population), but rather the detrimental impact of stigma and discrimination (Meyer 2003).

SEE ALSO: Cisgenderism; Heterosexism and Homophobia; Intersectionality; Sexual Identity and Orientation; Transphobia

REFERENCES

Barker, Meg. 2007. "Heteronormativity and the Exclusion of Bisexuality in Psychology." In *Out in Psychology: Lesbian, Gay, Bisexual, Trans and Queer Perspectives*, edited by Victoria Clarke and Elizabeth Peel, 95–117. Chichester: John Wiley & Sons.

Bigner, Jerry J., and R. Brooke Jacobsen. 1989. "The Value of Children to Gay and Heterosexual Fathers." *Journal of Homosexuality*, 18: 167–172.

Clarke, Victoria, Sonja J. Ellis, Elizabeth Peel, and Damien W. Riggs. 2010. *Lesbian, Gay, Bisexual, Trans and Queer Psychology: An Introduction*. Cambridge: Cambridge University Press.

Clarke, Victoria, and Elizabeth Peel. 2007. "From Lesbian and Gay Psychology to LGBTQ Psychologies: A Journey into the Unknown (or Unknowable)?" In *Out in Psychology: Lesbian, Gay, Bisexual, Trans and Queer Perspectives*, edited by Victoria Clarke and Elizabeth Peel, 11–35. Chichester: John Wiley & Sons.

Farr, Rachel H., Stephen L. Forssell, and Charlotte J. Patterson. 2010. "Parenting and Child Development in Adoptive Families: Does Parental Sexual Orientation Matter?" *Applied Developmental Science*, 14: 164–178.

Hooker, Evelyn. 1957. "The Adjustment of the Male Overt Homosexual." *Journal of Projective Techniques*, 21: 18–31.

Jorm, Anthony F., Ailsa E. Korten, Brian Rodgers, Patricia A. Jacomb, and Helen Christensen.

2002. "Sexual Orientation and Mental Health: Results from a Community Survey of Young and Middle-Aged Adults." *British Journal of Psychiatry*, 180: 423–427.

Kentlyn, Sue. 2006. "Adjusting Bass and Treble: The Continuously Modulated Performance of Gender." Social Change in the 21st Century Conference 2006, October 27, QUT Carseldine, Brisbane.

Kitzinger, Celia, and Adrian Coyle. 2002. "Introducing Lesbian and Gay Psychology." In *Lesbian and Gay Psychology: New Perspectives*, edited by Adrian Coyle and Celia Kitzinger, 1–29. Oxford: Blackwell.

Meyer, Ilan H. 2003. "Prejudice, Social Stress, and Mental Health in Lesbian, Gay, and Bisexual Populations: Conceptual Issues and Research Evidence." *Psychological Bulletin*, 129: 674–697.

Oerton, Sarah. 1998. "Reclaiming the 'Housewife'? Lesbians and Household Work." In *Living "Difference": Lesbian Perspectives on Work and Family Life*, edited by Gillian Dunne, 69–83. New York: Harrington Park Press.

Operario, Don, Toho Soma, and Kristen Underhill. 2008. "Sex Work and HIV Status among Transgender Women: Systematic Review and Meta-Analysis." *Journal of Acquired Immune Deficiency Syndromes*, 48: 97–103.

Ross, Lori, Cheryl Dobinson, and Allison Eady. 2010. "Perceived Determinants of Mental Health for Bisexual People: A Qualitative Examination." *American Journal of Public Health*, 100: 496–502.

Sausa, Lydia A., JoAnne Keatley, and Don Operario. 2007. "Perceived Risks and Benefits of Sex Work among Transgender Women of Color in San Francisco." *Archives of Sexual Behaviour*, 36: 768–777.

Sullivan, Maureen. 1996. "Rozzie and Harriet? Gender and Family Patterns of Lesbian Coparents." *Gender & Society*, 10: 747–767.

Tasker, Fiona, and Susan Golombok. 1997. *Growing Up in a Lesbian Family: Effects on Child Development*. New York: Guilford Press.

Tornello, Samantha, Rachel Farr, and Charlotte J. Patterson. 2011. "Predictors of Parenting Stress among Gay Adoptive Fathers in the United States." *Journal of Family Psychology*, 25: 591–600.

FURTHER READING

Clarke, Victoria, and Elizabeth Peel, eds. 2007. *Out in Psychology: Lesbian, Gay, Bisexual, Trans and Queer Perspectives*. Chichester: John Wiley & Sons.

Riggs, Damien W., and Gordon Walker, eds. 2004. *Out in the Antipodes: Australian and New Zealand Perspectives on Gay and Lesbian Issues in Psychology*. Perth: Brightfire.

Lesbian Performance

MARTINA WILLIAMS
University of Nottingham, UK

"Lesbian performance" conjures two main sets of meanings. The first is related to performativity, briefly, how a woman might act like a lesbian, act so that she will be recognized as a lesbian (particularly by lesbians), an idea that repeatedly falls prey to, and is rescued from, charges of essentialism by various critics. Butch/femme roles are perhaps the archetypal example of this type of lesbian performance, and Joan Nestle's funny, touching, erotic accounts of her life as a working-class lesbian woman and curator of the lesbian herstory archives provide particularly striking examples of how a shared and recognizable lesbian performance can form the basis for meaningful friendships, romantic relationships, and personal or political networks. This set of meanings may be best understood in the context of gender performance. The second set of meanings, which express what is more normally meant by lesbian performance, concern lesbian (stage) performance, a field that may appear simple to define, but which turns out to be quite slippery. First of all, performance is a deliberately vast term that may describe anything from dramatic plays to opera, dance, musical performance, one-woman shows (whether "straight" or comic), and everything in between. Trickier again is the question of how any particular performance may be classed as "lesbian": must it be written or performed by women who identify as lesbians, contain lesbian characters, concern lesbian themes (whatever these may be), have a largely or even wholly lesbian audience, or indeed fulfill several or all of these criteria? A generous response to this problem could be to adopt with Emily L. Sisley the formula that lesbian performances "implicitly or explicitly acknowledge that there are [lesbians] on both sides of the footlights" (Sisley 1981); they assume rather than hide lesbian experience, on or off the stage. It might be useful now to suggest something of the breadth of the area of lesbian performance so defined, and of the common characteristics of lesbian performances (if there are any), in part through closer examination of performances that fulfill the criteria established.

Lesbian performance remains a relatively small field, which often risks absorption into larger corpuses of queer or feminist performances, often dominated by works by homosexual men or heterosexual women, respectively. The same might be said of lesbian performance studies, although a number of critics prominent in the field have worked against this tendency toward marginalization. The most notable studies on lesbian performance appeared for the most part in the late 1980s and early 1990s: Jill Davis published two well-received anthologies of lesbian plays in 1987 and 1989; Lizbeth Goodman included a substantial chapter on lesbian performance in her survey of contemporary women's theater, and both Emily L. Sisley and Kate Davy did a good deal of work toward creating a definition of lesbian theater, looking particularly at the important role that the spectator might play. More recently, Sue-Ellen Case has published extensively and consistently on lesbian performance since the early 1990s, and focuses mainly on the lesbian theater scene in the United States, although she has worked on contemporary women's plays in Germany.

Vitally, at grassroots level, varied and often daring lesbian performances are being produced, although prominent lesbian theater writers have suggested that there is some resistance to producing lesbian works in traditional theater venues. The WOW café, located in New York's East Village, is perhaps the most influential dedicated lesbian performance space, and as such is one significant response to this stumbling block. The theater/café functions as a collective and aims to put on performances that reflect the diverse interests and concerns of the community (of lesbian women) that has grown up around it. Several leading lesbian performers began their careers there: Holly Hughes, the self-proclaimed "preeminent lesbian playwright of [her] generation," creates works that revel in lesbian sexuality without idealizing lesbian relationships in a way that she finds unhelpful; Lois Weaver and Peggy Shaw, the café's founders, are together the theater company Split Britches, whose most celebrated plays, *Dress Suits to Hire* (co-written with Holly Hughes, 1987) and *Upwardly Mobile Home* (with Deb Margolin, 1984), have received a great deal of critical attention. Their darkly comic performances tend to be concerned with relationships between women, playing with the tropes of popular culture and the conventions of the butch/femme roles that Shaw and Weaver also assume offstage.

There are few other dedicated, permanent lesbian performance spaces along this model. The result is that lesbian performance becomes decentralized; in Germany, for instance, quite a healthy lesbian theater scene exists as a number of small, often amateur theater groups, including Lesbithea in Hamburg and Theater HERstory in Dusseldorf. Festivals also play an increasingly important role in making room for lesbian performances. The International Dublin Gay Theatre Festival, which was founded in 2004 and is the largest festival of its type in the world, regularly debuts lesbian performances. In 2014, it awarded its Eva Gore Booth Award for Best Female Performance to the play *Lesbian Style*, which was also nominated for its prestigious Oscar Wilde Award for Best New Writing. The play, one of six lesbian performances produced at the festival, starred four women who recount and play out short scenes from their lives and relationships. Aside from gay theater festivals, which also program performances concerning gay men's experiences, there are a smaller number of festivals aimed particularly at lesbians. The two-week-long International Eressos Women's Festival on the island of Lesvos has a lineup that centers on musical performances. L-fest, which was established in 2011, has quickly grown to be the largest lesbian arts festival in the UK. It has a diverse arts program that includes poetry and literature readings, cabaret, plays, and film, although its main focuses are music and comedy. The prominence of comedy shows over traditional dramatic plays – a tendency that could also be noted in the programming at the WOW café – is one significant trend in contemporary lesbian performance. Lesbian comedy performers including Susan Calman, Zoe Lyons, Lea Delaria, and DeAnne Smith, whose work is otherwise very different, all use material drawn from their relationships and intimate lives in their comedy, and have achieved international recognition with lesbian and non-lesbian audiences, success that has proven to be elusive for most other forms of lesbian performance.

SEE ALSO: Butch/Femme; Gender Performance; Queer Performance

REFERENCE

Sisley, Emily L. 1981. "Notes on Lesbian Theatre." *TDR*, 25(1): 47–56.

FURTHER READING

Case, Sue-Ellen. 2009. *Feminist and Queer Performance: Critical Strategies*. Basingstoke: Palgrave Macmillan.

Davis, Jill, ed. 1987. *Lesbian Plays*. London: Methuen.

Goodman, Lizbeth. 1993. *Contemporary Feminist Theatres: To Each Her Own*. London: Routledge.

Nestle, Joan. 1998. *A Fragile Union: New and Selected Writings*. New York: Cleis Press.

Lesbian Popular Music

ANN M. SAVAGE
Butler University, USA

Lesbians have long been involved in the production of popular music. There is nonetheless no clear or generally accepted definition of "lesbian popular music" nor is it widely acknowledged as a distinct genre. Moreover, because certain artists associated with the genre did not or do not publicly identify as lesbian, classifying what exactly "lesbian popular music" is proves difficult. However, building on the definition of the 1970s "women's music" as music about, by, and for women, this entry focuses on music about, by, and for lesbians and specifically addresses English-speaking North American artists.

Contemporary lesbian popular music is indebted to the twentieth-century blues and folk traditions. Early blues artists associated with lesbianism include Gertrude "Ma" Rainey, Bessie Smith, and Big Mama Thornton. Formidable women with powerful voices, Rainey and Smith allude to same-sex desire in their lyrics (see Castle 2003) while Thornton was big, bold, and often masculine in her approach and style (see Spörke 2014). The lesbian activist group Daughters of Bilitis released lesbian renditions of two popular songs in 1960 from out lesbian folk singer Edith Eyde who used the pen name Lisa Ben (as in lesbian). Other early representatives of the genre include little-known Baltimore 1950s lesbian trio the Roc-A-Jets, and the Kansas City lesbian group The Rail Runners. Such artists laid the groundwork for the lesbian popular music of the second half of the twentieth century and beyond.

Lesbian music flourished in the context of the feminist and gay rights movements of the late 1960s and the 1970s. Feminists, many of whom were lesbians, began to launch women-centered music concerts and festivals under the banner "women's music," largely set up in protest of mainstream folk music and festivals that were heavily dominated by men. In 1973 Judy Dlugacz founded Olivia Records with a collective of feminist lesbians. Cris Williamson released the groundbreaking *The Changer and Changed* on the Olivia label in 1975. One of the best-selling independent releases of all time, the album, whose lyrics suggested same-sex desire, set the course for future feminist- and lesbian-inspired folk music. Other artists of this period include Margie Adams, Meg Christian, and June Millington. Feminist lesbian band Fanny was the first all-female band to be signed by a major label. They achieved two Top 40 singles *Charity Ball* and *Butter Boy* in the early 1970s. This rise of women's music led to the spawning of women-only or women-centered music festivals across the country, the largest and most widely known being the Michigan Womyn's Music Festival. Started in 1976, the Michigan Womyn's Music Festival is built, run, performed, and attended exclusively by women.

The 1980s saw the rise and success of two openly lesbian performers, "All-American Jewish Lesbian Folksinger" Phranc and Canadian folk-singer-songwriter Ferron. After years with various punk-inspired bands, Phranc went solo and signed with Island Records in 1989. Phranc released her first commercial album *I Enjoy Being A Girl* in 1989. In 1980, Ferron released her first professionally produced album *Testimony*. Both were profoundly influential for future lesbian and queer music artists.

Apart from Phranc and Ferron, the early 1980s did not produce many openly lesbian performers. This changed later in the decade when formerly closeted artists began to come out professionally. The late 1980s saw album releases from Tracy Chapman, the Indigo Girls, Melissa Etheridge, and k. d. lang. Self-identified "little folk singer" Ani DiFranco refused to sign with major labels because she was not willing to compromise her feminist and queer politics. DiFranco, who does not identify as lesbian (or straight) is a prolific artist who has released more than 20 albums on her own Righteous Babe Records.

Building on 1970s feminism and the punk bands of the era, riot grrrl music is an underground genre influenced by third-wave feminism that emerged in Olympia, WA, Portland, OR, and Washington, DC in the early 1990s. The genre prides itself on a Do It Yourself (D.I.Y.) ethic and privileges political over musical virtuosity. Riot grrrl music is characterized by an "in your face" attitude, and lyrics that challenge patriarchy, capitalism, and normative sexuality. Well-known bands include Bikini Kill, Bratmobile, Heavens to Betsy, Huggy Bear, Sleater-Kinney, and L7. Combining artistic practice with protest politics, riot grrrls organized political meetings and engaged in the production of zines. Defying the power of sexist slurs, some performers marked their bodies with words like "slut," "dyke," and "whore." Short-lived as a genre, the riot grrrl movement influenced many artists to come – especially of the queercore genre.

In the beginning of the twenty-first century, as more and more mainstream artists, athletes, politicians, and actors began to come out publicly as lesbian, gay, or queer, younger generations have come to embrace queer sexualities and flexible genders. Explicitly queer, political, and adopting somewhat of a punk style, queercore has emerged as a popular music genre with bands made up of both men and women. Queercore bands featuring lesbian artists include The Gossip, Team Dresch, Le Tigre, The Butchies, and Tribe 8.

SEE ALSO: Feminisms, First, Second, and Third Wave; Riot Grrrl; Sexual Rights

REFERENCES

Castle, Terry, ed. 2003. *The Literature of Lesbianism*. New York: Columbia University Press.
Spörke, Michael. 2014. *Big Mama Thornton: The Life and Music*. Jefferson: McFarland.

FURTHER READING

Darms, Lisa, Kathleen Hanna, and Johanna Fateman. 2013. *The Riot Grrrl Collection*. New York: The Feminist Press of CUNY.
Davis, Angela. 1999. *Blues Legacies and Black Feminism: Gertrude "Ma" Rainey, Bessie Smith, and Billie Holiday*. Vancouver: Vintage Books.
Leibetseder, Doris, and Rebecca Carbery. 2012. *Queer Tracks: Subversive Strategies in Rock and Pop Music (Popular and Folks Music Series)*. Farnham: Ashgate.
Morris, B. J. 2000. *Eden Built by Eves: The Culture of Women's Music Festivals*. New York: Alyson Books.
Whiteley, Sheila. 2000. *Women and Popular Music: Sexuality, Identity and Subjectivity*. New York: Routledge.

Lesbian Stereotypes in the United States

ANNA SORENSEN
University of California, Santa Barbara, USA

Stereotypes about lesbians are caricatures that reflect dominant expectations and beliefs about the characteristics of lesbians. Stereotypical images and ideas about lesbians tend to exaggerate their sexual experiences, portray lesbians as extremely feminine or extremely masculine, and oversimplify lesbians' historic and contemporary lives. Lesbian stereotypes attempt to reflect what typical lesbians wear, how they spend their leisure time, or how they act in their families and workplaces. Such images and ideas often draw on lesbians' identities and styles of self-presentation, but they are oversimplifications and exaggerations that are removed from the historical and sociopolitical contexts within which lesbians constructed their identities. These stereotypes are reproduced in ways that depict lesbianism as either a threat to heterosexuality or as a not-quite-good-enough mimicry of normative gender roles, desire, sexual behavior, and relationships.

The construction of lesbian identities and forms of self-presentation has occurred within the context of feminist, lesbian feminist, and LGBTQ (lesbian, gay, bisexual, transgender, and queer) social movements. Some stereotypes about lesbians that have become pervasive in popular culture are reflections of and contribute to the process by which lesbian feminists built collective identity, the "shared definition of a group that derives from members' common interests, experiences, and solidarity" (Taylor and Whittier 1992, 78), a process often marked by debates over the boundaries of acceptable and unacceptable forms of sexual and gender expression. Thus, stereotypes about lesbians have figured into lesbians' constructions of identity, as they continuously struggle to define themselves and achieve acceptance and visibility in a heteronormative world that assumes heterosexuality is the natural and superior way of organizing sexual relationships. These stereotypes have been used in religious texts, in legislation, in the media, and in literature and film to justify and perpetuate prejudice and discrimination against lesbians.

THE SOCIAL CONSTRUCTION OF LESBIAN IDENTITIES

Despite ample evidence that women have engaged in same-sex sexual behavior and relationships throughout history and across cultures, lesbianism as a category of social identity was not constructed until the late nineteenth century when sexologists began to categorize sexual practices as normal or abnormal based on cultural norms of masculinity and femininity (Rupp 2009). A woman whose appearance deviated from cultural norms of femininity was diagnosed as a female sexual invert, or as having a biological predisposition to masculine gender traits. Sexologists' theories were widely disseminated and the link between a "mannish" woman and lesbianism was established in the popular imaginary. In the post-World War II years when lesbians faced daily discrimination, from housing to employment to open hostility in public, masculine women, or butch women, and lesbians who embraced conventional norms of femininity, known as "femmes," built communities organized around the butch–femme dyad.

In the late 1960s and 1970s, lesbians played a central role in the emergence of the feminist movement, and they began to demand recognition and support for lesbian issues from the movement. Because women who challenge patriarchal gender norms are often discredited with the accusation of lesbianism, feminists were hostile toward lesbians, with some even referring to them as "the Lavender Menace." In response, lesbians formed a lesbian feminist social movement community and a politicized collective identity (Stein 1997; Taylor and Whittier 1992). Lesbian feminism set itself apart from heterosexual society by creating separate institutions and a "women's culture" marked by events that celebrated women's values. Lesbian feminists developed an oppositional consciousness that positioned lesbian relationships as the means of subverting patriarchy, and thus as the ultimate expression of feminism. They also consciously negotiated ways of expressing gender identity that would challenge oppressive patriarchal and heterosexist norms, including changing their names, rejecting hierarchical structures, and adopting ways of self-presentation such as wearing short hair, not shaving their legs, and walking and talking in ways that challenge conventional norms of femininity.

The lesbian community was never monolithic. Frequent debates over the boundaries of lesbian identity and lesbian self-presentation interrogated the ways that dominant culture represented lesbians and consciously used those images and ideas in the strategic deployment of identity (Bernstein 1997) in efforts to reduce the stigma faced by lesbians while simultaneously challenging sexism and heteronormativity. There was tension over the perceptions of the erasure of lesbian sexuality, accusations that butch sexuality and the butch–femme dyad were imitations of sexist gender roles, and critiques of femme lesbians as not "real" lesbians due to their expression of normative femininity. There were struggles over the exclusion of bisexuals, transgender individuals, and women of color. Many lesbians who had children from heterosexual relationships tried to retain custodial rights in discriminatory courts while others publicly pursued second-parent adoption rights and access to reproductive technologies (i.e., the "lesbian baby boom"). Recent decades have seen an increased presence of lesbians in the same-sex marriage movement and a proliferation of new lesbian identities (e.g., stone butch, softball lesbian, lipstick lesbian) with diverse styles of self-presentation.

STEREOTYPES OF LESBIANS IN POPULAR CULTURE

The images and ideas about lesbians that have become pervasive stereotypes are in part based on the ways that lesbians have consciously chosen to express gender identity. Stereotypical representations of lesbians are created from a heteronormative perspective that assumes heterosexuality is the "standard for legitimate sociosexual arrangements" and naturalizes norms of masculinity and femininity (Ingraham 1994, 204), an assumption that "shapes the production of identities, relationships, cultural expressions, and institutional practices" (Ward and Schneider 2009, 435). Thus, lesbian desire, gender identities, and relationships are presented as inferior replications of heterosexual desire, gender roles, and relationship norms.

Two of the most pervasive stereotypes about lesbians are that that they are either masculine *or* feminine, butch *or* femme. Butch lesbians have been depicted as unattractive, man-hating, masculine women who are sexually aggressive, unemotional, and sometimes athletic. Femme women have been depicted as women who are attractive to men or lesbians who are either dangerous seductresses or tortured souls due to their abnormal desires (Inness 1997). Butch women are typically assumed to be sexually attracted to and partnered with femme women.

Some scholars, such as Halberstam (1998), argue that butch sexuality challenges the idea that masculinity is attached solely to male bodies and therefore threatens the dominance of heterosexuality and patriarchy. Butch women are stereotyped as wanting to *be men* and images of butch women suggest that their appearance and sexual desire are designed to mimic heterosexual masculinity. However, because they are not "real" men, butch women are not granted the privileges of masculinity. As a result, butch women have been subject to significant discrimination and verbal and physical violence.

Because femme identities include elements of normative femininity, femme lesbians are often either assumed to be straight, or they are stereotyped as not "real" lesbians compared to butch or androgynous lesbians. Scholars such as Joan Nestle (1992) argue that femme lesbians' use of conventionally feminine dress, comportment, and accoutrements do not reflect the unconscious adoption of patriarchal gender norms. Rather, they consciously construct feminine identities within the context of non-heteronormative desires and relationships. By doing so, femme lesbians make same-sex sexuality visible and they transgress patriarchal gender norms.

Femme lesbians are also subject to unwanted male attention and are positioned as the objects of men's sexual fantasy. Heteronormativity assumes that women cannot achieve sexual satisfaction without the presence of men. This is illustrated in pornographic films that feature sex between femme women that does not result in sexual satisfaction until a man joins the scene. Same-sex sexual desire is staged and exploited for the benefit of men and the possibility of sexual gratification in the absence of male participation is erased. Representations in mainstream culture, such as the affair between Julianne Moore and Mark Ruffalo in the film *The Kids Are All Right* (2010), suggest that lesbian sexual desire may only be a phase in the life course and that lesbians will eventually find a man.

Stereotypes about lesbians develop from the perception that same-sex desire and sexual satisfaction are unimaginable, incomplete, or inferior outside the heteronormative male/female dyad (Wilton 1996). Stereotypes assume that lesbian sex must replicate, however poorly, heterosexual sex. Similarly, heteronormative expectations about relationships assume that lesbians will imitate heteronormative gender roles for men and women. For example, a common assumption is that one lesbian partner acts like a man and the other partner acts like a woman. Lesbians often are asked questions such as, "Which one's the man?," "Who takes out the garbage?," and "Who pays the check?" Furthermore, jokes popular among lesbians, such as the joke that lesbians bring U-Hauls to the second date, have been used to bolster mainstream stereotypes because they support the heterosexual sexual script that suggests women desire emotional connection over sex and prefer monogamous relationships (Gordon 2006). Thus, such stereotypes "explain" the existence of lesbian relationships by relying on traditional notions of women's innate need for deep emotional attachment.

With increasing lesbian visibility in the popular media in the 1990s and 2000s, representations of lesbians shifted to an emphasis on feminized women who were "chic and fashionable" (Ciasullo 2001). Lesbians were frequently depicted as stylish, feminine, white, and upper middle class, marginalizing the experiences of lower- and working-class lesbians and lesbians of color. There were few depictions of butch women and little suggestion of lesbian sexual desire and behavior. Television shows such as *The L Word* included some lesbians of color and lesbians with a variety of gender presentations, but lesbians are generally depicted as acceptably feminine, white, and economically advantaged (Farr and Degroult 2008). Ciasullo (2001) writes that such images present lesbians as consumable objects, available for heterosexual men to desire and women to emulate. Keegan (2006) used films such as *If These Walls Could Talk 2* (2000) and *What Makes a Family* (2001) to argue that the increase in visibility of lesbians in film and television comes with an emphasis on the achievement of normative female gender roles, such as motherhood. Lesbians are often positioned within monogamous relationships, in nuclear family units, dealing with parenting issues. Representations of lesbians as financially secure femmes or mothers highlight the ways in which lesbians "are just like heterosexuals" and therefore do not threaten the primacy of the heterosexual binary.

SHIFTING STEREOTYPES, SHIFTING IDENTITIES

Even though recent depictions of lesbians are more positive than the images of previous decades, they erase the diversity of lesbian experiences, desires, and identities by presenting a unidimensional figure. While some lesbians fit these stereotypes, far more do not. Recent research analyzes the ways that race, class, geography, and other factors affect lesbian identities and gender expression. For example, Kazyak (2012) found that female masculinity is less stigmatized in rural areas, allowing masculine lesbians to gain acceptance in rural locations. Other research finds that many black lesbians have historically and continue to organize their relationships around gendered presentations of self (Moore 2006), a finding that adds complexity to research that indicates that gender presentation, and particularly butch–femme dynamics, are an important part of lesbians' erotic lives (Inness 1997).

Similarly, depictions of lesbians as monogamous, marriage-seeking, motherhood-oriented women accurately represent many lesbians and reflect same-sex marriage's primacy as an LGBTQ movement goal. However, these representations are stereotypical because they suggest that *all* lesbians are desirous of such relationships and of same-sex marriage when in fact there are many debates within LGBTQ movements about whether lesbians should marry (Bernstein and Taylor 2013). Recent research indicates that many lesbians, including those who marry their partners, are critical of the institution of marriage and the notion that lesbians want to be the same as heterosexuals, and believe that their marriages will challenge and transform the institution of marriage (Kimport 2014).

Finally, research on the ways that women who love women are constructing their identities suggests that women's sexual identities are fluid (Diamond 2008) and that younger women are choosing from a wider variety of available identity labels (e.g., queer, fluid, pansexual) and ways of presenting themselves that challenge the heterosexual binary. Rupp et al. (2014) find that college-age women who participate in the hookup scene find space within that environment to "explore same-sex attractions and new sexual identities" (2). This suggests that young women are attuned to the stereotypes about lesbianism perpetuated in mainstream culture and within lesbian communities and actively negotiate those stereotypes in the formation of their identities and their modes of self-expression. Thus, we see that the creation of lesbian identities and mainstream stereotypes about lesbians are in constant tension. Just as second-wave feminists were not accepting of lesbians because of the stigmatization of lesbian identity and the association of lesbianism with feminism, younger women may be choosing new identities rather than identifying as lesbians because of the negative images of lesbians and the denigration of lesbianism in mainstream society. Future research should continue to explore the relationship between stereotypes, stigma, and lesbian identities.

SEE ALSO: Bisexuality; Butch/Femme; Compulsory Heterosexuality; Feminism, Lesbian; Lesbian Continuum; Stone Butch

REFERENCES

Bernstein, Mary. 1997. "Celebration and Suppression: The Strategic Uses of Identity by the Lesbian and Gay Movement." *American Journal of Sociology*, 103: 531–565.

Bernstein, Mary, and Verta Taylor. 2013. *The Marrying Kind? Debating Same-Sex Marriage within the Gay and Lesbian Movement*. Minneapolis: University of Minnesota Press.

Ciasullo, Ann M. 2001. "Making Her (In)Visible: Cultural Representations of Lesbianism and the Lesbian Body in the 1990s." *Feminist Studies*, 27: 577–608.

Diamond, Lisa. 2008. *Sexual fluidity: Understanding Women's Love and Desire*. Cambridge, MA: Harvard University Press.

Farr, Daniel, and Nathalie Degroult. 2008. "Understand the Queer World of the L-esbian Body: Using Queer as Folk and the L Word to Address the Construction of the Lesbian Body." *Journal of Lesbian Studies*, 12: 423–434.

Gordon, Liahna. 2006. "Bringing the U-Haul: Embracing and Resisting Sexual Stereotypes in a Lesbian Community." *Sexualities*, 9: 171–192.

Halberstam, Judith. 1998. *Female Masculinity*. Durham, NC: Duke University Press.

Ingraham, Chrys. 1994. "The Heterosexual Imaginary: Feminist Sociology and Theories of Gender." *Sociological Theory*, 12: 203–219.

Inness, Sherrie. 1997. *The Lesbian Menace: Ideology, Identity, and the Representation of Lesbian Life*. Amherst: University of Massachusetts Press.

Kazyak, Emily. 2012. "'Midwest or Lesbian?' Gender, Rurality, and Sexuality." *Gender & Society*, 26: 825–848.

Keegan, Cait. 2006. "Household Remedies." *Journal of Lesbian Studies*, 10: 107–123.

Kimport, Katrina. 2014. *Queering Marriage, Challenging Family Formation in the United States*. New Brunswick: Rutgers University Press.

Moore, Mignon. 2006. "Lipstick or Timberlands? Meanings of Gender Presentation in Black Lesbian Communities." *Signs: Journal of Women in Culture and Society*, 32: 113–129.

Nestle, Joan. 1992. *The Persistent Desire: A Butch–Femme Reader*. Boston: Alyson Publications.

Rupp, Leila. 2009. *Sapphistries: A Global History of Love between Women.* New York: NYU Press.

Rupp, Leila J., Verta Taylor, Shiri Regev-Messalem, Alison Fogarty, and Paula England. 2014. "Queer Women in the Hookup Scene: Beyond the Closet?" *Gender & Society*, 28: 212–235.

Stein, Arlene. 1997. *Sex and Sensibility: Stories of a Lesbian Generation.* Berkeley: University of California Press.

Taylor, Verta, and Nancy Whittier. 1992. "Collective Identity in Social Movement Communities, Lesbian Feminist Mobilization." In *Frontiers in Social Movement Theory*, edited by Aldon D. Morris and Carol M. Mueller. New Haven: Yale University Press.

The Kids Are All Right. Directed by Lisa Cholodenko. Universal City, CA: Universal Studios Home Entertainment, 2010.

Ward, Jane, and Beth Schneider. 2009. "The Reaches of Heteronormativity, An Introduction." *Gender & Society*, 23: 433–439.

Wilton, Tamsin. 1996. "'Which One's the Man?' The Heterosexualization of Lesbian Sex." In *Theorising Heterosexuality*, edited by Diane Richardson. Buckingham: Open University Press.

Lesbian and Womyn's Separatism

KATH BROWNE
University of Brighton, UK

Lesbian and womyn's separatism is adopting a way of life where womyn seek to be practically, emotionally, and sexually separated from men. This includes living apart from men, for example not relying on men for food, services, or any products, not listening to music by men, not reading literature by men, and not engaging with men's artistic productions. Lesbian and womyn's separatism is both a critique and reaction to heterosexisms and patriarchy and is built on the ideal that the personal is political.

Lesbian and womyn's separatism is closely related to lesbian feminisms, drawing on similar critiques of both patriarchal and heterosexist institutions that create everyday lives and understand the personal as political. Some radical lesbian feminists have argued that women should exist entirely apart from men. The use of the "y" in womyn (rather than women) and the "o" in womon (rather than woman) is used to indicate a separation from men and a celebration of womyn's independence. Similarly herstories, rather than histories, are discussed to indicate the masculinisms associated with the ways in which the past is narrated.

Lesbian and womyn's separatist communities emerged in the 1970s. Key to womyn's and lesbian separatism is the withdrawal from "masculinist" society, often to spatially live in separatist communities (Valentine 1997; Rudy 2001). Separatism illustrates that womyn are capable of being self-sufficient without men. However, separatism has various dimensions ranging from a complete separation from men, for example by living in womyn-only communes, to the exclusion of men from sexual relations.

Lesbianism itself can be read and used as a political act of separatism because it challenges accepted notions of gender and sexualities. In this way, identifying as a lesbian can be an act of resistance to patriarchy and heterosexism. Although not necessarily the case, womyn in separatist communities can identify as lesbian as a political act of separation from men, rather than associating this with desire or an innate trait/biological inevitability. Regardless of the modes of separation, the underlying arguments are the same, namely, that everyday life and/or sexual desires and practices have political effects. By living apart from men in various ways, lesbian and womyn's separatists highlight the taken-for-granted ways in which masculinist societies operate.

Commonly associated with rural areas in North America (see Bell and Valentine 1995, Browne, Lim, and Brown 2007), the siting of these separatist communities mainly in rural areas has enabled womyn to live more self-sufficiently, as well as resisting "man-made." Valentine (1997) has showed how some US lesbian separatists in the 1970s saw the rural as an opportunity not only to develop communities away from patriarchy, but also to exist closer to "Mother Nature." This links to the spiritual dimensions of womyn's and lesbian separatist communities. These relate not only to Wiccan, but also to other forms of female spiritualities, as well as reworking mainstream religious rituals such as celebrating the Sabbath at Michigan Womyn's Music Festival (Morris 1999; Browne 2009).

Communes and womyn's communities sought to rework the practices of everyday lives. Because patriarchy and compulsory heterosexuality are believed to be irrevocably intertwined, some lesbian feminists assert that feminism is only "true" when it is lesbian or separate from men. These staunch views have had divisive implications and the lived realities of lesbian feminist and womyn's lands in the 1970s were not straightforward. The multiple differences between womyn, including dis/abilities, made communal living something that needed to be carefully negotiated. Valentine contends that there were internal conflicts in women's spaces and suggests that "Many of these lesbian rural communes in the U.S. and the U.K. have folded as a result of political disputes and the ideals of the founders to reject all the trappings of the man-made city" (1997, 119).

Despite these issues, and contrary to Valentine's assertions, some womyn's lands still survive today. They can be characterized in at least two ways: first, as permanent settlements where womyn live separate from men for the majority of the year (for example the We'moon community in Oregon), and second, as temporary lands that arise during womyn's music festivals (such as Michigan Womyn's Music Festival; see Browne 2009). These contemporary spaces have addressed some of the issues of the 1970s and 1980s; however, they are not without their own controversies.

Whereas differences between women dominated debates in the 1970s and 1980s, the biggest challenge to womyn's lands has been the queering/questioning of the sign womyn. In particular, the assertion that womyn should live apart from men relies on a definition of "men" and "women"; whilst some have seen those who are female identifying as fitting in to womyn's lands, others have sought to police the boundaries more clearly. Specifically, policies such as "womyn-born-womyn" have elicited much debate and controversy at Michigan Womyn's Music Festival. The festival organizers ask for one week where womyn who have been brought up as girls might gather to the exclusion of all others (Morris 1999). Trans activists, and particularly trans women, argue that this policy denies their right to occupy women's space as womyn. The positioning of trans men is more ambiguous, with many attending Michigan Womyn's Music Festival on the basis of their female/girl herstories and links with feminist and lesbian communities (Browne 2009, 2011).

The future of womyn's and lesbian separatist spaces is in the balance as many of those who organize and run these spaces get older and are less able to live self-sufficiently outside of (masculinist) societies. This, in addition to queer critiques of rigid gender binaries, poses key challenges to these political, innovative, yet controversial spaces.

SEE ALSO: Feminism, Lesbian; Feminism, Radical; Mother Nature; Patriarchy; Personal is Political; Wicca

REFERENCES

Bell, David, and Gill Valentine. 1995. "Queer Country: Rural Lesbian and Gay Lives." *Journal of Rural Studies*, 11: 113–122.

Browne, Kath. 2009. "Womyn's Separatist Spaces: Rethinking Spaces of Difference and Exclusion." *Transactions of the Institute of British Geographers*, 34(4): 541–556.

Browne, Kath. 2011. "Beyond Rural Idylls: Imperfect Lesbian Utopias at Michigan Womyn's Music Festival." *Journal of Rural Studies*, 27(1): 13–23.

Browne, Kath, Jason Lim, and Gavin Brown. 2007. *Geographies of Sexualities: Theories, Practices and Politics*. London: Ashgate.

Morris, Bonnie J. 1999. *Eden Built by Eves: The Culture of Women's Music Festivals*. Los Angeles: Alyson.

Rudy, Kathy. 2001. "Radical Feminism, Lesbian Separatism and Queer Theory." *Feminist Studies*, 27(1): 191–222.

Valentine, Gill. 1997. "Making Space: Lesbian Separatist Communities in the United States." In *Contested Countryside Cultures: Otherness, Marginalization and Rurality*, edited by Paul Cloke and Jo Little, 109–122. London: Routledge.

Lesbians as Community Other Mothers

BRENDA HAYMAN
University of Western Sydney, Australia

Increasing visibility and social acceptance of various non-traditional constellations of family and kin have meant that some families consist of more than one mother, for example in the case of adoptive mothers, foster mothers, stepmothers, and non-biological mothers in lesbian-headed (*de novo*) families. Combined with the rise in alternate family constructions and the escalation in use of (and access to) assistive reproductive technologies, there has been an increase in the incidence of non-biological mothers engaging in mothering work. The term other mother is frequently used to describe the non-biological female parent in *de novo* lesbian families in academic literature. Alternate phrases include: non-birth mother, lesbian co-parent, lesbian co-mother, and social mother. Notably, the term "social mother" has been used more accurately in the literature when referring to the stepmother in lesbian-headed families where the children were born during the partner's previous heterosexual relationship. In the social context, as a child attempts to differentiate two female parents in *de novo* families, a variety of words and phrases are used to describe other mothers, for example: mum/mummy, ma, the woman's first name, "daddy," a name made up by their child, or a word that means "dad/daddy" in an alternate language that is culturally significant to the family.

A *de novo* lesbian family refers to a family constellation that consists of two partnered women and the child(ren) they planned, conceived, birthed, and are raising together in the context of their lesbian relationship. Since the 1970s, *de novo* families have become more visible in society. However, language (like other mother) to name various aspects, types, and members of *de novo* families continues to develop, and therefore a unique opportunity exists for other mothers and their families to construct their own identity, role, and title through language.

Other mothers challenge heteronormative ideologies about family and the need for biological connectedness to create a genuine family. Despite increased visibility, they are often required to justify their position as a legitimate parent. Other mothers, together with the biological mother and their children, often work together to create symbols of connectedness and relationship, to gain recognition as a genuine family and the acknowledgment of the other mother's position. Symbols of *de novo* family connection include the use of names, ceremonies, and other formal means of recognition. Lesbian parents choose names for their children that demonstrate a relationship between the other mother and the children. For example, the children are often given the other mother's surname. Parents also engage in ceremonies, like baby naming days and commitment ceremonies (where same-sex marriage is not permitted by law), which also attempt to show familial connectedness. Finally, any means of formal recognition, for example official documentation on birth certificates where the other mother is listed as a parent, is also used.

There is some contention about the use of the term other mother as it may not accurately or adequately describe the existent role and position of the non-biological mother in *de novo* families, and in fact it may further position the other mother outside of the family. Use of the word "other" may further marginalize her from the socially acceptable and heteronormative construct of "family" and detract from her role and position. "Others" are essentially defined as not ourselves, generally represent difference, and subsequently are vulnerable, excluded, and invisible. Use of the term other mother is not meant to infer exclusion or otherness in the context of academic literature, but in the absence of a more suitable term or until a more appropriate word or phrase is generated, this seems to be the term most reflective of the role and position of the non-biological mother in *de novo* families.

There is an abundance of research that has explored the outcomes for children of lesbian mothers compared to the outcomes for children raised in heterosexual families. Likewise, there is a significant amount of research that has explored the role of women in *de novo* families and, more recently, research exploring how lesbians make decisions about method of conception and donor status. Fewer studies have reported how lesbian women negotiate heteronormative spaces, for example healthcare services and schools. Much of this literature refers to the non-biological mother in *de novo* families as the other mother.

SEE ALSO: Families of Choice; Household Livelihood Strategies

FURTHER READING

Almack, Kathryn. 2005. "What's in a Name? The Significance of the Choice of Surnames Given to Children Born within Lesbian-Parent Families." *Sexualities*, 8: 239–254.

Bergen, Karla Mason, Suter, Elizabeth A., and Daas, Karen L. 2006. "'About as Solid as a Fish Net': Symbolic Construction of a Legitimate Parental Identity for Nonbiological Lesbian Mothers." *Journal of Family Communication*, 6: 201–220.

Brown, Rhonda, and Amaryll Perlesz. 2007. "Not the 'Other' Mother: How Language Constructs Lesbian Co-Parenting Relationships." *Journal of GLBT Family Studies*, 3: 267–308.

Brown, Rhonda, and Amaryll Perlesz. 2008. "In Search of a Name for Lesbians who Mother their Non-Biological Children." *Journal of GLBT Studies*, 4: 453–467.

Hayman, Brenda, Lesley Wilkes, Debra Jackson, and Elizabeth Halcomb. 2013. "*De Novo* Lesbian Families: Legitimizing the Other Mother." *Journal of GLBT Family Studies*, 9: 273–287. DOI: 10.1080/1550428X.2013.781909.

Millbank, Jenni. 2008. "Unlikely Fissures and Uneasy Resonances: Lesbian Co-Mothers, Surrogate Parenthood and Fathers' Rights." *Feminist Legal Studies*, 16: 141–167.

Morrow, Colette. 2001. "Narrating Maternity: Authorizing the 'Other' Mother in Lesbian Family Stories." *Journal of Lesbian Studies*, 5: 63–90.

Padavic, Irene, and Jonniann Butterfield. 2011. "Mothers, Father and 'Mathers': Negotiating a Lesbian Co-Parental Identity." *Gender & Society*, 25: 176–196.

Tasker, Fiona, and Susan Golombok. 1998. "The Role of Co-Mothers in Planned Lesbian-Led Families." *Journal of Lesbian Studies*, 2: 49–68.

Lesbos

VENETIA KANTSA
University of the Aegean, Greece

Lesbos – Lésvos in Modern Greek – is a Greek island located in the northeastern Aegean. It is also often called Mytilini after the name of its capital city and it is the third largest of the islands in Greece, with an area of 1636 sq. km and a population of approximately 86,000. Its male and female inhabitants are called *lesvios* and *lesvia*, respectively.

However, in the Greek language, *lesvia* not only connotes the female inhabitants of Lesbos but is also used as a descriptive and self-identificatory term for a same-sex desiring woman. This second meaning came into being in the late 1970s under the influence of the Anglo-Saxon feminist and lesbian movement that had been introduced into Greece. During the same period, Eressos, a village in the western part of Lesbos, became an international meeting point for lesbian women who have gradually established a seasonal lesbian community whose imaginary roots go back as far as the sixth century BCE, the time of Sappho's birth.

According to the prevailing evidence, the famous lyric poetess Sappho was born in Eressos into a prominent family. Souda, a Byzantine lexicon compiled in 1000 CE mentions her as "a Lesbian from Eressos," dating her birth between 612 and 609 BCE. In the nineteenth century, a revived interest in Sappho emerged. At the same time that her translators started to agree on the use of the feminine pronoun "her" instead of the masculine "his" when there is a reference to the beloved person, and while the classicists disputed over the true facts and the legends relating to her life, the doctors adopted terms such as "sapphism" and "lesbianism" to describe same-sex practices between women. The terms *sapphism* and *sapphic* officially appeared in the English language only in the last decade of the nineteenth century by British medical authorities who labeled with these terms what they judged as a psychopathological behavior. The terms *lesbian* and *lesbianism* have a different history. Their roots are in the Attic comedy of the fifth century BCE when the verb "lesbi[a]zein" (to act like one from Lesbos) was used to denote *fellatio* performed by females. The use of the noun lesbianism to suggest women's homosexuality dates back to 1870 (Lardinois 1989).

A few decades later, at the beginning of the twentieth century, and for the first time, women's literary potential was combined with the existence of lesbian relations. Women intellectuals who lived in Paris – not only French but also English, American, authors and poetesses – considered Sappho as their distant ancestor, an ancestor who encouraged them to take part in linguistic experiments. For the poetesses who believed that they did not have sufficient education, for the lesbian poetesses who looked for a lesbian tradition in vain, Sappho was a very special forebear. She was acclaimed a distant ancestor, mother, and sister, while the island of Lesbos, the island that gave Sappho the opportunity to express herself and create poetry, was related to the vision and the illusion of a society that would allow women to express themselves, enjoy love, and live without their existence being defined by men (Gubar 1984).

In the following decades, women from Europe and America traveled to the island of Lesbos in order to pay tribute to Sappho and to look for this mythical place. Eressos's inhabitants remember the place being visited by women alone or in couples long before the 1970s. Oral tradition in Eressos has it that these first visitors came with the vision and the illusion that they had found the ideal place – a place where Sappho lived and created her masterpieces, a place with tradition in homosexuality, a place where, as they (falsely) believed, men and women belonged to separate and mutually exclusive spheres of action.

The subsequent phenomenon of a massive arrival of women in Eressos after the 1970s, apart from being related to the development of a strong tourism current in Greece, especially from European countries, is directly linked to the boom of the lesbian–feminist movement in the Anglo-Saxon countries which encouraged the formation of separatist communities. In the context of a need to search for archetypal figures such as Sappho and Mother-Goddess and find isolated spaces, Eressos seemed to have all the prerequisites for becoming the ideal place for the establishment of a seasonal lesbian separatist community.

Although at the beginning local villagers were rather hostile towards lesbian women, since the mid-1990s no major quarrels among women and locals have been recorded. This change in attitudes is attributed mainly to economic reasons. Nowadays, a significant number of lesbian women visit Eressos every summer. They come from Greece and from other European countries – Germany, the United Kingdom, Italy, Italy, The Netherlands, Norway – but also from the United States, Australia, Canada, New Zealand, India and elsewhere. They come to see the place where Sappho was born, to meet other lesbian women, to have a vacation in a relaxed atmosphere, to see friends, to fall in love, and to participate in the annual International Eressos Women's Festival. Some of them have even bought houses in the village and are the owners of bars, restaurants, and small hotels. Still, for the locals the relation of Lesbos to "lesbians" continues to be a contested topic and a number of them persist in claiming the word *lesvia* only as a descriptive term for the female inhabitants of the island.

SEE ALSO: Lesbian and Womyn's Separatism

REFERENCES

Gubar, Susan. 1984. "Sapphistries." *Signs*, 10(1): 43–62.

Lardinois, Andre. 1989. "Lesbian Sappho and Sappho of Lesbos." In *From Sappho to de Sade. Moments in the History of Sexuality*, edited by Jan Bremmer, 15–35. London: Routledge.

FURTHER READING

Kantsa, Venetia. 2002. "'Certain Places Have Different Energy.' Spatial Transformations in Eressos Lesvos." *GLQ: A Journal of Lesbian and Gay Studies*, 8(1–2): 35–57.

Kantsa, Venetia. 2010. "*Lesvia*: (i) a same-sex desiring woman (ii) a woman inhabitant of Lesbos island. The re-introduction of a word of Greek origin into modern Greece." In *Language and Sexuality (Through and) Beyond Gender*, edited by Costas Canakis, Venetia Kantsa, and Kostas Yannakopoulos, 25–42. Newcastle upon Tyne: Cambridge Scholars Publishing.

LGBT Activism in Australia and New Zealand

GRAHAM WILLETT
University of Melbourne, Australia
CHRIS BRICKELL
Otago University, New Zealand

Australia and New Zealand have been separate countries since the early twentieth century when they began their transition from colonies to independence. Still, they are part of a cultural realm that binds them very closely. Both are settler states, founded on a colonization process that transplanted millions of people from the United Kingdom who brought with them laws, political institutions, social structures, and values. When the six British colonies of Australia federated in 1901, New Zealand's inclusion was not out of the question. The two countries have fought together in a variety of nation-defining wars and have a history of both progressive social policies and violent dispossession of the indigenous peoples. Both countries operated for a very long time on a two-party system, one of which was a Labor/Labour party that rested on the support of a vibrant trade union movement; the other being a center-right liberal party (in the British sense of that word). The term Australasia, coined to embrace both countries, is not in wide use, but is a useful way to draw attention to what they have in common.

At a deeper level still, the people and politicians and opinion-makers long thought of themselves as living in British outposts, looking "Home" for inspiration, guidance, leadership, and validation. It was no surprise that when the United Kingdom began to debate decriminalization of sex between men in the late 1950s, progressive forces in Australasia started to take up the cause.

The homosexual world was shaped in both countries by buggery laws that arrived with the colonists and by a deeply embedded social distaste. However, as elsewhere, a subculture was built. It was detectable in the major cities by the early twentieth century. In the smaller towns and regions, a different kind of homo-sociability associated with frontier notions of mateship and middle-class notions of romantic friendship (male and female) occasionally provided a vehicle for same-sex desire (Brickell 2008).

In the mid-1960s, the United States started to exercise a new influence on the political, social, and cultural imagination of Australasia and there is evidence of contact with American homophile politics via its media, The *Mattachine Review* and the *Ladder*, the magazine of the Daughters of Bilitis (see below), through travel, and through pen-pals.

The postwar economic boom of the 1950s and 1960s was experienced as intensely in Australia and New Zealand as it was elsewhere in the West, producing societies in which change was a matter of everyday experience – change that was strongly in the direction of liberal politics, social structures, and attitudes. At the parliamentary level, the election in 1972 of the Labor/Labour Party governments in both Australia and New Zealand, under Prime Ministers Gough Whitlam and Norman Kirk, respectively, was the culmination of a steady march of liberalism and social democracy into the mainstream and into the governmental realm.

Liberals regarded the laws and irrational attitudes directed against homosexuals as evidence of social and political backwardness, yet another aspect of society needing reform. In newspapers and magazines such as *Nation*, the *Bulletin*, and *Canberra Times* in Australia and the *Listener* and *Thursday* in New Zealand, liberal voices spoke out.

It helped that the United Kingdom was also moving on this issue. The government's Wolfenden Committee inquiry into homosexual offences had recommended in 1957 that homosexual acts committed by consenting adults in private be legalized. Their report was widely noted across the British world. In London, the Homosexual Law Reform Society (HLRS) spent the next decade campaigning for decriminalization and kept the issue alive in the press and in liberal circles.

Laurie Collinson – Jewish, communist, homosexual, poet – was inspired by reports in the *New Statesman* and his communication with the British HLRS. He attempted to found such an organization in Melbourne, but without success. It was not until 1969 that successful homosexual organizing began in Australia. In Melbourne, a group of lesbians founded the Daughters of Bilitis, based on and supported by the US organization of the same name. In Canberra, a Homosexual Law Reform Society was established by a group composed mostly of academics and journalists (few of them gay) to agitate for decriminalization. A year later, John Ware and Christabel Poll launched the Campaign Against Moral Persecution (CAMP, the word then most commonly used by homosexual women and men to name themselves). Intended as a small-scale lobby group, it rapidly became a national organization, with branches in all state capitals and on most university campuses. It provided a social life (via clubrooms and events such as dances, lectures, and libraries) and it was soon organizing protests and demonstrations of various kinds (Willett 2000).

In New Zealand, progress began much earlier. In 1962, a group of women in Wellington advertised the existence of the Radclyffe Hall Memorial Society, assuming that lesbians would recognize the name of the 1920s English lesbian novelist (Glamuzina 1993). In the same year, a number of men established a club, complete with clubrooms, called the Dorian Society, which brought together a wide cross-section of homosexual men for regular social events. In 1966, its legal affairs subcommittee adopted the name the Wolfenden Association to take up the task of lobbying for law reform. Like the British HLRS (with which it was in contact and whose name it adopted a year later), it presented itself as an organization open to anyone committed to a rational approach to a significant public issue. The participation of actual homosexuals was played down in order to appear respectable (Guy 2003).

All of these groups had one thing in common: a belief that existing laws and attitudes were unjust, given that homosexuals could not help the way they were and represented no threat to society. Left alone, they would soon cease to be a problem.

Something remarkable happened to this emerging homosexual politics in the early 1970s: it went gay. Reflecting more than a change in nomenclature, "gay" was an entirely new way of being. Lesbians and gay men threw off the shackles of respectability. Their tactics were no longer confined to polite lobbying and carefully calibrated educational activities; now these noisy gays were in the streets, on university campuses, in trade unions and professional associations, demanding that laws, policies, practices, and attitudes make space for them. The rallying cry was for equality, but many went beyond that and called for revolution and liberation, a transformation of society that would benefit not just gay but also straight people, allowing everyone to break out of their sex and gender straight-jackets.

Gay liberation politics arrived in both New Zealand and Australia chiefly from the United States, reflecting the ways in which young political activists – students, women, Aborigines and Māori – were shifting their focus from Britain to America. The word "gay" was American, as was the term "gay liberation." The radical dress, the protests and zaps, the demands and language of the movement were derived almost entirely from the United States, mostly from its lesbian and gay press (although Canada's *Body Politic* was probably the most respected of the newspapers).

Early on, divisions opened up between women and men. In response to male sexism, women-only groups were set up: Radicalesbians and the Camp Women's Association in Australia, and the Sisters for Homophile Equality in Christchurch, New Zealand. For many lesbians, working in the women's movement around issues such as rape, violence, abortion, and pornography proved more fruitful. Others remained committed to working with gay men.

After the high tide of gay liberation began to ebb after about 1973, both countries saw the emergence of lesbian and gay action groups, small organizations usually committed to taking on one part of the struggle against homophobia. They launched radio programs, newspapers and newsletters, election campaigns, speakers' bureaux, and national conferences. They campaigned for decriminalization and other legal reforms, ran pride marches and festivities, established gay and lesbian friendly churches, worked in trade unions and on university campuses.

These struggles sometimes rumbled along unobserved over extended periods and occasionally erupted into public view. They brought gay and lesbian people and their issues to the attention of public officials, professionals, and millions of ordinary citizens (as families, friends, workmates of gay men and lesbians), and eroded anti-gay prejudice at a remarkably rapid rate.

Even areas of controversy were not off-limits. In the field of education, for example, where discussions were usually clouded by homophobic anxieties, in the late 1970s, the three teacher trade unions in Victoria, Australia, all adopted policies in support of gay and lesbian members, teachers, and students, and condemned anti-gay laws and attitudes (Willett 1999). In New Zealand, young people disseminated sex education books and pamphlets that presented same-sex sexuality as valid and empowering (Brickell 2007).

The action groups provided a vehicle for change in society, but law reforms required politicians and other opinion-makers to take a stand. In the early years of the movement, it was often suggested it would be easier to change the law than to change attitudes, but this turned out not to be true. A majority of the public expressed support for decriminalization of sex between men (sexual relations between women had never been illegal) well before legislators were prepared to take the step.

The earliest reform efforts in the Australian states and territories (South Australia 1972 and 1975), the Australian Capital Territory (1976), Victoria (1980), and the Northern Territory (1984) were passed as a result of lobbying and public debate. Opposition was barely visible. The next clutch of states (New South Wales 1984, Western Australia 1989, Queensland 1990) were saddled with conservative governments which had to be pressured or replaced by more liberal parliamentary majorities. Tasmania, the last state to reform in Australia, experienced the nation's first serious homophobic mobilization. This bitterly contested struggle took 10 years to achieve its goal. New Zealand, which decriminalized sex between males over the age of 16 years in 1986, also encountered strong, organized opposition from right-wing Christians, a force that had emerged in both countries in the early- to mid-1980s (Carbery 2010).

As conservatives had warned, decriminalization proved to be the thin end of the wedge, and lobbying for further reform saw anti-discrimination and anti-vilification laws, relationship recognition, adoption and medically assisted reproduction, and official recognition of transgender people implemented. Same-sex marriage was legalized in New Zealand in 2013, but at the time of writing it is not permitted in Australia.

During the 1980s and 1990s, a visible and stable lesbian and gay community emerged, first in the major cities and then in smaller regional towns. This encompassed social venues, media, lobby and activist groups, and festivals. It became a kind of ethnic community at a time when cultural diversity ("multiculturalism") was all the rage. It took its place within the broader embrace of a tolerant, open, modern society. Gay and lesbian communities worked with governments, the public service, and the medical profession to respond to HIV/AIDS to bring the disease under control and ensure that social anxiety did not turn into a full-on assault on gay rights. In Australia, the openly gay politician Bob Brown led the Greens, and others played prominent ministerial roles. Penny Wong, an Asian Australian lesbian mother, held high office in the Labor government. The Chief Minister of the Australian Capital Territory, Andrew Barr, is proudly gay. There are numerous openly gay and lesbian members of parliament (MPs) in New Zealand, especially in the Labour and Green parties. Georgina Beyer, a New Zealand Labour MP between 1999 and 2007, was the world's first transgender MP.

At the same time, the gay and lesbian community became "queer," embracing its own diversity. Sexual identities proliferated, among them bisexuality, asexuality, pansexuality, and polysexuality. Age, ethnic, and racial differences were highlighted and incorporated. Gender identity came onto the field also, with transgender and intersex people raising demands for legal recognition and social acceptance of their gender(s). The "mainstream" gay and lesbian communities have generally welcomed these newly outspoken brothers and sisters, assuming that equality and acceptance ought to be extended to differences within the communities as well from those outside.

Like gay men and lesbians before them, and people living with HIV/AIDS, gender-diverse people have adopted as their key political strategies pride, visibility, and uncompromising demands for social, political, and legal changes and for acceptance and tolerance. They have organized themselves into support and advocacy groups and taken their demands onto the streets and into the media.

In both countries, the first peoples – Aboriginal and Torres Strait Islanders in Australia, Māori in New Zealand – have rich cultures, assailed by centuries of racism and exclusion. Struggles by these communities have often been focused on survival, basic rights, and well-being, but in recent years, queer indigenous activists have been placing demands on their own people, on the queer community, and the wider society. In doing so, they have brought Aboriginally inflected versions of LGBTI to the attention of the world, most notably in the rise of Sistagirls in Australia (Cook 2013). In New Zealand, the word *takatāpui* has been adopted by gay, lesbian, transgender, bisexual, and intersexual Māori women and men as an inclusive, indigenous name for themselves and their community (Aspin 2014; Schmidt, 2014).

SEE ALSO: Gender Belief System/Gender Ideology; Gender Variance; Sex Versus Gender Categorization

REFERENCES

Aspin, Clive. 2014. "Hōkakatanga – Māori sexualities." In *Te Ara – the Encyclopedia of New Zealand*. Accessed July 17, 2014, at www.TeAra.govt.nz/en/hokakatanga-maori-sexualities.

Brickell, Chris. 2007. "Sex Education, Homosexuality and Social Contestation in 1970s New Zealand." *Sex Education*, 7(4): 387–406.

Brickell, Chris. 2008. *Mates and Lovers: A History of Gay New Zealand*. Auckland: Godwit.

Carbery, Graham. 2010. *Towards Homosexual Equality in Australian Criminal Law – A Brief History*, 2nd ed. Parkville: Australian Lesbian and Gay Archives. Accessed September 8, 2015, at www.alga.org.au/files/towardsequality2ed.pdf.

Cook, Rachel. 2013. Out and Proud. Accessed December 2014 at http://gaynewsnetwork.com.au/feature/out-and-proud-12548.html.

Glamuzina, Julie. 1993. *Out Front: Lesbian Political Activism in Aotearoa, 1962 to 1985*. Hamilton: Lesbian Press.

Guy, Laurie. 2003. *Worlds in Collision: The Gay Debate in New Zealand, 1960–1984*. Wellington: Victoria University Press.

Schmidt, Johanna. 2014. "Gender Diversity." In *Te Ara – the Encyclopedia of New Zealand*. Accessed February 4, 2014, at http://www.TeAra.govt.nz/en/gender-diversity.

Willett, Graham. 1999. "Proud and Employed: the Gay and Lesbian Movement and the Victorian Teachers' Unions in the 1970s," *Labour History*, No. 76: 78–94.

Willett, Graham. 2000. *Living Out Loud: A History of Gay and Lesbian Activism in Australia*. Melbourne: Allen and Unwin.

LGBT Activism in the Caribbean

RACHEL E. NOLAN
University of Connecticut, USA

Lesbian, gay, bisexual, and transgender (LGBT) rights in the Caribbean region are complex and reflect the diversity of the entire region. Violence is both overt (state sanctioned, socially visible) and covert. Activism across the region is shaped by this diversity. Furthermore, histories of prejudice in the Caribbean are profoundly entangled with legacies of colonialism. The policies and legal infrastructures of European settler nations (Spain, United Kingdom, France, Portugal, The Netherlands) have had lasting impact and have remained partially or wholly in place after independence, depending on particular national political configurations. More recent interventions by twenty-first-century political and economic powers continue to restrict the autonomy of Caribbean nations. "Neocolonial" policies enforced by the United States, the United Nations, and the World Bank such as structural adjustment, gender mainstreaming, and "Shiprider" agreements directly or indirectly compromise the health, safety, and political well-being of LGBT populations. Attitudes toward LGBT communities are also deeply shaped by the entrenched authority of Catholicism, one of the largest religious denominations in the region, and one which has historically opposed progressive laws that would end the criminalization and persecution of LGBT populations. Although there are some pan-Caribbean initiatives to raise awareness about LGBT persecution, much activist work is nation-specific.

EUROPEAN COLONIAL LEGACIES

Long-standing cultures of violence targeting LGBT populations in specific nations across the Caribbean region are often linked to British colonial traditions that rejected homosexuality. Among the colonial powers, Britain is thought to have enacted the harshest societal and legal restrictions on homosexuality (Corrales and Pecheny 2010). British statutes in the nineteenth century grouped homosexual individuals with prostitutes, the deaf and dumb, and other populations considered "mentally deficient." This history is largely inscribed by the persistence of "anti-sodomy laws" in many postcolonial nations. A number of countries continue to enforce laws passed in the colonial era that make same-sex relations punishable by up to 25 years in prison. At least two Caribbean nations, Belize and the Republic of Trinidad and Tobago, maintain official immigration policies prohibiting the entry of gay people. Although not consistently enforced, global non-governmental organizations (NGOs) working on behalf of marginalized peoples have, since 2012, pressed for these laws to be overturned. The charity group Aids-Free World, supported financially and legally by the Tides Center, is vocal in this struggle.

As has been the case in other postcolonial nations around the world, popular anti-gay sentiment in some Caribbean nations perpetuates a belief that homosexuality is a "foreign contamination," originating with colonial oppressors. Human Rights Watch has urged the recognition that stigmatizing consensual homosexual conduct is a relic of colonial rule and has asked postcolonial national governments to affirm human rights as part of broader anti-colonial political programs. While colonial-era legislation has impacted all Caribbean nations, legacies of homophobia have proved more enduring in some localities than others. Jamaica has an especially notorious reputation for tolerating and promoting sexual violence, including murder.

JAMAICA

Homophobia across Jamaican popular culture has been viewed as especially virulent. Dancehall, a genre of Jamaican popular music that has roots in reggae, has become a particular focus of concern, with critics claiming that it promotes and normalizes sexual violence. Australian-born British political campaigner Peter Tatchell protested the pejorative content of dancehall music at the 2002 and 2003 MOBO (Music of Black Origin) awards, but received pushback from singers and their fans, who claimed that the content reflected Jamaican cultural values. Dancehall stars have been criticized for inciting violence with lyrics such as "(Its like) Boom bye bye/Inna batty bwoy head/Rude bwoy no promote no nasty man/Dem haffi dead." These lyrics describe, in Jamaican patois, shooting a gay man in the head. Criticism of sexuality-based violence in Jamaica has largely focused on discourses of masculinity that emphasize toughness and heterosexism.

Anti-gay "policing" impacts both men and women.

Activism in Jamaica has taken both legal and cultural reform. J-FLAG (the Jamaican Forum for Lesbians, All-sexuals and Gays) is one of the earliest human rights organizations in the nation's history and is described by some activists as the most pro-queer of Jamaican activist groups (Campbell 2014). J-FLAG serves as a mouthpiece for LGBT populations and agitates for legal aid and legal reform. Since 2012, struggles to overturn anti-buggery laws in Jamaica have been ongoing and have gained some traction. While the Jamaican government has claimed to be sympathetic toward LGBT struggles, restrictive laws remain in place. The documentary film *The Abominable Crime* (2013) addresses Jamaica's reputation as "one of the most homophobic places in the world." The documentary explores the impact of homophobia from the perspective of two gay Jamaicans. The film won the Trinidad and Tobago Film Festival's inaugural Amnesty International Human Rights Prize in 2014.

HAITI

The ongoing struggles of Haiti's LGBT community intensified in recent years in large part due to the rise of anti-gay sentiment and violence in the aftermath of the 2010 earthquake. The Inter-American Commission on Human Rights (IACHR) reported that in the days surrounding the event itself, lesbian, gay, bisexual, trans, and intersex persons were attacked with knives, machetes, cement blocks, rocks, or sticks in more than 47 separate incidents. During the post-earthquake reconstruction period, individuals living in "tent cities" were targeted for so-called "corrective" rapes and punishment. Although both the president and prime minister of Haiti denounced these outbreaks of violence at the time, violence continued to escalate as moral and religious groups publicly blamed the earthquake on what they called the "sins" of the country's gay population. In 2013, the Haitian Coalition of Religious and Moral Organizations (Coalition Haïtienne des organisations religieuses et morales) led a march against homosexuality in the nation's capital city, Port-au-Prince. The term "masisi" has been used more widely as a derogatory name for homosexual and transgender persons in Haiti.

Until very recently, the Haitian civil society group SEROvie was the only community-based, pro-LGBT organization in the country. Initially working to raise awareness about HIV and AIDS, the group has adopted a broader platform to help encourage LGBT networking and support. The political group Kouraj emerged out of the post-earthquake climate of persecution, declaring a platform for societal change through social action. The group has reclaimed the term "masisi" and aims to foster solidarity for those who are the victims of discrimination. Their goals include challenging negative discourses surrounding gay and transgender persons, establishing new media outlets, and fostering LGBT culture and arts in Haiti. Kouraj also works to develop international ties with LGBT allies in order to bring the human rights struggles of Haitian activists to the world stage.

CUBA

LGBT history in Cuba is deeply marked by the vicissitudes of political struggle, both between Cuban nationalists and the United States and intra-national struggles over ideological primacy. As the object of imperial campaigns in the nineteenth and twentieth centuries, Cuba was frequently cast by United States ideologues as an "effeminate" nation. Pejorative rhetoric such as this served to naturalize attempts to "Americanize" the population and annex the island. Furthermore, during the 1960s and 1970s, Fidel Castro's revolutionary government targeted gay populations for exclusion, and many gay people were sent by the state to UMAPs (Military Units to Aid Production/Unidades Militares de Ayuda a la Producción), agricultural labor camps for populations perceived as threats to collectivization.

Largely due to this legacy of hostility, advocacy for pro-LGBT laws and culture has proven both difficult and dangerous in Cuba. The Cuban writer Reinaldo Arenas, who was jailed in 1974, chronicled the treatment of gay men in his autobiography *Before Night Falls* (Arenas 1992), which was made into a movie with the same name in 2000. The visibility of pro-LGBT populations has, however, significantly increased since 2007 when Mariela Castro became the figurehead of a campaign to promote tolerance. While discrimination in the country continues, especially in the nation's provinces, advocates both within and outside the country have welcomed the shift toward egalitarian politics and social accommodation. In 2012, the Norwegian government expressed support for Mariela Castro's leadership by donating $230,0000 to her cause (*Sunday Review*). The city of Havana observed the International Day Against Homophobia and Transphobia for the first time in 2007.

The changes in Cuba can also be tracked by looking at the developments in national healthcare and social provisions for LGBT populations. The National Center for Sex Education (Centro Nacional de Educación Sexual, or CENESEX), founded in 1989, has expanded its work to tackle prejudices related to sexuality and gender. In addition to fostering relationships with institutions and medical professionals outside the country, part of the organization's work has involved developing the Lesbian and Bisexual Women

Network, which facilitates the training of LB women as health activists. State-financed gender reassignment surgery and hormone treatment for transgender people is also increasingly available.

THE REGIONAL PICTURE

The Caribbean Region of the International Resource Network (IRN) is an important pan-Caribbean organization. It is a resource for individuals and organizations both within and outside the region. While the Caribbean IRN supports academic and activist projects, a major objective is to connect individuals across the region and the world. In this respect the IRN serves as a clearinghouse. One of the Caribbean IRN's major projects has involved compiling oral histories recording the experiences of LGBT and intersex people across the Caribbean region. The IRN network and its regional projects are financially supported by the Ford Foundation and part of an initiative of the Center for Lesbian, Gay, Bisexual, Transgender, and Queer Studies (CLAGS) at the City University of New York.

Further efforts to cultivate pan-Caribbean solidarity have emerged out of the literary world. While the emergence of a Caribbean literary canon since the 1950s has played an important role in the construction of postcolonial national identities, writers and literary scholars have, in recent years, expressed concern over what they perceive as the overt promotion of hypermasculine and homophobic aesthetics. They have likewise expressed concerns that postcolonial literatures have sought to empower Black identity by celebrating heteronormative sexuality (Pecic 2013). Through scholarship on LGBT literatures of the Caribbean, writers have sought to bring activist efforts into conversation with the regional canon.

Following liberation movements of the 1950s, a number of Caribbean nations have become the target of neocolonial enterprises largely spearheaded by the United States. Interest groups such as corporations, structural adjustment programs, and financial organizations all contribute to cultural and political developments across the region, which have had a real impact on the trajectory of sexual liberation and rights-based activism. A particular issue of concern for activists in this respect is the emergence of gender mainstreaming, a global policy initiative aimed particularly at women's advancement in developing nations. Activists in the Caribbean have expressed concerned that the transformative potential of mainstreaming policies is limited.

The United Nations describes gender mainstreaming as a globally accepted strategy for promoting gender equality. Rather than representing an end in itself, mainstreaming is imagined by policymakers as a means of achieving the goals of gender equity. Emanating from the Beijing Declaration and Platform for Action (UN Fourth World Conference on Women) (United Nations 1995), the concept of mainstreaming provides a vocabulary and critical framework for bringing state operations in line with gender equity concerns. Critiques of mainstreaming have targeted the perceived paucity of institutional support within developing nations, the unevenness of implementation across regions, and the implicit ideological assumptions that homogenize genders rather than promote and protect difference.

Critics questioning its relevance as a strategy for promoting equity for all genders argue that the regulatory and disciplining impulses of developmental projects have made certain identities intelligible at the expense of others. It is claimed that mainstreaming policies have contributed to the marginalization of particular sexual subjects who do not fit the frameworks and evaluative mechanisms enforced to facilitate sustainable progress in developing regions. Despite feminist efforts to make visible a wide range of sexual practices, mainstreaming frameworks in the Caribbean continue to emphasize procreation, population control, and the stability of domestic spheres. Sexual autonomy and representation of sexual minorities is deemphasized (Rowley 2012).

CORPORATE INTERESTS AND SEX TOURISM

The impact of neocolonial interventions is especially evident in the phenomenon of sex tourism, a highly lucrative business in a number of Caribbean nations. It has been claimed that in some Caribbean nations, such as the Bahamas (where two-thirds of the nation's GNP is derived from tourism), corporate expansion has made citizenship coextensive with commodification (Alexander 1997). The exploitation of LGBT individuals in tourist zones has become the focus of recent scholarship in the field of sexual citizenship studies. In popular tourist destinations, female and male prostitution is common. Transgender prostitution has been observed in the Caribbean region but has received very little critical attention. Since the 1970s, organized sex tours have made monetized same-sex exchanges more available to visitors with the means to pay. In the Dominican Republic, "sanky-pankies" (male, bisexual gigolos) work almost exclusively with foreign clients (Kempadoo 1999). The developments in sex tourism in recent decades crystallize the ongoing interplay between sex, gender, race, and national identity.

SEE ALSO: Colonialism and Gender; Gender Violence; Sexual Citizenship in the Caribbean

REFERENCES

Alexander, M. Jacqui. 1997. "Erotic Autonomy as a Politics of Decolonization: An Anatomy of Feminist and State Practice in the Bahamas Tourist Economy." In *Feminist Genealogies, Colonial Legacies, Democratic Futures*, edited by M. Jacqui Alexander and Chandra Mohanty, 63–100. New York: Routledge.

Arenas, Reinaldo. 1999. *Before Night Falls: A Memoir*, trans. Dolores M. Koch. London: Serpent's Tail.

Campbell, Kofi Omoniyi Sylvanus. 2014. *The Queer Caribbean Speaks*. New York: Palgrave Macmillan.

Corrales, Javier, and Mario Pecheny. 2010. *The Politics of Sexuality in Latin America*. Pittsburgh: University of Pittsburgh Press.

Kempadoo, Kamala.1999. *Sun, Sex, and Gold: Tourism and Sex Work in the Caribbean*. Lanham: Rowman & Littlefield.

Pecic, Zoran. 2013. *Queer Narratives of the Caribbean Diaspora*. New York: Palgrave Macmillan.

Rowley, Michelle V. 2012. *Feminist Advocacy and Gender Equity in the Anglophone Caribbean: Envisioning a Politics of Coalition*. Hoboken: Taylor and Francis.

United Nations. 1995. "Beijing Declaration." In *UN Fourth World Conference on Women, Beijing*. Accessed September 8, 2015, at www.un.org/womenwatch/daw/beijing/platform/declar.htm.

FURTHER READING

Editorial Board. 2015. "Cuba's Gay Rights Evolution." *Sunday Review*, December 20, 2014. Accessed March 13, 2015, at http://www.nytimes.com/2014/12/21/opinion/sunday/cubas-gay-rights-evolution.html?_r=0.

Gaestel, Allyn. 2014. "Haiti's Fight for Gay Rights." *Al Jazeera*, November 8, 2014. Accessed March 13, 2015, at http://projects.aljazeera.com/2014/haiti-lgbt/.

Smith, Faith L., ed. 2011. *Sex and the Citizen: Interrogating the Caribbean*. Charlottesville: University of Virginia Press.

UN Women. 2015. United Nations Entity for Gender Equality and the Empowerment of Women. Accessed March 13, 2015, at www.unwomen.org/en.

LGBT Activism in Eastern Africa

ALIZA LUFT
University of Wisconsin-Madison, USA

Lesbian, gay, bisexual, and transgender (LGBT) activism in Eastern Africa operates in a heavily constrained and oppressive environment. Despite these obstacles, activists continue to mobilize on behalf of LGBT rights and create safe spaces for same-sex practicing individuals. This entry looks at the laws that shape Eastern African LGBT activism, the role of the West in both helping and hindering LGBT activism, how different LGBT organizations function with respect to the limitations they face, the relationship of LGBT activism to women's movements, and the impact of HIV/AIDS on LGBT individuals and activism. Recent successes are described as well.

Importantly, it is impossible to consider the status of lesbian, gay, bisexual, and transgender (LGBT) rights in Eastern Africa with any presumption of homogeneity. As a result, this entry looks at general patterns across countries while simultaneously recognizing that all countries have different governing structures, laws, and even different levels of institutional stability that secures the status of government and law, affecting how LGBT activism operates. Likewise, concepts such as lesbian, gay, bisexual, transexual, transgender, and queer, carry specific social meanings in different contexts. As Adam, Dyvendak, and Krouwel explain (1999, 2), "the context and meaning of 'gay' or 'lesbian' are contested terrain, varying within and among societies. How homosexually interested people come together, organize, and identify group objectives, then, differs immensely from place to place." Furthermore, Tamale (2011, 2) writes, "The notion of a homogenous, unchanging sexuality for all Africans is out of touch not only with the realities of lives, experiences, identities and relationships but also with current activism and scholarship." Eastern African sexualities have been shaped by each country's unique past and present, including, but not limited to, experiences of colonialism and globalization, and dynamics of gender, class, religion, ethnicity, and race. Finally, there is an enormous diversity of sexualities in Eastern Africa. This entry provides merely the contours of major dimensions of research on LGBT activism in this region.

To varying degrees, homosexuality is illegal in Kenya, Burundi, Tanzania, and Uganda, and there are also no laws in any of these countries to prohibit discrimination on the basis of sexual identity. In Rwanda, same-sex behaviors and relationships are legal, yet there are no laws to prevent same-sex discrimination. In many of the countries across Eastern Africa, existing laws that criminalize same-sex behaviors are remnants of colonialism and the legal systems they introduced (this was notably more common in British than French or other colonies). Of all the laws dealing with homosexuality in the region, Uganda's Anti-Homosexuality Act, which sought to revise an earlier act criminalizing homosexuality which was a remnant of British colonialism, is perhaps best known.

In 2013, Uganda's anti-homosexuality bill was revised to consider the death penalty for "repeat offenders" and even punishment for non-LGBT people who know of homosexual people and fail to report them to the authorities. Businesses that promote LGBT rights could be fined as well. The law ultimately passed in 2014 but with the provision that people convicted of same-sex acts be punished with life in prison as opposed to the death penalty originally proposed. A few months later, the Constitutional Court of Uganda ruled the law as invalid because it was not passed with the required quorum.

It is expected to be referred to the Supreme Court of Uganda for a hearing.

As in Uganda, sex acts between men are illegal in Tanzania and also carry the maximum penalty of life imprisonment. No law concerning sex acts between women is mentioned specifically in mainland Tanzanian law; however, the semi-autonomous region of Zanzibar outlaws same-sex acts between women with a maximum penalty of 5 years' imprisonment, as well as a 500,000 shilling fine.

Kenya also criminalizes homosexuality and in 2014 the Kenyan government introduced a law that would include the death penalty for "aggravated homosexuality," while a foreigner who commits a homosexual act would be stoned in public. At the same time, female same-sex marriage is practiced among some minority groups within the country (the Gikuyu, Nandi, Kamba, and Kipsigis). This is not understood in Kenya as homosexual behavior but rather as a way for women without sons to maintain their inheritance and keep it within the family. Sometimes, these marriages are also polygamous; however, only polygamy among men married to women is legal as of 2014.

These three examples point to a complicated relationship between state law and actual practices related to same-sex behaviors in Eastern Africa. As Epprecht notes:

> [M]any countries in Africa appear to have a *de facto* culture of tolerance (or indifference) to same-sex sexuality that amounts to freedom from discrimination, not withstanding sometimes harsh laws and elite homophobic rhetoric … The key provisio is that non-normative sexuality not be named as such, but take place under the umbrella of heteropatriarchal constructions of family, faith, and African identity. (Epprecht 2012, 226)

This statement is not meant to diminish the severity of laws regulating against same-sex behaviors and relationships in Eastern Africa, but rather to demonstrate that there is significant variation in how civilians understand and respond to these laws.

Partly resulting from the recent discourse surrounding LGBT rights in Eastern Africa, there has been renewed attention to questions of sexuality as well as to the laws criminalizing same-sex behaviors. This attention has resulted in a severe backlash towards many individuals who try to practice living openly as LGBT in Eastern Africa. In many places, the results of identifying as LGBT are severe: people are often disowned or evicted; they frequently lose their jobs; and they are subject to hostility, ridicule, and discrimination, which is occasionally even encouraged by political and religious authorities. Likewise, many LGBT individuals lack access to adequate medical care and sometimes have their confidentiality breached by health providers. When LGBT individuals have been assaulted by organized mobs, police have failed to come to their rescue. Such individuals are also often subject to arbitrary arrest. During these arrests, the police assault and harass them, and even sexually abuse them in some cases.

Sexual rights activists in Eastern Africa are often at risk of losing their jobs, being disowned by their families, and killed for their activism. According to Monica Tabengwa, an LGBT activist with Human Rights Watch in Kenya, it is impossible for individuals, especially women, to be lesbian, bisexual, or queer without it becoming political. Women who practice same-sex or have same-sex relationships in many Eastern African countries are often subject to what is called "corrective" or "curative" rape, sometimes even organized by their families, to make them "real women." In Tanzania and Uganda, well-known LGBT rights campaigners Maurice Mjomba and David Kato were murdered. Other activists are frequently derided with slurs such as *pédé* ("faggot") and sometimes described as "whore[s] to the West" (Epprecht 2012, 229).

Laws criminalizing homosexual behavior were first introduced by colonialist governments who imposed their own legal systems on Eastern African countries. Likewise, the introduction of Christianity or Islam by many of these governments led to the criminalization of same-sex practices and relationships as well as the negative stigma often associated with them. In recent years, there has been a significant influence on the extreme homophobic agendas of various Eastern African countries from American Christian Fundamentalist prostelytizers and "ex-gay" missionaries. This especially has been the case in Uganda, where in March 2009, a workshop opposing homosexuality took place in Kampala that featured three American evangelicals: Caleb Lee Brundige, a man who claims to heal homosexuality; Scott Lively, an author of several books against homosexuality; and Don Schmierer, a board member of Exodus International, an organization that claims to promote "freedom from homosexuality through the power of Jesus Christ." It was during this conference that a Ugandan attendant first announced the parliament's intention to restructure the bill criminalizing homosexuality.

Despite this, there is a widespread perception among opponents of LGBT activism that these movements are a form of Western neoimperialism. Recent controversies have only heightened this belief. For example, in 2011, UK prime minister David Cameron suggested that the UK may withhold or reduce aid to governments that do not reform their laws criminalizing homosexuality. In response, Bernard Membe, Tanzania's minister for foreign affairs and international cooperation, replied:

Tanzania will never accept Cameron's proposal because we have our own moral values. Homosexuality is not part of our culture and we will never legalise it.... We are not ready to allow any rich nation to give us aid based on unacceptable conditions simply because we are poor. If we are denied aid by one country, it will not affect the economic status of this nation and we can do without UK aid.

This backlash has led to a difficult situation for LGBT activists who not only are subject to harm, but also because threats made by donors to cut off aid has damaged LGBT organizations' relationships with other civil society movements. International sanctions to cut off aid in an attempt to assist LGBT organizations gain strength in their respective countries often have had the opposite effect. In many places, these organizations have become ostracized. As the "African statement to British government on aid conditionality" explains:

A vibrant social justice movement within African civil society is working to ensure the visibility of – and enjoyment of rights by – LGBTI people ... It has been working through a number of strategies to entrench LGBTI issues into broader civil society issues, to shift the same-sex sexuality discourse from the morality debate to a human rights debate, and to build relationships with governments for greater protection of LGBTI people. These objectives cannot be met when donor countries threaten to withhold aid. (African Social Justice Activists 2013, 92)

Additionally, and perhaps also because of the unique difficulties that many of these organizations face, there has been a backlash against attempts by Western organizations seen by some Eastern African activists as trying to co-opt local movements for their own purposes. For example, at the 2007 Nairobi Social Forum, the representatives of 20 LGBT groups across Africa signed a public statement against attempts by OutRage! to press the Nigerian government not to pass a same-sex marriage prohibition act. The signatories explained that OutRage!'s actions might create a backlash. They added:

> As African LGBTI Human Rights Defenders, we are working toward the recognition of our rights by our governments in Africa. We do not appreciate or accept the efforts of Western-based individuals or organizations who try to make our work for liberation into an ego-boosting publicity campaign for themselves. (African LGBTI 2007)

The signatories further described the behavior of OutRage! as a form of neo-colonialism. This is part of a more general shift towards questioning the purpose and usefulness of Western based and funded non-governmental organizations (NGOs). As Kenyan queer academic Keguro Macharia explains, "I want to resist the 'African homosexual' as an empirical figure waiting to be discovered or, through NGO and international interventions, to be created and saved'" (in Ekine, *New Internationalist Blog*).

The oppressive nature of states' laws and cultural attitudes towards LGBT individuals means that most organizations take the form of house gatherings and small networks of friends. Very rarely are activists able to meet in public spaces like restaurants or bars, and the ability for LGBT organizations to obtain formal meeting spaces is nearly impossible. Many organizations that exist to promote LGBT rights use coded language or neutral terms to label themselves, such as the Horizon Community Association in Rwanda, Minority Women in Action in Kenya, and the Uganda Health and Science Press Organization. However, not all organizations follow this trend and some, like the Coalition of African Lesbians, remain explicit about their intentions through their titles. It is important to note that the discreet names of LGBT organizations are not always due to the private interests of organizers. At times, organizations have changed their names in order to receive official accreditation as an NGO in their respective countries. For example, the former Burundian organization Groupe de Réflexion des Homosexuelles du Burundi (Group for the Reflection of Homosexuals in Burundi) recently changed its name to Humure ("Do not be afraid") for this purpose.

Despite widespread oppression, LGBT organizations in Eastern Africa continue to mobilize, in some cases increasing their efforts in the wake of violence against them. The main LGBT rights organization in Uganda is Sexual Minorities Uganda, which was founded in 2004 by Victor Mukasa. The current executive director and winner of several human rights awards is Frank Mugisha. Though increasingly severe measures against LGBT individuals have been introduced in Uganda, new forms of media have appeared such as the LGBT magazine, *Bombastic*, and the launch of an online platform, *Kuchu Times*. These publications are part of a campaign to reclaim the media, initiated by activist Kasha Jacqueline Nabagesera, who was awarded the Martin Ennals Award for Human Rights Defenders in 2011. Similarly, in Rwanda, members of the Horizons Community Association have experienced government harassment and been evicted from their offices, causing many staff to leave. Still, the organization continues to engage in public advocacy efforts on behalf of LGBT people. Executive director James Wandera Ouma of LGBT Voice Tanzania (formerly WEZESHA) was arrested by police in 2011 and ordered to stop his activism, but he and the organization continue their work to promote, protect, and support the interests of LGBT people in the country. Local organizations that take the risk of engaging in public activism have been instrumental in the movement to destigmatize LGBT individuals as they are started and run by Africans contributes to dismantling the notion that same-sex relationships are "un-African."

In addition to these organizations, some activism has been driven by academic initiatives, specifically African feminist scholarship and research. For example, since 2006, the African Regional Sexuality Resource Center has produced the magazine, *Sexuality in Africa*, whereas local publications, such as *Bombastic* in Uganda, have emerged in recent years. Academics have also organized seminars and intellectual forums around discussions of sex and sexuality, and there has been a move to create safe spaces for LGBT in Eastern Africa that are non-political in intention, such as gay-friendly faith groups and soccer clubs like Other Sheep East Africa in Kenya. The Internet has also provided a critical platform for the voices of LGBT activists. It has created a space for social networking that allows activists to create connections, communicate news and strategies, and share successes, helping to foster solidarity.

A number of global actors have had critical roles in funding new research and supporting LGBT movements in Eastern Africa. For example, the International Gay and Lesbian Human Rights Commission published a report in 2005 on how African countries were failing to help men who have sex with men (MSM) protect themselves against HIV. In 2008, the US-based Population Council sponsored a workshop in Nairobi on MSM and HIV/AIDS in Africa and the subsequent report urged governments to recognize the existence of MSM and promote their rights to health. In response to the recent attempts (and successes) of Eastern African governments to increase the severity of punishment for LGBT behaviors and relationships, many international donors have strengthened their solidarity with local organizations and increased their funding, though this tactic is not without contestation on the parts of governments and local activists.

Many LGBT organizations in Eastern Africa draw heavily from lessons of African women's movements and aim to promote an intersectional approach in their work that links homophobia and transphobia to sexism and patriarchy. This is not to say that women's movements have responded. Some LGBT women have reported experiencing harassment from women's movements that they belong to when they have suggested including same-sex practicing individuals as a "marginalized group" (Tamale 2003). Others report that individuals in the feminist movement struggle with responding to LGBT concerns (Kiragy and Nyong'o 2005). This is not only the result of homophobia, but also reflects tensions related to resource allocation and constraints within feminist movements and, occasionally, a lack of knowledge or capacity (Guma 2015). The result is that in many cases lesbian concerns are marginalized within broader feminist movements.

Finally, any review of LGBT activism in Eastern Africa is incomplete without a discussion of the high rates of HIV/AIDS in the region. Beginning in the late 1990s, it was found that men's secretive same-sex practices were a much greater factor in the spread of HIV in Africa than was previously assumed. In Kenya, a study found that over two thirds of MSM had unprotected sex with a woman in the previous year, whereas in Uganda 90 percent of MSM had female wives. The Kenyan government has estimated that at least 15 percent of all new HIV infections in the country occurred as a result of male–male sex. In turn, many organizations have fought for the decriminalization of same-sex behaviors and relationships particularly because they encourage many same-sex practicing people to remain private about their sexual identities and practices. The majority of same-sex practicing people in Eastern Africa keep a low profile and adhere to heteronormative social norms while using the Internet for private connections or secretly finding same-sex partners. In the context of the HIV/AIDS crisis in sub-Saharan Africa, this is dangerous. As a result, a number of LGBT organizations in Eastern Africa are motivated both by the desire to encourage political activism and support for LGBT people, and by the desire to organize for LGBT health rights. The challenges of the political context means that many of these organizations promote sexual rights and sexual health advocacy in a coded way, often embedding their agenda through the use of euphemisms or implicit language within the larger, and most often heterosexual-focused, public health campaigns in Eastern Africa.

Despite the severe repression of LGBT activists and same-sex practicing individuals, there are a few Eastern African political leaders who have vocalized their support for legal reform that would protect the rights of LGBT people. For example, Dr. Willy Mutunga, Chief Justice of the Kenyan Supreme Court, has expressed that "gay rights are human rights," and Health Secretary James Macharia has declared that "the Ministry… has a constitutional obligation to provide heath services to all who face discrimination." Likewise, in Uganda, former vice-president and UN special envoy for HIVA-AIDS in Africa has proclaimed, "I am in full solidarity with the LGBT community and I will defend their rights in Uganda and across Africa" (Human Rights First, *Report: The State of Human Rights for LGBT People in Africa*). In Rwanda, the government has signed the UN Human Rights Council statement towards "Ending Acts of Violence and Related Human Rights Violations Based on Sexual Orientation and Gender Identity." LGBT activism in Eastern Africa is heavily impeded by the national environments of their respective countries, but small gains continue to be made in the fight for equality.

SEE ALSO: Colonialism and Sexuality; Cross-Cultural Gender Roles; Gay and Lesbian Pride Day; Health, Healthcare, and Sexual Minorities; Human Rights, International Laws and Policies on; Lesbian and Gay Movements; Regulation of Queer Sexualities; Women's and Feminist Activism in Eastern Africa

REFERENCES

Adam, Barry D., Jan Willem Dyvendak, and André Krouwel, eds. 1999. *The Global Emergence of Gay and Lesbian Politics: National Imprints of a Worldwide Movement*. Philadelphia: Temple University Press.

African LGBTI, 2007. "African LGBTI Human Rights Defenders Warn Public Against Participation in Campaigns Concerning LGBTI Issues in Africa Led by Peter Tatchell and OutRage!" Accessed August 11, 2015, at http://mrzine.monthlyreview.org/2007/increse310107.html.

African Social Justice Activists. 2011. "Statement of African Social Justice Activists on the Threats of the British Government to "Cut Aid" to African Countries that Violate the Rights of LGBTI People in Africa, 27 October."

Epprecht, Marc. 2012. "Sexual Minorities, Human Rights and Public Health Strategies in Africa." *African Affairs*, 111 (443): 223–243.

Guma, Prince Karakire. 2015. "Feminist Solidarity: How Women are Shaping the Way We Think About Sex and Politics in Uganda." *Africa Review*, 7(1): 15–27.

Kiragu, Jane, and Zawadi Nyong'o. 2005. "LGBT in East Africa: The True Test Case for Human Rights Defenders." In *LGBTI Organizing in East Africa: The True Test for Human Rights Defenders*, edited by Madeleine Maurick. East Africa: UAF-Africa, Regal Press.

Tamale, Sylvia. 2003. "Out of the Closet: Unveiling Sexuality Discourses in Uganda." *Feminist Africa*, No. 2 (Changing Cultures). Cape Town: African Gender Institute.

Tamale, Sylvia, ed. 2011. *African Sexualities: A Reader*. Nairobi: Pambazuka Press.

FURTHER READING

Ekrine, Sokari, and Hakima Abbas, eds. 2013. *Queer African Reader*. Nairobi: Pambazuka Press.

Gevisser, Mark. 1999. "Homosexuality in Africa: An Interpretation." In *Africana: The Encyclopedia of the African and African American Experience*, edited by K.A. Appiah and H.L. Gates, 961–963. New York: Basic Civitas Books.

Johnson, Cary Alan. 2005. *Off the Map: How HIV/AIDS Programming is Failing Same-Sex Practicing People in Africa*. New York: IGLHRC.

Kaoma, Kapya. 2009. *Globalizing the Culture Wars: US Conservatives, African Churches, and Homophobia*. Somerville: Political Research Associates.

Kenya Human Rights Commission. 2011. *The Outlawed Amongst Us: A Study of the LGBTI Community's Search for Equality and Non-discrimination in Kenya*. Nairobi: Kenya Human Rights Commission.

Nyeck, S.N., and Marc Epprecht, eds. 2013. *Sexual Diversity in Africa: Politics, Theory, Citizenship*. Montreal: McGill–Queen's University Press.

Wieringa, Sakia. 2005. "Women Marriages and Other Same-Sex Practices: Historical Reflections on African Women's Same-Sex Relations." In *Tommy Boys, Lesbian Men and Ancestral Wives: Female Same-Sex Practices in Africa*, edited by R. Morgan and S. Wieringa, 261–280. Johannesburg: Jacana.

LGBT Activism in Eastern and Central Europe

SUSAN C. PEARCE
East Carolina University, USA

ALEXANDER COOPER
Central European University, Hungary

With the opportunities generated by the fall of state communist regimes in 1989 in Central and Eastern Europe, the collapse of the Soviet Union in 1991, and the dissolution of Yugoslavia beginning in 1991, new social movements are beginning to organize, including lesbian, gay, bisexual, and transgender (LGBT) activism. This overview of the post-1989 movements across the region situates their complex shared and diverse experiences in their pre- and post-1989 histories and cultures. These movements have faced barriers less common in their Western European counterparts, resulting in deep-seated backlashes and institutionally supported violence. However, the movements have also drawn upon an unprecedented political opportunity: they have emerged at a moment in history when transnational human rights instruments, governing bodies, donors, and watchdog groups have mainstreamed LGBT rights into their agendas. This entry outlines the relationships between the burgeoning movements and these transnational toolkits, as well as advances and retreats that activists face in public presentations such as Pride Parades. This general survey of the region's activism considers Eastern and Central Europe to include the Central European countries of the former "Eastern Bloc," including (former East) Germany, the Balkan countries of the former Yugoslavia, Albania, and the European countries of the former Soviet Union, including the Baltics and the Caucasus.

MOVEMENTS AND PRIDE PARADES

Prior to 1989, LGBT activism, if present at all, would have largely been underground in the region given the strictures on freedom to associate and the absence of a strong civil society with mechanisms to make claims on the state and other social institutions. As a result, the region had little experience with sustained grassroots organizing. LGBT activism in the post-socialist period has been concentrated within non-governmental organizations (NGOs), largely funded by international human rights groups, foundations, and governments in an effort to build sustainable civil societies. LGBT activism became ingrained into this "NGO-ization" of the region. Nevertheless, although concentrated through these organizations, there has been a steady growth of LGBT grassroots activism and positive outcomes. As the LGBT movement began to coalesce and make its presence known publicly, Pride Parades emerged as a key symbol of visibility and legitimation. Eastern and Central Europe experienced a mixed reaction to these parades and other Pride events (Pearce and Cooper 2014).

As of 2015, Albania, Azerbaijan, Belarus, Bulgaria, Croatia, Czech Republic, Estonia, Hungary, Latvia, Lithuania, Moldova, Montenegro, Poland, Romania, Serbia, Slovakia, and Ukraine have held Pride Parades. Although many had official parade permits, some took place despite a government ban, such as in Ukraine. The other countries in the region have hosted Pride events such as movie festivals and lectures, but due to the anti-LGBT cultural environment, have not been able to hold a Pride Parade successfully. The former East Germany has defied the norm, since it reunited with West Germany; Berlin Pride has occurred annually since 1979 and had become one of the largest in Europe. Backlashes continued, however, even when parades became established. Hungary, for example, saw counterprotests and a large police presence during its annual Pride in 2015. Poland has also faced difficulty in organizing Prides, with a center-right government opposing such events. Nevertheless, Poland and Hungary are continuing to hold Prides. In 2012, one openly gay and another openly trans candidate won parliamentary seats in Poland, representing a left-oriented opposition party marking a first for this predominantly Catholic country. Warsaw's 2015 parade drew thousands of marchers, with the support of 33 foreign embassies, and attracted a small nonviolent, but vocal, counter-protest.

Slovenia has held multiple Prides and has the longest track record of LGBT rights in the successor states of Yugoslavia. Croatia held a series of annual Pride Parades that were repeatedly attacked violently until peaceful events in 2013, as the country was joining the European Union (EU). Other countries have had less success. In 2001, Serbia's first Pride was organized but 40 participants were injured. In 2010, Serbia's Pride encountered more violence, finally succeeding in a 2014 parade after the government had cancelled the event for 3 years in a row. Montenegro's first Pride Parade in 2013 met with violent protests. Bosnia-Herzegovina, Kosovo, and FYR Macedonia have not been able to organize parades as of 2015. Similar patterns are seen in the Caucasus. Neo-Nazis aggressively tried to stop a Diversity march in Armenia in 2012 and fire-bombed a gay-friendly bar. In 2013, an attack on a small Pride march in Georgia included the throwing of stones by clergy.

While in most of these countries LGBT rights are inching forward, some LGBT activism still predominates over others. Trans* rights activism in the region has largely been marginalized, even within activist organizations claiming to be "LGBT." (The asterisk (*) designates a multiplicity of possibilities on the gender identity spectrum.) Several countries have no official classification for trans* individuals, and activists are working toward bringing trans* issues to the attention of governments and the wider society. Transnational organizations have also stepped up their work on trans* activism both globally and in this region, given that trans* lived experiences differ greatly from those of LGB people.

TRANSNATIONAL AND INTERNATIONAL SCENARIOS

Since 1989, the region's LGBT movements gained a set of tools that helped to bolster their efforts at change and legitimize their claims.

The growing globalizing context of their host societies provided activists with tools such as: (1) opportunities that resulted from negotiations between their host nation-states and the EU for membership; (2) international treaties and agreements; and (3) the increasingly transnational LGBT movement. LGBT activism has begun to achieve a modicum of gender identity and sexuality "mainstreaming" at global levels. This scenario has been central to activist work in a process that social movement scholars Keck and Sikkink (1998) call the "boomerang effect": activists reach for treaties, instruments, and agreements to place pressure the powers-that-be in their countries. Holzhacker (2013) describes this same dynamic through the metaphor of the ricochet for this "transborder, transinstitutional circulation of information and argumentation" (Holzhacker 2013, 2) in which there is a multi-directional influence.

EU accession has illustrated this opportunity. As of the time of writing this entry, countries from the post-socialist East–Central region fell within five categories of relationships with the EU:

1 Members: Bulgaria, Croatia, Czech Republic, Estonia, Germany, Hungary, Latvia, Lithuania, Poland, Romania, Slovakia, and Slovenia.
2 Candidates: Albania, Montenegro, Serbia, and the former Yugoslav Republic (FYR) of Macedonia.
3 Potential candidates: Bosnia and Herzegovina and Kosovo.
4 Partnered in an EU "European Neighborhood Policy": Armenia, Azerbaijan, Belarus, Georgia, Moldova, and Ukraine (with action plans for political and economic reform, including enhancement of human rights protection).
5 Outside of membership, negotiations, and neighborhood policy: Russia.

As each acceding country entered into negotiations, the EU included an expectation that members would provide legal protection for their citizens regardless of gender identity or sexual orientation. Although the EU published a toolkit on LGBT rights in 2010, it had not been binding (European Parliament's Intergroup on LGBT Rights 2013). In 2013, however, the EU foreign affairs ministers issued new rules on LGBT rights for all member countries, representing an unprecedented agreement across the member ministers on including LGBT rights. These rules were binding on member countries, and included:

(1) Eliminate discriminatory laws and policies, including the death penalty; (2) Promote equality and non-discrimination at work, in healthcare and in education; (3) Combat state or individual violence against LGBTI persons; and (4) Support and protect human rights defenders." (European Parliament's Intergroup on LGBT Rights 2013)

Despite the turmoil that the EU faced after the 2008 recession, EU membership is a particularly important boomerang in the toolkit for activists, and is known to require stricter compliance with expectations for new members, in contrast to other regional organizations such as NATO (North Atlantic Treaty Organization) (Pridham 2005). Countries such as Bosnia and Herzegovina are working to change their legal codes to protect sexual and gender minorities in the midst of EU accession negotiations; this country decriminalized homosexual acts in 1998, for example (Durkovic 2010, 8). In 2011, the Council of Europe introduced a new Council of Europe Convention on Preventing and Combating Violence against Women and Domestic Violence, the "Istanbul Convention." This convention explicitly applies to all women and girls regardless of sexual orientation or gender identity, and requires countries to provide a full range of services and legal remedies. By 2015, five Eastern and Central European countries had ratified and put the Convention into force and 11 had signed but not yet ratified.

Pressure on European countries also comes from watchdog groups such as ILGA-Europe (International Lesbian, Gay, Bisexual, Trans and Intersex Association, European division). Despite much progress across the continent since the 1980s, the organization's 2013 report stated that across all European regions, "Degrading, offensive, and defamatory language is being used by public officials at all levels – starting from heads of states to local councilors" (Kuyper, Iedema, and Keuzenkamp 2013). Further scrutiny and pressure on countries for their records on LGBT rights came from the Office for Democratic Institutions and Human Rights (ODIHR) of the Organization for Security and Co-operation in Europe (OSCE). Its annual hate crime report for 2013, gathered from NGOs across Europe, the Caucasus, and Central Asia, detailed violent attacks on LGBT individuals in the reporting countries, amounting to several thousand. One transgender woman was murdered in Hungary, a gay man was gang-raped in Lithuania, and an LGBT support center in FYR Macedonia was violently attacked. Russian organizations reported a range of LGBT hate crimes, including two murders. Countries in Western Europe also reported anti-LGBT hate crimes, some numbering in the hundreds for one country, but it was in Eastern and Central European countries that attacks on activist buildings and events, such as Pride parades, were more prevalent (OSCE ODIHR 2013). By 2015, LGBT issues and rights were mainstreaming within several high-level international bodies that could prove beneficial to activists, including the United States State Department, the United Nations, and the US Agency for International Development (USAID 2013).

BACKLASHES AND PUSHBACKS

Backlashes against LGBT activism are grounded in the region's particular historical and geographical contexts, including the legacies of state socialism. Although homosexuality had been decriminalized in some quarters such as the Soviet Union, Stalin had restricted rights on women and sexual minorities to improve the birth rate and as part of his general purge of nonconformists. Yugoslavian republics decriminalized homosexuality at varying times, but were the location of prisons and death sentences during World War II. Further, many citizens in the post 1989–1991 era viewed the work of LGBT activism as suspicious as in communist times such organizations were not allowed or did not define their agendas politically. By 2015, that suspicion was translated into the conditions of the new era, by suspecting that LGBT activists were working for foreign governments, were paid higher salaries, and incurred more notoriety. LGBT organizations and backlashes appeared in the context of the growing NGOization, where organizations such as Helsinki Watch began to establish local offices with paid staff.

Backlashes also took institutionalized forms. The revival of religious freedom and re-legitimacy of religious institutions across the region gave platforms for religious leaders who opposed LGBT communities on moral grounds. Russian Orthodox (Christian), Jewish, and Muslim leaders in Russia spoke forcefully against LGBT rights in public fora, echoing similar religious statements in countries such as Bosnia, Georgia, Latvia, and Poland. Religious leaders in the region used terms such as "perversion," "sin," "Satanic," "immorality," and "Sodom and Gomorrah," and some went so far as to call for thrashings. Latvia, the most conservative of the three Baltic nations and an EU member, did not outlaw discrimination against individuals based on sexual orientation until 2006. Organized opposition to LGBT activism included an organization, The Watchmen, which also operated among ex-pat Latvian communities in cities such as Sacramento, California, spurred on by an anti-gay Christian mega-church. In 2007, several Slavic men gay-bashed a man in Sacramento whom they presumed to be gay by his appearance; this man died from his injuries. Across Eastern and Central Europe, intersections between religious identity and nationalism strengthened the angry anti-gay sentiment in countries where religious and national identity are viewed as intertwined.

Economic and political institutions became centerstage in these controversies. Resistance came in the form of symbolic gestures in some cases, such as when a company in St. Petersburg, Russia, removed a public sculpture of an iPhone that it had installed to honor the late Steve Jobs, after the Apple Computer CEO Tim Cook publicly came out as gay in 2014. Further, LGBT activism in Russia has been hampered by the introduction to the "gay propaganda" bill that was signed into law in 2013, wherein perceived propaganda in support of LGBT rights and people (including displaying a rainbow flag) could be legally penalized. This helped to legitimize a growing trend of physical attacks on LGBT people in public places.

The EU accession process also unintentionally contributed to pushbacks against LGBT when politicians and citizens accused the EU as "forcing" the countries to accept LGBT rights. Some citizens in non-EU countries have cited the EU's LGBT rights agenda as a reason not to join the EU. After the 2013–2014 Euromaidan protest movement, Ukraine's new majority pro-EU parliament signed its visa liberalization agreement with the EU, but only after removing the anti-discrimination clause that would have protected LGBT people. Poland's signing of the Istanbul Convention stimulated right wing leaders, including Catholic Church leaders, to rail against "genderism" as a dangerous ideology worse than Nazism or communism. The EU's focus on LGBT rights was often seen as unwanted interference in the sovereignty of the state and a society's "tradition." This, coupled with the often heterosexual, masculine nationalisms present in these countries, confounded the issue. In Croatia for instance, as the country entered the EU, religious hardliners organized a referendum against marriage for same-sex couples, constitutionally declaring that marriage is between a woman and man. The referendum could be seen as against the EU accession process supporting LGBT rights in Croatia. A similar referendum was orchestrated in Slovakia, but failed because of a lack of sufficient turnout.

ACTIVIST GAINS

Despite this resistance, grassroots-level civil society organizations for LGBT rights have gradually proliferated. As these organizations' host countries transitioned toward stability and democratic governance at varying speeds, activists have seized the political opportunity of the moment to press for social and political change. Activists are working toward their own specific rights as LGBT people and contributing toward their societies' opportunities more broadly. In the Balkans, for example, two umbrella activist groups, the Southeastern European Queer Network of LGBT activists from the former Yugoslavia, and BABELNOR, a cross-continental network of organizations, signaled that cross-national and interethnic collaboration was the rule rather than the exception. Public officials have begun to join marchers in Pride Parades in some countries, and despite a strong anti-gay subculture Latvia's foreign minister came out publicly as gay in 2014. Also in 2014, Estonia became the first former Soviet country to legalize same-sex civil unions.

By 2015, 11 countries in the region have hate crime laws on the basis of sexual orientation, and 6 of these 11 include gender identity as a hate crime. In a few examples, Eastern and Central Europe are leading the way. Belgrade, Serbia, has become a hub for medical tourists seeking sex-change surgery (Bilefsky 2012). In 2015, ILGA-Europe included Croatia and Hungary in the handful of European countries that had reached above the 50% mark in achieving full human rights for LGBTI people (ILGA-Europe 2015). As of 2009, 16 European countries have granted asylum to individuals with a well-founded fear of persecution owing to sexual orientation or gender identity, including the Czech Republic, Hungary, and Poland (ILGA-Europe 2013). The region's countries fell on both sides of the equation: as both source and destination countries for those escaping such persecution (Pearce 2013). A 2013 decision by the Court of Justice of the EU ruled that EU countries cannot expect an asylum seeker who left their home country due to a fear of persecution based on sexual orientation to "conceal [their] homosexuality in [their] country of origin or exercise restraint in expressing it" (ILGA-Europe 2013).

In conclusion, LGBT activism in Eastern and Central Europe has experienced steady growth since the fall of state socialism. While many countries decriminalized homosexuality in the 1990s, hostility toward LGB and trans* people continued. As countries began the path of EU accession, activists used this process as well as support from other supranational entities to achieve their goals. Activism took shape mostly in NGOs, attempting to use state structures to create policy. Grassroots-level, non-institutionalized organizing was also in process, however. Despite pushbacks to LGBT rights promotion, an overall trend of better protections is in progress. Although trans* rights still seemed to be more marginal to activist goals, activists are working more intensely on decreasing transphobia. Overall, the activism in the region relies on the political institutional changes that rippled through the region in the 1990s as an opportunity in which to mobilize, resulting in accomplishments at cultural, social, and political levels.

SEE ALSO: Gay and Lesbian Pride Day; Gender Identification; Gender, Politics, and the State in Central and Eastern Europe; Human Rights and Gender; Human Rights, International Laws and Policies on; Lesbian and Gay Movements; Sexual Identity and Orientation; Sexual Minorities; Sexuality and Human Rights

REFERENCES

Bilefsky, Dan. 2012. "Serbia Becomes a Hub for Sex-Change Surgery." *The New York Times*. Accessed August 11, 2015, at http://www.nytimes.com/2012/07/24/world/europe/serbia-becomes-a-hub-for-sex-change-surgery.html.

Durkovic, Svetlana. 2010. "Study on Homophobia, Transphobia and Discrimination on Grounds of Sexual Orientation and Gender Identity." *Legal Report: Bosnia and Herzegovina*. Kongens Lyngby, Denmark: COWI, Danish Institute for Human Rights.

European Parliament's Intergroup on LGBT Rights. 2013. "EU Foreign Affairs Ministers Adopt Ground-Breaking Global LGBTI Policy." Accessed August 11, 2015, at http:// www.lgbt-ep.eu/press-releases/eu-foreign-affairs-ministers-adopt-lgbti-guidelines/.

Holzhacker, Ronald. 2013. "State-Sponsored Homophobia and the Denial of the Right of Assembly in Central and Eastern Europe: The 'Boomerang' and the 'Ricochet' between European Organizations and Civil Society to Uphold Human Rights." *Law and Policy*, 35(1–2): 1–28.

ILGA-Europe. 2013. "EU Court of Justice: LGBTI People are Eligible Group for Claiming Asylum in EU and they Cannot be Requested to Conceal their Sexual Orientation." Accessed August 11, 2015, at http://www.ilga-europe.org/home/news/for_media/media_releases/eu_court_of_justice_lgbti_people_are_eligible_group_for_claiming_asylum_in_eu_and_they_cannot_be_requested_to_conceal_their_sexual_orientation.

ILGA-Europe. 2015. "Rainbow Europe Package. International Lesbian, Gay, Bisexual, Trans and Intersex Association-Europe." Accessed August 11, 2015, at http://www.ilga-europe.org/home/publications/reports_and_other_materials/rainbow_europe.

Keck, Margaret E., and Kathryn Sikkink. 1998. *Activists Beyond Borders*. Ithaca: Cornell University Press.

Kuyper, Lisette, Jurjen Iedema, and Saskia Keuzenkamp. 2013. "Towards Tolerance: Exploring Changes and Explaining Differences in Attitudes Towards Homosexuality in Europe." Den Haag, The Netherlands: The Netherlands Institute for Social Research. Accessed August 11, 2015, at http://www.scp.nl/english/Publications/Publications_by_year/Publications_2013/Towards_Tolerance.

OSCE ODIHR. 2013. "Bias Against LGBT People." Accessed August 11, 2015, at http://hatecrime.osce.org/taxonomy/term/235.

Pearce, Susan C. 2013. "Out of Southeast Europe: Gender-Based Violence, Public Transitions, and a Search for Home." In *Advances in Gender Research*, vol. 18, edited by Vasilikie Demos and Marcia Segal. Bingley, UK: Emerald Group Publishing Unlimited.

Pearce, Susan C. and Alex Cooper. 2014. "LGBT Movements in Southeast Europe: Violence, Justice, and International Intersections." In *Handbook of LGBT Communities, Crime, and Justice*, edited by Dana Peterson and Vanessa R. Panfil. New York: Springer Publishing.

Pridham, Geoffrey. 2005. *Designing Democracy: EU Enlargement and Regime Change in Post-Communist Europe*. Basingstoke, UK and New York: Palgrave Macmillan.

USAID. 2013. "USAID Announces New Partnership to Promote LGBT Human Rights Abroad." Accessed August 11, 2015, at http://www.usaid.gov/news-information/press-releases/usaid-announces-new-partnership-promote-lgbt-human-rights-abroad.

FURTHER READING

Enguix, Begonya. 2009. "Identities, Sexualities and Commemorations: Pride Parades, Public Space and Sexual Dissidence." *Anthropological Notebooks*, 15: 15–33.

Jansen, Sabine, and Thomas Spijkerboer. 2011. "Fleeing Homophobia: Asylum Claims Related to Sexual Orientation and Gender Identity in Europe." A project of COC Netherlands and VU University Amsterdam. Accessed August 11, 2015, at http://www.academia.edu/900410/Fleeing_Homophobia._Asylum_Claims_Related_to_Sexual_Orientation_and_Gender_Identity_in_Europe.

Johnston, Lynda. 2005. *Queering Tourism: Paradoxical Performances of Gay Pride Parades*. London: Routledge.

Richard, Anne C. 2013. "LGBT: Equally Entitled to Human Rights and Dignity." *Forced Migration Review*, 42: 4.

Weller, Marc. 2008. "Introduction: The Outlook for the Protection of Minorities in the Wider Europe." In *The Protection of Minorities in the Wider Europe*, edited by Denika Blacklock and Katherine Nobbs. Basingstoke: Palgrave Macmillan.

LGBT Activism in Latin America

JOSÉ FERNANDO SERRANO-AMAYA
Colombia, Australia

GUSTAVO GOMES DA COSTA SANTOS
Federal University of Pernambuco, Brazil

The idea of Latin America as a homogeneous region has been a matter of intense discussion since the creation of the colonial structures that shaped the area. Language and religion have often been used to support the notion of common trends. Catholicism and Iberian colonization are offered as explanations of particular gender and sexual norms. However, behind this idea of communality there are complex and contradictory trends in social, political, and economic development. The result is a multiplicity of cultures, countries, and areas that share some global and regional trends but also have unique histories of interaction, contestation, and reaction to them. The politicization of groups and organizations around gender identities and sexual orientation needs to be framed in such heterogeneity.

ORIGINS OF LGBT POLITICAL ACTIVISM IN LATIN AMERICA

Latin American countries saw wide sociodemographic changes after the end of World War II. The process of import substitution and industrialization accelerated urbanization and contributed to the development of gay and lesbian subcultures in the major cities. These areas of homoerotic socialization were fundamental to the emergence of the social networks that were the bases for the first attempts to organize the struggle around same-sex desire in the region.

Initiatives to politically mobilize lesbian women and gay men have had parallel and interrelated paths in progressive social movements, leftist organizations, and communist parties since the early 1970s. Openly lesbian women have been part of women's and feminist organizations from their beginnings. They have also been involved in leftist parties and workers unions, challenging their patriarchal and misogynist structures.

Participation of gay activists in leftist movements did not mean that those organizations were open to issues of sexual orientation in Latin America. Activists in Brazil, Argentina, Chile, and Colombia had difficulties in bringing the discussion of discrimination and prejudice against homosexuals to their comrades in leftist parties and trade unions. Homosexuality was still seen by many leftists as a bourgeois vice, which would cease to exist in the new socialist era.

Other leftist activists regarded sexual orientation, as well as gender and ethnicity/race, as secondary issues that would prevent the working class from focusing their efforts on the primary struggle. Some small Trotskyist parties, such as Socialist Convergence (Brazil) and the Revolutionary Workers Party (Mexico), were more open to discussing issues of sexual orientation and were important in the politicization of homosexuality in the region.

These waves of organizations focused on deconstructing social ideas and stereotypes related to lesbian and gay people, but also on denouncing sexual oppression. The influence of counterculture and other cultural movements facilitated links with ideas of sexual liberation, cultural change, and ideological critique as could be seen in Colombia, Mexico, or Argentina. In Brazil, artists and performers such as Ney Matogrosso or the Dzi Croquettes questioned the sexist and macho Brazilian culture by blurring the boundaries of gender roles and identities.

In the 1970s, Latin American homosexual groups combined conscious-raising activities with political mobilization. The Argentinian *Frente de Liberación Homosexual* (Homosexual Liberation Front), and the Mexican group with the same name were founded in 1971. Beside their names, both groups struggled for homosexual liberation strongly influenced by Marxist ideology, but also by black and feminist movements. Other groups in the region, such as *Somos* in Brazil, were influenced by such patterns of activism. These homosexual groups operated in a very repressive environment, which explains their guerrilla-like organization style, for example following the structure of autonomous cells and copying underground patterns of organization.

At the same time, Latin American lesbian activism created regional alliances and positioned their needs in international arenas. In 1975, during the First World Conference on the Status of Women in Mexico City, a group of lesbian women from various countries organized and focused attention on their demands. Since then, Latin American lesbians have participated in international forums for the rights of women and have also connected them with local activism.

Travestis, and men and women socially and economically marginalized because of their gender and sexuality, have their own history of mobilization and politicization. The fight against police repression, exploitation, and criminality created collective organizations and informal networks of solidarity since the early twentieth century in cities in Brazil, Mexico, and Colombia. Their claims and initiatives were not always included in the more mainstream, but still marginalized, *movimientos de liberación homosexual* (homosexual liberation movements) that were emerging.

AIDS AND LGBT ACTIVISM IN LATIN AMERICA

The 1980s witnessed the beginning of political opportunities in some countries. Human rights activism was a key element in the struggle for redemocratization. For homosexual militancy, it was the beginning of a new wave of activism framed into rights discourses and fights for equality. The end of authoritarian regimes in the south was seen as the first step to the building of a society free from prejudice and discrimination on the grounds of sexual orientation. In countries that did not experience those regimes, democratization arrived later as part of structural adjustment reforms and post-conflict reconstruction. Increased democracy and demands for social change were pushed by a variety of social movements which created alliances, agendas, and learned lessons that oriented new trends for the politicization of gay and lesbian organizations in the 1980s.

Lesbian mobilization inside the feminist movement continued expansion at regional levels. Lesbian women publicly participated in the first *Encuentro Feminista Latinoamericano y del Caribe* (Latin American and Caribbean Encounter), in July 1981 in Bogotá, Colombia. Lesbianism as a political option was discussed as part of feminism and the political struggle.

It was also at this time that Latin America started to suffer the consequences of the HIV/AIDS epidemic. Concerns around human rights under authoritarian governments shifted to concern for other rights. AIDS reinforced old prejudices against homosexuality, fueling moral panics throughout the region. The struggle for a wide cultural transformation gave way to more specific, identity-based demands. Instead of relying on demands related to sexual liberation and cultural transformation, new activisms that emerged in Latin America were mainly focused on providing care to those affected by AIDS. Homosexual activists established health services, as many AIDS patients could not get assistance from public or private health services, or even from their own relatives, because of prejudice based on their sexual orientation.

The need to create policies to deal with the impact of AIDS forced a closer working relationship between gay men's organizations, international cooperation agencies, and health services. The struggle for HIV/AIDS prevention and for an anti-discriminatory approach to deal with the disease were the new topics on the political agenda of homosexual activism. AIDS helped in bringing sexuality to the core of public opinion and, consequently, was central to the politicization of homosexuality in Latin America. The joint work between Latin American activists and international cooperation resulted in the increasing professionalization of homosexual activism. The groups were reorganized primarily as non-governmental organizations (NGOs), with formal registration, offices, and relatively permanent funds. In many countries, these groups began to work together with state health services and helped to design a national public response to the AIDS epidemic.

HIV/AIDS activism was not the only concern that motivated claims for change in state policies. In Argentina, particularly in Buenos Aires, *travestis* and transsexuals organized throughout the 1980s to demand the abolishment of policy codes that were used against them, denounced discrimination in health services, and claimed recognition for their sexual identities.

The role of international cooperation was fundamental to the appropriation by Latin American activism of a militancy expertise developed by European and North American lesbian and gay organizations throughout the 1990s. Terms and concepts such as advocacy, empowerment, peer education, visibility, and vulnerability were increasingly present in AIDS prevention projects and in the daily political discourses and practices of Latin American activism. The influence of global AIDS cooperation and of globalized rights-based initiatives were important to the appropriation of the lesbian, gay, bisexual, and transgender (LGBT) identities by the homosexual militancy in the region.

The struggle against AIDS helped many LGBT activists forge regional and global mobilization networks that brought the issue of discrimination toward sexual minorities to regional and international notice. The actions of these networks and of women's organizations were central to the elaboration of the concept of sexual rights and to the inclusion of the demands of LGBT movements, both globally and locally, into the discourse of human rights.

AIDS also contributed to an increase in the number of academic studies related to sexual identities and practices in Latin America. Many of these studies analyzed the social construction of sexual identities in the region. They were initially oriented to demonstrate that many Latin American men who engaged in same-sex sexual intercourse did not identify themselves as *gay* or *homosexuales*. Academics showed that Latin American sexual identities were largely defined by sexual practices and gender roles rather than identity politics.

With globalized AIDS activism, categories such as "men who have sex with men" (MSM) were incorporated in AIDS prevention actions. The use of the MSM category allowed the inclusion of transgender populations in the efforts to combat AIDS and contributed to their participation in the political mobilization around sexuality. It was in such a context that "transgender" as a collective category and "sexual diversity" as a descriptive term were imported and translated to Latin American contexts.

Those translations caused reactions. These identities were seen by some Latin American activists as alien to their social and cultural realities. In Brazil, for instance, transgender identity was severely criticized by local transvestite and transsexual activists as a foreign importation that did not correctly represent their identities and experiences. Homosexual and lesbian activists contested the politics under such translations because of imposing knowledge and economic power relations channeled through cooperation agencies. Lesbian feminism also questioned mainstream feminism incorporated in international and regional cooperation agencies.

NEW TRENDS IN LATIN AMERICAN LGBT ACTIVISM

The beginning of the new century witnessed important changes in Latin American LGBT activism. In fact, it was then that "LGBT" became a common term to describe movements that have had their own developments and alliances.

The first change is the growing visibility of local LGBT movements in many countries. LGBT Pride Parades and other activities, such as "kiss-in" and institutional advocacy, contributed to a wider presence in public arenas of topics related to sexual orientation.

The second change is the replacement of HIV/AIDS as the main focus of Latin American LGBT activism. The struggle for rights using litigation strategies appeared as the new focus of militancy in the region. Together with demands for anti-discrimination legislation and policies, Latin American LGBT activism has recently obtained some recognition for same-sex couples' rights. In countries such as Argentina, Brazil, Chile, Colombia, Costa Rica, Mexico, and Uruguay, some protective measures for LGBT people have been recognized by state institutions, locally or nationally. In countries that have recently experienced processes of state reorganization, like Bolivia and Ecuador, the prohibition of discrimination based on sexual orientation and gender identity were included in their new constitutions.

However, those legal demands were not obtained in all countries at the same time nor in all countries facing wide political changes, as in the case of Venezuela or Bolivia. Backlashes in terms of violence coexisted with the enactment of protective measures, as in the case of Ecuador or Colombia, and Nicaragua still criminalizes homosexuality.

The third change is the inclusion of homophobia as a "social problem" demanding state intervention through public policies and anti-discriminatory measures. In countries like Argentina, Brazil, and Uruguay, national governments have been implementing anti-homophobic policies and including respect for sexual orientation and gender identities in policies such as education, health, and social security. Examples are national initiatives such as the Brazilian Human Right Secretary's Plan *Brasil Sem Homofobia* and the Uruguayan minister of social development's policies directed to the LGBT population. Capital cities in Argentina and Colombia have public policy schemes as a result of activists' demands for social services targeting LGBT people.

Groups of lesbians, transgender, and bisexual men and women have denounced the gay hegemony in the LGBT activism, demanding recognition of their particular experiences of discrimination and prejudice and challenging an assimilationist model of rights focused mainly on same-sex couples' rights. *Disidencia sexual* (sexual dissidence) is becoming a more common term to describe activism differentiated and in tension with LGBT-oriented activism.

In spite of some protective measures for transgender men and women in countries such as Cuba, Mexico, Panama, Colombia, Brazil, Argentina, and Uruguay, their needs are still underprotected and less represented in activism and litigation initiatives. Even more, legal changes in these topics are asymmetric and face problems of implementation.

These changes represent the configuration of new waves in Latin American LGBT activism. One is a more institutionalized, rights-based organization, with a closer relationship to state institutions. The other is a diversification and exponential increment in the number of groups, not only of gay men, but also of lesbians and transgender people, which can be identified as some of the new characteristics of LGBT activism in the region.

Despite much that has been written on the influence of US and European-based LGBT movements on Latin America and on migration toward the Global North and sexualities in diaspora, there has been less research on the role and contribution of Latin American activism to global trends on LGBT rights. Interchanges between Latin American countries and the Global South has been also a less examined area. The extensive literature on mobilizations around gender and sexuality in Latin America is still underrepresented in English-speaking academia. That situation presents a challenge not only in terms of translations, but also for cooperative work and alliance building.

Finally, the activism of LGBT people in transitions to democracy, peace building, and conflict resolution initiatives is still under-recognized by state institutions and by other social movements struggling for social justice.

SEE ALSO: AIDS-Related Stigma; Feminist Movements in Historical and Comparative Perspective; Gender, Politics, and the State in Latin America; Images of Gender and Sexuality in Latin America; Lesbian and Gay Movements; Pacifism, Peace Activism, and Gender; Transgender Movements in International Perspective; Women's and Feminist Activism in Latin America

FURTHER READING

Argüello Pazmiño, Sofía. 2008. *El Closet y el Estado: Ciudadanías sexuales en Ecuador y Bolivia*. Informe final del concurso: Las deudas abiertas en América Latina y el Caribe. Programa Regional de Becas CLACSO. Accessed August 20, 2015, at http://bibliotecavirtual.clacso.org.ar/ar/libros/becas/2008/deuda/argue.pdf.

Bazán, Osvaldo. 2006. *Historia de la Homosexualidad en la Argentina: De la Conquista de América al Siglo XXI*. Buenos Aires: Editorial Marea.

Bolaños, José Daniel Jiménez. 2014. "Temáticas en Construcción: El Desarrollo de los Estudios LGBT en Costa Rica, 1980–2013." *Cuadernos Inter.c.a.mbio sobre Centroamérica y el Caribe*, 11(2). DOI: 10.15517/c.a..v11i2.16311.

Careaga, Gloria, ed. 2003. *Orientación Sexual en la Lucha de las Mujeres*. México: El Closet de Sor Juana, ILGA.

Conselho Nacional de Combate à Discriminação. 2004. *Brasil sem Homofobia: Programa de Combate à Violência e à Discriminação contra GLTB e de Promoção da Cidadania Homossexual*. Brasilia, Ministério da Saúde. Accessed August 20, 2015, at http://www.biblioteca.presidencia.gov.br/publicacoes-oficiais-1/catalogo/orgao-essenciais/secretaria-de-direitos-humanos/brasil-sem-homofobia-programa-de-combate-a-violencia-e-a-discriminacao-contra-lgbt-e-de-promocao-da-cidadania-homossexual/view.

Contardo, Óscar. 2011. *Raro: Una Historia Gay de Chile*. Santiago: Editoral Planeta.

Corrales, Jorge, and Mario Pecheny, eds. 2010. *The Politics of Sexuality in Latin America: A Reader on Lesbian, Gay and Transgender Rights*. Pittsburgh: University of Pittsburgh Press.

Corrêa, Sonia, and Richard Parker, eds. 2011. *Sexualidade e Política na América Latina: Histórias, Interseções e Paradoxos*. Rio de Janeiro, ABIA. Accessed August 20, 2015, at http://www.sxpolitics.org/pt/wp-content/uploads/2011/07/dialogo-la_total_final.pdf.

Dehesa, Rafael de la. 2010. *Queering the Public Sphere in Mexico and Brazil: Sexual Rights Movements in Emerging Democracies*. Durham, NC: Duke University Press.

Facchini, Regina. 2005. *Sopa de Letrinhas? Movimento Homossexual e Produção de Identidades Coletivas Nos Anos 90*. Rio de Janeiro: Editora Garamond.

Green, James, and Renan Quinalha, eds. 2014. *Ditadura e Homossexualidade: Repressão, Resistência e a Busca da Verdade*. São Carlos: EDUFSCAR.

MacRae, Edward. 1990. *A Construção da Igualdade: Identidade Sexual e Política no Brasil da "Abertura"*. Campinas: Editora da Unicamp.

Martinez, Luciano. 2008. "Transformación y Renovación: Los Estudios Lésbico-Gays y Queer

Latinoamericanos." *Revista Iberoamericana*, 74(225): 861–876.

Ministerio del Desarrollo Social. 2014. *Diversidad Sexual en Uruguay: Las Políticas de Inclusión Social Para Personas LGBT del Ministerio de Desarrollo Social (2010–2014)*. Accessed August 20, 2015, at http://www.unfpa.org.uy/userfiles/publications/112_file1.pdf.

Robles, Victor Hugo. 2008. *Bandera Hueca: Historia del Movimiento Homosexual de Chile*. Santiago: Editorial Cuarto Próprio.

Sempol, Diego. 2013. *De los Baños a la Calle: Historia del Movimiento Lésbico, Gay, Trans Uruguayo (1984–2013)*. Montevideo: Editoral Sudamericana Uruguaya.

Wilson, Bruce M. 2007. "Claiming Individual Rights Through a Constitutional Court: The Example of Gays in Costa Rica." *ICON*, 5(2): 242–257.

LGBT Activism Among Māori

ELIZABETH KEREKERE
University of Wellington, New Zealand

Māori who identify as lesbian, gay, bisexual, trans, intersex, and queer (LGBTIQ) began forming networks from the 1950s and have featured prominently in LGBTIQ and other activism ever since. Since the early 1990s, Māori LGBTIQ have increasingly adopted the term "takatāpui" – a traditional Māori term meaning intimate companion of the same sex – as an indigenous and inclusive framework within which to identify personally and organize nationally.

Māori are the indigenous people of Aotearoa (Māori name) New Zealand. A process of British settlement, missionary influence, and military force culminated in the Treaty of Waitangi in 1840 and the establishment of a colonial government. Despite rights guaranteed within the Treaty, the major loss of Māori language, culture, and land occurred in the late 1800s. While homosexual and heterosexual identities only emerged in the late 1800s, examples of Māori same/both-sex attracted practices have been found within European and colonial records since the 1700s. The apparent casual sexuality embodied by Māori met with concerted efforts to suppress any expression or record of same/both-sex attracted or gender nonconforming behavior, even as colonists and missionaries engaged with it.

Dr. Ngahuia Te Awekotuku has been the primary scholar on this history, revealing several instances where such records were changed or subsequently removed. Te Awekotuku (2005) concluded that sexuality was enjoyed in many forms and that same-sex love was not condemned or vilified. Many Māori elders have confirmed that female and male homosexuality was common in pre-European times and that it was more readily accepted than in contemporary society. The cultural imperative of continuing one's line, however, was still expected, regardless of gender identity or sexual orientation.

Up until the 1940s, most Māori lived in rural areas of the country. Pressures to seek work and the enticement of city life created a national urban drift throughout the 1950s and 1960s. This contributed to the disconnection of Māori from their language and culture as they adjusted to living and working in non-Māori and often racist environments. Māori LGBTIQ coming into the cities congregated in networks of kamp/camp culture – the term for homosexual in pre-1970 New Zealand (Laurie 2003). Such networks are noted in the records of Carmen's (Māori trans icon) International Coffee Lounge, Wellington's Dorian Society (first homosexual organization 1962), and Auckland's KG Club (first lesbian organization 1971). In 1963, the Dorian Society formed a legal subcommittee to promote law reform which became the New Zealand Homosexual Law Reform Society in 1967.

By the 1970s, Māori LGBTIQ were involved in the many organizations formed to reflect the international influences of feminism, lesbian feminism, and gay liberation. One of the first was the Women's Liberation Front Club, 1970, at Victoria University of Wellington which hosted the first National Women's Liberation Conference in 1972. Groups were also established in Auckland, Dunedin, Christchurch, and Palmerston North. The United Women's Convention was held in 1973. Gay Liberation began in 1972 when a group of lesbians and gay men from the University of Auckland protested against the United States refusing a visa for Ngahuia Te Awekotuku because she was a known "homosexual" (Te Awekotuku 1991). Groups were also formed in Wellington, Christchurch, and Hamilton that same year. National conferences were held annually from 1972 to 1976 until the National Gay Rights Coalition (NGRC) was established in 1977 which hosted its own conferences.

The NGRC organized the first nationally coordinated Gay Pride Week with demonstrations in Wellington, Christchurch, and Auckland. Their goal was visibility and the transformation of heterosexual society, as opposed to law reform, and by 1978 the NGRC had around 30 affiliated groups. To balance the predominantly gay male membership of these groups, Māori lesbian, Alison Laurie, established the first lesbian feminist group, Sisters for Homophile Equality (SHE), in 1973. SHE established the first national lesbian magazine and worked to ensure that lesbian feminism was integrated into gay liberation.

Running parallel to these liberation movements was the growing strength of Māori protest, fueled by the poor state of Māori health, education, and employment and concern for the loss of language and culture. Māori LGBTIQ spread themselves across all sectors of struggle. In particular, Ngahuia Te Awekotuku was a member of Ngā Tamatoa which emerged from the inaugural Māori Leaders Conference, University of Auckland, in 1970. It was a Māori activist group that promoted Māori rights with a focus on Treaty of Waitangi violations and the promotion of Māori language. In September 1972, Ngā Tamatoa presented a petition with more than 30,000 signatures to the Crown to have Māori language taught in schools. They also organized the 1975 Land March, led by Dame Whina Cooper. Other initiatives led to the establishment of Te Kōhanga Reo (Māori language nests for preschool children). In 1987, the Māori Language Act was passed by the New Zealand government, making Māori an official language. The connections forged by Māori within LGBTIQ communities and organizations resulted in a visible LGBTIQ presence in marches and other protest actions organized by Māori activists.

This national level of organization and political awareness is one of the reasons given for the mobilization and cohesion with which Aotearoa met the AIDS epidemic when it hit New Zealand in the 1980s. The New Zealand AIDS Foundation (NZAF) was established in 1985 followed by the New Zealand Prostitutes Collective in 1987. The first Māori LGBTIQ-specific service, Te Roopu Tautoko Trust, in 1988 was run by takatāpui activist, Rex Perenara. National conferences – now known as Takatāpui Hui-a-Motu – have been held at least biannually since 1986 and Te Roopu Tautoko Trust hosted the first International Indigenous HIV Conference in 1991.

MP Fran Wilde took up the mantle in 1984 to ease the Homosexual Law Reform legislation through parliament. Gay task forces were formed in Wellington, Christchurch, Auckland, and Dunedin. The introduction of the Bill to parliament in 1985 created a massive backlash and 2,000 submissions were received, although very few from Māori individuals or organizations. In September, over 200,000 people marched throughout the country in support of the Bill. The so-called Nuremburg Rally against Law Reform presented a petition on the steps of parliament, one box being presented by a young Māori woman and man in traditional Māori costume. Only 350,000 of the 810,000 signatures were proved to be valid. On July 9, 1986 the Homosexual Law Reform Act was passed by Parliament by 49 votes to 44.

The term "takatāpui" came into currency in the late 1980s through promotion to Māori LGBTIQ organizations and networks by scholars Ngahuia Te Awekotuku and Lee Smith. They had separately found the term in the earliest manuscripts written by a Māori, scholar Wīremu Maihi Te Rangikāheke, in reference to the intimate relationship between two male friends, Tūtanekai and Tiki (Te Awekotuku 2005). The attraction of the term to Māori LGBTIQ is manifold in that it reinforces indigenous identity and a spiritual descent from "tūpuna takatāpui" (takatāpui ancestors) while replacing the inelegant "LGBTIQ" with an inclusivity of gender identities and sexuality similar to the term "rainbow." Most importantly, the term implies membership of a multi-tribal community where the different identities embodied by takatāpui can be unified and honored (Kerekere 2015).

The need to acknowledge the many lives lost to HIV/AIDS and to affirm takatāpui identity in the late 1980s and 1990s saw a flurry of takatāpui voices in print. Takatāpui trans women were at the forefront as Georgina Beyer made international headlines as the first trans mayor in the world in 1995 and the first trans MP in the world in 1999. That year former sex worker, Mama Tere Strickland, co-founded Te Aronga Hou Inaianei to provide services for takatāpui within the sex industry and those living on the street. Takatāpui increasingly came under discussion in Māori LGBTIQ networks and in women's studies departments at universities.

The dawn of the new millennium saw takatāpui groups addressing broader issues of health and well-being. Tīwhanawhana Trust, which was founded by Elizabeth Kerekere in Wellington in 2000, to "tell our stories, build our community and leave a legacy," addresses all aspects of takatāpui health and well-being, to advocate within LGBTIQ communities, and address homophobia and transphobia in Māori communities and New Zealand society.

The year 2004 was an auspicious one for takatāpui. It began with the launch of Māori Television on March 28 with a lineup that included the programme *Takatāpui*. It was the first free-to-air indigenous queer program in the world on the first free-to-air indigenous television channel in the world. Its successful magazine-style format went on to run for four seasons and was responsible for making the term "takatāpui" more of a household name in mainstream Māori society.

Christianity was adopted by most Māori during colonization and Christian prayer has often replaced or sits alongside *karakia* (traditional incantations) within traditional protocols, including at all takatāpui hui (gatherings/conferences). It was therefore devastating to many when takatāpui existence was called into question by a Māori Church leader. Appearing on the front page of the *New Zealand Herald*, June 5, 2004, was the banner: "*A World Without Gays.*" In opposition to the stated decision of the Anglican General Synod, Archbishop of Aotearoa and Polynesia, Te Whakahuihui Vercoe, announced that: "Homosexuality was not a part of traditional Māori society and that many people within the Māori community looked forward to the day when this would be the case again."

Takatāpui throughout the country were further appalled to watch the Destiny

Church-led march to Parliament on August 23, 2004 in protest against the proposed Civil Union legislation for same-sex couples. Under the banners of "Family Values" and "Enough is Enough," this predominantly Māori march intimated that takatāpui were not part of the whānau (family) – or should not be. Despite their best efforts, on December 9, 2004, the Civil Union Act was passed by Parliament by 65 votes to 55.

Sexuality and the Stories of Indigenous People (Hutchings and Aspin 2007) was the first non-fiction book devoted to takatāpui. Predominantly autobiographical, it arose partly as a positive and visibility-raising response to the 2004 Destiny Church march. Several of the 17 book contributors remarked on the march's negative impact on them personally and on Māori society generally.

Subsequent to the march, many takatāpui took part in the first national strengths-based study of lesbian, gay, and bisexual (LGB) people in New Zealand: *Lavender Islands: Portrait of the Whole Family*. The multidisciplinary interest areas included identity and self-definition, families of origin, relationships and sexuality, families of choice, immigration and internal migration, well-being, politics, income and spending, education, careers and leisure, community connections, challenges, and spirituality. The resulting report on Māori respondents found several statistically significant differences between them and non-Māori (Henrickson 2006):

1. Cultural affiliation was more significant for Māori than sexual orientation, and culture and spirituality had a more important role in negotiating takatāpui identities.
2. Contemporary takatāpui felt pressured to choose between being Māori and their sexuality, to marry and to have children.
3. Māori women were "developmentally remarkable" in that they were more likely to come out earlier and be out to everyone they knew.

Although the focus on LGB precluded many others who identified as takatāpui, the findings were consistent with anecdotal evidence within takatāpui communities.

The OUT THERE! National Queer Youth Project (Project) was a joint project between NZAF and Auckland-based group, Rainbow Youth. The Project organized the first National Queer Youth Hui in Wellington 2003, which was run by takatāpui Sarah Helm. Tīwhanawhana Trust was involved with the subsequent KAHA '07 and KAHA '09: National Hui for Takatāpui, Queer, and Trans Youth. As the national Kaimahi, Takatāpui Taiohi (Takatāpui youth worker), Elizabeth Kerekere organized KAHA '09 and provided cultural advice, political support, and leadership training. The Project was disestablished in 2009 and Rainbow Youth went on to organize KAZAM! National Hui, Auckland, 2010. Regional and national hui have been held annually ever since. The legacy of takatāpui activism can be seen in a queer and trans youth movement in New Zealand which holds the bulk of its gatherings at Marae (traditional Māori meeting houses) in adherence to Māori protocol and often with dedicated Māori/takatāpui positions or advisory roles within their organizational structures (Kerekere 2015).

While it existed, the Project funded the production of same/both-sex attracted reports for national surveys: Youth '01 and Youth '07. Youth '12 included data for transgender youth and shows that a greater proportion of "sexual minority" young people were "out" than in 2001 and 2007 (Lucassen et al. 2015). Most sexual minority youth reported good general health, liking school and having caring friends, and many contribute to their communities through volunteering. However, "sexuality minority" Māori are significantly more likely to experience bullying, unwanted sexual attention, and sexual and mental health problems than both their non-Māori and heterosexual counterparts. This has culminated in negative body image, increased risk-taking behavior, self-harm, and suicide. Tīwhanawhana Trust is among many Māori and LGBTIQ organizations working with government and community agencies to address these issues.

The second Asia Pacific OutGames was hosted in Wellington, March 2011 by Wellington 2011 Inc. The OutGames comprised a Human Rights Conference, and a range of sporting and cultural activities. Kevin Haunui of Tīwhanawhana Trust was a member of the organizing group which arranged a pōwhiri (traditional Māori welcome) at Te Papa Tongarewa (national museum) in place of the Opening Night dance party usually held at such events. The success of the week-long event saw Wellington 2011 Inc. win both the Sport and Leisure category and the Supreme Award at the Wellington City Council's 2011 Wellington Airport Regional Community Awards.

With support from most Māori MPs and Parliament's Rainbow Caucus, on April 18, 2013, marriage equality was passed into law by 77 votes to 44. Ongoing takatāpui priorities include keeping Māori values and worldviews at the forefront as the fight continues for the rights of trans and intersex people, anti-homophobic/transphobic bullying, and suicide prevention.

SEE ALSO: Gender, Politics, and the State, and the Māori; Images of Gender and Sexuality of Māori; LGBT Activism in Australia and New Zealand; Women's and Feminist Activism Among Māori

REFERENCES

Henrickson, Mark. 2006. "Ko Wai Rātou? Managing Multiple Identities in Lesbian, Gay and Bisexual Māori." *New Zealand Journal of Sociology*, 21(2): 248.

Hutchings, Jessica, and Clive Aspin, eds. 2007. *Sexuality and the Stories of Indigenous People*. Wellington: Huia.

Kerekere, Elizabeth. 2015. *"Part of the Whānau: The Emergence of Takatāpui Identity."* Unpublished doctoral thesis, Victoria University of Wellington.

Laurie, Alison J. 2003. *"Lady-Husbands and Kamp Ladies: Pre-1970 Lesbian Life in Aotearoa/New Zealand."* Unpublished doctoral thesis, Victoria University of Wellington.

Lucassen, Mathijs F.G., et al. 2015. "What Has Changed From 2001 to 2012 for Sexual Minority Youth in New Zealand?" *Journal of Paediatrics and Child Health*, 51(4): 410–418.

Te Awekotuku, Ngahuia. 1991. *Mana Wāhine Māori: Selected Writings in Māori Women's Art, Culture and Politics*. Auckland: New Women's Press.

Te Awekotuku, Ngahuia. 2005. "He Reka Anō: Same Sex Lust and Loving in the Ancient Māori World." In *Outlines: Lesbian and Gay Histories of Aotearoa*, edited by Alison J. Laurie and Linda Evans. Wellington: Lesbian and Gay Archives of New Zealand.

FURTHER READING

Laurie, Alison J. and Linda Evans, eds. 2009. *Twenty Years On: Histories of Homosexual Law Reform in New Zealand*. Wellington: Lesbian and Gay Archives of New Zealand.

LGBT Activism in the Middle East

SAMAR HABIB
School of Oriental and African Studies (SOAS), UK

INTRODUCTION

This entry is concerned with countries of Arabic-speaking populations, including those that fall outside the traditional Middle East, such as North Africa.

Although there is virtually no substantial scholarship on lesbian, gay, bisexual, transgender, intersex, and/or queer (LGBTIQ) activist clusters in this region (for exceptions see Anderson 2015 and Ake 2011), there is an active debate on whether LGBTIQ activism is imposed by Western political agendas and Western categories of sexuality, or whether it results from spontaneous agitations for greater civil liberties at a grassroots level. In this debate, Joseph Massad is the primary contender that LGBTIQ non-governmental organizations (NGOs) in the Middle East are extraordinary installments, seeking to alter local sexual epistemologies by participating in, and thus imposing, a Western taxonomy of sexuality (Massad, Éwanjé-Épée, and Magliani-Belkacem, 2013). Further Jasbir Puar (2007) has been critical of the phenomenon of "homonationalism," in which she dismantles the racial othering of Muslims through LGBT international rights organizing and the simultaneous construction of gay identity as a racial marker of white citizenship. Aleardo Zanghellini (2012) assesses whether Massad's and Puar's points of view lack the theoretical capacity to deal with Muslim (or even Islamic) homophobia and poses the question as to whether gay rights organizing is necessarily Islamophobic. Samar Habib's introduction to *Islam and Homosexuality* (Habib 2010) argues that rights discourses can be universally applicable with respect to torture and persecution, since these constitutionally affect human beings in similar ways, irrespective of cultural differences or social constructions. However, although all of these scholars grapple with theoretical concepts and origins of ideas, they do not substantiate their work with empirical information regarding the history of the formation of LGBTIQ NGOs and informal groups in the region, a matter that the remainder of this entry addresses.

Documented and organized LGBTIQ activism in the Arabic-speaking world began to emerge in the twenty-first century, and is frequently funded through an international development framework. It has become a profitable enterprise to seek funding through private donors from Europe, the United Kingdom and the United States to set up NGOs, whose logic and language center around LGBTIQ human rights discourse as it is fashioned in the United Nations and the European Union. LGBTIQ activists in this context are a mix of paid employees of NGOs and volunteer members. Nonetheless, unofficial groups that subsist purely on volunteer contributions of its members also exist. Most often, such organizations must remain clandestine because the contexts in which they operate are legally dangerous. This presents an ethical dilemma for the researcher, who, by publishing names of organizations and/or persons, puts such individuals and activities at a risk of persecution. For this reason, this entry limits the amount of information it releases on the groups and organizations it discusses and sometimes deliberately omits mention of certain groups and organizations.

Both Western donor-funded LGBTIQ rights NGOs in the Middle East and non-funded, unregistered groups have predominantly emerged organically as a result of local gender and sexual minority persons' efforts to reshape the cultural and legislative landscape of their nation states. The Internet has played a large role in facilitating the creation of online communities, which lead to non-virtual meetings and networking. These same virtual communities are used in police states, such as Egypt, to entrap (almost exclusively male) same-sex practitioners.

ALGERIA

Algerian LGBT activists struggle in a society that is closed to relations with Europe. Unlike

Tunisia and Morocco, Algeria's economy relies on oil rather than tourism, which has resulted in greater conservatism than in its neighbors. Homosexuals are prosecuted under Articles 333 and 338 of the penal code. The story of Algerian LGBT organizing began in 2007 with a 21-year-old woman who set up a mailing list forum asking if there were other same-sex-attracted people in her vicinity. The forum soon gained a substantial following and the virtual group decided to meet in person. These meetings led to the first interconnection beyond the virtual community. In 2007, Abu Nuwas was created. This group obtains international funding and its mission is centered around abolishing relevant penal codes and challenging social stigmatization. Founded in 2011, Alouen is another LGBT rights group that also seeks to abolish relevant penal codes under which homosexuals are prosecuted (Jean-Jacques 2014).

IRAQ

The Iraqi LGBT is an organization that operated a number of safe houses in Iraq until 2010 (Anderson 2015), and was primarily involved in facilitating asylum seeking cases for those fleeing persecution, after a violent spate of attacks targeting homosexuals in 2009 (Long 2009; Alzaid 2010). Given the volatility of the security situation, Iraqi LGBT operations are clandestine and little is known about the group. British journalist Peter Tatchell (2009) reported that the organization operated out of the United Kingdom.

ISRAEL/PALESTINE

al-Qaws is a well-known Jerusalem-based NGO that was founded in 2006. It began in 2001 as a project targeting Arabic-speaking citizens of Israel, under the initiative of the Jerusalem Open House, an LGBT center. Since 2006, al-Qaws has become entirely independent in philosophical and political orientation and actively leads a targeted Boycotts, Divestments and Sanctions campaign in response to Israeli-state violations of Palestinian human rights. Al-Qaws has been involved in active collaborations with a gay Palestinian women's group based in Haifa, Aswat, and has issued joint statements with Helem and Meem in Lebanon in response to Israeli incursions in Gaza and Lebanon.

Aswat is a group catering to "Palestinian gay women." The group is not registered with the Israeli government and obtains its funding from international donors such as the Global Fund for Women. It emerged out of the Feminist Coalition Complex in Haifa, when members of a Palestinian feminist group, named Kayan, began to organize around the issue of gay women's rights in Palestinian society. The group began operating in 2007 and runs workshops and meetings in Haifa and Tel Aviv. It shares responsibility for a counseling hotline with al-Qaws and periodically publishes books and newsletters.

LEBANON

Helem is the Arab world's first LGBT rights organization, and one that has been officially recognized in Lebanon since 2003. It makes strides toward repealing Article 534 of the Lebanese penal code under which homosexuals are persecuted (Makarem 2011). Helem began releasing the first LGBT magazine, *Barra*, in the Arab world in print and online in 2005. Uniquely, Helem commissions academic studies and reports around issues of legislative justice (Al Farchichi and Saghiyeh n.d.). In 2009, Helem organized an LGBT rights march of sorts, in Beirut.

Meem, a lesbian and transgender grassroots organization that obtained its funding from European non-governmental donors, has produced an autobiographical series of narratives published as an anthology entitled *Express Post/Barid Mista3jil* and the online magazine *Bekhsoos*. Meem's focus moved away from the gay and lesbian rights framework, and began to address women's and minority rights more broadly and focused on community building and engagement. It is unclear whether the group still continues to operate.

During the Israeli re-invasion of Lebanon in 2006, Meem, Helem and their counterparts in Jerusalem and Haifa (al-Qaws and Aswat, respectively) issued a joint statement condemning the violence. These groups continue to collaborate in order to counter incidents now termed "pinkwashing." Pinkwashing is often defined by LGBT activists as "a cynical attempt" on the part of the Israeli state to use LGBT rights to advance an image of itself as a progressive, democratic state, in order to obscure the reality of serious human rights breaches against Palestinians.

Proud, a recent NGO, founded in 2013, caters for populations of men who have sex with men, particularly focusing on Syrian refugees in Lebanon, who arrived as a result of the war in Syria. Proud provides healthcare services, sex education, and safety workshops and attempts to assist with asylum and immigration issues.

MOROCCO

The annual Sufi festival of Sidi Ali Bin Hamdoush attracts homosexuals from throughout Morocco, where marriage ceremonies for both male and female couples have been known to be performed. In 2008, 46 pilgrims were arrested on their way to the festival following a newspaper report in 2007 claiming that gay weddings were taking place in Morocco (Bergeaud-Blackler and Eck 2011). The authorities explicitly stated that the intention was to target and arrest homosexuals. These would-be participants were prosecuted under Article 489 of the penal code; their sentences ranged from 6 months' to 3 years' imprisonment.

In its early formation, LGBT rights organizing in Morocco began under the guise of HIV/AIDS healthcare initiatives as early as 1993, when the Moroccan Association for Combating AIDS/al-Jam'iyah al-Maghribiyah li-Muharabat al-AIDS (founded in 1988) ran its first campaign to address homosexual activity. An expedient route to funding in such instances had been to draft proposals for targeting male at-risk populations, such as "men who have sex with men," and similar initiatives began and continue in Egypt. In 2006, KifKif Moroc, an LGBT organization, was founded. On October 15, 2011, KifKif organized an LGBT rights demonstration in Ribat, which caused much controversy and the organization disbanded shortly afterwards. Activists involved in KifKif had a Spanish base of operations for the group.

TUNISIA

Like Algeria, in recent years public discourse about homosexuality has become common. After the popular uprising that saw an end to the despotic regime of Ben Ali, the conservative Islamic Party, An-Nahda, was democratically elected to government. In October 2011, Riad Chaibi, a spokesperson for An-Nahda, reassured Tunisians that governance there would remain secular. Pointedly, Chaibi asserted that individual freedoms and human rights are enshrined principles and that homosexuals in Tunis do exist, and have a right to this existence. Chaibi further asserted that alcohol consumption would not be prohibited, nor would the hijab be forced on women.

On January 28, 2012, a demonstration for LGBT rights took place. Less than 2 weeks later, Tunisia's minister for human rights, Samir Dilou, undermined this historic moment by making publicly scathing comments on national television. Essentially, Dilou asserted that freedom of speech should have its limits, that homosexuals are ill and require medical intervention, and that homosexuality is not a human right. Response to Dilou came from Tunisia's first gay magazine, *GayDay*, a magazine that had already stirred the anger of conservative elements of Tunisian society. Calling on the human rights minister, Palom Negra (an activist's pseudonym) wrote a letter in which they reminded him that homosexuality had ceased to be listed as an illness by the World Health Organization in 1990. In later comments delivered through his media representative, Chakib Darouiche, the minister, stood by his earlier comments and refused to apologize. Darouiche, however, conceded that the minister did consider it his responsibility to protect the rights of gender and sexual minority Tunisians as he would protect the rights of any other Tunisian citizen.

There is a registered human rights organization in Tunisia that was founded on August 19, 2011. It operates generally as an organization addressing rights of minorities, with specific goals toward addressing Penal Code 230 under which homosexuals may be prosecuted, in addition to raising awareness and challenging social stigmatization of LGBTIQ individuals. To date, the organization involves over 100 volunteers and 180 allies.

SUDAN AND EGYPT

In April 2011, Ahmad Badee', general director of the Muslim Brotherhood, remarked at a conference attended by over 25,000 members in Tanta, that the goal is to implement shari'a law in Egypt and to ensure that homosexuality is neither permitted nor tolerated. It would be misleading to think that only Islamist groups are seeking prosecution, and effectively persecution, of gender and sexual minorities in Egypt. For, under Mubarak, covert police operations began specifically to target and entrap gay men in online chatrooms and in real space. The arrest of 52 party goers on the *Queen Boat* in Cairo in 2001 has become a world-famous incident that attracted international media attention (Pratt 2007; Awwad 2010). This case, together with the aggressive surveillance and espionage tactics of the Egyptian police, has made LGBT activism in Egypt a virtual suicide mission.

An unofficial network of volunteers operates out of Sudan and Egypt, producing a local magazine and online podcasts. The group began in 2010 and has a virtually public presence; however, given the severity of the penal laws in the region, this entry will refrain from publishing the name of the group. The group deals pointedly with the relationship between Islam and gender and sexual variance, among other awareness-raising matters. It had conducted surveys on violence experienced by its members due to their sexual and gender orientations; however, the results remain unpublished. The group, like its counterparts in the countries we examined above, actively publishes articles and studies relevant to the repeal of penal codes. It also organizes workshops and participates in conferences in collaboration with queer Muslim initiatives in other regions of the world.

CONCLUSION

An unprecedented and unequivocal surge in LGBT rights organizing is now taking place. The religious right is simultaneously making homosexuality a public issue. It is unclear which of the two phenomena precedes the other. According to some, it is the visibility garnered by LGBTIQ organizing itself that is creating a right-wing backlash and activating persecution. However, there is no material evidence on which to substantiate that the opposite is not also true – that the religious trend toward conservatism has produced a civil society seeking to resist such oppressions, composed of sexual minorities, women, libertarians, and others. The role that the mainstream media plays in inciting hatred toward gender and sexual minorities also cannot be ignored and it is being countered at a grassroots level through the publication of books, articles, and magazines by gender and sexual minorities themselves.

See also: Gender, Politics, and the State in Northern Africa; Human Rights and Gender; Islam and Gender; Islam and Homosexuality

REFERENCES

Ake, Cassandra. 2011. *I Exist: Obstacles and Opportunities for GLBT Organizing in the Middle East*. Honors thesis, American University, Washington, DC.

Al Farchichi, Wahid, and Nizar Saghiyeh. n.d. *Homosexual Relations in the Penal Codes: General Study Regarding the Laws in the Arab Countries with a Report on Lebanon and Tunisia*. Beirut: Helem.

Alzaid, Barrak. 2010."Fatwas and Fags: Violence and the Discursive Production of Abject Bodies." *Columbia Journal of Gender & Law*, 19(3): 617–648.

Anderson, Jedidiah. 2015. *Sexual Intifada Now! Postcolonial Arab LGBTIQ Activism*. PhD thesis, Indiana State University.

Awwad, Julian. 2010. "The Postcolonial Predicament of Gay Rights in the *Queen Boat* Affair." *Communication and Critical/Cultural Studies*, 7(3): 318–336.

Bergeaud-Blackler, Florence, and Victor Eck. 2011. "Les 'Faux' Mariages Homosexuels de Sidi Ali au Maroc. Enjeux d'un Scandale Médiatique." *Revue des Mondes Musulmans et de la Méditerranée*, 129: 203–221.

Habib, Samar. 2010. "Introduction." In *Islam and Homosexuality*, edited by Samar Habib, vol. 1, xvii–lxii. Santa Barbara: ABC-CLIO.

Jean-Jacques, Sarah. 2014. "Gay & Lesbian Mobilization in Algeria: the Emergence of a Movement." *Muftah*, December 15, 2014. Accessed January 14, 2015, at http://muftah.org/gay-and-lesbian-mobilization-in-algeria/#.VLgYH0Y76c1.

Long, Scott. 2009. *"They Want Us Exterminated:" Murder, Torture, Sexual Orientation and Gender in Iraq*. New York: Human Rights Watch.

Makarem, Ghassan. 2011. "The Story of HELEM." *Journal of Middle East Women's Studies*, 7(3): 98–112.

Massad, Joseph, Félix Boggio Éwanjé-Épée, and Stella Magliani-Belkacem. "The Empire of Sexuality: An Interview with Joseph Massad." *Jadaliyya*, March 5, 2013. Accessed September 2014 at http://www.jadaliyya.com/pages/index/10461/the-empire-of-sexuality_an-interview-with-joseph-m.

Pratt, Nicola. 2007. "The Queen Boat Case in Egypt: Sexuality, National Security and State Sovereignty." *Review of International Studies*, 33: 129–144.

Puar, Jasbir. 2007. *Terrorist Assemblages: Homonationalism in Queer Times*. Durham, NC: Duke University Press.

Tatchell, Peter. "Iraq's Queer Underground Railroad." *The Guardian* online, February 25, 2009. Accessed September 15, 2014, at http://www.theguardian.com/commentisfree/2009/feb/25/iraq-gay-rights#comments.

Zanghellini, Aleardo. 2012. "Are Gay Rights Islamophobic? A Critique of Some Uses of the Concept of Homonationalism in Activism and Academia." *Social & Legal Studies*, 21: 357–374.

LGBT Activism in Native North America

BARBARA GURR
University of Connecticut, USA

Lesbian, gay, bisexual, and transgender (LGBT) activism among indigenous people in

North America is both similar to and different from LGBT activism among other racial and ethnic groups: similar due to a shared general oppression of sexual and gender minorities, but different due to the unique histories of colonization experienced by indigenous tribes and communities in what is now the United States, Mexico, Canada, the Caribbean islands, and other parts of North America. Important differences among these indigenous communities render generalizations challenging and potentially marginalizing; for example, there are currently over 560 federally recognized indigenous nations in the United States and over 600 in Canada, and in Mexico approximately 13% of the population is indigenous, speaking 62 languages. LGBT activism amongst indigenous peoples, therefore, must address not only sexual and gender oppressions, but also particular race and class oppressions in addition to diverse historical experiences, cultural practices, and community expectations. This entry focuses almost exclusively on indigenous LGBT in what is now the United States, although reference will also be made to indigenous communities in other parts of North America.

HISTORY

Historically in many indigenous cultures, gender was understood to be flexible and contextual, dependent more upon behavioral characteristics than on biology or sexual activities. Anthropological and other evidence suggests that widely varying social expressions of same-sex desires and behaviors, and also what might currently be referred to as transgender, transvestite, or genderqueer desires and behaviors, have likely always existed in Native American communities. For example, the Lakota *winkte*, the Piegan (and Canadian Blackfoot) *ninawaki*, the Diné (Navaho) *nádleehé* and *nádleehí*, and the Mohave *hwame* have long histories among their own people, corroborated by both local custom and anthropological and historical evidence. However, and importantly, not all of these roles refer to the same types of behaviors and/or desires; in some cases, they may refer to people with same-sex but different-gender erotic desires; in other cases they may be same-gender erotic desires, regardless of sex; and in still other cases (such as the *nádleehé* and *nádleehí*), they may reference a third or fourth gender, or a fluid and dynamic (possibly unfinished, or always-becoming) expression of sexual and/or gender behaviors and desires.

In many communities, such members would be understood as sacred or as having unique spiritual qualities that were useful to the community. Many precontact indigenous communities emphasized occupational roles as the determinant of gender category (as many continue to do in the twenty-first century); a person who took up occupational practices common amongst women would be understood as feminine and treated as such, whereas a person who took up occupational practices common to men would be understood as masculine. Whether or not their occupationally determined gender role extended to sexuality would depend on individual desires, perhaps as guided by community expectations. This is not to say that no precontact indigenous cultures of North America had fixed gender and sexuality boundaries or that they universally lacked particular expressions of heteropatriarchy and gender dualisms (there is some evidence that the Aztecs may had laws governing sexuality prior to contact with Europeans; see Lang 1998 and Spencer 1995), but rather to point out the vast variety of gender and sexuality expressions across the continent prior to the mass arrival of Europeans.

The imposition of Western (European) conceptualizations of gender and sexuality as fixed and binary, of female orientation as less valuable than male orientation, and of non-heterosexual desire and behavior as deviant began in the early contact period between settlers and local Native people. The arrival of Jesuit and other missionaries across North America slowly eroded many indigenous understandings of gender and sexuality, inserting European and Christian ideals into indigenous practices and communities (Gutiérrez 2007). Additionally to this, the rule of law eventually imposed by the United States, Canada, and Mexico further reified heteropatriachal community structures. For example, in the United States, the 1887 Dawes Allotment Act assumed that men were heads of households and discrete family units, and imposed primogeniture inheritance on these family units. In Canada, the 1876 Indian Act specified Indian identity for legal purposes (such as land ownership) and tied this directly to men, directly reducing women's agency in determining their Indian status and increasing their dependence on men as fathers and husbands.

The end result of centuries of colonization resulted in indigenous LGBT experiences being denied and buried, LGBT histories lost, and the historical acceptance and integration of LGBT people in many Native communities severely impacted. This damage has been further exacerbated by the scholarly record on LGBT Native Americans, which has focused almost exclusively on historical instances (neglecting contemporary experiences), largely ignoring the experiences of lesbians and female-bodied people who did/do not readily conform to mainstream conceptualizations of femininity.

EMERGENCE OF NATIVE LGBT ACTIVISM

With the rise of the Red Power movement in the 1960s (through, for example, the National Indian Youth Council, the American Indian Movement, and Women of All Red Nations) and LGBT activism in the United States and Canada, gay and lesbian Native Americans frequently found one oppression (for example, race) or another (for example, sexual minority status) recognized, but an intersectional understanding of their double oppressions as racialized gender and/or sexual minorities was neglected. To address this, the organization Gay American Indians (GAI) was formed in 1975 in San Francisco by Barbara Cameron (Lakota), Randy Burns (Paiute) and others. The organization met many social service needs for Lesbian and Gay Native Americans such as help with finding housing and employment, but just as importantly it provided a safe space for people who were both Native American *and* gay or lesbian, addressing specific cultural needs that more generic LGBT organizations or Native American organizations might miss (sometimes willfully). As GAI's membership grew through the 1980s, it also responded to the growing HIV/AIDS crisis by providing education and training for gay and lesbian Native Americans in the area, a much-needed effort given the limited resources and institutionalized homophobia of the Indian Health Service.

By providing resources such as these and also working for the recognition of the double oppression faced by gay and lesbian Native Americans, GAI lay the foundation for future LGBT activism in urban Native communities. The 1980s saw the formation of numerous organizations such as American Indian Gays and Lesbians in Minneapolis, Gays and Lesbians of the First Nations in Toronto, and increasing recognition on college and university campuses of lesbian and gay Native American students. Gay and lesbian Native people in rural and reservation-based communities frequently faced homophobia and intolerance, with fewer resources or avenues of support (Farrer 1997; Lang 1997).

EMERGENCE OF TWO SPIRIT

Although groundbreaking organizations such as GAI sought to address multiple oppressions for gay and lesbian Native Americans, many of them based their work on a fixed binary understanding of sexuality and primarily served homosexual Native Americans, neglecting transgender and other genderqueer experiences and needs. Two Spirit societies began to emerge in the 1990s partially in response to this lack, partially in response to the growing social and political recognition of sexual and gender minority people in general, and partially as an effort to restore and possibly reinvigorate historical indigenous understandings of gender and sexuality.

Prior to this time, the term *berdache* was most commonly used to refer to LGBT Native people, particularly by non-Native scholars. However, the term *berdache,* with both French and Persian roots meaning male prostitute or slave, was increasingly rejected by Native people. In 1989, First Nations LGBT people gathered in large numbers in Toronto to meet as a community. Despite great diversity in terms of sex, sexuality, gender expression, class, and other sociopolitical indicators, they established an organization called "Gays and Lesbians of the First Nations" and constructed a common mission, which was "To forge a link between our sexual identities and our identities as members of the First Nations' community; to provide a safe environment for our members to interact and share with each other; to strengthen and share our cultural knowledge (especially as it relates to Two-Spirited people); (and) to encourage a positive image and self-image of Native lesbians and gay men by reinforcing that traditional cultural knowledge" (Bear 1992). The term "Two Spirit," from the Ojibwa words *niizh manitoag* (meaning two spirit), was suggested as an alternative to *berdache* at the third international Native American/First Nations Gay and Lesbian conference in Winnipeg in 1990. Following this, two workshops in 1993 and 1994 sponsored by the American Anthropological Association and the Wenner-Gren Foundation brought together professional anthropologists and LGBT Native activists to discuss academic work on the history of LGBT Native Americans. Attendees focused heavily on the inappropriate use of the term *berdache* as an umbrella term for all LGBT Native people and the use of the term Two Spirit again emerged as a preferred alternative.

Although gay and lesbian Native people may use the term Two Spirit for self-identification, in the last 20 years it has come increasingly to refer to gender expression and identity rather than sexuality and provides an important point of distinction between commonly conflated gender and sexual statuses. At the same time, however, while the term has gained traction in many urban, multi-ethnic communities in both the United States and Canada, it may have less utility in reservation communities which may have adopted Western notions of gender as binary and fixed, and non-heterosexuality as deviant. Additionally, the term Two Spirit fails to capture the complexity of gender and sexuality experiences and expressions across Native North America; for example, it is commonly used to include Diné (Navaho) *nádleehé*, Lakota *winkte*, and the Zuni *Ihamana*, when in fact there are important emic differences between these cultures and their understandings and expressions of gender and sexuality. For all of these reasons, "Two Spirit" is a complex term and perhaps not entirely adequate. Nonetheless, the insistence by Native people on renaming and reclaiming their historical and contemporary experiences of sexuality and gender provided an important foundation for future activism.

TWO SPIRIT AND LGBT ACTIVISM AND ORGANIZATIONS

Beginning in the 1990s and continuing through the first decade and a half of the twenty-first century, the term Two Spirit gained wide acceptance among Native American LGBT activists and also among professional scholars. Perhaps due in part to the rising visibility of LGBT persons and issues in general, Native LGBT organizations have also increased both in number and in the scope of issues they address.

In 2015, several Two Spirit organizations exist across the United States and Canada, although their number is difficult to determine owing both to privacy issues and to the local, grassroots nature of many of these organizations. Most Two Spirit/Native LGBT organizations are located in urban areas, although they are increasingly found also on college campuses and in rural and reservation-based areas. These organizations tend to work primarily in three arenas: cultural and community support; social services such as housing and employment; and health and healthcare, particularly around HIV/AIDS and other sexually transmitted infections. Several Two Spirit societies and also individual Native activists have participated in the civil rights movement for marriage equality; for example, the Coalition for Navajo Equality, the leading LGBT organization in the Navajo (Diné) Nation, is working both at the grassroots level and in the Navajo court system to repeal the Diné Marriage Act of 2005, which voids and prohibits marriage between same-sex couples. However, other organizations and individuals feel that marriage equality is less important than decolonization and other issues facing LGBT Native people, and so have not acted on that issue.

In Canada, organizations such as the Dancing to Eagle Spirit Society focus on spiritual practices and community building for Two Spirit people; organizations such as Two Spirited People of the First Nations are primarily a social services agency and offers an online clearing house of primarily health-related information. Native people in the United States seem to have had more success building organizational structures than those in Canada. The Bay Area American Indian Two Spirits provides spiritual, cultural, and artistic support for Two Spirit people in and around San Francisco and Oakland, California, including organizing the first Two Spirit powwow open to the public (there are several other Two Spirit powwows held across the country throughout the year which are not open to the public). In 2015, this powwow gathered dancers, singers, and artists from across North America for the fourth time. The Northeast Two Spirit Society in New York City also organizes a powwow as part of its Annual Gathering, a three-day event which includes workshops, ceremonies, and speaker panels. In 2004, the Phoenix Two Spirit society was formed and later became NativeOUT. NativeOUT currently works to support Two Spirit organizations across North America by providing information, resources, and media coverage. The Native Youth Sexual Health Network works on a variety of fronts from the United Nations and social media to community workshops to address the gender and sexuality needs and rights of Native Youth in both Canada and the United States.

The diversity of LGBT experiences and identities among indigenous people across North America defies easy categorization, and ongoing debates over terminology reflect this. Nonetheless, the numbers of LGBT and/or Two Spirit Native people involved in local, national, and transnational activism have increased since the mid-1990s. While many issues of concern are similar to those for non-Native LGBT people (such as marriage equality, healthcare, and social services), many Native LGBT and/or Two Spirit activists and organizations also focus on specifically indigenous issues of decolonization.

SEE ALSO: Berdache; Gender Belief System/Gender Ideology; Gender Variance; LGBT Activism in North America; Sex Versus Gender Categorization

REFERENCES

Bear, Susan. 1992. We Are Part of a Tradition: A Report to the Royal Commission on Aboriginal Peoples. Accessed January 10, 2015, at http://www.2spirits.com/.

Farrer, Claire. 1997. "Dealing with Homophobia in Everyday Life." In *Two Spirit People: Native American Gender Identity, Sexuality, and Spirituality*, edited by Sue-Ellen Jacobs, Wesley Thomas, and Sabine Lang, 297–318. Chicago: University of Illinois Press.

Gutiérrez, Ramón. 2007. "Warfare, Homosexuality, and Gender Status Among American Indian Men in the Southwest." In *Long Before Stonewall: Histories of Same Sex Sexuality in Early America*, edited by Thomas Foster, 19–31. New York: New York University Press.

Lang, Sabine. 1997. "Various Kinds of Two-Spirit People: Gender Variance and Homosexuality in Native American Communities." In *Two Spirit People: Native American Gender Identity, Sexuality, and Spirituality*, edited by Sue-Ellen Jacobs, Wesley Thomas, and Sabine Lang, 100–118. Chicago: University of Illinois Press.

Lang, Sabine. 1998. *Men as Women, Women as Men: Changing Gender in Native American Cultures*. Austin: University of Texas Press.

Spencer, Colin. 1995. *Homosexuality in History*. London: Harcourt Brace.

FURTHER READING

Jacobs, Sue-Ellen, Wesley Thomas, and Sabine Lang, eds. 1997. *Two Spirit People: Native American Gender Identity, Sexuality, and Spirituality*. Chicago: University of Illinois Press.

Morgensen, Scott Lauria. 2011. *Spaces Between Us: Queer Settler Colonialism and Indigenous Decolonization*. Minneapolis: University of Minnesota Press.

Rifkin, Mark. 2011. *When Did Indians Become Straight? Kinship, the History of Sexuality, and Native Sovereignty*. New York: Oxford University Press.

Roscoe, Will. 1998. *Changing Ones: Third and Fourth Genders in Native North America*. New York: St. Martin's Press.

LGBT Activism in North America

MELINDA D. KANE and MARIANNE AYERS
East Carolina University, USA

The beginning of LGBT activism in North America is often attributed to the Stonewall Rebellion in New York City on June 28, 1969 (described below). However, the first modern North American activist organizations were started as early as the 1950s, both in the United States and in Canada, including the Mattachine Society (Los Angeles), the Daughters of Bilitis (San Francisco), and the Association for Social Knowledge (Vancouver) (Adam 1995; D'Emilio 1998; Smith 1999). There were a few organizational attempts even earlier, but they were quickly repressed (Adam 1995; Vaid 1995). Identified as homophile organizations, these groups defined homosexuals as an oppressed minority group rather than sexual deviants. The groups provided opportunities for people to gather, created publications to distribute information and connect members, and helped create a sense of collective identity among those who experienced same-sex attraction. While these organizations were still relatively hidden and emphasized modest goals such as education and inclusion, the framing of homosexuality as a form of inequality was a key ideological shift and the preliminary organizational infrastructure created by these groups was central in the development of subsequent LGBT activism (Vaid 1995; D'Emilio 1998).

During the 1960s, the North American LGBT movement grew and activists began to use more confrontational tactics, particularly in the United States, modeled after the tactics of the civil rights, women's rights, and student movements (Adam 1995; D'Emilio 1998). Examples of this transformation in strategies included annual pickets outside Independence Hall in Philadelphia, Pennsylvania, on the 4th of July, as well as active resistance to police raids in several cities (D'Emilio 1998; Adam 1995; Armstrong and Crage 2006). The best known of these events was the Stonewall Rebellion of 1969. The New York City police department raided the Stonewall Inn, a gay bar in Greenwich Village. Patrons usually fled during raids because arrests could lead to the publication of their names in the newspaper, with disastrous consequences, including outing them to family and friends or causing them to lose their jobs. In this case, however, patrons and neighborhood residents fought back, with the disturbance continuing for several days. The riot was labeled as the first time the LGBT community fought back and became commemorated by annual parades each June in cities throughout North America and the world (D'Emilio 1998; Armstrong and Crage 2006; Stryker 2008). (See Armstrong and Crage (2006) for a detailed analysis of the reasons for Stonewall's commemoration as the start of LGBT activism.)

While Stonewall was *not* the first instance of LGBT activism in North America or even the first riot in response to police harassment (the Compton Cafeteria riot occurred three years earlier), it did mark an important turning point in the movement's history both in size and strategy (Armstrong and Crage 2006). At the time of the Stonewall Rebellion, there were approximately 50 gay and lesbian organizations scattered throughout the United States, but just four years later there were over 800 (D'Emilio 1998, 238). Canada experienced a similar increase in the number and geographic dispersion of LGBT organizations and Mexico's first LGBT organizations were founded in the years immediately after Stonewall (Mogrovejo 1999; Smith 1999). Activists were able to draw upon the networks and organizations developed in the 1960s to capitalize on the energy and attention generated by Stonewall, creating a surge in mobilization (Armstrong and Crage 2006). Activism also shifted from a focus on social support and education to a movement focused on gay liberation, challenging dominant societal views about gender and sexuality, including the artificial distinction between homosexuality and heterosexuality (D'Emilio 1998). The movement envisioned itself "as a revolutionary struggle to free the homosexual in everyone" (Adam 1995, 84) and movement tactics reflected the radicalization of the movement, emphasizing direct action and more confrontational, flamboyant strategies. Even attempts within the formal political arena to change policy were seen as stepping stones for more radical, cultural change (Smith 1999). The ideology and strategies that predominated during this era were very much a reflection of the radical politics of the time.

By the mid-1970s, LGBT activism largely transitioned from gay liberation to a movement for civil rights emphasizing the similarities between those with same-sex attraction and the rest of society as a justification for equal treatment (Vaid 1995; Minter 2006). As the movement's primary ideology moved away from radical challenges of the gender and sexuality structures to a demand for rights, movement tactics also shifted, relying more heavily on mainstream political strategies such as lobbying, court challenges, and electoral politics, even as the larger LGBT movement also maintained a focus on identity, as evident through the continued use of pride parades and identity specific organizations (Armstrong 2002). The movement also became dominated by a few nationally focused, professionally staffed organizations, especially in the United States, such as the National Gay and Lesbian Task Force (e.g., the Task Force), Lambda Legal, and the Human Rights Campaign (HRC). Federally focused groups also emerged in Canada including the National Gay Rights Council and Egale Canada, though activism in Canada continued to be more regionally focused than activism in the United States (Vaid 1995; Smith 1999). That said, while there has been a general shift in movement ideology from liberation to rights, there has been ideological variation across organizations so that both radical and mainstream ideology often existed simultaneously (Armstrong 2002). While the HRC and the Task Force may be seen as defining organizations in the United States, direct action organizations more reflective of a liberation view continued to exist during this period as well, such as the Lesbian Avengers, Queer Nation, and Sex Panic (Adam 1995; Vaid 1995).

Another consistent theme throughout the modern history of LGBT activism is the presence of significant gender and identity based divisions within community. In both the homophile and liberation phases of the movement, groups throughout North America experienced sharp divisions between women and men. Early organizations were largely led by men and tended to emphasize male concerns and interests, treating women as auxiliary groups or support staff (D'Emilio 1998; Mogrovejo 1999; Smith 1999). For example, female members of the Mattachine Society complained that the organization focused on issues like cruising arrests, which were largely irrelevant to women, while ignoring family issues like child custody which mattered for many more women. Others charged that gay men were explicitly misogynistic. In Mexico, tensions between radical and reformist groups became gendered when giant plastic phalluses used during the Gay Pride Parade of 1986, and the subsequent hostility during the parade between movement factions, became interpreted to be symbols of the phallocentric nature of the gay movement (Mogrovejo 1999).

One way women responded to these gender-based tensions was to move their activism to feminist organizations (Adam 1995, 1999; Mogrovejo 1999). In fact, many women came out as lesbians through their activism in feminist organizations (Adam 1995; Smith 1999). "Lesbians had always been a tiny fraction of the [earlier] homophile movement. But the almost simultaneous birth of women's liberation and gay liberation propelled large numbers of them into radical sexual politics" (D'Emilio 1998, 236). Yet, involvement within the feminist movement was not without its challenges. Organizations like the National Organization for Women were concerned that having open lesbians within their ranks would diminish their respectability and distract the organization from achieving its "real" goals (Adam 1995; Smith 1999; Minter 2006). This helped contribute to women's second strategy – creating groups specifically for lesbians, such as OIKABETH and Lesbos in Mexico, the Radicalesbians in San Francisco, and Lesbians Against the Right in Canada (D'Emilio 1998; Mogrovejo 1999; Smith 1999).

In addition to the division between women and men, transgender and transsexual identified activists have also faced exclusion within the larger LGBT activist community. Transgender activists have always been part of the movement, yet their participation and contributions have not always been recognized. For example, one reason why the Compton Cafeteria riots of 1966 received such little attention, even within the LGBT community, is because the participants were seen as disreputable, mostly "queens" and "hustlers" (Armstrong and Crage 2006). There was also significant participation of transgender activists in the Stonewall Rebellion, with scholars identifying the involvement "drag queens," "transvestites," "dykes," and "feminine" gay men (D'Emilio 1998; Adam 1995; Stryker 2008). Yet, histories often appropriate these examples of transgender identities as gay or lesbian rather than recognizing the long standing, historical link between sexuality and gender nonconformity (Minter 2006). As LGBT activism moved from the gay liberation phase to the civil rights era, the link between sexuality and gender variance was explicitly challenged. Similar to feminist groups that were concerned about the stigma lesbians might bring, gay and lesbian organizations tried to downplay the role of transgender participants and concerns. The exclusion was very evident in the attempts to get anti-discrimination laws passed – activists consciously chose to leave out protection based on gender identity, either because it was seen as irrelevant, unconnected, or a hindrance to passage (Marcus 2002). (Scholars have documented similar divisions by race, ethnicity, and social class within the LGBT activist community. See Vaid 1995; Armstrong 2002; Marcus 2002; Minter 2006).

While divisions continue to exist today, the LGBT organizations of the civil rights era are more inclusive. The rise in AIDS in the 1980s contributed to bridging of gender divisions as gay men and lesbians came together to respond to the crisis and lesbians helped to fill the leadership void created by the epidemic. For example, the National Gay Task Force consciously chose to change its name to the National Gay and Lesbian Task Force in 1985 to demonstrate its commitment to inclusion. The needs of transgender members of the community are also increasingly included in the goals of national organizations. While gender tensions and questions about the relevance of transgender issues for the movement have not disappeared, organizations themselves are integrated and include goals specific to needs of the wider community (Vaid 1995; Smith 1999; Minter 2006).

Overall, the civil rights phase of the North American LGBT movement has achieved notable legal successes, though somewhat unevenly across issues and nations. Most legal successes involve sexual minority rights while much less progress has been made in transgender rights. Canada has been at the forefront, decriminalizing sodomy in 1969, granting anti-discrimination protection based on sexual orientation nationwide in 1982, and passing marriage equality in 2005. Progress on these issues has been much more inconsistent in the United States, where rights were initially granted state by state, with the decriminalization of sodomy finally achieved nationwide in 2003 and marriage equality in 2015. Anti-discrimination protection has yet to be granted at the national level, though several states provide protections (Smith 2008). The achievement of LGBT rights in Mexico falls somewhere in between Canada and the United States. Sodomy was decriminalized in the nineteenth century, anti-discrimination protection covering sexual "preference" was granted in 2003, and marriage equality was passed in the Federal District of Mexico (i.e., Mexico city) in 2009 (de la Dehesa 2010). Many of the substantive legislative successes in Mexico – including the first anti-discrimination law – have been attributed to the election of open lesbian activists Patricia Jimenez and Enoe Uranga to the Federal District Legislative Assembly (ADLF); a clear example of a rights-based strategy (de la Dehesa 2010). In contrast, none of the North American countries provides anti-discrimination protection based on gender identity at the national level, though Canadian provinces have provided this protection indirectly through laws covering gender (Egale 2013).

Activists continue to disagree over the preferred strategy for change, debating a liberationist view focused on large-scale cultural change versus a rights-based strategy emphasizing legal equality (Vaid 1995; Walters 2014). This debate can be seen in the current discussion around marriage equality. Critics within the LGBT movement highlight the inherently gendered and unequal nature of marriage as an institution, arguing that rights and benefits should not be dependent on marital status, but instead should address the full range of family forms and relationships (Walters 2014). However, a rights-based agenda appears to continue to be the primary, overarching framework of LGBT activism in North America.

SEE ALSO: Feminism, Lesbian; Gender Identity, Theories of; Identity Politics; Lesbian and Gay Movements; Lesbian and Womyn's Separatism; Sexual Orientation and the Law; Transgender Movements in the United States

REFERENCES

Adam, Barry D. 1995. *The Rise of a Gay and Lesbian Rights Movement*, rev. ed. New York: Twayne.

Adam, Barry D. 1999. "Moral Regulation and the Disintegrating Canadian State." In *The Global Emergence of Gay and Lesbian Politics: National Imprints of a Worldwide Movement*, edited by Barry D. Adam, Jan Willen Duyvendak, and Andre Krouwel, 12–29. Philadelphia: Temple University Press.

Armstrong, Elizabeth. 2002. *Forging Gay Identities: Organizing Sexuality in San Francisco, 1950–1994*. Chicago: University of Chicago Press.

Armstrong, Elizabeth, and Suzanne Crage. 2006. "Movements and Memory: The Making of the Stonewall Myth." *American Sociological Review*, 71(5): 724–751.

de la Dehesa, Rafael. 2010. *Queering the Public Sphere in Mexico and Brazil: Sexual Rights Movements in Emerging Democracies*. Durham, NC: Duke University Press.

D'Emilio, John. 1998. *Sexual Politics, Sexual Communities: The Making of a Homosexual Minority in the United States, 1940–1970*, 2nd ed. Chicago: University of Chicago Press.

Egale. 2013. FAQ – Gender Identity and Canada's Human Rights System, Canada Human Rights Trust. Accessed July 22, 2014, at http://egale.ca/all/faq-gender-identity/.

Marcus, Eric. 2002. *Making Gay History: The Half Century Fight for Lesbian and Gay Equal Rights*. New York: Perennial.

Minter, Shannon Price. 2006. "Do Transsexuals Dream of Gay Rights? Getting Real about Transgender Inclusion." In *Transgender Rights*, edited by Paisley Currah, Richard M. Juang, and Shannon Price Minter, 141–170. Minneapolis: University of Minnesota Press.

Mogrovejo, Norma. 1999. "Sexual Preference, the Ugly Duckling of Feminist Demands: The Lesbian Movement in Mexico." In *Female Desires: Same-Sex Relations and Transgender Practices Across Cultures* edited by Evelyn Blackwood and Saskia E. Wieringa, 308–335. New York: Columbia University Press.

Smith, Miriam. 1999. *Lesbian and Gay Rights in Canada: Social Movements and Equality-Seeking, 1971–1995*. Toronto: University of Toronto Press.

Smith, Miriam. 2008. *Political Institutions and Lesbian and Gay Rights in the United States and Canada*. New York: Routledge.

Stryker, Susan. 2008. *Transgender History*. Berkeley: Seal Press.

Vaid, Urvashi. 1995. *Virtual Equality: The Mainstreaming of Gay and Lesbian Liberation*. New York: Anchor Books.

Walters, Suzanna Danuta. 2014. *The Tolerance Trap: How God, Genes, and Good Intentions are Sabotaging Gay Equality*. New York: New York University Press.

LGBT Activism in Northern Africa

JUSTIN MCGUINNESS
American University of Paris, France

LGBT activism in North Africa, taken here as the five states of the Maghreb (Algeria, Libya, Mauritania, Morocco, and Tunisia), along with Egypt, was the concern of a vanishingly small proportion of those countries' populations in the 2000s. The aftermath of the 2011 Arab uprisings, marked by the return to authoritarian rule in Egypt, partial disintegration of the state in Libya, and a transitional period (2011–2014) in Tunisia with a government dominated by the Islamist Mouvement Ennahdha has not proved fertile ground for the emergence of structured LGBT groups. Nevertheless, there are slight indications that activist groups may yet appear in the public sphere, possibly on the model of civil society groups like the Lebanese LGBT activist organization Helem. Of the six countries discussed here, only Egypt has seen, from 2003, a concerted attempt by the regime to persecute self-identifying gays or men who have sex with other men. In the Maghreb states, though homophobic discourse is common, there has been little police persecution of the LGBT segments of the population. In the ever growing cities of the region, same-sex relationships are possible (and even tolerated in affluent social groups), provided the partners are discrete about their preferences. That said, flamboyant celebrity singers with supposed same-sex preferences are common media figures.

In premodern times, North African communities were largely tolerant of same-sex practices. From the mid-1990s, with the development and diffusion via the Internet of discourses and images of gay, lesbian, and trans lifestyles and sexualities, a dual shift took place: some clerics and politicians became more vehement in their condemnation of LGBT people, while certain filmmakers and writers became more open in their portrayals of them. In this cultural landscape, civil society activists were largely absent, Morocco being the exception. In that country, activists began to circulate a liberationist discourse of sorts in the early 2000s. Inspired in part by the visibility of kelma.org, a Paris-based non-profit association working to support French gays of North African extraction, and the politically aware discourse of the French gay leisure media like *Têtu*, in 2005 Samir Bargachi, a Moroccan activist based in Spain, established *Kifkif* ("same-same"), an online forum for gay and lesbian Moroccans. However, the Kifkif collective was never able to gain legal recognition as a civil society organization in Morocco.

Arabic is a language characterized by a marked difference between the formal written form and multiple spoken-only dialects. Formal media Arabic currently prefers the term *shudhudh jinsy* ("sexual deviation or anomaly") in discussions where other languages might use a cognate term from the Greco-Latin coinage "homosexual." The North African dialects of Arabic have a selection of highly derogatory terms to denote persons with same-sex preferences. The global term "gay" is also used, both as a positive label and as an insult in certain urban milieus. In the Maghreb, the term *lesbienne* is little known outside a small urban elite, though there are phrases like "worth a hundred men" (Egypt) to denote women perceived to have virile characteristics. The term "queer" is probably known only to a tiny urban elite in more Anglophone Egypt. To counter the negative charge of ordinary Arabic words used to designate gays and lesbians, organizations like Kifkif have promoted the non-judgmental neologism *mithliya* ("likeness") to refer to the practices of those preferring same-sex relations. The term can also be taken to mean "exemplarity." From this abstract noun equivalents for gay (*mithly*) and lesbian (*mithliya*) are derived. This family of terms was first promoted in Lebanon by the LGBT organization Helem before being taken up by both Arabic and French-using writers in the Maghreb, notably the liberal newsmagazines *Tel Quel* and *Nichane* in Morocco and on Kifkif's webzine *Mithly* which ran from 2010 to 2012. However, the term *mithliya* has yet to gain wide currency in North African Arabic usage.

In the Maghreb states, sexual relations between persons of the same sex are sanctioned by the law. In Egypt, on the other hand, the only sanction currently on the books is "offence against public morality." The Algerian and Tunisian criminal codes provide for prison sentences: in Algeria, of between two months and two years and in Tunisia of up to three years for sodomy, which may be accompanied by fines in both countries. Libyan judges can pass prison sentences of up to five years for homosexuality. In Morocco, an "indecent act against nature" carries a potential prison sentence of between six months and three years, plus a fine. In practice, these sentences are rarely applied. Paradoxically, it is in Egypt that the repression of gays is most severe, despite the apparent lenience of the legislation. The best known case started with mass arrests in Cairo in 2001: Egyptian police raided the *Queen Boat*, a floating nightclub on the Nile which attracted an essentially male clientele. Tens were arrested and put on trial for offending public morals. Given the centrality of Egypt in the Arab world and the growing influence of satellite television at the time, the case brought the question of what it might mean to have a "gay identity" out into the Arabic-speaking public sphere and beyond. The Egyptian judiciary decisively speared the country's reputation in liberal-minded countries for its heavy-handed sentencing.

In Morocco, the homophobia present in certain groups led, in the early 2000s, to isolated instances of persecution. In one case at the University of Fès, an Islamic rigorist group set up a kangaroo court which "sentenced" a student on account of his supposed sexual orientation. In 2007, the case of the so-called "gay wedding" in the provincial town of Ksar el Kébir in northwest Morocco generated much media coverage. There, a demonstration by residents against local men who had attended a lively all-male party with a distinctly gay tint nearly turned into a lynching. Nevertheless, in cases where local police and judges have been overzealous in their application of the law, orders have come down from high up in the Ministry of the Interior to overturn sentencing which might have a negative impact on Morocco's good standing with the liberal democracies.

In North America and Europe, LGBT activism gained focus and broader support due to civil society's role in publicizing cases of rank injustice. The work of strong-minded public figures was also crucial. To date, no such figures have emerged in Egypt, despite the regime's persecution of men who prefer sexual relations with men, whether they identify as gay or not. With the exception of writers Abdallah Taïa and Rachid O., there are almost no publicly self-identifying gays or lesbians in the Maghreb. (Resident in France and publishing in French, Rachid O. and Taïa's texts only reach a small North African audience.) While human rights activists may back gay campaigns publicly, the region has yet to see a major campaign for the decriminalization of homosexual practices. Broadly speaking, the cultural climate is unfavorable. In Egypt, the government uses the persecution of gays as a legitimation device, hoping to win the support of the conservative moral majority through well-publicized raids on gay meeting places. On social media and online news sites visited by Maghrebis and Egyptians, any piece on a gay issue is almost certain to attract highly homophobic comment. At a broader level, many commentators and activists consider that priority must be given to improving the legislation regulating the status of women and children before the question of gay rights reaches the politicians' agenda. Any push for such rights will probably follow once broader questions of social reform have been tackled.

While there is a growing body of qualitative and literary research on same-sex discourses and practices in Morocco (Bergeaud-Blackler and Eck 2011; Rebuccini 2011; McGuinness 2012; Zaganiaris 2013) and some publications on the persecution of gays in Egypt (El Menyawi 2006a,2006b), academic work on LGBT people and groups in the other North African states is almost nonexistent. Nevertheless, with researchers gaining greater access to the global corpus of social scientific research thanks to digital technology, this situation may yet change. Fundamentally, researchers will be observing how same-sex intimate relations are transformed if or when ideas about sexual identity as self-proclaimed membership of a global LGBT community take hold. With communications technologies being such powerful and fast moving vectors for exploring ideas about self and group, the way global LGBT modes of being may enter daily life in North Africa are by no means predictable.

SEE ALSO: LGBT Activism in Eastern Africa; LGBT Activism in Southern Africa; Same-Sex Marriage

REFERENCES

Bahgat, Hossam. 2001. "Explaining Egypt's Targeting of Gays." *MERIP*, 23 July. Accessed September 9, 2015, at www.merip.org/mero/mero072301.

Bergeaud-Blackler, Florence, and Victor Eck. 2011. "Les 'faux' mariages homosexuels de Sidi Ali au Maroc: enjeux d'un scandale médiatique." *Revue des mondes musulmans et de la Méditerranée*, 129: 203–221.

El Menyawi, H. 2006a. "Activism from the Closet: Gay Rights Strategizing in Egypt." *Journal of International Law*, 7, 28.

El Menyawi, H. 2006b. "Persecution of Homosexuals: The Egyptian Government's Trojan Horse against Religious Groups." *Human Rights Brief*, 14(1): 17–20.

McGuinness, Justin. 2012. "Représentation et résistance sur mithly.net: analyse du discours d'un site communautaire marocain." In *Les nouvelles sociabilités du Net en Méditerranée*, edited by Sihem Najar, 117–141. Paris: Karthala.

Rebuccini, Gianfranco. 2011. "Lieux de l'homoérotisme et de l'homosexualité masculine à Marrakech: Organisation et réorganisation des espaces dédiés." *L'Espace politique*, 13(1). Accessed September 9, 2015, at https://espacepolitique.revues.org/1830#ftn1.

Zaganiaris, Jean. 2013. *Queer Maroc: Sexualités, genres et (trans)identités dans la littérature*. Paris: Des Ailes sur un tracteur.

LGBT Activism in South Asia

KAREEM KHUBCHANDANI
University of Texas at Austin, USA

Dominant narratives about LGBT activism in South Asia have been shaped by the pervasive presence of non-governmental organizations (NGOs); these narratives center on working-class, trans-feminine people, and men who have sex with men (MSM), both of which are deemed at-risk populations in the fight against HIV/AIDS. These populations are also at risk of blackmail, harassment, and extortion by thugs and potential lovers, and also rape and abuse by partners, sex work clients, and police. LGBT activism in South Asia must be understood as much more than health advocacy, or organized policy work of NGOs that target these populations. Cultural performances, quotidian practices, support groups, and online networks also do the work of critiquing oppressive social systems, validating non-mainstream genders and sexualities, shifting public opinions, distributing relevant legal and medical information, and ensuring the safety of sexual and gender minorities.

Trans-feminine communities are highly visible in urban centers and some small towns across South Asia. In India, they are known variously as *hijra*, *aravani*, *jogappa*, and *dhurani*; in Nepal they are referred to as *meti*; and in Pakistan they are *khwaja sira*. These identities have different valences in their respective countries. For example, the identity of *khwaja sira* refers to intersex persons; however, many people with typically male genitalia identify as *khwaja sira* if they have a feminine spirit (Khan 2014). The visibility of trans-feminine communities stems not only from their displacement from family homes, but also because the few professions available to them – begging, sex work, dance – require them to circulate in public space more regularly. This leaves them subject to classist, transphobic, and misogynist harassment by passers-by and police alike. Several NGOs, run by English-speaking gay and bisexual men, have created work opportunities for trans people, often encouraging them to run community-based organizations (CBOs) in their respective neighborhoods, suburbs, or small towns. *Hijra*s are often tasked with distributing condoms, lubricant, and relevant literature in male cruising areas, roles seen as less desirable for middle-class gay men.

Activist networks have shaped identity categories, even as they attempt to adapt to local ideologies and customs. Relying on international health discourses and Western epistemologies, NGOs operationalize identities such as *hijra* and *kothi* (Dutta 2012a,b). In this context, *hijra* becomes a gender identity, whereas *kothi* is understood as more akin to a sexual orientation. Aniruddha Dutta's important research on West Bengal demonstrates that the subcultural networks that NGOs tapped into in the mid-1990s allowed for fluid forms of non-normative gender identification and presentation that NGOs do not currently accommodate. *Hijra*, *khwaja sira*, and *kothi* activists have strategically aligned themselves with "LGBT" in order to access foreign funding; at other times they have actively resisted the "MSM" outreach framework that hails them as male. In other cases, some individuals identify as "MSM," an NGO category specifically meant to circumvent identification.

LGBT activism in South Asia tends to coalesce through class-based affiliation. In Bangalore, LesBiT differentiates itself from the more elite women's group, "We're Here and Queer" (WHAQ), by insisting on its class inclusivity. It labors to avoid alienating non-middle-class members by avoiding English wherever possible, and translating meetings and minutes into relevant South Indian languages. Inclusivity through language has been an important debate in activist spaces, especially in cities with such linguistic diversity as Mumbai and Bangalore; in cities such as Kolkata, where Bangla can function as the lingua franca, more class integration has been observed. Alternatively, Stacy Pigg (2001) argues that English imports of NGO-based activism – terms such as "safe sex," "anal sex," and "sex worker" – are particularly efficacious because they create a critical distance from the intimacy associated with Nepali; they do not invoke the "moral density" associated with local language.

The naming of groups in English and non-English often reflects class differences: GayBombay (GB) vs. Humsafar Trust; Boys of Bangladesh (BoB) vs. Bhandu Social Welfare Society; Good As You (GAY) Bangalore vs.

Sangama. This, of course, does not hold true across the board; an organization developed in the smaller Indian town of Chandannagar chose the name *Amitié*, French for friendship. Organizations such as Dhaka-based BoB attract middle-class men who congregate for the purposes of sociality and support, whereas Bandhu focuses on safer sex education and human rights work amongst working-class MSMs, *kothi*s, and *hijra*s. Although Bandhu is committed to capacity-building and policy work, it also relies on various forms of cultural performances such as dance shows and pageants to foster community and support. Additionally, support and social groups that cater primarily to cisgender middle- and upper-class men such as GB, GAY, and BoB must not be deemed apolitical. They allow for sharing of resources around issues of marriage pressure, they engender social networks that have saved lives, and they provide an alternative to the medical industrial complex that adheres to outdated and problematic definitions of homosexuality.

LGBT activism in South Asia has had a distinctly transnational formation, not only in securing funding through the global NGO funders, but also through more intimate routes of cultural exchange and migration. Diasporic returnees have been instrumental in setting up activist organizations: Equal Ground in Colombo, Sahayatrika in Thrissur, Samapathik Trust in Pune. At conferences such as DesiQ in San Francisco, activists from various South Asian countries are able to share resources between themselves, and also source support from their diasporic counterparts. Lesbians in India have found their way to support groups via the New York-based South Asian Gay and Lesbian Association, diasporic queers have found useful resources in *Bombay Dost* magazine, and online spaces such as the Gay.com India chatroom and the Queer Kerala Facebook group have allowed for transnational flows of information, resources, and friendship.

Online forums have been an important space in which activism, at least amongst middle- and upper-class people, has been sustained. As Faris Khan (2014) argues, in moral climates where LGBT people are unable to acquire office space, virtual presence is all the more necessary. Parmesh Shahani (2008) models an online–offline framework for understanding groups such as GB, demonstrating that multi-method approaches are necessary for investigating activism. Often established as social, support, or dating spaces, online forums are used by some individuals to disseminate knowledge about STI/STD transmission, rally people to Pride events, and debate current LGBT issues. The place of "activism" in these online communities is often called into question, as Shuchi Karim (2014) describes in the Bangladeshi context. Online users in search of intimacy or sociality become resentful when they feel pressured into appearing at public venues. Despite this resistance to "activism" in online communities, they serve as essential forums for those experiencing marriage pressure, for members to find out information about parties as well as NGOs and support groups, and for people to make meaningful connections with others.

NGO-based activism privileges the health and safety of male-assigned persons, and women are rarely at the center of dominant narratives of activism. The institutional flow of funding for HIV/AIDS outreach and research has provided organizations serving "at-risk populations" – MSMs, gay men, transgender women – with a disproportionate share of funding, leaving cisgender women and transgender men at the periphery of activist discourses and with much less access to material resources.

Naisargi Dave's work is an important contribution to writing on LGBT South Asian activism, as it centers the formation of and challenges facing women-centered organizations: Campaign for Lesbian Rights (CALERI), Sangini, Prism, and Sakhi (Dave 2012). Dave recalibrates the issues that most visibly underlie queer activism in India by pointing to other incitements to activism: right-wing Hindu backlash against Deepa Mehta's1996 film *Fire*, the visceral desires of a variety of women to have sex with other women, the repetitious suicides of women-couples, feminist activisms, and the archiving tendencies of Giti Thadani. The voices and visibility of transgender men are disturbingly absent in media coverage of South Asian LGBT lives, despite their significant contributions to activism, community building, and cultural production across the subcontinent. With the efforts of trans activists this is very slowly shifting; in May 2014 in Mumbai, the Sampoorna Trans Masculine Meet was convened to share resources and build solidarity amongst Indian trans* masculine activists.

Law, specifically Section 377, has been central to many conversations about LGBT activism. An inheritance of British colonial law, Section 377 appears in the penal codes of India, Bangladesh, Sri Lanka, and Pakistan, criminalizing "acts against the order of nature," that include sex with children and penetrative sex between men. This law is both a relic of Victorian conservatism and a symbol of state-sanctioned homophobia. In Sri Lanka, it appears as Section 365 and 365A; efforts to decriminalize sodomy backfired and the language was broadened to criminalize sex acts between women. In Pakistan and Bangladesh, activists have not prioritized repealing Section 377 because it is not the primary law under which LGBT people are harassed, blackmailed, and detained.

In India also, Section 377 is not the primary edifice under which queers experience harassment at the hands of the state. Rather, police arrest, blackmail, and detain *hijras*, *kothi*s, and gay men for public indecency, begging, or even eve-teasing. Under detainment, many gender non-conforming people have reported being raped and assaulted by police.

In India, addressing Section 377 has become a *cause célèbre* of the LGBT movement, but not without controversy, and it has been a bumpy ride for the country's activists. Initial petitions (1994, 2005) to address Section 377 centered on hindrances to effective HIV/AIDS outreach. In preparation for the 2008 hearing by the Delhi High Court, a coalition of NGOs, Voices Against 377, convened to support its reading down; given the expansive scope of Section 377, which included child abuse, the strategy was to read it down instead of excise it completely. The scope of argumentation widened to a human rights framework that centered not only the efficacy of health outreach, but also individuals' rights to privacy. This rhetorical move raised significant conflicts between activists in the movement given working-class queers and transgender people lack of access to private space.

In 2009, the Delhi High Court delivered a judgment in favor of the Naz Foundation, decriminalizing consensual sex between same-gender adults. Immediately thereafter, coalitions of conservative parties filed petitions with the Indian Supreme court challenging the Naz judgment. In 2013, after a year of deliberation, two Supreme Court justices reversed the Delhi High Court decision, reasoning that the LGBT community is an interest group that is too small in number to merit amending the penal code, and criticizing the pro-LGBT lawyers for relying too much on non-Indian legal precedents. This has been a devastating blow to many LGBT activists and raises particular contradictions for the nature of "LGBT" activism in India – particularly given the National Legal Services Authority (NALSA) judgment following soon after.

In April 2014, the Indian Supreme Court returned a judgment on a petition filed by NALSA, recognizing the fundamental human and social rights of "third-gender" people. The governments of Bangladesh, Pakistan, and Nepal all recognize third-gender categories. *Hijra*s, *aravani*s, and other transgender people have had severe difficulty in accessing medical care, official identification, and legal services that recognize and respect their gender. This Supreme Court ruling recognizes transgender as a socioeconomically disenfranchised class that deserves affirmative actions in the realms of healthcare, welfare systems, and social standings. The NALSA judgment, pitted against the rescinding of the Naz judgment, suggests to many that "Westernized" ideas of an LGBT community are less favorable in the Indian public than more "indigenous" *hijra* identities. This by no means suggests that *hijra*s are better off in India than gay and lesbian people. Rather, it underscores perpetual discursive abjections of gay and lesbian identity as foreign, inauthentic, and adulterous imports.

Activism takes place not only in courtrooms, or at the level of policy, education, and quantifiable health outreach; cultural practices also function as critical means of advocating social change. At the 2014 Bangalore Queer Film Festival, a dance group performed a set that mocked the Supreme Court 2013 decision by fellating a banana pulled out of Justice Singhvi's pants. During the Global Day of Rage protests in response to the Supreme Court December 2013 decision, activists burned paper constructions inscribed not only with "Section 377," but also "Manusmriti," the Hindu text that is used to justify and institutionalize the caste system; burning both of these together implicates caste hierarchy and sex/gender oppression in one another. At a Pride march, two transgender activists dressed as policemen, satirizing the very policemen chaperoning the march; they did so with the intent of critiquing the Karnataka Police Act 36A that permits the arbitrary arrest of *hijra*s.

These cultural practices not only serve as symbolic critiques of systemic oppression but also have material effects, and function to hold those in power accountable. Pride marches across India, colorful and animated as they are, are coupled with a list of core demands for city and state officials and usually begin or conclude at politically significant sites. In West Bengal, Aniruddha Dutta (2012a,b) documents the use of particular forms of song and dance that *hijra* and *kothi* activists deploy to contest the class respectability of other activists and officials around them. At the more quotidian level, the signature open-palmed *hijra* clap and more spectacular flashing of castrated genitals are not only symbolic acts critiquing phallic patriarchy, they also facilitate soliciting money, and they protect *hijra*s by frightening possible abusers. Cultural tactics of survival are also employed by *khwaja sira*s, who use various forms of linguistic play to access NGO services, exclude unwanted listeners, and invoke solidarity between other *khwaja sira*s.

South Asia is home to successful and impressive LGBT activist organizations: the Humsafar Trust (Mumbai), Naz Male Health Alliance (Karachi), Bandhu Society (Dhaka), Equal Ground (Colombo), and the Blue Diamond Society (Kathmandu). The formidable work of these organizations in morally and politically challenging environments must be commended. However, to understand activism in South Asia, we must also attend to informal sites of social action, education, and community-making. It is in these settings that we might evidence the activist labor of women and transgender men in the movement, and also find critiques and learn the limits of the NGO industrial complex.

SEE ALSO: Arranged Marriages (in South Asia); *Hijra/Hejira*; Kathoey; NGOs and Grassroots Organizing

REFERENCES

Dave, Naisargi. 2012. *Queer Activism in India: A Story in the Anthropology of Ethics*. Durham, NC: Duke University Press.

Dutta, Aniruddha. 2012a. "Claiming Citizenship, Contesting Civility: The Institutional LGBT Movement and the Regulation of Gender/Sexual Dissidence in West Bengal, India." *Jindal Global Law Review*, 4(1): 110–141.

Dutta, Aniruddha. 2012b. "An Epistemology of Collusions: *Hijras*, *Kothis*, and the Historical (Dis)Continuity of Gender/Sexual Identities in Eastern India." *Gender and History*, 24(3): 825–849.

Karim, Shuchi. 2014. "Erotic Desires and Practices in Cyberspace: 'Virtual Reality' of the Non-Heterosexual Middle Class in Bangladesh." *Gender, Technology and Development*, 18(1): 53–76.

Khan, Faris. 2014. *Khwaja Sira: Culture, Identity Politics, and 'Transgender' Activism in Pakistan*. Dissertation, Syracuse University.

Pigg, Stacy Leigh. 2001. "Languages of Sex and Aids in Nepal: Notes on the Social Production of Commensurability." *Cultural Anthropology*, 16(4): 481–541.

Shahani, Parmesh. 2008. *Gay Bombay: Globalization, Love and (Be)Longing in Contemporary India*. New Delhi: Sage.

FURTHER READING

Khubchandani, Kareem. 2014. "Staging Transgender Solidarities at Bangalore's Queer Pride." *Transgender Studies Quarterly*, 1(4): 517–522.

Orinam.net. 2014. Orinam Section 377. Accessed January 31, 2014, at http://orinam.net/377.

LGBT Activism in Southeast Asia

ARPITA DAS
The Asian–Pacific Resource and Research Centre for Women, Malaysia

ALANKAAR SHARMA
University of Minnesota – Twin Cities, USA

The Southeast Asian geographic region comprises 11 countries, namely Brunei, Myanmar (Burma), Cambodia, Indonesia, Laos, Malaysia, the Philippines, Singapore, Thailand, Timor-Leste (East Timor), and Vietnam, and encompasses a wide diversity in sexual orientations and gender identities (SOGI), practices, expressions, and desires not only across the region but also within each country. Besides the widely used and understood categories of gay, lesbian, bisexual, and transgender, there are the *mak-nyahs* in Malaysia, the *baklas* in the Philippines, the *warias* and *bissus* in Indonesia, and many other SOGI coexisting in the Southeast Asian countries. Many of these communities and cultures cannot be easily translated or interpreted in simplified and recognized identities such as the lesbians, gays, and transgender people in the West. Historically, Southeast Asia is known to permit fluidity across genders without particularly strict gender codes in terms of behaviors and dress, although this cannot be claimed for all countries in the region. Simultaneously, however, there exists widespread discrimination and exploitation towards SOGI minorities, including LGBT.

LGBT activism in the Southeast Asian region is not a recent phenomenon; it has existed for decades and is as varied in its issues, approaches, and constituencies as the region itself. Diverse SOGI groups and communities in different contexts in the Southeast Asian region have collectivized on different occasions to fight against discrimination and violence and also to claim rights as equal citizens. Given such diversity, the idea of a monolithic and unified LGBT movement and activism within Southeast Asia is contestable. Some of the key issues that LGBT activism in the region has focused on are abolition of punitive and discriminatory laws against LGBT communities, better healthcare systems and social services for LGBT communities, and development of indigenous rights-based treaties and mechanisms that acknowledge and address the rights and concerns of SOGI minorities. Although a number of countries in the region have signed and/or ratified the various United Nations (UN) human rights documents and protocols, many have yet to enact laws and policies that protect the rights of LGBT people, punish violence and exploitation towards them, and extend healthcare facilities that cater to their unique needs.

One of the primary areas of focus of LGBT activism in Southeast Asia has been campaigning against various laws that are either punitive or discriminatory to diverse SOGI communities. The most common target of such activism are the laws that criminalize same-sex sexual behavior; such laws, commonly known as sodomy laws, are in force in several Southeast Asian countries. In this way, such laws have become a rallying point for LGBT activism against oppression and discrimination. Most of these sodomy laws are inherited through years of colonization. These laws typically frame any "carnal intercourse against the order of nature" as sodomy and could be interpreted to include acts such as oral sex and anal sex even among heterosexual people. Despite the presence of laws against sodomy, the prosecution rate is usually low. However, the presence of such laws has a negative impact on sexual minorities. Often, these laws are used as a threat against homosexual people. Although lesbians are not directly implicated under this law that considers penetration as sufficient to carnal intercourse, this has been used as a threat against all sexual minorities, including lesbian, bisexual, transgender, and transsexual persons. This legal prohibition exists in countries including Malaysia, Singapore, and Myanmar and a similar law also remains in force in Brunei. There also exist Syariah laws in some countries that criminalize same-sex sexual activities, such as in Brunei and certain parts of Malaysia, Indonesia, and the Philippines. Brunei, which has recently adopted the Syariah penal code into law, would allow for stoning to death for crimes of a sexual nature, including same-sex sexual relations. It is noteworthy that some countries in the region have actively removed sodomy laws (e.g., legal since 1956 in Thailand) whereas still others never had any such laws (e.g., Vietnam). Apart from sodomy laws, several countries also have laws that negatively impact transgender and transsexual communities. For example, there exist laws in Brunei, Indonesia, and Malaysia against "cross-dressing." In Malaysia, Thailand, the Philippines, and Vietnam, transgender and transsexual individuals are not allowed legally to change their name or gender. In Vietnam and Malaysia, rape laws leave out transgender or transsexual individuals, thereby offering them little or no protection. Laws also exist that negatively influence visibility and representation of LGBT communities in electronic and print media. In Indonesia, Malaysia, and Singapore, different laws are in place that censor, prohibit, or regulate content related to LGBT individuals, characters, and issues. Bringing attention to and seeking repeal of the aforementioned discriminatory and punitive laws have been a major focus area for LGBT activism in Southeast Asia.

In countries where laws against sodomy do not exist, discrimination against LGBT people may still be prevalent. Negative societal attitudes and media portrayal against LGBT people often affect how they are treated in their families, communities, and society. Many countries lack comprehensive sexuality education for adolescents and young people. In other contexts, sex education hardly includes issues and concerns of LGBT people, thus exacerbating misconceptions regarding LGBT people, and resulting in their non-acceptance by society, community members, and family. Discrimination may also take place in forms other than direct exploitation, bullying, and violence against LGBT people in terms of not being allowed rights on a par with heterosexual people. For example, in several countries LGBT people do not have the right to marry, to adopt children, or to inherit housing and property from their partners. In addition, there are also subtler forms of discrimination, such as non-recognition as equal entities. LGBT people and especially transgender and transsexual people are often restricted from employment opportunities in cases in which they are "out" about their identity. Transgender people are often forced to enter employment in massage parlors and beauty salons and as sex workers for lack of other opportunities. In addition to seeking removal of oppressive laws, LGBT activism in the Southeast Asian region has also made efforts to have laws enacted that would actively address such discrimination against SOGI minorities. For instance, in the Philippines, the struggle to introduce an anti-discrimination law to protect SOGI minorities has been in progress for nearly a decade. As part of this activism, an anti-discrimination bill to protect the rights of LGBT people has been filed again in the 16th Congress of the Philippines; a similar bill was also filed in the 15th Congress. The bill, if passed, will impose fines and imprisonment in cases of discrimination against LGBT people, including the disclosure of sexual orientation as a necessary criterion for the hiring, promotion, or dismissal of workers, refusal of admission to or expulsion from educational institutions on the basis of one's sexual orientation and gender identity, and denying access to LGBT people to health and other public facilities. Transgender and intersex people often face discrimination with regard to the use of public facilities such as toilets, and they may often be forced to use toilets that correspond to their assigned gender. There are usually no separate toilets for transgender people in schools, universities, workplaces, and other public places. Transgender people are often disallowed from using the toilets that they may be more comfortable in using because of societal attitudes and pressures. Further, public toilets are also a site for violence and assault on transgender, homosexual, and queer people. In a recent case in the Philippines, a transgender woman filed a case of discrimination when she was barred from using the women's toilet in her workplace, and the court decision in this case would bring to the surface the strength of the Quezon City Ordinance, which prohibits "all discriminatory acts against homosexuals in the workplace, whether in hiring, treatment, promotion or dismissal, in both the government and private sector." In June 2008, a school in the Kampang district of northeastern Thailand introduced "transvestite" toilets for male students who chose to dress like female students.

Organizing pride events has been an important part of activism in Southeast Asia in order to provide a platform for LGBT rights groups and allies to come together, acknowledge, and celebrate SOGI diversity, generate awareness, bring attention to issues of LGBT rights and oppression, and galvanize public support. Such events have taken place in many countries, including Thailand, the Philippines, Vietnam, Singapore, Cambodia, and Laos. Some of these events, typically annual, have started in the recent past (e.g., in Singapore, and Vientiane, Laos) whereas others have been running for decades (e.g., in Manila, the Philippines, and Bangkok, Thailand). State response to such events is varied across the region. Whereas certain governments have objected to such events and taken steps to prevent them from taking place (e.g., Malaysia), other governments have allowed them to go on but without offering any official recognition, sometimes despite prevailing laws that criminalize same-sex sexual activities (e.g., Singapore). Another prominent public awareness event that LGBT activists in the Southeast Asian region have rallied around is the International Day Against Homopohobia and Transphobia (IDAHOT). In 2014, IDAHOT was commemorated in around 17 cities in Indonesia during May 7–16 with a variety of activities, such as public discussions at universities, community gathering, movie screenings, and road rallies, and was organized by 29 organizations including LGBT groups, women's rights groups, students, researchers, religious groups, and the media. A series of events also took place in Myanmar in commemoration of the day between May 11 and 18, 2014, in Yangon. Similar events took place in the Philippines, Thailand, Vietnam, and Singapore. In Bangkok, Thailand, as a larger effort to prevent bullying on the basis of one's sexual orientation or gender identity, local and international groups organized the "school rainbow" campaign, encouraging communities to make chalk drawings of rainbows in city spaces symbolizing diversity in different schools and universities. A group of Vietnamese non-government organizations called the Sexual Rights Alliance also conducted an event in Hanoi with "free expression" as a key theme of action to urge the government to take more action to protect LGBT communities and to celebrate the progress made in reducing stigma and discrimination.

Negative representation and discrimination against LGBT people may also often translate into poor healthcare facilities for them. While healthcare facilities may exist in that region in general, healthcare professionals may lack an understanding of concerns and issues unique to LGBT people and they may be treated without empathy. For example, insistence by health authorities on transgender people sharing the same wards and cabins as males and females can lead to discrimination and often exploitation from other hospital inmates besides, of course, affecting their self-confidence. In certain instances they may also be subjected to outright discrimination and exploitation. Pathologization of SOGI is a key area that LGBT activism in Southeast Asia has targeted. Although homosexuality is no longer considered a mental illness according to the *Diagnostic and Statistical Manual of Mental Disorders* (DSM), many government officials and members of the public across the Southeast Asian region continue to consider it as such. Moreover, the DSM included Gender Identity Disorder until 2013 as a mental disorder; it has since been replaced by Gender Dysphoria, thereby arguably declassifying transgenderism as a mental disorder. Transgender, like homosexuality, continues to be considered a mental disorder by many despite the aforementioned advancements aimed at depathologization of diverse SOGI.

The HIV/AIDS epidemic has also played an important role in activism around homosexuality in Southeast Asia by drawing public, media, and state attention to diverse sexual orientations and their health concerns. The epidemic brought visibility to non-heterosexual communities and forced governments to acknowledge them and commit resources towards their health and well-being. These efforts, however, were primarily focused on gay men.

Activists have also been making efforts towards the acknowledgment of diverse SOGI and recognition of the rights of LGBT communities within international-, regional-, and national-level human rights instruments and mechanisms. For instance, activists have regularly sought greater visibility of LGBT issues in the international arena at the UN Commission on Population and Development by utilizing the provisions of the ICPD (International Conference on Population and Development) Programme of Action. At the regional level also, activism has focused on including LGBT issues in the language of human rights instruments. For example, the ASEAN (Association of Southeast Asian Nations) SOGIE (Sexual Orientation and Gender Identity/Expression) Caucus, a regional network of LGBT rights activists and organizations, has tenaciously attempted, albeit unsuccessfully thus far, to have sexual orientation and gender identity included in the language of regional human rights instruments such as the ASEAN Human Rights Declaration of 2012, ASEAN Declaration on the Elimination of Violence Against Women of 2013, and ASEAN Declaration on the Elimination of Violence Against Children of 2013.

LGBT activism in Southeast Asia has carefully attempted to tie regional activism to international rights-based discourses, policy instruments, and standards that countries in the region are legally or ethically required or expected to uphold, while at the same time emphasizing the uniqueness of SOGI identities and social, political, and cultural contexts of various countries in the region. For example, activists have urged their countries to be inclusive of diverse SOGI while discharging their obligations to the ICPD Programme of Action, UN Declaration of Human Rights, Convention on the Elimination of All Forms of Discrimination against Women, and UN Convention on the Rights of the Child; they have also asked their governments to commit to international rights-based instruments such as the Yogyakarta Principles on the Application of Human Rights Law in Relation to Sexual Orientation and Gender Identity. At the same time, activists have warned against the local SOGI identity categories such as *mak-nyahs*, *baklas*, and *warias* being subsumed by the largely West-defined umbrella term of LGBT.

LGBT activism is also in constant interaction with other rights-oriented activist communities in the Southeast Asian region, such as youth rights groups and women's rights groups. These interactions have produced both synergy and conflict. For instance, LGBT activists worked with youth rights activists during the 2014 ASEAN People's Forum held in Myanmar, and were encouraged by the ASEAN Youth Statement 2014 released during the event, which recognized SOGI minority youth as a vulnerable group and demanded special protections for them and repeal of oppressive and discriminatory laws against them. At the same forum, there were divergent opinions among women's rights groups about whether or not to include SOGI issues within their agenda; several women's rights activists expressed concern that LGBT rights issues may be too controversial within the Southeast Asian sociopolitical context to be included in women's rights agendas at the present time.

SEE ALSO: Gender Identification; Lesbian and Gay Movements; Sexual Identity and Orientation; Sexual Orientation and the Law; Sodomy Law in Comparative Perspective

FURTHER READING

Laurent, Erick. 2005. "Sexuality and Human Rights: An Asian Perspective." *Journal of Homosexuality*, 48: 163–225. DOI: 10.1300/J082v48n03_09.

Offord, Baden. 2011. "Singapore, Indonesia and Malaysia: Arrested Development!" In *The Lesbian and Gay Movement and the State: Comparative Insights into a Transformed Relationship*, edited by Manon Tremblay, David Paternotte, and Carol Johnson, 135–151. Farnham: Ashgate.

Slamah, Khartini. 2005. "The Struggle to Be Ourselves, Neither Men Nor Women: Mak Nyahs in Malaysia." In *Sexuality, Gender and Rights: Exploring Theory and Practice in South and Southeast Asia*, edited by Geetanjali Misra and Radhika Chandiramani, 98–112. New Delhi: Sage.

LGBT Activism in Southern Africa

MARY HAMES
University of the Western Cape, South Africa

In Southern Africa, the status of lesbian, gay, bisexual, transgender, and intersex (LGBTI) organizations is varied, with those located in South Africa perhaps the most advanced. Due to the prevalence of homophobia and transphobia and the respective prejudice attached, the organizing of same-sex and transgender issues that concentrated on the rights and concerns of individuals as well as minority groups never developed into broader social movements collectively. In South Africa, for instance, the claim to social and human rights as ensconced in the Constitution took the form of protracted litigation brought by individuals and non-government organizations (NGOs) such as the Gay and Lesbian Equality Project as class actions. In September 2014, South Africa was the only Southern African state to become a signatory to the United Nations clause on Human Rights, Sexual Orientation and Gender Identity (SOGI).

Homosexuality and sexual orientation in the Southern African region are mostly claimed from within the universal human rights framework and seldom from a feminist perspective. There are only four organizations in the region that lay claim to a feminist perspective in challenging sexual orientation and gender identity concerns, namely Sister Namibia in Namibia, and the Forum for the Empowerment of Women (FEW), Coalition of African Lesbians (CAL), and People Opposing Women Abuse (POWA) in South Africa. Only FEW and CAL work exclusively with lesbian women while Sister Namibia and POWA's work is deeply women-centered. There are a number of LGBTI organizations and coalitions in the region that are involved with advocacy work pertaining to the right to dignity, social justice, sexuality and sexual orientation, gender, gender identity, and gender performativity, as well as the right to healthcare and reproductive health.

Ironically, both governments and the LGBT movement premised their respective perceptions on the principles of universal human rights, but they have very different interpretations of what these rights entail. There is consistent pressure by homosexual people, organizations, and coalitions on their governments to align their attitudes with the universal human rights values and principles ensconced in their respective constitutions and to afford all inhabitants the right to inclusive citizenship. The Southern African states are signatories of various regional and international agreements, conventions, and protocols that accentuate dignity, human rights, and social justice for all. These include the Convention on the Elimination of All Forms of Discrimination against Women (CEDAW), the International Covenant on Civil and Political Rights (ICCPR), and the United Nations Human Rights Council (UNHRC), which conducts a system of universal periodic review (UPR) every four years to assess the progress countries have made with regard to their human rights track record.

Southern African statesmen are often quoted because of their vitriolic attacks on homosexual people. The former Namibian president Sam Nujoma said that gay men and lesbians were "un-African and unnatural" and that "homosexuality must be condemned and rejected" as a "foreign and corrupt ideology" that is "destroying the Namibian culture." Even the SWAPO Women's Council and the Ministry for Women strongly opposed lesbian and gay rights. The Zimbabwean president Robert Mugabe said that "homosexuals are worse than pigs and dogs," and in South Africa with its progressive Constitution, Jacob Zuma, the former deputy president, made the following remark: "When I was growing up an *ungqingili* [a gay boy] would not have stood in front of me. I would knock him out."

There is the perception that homosexuality is a disease and can be cured. Even in this oppressive context the LGBTI movement finds ways to network and challenge the draconian laws that still exist in the Southern African states. Even though South Africa has the most progressive laws in the region, it also reports the highest incidences of rape and murder of black lesbian women. Legal reform does not necessarily translate into societal transformation. South Africa, Namibia, Botswana, Lesotho, Malawi, Swaziland, Zambia, and Zimbabwe are governed by a dual legal system that consists of a combination of customary law, Roman Dutch law, and English common law. These postcolonial states have constitutions that guarantee progressive and fundamental human rights, such as the right of association, the right to privacy, and the right to gender equality. Paradoxically, however, the legal system also includes archaic colonial penal codes that criminalize homosexuality. The British colonial law's reference to "carnal knowledge against the order of nature" has been replicated in all the penal codes in the region, with South Africa as the only exception. South Africa has decriminalized sodomy.

On a theoretical level, the constitutions espouse the principles of equity and equality; in reality, however, there are constant violations of these institutionalized human rights by states. The punitive measures for perceived homosexuality and homosexual actions are extreme. In Zimbabwe, when found guilty of sodomy, the penalty is up to one year in prison, including a fine of $5,000. In Zambia a person could be incarcerated from 15 years to life for "unnatural acts" and 14 years for "gross indecency." The Tanzanian law is regarded as the most extreme and allows for a punishment of 30 years to life in prison for consensual same-sex intimacy. Whereas these penal codes were originally only applicable to sodomy between two men, the notions of gender mainstreaming and gender equality opened the window for the promulgation of laws that criminalized consensual sex between women. Malawi passed a new law in 2010 that criminalizes "indecent practices between females," arguing that it was done under the rubric of gender equality. Zambia too extended the law to include lesbians. Lesbian life became hypervisible after legislation was passed. The legal criminalization the LGBTI community experiences led to social exclusion, stigmatization, and rampant violence in all states. Many of the organizations do not operate publicly and a number of them function under the guise of "organizing and empowering women" or as health rights organizations. HIV and AIDS in particular carved the way for discursive debates on sexuality and sexual orientation.

National, regional, and international alliances and networks collectively campaign to have these oppressive laws repealed and societal homophobia and prejudice eradicated. South Africa is the only state on the continent where sexual orientation has been included in the Constitution as an inherent human right, and it became a safe haven for all who became sexual refugees. A number of the coalitions have their established head offices in South Africa from where they can organize across the continent. For example, People Against Suffering Oppression and Poverty (PASSOP) offers services and support to sexual refugees. In 2003 CAL was formed in Johannesburg as part of feminist movement building and to give lesbians in Africa a voice. The coalition is formed of 30 organizations in 19 African countries. CAL came into existence at a time when violence against lesbians escalated and when the states proposed and implemented laws that categorized lesbian women's same-sex activities as "indecent." The coalition lobbied the African Commission on Human and Peoples' Rights (ACHPR) for observer status. Their request was rejected because the ACHPR does not work with LGBT organizations. CAL remains committed to African radical feminist understandings and its goal is to transform Africa into a place where all lesbian women enjoy the full range of human rights and inclusive citizenship, and secure respect for the rich and diverse cultures from which they come.

CAL obtained the status of human rights defender and has systematically changed the way research has historically been conducted in the portrayal of sexually and gender non-conforming and marginalized people. In 2013 CAL co-published a report with African Men for Sexual Health Rights called "Violence Based on Real or Perceived Sexual Orientation and Gender Identity in Africa."

Because of the severe prosecution of gay and lesbian people in the region and in order to protect the identities of their members, some organizations work under the auspices of preventing and treating HIV and AIDS. Other organizations work exclusively with men having sex with men (MSM). These organizations play an important role in advocacy and lobbying for LGBTI rights. The regional MSM coalition African Men for Sexual Health Rights (AMSHeR) is located in South Africa and specifically addresses gay and bisexual men, male-to-female transgender women, and other MSM as well as HIV and AIDS. The countries that are represented in the AMSHeR coalition are Burundi, Cameroon, Côte d'Ivoire, Ghana, Kenya, Malawi, Mozambique, Namibia, Nigeria, South Africa, Tanzania, Togo, Uganda, Zambia, and Zimbabwe. It aims to increase the visibility of African MSM across policy, legislation, communities, and service delivery. AMSHeR's interest lies in the sexual and reproductive health rights of African MSM.

Although coalition politics are important in movement building as well as for regional and transnational solidarity, country-specific organization building and campaigning are essential. In research done by the International Gay and Lesbian Human Rights Commission (IGLHRC) there are numerous reports about blackmail and extortion of LGBT people in sub-Saharan Africa. In countries where there is a blatant contradiction between constitutional human rights and penal codes, the opportunities for blackmail abound. Blackmail and extortion depend on the shame and secrecy of victimization and it is in this regard that LGBT and human rights organizations play such a pivotal role (Thoreson and Cook 2011).

Angola is relaxed about LGBT issues. The Angolan Constitution is silent with regard to sexual orientation, and like the other states it has a penal code that states that "unnatural acts are punishable." However, there is no evidence that the law has ever been applied or that there has been any state persecution. The LGBT community is of the opinion that Angola is culturally not ready to recognize LGBT rights. Although the LGBT community openly socialize, there is no formal organization in the country. In 2008 the organization Lesbians, Gays, and Bisexuals of Botswana (LeGaBiBo) submitted a shadow report to the Human Rights Committee requesting that Botswana decriminalize all homosexual relationships and practices. It argued that the penal code violates the right to privacy as guaranteed by the ICCPR. In November 2014 LeGaBiBo was granted the right to formally register as an organization. The Rainbow Identity Association (RIA) was established in Botswana in December 2010 and focuses on transgender, gender non-conforming, and intersex concerns.

In 2010 the first LGBTI non-profit organization, Matrix, was registered in Lesotho. It offers psychosocial and other support services to the LGBTI community. In Malawi the Centre for the Development of People (CEDEP) conducts research and runs programs for MSM. CEDEP also undertakes advocacy and lobbying campaigns and its "Bring 2 Life" program provides a safe space for LGBT people. CEDEP is not an exclusive LGBT organization as it also focuses on other minority groups, such as prisoners and sex workers.

Mozambique is overall regarded as very tolerant to homosexual people, although there is no special constitutional protection for sexual orientation. The Constitution states that all citizens "enjoy the same rights and are subject to the same duties, regardless of color, race, sex, ethnic origin, place of birth, religion, level of education, social position, marital status of their parents, profession or political option," and it includes "any other status." The Mozambique Association for the Defense of Sexual Minorities (LAMDA) argues that the terms "sex" and "any other status" are too vague and that there is a need for the explicit inclusion of "sexual orientation."

The Rainbow Project (TRP) was founded in 1990 in Namibia and was the country's only lesbian and gay rights organization for a very long time. Sister Namibia is the oldest feminist NGO that fosters equality and human dignity. It was the first organization that advocated for human rights for lesbian women in Namibia. OutRights Namibia (ORN) was established in 2010 as a human rights organization that deals with LGTBI and MSM concerns.

House of Our Pride (HOOP) was established in 2009 in Swaziland with approximately 300 members. It offers services to the LGBT community and is especially concerned with access to healthcare as over a quarter of the population is HIV-positive.

In Tanzania legal discrimination similar to that in the other states of the region led to social exclusion and stigmatization. In October 2011 the UNHRC conducted its first UPR of Tanzania. The government under review is obligated to implement the recommendations made by the UPR. Tanzania did not accept the subsequent recommendations regarding sexual rights, which stipulated that the government take steps to protect the rights of all people irrespective of sexual orientation, adopt anti-discrimination legislation, and decriminalize same-sex activities. The network Wake Up and Step Forward Coalition (WASO) is located in Dar es Salaam and does work with MSM. Greater visibility has not necessarily translated to greater inclusion within the social fabric of society but has instead brought greater oppression.

Rainka in Zambia aims to protect, advance, and promote human rights for Zambian sexual minorities and strives to engage legislators and policymakers in the process of reforming the law. While the penal code was particularly designed to address men caught in the act of sodomy, the law has been extended to include both men and women. Women can now be charged for soliciting and imprisoned for a period of 14 years. In November 2013 the First Lady, Christine Kaseba-Sata, surprised the LGBTI community when she said that there should be an end to discrimination against sexual minorities and that homosexuality should be decriminalized. Gays and Lesbians of Zimbabwe (GALZ) is one of the oldest and most established organizations in the region. Members of GALZ are consistently persecuted by state-sponsored violence.

South Africa has the advantage that sexual orientation is included in the Constitution and individuals and organizations have consistently petitioned for the repeal or amendment of discriminatory laws. Lesbian women have been pivotal in politicizing embodiment and have transformed jurisprudence to become inclusive for all. The Lesbian and Gay Equality Project (LGEP), formerly the National Coalition for Gay and Lesbian Equality, played an instrumental role in mobilizing the LGBT community to lobby the African National Congress (ANC) to include sexual orientation in the equality clause. The Triangle Project is the oldest organization in the country. While its primary focus remains health and counseling, it is involved in a variety of outreach and empowerment projects. There are a number of LGBTI organizations across the country. The Durban Lesbian and Gay Community and Health Centre located in KwaZulu-Natal offers services that range from health to legal advice to the LGBTI community. FEW was founded to work with black lesbians and bisexual and transgender women. The OUT LGBT and Well-Being Organization concentrates on health education. The Inner Circle (TIC) offers services to Muslim LGBTI people. GenderDynamiX was the first human rights organization on the continent to work exclusively for the recognition of expression of gender identity and the rights of transgender, transsexual, and gender non-conforming people. Intersex South Africa (ISSA) is the only organization of its kind in the region. Gay and Lesbian Memory in Action (GALA), based at the University of the Witwatersrand, conducts research and collects archival material.

Various community-based organizations exist and focus on LGBTI concerns in a particular community. They advocate, lobby, and build coalitions with like-minded organizations as the need arises. Free Gender and Luleki Sizwe are organizations that specifically advocate and lobby for the introduction of hate-crime legislation in response to the rape and murders of black lesbian women. Transgender Intersex Africa (TIA) raises awareness with regard to the black transgender and intersex community. Oranti-org is a queer human rights visual media organization that challenges all discrimination premised on gender, sexuality, sexual orientation, and gender nonconformity. Several South African universities have LGBTI student organizations that network and campaign across universities and civil society organizations to ensure homophobia-free higher education institutions.

SEE ALSO: Black Feminist Thought; Convention on the Elimination of All Forms of Discrimination against Women (CEDAW); Feminism, Lesbian; Gender Equality; Gender Mainstreaming; Gender Transgression; Intersex Movement; Lesbian and Gay Movements; Sexual Identity and Orientation; Sexual Rights; Sexualities; Sexuality and Human Rights; Transgender Movements in International Perspective; Women's and Feminist Activism in Southern Africa; Universal Human Rights

REFERENCE

Thoreson, Ryan, and Sam Cook, eds. 2011. *Nowhere to Turn: Blackmail and Extortion of LGBT People in Sub-Saharan Africa*. New York: International Gay and Lesbian Human Rights Commission.

FURTHER READING

Epprecht, Marc. 2008. *Heterosexual Africa? History of an Idea from the Age of Exploration to the Age of AIDS*. Athens: Ohio University Press.
Fester, Gertrude. 2006. "Some Preliminary Thoughts on Sexuality, Citizenship and Constitutions: Are Rights Enough?" *Agenda*, 67: 100–111.
Gays and Lesbians of Zimbabwe. 2008. *Unspoken Facts: A History of Homosexualities in Africa*. Harare: GALZ.
Gevisser, M., and E. Cameron, eds. 1995. *Defiant Desire: Gay and Lesbian Lives in South Africa*. New York: Routledge.

Hames, Mary. 2007. "Sexual Identity and Transformation at a South African University." *Social Dynamics*, 33(1): 53–77.

Judge, Melanie, Anthony Manion, and Shaun de Waal, eds. 2008. *To Have and To Hold: The Making of Same-Sex Marriage in South Africa*. Auckland Park: Jacana Media.

Mkhize, Nonhlanhla, et al. 2010. *The Country We Want to Live In: Hate Crimes and Homophobia in the Lives of Black Lesbian South Africans*. Cape Town: HSRC Press.

Morgan, Ruth, Charl Marais, and Joy Rosemary Wellbeloved, eds. 2009. *Trans: Transgender Life Stories from South Africa*. Auckland Park: Gay and Lesbian Memory in Action (GALA).

Morgan, Ruth, and Saskia Wieringa. 2007. *Tommy Boys, Lesbian Men and Ancestral Wives: Female Same-Sex Practices in Africa*. Auckland Park: Jacana Media.

Queer Malawi: Untold Stories. 2010. Malawi and Johannesburg: Centre for the Development of People (CEDEP) and Gay and Lesbian Memory in Action (GALA).

Reddy, Vasu, Theo Sanfort, and Laetitia Rispel, eds. 2009. *From Social Silence to Social Science: Same-Sex Sexuality, HIV & AIDS and Gender in South Africa*. Cape Town: Human Sciences Research Council.

Tucker, Andrew. 2009. *Queer Visibilities: Space, Identity and Interaction in Cape Town*. Oxford: Wiley Blackwell.

Van Zyl, Mikki, and Melissa Steyn, eds. 2005. *Performing Queer: Shaping Sexualities 1994–2004*, vol. 1. Roggebaai: Kwela Books.

LGBT Activism in Western Europe

HELMA G.E. DE VRIES-JORDAN
University of Pittsburgh at Bradford, USA

In Western Europe, important strides in lesbian, gay, bisexual, and transgender (LGBT) activism have occurred at both the supranational and domestic levels. European integration has shifted the political opportunity structure (POS) for activists, creating new targets around which to mobilize at the supranational level and contributing to the Europeanization of LGBT rights (Ayoub 2013). The European Union (EU) and the Council of Europe (CoE) have helped to establish rules and procedures regarding LGBT rights and contributed to the spread of norms regarding equality, with policy spillover occurring from the supranational to the domestic level. Activists involved in both domestic and international non-governmental organizations (NGOs) and social movement organizations (SMOs) have increasingly targeted European institutions for lobbying and litigation. Transnational advocacy networks (TANs) have emerged that serve as umbrella groups linking together domestic NGOs and SMOs, coordinating their advocacy at the supranational level. The diffusion of LGBT rights as human rights and the emergence of shared understandings of equality at the European level have enabled TANs to help domestic NGOs and SMOs in linking supranational norms with domestic appeals for policy change regarding LGBT rights.

At the supranational level, lobbying has enabled activists to build cooperative relationships with government officials and policymakers, sharing their expertise, advocating for policy change, and helping to draft proposals for improving the recognition of LGBT rights. For example, in the 1980s and early 1990s, advocates who lobbied the European Parliament were informally involved in drafting a report calling for equal rights for gays and lesbians and the opening up of marriage to lesbian and gay couples (Kollman 2009). After that report was published, annual European Parliament reports concerning human rights included a discussion of sexual orientation, setting LGBT rights on the agenda in the European Commission and EU Council. These earlier successes were instrumental in building support for including an anti-discrimination clause in the Amsterdam Treaty of 1997, the first legally binding international treaty to include sexual orientation as a type of protected category.

The Amsterdam Treaty helped set the stage to pass the Employment Equality Directive of 2000, which prohibited employment discrimination based on religion, disability, age, or sexual orientation (Kollman 2009, 2013). The Netherlands and Scandinavian states were among the early adopters of such anti-discrimination laws. As a result of the Employment Equality Directive, national LGBT activists were able to get all EU member states to develop anti-discrimination laws with sexual orientation as a protected class, successfully transposing the directive into national law. While sexual orientation has been added as a protected class in most countries, discrimination protections regarding gender identity are still rare.

Activists have also relied on litigation to advance LGBT rights, particularly in venues such as the CoE's European Court of Human Rights (ECtHR) and the EU's European Court of Justice (ECJ) (Kollman 2009; Kollman 2013). For instance, David Norris, an "out" senator and gay rights activist, first unsuccessfully challenged domestic laws criminalizing homosexuality in Ireland, but subsequently successfully appealed the Irish court decision in the ECtHR. The ECtHR judgment outlawed the criminalization of homosexuality in Europe, leading Ireland to repeal the legislation in 1993, several years later. The growing strength and formal organization of LGBT rights movements in many countries contributed to the decriminalization of homosexuality in nearly all Western European states by the time the ECtHR ruled in the Norris case. Since then, the remaining countries have decriminalized homosexuality, and the ECtHR decision was instrumental in driving forward this policy diffusion.

Other litigation has touched on a range of LGBT rights issues. Decisions in other cases by both the ECtHR and ECJ have prohibited discrimination targeting LGBT individuals (Kollman 2009). Further, decisions by the ECtHR in other types of cases ended the ban on homosexuality in the British military and protected parental rights of LGBT citizens in Portugal. A 2003 ECtHR decision required the Austrian government to grant the same benefits to unmarried cohabitants, regardless of whether they are same-sex or opposite-sex couples, imposing a minimal relationship recognition law in Austria. Similarly, a 2008 ECJ decision in the EU protected pension benefits for surviving same-sex spouses or partners of employees in countries with domestic policies recognizing same-sex unions (SSUs). The courts have been reluctant to rule in favor of opening up civil marriage for same-sex couples in countries that lack SSU recognition entirely or only have registered partnerships, allowing states to retain the power to grant or deny benefits to same-sex couples.

TANs advocating for LGBT rights have emerged at the European level due to the increasing importance of supranational institutions in advancing LGBT rights as well as the need to coordinate the work of activists cross-nationally (Ayoub 2013). In particular, the European section of the International Lesbian, Gay, Bisexual, Trans and Intersex Association (ILGA-Europe) has had a prominent role, drawing together hundreds of organizations from across Europe. The primary source of funding for ILGA-Europe is the European Commission, as the EU has historically provided generous financial support for civil society organizations. ILGA-Europe collaborates closely with Members of the European Parliament in the Intergroup on LGBT Rights. Additionally, it has achieved a participatory status at the CoE and a consultative status with the Economic and Social Council of the United Nations. Insider activism including lobbying helps transnational LGBT activists to cultivate relationships with civil servants and policymakers. EU officials can serve as valuable allies in dealing with member states' national governments, particularly at times when domestic officials are more reticent in responding to LGBT rights claims and the domestic POS is perceived as closed. LGBT and human rights NGOs have to be receptive to changes in the POS, both domestically and at the international level, and adjust their tactics in conjunction with activists in other member states. The range of issues that groups such as ILGA-Europe are currently focused on include seeking asylum for refugees who fear persecution based on their sexual orientation or gender identity; combating discrimination of LGBT and intersex people and their families regarding education, employment, healthcare, and legal rights; promoting trans* (including the entire spectrum of gender identities) and intersex rights; and opposing hate crime and hate speech.

The EU has helped to create an understanding of LGBT rights as human rights, and the dissemination of this norm may have been instrumental in the diffusion of domestic SSU adoption in Western Europe (Kollman 2009, 2013). TANs have encouraged domestic NGOs and SMOs to use policy changes promoting equality at the European level to argue a norm has emerged for the legal recognition of SSUs as a human rights concern. Further, activists have utilized this norm in lobbying policymakers to place SSU recognition on the domestic policy agenda. SSU adoption started with Nordic states in the early 1990s, before this norm was fully internalized. Subsequently, advocates have been able to use European norms in mounting pressure to reform additional member states' policies. Accordingly, the number of member states who have enacted domestic policies regarding SSUs has increased considerably. Further, most governments that have legalized same-sex marriage or civil unions in the past two decades, have justified such laws using examples from the EU, ECtHR, and from other states.

Western European states that have opened up civil marriage to same-sex couples include the Netherlands, Belgium, Spain, Norway, Sweden, Portugal, Iceland, Denmark, France, England, Wales, Scotland, Luxembourg, and Finland (Kollman 2013). Almost all of these states had previously taken steps in adopting registered or unregistered partnerships. Some states, which adopted registered partnerships, have been reluctant to legalize same-sex marriage. Finally, Cyprus, Greece, Italy, and Monaco do not recognize SSU. Some of the laggard countries are highly religious, and the European norm for SSU may not be perceived as legitimate in certain national contexts. However, several countries are developing legislation for registered partnerships, and many states are in the midst of ongoing campaigns for marriage equality.

Domestic LGBT rights activists have had an important role in advocating for SSU recognition and in securing international media coverage of both partnership and wedding ceremonies (Kollman 2013). In Western Europe, marriage equality has been advanced via legislation, and thus activists have conducted campaigns that relied heavily on lobbying and raising public awareness. In Ireland, a referendum on this issue is forthcoming in Spring 2015, making grassroots mobilization of particular importance in turning out voters. Additionally, litigation in domestic courts has also been used to challenge the discrimination experienced by LGBT couples in some of these countries.

The prominence of SSU recognition in activists' grievances has raised important debates about which LGBT rights concerns ought to be prioritized, how these issues should be linked together in activists' framing of grievances, and whether a progressive policy change concerning one issue leads to policy diffusion or damaging backlash in passing subsequent equality policies. Some scholars have argued that an incremental approach led to the legalization of same-sex marriage in the Netherlands, making it the first country to open up civil marriage to same-sex couples (Waaldijk 2004). In the incremental approach, small steps are sequentially taken and used to build up to the legalization of same-sex marriage. The Dutch process started with the decriminalization of homosexuality. In the 1970s, the Dutch government developed laws that applied to both married couples and to couples who are informally cohabiting, regardless of gender. Hence, it was possible for same-sex couples to foster children, but they continued to face difficulty in establishing their parenting rights. Due to pressure that built up in the 1990s, registered partnerships and adoption legislation came into effect in 1998, available to same-sex and opposite-sex cohabiting couples alike. In response to a report by a commission recommending the legalization of same-sex marriage, two bills were passed that opened up marriage and adoption to same-sex couples. Additionally, two subsequent bills were passed replacing gender-specific language with gender-neutral language in legislation and granting automatic joint parental authority to both parents when a child is born to one partner in a couple, yet requiring adoption to obtain legal parental status. As predicted by the incremental approach, many countries that first introduced registered partnerships have subsequently created legislation allowing same-sex couples to marry.

However, the incremental approach, which focuses on securing registered partnerships, in advance of marriage or instead of marriage, has also been criticized for having delayed legal victories in securing same-sex marriage (Aloni 2010). Because most European civil unions conferred the same rights and obligations as civil marriage, the public perceived these institutions as having mitigated discrimination with remaining differences largely semantic. Some of the economic incentives that previously motivated activists to organize were diminished. Further, many European LGBT organizations were reluctant to advocate for same-sex marriage because LGBT communities often perceived marriage as promoting patriarchy and discrimination. In fact, major movement organizations in the United Kingdom, Germany, and France advocated for civil partnership over marriage, although some have since shifted standpoints while advocating for marriage equality.

Scholars and activists argue that viewing civil marriage as the end stage in a progression toward equality risks viewing same-sex marriage as the endpoint of LGBT activism and defining the acceptance of homosexuality via the extension of a heteronormous institution like marriage (Aloni 2010). Critics have suggested that some activists advancing marriage equality have embraced homonormativity and the status quo in society, without critiquing the privilege that marriage has been used to attain, socially, politically, and economically. Presenting marriage as the final step in achieving equality may result in misconceptions amongst the public about ongoing discrimination, even in states with SSU recognition. In countries like France, parenting rights are a much stronger wedge issue amongst the public than marriage is, contributing to laws prohibiting same-sex couples from using in vitro fertilization and surrogacy to have children. Accordingly, LGBT activists in many European countries have tended to focus on achieving legal recognition of relationships and equal rights as opposed to same-sex marriage. Key rights issues that have been advocated for concern are issues such as adoption, child custody, tax laws, and pension laws.

There have been several historical debates regarding rights-related framing within the LGBT movement in Europe (Kollman 2013). Although LGBT activists have historically adopted civil rights frames, the underlying assumptions of the movement were challenged in the 1970s, with the rise of sexual liberation movements. Liberation activists felt that rights-related approaches to LGBT rights were too strongly grounded in promoting the status quo in society, including the entrenched patriarchy and bourgeois values. In the 1980s, the growth of the international human rights regime, the spread of neoliberalism, as well as the dire impact of the HIV/AIDS epidemic, shifted the movement back toward human rights framing of grievances. Moreover, these developments were instrumental in the formation of several prominent SMOs that were rights-oriented and helped drive forward national campaigns for LGBT rights. In the late 1980s, a new generation of activists reappropriated and embraced the term "queer" in their sense of identity, organization names, and slogans. Queer activists have criticized rights-related approaches for being too conservative and homonormative and for failing to challenge social institutions that are discriminatory.

In each national context, a range of specialized NGOs and SMOs emerged to advocate for LGBT rights. Further, varied political, cultural, and historical influences have led to both cooperation and conflict amongst these organizations, which have in turn shaped their sense of identity, framing of grievances, and selection of tactics. In Britain, the liberation movements of the 1970s led radical activists to branch off, forming organizations such as the Gay Liberation Front (GLF) (Plummer 1999). Grassroots organizations such as GLF were committed to radical critiques of the status quo, using more militant tactics like direct action in order to advocate for a revolutionary restructuring of society, not just equal rights and acceptance of the LGBT community. GLF espoused socialism as the means to end all types of oppression and was characterized by many internal divides, limiting the duration of its existence. During this period, there was a departure of lesbians from the gay movement, with the emergence of a lesbian feminist movement. Lesbians critiqued the misogyny and sexism in the GLF and formed their own SMOs, but also encountered organizing challenges as a result of fractures in the feminist movement and backlash against feminism.

The need to respond effectively to HIV/AIDS helped to remobilize the British LGBT movement in the 1980s, with organizations such as the Terrence Higgins Trust adopting a more professionalized form of advocacy, which involved greater cooperation with the government and service providers (Plummer 1999). Proposed laws or reforms involving the LGBT community have also provided activists with useful targets around which to organize, but have sometimes led to schisms within the movement. In 1987, the Conservative government's introduction of Section 28, prohibiting local governments from promoting homosexuality, facilitated renewed cooperation between gays and lesbians in the movement and the overall remobilization of a more unified movement. Some queer activists were angry at the political climate and started to adopt more radical tactics, challenging the status quo. In the 1980s, many associations involved in LGBT rights activism became more formally organized and focused on advancing rights-based claims via professionalized lobbying. For example, the organization Stonewall was set up in 1989 and has been very successful in mobilizing resources, helping to draft equality legislation, lobbying politicians to support bills, and gaining the support of prominent allies such as celebrities. Sometimes such organizations have been criticized for their assimilationist approach and rights-based framing. The heightened visibility of the LGBT community, in both media coverage and Pride Marches, has accompanied this shift in LGBT organizing.

Although both insider and outsider tactics have been used to advocate for LGBT rights in different domestic contexts, the adoption of new equality policies, legislation, and government agencies may have created an opening in the POS for additional insider activism. In the United Kingdom, legislative reform such as the 2010 Equalities Act which added sexual orientation and gender identity as protected categories, created opportunities for insider activism within the state (Browne and Bakshi 2013). As a result, some activists, especially those who are involved in public sector services, have moved away from outsider activism and have started to work in close partnership with state organizations in implementing the new equality policies. Some scholars and activists have suggested that this cooperation with the state may have co-opted the movement, contributing to the deradicalization of certain factions, encouraging the adoption of an assimilationist approach, and limiting the usage of more oppositional tactics and critiques of mainstream politics.

The presence of "out" LGBT legislators and executives has also created openings in the POS for insider activism to advance LGBT rights, and in some cases, the representation of the LGBT community in the government is also a reflection of the changing status of LGBT rights and shifts in public opinion. In research on national legislatures from 1976 to 2011, the majority of out legislators were located in Western Europe (Reynolds 2013). Further, in Belgium, Iceland, Luxembourg, and Norway, gay or lesbian individuals have served as prime minister. Equality laws concerning six areas were explored: the decriminalization of homosexuality; marriage, civil unions, and registered partnerships; adoption rights; antidiscrimination; hate crimes; and bans against military service. Interestingly, the countries with the best equality law scores were predominantly located in Western Europe and were included among the first countries to open marriage to same-sex couples. States with LGBT legislators were considerably more likely to have SSU recognition laws. In addition, the presence of LGBT legislators increased the likelihood of passing progressive LGBT laws. Out legislators may influence their colleagues and thus impact legislation that is drafted, and the visibility of out politicians influences public opinion concerning the LGBT community and equal rights.

Although many European states have legal procedures for gender recognition, there are various conceptual and human rights concerns regarding these laws (Hines 2009). Most states require extensive psychological counseling and a diagnosis of gender identity disorder, and some states require gender reassignment surgery, sterilization, and either single-status or divorce. Some states prohibit individuals who have transitioned from marrying. Advocates have campaigned to challenge trans* pathologization, removing gender identity disorder as a diagnosis, demedicalizing the requirements for transitioning, and enabling individuals to remain married or marry after transitioning. The Gender Recognition Act in the United Kingdom did not impose a surgery requirement, but essentially required married individuals to divorce in order to receive a full gender recognition certificate. Officials argued that couples seeking legal recognition of their families could instead pursue civil partnerships. Hence, the law is critiqued for its emphasis on medical interventions as a mechanism for altering bodily appearance and presentation and assumptions that gender identity and sexual orientation are binary, not fluid concepts.

Increasing numbers of European SMOs have incorporated trans* identity into their names and advocacy objectives. However, this shift may sometimes reflect international pressure to embrace the LGBT acronym and the desire to provide resources to trans* advocates, more so than a change in grassroots support (Eeckhout 2011). In some cases, lesbian, gay, and bisexual (LGB) organizations decided on their own to be more inclusive and advocate for trans* rights, but were critiqued for not adequately being guided by and inclusive of trans* voices. Internally, some organization members have been resistant to making changes due to different understandings of distinctions between gender versus sexuality and the history of LGBT and liberation movements. As the trans* community has often felt excluded by LGB movements in Europe, NGOs and SMOs devoted to trans* rights were established to advocate for equality. However, many trans* organizations lacked in resources and longevity, and similar challenges have arisen in facilitating cooperation amongst these groups. At the European level, Transgender Europe has emerged as an important TAN linking domestic organizations together and targeting European institutions to advocate for trans* rights.

SEE ALSO: Civil Rights Law and Gender in the United States; Heteronormativity and Homonormativity; Human Rights, International Laws and Policies on; Identity Politics; Lesbian and Gay Movements; NGOs and Grassroots Organizing; Same-Sex Marriage; Sexual Orientation and the Law; Transgender Movements in the United States

REFERENCES

Aloni, Erez. 2010. "Incrementalism, Civil Unions, and the Possibility of Predicting Legal Recognition of Same-Sex Marriage." *Duke Journal of Gender Law and Policy*, 18(1): 105–161.

Ayoub, Phillip M. 2013. "Cooperative Transnationalism in Contemporary Europe: Europeanization and Political Opportunities for LGBT Mobilization in the European Union." *European Political Science Review*, 5(2): 279–310. DOI: 10.1017/S1755773912000161.

Browne, Kath, and Leela Bakshi. 2013. "Insider Activists: The Fraught Possibilities of LGBT Activisms From Within." *Geoforum*, 49: 253–262. DOI: 10.1016/j.geoforum.2012.10.013.

Eeckhout, Bart. 2011. "Queer in Belgium: Ignorance, Goodwill, Compromise." In *Queer in Europe*, edited by Lisa Downing and Robert Gillett, 11–24. Surrey: Ashgate.

Hines, Sally. 2009. "A Pathway to Diversity?: Human Rights, Citizenship and the Politics of Transgender." *Contemporary Politics*, 15(1): 87–102. DOI: 10.1080/13569770802674238.

Kollman, Kelly. 2009. "European Institutions, Transnational Networks and National Same-Sex Unions Policy: When Soft Law Hits Harder." *Contemporary Politics*, 15(1): 37–53. DOI: 10.1080/13569770802674204.

Kollman, Kelly. 2013. *The Same-Sex Unions Revolution in Western Democracies: International Norms and Domestic Policy Change*. Manchester: Manchester University Press.

Plummer, Ken. 1999. "The Lesbian and Gay Movement in Britain: Schisms, Solidarities, and Social Worlds." In *The Global Emergence of Gay and Lesbian Politics: National Imprints of a Worldwide Movement*, edited by Barry D. Adam, Jan Willem Duyvendak, and André Krouwel, 133–157. Philadelphia: Temple University Press.

Reynolds, Andrew. 2013. "Representation and Rights: The Impact of LGBT Legislators in Comparative Perspective." *American Political Science Review*, 107(2): 259–274. DOI: 10.1017/S0003055413000051.

Waaldijk, Kees. 2004. "Others May Follow: The Introduction of Marriage, Quasi-Marriage, and Semi-Marriage for Same-Sex Couples in European Countries." *New England Law Review*, 38: 569–589.

FURTHER READING

Ayoub, Phillip, and David Paternotte, eds. 2014. *LGBT Activism and the Making of Europe: A Rainbow Europe?* Basingstoke: Palgrave Macmillan.

Beger, Nico J. 2004. *Tensions in the Struggle for Sexual Minority Rights in Europe: Que[e]rying Political Practices.* Manchester: Manchester University Press.

Blasius, Mark, ed. 2001. *Sexual Identities, Queer Politics.* Princeton: Princeton University Press.

Tremblay, Manon, David Paternotte, and Carol Johnson, eds. 2011. *The Lesbian and Gay Movement and the State: Comparative Insights into a Transformed Relationship.* Farnham: Ashgate.

Life Expectancy

YUEJEN ZHAO

Department of Health, Northern Territory, Australia

CALCULATION

The period life table remains a commonly used instrument for measuring the overall health status of a population or a country. Let e_x^0 designate the life expectancy at age x, which is calculated as $e_x^0 = T_x/l_x$, where l_x is the number of persons left alive at age x, and the person-years lived above age x is

$$T_x = \sum_{i=x}^{\infty} {}_nL_i$$

in the hypothetical cohort. The person-years lived between ages x and $x + n$ is

$${}_nL_x = n \cdot l_{x+n} + {}_na_x \cdot n \cdot {}_nd_x$$

where $l_{x+n} = l_x - {}_nd_x$
${}_nd_x = l_x \cdot {}_nq_x$
${}_nq_x = \frac{n \cdot {}_nm_x}{1+(1-{}_na_x) \cdot n \cdot {}_nm_x}$
${}_nm_x = \frac{{}_nD_x}{{}_nN_x}$

${}_na_x$ = Average fraction of the age interval lived by individuals who die in the interval
${}_nD_x$ = Deaths between ages x and $x + n$
${}_nN_x$ = Mid-year population between ages x and $x + n$.

For technical details of the period life table calculations, especially for the first and last age groups, see Preston, Heuveline, and Guillot (2001). Life expectancy is a product of many physical, environmental, and social factors. It cannot be attributed solely to any single risk or contributing factor.

Differences in life expectancy can be broken down by age, cause of death, and health risks (Preston, Heuveline, and Guillot 2001; Zhao et al. 2013). Life expectancy patterns among selected populations are apparent.

PATTERNS

Time trends

Globally, life expectancy has improved progressively over recent decades (Figure 1) (World Health Organization 2013; World Bank 2014). The total life expectancy at birth has steadily increased from 52.5 years in 1960 to 70.5 years in 2011 worldwide, so by 18 years in 50 years (World Bank 2014).

Sex

Females tend to survive better than males in all age groups, even prenatally, and in nearly all species (Kalben 2001). Worldwide, men's life expectancy at birth averages 4.2 years less than women's (World Bank 2014), with a maximum difference of 12 years in Russia (World Life Expectancy 2014b). About 90 percent of people aged over 110 years are female. The reason remains unclear. There is strong evidence to suggest that all genetic, environmental, and behavioral factors are associated with gender inequality in human life expectancy (Kalben 2001).

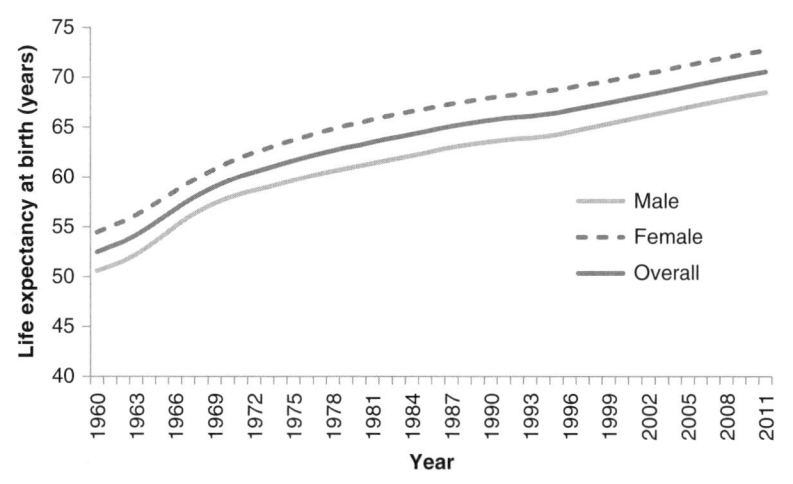

Figure 1 Global life expectancy at birth by sex, 1960–2011. Data source: World Development Indicators 2014 by World Bank Publications. Accessed September 02, 2015, at http://data.worldbank.org/data-catalog/world-development-indicators/wdi-2014.

Research indicates that mitochondrial mutations that shorten lifespan are more likely to be expressed in males than in females, because mitochondria are inherited only through the mother (Camus, Clancy, and Dowling 2012). Although the discovery of genes affecting longevity will lead to longer lives, non-genetic changes likely explain the human lifespan increases to date (Vaupel et al. 1998). A much greater socioeconomic gradient was found in life expectancy among men than among women. Cultural, social, environmental, health risk behavioral factors, and health service use are believed to have a major role in the sex differences.

Age

The life expectancy at different ages is the number of additional years a person can expect to live, obtained directly from the life tables. After birth, life expectancy initially increases with age as individuals survive high infant mortality. As age increases, life expectancy converges (Preston, Heuveline, and Guillot 2001). Aging arises from improved longevity and decreasing fertility. Globally, the number of elderly people aged 60 years and older was projected to double, from 841 million in 2013 to 2 billion in 2050 (United Nations 2014). The elderly population is predominantly female. In 2013, there were 85 men per 100 women in the age group 60 years or over globally, and 61 men per 100 women in the age group 80 years or over (United Nations 2014).

Countries and regions

There is a high level of inequality in life expectancy among different countries. The four countries with the highest life expectancy at birth (combined male and female) in 2011 were Switzerland (82.7 years), Japan (82.6), Iceland (82.4), and Spain (82.3). The countries with the lowest life expectancy at birth were Sierra Leone (45.1), Botswana (46.7), Lesotho (48.2), and Swaziland (48.7) (World Bank 2014). The life expectancy differences by country relate to economic circumstances, public health, and human behavior. Regional and geographic variations in life expectancy within a country were also evident.

Race

The life expectancy gap between white and black populations in the United States was 5.3 years (77.9 and 72.6 years) in 2003. The indigenous and non-indigenous life expectancy gap in Australia was 12 years for men and 10 years for women in 2005–2007. The racial life expectancy gap is believed to be mainly driven by socioeconomic disadvantage and behavioral health risks (Zhao et al. 2013).

Education

Difference in life expectancy at age 25 between high and low education was 5.4–8.4 years (Meara, Richards, and Cutler 2008). The life expectancy educational gap increased by 30 percent between the 1980s and 1990s.

Income, unemployment, and economic circumstances

In 2012, life expectancy at birth ranged from 62 years in low income countries to 79 years in high income countries (World Health Organization 2014a). Life expectancy gain was of the same order as income gains. Generally, areas with higher life expectancy and lower infant mortality tended to have higher social class for both males and females (Department of Health 2005). Areas with higher male life expectancy tended to have higher male employment rates. There is also a growing consensus that improving health can have equally large indirect payoffs for accelerating economic growth.

RISK FACTORS

Tobacco, alcohol, and other drugs have been found to have an impact on life expectancy. Long-term tobacco smoking reduces life expectancy, on average, by 10 years (Doll et al. 2004). However, life expectancy can be increased by 4–10 years by smoking cessation. In Finland, alcohol-related deaths were responsible for a 2-year loss in life expectancy at age 15 years among men and 0.4 years among women in 1987–1993 (Mäkelä 1998). However, long-term light alcohol intake possibly increased life expectancy (Streppel et al. 2009). Illicit drugs have a severely negative impact on life expectancy. Depending upon the drug, the life expectancy is 15–20 years after becoming a drug addict (Smyth, Fan, and Hser 2006; World Life Expectancy 2014a). Cocaine addicts often die within 5 years from the time they begin heavy usage. In a cohort study, heroin addiction contributed to a reduction in life expectancy of 15 years (Smyth, Fan, and Hser 2006).

Of risk factors relating to the body, overweight and obesity are associated with 3–7 years loss in life expectancy (Peeters et al. 2003). Research suggests that sexual activity seems to improve life expectancy for middle-aged men (Smith, Frankel, and Yarnell 1997). A life table analysis noted that life expectancy at age 20 years for gay and bisexual men was 8–20 years less than for all men (Hogg et al. 1997).

Other risk factors

The negative effect of famine on life expectancy was stronger for boys than for girls. Boys and girls lost on average 4 and 2.5 years of life, respectively, after exposure at birth to famine. Lower social classes appeared to be more severely affected by early exposure to famine than higher social classes.

UNDERLYING CAUSES OF DEATH

Infectious diseases

Infectious diseases adversely affect life expectancy. Between 1944 and 1972, human life expectancy jumped by 8 years, largely attributed to the introduction of antibiotics against bacterial infections. According to estimates made by the United Nations, HIV/AIDS reduced life expectancy at birth by 9.5 years in 38 affected countries in Africa in 2000–2005 (United Nations 2004). The life expectancy of patients with HIV/AIDS was around 47 years in 1996–2008 (Wada et al. 2013).

Non-infectious diseases

Cardiovascular disease reduced life expectancy by 6.4–7.1 years. Eliminating heart disease would increase life expectancy at birth by 3.7 years, ischemic heart disease by 2.5 years, and cancer by 3.2–3.9 years (Arias, Heron, and Tejada-Vera 2013).

The data from the Framingham Heart Study showed diabetic men and women aged 50 years and older lived on average 7.8 and 8.4 years less than their non-diabetic counterparts (Franco et al. 2007). The life expectancy of people with diabetes was likely to be reduced by 10 years (Diabetes UK 2010) as a result of the condition.

SPECIAL APPLICATIONS

Healthy life expectancy

Healthy life expectancy summarizes mortality and non-fatal outcomes, and compares health between countries. Compared with substantial progress in the reduction of mortality over the past two decades, relatively little progress has been made in the reduction of the overall effect of non-fatal disease and injury on population health.

Active and inactive life expectancies

Inactive life expectancy is often used in measuring disabilities. It defines the period of life individuals can expect to live with severe disability, being unable to provide independent living or personal care. The inactive life expectancy for females was about twice that for males.

SEE ALSO: Aging, Ageism, and Gender; Cardiac Disease and Gender; Disease Symptoms, Gender Differences in

REFERENCES

Arias, Elizabeth, Melonie Heron, and Betzaida Tejada-Vera. 2013. "United States Life Tables Eliminating Certain Causes of Death, 1999–2001." *National Vital Statistics Reports*, 61(9): 1–128.

Camus, M. Florencia, David J. Clancy, and Damian K. Dowling. 2012. "Mitochondria, Maternal Inheritance, and Male Aging." *Current Biology*, 22(18): 1717–1721.

Department of Health. 2005. *Tackling Health Inequalities: Status Report on the Programme for Action*. London: Department of Health.

Diabetes UK. 2010. *Diabetes in the UK 2010: Key Statistics on Diabetes*. London: Diabetes UK.

Doll, Richard, Richard Peto, Jillian Boreham, and Isabelle Sutherland. 2004. "Mortality in Relation to Smoking: 50 years' Observations on Male British Doctors." *British Medical Journal*, 328: 1519.

Franco, Oscar H., Ewout W. Steyerberg, Frank B. Hu, Johan Mackenbach, and Wilma Nusselder. 2007. "Associations of Diabetes Mellitus With Total Life Expectancy and Life Expectancy With and Without Cardiovascular Disease." *Archives of Internal Medicine*, 167(11): 1145–1151.

Guinness World Records. 2014. "Oldest Person." Accessed September 2, 2015, at http://www.guinnessworldrecords.com/records-5000/oldest-person/.

Hogg, Robert S., Steffanie A. Strathdee, K.J. Craib, Michael V. O'Shaughnessy, J.S. Montaner, and Martin T. Schechter. 1997. "Modelling the Impact of HIV disease on Mortality in Gay and Bisexual Men." *International Journal of Epidemiology*, 26(3): 657–661.

Kalben, B.B. 2001. *Why Men Die Younger: Causes of Mortality Differences by Sex*. Illinois: Society of Actuaries.

Mäkelä, Pia. 1998. "Alcohol-Related Mortality by Age and Sex and its Impact on Life Expectancy Estimates Based on the Finnish Death Register." *European Journal of Public Health*, 8(1): 43–51.

Meara, Ellen R., Seth Richards, and David M. Cutler. 2008. "The Gap Gets Bigger: Changes in Mortality and Life Expectancy, by Education, 1981–2000." *Health Affairs*, 27(2): 350–360.

Peeters, Anna, Jan J. Barendregt, Frans Willekens, Johan P. Mackenbach, Abdullah Al Mamun, and Luc Bonneux. 2003. "Obesity in Adulthood and its Consequences for Life Expectancy: A Life-Table Analysis." *Annals of Internal Medicine*, 138(1): 24–32.

Preston, S., P. Heuveline, and M. Guillot. 2001. *Demography: Measuring and Modeling Population Processes*. Victoria: Blackwell.

Shryock, H.S., J.S. Siegel, and E.A. Larmon. 1980. *The Methods and Materials of Demography*. Washington, DC: Department of Commerce, Bureau of the Census.

Smith, George Davey, Stephen Frankel, and John Yarnell. 1997. "Sex and Death: Are They Related? Findings from the Caerphilly Cohort Study." *British Medical Journal*, 315: 1641–1644.

Smyth, Breda, Jing Fan, and Yih-Ing Hser. 2006. "Life Expectancy and Productivity Loss Among Narcotics Addicts Thirty-Three Years After Index Treatment." *Journal of Addictive Diseases*, 25(4): 37–47.

Streppel, Martinette T., Marga C. Ocké, Hendriek C. Boshuizen, Frans J. Kok, and Daan Kromhout. 2009. "Long-Term Wine Consumption is Related to Cardiovascular Mortality and Life Expectancy Independently of Moderate Alcohol Intake: The Zutphen Study." *Journal of Epidemiology and Community Health*, 63(7): 534–540.

United Nations. 2004. *World Population Prospects: The 2002 Revision*. New York: United Nations.

United Nations. 2014. *World Population Aging, 2013*. New York: United Nations.

Vaupel, James W., et al. 1998. "Biodemographic Trajectories of Longevity." *Science*, 280: 855–860.

Wada, Nikolas, Lisa P. Jacobson, Mardge Cohen, Audrey French, John Phair, and Alvaro Muñoz. 2013. "Cause-Specific Life Expectancies After 35 Years of Age for Human Immunodeficiency Syndrome-Infected and Human Immunodeficiency Syndrome-Negative Individuals Followed Simultaneously in Long-Term Cohort Studies, 1984–2008." *American Journal of Epidemiology*, 177(2): 116–125.

World Bank. 2014. "World Development Indicators: Data 2014." Accessed September 2, 2015, at http://data.worldbank.org/data-catalog/world-development-indicators?cid=GPD_WDI.

World Health Organization. 2013. *World Health Statistics 2013*. Geneva: WHO.

World Health Organization. 2014a. "*Global Health Observatory*." Accessed September 2, 2015, at http://www.who.int/gho/mortality_burden_disease/life_tables/situation_trends_text/en/.

World Health Organization. 2014b. "Life Expectancy." Accessed September 2, 2015, at http://www.who.int/topics/life_expectancy/en/.

World Life Expectancy. 2014a. "Addiction and Your Brain." Accessed September 2, 2015, at http://www.worldlifeexpectancy.com/addiction-and-your-brain.

World Life Expectancy. 2014b. "Life Expectancy Gender Ratio 2014." Accessed September 2, 2015, at http://www.worldlifeexpectancy.com/gender-ratio-by-country.

Zhao, Yuejen, Jo Wright, Stephen Begg, and Steven Guthridge. 2013. "Decomposing Indigenous Life Expectancy Gap by Risk Factors: A Life Table Analysis." *Population Health Metrics*, 11(1): 1.

Lookism

JACQUELINE GRANLEESE
University of East Anglia, UK

Lookism, a term coined in the late 1970s (Ayto 1999), describes a form of discrimination based on an individual's physical appearance. It is underpinned by social science research that explores cultural stereotypes of beauty and physical attractiveness such as Langlois et al.'s (2000) meta-analytic study of facial attractiveness findings from 1932 to 1999. They found a common standard of beauty both within and across cultures, with attractive adults and children being judged more favorably and tending to demonstrate more positive behaviors and traits than those judged unattractive. Lookism occurs when individuals are compared to the stereotype either to their detriment or advantage. Rhode (2010) argues that lookism occurs across a range of inherent characteristics that are "fixed" at birth, such as face and body morphology, to those that may be considered more "mutable" in nature (e.g. clothes, make-up, grooming).

Individuals' physical appearance has been researched in the economic literature linking physical characteristics such as beauty, hair color, obesity, and height to labor market outcomes. Evidence to date suggests that in the United States there is a wage premium for some physical characteristics of 1–13 percent for above average looking people and a penalty of 1–15 percent for below average looking people. Controlling for factors such as intelligence levels, a longitudinal study of 11,000 UK people born in 1958, found unattractive men's pay penalty is 4–15 percent, and approximately 11 percent for unattractive women (Harper 2000). Individuals, irrespective of gender, who are judged as more beautiful or attractive than average, blonde women, and taller men earn more money during their working life and are more likely to be promoted than their less attractive, brunette, and shorter colleagues. Women in male-dominated jobs/professions, however, may find their attractiveness counts against them in the promotion stakes. Moreover, an individual is less likely to be employed, or, when employed, less likely to be promoted if they are obese.

There is a paucity of legislation to protect individuals against lookism. In the United States, Michigan became the first state to explicitly prohibit discrimination based on weight and height, as do the cities of Santa Cruz, Binghampton, and San Francisco. Washington D.C. prohibits all forms of personal appearance discrimination, while Urbana, Illinois, and Madison, Wisconsin have ordinances banning discrimination based on "personal appearance" and "physical appearance," respectively. The Equal Employment Opportunity Commission now views the extremely obese, or those whose obesity results in physical ailments, as disabled. Such individuals are thus protected by the Americans with Disabilities Act 1990. Where there is no legislation to protect against lookism in the United States, cases as applicable are cobbled onto other civil rights legislation (see Cavico, Muffler, and Mujtaba 2012 for a fuller discussion). Most US jurisdictions, however, do not consider lookism as unlawful.

In the United Kingdom, also subject to the jurisdiction of the European Union, there is no legislation covering discrimination on the grounds of physical appearance other than where such discrimination is covered in the Equality Act 2010 by the protected categories of sex, race, age, sexual orientation particularly transgender individuals, religious belief, and disability. Following the *Eweida v. British Airways plc* case, the airport worker who took her case to the European Court of Human Rights and won the right to wear a religious cross to work, some aspects of personal appearance bias may be covered by the Human Rights Act 1998.

The state of Victoria, Australia, remains the only jurisdiction outside the United States that places an explicit ban on appearance-related bias. Since the law's introduction in 1995, now covered by the state's Equality Act 2010, the protected category of "physical features" (a person's height, weight, size, or other bodily characteristics) has resulted in thousands of lookism complaints being dealt with by the Victorian Equal Opportunity and Human Rights Commission. In other Australian states, where applicable, lookism cases are considered under other discrimination legislation.

Increasingly, companies, especially in the retail industry, are employing individuals who exemplify their brand and or image, such as Abercrombie & Fitch's desire to employ an "all American" workforce, or Google's youthful corporate culture. Such lookist branding activities may result in discrimination cases being brought against employers, if no defense can be made for a Genuine Occupational Characteristic (UK) or a Bona-fide Occupational Qualification (United States). Indeed, Abercrombie & Fitch were sued by employees of color in the US federal court under civil rights laws, reaching an out of court settlement at a cost of $50 million.

Employees who suffer lookism may take cases under other discrimination legislation not just because there is a lack of legislative support, but because lookism is associated with other forms of discrimination. Granleese and Sayer (2006) argue that you look old or young, male or female, and white or of color. Hence, lookism is inextricably linked to the "fixed" elements of physical appearance which may give rise to agism, sexism, and racism. Moreover, some forms of body gloss (e.g., turbans, burkas, i.e., "mutable" forms of physical appearance) are associated with religious beliefs. Hence, you look like a Sikh man or a Moslem woman which may result in individuals being discriminated against on the basis of lookism *and* religious beliefs.

Lookism is a growing area of research interest in economics, termed "pulchronomics": focus being given to the need to disentangle the confounding variable of levels of productivity from pay penalty and pay premium measures. In employment law, in what has been called the "new frontier" of employment discrimination, opinion is more divided. Tietje and Cresap (2005) argue against state intervention, stating that policy interventions to redress lookism cannot be justified on moral grounds until it is shown that beauty discrimination is unjust. Malos (2007) argues that given court treatment of discrimination cases based on physical appearance is inconsistent, employers should develop their own policies to limit their legal liability. Most researchers support the need for future research to identify apposite discrimination laws to provide adequate remedies for those discriminated against on the grounds of lookism.

SEE ALSO: Appearance Psychology; Beauty Industry; Visual Culture; Visual Culture and Gender

REFERENCES

Ayto, John. 1999. *Twentieth Century Words*. New York: Oxford University Press.

Cavico, Frank J., Stephen C. Muffler, and Bahaudin G. Mujtaba. 2012. "Appearance Discrimination in Employment: Legal and Ethical Implications of 'Lookism' and 'Lookphobia'." *Equality, Diversity, and Inclusion: An International Journal*, 32(1): 83–119.

Granleese, Jacqueline, and Gemma Sayer. 2006. "Gendered Ageism and 'Lookism': A Triple Jeopardy for Female Academics." *Women in Management Review*, 21(6): 500–517.

Harper, Barry. 2000. "Beauty, Stature and the Labour Market: A British Cohort Study." *Oxford Bulletin of Economics and Statistics*, 62: 771–800.

Langlois, Judith H., et al. 2000. "Maxims or Myths of Beauty? A Meta-analytic and Theoretical Review." *Psychological Bulletin*, 126: 390–423.

Malos, Stan. 2007. "Appearance-based Sex Discrimination and Stereotyping in the Workplace: Whose Conduct Should we Regulate?" *Employees Responsibilities and Rights Journal*, 19: 95–111.

Rhode, Deborah L. 2010. *The Beauty Bias: The Injustice of Appearance in Life and Law*. New York: Oxford University Press.

Tietje, Louis, and Steven Cresap. 2005. "Is Lookism Unjust?: The Ethics of Aesthetics and Public Policy Implications." *Journal of Libertarian Studies*, 19(2): 31–50.

FURTHER READING

Hamermesh, Daniel S. 2011. *Beauty Pays: Why Attractive People Are More Successful*. Princeton: Princeton University Press.

Mail-Order Brides

LAURA V. HESTON
University of Massachusetts Amherst, USA

International Marriage Agencies (henceforth, IMAs) insist, "There is no such thing as a 'mail-order bride.'" Men do not simply pick women out of catalogs, send money, and have wives show up on their doorsteps. However, in the popular imagination, "mail-order bride" refers to women of the Global South engaged in the market for commercially arranged marriage migration which pairs them with men from the Global North. Unlike other international dating websites, IMAs showcase pictures of available women often without requiring men to produce similar profiles, leaving the prerogative to initiate contact, often for a fee, in the hands of men. However, women maintain the option of accepting or rejecting any contact with men, let alone marriage proposals. Thus, "mail-order bride" is a misnomer for a complex, negotiated courtship between women of the Global South and men of the Global North. A less inflammatory term for this process is *commercial marriage migration* (Constable 2003), thus "mail-order bride" has been put in quotes to denote the term's contested nature. Still, the commercial marriage process, with its mixing of money and intimacy, older men with younger women, and the geopolitical inequities that serve as a necessary context, continues to inspire uneasy feelings.

The term "mail-order bride" originated in the early nineteenth century when Japanese men working in the United States received pictures of available women from matchmakers in their home country. Later, US servicemen met and married women during wars and military interventions in the Philippines, Korea, and Vietnam paving the way for intercultural, international marriages (Constable 2003). Returning veterans raved to other men about the superiority of foreign women. Whereas women of the Global North were seemingly abdicating their roles as wives and mothers by entering the labor force and organizing for equal rights, women of the Global South were framed as "more traditional" and better marriage material. After the dissolution of the Soviet Union, IMAs began listing women from former Soviet states which vastly increased the number of IMA websites. IMAs position these women "between East and West," possessing both traditional values and "modern" sensibilities (read: whiteness) (Taraban 2006). Overall, the idea that better wives existed elsewhere combined with well-established trade networks and immigration flows lead to the "global outsourcing of the family" that commercial marriage represents as well as the anxieties it stirs in residents of the Global North (Schaeffer-Grabiel 2006; So 2006).

Since the early 1990s, bride catalogs have moved, *en masse*, online and marriage agencies have proliferated; over 350 such websites were cataloged in 2003 (Constable 2003). With the help of IMAs, men have the opportunity to sift through thousands of women's pictures and profiles. This gives those already in structurally privileged positions – being from the Global North, often much older, and always men – the opportunity to "shop" for potential wives, by purchasing email addresses, expanded profiles, and risqué pictures. Reflecting on the process, one researcher states, "I had read the reassurances from the company's site that I was only buying addresses … but it still felt as if I were buying *them*" (Johnson 2007, 15, emphasis in original).

Marriage agencies situate women as objects to peruse and facilitate racial and ethnic stereotyping of the women on their websites by characterizing them as exotic, submissive, and family-focused (Schaeffer-Grabiel 2006). For instance, IMAs listing the profiles of Asian women routinely call upon the controlling image of the "Lotus Blossom" – quiet, docile, and submissive – to enforce what men in the Global North "already know" about Asian women (Tajima 1989). Universally, women of the Global South involved in commercial marriage are framed as focused on caring for their future husbands and children, not minding large age differences with their spouses, and being uncorrupted by feminism (Schaeffer-Grabiel 2006). These stereotypes also dominate media representations of "mail-order brides" in film and literature informing men's expectations (So 2006; Zare and Mendoza 2011).

On the contrary, women of the Philippines, China, Columbia, Russia, Ukraine, and other countries ready and willing to immigrate to the United States and other nations of the Global North do so for increased financial opportunities, often so they can become fully employed and send remittances back to their families (Constable 2003). These women are ready to relocate to a new country (hardly a "traditional" decision), and, contra men's expectations, global and local feminist movements are present in all these countries. They are also fed stereotypes of men of the Global North as progressive and comfortable with their wives being employed, though they are more likely to meet conservative men looking for housewives (Johnson 2007; Schaeffer-Grabiel 2006).

For those outside the union, the "mail-order bride" is the crystallization of commercialized intimacy and the supposed creeping of global capital into domestic life. Ultimately, the specter of the "mail-order bride" is so feared because it threatens to expose the commercial nature of all marriages (So 2006).

SEE ALSO: Arranged Marriages (in South Asia); Human Trafficking, Feminist Perspectives on; Immigration and Gender; Orientalism; Visual Culture and Gender

REFERENCES

Constable, Nicole. 2003. *Romance on a Global Stage*. Berkeley: University of California Press.

Johnson, Ericka. 2007. *Dreaming of a Mail-Order Husband*. Durham, NC: Duke University Press.

Schaeffer-Grabiel, Felicity. 2006. "Planet-love.com: Cyberbrides in the Americas and the Transnational Routes of U.S. Masculinity." *Signs*, 31(2): 331–356.

So, Christine. 2006. "Asian Mail-Order Brides, the Threat of Global Capitalism, and the Rescue of the U.S. Nation-State." *Feminist Studies*, 32(2): 395–419.

Tajima, Renee E. 1989. "Lotus Blossoms Don't Bleed." In *Making Waves*, edited by Asian Women United of California. Boston: Beacon Press.

Taraban, Svitlana. 2006. "Birthday Girls, Russian Dolls, and Others: Internet Bride as the Emerging Global Identity of Post-Soviet Women." In *Living Gender after Communism*, edited by J. E. Johnson and J. C. Robinson. Bloomington: Indiana University Press.

Zare, Bonnie, and S. Lily Mendoza. 2011. "'Mail-Order Brides' in Popular Culture: Colonialist Representations and Absent Discourse." *International Journal of Cultural Studies*, 15(4): 365–381.

FURTHER READING

Lu, Melody Chia-Wen. 2005. "Commercially Arranged Marriage Migration: Case Studies of Cross-Border Marriages in Taiwan." *Indian Journal of Gender Studies*, 12(2–3): 275–303.

Thai, Hung Cam. 2008. *For Better or For Worse*. New Brunswick: Rutgers University Press.

Male Circumcision

LAUREN M. SARDI
Quinnipiac University, USA

Male circumcision is the removal of the prepuce, or foreskin, from the glans, or head, of the penis. In the United States and other Western countries, this surgical procedure is usually performed for non-religious reasons in a hospital setting shortly after birth, although the procedure is also performed outside of the hospital for religious reasons as well. Male neonatal circumcision is considered to be the most common medical procedure practiced in the United States. Male circumcision is also performed in other English-speaking countries such as Canada, Australia, and England, but to a much lesser extent (Gollaher 2000; Darby 2005).

Male circumcision is also performed for religious reasons among both the Muslim and Jewish communities. In the Muslim community, circumcision is not religiously mandated and there is no fixed age for the procedure to be completed; however, it is ritualized in a way to welcome the boy into the faith and into the larger religious community. For Jews, a boy is circumcised on his eighth day of life in a ceremony known as *brit milah*, or "Covenant of Circumcision." While male circumcision has been practiced among numerous societies for thousands of years for various reasons, the procedure became increasingly medicalized and also popularized within the United States and Great Britain, coinciding with the advent of germ theory as well as the rise of the Victorian era. Circumcision was seen as a "self-protective" measure against masturbation, which was once believed to have caused a variety of "social illnesses" such as insanity, hysteria, clumsiness, and even death. As the link between masturbation and such issues became weaker over time, many in the medical community blamed the foreskin itself for a number of illnesses, such as paralysis, epilepsy, blindness, gout, gangrene, tuberculosis, and phimosis (Wallerstein 1980; Goldman 1997; Gollaher 2000; Darby 2005).

As circumcision has popularly been called "a cure in search of a disease" by filmmaker Eli Ungar-Sargon and by many other anti-circumcision scholars and historians, the "fear of the foreskin" has been maintained through a host of new medical theories which state that circumcision substantially lowers the risk of HIV/AIDS transmission from females to males. Such studies performed over the past decade in sub-Saharan Africa have added to this argument, although many of these studies have been criticized for their methodology, ethics, lack of demographic similarity, and overall inability to make cross-cultural comparisons (Boyle and Hill 2011).

Currently, many scholars have noted that parents choose to circumcise their boys for non-medical reasons, such that cultural or social factors play a much more prominent role in their decisions (Tiemstra 1999; Adler, Ottaway, and Gould 2001; Binner et al. 2002).

Parents often choose to circumcise based on a number reasons including the desire to have their sons "match" their fathers, the notion that the circumcised penis "looks better," and the fear that if their son is left uncircumcised, he will be teased by other boys for having a "different appearance" (often referred to as the "locker room argument").

Numerous scholars, activists, medical providers, and parents have begun to challenge male neonatal circumcision, which until recently was routinely performed on the majority of all boys born in the United States (Owings, Uddin, and Williams 2013) without much question – or even informed consent. Not only have such individuals questioned the necessity of the procedure, but they have also questioned the ethical and legal issues surrounding male circumcision. Such people often call themselves "intactivists," which combines the terms "intact," or uncircumcised penis, with "activist," although not all people who are against the procedure would consider themselves intactivists.

Opponents of circumcision argue that the procedure is cosmetic and medically unnecessary at best, and at worst, is permanently mutilating and can cause death. Thus, performing a cosmetic surgery on an infant who is too young to give consent on his own behalf is a violation of the Hippocratic Oath and is also a violation of the standards of informed consent. While parents or legal caregivers are able to provide proxy consent for a medically necessary procedure on behalf of a child who is too young to consent on his own, anti-circumcision activists argue that proxy consent cannot apply in a situation where a child is undergoing a cosmetic and medically unnecessary procedure. Therefore, such opponents argue that the decision to circumcise must be left up to the child himself once he is legally able to provide informed consent on his own behalf (Goldman 1997; Sardi 2011). Scholars also note that while girls are legally protected against any type of circumcision or genital cutting, often referred to as female genital mutilation/cutting, boys are not protected against what is often considered by some to be the gendered equivalent of Type I FGM/C, which includes the removal of female foreskin from the clitoris (Bell 2005; Sardi 2011).

Another controversy surrounding circumcision is that a male's circumcision status may also permanently alter his sexual experiences. Foreskin is noted as having a number of beneficial functions, as it is a healthy and normal part of all mammalian genitalia. Some studies note that foreskin is considered to be the most erogenous part of the penis with thousands of nerve endings that enhance sexual experience (Sorrells et al. 2007; Bronselaer et al. 2013). When not erect, the foreskin may also cover the glans completely, keeping the skin moist and soft. Otherwise, over time, an exposed glans leads to dry, tough, and calloused skin. Foreskin contains the frenulum, a band of tissue on the underside of the shaft of the penis that connects the foreskin to the glans and is particularly sensitive to stimulation. The foreskin also houses a rigid band of tissue that assists in the "gliding" motion of the penis during heterosexual sexual intercourse. This gliding allows the penis to move more easily and with less friction within the vagina. Such friction can cause vaginal pain, dryness, and bleeding after intercourse. However, other studies have noted that there is no change or decrease of sexual function as a result of circumcision.

Circumcision status also serves as a way for the male body to be "marked." Depending upon the culture in which a male lives, his genitals are labeled by his circumcision status in that his body may demonstrate religious or hegemonic masculine norms, or he may stand out due to whether or not his foreskin is still present (Glick 2005). For example, in the United States, the hegemonic norm for a male is to be circumcised, such that in some instances, the masculinity of a male who is uncircumcised may be called into question in that his body is considered "deviant," or not within the culturally inscribed norms of American culture. These norms, however, are slowly changing over time as fewer boys are circumcised at birth.

SEE ALSO: Masculinities; Medicine and Medicalization; Sexual Regulation and Social Control

REFERENCES

Adler, Robert, Sandra Ottaway, and Stacey Gould. 2001. "Circumcision: We Have Heard from the Experts; Now Let's Hear from the Parents." *Pediatrics*, 107: e20.

Bell, Kirsten. 2005. "Genital Cutting and Western Discourses on Sexuality." *Medical Anthropology Quarterly*, 19: 125–148.

Binner, Sharon L., Joan M. Mastrobattista, Mary-Clare Day, Laurie S. Swaim, and Manju Monga. 2002. "Effect of Parental Education on Decision-Making About Neonatal Circumcision." *Southern Medical Association Journal*, 95: 457–461.

Boyle, Gregory L., and George Hill. 2011. "Sub-Saharan African Randomised Clinical Trials into Male Circumcision and HIV Transmission: Methodological, Ethical, and Legal Concerns." *Journal of Law and Medicine*, 19: 316–334.

Bronselaer, Guy A., et al. 2013. "Male Circumcision Decreases Penile Sensitivity as Measured in a Large Cohort." *BJU International*, 111: 820–827. DOI: 10.1111/j.1464-410X.2012.11761.x.

Darby, Robert. 2005. *A Surgical Temptation: The Demonization of the Foreskin and the Rise of Circumcision in Britain*. Chicago: University of Chicago Press.

Glick, Leonard B. 2005. *Marked in Your Flesh: Circumcision from Ancient Judea to Modern America*. New York: Oxford University Press.

Goldman, Ronald. 1997. *Circumcision: The Hidden Trauma*. New York: Vanguard.

Gollaher, David L. 2000. *Circumcision: A History of the World's Most Controversial Surgery*. New York: Basic Books.

Owings, Maria, Sayeedha Uddin, and Sonja Williams. 2013. "Trends in Circumcision for Male Newborns in U.S. Hospitals: 1979–2010." Centers for Disease Control and Prevention. Accessed August 9, 2015, at http://www.cdc.gov/nchs/data/hestat/circumcision_2013/circumcision_2013.pdf.

Sardi, Lauren M. 2011. "The Male Neonatal Circumcision Debate: Social Movements, Sexual Citizenship, and Human Rights." *Societies Without Borders*, 6: 304–329.

Sorrells, Morris L., et al. 2007. "Fine-Touch Pressure Thresholds in the Adult Penis." *BJU International*, 99: 864–869. DOI: 10.1111/j.1464-410X.2006.06685.x.

Tiemstra, Jeffrey D. 1999. "Factors Affecting the Circumcision Decision." *Journal of the American Board of Family Practitioners*, 12: 16–20.

Wallerstein, Edward. 1980. *Circumcision: An American Health Fallacy*. New York: Springer.

Maquiladora

JAMES D. WILETS
Nova Southeastern University, USA

A "maquiladora" or "maquila" is a term for a manufacturing plant, traditionally in Mexico, that assembles components, usually from foreign countries, into finished products for export back to industrially developed countries, usually the United States. The term is sometimes also used to refer to foreign-owned assembly plants in other developing countries, although this use of the term is more colloquial than technically accurate because maquiladoras have been tied to specific tax provisions in US and Mexican law. Maquiladoras, however, share many of the characteristics of these other export-oriented assembly plants. Maquiladoras were originally created as free trade zones taking advantage of provisions of US and Mexican tax law that permitted components from the United States or other countries to be imported into the maquiladoras duty free for assembly into the finished product for re-export to the United States. In this manner, US companies could use, and in many cases exploit, cheaper Mexican labor to assemble US components into finished products without incurring any duty upon export of the US components to Mexico, or upon re-export of the assembled product back to the United States. The United States as a whole enjoyed an economic benefit because it allowed the components to continue to be manufactured in the United States without having to manufacture the component in the country of manufacture to avoid duty. Mexico arguably benefited because it increased employment opportunities, particularly near the border with the United States, although there is an enormous literature on the extent to which these maquiladoras, and similar export-oriented assembly plants in other countries, were subject to egregious labor abuses, particularly of women. Strictly, "maquiladoras" were originally only those assembly plants that utilized the specific maquiladora provisions in US and Mexican tax law, but the term has come to encompass assembly plants in low-wage countries that take foreign components and assemble them into finished products for duty-free export to a developed country such as the United States.

Although maquiladoras increased in number after the implementation of the North American Free Trade Agreement (NAFTA) in 1994, NAFTA in fact largely eliminated the need for most of the maquiladora provisions in US and Mexican law because it eliminated duties on most components previously covered by those tax provisions. The elimination of these provisions did not eliminate this kind of maquiladora export assembly plants, however, simply the need for the specific tax provisions under which the original maquiladoras were created. Nevertheless, it took a number of years for the elimination of duties on the components covered under NAFTA to become completely eliminated. Even after the elimination of almost all duties on components under NAFTA, the growth of maquiladora assembly plants has paradoxically increased. This has been because the wage differentials and weaker labor protections have still provided incentives for manufacturing plants in low-wage countries to assemble foreign components into finished products for export. Moreover, to the extent that the components are not from the United States, having the assembly plants in Mexico frequently allows the finished product to enter the United States duty free under NAFTA. Otherwise, a company from a foreign developed country such as Japan would have to pay duty on the export of its finished products to the United States, regardless of whether it took advantage of lower cost labor in other countries prior to export to the United States.

Assembly plants, regardless of their location, have generally preferred to hire young women to do the assembly work, regardless of location. This is because women are usually perceived as a more compliant and reliable workforce, and are perceived as having more patience and the fine motor skills necessary in the assembly of components into finished products (Kopinak 1995). In the case of Mexico, the maquiladora plants have favored single women with no children, usually between 14 and 24 years of age (Plumtree 1999). This is consistent with patterns of gendered labor force participation in other developing countries, particularly those engaged in assembly manufacturing, such as China (BSR 2013).

Although some commentators have praised the contribution of maquiladoras to developing and developed economies, they have generally been characterized by poor oversight of working conditions, including occupational hazards, violation of human rights, and exposure to dangerous or even life-threatening situations (Kagan 2005). In the case of Mexico, these conditions are consistent with the frequently lax or non-enforcement of Mexican labor law generally. Although Mexican labor law is substantively more progressive than US labor law in many respects, its lax and inconsistent enforcement results in numerous opportunities for labor exploitation. Moreover, maquiladoras provide an opportunity for US corporations to practice gender- and age-related discriminatory employment that would be unlikely to succeed in the United States. Such practices may include pregnancy testing and the firing of workers beyond the preferred age.

The existence of gendered human rights violations has been well documented in maquiladoras, whether they be the traditional Mexican maquiladora or the equivalents in numerous other developing countries. The large-scale displacement of women workers from their traditional homes to assembly manufacturing plants in sometimes distant cities has both enabled and aggravated these abuses. Many commentators have attributed these violations to the process of economic globalization generally, in which the elimination of barriers to trade has made it possible for companies to manufacture or assemble products in countries with few or no protected health or working conditions, but still export those products back to economically developed countries with few of the previously existing barriers.

SEE ALSO: Division of Labor, Gender; Feminization of Labor; Free Trade Zones; Gender, Politics, and the State in Latin America; Third World Women

REFERENCES

BSR. 2013. "Between the Lines: Listening to Female Factory Workers in China." Accessed June 3, 2015, at http://www.bsr.org/reports/bsr_female_factory_workers_china_en.pdf.

Kagan, Joshua. 2005. "Workers' Rights in the Mexican Maquiladora Sector: Collective Bargaining, Women's Rights, and General Human Rights Law, Norms, and Practice." *Journal of Transnational Law and Policy*, 15(1): 153–180.

Kopinak, Kathryn. 1995. "Gender as a Vehicle for the Subordination of Women Maquiladora Workers in Mexico." *Latin American Perspectives*, 22(1): 30–48.

Plumtree, Maria. 1999. "Maquiladoras and Women Workers: The Marginalization of Women in Mexico as a Means to Economic Development." *Southwestern Journal of Law and Trade in the Americas*, 6: 177.

FURTHER READING

Anderson, Rachel. 2010. "Women, Law, and the Economy: Promoting Distributional Equality for Women: Some Thoughts on Gender and Global Corporate Citizenship in Foreign Direct Investment." *Women's Rights Law Reporter*, 32: 1.

Arriola, Elvia. 2000. "Voices from the Barbed Wires of Despair: Women in the Maquiladoras, Latina Critical Legal Theory, and Gender at the U.S.-Mexico Border." *DePaul Law Review*, 49: 729–815.

Arriola, Elvia. 2007. "Sociocultural Consequences of Free Trade: Accountability for Murder in the Maquiladoras: Linking Corporate Indifference to Gender Violence at the U.S.-Mexico Border." *Seattle Journal of Social Justice*, 5: 603–797.

Cravey, Altha. 1998. *Women and Work in Mexico's Maquiladoras*. Lanham: Rowman & Littlefield.

Goergen, Elizabeth. 2008. "Women Workers in Mexico: Using the International Human Rights Framework to Achieve Labor Protection." *Georgetown Journal of International Law*, 39: 407–438.

Tanner-Rosati, Corey. 2010. "Is There a Remedy to Sex Discrimination in Maquiladoras?" *Law & Business Review of the Americas*, 16: 533–557.

Masculinism

ULLA HAKALA
University of Turku, Finland

The masculinist movement, which arose in the 1980s and attracted white North American and European heterosexual men, is based on scapegoat theory. Its evolution was primarily blamed on the second-wave feminism that originated in the United States in the early 1960s. Masculinists further believe that women, and particularly feminists, seek to dominate men and to worsen their position, and they feel insecure in carrying out the tasks they regard as their own. The term "masculinism" derives from its French usage as a constituent of antifeminism. "Men's movement" and "fathers' rights movement" are used interchangeably in English. The members of these movements include activists, even radicals, who engage in spectacular activities in order to attract sensational media coverage promoting the rights of men and fathers because they feel women have deprived them of their manhood. Masculinists have targeted women on issues such as divorce and child support, and have made more militant calls for the total abolition of women's rights (Blais and Dupuis-Déri 2012).

The concept of masculinity has changed since the rise of the masculinist movement, feminism as well as the gay movement being largely responsible for the crisis facing traditionalists: men are said to be becoming more woman-like and women more man-like. Masculinists still cherish the traditional ideals: a real man does not resemble a woman; a man is someone who has the ability to obtain wealth, success, and status; a man's man is to be relied upon but is not reliant on others; and men use aggression and violence to dominate women and to obtain sex from them. The physical male body potentially offers the concrete means for achieving and asserting "manhood." Heterosexual masculinity, which masculinists value, even embodies personal characteristics such as success and status, toughness and independence, and aggressiveness and dominance. It could also be defined in terms of what it is not, that is, not feminine and not homosexual. Femininely charged symbols and values related to femininity such as domestic life, children, verbal ability, and relationships are devalued among men's men whereas work, independence, strength, power, action, control, and self-sufficiency are values that are appreciated. Nevertheless, along with the changing gender ideals, hard-core masculine values are being questioned, and traditional gender boundaries are becoming obscured (Hakala 2006).

SEE ALSO: Child Custody and the Father Right Principle; Fatherhood Movements; Feminisms, First, Second, and Third Wave; Gender Equality; Masculinities; Masculinity and Femininity, Theories of; Patriarchy

REFERENCES

Blais, Melissa, and Francis Dupuis-Déri. 2012. "Masculinism and the Antifeminist Countermovement." *Social Movement Studies*, 11(1): 21–39. DOI: 10.1080/14742837.2012.640532.

Hakala, Ulla. 2006. *Adam in Ads: A Thirty-Year Look at Mediated Masculinities in Advertising in Finland and the US*. PhD dissertation, Turku School of Economics.

FURTHER READING

Connell, Bob. 2002. "Hegemonic Masculinity." In *Gender: A Sociological Reader*, edited by Stevi Jackson and Sue Scott, 60–62. London: Routledge.

Flood, Michael. 2012. "Separated Fathers and the 'Fathers' Rights' Movement." *Journal of Family Studies*, 18(2–3): 235–245.

Herek, Gregory M. 1987. "On Heterosexual Masculinity: Some Psychical Consequences of the Social Construction of Gender and Sexuality." In *Changing Men: New Directions in Research on Men and Masculinity*, edited by Michael S. Kimmel, 68–82. Newbury Park: Sage.

Hirschman, Elisabeth. 1999. "The Meanings of Men." *Semiotica*, 126(1/4): 161–178.

Hirschman, Elisabeth. 2003. "Men, Dogs, Guns, and Cars: The Semiotics of Rugged Individualism." *Journal of Advertising*, 32(1): 9–22.

Jordan, Ana. 2009. "'Dads Aren't Demons. Mums Aren't Madonnas': Constructions of Fatherhood and Masculinities in the (Real) Fathers 4 Justice

Campaign." *Journal of Social Welfare and Family Law*, 31(4): 419–433.

Kimmel, Michael. 1987. "Rethinking Masculinity: New Directions in Research." In *Changing Men: New Directions in Research on Men and Masculinity*, edited by Michael S. Kimmel, 9–24. Newbury Park: Sage.

Kimmel, Michael. 2004. "Masculinities." In *Men and Masculinities: A Social, Cultural, and Historical Encyclopedia*, edited by Michael Kimmel and Amy Aronson, vol. 2, 503–507. Santa Barbara: ABC-Clio.

Kimmel, Michael, and Amy Aronson, eds. 2004. *Men and Masculinities: A Social, Cultural, and Historical Encyclopedia*. Santa Barbara: ABC-Clio.

Messner, Michael A. 1997. *Politics of Masculinities: Men in Movements*. Thousand Oaks: Sage.

Newton, Judith. 2005. *From Panthers to Promise Keepers: Rethinking the Men's Movement*. Lanham, MD: Rowman & Littlefield.

Masculinities

MURRAY DRUMMOND
Flinders University of South Australia, Australia

While the critical study of men and masculinities has burgeoned in recent times, as Beasley (2012) has aptly identified, it can also be argued that the term "masculinity" and its plural "masculinities" remain very difficult to describe. Research conducted by Drummond (2002, 2005, 2006, 2008, 2012) affirms the lack of clarity about the terms amongst men themselves. In interviews with males from a range of ages and demographics including young boys, adolescent males, young adults, middle-aged and elderly men, and including men from populations such as elite-level athletes, young males attending school, gay men, men overcoming illness such as HIV/AIDS, or mental health issues including body image concerns and eating disorders, Drummond has identified a common difficulty in articulating what masculinity means. Interestingly, the group who arguably had the greatest capacity to articulate the term was younger gay males. Drummond (2005) has argued that such a cohort of young males has had to think deeply about their sexuality and their sense of "masculinity" in terms of what is seen as normalized within contemporary Western society. Most of the other populations listed framed their responses around the visual aspects of males, such as large muscular bodies, and traditional stereotypical "masculinized" roles including financial provider, along with the heteronormative construction of being a protector of families and females. It is these responses that provide an important backdrop to any discussion on masculinities.

Hegemony is a concept arising from Antonio Gramsci's early works in relation to the formation and destruction of social groups based on winning and holding of power. Donaldson (1993) suggested that "hegemony involves persuasion of the greater part of the population, particularly through the media, and the organisation of social institutions in ways that appear 'natural', 'ordinary', 'normal'"(1993, 645). Further, Donaldson claimed that "hegemonic masculinity" was a term developed to emphasize a critique of masculinity. Some fundamental tenets of masculine hegemony are heterosexuality, homophobia, and men's sexual objectification of women. However, Carrigan, Connell, and Lee (1987) argued that despite women providing heterosexual men with sexual validation, and men competing for this, it does not inevitably involve men being aggressive towards women. They suggested that some women become comfortable with the masculine hegemonic pattern in place and therefore may feel as oppressed by non-hegemonic forms of masculinity.

Connell (1995) provided a forum that enabled masculinities to be discussed not only in academic circles, but also within the wider community. Connell's formulation of the concept of "hegemonic masculinity" represents her most influential and indeed most well-known part of her work. Essentially, hegemonic masculinity in Western society is equated to male dominance and the oppression of femininities, and subordinated and marginalized masculinities. Its qualities were richly described by Donaldson (1993) when he stated that it is:

> A culturally idealised form, it is both a personal and a collective project, and is the common sense about breadwinning and manhood. It is exclusive, anxiety-provoking, internally and hierarchically differentiated, brutal and violent. It is pseudo-natural, tough, contradictory, crisis-prone, rich, and socially sustained. While centrally connected with the institutions of male dominance, not all men practice it though most benefit from it. Although cross-class, it often excludes working class and black men. It is a lived experience, and an economic and cultural force, and dependent on social arrangements. It is constructed through difficult negotiation over a life-time. Fragile it may be, but it constructs the most dangerous things we live with. Resilient it incorporates its own critiques, but it is nonetheless, unravelling. (Donaldson 1993, 645–646)

The notion of hegemonic masculinity has developed and maintained its privileged position within Western society. Domains such as sport have played a major part in the formation and perpetuation of masculine hegemonic ideology. Organized team sports in particular have often been revered as a central site for the construction of masculinity (Messner and Sabo 1990). It has been speculated that organized sport develops a sense of male solidarity, which encourages men to identify with one another thus providing a medium for the regular rehearsal of masculine identification (Whitson 1990). The playing arena at training or in competition, the locker room, or social settings beyond the sporting context, such as bars or night clubs, are all locations in which this masculine identification and solidarity is reinforced. Boys' sport has been cited as a testing ground for uncomplicated admission into adult society. It has been argued that boys who do not participate in sport will be void of a primary character-building institution and may find it difficult to cope in adult life. Thus, sport becomes a primary site for the production of hegemonic masculinity in childhood and a site for perpetuating hegemonic masculine ideals later in life (Messner and Sabo 1990, 1994).

In contemporary Western society, the body has come to represent an important part of hegemonic masculinity. It is increasingly evident from empirical research that men emphasize the way in which the male body looks, and its aesthetic is closely aligned to perceived positional power. Filiault and Drummond (2007) have argued, based on Connell's notion of hegemonic masculinity, that only men who possess both the right attitude and the right "look" have access to power. Those men who are found to be lacking in either dimension are therefore thought to be marginalized. If that preposition is accurate, then it should be that some men – those in power – are hegemonic in that they have both the look and the attitude. Filiault and Drummond went on to claim:

> The most obvious way to deconstruct hegemonic masculinity may be to break it down to its two component parts described above: attitude and somatotype. A man may gain prestige and power by exhibiting either the right kind of attitudes – namely, a stoic homophobia (however paradoxical that may seem), or by having the right kind of body – big, hard, and muscular. Thus, there is both a hegemonic attitude and a hegemonic somatotype. (Filiault and Drummond 2007, 176)

Certainly there may be differences that exist with respect to the male body and masculine hegemony among gay and heterosexual men. In terms of masculine hegemony among heterosexual men, it could be argued that muscularity has a key role in the development of a masculine hierarchy. Those men who are afforded the privilege of attaining and maintaining a muscular and athletic-looking physique are often perceived as more masculine (Pope, Phillips and Olivardia 2000). In his groundbreaking text on the bodybuilding subculture, Klein (1993) identified that due to the backlash that confronted gay men around HIV/AIDS in the mid and late 1980s, many gay men began bodybuilding to make themselves appear both "heterosexual" (and therefore "pass" as straight), as well as healthy (Leary 1999). Prior to this point in time, the archetypal gay male physique was that of being thin. With the advent of the perceived HIV/AIDS epidemic, being a thin gay man heightened the possibility of being stigmatized as "contagious" while further marginalizing an already marginalized group (Drummond 2005). The interesting historical element to this is that over time, as gay men came to see the cultural benefits of looking "heterosexually muscular," the increased numbers of gay men entering the bodybuilding subculture led to bodybuilding and hypermuscularity being perceived as the antithesis of heterosexuality. Hence, the archetypal heterosexual male physique is now one that is muscular, yet with a high degree of athleticism. It has distanced itself from the "protest muscularity" (Drummond 2005) adopted by the gay male community, and is now seen as a physique that is athletic, aesthetic, and functional.

Clearly, masculinity is a fluid concept (Connell 1995) and will vary from place to place and from one generation to the next. The body plays a significant part in how masculinity is conceived, constructed, and enacted. In Western culture it is arguable that the past decade has seen a shift in the ideological construction of masculinity "through" the male body. As we become increasingly global and diverse, particularly within metropolitan cities, an array of "accepted" male body images are becoming tolerated. Nonetheless, it is evident in research with young males that the hegemonic form of masculinity associated with heterosexuality and the body is still that of athletic muscularity.

The school environment is a heteronormative one in which gender and sexual divisions of labor are both reflected and actively produced and reproduced (Mac an Ghaill 1996). Heterosexuality, including the traditional ideologies of femininities and masculinities, is made available to students at various hierarchical levels, but it is generally left unquestioned and rarely deconstructed. Indeed, Epstein (1997) claims that despite the efforts of teachers who do important cultural work on the construction of identity, including sexuality, their efforts are thwarted given the compulsory heterosexual context in which schools are positioned.

According to Pascoe (2005), who studied masculinity in adolescent boys in a US high school, masculinity is based on a fundamental "fag discourse." The notion of "the fag" is closely aligned symbolically with being penetrated, and therefore relinquishing power. Since power is inextricably linked to masculine ideology, loss of power (as a consequence of being labeled a faggot) affects the way an adolescent male constructs his gender identity. As Pascoe (2005) notes, with its homophobic jokes and banter, "fag talk" provides a discourse and a form of masculine discipline for young males. Given that any male can move in and out of such banter in any given social setting or space, the notion of fag is a fluid construct. Irrespective of one's perceived sexuality, fag talk is premised on a failure to have achieved a particular level of masculinity. This may be related to competency associated with masculinized features, including strength and heterosexual prowess, as well as revealing weaknesses. Kehily and Nayak (1997) concur when they suggest that there is indeed a struggle to fashion dominant heterosexual masculinities through the use of jokes and humor among boys in schools. Additionally, they claim, women and subordinate males are the butt of many of these jokes, which in turn blurs the boundaries of harassment and humor. The authors add that homophobic humor is a means by which heterosexual masculinity can be overtly displayed. Kimmel and Mahler (2003) also identify homophobia as central to the characterization of masculinity in schools.

The school environment is a contested arena in which many ambiguities and tensions exist (Mac an Ghaill 1996). Jones and Mahony (1989) discussed the culture of Western-based schools that exists within the boundaries of compulsory heterosexuality. Almost two decades later, compulsory heterosexuality still exists, and is produced and reproduced through the moderate mainstream schooling structure. Difference is rarely embraced within such a structure, while sexual difference is even admonished in the heteronormative environment that schools sustain.

Conceptions of masculinity vary according to the person, society, or class in question. Associations of masculinity are limitless, which is why attempting to define masculinity is fraught with difficulties. The theoretical definition of masculinity is not a problem. However, in practice, understanding masculinity is proving to be a major dilemma for men in Western culture. These are several issues confronting contemporary men as they move into an era of uncertainty away from the traditional masculine discourse that has underpinned men's masculine ideology.

Masculine ideology has traditionally enabled men to exude an air of public and private dominance over women and over other men. Both of these domains of dominance are gradually being eroded as the feminist movement increases momentum.

The feminist movement has given women the confidence to speak out and state how they want to be treated by men, even in historically taboo areas such as sex. Men are now having their private activities assessed and scrutinized by women in candid and open descriptions, particularly in women's magazines. As a consequence, men are feeling the need to "measure up," as they believe their sexual performance will be judged according to other men's and women's standards. According to Reilly (1993, 5): "While not denying that many men benefit from the privileges of manhood, many masculinist authors argue that men's public power is matched by private disadvantage."

Not only are men experiencing pressure to change work and family roles, but they are also feeling the pressure of having to change their physical appearance. Women, media, advertising, and even other men are all areas of intensifying pressure. The feminist movement has been an influencing factor in the reassessment of men's physiques, because it has provided women with the confidence to verbalize publicly their perceptions of positive and negative aspects of men's bodies.

Change is a big factor in the conception of contemporary masculinity. For example, men have traditionally perceived their patriarchal duties as being the authoritative figurehead and financial provider for their family, while at the same time acting as role models for the perpetuation of hegemonic masculinity in boys, particularly their own sons. Fathers often believe their duty is to demonstrate masculine-oriented traits to their sons. Such hegemonic characteristics are based around the notion of male domination over women and over subordinate and marginalized men – that is, gay men and men who are smaller and less physically capable (Connell 1987).

Contemporary societal ideals concerning patriarchal duties are changing. In the past, parents' roles have been easily defined and clearly delineated, particularly with respect to raising children. In Western societies over the past few hundred years, a mother's task was to nurture the children during the developmental stages of childhood through to adolescence. At this point, with a major part of the caregiving duties having been fulfilled, the children were able to make informed personal decisions and begin looking after themselves. The father's role during this developmental period was primarily one of financial provider, colloquially known as "breadwinner," allowing the mother to fulfill her childrearing function. His task was crucial, because without sufficient money the mother could not adequately clothe and feed the children thereby compromising their health. A father's role was also symbolic of authoritarianism. He was the perceived leader of the family unit who commonly devised rules and implemented punishments for breaching them. As figurehead and a role model of dominance, children identified him as the protector of the family. Categorically dissimilar to their mother, he carried out few traditional nurturing duties.

Like changing societal ideals, so too is contemporary fatherhood in Western societies. Increasingly, more fathers are remaining at home and taking care of the children while carrying out traditionally female-oriented tasks. On the other hand, many mothers are pursuing careers and providing financial support for their families. Dominant cultural, economic, and social changes as well as intrinsic and extrinsic reasons may account for mother/father role reversal. Some men want to change roles to fulfill intrinsic desires, while others have to change as a consequence of unemployment. These are important conceptual issues, which must be understood in coming to terms with these changes.

Of course, what is considered "masculine" or a "masculine family role" varies between and within cultures and societies. What is considered masculine in one country might be considered feminine in another. So too do constructions of masculinity vary between different racial, ethnic, and socioeconomic groups in a given society. This speaks to the fact that gender, masculinity, and femininity are all social constructs that vary across time, space, and culture.

SEE ALSO: Family Wage; Gender Stereotypes; Hegemonic Masculinity; Hypermasculinity; Masculinism; Masculinity and Femininity, Theories of; Military Masculinity; Patriarchy; Social Constructionist Theory

REFERENCES

Beasley, C. 2012. "Problematizing Contemporary Men/Masculinities Theorizing: The Contribution of Raewyn Connell and Conceptual-Terminological Tensions Today." *British Journal of Sociology*, 63(4): 747–764.

Carrigan, Tim, Bob Connell, and John Lee. 1987. "Toward a New Sociology of Masculinity." In *The Making of Masculinities: The New Men's Studies*, edited by Harry Brod, 99–118. Boston: Allen & Unwin.

Connell, Raewyn W. 1987. *Gender and Power*. Sydney, Australia: Allen & Unwin.

Connell, Raewyn W. 1995. *Masculinities*. St. Leonards, New South Wales: Allen & Unwin.

Donaldson, Mike. 1993. "What is Hegemonic Masculinity?" *Theory and Society*, 22: 643–657.

Drummond, Murray J.N. 2002. "Men, Body Image and Eating Disorders." *International Journal of Men's Health*, 1(1): 79–93.

Drummond, Murray J.N. 2005. "Men's Bodies: Listening to the Voices of Young Gay Men." *Men and Masculinities*, 7(3): 270–290.

Drummond, Murray J.N. 2006. "Ageing Gay Men's Bodies." *Gay and Lesbian Issues and Psychology Review*, 2(2): 60–66.

Drummond, Murray J.N. 2008. "Sport, Aging Men, and Constructions of Masculinities." *Generations*, 32(1): 32–35.

Masculinity and Femininity, Theories of

MIMI SCHIPPERS
Tulane University, USA

Most social science theorizing about masculinity and femininity, prior to the women's movement of the 1960s and 1970s, conceptualized masculinity and femininity in one of the following ways: (1) what men and women do (positivist/normative theories); (2) a fixed personality type resulting from socialization (psychoanalytic, behaviorist, socialization theories); and/or (3) an evolved and thus largely inherent or biological set of personality characteristics reflecting men's and women's respective roles in reproduction (functional, sociobiological, evolutionary anthropological theories).

FEMINIST THEORY AND THE CRITIQUE OF MASCULINITY AND FEMININITY

Feminist theories in the United States and Europe introduced theoretical challenges to these conceptualizations of masculinity and femininity. Several feminist theories asserted that biological sex is distinct from gender. Gayle Rubin's essay, "The Traffic in Women," published in 1975, for instance, distinguished between sex and gender by asserting that sex refers to biological differences between males and females and gender is the social and cultural expectations and rules assigned to each sex as masculine and feminine roles. Like normative and positivist definitions, feminist theorists focused their attention on masculinity and femininity as personality types and behavior embodied by individual men and women. However, unlike the normative/positivist definitions of masculinity and femininity, these theories highlighted how gender expectations and the embodiment

Drummond, Murray J.N. 2012. "Boys Bodies in Early Childhood." *Australasian Journal of Early Childhood*, 37(4): 107–114.

Epstein, Debbie. 1997. "'Boyz' Own Stories: Masculinities and Sexualities in Schools." *Gender and Education*, 9(1): 105–116.

Filiault, Shaun M., and Murray J.N. Drummond. 2007. "The Hegemonic Aesthetic." *Gay and Lesbian Issues and Psychology Review*, 3(3): 175–184.

Jones, Carol, and Pat Mahony, eds. 1989. *Learning Our Lines: Sexuality and Social Control in Education*. London: Women's Press.

Kehily, Mary Jane, and Anoop Nayak. 1997. "'Lads and Laughter': Humour and the Production of Heterosexual Hierarchies." *Gender and Education*, 9(1): 69–88.

Kimmel, Michael S., and Matthew Mahler. 2003. "Adolescent Masculinity, Homophobia and Violence. Random School Shootings, 1982–2001." *American Behavioral Scientist*, 46(10): 1439–1458.

Klein, Alan. 1993. *Little Big Men: Bodybuilding Subculture and Gender Construction*. Albany: SUNY Press.

Leary, Kimberlyn. 1999. "Passing, Posing, and 'Keeping it Real'." *Constellations*, 6(1): 85–96.

Mac an Ghaill, Maírtín. 1996. "Deconstructing Heterosexualities Within School Arenas." *Curriculum Studies*, 4(2): 191–209.

Messner, Michael A., and Donald F. Sabo, eds. 1990. *Sport, Men and the Gender Order: Critical Feminist Perspectives*. Champaign: Human Kinetics.

Messner, Michael A., and Donald F. Sabo, eds. 1994. *Sex Violence and Power in Sports: Rethinking Masculinity*. Freedom: Crossing Press.

Pascoe, C.J. 2005. "'Dude, you're a fag': Adolescent Masculinity and the Fag Discourse." *Sexualities*, 8(3): 329–346.

Pope, Harrison, Katherine A. Phillips, and Roberto Olivardia. 2000. *The Adonis Complex: The Secret Crisis of Male Body Obsession*. New York: Free Press.

Reilly, G. 1993. "What Makes a Real Man?" *The West Australian You Supplement*, 4–5.

Whitson, D. 1990. "Sport in the Social Construction of Masculinity." In *Sport, Men and the Gender Order: Critical Feminist Perspectives*, edited by Michael Messner and Donald Sabo, 19–29. Champaign: Human Kinetics.

of masculinity and femininity are not just deeply cultural; they are also political. These theorists were generally critical of masculinity, arguing that, within a male dominant or patriarchal social structure, masculinity is the embodiment of dominance and authority at the expense of others.

While masculinity was conceptualized as a socially constructed personality type and the source of social ills and women's oppression, feminist theories defined femininity as either (1) a personality type that is forced onto girls through socialization and, for adult women, required and enforced by men to serve men's interests (e.g., Daly 1984; Frye 1983; MacKinnon 1989), or (2) women's internalization and embodiment of their inferior and subordinate status in relationship to men (e.g., Young 1990). In most of this work, masculinity and femininity were defined as the behaviors and personality types of men and women respectively and as embedded within and constitutive of structural gender inequalities.

This body of feminist theory has had a profound impact on how sociologists in the United States theorize masculinity and femininity. Masculinity and femininity could no longer be assumed to be essential, biological, or even complementary personality types. Instead, femininity and masculinity are understood to be deeply embedded in culture and politics and reflective and productive of power relations that systematically benefit men and are disadvantageous to women.

MASCULINITY, FEMININITY, AND THE SOCIAL ORGANIZATION OF SOCIETY

With this new formulation of the role of masculinity and femininity in relations of inequality, sociological theories shifted from a taxonomy of the personality characteristics of men and women and instead focused on understanding masculinity and femininity as both an outcome of and contributing factor to interpersonal and structural gender inequalities.

For instance, Kimmel (1996, 2008) theorized how masculinity is grounded in homophobia and a violent opposition to femininity. Kimmel defined masculinity not as individual personality types, but as a set of ideological tools or constructs available to boys and men that define gay men, girls, and women as the inferior feminine other. Masculinity is first and foremost defined as *not* femininity. As such, masculinity allows/compels boys and men to see girls, women, and gay men as inferior and act toward them accordingly. Men's violence, according to Kimmel, is not an expression of their personalities, but instead, a set of practices and ideas available to men so that they can feel and act as the dominant class in relationship to girls, women, and gay men. This idea was a subtle but important shift. If conceptualized as personality, masculinity is something that men carry around with little choice but to express that personality in interactions with others and in their activities. In contrast, Kimmel's definition of masculinity emphasized the social rather than psychological aspects of masculinity and, importantly, argued that masculine behavior is optional, not a biological or psychological inevitability.

While Kimmel placed homophobia at the center of masculinity, more recently Anderson (2011) argued that the gay and lesbian rights movement has resulted in a new *inclusive masculinity* that accepts gay men and lesbians and does not hinge on homophobia or heterosexism. With a similar emphasis on how masculinities have changed due to feminism and the lesbian and gay rights movement, Heasley (2005) identified what he calls *queer straight masculinities*. These are the various ways in which heterosexual men embody masculinity to challenge sexism, homophobia, and heterosexism as central to heterosexuality. Others, including

Kimmel, argued that, although heterosexual men might not overtly express heterosexism, heterosexual masculinity is still defined in terms of a disavowal and distancing from homoerotic desire, gay men, and women.

Building on the feminist assertion that masculinities are deeply social, political, and harmful, Messner (1992) emphasized the way in which the embodiment of masculinity is harmful not just to girls and women but also to boys and men. Focusing on sports, Messner argued that embodying masculinity leads to men's violence against women, men's violence against each other and, in the pursuit of masculinity, men's violence toward themselves.

Emphasizing the intersection of gender and race, Patricia Hill Collins (2005) situated racially specific constructions of masculinity and femininity as central to not just masculine dominance, but also white supremacy and the new racism. According to Hill Collins, controlling images of African American women and men, especially in terms of sexualized masculinities and femininities, construct African American sexualities as deviant or pathological in comparison to white masculinities and femininities.

HEGEMONIC MASCULINITY

Connell, in her groundbreaking books, *Gender and Power* (1987) and *Masculinities* (1995), offered a new definition of masculinity, not as a personality type or essence, but instead as a location or place in social relations (the masculine position), embodied practice (embodying masculinity), and an idealized set of valued characteristics, called hegemonic masculinity. Connell's term *hegemonic masculinity* was defined as the characteristics and practices that, when embodied by men, secure their dominance and superiority over women. Connell offered *emphasized femininity* as the place in social relations, embodied practices, and idealized set of characteristics associated with and expected of women. By embodying emphasized femininity, women occupy a subordinate and inferior position in relationship to men, thereby upholding the dominance and superiority of hegemonic masculinity.

Connell argued that men's dominance over women relies upon not just the hierarchical relationship between masculinity and femininity, but also between different forms of masculinity. According to Connell, hegemonic masculinity secures its dominance by situating other masculinities as subordinate and marginalized. Some kinds of men, most notably gay men, are defined as inferior in relationship to heterosexual men. This sets up a hierarchical relationship of dominance and subordination between hegemonic masculinity and what Connell calls "gay masculinities" or *subordinate masculinities*. Race and class intersect with hegemonic masculinity to reflect race, ethnic, and class stratification. Specifically, the relationship between hegemonic masculinity and what Connell called *marginalized masculinities* is one of marginalization, not inferiority as was the case with subordinate masculinities. Masculinities associated with men of color and working-class white men are marginalized from the center of power and authority whereas white masculinities are constructed as authoritative. The hierarchical relationship between hegemonic masculinity and other subordinate or marginalized masculinities secures and legitimates power and authority in the hands of heterosexual, white, and middle and upper-middle-class men. Finally, although most men do not embody the idealized characteristics of hegemonic masculinity, by going along with normative gender relations they maintain the central and authoritative position of hegemonic masculinity and, therefore, are complicit in maintaining men's dominance over women.

Taking up Connell's concept of hegemonic masculinity, sociologists empirically focused on men and boys' behavior in specific, localized settings. A large body of ethnographic research on men and boys and their behavior in sports, crime, employment, education, and other institutionalized settings dominated empirical understanding of masculinity. Along with this large empirical literature on boys and men, a smaller, yet significant, theoretical and empirical literature on masculine girls and women emerged as well. For instance, James Messerschmidt (1993) developed a theoretical framework for explaining female delinquency and crime as attributable to girls' and young women's masculine identification and behavior. Pascoe (2011) found that masculine girls in high school were high in status and suggested that, in that particular setting, power and status were attached to masculinity more than to men or boys. In other words, hegemonic masculinity is, as Connell suggested, a place in social relations as much as it is a set of practices that subordinate the feminine as well as subordinate and marginalized masculinities, even when embodied by girls or women.

CRITIQUE OF EMPIRICAL RESEARCH ON HEGEMONIC MASCULINITY

While all of this research provides invaluable insight into the workings of hegemonic, marginalized, and subordinate masculinities within specific settings, Connell and Messerschmidt (2005) argue that, in much of this research, hegemonic masculinity was reduced to the behavior of high-status boys and men in face-to-face interaction with other boys and men and with girls and women. To clarify the concept, Connell and Messerschmidt (2005) emphasized that, in Connell's original conceptualization, the superiority and dominance of hegemonic masculinity depends on the hierarchical relationship between hegemonic masculinity and emphasized femininity, subordinate masculinities, and marginalized masculinities. Much of the empirical work, they suggested, focused less on the relationships between and among masculinities and femininities, and instead on the behavior of men during interpersonal interaction. They also reiterated that hegemonic masculinity is the organizing and legitimating logic for men's dominance not just in interpersonal relationships, but also in establishing and legitimating the division of labor, the distribution of power and resources, desire and sexuality, and the symbolic realm of media production and distribution at all levels of social organization from the most micro (e.g., the gendered self/identities, gendered embodiment), to the interactional (interpersonal relations), to the regional, and to the macro dynamics of global economies, politics, and media.

THEORIZING FEMININITIES

Though Connell's and Connell and Messerschmidt's conceptualization of hegemonic masculinity is paradigmatic in the sociology of gender, several critics pointed out that the concept of hegemonic masculinity, even in Connell's and Messerschmidt's reworking, severely under-theorizes and is not applicable to femininity. Connell's "emphasized femininity" does not provide a way to identify multiple and hierarchical femininities and juxtaposing hegemonic masculinity with emphasized femininity leaves little room for embodiments of femininity that are not complacent or supportive of hegemonic masculinity. These critics argued that, because of the centrality of masculinity in Connell's theory, femininities as multiple and hierarchical remain undertheorized and absent from empirical research.

To begin thinking about multiple and hierarchical femininities across race and ethnicity,

Pyke and Johnson (2003) defined hegemonic femininity as the characteristics associated with or attributed to white women. Based on their research on Korean and Vietnamese American women, they defined subordinate femininities as the specific attributes attached to racial and ethnic minority women that, in comparison to the characteristics of white women, are defined as inferior. Hegemonic masculinity is a superstructure of domination that subordinates all femininities, but hegemonic femininity privileges white women in power relations among women.

Bettie (2003) also focused on femininities and racial/ethnic inequality by suggesting all women embody racially, ethnically, and classed forms of femininity. Race–class femininities emerge within, reinforce, and legitimate racial and ethnic hierarchies and stratification among women while also reinforcing gender inequalities between women and men.

Schippers's (2007) theory focused specifically on the relationship between masculinity and femininity as complementary and hierarchical opposites. According to Schippers, hegemonic masculinity is defined as the characteristics associated with boys and men that, when situated as dominant and superior to complementary, feminine characteristics, ensure and legitimate men's dominance over women. Hegemonic femininity consists, then, of the characteristics associated with girls and women that, when situated as inferior and subordinate to complementary, masculine characteristics, ensure and legitimate men's dominance over women. The relationship between hegemonic masculinity and femininity is sociologically significant, according to Schippers, because it is an organizing rationale or blueprint for setting up social relations.

A refusal by women to complement hegemonic masculinity as superior and dominant, Schippers suggested, disrupts the hierarchical and complementary relationship between hegemonic masculinity and hegemonic femininity and is constructed as contaminating to normal social relations. When women refuse to play the part of hegemonic femininity *in relationship to hegemonic masculinity*, they are labeled and socially sanctioned. These are called *pariah femininities* (e.g., bitch, slut, prude, dyke, etc.) and are based on social exclusion, not subordination. Multiple and hierarchical femininities, then, are defined by how they complement hegemonic masculinity, not each other. Schippers posited that, within race, ethnic, and class groups, there are forms of hegemonic masculinity and femininity specific to those groups. The ascendancy of white, middle-class, hegemonic masculinity and femininity relies on the negative evaluation of real or imagined gender practices of subordinate race, ethnic, and class groups but serves class and race interests, not gender.

Messerschmidt (2010) disagreed with Schippers and argued that there are multiple masculinities that cut across race, class, religion, and nationality and are, indeed, hierarchical on the basis of gender. Messerschmidt offers *toxic masculinities* as the discursive construction of dangerous kinds of men (e.g., the Muslim other) that bolster and legitimate the dominance and superiority of hegemonic masculinity.

A second critique is that Connell's definitions of subordinate and marginalized masculinities constituted a static typology of groups of men rather than a way to characterize dynamics of power and stratification. Demetriou (2001), for instance, argued that the concept "hegemonic masculinity" under-theorized the plasticity of hegemonic masculinity and ability to not only subordinate but also absorb other masculinities to serve not just gender interests, but also race and class interests. Demetriou offered the concepts *external hegemony* and *internal hegemony* to distinguish between the dynamics between masculinity and femininity and those among masculinities respectively.

TRANSGENDER MASCULINITIES AND FEMININITIES

More recently, theory and research on transgender identities and individuals further expanded the ways in which sociologists think about and research masculinities and femininities. Schilt and Westbrook (2009), for instance, suggested that heterosexual women's and men's attitudes and behavior toward transgender individuals reveal the centrality of heterosexual desire in defining and embodying hegemonic masculinities and femininities. Research on transgender individuals and their experiences of transitioning has led to better understanding of the role of masculinities and femininities in gender inequality. For instance, individuals who transition from man to woman consistently report that embodying femininity results in being treated as subordinate and inferior by cisgender men, and those who transition from woman to man experience increased social status and authority among cisgender women and men.

Some sociologists suggest that too great an emphasis on how people perform masculinity and femininity in localized settings overstates the performance of gender and understates the structural institutionalization of gender, race, and class inequalities, especially when considering the global division of labor, distribution of resources and power, and the proliferation of controlling images through global media. Others suggest that this is not an "either performance or structure" question and that understanding the construction and distribution of masculinities and femininities can have explanatory power at all levels of social organization.

SEE ALSO: Feminisms, First, Second, and Third Wave; Gender Difference Research; Gender Identities and Socialization; Masculinities; Structuralism, Feminist Approaches to; Transgender Movements in the United States

REFERENCES

Anderson, Eric. 2011. *Inclusive Masculinity: The Changing Nature of Masculinities*. New York: Routledge and Kegan Paul.

Bettie, Julie. 2003. *Women without Class: Girls, Race, and Identity*. Berkeley: University of California Press.

Connell, R.W. 1987. *Gender and Power: Society, the Person, and Sexual Politics*. Stanford: Stanford University Press.

Connell, R.W. 1995. *Masculinities*. Berkeley: University of California Press.

Connell, R.W., and James W. Messerschmidt. 2005. "Hegemonic Masculinity: Rethinking the Concept." *Gender & Society*, 19(6): 829–859.

Daly, Mary. 1984. *Pure Lust: Elemental Philosophy*. Boston: Beacon Press.

Demetriou, Demetrakis Z. 2001. "Connell's Concept of Hegemonic Masculinity: A Critique." *Theory and Society*, 30(3): 337–361.

Frye, Marilyn. 1983. *The Politics of Reality: Essays in Feminist Theory*. New York: Crossing Press.

Heasley, Robert. 2005. "Queer Masculinities of Straight Men: A Typology." *Men and Masculinities*, 7(3): 310–320.

Hill Collins, Patricia. 2005. *Black Sexual Politics: African Americans, Gender, and the New Racism*. New York: Routledge and Kegan Paul.

Kimmel, Michael. 1996. *Manhood in America*. New York: Free Press.

Kimmel, Michael. 2008. *Guyland: The Perilous World Where Boys Become Men*. New York: HarperCollins.

MacKinnon Catharine. 1989. *Toward a Feminist Theory of the State*. Cambridge, MA: Harvard University Press.

Messerschmidt, James W. 1993. *Masculinities and Crime: Critique and Reconceptualization of Theory*. Lanham: Rowman & Littlefield.

Messerschmidt, James W. 2010. *Hegemonic Masculinities and Camouflaged Politics: Unmasking the Bush Dynasty and Its War Against Iraq*. London: Paradigm Publishers.

Messner, Michael A. 1992. *Power at Play: Sports and the Problem of Masculinity*. Boston: Beacon Press.

Pascoe, C.J. 2011. *Dude You're a Fag*, 2nd ed. Berkeley: University of California Press.

Pyke, Karen, and Denise Johnson. 2003. "Asian American Women and Racialized Femininities: 'Doing' Gender across Cultural Worlds." *Gender & Society*, 17(1): 33–53.

Rubin, Gayle. 1975. "The Traffic in Women: Notes on the 'Political Economy' of Sex." *In Toward an Anthropology of Women*, edited by Rayna Reiter. New York: Monthly Review Press.

Schilt, Kristin, and Laurel Westbrook. 2009. "Doing Gender, Doing Heteronormativity 'Gender Normals,' Transgender People, and the Social Maintenance of Heterosexuality." *Gender & Society*, 23(4): 440–464.

Schippers, Mimi. 2007. "Recovering the Feminine Other: Masculinity, Femininity, and Gender Hegemony." *Theory & Society*, 36(1): 85–102.

Young, Iris Marion. 1990. *Throwing Like a Girl and Other Essays in Feminist Philosophy and Social Theory*. Bloomington: Indiana University Press.

Masturbation

ELENA FRANK
Arizona State University, USA

The touching or other stimulation of one's own genitals or other erogenous zones for sexual purposes, masturbation has a long and complex record as a social, moral, and medical problem. Denigrated as a sign of immorality or illness for most of Western history, as the "radical other of coitus," masturbation has consistently been perceived as a manifestation of cultural anxieties (Laqueur 2003, 371). Autonomous and non-reproductive in nature, lacking public punitive and health consequences, masturbation has principally been conceived as the quintessential invisible sexual behavior. Despite being a largely private practice, however, masturbation has played an important public role in Western society, posing both a physical and symbolic challenge to societal attempts to control private behavior.

Branded as the solitary vice or self-polluting, masturbation has long provoked religious fears. Dominant Christian discourses condemned masturbation as a "morally disordered act" and a sin, primarily because of the challenge it posed to the institution of marriage (Van Driel 2012, 156). With procreation considered to be the "ultimate function" of sex, masturbation was considered taboo, along with other forms of non-reproductive sex, such as homosexuality and prostitution (Abramson and Pinkerton 2002, 6).

With the term masturbation first appearing in English in John Marten's (1708) treatise on venereal disease, and then more significantly entering Western public discourse with the publication of Samuel-Auguste Tissot's *Onanism* (1766), the cultural view of masturbation evolved from a moral problem to a medical problem. As such, the dangers of onanism were heavily emphasized in eighteenth-century medical and popular health literature, with a strong focus on surveillance, prevention, and treatment.

While there is a long documented history of masturbation, up to this point most of the prevailing discourse pertained solely to men. Physicians' records have served as the primary historical source of information on female masturbation, because it was often perceived as indicative of physical or mental illness. Rooted in widespread fears about the socially and economically independent woman, masturbation was considered more morally and physically dangerous for women than men; consequently, the majority of female disorders were ascribed to masturbation or related transgressions as a mechanism for controlling and disciplining female behavior (Maines 1999).

Prominent sexologists brought the concept of masturbation under the psychoanalytic lens in the nineteenth century. Havelock Ellis introduced the concept of auto-eroticism, as self-generated sexual stimulation, into medical and popular discourse. Regarding masturbation as natural in the young, as a normative and useful stage in psychosocial development, Sigmund Freud (1933) helped to deconstruct the prevailing medical understanding of masturbation as necessarily harmful. However, Freud's belief that masturbation was a sign of stunted development in adults, in particular that the clitoris should hand over sexual sensitivity and importance to the vagina as a young woman matures, set a long-standing precedent for the pathologization of female pleasure and orgasm.

By the twentieth century, while masturbation was considered healthy within the medical community, little knowledge existed regarding the frequency and variation in individual masturbatory behavior. Academic researchers Alfred Kinsey, William Masters and Virginia Johnson, and Shere Hite, however, in the 1950s, 1960s, and 1970s respectively, understood that a comprehensive psychological and physiological understanding of masturbation could be key to unlocking the secrets of a diversity of sexual attitudes and behaviors, especially for women. Not only did their results illuminate how many women and men actually masturbate, but their consistent findings that the majority of women prefer clitoral to vaginal stimulation during masturbation also helped to challenge the myth of the vaginal orgasm propagated by Freud. As such, it is these three pioneering studies that have provided the primary basis for masturbation research worldwide.

Moving forward with this knowledge that masturbation was in fact a healthy and common practice for women and men, masturbation was later adopted and advocated by various social liberation movements (i.e., women's rights, gay rights) as a political act, as a practice which signified the embodiment of individual autonomy, knowledge, and power, as well as a larger symbolic challenge to traditional gender and sexuality ideals that situated heterosexual, penile–vaginal intercourse, and female sexual passivity and purity as the norm. Books like *Our Bodies, Ourselves* and Betty Dodson's *Liberating Masturbation*, in particular, promoted female masturbation as a path to individual personal and political liberation.

Despite the advances garnered as a result of the sexual revolution, and a shift in the conceptualization of masturbation from a medical or psychological problem to a natural and healthy sexual behavior, masturbation remains a controversial, and even taboo, issue today, especially for women. Due to its perceived sensitivity and stigma, recent research on masturbation has largely been limited to written questionnaires administered by psychologists or other medical professionals. However, we are gradually seeing an increase in qualitative and multi-method research that aims to examine the complexity of individuals' masturbation ideologies, feelings, and experiences. Investigating the interplay between technology and masturbation is another significant new avenue for research, as more convenient, private, and inexpensive access to sexual information, sex toys, and pornography through the Internet, as well as the increased capacity to participate in virtual sex via instant multimedia communication, has opened up a multitude of new possibilities for engaging in masturbation for women and men.

SEE ALSO: Female Orgasm; The Hite Report on Female Sexuality; Internet Sex; Sex Toys; Sexology and Psychological Sex Research; Taboo

REFERENCES

Abramson, Paul R., and Steven D. Pinkerton. 2002. *With Pleasure: Thoughts on the Nature of Human Sexuality*. New York: Oxford University Press.

Freud, Sigmund. 1933. New Introductory Lectures on Psychoanalysis. In *The Standard Edition of the Complete Psychological Works of Sigmund Freud*, trans. James Strachey, vol. 22, 136–157. London: Hogarth.

Laqueur, Thomas W. 2003. *Solitary Sex: A Cultural History of Masturbation*. New York: Zone Books.

Maines, Rachel P. 1999. *The Technology of Orgasm: "Hysteria," the Vibrator, and Women's Sexual Satisfaction*. Baltimore: Johns Hopkins University Press.

Van Driel, Mels. 2012. *With the Hand: A Cultural History of Masturbation*, trans. Paul Vincent. London: Reaktion Books.

FURTHER READING

Bennett, Paula, and Vernon A. Rosario II, eds. 1995. *Solitary Pleasures: The Historical, Literary, and Artistic Discourses of Autoeroticism*. New York: Routledge.

Juffer, Jane. 1998. *At Home with Pornography: Women, Sex, and Everyday Life*. New York: NYU Press.

Maternal Activism

ELVA F. OROZCO MENDOZA
Drexel University, USA

The term maternal activism has been used to denote women's deployment of the mother identity in their campaigns for economic, social, and political change. Although it is oftentimes assumed that mothers' participation in politics and the public sphere is an exception, historically women have found that mothering is not only a private endeavor, but also a political one. For example, in Greek antiquity, as Jacqueline Rose notes, becoming a mother signaled a woman's incorporation into civic life (Rose 2014). Maternity provided women with a new economic and affective power, allowing them to stop being an object of exchange. In other words, through maternity women gained public recognition. They became more, rather than less, engaged in the *polity* thanks to the moral authority and prestige that is commonly attributed to motherhood, particularly in those societies that value mothers above all other women (Taylor 1997).

It should be noted, however, that maternal activism arises not, as it is commonly assumed, from the actual experience of giving birth, but rather from systematic experiences of social and political neglect, economic deprivation, physical injury, and even death. Accordingly, maternal activism denotes the process whereby a woman, or a group, adopts the figure of the mother to make claims on behalf of her sons, daughters, and community. As such, the central aim of maternal activism is to pursue a politics of visibility – a series of actions as well as performances seeking to raise awareness about a particular concern in order to reestablish peace and/or justice. The politics of visibility is the driving force behind maternal activism and it is deployed through diverse practices such as direct action, public protests, teaching rallies, press conferences, community work, and others.

Historically, maternal activism has been preoccupied with a wide range of issues, including free access to education, social welfare, the environment, affordable healthcare, housing, recreation spaces for the youth, prevention of drug consumption and alcoholism, and, increasingly, violence (see, for example, Naples 1998a,b). The emphasis on this issue indicates that mothering practices and community work are not always mutually exclusive, even if they are historically, geographically, and culturally specific. In fact, as Nancy Naples notes, women who engage in community work see this kind of involvement as a way to improve the lives of their own family members and their neighbors. Furthermore, by drawing on the experiences of African American and Latina community activists in New York City and Philadelphia, Naples rightly destabilized the boundaries between home and community, paid and unpaid work, and private and political goals (Naples 1992, 1998a,b).

Maternal activism is a transformative human activity and practice that takes many forms. An example is community work in (mostly, albeit not exclusively, poor) neighborhoods and communities. In this case, maternal activism is an ethic of care as Joan Tronto envisions it: "everything that we do to maintain, continue, and repair our 'world' so that we can live in it as well as possible. That world includes our bodies, our selves, and our environment, all of which we seek to interweave in a complex, life-sustaining web" (Tronto 1998, 16). An ethic of care demands not only thoughtful judgments about care and caring, but also active involvement. Therefore, an ethic of care is more than attitude toward others. It is both an action and a practice that "occur[s] in a variety of institutions and settings. Care is found in the household, in services and goods sold in the market, in the workings of bureaucratic organizations, in contemporary life" (Tronto 1998, 16).

As an ethic of care, maternal activism finds inspiration in the experiences of grandmothers, mothers, aunts, and many women who fought for equality, fairness, and justice. To be sure, in the early 1990s, Naples found that women's negative experiences with racism, classism, and sexism sparked their interest in community work, which they approached as a way to address basic problems such as childcare, voter registration, and elder care (Naples 1998, 109). Such experiences of discrimination and injustice led them to do "what needed to be done" to demand better living conditions for African American and Latino communities. This indicates that mothers, even those women with no children of their own, stand at the forefront of contemporary struggles for social justice not only because they seek a personal benefit, but also because of their desire to improve the living conditions of the whole community (Naples 1992). Thus, with its role in making visible everyday social injustices, maternal activism is significant in transforming persisting race, class, and gender structures.

Another example of maternal activism is found in regions with frequent political unrest such as Latin America and the Middle East, where mothers have been at the forefront of struggles for social justice (see, for example, Wright 2006; Staudt 2008; Fregoso and Bejarano 2010). In these cases, women have found that motherhood provides them with a moral voice to denounce injustice and promote political change. Maternal activism has been central in states undergoing extraordinary rates of violence. In such cases, it has been widely demonstrated that women take a central role in the process of denouncing torture, systematic murder, or enforced disappearance – the kidnapping of young women and men by state forces or criminal organizations. As historian Thomas Laqueur has argued, the mother is the paradigmatic figure of mourning (Laqueur 2002). Thus, when a mass campaign of murder, massacre, or genocide takes place, mothers gain prominence because they take on the task of mourning and commemorating the dead. In the sexual division of labor, mourning is a task overwhelmingly given to women. As a result, maternal organizations are oftentimes portrayed as the guardians of memory. The public display of maternal pain reminds us that the victims of catastrophic violence had a name and a story and that they belonged to a family and a community. In this sense, maternal activism functions as the archetype of a universal ethic of care and love in search of rightful retribution. Some of the most representative examples of maternal activism around the world are The Mothers of the Plaza de Mayo in Argentina, the mothers of femicide and disappeared women in Ciudad

Juárez and Chihuahua, Mexico, and the Mothers for Peace in Palestine.

One of the first groups to organize in order to denounce state violence in Latin America was the Argentinean organization best known as Las Madres de la Plaza de Mayo (the Mothers of the Plaza de Mayo). Since 1985, Las Madres began a persistent campaign to demand the return of the disappeared women and men and to name the skeletal remains of those who were murdered during the military dictatorship, or the Dirty War (1976–1983). The mothers began denouncing human rights violations (kidnappings, illegal detentions, torture, and mass murder) as a single group in 1977. However, conflicts having to do with issues of leadership, representation, financial resources, commemoration, and even the meaning of motherhood resulted in the organization's split in 1986. As a result, two separate groups were created: (1) La Línea Fundadora (The Founding Line of the Mothers) and (2) and the Asociación Madres de Plaza de Mayo (The Association of Mothers of the Plaza de Mayo). The split in the organization can be characterized as the public–private divide oftentimes associated with maternal activism.

Whereas La Línea Fundadora regarded motherhood as personal and individual, the Asociación Madres de Plaza de Mayo began redefining motherhood as public and collective. In doing so, they sought to represent all those women and men who were affected by the violent events that took place during the military dictatorship. Such a conception of motherhood enabled the construction of a broader struggle for social change that sought to move away from individual demands for justice. However, despite the differences between the two separate groups of Mothers of the Plaza de Mayo, their weekly marches at 3:30 p.m. in the Plaza de Mayo have inspired similar groups in Chile, Brazil, Nicaragua, Guatemala, Mexico, El Salvador, and many other countries around the world. One such group inspired by Argentinean mothers emerged in Ciudad Juárez, Mexico, during the last decade of the twentieth century. This group of activist mothers arose in response to nearly 500 murders and more than 1,000 disappearances of women.

In Mexico, maternal activism became prominent after the mothers of the murdered and disappeared women launched a permanent campaign to make femicide – the murder, with state impunity, of women and girls because they are female – visible and to demand justice. Mothers and relatives of the victims formed human rights organizations such as Voces sin Eco (Voices Without Echo), Nuestras Hijas de Regreso a Casa (May Our Daughters Return Home), and Justicia para Nuestras Hijas (Justice for Our Daughters) to call people's attention to the fact that an increasing number of women were being brutally murdered. In addition, maternal activism in Ciudad Juárez offered a powerful critique against the state institutions that reproduce a culture of impunity by failing to provide adequate solutions to the problem of gender-based violence. Maternal activism has emerged in Ciudad Juárez alongside the implementation of new forms of social and political organization, including transnational solidarity, human rights discourse and practice, and the ethic of care.

Maternal activism has also emerged around the Israel–Palestine conflict. In particular, maternal activism has played a crucial role in the national struggle for liberation. This happened since 1987, after the occupation of the West Bank, Gaza Strip, and East Jerusalem when motherhood was raised to the level of national duty. Palestinian women received worldwide attention for using motherhood to make visible the hundreds of deaths resulting from the continuing Israeli–Palestine conflict and other occupation-related violence such as targeted arrests, house demolitions, and family disintegration. Because of this, maternal activism is regarded as a central part of the liberation movement. Palestinian mothers bear witness to the persistent injustice resulting from the occupation. In addition, maternal activism in Palestine has revolved around food and goods boycotts of Israeli imports seeking to make visible the violence of the occupation.

An important aspect to note in all the aforementioned examples of maternal activism is the role of symbolic mothers, also known as community mothers, a practice that extends mothering to those women who embrace communal responsibility even in those cases when women who act as community mothers do not have children of their own. As African American intellectuals have shown, grandmothers, sisters, nieces, aunts, and friends who assist biological mothers have played a fundamental role in the struggle for liberation and political change understood in its broad sense (Collins 2000).

While the aforementioned examples of maternal activism show that political mobilization through the figure of the mother crosses ethnic, class, and racial divides, it is also important to emphasize that, in a very real sense, a great number of mothers who became politically active after losing a son or a daughter are working-class women. This is particularly evident in Ciudad Juárez, where the overwhelming majority of murdered and disappeared women were poor. In fact, former activist Ester Chávez Cano once declared that the impunity surrounding femicide cases in Juárez is due to the fact that the victims were both women and poor (Chávez Cano et al. 2010). In this respect, maternal activism is deployed to highlight the humanity of both the victim and the mother, whose right to justice is not guaranteed given that poverty relates them to a second-class citizen status.

Finally, although maternal activism is frequently celebrated, the adoption of maternalism to make political claims is not without problems, as prominent feminist Mary Dietz has repeatedly claimed (Dietz 1985). In fact, there is a prominent debate within feminist theory about the political significance of maternal activism. This debate has sought to interrogate the relevance of maternal activism for a more radical project of female emancipation given that women's traditional position within the family has been the main source of their subordination. In other words, for radical feminists, it is important to maintain a critical stance with respect to maternal activism to the extent that the sexual division of labor has been the basis to relegate women to the domestic sphere and to ban them from politics. In such cases, maternal activism may help to reproduce, rather than challenge, traditional gender roles (Dietz 1985). Two central figures in this debate are Jean Bethke Elshtain and political and feminist theorist Mary G. Dietz.

Using the Argentinean Mothers of the Plaza de Mayo as her model, Elshtain has defended maternal values and maternal thinking as a model for political life. With respect to the mothers, Elshtain claims that their activism indeed challenged traditional gendered roles. They did this by taking to the plaza where they created a space for anti-repressive politics (Elshtain 1982). In doing so, they helped to bring about the fall of the dictatorship in Argentina. Thus for Elshtain, the Mothers questioned the political excesses of the military junta and denounced the disappearances of thousands of dissidents despite the fact that their challenge came from the ethical stance of a caring maternity preoccupied with "moral protest and democracy." Critics such as Dietz claim, however, that although the Mothers' ethics of lamentation might be politically salient, the movement itself was not primarily political. In fact, from the standpoint of radical feminism, it seemed strikingly apolitical. Accordingly, Dietz has challenged Elshtain's defense of maternal activism, arguing that this form of activism distorts the meaning of politics and political action by reinforcing a one-dimensional view of women as creatures of the family (Dietz, 1985).

Although there is some truth to both sides of the debate, it is important to emphasize that the major lesson we learn by looking at maternal activism is that this type of activism has indeed demonstrated that the boundaries dividing the private from the public sphere are inoperable in practice. For one thing, the mothers have had to rely on their private roles as mothers revealing publicly the immense pain of having lost a son or a daughter in order to denounce state and criminal violence. Furthermore, nothing inherent in the experience of mothering dictates that a mother should always assume the responsibility of denouncing the death or disappearance of a child. In fact, the mothers' criticism of the state makes it clear that justice is the responsibility of the state and its political institutions. Regardless, mothers continue to be the ones who organize all over the world to demand justice on behalf of their children. Because of this, one is able to see that activists' adoption of motherhood is indeed performative and depicts not a biological experience but a public and collective one seeking to instill social justice.

SEE ALSO: Activist Mothering; Consciousness-Raising; Ethic of Care; Femicide; Gender Performance; Gender, Politics, and the State: Overview; Gender Violence; Maternalism

REFERENCES

Chávez Cano, Esther, Gloria Ramírez, and Ignacio Hernández. 2010. *Construyendo Caminos y Esperanzas*. Ciudad Juárez: Casa Amiga Centro de Crisis.

Collins, Patricia H. 2000. *Black Feminist Thought: Knowledge, Consciousness and the Politics of Empowerment*. New York: Routledge.

Dietz, Mary G. 1985. "Citizenship with a Feminist Face: The Problem with Maternal Thinking." *Political Theory*, 13: 19–37.

Elshtain, Jean Bethke. 1982. "Antigone's Daughters." *Democracy*, 2, 46–59.

Fregoso, Rosa-Linda, and Cynthia L. Bejarano, eds. 2010. *Terrorizing Women: Feminicide in the Américas*. Durham, NC: Duke University Press.

Laqueur, Thomas W. 2002. "The Dead Body and Human Rights." In *The Body*, edited by Sean T. Sweeney and Ian Holder, 75–93. Cambridge: Cambridge University Press.

Naples, Nancy A. 1992 "Activist Mothering: Cross-generational Continuity in the Community Work of Women from Low-income Urban Neighborhoods." *Gender and Society*, 6(3): 441–463.

Naples, Nancy A. 1998a. *Grassroots Warriors: Activism Mothering, Community Work and the War on Poverty*. New York: Routledge.

Naples, Nancy A., ed. 1998b. *Community Activism and Feminist Politics: Organizing Across Race, Class, and Gender*. New York: Routledge.

Rose, Jacqueline. 2014. "Mothers." Review of *The Conflict: How Modern Motherhood Undermines the Status of Women*, by Elisabeth Badinter, trans. Adriana Hunter; *Are You My Mother?*, by Alison Bechdel; *A Child of One's Own: Parental Stories*, by Rachel Bowlby; *Mothering and Motherhood in Ancient Greece and Rome*, by Lauren Hackworth Petersen and Patricia Salzman-Mitchell; *Sinners? Scroungers? Saints? Unmarried Motherhood in 20th-Century England*, by Pat Thane and Tanya Evans; and *I Don't Know Why She Bothers: Guilt-Free Motherhood for Thoroughly Modern Womanhood*, by Daisy Waugh. *London Review of Books*, 36: 17–22. Accessed September 10, 2015, at http://www.lrb.co.uk/v36/n12/jacqueline-rose/mothers.

Staudt, Kathleen. 2008. *Violence and Activism at the Border: Gender, Fear, and Everyday Life in Ciudad Juárez*. Austin: University of Texas Press.

Taylor, Diana. 1997. *Disappearing Acts: Spectacles of Gender and Nationalism in Argentina's "Dirty War."* Durham, NC: Duke University Press.

Tronto, Joan C. 1998. "An Ethic of Care." *Generations*, 22(3): 15–20.

Wright, Melissa W. 2006. *Disposable Women and Other Myths of Global Capitalism*. New York: Routledge.

FURTHER READING

Bayard de Volo, Lorraine . 2001. *Mothers of Heroes and Martyrs: Gender Identity Politics in Nicaragua, 1979–1999*. Baltimore: Johns Hopkins University Press.

Bejarano, Cynthia L. 2002. "Las Super Madres de Latinoamerica." *Frontiers: A Journal of Women Studies*, 23: 126-150.

Bergman, Marcelo, and Szurmir Mónica. 2001. "Gender, Citizenship, and Social Protest: The New Social Movements in Argentina." In *The Latin American Subaltern Studies Reader*, edited by Ileana Rodríguez, 383–401. Durham, NC: Duke University Press.

Bosco, Fernando J. 2007. "Mother-Activism and the Geographic Conundrum of Social Movements," *Urban Geography*, 28: 426–431.

Elshtain, Jean Bethke. 1994. "The Mothers of the Disappeared: Passion and Protest in Maternal Action." In *Representations of Motherhood*, edited by Donna Bassin, Margaret Honey, and Meryle Mohrer Kaplan. New Haven: Yale University Press.

Feijoo, Maria del Carmen, and Marcela Maria Alejandra Nari. 1994. "Women and Democracy in Argentina." In *The Women's Movement in Latin America: Participation and Democracy*, edited by Jane S. Jaquette, 109–130. Boulder: Westview Press.

Molyneux, Maxine. 1985. "Mobilization Without Emancipation?: Women's Interests, the State, and Revolution in Nicaragua." *Feminist Studies*, 11: 227–254.

Tronto, Joan C. 1993. *Moral Boundaries: A Political Engagement for an Ethic of Care*. New York: Routledge.

Maternalism

CLEMENCE DUE
University of Adelaide, Australia

Maternalism refers to the concept that women possess particular characteristics that make them uniquely suited to care for children (such as compassion, empathy, and patience) as well as to a movement going by the same name that sought to apply those characteristics within a broader political arena, while also ensuring that the state was responsible for the care of women and children. As such, there is no succinct definition of maternalism. Indeed, the movement itself was characterized by contradictions and tensions between those who thought that mothering was primarily a private role (and the primary role for women), and those who felt that the state ought to be responsible for the welfare of women and children, and who fought for increasing women's participation in the workforce.

Maternalism spans a broad range of scholarship. Within a large number of disciplines (including psychology, gender and cultural studies, and anthropology), there has long been attention paid to women's relationship to motherhood. For example, scholars have argued that women are only satisfied as "mothers," or that women possess innate characteristics such as compassion and empathy that are essential to the mothering role (Ruddick 1980). On one level, then, a broad definition of maternalism includes a focus on those characteristics thought to be essential or innate to women, and which therefore influence women's "unique" ability to mother. Such a position arguably conflates the categories of "women" and "mother" to make them intertwined and normatively related to one another.

However, the term maternalism refers to more than a consideration of the sociobiological ability of women to be mothers, with the attendant characteristics that ability brings. Instead, maternalism also refers to a broader paradigm or sociopolitical movement, in which those same "maternal" characteristics are positioned as important considerations in policy and welfare development, and make women important contributors to decisions at a state level. Indeed, maternalism is typically seen within the literature as emerging in relation to modern welfare states (Plant and van der Klein 2012), when attention began to be paid to the welfare of women outside the paid workforce.

In brief, then, the paradigm of "maternalism" refers to ideologies that highlight and support women's ability to mother (together with characteristics that are typically assigned to the mothering role), as well as the potential application of those characteristics at a policy development level (see Skocpol 1992; Koven and Michel 1993). More specifically, Koven and Michel (1993, 107–109) state that maternalism describes "ideologies that exalted women's capacity to mother and extended to society as a whole the values of care, nurturance, and morality. Maternalism always operated on two levels: it extolled the private virtues of domesticity while simultaneously legitimating women's public relationships to politics and the state, to community, workplace, and marketplace."

However, while there is a consensus that a broad definition of maternalism such as that presented above is typically considered to be centered around a valuing of motherhood and the mothering role, there is less agreement in relation to the objectives and ideologies within the movement of maternalism itself, and this is also highlighted by various manifestations of maternalism in different cultures (Michel and Rosen 1992; Curran 2005; Manning 2005). For example, some scholars argue that the maternalism movement in Western countries saw middle- and upper-class white women fighting for assistance for "all" women, including those from lower socioeconomic statuses, in relation to employment and welfare provision. However, other scholars argue that the movement largely saw women fighting for the maternal role itself with little consideration to allowing women access to the paid workforce or influence at a state or political level. Scholars adopting this latter view of maternalism argue that the movement essentialized women's roles to align with that of mothering, and therefore limited women's roles to that of the private or domestic (Boris 1993; Gentry 2009). As Curran (2005) argues, such contradictions are typically seen as being somewhat inherent to maternalism, thereby positioning maternalism as less effective in relation to reform than it could have been had it presented a more united movement to further women's rights.

Despite the contradictions mentioned above, much of the scholarship in the area of maternalism focuses on the political movement associated with the paradigm (Weiner 1993). The maternalist movement can broadly be positioned within first-wave feminism (stemming from the late nineteenth century), in that in many instances it posited philosophies that allowed women's caregiver roles and abilities (previously seen as private) to enter the public arena and begin reforming areas of politics, particularly in the area of welfare provision (Koven and Michel 1993). Women such as Nobel Peace Prize winner Jane Addams sought to reform government policies in accordance with the ideologies of maternalism, foregrounding issues related to the realm of the maternal such as health, education, and the well-being of babies and children (Fischer 2006), as well as promoting state support for mothers who were full-time caregivers, and protection for women in the paid workforce (Orloff 2006). This was also carried through in the work of women who were successful in obtaining positions of relative power, such as Julia Lathrop, whose role as chief of the United States Children's Bureau meant that the work of women in private organizations could be extended into the public arena (Michel and Rosen 1992).

However, the role of the state in advancing women's rights was an issue that divided the maternalism movement, with some commentators arguing that the welfare of women and children was a concern that should fall within the realm of private or philanthropical organizations rather than the government (see Michel and Rosen 1992). This debate therefore echoed the contradictions at the heart of maternalism: that is, whether the movement represented a conservative approach to women that recognized them essentially as mothers, or whether the movement was successful at fighting for the rights of women to participate in the paid workforce and hold positions of power.

One issue that could arguably be seen as going the furthest to unite the maternalism movement is that of women's suffrage. Maternalism was particularly prominent during the women's suffrage movement, contributing arguments around women's rights to vote on the basis of their knowledge and experience rather than fighting for equal rights or minimizing differences between men and women. As such, maternalism fought for suffrage for women on the basis of women's ability to contribute to politics by virtue of their maternal qualities. As maternalism's contribution to women's suffrage indicates, the political paradigm of maternalism can broadly be characterized as encouraging women's political engagement as a consequence of their status and knowledge as (potential) mothers, rather than directly challenging male dominance or inequalities, and therefore stands in contrast to the feminist movement (see Woollacott 1994; Orloff 2006). Orloff (2006) argues that this meant that the maternalism movement promoted a discourse of gender difference while fighting for equality: a potential contradiction for which it has been criticized. Some scholars have argued that it was only after women's suffrage was no longer an issue in Western countries that the maternalism and feminist movements diverged, with feminism largely becoming more prominent (Ladd-Taylor 1993).

While the maternalism movement was strong in the beginning of the nineteenth century and throughout the women's suffrage movement, Orloff (2006, 230) has suggested that so-called developed countries are currently in what she calls a "farewell to maternalism," in which it is becoming increasingly uncommon for women to be seen primarily as caregivers for children and more the case that women are also expected to be engaged in paid work, with a corresponding decline in arguments centering on women's maternal characteristics. Orloff argues that this shift stems from both cultural changes (such as norms around the acceptability of working whilst also caring for children) and economic pressures (related to the need for individual families to earn two incomes as well as the increasing need for women's participation in the workforce at a broader economic level). These shifts away from maternalism may be seen as directly leading to equal workforce participation for men and women and therefore greater equality. However, as Orloff argues, the movement away from maternalism contains just as many contradictions as maternalism itself, with the increase in women's workforce participation in many countries leading to a situation in which women remain primary caregivers while *also* undertaking paid work, thus doing little to challenge inequalities. In this way, both feminism (which broadly argued for decreasing differences between men and women) and maternalism (which broadly foregrounded such differences) have so far fallen somewhat short of reaching full equality for men and women, despite important successes.

Indeed, while maternalism has had (perhaps limited) success in some areas of policy reform, there remain a number of critiques of the ideologies of maternalism. One such critique is that scholarship of maternalism has typically focused primarily on white women, with less attention paid to women from non-Western backgrounds (Boris 1993). While there is a body of work that focuses on maternalism from a range of countries (see, for example, Uno 1993 in relation to maternalism in Japan, and Gentry 2009 in relation to maternalism and Palestinian women who engage in suicide attacks), this work is less cohesive.

Political movements concerning mothers engaged in political activity that have received some scholarly attention include the Mothers of the Plaza de Mayo and the Women in Black movements. The first of these concerns a group of women who began fighting for human rights in Argentina after the abductions of their adult children by the military in the early 1970s (Burchianti 2004). Similarly, the Women in Black movement, begun in Israel, saw women protesting through silent vigils over political issues such as the ongoing conflict between Israel and Palestine (Blumen and Halevi 2009). In both these cases, it is arguably women's position as mothers that provided the catalyst for women to become engaged at a political level.

More broadly, the Marxist maternalism movement in China saw policies implemented in the late 1920s aimed at assisting women to gain equal workforce participation in order to increase equality between men and women (Manning 2005). Nevertheless, at the heart of some of these reforms was protection for women in relation to mothering, together with continuing assumptions that housework was the responsibility of the woman. As such, the Marxist maternalism movement can be seen as maintaining similar contradictions to the movement elsewhere in relation to the potentially conflicting aims of maintaining gender divisions while also attempting to gain equality for women.

Indeed, a further critique of maternalism relates to the movement being a type of "feminism for hard times" (Brush 1996, 430), with particular critiques of the ideology of maternalism due to its focus on gender differences. For example, Orloff (2006) argues that the maternalism movement did not highlight the feminist ideals of women's independence and instead focused on differences between males and females and the resulting inequalities. More recently, scholars such as Mezey and Pillard (2012) have supported this argument in relation to what they term the "new maternalism," stating that more recent maternalism movements, particularly from conservative politics, fight to "reposition" motherhood as being culturally valid and a source of pride and therefore risk building on existing inequalities. Mezey and Pillard (2012) argue that whilst scholarship concerning mothers and motherhood is important, the foregrounding of gender differences within recent manifestations of maternalism not only leads to stereotypes based on gender, but also posits a narrow identity for women that effectively defines them primarily (or even solely) as mothers. They argue that this leads to the ironic situation in which new maternalism may "powerfully spea[k] to women's current circumstances, and in some cases seek to make mothers' caretaking burdens a subject of political action, yet simultaneously hel[p] to reinforce those burdens by naturalizing and celebrating the maternal role" (2012, 296). Indeed, many scholars argue that one of the main critiques of maternalism is that it offers little in relation to how to increase men's caretaking roles, with a narrow focus instead on women. Further, critics of maternalism typically highlight the stigmas of childlessness associated with a conflation of "women" and "motherhood." As such, and given frequent critiques of feminism in relation to overlooking women's role as mothers, it has been argued that maternalism and feminism need to meet to ensure that women have the full range of choices available to men, whilst also ensuring that motherhood is a valued and supported choice for women to make (Kawash 2011).

SEE ALSO: Feminist Activism; Gender as a Practice

REFERENCES

Blumen, Orna, and Sharon Halevi. 2009. "Staging Peace through a Gendered Demonstration: Women in Black in Haifa, Israel." *Annals of the Association of American Geographers*, 99(5): 977–985. DOI: 10.1080/00045600903202848.

Boris, Eileen. 1993. "What About the Working of the Working Mother?" *Journal of Women's History*, 5(2): 104–107. DOI: 10.1353/jowh.2010.0400.

Brush, Lisa D. 1996. "Love, Toil, and Trouble: Motherhood and Feminist Politics." *Signs*, 21(2): 429–454.

Burchianti, Margaret E. 2004. "Building Bridges of Memory: The Mothers of the Plaza de Mayo and the Cultural Politics of Maternal Memories." *History and Anthropology*, 15(2): 133–150.

Curran, Laura. 2005. "Social Work's Revised Maternalism: Mothers, Workers, and Welfare in Early Cold War America, 1946–1963." *Journal of Women's History*, 17(1): 112–136. DOI: 10.1353/jowh.2005.0005.

Fischer, M. 2006. "Addams' Internationalist Pacificism and the Rhetoric of Maternalism." *National Women's Studies Association Journal*, 18(3): 1–19.

Gentry, Caron E. 2009. "Twisted Maternalism." *International Feminist Journal of Politics*, 11(2): 235–252. DOI: 10.1080/14616740902789609.

Kawash, Samira. 2011. "New Directions in Motherhood Studies." *Signs*, 36(4): 969–1003.

Koven, Seth, and Sonya Michel, eds. 1993. *Mothers of a New World: Maternalist Politics and the Origins of Welfare States*. New York: Routledge.

Ladd-Taylor, Molly. 1993. "Towards Defining Maternalism in US History." *Journal of Women's History*, 5(2): 110–113. DOI: 10.1353/jowh.2010.0401.

Manning, Kimberley. 2005. "Marxist Maternalism, Memory and the Mobilization of Women in the Great Leap Forward." *China Review*, 5(1): 83–1110.

Mezey, Naomi, and Cornelia Pillard. 2012. "Against the New Maternalism." *Michigan Journal of Gender and Law*, 18: 229–296.

Michel, Sonya, and Robyn Rosen. 1992. "The Paradox of Maternalism: Elizabeth Lowell Putnam and the American Welfare State." *Gender and History*, 4(3): 364–387. DOI: 10.1111/j.1468-0424.1992.tb00155.x.

Orloff, Ann Shola. 2006. "From Maternalism to 'Employment for All': State Policies to Promote Women's Employment Across the Affluent Democracies." In *The State after Statism: State Activities in the Age of Liberalization*, edited by Jonah Levy, 230–270. Cambridge, MA: Harvard University Press.

Plant, Rebecca, and Marian van der Klein. 2012. "Introduction: A New Generation of Scholars on Maternalism." In *Maternalism Reconsidered: Motherhood, Welfare and Social Policy in the Twentieth Century*, edited by Marian van der Klein, Rebecca Plant, Nichole Sanders, and Lori Veintrob, 1–21. New York: Berghahn Books.

Ruddick, Sara. 1980. "Maternal Thinking." *Feminist Studies*, 6(2): 342–367.

Skocpol, Theda. 1992. *Protecting Soldiers and Mothers: Political Origins of Social Policy in the United States*. Cambridge, MA: Harvard University Press.

Uno, Kathleen. 1993. "Maternalism in Modern Japan." *Journal of Women's History*, 5(2): 126–130. DOI: 10.1353/jowh.2010.0410.

Weiner, Lynn Y. 1993. "Maternalism as a Paradigm: Defining the Issues." *Journal of Women's History*, 5(2): 96–98. DOI: 10.1353/jowh.2010.0404.

Woollacott, Angela. 1994. "Maternalism, Professionalism and Industrial Welfare Supervisors in World War I Britain." *Women's History Review*, 3(1): 29–56. DOI: 10.1080/09612029400200043.

Matriarchy

DIEDERIK F. JANSSEN
Independent Researcher, The Netherlands

The assumption of either pre-Hellenic or non-Western female-dominated forms of society can be found in Western European scholarly debate from the mid-nineteenth century onward. As an empirical question it has notably appealed to historical reflections on social and state evolution. As such, it has intrigued many late nineteenth-century evolutionist anthropologists, ethnologists, and social theorists, before being taken up by twentieth-century archeologists and classicists. Matriarchy was made to speak centrally to shifting ideas of gender relations. It enjoyed wide appeal in anti-patriarchal, socialist, Jungian, Reichian, spiritualist, environmentalist, Africanist, and otherwise progressive – but also fascist – movements.

In the 1970s, in attempts to distinguish probability from postulation, these movements have been described as having cultivated a doctrinal or mythopoetic *matriarchalism* suiting their respective political or psychological needs. Moreover, most of the criticism long leveled against notions of "patriarchy" would seem to have immediate purchase on contemporaneous constructions of matriarchy. Most historians of the largely Western European matriarchy motif (Wesel 1999; Davies 2010; Eller 2011; Fehlmann 2011; Laugsch 2011), however, suggest that the possibility of distant non-patriarchal worlds made sense across many planes of cultural debate. The matriarchal myth's conduciveness to social theorizing on the political left as well as the political right – even among the Nazi leadership, despite the Third Reich celebration of Aryan manliness – raises questions about the political uses of myth in general. Focusing on its feminist appropriations should not distract one from appreciating its much wider historical intrigues and resonance.

ETYMOLOGY AND TERMINOLOGY

The canonical thesis of a primeval *maternal or mother right*, or *gynocracy*, was presented in 1856 lectures and the eventual 1861 tome, *Das Mutterrecht,* by Swiss professor of Roman law and Indo-Europeanist Johann Jakob Bachofen (1815–1887). *Mutterrecht* (mother right or law), distinguished from *Vaterrecht* (paternal right or law), referred to a legal principle and social structure inferred primarily from Greco-Roman mythology and historiography.

The idea was not particularly new. The Greek word and concept of *gunaikokratia* ("rule by women") can be traced back to the fourth century BCE. The English adjective *matriarchal* had been used sporadically in anthropological texts from the 1840s onward, while the term *matriarch* goes back to at least the early seventeenth century. Neither were used by Bachofen, however. The German term *Matriarchat* (notably in French and English texts) and the French *matriarcat* (seemingly entering the English language in an article by later secretary general of the Anthropological Society of Paris, Girard de Rialle), do not seem to appear until 1876 and 1877, respectively. They appear as synonyms of Bachofen's *Mutterrecht*, a usage subsequently consolidated by Leiden ethnologist George Alexander Wilken's Dutch work *Het Matriarchaat bij de Oude Arabieren* (1884) and its translations, as well as by a similarly themed conference address of that year by E.B. Tylor (president of the Anthropological Section of the British Association for the Advancement of Science), entitled "Arabian Matriarchate." The latter spelling variant occurs first in commentaries on this address published later that year.

Definitions of matriarchy have varied widely, with a range of alternative terms (*matrism, gylany, matrix*) coined to avoid connotations of earlier terms. Already in 1924, social anthropologist Alfred Radcliffe-Brown could report "a great deal of looseness" in the use of the terms *matriarchal* and *patriarchal*, and for that reason many anthropologists refused to use them. Moreover, he argued that a great many societies were neither, but rather tended to incline toward one or the other side – if defined in strict technical terms of descent, inheritance, succession, residence after marriage ("locality"), and authority over children. *Gynocentric* (matristic), *gynecocratic*, or *matriarchal* social systems have been related to, but also distinguished from mere *matrilinearity* and *matrifocality*, concepts that refer to descent, inheritance, and household governance following the female/maternal rather than the male/paternal line. *Matrilocality* (*uxorilocality*) refers to residence with the wife's, rather than husband's, parents after marriage. Matriarchy has also been closely associated with either preponderant or notable veneration of female-identified, rather than male-identified, divinities (goddesses rather than gods) and relatedly to the place of women in religious office (e.g., as priestesses), myth, and ritual.

THE "MATRIARCHAL MYTH"

Although fully aware that he was entering "virgin territory" at the time, Bachofen postulated a three-stage trajectory of human sociocultural evolution. In *hetaerism* (associated with Greek goddess Aphrodite), a fully "earth-centric," nomadic, and promiscuous stage, men communally own women outside structures of paternity, family ties, or private property. *Gynocracy*, the middle stage associated with Demeter, entails the conscious and continuous resistance of women against demeaning hetaerist exploitation and disorder. This would bring about the extension of the material experience of motherhood into an ethical principle guiding the female-governed institutions of family life, agriculture, matrilineal inheritance (inheritance via the maternal line), and monogamous marriage. This "conjugal-maternal" revolution, Bachofen argued, would have come about by a transitional stage of Amazonism expressive of the revolt of maternity against male sexual violence, resulting in the rebellious Amazon settling into a more vocational mode of married motherhood. What had thus been initiated was a winding conflict between female (motherly, earthly, and corporeal) and male (fatherly and spiritual) principles, finally resulting (after a "Dionysian" and a second Amazonian interlude) in a "patriarchal-Apollonian" end stage.

Although poorly received in some circles, Bachofen's thesis was taken up seriously, at times axiomatically, in the decades to come through reference, and by the 1880s even fieldwork, by notable ethnologists. In formulating his theory of social evolution, Bachofen had been inspired by a rather heterogeneous corpus of allusions to female rule or high female status. These include popular classical myths, notably that of Amazons, as discussed by Herodotus and Aristophanes among others; more or less elaborate propositions of a prehistoric matriarchal heyday and subsequent decline of female status by a number of eighteenth-century evolutionists, by Scottish moral philosophers (after Hobbes, especially John Millar and Adam Ferguson), early ethnographers (particularly Joseph François Lafitau, in his 1724 description of the Iroquois), and finally socialist utopists (notably Charles Fourier). The most substantial influences on Bachofen, however, were close-by colleagues working in classical and legal studies.

Historians observe that core elements of (Hegelian) dialectic (resolution through confrontation of opposing, in this case male and female, forces), repression and revolution in Bachofen's writings made them attractive, although for different reasons, to Marxists, psychoanalysts, and many feminists. To Bachofen, "gynocracy" extended across kinship, legal, and religious dimensions.

Moreover, it effectively *established* these dimensions for the first time, thus making possible mankind's next and final step away from nature and chaos toward societies based, ultimately, on masculine leadership. Bachofen associated the idea of a primal or original motherhood (*Urmuttertum*) to that of original or foundational religion (*Urreligion*). Early Marxists connected it to postulations of a primeval communism (*Urkommunismus*).

Matriarchy scholarship has waxed and waned along with the waxing and waning of its sponsoring frames, particularly Marxism and second-wave feminism. Moreover, it was never without its critics. Some first-hour evolutionists contemporary to Bachofen assumed not an original matriarchal but an original patriarchal rule. Colleague Indo-Europeanist Henry Sumner Maine's 1861 *Ancient Law* is a case in point, but also Charles Darwin's later allusions (inspiring Sigmund Freud) to what he called the "primal horde," in *The Descent of Man* (1871). Bachofen's *Mutterrecht* did strike a chord with notable intellectuals including Lewis Henry Morgan, Friedrich Engels (1884) – and hence, twentieth-century Marxist thought – and Friedrich Nietzsche (one of Bachofen's students) but became marginalized after posthumous criticism by Finnish sociologist Edvard Westermarck. A revival of Bachofen's ideas was seen in the 1920s among a circle of creative artists, psychoanalysts (including Carl Jung, Otto Rank, Wilhelm Reich, and Erich Fromm), and literary men, leading to a reprint of excerpts of *Mutterrecht* in a 1926 volume.

A second revival occurred under second-wave feminism of the 1960s–1980s, leading to the first translation of Bachofen's ideas into English in 1967 (of the previously mentioned 1926 German volume). A translation of *Mutterrecht* was ultimately published by Edwin Mellen Press in five volumes, in 2003–2007. Matriarchy became an important, if not foundational, assumption to proponents of feminist theology and spiritualism, across neopagan religions such as Wicca, and, from the mid-1970s onward, in comparative scholarship on "goddess religions" spearheaded by archeologist Marija Gimbutas (1921–1994). An International Academy for Modern Matriarchal Studies and Matriarchal Spirituality (HAGIA, www.hagia.de) was founded in 1986 by German researcher Heide Göttner-Abendroth. Challenging what she characterized as a "modern witch hunt" on matriarchy studies, in a 2012 magnum opus, she sums up world evidence for the matriarchal case across myths, customs, and social structures.

LEGACY

The anthropological components of matriarchy have been variably but widely and sometimes critically extrapolated to more abstract and generalizing accolades of social harmony, freedom, unity, equality, peace, justice, familism, authenticity, sustainability, natural order, even utopia. Taking note of these generous extrapolations, historians including Peter Davies (2010) do well to examine how Bachofen's work was read and re-read across generations of debate about modernity, myth and history, feminism and anti-feminism, rationalism, and utopianism. Davies takes inventory of the parallels and contrasts between Bachofen's own conception of the work of scholarly observation (requiring a personal, spiritual and hard-won encounter with past symbols for assimilation into a narrative, and vision, of progress), the species of working through accomplished in psychoanalysis (echoing Bachofen, centralizing the male Oedipal struggle with Mother and its destined resolution through identification with the Law of Father), and finally the kind of spiritual mining, archaeology, and origin-seeking inherent in women's struggle with millennia of male rule.

The usefulness and necessity to feminists of matriarchal origin stories continues to be professed but was doubted by, among other early commenters, Simone de Beauvoir and Kate Millet. Young and Nathanson (2010) have more recently interpreted grand narratives of what they call "goddess ideology" as attempts to "sanctify misandry" that go well beyond mere, and arguably due, anti-androcentrism.

In ongoing archeological allusions to "matriarchies," meanwhile, the critical issue remains the limited, scattered, and enduringly disputable base of evidence for the kind of sociocultural evolution envisioned by the early, and maintained by some recent, matriarchy theorists. Furthermore, it is a matter of ongoing dispute whether – and if so, to what extent – either side of the debate or indeed the form of the debate itself must be seen as an articulation of masculine, "logocentric," or rationalist views of gender, of social status, of *history* as it relates to *myth*, and ultimately of knowledge as it relates to social politics. For generations, anthropologists have asked whether the matriarchy–patriarchy debate relies too much on ethnocentric juxtapositions of male and female rule. In early twentieth-century anthropology, the sweeping evolutionism of the nineteenth was rejected in favor of structural-functionalist and relativist approaches to kinship, the nuclear family, and social power in stateless societies. Even here, there remained the risk of making too much of principles of social organization such as descent. Still, kinship and gender became more and more construed in social constructionist and emic (native) terms.

One-time co-editor of a book on matrilineal kinship, anthropologist David M. Schneider drew the hasty conclusion in 1972 that from this vantage point, "'kinship,' like totemism, the matrilineal complex and matriarchy, is a non-subject, since it does not exist in any culture known to man." Defining matriarchy either in terms of "female rule" or by reference to mother goddesses need not reflect the complexities of women's standing in social life, Schneider argued – particularly across widely differing ethnographic contexts. Considerations of patriarchy, matriarchy, or "diarchy" should not be about which sex rules over the other but about how gender gets to be represented across key texts in society (such as origin myths), and ultimately how gender gets to be reflected in social practices. Matriarchy's *mythic* status, in this sense, refers less to its centrality to ancient belief systems than to its usefulness as a blueprint for current (gender) sensibilities. Work by Peggy Reeves Sanday (2002) among matrilineal Minangkabau (Indonesia), some of whom recognize *adat matriarchaat* ("customary matriarchy") in local parlance, would be a case in point. It appears to be at odds, incidentally, with Schneider's conclusion that *matriarchy* nowhere exists as a native concept. This term and concept would probably go back to Dutch colonial officials – including Wilken, who published a monograph on "matriarchy" in Sumatra in 1888.

For many, anthropologic considerations resolved much of the quarrel over matriarchical prehistory. The quarrel hardly survived into contemporary evolutionist thought about gender, with its research niches of "mating psychology," Darwinian or "evolutionary feminist psychology," and "sexual economics" theories. *Mutterrecht* appeared two years after Darwin's *On the Origin of the Species*. The replacement of social evolutionism by evolutionary psychology and comparative zoology has not ended the problems concerning methodology and interpretation that critically haunted the matriarchy debate. Yet, as Sarah Hrdy (1981) suggested, it does shed a new empirical light on how to proceed beyond what she called the "matriarchal fallacy." In non-human primate kinship, matriarchies are sometimes defined as adult females sharing ranges with their mother and/or sisters. They are prevalent in some, not all, primates. Of evolutionary note, chimpanzees and bonobos, closely related hominoid primates, differ markedly in female gregariousness and dominance style, with chimps displaying a male-conflict-driven and bonobos a rather more female-centered, pacifist style of sociality (Sommer et al. 2011). Research might be able to show what causes this seeming dichotomy, for instance whether it answers to local ecologic differences. Refined questions of "female dominance" and "intersexual competition" in the primatologic context may eventually come very close to those posed today in social anthropology and psychology (Fisher, Garcia, and Chang 2012). If so, the trope of matriarchy may come to animate social utopianism once again. On the back cover to Frans de Waal's *Bonobo: The Forgotten Ape* (1998) one reads that: "Bonobos form a gentle matriarchy, offering a provocative alternative to the male-based model of human evolution that emphasizes man the hunter and tool maker."

SEE ALSO: Feminisms, First, Second, and Third Wave; Feminist Utopian Writing; Patriarchy; Wicca

REFERENCES

Bachofen, Johann Jakob. 1861. *Das Mutterrecht: Eine Untersuchung über die Gynaikokratie der Alten Welt nach ihrer Religiösen und Rechtlichen Natur*. Stuttgart: Krais & Hoffmann.

Bachofen, Johann Jakob. 1967. *Myth, Religion, and Mother Right; Selected Writings of J.J. Bachofen*, edited by Ralph Mannheim. Princeton: Princeton University Press.

Davies, Peter J. 2010. *Myth, Matriarchy and Modernity: Johann Jakob Bachofen in German Culture, 1860–1945*. Berlin: Walter de Gruyter.

de Rialle, Girard. 1877. "La Famille et le Mariage dans les Sociétés Primitives." *La Revue Scientifique de la France et de l'Étranger*, 46: 1077–1083.

Eller, Cynthia. 2011. *Gentlemen and Amazons: The Myth of Matriarchal Prehistory, 1861–1900*. Berkeley: University of California Press.

Engels, Friedrich. 1884. *The Origin of the Family, Private Property and the State*. New York: International Publishers.

Fehlmann, Meret. 2011. *Die Rede vom Matriarchat. Zur Gebrauchsgeschichte eines Arguments*. Zürich: Chronos.

Fisher, Maryanne, Justin R. Garcia, and Rosemarie Sokol Chang, eds. 2012. *Evolution's Empress: Darwinian Perspectives on the Nature of Women*. Oxford: Oxford University Press.

Hrdy, Sarah Blaffer. 1999. *The Woman That Never Evolved*. Cambridge: Harvard University Press. First published 1981.

Laugsch, Helga. 2011. *Der Matriarchats-Diskurs (in) der Zweiten Deutschen Frauenbewegung*, 2nd ed. Munich: Herbert Utz Verlag.

Sanday, Peggy Reeves. 2002. *Women at the Center: Life in a Modern Matriarchy*. New York: Cornell University Press.

Sommer, Volker, Jan Bauer, Andrew Fowler, and Sylvia Ortmann. 2011. "Patriarchal Chimpanzees, Matriarchal Bonobos: Potential Ecological Causes of a Pan Dichotomy." *Developments in Primatology: Progress and Prospects*, 35: 469–501.

Wesel, Uwe. 1999. *Der Mythos vom Matriarchat: Über Bachofens Mutterrecht und die Stellung von Frauen in Frühen Gesellschaften vor der Entstehung Staatlicher Herrschaft*. Frankfurt am Main: Suhrkamp. First published 1980.

Young, Katherine K., and Paul Nathanson. 2010. *Sanctifying Misandry: Goddess Ideology and the Fall of Man*. New York: McGill-Queen's University Press.

FURTHER READING

Gewertz, Deborah, ed. 1988. *Myths of Matriarchy Reconsidered*. Sydney: University of Sydney Press.

Göttner-Abendroth, Heide. 2012. *Matriarchal Societies: Studies on Indigenous Cultures across the Globe*. New York: Peter Lang.

Röder, Brigitte, Juliane Hummel, and Brigitta Kunz, eds. 1996. *Göttinnendämmerung. Das Matriarchat aus Archäologischer Sicht*. Munich: Droemer Knaur.

Ruether, Rosemary. 2005. *Goddesses and the Divine Feminine: A Western Religious History*. Berkeley: University of California Press.

Wagner-Hasel, Beate, ed. 1992. *Matriarchatstheorien der Altertumswissenschaft*. Darmstadt: Wissenschaftliche Buchgesellschaft.

Matrilineal and Matrilocal Systems

SIOBHÁN M. MATTISON
Boston University, USA

Matriliny refers to a relatively rare system of kinship where ties on the maternal side are recognized more than those on the father's in defining the social group. *Matriarchy* – where women have power over men – is often conflated with matriliny, but there are no known societies, matrilineal or otherwise, that have been shown convincingly to be matriarchal (although matrilineal societies tend to be more gender egalitarian than societies organized according to other forms of kinship). In contrast, *matrifocal* systems – where women and daughters exist at the core of a household's structure and function – are probably more common than matriliny, per se, and would seem to involve many similar norms, if not institutions.

There are a number of interrelated concepts that are important to distinguish in thinking about matrilineal and matrilocal systems. First, *descent* is distinct from a more general sense of *kinship*. Most societies recognize both maternal and paternal kin, but descent refers to a form of social grouping – in other words, descent typically determines the group to which an individual belongs. In systems of matrilineal descent, children belong to their mother's lineage. *Inheritance* refers to the intergenerational [although not necessarily post-mortem (i.e., after death); see Goody (1976)] transmission of property and assets. In systems of matrilineal inheritance, property is transmitted from a senior member of the matrilineal lineage to a more junior member or members. *Postmarital residence* is the place of residence taken up by a couple following marriage or cohabitation. *Matrilocal* postmarital residence stipulates that a married or cohabitating couple resides with the wife's descent group. Note that this is often considered synonymous with *uxorilocal* residence, but usage of the former is, in fact, slightly stricter: uxorilocal implies only that a man resides in his wife's residence and implies nothing about the presence of the larger kin group.

There is not just one form of matrilineal kinship, but many common variants. Matrilineal kinship systems are variable at both the population level and among households within larger normative systems. Beginning with the population level, the most common form of matrilineal kinship involves succession (i.e., inheritance of title, office, etc.) and transmission of property from the mother's brother (MB) to the sister's son (ZS) (Figure 1A). This mode of transmission is apparent in many African societies and the special relationship often evident between these classes of kin (MB and ZS) is not exclusive to matrilineal systems (e.g., Goody 1959). Transmission of rights and property less commonly occurs from several members of one generation of matrilineal relatives to several members of the next (Figure 1B). In such cases, as seen among the Mosuo of China (Mattison 2011), property is owned communally and all members of the senior generation contribute to making important household decisions with or without deference to a particular senior member of the household (e.g., the MB). A third variant involves parents transmitting their property to their daughters, as shown in Figure 1C. This is the mode of matrilineal inheritance among the Chewa (Holden, Sear, and Mace

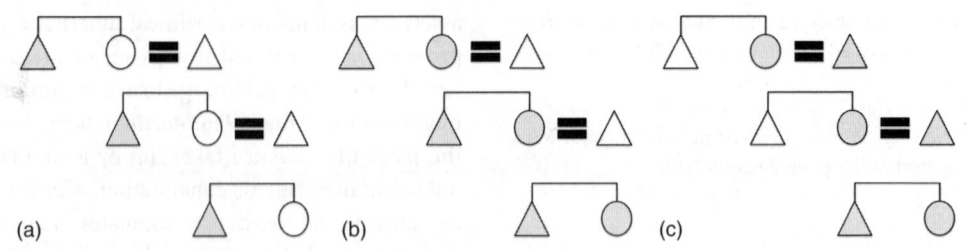

Figure 1 Variants of ideal forms of matrilineal inheritance and descent. Triangles represent males and circles females. Equal signs indicate affinal (i.e., marital) relationships and siblings are linked by single line brackets, and are descended from the couple drawn above them. Ascendant generations are thus drawn at the top of the image and descendant generations at the bottom. Filled shapes indicate who, officially, owns or transmits descent and inheritance. In A, the MB transfers his title and assets to ZS. This is the most common form of matrilineal kinship system; some rights and property may also be transmitted directly to female descendants (see Goody 1976). In B, any children of a matrilineage stand to inherit rights and assets. This is the system in place among the Mosuo of China. In C, transmission is from parents to their children. This system is common among many matrilineal populations in Africa, such as the Chewa. Source: Mattison 2011.

2003) and Khasi (Nongbri 2000) and has been described in many cases where the mode of postmarital residence is matrilocal. Note that these ideal forms are somewhat male-centric and obscure ever-present variation in the transmission of property and rights according to the specifics of which rights and property belong to males versus females (see, e.g., Goody 1976). It is also important to note that matrilineal inheritance arises in many isolated cases within non-matrilineal contexts (e.g., via adopting biologically unrelated boys to serve as sons to perpetuate a lineage in an otherwise patrilineal system) and significant variation among households within matrilineal systems is always evident as family structure changes across generations (Goody 1962).

Worldwide, matrilineal systems are comparatively rare. The last published statistic attempting to enumerate the frequency of kinship systems is found in the *Standard Cross-Cultural Sample* (Murdock and White 1969). Only 17 percent of societies from this sample were deemed matrilineal and the percentage is almost certainly lower today. The predominant mode of postmarital residence among matrilineal societies is matrilocal (Aberle 1961), but many other residence patterns, including avunculocal, patrilocal, and duo- or nata-local, have been observed. Briefly, *avunculocal* residence involves the children (i.e., not the couple) of a matrilineage leaving their parents to co-reside with their MB and, if not the most common form of postmarital residence, lies at the center of many classical studies of matrilineal societies (see Harrell 1997, especially Chapter 9). *Patrilocal* residence stipulates residence of a couple with the husband's kin (cf., *virilocal*). In *duo-* or *nata-local* residence, husbands and wives live separately (*duolocal*), often remaining with their natal kin (*natalocal*).

In addition to postmarital residence, several other social and ecological conditions have been associated with matriliny or matrilocal residence in cross-cultural studies, including horticulture, significant warfare, and frequent or prolonged male absences. Unsurprisingly, changes in these variables are thought to erode matrilineal systems. Matriliny is only rarely found in association with plow agriculture and often gives way to other forms of social organization under conditions of economic prosperity (but see Harrell 1997). Ethnographic evidence has shown the loss of matriliny in numerous isolated cases (Douglas 1969). Linguistic phylogenetic reconstructions have lent broader support to the hypothesis that intensification of production (e.g., intensification of agriculture), including adopting cattle for consumption and use in subsistence, leads to the loss of matriliny (Holden and Mace 2003), but there is debate among social scientists about the extent to which matriliny is likely to persist in connection with modernization (Nongbri 2000). "Disintegration" theorists posit instability of matriliny and an unlikely persistence in the face of economic and social reforms whereas "resilience" theorists focus on the strengths of matrilineal systems and their relative adaptability (see Nongbri 2000). Interestingly, matrifocality is often present in economically stressed modern populations, suggesting overlap in the socioecological conditions generating female-centered social systems and undermining the view that there is necessarily a progressive retreat from matriliny over time and under circumstances of socioeconomic reforms.

The unusual features of matrilineal systems have generated significant interest in explaining why such systems are so rare. More than a century ago, unilineal evolutionists such as Bachofen, Morgan, and others posited that matriliny was one step along a progressive pathway from less to more advanced societies. In this light, matriliny was considered "primitive" and common features of matriliny seen in other societies (e.g., the special relationship between MB and ZS) were seen as "survivals" (i.e., vestiges) of a former matrilineal state (see Goody 1959). In the mid-twentieth century, Audrey Richards (1950) problematized matrilineal systems differently: her "matrilineal puzzle" emphasized the difficulties inherent to matriliny due to non-overlapping descent (female) and authority (male). Viewed from the male perspective, matrilineal kinship would seem to constitute a "problem" because men are interested in the reproductive activities of their sisters, who perpetuate their lineages, but whose reproductive activities are otherwise tabooed subjects (Schneider and Gough 1961). There have been various interpretations of this "problem", from anthropological and sociological perspectives to sociobiological (Mattison 2011). All posit fundamental tensions between men and their affinal (i.e., marital) relations over who holds authority in the domestic sphere and in the larger matrilineage [see Harrell (1997) for discussion of avunculocal systems].

More recent accounts of matriliny have emphasized its more harmonious features. Shih (2010), in describing duolocal residence patterns among the Mosuo of China, emphasized harmonious relations among natal, matrilineal kin, that are unperturbed by affinal tensions. Sociologists have also been interested in the association between female autonomy, as evident in many matrilineal systems, and improved health and well-being (e.g., Dyson and Moore 1983). Indeed, matrilineal societies are often more gender egalitarian than societies practicing other forms of social organization, perhaps because norms of gender egalitarianism are stronger where women dominate in domestic spheres and contribute significantly to subsistence activities, as they do in many matrilineal societies (Harrell 1997). In that vein, new research has shown that matrilineal systems are sometimes associated with more prosocial behavior, especially among men, than patrilineal kinship systems. Using economic games, Binglin Gong and her colleagues have shown that men engage in more prosocial behavior among the matrilineal Mosuo than among the patriarchal Yi; their review of the relevant literature suggests fewer gender disparities in economic behavior in matrilineal societies (Gong, Yan, and Yang 2015). Evolutionary approaches have elucidated some of the ways in which women act to support each other in matrilineal systems. For example, Donna Leonetti and her colleagues have shown that matrilineal households offer women protection from the rapidly paced reproductive agendas of their spouses, leading to better health outcomes for women and children (Leonetti, Nath, and Hemam 2007).

In general, scholars using an evolutionary approach [see Mattison (2011) for a recent review] have focused on the ways in which matriliny might be construed as "adaptive" rather than problematic. The prevailing view at present sees matriliny [and indeed matrifocality; see Quinlan (2006)] as an adaptive means of transmitting resources if such resources benefit daughters more than sons (Holden, Sear, and Mace 2003; Mattison 2011). Matrilineal kinship systems are also of significant interest to scholars attempting to reconstruct our evolutionary history – in particular, how we diverged from an ape ancestor to a long-lived species with large brains and yet rapid reproduction. A leading hypothesis posits a large role for maternal grandmothers in supporting the rapid pace of human reproduction, allowing for the evolution of other unique aspects of our life history (see Leonetti et al. 2005). This view is not without its detractors, but would seem bolstered by the existence of matrilineal systems in several other long-lived, intelligent, and highly social species, including certain macaques (Old World monkeys), whales, and elephants.

Matrilineal and matrilocal systems have applications in areas beyond the humanities and social sciences. In particular, because mitochondrial DNA (mtDNA) is inherited intact via the maternal line, population biologists have been able to reconstruct archaic population structure and migratory history via examinations of changes (mutations) in mtDNA. These analyses have repeatedly (although not unequivocally) supported an "out-of-Africa" view of human evolution, in which all modern human populations are derived ultimately from a single woman ("mitochondrial Eve") in Africa some 1.5–2 million years ago. Similar analyses (phylogenetic reconstructions) have also lent support to hypotheses regarding the sequence of changes as societies transition between forms of kinship. For example, Fiona Jordan and Ruth Mace have shown that residence patterns tend to precede changes in inheritance (Jordan and Mace 2007; see also Richards 1950 and Harrell 1997, Chapter 9), consistent with the view that propinquity among natal men erodes matrilineal norms and institutions (e.g., Murdock 1949).

There are several areas of relevance to matrilineal systems that cannot be addressed systematically in this short review. In particular, there are many insightful historical treatises on matriliny that are not discussed here: some readers will be interested in how matrilineal systems have been used to foster understandings of cultural relativism, for example, or in the challenges posed to psychoanalytic theory and other areas of traditional psychological research by scholars such as Brownislaw Malinowski. This entry has touched only briefly on a large and influential body of theory that questions the legitimacy of typological treatments of "kinship," including matriliny, and views gender as indispensable to any effort to make sense of kinship (e.g., Yanagisako and Collier 1987). It has also overlooked to some extent the importance of *history* in defining the spheres of dominance and how those spheres feed into the productive and reproductive domains of matriliny and its resilience in the face of acculturation and market integration (see, e.g., Peters 1997). Undoubtedly, there are still other areas of inquiry (e.g., assisted reproductive technology) that are foci of current kinship studies and could be fruitful pursuits to understanding matrilineal and matrilocal kinship. In recognizing the centrality of matrilocal residential patterns to many arguments pertaining to matriliny, it is also not meant to trivialize the critical importance of other forms of residential arrangement to matrilineal systems.

Several challenges remain to be addressed in studies of matrilineal and matrilocal systems. First, matrilineal systems are increasingly rare; thus, systematic study is necessary before their possible disappearance. Second, there needs to be a stronger understanding of the links between matrifocal, matrilineal, and matrilocal systems. Although matrilineal systems would seem to be on the verge of extinction, there is nothing precluding their reemergence if and when conditions make matriliny more desirable. Matrifocality is an intriguing means of creating strong female linkages within larger systems of patriarchy and or patrilocality, yet systematic study about how such systems impact gender norms, cooperation, and related outcomes is lacking. Third, several bodies of literature pertaining to matrilineal and matrilocal systems remain disconnected despite obvious areas of overlap. Future research would benefit from linking feminist, anthropological, sociological, demographic, and evolutionary perspectives to generate a more holistic understanding of a somewhat under-studied topic that has a broad set of implications only briefly touched on in this entry.

SEE ALSO: Kinship

REFERENCES

Aberle, David. 1961. "Matrilineal Descent in Cross-Cultural Perspective." In *Matrilineal Kinship*, edited by David M. Schneider and Kathleen Gough, 655–727. Berkeley: University of California Press.

Douglas, Mary. 1969. "Is Matriliny Doomed in Africa?" In *Man in Africa*, edited by Mary Douglas, Phyllis Mary Kaberry, and Cyril Daryll Forde, 121–135. London: Tavistock Publications.

Dyson, Tim, and Mick Moore. 1983. "On Kinship Structure, Female Autonomy, and Demographic Behavior in India." *Population and Development Review*, 9(1): 35–60.

Gong, Binglin, Huibin Yan, and Chun-Lei Yang. 2015. "Gender Differences in the Dictator Experiment: Evidence from the Matrilineal Mosuo and the Patriarchal Yi." *Experimental Economics*, 18: 302–313. DOI: 10.1007/s10683-014-9403-2.

Goody, Jack. 1959. "The Mother's Brother and the Sister's Son in West Africa." *The Journal of the Royal Anthropological Institute of Great Britain and Ireland*, 89(1): 61–88. DOI: 10.2307/2844437.

Goody, Jack. 1962. *The Developmental Cycle in Domestic Groups*. Cambridge: Cambridge University Press.

Goody, Jack. 1976. *Production and Reproduction: A Comparative Study of the Domestic Domain*. Cambridge: Cambridge University Press.

Harrell, Stevan. 1997. *Human Families*. Boulder: Westview Press.

Holden, Clare Janaki, and Ruth Mace. 2003. "Spread of Cattle Led to the Loss of Matrilineal Descent in Africa: A Coevolutionary Analysis." *Philosophical Transactions of the Royal Society of London, Series B, Biological Science,s* 270: 2425–2433.

Holden, Clare Janaki, Rebecca Sear, and Ruth Mace. 2003. "Matriliny as Daughter-Biased Investment." *Evolution and Human Behavior*, 24: 99–112.

Jordan, Fiona M., and Ruth Mace. 2007. "Changes in Post-Marital Residence Precede Changes in Descent Systems in Austronesian Societies." Presented at the European Human Behaviour and Evolution Conference 2007 (EHBE 2007), March 28–30, 2007, London School of Economics, London.

Leonetti, Donna L., Dilip C. Nath, Natabar S. Hemam, and Dawn B. Neill. 2005. "Kinship Organization and Grandmother's Impact on Reproductive Success among the Matrilineal Khasi and Patrilineal Bengali of N.E. India." In *Grandparenthood – The Second Half of Life*, edited by Erik Voland, Athanasios Chasiotis, and Wulf Schiefenhoevel, 194–219. Piscataway: Rutgers University Press.

Leonetti, Donna L., Dilip C. Nath, and Natabar S. Hemam. 2007. "In-Law Conflict: Women's Reproductive Lives and the Roles of Their Mothers and Husbands Among the Matrilineal Khasi." *Current Anthropology*, 48: 861–890.

Mattison, Siobhán M. 2011. "Evolutionary Contributions to Solving the 'Matrilineal Puzzle': A Test of Holden, Sear, and Mace's Model." *Human Nature*, 22: 64–88. DOI: 10.1007/s12110-011-9107-7.

Murdock, George P. 1949. *Social Structure*. New York: Macmillan.

Murdock, George P., and Douglas R. White. 1969. "Standard Cross-Cultural Sample." *Ethnology*, 8: 329–369.

Nongbri, Tiplut. 2000. "Khasi Women and Matriliny: Transformations in Gender Relations." *Gender, Technology, and Development*, 4: 359–395.

Parkin, Robert, and Linda Stone, eds. 2004. *Kinship and Family: An Anthropological Reader*. Blackwell Anthologies in Social and Cultural Anthropology, vol. 4. Malden: Blackwell.

Peters, Pauline E. 1997. "Against the Odds Matriliny, Land and Gender in the Shire Highlands of Malawi." *Critique of Anthropology*, 17(2): 189–210. DOI: 10.1177/0308275X9701700205.

Quinlan, Robert J. 2006. "Gender and Risk in a Matrifocal Caribbean Community: A View from Behavioral Ecology." *American Anthropologist*, 108: 464–479.

Richards, Audrey I. 1950. "Some Types of Family Structure amongst the Central Bantu." In *African Systems of Kinship and Marriage*, edited by Alfred Reginald Radcliffe-Brown and Cyril Daryll Forde, 83–120. London: Oxford University Press.

Schneider, David M., and Kathleen Gough. 1961. *Matrilineal Kinship*. Berkeley: University of California Press.

Shih, Chuan-Kang. *Quest for Harmony: The Moso Traditions of Sexual Union & Family Life*. 2010. Stanford: Stanford University Press.

Yanagisako, Sylvia Junko, and Jane Fishburne Collier. 1987. "Toward a Unified Analysis of Gender and Kinship." In *Gender and Kinship: Essays Toward a Unified Analysis*, 14–50. Stanford: Stanford University Press.

FURTHER READING

Stone, Linda. 2010. *Kinship and Gender*. Boulder: Westview Press.

Matrix of Domination

CIRILA P. LIMPANGOG
Victoria University, Australia

Matrix of domination is a groundbreaking theory proposed by Patricia Hill Collins in her influential 1990 book, *Black Feminist Thought: Knowledge, Consciousness and the Politics of Empowerment*. It offers a postcolonial approach to understanding systems of oppression that are situated on the intersections of gender, race, class, and other social identities (see also Collins 1998). By giving voice to those who have been systematically silenced or ignored in knowledge production, the matrix of domination deploys an analysis that is not only a corrective to the dominant Eurocentric white male knowledge and an alternative to white female knowledge; it is also one that legitimizes black feminist epistemology. Twenty-five years since its first use, matrix of domination has since been applied to the understanding and empowerment processes of marginalized and othered categories such as trafficked people, persons with disability, sexually deviant identities, transgender people, juvenile delinquents, welfare recipients, indigenous peoples, small entrepreneurs, residentially segregated citizens, and migrants.

Matrix of domination is akin to *intersectionality theory* introduced by another black American feminist scholar, Kimberlé

Williams Crenshaw, in the late 1980s. In fact, academics and professionals would use these theories interchangeably because of their identical aims of unmasking cultures of oppressions, and their assertions of differences in feminist projects. Collins herself built her idea of matrix of domination from intersectionality. Influenced by the works of Weber and Foucault, she lifted the theory of power by problematizing its key domains. Both matrix of domination and intersectionality emphasize the racialization of gender, and the necessity of black feminist thought in analyzing the interconnection between gender and racial inequality from women's lived experienced. But while both theories would gain critical prominence in feminist theorizing worldwide, matrix of domination easily found currency outside the black feminist category, due in part to Collins's modernist and postmodernist sociological applications.

Even the most oppressed have agency. They can transform power through resistance in ways that are not readily discernible through the hegemonic surveillance and knowledge production of the racially dominant group. Even black men did not readily share power with black women, thus sustaining the latter's subordinate position in their own household and community. Black women's resistance against being accommodated in the radical feminism of their white sisters during the 1960s was symbolic of their struggle against interlocking oppressions. The unequal social status of these women, made explicit through housing and job segregations and welfare access, helped rationalize the unique contribution of black feminist epistemology in understanding the matrix of domination.

The theory does not merely serve as a lens to multidimensional systems of oppressions that reify black women's victim identity. Equally important, it posits new ways of understanding women's (or other marginalized person/s) self-identity, as opposed to externally imposed identity, through individual and collective activism, with the central goal of achieving social justice. By producing situated knowledge based on and that feeds into the analysis of interlocking systems of oppression, it inspires change at personal, local, and transnational dimensions.

Collins reflects on the historic racial segregation in America and the rise of the African American civil rights movement as impacting black women, in her theorization. The severity of discrimination they faced in public and private domains prevented them from participating in formal and organized ways of resisting. Yet, to Collins, black women performed resistance in two distinctive ways, *group survival* and *institutional transformation*, subsequently disturbing the matrix of domination. By group survival, black women did not directly confront the oppressive structures, for they needed the domestic service jobs to sustain their families. They projected obedience and conformity to the rules of the dominant holders of power, for instance, by accepting handouts in lieu of salary raise, but deep within they consciously rejected being objectified. So they lived oppositional identities in the private sphere. For instance, they raised their children with alternative values that foster self-worth. They resisted passing on to them externally defined images of themselves as "mules, mammies, matriarchs, and jezebels" (Collins 1990, 209). In their jobs, they developed alternative tools that undermine the rules of domination, for instance, by refusing to be called "girl" and binning hand-me-down clothes, in subtle yet conscious ways. By institutional transformation, black women used the limited entitlements they have in public spaces where they are permitted. They challenged the dominant oppressive knowledge and provided alternative knowledge, in the churches, media, and schools. They resisted against slavery, and advocated for inclusion in social and political spheres. All these incrementally created critical consciousness and political strategies to empowerment.

The theory therefore is a tool to dismantling discrimination. It espouses a transformational change approach in four domains: *structural, hegemony, disciplinary*, and *interpersonal*. Given the massive and deeply entrenched nature of oppression, a multistrategy comparable response is needed. Oppression is organized in the structural domain, and it is the disciplinary domain that manages it. The hegemonic domain works to legitimize oppression, while it is the interpersonal domain that the dominant group's ideology gets embedded through everyday lived experiences and interaction. Collins's scholarship significantly explores how power intersects, gets challenged, and is reconstituted in these domains (see, for instance, Collins 2006, 2013).

Matrix of domination rejects the additive and dichotomous model of oppression that forces an "either/or" identification. For example, it acknowledges that gender is a complex category that should not only focus on differences between men and women, but also on their similarities. When deployed to race, it disrupts the essentialist "black/white" categories and recognizes diverse shades of blackness. It therefore examines power and oppression firstly within race and gender, and then across other social terrains such as ethnicity, class, age, religion, sexuality, and disability. It acknowledges the fluid and at times contradictory systems of oppression, as well as power and privileges of these women and the diverse actors surrounding them.

SEE ALSO: Feminist Standpoint Theory; Gender Equality; Intersectionality

REFERENCES

Collins, Patricia Hill. 1990. *Black Feminist Thought: Knowledge, Consciousness, and the Politics of Empowerment*. Boston: Unwin Hyman.

Collins, Patricia Hill. 1998. "It's All in the Family: Intersections of Gender, Race, and Nation." *Hypatia*, 13(3):62–82.

Collins, Patricia Hill. 2006. *From Black Power to Hip Hop: Racism, Nationalism, and Feminism*. Philadelphia: Temple University Press.

Collins, Patricia Hill. 2013. *On Intellectual Activism*. Philadelphia: Temple University Press.

FURTHER READING

Connor, David J. 2006. "Michael's Story: 'I Get Into so Much Trouble Just by Walking': Narrative Knowing and Life at the Intersections of Learning Disability, Race, and Class." *Equity & Excellence in Education*, 39(2): 154–165. DOI: 10.1080/10665680500533942.

Zinn, Maxine Baca, and Bonnie Thornton Dill. 1996. "Theorizing Difference from Multiracial Feminism." *Feminist Studies*, 22(2): 321–331.

Media and Gender Socialization

AUDREY GADZEKPO
University of Ghana, Ghana

INTRODUCTION

Feminist media studies have since the 1960s raised fundamental questions about the structure of gender in society and the complicity of mass media in social and cultural constructions of and constrictions relating to gender identity. The dominant research preoccupation has been to highlight the multifarious ways in which media images and representations reinforce how individuals are socialized to understand and "do" gender.

Feminist theorists have differing definitions for the term "gender" but the broad understanding is that gender refers to social factors that determine what it means to be a woman or man and is different from biological sex. All societies are gendered, although how gender marks social relations can differ across the world. As "a mechanism that structures material and symbolic worlds and [people's] experiences of them" (van Zoonen 1996, 31) gender is constantly being constructed and negotiated. Gender has been operationalized in this entry as an analytic category that conveys the cultural meanings, values, norms, and roles assigned to women and men, and how, based on that, they are treated within society.

The learning of culturally defined gender roles results from the process of socialization. Social learning theorists have argued that gender role differences are understood very early on in life because they are socially constructed through various cognitive factors such as family, religion, education, peers, and the media (Mischel 1966; Bandura 1977). Boys and girls learn what it means to be masculine and feminine from observing the behaviors of others, imitating them, and being validated for their behaviors. The central concern has been that children imitate what they watch on television or see in films, as well as what they read and hear from other socializing agents. The perceived influence of the media in the process of socialization and in "our gendered lives" (Wood 1994) has led feminist media theorists and activists to focus on the media/gender nexus.

The media of mass communication encompasses an array of print and electronic instruments of communication that carry messages to diverse and widespread audiences and pervade all areas of contemporary society – from family life, to education, to politics and entertainment. The definition includes traditional or old media forms (books, newspapers, magazines, radio, television, film, and music) as well as new media – Internet-based social media (e.g., Facebook and Twitter), mobile telephones, and video games. In the last two decades especially the range of media technologies has expanded dramatically and altered the manner in which people access, consume, and participate in media, as well as respond to media content.

MEDIA AS SOCIALIZING AGENT

In many societies the media is considered one of the key socializing agents because it is ubiquitous and central to the daily lives of people. Media theorists argue that the media has now largely replaced other socializers such as family, church, and schools and has become "caretaker," "arbiter of cultural values," "site of education," and "public agenda-setter" (Ott and Mack 2009). The media's socializing role includes enforcing societal norms and reinforcing proper behavior by highlighting what happens when people go against sanctioned behavior, although it sometimes affirms wrongdoing. It also regulates opinion by defining issues and shaping people's perceptions of them as well as conferring status on individuals, organizations, and public issues when these are singled out for portrayal.

The media is regarded as an ideological institution that perpetuates, reinforces, and challenges hegemonic perspectives. The media reproduces inequalities when what it produces reflects and distorts cleavages in society (e.g., gender, race, ethnicity, sexual orientation, economic status, social class) and promotes change when it defies the status quo. As a socializing agent, the media's power is perceived as deepening because of what media analysts term supersaturation of cultural life (Gitlin 2002), a situation where the media has become pervasive and so embedded in people's lives that their mediated experiences essentially determine how they perceive the world and themselves.

There are different theoretical positions on the extent of influence the media exerts on people's realities and behaviors. Some posit that the media has powerful effects on audiences (hypodermic syringe/magic bullet theory; cultivation theory), while others suggest minimal or more subtle influences (social action theory). Counter-perspectives suggest media effects are neither all powerful nor minimal. Agenda-setting theory (McCombs and Shaw 1972), for example, submits that the media may not necessarily tell us what to think but it influences what we think about, while framing theory posits that media messages influence perceptions because they are constructed to "promote a particular problem definition, causal interpretation, moral evaluation and/or treatment recommendation" (Entman 2002, 391).

PERSPECTIVES ON MEDIA AND GENDER

The dominant perspectives on media and gender socialization have been shaped by feminist thought within academia as well as gender activists working to change representations of women in the media. The thrust of scholarship is premised on the notion that the media legitimizes existing gender disparities through its portrayal, representation, and framing of issues relating to women and men. The media have become a dominant force in conveying stereotypical and hegemonic messages that reinforce patriarchy and define femininity (van Zoonen 1994). Consequently scholarship has tended to focus on examining how gender is constructed in the media and the manner in which, as a socializing institution, media support and/or challenge various forms of sexism.

The trajectory of research on media and gender has focused on the deleterious effects of media content and practices on women principally. Academic interest has only recently (since the 1980s and 1990s) begun to explore the intersection between media and masculinities and the harmful concepts media transmits regarding the characteristics to which boys and men must conform.

Most studies on media and gender demonstrate that media content reinforces popular gender stereotypes by constantly depicting men as visible, forceful, independent, competent, and breadwinners, and women as largely invisible, submissive, caregivers, incompetent, and dependent. Gaye Tuchman (1978) has described the media's stereotyping, trivialization, and marginalization of women and their related issues as a form of "symbolic annihilation."

The media is seen as perpetuating subtle and harmful forms of gender bias through framing practices in the coverage of women, for example when it uses conventional frames that suggest women belong in traditional roles (e.g., cooking) or implies they are straying into "male preserves" such as politics. The media objectifies women when it portrays them in ways and contexts that suggest they are objects to be ogled, touched, or used, and commodifies women when it projects them as products to be acquired for male pleasure and consumption in advertisements aimed primarily at male consumers (e.g., cars and alcohol). Related to objectification and commodification is how the media sexualizes women, particularly in advertisements and films. Laura Mulvey (1975) theorizes that in films the camera lens subjects women to the "male gaze" by depicting them as objects for sexual use and maintaining an asymmetric power relationship between viewer (male) and viewed (female).

Those concerned about the media's negative socializing effects on children argue that media images and messages encourage people to be valued by their level of sexual attractiveness and impose adult sexuality on girls who are not mature enough to handle it.

Television and magazines, which rank among the top informants of adolescent sexuality, are accused of being a source of teenage body dysmorphia. Critics also perceive the media as encouraging violent behavior and as a contributory factor to gender-based violence.

Much of the literature informing the dominant understandings of gender construction in the media has emerged from research on a vast range of media products, including children's books, magazines, newspapers, radio and television programs, films, popular culture, advertisements, and increasingly online content and video games. Betty Friedan's seminal book, *The Feminine Mystique* (1963), represents one of the earliest attempts at revealing how the media – specifically women's magazines and advertisements – socializes women by creating the illusion that they are happy housewives.

Children's literature and films contain examples of the earliest forms of mediated gender socialization. Fairy tales from Western societies carry stereotypes portraying women and girls as damsels in distress rescued by handsome princes who accord them high social status through marriage. Such children's stories reinforce an obsession with physical appearance and women's subordination and dependence on men for social and financial security. In non-Western societies such as Africa, oral literature aimed at children tends to emphasize motherhood and girls' domesticity and passivity. The socialization of children into gendered roles and behaviors is continued in school texts that typically represent men in prestigious jobs as presidents, doctors, engineers, and so on and women in less influential positions (e.g., secretaries, nurses, receptionists). The effect of such media exposure is that boys learn to be independent and to aspire to positions of power, while girls are encouraged to tame their ambitions and be dependent on men. The advent of video games targeted at children has provided gender researchers and activists with a new area of concern. Like literature and film, children's video games have come under attack for repeating similar sexist stereotypes and also for producing violent sexualized content that promotes tolerance for sexual harassment and violence against women.

Research on news content in newspapers, radio, and television similarly indicts the media for perpetuating gender inequalities. Women's invisibility on prominent news pages (e.g., front pages) and general underrepresentation in news have been buttressed by diachronic research from the Global Media Monitoring Project (GMMP). GMMP research, conducted in five-year cycles (1995, 2000, 2005, 2010) worldwide, consistently shows women are severely underrepresented in news coverage in contrast to men, and that in news stories men outnumber women in almost all occupational categories, especially in the professions. According to the findings, when women appear in the news they are more likely to be interviewed as ordinary persons rather than expert commentators (World Association for Christian Communication 2010).

Academic interest in the television and film industries continues to highlight how television programs and Hollywood films underrepresent women as main characters and portray images of men and women that promote sexism. On the screen boys and men are often powerful, physically active, sexually aggressive, and emotionally detached; girls and women are beautiful, thin, dependent, vulnerable, passive, and less intelligent and capable than men. The roles that men and women play are equally gendered, with men more likely to be depicted as breadwinning career husbands and bosses, and women as caregivers who hold less important jobs. The increasingly influential cinema industries in

India (Bollywood) and Nigeria (Nollywood) are similarly gendered, although some portrayals betray cultural norms quite different from those of Hollywood. Nollywood plots, for example, often revolve around mysticism and redemption, so women are portrayed as diabolical and manipulative witches or caught between two extremes – the traditional, virtuous, long-suffering wife, and the glamorous, power-hungry Jezebel. Over time these stereotypical screen representations of men and women have undergone some change, with more TV programs and Hollywood films offering gendered representations that challenge popular stereotypes, sometimes depicting countercultures of "girl power."

Advertising images and messages found on TV, billboards, and radio and in magazines are considered just as culpable in purveying traditional gender biases as well as carrying in particular recursive depictions of adolescents and women that objectify, commodify, and sexualize them.

The expansion in new media, characterized by a shift from "one-to-many" communication to "many-to-many," more interactive, and less controlled means of communicating, has attracted two schools of feminist thought. One holds that information and communication technologies (ICTs) are potentially liberating for women because they reformulate relationships between the public and private as well as disrupt hierarchies of information production by allowing women to create and control their own content more easily on websites, through blogs, and in social media. An alternative, more pessimistic view argues that ICTs manifest some of the old gendered inequalities that have preoccupied feminists for a while, and in addition exacerbate sexual harassment as well as access to pornography and denigratory images of women.

Feminist activism aimed at addressing the "sins" of the media globally dates back to the First United Nations (UN) World Conference on Women in Mexico City in 1975, where the media was identified as a site for action. Focus on the media increased when in 1995, at the Fourth UN World Conference on Women in Beijing, China, media was declared one of 12 critical areas of concern. There were calls for an increase in women's participation and access to expression and decision-making in the media, and for a more balanced and non-stereotyped portrayal of women by the media (United Nations 1995).

Traditional feminist responses aimed at redress have encouraged the establishment of women-controlled media, creation of gendered spaces, and increasing women in decision-making postions, although such strategies have been criticized for either ghettoizing women or failing to account for media cultures that gender media practices. Studies suggest masculinity is integral to newsroom culture, and rather than gender, it is that which influences journalists' professional values and the kind of content they produce. More recently there has been a push to en-gender newsrooms by reconceptualizing journalistic norms and removing the cultural and structual impediments that gender media production. The debate on gendered mediation is likely to continue as further research, media monitoring, and activism produce new evidence on how the media constructs gender relations and how, through media agency, gender can be deconstructed to promote equality between women and men.

SEE ALSO: Children's Literature and Gender; Digital Media and Gender; Fairy Tales; Gaze; Gender Bias; Gender Identities and Socialization; Images of Gender and Sexuality in Advertising; Socialization and Sexuality

REFERENCES

Bandura, Albert. 1977. *Social Learning Theory*. New York: General Learning Press.

Entman, Robert. 2002. "Framing: Towards Clarification of a Fractured Paradigm." In *McQuail's Reader in Mass Communication Theory*, edited by Denis McQuail, 391–397. Thousand Oaks: Sage.

Friedan, Betty. 1963. *The Feminine Mystique*. New York: Dell.

Gitlin, Todd. 2002. *Media Unlimited: How the Torrent of Images and Sounds Overwhelms Our Lives*. London: Picador.

McCombs, Maxwell, and Donald Shaw. 1972. "The Agenda-Setting Function of Mass Media." *Public Opinion Quarterly*, 36(2): 176–187.

Mischel, Walter. 1966. "A Social-Learning View of Sex Differences in Behavior." In *The Development of Sex Differences*, edited by E. E. Maccoby, 56–81. Stanford: Stanford University Press.

Mulvey, Laura. 1975. "Visual Pleasure and Narrative Cinema." *Screen*, 16(3): 6–18.

Ott, Brian, and Robert Mack. 2009. *Critical Media Studies: An Introduction*. Oxford: Wiley Blackwell.

Tuchman, Gaye. 1978. "Introduction: The Symbolic Annihilation of Women by the Mass Media." In *Hearth and Home: Images of Women in the Mass Media*, edited by Gaye Tuchman, Arlene Kaplan Daniels, and James Benet, 3–38. New York: Oxford University Press.

United Nations (UN). 1995. Beijing Declaration and Platform for Action, para. 234. Accessed October 19, 2013, at www.un.org/womenwatch/daw/beijing/platform/plat1.htm.

van Zoonen, Lisbeth. 1994. *Feminist Media Studies*. London: Sage.

van Zoonen, Lisbeth. 1996. "Feminist Perspectives on the Media." In *Mass Media and Society*, edited by James Curran and Michael Gurevitch. London: Arnold.

Wood, Julia T. 1994. *Gendered Lives: Communication, Gender, and Culture*. Belmont: Wadsworth.

World Association for Christian Communication (WACC). 1995, 2000, 2005, 2010. *Global Media Monitoring Project*. London: WACC.

FURTHER READING

Cameron, Deborah, ed. 1998. *The Feminist Critique of Language: A Reader*. New York: Routledge.

Tuchman, Gaye. 1996. "Representation: Image, Sign, Difference." In *Turning It On: A Reader in Women and Media*, edited by Helen Baehr and Ann Gray. London: Arnold.

Medical and Scientific Experimentation and Gender

ELIZABETH VICTOR
William Paterson University, USA

Gender refers to the social and cultural, as opposed to biological roles and behaviors prescribed for different sexes. Aspects of gender vary widely across and within cultures to mark differences between persons. Although contemporary literature is more attentive to the difference between sex and gender, there is still a tendency for researchers to equivocate the two. While feminist theorists and feminist philosophers are among the most prolific, researchers across disciplines who do not pursue specifically feminist research agendas have explored the degree to which gender has influenced medical and scientific experimentation. Broad topics of inquiry include whether medicine and science construct and perpetuate norms of femininity and masculinity, the influence of gender on how society constructs the institution of medicine and science, as well as whether gender has an influence on particular aspects of medical and scientific experimentation. Specific research topics include but are not limited to whether the ideals of scientific experimentation are fundamentally masculine and exclusionary, whether gender plays a role for those pursuing careers in science and medicine, which projects are publically funded in medicine and science, which methodologies are used to investigate and test hypotheses, which populations are perceived to be acceptable research subjects, how a researcher interprets outcomes, or how outcomes shape policies in a way that disproportionately affects one gender rather than others.

Within the context of medical and clinical research in the United States, it was not until December of 1990 that the National Institutes of Health mandated equal inclusion of minorities and women in study populations. Some examples of studies that were comprised of all white male research participants included the possible relationship between caffeine and heart disease, the effects of aspirin on heart attack prevention and migraine relief, and a pilot project studying the effect of obesity on breast and uterine cancer (Dresser 1992). Some theorists argue that the exclusion of women is explained, at least in part, by the Western cultural assumption that (white) men function as a stand in for all persons and a related cultural association between weakness and femininity. These two cultural misconceptions affect clinical judgments about which members of the population are higher risk research participants, resulting in a substantially lower rate of recruiting women for clinical research (Dresser 1992; Lyerly et al. 2009).

More contemporaneously, there is evidence that the representation of women in clinical research is approaching parity, but researchers persist in failing to analyze data findings in terms of sex and gender (Rogers and Ballantyne 2008). Such pervasive failure to attend to differences has an effect on medical practice where, despite the data, sex and gender difference is regularly not taken into account in diagnosis, treatment, or disease management (Oertelt-Prigione and Regitz-Zagrosek 2012). Finally, there continues to be systematic exclusion of pregnant women and increased caution when including women of childbearing potential (WOCBP is the common acronym in the biomedical and bioethics literature) in clinical research (Dresser 1992; Lyerly et al. 2009).

Feminist bioethicists in particular have been advocates for outlining what responsible inclusion of pregnant women in clinical research entails. Even though researchers are expected to take precautions when involving vulnerable populations in medical experimentation, there is an argument to be made that the exclusion of all pregnant or potentially pregnant women violates the principle of benefice (Dresser 1992). The principle of benefice is one of the ethical principles governing human experimentation research. The principle of benefice states that researchers should minimize harm and maximize benefits for all persons. By excluding women from clinical and biomedical as possible participants, researchers are directly ensuring that any benefits related to experimental interventions are conferred on only a select few (male participants, specifically). Additionally, the reasoning used to justify the exclusion of all pregnant or potentially pregnant persons from medical research appears to be less about the risks of medical intervention during pregnancy and more about fear and control of women's bodies (Lyerly et al. 2009). Fear, moral approbation, or moral censure, as opposed to evidence-based practices, is also found outside of the clinical setting in the social advice found in self-help books and public health campaigns given to women on how to stay healthy and act in the best interest of one's children (Kukla 2006; Lyerly et al. 2009).

Recent analyses of medical advice and public health campaigns targeted at women highlight the ways in which social values about gender influence the interpretation of medical research. For instance, one criticism of a recent breastfeeding campaign sponsored by the United States Department of Health and Human Services, argues that a campaign focused on presenting a woman's failure to breastfeed as a moral failure (e.g., a failure on par with smoking while pregnant) is more likely to produce shame than substantially increase breastfeeding rates (Kukla 2006). Other research on the effects of gender and medical and scientific experimentation attend to the ideals underlying the shared methodologies of both. The ideals that have been brought under scrutiny in the last several decades include the focus on attaining universalized, general, and abstract knowledge.

The methods of medical and scientific experimentation have historically been grounded by the aim of producing knowledge that is general, universal, and abstract. This aim entails developing methods which take as a starting point that it is both possible and preferable to remove the particularities of a researcher's and study participant's identity (identity particularities might include, e.g., social location, gender, religion, age, differences in mobility or motility) within the context of testing a given hypothesis, and the result will be abstracted and generalizable knowledge. The most notable criticisms of the ideals governing medical and scientific experimentation have their origins in feminist standpoint theory.

Feminist standpoint theory has its historical roots in the philosophical and political writings of Georg Hegel, Karl Marx, and Friedrich Engels. Feminist standpoint theory begins with the belief that knowledge is socially situated, which means that if persons have differences in, for instance, social and political power, these differences will influence who is socially located such that she or he will have access to certain kinds of experiences and knowledge. This belief entails that marginalized groups are socially situated such that they have distinctive insights compared with non-marginalized groups, and to the extent that researchers aim to measure differences between persons, they should begin with the experiences of the marginalized.

Notable figures in feminist standpoint theory include but are not limited to Dorothy Smith, Donna Haraway, Sandra Harding, Alison Jaggar, and Patricia Hill Collins. The discourse between theorists have resulted in a formidable body of literature. Some theorists put forward conceptual alternatives to the classical concept of objectivity. One early example of one such alternative is the concept of situated knowledge (Haraway 1988). As a concept, situated knowledge takes seriously the limits of knowledge as necessarily local. The aim for science then should not be absolute, universal knowledge, but rather forms of knowledge that are translatable across epistemic positions (Haraway 1988). Another formative concept in feminist standpoint theory is feminist empiricism. There are different interpretations and nuances that fall under the term feminist empiricism. Empiricism holds that knowledge is derived from sense experience. Feminist empiricism builds on this classical understanding by pointing out, for instance, that a person's sense experiences are defined in part by aspects of a person's identity. Thus, one earlier formulation of feminist empiricism relied on the concept of situated knowers (Harding 1991). One definition of a situated knower holds that knowledge is differentiated according to social location, and researchers should engage in reflexive analysis about how their own social location could shape their research (Harding 1991). From the perspective of feminist empiricism, those engaging in medical and scientific experimentation are situated knowers, which entails that there will be limits to what can be asked, analyzed, and derived knowledge. One suggestion to help overcome this limitation in perspective might be to engage in reflexive analysis combined with engaging the perspectives of marginalized or oppressed groups, the resulting knowledge will be a form of strong objectivity (Harding 1991). This strong objectivity will be less distorted, less partial, and hence, more objective in a robust sense.

Feminist philosophers of science have also taken up the question of whether and to what degree gendered social values influence scientific experimentation. Feminist philosophers of science have a strong tradition of defending the idea of scientific experimentation with the aim of producing knowledge that is reliable, repeatable, and aids in the progress of science. For example, the concept of contextual empiricism holds that social values play a role in each step of the scientific process (Longino 1990, 2002). Contextual empiricism claims that science should be understood to be a social rather than individual enterprise, and is an enterprise that necessitates dialogue between methodologists and critics. However, this need not threaten the objectivity of science and can help scientists to maintain a meaningful concept of knowledge in the face of uncertainty and pluralism (Longino 1990).

Taken seriously, feminist criticisms of scientific ideals have significant consequences for research methodology and design within medicine and scientific experimentation. For example, if a researcher is seeking to study the health of women that regularly employ public assistance or welfare, and the researcher takes seriously the claim that she or he might have a limited epistemic position, the researcher might change how the collection of information is structured. She or he might, in addition to gathering information pertaining to health-related outcomes (e.g., obesity, risk for diabetes or heart disease), begin by asking the women themselves about their lived experiences and challenges they face in their daily lives. This shift in methodology could help identify barriers to access health-related services, limitations in accessing reliable modes of transportation, residing in a food desert, or other specific life experiences that provide a more nuanced picture of the lives of this population, challenge misconceptions or harmful stereotypes, and identify public policy options to alleviate barriers to well-being.

There has been a wealth of literature on the degree to which criticisms arising from feminist standpoint theory and feminist philosophy of science are applicable to different branches within science and medicine. In the contemporary scholarship, there is an ongoing debate about whether values influence the natural sciences, such as physics, chemistry, or biology. Elizabeth Potter (2001) argues that science can be both good science and influenced by gender and class politics. Potter provides an in-depth analysis of Robert Boyle's gas law to demonstrate that even as Boyle's gender and class politics influenced his mechanistic research, it was good science nonetheless. Ágnes Kovács (2012a,b) provides a comprehensive analysis of whether gender affects the substance of chemistry, particularly the model of the ideal gas. Kovács argues in her two-part article that this "cornerstone of the theory of matter in chemical thermodynamics" (2012a) is dependent upon problematic philosophical assumptions critiqued by feminist philosophers, most notably a negligence of the interrelationships among parts and their embodiment. Kovács suggests an alternative theoretical model that relies on feminist philosophical non-ideal "virtues" espoused by feminist philosopher of science, Helen Longino (Kovács 2012a,b). Megan Urry (2008) analyzes whether gender has an effect on how we understand the function of photons. Urry implies that while gender might play a role in what questions a scientist might pursue, "gender does not affect the results in physics, astronomy, or mathematics. *In short, photons have no gender*" (2008, emphasis added).

Explicit forms of discrimination kept women out of the fields of science and medicine, with rare exceptions, for at least hundreds of years. It has been argued, for example, that women were unfit to pursue the intellectual rigors necessary for a career in science or medicine, that intellectual pursuits would make a woman unfit to be a wife and mother, and suggested that the difference in biological function (i.e., the potential to bear children) explained the dearth of women in the fields of science and medicine more generally. In the context of the United States and the United Kingdom, current research has shifted to focus on the effect of implicit, rather than explicit, biases in medical and scientific experimentation. Implicit biases refer to subconscious or unconscious associations that influence a person's judgments of another's competence, trustworthiness, authority, and likelihood to succeed or make an impact on future research. Implicit bias explains how science faculty can favor male students while not realizing they are doing so (Moss-Racusin et al. 2012). By studying the effects of implicit bias some universities, private and public research centers, and laboratories have adjusted how individuals are evaluated, how standards of merit are assessed, and who is promoted within their field of specialization.

SEE ALSO: Clinical Trials and Experimental Science, Bias Against Women in; Feminist Studies of Science; Gender Analysis; Gender Bias in Research; Medicine and Medicalization; Scientific Sexism and Racism; Traditional and Indigenous Knowledge; Women in Science

REFERENCES

Dresser, Rebecca. 1992. "Wanted Single, White Male for Medical Research." *The Hastings Center Report*, 22(1): 24–29. DOI: 10.2307/3562720.

Haraway, Donna. 1988. "Situated Knowledges: The Science Question in Feminism and the Privilege of Partial Perspectives." *Feminist Studies*, 14: 575–599.

Harding, Sandra. 1991. *Whose Science? Whose Knowledge? Thinking from Women's Lives*. Ithaca: Cornell University Press.

Kovács, Ágnes. 2012a. "Gender in the Substance of Chemistry, Part 1: The Ideal Gas." *Hyle*, 18(2): 95–120.

Kovács, Ágnes. 2012b. "Gender in the Substance of Chemistry, Part 2: An Agenda for Theory." *Hyle*, 18(2): 121–143.

Kukla, Rebecca. 2006. "Ethics and Ideology in Breastfeeding Advocacy Campaigns." *Hypatia*, 21(1): 157–180. DOI: 10.1111/j.1527-2001.2006.tb00970.x.

Longino, Helen E. 1990. *Science as Social Knowledge: Values and Objectivity in Scientific Inquiry*. Princeton: Princeton University Press.

Longino, Helen E. 2002. *The Fate of Knowledge*. Princeton: Princeton University Press.

Lyerly, Anne D., et al. 2009. "Risk and the Pregnant Body." *Hastings Center Report*, 39(6): 34–42. DOI: 10.1353/hcr.0.0211.

Moss-Racusin, Corinne A., John F. Dovidio, Victoria L. Brescoll, Mark J. Graham, and Jo Handelsman. 2012. "Science Faculty's Subtle Gender Biases Favor Male Students." *Proceedings of the National Academy of Sciences*, published ahead of print. DOI:10.1073/pnas.1211286109.

Oertelt-Prigione, Sabine, and Vera Regitz-Zagrosek, eds. 2012. *Sex and Gender Aspects in Clinical Medicine*. London: Springer.

Potter, Elizabeth. 2001. *Gender and Boyle's Law of Gases*. Bloomington: Indiana University Press.

Rogers, Wendy A., and Angela J. Ballantyne. 2008. "Exclusion of Women from Clinical Research: Myth or Reality?" *Mayo Clinic Proceedings*, 83(5): 536–542. DOI: 10.4065/83.5.536.

Urry, Megan C. 2008. "Are Photons Gendered? Women in Physics and Astronomy." In *Gendered Innovations in Science and Engineering*, edited by Londa Schiebinger, 150–164. Redwood City: Stanford University Press.

Medicine and Medicalization

MIRANDA R. WAGGONER
Florida State University, USA

Medicalization, now a familiar term in social science and medicine, generally refers to the process by which a problem is defined in medical terms, described using medical language, understood through the adoption of a medical framework, or "treated" with a medical intervention. While the medicalization framework may orient studies on any non-medical phenomenon that comes to be treated as a medical one, feminist scholars have been at the forefront of using a medicalization framework to unearth the gendered and heteronormative discourses and expectations underlying the ways in which bodies and behaviors come to be deemed medical issues. The medicalization of "problems" such as menstruation, pregnancy, childbirth, menopause, or gender identity starkly reveals the transformation of "natural" conditions of life and the body into medical events.

Medicine has long intersected with conversations about social or behavioral problems, yet social scientists and social theorists involved in leveling medicalization critiques prior to the 1970s did not always use the term "medicalization" and, with a few exceptions, were not always concerned with topics of gender, sex, the body, or sexuality. The initial focus in the first empirical studies on "medicalization" processes (from the 1970s and 1980s) could be characterized as "top-down." Research during this time highlighted the cultural influence and imperialistic qualities of the expanding medical profession – and its professional activities – as serving a major part in defining human problems as medical problems. Studies attended to the ever-expanding medical gaze, the encroachment of medicine into other arenas of social life, and the social construction of novel medical categories. Canonical in the early trajectory of medicalization theory was Irving K. Zola's article "Medicine as an Institution of Social Control" (1972), which elucidated the emergence of medicine as a key institution of social life – akin to, but even superseding, the social power of religion and law.

Also central to early sociological studies of medicalization were investigations into how deviant behavior became considered within the purview of medicine. Peter Conrad's work on hyperkinesis (now labeled attention deficit hyperactivity disorder, or ADHD) in 1975 served as a benchmark empirical case in the development of medicalization theory. Analysis of how certain behaviors became understood in medical categories, such as alcoholism, addiction, or mental illness, revealed the medicalization of social problems. Conrad and Joseph Schneider, in their influential text *Deviance and Medicalization* (1980/1992), conceptualized this process as moving from "badness to sickness." This framework facilitated the work of scholars who studied how gendered behaviors deemed "deviant" or outside normative strictures transitioned to be considered within the realm of recognizable medical "fixes."

Inspired by the women's health movement of the 1970s, which in part sought to expose the ways in which female patients lacked authority and autonomy in medical encounters, feminist work in medicalization studies highlighted the overmedicalization and surveillance of women's bodies. Reproduction and reproductive events served as especially illustrious examples of the medicalization process. At the beginning of the twentieth century, women in the United States, for instance, did not seek prenatal care and gave birth at home. In contemporary US society, almost all women receive clinical care throughout their pregnancies and travel to a hospital to give birth. The medicalization of pregnancy followed the rise in medical interpretations of pregnancies, such as in the dissemination of health and behavioral advice to pregnant women, and in medical interventions during pregnancy, such as with the advent of prenatal screening techniques. Medicalization of pregnancy extends now to every potentially pregnant woman. The ascendant framework of pre-conception health and healthcare positions "normal" women's bodies as potentially hostile to future fetuses and thus in need of medical attention. The medical surveillance of the lives of virtually all women of childbearing age signals an exceedingly gendered expansion of medicalization. Childbirth today reflects a highly medicalized event as well, with continual medical monitoring of birthing women. Some advances in medical technology, such as the cesarean section, have saved the lives of many women and children. However, the overuse of interventions has also been linked to loss of autonomy and respect in the birthing process as well as to adverse outcomes such as increased maternal and infant mortality and morbidity.

There remains ongoing concern about whether medicalization has positive or negative effects vis-à-vis gendered experiences, yet this normative focus is not inherent to a medicalization analysis. Often written about as a negative social process (e.g., the "overmedicalization" of society), medicalization sometimes provides social and practical benefits to certain populations. While the early feminist scholarship on medicalization focused on the ways in which women have historically been mistreated by the paternalistic medical establishment, over time it has become clear that women are not always victims of medicalization but rather participate actively in its process. Medicalization has at times been agitated for – and achieved – through patient advocacy for changes in medicine and medical practice. With "conditions" such as infertility, premenstrual syndrome, depressive symptoms, or chronic fatigue, social acceptance of the issue as a medical problem may offer relief and social benefits as well as expand women's options regarding embodied processes and reproductive decisions.

Historically, women's conditions or problems have disproportionately been medicalized more than men's, arguably because women's bodies and their processes are more visible and thus subject to more social surveillance than men's bodies. Nevertheless, scholars have noted how men's bodies and men's health are increasingly medicalized. In this vein, studies have begun to highlight the ways that men's "normal" bodily processes – especially those of aging males – have been medicalized just as women's have. Topics such as hair loss, erectile dysfunction, or testosterone therapy are the focus of medical studies and pharmaceutical development. As one example, the promotion of the drug Viagra for erectile dysfunction facilitated the redefinition of men's sexuality as a medical phenomenon, emancipating many men from impotence yet at the same time framing aging sexuality in unrealistic terms.

Increasingly, sexuality is medicalized as pharmaceuticals enable the medicalization of sex acts. While erectile dysfunction and Viagra have received much scholarly and popular attention, scholars have also noted how "big pharma" is targeting women's sexuality by working to develop drugs that treat the medicalized notion of "female sexual dysfunction" (FSD). The rise of elective cosmetic genital surgeries (e.g., labiaplasty) also reveals the medicalization of the body in a way that aims to alter the material and aesthetic experience of sex. Sexuality is further medicalized through the realm of reproduction, with the pervasive uptake of pharmaceutical contraceptives and assisted reproductive technologies. Additionally, sexuality is medicalized through the continued medical and scientific search for physiological indicators of sexual orientation. This comes despite the documented demedicalization of homosexuality over time. In the middle of the twentieth century, psychiatrists established homosexuality as a medical problem, one that was seemingly amenable to clinical, behavioral, or pharmaceutical intervention. Homosexuality was defined as a psychiatric pathology in the second edition of the *Diagnostic and Statistical Manual of Mental Disorders* (DSM), published by the American Psychiatric Association. Public challenges to this designation led to the formal removal of "homosexuality" in the DSM starting in 1973.

Sex and gender too are deeply medicalized. As another historical case in point, the medicalization of "transsexualism" started in the 1960s as a clinical endeavor to "correct" the relationship between self and the sexed body, rendering parallel genitalia and gender identity. The transsexual body, as an ostensibly deviant body, was depicted as being "cured" by medicine through the advent of sex reassignment surgery, and many transsexual individuals embraced this medicalization, as it aligned the body with the lived experience. As part of the process of medicalization, the term "gender dysphoria syndrome" was coined in the 1970s to refer to cases in which an individual sought sex reassignment surgery. Recent studies have documented the practice of transgender individuals seeking or receiving cross-sex hormones in order to actualize, express, and/or balance sex and gender.

Surgical "solutions" for individuals born intersex reflect the process of medicalizing a natural condition that is not necessarily accompanied by any medical complication. While some individuals and social commentators laud the biomedical advances regarding sex surgery and hormonal therapy, there are potentially devastating consequences. For instance, intersexed infants who undergo surgery may suffer iatrogenic complications of the medical intervention that last throughout their lives. The medicalization of sex and gender can be viewed as deeply degrading ("fixing" bodies to align with a dichotomous gender system), as intensely worrisome (inflicting harm through medical procedures), or as profoundly compassionate (allowing for the realization of the body one desires).

As an analytic matter, the process of medicalization is not uniform. For example, childbirth, as a mundane life event that today usually takes place in the hospital rather than in the home, represents a human condition that is fully medicalized. Eating disorders, with both social and medical explanations for cause and treatment, are semi-medicalized, whereas a contested condition such as fibromyalgia exposes the social struggles between patients and doctors within the medicalization process. Medicalization is also bi-directional; as the paradigmatic example of demedicalization, homosexuality has undergone changes in degree of medicalization and demedicalization throughout history. More recently, scholarly work has pointed to the process of remedicalization. For instance, male circumcision epitomizes a historically demedicalized practice that is accompanied by a reenergized medicalization discourse invoked by certain social groups and medical researchers. Furthermore, recent scholarship highlights the ways in which health professionals may concurrently medicalize and demedicalize phenomena through their work.

Moreover, while medicine as a social institution was pivotal in early theorizing about medicalization, the social organization of medicine has changed markedly since these writings. The power and authority of physicians in deciding whose and which conditions are to be medicalized has long been recognized, yet physicians have become less important to the medicalization process. Hospitals, government, and the pharmaceutical industry have usurped this once-dominant authority. Medicalization today is characterized less by influential claims-makers in medicine and more by medical consumers and market interests. Still, medicine maintains a huge economic force, making up a significant portion of US gross national product. It is also a hefty cultural force, especially with the advent of direct-to-consumer drug marketing, personalized medicine, and the growth of health information on the Internet. Given the evolution in the structure and visibility of medicine and the impact of new technologies, recent scholars have argued that the twenty-first-century manifestation of medicalization is "biomedicalization," a concept that pays much attention to the rise of biomedicine and technoscience. Advances in technoscience allow for novel understandings of gender, sex, and embodied experience through, for instance, the uptake of new reproductive technologies. Amid rapid transformation in medical technology and in the production of knowledge concerning matters of reproduction and the body, there is recognition of the interlocking relationship between medical practices and configurations of bodies, families, and relationships. Embodied experiences of medicalization constitute a ripe area for future scholarship on the process and effect of medical encroachment into topics such as reproduction and kinship that are consistently germane to the human experience.

Medicalization remains a persistent and potent force in culture and in medicine. It continues to be one of the most prevalent and useful analytic themes in scholarship about health and medicine as well as in studies focused on the cultural dimensions of gender and sexuality. There is strong evidence of the expansion of medicalization in society, as scholars have found that disorders or conditions that have been medicalized define a significant chunk of healthcare expenditures in the United States. Moreover, there is growing indication of the globalization of medicalization. With this reality in view, it is imperative for medicalization studies to continue to examine and understand the social sources and ethical ramifications of defining human problems as medical ones. Given that gendered and sexual norms of behavior and identity are so often tied to medicalization processes, future studies of medicalization that employ the critical analytic lenses of sexuality, reproduction, and embodiment will serve a central role in documenting the intersection of society and medicine.

SEE ALSO: Aging, Ageism, and Gender; Male Circumcision; Premenstrual Syndrome (PMS); Reproductive Health; Sexual Regulation and Social Control

FURTHER READING

Barker, Kristin K. 1998. "A Ship Upon a Stormy Sea: The Medicalization of Pregnancy." *Social Science and Medicine*, 47: 1067–1076.

Bell, Susan E. 1987. "Changing Ideas: The Medicalization of Menopause." *Social Science and Medicine*, 24: 535–542.

Carpenter, Laura M. 2010. "On Remedicalisation: Male Circumcision in the United States and Great Britain." *Sociology of Health and Illness*, 32: 613–630.

Clarke, Adele E., Laura Mamo, Jennifer R. Fosket, Jennifer R. Fishman, and Janet K. Shim, eds. 2010. *Biomedicalization: Technoscience, Health, and Illness in the US*. Durham, NC: Duke University Press.

Conrad, Peter. 2007. *The Medicalization of Society: On the Transformation of Human Conditions into Treatable Disorders*. Baltimore: The Johns Hopkins University Press.

Hartley, Heather. 2003. "'Big Pharma' in our Bedrooms: An Analysis of the Medicalization of Women's Sexual Problems." In *Gender Perspectives on Health and Medicine: Key Themes. Advances in Gender Research*, vol. 7: 89–129. London: Elsevier.

Loe, Meika. 2004. *The Rise of Viagra: How the Little Blue Pill Changed Sex in America*. New York: NYU Press.

Markens, Susan. 1996. "'The Problematic of 'Experience': A Political and Cultural Critique of PMS." *Gender and Society*, 10: 42–58.
Preves, Sharon E. 2003. *Intersex and Identity: The Contested Self*. New Brunswick: Rutgers University Press.
Riessman, Catherine Kohler. 1983. "Women and Medicalization: A New Perspective." *Social Policy*, 14: 3-18.
Riska, Elianne. 2010. "Gender and Medicalization and Biomedicalization Theories." In *Biomedicalization: Technoscience, Health, and Illness in the US*, edited by A.E. Clarke, L. Mamo, J.R. Fosket, J.R. Fishman, and J.K. Shim, 147–170. Durham, NC: Duke University Press.
Rosenfeld, Dana, and Christopher A. Faircloth. 2006. *Medicalized Masculinities*. Philadelphia: Temple University Press.
Torres, Jennifer M.C. 2014. "Medicalizing to Demedicalize: Lactation Consultants and the (De)medicalization of Breastfeeding." *Social Science and Medicine*, 100: 159–166.

Men's Magazines

DAVID FREDERICK
Chapman University, USA

JUSTIN LYNN
California State University, USA

BRANDON RONNE
Chapman University, USA

Men's magazines are publications that are printed or published electronically and marketed specifically to heterosexual men. These magazines focus on men's lifestyle issues, particularly as they relate to sex, relationships, physical fitness, and sports. They contain humorous articles as well as articles covering social or political issues perceived to be of interest to heterosexual men. Men's magazines provide one example of what it takes to be considered a masculine man, and often feature conventionally attractive women photographed in sexual poses with little clothing. In the United Kingdom, they are commonly referred to as "lads' magazines" or "lads' mags" (Ricciardelli, Clow, and White 2010).

Historically, lifestyle magazines were primarily targeted at women. Men's lifestyle magazines, however, started to gain popularity following the launch of the magazine *Loaded* in the United Kingdom in 1994. The popularity of *Loaded* led to the development of many similar magazines and periodicals, including *Minx, Zoo, Maxim, Stuff*, and *FHM* (*For Him Magazine*). The magazines typically feature raunchy jokes, explicit commentary on sexuality, and celebration of aggressive masculinity. Men's lifestyle magazines also emerged that were targeted at different ethnic groups. For example, *King, BlackMen*, and *Smooth* magazines are targeted at African Americans in the United States. The emergence of these magazines may have been driven by the perception that men's magazines such as *Maxim* cater primarily to white men and portray white men as the norm. In an interview, the editor of *Smooth*, Sean Cummings, stated: "We've positioned ourselves to be the black *Maxim* … These books allow us to celebrate the beauty of our women without compromise. For years, magazines like *FHM, Maxim*, and *Stuff* have showed you their idea of beauty – a blond and blue-eyed 110-pound woman. Now we're showing you ours."

A related set of magazines also emerged during this time that emphasized physical fitness and health as the primary content, but then surrounded this with content related to sex, dating, and other issues perceived to be of interest to men. In the United States, popular examples of these include *Men's Health* and *Men's Fitness*.

Many men's magazines now have substantial reader bases and subscribers, with some publications exceeding 2 million monthly readers/subscribers. A number of men's magazines (e.g., *Men's Health, Maxim, FHM, Fitness*, etc.) can also be found listed in the most circulated publications in the United

States (Alliance for Audited Media 2013). Some magazines, such as *Maxim*, have international versions in a wide variety of other countries as well.

One explanation for the rise in lads' magazines is that these publications began to emerge in order to address a growing number of men's questions and/or possible anxieties about masculinity and what it means to be "manly" in the twentieth century (Ricciardelli, Clow, and White 2010). These magazines filled a niche that was not covered by some of the longer running men's magazines such as *Details* and *GQ* (formerly *Gentleman's Quarterly*), which emphasize men's fashion and lifestyle but also cover social and political issues, and are sometimes more associated with the "metrosexual" lifestyle (metropolitan + heterosexual). The term "metrosexual" stereotypically refers to men who are meticulous about grooming and maintaining their appearance and who spend a significant amount of money and time on shopping and appearing fashionable (Segal 1993). Lads' magazines were able to distinguish themselves by celebrating a version of masculinity that, while still embracing consumerism, targets a less affluent readership and a form of masculinity that celebrates aggression, sports, and being explicitly sexual. The different men's magazines present different forms of masculinity as ideal depending on the social class position of the readers, with *GQ* targeting men with a higher socioeconomic status.

The content of these publications has recently received attention from researchers and social commentators regarding the potential effects that these magazines might have on readers. Men's magazines are largely similar to women's magazines in terms of their structure and focus on consumerism (Mooney 2008). Like women's magazines, they emphasize how one can attain the perceived social ideals for their gender through purchasing different consumer products.

One common theme in men's magazines is the focus on attaining sexual gratification outside of committed relationships. Exposure to these magazines provides men with a particular view of sex and how they should act toward women. In these magazines, tips on how to "score" with women are common, as are tales of sexual exploits (Tinknell et al. 2003). This emphasis on attaining sexual partners with minimal time or resources may be a popular theme in these magazines because it taps into an evolved predisposition in men to seek short-term affairs as one way to maximize reproductive fitness (Schmitt 2005). Alternatively, this may reflect one way for men to achieve higher social status as part of a socially constructed gender system that encourages men to define their masculinity, in part, through their sexuality. In one correlational study, men who reported reading men's magazines more often also indicated more interest in casual sex outside of committed relationships, and also expected a greater variety of sexual activities to occur within a committed relationship (e.g., sex, group sex, bondage). This, however, does not necessarily mean that reading the magazines causes these attitudes to form. It is possible that men with these attitudes are more likely to choose to read men's magazines. Increased consumption of men's magazines was not related to acceptance of "rape myths" such as the idea that women are to blame if they are sexually assaulted (Taylor 2006).

One concern that has been raised regarding these magazines is how they represent male and female bodies. In male-oriented publications, it has been found that women are routinely sexually objectified: women are typically photographed in sexual poses with little clothing and men are expected to value them for their appearance rather than other aspects of their identity. Some of these photos, however, are accompanied by interviews with the women that allow men to feel more of a connection with the woman's personality (or, at least, her representation of her views and personality). Objectification, however, is often explicit, with photographs commonly featuring partially exposed breasts or buttocks (Krassas, Blauwkamp, and Wesselink 2003).

There has also been concern raised regarding the messages in men's magazines regarding fitness and health, in particular as this relates to the publications *Men's Health* and *Men's Fitness*. These magazines routinely present men who are very toned and muscular as ideal (Frederick, Fessler, and Haselton 2005), along with advertisements for protein shakes and other dietary regimes (Ricciardelli, Clow, and White 2010), suggesting that men can attain this masculine ideal through use of consumer products. The extent to which reading these magazines actually impacts men's attitudes and behaviors remains largely speculative and untested.

SEE ALSO: Images of Gender and Sexuality in Advertising; Masculinism; Media and Gender Socialization; Popular Culture and Gender; Representation; Sexual Objectification; Visual Culture

REFERENCES

Alliance for Audited Media. 2013. "Consumer Magazine Circulation Averages 2013." Accessed August 20, 2015, at http://abcas3.auditedmedia.com/ecirc/magtitlesearch.asp.

Frederick, David. A., Dan M. T. Fessler, and Martie G. Haselton. 2005. "Do Representations of Male Muscularity Differ in Men's and Women's Magazines?" *Body Image*, 2: 1407–1415.

Krassas, Nicole R., Joan M. Blauwkamp, and Peggy Wesselink. 2003. "'Master Your Johnson': Sexual Rhetoric in *Maxim* and *Stuff* Magazines." *Sexuality and Culture*, 7: 98–119.

Mooney, Annabelle. 2008. "Boys Will Be Boys: Men's Magazines and the Normalisation of Pornography." *Feminist Media Studies*, 8: 247–265.

Ricciardelli, Rosemary, Kimberly A. Clow, and Philip White. 2010. "Investigating Hegemonic Masculinity: Portrayals of Masculinity in Men's Lifestyle Magazines." *Sex Roles*, 63: 64–78.

Schmitt, David P. 2005. "Sociosexuality from Argentina to Zimbabwe: A 48-nation Study of Sex, Culture, and Strategies of Human Mating." *Behavioral and Brain Sciences*, 28: 247–275.

Segal, Lynne. 1993. "Changing Men: Masculinities in Context." *Theory and Society*, 22: 625–641.

Taylor, Laramie D. 2006. "College Men, Their Magazines, and Sex." *Sex Roles*, 55: 693–702.

Tincknell, Estella, Deborah Chambers, Joost Van Loon, and Nichola Hudson. 2003. "'Begging for It': New Femininities, Social Agency, and Moral Discourse in Contemporary Teenage and Men's Magazines." *Feminist Media Studies*, 3: 47–63.

Menarche

DANIELLE V. SAMUELS and MISAKI N. NATSUAKI
University of California, Riverside, USA

Menarche, the onset of menstruation, is an abrupt event that is particularly salient against the backdrop of the more gradual and continuous processes of pubertal development. It is conferred unique status as the harbinger of reproductive fertility in females and symbolic shift from girlhood to womanhood, a biological transition that requires psychological and social adjustment. Although the meaning and psychosocial experience of menarche vary across individuals and cultures, the sequence of biological events that precede and define it unfold in uniform fashion.

Menarche is a relatively late event in the course of female pubertal development. It comes at the end of a complex series of biological developments at the neuroendocrine level that involve two independent but overlapping components, adrenarche and gonadarche (Styne and Grumbach 2008). Adrenarche, which typically occurs between ages 6 and 9, refers to the maturation of the hypothalamic-pituitary-adrenal (HPA) axis, during which levels of adrenal androgens begin to increase. These contribute to the growth of pubic and axillary hair. Gonadarche, which begins at approximately ages 9 to 11, involves the maturation of the ovaries and corollary increases in gonadal hormones (e.g., estradiol) spurred by the reactivation of the gonadotropin-releasing hormone (GnRH) pulse generator in the brain. Inhibited since infancy, the first signal of its reactivation is breast development followed by menarche. The mean age of menarche among American women born between 1980 and 1984 is 12.4 years, a secular decline from a mean age of 13.3 years among those born prior to 1920 (McDowell, Brody, and Hughes 2007).

Whereas the term menarche refers to a biological event in the body, interest in the topic has historically focused on the psychological and social aspects of the transition. The majority of early research on the psychological experience of menarche was conducted in Western countries in the 1970s and 1980s. These studies revealed problematic dimensions of menarche as an embodied experience accompanied by negative feelings including shame, confusion, and anxiety, particularly when girls were unprepared or ahead of their peers (Ruble and Brooks-Gunn 1982). Ongoing investigations have confirmed these negative reactions, but increasing attention is being paid to ambivalent and positive reactions to menarche (Lee 2008), and to cross-cultural comparisons (Uskul 2004). Current emphases in research include factors that influence the experience of menarche, their implications for adjustment, and the timing of menarche in relation to one's same-age peers.

Psychologists and anthropologists who study menarcheal experience often draw on narrative accounts to explore how girls experience it in relation to the larger sociocultural meaning of the event. In most cultures, communities, and families, menstruation and menarche remain somewhat taboo topics (Uskul 2004). For instance, some religious practices (e.g., Orthodox Jewish laws of niddah) consider menstruating females as impure. As such, a defining feature of menarche across cultures is secrecy and discourses of concealment. Females describe leaking or visible blood as a humiliating event, and elaborate systems of concealment (e.g., wearing dark-colored pants, special pouches for tampons) are common practice (Uskul 2004).

Positive reactions to menarche among females across cultures are associated with preparedness and prior information (Orringer and Gahagan 2010) and maternal support (Lee 2008). Girls from various cultural backgrounds express a salient need for reassurance that menstruation is a normative part of being a female, and a cognitively coherent explanation for its occurrence. Further, some contemporary movements such as menstrual health activism reclaim menstruation as empowering (Bobel 2010).

Contemporary researchers find that the effect of menarche on psychological adjustment is influenced by its timing. Specifically, there is a robust association between early menarche (as opposed to on-time or late) and negative psychological outcomes, including depression, anxiety, delinquency, and substance abuse (Ge and Natsuaki 2009). Moreover, early menarche may be a risk factor for adult breast cancer (Apter, Reinilä, and Vihko 1989). Recently, emerging research on antecedents of early menarche has focused on environmental stressors, including family conflict, paternal absence, stepfather presence, and sexual abuse (Allison and Hyde 2013).

Future directions in theory and research will continue to focus on elucidating specific mechanisms by which early menarche arises and leads to negative psychological and health outcomes. Age at menarche is a crucial marker in such investigations yet it relies on self-report and shows moderate reliability (Dorn et al. 2013). As such, a focus in methodology will be on finding multiple and more reliable measures for age at menarche.

SEE ALSO: Menopause; Menstrual Activism; Menstrual Rituals; Niddah; Reproductive Health

REFERENCES

Allison, Carlie M., and Janet S. Hyde. 2013. "Early Menarche: Confluence of Biological and Contextual Factors." *Sex Roles*, 68: 55–64. DOI: 10.1007/s11199-011-9993-5.

Apter, Dan, M. Reinilä, and Reijo Vihko. 1989. "Some Endocrine Characteristics of Early Menarche, a Risk Factor for Breast Cancer, are Preserved into Adulthood." *International Journal of Cancer*, 44: 783–787.

Bobel, Chris. 2010. *New Blood: Third-Wave Feminism and the Politics of Menstruation*. New Brunswick: Rutgers University Press.

Dorn, Lorah D., Stephanie Pabst, Lisa M. Sontag-Padilla, Abbigail Tissot, and Elizabeth J. Susman. 2013. "Longitudinal Reliability of Self-Reported Age at Menarche in Adolescent Girls: Variability across Time and Setting." *Developmental Psychology*, 49: 1187–1193. DOI: 10.1037/a0029424.

Ge, Xiaojia, and Misaki N. Natsuaki. 2009. "In Search of Explanations for Early Pubertal Timing Effects on Developmental Psychopathology." *Current Directions in Psychological Science*, 18: 327–331. DOI: 10.1111/j.1467-8721.2009.01661.

Lee, Janet. 2008. "A Kotex and a Smile: Mothers and Daughters at Menarche." *Journal of Family Issues*, 29: 1325–1347.

McDowell, Margaret A., Debra J. Brody, and Jeffrey P. Hughes. 2007. "Has Age at Menarche Changed? Results from the National Health and Nutrition Examination Survey (NHANES) 1999–2004." *Journal of Adolescent Health*, 40: 227–231. DOI: 10.1016/j.jadohealth.2006.12.019.

Orringer, Kelly, and Sheila Gahagan. 2010. "Adolescent Girls Define Menstruation: A Multiethnic Exploratory Study." *Health Care for Women International*, 31: 831–847. DOI: 10.1080/07399331003653782.

Ruble, Dianne N., and Jeanne Brooks-Gunn. 1982. "The Experience of Menarche." *Child Development*, 53: 1557–1566.

Styne, Dennis M., and Melvin M. Grumbach. 2008. "Puberty: Ontogeny, Neuroendocrinology, Physiology, and Disorders." In *Williams Textbook of Endocrinology*, edited by Henry Kronenberg, Shlomo Melmed, Kenneth Polonsky, and Reed Larsen, 969–1104. Philadelphia: Saunders.

Uskul, Ayse. 2004. "Women's Menarche Stories from a Multicultural Sample." *Social Science and Medicine*, 59: 667–679. DOI: 10.1016/j.socscimed.2003.11.031.

Menopause

HEATHER DILLAWAY
Wayne State University, USA

Most women experience menopause in their late 40s or early 50s. There is continued debate about whether male menopause exists and what it entails, but the vast majority of published research still focuses on women's menopause. Clinically, "menopause" refers to the cessation of menstruation at midlife, or the final menstrual period (FMP). The FMP is one point in a much longer physiological process, however (Harlow et al. 2008). In fact, the menopausal transition can include multiple stages. "Perimenopause" refers to the transitional time surrounding the end of menstruation (including the year following the FMP). "Premenopause" is the time before perimenopause, when women might start to notice some bodily changes such as breast tenderness, hot flashes, and changes in menstrual bleeding (Prior 1998). Menopause is defined retrospectively as the moment at which women have reached a full 12 months past their FMP. "Postmenopause" does not start until 12 months after the FMP. While these clinical definitions exist, the signs and symptoms of menopause and the timing or length of each stage can vary significantly from woman to woman (Harlow et al. 2008). Women also have their own ways of referring to certain stages of this transition. For instance, perimenopause is often what individual women refer to as "menopause," since it is in perimenopause that women will experience signs and symptoms. Other common terms for the entire transition are reproductive aging, the climacteric, the change, or the change of life, and the word "menopause" may be used to refer to the entire transitional process.

Biomedical researchers have suggested that menopause is a "deficiency disease" (Lyons and Griffin 2003). The traditional biomedical model assumes that when estrogen levels decline below those of the reproductive years, a woman becomes vulnerable to a range of chronic illnesses, including heart, bone, and brain disease (Murtagh and Hepworth 2003). This estrogen deficiency perspective is reflected in the original name given to prescription estrogen supplements in the United States – namely, "hormone replacement therapy" or HRT. Prescriptions for HRT soared in the 1980s and 1990s as a result of this "deficiency" mindset (Hersh, Stefanick, and Stafford 2004). Over the last few decades biomedical opinion has diversified, however. It has become more common among health professionals to state that menopause is "perfectly natural," although professionals remain divided about whether menopause is related to negative health effects or necessitates medical treatment. Additionally, there is a broader range of medical and alternative treatments for menopause now than there were several decades ago, and the emphasis on "replacement" of estrogen in medical treatment has lessened.

Anthropologists and behavioral biologists remind us that menopause is a human universal, ensuring that humans have a life stage during which women are post-reproductive and healthy – that precedes their old age – and this may reflect the working of evolutionary forces (Derry 2006). Perhaps a postmenopausal life stage was adaptive because human groups benefited from older members with social and technical skills (Derry 2006). Anthropologists and other social scientists have also documented the variations in menopausal attitudes and experiences across countries, racial-ethnic groups, and social classes. Anthropologists have specifically explained how the meanings and experiences of menopause differ depending on where and when we research these topics (Melby, Lock, and Kaufert 2005). Hot flashes, for instance, are not so widely reported in countries such as India, Japan, and China, yet most women in Europe and North America report this vasomotor symptom (Ayers, Forshaw, and Hunter 2010). Differences in symptom reporting may result from varied diets and levels of exercise, availability of medical treatment, and wide-ranging attitudes toward menopause and aging.

Until recently, in the United States, cultural attitudes toward older women and menopause have been fairly negative (Komesaroff, Rothfield, and Daly 1997). Feelings of negativity sometimes come from women's thoughts about whether menopause means that they are "old" or aging or how they feel about the loss of fertility. On the other hand, feminist scholars suggest that increasing numbers of women see menopause as positive or neutral, even in the United States (Komesaroff, Rothfield, and Daly 1997; Lyons and Griffin 2003). Women may view menopause as ushering in a good life stage, better and more carefree than the one before it, because it represents relief from the burdens of pregnancy, menstruation, and contraception. Ultimately, menopause can be positive, negative, or mixed in meaning, depending on the various everyday contexts of women's lives and cultural attitudes toward older women in any particular society.

SEE ALSO: Aging, Ageism, and Gender; Body Politics; Menarche; Reproductive Health; Senior Women and Sexuality in the United States

REFERENCES

Ayers, Beverly, Mark Forshaw, and Myra Hunter. 2010. "The Impact of Attitudes Towards the Menopause on Women's Symptom Experience: A Systematic Review." *Maturitas*, 65: 28–36.
Derry, Paula. 2006. "A Lifespan Biological Model of Menopause." *Sex Roles*, 54: 393–399.
Harlow, Sioban, Ellen Mitchell, Sybil Crawford, Bin Nan, Roderick Little, and John Taffe. 2008. "The ReSTAGE Collaboration: Defining Optimal Bleeding Criteria for Onset of Early Menopausal Transition." *Fertility and Sterility*, 89: 129–140.
Hersh, Adam, Marsha Stefanick, and Randall Stafford. 2004. "National Use of Postmenopausal Hormone Therapy: Annual Trends and Response to Recent Evidence." *Journal of the American Medical Association*, 291: 47–53.
Komesaroff, Paul, Philipa Rothfield, and Jeanne Daly, eds. 1997. *Reinterpreting Menopause: Cultural and Philosophical Issues*. London: Routledge.
Lyons, Antonia C., and Christine Griffin. 2003. "Managing Menopause: A Qualitative Analysis of Self-Help Literature for Women at Midlife." *Social Science and Medicine*, 56: 1629–1642.
Melby, Melissa, Margaret Lock, and Patricia Kaufert. 2005. "Culture and Symptom Reporting at Menopause." *Human Reproduction Update*, 11(5): 495–512.
Murtagh, Madeleine J., and Julie Hepworth. 2003. "Menopause as a Long-Term Risk to Health: Implications of General Practitioner Accounts of Prevention for Women's Choice and Decision-Making." *Sociology of Health and Illness*, 25: 185–207.
Prior, Jerilynn. 1998. "Perimenopause: The Complex Endocrinology of the Menopausal Transition." *Endocrine Reviews*, 19: 397–428.

FURTHER READING

Voda, Ann. 1992. "Menopause: A Normal View." *Clinical Obstetrics and Gynecology*, 35: 923–933.

Menstrual Activism

BREANNE FAHS
Arizona State University, USA

Menstruation has a long history of constructing the menstruating body as shameful, taboo, silent, and even pathological. From the historic separation of women's menstruating bodies into menstrual huts to the idea that the premenstrual and menstrual body is disgusting and disordered, women face a plethora of challenges to accepting and even celebrating their menstrual cycles. From the mental health diagnosis of premenstrual dysphoric disorder and popular culture depictions of menstruation, women have had to confront their internalized body shame alongside cultural expectations that menstruation remain in the closet. Menstrual activists, on the other hand, have developed a variety of ways to combat these trends. These activists have helped women to feel more open and accepting toward their menstrual cycle and have focused on changing institutions that either promote harmful products or encourage women to construct their menstrual cycles as a source of mental illness, psychological distress, or physical pain. Menstrual activists also promote anti-consumerism via alternative menstrual products, critiques of commercials and advertising about menstrual products, and by encouraging collective resistance to the corporate interests connected to menstrual management.

THE TABOO OF MENSTRUATION

Women's bodies in their natural state have long been treated with disdain and disgust, as routine processes of the body such as growing body hair, breastfeeding (especially in public), having natural body odors, weight gain, sweating during exercise, eating (especially in public), masturbating, and menstruating each month have become more tightly controlled, monitored, and, in some cases, eliminated by the ever-narrowing cultural ideas of modern womanhood. Women are advised against hairiness, to only breastfeed in the confines of their own home, to cover their natural scents with deodorants and perfumes, to avoid weight gain at all costs, to avoid sweating during exercise and to avoid exercise altogether, to never eat in excess and certainly not eat in public, to keep silent about masturbating, and to manage their menstrual cycles in careful ways. As such, women routinely engage in a variety of practices that manage their bodies, whether via shaving or waxing, covering themselves while breastfeeding or never breastfeeding in public spaces, avoiding exercise altogether, or hiding their tampons, pads, and menstrual fluids from public view. While women often struggle with accepting their leaky and viscous bodies – historically, women's bodies have been seen as more difficult to manage than men's bodies – menstruation represents a difficult union between external appraisals of women's bodies and women's negotiations of bodily taboo.

Traditional gender scripts dictate that women keep menstruation hidden from view and that they manage their menstrual cycles without talking about menstruation. Though there are a few socially acceptable environments where talk of menstruation is permitted (for example, doctor's offices, health class in school, or conversations with one's mother or sister(s) when first starting menstruation), most social contexts dictate silence and secrecy around menstrual cycles. When women worry about revealing their menstrual status, they access deep-seated historical beliefs about menstruation. Historically, women were taught to look at their menstrual cycles as something in need of control and discipline, as menstrual blood implied disease, social violations, and spiritual corruption. Western narratives of menstruation today treat it as failed reproduction in large part because women's bodies are still treated as machines of reproduction, perhaps signaling the capitalistic priorities of productivity and total lack of cyclic behavior (e.g., leisure, sleeping, resting). In spite of all of this menstrual negativity that permeates the West, some cultures, particularly African tribes, value menstruation and see it as a powerful and revered practice deserving of respect and admiration. Some African tribes in sub-Saharan Africa believe that women's menstrual blood will help with that year's crops and weather patterns, while others believe that menstruating women have special powers.

Menstrual activists have expressed concern that women face an onslaught of images and ideas that treat menstruation as disgusting, tainting, and even disabling. Films typically portray menstruation as a "horrifying" discovery, the butt of a joke (e.g., *Superbad*), or as a coming-of-age moment for girls when they first discover their menstrual cycles have begun. This ignores the basic adult experience of menstruation and instead focuses on the menstruating teenager or adolescent as the normative menstruating body. Other media-generated stories promote to women the idea that menstrual cycles could halt participation in sports, career, or family life, prevent full range of movement, and impact sexual contact. Negative rhetoric surrounding menstruation has even circulated as justification for preventing women from becoming president ("You cannot trust something that bleeds for seven days and doesn't die!" is a popular joke in the United States targeting menstruating women) or holding serious positions of power and decision-making. The notion that menstrual cycles impede women's accurate judgment and rationality exists throughout the media.

Further, the menstruating body today is also treated as a nuisance, so much so that many women now express a desire to rid themselves of their menstrual cycles via pharmaceutical interventions like the oral contraceptive Seasonale, which creates four periods per year, or Lybrel, which eliminates all periods. These birth control pills allow for occasional or no menstrual cycles rather than monthly cycles, placing value on the non-menstruating body over that of the menstruating body. This surge in menstrual suppression products idealizes the non-menstruating body as having the ultimate cultural value. Similarly, when selling disposable menstrual products, advertisers typically depict women as unclean, unfeminine, and dirty in order to effectively market panty liners, pads, and tampons. These advertisements almost never discuss the environmental consequences of disposable, one-time-use products while also encouraging women to see menstruation as taboo and worrisome. The phrase *feminine hygiene* – a relic from the 1930s advertisements for birth control – still suggests the dirtiness of the natural female body in contrast to the cleanliness one can obtain through the use of menstrual products.

In psychological studies of menstruation, girls face negative messages about menstruation quite early on as they learn to dislike menstruation even before it happens. Older girls, those prone to body image problems, those with less sexual experience, and those who did not communicate with their mothers about menstruation are particularly at risk for negative menstrual attitudes. As adults, this pattern of menstrual negativity continues, as roughly half of adult women largely avoid having sex during their menstrual cycles and a third of adult women state that they would never want to have sex while menstruating. Lesbian and bisexual women (regardless of whether they had a male or female partner) described menstrual sex more positively than did heterosexual women, perhaps suggesting the impact of sexual identity on menstrual attitudes.

FIGHTING BACK WITH MENSTRUAL ACTIVISM

In response to this overwhelming negativity expressed toward menstruation throughout our contemporary culture, menstrual activists – typically a mix of feminist activists, environmental activists, and youth/punk activists – have designed ways to fight back. Taking up an often controversial and confrontational approach, menstrual activists have a range of goals and practices that they have enacted in order to change the culture of menstruation and to combat the consumerist, shame-based, patriarchal, and sexist basis of menstrual management and menstrual hygiene today.

Menstrual activism, also known as menarchy (a combination of *menstrual* and *anarchy*) first appeared during the early 1970s when radical feminists taught classes to women about how to perform menstrual extraction upon themselves. This procedure, first introduced by Lorraine Rothman in 1971, allowed women to extract their menstrual blood for the purposes of early abortion or to shorten the length of their menstrual cycles. It also functioned to allow women to take menstruation into their own hands and menstruate on their own terms. Since then, menstrual activism has grown into a larger movement that uses media campaigns, consciousness-raising, educational campaigns, and assaults on mainstream representations of menstruation. Menstrual activists include a range of people interested in reimagining the menstruating body: student activists, do-it-yourself advocates, health experts, scholars, teachers, public health researchers and practitioners, anarchists, anti-consumerist advocates, and a host of others.

One common aim of menstrual activism includes the depathologization of menstruation as a "disorder" or a problem. This has resulted in campaigns to fight against "premenstrual syndrome" (PMS) as a diagnosable problem, as feminist scholars have called into question how we can continue to promote a "syndrome" with no reliable symptoms across women (each woman typically reports an array of symptoms that differ greatly from person to person and that can encompass just about anything distressing or physically upsetting). Menstrual activists have also fought against the inclusion of "premenstrual dysphoric disorder" (PMDD) as a diagnosable mental illness, citing that psychiatrists and doctors typically treat PMDD with the same medications as used to treat major depressive disorder (they use Prozac in a pink package) and that there are no reliable data showing support for PMDD as an actual mental illness. Rather, PMDD promotes the idea that women are "ill" or "sick" in their natural states, and that cycling is a problem rather than something to be embraced.

Additionally, menstrual activists have fought against mainstream menstrual products that typically use toxic chemicals (dioxin, rayon), bleached cotton, and other irritants that harm the vaginal lining and disrupt the natural flow of the body. Along these lines, menstrual activists have advocated for the use of alternative products like organic cotton tampons, the menstrual cup (a device that catches menstrual fluid and can be reused and worn for up to 12 hours), sea sponges (natural absorbers of menstrual fluid that can be washed and reused), reusable menstrual pads (these can typically be used for three years or more), and make-it-yourself menstrual products that avoid conflating menstrual management with consumerism. Activists have also historically fought to have toxic shock syndrome recognized and to get warning labels placed on tampons; currently, activists are fighting to have the chemical bleaching process changed for commercial tampons.

Activists have also brought a critical voice to menstrual suppression products and encouraged women to develop more positive feelings about menstruation by seeing it as affirming of womanhood, a sign of nonpregnancy, a symbol of overall health and well-being, a natural part of the cycles of life, and as a marker of change and growth. Rather than promoting menstruation as a hidden and secretive part of life, menstrual activists advocate for more education about the menstrual cycle and more openness about discussing menstruation in health settings, classrooms, and within the home. Working on cross-gender health classes (where boys learn about menstruation too), open dialogues on college campuses, and more education about the connections between menstrual shame and menopausal shame are new areas of activism that menstrual activists have begun to take up.

Most importantly, menstrual activists want both men and women to develop a stronger and more nuanced critical consciousness about the social constructedness of menstruation and the links between gender, power, and menstruation. In particular, menstrual activists almost all embrace the notion that menstruation should be treated as less of a taboo and as less shame-based, sometimes using humor, songwriting, and subversion as tactics to combat the menstrual taboo. Menstrual activists strive for more positive representations of menstruation along with safer products and more comprehensive education about the menstrual cycle. Having more honest and forthcoming dialogue about women's menstrual cycles, along with encouraging more accurate and honest information about menstruation and the available alternatives to mainstream menstrual products, all represent key goals for menstrual activists. From advocating herbal remedies for cramps to celebrating the power of women and their bodies to showcasing connections between the personal and the political to teaching women to track and understand their menstrual cycles in humorous or irreverent ways, the goals of menstrual activists are multiple. Some menstrual activists are questioning why many women hate their periods and how culture, gender, and consumerism have shaped these reactions. Still other menstrual activists are taking on a host of other activist projects: tackling negative menstrual language, intervening about how to teach girls and boys about menstruation in health classes, developing modules for how to better account for and involve the trans and queer community in menstrual activism, and how to assess "knowledge gaps" about menstruation. Songs like Robyn Archer's "Menstruation Blues" and the famed event where lead singer of the band L7, Donita Sparks, threw her tampon into the crowd mid-show are examples of how musicians can (perhaps unwittingly) become icons of menstrual activism.

Menstrual activists also emphasize that everyday acts of resistance – from not using commercial pads and tampons, consuming less television, talking to one's partner(s) about menstruation and menstrual sex, insisting on better menstrual education, fighting back against toxic shock syndrome and dioxin in tampons, and publicly discussing menstruation – play a particularly powerful role in upending traditional ideas about menstrual silence and taboo. With multiple goals, many faces, and a strong commitment to challenging personal and political ideologies about menstruation, menstrual activists are working to change the culture and politics of menstruation.

SEE ALSO: Body Politics; Feminist Activism; Feminist Movements in Historical and Comparative Perspective; Menstrual Rituals; Niddah; Patriarchy; Politics of Representation; Premenstrual Syndrome (PMS); Taboo; Women's Health Movement in the United States

FURTHER READING

Bobel, Chris. 2006. "'Our Revolution Has Style': Contemporary Menstrual Product Activists 'Doing Feminism' in the Third Wave." *Sex Roles*, 54(5–6): 331–345.

Bobel, Chris. 2010. *New Blood: Third Wave Feminism and the Politics of Menstruation*. New Brunswick: Rutgers University Press.

Chrisler, Joan C. 1996. "PMS as a Culture-Bound Syndrome." In *Lectures on the Psychology of Women*, edited by Joan C. Chrisler, Carla Golden, and Patricia D. Rozee, 106–121. New York: McGraw-Hill.

Fahs, Breanne. 2011. "Sex During Menstruation: Race, Sexual Identity, and Women's Qualitative Accounts of Pleasure and Disgust." *Feminism & Psychology*, 21(2): 155–178.

Kissling, Elizabeth A. 2006. *Capitalizing the Curse: The Business of Menstruation*. Boulder: Lynne Rienner.

Mansfield, Phyllis K., and Margaret L. Stubbs. 2007. "The Menstrual Cycle: Feminist Research from the Society for Menstrual Cycle Research." *Women & Health*, 46(1): 1–5.

Rosewarne, Lauren. 2012. *Periods in Pop Culture: Menstruation in Film and Television*. New York: Lexington Books.

Menstrual Rituals

CARINE PLANCKE
Roehampton University, UK

Anthropological literature reveals a widespread occurrence of ritual practices related to women's cyclical bloodshedding, or menstruation, in cultures and religions throughout the world. Foremost among these are menarche (first menstruation) rituals; regular instances of ritual seclusion of menstruating women in special shelters, called "menstrual huts"; and ritual prohibitions and rules regarding food preparation, bathing, sexual contact with men, entrance to sacred places, etc., known as "menstrual taboos." In order to convey the diversity of these rituals, this entry provides a few examples of each type of practice from a variety of cultures, including rituals in traditional settings, those prescribed by monotheistic religions and practices from New Age or Neopagan movements. Adopting a gender-sensitive approach, it highlights evolving interpretations of these rituals in terms of female subordination, power, agency, and creativity.

Beginning in the 1960s, systematic scholarly attention to menstrual rituals developed as a consequence both of the emergence of female anthropologists and of critical interrogations on the place of women in society and their presumed worldwide subordination by men. A highly influential book in this regard was Mary Douglas's *Purity and Danger* (1966). Redefining pollution as disorder, as "matter out of place," Douglas advances that instead of expressing hygienic concerns, cultural views on pollution uphold social rules or confirm the social order, particularly addressing the underlying tensions therein. Accordingly, she states, views on menstrual pollution symbolically encode an underlying social structural ambiguity regarding women and things female; these views flourish most when male domination cannot be fully exercised and domains of female power remain present. Inspired by this theory, Sherry Ortner and Harriet Whitehead interpret beliefs and practices related to menstrual pollution as a cornerstone for maintaining a social order based on male superiority and ceremonial prestige but dependent on female productive labor (Ortner and Whitehead 1981, 20).

This interpretation of menstruation as pollution and of menstrual restrictions as an expression of the inferiorization of women has met with severe criticism. In their work *Blood Magic*, Thomas Buckley and Alma Gottlieb bring together essays on menstrual beliefs and rituals from diverse societies that depict a wide range of rules for conduct regarding menstruation and denote a variety of purposes and meanings (Buckley and Gottlieb 1988). They target the male-focal vision of culture that underlies analyses of pollution, noting how typical ethnography rarely tells the readers what women of the culture at hand think of menstrual periods – either their own or those of other women. This is notably the case with regard to a menstrual custom that has often been singled out as indicative of "low female status:" that of menstrual "seclusion" in special shelters.

An essay by Thomas Buckley (1988) on the Yurok Indians native to California is highly telling in this regard. In Yurok culture, the expression "on moontime" refers to a 10-day seclusion period for women during and after menstruation. When a young Yurok woman explains to Buckley that this is the time when a woman is at the height of her powers, a time of concentrated meditation where women can discover their life purpose and accumulate spiritual energy, he is initially highly skeptical. Having studied the established ethnographies that entail an entirely negative coding of menstruation, he presumes that this is a recent reinterpretation of the traditional custom. However, to his great surprise, he discovers a set of notes by the anthropologist Kroeber that document an unpublished conversation with an old Yurok woman in 1902 and confirm the first woman's account. These notes suggest that the collective 10-day retreat for Yurok women, who share their menstrual periods in synchrony with the moon phases, can be compared to the sweathouse retreats of men and are both considered periods of spiritual advancement.

In a special journal issue entitled *Blood Mysteries: Beyond Menstruation as Pollution*, Janet Hoskins further argues for a complex approach to understanding cultural responses to menstruation in a variety of contexts (Hoskins 2002a). Like Buckley (1988), she incisively questions the simplistic negative reading of menstrual huts as a socially restrictive custom for women. Among the Huaulu of Seram in Eastern Indonesia, where she conducted fieldwork (Hoskins 2002b), women are proud of controlling dangerous blood taboos. Rather than feeling restricted, they feel a sense of empowerment and responsibility from the highly important task of protecting their menfolk, who risk illness and death when approaching a menstruating woman. Instead of considering menstrual seclusion as a burden, they welcome it as a time of extra leisure with the opportunity for activities such as storytelling and singing. By introducing a second case study of another Eastern Indonesian people, the Kodi, Hoskins further undermines the simplistic idea that the existence of menstrual taboos necessarily entails a negative view of menstruation, whereas its absence would reveal a positive or neutral view. The Kodi do not have any overt menstrual taboos; however, they view menstrual blood from a negative perspective, as they fear deliberate menstrual poisoning of men by women who can trick them into sex acts that could make them infertile and impotent.

In addition to criticizing the application of cross-cultural generalities onto menstrual taboos, these studies have also questioned the idea that ritual regulations of menstruation presuppose an ambiguous status for women. In Yupik society in Southwest Alaska, a long list of rules applies to women at menarche, for the year after menarche, and during subsequent menstrual periods. These rules are primarily intended to distance menses, menstrual odor, or the gaze of a menstruating woman from community resources in order to avoid bad luck. However, according to Phyllis Morrow (2002), these rules do not imply that women are considered inferior; indeed, they are viewed as relatively equal partners with men. The overarching principle behind these rules is a need to avoid the inadvertent use of women's powerful bodily substances and to promote an awareness that is essential for maintaining correct reciprocal relationships among people and non-human entities (plants, fish, game, and weather conditions), hence ensuring the community's well-being.

Since the late 1990s, in a context of advancing modernization, westernization, and globalization, anthropologists have addressed the issue of the continuing survival of traditional menstrual rituals, and also the transformations that these rituals undergo in contemporary settings. This has especially been the case for rituals at menarche. Yumiko Tokita-Tanabe (1999) shows how, in the Indian state of Orissa, a girl's menarche ritual is conceived in close parallel to the *raja parba* festival celebrating the menstruation of Mother Earth. Both entail a celebration of female sexual power (*sakti*), which is conceptualized as being related to heat that must be cooled down in order to produce fertility. During the festival, the celebration of female power is paramount; however, in the first menstruation ritual, which consists of the girl's three-day confinement in a room and a subsequent bath ritual, the need to control her nascent fertility is predominant. After the ritual, the girl is restricted: she is not allowed to venture far outside her neighborhood, and she is protected and watched over by male members of her household lest she have sexual relations with men before marriage. Interestingly, Tokita-Tanabe (1999) argues, downplaying the celebratory aspects of female reproductive powers during the menarche ritual and emphasizing women's spatial containment and control over their bodies is a relatively recent phenomenon that is directly related to the modernization of Indian society. Faced with an increasing Western influence that is commonly believed to break down customary morals and norms and affect India's spiritual identity, women have become the bearers of traditional values and have come to symbolize the space of "home" and tradition that must be preserved from the exterior world.

Thera Rasing's analysis of the *chisungu* ritual of the matrilineal Bemba in Zambia further demonstrates that menarche rituals can be sites for maintaining traditional values in a context where female power derived from women's reproductive capacities progressively decreases (Rasing 2004). After her first menstruation, the girl is secluded and receives instructions that are carried out by singing, dancing, and displaying clay models which express traditional values. The instructions are given by a priestess, *nacimbusa*, who as "blood chief" is thought to communicate with the "blood spirit" that activates a girl's menstruation and, consequently, her fertility. Although authorities in the Zambian Roman Catholic Church have repeatedly attempted to adapt the ritual and make it conform to the values of the male-dominated church as part of their policy of inculturation, it continues to be performed in an exclusively female sphere. This is also the case in urban contexts, notwithstanding the deconstruction of traditional womanhood through westernization and the disappearance of women's significant role in religion. Bemba women continue to perform the rite because to them, a woman's role in sexuality is as important today as it was in the past. As imprinted by the rite, the construction of female identity remains central, albeit in new ways.

While the last two accounts demonstrate examples of the recent cultural erosion of women's self-determination and the esteem in which women were traditionally held, studies on menstrual regulations in monotheistic religions, such as Judaism and Islam, frequently emphasize women's growing agency within longstanding patriarchal systems. These studies highlight how, in contemporary contexts, these religious women deal with a difficult dichotomy: compliance with orthodox practice, on the one hand, and a modern life that promotes autonomy and independence, on the other. The opposite outcomes that may result from the negotiation of this tension are explored in the study by Hartman and Marmon (2004) on orthodox Jewish women's perceptions of the *niddah*, the 12-day period of ritual impurity during and after menstrual flow when sexual intercourse and physical intimacy between husband and wife are forbidden. Some women in the study experience the ritually imposed cycle of separation and closeness as a series of deprivations and degradations. They feel especially humiliated by a certain obligation: upon observing a bloodstain during the seven clean days before the final ritual immersion, they must consult a rabbi and show him the undergarment so that he may discern whether this stain renders them unclean. While one woman in the study, as a consequence, simply decides that she has enough sense to make her own decision, another one "shops around" to see which rabbi will offer her the most lenient opinion. In stark contrast with these experiences, other orthodox Jewish women consider the *niddah* deeply empowering: they enjoy the authority inherent in being responsible for both their own and their husbands' observance of the laws. Moreover, they may find a benefit in the constant renewal of sexual interest or appreciate the legislation of a non-sexual sphere within married life that corresponds to the needs of women's bodies.

A similar diversity of experiences is assessed in a study by Nitzan Ziv (2006) on the understanding of menstrual regulations among educated, middle-class Muslim women from urban Morocco. Islamic law exempts menstruating women from praying and participation at Ramadan. While some women therefore view menstruation as a fact of their impurity which prohibits them from participating in sacred religious performances, others develop new interpretations of this law: they are relieved to be provided with a break from praying or fasting all month and believe that the law is a sign of Allah's mercy for the physical weakness of women.

Finally, it should be noted that in contemporary Euro-American settings, some groups of women who do not or not fully identify with mainstream monotheistic religions because of these religions' negative views of the female body instead recreate menstrual rituals in line with traditional or pagan practices perceived as revitalizing and empowering for women in developing their female identity. These rituals are highly variable from one community to another and creatively blend diverse symbols and practices. In a discussion of Neopagan and New Age menarche rituals, Michael Houseman (2007) elucidates a number of recurrent features: the relinquishment of a childhood toy, the prevalence of the color red, bathing, seclusion, a moment of privileged communication between mother and daughter, episodes connoting transition (such as crossing a line, entering a circle, or passing under spread legs or raised arms), adult women telling stories about menstruation and womanhood, gift-giving, and so on. However, he stresses that these rites are only deemed effective when consciously adapted to the peculiarities of the situation at hand and the individual participants concerned.

A similar creative reconfiguration of a diversity of elements, originating in traditions and religions from different regions and periods, characterizes a menstrual ritual that is part of contemporary pilgrimages for Mary Magdalene in Southern France (Fedele 2014). This ritual, which takes place in a cave dedicated to Mary Magdalene, conflates shamanic, pagan, and Christian elements. It involves the invocation of spirits, the creation of an altar, and the ingestion of homeopathically diluted menstrual blood mixed with wine in a chalice. As such, it enacts a transformation of Christian symbols and actions, inverting their original meaning. The figure of Mary Magdalene in particular is radically altered: appearing both as Jesus's lover and as a priestess of the pre-Christian Goddess, she is defined as the guardian of menstrual blood, allowing the ritual to be experienced as a way to change the world order created by patriarchal Christianity.

SEE ALSO: Androcentrism; Initiation Rites; Menarche

REFERENCES

Buckley, Thomas. 1988. "Menstruation and the Power of Yurok Women." In *Blood Magic: The Anthropology of Menstruation*, edited by Thomas Buckley and Alma Gottlieb, 182–209. Berkeley: University of California Press.

Buckley, Thomas, and Alma Gottlieb. 1988. *Blood Magic: The Anthropology of Menstruation*, Berkeley: University of California Press.

Douglas, Mary. 1966. *Purity and Danger: An Analysis of the Concepts of Pollution and Taboo*, London: Routledge and Kegan Paul.

Fedele, Anna. 2014. "Reversing Eve's Curse: Mary Magdalene, Mother Earth and the Creative Ritualization of Menstruation." *Journal of Ritual Studies*, 28(2): 23–35.

Hartman, Tova, and Naomi Marmon. 2004. "Lived Regulations, Systemic Attributions: Menstrual Separation and Ritual Immersion in the Experience of Orthodox Jewish Women." *Gender and Society*, 18(3): 389–408.

Hoskins, Janet. 2002a. "Introduction: Blood Mysteries: Beyond Menstruation as Pollution." *Ethnology*, 41(4): 299–301.

Hoskins, Janet. 2002b. "The Menstrual Hut and the Witch's Lair in Two Eastern Indonesian Societies." *Ethnology*, 41(4): 317–333.

Houseman, Michael. 2007. "Menstrual Slaps and First Blood Celebrations." In *Learning Religion: Anthropological Approaches*, edited by David Berliner and Ramon Sarro, 31-48. Oxford: Berghahn Books.

Morrow, Phyllys. 2002. "A Woman's Vapor: Yupik Bodily Powers in Southwest Alaska." *Ethnology*, 41(4): 335–348.

Ortner, Sherry, and Harriet Whitehead. 1981. "Introduction: Accounting for Sexual Meanings." In *Sexual Meanings. The Cultural Construction of Gender and Sexuality*, edited by Sherry Ortner and Harriet Whitehead, 1–27. Cambridge: Cambridge University Press.

Rasing, Thera. 2004. "The Persistence of Female Initiation Rites: Reflexivity and Resilience of Women in Zambia." In *Situating Globality. African Agency in the Appropriation of Global Culture*, edited by Wim Van Binsbergen and Rijk van Dijk, 277–310. Leiden: Brill.

Tokita-Tanabe, Yumiko. 1999. "Women and Tradition in India: Construction of Subjectivity and Control of Female Sexuality in the Ritual of First Menstruation." *Senri Ethnological Studies*, 50: 193–220.

Ziv, Nitzan. 2006. "Interpreting Their Blood: The Contradictions of Approaches to Menstruation Through Religious Education, Ritual and Culture in Rabat, Morocco." *Independent Study Project (ISP) Collection*, Paper 331. Accessed October 27, 2014, at http://digitalcollections.sit.edu/isp_collection/331.

Mentoring

MARIANNE COLEMAN
University of London, UK

Mentoring is usually a one to one relationship between a younger less experienced person and an older more experienced person who is charged with guiding, supporting, and teaching them. The term is said to originate from the name of Mentor, an older man, deputed by Odysseus to guide the young Telemachus in his father's absence. Mentoring usually takes place in a work context and has two functions. The first is to support career progress and includes the inculcation of skills, technical knowledge, and social capital; and the second is the provision of psycho-social support. It is commonly part of a formal program, but can be arranged informally.

The career progress aspect of mentoring might include elements of being a coach or a sponsor. Although coaching may occur within the relationship, it is differentiated from mentoring as it tends to relate to specific skill development, while mentoring is a general developmental process. Mentoring is therefore likely to be a longer term relationship and coaching to be linked to short-term aims (Clutterbuck 2001). Sponsorship is a potential aspect of the career progress function of mentoring and occurs where the mentor actively supports the mentee for promotion and ensures that they are considered for job opportunities. Mentors with more power and influence therefore tend to be better able to act as sponsors. The psycho-social aspect of mentoring might include elements of counseling where the mentor acts as a sounding board. It also includes mentors acting as role models to mentees.

The benefits to the individual being mentored, who is known as the mentee or protégé(e), are generally seen as the main object of mentoring and they include learning new facts and skills and developing in confidence, especially in regard to career progress. Mentoring may be particularly helpful in learning political skills. Mentors also benefit from mentoring as a form of professional development allowing them to update their knowledge and providing them with opportunities to improve skills such as problem analysis. It may also enhance their personal reputation and increase self-esteem and job satisfaction. Mentoring is of benefit to the organization as it facilitates the learning and development of employees, increases retention, motivation, and commitment and strengthens the work culture.

Successful mentoring occurs where there is clarity and agreement about the purpose of the relationship, where the results are measured, and there is training for those concerned (Clutterbuck 2001). Mentors need particular skills in building interpersonal relationships and the relationship may suffer where the two parties have different expectations or where there has not been sufficient discussion and agreement within the pairing about confidentiality and discretion and on the boundaries to the relationship.

Mentoring along with networking is seen as particularly important in supporting and furthering the career progress of women and individuals from ethnic minorities (Burke and Mattis 2005). Cross-gender and cross-race mentoring are likely to occur as there are shortages of senior women and individuals from ethnic minorities to act as mentors and white males are likely to be the more powerful sponsors. In cross-race and cross-gender mentoring it is important that potential sensitivities and differences are part of the initial discussion to ensure good communication between the pair (Clutterbuck and Ragins 2002). Cross-gender mentoring is open to a range of difficulties including that: men and women are likely to adopt stereotypical roles within the relationship; role modeling may be less satisfactory; there may be concerns about intimacy and sexuality in the relationship; the relationship receives more public scrutiny than a same-sex pairing and the mentee may be subject to peer resentment as being specially favored (Kram 1985).

Mentoring can occur at different stages in a career. Most often it is associated with a period of induction into a new role at the start but it may occur later in the career as an individual is promoted to a higher level. Mentoring progresses through stages, for example, those identified by Kram (1985) of initiation at the start of the relationship, cultivation when the relationship is working smoothly, followed by separation as the relationship begins to be less important, and finally a possible re-definition where a different sort of relationship develops or else the relationship ends completely.

There are alternatives to the traditional model of mentoring which has been criticized by feminists and others who see it as limited and functionalist. Feminists view traditional mentoring as supporting the status quo of a system dominated by an underlying masculinist perspective. Thus mentoring is seen as helping to perpetuate an exclusive system, ensuring that positions of power and influence remain in the hands of white, able-bodied, middle-class, middle-aged, heterosexual men.

The feminist critique of mentoring incorporates postmodern feminist values and advocates a more equal, non-hierarchical relationship of power sharing, co-leading, and reciprocal learning, where emotion might be brought into the discussion, personal experience is valued, and where power and privilege are problematized. The roles of mentor and mentee are therefore not clearly defined in feminist mentoring and the relationship becomes one of collaboration or the interchange of roles between what might be seen as a primary and a secondary mentor. Feminist inspired mentoring is not limited to a dyadic relationship but is distributed and includes collaborative approaches such as co-mentoring and network or mosaic mentoring. Kram (1985) refers to a "relationship constellation" where different mentors might have different functions. Feminist mentoring is orientated toward activism and change to empower women and others normally excluded from power.

SEE ALSO: Feminist Theories of Organization; Gender Equality; Gender Stereotypes; Leadership and Gender; Sexism

REFERENCES

Burke, Ronald J., and Mary C. Mattis. 2005. *Supporting Women's Career Advancement:*

Challenges and Opportunities. Cheltenham: Edward Elgar.

Clutterbuck David. 2001 *Everyone Needs a Mentor: Fostering Talent at Work*. London: Chartered Institute of Personnel Development.

Clutterbuck, David, and Belle Rose Ragins, eds. 2002. *Mentoring and Diversity*. Oxford: Butterworth Heinemann.

Kram, Kathy E. 1985. *Mentoring at Work*. Glenview: Scott, Foresman.

FURTHER READING

Fletcher, Sarah. J., and Carol A. Mullen, eds. 2012. *The Sage Handbook of Mentoring and Coaching in Education*. London: Sage.

Mestiza Consciousness

VALORIE THOMAS
Pomona College, USA

"Mestiza consciousness," or *mestizaje*, is the central concept of Gloria Anzaldúa's 1987 book, *Borderlands/La Frontera: The New Mestiza*. Anzaldúa's theory of *mestizaje* reclaims indigenous spirituality as a means of resisting colonial and patriarchal erasure, using it as a basis for revaluing the experience of those marginalized by race, class, gender, sexual discrimination, and nationalism. The theory of *mestiza* consciousness tracks the path of the indigenous woman ancestor, *la indigena*, as a bridge to that suppressed inner life which is, Anzaldúa declares, the source of agency. This critical reclamation of spiritual and political agency through indigeneity, intersectional analysis, and remapping border space constitutes a paradigm shift in Chicana and women-of-color feminisms.

Anzaldúa argues that *mestiza* border space operates as "a third country" of psychological, sexual, and spiritual terrain "wherever two or more cultures edge each other, where people of different races occupy the same territory, where under, lower, middle and upper classes touch, where the space between two individuals shrinks with intimacy." This cultural and spiritual third space invites mutual understanding of "our Indian lineage, our afro-*mestizaje*, our history of resistance … Chicano, *indio*, American Indian, *mojado*, *mexicano*, immigrant Latino, Anglo in power, working class Anglo, Black, Asian – our psyches resemble the bordertowns and are populated by the same people. The struggle has always been inner, and is played out in the outer terrains." The *mestiza* is the definitive border dweller.

The multiplicity of identities embodied by the *mestiza*, or multiracial woman, challenges hierarchies and dualisms such as white/other, civilized/savage, and virgin/whore; categories which have been controlling themes in Western colonialism. *Mestiza* consciousness places Chicanas at the fulcrum of their own narratives of history and culture, challenging borders literal and figurative while reclaiming the critical value of indigenous thought, language, and spiritual archetypes. *Mestiza* consciousness then becomes an instrument of critical inquiry that breaks out of dominant structures of knowledge, memory, and imagination that have historically subjugated indigenous women. The ethos of *mestizaje* emerges in Anzaldúa's style of writing across genres as *Borderlands* shifts between prose, poetry, memoir, and myth, just as the language of the text shifts between Standard English, Spanish, Spanglish, and Nahuatl.

As a writer concerned with the politics of language, Anzaldúa deconstructs the term *mestiza*. Under Spanish colonial regimes in Mexico the term "*mestiza*," which translates in English to "half-breed," "mixed-breed" or "mongrel," was part of a racial caste system that categorized people with European, indigenous, and African ancestry. The *mestiza* was regarded as racially impure, morally corrupt, and sexually deviant. In Anzaldúa's view the *mestiza* represents resilience and "the Indian woman's history of resistance." Reclaiming memory and culture reconstructs *mestiza* identity.

Mestizaje methodology reimagines familiar icons such as Our Lady of Guadalupe, La Malinche, and La Llorona, whom Anzaldúa terms "the three mothers" of Chicana culture. Her account of *mestiza* iconography tracks the suppression of qualities unacceptable to patriarchal Aztec and later Christian orthodoxies. *Mestizaje* advocates reclaiming the repressed feminine power of sexuality, darkness, and transformation. Anzaldúa identifies Our Lady of Guadalupe as "the central deity who connects us to our Indian ancestry." Two of her ancient names are Coatlalopeuh and Tonantsi, aspects of Coatlicue, a Meso-American Serpent-Creator goddess associated with sexuality, death, darkness, light, balance, and fertility. Following the Spanish conquest, Guadalupe became an asexual, more palatable version of Tonantsi/Coatlalopeuh. La Malinche/Malintzin represents the mother, but as sexual outlaw. Malintzin is vilified as Cortés's lover, betrayer of her native people. But Anzaldúa refigures Malintzin as a foremother of contemporary *mestizaje*, raped by conquerors but also the origin of Aztlan, the mythic homeland of Chicana/o culture. La Llorona, the grieving woman associated with lost and murdered children, embodies the good mother gone bad. Anzaldúa connects La Llorona to Cihuacoatl, a Meso-American deity who presides over motherhood. Critic Sonia Saldívar-Hull (1987) writes that "Part of the work of *mestiza* consciousness is to break down dualities that imprison women … the ultimate rebellion for Chicanas is through sexuality, and in Anzaldúa's version of queer theory, this is specifically true for lesbians of color."

The transnational feminist sociopolitical awareness of *mestiza* consciousness provides a critical methodology, a means to remap identity between and across borders, and an invitation to activism. By excavating *mestiza* consciousness through Coatlicue, Anzaldúa reconfigures the origins of Chicana political agency and feminism as a spiritual path that begins with confronting one's deepest fears and inadequacies. If the serpent, Coatlicue, is the image of *mestiza* consciousness, "the Coatlicue state" is the in-between space and time in which subjects become immersed in the lessons of *mestizaje*, a new yet ancient literacy.

Anzaldúa's encounter with ancient archetypes relocates Chicana feminist consciousness in *una cultura mestiza*. In the process of articulating *mestizaje* as a basis for imagining a self-determined future *sin fronteras*, without borders, Anzaldúa re-envisions the *India-Mestiza* whose home is "this thin edge/of barbwire" as a source of inspiration. *Mestiza* consciousness thus aligns feminism with indigeneity, self-determination, shifting subjectivity, and a revolutionary declaration of decolonized agency in the global crossroads.

SEE ALSO: Feminism, Chicana; Intersectionality; Nationalism and Gender

REFERENCES

Anzaldúa, Gloria. 1987. *Borderlands/La Frontera: The New Mestiza*. San Francisco: Aunt Lute Books.

Saldívar-Hull, Sonia. 1987. "Introduction." In Gloria Anzaldúa, *Borderlands/La Frontera: The New Mestiza*. San Francisco: Aunt Lute Books.

FURTHER READING

Arredondo, Gabriela, Aida Hurtado, Norma Klahn, and Olga Najera-Ramirez, eds. 2003. *Chicana Feminisms: A Critical Reader*. Durham, NC: Duke University Press.

Delgadillo, Theresa. 2011. *Spiritual Mestizaje: Religion, Gender, Race and Nation in Contemporary*

Chicana Narrative. Durham, NC: Duke University Press.

Koegeler-Abdi, Martina. 2013. "Shifting Subjectivities: Mestizas, Nepantleras, and Gloria Anzaldúa's Legacy." *MELUS*, 38(2), Summer.

Pérez-Torres, Rafael. 2006. *Mestizaje: Critical Uses of Race in Chicano Culture*. Minneapolis: University of Minnesota Press.

Saldívar-Hull, Sonia. 2000. *Feminism on the Border: Chicana Gender Politics and Literature*. Berkeley: University of California Press.

Metrosexual

DAVID COAD
University of Valenciennes, France

In its original conception, the metrosexual was, and fundamentally still is, an Anglo-American or Western European urban male, of any sexual orientation, who imitates or adopts a number of self-care and sartorial behaviors that in some cultures have traditionally been associated with women or gay men. The term was first coined by British cultural writer Mark Simpson, in 1994, in an attempt to describe a combination of homoeroticism and narcissism that he had been observing in contemporary Western European and American advertising and commoditization (Simpson 1994). Simpson's term came at the end of a 10-year period which saw marked changes in the way men's bodies were represented in advertising. The precursor of this change was Nick Kamen's "Launderette" television commercial for Levi's 501 jeans. First shown in 1985, the commercial displays Kamen stripped to his boxer shorts while waiting in a crowded laundry for his jeans to wash. In an appeal to both women and gay men, the male body was thus shown on mainstream television, and later in cinemas, as an object of desire in an overtly (homo)erotic manner. In recent decades, advertising strategy based on showing a male as the object of the gaze has become increasingly normalized and progressively more explicit on a worldwide scale.

Given the Western context of its creation, it is useful to go further back in time to the term's predecessor, the dandy. Indeed, this term has always been the one most commonly used by journalists in an attempt to find a synonym for the metrosexual. Dandyism has a long history in Europe and the United States that extends throughout the nineteenth-century. Dandies and metrosexuals share an interest in style, being fashion conscious and fanatic about their appearance. In a word, both the dandy and the metrosexual are linked by a key attribute of metrosexuality, vanity. Likewise, a foreshadowing of the term metrosexual can also be found in a certain lineage of American male urban consumers. The research of Bill Osgerby into masculinity and men's lifestyle magazines reveals a pedigree of the American male consumer that after the mid-1990s would be called the metrosexual (Osgerby 2001). Historic types such as the dude, the "Arrow Man," the Jazz Age Gatsby buck and the gangster predate and find distinct parallels with their twenty-first-century counterpart, the metrosexual.

Although coined in 1994, the term metrosexual did not go global until after an online publication by Mark Simpson in July 2002. In "Meet the Metrosexual," Simpson drew attention to the fact that metrosexuality was a lifestyle rather than a sexuality in the normal sense of the term (Simpson 2002). He highlighted "looked-at-ness" as a major attribute of metrosexuality. He also attached the concept to sports culture by identifying David Beckham, the then captain of the England soccer team, as the country's leading metrosexual. Beckham successfully queered the codes of hegemonic masculinity by appearing to be desired rather than desiring, passive rather than active and, finally, looked at instead of looking.

Identifying the relationship between metrosexuality and sports culture is of crucial importance. First, because it acknowledges the role that sports culture has played in fashion photography, designer fashions, and men's lifestyle magazines, and second, it shows how these mediums have been, and continue to be, at the center of promoting metrosexuality, or what would become known as metrosexuality, as a lifestyle. David Coad's *The Metrosexual: Gender, Sexuality, and Sports* (Coad 2008), the first full-length study of metrosexuality, further demonstrates how athletes and sports culture have been vital in promoting a positive image of the metrosexual ever since the 1960s. On a global level, Coad also investigates how the symbiotic relationship between stellar athletes and European fashion designers such as Armani has been essential in providing models of metrosexuality internationally.

In addition to sports culture, the cinema has also been influential in promoting the normalization of metrosexual masculinity. Not only Hollywood, but increasingly, alternative sites of the film industry such as Bollywood, provide role models for millions of cinemagoers, thus demonstrating the transnational appeal of metrosexual men.

An ever-increasing number of males from Western and Eastern countries are consequently imitating sports icons and famous actors by taking an accrued interest in their personal appearance. This can be observed in the successful commercialization of grooming and self-care products designed specifically for men. The magazine *Men's Health*, for example, has been attributing annual Grooming Awards since 2004. In 2014, the magazine had 600 products tested in areas such as hair, face, body, shaving, teeth, fragrance, and tools.

Rather than being restricted to self-care products or items of clothing that are put on the body, metrosexuality also refers to body modification practices such as muscle toning, tattooing, and body piercing. Many athletes overtly and unashamedly display their toned, tattooed, and pierced bodies on and off the field. While sports nudity may have been normalized for the Greeks, and may have had a brief comeback in mid-twentieth-century America when physique iconography blossomed, it is now vigorously being brought back into the mainstream by metrosexuality.

In the last 20 years, the term metrosexual has become useful in a variety of disciplines such as sociology, gender studies, media studies, and cultural studies. In addition, it has evolved from its original Eurocentric and US-centric focus to gradually occupy the attention of cultural critics, academics, and journalists working in Asia. India, South Korea, Thailand, and especially China are the new market areas targeting men that transnational companies have set out to conquer.

SEE ALSO: Images of Gender and Sexuality in Advertising; Masculinities

REFERENCES

Coad, David. 2008. *The Metrosexual: Gender, Sexuality, and Sport*. Albany: State University of New York Press.

Osgerby, Bill. 2001. *Playboys in Paradise: Masculinity, Youth and Leisure-Style in Modern America*. Oxford: Berg.

Simpson, Mark. 1994. "Here Comes the Mirror Men." *The Independent*, 15 November, Metro Page, 22.

Simpson, Mark. 2002. "Meet the Metrosexual." Accessed June 22, 2015, at http://www.salon.com/2002/07/22/metrosexual/.

FURTHER READING:

Simpson, Mark. 2013. *Metrosexy: A 21st Century Self-Love Story*. North Charleston: CreateSpace Independent Publishing Platform.

Microcredit and Microlending

JULIE L. DROLET
University of Calgary, Canada

Microcredit is a term used to describe the provision of small loans to people who are totally or partially excluded from the formal banking system. In developing countries, microcredit programs aim to reduce poverty and empower socially excluded persons. This is particularly important for gender and development, as the majority of microcredit recipients worldwide are low-income women. In industrialized or developed countries, microcredit initiatives aim to reduce poverty by encouraging or facilitating self-employment. Microcredit and microlending programs serve an important function by providing an alternative to the oppressive "moneylender" who charges exorbitant interest rates for small loans.

The concept of microcredit was popularized through the Grameen Bank, and the work of Muhammad Yunus who launched an action research project in 1976 to examine the possibility of designing a credit system to provide banking services targeted at the rural poor. The project evolved into the Grameen Bank, which promotes microenterprise among women and encourages economic self-reliance. In 2006 Muhammad Yunus was awarded the Nobel Peace Prize for his pioneering work in fighting global poverty through loans and other financial services for the poor (Grameen Foundation 2014).

Traditional formal banks claimed they could not meet the credit needs of the poor due to relatively high transaction costs and operating expenses, as loans are often repaid in weekly or biweekly installments. Many of the world's poor work in the informal and unregulated sectors of the economy, and lack collateral for bank loans. Microfinance institutions (MFIs) were developed to address these concerns. From 1950 to the 1970s, governments and donors provided subsidized agricultural credit to farmers in order to raise productivity and incomes. During the 1980s, microcredit provided loans to poor women to invest in small businesses, enabling women to accumulate assets and raise household income and well-being. Non-governmental organizations (NGOs) delivered microcredit programs to meet social development needs. Today, MFIs are providing a range of financial services.

The group lending models include village banking, ROSCAs, and credit unions, which share similar characteristics and approaches. Typically, the group lending model administers a single loan to a group of women, and then disperses portions of the loan among individual members of the group for their specific needs. Each member gets a portion of the loan for their own business activity, and if one member fails to repay an installment, the other members are required to cover their payment. The group lending model is known for high repayment rates, using social pressure to deter missing payments. Microcredit programs often build on women's social networks in the community by reinforcing ties between women and collective responsibility to ensure repayment. The individual lending model is the most prevalent type of microfinance in Latin America. In recent years, individual loans for microenterprise and consumer purposes have increasingly been offered by MFIs. In this model an individual is solely responsible for the payment of their own loan, and the procurement of credit is usually based upon past credit history, references, collateral, and the type and validity of business venture. In this system MFIs are generally less discerning than a typical commercial bank, and primarily operate in urban settings.

The feminization of poverty is a concept that refers to how women are more likely to be affected by poverty than men (UN Women 2000). There are several reasons why microcredit programs have focused almost exclusively on women. It is widely believed that women use the profits of income-generating activities supported by microcredit to improve the welfare of the household, whereas men are more likely to spend their earnings on personal expenses. Women are also considered more reliable than men in repaying loans. Studies have documented how access to financial services improves the status of women in the family. Women are more assertive, confident, and play a greater role in decision-making. Women own assets, including land and housing. Advocates of microcredit programs argue that credit provision can help combat gender inequality, improve women's financial independence, increase women's bargaining power and status in the household and larger community. Scholars and critics have raised important questions about microcredit's potential for poverty reduction in the developing world, given all of the structural challenges women face in their households and communities. According to Bagati (2003), the pursuit of empowerment is an ongoing "journey" for the microcredit loan recipients – a journey that originates from different starting points and cultural contexts for each woman. Some women face challenges in accessing economic opportunities and the necessary resources due to their gender (Kabeer 2001). At the same time, women are reproduced as "financially responsible moral" women or gendered subjects in such programs designed for bottom billion capitalism (Roy 2012).

It is important to consider that microcredit is one of many tools available to reduce poverty and empower women. Microfinance is not a silver bullet. The popularity of microcredit is aligned with recent global transformations brought about by neoliberalism and the consequences of globalization (Isserles 2003). For example, a number of microfinance NGOs have adopted neoliberal market principles to shape the conduct of their borrowers as entrepreneurial subjects (Karim 2011). For microcredit to be appropriate, however, clients must have the capacity to repay the loan and engage in business. Otherwise, clients risk being pushed into chronic debt problems. Microcredit is viewed by some as a "one-size-fits-all" approach yet there is a need to consider the local context. Populations that are geographically dispersed or have a high incidence of ill health may not be suitable. Alternative interventions such as cash grants, public work projects and infrastructure improvements, health services, or education and training programs may be more effective. There is great promise in social protection initiatives to provide a "floor" for many social and economic activities (Drolet 2014).

Because power is deeply rooted in social, economic, political and cultural systems and values, and permeates all aspects of life, it is unlikely that one intervention is capable of transforming power and gender relations in society and in the economy (Drolet 2011a). The many ways that women and men work and contribute to the economy, their family, and society must be included in the analysis. Future directions include holistic and integrated approaches that bring microcredit together with social protection floor initiatives, and other education, social and health services, to contribute to meeting women's gendered needs (Drolet 2011b).

SEE ALSO: Empowerment; Feminization of Poverty; Gender and Development; Informal Economy; Poverty in Global Perspective

References

Bagati, D. 2003. "Microcredit and Empowerment of Women." *Journal of Social Work Research and Evaluation*, 4(1): 19–35.

Drolet, Julie L. 2014. *Social Protection and Social Development: International Initiatives*. Dordrecht: Springer.

Drolet, Julie L. 2011a. "Women, Micro Credit and Empowerment in Cairo, Egypt." *International Social Work*, 54(5): 629–645. DOI: 10.1177/0020872810382681.

Drolet, Julie L. 2011b. "Women's Micro Credit Loans and *gam'iyyaat* Saving Clubs in Cairo, Egypt: The Role of Social Networks in the Neighborhood." *Journal of Human Security*, 7(2): 20–31.

Grameen Foundation. 2014. "Awards & Recognition: 2006 Nobel Peace Prize Muhammad Yunus and Grameen Bank." Accessed February 13, 2014, at: http://www.grameenfoundation.org/about/awards-recognition.

Isserles, Robin G. 2003. "Microcredit: The Rhetoric of Empowerment, the Reality of 'Development as Usual.'" *Women's Studies Quarterly*, 31(3/4): 38–57.

Kabeer, Naila. 2001. "Conflicts over Credit: Re-Evaluating the Empowerment Potential of Loans to Women in Rural Bangladesh." *World Development*, 29(1): 63–84.

Karim, Lamia. 2011. *Microfinance and its Discontents: Women in Debt in Bangladesh*. Minneapolis: University of Minnesota Press.

Roy, Ananya. 2012. "Subjects of Risk: Technologies of Gender in the Making of Millennial Modernity." *Public Culture*, 24(1): 131–155.

Further Reading

Consultative Group to Assist the Poor. Accessed August 24, 2015, at: www.cgap.org.

Hulme, David, and Paul Mosley. 1996. *Finance Against Poverty*. London: Routledge.

Microcredit Summit Campaign. Accessed August 24, 2015, at: www.microcreditsummit.org.

Rahman, Aminur. 1999. Women and Microcredit in Rural Bangladesh. *An Anthropological Study of Grameen Bank Lending*. Boulder: Westview Press.

UN Women. 2000. "The Feminization of Poverty." Accessed February 13, 2014, at: http://www.un.org/womenwatch/daw/followup/session/presskit/fs1.htm.

Midwifery

ALISON HAPPEL-PARKINS
University of Memphis, USA

Midwifery is the practice of caring for women during pregnancy, labor, birth, and post-partum. Midwives are the primary providers of care for childbearing women around the world (Hatem et al. 2009). Although contextually varied, cross-culturally midwives have played prominent roles in childbearing women's lives throughout different international contexts. Within many indigenous cultures, birth is considered to be within the domain of women.

Many indigenous and non-Western cultures regularly utilize and depend upon midwives for the care of and assistance to pregnant, laboring, and post-partum women. For example, in indigenous Mayan communities, midwives are referred to as "the mother of the village" (Gonzales 2012). Many indigenous cultures conceptualize childbirth as natural and sacred. Some indigenous cultures honor and celebrate pregnancy, childbirth, and delivery with ceremonies and rituals in order to denote the importance of the life event for both the woman and the community. In contrast, within medicalized Western cultures, pregnancy and childbirth are understood as medical conditions that are inherently risky and in need of medicalized management.

Sociologist Barbara Katz Rothman (1979) was the first to academically delineate a difference between the midwifery model of care and the medical or obstetrical model of care. The midwifery model of care is a wellness model that is woman-centered, holistic, and non-interventionist. A woman's social, cultural, and emotional context are centered and understood as integral to the woman's experiences of health, pregnancy, labor, and delivery. Within this model, pregnancy and childbirth are viewed as natural and normal, and pregnant women are continuously observed by midwives but not intervened upon unless complications arise. It is assumed that women should be in charge of their own pregnancy, labor, and birth; midwives provide individualized education while being responsive to individual women's needs. Technology and technological interventions are minimized within the midwifery model of care. In addition to supporting women during pregnancy and childbirth, midwives often help women post-partum. For example, midwives often make home visits in order to ensure that women have the support they need after the birth of their baby.

In contrast to the midwifery model of care, the medical or obstetrical model of care focuses on the management of pregnancy, labor, and delivery. Within this conceptualization of pregnancy and childbirth, pregnancy is understood as a condition that must be managed and controlled by technologically trained professionals. The medical model of care depends upon technology and physician expertise to prevent, diagnose, and/or treat complications that may arise during pregnancy, labor, and delivery. This model consequently facilitates medical interventions that utilize medication, instruments, and surgery for laboring women.

The decreased usage of and reliance upon midwives in countries such as the United States can be attributed to the deliberate efforts of male physicians and medical institutions (such as the American Medical Association) to introduce and perpetuate the medical model of pregnancy and childbirth. Midwifery was routinely denigrated within the media and within prominent social institutions, which led to the subsequent dominance of the medical model. The denigration of midwives and midwifery was facilitated by sexism, xenophobia, and racism, since many of the practicing midwives in the early 1900s were women newly immigrated to the United States. Despite the denigration of midwifery, midwives and childbearing women have resisted the medical model by insisting that the midwifery model of care be accepted and offered as a valid choice for pregnant women. Countries that have given continual support to midwives, such as the Nordic countries in Western Europe and Japan, have continued to exist within and benefit from the midwifery model of care.

Women who are cared for by midwives tend to have lower rates of medical and technological interventions, including but not limited to ultrasounds, inductions, epidurals, and caesarean sections. For example, as of 2011, midwives attended over 80 percent of all births in the Nordic countries of Western Europe. Caesarean section rates in these countries range from 14 percent to 17 percent. In contrast, China has been aggressively discouraging midwifery, and the national caesarean rate is currently over 42 percent, which is one of the highest in the world. Additionally, caesarean sections are considered a marker of class and social status in some countries such as Brazil; consequently, caesarean sections rates are 82–90 percent in private hospitals in Brazil (Lumbiganon et al. 2010; OECD 2011).

Women with low-risk pregnancies who have access to skilled midwives have better birth experiences and outcomes. Organizations such as the World Health Organization and the United Nations are committed to increasing childbearing women's access to skilled midwives in order to prevent complications during pregnancy and unnecessary maternal deaths. It is suggested that more women be provided skilled midwifery options and services during pregnancy, birth, and post-partum.

SEE ALSO: Reproductive Health

REFERENCES

Gonzales, Patrisia. 2012. *Red Medicine: Traditional Indigenous Rites of Birthing and Healing*. Tucson: University of Arizona Press.

Hatem, Marie, et al. 2009. "Midwife-led Versus Other Models of Care for Childbearing Women (Review)." *The Cochrane Collaboration*. Chichester: John Wiley & Sons, Ltd.

Katz Rothman, Barbara. 1979. *Two Models of Maternity Care: Defining and Negotiating Reality*. New York: New York University

Lumbiganon, Pisake, et al. 2010. "Method of Delivery and Pregnancy Outcomes in Asia: The WHO Global Survey on Maternal and Perinatal Health 2007–08." *Lancet*, 375(9713): 490–499. DOI: 10.1016/S0140-6736(09)61870-5.

Organisation for Economic Cooperation and Development (OECD). 2011. "Caesarean Sections." In *Health at a Glance 2011: OECD Indicators*. Paris: OECD Publishing.

FURTHER READING

Gaskin, Ina May. 2011. *Birth Matters: A Midwife's Manifesta*. New York: Seven StoriesPress.

Goldsmith, Judith. 1990. *Childbirth Wisdom from the World's Oldest Societies*. Brookline: East West Health Books.

Johnson, Kenneth C., and Betty-Anne Daviss. 2005. "Outcomes of Planned Home Births with Certified Professional Midwives: Large Prospective Study in North America." *BMJ*, 330: 1416–1419.

United Nations Population Fund (UNFPA). 2011. *The State of the World's Midwifery 2011: Delivering Health, Saving Lives*. New York: UNFPA.

Militarism and Gender-Based Violence

SIMONA SHARONI
State University of New York at Plattsburgh, USA

Militarism and gender-based violence are major human rights issues, involving particular understandings of "violence" and "security." Militarism is the belief of governments and people in the importance of maintaining a strong military capability and being ready to use violence and other military methods to gain power and to promote national interests. Fear and narrow understandings of security are often deployed to mobilize support among citizens for the use of aggression, violence, and military interventions for settle disputes and to enforce economic and political interests.

The Declaration on the Elimination of Violence against Women, adopted by the United Nations General Assembly in 1993, defined violence against women as "any act of gender-based violence that results in, or is likely to result in, physical, sexual, or psychological harm or suffering to women, including threats of such acts, coercion, or arbitrary deprivation of liberty, whether occurring in public or private life" (UN News Center 1994). The definition encompasses, but is not limited to, physical, sexual, and psychological violence occurring in the family, including battering, sexual abuse of girls in the household, dowry related violence, marital rape, female genital mutilation, and other traditional practices harmful to women, non-spousal violence, and violence related to exploitation; physical, sexual, and psychological violence occurring within the general community, including rape, sexual abuse, sexual harassment, and intimidation at work, in educational institutions and elsewhere; trafficking in women and forced prostitution; and physical, sexual, and psychological violence perpetrated or condoned by both state and non-state actors.

Gender-based violence resulting from militarism and war can also be viewed as one component of a broad spectrum of violence that women encounter throughout their lives. The implications of militarism are far-reaching as it often leads to multiple forms of violence, including physical violence (intimate-partner violence and war violence), structural violence (environmental degradation, health and safety), and cultural violence (discrimination, prejudice, segregation, and binaries that reinforce systems of power and privilege). The levels and types of violence affecting women's lives are often more acute in conflict-torn regions. Understanding the relationship between militarism and gender-based violence requires attention to structural hierarchies that perpetuate violence as well as to context-specific social and cultural norms that legitimize the use of aggression and military force. Another key factor impacting the relationship between militarism and violence against women involves the political and psychological processes used by leaders to mobilize support for military action and to silence dissent. These processes, norms, and hierarchies are often present during peace times but become more visible when a political conflict escalates. Levels of militarism and rates of sexual assault, rape, and intimate-partner violence in a particular society prior to the conflict may impact gender-based violence during conflict. Similarly, the prevalence of violence against women during conflict often impacts the life experiences and safety of women in post-conflict societies (Cockburn 2012). Whereas women are vulnerable to various forms of violence emanating from militarism, their involvement at the forefront of anti-militarism and peace movements has called into question their stereotypical depiction as mere victims of political violence (Anderlini 2007; Confortini 2012).

Nowadays there is a consensus among feminists that women's relationship to militarism is complex and multifaceted. In conflict zones, women have worked to both promote and confront militarism and while most gender-based violence is male-led and targets women, under some conditions, women have participated, directly or indirectly, in the perpetration of sexualized violence against noncombatants (Cohen 2013). Feminist scholarship on the relationship between militarism and gender-based violence encompasses the following key themes:

1. the militarization of masculinities and femininities;
2. the relationship between political violence and gender-based violence;
3. women's resistance to militarization and war;
4. political participation, militarism, and gender-based violence.

THE MILITARIZATION OF MASCULINITIES AND FEMININITIES

Gender relations are deeply implicated in the lived experiences of men and women before, during, and in the aftermath of political violence. Though gender roles and relations vary from society to society, and change over time, in most contemporary societies boys and men are socialized to be independent, competitive, combative, physically tough, courageous, and dominant. The valorization of dominance and aggression as core masculine traits, even in peacetime, incline males to accept fighting as a key aspect of their identity and role in society. Girls, on the other hand, are socialized to be dependent, vulnerable, collaborative, empathetic, and nurturing. In most patriarchal societies, the socially constructed distinctions between boys and girls are taken for granted and presented as natural. Long before men are recruited into armed forces, their sense of masculine identity has been shaped by a choice of toys, activities, and media and popular culture content that reflect qualities associated with militarized masculinity. In most societies, militarism impacts dominant conceptions of masculinity and femininity by casting men as protector and girls and women as needing protection. Another gendered distinction enhanced by militarism is that between men as agents, utilizing violence to achieve various ends and girls, and women as victims of violence. These gendered dichotomies are further reinforced when political violence escalates (Sharoni 2001).

Exploiting and building upon existing stereotypical sociocultural distinctions between men and women within a given society, militarism is not merely an ideology or a political project but rather a cultural phenomenon, built over time. Militarism is bolstered by the distinction between "Us" and "Them," the construction of the "enemy," and the systematic creation and dissemination of gendered myths about the nation as well as "the other." Through massive indoctrination and fear-mongering campaigns, leaders who seek to use militarism for their personal and political gains present their narrow understanding of security as the only credible mechanism to safeguard the national collectivity (Enloe 2007).

As a system of domination, militarism depends on particular forms of militarized masculinities and femininities. The prevailing meanings of the practices associated with being a man or a woman in a militarized society are greatly influenced by and depend on patriarchy. As a system of domination, patriarchy normalizes the male dominance and the subordination of women and reinforces the unequal division of power and labor between the sexes. Other such systems of domination like racism, homophobia, and capitalism are also often deployed when masculinities and femininities become militarized (Whitworth 2004; Sharoni 2008).

Although the militarization of masculinities is readily evident when political conflicts escalate, governments and political leaders cannot militarize their policies and operations without affecting both men's and women's identities and roles. When violence erupts, men are called upon to assume their roles as protectors, which usually involves taking up arms. Women and children on the other hand are portrayed as weak, vulnerable, and in need of protection. Though at times, women are called to temporarily assume the responsibilities of men while they are on the battlefield, their designated roles are primarily as keepers of the home front and supporters of the men on the battlefield and the war more generally (Enloe 2007).

THE RELATIONSHIP BETWEEN POLITICAL VIOLENCE AND GENDER-BASED VIOLENCE

The unequal treatment and abuse of women and girls are effectively condoned in almost every society of the world. Prosecution and conviction of men who beat or rape women or girls is rare when compared to numbers of assaults. Gender-based violence therefore operates as a means to maintain and reinforce women's subordination, which is reinforced through socialization. Militarism and the role it plays in the socialization of boys and girls builds upon and offers another layer of legitimacy for gender-based violence (Reardon 1985).

Political violence impacts both men's and women's lives because it can lead to injuries, malnutrition, infectious diseases, reproductive problems, chronic pain, depression, post-traumatic stress disorder, disability, and death. However, women are often more vulnerable than men when a political conflict escalates as they can become victims of gender-based violence including sexual assault, rape, sexual slavery, human trafficking, and intimate-partner violence. Additionally, women usually bear a heavy burden during and after political violence as they often assume the primary responsibility to support their families and to safeguard their communities while men are on the battlefield, killed, imprisoned, or exiled. In addition to the workload and stress associated with safeguarding the home front during wartimes, women themselves may be killed, imprisoned, and tortured. While militarism and political violence often have negative impact on most women's lives, women's vulnerability to political violence increases among the poor and marginalized groups; women from national and ethnic minorities and economically disempowered and tend to suffer greatly when political violence erupts (Sachs, Sa'ar, and Aharoni 2007). At the same time, new evidence from conflict zones indicates that men too have been targets of sexualized violence and that women have been among perpetrators of wartime gender-based violence (Cohen 2013).

The use of rape during war, sexual assault within militaries and militias, and the rise in reported cases of intimate-partner violence are particular manifestations of the impact of political violence on women. Though the extensive use of rape during wartimes did not receive much scholarly and media attention until the early 1990s, there is ample historical evidence that the use of mass rape is not merely a modern phenomenon (Buss 2009). Throughout time, militarism has enabled and normalized gender-based crimes perpetrated against women during fighting. While sexual assault and rape are present in many societies in peacetime, the prevalence and magnitude of sexual attacks on women increases dramatically in wartimes, with some cases involving the deliberate and systematic rape of thousands of women. Accounts from Africa, Asia, the Americas, the Middle East, and Europe reveal that large-scale sexual violence was present in 51 countries over the last 20 years. (Bastick, Grimm, and Kunz 2007).

Detailed accounts by UN agencies and by international humanitarian and human rights non-government organizations, which focused on the impact of armed conflict on women, confirm the prevalence of multiple rapes of individual women in many conflict zones (Leatherman 2011; Kirby 2013). The systematic sexual violence was sometimes carried out by various groups of men, including gangs of boys and men, local and regional militias, and organized armed forces, including UN peacekeepers (Whitworth 2004). Women were raped in their homes, in refugee camps, and in prison. In some militias that included women, they were held in sexual servitude by the fighting men. In other cases, sexual slavery was institutionalized (Yoshimi 2000). The prevalence of sexual assault in the military and the lack of accountability for perpetrators is now a noted area of concern in the United States (Hunter 2007).

Feminists have long pointed out that violence against women is a result of complex sociopolitical and cultural institutions that normalize the use of violence (Reardon 1985). However, discussions on the proliferation of small arms and their role in intimate-partner violence revealed higher rates of violence against women in militarized societies, often during and in the aftermath of wars. More often than not, militaristic interpretations of "national security" and the massive presence of armed military and police personnel paradoxically heighten the sense of insecurity of both women and minority groups (Sharoni 2008).

Though rape and sexual violence have been prevalent aspects of war throughout history, the phrase "rape as weapon of war," became widely used by researchers, policymakers, and media analysts only during the 1990s, as evidence surfaced about widespread use of rape and sexual assault in Bosnia (Salzman 1998). Attention to this issue revealed the prevalence of gender-based sexualized violence in other conflict zones including Liberia, Rwanda, the Democratic Republic of Congo (DRC), and Sierra Leone, among others (Bastick, Grimm, and Kunz 2007; Cohen 2013). The recognition by foreign policy establishments that rape and other forms of gender-based violence are in fact tactics of war led to the categorization of these crimes as war crimes. As a result, gender-based violence has been a prominent issue, in recent years, on the agenda of both the United Nations and numerous human rights organizations (Sharlach 2000; Kirby 2013).

Research on gender-based violence, especially rape and sexual assault in war times, points to two overlapping discourses that shape and grant legitimacy to soldiers' crimes. The first discourse is based on the premise that rape is essentially sexual, driven by the male libido and that satisfying that need is essential to the success of the military campaign. The second discourse treats rape and sexual assault as an expression of rage and hatred, rather than a sexual desire (Aroussi 2011). The discourses determine both the nature of the assault and the target. While gender-based violence perpetrated by soldiers who are presumed to act on sexual desires can target women on both sides of a political divide, sexualized violence fueled by hatred and rage toward "the enemy" tends to target noncombatants, (predominantly but not exclusively women and girls) associated with the opposing political party (Baaz and Stern 2009; Cohen 2013).

Whereas early analyses of gender-based violence in conflict zones attributed the phenomenon primarily to violent socialization of boys, and saw sexual assault and rape as practices stemming from militarized masculinities, the fact that these crimes occur in some places and not others led to research on the context-specific conditions that may act as catalysts for sexualized violence in wartime (Sharlach 2000; Skjelsbæk 2001; Mackenzie 2010). This research uncovered several key patterns. First, it appears that most sexualized violence perpetrated against noncombatants was carried out by groups rather than by lone soldiers. Second, the prevalence and severity of gender-based violence were greater in places where fighters were forcibly recruited through coercion and abduction compared to armed forces comprised of volunteers. Based on this new evidence, researchers concluded that intergroup social dynamics were often a catalyst for sexualized violence in wartime. At times, soldiers who were forced to join militias were under pressure to participate in gang rapes in order to survive (Cohen 2013). Traditionally, feminists viewed militarism as an ideology that legitimized the use of aggression as a practice of male bonding. However, new evidence suggests that under some circumstances many men and some women may take part in male-led sexualized violence against noncombatants. In this case, the combatants' participation in perpetrating violence reflects a new form of militarism that is not an ideology but rather a mode of survival.

Although women have been implicated in both militarism and gender-based violence, their involvement has been for the most part in support rather than in leadership roles. At the same time, women have taken more initiative than men in resistance to militarism and political violence (Anderlini 2007).

WOMEN'S RESISTANCE TO MILITARIZATION AND WAR

Though women's lives have been severely affected by militarism, their response to war has been far from passive. The prevalent tendency to highlight women's vulnerability by depicting them as victims of militarism overlooks the fact that women's relationship to war is far more complicated. In some societies, women are active combatants and in many places across the world, women have played a leading role in resistance to militarism and war. For centuries, women have been at the forefront of anti-war and peace movements. During World War I and II, women in Europe and North America mobilized across borders to protest the destruction wrought by war and to discuss ways of building a sustainable peace (Sharp 2013). Such organizations as Women's International League for Peace and Freedom and Women's Strike for Peace have combined protest with legislative work, lobbying for alternatives to militarism and war (Confortini 2012). Less known are local and regional protest activities, led by women with no prior political experience. A case in point is Women in Black, a weekly women's vigil, which started in Israel in 1990, during the early days of the first Palestinian uprising, known as the *intifada*. The group's anti-war message was later adopted by women peace activists in other parts of the world including the former Yugoslavia and India (Sharoni 2008).

With few exceptions, women's anti-militarism and peace efforts around the world have been both trivialized and marginalized, even when they included explicit policy relevant recommendations. Nevertheless, women continue to search for creative ways to make visible their widespread involvement in conflict transformation and peacebuilding efforts around the world (Anderlini 2007; Sharp 2013). A case in point is the 1,000 Women for the Nobel Peace Prize campaign, which nominated 1,000 women from around the world to receive collectively the Nobel Peace Prize in 2005. The women nominated came from more than 150 countries (Shun-hing 2011).

Most feminist critiques of militarism and its effect on women equated war with patriarchy, militarism with sexism, and peace and world order with feminism (Reardon 1985). Feminist scholars and activists exposed the gendered dimensions of militarism as they analyzed the national, racial, and ethnic conflicts characterized by high levels of militarization and political violence (Zarkov 2007; Shalhoub-Kevorkian 2009). Others focused on theorizing peace, searching for definitions that go beyond viewing peace as the absence of war, insisting that feminist approaches to peace are qualitatively different than men's (Reardon 1985). Feminist scholars sought to highlight women's resistance to militarism by suggesting that because women experience sexism and violence they can empathize with other victims and support movements for justice and peace. Others insisted that it was women's experiences as nurturers, and especially the practice of mothering, that provides the basis for a unique approach against militarism (Ruddick 1989).

Over the years, the tendency to associate men with war and militarism and view women primarily as victims of violence and as peacemakers was replaced with more nuanced feminist theorizing about militarism, violence, and security. Postcolonial and post-structural feminists viewed men's and women's relationship to militarism as socially constructed, rather than rooted in biological differences. Grounding their analyses in particular case studies, feminists examined linkages between violence in public and private domains, including the interplay between the violence of war and violence against women, and militarism and sexism (Sachs, Sa'ar, and Aharoni 2007; Shalhoub-Kevorkian 2009). While early feminist theorizing on violence focused mainly on direct, physical violence, and associated violence with men and non-violence with women, the shift in feminist theorizing examined not only gender-based violence but also other systemic violations of people's rights and dignity based on race, ethnicity, class, and sexual orientation. Feminist theorizing about gender-based violence in conflict zones points to the need to look beyond the symptoms, by focusing on the socioeconomic and political conditions that may contribute to the escalation of violence in a given society (Shalhoub-Kevorkian 2009; Leatherman 2011). One of the main critiques articulated by women's peace movements involves the absence of women and feminist perspective from the political arena, especially within bodies charged with making important decisions about security, war, and peace.

POLITICAL PARTICIPATION, MILITARISM, AND GENDER-BASED VIOLENCE

Feminists have argued that women's experiences as both victims of militarism and advocates for peace should be recognized and inform key policy recommendations. Accordingly, the increased women's participation at all levels of the political system may result in the exploration of alternatives to militarism and drop in the rates of gender-based violence (Chinkin and Charlesworth 2006; Cohn 2013).

The United Nations has long been concerned with the situation of women in armed conflict. In 1969, the Commission on the Status of Women considered whether special protection should be accorded to women and children in conflict zones. In 1974, the General Assembly adopted the Declaration on the Protection of Women and Children in Emergency and Armed Conflict. The linkages between gender equality, development, and peace were a central theme in all United Nations World Conferences on Women (Mexico in 1975, Copenhagen in 1980, Nairobi in 1985, Beijing in 1995). Over the years, the focus of the discussions on women and peace shifted from overall political issues to the impact of war on women and girls and their role in peacebuilding (Sharp 2013). The vision of peace that emerges with the Platform for Action formulated at Beijing led to the adoption of United Nations Security Council Resolution 1325 in October 2000.

A direct result of advocacy efforts by women's organizations, UNSCR 1325 was the culmination of several decades of statements recognizing women's involvement in conflict resolution and peacebuilding initiatives around the world. The important resolution began with the premise that gender equity, social justice, and respect for human rights are crucial elements to nurturing a sustainable peace. The resolution also articulated concerns for women and girls whose lives have been disrupted by war, displacement, sexual violence including rape, forced pregnancy, and exploitation (Cohn 2008; Sharp 2013). UNSCR 1325, which has become one of the best known and the most translated resolutions of the UN Security Council, invigorated the commitment of various UN bodies, including member states and civil society organizations to address two interrelated issues: gender-based violence in times of war and the lack of women's representation at the negotiation tables. The Inter-Agency Taskforce on Women, Peace and Security of the Inter-Agency Network on Women and Gender Equality was one of the bodies within the UN charged with coordinating the implementation of UNSCR 1325 (Sharp 2013).

Despite the growing awareness in the international arena of gender-based violence in times of war and the importance of including women in decision making and negotiation teams dealing with questions of security, peacemaking, and conflict transformation, implementation of other aspects of UNSCR 1325 has been slow and uneven. Women continue to be conspicuously underrepresented at the negotiations table where community leaders formulate key plans for post-conflict reconstruction and peacebuilding. Moreover, in many conflict zones, cultural excuses have been used to legitimize the ongoing violation of the human rights of women and girls and very little has been done regionally and internationally to protect noncombatants, especially women and girls, from gender-based violence. In many conflict zones, women and girls' vulnerability is heightened by economic, health, and food insecurity (Cohn 2008; Sharp 2013).

A 2010 UNIFEM report noted that women's participation in peace processes remains one of the least implemented elements of the plan outlined in UNSCR 1325 and related resolutions. According to the report, less than eight percent of negotiating parties were women. Political bodies charged with negotiating the aftermath of wars continue to be male-dominated and reflect militaristic thinking. By failing to comply with UNSCR 1325 and include women with peacebuilding experience in peace negotiations, political parties undermine the potential of women peace leaders to introduce alternatives to militarism and to dramatically transform the landscape of and post-conflict recovery (Sharp 2013). A study commissioned by the UN's secretary-general in 2001 under the title "Women, peace and security" analyzed the impact of armed conflict on women and girls, providing context-specific examples of the experiences and struggles of women in conflict regions to safeguard their own lives and to ensure the safety and well-being of their families and broader community. Authored by independent experts, the study also included a critical review of existing literature on gender perspectives on war, peace, humanitarian efforts, and post-conflict reconstruction (United Nations 2002).

UNSCR 1325 made the relationship between militarism and gender-based violence visible and outlined a plan to guarantee greater involvement of women in peacebuilding efforts as well as in other key political bodies governing the well-being of their communities. Far from being an instrument capable of altering the negative effects of militarism, the important UN resolution introduced a framework that placed human needs above national self-interests, highlighted the prevalence of gender-based violence during wartime, and recognized women's agency as peacemakers. Feminist scholars as well as human rights and women's advocacy groups continue to raise concerns over the gap between international treaties and the insecurity and threats faced by women and girls, and other noncombatants, in conflict zones around the world (Cohn 2013). A major area of concern involves the lack of accountability for perpetrators of sexual and gender-based violence and the impunity of state and non-state actors alike. In addition to continuing to monitor the implementation of UN resolutions and international treaties concerning gender-based violence during war, the international community should focus on mechanisms to ensure accountability for perpetrators of gender-based violence as a crucial aspect of the ongoing struggle to confront both militarism and its negative impact on women and girls.

SEE ALSO: Gender-Based Violence; Leftist Armed Struggle, Women in; Sexual Assault/Sexual Violence; Violence Against Women in Global Perspective

REFERENCES

Anderlini, Sanam. 2007. *Women Building Peace What They Do, Why it Matters*. Boulder: Lynne Riener.

Aroussi, Sahla. 2011. "'Women, Peace and Security': Addressing Accountability for Wartime Sexual Violence." *International Feminist Journal of Politics*, 13(4): 576–593.

Baaz, Maria, and Maria Stern. 2009. "Why Do Soldiers Rape? Masculinity, Violence, and Sexuality in the Armed Forces in the Congo (DRC)." *International Studies Quarterly*, 53: 495–518.

Bastick, Megan, Karin Grimm, and Rahel Kunz. 2007. *Sexual Violence in Armed Conflict: Global Overview and Implications for the Security Sector*. Geneva: Geneva Centre for the Democratic Control of Armed Forces. Accessed August 25, 2015, at http://www.essex.ac.uk/armedcon/story_id/sexualviolence_conflict_full%5B1%5D.pdf.

Buss, Doris. 2009. "Rethinking 'Rape as a Weapon of War.'" *Feminist Legal Studies*, 17(2): 145–163.

Chinkin, Christine, and Hilary Charlesworth. 2006. "Building Women into Peace: The International Legal Framework," *Third World Quarterly*, 27(5): 937–957.

Cockburn, Cynthia. 2012. *Antimilitarism: Political and Gender Dynamics of Peace Movements*. New York: Palgrave Macmillan.

Cohen, Kay. 2013. "Female Combatants and the Perpetration of Violence Wartime Rape in the Sierra Leone Civil War." *World Politics*, 65(3): 383–415.

Cohn, Carol. ed. 2013. *Women and Wars: Contested Histories, Uncertain Futures*. Cambridge: Polity.

Confortini, Catia. 2012. *Intelligent Compassion: Feminist Critical Methodology in the Women's International League for Peace and Freedom*. Oxford: Oxford University Press.

Enloe, Cynthia. 2007. *Globalization and Militarism: Feminists Make the Link*. Lanham: Rowman & Littlefield.

Hunter, Mic. 2007. *Honor Betrayed: Sexual Abuse in America's Military*. Fort Lee: Barricade Books.

Kirby, Paul. 2013. "How Is Rape a Weapon of War? Feminist International Relations, Modes of Critical Explanation and the Study of Wartime Sexual Violence." *European Journal of International Relations*, 19(4): 797–821.

Leatherman, Janie. 2011. *Sexual Violence and Armed Conflict*. Cambridge: Polity Press.

Mackenzie, Megan. 2010. "Securitizing Sex? Towards a Theory of the Utility of Wartime Sexual Violence." *International Feminist Journal of Politics*, 12(2): 202–221.

Reardon, Betty. 1985. *Sexism and the War System*. New York: Teachers College, Columbia University.

Ruddick, Sara. 1989. *Maternal Thinking: Toward a Politics of Peace*. Boston: Beacon Press.

Sachs, Dalia, Amalia Sa'ar, and Sarai Aharoni. 2007. "'How Can I Feel for Others When I Myself Am Beaten?' The Impact of the Armed Conflict on Women in Israel." *Sex Roles*, 57(7–8): 593–606.

Salzman, Todd. 1998. "Rape Camps as a Means of Ethnic Cleansing: Religious, Cultural, and Ethical Responses to Rape Victims in the Former Yugoslavia." *Human Rights Quarterly*, 20(2): 348–378.

Shalhoub-Kevorkian, Nadera. 2009. *Militarization and Violence against Women in Conflict Zones in the Middle East: A Palestinian Case-Study*. Cambridge: Cambridge University Press.

Sharlach, Lisa. 2000. "Rape as Genocide: Bangladesh, the Former Yugoslavia, and Rwanda." *New Political Science*, 22(1): 89–102.

Sharoni, Simona. 2001. "Rethinking Women's Struggles in Israel-Palestine and in the North of Ireland." In *Victims, Perpetrators or Actors? Gender, Armed Conflict and Political Violence*, edited by Caroline Moser and Fiona Clark, 85–98. London: Zed Books.

Sharoni, Simona. 2008. "De-militarizing Masculinities in the Age of Empire." *The Austrian Political Science Journal* (special issue: "Counter/Terror/Wars: Feminist Perspectives,"), 37(2): 147–164.

Sharp, Ingrid. 2013. "Feminist Peace Activism 1915–2010: Are We Nearly There Yet?" *Peace & Change*, 38(2): 155–180.

Shun-hing, Chan. 2011. "Beyond War and Men: Reconceptualizing Peace in Relation to the Everyday and Women." *Signs*, 36(3): 521–532.

United Nations. 2002. *Women, Peace, and Security: A Study Submitted by the Secretary-General Pursuant to Security Council Resolution 1325 (2000)*. New York: United Nations. Accessed August 25, 2015, at http://www.un.org/womenwatch/daw/public/eWPS.pdf.

UN News Center. 1994. "A/RES/48/104. Declaration on the Elimination of Violence against Women." Accessed September 13, 2014, at http://www.un.org/documents/ga/res/48/a48r104.htm.

Whitworth, Sandra. 2004. *Men, Militarism, and UN Peacekeeping: A Gendered Analysis*. Boulder: Lynne Rienner.

Yoshimi, Yoshiaki. 2000. *Comfort Women: Sexual Slavery in the Japanese Military During World War II*. New York: Columbia University Press.

Zarkov, Dubravka. 2007. *The Body of War: Media, Ethnicity, and Gender in the Break-up of Yugoslavia*. Durham, NC: Duke University Press.

FURTHER READING

Center for Global Leadership. 2011. *Intersections of Violence Against Women and Militarism Meeting Report*. New Brunswick: Rutgers University.

United Nations Security Council. 2010. *Resolution 1325 on Women, Peace and Security*. New York: United Nations Security Council, October 31, 2000. Accessed August 25, 2015, at http://daccess-dds-ny.un.org/doc/UNDOC/GEN/N00/720/18/PDF/N0072018.pdf?OpenElement.

Militarism and Sex Industries

JIN-KYUNG LEE
University of California, San Diego, USA

The decisive and persistent convergence of militarism and sex industries is a modern phenomenon, historically distinct from its premodern counterpart where the circumstances of war and soldiering produced military prostitution. This modernity of militarized-industrialized sex work stems from two broader sets of transnational and national systems and ideologies: the late nineteenth-century neo-imperialism and its attendant militarism, on the one hand, and the globalizing capitalism, industrialism, and developmentalism, on the other. These differentiated politico-military and economic institutions exist, in turn, as an interdependent nexus with each other and in fact as an enmeshed entity. While military sex work in the first half of the twentieth century had much closer ties to territorial colonialism and military expansionism by European and Japanese empires (Barry 1996), the postwar sexual proletarianization of third world women came to be propelled, most importantly, by the economic conditions and motivations produced under the neocolonial hegemony of the United States. The postwar American empire has been termed an "Empire of Bases" (Johnson 2004), one that is economically driven and militarily backed through the stationing of its troops on a global scale. The US military bases are scattered across multiple continents and oceans including the Middle East, Asia, Europe, and Latin America and the Pacific, Atlantic, and Caribbean oceans. While the United States has had the largest military presence worldwide in the postwar era, other countries such as the United Kingdom, France, Australia, the Soviet Union/Russia, and South Korea among others have stationed their troops in strategic locations.

Cynthia Enloe has argued that "sexual imperialism," manifested and institutionalized as military sex industries, is a product of such intersecting dominant ideologies and systems that operate both intra-nationally and transnationally as patriarchy/masculinism, nationalism/imperialism, class hierarchy, and a racially segmented global labor market. She has also explained that a conglomeration of more concrete factors such as politico-military decisions, organizational strategies, calculations of profitability for hosting and occupying governments and military authorities, a surplus of cheapened working-class women's labor, and patriarchal-military assumptions about male sexual "needs" and their relation to troop morale and combat readiness give rise to military sex industries (Enloe 2000a). What Kathleen Barry has called the "industrialization of sex" – that is, the development of well-organized and interrelated businesses that support and profit from prostitution – is a structural dimension of the postwar military prostitution (Barry 1996). However, militarized industrialization of sex is a more complex institution than non-military commercialization of sex, as the occupying and hosting countries' governments and the occupying military intervene in the process of commercialization of sex through legislation, medicalization, and other kinds of governmental and military power, control, and discipline at their disposal. While taking note of its particularity without exceptionalizing it, we must situate military sex work in the broader continuum of various kinds of working-class women's labor that are devalued and exploited – again, as a result of the compounding set of ideologies and systems mentioned above, that is, in relation to other kinds of service and manufacturing industries that commodify the third world working-class female body, labor, and sexuality.

THE STATE, CAPITAL, AND MILITARY PROSTITUTION

Because modern military prostitution came into existence with (neo-)imperial capitalization and modernization seeking global expansion, it is, in fact, difficult to separate out the forces of the (imperial) states and those of capital. They tended to operate, in significant ways, in conjunction with each other. And yet the powers of the imperial states must be carefully delineated from the more "privatized" aspects of the capitalist market at large and (military) sex industries in particular. The two most prominent examples of state intervention in military prostitution are Japan during World War II and the United States in the postwar era.

In the case of Japan's military sexual slavery, the fact of the state's official role as an organizing agent has been traced back to premodern Japan's licensed public prostitution system, while the imperial state exercised its distinctly modern power of various kinds over the vast occupied territories in Asia in recruiting and maintaining the military sexual prostitution corps (Soh 2009). As the "comfort women" system enslaved Korean, Chinese, Taiwanese, Southeast Asian, Dutch, and Japanese women, the pattern of its state-directed imperialist "sexploitation" based upon hierarchized intersectionality of gender, class, race, and nationality cannot be dissociated, in any absolutist manner, from the kind of state power that the United States practiced over military prostitution in the postwar era. The shift was from the (Japanese) state's more obvious physical coercion backed by its military force to the (American) state's embedded, institutionalized, and differentiated function in its tacit alliance with the largely privatized industry of military prostitution.

There are three broad areas over which the US government exercises its power: first, where (which particular nation-states and regions) it stations its military for the purpose of protecting and promoting its geopolitical interest; second, the medicalized control over the body and sexuality of military sex workers; third, the impact of military prostitution on the hosting countries' local and national economies. The power relations between the governments of the United States and other occupying countries and the hosting countries' governments vary according to a set of multiple factors, political, economic, and military relations between the two respective states, their economies, and other kinds of strategic leverage that each has against the other. The legal arrangements made between the governments of the occupying military and those of the hosting countries, which concern, most centrally, issues of the military personnel, their conduct, civil and criminal liabilities, and property, are known as SOFA, the Status of Forces Agreement. The diverse versions of SOFA that have existed in postwar global history reflect the complex and changing relations of power between the governments of the occupying military and those of the hosting countries. For example, the local US military authorities in South Korea exercise the most pervasive kind of control over the military sex industries and their workers via medicalization of their bodies through regular examination for STDs and use of an identification system for the purpose of screening sex workers. They also possess the legal-medical authority to quarantine those who are infected (Moon 1997). This aspect of the occupying military's power also functions implicitly as a broader mechanism of governing the "camp towns," the local civilian areas surrounding the bases that depend economically on the presence of the troops. In sum, the governmentality of the occupying countries and their military in multiple national-local contexts is an articulation of a complex convergence of contradictory and yet necessarily complementary forces, representing state racism, biopower and necropolitics, and humanitarianism, while the hosting countries also exercise these powers of (auto-)racialism, classism, and sexism, along with the occupying empire and its military, by helping to control, regulate, and manage its own laboring population.

The intersectionality of patriarchal familism, masculinist nationalism, racialist and gendered international division of labor, and both national and global class stratifications has subjected, en masse, third world working-class women's sexuality and sexualized labor to devalued and commodifying wage relations for military prostitution (Bell 1994). These ideological forces articulate themselves in concrete ways as discriminatory social and economic inequities in education, job availability, and pay, which produce in turn a military (and non-military) prostitution labor market. The hosting countries' developing economies benefit from the profitability and exploitability of the sex work provided by their working-class female population. In addition to contributing directly to the state revenue, their artificially low-waged labor maintains and supports, in a serial manner, other sectors of the national economy.

The economic relations around militarized sex industries between the hosting and occupying countries and their central and local governmental authorities are generally cooperative, collusive, and comprador in the context of dependent developmentalism, as the capital accumulation in a "national" economy that military sex work contributes to benefits, in an un-egalitarian fashion, the elite classes whose socioeconomic interests are aligned with those of the US empire and its allies. We should note that military sex work performed for US soldiers largely by third world working-class women does not simply serve the economic interests of the United States, although it certainly does, but rather, it supports the interests of a much larger network of capitalist nation-states and transnational capitalism as a global system, against its enemies, those recalcitrant non-capitalist economies, rogue states, and post-socialist regions. Militarism serves capitalism and capital serves militarism, as militarized sex industries serve both. In the context of the intensifying ubiquity of modern sexual proletarianization, military sex work exemplifies the economic and ideological coerciveness and the structural violence built into the conglomerated nexus of the state(s), capital, and militarism. Military sex work along with tourist sex work in places like Okinawa, South Korea, the Philippines, and Thailand has been one of the most important and yet least visible types of labor that has served the global capitalization process.

RESISTANCE AND ACTIVISM

As military prostitution as an industry establishes itself at the point of the complex convergence of these historical, ideological, geopolitical, and economic forces, how we might conceptualize "resistance" and understand "activism" is consequently a complicated matter. Critical scholarly work and activism on military prostitution must take into account larger factors such as US military hegemony, state involvement, and legal and medical issues as outlined above. The voices and perspectives that are critical of military prostitution and various dimensions of it as a state-related institution come from varied, overlapping, and yet often conflicting positions. For example, in the case of Okinawa, a major base in Asia for the United States since the end of the World War II, and the US territories in the Pacific such as Guam and Samoa, strategically buttressing US military domination, complex questions of de-neocolonization and demilitarization intersect with the issues of anti-military prostitution resistance and activism. These varying and diverse perspectives include, for example, the local and central governments of the hosting countries, local business owners in camp towns, anti-neo-imperialist/nationalist activists, and anti-prostitution activists, who may be Christian, secular, feminist, and/or anti-feminist/masculinist. At the same time, military sex workers represent their own interests as activists, although their "own" interests may not coincide wholly or even partially with (any of) the other agents who "oppose" and "critique" different dimensions of military prostitution as an institution and business. For example, in the context of South Korea, former sex slaves of the Japanese imperial army from World War II as well as military sex workers from the postwar era up to the late 1980s were compelled to perform ideological labor in order to continue to hold up the postcolonial and anti-neocolonial androcentric nationalist narrative: their sexual labor was once more exploited, this time in the cultural sphere, as an allegory for the masculinist nation whose sovereignty (read as rights to protect their women) was violated by imperial and neo-imperial military encroachment.

CONCLUSION: ADDITIONAL ISSUES

Continuities and discontinuities

Rather than exceptionalizing military prostitution, we can think through the continuities and discontinuities among multiple categories and phenomena where there is a slippage and overlap. For example, we might consider the dis/continuity between imperial military prostitution (for US troops in global locations) and national military prostitution (for national military in respective national contexts), between military prostitution and "industrial" (non-military, market or peace-time) prostitution, between military tourism and sex tourism, between militarized sex workers and other militarized women workers (as mothers and wives of soldiers, diplomats, nurses, etc.) (Enloe 2000b), between female sexploitation and male sexploitation in military prostitution, between male military labor and military sex work, respectively as masculinized and feminized versions of racialized and proletarianized labor, between military prostitution that takes place "over there" and military brides who immigrate "over here" and continue to work in the domestic militarized sex industries (i.e., between overseas transnational labor and domestic immigrant labor), between militarism/military tourism and market tourism, between female (military) sex work and female non-sex work, as proletarian labor available to third world women situated in the context of educational, social, and economic inequities.

Contemporary changes

The intensifying globalization of the late twentieth and early twenty-first centuries has also brought changes to US-related military prostitution. While military sex work has always been migratory throughout modern history, the patterns of migration became more complex. For example, South Korean military sex workers served US soldiers who were fighting in the Vietnam War in the 1960s and 1970s, while Filipina and Russian women serve the US troops in South Korean and Okinawan camp towns as migrant military sex workers. Although the United States remains a global military empire, the contemporary wars it is engaged in are no longer conventional, in multiple ways. As the conditions and necessity for deployment of troops change, we can safely assume that military prostitution in the future will also undergo transformation.

Pioneering feminist works by Enloe and others have deconstructed what had been obscured by the language and discourse of "international politics" and "national security," that is, the nexus of power that interweaves global capitalism, ideologies of racialization and sexism, and (neo-) imperialism, placing militarism at its center. Their critical works have illustrated that militarism, in turn, has premised itself upon third world women's proletarianized sex work that functions as the material basis of the complex global system. Their work makes it possible for us to pay attention to and to be able to locate this foundational labor at the heart of the global order, as it moved through periods of successive change from World War II, the period of expanding empires and capitalism, the postwar era of the Cold War/Hot War confrontations of communism and anti-communism, the postsocialist capitalization in the post-Cold War era, and the ongoing "war on terror," the latest manifestation of imperial militarism.

SEE ALSO: Comfort Women; Militarism and Gender-Based Violence; Prostitution/Sex Work; Sex Tourism; Sexual Violence and the Military

REFERENCES

Barry, Kathleen. 1996. *The Prostitution of Sexuality*. New York: NYU Press.

Bell, Shannon. 1994. *Reading, Writing, and Rewriting the Prostitute Body*. Indianapolis: Indiana University Press.

Enloe, Cynthia. 2000a. *Bananas, Beaches and Bases: Making Feminist Sense of International Politics*. Oakland: University of California Press.

Enloe, Cynthia. 2000b. *Maneuvers: The International Politics of Militarizing Women's Lives* Oakland: University of California Press.

Johnson, Chalmers. 2004. *The Sorrows of Empire: Secrecy, Militarism and the End of the Republic*. New York: Metropolitan Books.

Moon, Katharine H. S. 1997. *Sex Among Allies: Military Prostitution in U.S.–Korea Relations*. New York: Columbia University Press.

Soh, Sarah, C. 2009. *The Comfort Women: Sexual Violence and Postcolonial Memory in Korea and Japan*. Chicago: University of Chicago Press.

FURTHER READING

Enloe, Cynthia. 2007. *Globalization and Militarism: Feminists Make the Link*. Lanham: Rowman & Littlefield.

Hohn, Maria, and Seungsook Moon. 2010. *Over There: Living with the U.S. Military Empire from World War Two and to the Present*. Durham, NC: Duke University Press.

Shigematsu, Setsu, and Keith L. Camacho. 2010. *Militarized Currents: Toward a Decolonized Future in Asia and the Pacific*. Minneapolis: University of Minnesota Press.

Military Masculinity

RYAN S. OGILVY
United States Air Force, Biomedical Science Corps, USA

Essential to any definition of military masculinity is recognition of the fact that it is embedded in military institutions in which the individual military member exists. The military is known to offer access to unique benefits, including training, which construct a masculine ideal defined by self-discipline, respect for authority within the ranks, self-reliance, a willingness to use violence, willingness to place service before self, and risk-taking capacity when faced with life-threatening decisions. All of these characteristics underpin modern soldiers, sailors, and airmen and therefore define broadly military masculinity.

Nonetheless, it is important to acknowledge that despite the establishment of a broad set of traits that define masculinity in the military, the relationship between masculinity and the military is far more complex than one single set of established traits or ideals. Despite the fact that the above traits are considered important across military branches, there is evidence to suggest that each branch is predisposed to a dominance of particular traits. Brown (2012) argues that there is not a dominance of traits amongst branches of the military; rather, there is a disaggregate construction of military masculinity. In particular, the Marine Corps promotes a culture of competence with violence and superior ability within the profession of arms, while the Navy promotes the ideal of service before self, while differently again the Air Force promotes dominant traits of intelligence, and finally the Army a service of submission to authority that is unquestioned in its agenda. This is not to argue that the other traits identified in the broad definition of military masculinity do not exist within the subcultures or branches of military. Rather, it is argued that military masculinity is dynamic in nature with many complexities.

As described above, military masculinity may be seen as comprised of a relatively unique set of components that distinguish it from other forms of masculinity. Most obvious is the relationship between ideas of masculinity and militarism, which have become so closely aligned that in many cultures and countries throughout history, assuming a military role has been and will continue to be seen as a normative pathway into manhood (Cockburn 2001). In contrast to this, however, is the argument that military masculinities are dynamic and contradictory. This has been especially true since the turn of the twenty-first century, as social and policy change has led to the modern military member coming from varied gender, transgender, sexual preference, race, and cultural backgrounds. Repeals of policies such as "Don't Ask, Don't Tell" (a policy banning the disclosure of sexual orientation for homosexual military members) have led to an understanding of military masculinity that, while maintaining some tradition, also embraces a wider range of qualities.

Prior to these more recent changes, and especially during times of war, traits such as strength, sacrifice, submission to superiors, courage, and intelligence have been considered central to the definition of military masculinity. Whilst militaries from all over the world have notionally been comprised of men from different races, classes, and gendered preferences, depictions of white, middle-class, strong, physically superior individuals have been the norm. As a result, individuals who did not meet this ideal, including homosexual, racially diverse, and/or lower-class men, were often denied the entitlements that came with military service, or, in the case of homosexual men, excluded from service upon speaking of their sexuality. Belkin (2012) has argued that the military's treatment of masculinity and heterosexuality as corollaries became a tool to discard the ugliness of war and the military-industrial complex by emphasizing flawless military men of perfect moral standing.

Significant changes to military masculinity have occurred since the 1960s. Civil rights movements, and especially the legal abolishment of class, gender, and racial separation, brought with them a new era in which traction was gained in the challenge to hegemonic definitions of military masculinity. For the first time equality was considered for those whose service had for decades been undervalued. Nonetheless, while such social movements have empowered marginalized races, genders, lesbian, homosexual, transgender, and bisexual individuals, hegemonic definitions of military masculinity have arguably been modified rather than replaced completely. For example, whilst military policies are no longer sexist, sexually biased, or middle-class driven, in practice many prejudices remain. Within the frameworks of gender realignment and theories of modern masculinity, emotional awareness and willingness to embrace emotions are being viewed as essential to the ongoing success of military members. Large numbers of individuals presenting with post-traumatic stress disorder (PTSD) are being forced to confront their past trauma, under the understanding that to do so is heroic and valorous, drawing on the original definition of military masculinity.

As major conflicts around the world are coming to an end and peacekeeping roles have become important, it is essential to consider military masculinity in this context. Duncanson (2009), in her analysis of soldier accounts of war, found evidence that peacekeeping is as definably masculine as wartime activities. There is toughness about peacekeeping that does not exist in large-scale conflicts, where soldiers are more autonomous, promoting bravery and self sufficiency, characteristics often found in hegemonic definitions of masculinity. The role of the peacekeeper allows military members to use force only when threatened, suggesting a high level of self-discipline is required. This is again consistent with hegemonic traits discussed in terms of military masculinity. Despite the differences in roles between war fighting and peacekeeping, the underlying traits of military members required to perform both are undeniably similar. There is significant scope for future research to explore military masculinity further in the context of the lateral role of peacekeeping.

SEE ALSO: "Don't Ask, Don't Tell" Policy in the United States; Hegemonic Masculinity; Hypermasculinity; War, International Violence, and Gender

REFERENCES

Belkin, Aaron. 2012. *Bring Me Men: Military Masculinity and the Benign Façade of the American Empire, 1898–2001*. New York: Columbia University Press.

Brown, Melissa. 2012. *Enlisting Masculinity: The Construction of Gender in US Military Recruiting Advertising During the All-Volunteer Force*. Oxford: Oxford University Press.

Cockburn, Cynthia. 2001. "The Gendered Dynamics of Armed Conflict and Political Violence." In *Victims, Perpetrators or Actors? Gender, Armed Conflict and Political Violence*, edited by Caroline O. N. Moser and Fiona C. Clark, 13–29. London: Zed Books.

Duncanson, Claire. 2009. "Forces for Good? Narratives of Military Masculinity in Peace Keeping Operations." *Journal of International Feminist Politics*, 11(1): 63–80.

Mind/Body Split

K. J. WININGER
University of Southern Maine, USA

The intellectual conception of a split between mind and body has had a profound effect on both conceptions of gender and views of sexuality. The European association of mind with brain and soul, and the idea that mind is both the governing faculty and the spiritual home, form the foundation for human authority. The power of the mind is the underpinning of most European intellectual views of human exceptionalism. The conceptual activity of the mind is what makes humans different from other animals: we are *Homo sapiens*. Far more pernicious for human gender issues is the association of mind and its properties with men and masculinity, and body with femininity and animality.

This simple division between the mind and body, conceived of in antiquity and having a lively afterlife, helped form the rationale for the subordination of women and feminine men, and contempt for sexuality and sexual desire. Even in antiquity, radical ideas of mind–body differences, dualisms of mind and body, sun and moon, white and black, male and female are not innocent categories of differentiation; they are hierarchical. It is these notions that entered European thought and have formed the intellectual substructure which kept women from libraries and slaves from learning to read. This dualism is so pronounced in the case of gender that some thinkers concluded that women do not really exist; they are simply non-men. The postulation of the non-existence of women can be seen from pre-Socratic to Lacanian thought. Lacan's peculiar denial of woman's existence is just a continuation of the idea that women do not occupy the public spheres of intellectual power and discourse (Lacan 1983).

The idea of a radical differentiation between mind and body is of ancient origin, and can be found in many forms of dualism – not only those coming from Europe. The mind–body split was not simply a division, it almost always functions as a hierarchy, as is the case with other traditional dualities in the European tradition. Mind is the more important element, the governor of the self, that which is capable of development and formal education. The idea that there might be an immaterial soul or mind (psyche) in addition to the material body had an obvious attraction to philosophies which believed in a variety of types of afterlives, especially those including the immortality of or the transmigration of a soul. These ideas predate Christianity and Islam; Pythagoras advocated the immortality of the soul. Anaxagoras's (*c*.510–428 BCE) cosmology maintains a dualism where there are two radically distinct ultimate things: mind and matter. Early pre-Socratic philosophy was influenced by North Africa and the East, and this division was eventually incorporated into canonical monotheism. The direct links between Plato in the West and Aristotle in the East ensured that a version of these philosophies entered into Christianity and Islam. The subordination of women, ruled as they are by ungoverned bodies and passions rather than circumspection and reason, formed the basis of their exclusion from many aspects of life. Not being able to participate in public political life due to their lack of reason, women were excluded from religious leadership, economic development, and educational advancement. In most of the Islamic world women could inherit wealth, but if they were excluded from banks and other financial sectors, it did not really allow them that much more autonomy.

In its most virulent form, for example, that of René Descartes (1596–1650), mind–body dualism even poses a paradox concerning the possibility of mind–body interaction. If mind is entirely immaterial and body entirely material and mechanical, then how does the mind move the body? Princess Elisabeth of Bohemia (1618–1680), who pointed this problem out to Descartes, was puzzled by this issue and his answer was that it occurred through the pineal gland, an unsatisfactory answer since the gland is corporeal. Descartes's mind–body dualism placed the mind outside nature by rendering it as an immaterial substance. In the case of most mind–body dualisms, the body was considered transient; it came into being and went out of existence. It belonged to an unstable world. In this, Descartes is in a philosophical tradition that dates back to Parmenides; the body comes into being and passes away. Women lacking a mind or soul were by association considered to be ruled by their bodies and therefore not able to engage in moral reasoning or civil life. To be properly governed, they must be controlled by a man who has a mind and reason (Descartes 1988).

In this European tradition, sexuality is seen as corporeal and thus pulling us away from the distinctive feature of humanity: the mind. Sexuality is shared with lower animals; it is considered the base. In this view, sexuality of any kind is considered ignoble and animal-like, but even the greatest enemies of body conceive of an exception in the case of sexuality that leads to procreation. This does not elevate the bodily nature of the deed, but reproduction logically requires carnal activity. While heterosexual intercourse is required for the continuation of the species, it does not elevate the corporeal in the mind–body split.

SEE ALSO: Embodiment and the Phenomenological Tradition; Feminist Theories of Experience

REFERENCES

Descartes, René. 1988. *The Philosophical Writings of Descartes*, trans. J. Cottingham, R. Stoothoff, A. Kenny, and D. Murdoch. Cambridge: Cambridge University Press.

Lacan, Jacques. 1983. *Feminine Sexuality: Jacques Lacan and the école freudienne*, edited by Juliet Mitchell and Jacqueline Rose, trans. Jacqueline Rose. New York: Norton.

FURTHER READING

Aquinas, Thomas. 1981. *The Summa theologica*, repr, 5 vols. Westminster, MD: Christian Classics.

Bordo, Susan. 1987. *The Flight to Objectivity: Essays on Cartesianism and Culture*. Albany: SUNY Press.

Kirk, G. S., J. E. Raven, and M. Schofield. 1983. *The Presocratic Philosophers: A Critical History with a Selection of Texts*. Cambridge: Cambridge University Press.

Nye, Andrea. 1999. *The Princess and the Philosopher: Letters of Elisabeth of the Palatine to René Descartes*. Lanham: Rowman & Littlefield.

Misogyny

JANE M. USSHER
University of Western Sydney, Australia

Misogyny is defined as hatred of women or girls, expressed as disgust, intolerance or entrenched prejudice, serving to legitimate women's oppression. Misogynist beliefs and practices are conceptualized by some as "a potential in all men," called out by "particular circumstances" (Jukes 1993, xxix). However, women can also adopt misogynistic beliefs, through self-hatred or self-objectification.

Misogyny is manifested through religious and cultural beliefs which represent women as dangerous, defiled, or polluting; hostile folklore and jokes; the sexualization and objectification of women through art, film, literature, the mass media and pornography; hostility towards women in positions of power; sexual violence and domestic despotism; female genital surgery and footbinding; and the visceral horror held towards women's secretions, including menstrual taboos and phobias (Jeffreys 2005; Gilmore 2009; Summers 2013).

Misogyny damages the physical and mental health of women. In 2007 the World Bank concluded that "unequal treatment of women – by the state, in the market and by their community and family – puts them at a disadvantage throughout their lives and stifles the development of their societies." Women significantly outnumber men amongst the world's poor and dispossessed; if they are in paid work, they earn significantly less than men; and are absent or underrepresented in positions of social and commercial power. Across the world millions of women are also systematically denied reproductive rights, through forced sterilization, denial of access to safe and effective methods of fertility control, and safe care in pregnancy and child birth (Ussher 2011).

The misogynistic continuum of objectification and abuse against women and girls starts with the sexualized imagery that is endemic in Western culture, documented in a report published by the American Psychological Association (2007). For example, in one study of prime-time television, 84% of programs contained incidents of sexual harassment, including sexist and sexual comments about women, sexualized body language, and depictions of men or boys leering at women. Advertising depicts women as sexual objects more frequently than it depicts men in such a way, at a rate of 2:1–3:1, with women represented as attractive, and men as authoritative. The absence of alternative roles for women reinforces their positioning as sexual objects, to be desired and derided in equal proportions.

Objectification of women is enacted on a daily basis through sexual violence and abuse, affecting between 12% and 46% of girls and women. For example, a survey of US women reported that 44% had experienced rape or attempted rape and a World Health Organization (WHO) report published in 2002 found reported rates of attempted or completed forced sex by an intimate partner in 15.3% (Canada), 21.7% (Nicaragua), 23% (Mexico; London, UK), 25% (Zimbabwe), 29.9% (Thailand), 46.7% (Peru), and 51.9% (Turkey) of women. Sexual violence is often accompanied by physical violence, or threats of violence, particularly in the context of partner or child sexual abuse.

There is also a long history of rape being used as a strategy of war – from the mythical rape of Troy, to recent conflicts in Syria, Rwanda, East Timor, or the former Yugoslavia, a practice recognized by the WHO as a deliberate strategy to subvert community bonds. At the same time, sexual trafficking of girls and women is occurring at epidemic proportions – a new slave trade predicated on objectification and exploitation, which results in hundreds of thousands of women and girls being sold into prostitution or sexual slavery every year. For example, it has been estimated that more than 200,000 Bangladeshi women were trafficked between 1990 and 1997, and approximately 7,000 Nepali women and girls are trafficked to India each year (Ussher 2011).

Sexual harassment in a public setting is another manifestation of misogyny. For example, in a study conducted in Canada, 23% of girls reported having experienced sexual harassment at school; whilst in a study conducted in the United States, the rate was 63%, including being the object of sexual jokes, comments, gestures or looks, and being touched, grabbed or pinched in a sexual way. Sexual harassment at work has been reported by 25% of women in Poland and in the Czech Republic, 22% of women in Australia, 50% of women in the United Kingdom, and 25–58% of women in the United States.

Misogyny is internalized by women and girls through a process of self-objectification; self-judgement in relation to unrealistic societal norms of sexual attractiveness (Jeffreys 2005). Self-objectification is associated with reports of low self-esteem, impairments in cognitive functioning, feelings of shame about the body, and anxiety about appearance. It has been linked to the relatively high rates of cosmetic surgery in girls living in the United States and to eating disorders, such as excessive dieting and exercising, anorexia nervosa or bulimia nervosa (APA 2010/2007).

The more girls and women objectify their bodies, the more likely they are to report depression. The attribution of women's depression to an internal pathology, in particular to the reproductive body, rather than to cultural norms and social practices, is a further manifestation of misogyny – women blamed for their own distress (Ussher 2011).

There are many psychological explanations for misogyny, including men's envy of women's capacity to reproduce; castration anxiety leading to fear of menstrual blood; frustration-aggression, resulting from unfulfilled sexual desires for women; and psychic imbalance resulting from men's dependency on women, combined with regressed fear and longing of being physically consumed (see Gilmore 2009). Misogyny also serves to maintain women's position as the "second sex," which benefits men financially, politically, and socially. Misogyny means women serve as scapegoats during times of social hardship, such as during the witch trials of the Middle Ages. Misogyny thus underpins gendered power imbalances in patriarchal society, to the detriment of all women. While patriarchy prevails, so will misogyny.

SEE ALSO: Beauty Industry; Child Sexual Abuse and Trauma; Depression; Eating Disorders and Disordered Eating; Patriarchy; Sexual Assault/Sexual Violence; Sex Trafficking; Witches

REFERENCES

American Psychological Association (APA). 2010 [2007]. American Psychological Association Task Force on the Sexualization of Girls. Accessed August 30, 2015, at: www.apa.org/pi/wpo/sexualization.html.

Gilmore, David D. 2009. *Misogyny: The Male Malady*. Philadelphia: University of Pennsylvania Press.

Jeffreys, Sheila. 2005. *Beauty and Misogyny: Harmful Cultural Practices in the West*. London: Routledge.

Jukes, Adam. 1993. *Why Men Hate Women*. London: Free Association Books.

Summers, Anne. 2013. *The Misogyny Factor*. Sydney: New South Wales University.

Ussher, Jane M. 2011. *The Madness of Women: Myth and Experience*. London: Routledge.

World Bank. 2007. *Global Monitoring Report: Millennium Development Goals: Confronting the Challenges of Gender Inequality and Fragile States*. Washington: The World Bank.

World Health Organization. 2002. World report on violence and health. Accessed August 30, 2015 at: www.who.int/violence_injury_prevention/violence/world_report/en/.

Monasticism

STEPHEN J. DAVIS
Yale University, USA

The word "monasticism" derives from the Greek word *monos*, meaning "solitary," but the practice of monasticism in fact encompasses a range of social configurations. Some monastics are sedentary hermits or itinerant mendicants. Others form various communities: from consecrated women living in converted households, to loosely organized clusters of monastics living independently but worshiping together, to larger groups of monks or nuns living in walled compounds and governed by a common rule.

As a cultural and religious phenomenon, monastic retreat was first attested in ancient India, where sometime in the first millennium BCE different religious groups began to promote renunciation from the world. The beginnings of monasticism can be seen in the Upanisads and in the "heterodox" traditions of Jainism and Buddhism.

Both Jainism and Buddhism critiqued the Indian caste system and orthodox cults of sacrifice, instead emphasizing detachment, non-violence, and celibacy. Jain monastics (both male and female) committed themselves to a life of perpetual wandering, traveling in small groups, begging for food and lodging in order to subsist, and forming lineages with disciples. At an early period, elaborate sets of rules developed, governing every aspect of a monk's or nun's life. Some monks, from both the major sectarian divisions in Jainism – the Svetambara ("White Robed") and Digambara ("Sky Clad"), lived in settled monasteries, although reform-minded leaders frequently called for a return to the peripatetic way of life.

In Buddhism, a less austere monastic path emerged, following a "middle way" that sponsored not only itinerant forms but also temporary and more permanent communal living arrangements for monks and nuns, sometimes in gardens and retreats donated by lay supporters. Unlike the Jains, the Buddhists had separate rules for nuns. Buddhist monks were successful proselytizers and Buddhism would eventually spread throughout Asia, including Southeast Asia, Sri Lanka, Central Asia, Afghanistan, Tibet, China, and Japan.

In the Mediterranean world, forms of monastic practice emerged as alternative social options for Christians in the fourth century CE, perhaps partly in reaction to institutional changes brought about by imperial support for Christian churches. While solitary hermits were celebrated as models of piety in literary *vitae* such as Athanasius' *Life of Antony*, coenobitic ("communal") monasteries were founded and organized around common rules. Early examples include the canons of Pachomius and Shenoute in Egypt, Basil in Asia Minor, and Benedict in Italy. As in the case of Buddhist foundations, Christian monasteries became economic centers: in many places monasteries came to function as universities with well-equipped libraries and scriptoria and as hospitals with state-of-the-art healthcare facilities (Schopen 2004, 6–12; Crislip 2005).

What these diverse expressions have in common is the decision to withdraw from everyday society and to engage in an ascetic life of renunciation. Withdrawal and renunciation are ways in which monastics differentiate themselves – both spatially and bodily – from typical familial and civic conventions within a given culture. The construction of gender in monastic communities therefore is regularly framed by discourses of sexual differentiation and segregation. These discourses function as mechanisms of social control within communities, but they are sometimes complicated and contested in practice.

In the Hindu, Jain, Buddhist, and Christian traditions, most literature has been produced by monks, whether the intended audience was male or female, monastic or lay. Not surprisingly, monastic texts frequently articulate patriarchal/misogynist assumptions portraying women as radically "other" and authorizing social policies of segregation. Thus, for example, in early Indian texts advocating ascetic discipline, women are viewed as "the flame of sin" and "the fuel of hellfire" and their private parts are described as "a deep festering ulcer" (Olivelle 1992, 77–78), and in Christian stories about monks in the Egyptian desert the demon of fornication is envisioned as a female temptress. To guard against being contaminated or seduced by such threats, male monks are counseled to avoid all contact with women. Thus, one Jain codebook, the *Acaranga Sutra*, enjoins its monastic readers to avoid talking to, looking at, thinking about, or being in physical proximity to women (Sethi 2012, 59–60). In the Christian monasteries on Mount Athos in Greece, an even stricter policy of segregation pertains: all women (including female animals) are banned from the entire peninsula.

The rigorous application of such rules helps construct and reinforce a binary opposition between male and female bodies; and yet, in monastic literature, one observes how these boundaries are sometimes curiously subverted, fragmented, crossed, and/or contested. For example, Jain monastic teachings subtly theorize a threefold division of biological gender – male, female, and indeterminate – while also distinguishing between three different "psychological sexual inclinations" (Jaini 1991, 11). In Digambara Jain circles and in some early Buddhist traditions, women must be reborn as men before they can be eligible for liberation. In early Christianity, monks wrote tales about women who attained salvation by disguising themselves as men, becoming monks, and living in male monasteries undetected until death (Davis 2002). In these ways, monasticism historically has proven to be a complex social terrain not only for ascetic practices of renunciation and withdrawal but also for a diverse range of gendered polities designed to reconfigure and regiment human bodies and communities.

SEE ALSO: Patriarchy; Sexualities

REFERENCES

Crislip, Andrew T. 2005. *From Monastery to Hospital: Christian Monasticism and the Transformation of Health Care in Late Antiquity*. Ann Arbor: University of Michigan Press.
Davis, Stephen J. 2002. "Crossed Texts, Crossed Sex: Intertextuality and Gender in Early Christian Legends of Holy Women Disguised as Men." *Journal of Early Christian Studies*, 10(1), 1–36.
Jaini, Padmanabh S. 1991. *Gender and Salvation: Jaina Debates on the Spiritual Liberation of Women*. Berkeley: University of California Press.
Olivelle, Patrick. 1992. *Saṃnyāsa Upaniṣads: Hindu Scriptures on Asceticism and Renunciation*. New York: Oxford University Press.
Schopen, Gregory. 2004. *Buddhist Monks and Business Matters: Still More Papers on Monastic Buddhism in India*. Honolulu: University of Hawai'i Press.
Sethi, Manisha. 2012. *Escaping the World: Women Renouncers Among Jains*. New Delhi: Routledge.

FURTHER READING

Crosby, Kate. 2014. *Theravada Buddhism: Continuity, Diversity, and Identity*. Malden, MA: Wiley Blackwell.
Johnston, William M., ed. 2000. *Encyclopedia of Monasticism*. 2 vols. Chicago: Fitzroy Dearborn. See especially "Gender Studies," "Rules, Buddhist (Vinaya)," and "Women's Monasteries."

Monogamy, Biological Perspectives on

DAVID P. BARASH
University of Washington, Seattle, USA

Unlike asexual species, in which each individual reproduces on its own, among sexual species there must be some sort of association between male and female. In some cases, there is essentially no social bond connecting the two biological parents; this is true, for example, among the many marine invertebrates in which gametes (eggs and sperm) are simply discharged into the surrounding water, after which fertilization and eventually development occurs. Even in such cases, however, there is typically a degree of coordination between male and female, either via chemical signals (pheromones) or shared sensitivity to environmental cues such as day length, ambient temperature, and so forth. But among nearly all vertebrates – and all birds and mammals – sexual reproduction occurs in the context of direct behavioral communication and physical coordination between the parents.

The union of egg and sperm requires that each parent makes a comparable genetic contribution to the next generation. However, the union of egg and sperm can occur as a result of a variety of interaction patterns between male and female. Biologists have accordingly identified various "breeding systems," depending on the social dynamics between the two parents. When reproduction involves an association of one male and one female, in a relationship that is at least identifiable and persistent – if only briefly – we speak of "monogamy." When the association is so brief as to constitute mating only, the preferred term is "promiscuity," although without the negative connotations typically involved when speaking of human beings. There are also mating systems in which one male or one female remains simultaneously associated with several individuals of the opposite sex; these are generally identified as various forms of "polygamy," which in turn is subdivided into "polygyny" – one male associated with multiple females (also known as a harem system) – and "polyandry," in which one female associates reproductively with more than one male.

An alternative way to characterize mating systems, and one that is actually more biologically meaningful, is to examine the variance in reproductive success of males and females. When the variance of male and female reproductive success is essentially equal, this offers a more precise definition of monogamy than does one involving an assessment of the duration or intensity of male–female social bonding. Similarly, polygyny obtains when male variance in reproductive success exceeds female variance, and polyandry is defined as occurring when female variance exceeds its male counterpart. This result occurs because in polygyny, with one male mated to multiple females, each female experiences approximately the same breeding success (therefore, female variance is relatively low), whereas male variance is high – since with a typically equal sex ration, the success of one male as a "harem-master" necessitates the failure of numerous other males. The inverse obtains during polyandry.

The different patterns of social bonding found between male and female – rather than differences in variance of breeding success – are nonetheless typically employed in distinguishing mating systems, simply because it is generally easier to identify bonding patterns than to quantify individual reproductive success for males and females. However it is defined, polygyny is by far the most common mating system among mammals, with polyandry the rarest. Monogamy, by contrast, has long been known to be unusual among vertebrates, although it had been thought to be the predominant system employed by birds, until DNA fingerprinting techniques revealed that there is a substantial difference between "social monogamy" and "sexual monogamy." Social monogamy refers to the behavioral interactions within a "mated pair." By contrast, "sexual monogamy" is more attuned to the biologically relevant dimension of variance in reproductive success – more specifically, the question of who is actually a genetic parent in each case. It is now known that even though many species show social monogamy, the male partner is often not the genetic parent of the offspring in question.

Actual numbers vary with the species and circumstances, but even among birds – widely considered the most monogamous of vertebrates – it is not unusual for 10 to 50 percent of offspring to have been fathered by a male other than the social partner of the mother. Of course, such departures from expectation are much rarer among females, simply because with internal fertilization, offspring emerging from a mother's body are guaranteed to be her genetic offspring. In short, "Mommy's babies, Daddy's maybes."

Biologists have long understood why, from the perspective of males, monogamy is relatively rare. Essentially, because sperm are cheap and eggs are expensive, males of many species are more likely to experience evolutionary success (to be more "fit" in the technical sense) if they seek out and obtain additional, extra-pair copulations, or EPCs. It had long been assumed that the situation for females is different, since for egg-makers and placenta-producers, additional copulations are unlikely to generate additional reproductive success, given that each female's male partner has already been selected to produce very large numbers of sperm. Along with the discovery of EPCs, however, has come recognition of the various evolutionary benefits that females can derive from such behavior. These include obtaining additional resources (notably food), getting one's eggs fertilized by a male of better genetic quality than one's social partner, "moving up" to a more productive mateship, and so forth.

At the same time, it must be emphasized that monogamy – despite its rarity in the biological world – is a viable evolutionary option for at least some species. Females are more likely to adhere to monogamy when their male partner is of desirable (or at least, acceptable) quality, both genetically and behaviorally. Males are more inclined toward monogamy when they have relatively high confidence in the sexual fidelity of their partners, such that further investment in their offspring is unlikely to benefit the evolutionary fitness of a rival male. An additional consideration – and perhaps an overwhelming one from a strictly evolutionary perspective – is that monogamy is typically enhanced when there is a payoff to biparental care; that is, when the success of jointly produced offspring is considerably greater when male and female cooperate to provision, protect, and provide learning experiences for the next generation.

SEE ALSO: Monogamy, Sociological Perspectives on

FURTHER READING

Barash, David P. 2016. *Out of Eden: Surprising Consequences of Human Polygamy*. New York: Oxford University Press.

Barash, David P., and Judith E. Lipton. 2002. *The Myth of Monogamy: Fidelity and Infidelity in Animals and People*. New York: Henry Holt.

Barash, David P., and Judith E. Lipton. 2009. *Strange Bedfellows: the Surprising Connection between Sex, Evolution and Monogamy*. New York: Bellevue Literary Press.

Dixson, Alan F. 2009. *Sexual Selection and the Origin of Human Mating Systems*. New York: Oxford University Press.

Reichard, Ulrich H., and Christophe Boesch, eds. 2003. *Monogamy: Mating Strategies and Partnerships in Birds, Humans and Other Mammals*. New York: Cambridge University Press.

Ridley, Matt. 2003. *The Red Queen: Sex and the Evolution of Human Nature*. New York: HarperCollins.

Monogamy, Sociological Perspectives on

ABBEY WILLIS
University of Connecticut, USA

There is debate within the field as to whether humans are *biologically* oriented toward monogamy or non-monogamy (for an exchange within this debate, see Ellsworth's (2012) review). Scholars (Frank and DeLamater 2010) have also suggested that labeling relationship formations as either "monogamous" or "non-monogamous" paints with too wide a brush. With scholars frequently writing on non-monogamies, Frank and DeLamater (2010) suggest that scholars might likewise understand different forms of monogamies, writing that monogamy is lived and practiced in a variety of ways and which factors demarcate "exclusivity" will differ among partners. For example, some people form monogamous relationships that are intended to last a lifetime, and others engage in "serial monogamy," which refers to separate and sequential monogamous pairings. Within the several different forms monogamy may take, agreed upon boundaries will vary when it comes to additional romantic, emotional, and sexual ties that partners may form.

From a social constructionist perspective within sociology, monogamy (defined as the practice of having one exclusive sexual and/or romantic relationship at a time) can be studied as a normative, institutional, and compulsory relationship formation. Monogamy, like other normative expectations and practices, becomes normative and enforced through the complex social relations that make up and reproduce daily life. At the institutional level, sexual and romantic relationships are regulated not only through marriage but also through regulations of living arrangements filtered through zoning laws (for a recent example, see this story from Hartford, Connecticut, USA: http://www.courant.com/community/hartford/hc-hartford-scarborough-zoning-1121-20141120-story.html). At a cultural level, monogamy is often constructed as the sole normative expectation for loving and sexual adult relationships – this is referred to by scholars as *mononormativity* (Piper and Bauer 2006).

Mononormativity (Piper and Bauer 2006) refers to the dominant discourse of monogamy which serves as a basis from which rules, expectations, and assumptions are built upon, with examples including the primacy of couples (coupledom), exclusivity, and the privileging of romantic love over other forms of intimate connections (Barker and Langdridge 2010). Even when communities and scholars attempt to create and theorize about alternative relationship formations, the primacy of coupledom, for example, often continues to be reinforced. These residual assumptions about human sexuality and intimacy continue to lace "alternative" sexualities. For example, while based on critiques of heteronormativity, the construction of separated spheres of romantic and platonic love, the various borders erected around the "good" and "bad" queer, or the primacy given to coupledom and the longevity/permanence/linearity of sexual relationships, these critiques often tend to reinforce and extend heteronormativity rather than moving beyond it. On the other hand, it has also been demonstrated that some communities and scholars have assumed and argued for an inherent "radical" potential embedded in alternative relationship formations such as non-monogamy or polyamory (Klesse 2006; Barker and Langdridge 2010). Both of these tendencies tend to re-center monogamy as the dominant sexual relationship formation.

Influenced by Adrienne Rich's (1980) work on compulsory heterosexuality, scholars have theorized and studied monogamy as a distinctively *compulsory* relationship formation (Heckert 2010), as well as a central component of heteronormativity. To understand the compulsory aspect of monogamy, scholars have looked at the ways feminists have theorized and studied how gender is reproduced in daily life (Chodorow 1978, 1979; West and Zimmerman 1987), forming the basis for critical replies and debates within feminist scholarship (Benson 1980; Rich 1980; Lorber 1981; Smith 2009). Feminist theories and analyses of the reproduction of gender in regards to mothering (Chodorow 1978, 1979), institutions (Lorber 1981), and other areas of investigation have also provided lenses through which to explore the reproduction of heterosexuality (Rich 1980). In response to feminists writing on the reproduction of gender, Rich (1980, 637) made a call to encourage heterosexual feminists to examine "heterosexuality … as a political institution" which disempowers women. Rich suggests that this missing analysis is a result of compulsory heterosexuality. Lesbian existence, according to Rich, is not just routinely erased from literature and left ignored and un-analyzed. Rather, heterosexuality "needs to be recognized and studied as a political institution" (Rich 1980, 637). Rich demonstrates that theories of social reproduction and gender are missing analyses of sexuality and compulsory heterosexuality, as integral parts of the reproduction of gender difference and inequality. Yet, more recent scholars (Heckert 2010) have pointed out that Rich's arguments are also based on assumptions of monogamy and monogamous pairings.

Like most enforced behaviors, compulsory monogamy is so effectively naturalized that it is difficult to detect. Rather, compulsory monogamy is an underlying social expectation that is produced through media, language, culture, laws, regulations, and in some cases, particularly in regards to openly non-monogamous women, violence (Heckert 2010). Understanding the institutionalized and *compulsory* aspects of monogamy allow for new questions to be asked about all forms of sexuality, including questions about identity, sexual orientation, and how we understand ourselves as *sexual* selves. This also allows scholars the opportunity to ask questions about the political and economic forces that make loving relationships outside of exclusive, dyadic coupledom difficult or impossible, and how these forces influence the cultures around monogamy and non-monogamy. More generally, a sociological perspective will often tend to ask what the status quo is and whose interests it serves – in this case, monogamy is the status quo and sociologists are left with myriad questions and potential research as to how monogamy upholds the status quo, which groups this status quo privileges, and how and by whom it is being challenged.

SEE ALSO: Compulsory Heterosexuality; Families of Choice; Heteronormativity and Homonormativity; Monogamy, Biological Perspectives on; Polyamory; Polygamy, Polygyny, and Polyandry; Queer Theory; Sexual Identity and Orientation; Sexualities

REFERENCES

Barker, Meg, and Darren Langdridge. 2010. *Understanding Non-Monogamies*. New York: Routledge.

Benson, Leonard. 1980. "Chodorow, the Reproduction of Mothering: Psychoanalysis and the Sociology of Gender (Book Review)." *Social Science Quarterly*, 61(2): 364.

Chodorow, Nancy. 1978. *The Reproduction of Mothering: Psychoanalysis and the Sociology of Gender*. Los Angeles: University of California Press.

Chodorow, Nancy. 1979. "Feminism and Difference: Gender, Relation, and Difference in Psychoanalytic Perspective." *Socialist Review*, 9(46): 51–69.

Ellsworth, Ryan M. 2012. "The Myth of Promiscuity: A Review of Lynn Saxon, Sex at Dusk: Lifting the Shiny Wrapping from Sex at Dawn." *Evolutionary Psychology*, 10(3): 611–616.

Frank, Katherine, and John DeLamater. 2010. "Deconstructing Monogamy: Boundaries, Identities, and Fluidities across Relationships." In *Understanding Non-Monogamies*, edited by Meg Barker and Darren Langdridge. New York: Routledge.

Heckert, Jamie. 2010. "Love Without Borders? Intimacy, Identity and the State of Compulsory Monogamy." In *Understanding Non-Monogamies*, edited by M. Barker and D. Langdridge, 255–266. New York: Routledge.

Klesse, Christian. 2006. "Polyamory and Its 'Others': Contesting the Terms of Non-Monogamy." *Sexualities*, 9(5): 565–583.

Lorber, Judith, Rose L. Coser, Alice S. Rossi, and Nancy Chodorow. 1981. "On 'The Reproduction of Mothering': A Methodological Debate." *Signs: Journal of Women in Culture and Society*, 6(3): 482.

Pieper, Marianne, and Robin Bauer. 2006. "*Polyamory and Mononormativity: Results of an Empirical Study of Non-Monogamous Patterns of Intimacy*." Unpublished paper.

Rich, Adrienne. 1980. "Compulsory Heterosexuality and Lesbian Existence." *Signs*, 5(4): 631–660.

Smith, Dorothy. 2009. "Categories are Not Enough." *Gender & Society*, 23(1): 76–80.

West, Candace, and Don Zimmerman. 1987. "Doing Gender." *Gender & Society*, 1(2): 125–151.

FURTHER READING

Barker, Meg. 2005. "This is My Partner, and This is My … Partner's Partner: Constructing a Polyamorous Identity in a Monogamous World." *Journal of Constructivist Psychology*, 18(1): 75–88.

Barker, Meg, and Darren Langdridge. 2010b. "Whatever Happened to Non-Monogamies? Critical Reflections on Recent Research and Theory." *Sexualities*, 13(6): 748–772.

Emens, Elizabeth F. 2004. "Monogamy's Law: Compulsory Monogamy and Polyamorous Existence." *Review of Law and Social Change*, 29(2): 277–376.

Klesse, Christian. 2007. "'How to be a Happy Homosexual?!' Non-Monogamy and Governmentality in Relationship Manuals for Gay Men in the 1980s and 1990s." *The Sociological Review*, 55(3): 571–591.

Klesse, Christian. 2008. *The Spectre of Promiscuity: Gay Male and Bisexual Non-Monogamies and Polyamories*. Farnham: Ashgate.

Overall, Christine. 1998. "Monogamy, Non-monogamy, and Identity." *Hypatia*, 13(4): 1–17.

Otto, Katy. 2001. "Multiple Partners, Multiple Choices: A Feminist Exploration of Monogamy vs. Non-Monogamy." *Off Our Backs*, 31(7): 10–16.

Monstrous-Feminine

BARBARA CREED
University of Melbourne, Australia

The idea of the monstrous-feminine focuses attention on the significance of gender in the construction of female monstrosity. The concept of the "monstrous-feminine" holds that all human societies have patriarchal representations of female monsters, which are ultimately related to women's sexual desires and reproductive functions. In other words, patriarchal discourses have represented woman as monstrous through the abjection of her sexuality and reproductive bodily functions. Rather than accept these abject stereotypes, women artists, filmmakers, writers, and theorists have celebrated woman's potential to disrupt the patriarchal symbolic order through a positive focus on woman's terrifying and abject powers. This approach has taken two forms. Practicing writers and artists have created works that revel in the abject female body, transforming the monstrous-feminine into a deliberately provocative figure. Theorists and critics have drawn on the concept of the monstrous-feminine to retheorize abject representations of woman, emphasizing her traditional status as a figure designed to fulfill patriarchal fantasies and fears about female sexuality.

The term was first proposed by Barbara Creed in her 1986 article, "The Monstrous-Feminine: An Imaginary Abjection," which analyzed the patriarchal depiction of female monstrosity. Her later monograph (Creed 1993) drew on psychoanalytic theory to analyze six "faces" of the monstrous-feminine in cultural discourse and popular cinema. These were the monstrous-feminine as archaic mother (*Alien*), possessed monster (*The Exorcist*), monstrous womb (*The Brood*), vampire (*The Hunger*), witch (*Carrie*), and castrating monster (*I Spit On Your Grave* and *Psycho*). Two psychoanalytic approaches that offered key insights into the cultural production of the monstrous-feminine were drawn from the writings of Julia Kristeva and Sigmund Freud.

Freud's writings produced a passive image of female monstrosity. He related female monstrosity to male castration anxiety and woman's so-called castrated genital. According to Freud, "no human male being is spared the fright of castration at the sight of the female genital" (Freud 1953–1966, 154). Woman terrifies because of her appearance – not because she is an actively terrifying monster. The prevalence of images of the castrating mother in myth, legend, and popular culture, however, reveals a different picture. Creed argues that Freud repressed evidence that the mother, not just the father, also posed a threat of castration. Evidence that man fears woman's powers of castration is found in widespread myths of the vagina dentata and taboos placed on menstruating women. The monstrous-feminine as castrator is present in the vampire film as an oral sadistic figure, in the rape-revenge film as a castrating avenger, and in gothic horror as the castrating mother.

Kristeva's theory of abjection is of particular relevance to an understanding of the monstrous-feminine. In *Powers of Horror* Kristeva (1982) explores the role played by abjection in the formation of human society and the constitution of the subject. She focuses on woman's mothering and reproductive functions as offering a powerful threat of abjection central to these processes. The abject offers a means by which an imaginary line can be drawn between civilized society and those things that threaten its identity. The abject does not "respect borders, positions, rules"; it "disturbs identity, system order" (Kristeva 1982, 4). Those things that threaten the integrity of the subject, such as bodily wastes, must be ejected from the body. The ultimate in abjection is the corpse, which is "the most sickening of wastes … a border that has encroached upon everything" (Kristeva 1982, 3–4). The abject must be located on the other side of an imaginary border, and separated from the subject. The subject, however, can never feel free of the abject because the former remains drawn to what the abject represents – that which is forbidden, marginal, taboo.

The maternal figure is particularly abject insofar as she threatens the formation of the properly constituted subject. She has the power to overwhelm the infant as it attempts to assert its independence. "Rituals of defilement" are instituted to "ward off the subject's fear of his very own identity sinking irretrievably into the mother" (Kristeva 1982, 64). A particularly powerful image of abjection is of woman as a suffocating, smothering figure. The maternal figure is also more aligned than the paternal figure to a range of abject bodily fluids and wastes. Her body is less stable; its boundaries are more porous. Woman menstruates and lactates. During pregnancy her body changes shape, during birth she sheds the bloody placenta. Furthermore, during toilet-training, the mother is again closely aligned with bodily waste – urine, feces, mucus. The monstrous-feminine as an abject figure in terms of woman's reproductive functions is present in horror films about woman as menstrual monster, and woman as monstrous-womb capable of giving birth to alien creatures. As the concept of the monstrous-feminine has entered public discourse, both popular and academic, artists and filmmakers have made the monstrous-feminine central to their artistic production. The teen film *Ginger Snaps* knowingly has the young girl transform into a female werewolf when she first menstruates. The black comedy *Teeth* focuses on a sexually innocent heroine, who wears a purity ring, but unknowingly possesses a vagina dentata. Cindy Sherman's grotesque but darkly humorous mannequins in *Untitled #250* and *Untitled #263* celebrate the monstrous-feminine.

Although originally theorized in relation to film and popular culture, the monstrous-feminine has exerted strong interdisciplinary appeal. Discussions of the monstrous-feminine have been taken up in art history, literature, cultural studies, and women's health. International scholars have drawn on the concept to explore representations of female monstrosity in their own cultures. There has been particular interest in Korea and Singapore, which has its own tradition of female ghosts and vampires. The monstrous-feminine also lends itself to posthuman studies in relation to issues of science, cloning, and the creation of female/animal forms of life, as in the film *Splice* and the practice of the Australian artist Patricia Piccinini. More recently the concept has been employed in women's health with the appearance of Jane M. Ussher's 2006 book, *Managing the Monstrous-Feminine: Regulating the Reproductive Body*. Ussher examines the different ways in which medicine, the law, science, and popular culture have constructed fictions about woman's reproductive body. In its power to speak across a range of disciplines, the concept of the monstrous-feminine continues to inform both artistic practice and scholarly debate – particularly in a postfeminist era where the opportunity for parody and black humor have informed new approaches to the monstrous-feminine.

SEE ALSO: Feminist Film Theory; Feminism and Psychoanalysis; Postfeminism; Taboo

REFERENCES

Creed, Barbara. 1986. "The Monstrous-Feminine: An Imaginary Abjection." *Screen*, 27(1): 44–71.
Creed, Barbara. 1993. *The Monstrous-Feminine: Film, Feminism, Psychoanalysis*. New York: Routledge.
Freud, Sigmund. 1953–1966. "Fetishism." In *The Standard Edition of the Complete Psychological Works of Sigmund Freud*, trans. James Strachey, vol. 21, 147–158. London: Hogarth.
Kristeva, Julia. 1982. *Powers of Horror: An Essay on Abjection*, trans. Leon S. Roudiez. New York: Columbia University Press.

FURTHER READING

Gear, Rachel. 2001. "All Those Nasty Womanly Things: Women Artists, Technology and the Monstrous-Feminine." *Women's Studies International Forum*, 24(3): 321–333.

Mormonism

CLAUDIA L. BUSHMAN
Claremont Graduate University, USA

Mormons believe earth life is a testing period between a long premortal and postmortal existence. A major purpose of life on earth is to receive bodies and to form marital relationships prior to higher stages of being. Mormons believe that they will find their greatest happiness and satisfaction in family life on earth and in heaven. The family, not the individual, is the essential unit. Eternal marriage, enacted through ordinances performed in temples, allows the perpetuation of the marital unit, including procreation, into eternity. The eternal family will continue gender-related earth activities, the male providing and presiding and the female nurturing the young. The plan was the same during the 50 years after polygyny was publicly announced in 1852, and in 1890 when it was discontinued. In the 1995 Proclamation on the Family, issued but not canonized by church leaders, these roles are laid out for earth life and for the future. This document asserts that gender is eternal, a claim not made previously, though widely assumed.

The church teaches a traditional, conservative, family life, including premarital chastity, and complete marital fidelity. Mormons believe that marriage is blessed by children and in the past have preached early and large families. They now take no official stand on birth control, bedroom behavior, or family size, but counsel that these decisions should be made prayerfully between husband and wife and that husbands should be considerate of their wives. Abortion is discouraged with exceptions for incest, rape, and the mother's health. Adoption is encouraged, and adopted children take full eternal membership in adoptive families.

Traditional Mormon teaching that homosexuality and other non-normative sexual behaviors were chosen rather than innate has recently been modified. Therapy to change orientation is no longer widely practiced, and the church teaches that those attracted to the same sex should be treated with warmth and understanding, but they are discouraged from same-sex marriage and should be celibate to be in good standing. Mormons favor civil benefits for same-sex couples. The church has been active in political movements to reserve the title "marriage" for the union of a man and a woman. Mormon contributions of organization and funds against Proposition 8 in California in 2008 led to public backlash.

The organization of the church is patriarchal; males ascend to higher priesthood levels at regular intervals beginning at age 12. The high leadership of congregations, groups of congregations, and the church itself is entirely male. Women do not hold the priesthood and are not ordained. They are, nevertheless, very active in congregational life, preaching, praying, and performing in church meetings, running organizations that teach children, girls, and women, caring for the poor, and providing activities and social life. Husbands are designated to "preside" in the family, but while roles are marked out, family life is notably egalitarian with wives active in decision-making and husbands often engaged in childcare and housekeeping tasks. Theologically, men and women have equal access to God through prayer. Women have equal agency to make decisions. Mormons believe in a heavenly Mother to whom they have prayerful access.

Mormon couples marry earlier and have larger families than other Americans; they have fewer divorces and less intermarriage. But differences are not large and the fluctuations reflect national trends. Education is encouraged for both sexes, but Mormon mothers are encouraged to stay at home to raise their families rather than work outside for pay. Despite this stereotype, Mormon women are remarkably able. Experience in public speaking and performing in classes and organizations makes them competent leaders. They were the first women in the United States to vote in 1869, although Wyoming first approved woman suffrage. In early Utah they served as legislators, doctors, telegraphers, and shopkeepers. Polygamous wives often ran family farms.

Despite emphasis on marriage, many Mormons do not fit the happy family stereotype. A significant percentage of Mormons never marry. Others are divorced, widowed, or abandoned. The church provides special programs for its singles, but the aim of this activity – to marry – frequently eludes singles who often report feeling deficient by church standards.

Members and leaders of the church are sometimes threatened by the word feminism, even though they support feminist educational and career ambitions. Some feel that such achievements are hollow without marriage. Many women insist that they have all the rights and privileges they want. A minority group of Mormon feminists is vocal in calling for reforms: the extension of the priesthood to women and the rewriting of patriarchal temple ceremonies. The church, despite Utah's early suffrage history, opposed the Equal Rights Amendment and punished some women for their public vocal support. Such political punishment, much less frequent in recent years, consists of loss of church membership or privileges.

The church is remarkable for the many faithful and dedicated men who serve in leadership positions, many filling nearly full-time church jobs without pay in addition to their regular work. Women also devote time and effort to the church, but are not to do so at the expense of their homemaking duties. A recent expansion of missionary opportunities has had wide repercussions. Previously, 19-year-old men and 21-year-old women were called to serve 2-year or 18-month missions. Since 2012, men may serve at 18 and women at 19. The announcement brought hope and cheer to young women who want to serve missions before they are limited by career plans and family responsibilities. The tremendous surge of girls who wish to be missionaries has made this Mormon rite of passage a more egalitarian effort.

SEE ALSO: Polygamy, Polygyny, and Polyandry; Religion and Homophobia; Suffrage

FURTHER READING

Bushman, Claudia L. 2006. "Gender and Sexual Orientation." In *Contemporary Mormonism: Latter-Day Saints in Modern America*, 111–129. Westport: Praeger.

The First Presidency and Council of the Twelve Apostles of the Church of Jesus Christ of Latter-Day Saints. 1995. "The Family: A Proclamation to the World." Accessed June 15, 2015, at https://www.lds.org/topics/family-proclamation?lang=eng.

Ludlow, Daniel H., ed. 1992. *Encyclopedia of Mormonism: The History, Scripture, Doctrine, and Procedure of the Church of Jesus Christ of Latter-Day Saints*, 5 vols. New York: Macmillan.

Mother Nature

STEVEN DOUGLAS
Monash University, Australia

"Mother Nature" is a concept common to many cultures, races, languages, and times, and is generally synonymous with "Mother Earth" and "Earth as our Mother."

"Nature" in the sense of Earth, or more specifically, the biosphere, is most often seen as feminine. The basis for this is believed to be that the feminine is associated with birthing the material world and its boons. This view may have deepened in agrarian cultures where much attention and devotion was directed to maintaining or increasing the fecundity of the land and water. Such an association is evident in ancient Greek (*Gaia* or *Ge Mater*), Roman (*Terra Mater* or *Tellus*), Inca (*Pachamama*), and Vedic (*Bhumi Devi, Bhu Devi, Bhuvaneswari, Prithvi Mata, Narayani Devi*) belief in which the Earth goddess is often depicted holding crops, flowers, healing herbs, and sometimes in the company of lesser deities of fecundity such as *Ceres* (Roman) and *Demeter* (Greek) – both of whom relate to agricultural productivity.

"Mother Nature" is primarily used with reference to Earth or its biosphere, but at its broadest, the term is cosmological and synonymous with "the Universe" or the universal feminine creative principle associated with materiality. In contrast, the sky is often separated from the earlier notions of Mother Nature or Earth, and is generally associated with the masculine principle, for example, Father Sky or *Uranus* (ancient Greek); *Caelus* or *Jupiter* (ancient Roman); *Inti* (Inca); *Dyaus Pita* (Vedic). In its most cosmological form, this masculine counterpart to Mother Nature extends to a universal scale and is equated with space, the void, ether, light, the sun, and consciousness. The differences in scale of the Mother Earth or Father Sky dichotomy are determined by the cosmology of the culture in which the belief is founded. Generally, earlier cultures based this dichotomy of Earth or Nature on the physical realm that yields food, water, fiber, tools, shelter, etc.; with Sky or Heaven seen as the etheric realm of spirit, the home of the highest gods, the Otherworld (see, for example, Campbell and Moyers 1988). Cultures with an understanding closer to that of modern science tend to take a larger view by extending the feminine principle to that of the cosmic creative force or Creation itself, and extending the nominally masculine sky or air to equate to space, ether, the sun, or the stars.

Christianity, Judaism, and Islam differ from the earlier polytheistic traditions in that their overall model is of a Divine patriarchy. In normative versions of these faiths, a paternalistic God is the Creator of all, including the Earth. Earth is not assigned gender or necessarily divinity, but is recognized as being "good" because the Creator approved of His work. Within these traditions, there are polar views in which Earth or components of it are praised and mandated for protection or at least stewardship; or dismissed as existing only to serve and be modified by "Man," and where veneration of Earth is seen as sinful. Some variants of these traditions, particularly Christianity, also dismiss Earth and Nature as delusory or at best very temporary and not of any ultimate divine merit. In the Orthodox and Roman Catholic variants of Christianity, there can be a notion of the Divine feminine, which is generally understood through the figure of Mother Mary. Campbell and Moyers (1988) believe that Mother Mary is a derivative concept of the ancient Egyptian goddess Isis and her son Horus. The patriarchal nature of Abrahamic faiths and their often profound inconsistency in prescribing how to relate to Nature has been widely argued to be a key factor in driving what has become the global ecological crisis (see, for example, White 1967).

Older, agrarian notions of Mother Nature or Earth fell away to some degree in the West through the paradigm shift of the so-called Enlightenment and the later Industrial Revolution. Early scientists in the Natural Science tradition believed that scientific understanding of Nature is a spiritual process that could bring the practitioner closer to knowing God. However, a wider trend is evident in which science was seen as antithetical to religion, and where Nature was seen as having to be separated from God in order to be studied so as to not cross into the realm of religion (see, for example, Keller 2001). Combined with industrialization, these processes promoted the desacralization of Nature, and an increasingly exploitative perspective. Merchant (1980) termed this "the death of Nature."

Feminists, and ecofeminists in particular, sometimes argue that the desacralization of Nature is linked to the concept of Nature as female. In that period, women were viewed as being owned by men. Feminization is seen as serving the interests of predominantly male scientists, industrialists, and political elites who viewed the natural world as a chattel – a mere possession of Man and Science, to be dissected, understood, controlled and used for economic gain (see Merchant 1980, 2001, and Keller 2001). Such a case may be valid but gives insufficient weight to much earlier influences including those of normative Christianity, which itself was influenced by earlier patriarchal interests (see, for example, White 1967).

Ecofeminism is a diverse field of thought, and extends to ecotheology that criticizes the influence of patriarchy and sexism, whether religious or secular, as key factors in the societal and institutionalized abuse of Earth. Ecofeminism holds that patriarchy is responsible for the rape and pillage of Mother Nature. A core tenet of ecofeminism is that the Earth or Mother Nature will not be protected and healed until patriarchy and the forces that support it are replaced with a paradigm that places more moral and spiritual weight on care for Nature rather than on its exploitation for material gain. Patriarchy is problematic but arguably, matriarchy could be equally so were it to dismiss Nature as a mere commodity.

Whether or not Nature is perceived as feminine, as a gift from the Divine, or as being inherently divine, ultimately seems of secondary importance to how humans choose to interact with it. Gender is at least in part a cultural lens through which we seek greater understanding or connectivity. The more substantial issue is whether Nature is perceived as warranting care.

SEE ALSO: Climate Change and Gender; Deep Ecology; Ecofeminism; Environment and Gender; Environmental Justice; Ethic of Care; Gyn/Ecology; Hinduism; Mysticism

REFERENCES

Campbell, Joseph, and Bill D. Moyers. 1988. *The Power of Myth*. New York: Doubleday.
Keller, Evelyn Fox. 2001. "Secrets of God, Nature and Life." In *The Gender and Science Reader*, edited by Muriel Lederman and Ingrid Bartsch, 98–110. New York: Routledge.
Merchant, Carolyn. 1980. *The Death of Nature: Women, Ecology and the Scientific Revolution*. San Francisco: Harper & Row.
Merchant, Carolyn. 2001. "Dominion over Nature." In *The Gender and Science Reader*, edited by Muriel Lederman and Ingrid Bartsch, 68–81. New York: Routledge.
White Jr., Lynn. 1967. "The Historical Roots of our Ecologic Crisis." *Science*, New Series, 155(3767): 1205.

FURTHER READING

Arnold, Philip P., and Ann G. Gold, eds. 2001. *Sacred Landscapes and Cultural Politics*. Aldershot: Ashgate.
Badiner, Alan H., ed. 1990. *Dharma Gaia: A Harvest of Essays in Buddhism and Ecology*. Berkeley: Paralax Press.
Barnhill, David L., and Roger S. Gottlieb. 2001. *Deep Ecology and World Religions: New Essays On Sacred Grounds*. Albany: SUNY Press.
Gottlieb, Roger S., ed. 2010. *Religion and the Environment*. New York: Routledge. [esp. Volume IV: Connections: Science, Ethics, Eco-Feminism, Consumerism, Sustainability, Spirituality]
Lovelock, James E. 2000. *Gaia: A New Look at Life on Earth*, 3rd ed. Oxford: Oxford University Press. First edition 1979.
McFague, Sally. 1993. *The Body of God: An Ecological Theology*. Minneapolis: Fortress.
Merchant, Carolyn. 1980. *The Death of Nature: Women, Ecology and the Scientific Revolution*. San Francisco: Harper & Row.
Ruether, Rosemary R. 1993. *Gaia & God: An Ecofeminist Theology of Earth Healing*. London: SCM Press.

Mysticism

CALVIN MERCER
East Carolina University, USA

The topic of mysticism can be approached historically and via social scientific study. Mysticism is here understood generally as a religious experience that entails a sense of oneness with God or the divine. This understanding of mysticism is distinct from paranormal or psychic experiences, e.g., extrasensory perception, clairvoyance.

HISTORY

Female mystics are found in various religious traditions, although they have not always received the same scholarly attention as devoted to male mystics. In Christianity, the thirteenth and fourteenth centuries saw a significant increase in mystical writings with feminine themes. Female mystics of this period challenged authority with their experience-based writings, expressed themselves in visions, and utilized erotic imagery (McGinn 1998).

Feminist analysis has suggested new ways of thinking about Christian medieval female mystics and about erotic imagery found in both female and male mystics of the Christian Middle Ages. Caroline Walker Bynum's reframing of Christian medieval women's mysticism has been generally accepted. She emphasized the bodily nature of their spirituality, contending that female mystics moved more fluidly between the spiritual and physical, unlike male mystics who generally separated physical and spiritual love (Bynum 1991). In effect, embodied mysticism allowed women to find a path to the divine in a patriarchal society and religion.

English mystic Julian of Norwich (1342–1416), in her *Revelations of Divine Love*, speaks of God as both father and mother and of the "Wisdom of the Motherhood." She says Jesus is our mother in nature and grace (Book LIX). St Theresa of Avila (1515–1582) was a Spanish mystic in the Roman Catholic tradition. Associated with St John of the Cross (1542–1591), one of the most renown mystics in the Christian religion, St Theresa articulated the mystic journey as the ascent of the soul to God in four stages. Her well-known *Interior Castle* pictures seven mansions, each bringing one a step closer to God. Other prominent female Christian mystics include St Hildegard of Bingen (1098–1179), Mechtild of Magdeburg (1210–1282), Angela of Foligno (1248–1309), Hadewijch of Antwerp (thirteenth century), and Margery Kempe (1373–1439).

Erotic mystical imagery, by both female and male mystics, can be quite explicit, e.g., lie in your bed with you (Kempe), breastfeeding the Christ-child, and vulvic imagery of the side-wounds at the crucifixion (Waller 2012, 52–53).

Sufism, the mystical branch of Islam, and other mystical traditions from the Indian subcontinent have attracted many Westerners. Sufism venerates Rabia Basri (c.717–801), who, according to tradition, from humble beginnings ended up as a desert ascetic, spending long hours in prayer and meditation to her "Beloved." She spontaneously achieved self-realization and articulated in mystical poetry the Divine Love, which became an important Sufi concept. She attracted many followers and is one of the earliest of a long line of Sufi mystics.

Sarada Devi (1853–1920) was the wife and spiritual companion of the great Bengali Hindu mystic Ramakrishna (1836–1886), who saw his wife as a manifestation of Shakti, the dynamic, creative, and potent Divine Mother feminine energy. Following the guru's death, "Holy Mother" provided advice and direction to the growing Ramakrishna monastic order.

Buddhist mystic Yeshe Tsogyal (757–817) was the consort of Padmasambhava, a great eighth century tantric teacher and founder of the Nyingma tradition of Tibetan Buddhism. She is venerated as a female Buddha by the Nyingma and Karma Kagyu Tibetan Buddhist schools. Legend has it that miracles surrounded her birth and life and that she came in the form of an ordinary woman in order to be accessible to lay people.

SOCIAL SCIENCES

An important social scientific study of mysticism and gender orientation is a 1999 study (Mercer and Durham, 1999) that utilized the Bem Sex Role Inventory (BSRI) and a modified version of the Hood Mysticism Scale, developed by psychologist Ralph Hood and the most widely used instrument to study mysticism. The Hood Mysticism Scale is based on the criteria for mysticism of philosopher W. T. Stace. These criteria include an experience that is noetic, ineffable, holy, characterized by a positive affect, perceived as timeless and spaceless, and characterized by a perception of unity in all things. The BSRI categorizes people as high on both masculine and feminine scales (androgynous), low on both (undifferentiated) or high on one and low on the other (masculine or feminine).

The study showed a clear correlation between mysticism and gender orientation. Those categorized as high femininity scored higher on mysticism than those with low femininity scores. Although the direction of causality cannot be shown from the study, the authors speculate that femininity is primary and situates one to be receptive to mystical experience. The sense of unity is usually seen as fundamental to the mystical experience. A sense of unity can involve loss of self and is compatible with important aspects of femininity, such as a communal nature. Sensitivity to others and the importance of interpersonal relationships can be viewed as akin to an experience of oneness.

SEE ALSO: Buddhism; Christianity, Gender and Sexuality; Hinduism

REFERENCES

Bynum, Caroline Walker. 1991. *Fragmentation and Redemption: Essays on General and the Human Body in Medieval Religion*. New York: Zone Books.

McGinn, Bernard. 1998. *The Presence of God: A History of Western Christian Mysticism*. Volume 3: *The Flowering of Mysticism: Men and Women in the New Mysticism, 1200–1350*. New York: Crossroad.

Mercer, Calvin, and Thomas Durham. 1999. "Religious Mysticism and Gender Orientation." *Journal for the Scientific Study of Religion*, 38(1): 175–182.

Waller, Gary. 2012. *The Virgin Mary in Late Medieval and Early Modern English Literature and Popular Culture*. New York: Cambridge University Press.

FURTHER READING

Changchub, Gyalwa, and Namkhai Nyingpo. 1999. *Lady of the Lotus-Born: The Life and Enlightenment of Yeshe Tsogyal*, transl. Padmakara Translation Group. Boston: Shambhala Publications.

Harish, Ranjana, and V. Bharathi Harishankar, eds. 2003. *Shakti: Multidisciplinary Perspectives on Women's Empowerment in India*. New Delhi: Rawat.

Theresa of Avila. 2007. *Interior Castle: The Classic Text with a Spiritual Commentary by Dennis J. Billy C.Ss.R*. Notre Dame, IN: Ave Maria Press.

N

Nationalism and Gender

JOANE NAGEL

University of Kansas, USA

Gender and sexuality have important places in the nation, but all genders and sexualities are not socially approved, legal, or equal within a nation or a state. A "state" generally is considered synonymous with a "country" – an area of land controlled by its own government. A "nation" refers to the people considered to be members or "citizens" of a state or country. Nationalism is the ideology that defines a particular nation. There are sometimes quarrels within nations about the exact content of the national ideology. Are we a Christian or a Muslim or a Hindu nation? Are we a monarchy or a democracy or some combination? What does it mean to be an American or a Russian or a Pakistani?

The idea of the nation and the history of nationalism are intertwined with particular ideas of manhood, womanhood, and approved sexualities. Heterosexual males hold an honored place in most nations. This is not to say that women or homosexuals do not have roles to play in the making and unmaking of nations: as citizens, as activists, as leaders. But women and homosexuals often are the foils against which national manhood is defined: they are what real men of the nation are NOT. Most nationalist scripts are written primarily by men, for men, and about men. In these national dramas women are relegated to mainly supporting roles – as mothers of the nation, vessels for reproducing the nation, agents for inculcating national culture into new members, and national housekeepers responsible for maintaining home and hearth for the nation's men who are out and about on important official business – fighting wars, defending homelands, representing the nation abroad, *manning* the apparatus of the state. Homosexuals typically do not occupy even these supporting roles in national sagas. They often are relegated to places on the margins of national cultural or legal systems or even cast as outsiders or traitors. The starring actors in nationalist productions are men defending their freedom, their honor, their homeland, and their women.

The culture and ideology of heterosexual masculinity go hand in hand with the culture and ideology of nationalism. The modern form of Western masculinity emerged at about the same time and place as modern nationalism in the nineteenth century. George Mosse (1996, 7) describes modern masculinity as a centerpiece of all varieties of nationalist movements:

> The masculine stereotype was not bound to any one of the powerful political ideologies

The Wiley Blackwell Encyclopedia of Gender and Sexuality Studies, First Edition. Edited by Nancy A. Naples.
© 2016 John Wiley & Sons, Ltd. Published 2016 by John Wiley & Sons, Ltd.

of the previous century. It supported not only conservative movements ... but the workers' movement as well; even Bolshevik man was said to be "firm as an oak." Modern masculinity from the very first was co-opted by the new nationalist movements of the nineteenth century.

Nationalist politics are a major venue for "accomplishing" masculinity for at least two reasons. First, as noted above, the national state is essentially a masculine institution. Feminist scholars point out the typical state's hierarchical authority structure, emphasis on competition and domination, male monopoly over decision-making positions, the male superordinate/female subordinate internal division of labor, and the male legal regulation of female rights, labor, and sexuality. A second reason that nationalist politics provide men a means of enacting their manhood is that the culture of nationalism is constructed to emphasize and resonate with masculine cultural themes. Terms like *honor*, *patriotism*, *cowardice*, *bravery*, and *duty* are hard to distinguish as either nationalistic or masculinist since they seem so thoroughly tied both to the nation and to manhood. The "microculture" of masculinity in everyday life articulates very well with the demands of nationalism, particularly its militaristic side. Local masculine cultures can differ from one another around the world in terms of the class, race, ethnicity, or nation of the men involved. In all societies, however, there are distinct gender cultures shaping the lives of boys and girls and of men and women, and it is male gender culture that tends to dominate nationalism everywhere. As Cynthia Enloe (1990, 45) observes, "nationalism has typically sprung from masculinized memory, masculinized humiliation and masculinized hope."

Nationalism, coupled with masculinist heterosexuality, tends to embrace patriarchal forms of social organization that create different and unequal places for men and women in the nation and that often exclude homosexuals completely except as "examples" to remind citizens of proper gender and sexuality. Traditional patriarchal systems generally are unsympathetic to feminist efforts to eliminate gender inequality, and see women's rights as secondary and subversive to nationalist goals and struggles. Standards for national conduct that reflect masculinized heteronormativity tend also to be homophobic, and are intolerant of sexual diversity, particularly homosexuality.

The sexist nature of much nationalism has led some scholars to argue that "woman nationalist" is an oxymoron, a self-contradictory status that reflects the historic opposition between the goals and needs of women and those of nationalists. Feminists often find themselves attempting to negotiate the difficult, some would say impassable, terrain that separates the interests of women and the interests of nationalists. Discussing Hindu and Muslim nationalism in Indian politics, Zoya Hasan (1994, xv) notes the tension between feminist principles and communal religious solidarity: "Forging community identities does not imply or guarantee that women will always identify themselves with or adhere to prevailing religious doctrines which legitimize their subordination."

Whatever the problems facing a feminist/nationalist alliance, women often have supported men's nationalist efforts in the name of a united nation, even involving themselves in revolutionary cadres and military units. Despite their bravery, their taking on of traditional male military roles, or the centrality of their contribution to many nationalist struggles, feminist nationalists often find themselves once again under the thumb of institutionalized patriarchy when national independence is won. A nationalist movement that encourages women's participation in the name of national liberation often balks at feminist demands for gender equality in the new state. Women who press their case face challenges to their loyalty, their sexuality, or their ethnic or national authenticity. In many non-Western countries, feminists who oppose patriarchal national systems are said to be "carrying water" for colonial oppressors, or they are labeled lesbians, or they are accused of being unduly influenced by Western feminism.

Despite efforts to build feminism into nationalist movements, many feminist nationalist movements fail to overthrow the patriarchal *ancien régime*. Indeed, patriarchal, masculinist notions of men's and women's roles often become more entrenched during nationalist mobilizations; an example is the human rights violations of Afghani women by the masculinist nationalism of Afghanistan's former ruling Taliban party. The Taliban government initially was widely supported when it came to power in 1996, partly because it was reputed to provide protection for women who had become targets of sexual abuse under the previous government. After they gained national power, the Taliban's draconian measures against women, who were required to wear head-to-toe coverings and were forbidden to work outside the home or to attend school, became an international scandal (Rashid 2000).

GENDER, SEXUALITY, AND NATIONALISM

The interest of nationalists in "their" women's sexuality is not unique to Muslim nationalists. Women's sexuality turns out to be a matter of prime national interest around the world for at least two reasons. First, women as mothers are exalted icons of nationalism, and efforts in many countries to restrict contraception or abortion reflect this connection. Women's sexuality is a second concern to nationalists because, as wives, sisters, mothers, and daughters, women often are considered to be the bearers of national and masculine honor. For instance, the physical assaults and murders of women suspected of adultery by jealous husbands tend to be taken less seriously or ignored by law enforcement in many countries including the United States (Feder 1999). While there certainly are variations across history and around the world in the extent to which such "honor killings" are tolerated, Camilla Fawzi El-Solh and Judy Mabro (1994, 8) identify a common connection between men's and family honor and women's sexual respectability as a situation where honor is for men to gain and women to lose: "honour is seen more as men's responsibility, and shame as women's … honour is seen as actively achieved while shame is seen as passively defended."

Just as feminism has the capacity to challenge the stability of the masculinist heterosexual order that underlies nationalist boundaries, so too does homosexuality. Both queers and feminists are problems for nationalists. This is partly because nationalists almost always are traditionalists. Nationalism, even "revolutionary" nationalism, is inherently conservative because nationalists tend to fix their gaze backward to real or imagined pasts for their legitimation and to mark their paths to the future. Feminists and homosexuals are among the most vocal critics of these histories, and they oppose many "retraditionalizing" aspects of contemporary nationalist movements since these steps backward usually do not lead to improvements in the rights and options of women and gay men. Feminists frequently raise questions about the accuracy and justice of patriarchal "golden ages" so often celebrated by nationalist leaders, and homosexuals contradict the core nationalist project of reproducing the nation. Both feminists and homosexuals also tend to be seen by nationalists as potential sources of disloyalty, since their commitment to gender and sexual equality raises doubts in the minds of nationalists about the strength of their allegiance to the nation as their primary unit of identification.

In recent years lesbian and gay rights groups around the world, but particularly in the West, have mounted assaults on sexuality exclusionary policies and have claimed equal rights to be members of the nation. During the past few decades both straight and queer sexual rights advocates have asserted equal rights and membership in countries around the world, including recent court decisions and policy changes in favor of gay rights in the United States. The integration of Europe is playing an important role in efforts to liberalize conservative nationalism inside European states. In the Republic of Ireland, for instance, both feminist and gay rights groups have appealed *outside* Irish national boundaries, to the European Union (EU), to claim rights within the Irish state. Irish gay and lesbian rights groups have appealed to the European Convention on Human Rights to force the decriminalization of same-sex acts between consenting adults in Ireland. In Eastern Europe, there has been pressure on states seeking admission to the Council of Europe to abandon codes outlawing homosexuality; for instance, in 1993, Lithuania repealed its laws against same-sex acts. These and other advances of women's and gay rights within national systems tend to be rarer outside the West. For instance, in 2013 legislation in Russia restricted public discussion of homosexuality. Such regulation of gender, sexuality, and nationalism is testimony to their intimate interconnections.

Contemporary nationalist ideologies define proper places for men and women, and valorize the heterosexual family as the bedrock of the nation. This uniformity in sexualized nationalist discourse is a striking and surprising feature of the global system of more than 200 national states. Whether national sexual ideologies are spoken by nationalists from former ruling colonial powers or by nationalists in former ruled colonies, the similarities easily can be heard. The tendency for many national governments to exclude women and homosexuals from the most important national institutions, such as those involved in war-making and governance, illustrates the gendered, sexualized face of nationalism.

The points of convergence among gender, sexuality, and the nation can be dangerous intersections. The imposition of strict controls on the national meanings and enactments of gender or sexuality can reinforce national identities and intolerance movements. Restrictions and discrimination, however, can backfire by generating resistance movements and can become the nation's undoing. If masculinist heterosexuality is a central element of the bedrock upon which nationalist boundaries rest, movements for women's and gay rights are cracks in that foundation. Contemporary states must manage both the frontiers of international borders and their internal gender and sexual frontiers. Managing restlessness on these frontiers represents one of the most enduring challenges facing contemporary nations and states in the global system.

SEE ALSO: Gender Stereotypes; Heteronormativity and Homonormativity; Sexuality and Human Rights

REFERENCES

El-Solh, Camilla Fawzi, and Judy Mabro. 1994. "Introduction: Islam and Muslim Women." In *Muslim Women's Choices: Religious Belief and Social Reality*, edited by Camilla Fawzi El-Solh and Judy Mabro, 1–32. Providence: Berg.

Enloe, Cynthia. 1990. *Bananas, Beaches, and Bases: Making Feminist Sense of International Politics*. Berkeley: University of California Press.

Feder, Lynette. 1999. *Women and Domestic Violence: An Interdisciplinary Approach*. New York: Haworth Press.

Hasan, Zoya. 1994. "Introduction: Contextualizing Gender and Identity in Contemporary India." In *Forging Identities: Gender, Communities and State in India*, edited by Zoya Hasan, vii–xxiv. Boulder: Westview Press.

Mosse, George L. 1996. *The Image of Man: The Creation of Modern Masculinities*. New York: Oxford University Press.

Rashid, Ahmed. 2000. *Taliban: Militant Islam, Oil, and Fundamentalism in Central Asia*. New Haven: Yale University Press.

FURTHER READING

Banerjee, Sikata. 2004. *Muscular Nationalism: Gender, Violence, and Empire in India and Ireland, 1914–2004*. New York: NYU Press.

Mayer, Tamar. 1999. *Gender Ironies of Nationalism: Sexing the Nation*. New York: Routledge.

Nationalism and Sexuality

ALEXANDER MAXWELL
Victoria University of Wellington, New Zealand

Sexuality has played a central role in patriotic imaginations since the age of nationalism began in the late eighteenth century. The unstated assumption that national women are the collective property of a masculine nation, the "national brotherhood," permeates diverse nationalist practices.

Enlightenment patriots imagined a sovereign nation defined by a "social contract," an idea that featured prominently in both the American and French revolutions. Both American and French revolutionaries posited a sexual basis to the social contract, which Carol Pateman (1988) has memorably analyzed as a "sexual contract." The sexual contract allows patriot men to regulate their collective access to women. Pateman thus highlighted the masculinity of the French Revolutionary ideal of *fraternité* [fraternity]: the nation is a brotherhood of men and exists to promote their collective interests as men. The national interest thus protects explicitly masculine and implicitly heterosexual erotic desires.

Pateman's analysis applies primarily to governments, but the notion that a male brotherhood enjoyed collective ownership of national women persisted and proliferated during the nineteenth century, as national communities were increasingly imagined independently of the state. Patriots often promote national sexual endogamy by sanctioning or stigmatizing women who marry non-national men (Schaefer 1980; Maxwell 2007). Enforcing national endogamy can help an endangered or threatened community maintain its distinctiveness, but patriot men often treat control of women's sexuality as an end in itself. The widespread belief that patriot men nationalize women by establishing a sexual bond with a chosen partner partly explains why the nationalist regulation of sexual practices treats men and women differently. Hegemonic views of national sexuality typically allow men greater freedom to choose a foreign spouse or sexual partner. Male seduction of women implies national ownership: women who marry outside the nation become denationalized, but men instead bring foreign women into the national community. Patriots see female promiscuity as a national risk, particularly if the promiscuity may involve national exogamy. Male promiscuity or infidelity, by contrast, is generally treated leniently: promiscuous men may recruit additional women to the national cause. Male homosexuality, meanwhile, sometimes attracts more patriotic opprobrium than lesbianism. Homosexual men, by not seeking to seduce women, neglect their patriotic duty. Meanwhile, the sexuality of women without male partners, particularly adult women without fathers, may lie beyond the scope of the national imagination.

Patriots routinely discuss national women using imagery of protection or guardianship. Much as states have treated women as the dependants of their fathers or husbands, so too do they make national women dependent on the male brotherhood for protection. The brotherhood sometimes protects women as male possessions, not as individuals with independent interests. The masculine desire to defend the purity or virtue of national women may, for example, contribute to honor killing.

Patriots often view women's sexuality, and particularly women's fertility, as a collective national resource. When population growth is a source of concern, for example, national states may adopt policies that encourage population growth. Nationalist anxieties may inform government policy toward birth control or abortion. States may restrict women's fertility to cut the birth rate. States may also set different policies for national minorities. The Chinese government, for example, excluded national minorities from its "one-child" policy, partly to acknowledge and protect the cultural distinctiveness of minorities. Other states specify distinct policies for national minorities as a form of discrimination. Forced sterilizations of minority women have taken place in several countries, though often such policies are more racial than national. Children of mixed parentage have often faced serious discrimination, particularly when conceived in wartime and born to a local mother and a father from an occupying army.

In wartime, male patriots often feel a need to defend "their" women. Propaganda often depicts enemy men as sexual predators, rapists, or sadists. The perceived need to defend national sexual purity can inspire moral panic (Hirschfeld 1943). Patriots have not been immune to fears that youthful masturbation may cause illness or weakness. Patriotic passions also interact with the struggle against venereal disease. Prostitution policies can also acquire a national or racial aspect: in wartime, armies recruit prostitutes from foreign nationalities to protect national sexual virtue. War often leads to sexual violence. Military masculinity prizes toughness and dominance, and often contempt for and disinterest in women (Theweleit 1987). Soldiers often use rape as a means of asserting national supremacy or vengeance. Somewhat counterintuitively, wartime rape is often directed not at women but at enemy men: soldiers may humiliate enemy men by sexually possessing or defiling "their" women (Banerjee 2012). Perceived threats to national virility may also inspire violence, including sexual violence against men.

Patriots often associate national rivals or enemies with stigmatized sexual practices, typically homosexuality or promiscuity. In France, to give a less typical example, sexual masochism and particularly flagellation is often described as "the English vice" [*le vice anglais*]. Even relatively benign stereotypes, however, can reify national differences. In the multinational Habsburg Empire, for example, one patriotic author proclaimed ethnic Hungarian men more passionate, but Slavic men more dependable: "the Hungarian would therefore make the better lover, but the Slav is more desirable as a husband." The desire to associate sexual characteristics with different nationalities is apparently ubiquitous and powerful, and features prominently in popular culture.

The ideal of the national brotherhood implicitly assumes that women participate in national life as men's wives, mothers, or daughters. The marital bond generally trumps other relationships: girls are born with the nationality of their fathers, but then acquire the nationality of their husbands. During the nineteenth century, for example, several citizenship laws specified that women lose the nationality of their birth if they marry a foreign man and acquire that of their husband. Since the 1957 United National Convention on the Nationality of Married Women, national states generally grant women and men an equivalent ability to extend citizenship through marriage. Nevertheless, ideas of sexual propriety continue to inform modern citizenship laws. Most states refuse to acknowledge same-sex marriage, and thus do not allow same-sex couples to pass citizenship to their chosen partners the way opposite-sex couples can.

Women have also exploited national heterosexuality as a tool of protest. The sex strike or sex boycott, first described in ancient Greece by Aristophanes, involves women refusing to have sex with their husbands or boyfriends until political demands are met. In recent years, sex boycotts have enjoyed some success in Liberia and Colombia. In wartime, furthermore, female patriots may threaten to boycott foreign men. The gender logic of nationalism, apparently, does not give men an equivalent ability to launch a sex strike. Seen as a form of female empowerment, sex strikes emphasize the importance of sexuality to women's imagined role in national life.

In fact, women have always participated in national life in a variety of ways, but generally won recognition primarily as wives, mothers, or symbolic figures (Yuval-Davis 1997). Since chivalric self-perceptions sometimes accompany masculine hegemony over the nation, women working as political activists have long employed national rhetoric in service of feminist goals. During the nineteenth century, for example, female activists successfully influenced government policy by depicting prostitution as a national shame and appealing to male political leaders for protection. In recent times, furthermore, even male patriots have begun imagining a national community in which women participate equally in the nation in their own right, rather than through their relationship with a national man.

Nationalist authors have linked patriotism to sexuality in a variety of literary genres. Poets and novelists use sexual metaphors to depict patriotic emotions. A male hero pining for a beautiful woman may signify patriotic love for the nation, for example, or a woman's self-sacrifice or devotion to her lover may symbolize her national devotion. Ethnographers may rank racial or national beauty, providing a pseudo-scientific justification for national or racial prejudices. Self-glorification is a common theme in nationalist texts of any genre: patriots extoll the superiority of all things national. As concerns sexuality, patriots extoll the national sexual virtues of both genders. The beauty of the national woman, the virility of the national man, or the sexual purity or virtue of both genders may inspire songs, poetry, or other forms of public celebration.

Collective pride in national female beauty is widespread. Beauty pageants have even turned pride in national beauty into an arena for ritualized national competition (Banet-Weiser 1999). Patriots generally associate the national community with attractive sexual characteristics. Postcolonial national movements may extoll the beauty of national women as a political act, seeking counterbalance to racist beauty standards from the colonial era (Mayer 2012). Such phenomena suggest that national pride depends partly on sexual self-esteem. Patriots may also contest cultural values by seeking to nationalize different sexual characteristics. Conservative or religious patriots may proclaim national sexuality particularly virtuous and freethinking patriots may boast of national sexual liberty. Stereotypes of the national man may differ from those of the national women, or be contested by various social constituencies, but patriots generally encourage endogamy, and particularly want national women to partner with national men. Pride in national sexuality can reinforce distinct gender roles. Patriots may praise national women as virtuous and chaste, while simultaneously boasting of national men's sexual prowess.

However patriots may imagine national sexuality, individuals who do not conform to expectations may suffer sanction. Men who insist on sexual practices deemed nationally inappropriate may find their membership in the nation contested or restricted. Since hegemonic national sexuality usually presupposes heterosexuality and monogamy, collective nationalism generally treats alternate forms of sexuality as deviant or perverse. The systematic murder of homosexuals in Nazi Germany most spectacularly illustrates the link between nationalism and compulsory heterosexuality, but the persecution of same-sex sexuality appears in nationalist movements in many parts of the world (Mosse 1985; Peterson 2010).

While members of sexual minorities may experience hegemonic national sexuality as oppressive, progressive activists sometimes link the defense of sexual subcommunities to patriotism. In Scandinavia and the Netherlands, progressive politics features so strongly in the nationalist self-image that tolerance for sexual diversity has become not only a sign of patriotism, but the basis for anti-immigrant politics. Openly gay Dutch Politician Pim Fortuyn notably opposed multiculturalism in the Netherlands because he feared that Muslim minorities would endanger the country's liberal attitude toward homosexuality. The American activist group Queer Nation, to give another example, invoked nationalist rhetoric in the service of homosexual rights. Nationalism is a diverse phenomenon, taking different forms in different contexts. As sexual subcultures proliferate, they can be expected to adopt new connections to various expressions of nationalism.

SEE ALSO: Colonialism and Gender; Compulsory Heterosexuality; Nazi Persecution of Homosexuals; Orientalism; Patriarchy; Privilege; Scientific Sexism and Racism; Sexual Contract; Sexualizing the State

REFERENCES

Banerjee, Sikata. 2012. *Muscular Nationalism: Gender, Violence, and Empire in India and Ireland, 1914–2004*. New York: NYU Press.

Banet-Weiser, Sarah. 1999. *The Most Beautiful Girl in the World: Beauty Pageants and National Identity*. Berkeley: University of California Press.

Hirschfeld, Magnus. 1943. *The Sexual History of the World War*. New York: Panurge.

Maxwell, Alexander. 2007. "National Endogamy and Double Standards: Sexuality and Nationalism in East-Central Europe during the 19th Century." *Journal of Social History*, 41(2): 413–433. DOI: 10.1353/jsh.2008.0021.

Mayer, Tamar, ed. 2012. *Gender Ironies of Nationalism: Sexing the Nation*. London: Routledge.

Mosse, Lachman. 1985. *Nationalism and Sexuality: Respectability and Abnormal Sexuality in Modern Europe*. New York: Fertig.

Pateman, Carole. 1988. *The Sexual Contract*. Stanford: Stanford University Press.

Peterson, Spike. 2010. "Political Identities/Nationalism as Heterosexism." *International Feminist Journal of Politics*, 1(1): DOI: 10.1080/146167499360031.

Schaefer, R. T. 1980. "Racial Endogamy in Great Britain: A Cross-National Perspective." *Ethnic and Racial Studies*, 3(2): 224–235. DOI: 10.1080/01419870.1980.9993301.

Theweleit, Klaus. 1987. *Male Fantasies. Volume 1: Women, Floods, Bodies, History*. Minneapolis: University of Minnesota Press.

Yuval-Davis, Nira. 1997. *Gender and Nation*. London: Sage.

Nature–Nurture Debate

TORA HOLMBERG
Uppsala University, Sweden

INTRODUCTION

If one searches the web for "gender and genetics" the most likely articles found are on the genetic basis of gender identity, sex determination, and the genetics and gender of the brain. This flags a connection between the concepts of gender and genes that is more than etymological. But, contrary to this first impression, gender studies and biology have not, to say the least, lived in harmony. On the contrary, biologically based explanations of human behavior have been put forward in public throughout history, and have been fiercely contested by gender scholars. This entry explores the so-called nature–nurture debate and its effects on contemporary feminist theory, in particular in the area of feminist science studies and feminist epistemology.

DEBATES IN THE PLURAL

From the feminist perspective, there are several reasons for the contestations of biological accounts of sex differences. The first is because arguments for the biological and unconditional base of women's subordination have historically found legitimacy in genetics. Geneticists have, since the founding of the field in the early twentieth century, tried to find differences between humans and other animals as well as among humans, including race and sex differences. In 1975, Edward O. Wilson's controversial book on sociobiology fueled an already heated debate concerning the nature of human sexual and gendered behavior. In the late 1970s and 1980s, the debate came to involve advocates from disciplines such as psychology, anthropology, and sociology, and extended from scientific arenas to almost every tabloid magazine, newspaper, and, more recently, social media such as research blogs and chat rooms. The most active academic discussants were and still are evolutionary biologists and neuroscientists, debating with, among others, gender studies scholars from a wide range of disciplines including the biological ones mentioned. It is not surprising that media discussions concern such politically sensitive topics as gender relations, violence, and sexuality, and in the heated debate over these issues, discussants sometimes adopt polarized positions.

A second reason for the debates is that science has reproduced a male norm of the research subject: the scientist. The overrepresentation of men has become more and more embarrassing for science, and thus historical analyses can shed light over some of the dynamics at work in excluding women. It also makes visible the discriminatory structures of academia, and the networks and strategies that enable women scientists to succeed, despite the harsh conditions. Moreover, biology, including genetics, has reproduced the male norm of research objects: humans equal men. Thus the feminist claim to widen the category of "human" to include women has led feminist science studies scholars and philosophers of science to critically examine scientific facts and practice. In fact, the introduction of the concept "gender" was due to the wish to be able to hold apart the biological body ("sex") – including genes, hormones, and anatomy – from the societal power relations that produce women's subordination, thus enabling feminists to critically scrutinize the ways in which gender influences how science produces knowledge of sex (Keller and Longino 1996). For more than three decades, feminist science studies scholars from a range of disciplines have developed insights through thorough critical analyses of genetics, from Hilary Rose's groundbreaking critique of sociobiology, through Ruth Hubbard, Evelyn Fox Keller, Donna Haraway, and Sarah Franklin, to name just a few. This has been done with analytical strength and has yielded results in terms of the ways it has changed science, for example when it comes to medical and reproductive genetics (see Schiebinger 2001).

Third, science is supposed to deal with nature in objective ways, while feminist theory has a critical and normative approach. Thus, epistemological ideals such as objectivity, rationality, and detachment have been scrutinized in terms of their implicit masculinity, as well as the effect of gender-stereotypical discourse on scientific knowledge and facts. This is the context of the so-called science wars of the 1990s and early 2000s. These are often described as the reaction of American scientists to an academic trend of so-called postmodernist attacks on science. The impetus for this reaction is not entirely clear, but one formation came to *defend* science from what it described as attacks in terms of relativism, psychoanalysis, feminist epistemologies, cultural studies, sociology of science, and other "pseudoscience." Science was under attack from within academia, but the attack was said to go hand in hand with other anti-scientific trends. The advocates further opined that science, as it is among other things objective and rational, is a special kind of knowledge that no outsider can really understand. Sociologists of science and others can study controversies and the like, but they will never understand true science and the core of scientific knowledge: to talk about science as socially constructed is nothing but rubbish. The "other side," then, those who through science studies had *challenged* science, repeated their right to study science as a cultural, social, and thus gendered activity among others. Renowned advocates like Sandra Harding asserted the prevalent lack of knowledge in the philosophy and theory of science, revealed for example by the defenders' quotation techniques, which indicated that they really did not know what they were talking about. The science wars made a great impact and became widespread in the United States, and to a lesser extent in the United Kingdom and other Western countries. Conferences were organized, anthologies produced, and research grants and chair appointments became contested. Scholars on all sides of the war were affected, as well as the way science and the relation between science and society were viewed and conceptualized, both within academia and in a more public context.

SEX(UAL) DIFFERENCE

The analytical sex/gender distinction that was productive for challenging science in the 1970s and 1980s began to render some serious critiques, mainly for two reasons. The first was by widening the scope of the cultural, of "nurture" to include "nature." Judith Butler (1990) seriously questioned the distinction between biological sex and social gender, and would come to say that biological sex is also characterized by contingent, situated, and socially accepted differences and, thereby, can be seen as an additional construction. In later work, Butler deepened the analysis of the material body, saying that societal norms and discourses at once make biological bodies comprehensible and produce or *materialize* them. Second, the analytical separation of sex and gender has been criticized for contributing to the feminist "black-boxing" of the biological, gendered body (Haraway 1991, 197). This means that too little attention has been paid to analyzing the biological body through a critical gender approach, resulting in the situation that the scientific view of the body one was so critical of is still left to the natural sciences to understand. The sex/gender distinction has also been criticized on the grounds that, in practice, it pays too much attention to biological differences, meaning that the sex/gender distinction per se could fuel the very thing feminists wish to avoid, namely a biologistic view of the body. Thus, by referring sex to the biological sphere, it is constructed as unchangeable and static. This constitutes the background of a new strand of "material feminisms" (Alaimo and Hekman 2008). In addition, it is argued that most feminists have attended to reproductive genetics and technologies, but there is more to a body than X and Y chromosomes, hormonal glands, and sexual organs. What appear as more gender-neutral organs and parts of the body are in need of feminist attention, too (Birke 1999). A feminist intervention would be to challenge the reductionist idea of free-floating organs altogether, and theorize the interconnectedness of processes and organs within as well as between bodies. Further, a central argument of material feminisms is that the material part of the world – whether living or non-living, environmental or technological – needs feminist attention and can be understood in terms of material performativity and agency (Barad 2007). Thus, moving beyond traditional agendas, a material feminist approach may well include serotonin or blood sugar levels, bacteria, waste, and storms.

REPRODUCTION GENETICS

Several researchers within the field of feminist science studies have in different ways problematized how scientific knowledge production and cultural imagination become intertwined in reproduction genetics. Heteroromantic stories of the communion of the active sperm and the passive egg, or, as in plant biology, of the brave stamen and the coy pistil, have been uncritically reproduced by science since Linnaeus's botany (Schiebinger 2001). But reproduction genetics has changed profoundly with new knowledge and technologies, and so have some of the stories connected to it. One influential scholar in the feminist science studies strands is Sarah Franklin. She has devoted much of her scholarly work to reproduction genetics and in particular a specific field: the cloning of non-human animals (Franklin 2007). From this work, she has developed the concept of "transbiology." In Franklin's version, transbiology describes the contemporary reorganization of living matter, of life itself. Transbiology is more than a description of laboratory practice, it also captures the postmodern diffusion of science into all imaginable spheres of society, including popular culture, politics, and economics. Transbiological offspring – such as Dolly the cloned sheep – were at first miraculous because they seemed so normal. What made Dolly a successful clone is, paradoxical as it may seem, that she was both common and unique. The concept helps to highlight the transgressive intervention occurring in which traditional views of sexuality, genealogy, body, and reproduction become challenged.

EVOLUTIONARY GENETICS

In recent years, there has been what can be understood as a small revolution within feminist evolutionary biology. However, we should not forget that already in the early twentieth century women biologists worked consciously to change the androcentric bias of evolutionary theories. In 1981, Sarah Blaffer Hrdy published her highly influential *The Woman That Never Evolved*, claiming that females too lead interesting lives, however ignored they are by science. Hrdy also claimed that primate females compete fiercely over status and resources, a viewpoint very much in opposition to the by then fashionable idea of certain female characteristics such as care and emotion. Her standpoint could be categorized as that of a liberal feminist sociobiologist, also called Darwinian feminism. Others have followed, engaging closely with evolutionary genetics, especially in sexual selection theory. Patricia Gowaty (1997), for example, has engaged in conversations with feminism, asking how evolutionary biology and feminism can benefit from one another. Other scholars have stressed how truths about human nature seem so nicely to be extrapolated from animal research and how (other) animals are interpreted in order to fit preconceptions about the same human nature. Some of the most interesting work done in this field of biology/gender involves a problematization of other animals, who are not such simple beings as feminists outside of biology might think.

Most scholars concerned with feminism and biology have their background in biology. But there are some examples of well-established philosophers who have lately become more interested in genetics and biology. Elisabeth Grosz (2011) is one feminist scholar without a biological background, who stands out as intimately concerned with evolutionary biology. Her main argument is that Darwin's theories on natural and sexual selection are well worth a feminist inquiry, because this may prove useful. By this Grosz does not embrace the whole package, but means that Darwinian feminism is too much of a "liberal reformism" that aims at correcting male bias. But, says Grosz, what if Darwinism, instead of being in need of correction, proves to provide an explanation of the power asymmetries and structures that exist? The area of Darwinian feminism is a growing and vivid one, and it will be very interesting to see which directions it will take and the impact it will have on mainstream feminist science studies, and vice versa.

DISCUSSION

The nature–nurture debate and contemporary conversations and transgressions over the nature–culture divide, when it comes to feminist studies, are certainly diverse and fruitful. However, critics have argued that attempts to breach the nature–culture divide in science and to build alliances between biology and feminism will result in a neglect of the critical agenda and an emptying of the "culture" category. Moreover, debates are themselves essential to critical academic work, and thus are productive of knowledge. It is probably uncontroversial to say that critique is needed both from the outside and from within. Nevertheless, while the nature–nurture debate is still in many regards flourishing, unrecognized alliances and transgressive, collaborative work are also occurring in many areas, some of which are mentioned briefly below.

The field of nature and environmental studies has for long been a central one for ecofeminist concerns and interventions, and has recently been revitalized with a new generation of more interdisciplinary research, rendering gender, if not a fully integrated perspective, at least with some influence on and in environmental studies. This area will expand even more as climate and environmental concerns grow and the need for even greater interdisciplinarity becomes more pressing. Bioethics is also a related area where feminist and gender perspectives have developed and is slowly moving toward an integrated position. Ethics has also become an integrated part of mainstream feminist theory, as established scholars explicitly engage in the bioethical debate.

When it comes to gender studies and neuroscience, which is obviously a burning relationship, there is a rather long tradition of feminist critique, but not much of conversation. Scholars speak of how we are witnessing an era of cerebralization: the brain has become the true source of understanding complex issues such as gender and sexual differences, and as an object of inquiry the brain is very much understood as static, rather than as processual. However, there are some promising examples of how this could take shape. Dussauge and Kaiser (2012), for example, argue for a queer neuroscience in which the ontological understanding of the plasticity of the brain and of gender as performative is built into the methodologies used.

The paradigm of sexual selection theory, of the genetic makeup as framing environmental contributions to personality and behavioral traits, hand in hand with personification metaphors such as the "selfish gene," have become well established within socioevolutionary biology discourse. This scientific practice has been widely contested – and, of course, also widely appreciated – for almost 40 years, and its critical gender scholars are slowly moving into the mainstream. The cultural landscape that represents the gene, labeled the genetic imagery, has been analyzed within feminist cultural science studies. There are many connections made between genes and gender in this imaginary, in which taken-for-granted notions of sex, kinship, genealogy, reproduction, and sexuality become questioned. Genetics as well as other biological sciences, in this respect, certainly connect with contemporary gender theory and feminist concerns, and future conversations may well be both fiery and productive.

SEE ALSO: Biochemistry and Physiology; Biological Determinism; Cognitive Sex Differences, Debates on; Ethics, Moral Development, and Gender; Feminism, Material; Feminist Objectivity; Feminist Sex Wars; Feminist Studies of Science; Gender, Definitions of; Genetics Testing and Screening; Human–Animal Studies; Neuroscience, Brain Research, and Gender; Women in Science

REFERENCES

Alaimo, Stacy, and Susan Hekman, eds. 2008. *Material Feminisms*. Bloomington: Indiana University Press.

Barad, Karen. 2007. *Meeting the Universe Halfway*. Durham, NC: Duke University Press.

Birke, Lynda. 1999. *Feminism and the Biological Body*. Edinburgh: Edinburgh University Press.

Butler, Judith. 1990. *Gender Trouble: Feminism and the Subversion of Identity*. New York: Routledge.

Dussauge, Isabelle, and Annelis Kaiser. 2012. "Re-Queering the Brain." In *Neurofeminism*, edited by Robyn Bluhm, Anne Jacobsen, and Heidi Maibom. Basingstoke: Palgrave Macmillan.

Franklin, Sarah. 2007. *Dolly Mixtures: The Remaking of Genealogy*. Durham, NC: Duke University Press.

Gowaty, Patricia A., ed. 1997. *Feminism and Evolutionary Biology: Boundaries, Intersections and Frontiers*. London: Chapman and Hall.

Grosz, Elisabeth. 2011. *Becoming Undone: Darwinian Reflections on Life, Politics, and Art*. Durham, NC: Duke University Press.

Haraway, Donna J. 1991. *Simians, Cyborgs and Women: The Reinvention of Nature*. New York: Routledge.

Hrdy, Sarah Blaffer. 1981. *The Woman That Never Evolved*. Cambridge, MA: Harvard University Press.

Keller, Evelyn Fox, and Helen E. Longino, eds. 1996. *Feminism and Science*. Oxford: Oxford University Press.

Schiebinger, Londa. 2001. *Has Feminism Changed Science?* Cambridge, MA: Harvard University Press.

FURTHER READING

Ah-King, Malin, and Søren Nylén. 2010. "Sex in an Evolutionary Perspective: Just Another Reaction Norm." *Evolutionary Biology*, 37: 234–246.

Fausto-Sterling, Anne. 2000. *Sexing the Body: Gender Politics and the Construction of Sexuality*. New York: Basic Books.

Giffney, Noreen, and Myra Hird, eds. 2008. *Queering the Non/Human*. Aldershot: Ashgate.

Haraway, Donna, J. 1989. *Primate Visions: Gender, Race and Nature in the World of Modern Science*. New York: Routledge.

Hubbard, Ruth. 1979. "Have Only Men Evolved?" In *The Politics of Women's Biology*, 87–106. New Brunswick: Rutgers University Press.

Jordan-Young, Rebecca, M. 2010. *Brain Storm: The Flaws in the Science of Sex Differences*. Cambridge, MA: Harvard University Press.

Oakley, Anne. 1972. *Sex, Gender and Society*. London: Temple Smith.

Roberts, Celia. 2007. *Messengers of Sex: Hormones, Biomedicine and Feminism*. Cambridge: Cambridge University Press.

Zuk, Marlene. 2003. *Sexual Selections: What We Can and Can't Learn about Sex from Animals.* Berkeley: University of California Press.

Nazi Persecution of Homosexuals

ERIK JENSEN
Miami University, USA

Over the course of its existence, from 1933 to 1945, Nazi Germany investigated as many as 100,000 men on suspicion of homosexual behavior. It convicted about half of those men in criminal proceedings, sentencing them to prison, the workhouse, and – for an estimated 10,000 – indefinite incarceration in concentration camps, where between 5,000 and 7,000 of them died. The Nazis viewed homosexuality as a detriment to the birth rate and to the national health and thus sought its eradication. To this end, the regime imposed solitary confinement, hard labor, and, in some cases, castration and hormone treatments on men convicted of homosexual behavior, although it did not persecute women for same-sex sexual attraction. Unlike the Nazis' expansive and relentless persecution of Jews throughout occupied Europe, the regime also did not target non-German homosexuals, nor did it pursue German homosexuals with the same exterminationist zeal that it did the Jews and other racially targeted groups. Nevertheless, thousands of men who were convicted of homosexual behavior suffered tremendously under the Nazi regime, and even the hundreds of thousands who escaped detection during this period did so only within a climate of fear, suspicion, and self-repression. Furthermore, and unlike the survivors of other victimized groups, men imprisoned and tortured for homosexual activity during the Nazi period were denied official recognition of their suffering for decades after 1945, and most died without exoneration, compensation, or even an apology.

The criminalization of homosexual acts between men in Germany predated the Nazi regime and existed throughout much of Europe in the first half of the twentieth century. Paragraph 175 of the German criminal code had made fornication between men a prosecutable offense since 1872. Enforcement of the law, however, varied widely over time and between regions. By the 1920s, an organized homosexual emancipation movement was actively lobbying for the repeal of Paragraph 175 at the same time as the most lively and visible homosexual subculture that the world had yet seen was establishing itself in Berlin, Hamburg, Cologne, and other German cities, with bars, publications, and organizations catering to every taste and fetish. The relative openness and acceptance of homosexual life in Germany in the decades prior to 1933 made the subsequent persecutions both especially shocking and – from the perspective of the Nazi authorities targeting homosexual men – logistically easier.

Within months of coming to power in January 1933, the Nazis had begun shutting down the gathering spots for homosexuals and transvestites and banning publications that addressed that subculture. In early May, Nazi supporters stormed Magnus Hirschfeld's Institute for Sexual Science – a pioneer in the study of sexuality and the advocacy of homosexual rights – and fed most of its valuable library to a bonfire in the center of Berlin several days later. This targeting of institutions and gathering places during the regime's first 18 months in power formed part of a larger and ongoing effort to bring every facet of German society under Party control and to restrict sites of independent gathering, especially those perceived to be secretive and "cliquish," which included gay bars as well as

Masonic lodges. Authorities also prosecuted individual men for homosexual acts during this period, but they did so at only a slightly greater rate than during the last years of the Weimar Republic, just under 700 convictions annually.

The turning point in the Nazi persecution of homosexuals occurred during the night of June 30 to July 1, 1934, the so-called "Night of the Long Knives," when Hitler purged hundreds of potential political rivals within the Nazi Party and among the German elite. The principal target in this purge was his erstwhile second in command, Ernst Röhm, whose socialist leanings threatened German business leaders and whose 3 million man strong SA paramilitary organization threatened the military establishment. If those threats provided the real motivation behind the Hitler-directed murder of Röhm, his widely known homosexual relationships provided a convenient public pretext. Röhm's purge removed the one potential internal voice for restraint in Nazi policy toward homosexuals, and it also freed the way for the virulently homophobic head of the SS, Heinrich Himmler, to consolidate the state's policing and security apparatus under his command. Moreover, a fierce press campaign justified Röhm's purge in terms of eradicating the "pestilence" of homosexuality at the heart of the Nazi Party. Articles throughout the summer and fall whipped up societal animosity toward homosexuals, while municipal and state authorities raided the remaining gay bars and arrested hundreds of men. The Gestapo simultaneously began compiling lists of homosexuals in Germany, based on the interrogations of those already in custody, on apartment searches, on denunciations by neighbors and colleagues, and on the records of court cases involving violations of Paragraph 175 over the previous two decades.

While Röhm's purge precipitated the regime's increased targeting of homosexuals, deeper ideological preoccupations underpinned it. The quantitative expansion of the "Aryan race" was central to Nazism's vision for a future Germany, and homosexuals were seen as shirking their reproductive duties. "Reorienting" homosexuals toward heterosexual reproduction thus formed part of a larger Nazi program of population growth that also included pro-natal propaganda, a government subsidy for large families, the restriction of birth control, and the destigmatization of out-of-wedlock childbirth. The 1936 creation of the Reich Central Office for Combatting Homosexuality and Abortion, under Himmler's direct control, illustrated the close connection between Nazism's concern over the "Aryan" birth rate and its persecution of homosexual men.

In addition, the Nazi regime viewed homosexuality itself as a threat to the qualitative preservation of the "Aryan race." Homosexuality ostensibly undermined German manhood and contributed to an inexorable "degeneration" of the racial stock, and Nazi propaganda regularly referred to homosexuality as a contagion that would proliferate if left unchecked. The Nazis imagined predatory homosexual men "infecting" susceptible populations, particularly youth and those of subordinate rank in hierarchical organizations, in much the same way as a pandemic would spread through the population. In this respect, Nazi officials viewed homosexuality's eradication within a larger eugenic project that included the elimination of alcoholism, criminality, indolence, and other purportedly infectious threats to the health of the race.

Finally, from the perspective of a regime that sought control over every aspect of German society, a population perceived as secretive and cliquish, such as homosexuals, appeared inherently subversive. The Nazis imagined networks of homosexual men who traveled widely, exchanged information surreptitiously, "recruited" new men into their fold, and skillfully avoided detection. Within this imaginary, the same networks that spread homosexuality and eroded racial health also spread uncensored information and undercut state authority. The pursuit of social control largely prompted the crackdown on bars and publications in the first months of the regime, even as the Nazis publicly justified those actions on moral grounds. The regime proved quite willing to defy moral convention in other areas of sexual regulation, including a toleration of brothels, out-of-wedlock childbirth (when the parents were "Aryans"), and abortion (when they were not). The desire to monitor the putative network of homosexual men also explains the regime's continued toleration of a selected number of bars and cruising spots frequented by men seeking other men, all of them kept under the Gestapo's watchful eye.

The intensity of the persecution varied over the course of the regime, with the number of convictions increasing steadily between 1934 and 1938, when it peaked at over 8000. The increase stemmed both from Himmler's priorities and from the passage in June 1935 of a tougher version of Paragraph 175, known as Paragraph 175a, which made convictions easier and penalties more severe. Henceforth, even the suspicion of homosexual behavior, such as a hug or a "lustful glance," could result in 10 years' imprisonment. In fact, many men convicted under Paragraph 175a were sent to concentration camps instead of or immediately upon completion of their prison sentences, especially if they had "seduced" more than one partner. Men who did not conform to masculine norms also faced more severe punishment, since they represented acute "degeneracy" and a diminution of German manhood.

The Nazi regime sent perhaps 10,000 men convicted of violating Paragraph 175 or 175a to a concentration camp. In the camps, these men wore a special marking on their uniform, initially a large "A" and later a pink triangle, which exposed them to some of the harshest treatment and humiliations from the camp guards and fellow inmates, as a consequence of which those convicted of homosexual acts had a higher death rate in the camps – over 50 percent – than any victim group not persecuted on racial grounds. Determining the exact number who died in the camps, however, has challenged historians for decades. Many records disappeared or were destroyed during the war, others have only recently attracted scholarly attention, and the vast empire of satellite camps that fell under the jurisdiction of each main camp adds to the complexity. In 1977, Rüdiger Lautmann (1977) estimated that 5,000–15,000 men convicted of homosexuality perished in the camps, an estimate that subsequent research has supported, albeit decidedly at the lower end of that range. Where relatively extant records exist, historians have compiled tentative totals for certain concentration camps, including Neuengamme, where 33 men who were interned under Paragraph 175 and 175a died; Dachau, where 120 died; Buchenwald, where 400 died; and Sachsenhausen, where about 1,000 of these men died between 1936 and 1945, more than at any other camp. Most died from starvation, disease, forced labor, and the abuse to which they were subjected on a daily basis.

The Nazis envisioned forced labor as both punishment and therapy. The 14-hour days of back-breaking work – including the infamous shoe-testing commando in Sachsenhausen, in which undernourished inmates shouldered heavy packs while walking the equivalent of a marathon – would, Nazi officials surmised, toughen the men and potentially "cure" them of their homosexuality. In addition to the labor, camp officials carried out more invasive forms of "therapy," including the castration of nearly 800 men during the Nazi period, coerced through promises of early release that were rarely honored. Inmates also underwent other painful and dangerous medical experiments, which sought both the cause of homosexuality and cures for it. In the Buchenwald camp, for example, Carl Vaernet implanted men with artificial sex glands and injected them with dangerous levels of hormones. Some camps also organized mandatory brothel visits, carefully observed by SS doctors, for men convicted of homosexual acts, again with the goal of reorienting them to heterosexuality.

For men in uniform who were caught engaging in homosexual activity, special procedures applied, which varied over time and between the different branches. The SS and police meted out the most serious punishment, since both fell under Himmler's direct jurisdiction and since the SS, in particular, saw itself as the pinnacle of German manhood. At Himmler's insistence, Hitler decreed the death penalty in November 1941 for any member of the SS or police caught engaging in homosexual activity. The regular branches of the German armed services, on the other hand, did not carry out a single death sentence for homosexual activity and offered relatively light punishment for "first-time offenses," which they often applied to second and third "offenses" as well. Officers who "seduced" enlisted men, however, faced more severe consequences. Over the course of the war, the military sentenced nearly 7,00 men to Wehrmacht prison, one of the Emsland concentration camps, or front-line combat. Historian David Raub Snyder (2007) notes that sentences rarely exceeded 6 months and were often suspended with parole to the front. Even those incarcerated in camps could be mobilized into regular or penal units at any time, and only those men deemed "incorrigibles" were handed over to the SS. The increasingly acute shortage of men helps to explain the army's relatively benign treatment and also the overall drop in convictions in the civilian German population over the course of the war. Convictions for violating Paragraph 175 and 175a declined from over 3,000 in 1940 and 1941 to about 2,500 in 1942 and under 2,000 in the last 3 years of the war.

Regarding the fate of homosexual women in Nazi Germany, historian Claudia Schoppmann (1995) and others have concluded that they did not face systematic persecution comparable to that of homosexual men. Beginning in the 1980s, some historians and political activists speculated that the Nazis used the charge of "asocial behavior" to prosecute women for homosexual activity, since Germany's legal prohibition against homosexual acts applied only to men. Subsequent research, however, has disproved that theory. Lesbians certainly faced hardships under the Nazi regime, including economic discrimination, ideological pressure to marry and have children, and the destruction of their institutions and social networks, but they never faced targeted persecution as a group. Even in Austria, where the sex-neutral prohibition of homosexual activity, Paragraph 129, retained force even after Austria's absorption into Greater Germany, historians have not found a case in which a court imposed even the minimum sentence on a woman.

The persecution of homosexuals contained a tragic post-1945 coda, since Paragraph 175a, the tougher version of Germany's anti-homosexual law imposed by the Nazis, retained its legal force in West Germany for another two decades. Between the end of the war and 1969, courts in that democratic postwar German state convicted another 50,000 men for engaging in homosexual activity, resulting in prison sentences, criminal records, ruined careers and families, and social ostracism. Only in 1969 did West Germany liberalize Paragraph 175 so that men over the age of 21 years could legally engage in sex, and only in 1994, after just over 122 years on the books, did reunified Germany strike Paragraph 175 from its criminal code altogether.

SEE ALSO: Compulsory Heterosexuality; Heterosexism and Homophobia; Militarism and Gender-Based Violence; Sexual Orientation and the Law; Sexuality and Human Rights

REFERENCES

Lautmann, Rüdiger. 1977. "Der rosa Winkel in den nationalsozialistischen Konzentrationslagern" ["The Pink Triangle in National Socialist Concentration Camps"]. In *Seminar: Gesellschaft und Homosexualität* [Society and Homosexuality]. Frankfurt am Main: Suhrkamp.

Schoppmann, Claudia. 1995. "The Position of Lesbian Women in the Nazi Period." In *Hidden Holocaust? Gay and Lesbian Persecution in Germany, 1933–1945*, edited by Günter Grau, trans. Patrick Camiller. London: Cassell.

Snyder, David Raub. 2007. *Sex Crimes Under the Wehrmacht*. Lincoln: University of Nebraska Press.

FURTHER READING

Giles, Geoffrey. 2001. "The Institutionalization of Homosexual Panic in the Third Reich." In *Social Outsiders in Nazi Germany*, edited by Robert Gellately and Nathan Stoltzfus. Princeton: Princeton University Press.

Herzog, Dagmar. 2005. *Sex After Fascism: Memory and Morality in Twentieth-Century Germany*. Princeton: Princeton University Press.

Neuroscience, Brain Research, and Gender

ROBYN BLUHM
Michigan State University, USA

Although scientific interest in the differences between women and men is long-standing, during the twentieth century a number of technological and methodological advances in the neurosciences have sparked a new interest among scientists in relating purported sex/gender differences in characteristics and behavior to differences in neuroanatomy and physiology.

The distinction between sex and gender is central to feminist thought, though also controversial. "Gender" was originally used to refer to the social roles and behaviors associated with femininity and masculinity and was intended to be opposed to "sex," which referred to the biological state of being male or female. Whereas gender was thought to be the result, at least in large part, of socialization, sex was viewed as a biological given. The brain, however, is highly plastic, changing in response to experience. This means that even though observed differences between women and men are clearly biological, that does not mean that they are not affected by experience, including the processes of socialization. The compound term "sex/gender" is used to indicate that the distinction between sex and gender cannot be maintained in the case of differences in brain structure or brain activity (even if it may still be useful in other areas).

METHODS FOR INVESTIGATING SEX/GENDER DIFFERENCES IN THE BRAIN

Researchers examining the question of whether (and where) there are sex/gender differences in the brain use a variety of methods. The one with the longest history is the measurement of gross anatomy; researchers look for differences in the size or, less frequently, the shape of particular areas of the brain. These areas may be "gray matter," i.e., the parts of the brain that contain cell bodies, or "white matter," which consists of fiber tracts connecting different parts of the gray matter. Many investigators focus on the cerebral cortex, which is the thin layer of gray matter on the outside of the brain, but there is also some interest in subcortical nuclei, which are also cellular structures.

Traditionally, measurement of gross anatomy and morphology has been conducted post mortem. Although new neuroimaging techniques make it possible to measure the living brain, this research is generally done on a smaller spatial scale, which will be described below. Measuring the post mortem brain requires making decisions specifically about how and where to measure. Since the brain is a complex, three-dimensional object, as are the specific parts that might be the focus of a study, researchers must choose a particular way to slice and measure the structure(s) of interest. This task is further complicated by individual variability of brain structures.

Although much post mortem research looks at gross anatomical features, some examines the microscopic structure of brain areas of interest. In the studies, researchers must also decide how to fix and to stain their samples. These procedures, as well as changes related to tissue death, may themselves alter the microstructure of the brain, complicating the interpretation of results relevant to the relationship between brain and behavior.

With the development of new techniques for imaging the living brain, researchers have brought new methods to bear on the question of sex/gender differences. Magnetic resonance imaging (MRI) can be used to create detailed, three-dimensional images of the brain. Researchers can then use techniques such as voxel-based morphometry (VBM) to examine neuroanatomy. VBM involves dividing a brain area of interest into voxels, small cubes (or near-cubes), and then counting the number of voxels in the structure. The average number of voxels can then be compared between female and male study participants. VBM does not provide as small scale a view of the brain as do microscopy studies, but it has the advantage of using the living brain as data. It also has advantages over gross measurements, since it is more precise at a small scale and can also be used to measure brain structures in all three dimensions.

The new technologies that have received the most attention by the public and the media are various methods of imaging brain function. These include functional MRI (fMRI) and positron emission tomography (PET). Both of these techniques measure changes in the blood at specific areas of the brain (though what exactly is measured is slightly different for each technique); these changes are a proxy for changes in neural activity, which cannot be measured directly in the whole brain. (Moreover, techniques for measuring brain activity directly are invasive and can therefore only rarely be used in human beings.) Both PET and fMRI are generally used to compare patterns of brain activity in an experimental condition with activity in a control condition. For example, to find where in the brain information about color is processed, researchers would show study participants both color pictures (the experimental condition) and black-and-white pictures (the control condition). Activity in the control condition is then "subtracted" from activity in the experimental condition, which will show which areas of the brain are significantly more active in the experimental than in the control condition.

In addition to research on human beings, animal models are used in neuroscientific research on sex/gender differences. These approaches allow experimentation (e.g., increasing or decreasing exposure to hormones and determining the effect on behavior and on the brain); however, certain assumptions must be made before extrapolating the results of this research to human beings. For example, operationalized measures of animal behavior may or may not be close enough analogues to human behavior to justify using animal research to explain human behavior. Moreover, anatomical differences between humans and other animals (including the much larger cerebral cortex in human beings) must be taken into account.

Finally, hormone effects on the brain can sometimes be studied in human beings who have been exposed to abnormal levels of hormones in utero. These studies avoid the extrapolation problems inherent in animal research. The main group studied here are girls and women with congenital adrenal hyperplasia (CAH), which results in exposure to higher than normal levels of prenatal androgens. These hormones have been thought to "organize" development of the brain along more masculine lines. As a result of this hormonal influence, women and girls with CAH are thought to exhibit more masculine characteristics. (These characteristics include being sexually attracted to women, reflecting a tendency to view sexual preference as also resulting from the influence of fetal hormones.) Although for some time research on this group was limited to examining behavior (e.g., "masculine" play style and toy preferences in girls), some neuroimaging studies have been conducted to examine brain structure and function in this group compared with girls/women without CAH and with men.

RESEARCH ON THE NEURAL CORRELATES OF BEHAVIORAL DIFFERENCES

One important point about research on sex/gender differences in the brain is that researchers look for brain differences that underlie sex/gender differences in characteristics, traits, and abilities. In other words, if there is no sex/gender difference at a behavioral level, researchers do not tend to look for brain differences associated with a task. Critics of sex/gender difference research have pointed out that these purported behavioral differences may not be observed consistently in psychological research; however, the belief that there are such differences is firmly entrenched and has at least some empirical support. Conversely, the endocrinologist Geert de Vries has suggested that sex/gender differences in brain structure may actually serve to *prevent* differences in behavior by compensating for differences in brain function that are caused by gonadal hormone levels and sex chromosome gene expression (de Vries 2004). Thus, differences in the brain may actually be responsible for the *same* behaviors in women and in men. This suggestion, however, has not influenced research as much as has evidence for behavioral differences.

Research on sex/gender differences in the brain appears to have coincided with periods of social change. During the first wave of feminism, in the later nineteenth and early twentieth centuries, scientists measured the relative size and shape of men's and women's brains and skulls, hoping to establish a biological basis for the (supposed) intellectual superiority of men (see Sayers 1982 for a discussion of sex/gender difference research during this time period). In the 1960s and 1970s, the period of second-wave feminism, research was less overtly sexist, coming to emphasize the relative strengths and weaknesses of women and men, though it should be noted that the specific characteristics assigned to each sex reflected gender stereotypes. In particular, men were thought to be better at tasks that required visuospatial skills, while women had stronger language skills.

As with the earlier period of sex/gender difference research, scientists focused on gross anatomical characteristics, using post mortem brains and, later, MRI. Instead of looking at the whole brain, however, much of the research at this time focused on the corpus callosum, which is a large bundle of fibers that connects the left and right hemispheres of the brain. The guiding hypothesis of this research was that women would have, on average, larger corpora callosa than men. This hypothesis was based on the theory that women's brains were less lateralized than men's. That is, in women the (closely connected) hemispheres tended to work together, while in men they functioned largely separately. In other words, the two hemispheres in men were each specialized for different functions. Much of the discussion about corpus callosum differences focused on the splenium, which is the most posterior subpart of the corpus callosum and connects across hemispheres those areas of the cerebral cortex that process visual information. Women had been reported to have a larger splenium, and were therefore less lateralized for processing visuospatial information (DeLacoste-Utamsing and Holloway 1982). Men had also been shown to perform better on visuospatial tasks in standardized tests, which was thought to explain their superiority at mathematics and science.

Despite the publication of a number of studies reporting on sex/gender differences in the corpus callosum, the question of whether there really were such differences remained unsettled. The studies that did report differences tended to have small sample sizes, which may lead to false positive results. Moreover, the specific locations at which the structure was measured, as well as the methods used to make the measurements, varied between studies. A meta-analysis published in 1997 reported that, combining the results of 49 studies, there was no difference in corpus callosum size between women and men. Looking only at more recent studies, most of which used MRI, the combined results suggest that, in fact, men had larger corpora callosa, on average, than women but that this was proportionate to their larger overall brain size. The authors also conclude that there is no evidence for the claim that women have a larger splenium (Bishop and Wahlsten 1997).

Anne Fausto-Sterling notes in her critique of research on sex/gender differences in the corpus callosum that, despite the lack of clear evidence in support of sex/gender differences in the structure, both the hypothesis that the corpus callosum was large in women and the attempt to demonstrate this difference persisted for some time (Fausto-Sterling 2000). Now, however, researchers seem to have largely abandoned this line of inquiry. This may be in part due to the rising popularity of functional neuroimaging and a relative decrease in research on purely structural differences. In fact, functional neuroimaging research does still investigate the possibility of sex/gender differences associated with the characteristic strengths assigned to women and to men. A lot of research has been done, in particular, on sex/gender differences in language processing. This may, in part, be because language processing is one of the few types of cognitive processing that has been shown to have (in most people) a clear hemispheric specialization; in the majority of people (both women and men), language is processed mainly in the left hemisphere. An early neuroimaging study examining sex/gender differences reported, however, that while men processed language in the left hemisphere, women tended to use both hemispheres, a result that echoed the earlier lateralization hypothesis. Later studies, however, have not decisively confirmed these findings. Similarly, there is a small body of research examining sex/gender differences in visuospatial ability, which draws primarily on mental rotation tasks. Here again, the evidence of sex/gender differences is inconclusive.

In addition to work examining cognitive tasks, there are a number of studies that have looked at whether there are sex/gender differences in emotion processing. Here, the guiding hypothesis is that women are more emotional than men and that this will be reflected in (usually) greater brain activity in response to emotional stimuli in women compared with men. Some of these studies also note that women are more likely than men to experience depression and suggest that understanding sex/gender differences in emotion processing in healthy individuals may lead to a better understanding of women's greater risk of depression. Some research examining emotions uses neuroimaging to look at the whole brain in order to find areas that show differences in activity, while others focus specifically on areas of the brain that have been previously shown to be involved in emotion processing. Again, there have been no conclusive sex/gender differences identified by this research.

CRITICISMS OF SEX/GENDER DIFFERENCE RESEARCH IN NEUROSCIENCE

As noted above, interest in conducting research on sex/gender differences has increased with the increasing questioning of, and changes to, traditional gender roles. Critics of this research have worried that evidence of sex/gender differences in the brain would be interpreted as showing that gender roles are biologically determined and that efforts at social change were therefore destined to fail. For example, the idea that the developing brain is organized by hormones and thereby becomes either "male" or "female" may be taken as evidence that neural differences between women and men are biologically determined rather than, or at least to a larger extent than, being the result of cultural and social influences.

Daphna Joel (2012) has pointed out, however, that even in areas of the brain that are thought to be sexually dimorphic, individuals tend to have the "male" form of some structures and the "female" form of others. She concludes this undermines the very idea that brains can be identified as having the form of one sex or the other, and suggests that they are best viewed as "intersex."

In addition to querying the motives of this research, scholars have also criticized the methods used and the interpretation of the results. Methodological problems include the tendency of investigators to shift to new measurement strategies when previous strategies fail to show a sex/gender difference. Anne Fausto-Sterling has documented this kind of issue in her critique of corpus callosum research and notes that it is evidence that researchers are convinced that there must be a sex/gender difference *somewhere*, which they could find if they only chose the right way to measure. Another common methodological problem is the use of within-group statistical analyses in men and in women separately, rather than direct comparison of the two groups. This is problematic because there is a great deal of variability across individuals in both brain structure and brain function. This means that a difference between women and men in the average value of a measured variable (e.g., size or activity level of a brain area) may not be statistically significant, since the differences between individuals are greater than the differences between groups.

The interpretation of observed sex/gender differences has also been criticized. Any difference can be interpreted as supporting the specific hypothesis being tested. For example, Bluhm (2013) and Kaiser et al. (2009) have shown that sex/gender difference neuroimaging research (on emotion and linguistic processing, respectively) tends to support the hypothesis of sex/gender differences, regardless of the actual data obtained experimentally (see also Fine 2010). Rebecca Jordan-Young (2010) has argued that the entire research program based on brain organization theory is also largely unsupported by evidence and persists primarily because of the tendency of researchers to interpret their results as confirming the theory.

SEE ALSO: Biological Determinism; Cognitive Sex Differences, Debates on; Gender Bias in Research

REFERENCES

Bishop, Katherine M., and Douglas Wahlsten. 1997. "Sex Differences in the Human Corpus Callosum." *Neuroscience and Biobehavioral Reviews*, 21(5): 581–601.

Bluhm, Robyn. 2013. "Self-Fulfilling Prophecies: The Influence of Gender Stereotypes on Functional Neuroimaging Research on Emotion." *Hypatia*, 28(4): 870–886.

De Lacoste-Utamsing, C., and R. C. Holloway. 1982. "Sexual Dimorphism in the Human Corpus Callosum." *Science*, 216(4553): 1431–1432.

De Vries, Geert J. 2004. "Minireview: Sex Differences in Adult and Developing Brains: Compensation, Compensation, Compensation." *Endocrinology*, 145(3): 1063–1068.

Fausto-Sterling, Anne. 2000. *Sexing the Body: Gender Politics and the Construction of Reality*. New York: Basic Books.

Fine, Cordelia. 2010. *Delusions of Gender: How Our Minds, Society, and Neurosexism Create Difference*. New York: Norton.

Joel, Daphna. 2012. "Genetic-Gonadal-Genitals Sex (3G-sex) and the Misconception of Brain and Gender, or, Why 3G-males and 3G-females Have Intersex Brain and Intersex Gender." *Biology of Sex Differences*, 3(27). DOI: 10.1186/2042-6410-3-27.

Jordan-Young, Rebecca M. 2010. *Brainstorm: The Flaws in the Science of Sex Differences*. Cambridge, MA: Harvard University Press.

Kaiser, Anelis, Sven Haller, Sigrid Schmitz, and Cordula Nitsch. 2009. "On Sex/Gender Related Similarities and Differences in fMRI Language Research." *Brain Research Review*, 61(2): 49–59.

Sayers, Janet. 1982. *Biological Politics: Feminist and Anti-Feminist Perspectives*. London: Tavistock.

Neuroscience, Brain Research, and Sexuality

ANELIS KAISER
University of Bern, Switzerland

SIGRID SCHMITZ
University of Vienna, Austria

With the decade of the brain (1990 to 2000) and the emergence of highly elaborated methods of in vivo brain imaging, neuroscience has grown to become a leading, powerful, and culturally significant field. Today, brain research profoundly frames notions of human subjectivity. Since sex/gender is an important aspect of personhood, neuroscience has directed its focus to examining the neurobiological foundations of sexuality, too. Thinking about sexuality in relation to the brain leads to different questions depending on which disciplinary perspective is formulating the questions, that is, gender/queer studies or neuroscience.

Within gender and queer studies, the neuroscientific approach to sexuality applies theories from cultural studies, the humanities, and social sciences and formulates questions such as, "How does brain research construct sexuality?" or "Which discourses about (a largely normative) sexual identity do neuroscientific studies (re)produce?" Since the 2000s, a considerable amount of attention has been devoted to examining the ways in which neuroscience explains sexual performance, behavior, and desire as being a part of the brain (Dussauge and Kaiser 2012). In addition to analyzing how knowledge is produced about individual brains, gender and queer studies have also queried how notions of sexed/gendered brains and sexual identity are governed by and reciprocally impact cerebral biopolitics (Dussauge 2014; Schmitz and Höppner 2014).

Within neuroscience, the topic of sexuality is addressed using laboratory studies carried out on humans and animals. Taking a closer look at such empirical analyses, we find innumerable studies that examine slightly different aspects of what neuroscience regards as being part of sexuality, sex, and sexual desire, for example, the structures and activation of the brain when people are sexually aroused. Most neuroscientific studies of sexuality are confined to researching heterosexual sex. However, persons categorized as lesbians and gays – always compared to those of heterosexual groups – have become a topic of interest when functional brain imaging started to examine different activation patterns of sexual arousal based on "sexual orientation." The classification of participants along the axes of sexuality has been performed using questionnaires of self-identification, such as the Kinsey Scale.

In order to further understand how neuroscience deals with sexuality and sexual desire, it is indispensable to first critically reflect on the empirical settings and underlying principles that neuroscience applies when studying sex/gender. In other words, it is crucial to first clarify how brain research construes differences between categorized groups, such as women and men, or their brains, respectively, before conclusive investigations on the neuroscientific knowledge production concerning sexuality can be presented.

Since the 1980s, feminist research within and outside the neurosciences has worked to deconstruct the naturalized "evidence" of a brain that is per se "sexed." Gender studies and feminist scholars have highlighted flaws and inaccuracies within the processes of creating knowledge through neuroscience (for an overview, see Rippon et al. 2014; Schmitz and Höppner 2014), which include:

1 *Overemphasizing sex/gender differences* in the brain, as compared to sex/gender similarities. In brain research, there is an inherent entanglement between examining sex/gender and searching for difference(s). This axiomatic approach is based on a general difference-oriented methodology, in which two groups (women and men) are assumed to be homogeneous and the categorical borders between the groups are considered to be truly distinct. Differences in women's and men's brains are thus a point of departure and not a point of arrival, that is, one begins by assuming there is a difference and, unsurprisingly, ends up also discovering difference.

2 The *inconclusiveness of results* when examining women's and men's brains. Findings based on brain imaging are by no means void of ambiguity. Besides results showing sex/gender differences in specific areas of the brain, research has also come up with examples that suggest similarities between the sexes/genders, while other research shows that the variability within a single sex/gender exceeds the differences between women and men. This holds true for numerous studies of cognitive abilities, for instance investigations of linguistic ability or spatial orientation.

3 *Methodological uncertainties*. Variations regarding data selection, statistical analysis, and neuroimaging computations challenge inaccurate generalizations of results based on a binary categorization of sex/gender. Scientific articles focusing on the impact of the methods chosen in studies that have come to reveal sex/gender difference are proof that there is indeed an increasing sensitization in the

neuroscientific community toward the critical reflection of sex/gender.

4. *Contextual influences* during experimentation. Negotiations within and outside a lab (for instance, funding that supports the explicit examination of sex/gender difference), the pragmatic aims of research procedures, conscious and unconscious beliefs of researchers about sex/gender (for instance, women and men are profoundly different), and especially cultural norms and sexed/gendered assumptions are inscribed into empirical processes where the experiments take place and research questions are operationalized to create measurable variables.

5. The bias toward a *perceived abundance of sex/gender differences* within scientific publications. Studies that show similarities most often get stuck in the publication pipeline as they are regarded as "non-results," and scholarly journals predominantly publish papers that provide proof of dissimilarities. Overemphasizing sex/gender difference has resulted in the unscientific and inaccurate conclusion that regards differences as the only proper outcome. This, along with the popular media's general lack of interest in no-difference papers, clearly shows why the notion of difference remains dominant in both neuroscience and society.

6. The *disregard of the concept of neuronal plasticity*. Neurofeminism has long stressed the importance of neuronal plasticity in changing brain structures and functions based on learning and social experience. Neuronal plasticity provides explanations for inter-individual variation, such as differences between individuals, and the intra-individual variability throughout life. The notion of plasticity enables the interpretative value of brain images to be regarded as "snapshots" of a current state of an individual's development. The image does not allow for determinations of cause and effect within the inseparable network of biological processes and social influences. Despite the overall uncontested acceptance of plasticity theory in neuroscience, it is still left on the sidelines when it comes to analyses of sex/gender. Instead, examinations follow the snapshot approach that we are born with a fixed and unchangeable sexed brain.

7. The distortion of treating *sex/gender as a clear-cut category*. In the 1990s, it was demonstrated that sex/gender is highly intersected with other important social identities such as ethnicity, social class, and disability and that these categories mutually constitute each other. This certainly applies for the scientific process in human neuroscience too, where sex/gender and "race" have often been brought together in the brain, for instance in studies on prejudice, stereotypes or face perception. Research on "race"–gender power relations and on the race(ism) of neuroscience has shown how "race" and sex/gender are used to naturalize what in fact is an intersected cultural classification.

Following these critiques of neuroscientific research paradigms on sex/gender, categories developed and applied in the neurosciences, for instance, of distinct groups based on sexuality and sexual desire, have been critically assessed. Neuroscientific research on lesbians and gays has been shown to be limited through its "2×2" (women/men × hetero/homo) modes of categorization. In seeking to examine desire, most 2×2 neuroscientific studies strongly adhere to a deterministic and biologically essentialized understanding of so-called sexual orientation without any consideration of the influence of history, socialization, or the effects of a self-affirmed sex/gender and sexual identity (Dussauge and Kaiser 2012). The following outline of the development of neuroscientific research of sexuality can show how this understanding of a biologically determined 2×2 categorization has been manifested.

Although the linkage between neuroscientific research and heteronormativity can be traced back to earlier centuries, it was in the 1990s that LeVay explicitly suggested, on the basis of post mortem brain experiments on gay and heterosexual men, that "sexual orientation has a biological substrate" (LeVay 1991, 1034) and that it is situated in a particular part of the brain – the hypothalamus and, more specifically, in the INAH3, which is the third interstitial nucleus of the anterior hypothalamus. The size of this area was found to be similar in gay men and heterosexual women – a juxtaposition or assimilation that has since remained part of neuroscientific interpretation and is still frequently used to explain that gay men are more like heterosexual women instead of more like heterosexual men. Independent of the fact that INAH3 was previously found to be involved in the regulation of (heterosexual) sexual behavior (Allen et al. 1989), several activists and scholars found the neurological naturalization of male homosexuality necessary, and even emancipatory, so as to reduce stigmatization during the era of the HIV epidemic.

Particularly during the 1990s, such studies of the "gay brain" were accompanied by examinations of the conditions that led to its emergence in both science and culture. The claim that the male homosexual brain was a sexually inverted brain was only made possible because of the underlying assumption that the brain has (to have) a sex. Additionally, neuroscientific studies on sexual orientation in the 1990s supported the heteronormative matrix insofar as it was assumed that sex/gender was based on sexual attraction toward the opposite sex/gender. The androcentric bias toward the *male* gay brain again is traced back to the discussion along with the HIV epidemic, which affected male homosexuals to a much greater extent than female homosexuals.

Since the 1990s, innumerable data on sexuality and its neurological basis have been amassed in the various neuroscientific laboratories worldwide. The global brain is, however, far less international, as it only continues to represent what Western societies are keen to research in it. Therefore, when discussing brain research on sexuality, it should always be clearly noted where in the world these results have been generated, and where critique is being formulated. The latest (Western) research methodologies of structural and functional brain imaging have become more dominant, such as (f)MRI (functional magnetic resonance imaging), TMS (transcranial magnetic stimulation), or DTI (diffusion tensor imaging) – leaving the less resource-intensive methods, like electrophysiological or post mortem studies, with less importance altogether. As a result, research communities with limited access to high-tech methods are less visible in the output of neuroscientific knowledge on sexuality and the brain.

Analyses of brain imaging unearth five major approaches that currently frame the field of "neuroscientific research and sexuality" and show how sexuality is constructed in today's cerebral era. These are described below.

1. In the early years, when empirical research in neuroimaging laboratories began to use techniques such as PET (positron emission tomography) and fMRI to capture increases in cerebral blood flow, research was not sex/gender-balanced and predominantly focused

on *male sexual excitability*. Inside the scanner, men were asked to become sexually aroused or invited to have an orgasm with the help of their female partners, erotic stimuli (video clips or pictures), or their own manual skills. Drawing on studies conducted on animals, researchers had expected the sexual responses to appear in the hypothalamus. Although several studies provided evidence for *hypothalamic activation* in men, in general, the activation turned out to be low or even nonexistent. Instead, responses were often found elsewhere, for instance in the right-sided neocortex, in mesodiencephalic structures and in the cerebellum (Holstege et al. 2003).

2 Neuroimaging research focusing specifically on *female sexual arousal* began later and also resulted in brain activation appearing in several cortical and subcortical regions. In some studies there was no activation in the hypothalamus at all, while other cases with a direct sex/gender comparison found hypothalamic responses in women (Karama et al. 2002) – although significantly less prominent than in the hypothalamus of male participants. Despite such conflicting research results, the notion that men's hypothalamic activation is greater in sexual encounters remains prominent, which is largely based on the presumption that men are more willing and/or susceptible to experiencing sexual arousal (Karama et al. 2002).

3 The investigation of *functional neuroimaging of homosexuality* started with Kinnunen et al.'s (2004) study. Following LeVay, this study, and most research that followed, continued to present similarities between the brains of lesbians and heterosexual men and between the brains of gays and heterosexual women, that is, professed the existence of a neural likeness between homosexuals and the "opposite sex." Others have attempted to link the sex/gender of the stimulus to sexual preference and aimed to show a stronger neural response to erotic images of the preferred sex/gender, irrespective of the participants' own sex/gender. These efforts must be regarded as a crucial step, since a great part of research has been conducted under heterosexual conditions (i.e., exposing men to erotic pictures of women and women to erotic pictures of men) but without explicitly naming them, thereby imposing heterosexuality as the "norm" for sexuality. In recent years, awareness has increased and the prefix "hetero-" has been added to studies of heterosexuality, thus making the neuroscience of sexuality – at least terminologically – less heteronormative.

4 Since the 1990s, *transsexuality* has also become a topic of interest in neuroscientific investigations. From the first post mortem studies to brain imaging methodologies, the approach is once again familiar. Studies have highlighted structural similarities between male-to-female (MtF) trans persons and heterosexual (cis) women as well as between female-to-male (FtM) trans persons and heterosexual (cis) men. Similar to neuroscientific research on homosexuals, a close relation is drawn between "MtF resembling cis women" and "FtM resembling cis men." However, most recent functional and structural brain imaging studies have started to open up the space for the interpretation of FtM and MtF persons as being sex/genders on their own (e.g., Kranz et al. 2014).

In general, the topic of transition in sex/gender identity has been embedded in clinical settings of investigating transsexual participants in neuroscience, thus leading to a pathologization of trans identities. Up to now, there has not been one neuroscientific study published engaging with trans*, transqueer, transgender, sexual dissident or intersex participants that approaches the issue differently than in terms of a pathology or gender dysphoria. Thus, a more complex and attentive, less binary and more fluid approach to issues of sex/gender and sexual and sex/gender identity is yet to be applied to research on sex/gender and sexuality in neuroscience.

5   The youngest phenomenon observed in the neuroscientific depiction of sexuality can be called the *neuroeconomization of sexuality* (Dussauge 2014). Despite the fact that this kind of research is part of social neuroscience, current studies are searching for areas in the brain that respond to sexual excitability or sexual arousal, thereby ignoring an understanding of "the social" in human sexuality. With reference to recent studies, components in the neuroscience of human sexuality, such as social emotions, are regarded as unwanted, because only those activations that are supposed to be "purely sexual" are of real interest. In contrast to a call for researching the social entanglement of sexual desire, what seems to count in today's neuroscientific experiments on human sexuality is the individualistic economics of reward systems, thus making the brain an object of neuroeconomics.

Numerous feminist and queer approaches to neuroscientific knowledge production, some of which already provide up-to-date and critical analyses of sexuality, intersectionality, and ethnicity, have convincingly outlined evidence that humans are not neurologically "hardwired" to be women *or* men, gay *or* straight. The same holds true for categorizations of "race"/ism, as Emily Ngubia Kuria has pointed out, arguing for the reflection of "white" norms as an "act of decolonizing knowledge" (see Schmitz and Höppner 2014) and claiming for the necessity of integrating "race" as a mandatory category in neuroscience and *NeuroGenderings*.

Neither human brain organization theories nor the concept of "sex hormones" provide solid explanations for why women and men, gay and straight people are the way they are. Current reviews of neuroscientific knowledge production outline a remarkable *overlap* between categorized experimental groups, a *mosaicism* of sexed or sexualized features in the brain instead of binary models, a *contingency* between biological and social factors (including self-schemata) influencing the development of sex/gender and sexuality, and an incorporation and *entanglement* of sociocultural experiences within brain-behavior formations via plasticity (Rippon et al. 2014). Considering that sexuality is cultural, behavioral, self-identified, and not necessarily static over a lifetime (Cipolla 2012), brains must be regarded as much more receptive, much more "in the doing," and much queerer than today's neuroscientific experiments demonstrate (Dussauge and Kaiser 2012).

Following these evaluations, over the past decade a framework for improving empirical neuroscientific research, explicitly examining sexuality and sex/gender and advocating feminist neuroscientific studies, has been established (for an overview, see Schmitz and Höppner 2014). Going beyond a mere evaluation or critique of the existing research, these neurofeminism and queer studies scholars emphasize the importance of empirical work in the scientific laboratories but also call for the integration of similarity studies and multi-categorical approaches to remultiply sex/gender expressions and sexual desires. However, the integration of neurofeminist and critical gender/queer studies into neuroscientific research has been realized only on the margin. The potential of feminist and queer approaches to "repoliticize" the brain could spark research that explores the limits and contingencies of neuroscientific claims as part of a queer, trans*, intersex or feminist struggle.

SEE ALSO: Feminist Studies of Science; Gender Difference Research; Genderqueer; Heteronormativity and Homonormativity; Heterosexism and Homophobia; Intersexuality; Kinsey Scale; Lesbian and Gay Movements; Medical and Scientific Experimentation and Gender; Neuroscience, Brain Research, and Gender; Sexualities; Trans Identities, Psychological Perspectives

REFERENCES

Allen, Laura S., Melissa Hines, James E. Shryne, and Roger A. Gorski. 1989. "Two Sexually Dimorphic Cell Groups in the Human Brain." *Journal of Neuroscience*, 9(2): 497–506.

Cipolla, Cyd. 2012. "Sex/Gender, Sexuality, and Neuroscience." *The Neuroethics Blog*. Accessed September 10, 2013, at http://www.theneuroethicsblog.com/2012/03/sexgender-sexuality-and-neuroscience.html.

Dussauge, Isabelle. 2014. "Sex, Cash and Neuromodels of Desire." *BioSocieties*, August 11. DOI: 10.1057/biosoc.2014.23.

Dussauge, Isabelle, and Anelis Kaiser. 2012. "Re-Queering the Brain." In *Neurofeminism: Issues at the Intersection of Feminist Theory and Cognitive Neuroscience*, edited by Robyn Bluhm, Anne J. Jacobson, and Heidi L. Maibom, 121–144. Basingstoke: Palgrave Macmillan.

Holstege, Gert, et al. 2003. "Brain Activation during Human Male Ejaculation." *Journal of Neuroscience*, 23(27): 9185–9193.

Karama, Sherif, et al. 2002. "Areas of Brain Activation in Males and Females during Viewing of Erotic Film Excerpts." *Human Brain Mapping*, 16: 1–13.

Kinnunen, Leann H., Howard Moltz, John Metz, and Malcolm Cooper. 2004. "Differential Brain Activation in Exclusively Homosexual and Heterosexual Men Produced by the Selective Serotonin Reuptake Inhibitor, Fluoxetine." *Brain Research*, 1024(1–2): 251–254.

Kranz, Georg, et al. 2014. "White Matter Microstructure in Transsexuals and Controls Investigated by Diffusion Tensor Imaging." *Journal of Neuroscience*, 34(46): 15466–15475.

LeVay, Simon. 1991. "A Difference in Hypothalamic Structure between Heterosexual and Homosexual Men." *Science*, 253(5023): 1034–1037.

Rippon, Gina, Rebecca Jordan-Young, Anelis Kaiser, and Cordelia Fine. 2014. "Recommendations for Sex/Gender Neuroimaging Research: Key Principles and Implications for Research Design, Analysis, and Interpretation." *Frontiers in Human Neuroscience*, 8. DOI: 10.3389/fnhum.2014.00650.

Schmitz, Sigrid, and Grit Höppner. 2014. "Feminist Neuroscience: A Critical Review of Contemporary Brain Research." *Frontiers in Human Neuroscience*, 8. DOI: 10.3389/fnhum.2014.00546.

FURTHER READING

Bluhm, Robyn, Anne J. Jacobson, and Heidi L. Maibom, eds. 2012. *Neurofeminism: Issues at the Intersection of Feminist Theory and Cognitive Science*. Basingstoke: Palgrave Macmillan.

Hegarty Peter. 1997. "Materializing the Hypothalamus: A Performative Account of the 'Gay Brain'." *Feminism Psychology*, 7(3): 355–372.

Jordan-Young, Rebecca. 2010. *Brain Storm: The Flaws in the Science of Sex Differences*. Cambridge, MA: Harvard University Press.

Schmitz, Sigrid, and Grit Höppner, eds. 2014. *Gendered Neurocultures: Feminist and Queer Perspectives on Current Brain Discourses*. Vienna: Zaglossus.

NGOs and Grassroots Organizing

MANGALA SUBRAMANIAM
Purdue University, USA

The term "non-governmental organization" (NGO) was first coined by the United Nations (UN) in 1946. Selected "tax-exempt" (charitable) organizations were granted consultative status by UN's Economic and Social Council ("consultative" status refers to NGOs which have registered with ECOSOC and have access not only to ECOSOC but also its many subsidiary bodies, as well as special events organized by the President of the General Assembly). In 1946, 41 NGOs were granted consultative status by the council; by 1992 more than 700 NGOs had attained consultative status and the number has been steadily increasing ever since to 3,400 organizations. The context for NGOs in the 1990s and well into the twenty-first century continues to change rapidly in a variety of ways and for a multiplicity of interacting reasons. In February 1993, the UN's Economic and Social Council (ECOSOC) established an Open-Ended Working Group (OEWG) to update, if necessary, its arrangements for consultation with NGOs and to introduce coherent rules to regulate the participation of NGOs in international conferences organized by the UN.

This entry uses the NGO label to refer to voluntary organizations that are independent of both government and private business sectors but may receive support from the state. Autonomous women's organizations – those that exist independent of state support and have no official role in state decision-making – may or may not be feminist. Among the autonomous feminist organizations active today are many that are international in scope. They are NGOs that draw their membership and define their goals more broadly than the boundaries of individual nation states. This entry first focuses on NGOs and explains their growth, connects them to social movements, and then discusses the significance of grassroots organizing. Intertwined in this discussion is the tension between NGOs and grassroots groups.

NGOs vary in size and differ by the scope of geographic area covered, within communities, regions, nations, and globally. Most NGOs are actively involved in mobilizing and organizing people for social change. While these activities often take the shape of specific "development" initiatives such as providing health services or setting up schools, they indirectly facilitate the raising of issues about social justice and the rights of the less privileged. Therefore, NGO research has been a major area of interest to scholars of development studies. As NGOs have increasingly become prominent actors in international forums and engaged in forming or in becoming constituents of transnational networks, they have drawn the attention of feminist and social movement scholars.

The increasing involvement of NGOs in transnational networks has been facilitated by processes of globalization (Naples and Desai 2002; Moghadam 2005). The involvement of NGOs, specifically feminist organizations, in UN-sponsored global forums has also changed the UN. It has led to the UN establishing several agencies focused on women's issues and change for women. In July 2010, the UN General Assembly created UN Women, the UN Entity for Gender Equality and the Empowerment of Women. In doing so, UN member states took a historic step in accelerating the organization's goals on gender equality and the empowerment of women. The creation of UN Women came about as part of the UN reform agenda, bringing together resources and mandates for greater impact. It builds on the work of four previously distinct parts of the UN, which focused exclusively on gender equality and women's empowerment: Division for the Advancement of Women (DAW), International Research and Training Institute for the Advancement of Women (INSTRAW), Office of the Special Adviser on Gender Issues and Advancement of Women (OSAGI), and United Nations Development Fund for Women (UNIFEM).

Arguably the most far-reaching of the UN–NGO relationships is the role that NGOs have assumed in relation to UN intergovernmental conferences. The participation of NGOs, as members of states' delegations and in activities run parallel to the governmental conferences, has snowballed over the last 20 years. For instance, the 1995 Fourth World Conference on Women proved to be the largest UN conference ever held. In addition to 400 participating NGOs with ECOSOC accreditation, there were almost 2,500 other NGOs accredited to the conference (Otto 1996). Echoing earlier conferences, the Declaration and Platform for Action identified the participation of women's groups and networks and other NGOs as critical to the follow-up and implementation of conference commitments.

The NGO forum spaces at the UN conferences have facilitated the circulation of feminist discourse and made gender-specific claims targeting the state and international institutions such as the World Bank. Alvarez (1997) referred to the NGO-ization of movements in her early analysis of the emergent international feminist presence in Latin America. According to Alvarez (1997), diverse groups within movements have become more "NGO-ized," that is, they have become professionalized and specialized and won a certain degree of legitimacy as experts both nationally and internationally. In her later work, Alvarez (2009) observes that even in the height of professionalization, many NGOs "often played a critical role in grounding and articulating the expansive, heterogeneous Latin American feminist fields of the 1990s and 2000s" (2009, 177). These NGOs contribute as producers of feminist knowledge and disseminators of feminist discourse. In this sense, NGOs mobilize ideas and not just people.

The processes of globalization have eased the movement of resources for NGOs that has increasingly become a mechanism to manage activities and programs in the so-called "third" world by resource providers or donors. However, there is uncertainty in continued funding as donors may not commit to a continuous stream of resources, have unrealizable goals, and often know little about the communities and people they support as beneficiaries (Subramaniam 2007; Watkins et al. 2012). NGOs – local (within nations) or international – are not grassroots groups, but grassroots groups may over a period of time become NGOs. Studies of grassroots groups started by volunteers that beat the survival odds show a consistent pattern. The volunteers begin by providing practical help to needy or sick people whom they know or the volunteers may have been inspired by the international women's movement to help poor women on the economic front. Over time, however, they become more ambitious in their goals and form an NGO to access outside funding (Watkins et al. 2012).

Scholars have pointed out the limits to the term "grassroots"; particularly who should be considered as grassroots and whether that should include marginalized groups or coalitions. In addition, studies draw attention to the negative use of the term "grassroots." For example, white and middle-class women used the term "grassroots" to refer to black and rural women in discussions of interventions by NGOs in South Africa (Mindry 2001). However, as noted by Naples (2002, 7–8), "This construction of the 'grassroots' fails to capture the politics of accountability and the extent to which so-called grassroots groups are inclusive and encourage participatory democratic practices."

Grassroots groups, sometimes known as base groups, peoples' organizations, or local organizations (Bystydzienski and Sekhon 1999), emerge and work at the local level to improve and develop their communities either through community-wide or more specific memberships, such as women or farmers. Grassroots groups are community-based, generally small in scope and scale, and often focus on feminist issues that directly impact members' lives. They often perform a mediating role between the private and the public; the state, the local community, and the family. The context within which grassroots groups emerge, such as the life experiences of members and program goals, can also shape group structure. Older groups may develop the potential to influence and even alter state policies and structures at the local community level.

Grassroots groups are neither bureaucratically structured nor entirely collectivist in form because of the ways in which they engage in power sharing and distribution of authority; they are similar to hybrid forms of organizations. Feminist scholars have persuasively argued for considering informal and hybrid forms of organizations (Purkayastha and Subramaniam 2004; Ferree and Martin 1995). In doing so, they highlight the importance of the process that is the "means" as well as the ends for change (Ferree and Martin 1995). In a similar vein, Martin (1990) calls for examining the concrete forms and practices of feminist organizations and their transformative impact on members. Such transformative impact is possible in feminist grassroots organizations.

Feminist organizations actively promote the mobilization of grassroots women in defining their own needs and speaking out in their own cause. Such empowerment implies not only engagement in the formal organizations of politics, but in confronting institutional power expressed in family, religion, and other social institutions. In order to challenge paternalistic assumptions, women's movements need specifically to empower the most marginalized women. For example, in rural India, efforts have been made to organize women's groups or collectives at the village level which serve as institutions which women call their own (Subramaniam 2006, 2012).

Grassroots organizing creates and expands spaces to enable a process that redefines the form and content of politics (Bystydzienski and Sekhon 1999; Purkayastha and Subramaniam 2004). For instance, grassroots groups may aim to gain greater representation for the disadvantaged, such as women, in local political institutions. The groups provide a space for women to articulate their experiences, listen to others, and consider individual and collective challenges to injustices. In fact, such groups are particularly effective in consciousness-raising and promoting group solidarity through participation. Participation in such groups can be critical for the deeply disadvantaged, such as poor women, who have accepted silence and repression as part of their lives (see, for instance, cases in Naples and Desai 2002; Subramaniam 2012).

Participants in grassroots groups benefit from capacity building initiatives made possible through development aid. Capacity building entails actions to create, reform, or support activities that facilitate sharing of experiences, knowledge, and strategies. Capacity building includes training of members of feminist grassroots groups to seek formal power such as representation in formal political institutions. It may also include training scholars and practitioners to enhance skills to conduct research, contribute to policy-making, and document change and simultaneously enable interaction among feminists at the local and national level. Initiatives directed towards capacity building inevitably reflect specific interests, particularly when donors predetermine activities to be pursued to promote their own ideology and goals (Ferree and Subramaniam 2001).

An important point is the role of the state in facilitating grassroots organizing. Typically, development interventions in the "third world" view women as beneficiaries but in many developing countries NGOs have become the vehicle for social development (Watkins et al. 2012), particularly as the state has withdrawn services (such as education and health) often in rural areas. The state has simultaneously facilitated the creation of NGOs to maintain access to international aid and to oversee development programs. Such an initiative addresses the criticism of the "top-down" clientalistic approach often adopted by the state but fails to directly enable grassroots organizing. With new trends in multi-level power sharing local democracy will increasingly have to be reconsidered in terms of a strictly delineated political sphere to one of social relations in a global civil society.

SEE ALSO: Anti-Globalization Movements; Economic Globalization and Gender; Third World Women; Universal Human Rights

REFERENCES

Alvarez, Sonia E. 1997. "Altered States? Dilemmas of Gendered Citizenship in Post-Authoritarian Latin America." Paper presented at the Conference on Gendered Citizenships, European and Latin American Perspectives, Minda de Gunzburg Center for European Studies, Harvard University, March 14–15, 1997.

Alvarez, Sonia E. 2009. "Beyond NGO-ization? Reflections from Latin America." *Development*, 52(2): 175–184.

Bystydzienski, Jill M. and Joti Sekhon. 1999. "Introduction." In *Democratization and Women's Grassroots Movement*, edited by Jill M. Bystydzienski and Joti Sekhon, 1–21. Bloomington: Indiana University Press.

Ferree, Myra Marx, and Patricia Yancey Martin, eds. 1995. *Feminist Organizations: Harvest of the New Women's Movement*. Philadelphia: Temple University Press.

Ferree, Myra Marx, and Mangala Subramaniam. 2001. "The International Women's Movement at Century's End." In *Gender Mosaics: Social Perspectives*, edited by Dana Vannoy, 496–506. Roxbury Press.

Mindry, Deborah. 2001. "NGOs, 'Grassroots', and the Politics of Virtue." *Signs*, 26(4): 1187–1211.

Moghadam, Valentine. 2005. *Globalizing Women: Transnational Feminist Networks*. Baltimore: Johns Hopkins University Press.

Naples, Nancy. 2002. "Changing the Terms: Community Activism, Globalization, and the Dilemmas of Transnational Feminist Praxis." In *Women's Activism and Globalization: Linking Local Struggles and Global Politics*, edited by Nancy Naples and Manisha Desai, 3–14. New York: Routledge.

Naples, Nancy and Manisha Desai, eds. 2002. *Women's Activism and Globalization: Linking Local Struggles and Global Politics*. New York: Routledge.

Otto, D. 1996. "Nongovernmental Organizations in the United Nations System: The Emerging Role of International Civil Society." *Human Rights Quarterly*, 18(1): 107–141.

Purkayastha, Bandana, and Mangala Subramaniam. 2004. *The Power of Women's Informal Networks: Lessons in Social Change from South Asia and West Africa*. Lanham: Lexington Books.

Subramaniam, Mangala. 2006. *The Power of Women's Organizing: Gender, Caste, and Class in India*. Lanham: Lexington Books.

Subramaniam, Mangala. 2007. "NGOs and Resources in the Construction of Intellectual Realms: Cases from India." *Critical Sociology*, 33(3): 551–573.

Subramaniam, Mangala. 2012. "Grassroots Groups and Poor Women's Empowerment in Rural India." *International Sociology*, 27(1): 70–93.

Watkins, Susan Cotts, Ann Swidler, and Thomas Hannan. 2012. "Outsourcing Social Transformation: Development NGOs as Organizations." *Annual Review of Sociology*, 38: 285–315.

Niddah

ILANA COHEN
Brandeis University, Waltham, USA

Niddah (Hebrew "a menstruating woman" or "time of menstruation"; literally, "isolation" or "condition of uncleanness") is a term used within Jewish law to refer to a woman who is menstruating, or who has a vaginal discharge of blood, and is thus considered ritually impure. The term originates from the book of Leviticus and is part of a larger biblical code on ritual impurity. This code proscribes specific observances and purifying behaviors for various bodily emissions and conditions, including menstruation and childbirth; these observances are elaborated upon and discussed in great detail in the Talmud, the codified body of Jewish law. The laws of Niddah are closely observed in Orthodox Jewish communities and prohibit contact, sexual or otherwise, between a menstruating woman and her husband during the days of her period and for another 7 days until she immerses in a mikvah (ritual bath) and is then considered ritually pure again.

Chapters 11–15 of the book of Leviticus describe different conditions and encounters that can cause ritual impurity for the Israelite people. In the biblical context, impurity is not sinful; it renders a person unfit to approach the holy alter and to engage in religious ritual. There are broadly three categories of sources that cause ritual impurity: encountering corpses, bodily emissions, and skin diseases. Within the biblical system, when a woman has a discharge of blood, commonly understood as menstruation, she remains in her impurity (literally "in her Niddah") for 7 days; anything she lies on during this time becomes impure, and anyone who touches her or what she has lain on becomes impure until the evening. If a man lies with her, her impurity is passed to him, and he is impure for 7 days, and any bedding on which he lies becomes impure. On the eighth day she must bring two turtledoves or two pigeons to the priest at the Tent of Meeting; one is offered as a sin offering and one is offered as a burnt offering to make expiation on her behalf (Leviticus 15:19). If a woman has a discharge of blood for many days beyond, or not during, her time of Niddah she, along with her bedding and anything on which she sits, is impure for the duration of the bleeding; a woman with bloody discharge of this nature is considered a "Zavah" (literally, "oozer"). A woman with this condition must wait 7 days in which there is no blood, bring two turtledoves or pigeons in sacrifice, and then she is pure.

A state of ritual impurity also applies to a woman who has given birth: when a woman gives birth to a male she is impure for 7 days (remaining in a state of blood purification for 33 days) and when a woman gives birth to a female, she is impure for 14 days (remaining in a state of blood purification for 66 days). At the end of the 33 or 66 days, the parturient must bring a lamb for a burnt offering and a pigeon or turtledove for a sin offering, and then she is pure (Leviticus 12:1–8). In Leviticus 18:19, men are instructed not to come near a woman to uncover her nakedness during her time of Niddah; this instruction is embedded within a list of prohibited sexual behaviors and sexual partners.

Menstrual blood, and other vaginal discharges, are not the only bodily fluids that render a person ritually impure; any discharge from a man's member, seminal or non-seminal, renders him temporarily impure. An emission of semen renders a man impure until the evening and until he has bathed in water. After intercourse, both the man and woman must bathe in water and are impure until the evening. If a man has non-seminal continuous discharge his impurity parallels that of a Zavah; anything that he touches or sits upon becomes contaminated and can communicate, along with the man himself, impurity. At the end of the discharge he must wait 7 days, after which he must bathe and bring two turtledoves or pigeons as a sacrifice.

Eilberg-Schwartz (1990) suggests three systems of relation for understanding why certain bodily fluids (menstrual blood, bloody vaginal discharge, seminal and non-seminal emissions) are polluting, while others, such as sweat and tears, are not: gender, demarcation of life and death, and uncontrollability. According to a system of relations revolving around gender, menstrual blood causes impurity simply because it comes from a woman (men's blood, even blood from ritual circumcision is not contaminating). A gender system of relations might also explain why the birth of a daughter makes a woman impure for twice as long as the birth of a son. The priestly rules governing bodily emissions seem to constitute a system that associates certain fluids with death, an underlying source of impurity. Menstruation and semen can be considered to represent missed opportunities for conception – symbolic death. The last system relates uncontrollability with impurity: the less controllable a bodily fluid, the more polluting it is. Menstrual blood and non-seminal discharge, released passively, render the woman or man impure for 7 days. Tears, sweat, and mucus which are thought to be more controllable are thus not polluting and do not cause impurity.

These systems of relation work together both symbolizing and actually constituting gender differences, often resulting in positions of inferiority for women in the biblical context. Such views and fears towards menstruation and bodily fluids were common in the ancient Near East and are found in cultures worldwide. Though the destruction of the Second Temple in 70 CE essentially rendered the ritual purity system and laws irrelevant, a modified version of the laws of the Niddah continue to inhabit a critical place in the daily lives of Orthodox observers of Halacha, Jewish law, who consider the laws commandments and essential to a religious way of life.

In late antiquity and the Middle Ages, Jewish sages paid a great deal of attention to transcribing and debating accurate, detailed instructions for following the biblical laws of Niddah within the context of the development of the Oral Torah, made up of the Mishnah and the Talmud. The Mishnah is a systematic codification of Jewish laws, derived from the Bible, first recorded around 200 CE. It is comprised of six orders, and the laws of Niddah are codified in the sixth order, Taharot, which contains all the laws of purity and impurity. The Babylonian Talmud, a body of lengthy commentary on each order of the Mishnah, discusses the laws and practices of Niddah in Tractate Niddah (2a–76b). The discussion of laws found in Tractate Nidddah presents three practical changes to the biblical text, producing the version of laws that are widely observed in the modern day: women must immerse in a ritual bath of naturally collected water known as a mikvah (literally, "pool") after menstruation to be considered pure; women must wait 7 clean days after menstruation has ended before immersing and becoming pure; and a husband and wife are to have no physical contact during menstruation (so as to avoid sexual arousal, the underlying concern being that ritual impurity can be communicated from the woman to the man during intercourse).

The practice of immersing in a mikvah has become the hallmark of the laws of Niddah for observant Jewish woman, completely replacing the turtledove or pigeon sacrifice no longer possible after the destruction of the Temple. Scholars observed that the Talmudic discussion and laws produce an ironic phenomenon in which men serve as authorities for matters of menstruation and other vaginal discharges; the Talmudic laws can thus be seen as men insisting on their authority to interpret and control women's bodies. However, in the late twentieth century, Nishmat, a center for advanced Torah study for women, pioneered a new leadership role called Yoetzet Halcha, Women Halachic

Advisors. These advisors serve as a resource and legal council for women with questions regarding the laws of Niddah including marriage, sexuality, and women's health. Whereas the Talmudic text primarily locates authority on issues of Niddah with male rabbis, the end of the twentieth and early twenty-first centuries have started to claim Niddah as a women's authoritative realm. Nishmat also runs an online project, Women's Health and Halacha, devoted to making the laws of Niddah accessible to twenty-first-century women worldwide.

In modern day Orthodox communities, observing the laws of Niddah is an essential commandment for married women. Ethnographic studies of women who observe Niddah in Israel (Avishai 2008) demonstrate that adherence to them becomes a site for expressing religious Jewish identity and serves to differentiate the self from a secular other. Though compliance with the laws of Niddah, also called Taharat HaMishpacha (family purity), is primarily motivated by the fact that they comprise a core commandment, they also offer some perceived benefits to women and their families that help to justify the strict prescriptions, such as improved gynecological health, a prolonged "honeymoon" period between a couple when they reunite after temporary monthly separation, increased communication between spouses, and overall harmony in the home. Naturally, women internalize and relate to the implications of following the laws in many different ways. Taking issue with label of "impurity," a concept that feels inaccurate, some women like to think of themselves in terms of "permissible" or "forbidden." Traditionally, only married women observe the laws of Niddah, immersing in the mikvah for the first time before their wedding after being counseled by an older woman, usually a rabbi's wife or Yoetzet Halacha, in how to follow the laws of Niddah.

Most liberal Jewish communities have rejected compulsory observance of the laws of Niddah, finding them archaic in addition to the fact that commandments are not observed as strictly. Still, the past decade has seen a small reclaiming of the practice of monthly immersion in the mikvah in these communities for married and even sexually active unmarried women, highlighting the renewal and personal reflection the practice can offer an individual. Two community mikvaot, Mayhim Hayim, in Boston, and ImmerseNYC in New York are inclusive and open to Jews of all denominational backgrounds and all sexual orientations. These community mikvaot offer opportunities for immersion following menstruation and for many other times throughout the life cycle as well, as the mikvah can be used to mark moments of transition and change. In all contexts, the laws of Niddah and preparation for mikvah (including awareness of the menstrual cycle, monitoring the body for onset of menstruation, examining to see if menstruation has stopped, and thoroughly cleaning the body before immersing in the mikvah) create a space for a woman to be grounded in and in touch with her body and, for women from more conservative Orthodox communities, to open a door onto sexual identity within a religious context.

The laws of Niddah occupy an important place in Jewish law, history, and culture, and there is a wide body of literate and critical scholarship engaging various facets of the laws of Niddah, from exegetical, anthropological, sociological, gender studies, and rabbinic points of view.

SEE ALSO: Judaism and Gender; Judaism and Sexuality; Menstrual Rituals

REFERENCES

Avishai, Orit. 2008. "'Doing Religion in a Secular World': Women in Conservative Religions and the Question of Agency." *Gender and Society*,

22(4): 409–433. DOI: 10.1177/0891243208321019.

Eilberg-Schwartz, Howard. 1990. *The Savage in Judaism: An Anthropology of Israelite Religion and Ancient Judaism.* Bloomington: Indiana University Press.

FURTHER READING

Cohen, Shaye. 1991. "Menstruants and the Sacred in Judaism and Christianity." In *Women's History and Ancient History*, edited by S. Pomeroy, 273–299. North Carolina: University of North Carolina Press.

Cohen, Shaye. 1999. "Purity, Piety, Polemic: medieval Rabbinic Denunciations of 'Incorrect' Purification Practices." In *Women and Water: Menstruation in Jewish Life and Law*, edited by Rahel R. Wasserfall, 82–100. Hanover: University Press of New England.

Collins, John J. 2004. *Introduction to The Hebrew Bible.* Minneapolis: Fortress Press.

Jewish Women's Archive. 2009. "Tractate Niddah." Accessed August 12, 2015, at http://jwa.org/encyclopedia/article/niddah-tractate.

Ta-Shma, Israel Moses, and Judith R. Baskin. 2007. "Niddah." *Encyclopaedia Judaica*, 2nd ed., vol. 15, edited by Michael Berenbaum and Fred Skolnik, 253–258. Detroit: Macmillan Reference.

Nomadic Subject

LEONIE ROWAN
Griffith University, Australia

In gender and sexuality studies the concept of nomadic subjectivity is most closely associated with three texts: "Nomad Thought" (1973/1985) by Gilles Deleuze; *A Thousand Plateaus: Capitalism and Schizophrenia* (1987) by Gilles Deleuze and Felix Guattari, and *Nomadic Subjects: Embodiment and Sexual Difference in Contemporary Feminist Theory* (1994/2011) by Rosi Braidotti.

The authors use the term to contribute to the broader, anti-essentialist project of critiquing Western, phallogocentric understandings of philosophy, subjectivity, and self. The individual self at the heart of traditional representations of the subject is an autonomous, rational, coherent agent governed by logic and reason. This view of self (or subjectivity) has historically been mobilized to naturalize an artificial association between very particular kinds of bodies (generally those of white, Christian, financially secure and, often, heterosexual and able-bodied men) and access to the kinds of social, physical, economic and political power that allow these rational performances of agency in the first place.

Deleuze and Guattari's philosophy of difference challenges this approach to theorizing subjectivity. Conceptualizing the subject as *assemblage*, they employ the concepts *nomad* and *nomadic subjectivity* to argue subjectivity as a process of *becoming*, not a state of being. They distinguish between dominant systems (the *arboreal*) that construct and police territories, behaviors, and bodies, and *rhizomatic lines of flight* that transgress arboreal, regulated ways of "being." Lines of flight are *becomings* that enact a *deterritorialization* (however temporary). Similarly, a deterritorialized nomadic subjectivity cuts across territories (such as public/private; masculine/feminine) and links together characteristics and ways of being that have historically been positioned in a binary or oppositional relationship.

Deleuze and Guattari have been critiqued by many feminists for their claim that all becomings begin with *becoming-woman* (even for women) but although recognizing these critiques many nevertheless draw carefully upon Deleuzian theoretical resources while pursuing explicitly feminist, anti-racist, and postcolonial agendas.

The best-known feminist use of the term *nomadic subject* is found in the writings of Rosi Braidotti. Braidotti critiques traditional notions of self that consistently position women as a homogenous group understood as "other" to a natural, dominant, white male subject. Like many feminists working with postmodern resources, Braidotti argues that these representations are sustained by powerful stories about what is possible and desirable for a woman to "be." For Braidotti, these stories can be disrupted, denaturalized and consumed by the circulation of politically powerful *feminist figurations*.

Figurations demonstrate the potential for freedom from dominant narratives (such as those relating to masculinity and femininity). Mapping the diverse ways in which individuals display this freedom as they negotiate and perform their own (fluid) subjectivity, unsettles and contests the power long accorded to traditional representations of self and the subordination of women that results. The nomadic subject thus helps to create an understanding of the possibilities of becoming, in Braidotti's terms, *post-Woman women*.

Braidotti cites several examples of feminist figurations in the work of other writers (such as Trinh T. Minh-ha's, "in/appropriated other" and Teresa de Lauretis's "eccentric subject"). The central figuration she herself draws upon is the nomadic subject. Like Deleuze and Guatarri, Braidotti does not link nomadic subjectivity to literal movement. Rather the nomadic subject inhabiting a woman's body acts, thinks, or moves in ways that challenge the traditional discursive boundaries linked to constructions of femininity. Thus an individual's sense of self is represented as multiple and weblike: going, processing, passing through; able to make connections between what is (an embodied, historically situated subject) and what may be.

Escaping representations that depend upon notions of a female "nature" or "essence," the nomadic subject also relinquishes a nostalgic desire for an "origin" or "home" and does not seek a final place of belonging: the subject is always becoming, not being. However, while a nomadic subject is forever in transit, it is sufficiently aware of its historical position to recognize the politics of location, and to accept responsibility for local and global decisions (such as those relating to the environment or refugees). Thus nomadic subjectivity is central to Braidotti's writing about ethics in a global context.

The nomadic subject also acknowledges the realities of embodiment. Attention is closely focused on sexed, raced, classed bodies – bodies ascribed with specific meanings in specific cultural and historical contexts – and the role these differences (including those associated with migration, movement, and literal nomadism) might play in how any nomadic journey develops.

Concerns raised about the political significance of the use of the term "nomad" within feminist, postcolonial and anti-racist writings include the potential for it to misrepresent or romanticize the experiences of literally nomadic peoples; the risk of sentimentalizing or essentializing nomadic people or groups; and the danger that the term could become a celebratory label for the kind of literal mobility afforded to individuals with sufficient cultural and economic capital to pursue "legitimate" modes of travel while overlooking the vastly different experiences of those undertaking forced migration, particularly given contemporary negative representations of immigrants and refugees.

These criticisms have informed careful use of the term within diverse feminist, profeminist and postcolonial projects spanning fields such as literature, film, geography, history, education, art, and politics. The term continues to inform critical projects mapping conceptualizations of the self that exceed eurocentric and/or phallogocentric perspectives on the subject, "Woman" and man.

SEE ALSO: Embodiment and the Phenomenological Tradition; Essentialism; Feminisms, Postmodern; Feminism, Postcolonial; Feminism, Poststructural; Feminist Theories of the Body; Phallocentrism and Phallogocentrism

REFERENCES

Braidotti, Rosi. 2011 [1994]. *Nomadic Subjects: Embodiment and Sexual Difference in Contemporary Feminist Theory*, 2nd ed. New York: Columbia University Press.
Deleuze, Gilles. 1985 [1973]. "Nomad thought." In *The New Nietzsche*, edited by Donald B. Allison, 142–149. Cambridge, MA: MIT Press. [Original edition, "La Pensée nomade" in *Nietzsche Aujourd'hui?* vol. 1. Paris: 10/18, 1973.]
Deleuze, Gilles, and Felix Guattari. 1987. *A Thousand Plateaus: Capitalism and Schizophrenia*, trans. Brian Massumi. Minneapolis: University of Minnesota Press.

FURTHER READING

Braidotti, Rosi. 2006. *Transpositions: On Nomadic Ethics*. Cambridge: Polity.

Nomadic Theory

ARTHUR LAING MING WONG
The Chinese University of Hong Kong, People's Republic of China

Nomadic theory insists on a loss of the notion of a single subject position as marked by a Cartesian identity that exists beyond location and situation. Becoming nomadic is a process of active displacement of dominant formations of identity, memory, and identification thus making oneself by "becoming minoritarian," that is, unhinged from the binary system that is traditionally opposed to sameness. Alterity or difference is a positive force that entails multiple processes of transformation and transposition, creative tools that express the principle of "not-one" that displaces the centrality of "ego-indexed" notions of identity. Nomadic theory, then, is a political project that creates an agency which looks into the decline of the metaphysical fixed and steady identities in which one has to de-familiarize an active knowing subject evolving from the normative engagement of the self to that which one can get accustomed. Contrary to this, one has to become an open-ended, interrelational, multi-sexed, and trans-species vitalist by interacting with multiple others that one get into contact with in this globalized mediated world.

Rosi Braidotti has created from her nomadic existence a politically motivated philosophy that provides a new framework for reinventing the female subject in our globalized age. She was born in 1954 in Italy and raised in Australia, where she received degrees from the Australian National University in 1977 and a doctorate in philosophy in 1981 from Sorbonne. She has taught at Utrecht University in the Netherlands since 1988, where she was appointed as the founding professor in women's studies. Braidotti is currently Distinguished University Professor at Utrecht University and founding Director of the Centre for the Humanities. Her first publication of her doctoral dissertation *Patterns of Dissonance: An Essay on Women in Contemporary French Philosophy* (1991), which was developed into a trilogy on nomadic theory, namely *Nomadic Subjects* (1994), *Metamorphoses* (2002), and *Transpositions* (2006). *Nomadic Subjects*, a seminal work for Braidotti, has been reissued by Columbia University Press in a totally revised second edition 17 years after its original publication (2011). It has more polemical discourse on contemporary issues pertaining to cultural and social criticism that crept into continental philosophy, queer theory, and feminist, postcolonial, technoscience, media, and race studies, as well as into architecture, history, and anthropology.

Rosi Braidotti portrayed the definition of the nomadic subject as

> [a] piece of meat activated by electric waves of desire, a text written by the unfolding of genetic encoding. Neither a sacralised inner *sanctum* [italics in original], nor a pure socially shaped entity, the enfleshed Deleuzian subject is rather an "in-between": it is a folding-in of external influences and a simultaneous unfolding outwards of affects. A mobile entity, an enfleshed sort of memory that repeats and is capable of lasting through sets of discontinuous variations, while remaining faithful to itself. The Deluezian body is ultimately an embodied memory. (Rosi Braidotti, "Teratologies," in Buchanan and Colebrook 2000, 159.)

Influenced greatly by Gilles Delueze, Michel Foucault, and Luce Irigaray, but restraining from limiting herself by overly loyal attachment to any one philosophical figure or school, Braidotti seeks to develop a "non-unitary" subject which is split, in process, knotted, rhizomatic, transitional, and in relation with issues of fragmentation, complexity, and multiplicity.

Braidotti defines the nomadic subject as a creative entity that creates for itself a new brand of materialism that is fluid and productive, seeking for alternative differences as it moves within and across multiple boundaries – virtual, philosophical, and embodied locations. She attempts to be critical on the representation of the lived existence in theoretical terms and discourses pertaining to the multiple bodies living in globalized societies, overshadow by advanced technologies and high-speed telecommunication, free borders for the privileged, increased border controls for the subaltern, and security controls for the racial others. The body is the "threshold of subjectivity; it is to be thought of as the point of interaction, as the interface between the biological and the social" (Braidotti 1994, 182), defining differences in terms of sexualized, racialized, and naturalized others and the irreducibility of sexual difference and sexuality.

The nomadic subject thus, within the logic of the globalization, is centripetal and centrifugal, drawing the subject to its core or norms and at the same time spreading outwards across the world creating contestation of different cultural, social, and political forms and their power relationships. It provokes and sustains a critique of dominant visions of the subject, identity, and knowledge from within one of the many "centers" that form the contemporary globalized world. The hierarchical nomads produce different subjectivities that engage with the boundaries between the so-called universal and particular within the Eurocentric universalism, without ignoring the encounters that create eventful actions and behaviors that a subject can undertake, and shape the types of interactions that the subjects can have with each other. Subjectivity is a process of ontological self-styling, which involves complex and continuous negotiation with dominant norms and values and hence also multiple form of accountability. The body becomes a vital "machinic" entity in contemporary culture, which is enfleshed with highly eroticized space that conveys a transsexual/racial social imagery that is dominated by advanced capitalism. The "machinic" concept for Braidotti following Deleuze is a figuration that expresses the non-unitary, radically materialistic, and dynamic structure of subjectivity. It expresses the subject's capacity for multiple, non-linear, outward-bound interconnections with a number of external forces (to use the term by Deleuze). The nomadic subject identifies lines of flight, that is to say, a creative alternative space of becoming that defies the duality between mobile/immobile, resident/foreigner distinction but still within those categories.

SEE ALSO: Ecofeminism; Sexualities; Technosexuality

REFERENCES

Braidotti, Rosi. 1994. *Nomadic Subjects: Embodiment and Sexual difference in Contemporary Feminist Theory*. New York: Columbia University Press.

Buchanan, Ian and Claire Colebrook, eds. 2000. *Deleuze and Feminist Theory*. Edinburgh: Edinburgh University Press.

FURTHER READING

Blaagaard, Bolette, and Iris van der Tuin, eds. 2014. *The Subject of Rosi Braidotti: Politics and Concepts*. London: Bloomsbury Publishing.

Braidotti, Rosi. 1991. *Patterns of Dissonance: A Study of Women and Contemporary Philosophy*. Cambridge: Polity.

Braidotti, Rosi. 2002. *Metamorphoses: Towards a Materialist Theory of Becoming*. Cambridge: Polity.

Braidotti, Rosi. 2011. *Nomadic Subjects: Embodiment and Sexual Difference in Contemporary Feminist Theory*, 2nd ed. New York: Columbia University Press.

Braidotti, Rosi. 2011. *Nomadic Theory: The Portable Rosi Braidotti*. New York: Columbia University Press.

Braidotti, Rosi. 2013. *The Posthuman*. Cambridge: Polity.

Non-Sexist Education

NANCY GROPPER
Bank Street Graduate School of Education, USA

In 1920, women in the United States achieved suffrage with the passage of the Nineteenth Amendment to the Constitution prohibiting voting restrictions based on gender. Dormant in the subsequent decades, the women's movement was reignited in the late 1960s in the wake of the civil rights movement.

In the public arena in 1972, well-known actors Marlo Thomas, Harry Belafonte, Alan Alda, Mel Brooks, and others created a record, book, and eventually a television special entitled *Free to Be You and Me* (Rotskoff and Lovett 2012). Reaching an audience of countless children, parents, and teachers, it communicated a strong message about the limitations of gender stereotypes. At the same time, in the educational arena concerns were voiced about long-standing, unquestioned discriminatory practices that deprived girls of equal education opportunities including those related to sports and college admission. As gender issues entered the public consciousness, the groundwork was laid for passage of Title IX of the Education Amendments, signed into law in 1972, which prohibited discrimination of the basis of sex in any federally funded education program or activity. Accompanying its passage and continuing to this day, non-sexist education has been a constant theme but with shifting foci over time.

Early research that lent support to non-sexist education included a systematic analysis of award winning picture books for young children which showed that girls and women were far less visible than men and boys and even when visible were depicted in far less interesting roles (Weitzman et al. 1972). Over time changes in children's literature occurred and by 1987 a replication study showed a greater balance in the visibility of females and males in picture books. However, the roles they were afforded were still less interesting than those of males who were almost all shown as independent, persistent, and active (Williams et al. 1987).

Other efforts to promote non-sexist early childhood education focused on the gender messages conveyed in classroom activities and materials. For example, the omnipresent housekeeping area in preschool and kindergarten classrooms were found to support gender stereotypes (Sprung 1975). Designed to enable children to engage in dramatic play related to family life, housekeeping areas were typically equipped with toy kitchen appliances, dolls, and dress-up clothes such as neckties, fedora-type hats, suit jackets, briefcases, aprons, jewelry, frilly dresses, high heels, and handbags. While teacher training programs normalized the possibility that children might don the accoutrements associated with the opposite sex, most children tended to wear the clothing stereotypically associated with their own gender; those who chose clothing associated with the opposite gender ran the risk of being teased by their peers or raising parental alarm. Today the housekeeping area can still be found in some classrooms but the dress-up materials in many are more neutral. Indeed in many classrooms the housekeeping area has been replaced by a more flexible dramatic play area where children can use materials such as large wooden blocks to create the set of their choice, be it a doctor's office one day or a construction site the next. Today, the gender signals conveyed by dress, hairstyle, or activity are themselves being challenged and there is a growing body of literature on how to support children to think beyond a binary view of gender (MacNaughton 2000).

Studies also showed that boys dominated the block areas in early childhood classrooms so this too became a focus for promoting non-sexist education. Because block play offers rich opportunities to learn about mathematics and physics and to represent social experience in miniature, teachers were offered a multitude of strategies for bringing girls into the block area (Cuffaro 1974; Sprung 1975; MacNaughton 2000).

At the elementary through post-secondary level, concerns about gender inequities in achievement in mathematics and science emerged soon after the passage of Title IX and continue to this day with an expanded focus on what is now referred to as STEM (Science, Technology, Engineering, and Mathematics). A body of research shows that girls feel less confident than boys in their math abilities and are less interested in careers in math and science and strategies for redressing this have been generated (Halpern et al. 2007).

In recent years, concerns about inequities for boys have been raised with evidence that girls do better than boys in language arts and literacy and that boys are more likely than girls to be suspended or expelled from school or referred for special education evaluations (Gilliam 2005). In response, there is a growing body of literature on ways to better meet the needs of boys in school settings (Tyre 2008; Sprung, Froschl, Gropper 2010).

Clear evidence of expansive views of gender roles was the appointment in August 2014 of the first female assistant coach to serve in the National Basketball Association. Without Title IX and the accompanying efforts to promote non-sexist education, girls would have continued to be restricted to playing girls rules in basketball; there would have been little or no financial support for women's teams in high schools and colleges; there would have been no professional women's basketball teams or leagues and it would have remained inconceivable that a woman could achieve a leadership role in a sport so dominated by men.

Still there continues to be good reason for educators to adopt non-sexist practices in order to achieve gender equity. In every culture, the gender label is used to define and distinguish perceptions about males and females, albeit in varying ways, and while gender-stereotyped distinctions may abate they are not likely to disappear.

SEE ALSO: Gender Equality; Gender Equity in Education in the United States

REFERENCES

Cuffaro, H. 1974. "Blocks." In *The Women's Action Alliance Guide to Nonsexist Early Childhood Education*, edited by B. Sprung, 49–60. New York: Women's Action Alliance.

Gilliam, W. S. 2005. *Prekindergarteners Left Behind: Expulsion Rates in State Prekindergarten Programs*, Policy Brief, Series No. 3. New York: Foundation for Child Development.

Halpern, D., et al. 2007. *Encouraging Girls in Math and Science: IES Practical Guide*. Washington, DC: National Center for Education Research, Institute of Education Sciences. US Department of Education. Accessed August 11, 2015, at http://ncer.ed.gov.

MacNaughton, G. 2000. *Rethinking Gender in Early Childhood Education*. St. Leonards: Allen and Unwin.

Rotskoff, L., and L. Lovett. 2012. *When We Were Free to Be: Looking Back at a Children's Classic and the Difference It Made*. Chapel Hill: University of North Carolina Press.

Sprung, B. 1975. *Non-Sexist Education for Young Children: A Practical Guide*. New York: Citation Press.

Sprung, B, M. Froschl, and N. Gropper. 2010. *Supporting Boys' Learning: Strategies for Teacher Practice, Pre-K-Grade 3*. New York: Teachers College Press.

Tyre, P. 2008. *The Trouble with Boys: A Surprising Report Card on Our Sons, Their Problems at School and What Parents and Educators Must Do*. New York: Crown Publishers.

Weitzman, L., D. Eifler, E. Hokada, and C. Ross. 1972. "Sex-Role Socialization in Picture Books for Preschool Children." *American Journal of Sociology*, 77: 1125–1150.

Williams, J., J. Vernon, M. Williams, and K. Malecha. 1987. Sex Role Socialization in Picture Books: An Update. Lincoln: DigitalCommons@University of Nebraska. Accessed August 11, 2015, at http://digitalcommons.unl.edu/sociologyfacpub/8.

Non-Sexist Language Use

ANN WEATHERALL
Victoria University of Wellington, New Zealand

The issue of non-sexist language arose from criticism of women's secondary social status and its manifestation in language. Feminists highlighted the various ways language is androcentric or encodes a male worldview. For example, historically grammarians have been men so they prescribed rules for language that reflected their sexist perspective. Non-sexist language is about changing the unequal ways in which language use and language structures represent women and men. One central aspect of the topic is documenting what the forms of gender bias are in language. Another is the kind of strategies implemented to correct that bias and how they are enforced. An important question is how political awareness of the issue, in terms of the salience of women's rights, impacts on the success of interventions that aim to reform language.

There is tremendous variation across languages in the ways gender is encoded. A challenge is to document gendered structures in different languages and to get agreement on what aspects are sexist. Hellinger and Bussmann (2001–2003) provide a survey of languages worldwide. Four general areas are considered for each: grammatical gender marking for nouns and adjectives; lexical gender or the ways words are used to refer differently to women and men; referential gender, for example the ways women and men are addressed in practice; and social gender or the kinds of idiomatic expressions and metaphors that reflect beliefs and attitudes about women and men.

An early and ongoing aspect of sexism in language is the use of male terms to designate human beings in general whereas female terms refer to women only. Supposed masculine generics include *man* in English and *homme* in French but are also evident across many languages in words for occupations. For example, in French *étudiants* can refer to a group of all men or a group of men and women. In contrast, the feminine form *étudiantes* refers only to an all-female group. A different but related matter is that feminine forms are marked forms of masculine words – *host/hostess, actor/actress*, or in German *Lehrer/Lehrerin* (teacher), *Student/Studentin*.

Feminist linguistic activists in English have exposed the male-centeredness of supposed generics and occupational terms by the creative coining and use of new terms such as *herstory* for history and *wimmin* or *womyn* for *women*. However, a more widespread and perhaps measured strategy has been promoting the adoption of gender-neutral terms, for example *humankind, chairperson*, and *police officer*. In some cases the use of the unmarked masculine term has been promoted – for example using *actor* to refer to both women and men.

In languages other than English, different solutions have been proposed. For example, in French a feminization rather than a neutralization strategy has been employed. In written language, feminine gender forms are used in addition to the masculine forms as a way of making women more visible in places they would have been previously hidden. The feminization strategy maintains a binary categorization of gender, which is the target of critique in queer theory. An increasing awareness of the multiplicity of genders and sexualities is reflected in a proliferation of English terms for cis-gender or within-gender reference terms, such as *boi, butch*, and *female bodied*.

The coining of new terms and the promotion of language changes may not always go as planned. A feature of naming conventions in English that has undergone feminist reform is titles preceding women's names that can vary according to whether they are married or not (Mrs. or Miss). In contrast, the equivalent title (Mr.) comes before men's names regardless of their marital status. A language planning strategy to remove the inequity of titles has been the introduction of the unmarked title "Ms." However, Ms. does not function as the intended equivalent of Mr. but as a third alternative to Miss or Mrs. Furthermore, it carries connotations of being used by marginalized women such as lesbians or divorcees.

Language change can occur from top-down processes – as a result of institutionalized guidelines, policies, or laws – or from the bottom up. Research tends to point to bottom-up or grassroots processes as more effective and engendering change. Even international bodies responsible for the elimination of inequalities between men and women on a global scale have a chequered history of non-sexist language use. Spain is an interesting case (see Bengoechea 2011). It has long campaigned for the use of neutral forms in Spanish. The changes have not received universal support, which may account for their limited success. In contrast, a grassroots practice, not even mentioned in official policy documents, that has been successful is the use of @s as an ending to represent both the masculine and feminine forms: *abogad@s* (lawyers) means both *abogados* (masc.) and *abogadas* (fem.).

The dynamism of issues concerning sexist and non-sexist language is closely tied to public political consciousness about gender. Research in this area importantly documents the close relationships between the organization of society around gender and how this is manifest in language.

SEE ALSO: Androcentrism; Discourse and Gender; Language and Gender; Sexism in Language

REFERENCES

Bengoechea, Mercedes. 2011. "Non-Sexist Spanish Policies: An Attempt Bound to Fail?" *Current Issues in Language Planning*, 12(1): 35–53.

Hellinger, Marliss, and Bussmann, Hadumod, eds. 2001–2003. *Gender Across Languages*, vols. 1–3. Amsterdam: John Benjamins.

FURTHER READING

Liddicoat, Anthony J. 2011. "Feminist Language Planning." *Current Issues in Language Planning*, 12(1): 1–7.

Pauwels, Anne. 1998. *Women Changing Language*. London: Longman.

Non-Violence

ANNE N. COSTAIN and W. DOUGLAS COSTAIN
University of Colorado, USA

Research on non-violence commonly defines non-violent practices as the "avoidance of the use of violence, especially as a principle" (Oxford University 2003). Academic literature identifies these actions as including boycotts, non-cooperation with government, public rallies, demonstrations, strikes, and dissent. All, along with other peaceful staged events, commonly fit into this category. In modern times, non-violence is most often employed by social movements advocating for major shifts in policy, regime change, empowerment of individuals, and mobilization of groups. Non-violence is important to the study of sex and gender because, globally, women more often than men prefer its use (Shapiro and Mahajan 1986; Conover and Sapiro 1993; Eichenberg 2003). In practice, this means that women engage in non-violent political activities more often than violent ones and largely avoid causes employing significant use of force. The unanswered question is whether non-violent tactics are as effective in bringing about political change.

In most nations, non-violence is linked to Mohandas Gandhi and his successful campaigns against colonial rule. Gandhi inspired liberation movements including British women's suffrage, South African anti-apartheid, and, more recently, the democracy movement in Myanmar/Burma led by Aung San Suu Kyi (Zahniser and Fry 2014). Gandhi in his writings and teachings laid out a philosophy of non-violence that continues to guide global discussions about how best to achieve social change.

Many countries interpret and apply Gandhian principles within their own cultural contexts. In the United States, Henry David Thoreau's (1983) writings of the mid-nineteenth century have strongly influenced how Gandhi's teachings have been read and acted upon. Like Thoreau, American non-violence has focused largely on the individual of conscience choosing to separate him/herself from a government that acts unjustly. In Thoreau's time, slavery and war with Mexico embodied an unjust government. In more recent times, movements challenge state injustices that range from the Occupy movement's condemnation of economic inequality to the pro-democracy protests in China's Tiananmen Square and later in Hong Kong. Each of these movements has used culturally resonant themes to mobilize the populace. Gandhi's combination of idealism and pragmatism in advocating and employing non-violence allows global application (Mantena 2012).

Examinations of women's movements across the world observe that domestic and societal violence have a chilling effect on women's willingness to use aggressive means to bring about changes in their own condition (Weldon 2002; Skrentny 2009). Sociologist William Gamson's *The Strategy of Social Protest* (1975) uses a random sample of challenging groups in the United States spanning the period from 1800 to 1945 to analyze group success in altering public policies. He concludes that movement groups employing non-violence were less likely to bring about change than ones that engaged in violence. The least successful of all movements were those that both used non-violence and endured repression. Subsequent studies have generally supported Gamson's findings (Tarrow 2011, 215–233).

In Britain, one of the most prominent suffrage groups, the Women's Social and Political Union (WSPU), engaged in violent activity to promote its cause. Although the violence was primarily directed at property (including smashing windows and throwing stones at historic buildings), it extended to physically confronting politicians and elected officials, breaking through police lines, and resisting arrest. Activists in the United States communicated regularly with the radical suffragettes in Britain, but although accused of promoting disorder, did not vandalize public buildings nor fight being sent to jail for their protests (Zahniser and Fry 2014).

The American woman suffrage movement relied heavily on non-violent tactics. With the onset of America's participation in war in 1917, however, women's organizations split over whether to support US entry into the war or oppose it. The National American Woman Suffrage Association (NAWSA) actively assisted the government's efforts to mobilize troops for the war effort. NAWSA president Dr. Anna Howard Shaw, in fact, resigned from her position to take a government position chairing the Woman's Committee of the Council of National Defense. The National Woman's Party (NWP), by contrast, intensified its efforts to confront President Wilson, challenging the legitimacy of his pursuit of war by picketing the White House. Ultimately, after being jailed, members carried out hunger strikes to protest what they saw as their unjust imprisonment.

One of the likely reasons that American suffragists pursued a non-violent path is the presence of leaders raised in – and in many cases practitioners of – the Quaker (Society of Friends) religion. By the end of the eighteenth century, Quaker women were expected to speak up at local meetings and accept local leadership positions, and by the 1820s women participated in regional quarterly and yearly meetings, although not proportionate to their numbers. Their faith taught the spiritual equality of each person before God, without racial and gender distinction. Quaker theology combines individual search for truth within one's own soul, similar to Thoreau, but guided by weekly meetings of Friends to encourage adherence to explicit practices and values (Religious Society of Friends 1999).

Recent work in international relations by Maria J. Stephan and Erica Chenoweth (2008) has questioned whether, in a global context, non-violence is less effective as a tactic than violence. They have created a data set reanalyzing this question. They come to a very different conclusion from Gamson, finding that 53 percent of non-violent groups were successful in achieving significant goals, in contrast to just 26 percent of the groups employing violence. Their studies have obvious differences in approach from Gamson's. Stephan and Chenoweth (2008, 35ff.) exclude challenges to social and/or economic structures (e.g., the US Civil Rights or European anti-immigrant movements) while including "campaigns for domestic regime change, against foreign occupations, or for secession or self-determination." By contrast, Gamson's research uses only US cases, including many movements that would be omitted from Stephan and Chenoweth's data. Differences in their findings are so significant as to warrant ongoing research on this question.

Debates continue over the ethics and effectiveness of violence versus non-violence as a tactic to drive change. Empirical studies have shown that gender differences occur along a continuum. Women as a group are rarely pacifist, nor are men consistently in favor of using force (Eichenberg 2003). Research suggests that the context in which wars are declared and fought influence the sexes differently. Women are more likely to consent to wars that the United Nations has authorized.

Women will often accept prolonged conflict to achieve humanitarian goals. By contrast, men are more supportive of wars justified on strategic and economic grounds (Brooks and Valentino 2011). Within each gender category variables such as race, class, religiosity, and education may be more influential in shaping attitudes than sex alone (Howell and Day 2000; Gidengil 2007).

Can persistent non-violent action create change? How do social, economic, gendered, and cultural contexts shape outcomes? Non-violent and violent social movements have arisen with great frequency in this century. As their experiences are shared and analyzed, the debate intensifies over which path to change is more likely to bring success.

SEE ALSO: Feminist Activism; Pacifism, Quakers, and Gender; Pacifism, Peace Activism, and Gender; Women's Movements: Early International Movements; Women's Political Representation

REFERENCES

Brooks, Deborah Jordan, and Benjamin A. Valentino. 2011. "A War of One's Own." *Public Opinion Quarterly*, 75: 270–286.

Conover, Pamela Johnston, and Virginia Sapiro. 1993. "Gender, Feminist Consciousness, and War." *American Journal of Political Science*, 37: 1079–1099.

Eichenberg, Richard C. 2003. "Gender Differences in Public Attitudes toward the Use of Force by the United States, 1990–2003." *International Security*, 28: 110–141.

Gamson, William A. 1975. *The Strategy of Social Protest*. Homewood, IL: Dorsey.

Gidengil, Elisabeth. 2007. "Beyond the Gender Gap." *Canadian Journal of Political Science*, 40: 815–831.

Howell, Susan E., and Christine L. Day. 2000. "Complexities of the Gender Gap." *Journal of Politics*, 62: 858–874.

Mantena, Karuna. 2012. "Another Realism." *American Political Science Review*, 106: 455–470.

Oxford University. 2003. "Non-Violence." Accessed August 21, 2015, at http://www.oed.com.

Religious Society of Friends. 1999. *The Old Discipline: Nineteenth-Century Friends' Disciplines in America*. Glenside: Quaker Heritage.

Shapiro, Robert Y., and Harpreet Mahajan. 1986. "Gender Differences in Policy Preferences." *Public Opinion Quarterly*, 50: 42–61.

Skrentny, John David. 2009. *The Minority Rights Revolution*. Cambridge, MA: Harvard University Press.

Stephan, Maria J., and Erica Chenoweth. 2008. "Why Civil Resistance Works." *International Security*, 33: 7–44.

Tarrow, Sidney G. 2011. *Power in Movement*. New York: Cambridge University Press.

Thoreau, Henry David. 1983. *Walden and Civil Disobedience*. New York: Penguin.

Weldon, S. Laurel. 2002. *Protest, Policy, and the Problem of Violence against Women*. Pittsburgh: University of Pittsburgh Press.

Zahniser, J. D., and Amelia R. Fry. 2014. *Alice Paul*. New York: Oxford University Press.

FURTHER READING

Brooks, Deborah J., and Benjamin A. Valentino. 2011. "A War of One's Own: Understanding the Gender Gap in Support for War." *Public Opinion Quarterly*, 75: 270–286.

DuBois, Ellen C. 1999. *Feminism and Suffrage: The Emergence of an Independent Women's Movement in America, 1848–1869*. Ithaca, NY: Cornell University Press.

Mantena, Karuna. 2012. "Another Realism: The Politics of Gandhian Nonviolence." *American Political Science Review*, 106: 455–470.

Normalization

STEPHEN VALOCCHI
Trinity College, Hartford, USA

Normalization was first used by Michel Foucault to refer to the changing nature of power and subjectivity in modern societies (Foucault 1990, 1991). The growth of the nation-state, the development of science, and the rise of the factory system led to a new and more efficient way of controlling populations. Modern societies entailed greater attention to the challenges of population growth, migration, fertility, public health, and large-scale labor systems. Rather than regulate these problems on an individual basis through prohibition, censorship, and punitive law, Foucault asserts that society shifted its form of social control from one based on a juridico-political discourse to one based on norms. This normative form of control, however, is more thoroughgoing and pervasive than the standard sociological concept of norms. Foucault's concept of normalization requires an epistemological shift from the idea of the social self as partly autonomous from the forces that shape and control it (i.e., institutions and the norms embedded in those institutions) to the social subject whose very existence is due to the operation of norms (i.e., discursive forces that are both external and internal to the individual). Norms are not imposed on but are constitutive of the self. These norms operate to both produce and regulate the subject and these two dynamics are inseparable from one another. The process of normalization then is done by the constitution of persons who reiterate norms in order to become knowing and knowable, recognized and recognizable to others. In this way, the work of social control is accomplished.

Foucault's treatment of sexuality figures centrally in the dynamics of normalization. Foucault's *History of Sexuality, Volume 1* (1990) not only traces the shift in the nature of prohibition from acts to persons but also demonstrates how this shift created a thoroughgoing system of classification which turned sexuality into a mechanism of power. The psyche and the body become the site of social control. Social control is not accomplished through the operation of some external force which constrains individuals' sexual behaviors and thoughts. In this way, one's subjectivity is partly constituted through sexual regimes of the normal/abnormal. Of course, social institutions are not absent in this theory of normalization. Foucault's reference to institutions is embedded in the language of discourse. Specifically, he references the Christian pastoral of the seventeenth century and its incitement to discourse through confession (Foucault 1990) to illustrate the psychic implantation of the normal. Others (Dreger 1998) have noted that this religious discourse was "taken up" by and partially transformed with the rise of science and the medical profession in the nineteenth century so as to attach a therapeutic language to normalization. Finally, the state uses these classification systems in the twentieth century (Canaday 2009) to install the language of normalization into legal codes and political practices. Although sociologists frequently foreground the rules, roles, and resources of institutions that enable these classificatory systems, Foucault chooses to focus on the discourses or systems of knowledge that circulate from these institutions. These systems of knowledge constructed by institutions are more important than the legal prohibitions of these institutions since these systems construct the normal, the natural, the orderly, and the healthy, and thus make the legal prohibitions the social control "of last resort." Foucault describes sexuality as a "transfer point for relations of power" deployed to control "children, women, perverts, and populations." Individuals embody the norms developed in these knowledge systems and monitor themselves in an effort to conform to these norms.

Normalization is also important in understanding gender and the imbrication of the gender binary with the associated binaries of anatomical sex (male/female) and sexuality (heterosexuality/homosexuality). In *Gender Trouble* (Butler 1990) and elsewhere (Butler 1991, 1993), Judith Butler builds on and extends Foucault's focus on normalization by demonstrating how the discourses produced by science, medicine, family, school, and the state simultaneously inscribe norms regarding heterosexuality and male/female gender differences. Butler says the gendered self is constituted though the heterosexual family idiom implemented by the medical profession which assigns gender to bodies based on assumptions regarding "normal looking" and normative (i.e., assumptions regarding heterosexual penetration) penises, vaginas, and clitorises. We then "come into being" through gender enacted through the reiteration and repetition of norms. This involves the citation of a set of "oughts" and "ought nots" that we take on in order to make sense of ourselves and to be readable to others. This is what Butler means by gender performativity. Normalization then is experienced not as coercive but as a somewhat insidious method of becoming human. In this context, normalization is fraught with dangers and risks since these ideals of heterosexuality and gender difference can never be fully realized; they are in a sense "copies of copies." Thus, they come into existence through an anxious process of impersonation and approximation. Similar to Foucault's discussion of sexuality as a normalizing regime, gender also works in similar ways whereby the normal becomes inscribed as the normative, and classification systems develop to accomplish that shift and thus serve as an implicit regulatory mechanism.

Changing relations of power and the use of normalization as a technique of power are also central concerns of Foucault in his genealogy of the prison, *Discipline and Punish* (1991). For Foucault, the development of the modern prison or penitentiary embodies as well as signals a profound shift in the nature of power beginning in the eighteenth century. In the penitentiary the body is "arranged, regulated, and supervised rather than tortured." Similar to sexuality, these changes in the nature of punishment in prisons emerge as more "efficient" responses to the many developments in mass society. For example, the monitoring, measuring, evaluating, and classifying used by medicine in creating sexual subjectivities are also used in many other institutional arenas: the army, the hospital, the asylum, the school, the office. The development of "idealized norms of conduct" within each of these areas enables the establishment of the standard and the deviations from that standard. The effects of the nearly constant observation and imposition of the proper rules of conduct are not only the desire to belong but also the associated desire to discipline oneself to ensure that belonging. Thus, the school examination, scientific management techniques in factories, and bureaucratic procedures in the office work to produce the normal citizen just as the act of confession and the medical examination work to produce the normal sexual subject. Again, constraint is not external to the individual but is tied into the exercise of freedom in the liberal state. In some sense, normalization is the "dark vision" of modernity. Normalization enables individuals to be "free" to assume from the state the burden of some of its regulatory functions and we, in turn, impose those regulations on ourselves of our own accord.

SEE ALSO: Gender Difference Research; Queer Theory; Sexualities

REFERENCES

Butler, Judith. 1990. *Gender Trouble: Feminism and the Subversion of Identity*. New York: Routledge.

Butler, Judith. 1991. "Imitation and Gender Insubordination." In *Inside/Out: Lesbian Theories, Gay Theories*, edited by Diane Fuss, 13–32. New York: Routledge.

Butler, Judith. 1993. "Critically Queer." *GLQ* 1: 17–32.

Canaday, Margot. 2009. *The Straight State: Sexuality and Citizenship in Twentieth Century America*. Princeton: Princeton University Press.

Dreger, Alice Domurat. 1998. *Hermaphrodites and the Medical Invention of Sex.* Cambridge, MA: Harvard University Press.

Foucault, Michel. 1990. *The History of Sexuality. Volume 1: An Introduction.* New York: Vintage Books.

Foucault, Michel. 1991. *Discipline and Punish: The Birth of the Prison.* New York: Vintage Books.

Nuns, including Taiwan Buddhist

HWEI-SYIN LU

Tzu Chi University, Hualien City, Taiwan

A Buddhist nun connotes a woman who renounces marriage and family, receives formal ordination, and leads a celibate religious life. She follows Vinaya rules set out by the Buddha, pursues enlightenment, and liberation from the cycle of existence. Nuns take residence in sanghas which may include monks or be unisex. The appearance of nuns differs from other women in that their heads are shaved and they wear robes as monks do, and as such are deprived of femininity. Buddhist nunneries accord women a spiritual and residential refuge which frees them from domestic and male bondage. Nuns have prevailed in Theravada, Mahayana and Tibetan Buddhism in Asia. Nowadays, the number of Western women who are attracted to Buddhism and become nuns is increasing.

According to the Buddhist ideal, women and men have equal potential for enlightenment and gender distinction is but a matter of illusion. Nevertheless, nuns in most Asian countries fare worse than monks because of religious, historical, and social factors. In the history of Buddhism, female renunciants encountered discrimination in their social image, education, precepts, monastic status, and ordination. Today, monks still outnumber and outrank nuns in most Buddhist areas. Nuns have not received equal opportunities for monastic leadership and doctrinal studies until recent decades when equal rights for women became an activist issue.

Gender distinction in Buddhist clergies traces back to the early age of Buddhism. The first nun was Mahaprajapati, maternal aunt and foster mother of Sakyamuni, the Buddha. She asked three times before the Buddha permitted women to enter the sangha. He prescribed for them to follow Eight Rules of Respect, which institutionally subordinated nuns to monks:

1. A nun, even though a hundred years old, must pay respect to a newly ordained monk and offer a seat to him.
2. A nun must never scold or admonish a monk.
3. A nun must never accuse or speak of a monk's misdeeds.
4. A nun obtains reception into the order at a monk's hands.
5. A nun confesses sin before the assembly of monks and nuns.
6. A nun must ask the fraternity for a monk as preceptor.
7. A nun must never share the same resort with monks.
8. After the summer retreat, a nun must report and ask for a responsible confessor before both orders.

The Eight Rules were established in ancient Indian society where women were subordinate to men. Considering the social milieu, the Buddha assigned monks to guide nuns' learning and activities. As for respective rules of housing and communications, the Buddha might have intended to prevent sexual temptation among monks and nuns. In the earliest scriptures, women were often depicted as immoral, lustful, and thus dangerous in distracting monks from their duties. There were repeated warnings in sutras and prophetic statements, claiming that women's admission to the order would shorten the life of the Dharma. In addition, women were seen as weaker than men at physical, emotional, and intellectual levels and thus incurred bad karmas, which hindered them from attaining Buddhahood. Unless reborn as a man, a woman's enlightenment was rarely fulfilled, a view widespread in Theravada Buddhism (i.e., Small Vehicle school which aims for self-salvation). Only in Mahayana Buddhism (i.e., Great Vehicle school which helps humanity in self-cultivation to become a Bodhisattva and finally a Buddha), could women reach Buddhahood without transforming genders.

According to the Vinaya precepts of monastic rules, a woman has to receive dual ordination to become a nun. She is called in Pali, Sanskrit, and Chinese, respectively, *bhikkhunī*, *bhiksunī*, and *bǐqiūní*. Dual ordination is bestowed first by 10 fully ordained nuns and then by 10 fully ordained monks. Nuns alone are not eligible to give full ordination. Monks carry out a higher ordination because they are considered advanced in knowledge and spiritual practice. Full ordination may last for a month for the novice to learn precepts. It may take several years of training before a novice receives ordination, including learning chanting, disciplines, scriptures, and duties in the order. The novice is first shaved and becomes a samaneri which is the preliminary stage of nunhood.

Today, full ordination is available only in Mahayana Buddhist areas such as Taiwan, China, Korea, and Vietnam. In South Asia, although the nun sangha system originated in India, it disappeared after the thirteenth century with the demise of Buddhism there. Despite the fact that a group of Sri Lankan nuns in the fifth century had brought the nun system to China, the Sri Lankan nun lineages became extinct at the end of the tenth century. In Tibetan Buddhist areas, formal nuns' ordination has also ceased for centuries. In Sri Lanka, Thailand, and Burma at present, women are not allowed to go beyond the status of samaneri. They are regarded simply as Buddhist practitioners called "ten-precept mothers." Shaved and wearing garments with different colors and styles from monks, they receive fewer alms and monetary donations than monks. People think offering to nuns accumulates less merit.

Since the time of early Buddhism, nuns do not acquire the same status as monks even after full ordination. According to the books of rules of discipline for monastics, nuns have been required to observe up to 500 precepts, twice that of monks' 250. Some precepts are considered trivial and not enforced, yet rules for a nun passing down the ages are virtually intact and may even get stricter. In Chinese Buddhism, to be a monastic is likened "to become a heroic man (*dà zhàngfū*)." Chinese nuns identify themselves with that description and dismiss the meek gender identities of the past. In monasteries where monks and nuns co-reside, monks usually take the lead in preaching, teaching, and management. Monks can ordain and recruit disciples of both sexes, but nuns are not allowed to ordain monks. While monks can revert to lay life and receive repeated ordination up to seven times, nuns are only permitted one ordination. Social contempt of nuns returning to secular life is prevalent. They are disparaged as being defective in following the precepts.

In monastic communities where the power is in the hands of monks, nuns keep a low profile. The routine activities of nuns resemble those of monks; chanting sutras in morning and evening lessons, meditation, confessions, and retreating at least once for three months in summer for self-cultivation. Nevertheless, nuns are additionally charged with taking care of the livelihood of the monastic community. Through preaching and giving spiritual guidance, monks have privileged access to education and financial support from lay followers. Nuns, generally being less educated, lack such access and opportunities and they support themselves by performing penitential rituals on request by devotees who want to avert misfortunes and ameliorate the sufferings of their deceased family members.

Economic factors have a significant influence on whether women dedicate themselves to spiritual realization. For instance, in Thailand, a woman takes vows to become a samaneri for some period of time if her certain wish is fulfilled, such as recovery from an illness or respite from some personal difficulties. Yet she cannot afford to stay in robes for long because the educational and material resources to sustain her are slim. Rather, she would support a male sangha and nurture a son to become a monk.

Gender stereotyping dominates historical accounts of nuns. In dynastic chronicles of China, nuns were often depicted as "old nuns," implying infirmity and decline. It was largely due to the fact that Confucianism limited women's roles and duties in the patriarchal family. A woman renouncing marriage and family was generally considered selfish, unfilial, and a failure. In popular literature, nuns were often caricatured as unattractive or being traumatized by problems of love and marriage. Classified as "escapers" from and thus a threat to society, they were often accused of troublemaking and being meddlesome in eliciting alms and enticing illicit affairs.

Biographies of Chinese nuns were few and sketchy. Some nuns were cast in positive terms: intelligent, ascetic, scrupulous in observing monastic rules, proficient in scriptures and meditation. They were known for their expertise in sutra exposition and eloquence in discussing the Dharma with the elites. They preached in front of royalty and were highly respected among the gentry.

They were socially active in promulgating Buddhist ideas. In historical records, a nun had even been commissioned to be a high-ranking official in charge of Buddhist affairs. Given the rich life stories of countless nuns, there was only one compilation extant prior to the twentieth century, a book published in the sixth century. By comparison, there have been many collections of biographies of eminent monks.

Despite discrimination within Buddhist monasteries and in the wider society, many women have sought autonomy and comfort by becoming nuns. Nunneries have provided women with protection, particularly attracting the disempowered such as widows or the poor. Monasteries have been a final shelter for women resisting marriage and the patriarchal family system.

In Buddhist areas, nunneries vary: there are celibate women who simply gather to live in vegetarian halls; others may ordain themselves and observe a subset of precepts. Many nuns are patronized by their natal families. In China, it has been common since the fifth century for parents to send their daughters to nunneries. They entrusted their children to nuns for the mundane purpose of reducing the family's economic burden, or hoping for a better fate for their daughter's future. In the families of traditional Chinese gentry, a woman who chose to renounce the worldly life after her husband died was considered chaste. She could receive an honor from the court whose mandate was to uphold Confucian virtues.

Nuns in contemporary societies have rather different roles than those of traditional nuns in respect of the motivation, goals, and avenue of spiritual cultivation. Where Mahayana Buddhism prospers in areas like Taiwan, Korea, and Vietnam, nuns are proactive to unprecedented degrees. Rather than seeking refuge in Buddhist temples as most of their traditional counterparts did, they take the vow as a career choice, provide social services, and promote Buddhist thought.

Buddhist nuns in Taiwan provide remarkable examples. The first ordination of nuns was introduced by refugee monks from mainland China in 1953. By the end of the twentieth century more than 12,000 nuns had received full ordination. They made up 75 percent of the total ordained monastics on the island. It is estimated that there are more than 15,000 nuns who are active in Taiwan. Their ratio to monks is four to one or even higher. For the first time in Chinese history, nuns have greatly outnumbered monks. Many Taiwanese nuns use mass media to impart knowledge of Buddhism to society and set personal examples of cultivation on a par with monks. Many have earned overseas doctoral degrees and teach in universities and Buddhist institutions. With academic and business experience before renunciation, they write articles, carry out research, edit magazines, and produce radio and television programs. They employ modern business techniques in running the temples. Several large organizations for humanistic Buddhism (*rénjiān fójiào*) are mainly managed by nuns. For example, nuns of the Buddhist sangha Fo Guang Shan have taken on the bulk of the work in establishing overseas temples and educational institutions.

Numerous nuns dedicate themselves to purifying the society and improving the welfare of humankind by means of philanthropy, education, and culture. Among them, Dharma Master Cheng Yen (*Shì Zhèngyán*) is arguably the most famous. She founded the Merit Association of Compassion Relief in 1966 when she was in her late twenties. The Association and later the Buddhist Compassion Relief Tzu Chi Foundation (Tzu Chi, *Ciji*) have since extended their services to cover medical care, international relief, education, community services, environmental protection, and mass communication. Tzu Chi owns a television station whose programs are broadcast worldwide. Considered to be the most influential Buddhist community in Taiwan, Tzu Chi has established branches in 50 countries and recruited volunteers of different ethnicities and religions. Cheng Yen has been hailed as "Mother Teresa of Taiwan" and has won many international honors (e.g., one of the Time 100 for 2011). She continues to lead her nun sangha and the Tzu Chi organizations which retain over 100,000 commissioned lay followers, both women and men volunteers.

Another noted Taiwanese nun is Dharma Master Hiu-Wan (Hsiao Yun, *Shì Xiǎoyún*), an artist and educator, who established a monastic training center for nuns. At the age of 76 she founded the Hua Fan University. Dharma Master Chao Hui (*Shì Zhàohuì*), a well-known feminist nun and professor at the Hsuan Chuang University, has openly challenged structural gender inequalities of Buddhism. In 2001, during the opening ceremony of a conference that celebrated the 97th birthday of Dharma Master Yin Shun, a monk esteemed to be "the tutorial master of Humanistic Buddhism," she declared her wish to abolish the Eight Rules of Respect as they were an epitome of gender discrimination. Together with seven other monks, nuns, lay men, and lay women, she read aloud the Rules written on posters and tore them up. This symbolic action ignited a storm of controversy. Although leading monastics like Yin Shun acknowledged the incongruity of the Rules in modern times, they thought that obliterating them should be approved by the grand council of monastic communities of Taiwan. Many nuns also regarded Chao Hui's overt act as unnecessary, given that the nun orders were already strong and flourishing, that the degree of gender equality was already high in Taiwan, and that the Eight Rules had not been universally observed.

Taiwanese nuns' achievements can be ascribed to their high educational backgrounds, economic independence, business competence, and consciousness-raising of self-reliance. Democratic theory and praxis of equity in Taiwanese society also bear on the blooming of Buddhist communities, which are conducive to personal fulfillment through spiritual realization. Notably, Taiwanese nuns have successfully propagated Buddhism by drawing upon their feminine nature – compassion, nurturing, gentleness, and endurance. Femininity is denied once they become monastics, but it implicitly advantages them to conduct religious performances in correspondence with Buddhist virtues, in particular, the Bodhisattva's spirit in the Mahayana Buddhism. The popular Bodhisattva Guanyin (the goddess of mercy) in the Chinese belief system has set a glorious model for the Mahayana nuns.

As Buddhism spreads in the West, its beliefs and practices have been modified to accommodate prevailing Western values – individuality, social justice, and happiness in this life. Feminist nuns scrutinize sexist tenets and interpretations of Buddhist texts and canons. Intellectual growth and the rise of women's consciousness inspire nuns to work for the betterment of women's status and welfare. Buddhist women including nuns have taken the lead in establishing centers of training and education, shelters for refugee relief, healthcare centers, and counseling services. All such efforts have dramatically benefited women, especially those in developing countries. In this progressive vein, nuns are acquiring new social roles, finding resources and establishing strongholds to empower themselves.

International coalitions among Buddhist nuns and lay women have been formed in recent decades. A notable case is Sakyadhita (daughters of the Buddha), the International Association of Buddhist Women, which was organized in 1987 in India by American nun scholars Ayya Khema and Karma Lekshe Tsomo, and Thai scholar Chatsumarn Kabilsingh. It is a forum for Buddhist women to exchange views on ways to educate women as Buddhist teachers and to restore Buddhist nun sanghas in Theravada Buddhist countries. It holds biennial international conferences in Asia. The conferences highlight Buddhist cultural expressions and concerns pertaining to the personal lives and social actions of nuns. Members of Sakyadhita include lay and ordained Buddhists of any gender or age. The sharing of experiences encourages women to achieve spiritual enlightenment on equal terms with men, and in so doing revitalizes Buddhism in the world.

Networking influences the lives and identities of Buddhist nuns today. Multiple voices and practices of Buddhist cultivation have emerged while mutual support among nuns and Buddhist women in the East and the West has grown. Many female renunciants in Theravada and Tibetan Buddhist areas have gone to Taiwan, Korea, Hong Kong, and Vietnam to receive full ordination. Nevertheless, their new identities acquired abroad may not be accepted by monasteries in their native countries. For example, in Sri Lanka Theravada Buddhism is taken as the most authentic whereas Mahayana Buddhism is thought to be deficient in spiritual enlightenment and too this-worldly. As this purist stance is maintained even among women in Sri Lanka, nuns who lead the few indigenous educational centers for Buddhist women are still struggling to attain the goal of re-establishing the order of nuns in Theravada tradition.

In Western countries such as the United States, Buddhist nuns are growing in number. Mostly being adult converts, they are less concerned with issues of ordination than spiritual practice and interpersonal relationships. Intellectuals and activists among them integrate Buddhist cultivation with sociopolitical engagements such as seeking to ban nuclear power and protect ecological systems from climate change disasters. Whether new practices involving matrixes of secular affairs could ultimately liberate Buddhist nuns remains to be seen.

SEE ALSO: Buddhism; Feminist Theology

FURTHER READING

Cheng, Wei-Yi. 2007. *Buddhist Nuns in Taiwan and Sri Lanka: A Critique of the Feminist Perspective.* London: Routledge.

DeVido, Elise A. 2010. *Taiwan's Buddhist Nuns.* Albany: SUNY Press.

Gross, Rita M. 1993. *Buddhism After Patriarchy: A Feminist History, Analysis, and Reconstruction of Buddhism.* Albany: SUNY Press.

Horner, I.B. 1930. *Women Under Primitive Buddhism.* Motilal Banarsidass, Delhi.

Paul, Diana. 1979. *Women in Buddhism.* Berkeley: Asian Humanities Press.

Tsomo, Karma L., ed. 2000. *Buddhist Women Across Cultures: Realizations.* Delhi: Sri Satguru.

Yu, Chun-fang. 2013. *Passing the Light: The Incense Light Community and Buddhist Nuns in Contemporary Taiwan.* Honolulu: University of Hawai'i Press.

Obscenity Laws in the United States, Canada, and Europe

KEVIN W. SAUNDERS
Michigan State University, USA

Censorship is the suppression of expression through a prepublication prohibition or the threat of a postpublication punishment. When governments engage in censorship, they may be motivated by a number of reasons. A government may try to protect itself by placing limits on political dissent, an approach inconsistent with the democratic principle of freedom of expression. Alternatively, even democratic governments may try to limit expression as a way of furthering societal morality. Laws that seek to impose such morality-based limits are generally classified as obscenity laws.

Obscenity is not simply sexual content. All material with sexual content, of a somewhat explicit variety, may properly be labeled as pornography. However, not all pornography is legally defined as obscene. Finding material to be obscene is a legal conclusion that allows the material to be suppressed. In US law, since *Swearingen v. United States* (1896), obscenity has focused on sexual depiction, but it was a broader concept in earlier US law and remains so in some countries.

In the United States, expression is protected by the strong, seemingly absolute, language of the First Amendment to the Constitution: "Congress shall make no law … abridging the freedom of speech, or of the press." The First Amendment applies to more than just Congress and reaches all Acts of the federal government. The amendment also applies to the states, through the Due Process Clause of the 14th Amendment.

Despite the language of the First Amendment, the US Supreme Court, in *Roth v. United States* (1957), recognized an exception to the First Amendment that leaves obscene materials unprotected. The Court did not view itself as creating a new exception but as recognizing an exception that had existed from the colonial era, through the era of the Constitution and Bill of Rights, to the present. Such material was seen as having "no essential part of any exposition of ideas" with any slight social value outweighed by a societal interest in order and morality. As a result of this ruling, the sale and distribution of obscene materials could be subject to criminal sanction. In *Paris Adult Theatre I v. Slaton* (1973), bans on showing obscene films to consenting adults were also upheld. In contrast, in *Stanley v. Georgia* (1969), the

Court concluded that possession of obscene materials in one's own home enjoyed the protection of the First Amendment.

After a series of attempts, the Court set out the current test for obscenity in *Miller v. California* (1973), with some later minor modification. The test asks "(a) whether 'the average person, applying contemporary community standards' would find that the work, taken as a whole, appeals to the prurient interest; (b) whether the work depicts or describes, in a patently offensive way, sexual conduct specifically defined by the applicable state law; and (c) whether the work, taken as a whole, lacks serious literary, artistic, political, or scientific value."

The strong protection the First Amendment provides for expression, and the narrow definition of obscenity, have required the Court to modify the test and to add an additional, related, exception. In *Mishkin v. New York* (1966), the Court had to consider a publication intended to appeal to sadomasochists. The defense argued that the material at issue did not meet what was then the test for obscenity, because it did not appeal to average prurient interests. The Court refused to accept the defense, saying that, when material is marketed or distributed to a particular audience with different sexual interests, it will be judged by the prurient interest of that group.

A similar modification was required in a later case involving the sale of "girlie" magazines to a minor. The magazines would not have been obscene for an adult audience. In *Ginsberg v. New York* (1968), the Court held that when materials are sold to juveniles, the standard will be the more easily appealed to the prurient interest of juveniles. In a still later case, *New York v. Ferber* (1982), the Court created a new, related, exception for materials depicting sexual acts, or photographs of a sexual nature, involving children. Such materials may be banned, even if they fail to be obscene under the *Miller* test, and in the sense of "legally proscribable" are obscene nonetheless.

The United Kingdom's statute addressing obscenity, the Obscene Publications Act of 1964, is broader than the *Miller* definition. Material is obscene in the United Kingdom "if its effect ... is, if taken as a whole, such as to tend to deprave and corrupt persons who are likely, having regard to all relevant circumstances, to read, see or hear the matter contained or embodied in it." It may not need sexual explicitness or an appeal to the prurient interest to come within the scope of the statute.

This more expansive definition allowed the prosecution of *The Little Red Schoolbook*, a work lacking explicit sexuality but discussing sexual activity and drugs and intended for a youthful audience. The UK court said that the book's mix of "one-sided opinion" and fact in what claimed to be a reference book would "tend to undermine, for a very considerable proportion of children, many of the influences, such as those of parents, the Churches and youth organizations, which might otherwise provide the restraint and sense of responsibility for oneself which found inadequate expression in the book." Furthermore, the court concluded that the book was "inimical to good teacher/child relationships" and was subversive not only to authority generally, but to the influence of and trust between children and teachers.

The concerns expressed clearly went beyond the exposure to sexual images and were based on a far broader tendency to corrupt. For example, the book seemed to approve of the use of marijuana and of sexual activity. The court noted that there was no mention of the illegality of such drug use or underage sex. While the book itself was not pornographic, it suggested that the use of pornography might give the reader ideas regarding acts that might prove enjoyable.

This, too, was objectionable without being pornographic.

It seems clear that the UK statute was applied based on the ideas conveyed. The UK court expressed concern that the book would undermine, for many of its young readers, the influences that lead to a well-adjusted and law-abiding child or adult. Such positive influences, those that might provide moral strength and a sense of responsibility for one's actions, were seen as lacking in the book.

The European Court of Human Rights, in *Handyside v. United Kingdom* (1979–1980), held the book's suppression to be consistent with the European Convention on Human Rights. The European Convention, in Article 10(1), protects the freedom of expression: "Everyone has the right to freedom of expression. This right shall include freedom to hold opinions and to receive and impart information and ideas without interference by public authority and regardless of frontiers." However, section 2 of the same Article provides: "The exercise of these freedoms, since it carries with it duties and responsibilities, may be subject to such formalities, conditions, restrictions or penalties as are prescribed by law and are necessary in a democratic society … for the protection of health or morals."

This more general exception addresses more than that which would be seen as obscene under US law; it allows protection for morality in general. The action in *Handyside* was motivated, essentially, by the perceived corrupting impact of the ideas presented in the book, rather than an explicit sexuality appealing to the prurient interest. This would be completely inconsistent with the view in the United States, where the Supreme Court held, in *Kingsley International Pictures Corp. v. New York* (1959), that obscenity cannot be based on the ideas conveyed but only on the explicitness and offensiveness of the sexuality.

Returning to the *Miller* test, the test employs community standards with regard to the prurient interest and to offensiveness. In contrast, *Pope v. Illinois* (1987) held that the standard for "serious value" should be of a "reasonable person," rather than being tied to a particular community's standards. With regard to community standards for prurience and offensiveness, the Court explained that it was not reasonable to require the people of Maine or Mississippi to accept what was acceptable in Las Vegas or New York City. That, of course, has led to material being obscene in some areas and not in others. The European Court has also recognized differences from country to country, with no single unified concept of obscenity or standard of morality. The *Handyside* case stated that member states are due a "margin of appreciation" in the application of laws intended to protect morality that will lead to differences from country to country.

These locality-based approaches work reasonably well when applied to the sale of magazines and films, where the dealer could be expected to understand the community standard or national – in the case of Europe – norm. The Internet has, however, raised problems regarding the application of community values, because material that is posted to the Internet is available everywhere. In the United States, there is a split among the courts, with some allowing prosecutions to be based on local standards where the material was accessed and others applying a national test based on the Internet community. Europe would seem required also to consider the issue in applying the margin of appreciation.

The serious value aspect of the *Miller* test serves to protect material that might have an appeal to the prurient interest and might be found patently offensive but, nonetheless, has serious value. This factor is not based on community standards but rather on the reasonable person. The savings clause would allow the display of, for example, the homoerotic work of the acclaimed photographer Robert Mapplethorpe, despite the morality concerns of a local population. It has, historically, also protected works of literature from those who would ban erotic literary work.

However, there are countries in which serious value does not necessarily protect a publication. In a Japanese case, *Expression (The Lady Chatterley's Lover Decision)*, a prosecution based on D.H. Lawrence's book, *Lady Chatterley's Lover*, the Court said that artistry and obscenity have different dimensions and can exist side by side; even high artistic merit may not dissipate the work's obscene nature.

There have been attempts to treat other sorts of depictions as obscene or, at least, to treat them in the same way that obscene materials are treated. In the 1980s, the feminists Catherine MacKinnon and Andrea Dworkin inspired a number of ordinances and statutes aimed at what they called "pornography." As the material they addressed had sexual content, it is properly labeled as pornographic, but because they were seeking a ban, the argument was really that it should be considered obscene. Their approach was to ban material depicting sexually explicit subordination of women. It required not just sexual explicitness but the degradation of its characters. An Indianapolis ordinance of this nature was struck down as unconstitutional in *American Booksellers Association v. Hudnut* (1985). Basing prosecution on the work's message was seen as a violation of First Amendment protection.

In contrast, Canada enacted a similar ordinance that was, in *Regina v. Butler* (1992), found not to violate the Canadian Charter of Rights and Freedoms. The Charter guarantees free expression in Article 2: "Everyone has the following fundamental freedoms: ... (b) freedom of thought, belief, opinion and expression, including freedom of the press and other media of communication." But, Article 1 provides "The *Canadian Charter of Rights and Freedoms* guarantees the rights and freedoms set out in it subject only to such reasonable limits prescribed by law as can be demonstrably justified in a free and democratic society." As with the European Convention, there is an invitation to balance expression against other concerns and values. Taking up this invitation, the Canadian Court balanced the values behind freedom of expression with the harm thought to be done. The Court saw the material as being far removed from the core of the guarantee of free expression, while the avoidance of harm and furtherance of respect were held to be of fundamental importance.

The Canadian experience also demonstrates an issue that may arise in applying this sort of statute based on degradation. In the case *Little Sisters Book & Art Emporium v. Canada* (2000), Little Sisters, a gay and lesbian bookstore, sued Canadian Customs over the impoundment of its materials, while heterosexual erotica, and even the same material imported to more mainstream bookstores, was allowed entry. It appears that heterosexual customs officials had difficulty in distinguishing gay and lesbian material from degrading or dehumanizing material.

More recent attempts to limit expression have involved children and violent video games. A number of state and local governments have tried to limit the sale, rental, or arcade play of these games by children. Some rested on an argument that such play was sufficiently harmful to override the protections of the First Amendment. Others argued that *Ginsberg* and its "obscenity as to children" analysis should apply to violent materials as well as to sexual matter. The Supreme Court rejected these attempts in *Brown v. Entertainment Merchants Association* (2011). The result has been to shield children from sexual material, without real evidence of negative impact, while allowing them access to violent material, despite evidence of negative impact. Given the broader exceptions to the protection granted for freedom of expression in the European Convention and in the constitutions of many countries, most other countries have been able to provide this shielding of children.

SEE ALSO: Media and Gender Socialization; Pornography, Feminist Legal and Political Debates on

REFERENCES

American Booksellers Association v. Hudnut, 771 F.2d 323 (7th Cir.), 1985.
Brown v. Entertainment Merchants Association, 131 S.Ct. 2729, 2011.
Expression (The Lady Chatterley's Lover Decision), Hanreishu, XI, No. 3, 997 (Criminal).
Ginsberg v. New York, 390 U.S. 629, 1968.
Handyside v. United Kingdom, 1 E.H.R.R. 737, 1979–1980.
Kingsley International Pictures Corp. v. New York, 360 U.S. 684, 1959.
Little Sisters Book & Art Emporium v. Canada, 2000 S.C.C. 69, 2000.
Miller v. California, 413 U.S. 15, 1973.
Mishkin v. New York, 383 U.S. 502, 1966.
New York v. Ferber, 458 U.S. 747, 1982.
Paris Adult Theatre I v. Slaton, 413 U.S. 49, 1973.
Pope v. Illinois, 481 U.S. 497, 1987.
Regina v. Butler, 89 D.L.R. 4th 449, 1992.
Roth v. United States, 354 U.S. 476, 1957.
Stanley v. Georgia, 394 U.S. 557, 1969.
Swearingen v. United States, 161 U.S. 446, 1896.

FURTHER READING

Clor, Harry M. 1985. *Obscenity and Public Morality: Censorship in a Liberal Society*. Chicago: University of Chicago Press.
De Grazia, Edward. 1993. *Girls Lean Back Everywhere: The Law of Obscenity and the Assault on Genius*. New York: Vintage.
Saunders, Kevin W. 1996. *Violence as Obscenity: Limiting the Media's First Amendment Protection*. Durham, NC: Duke University Press.
Schauer, Frederick F. 1976. *The Law of Obscenity*. Arlington: Bureau of National Affairs.

Occupational Health and Safety

HIROAKI MATSUURA
University of Oxford, UK

The proportion of women in the workforce has increased dramatically over the last 40 years. Today, women make up about 39.5 percent of estimated global employment, making them indispensable contributors to the world economy (ILO 2014). This increasing trend raises a wide variety of public health questions on the different effects of occupational exposure on men and women, including (1) the impact of choosing physically demanding work and longer working hours, especially when women are often not exempted from the traditional domestic and family duties in households, (2) the heterogeneous health effects of the same chemical, physical, and psychological hazards in the workplace on gender, and (3) the impact of such hazards on reproductive outcomes. Globally, occupational risk factors accounted for 102,250 deaths and 1.3 percent of global disability adjusted life years (DALYs) among women, compared to 749,857 deaths and 3.5 percent of global DALYs among men in 2010 (Lim et al. 2013). Worldwide, women still represent a small fraction of the total burden of disease due to occupational risk factors.

In many situations, working and employment conditions may differ by sex. Due to the persistent ideology of the sexual division of labor, domestic chores and childcare are typically assigned to women and working women are not exempted from these expectations. This division of labor explains much of the gender differences in occupational choice, the time spent in the labor market, and other working conditions. The pattern of women's employment is very different from country to country. In sub-Saharan Africa where formal sector employment is limited for women, many women are engaged in agricultural production, domestic labor, and informal sector activities. This type of work environment increases women's exposure to household air pollution, toxic wastes, organic dusts from food processing, and other occupational and environmental risk factors (Howson and Institute of Medicine's Committee to Study Female Morbidity and Mortality in Sub-Saharan Africa 1996). In the European Union and the United States where women are mostly engaged in formal employment, women are less likely to engage in sectors such as construction, mining, and agriculture and fishery where workers are more exposed to noise, environmental hazards, and work-related injuries. They are more likely to engage in health and education-related sectors where workers are more exposed to psychological hazards in the workplace. Moreover, employed women typically have less job security, lower control of their working environment, worse contractual working conditions, and lower job status, but experience less exposure to physically demanding work, while receiving higher social support and lower levels of effort–reward imbalance than men do (Campos-Serna et al. 2013). Furthermore, there are other issues attributed to the gender difference in working and employment conditions. Some of these examples are sex discrimination, sexual harassment, and unequal wages for equal work in the workplace, which exist within the scope of traditional anti-discrimination and labor laws rather than occupational health and safety laws.

There is a growing concern that the health effects from the same occupational exposure may differ for men and women. Most epidemiological research have either ignored or merely controlled for gender. The limited numbers of studies have investigated the heterogeneous effect of the same chemical, physical, and psychological hazards by gender in the workplace. Most of these studies focus on specific occupations and industries and suggest that females are at a higher risk than males for work-related injuries, particularly those with musculoskeletal symptoms (MacRae 2005). The studies also suggest that women typically experience worse self-reported physical and mental health than men. Although there is still a possibility that the exposure to occupational hazards differ by gender under the same job title, some of these differences can be attributed to the gender difference in terms of susceptibility to occupational hazards or women's exposure to additional hazards at home. Moreover, much of the exposure limits and ergonomic designs are still based on average male physical capacity. As a result, it is possible that females may be at a greater risk of specific types of injuries and illnesses in specific occupations.

As many women work during their reproductive years, they are exposed to a wide variety of chemical, physical, and psychological hazards at the workplace that potentially cause problems such as infertility, miscarriage, birth defects, and developmental disorders in children. Not surprisingly, the epidemiological research on the reproductive effects of occupational hazards has been intensively studied among women (Walsh and Kelleher 1987). Some of the findings have been successfully translated into regulations (cf. lead and ethylene oxide). In the 1970s, research focused on the effects of maternal exposure on pregnancy outcomes, but has expanded to include male-mediated reproductive effects and a wide scope of outcomes over time (Goldman, Troisi, and Rexrode 2013).

Further research is needed for all three areas discussed above, but certainly, research on the heterogeneous effects of chemical, physical, and psychological hazards by gender are most needed. This will overcome the current situation whereby much of the exposure limits and ergonomic design are based on average male physical and biological capacity. Moreover, current research on occupational health and safety has been disproportionally concentrated in the context of developed countries. Thus, further research is needed in the context of developing countries. The failure to take gender into account constitutes a barrier to effective occupational health and safety policies and creates major obstacles to equal work opportunities for women. Incorporating gender issues in epidemiologic research may be useful for regulatory agencies seeking effective regulation as well as health professionals aiming to increase their understanding of the social determinants of health.

SEE ALSO: Biochemistry and Physiology; Depression; Health Disparities; Hostile Work Environment in the United States; Occupational Segregation

REFERENCES

Campos-Serna, Javier, Elena Ronda-Perez, Lucia Artazcoz, Bente Moen, and Fernando Benavides. 2013. "Gender Inequalities in Occupational Health Related to the Unequal Distribution of Working and Employment Conditions: A Systematic Review." *International Journal for Equity in Health*, 12(1): 57.

Goldman, Marlene B., Rebecca Troisi, and Kathryn M. Rexrode. 2013. *Women and Health*, 2nd ed. Amsterdam: Elsevier/Academic Press.

Howson, Christopher Paul, and Institute of Medicine's Committee to Study Female Morbidity and Mortality in Sub-Saharan Africa. 1996. *In Her Lifetime: Female Morbidity and Mortality in Sub-Saharan Africa*. Washington, DC: National Academy Press.

ILO. 2014. *Global Employment Trends 2014: Risk of a Jobless Recovery?* Geneva: International Labour Office.

Lim, Stephen S., et al. 2013. "A Comparative Risk Assessment of Burden of Disease and Injury Attributable to 67 Risk Factors and Risk Factor Clusters in 21 Regions, 1990–2010: A Systematic Analysis for the Global Burden of Disease Study 2010." *The Lancet*, 380(9859): 2224–2260.

MacRae, Nancy. 2005. "Women and Work: A Ten Year Retrospective." *Work*, 24(4): 331–339.

Walsh, Diana C., and Susan E. Kelleher. 1987. "The 'Corporate Perspective' on the Health of Women at Work." In *Women and Work: An Annual Review*, edited by Ann H. Stromberg, Laurie Larwood, Barbara A. Gutek. Newbury Park: Sage.

Occupational Segregation

EVA SIERMINSKA
LISER (Luxembourg Institute of Socio-Economic Research), Luxembourg

Occupational segregation is the distribution of people based upon demographic characteristics (such as gender, race or ethnicity, or education), both across and within occupations and jobs. Occupational gender segregation refers to the tendency of men and women to work in different occupations or the fact that men (women) are overrepresented in some occupations, while women (men) are overrepresented in others. Racial (ethnic) occupational segregation (more common in the United States than in Europe) refers to the division of paid labor according to racial or ethnic characteristics. Perfect segregation indicates that any given occupation employs only one group. Perfect integration, on the other hand, occurs when, in an occupation, each group holds the same proportion of positions as it holds in the labor force.

The literature distinguishes between two types of segregation: horizontal and vertical. Horizontal segregation refers to the distribution of individuals across occupation groups, for example with similar skill requirements. In this case, women and men most commonly work in different types of occupations. For example, during the postindustrial period many women entered into service sector jobs, where part-time and flexible schedules were available.

The term vertical segregation refers to either the distribution between hierarchically ordered occupations (inter-occupational segregation) or the separation of men and women on the career ladder in the same occupation (intra-occupational segregation). In other words, vertical segregation exists when one group is working in higher-grade occupations, while the other group is in lower-grade occupations.

Horizontal segregation is more resistant to change than vertical segregation because it plays to our basic understandings of gender roles. The idea that certain occupations are female or male is an example of how horizontal segregation is ingrained in our society.

Generally, the more present horizontal segregation is in a country, the less present is vertical segregation because as the share of employment of women (or men) in a given occupation increases, they have a better chance of obtaining the highest positions in that occupation.

One of the many ways to measure (horizontal) occupational segregation is by using Duncan's D, or the dissimilarity index or index of segregation (Duncan and Duncan 1955). It gives the percentage of female (or male) workers who would have to change jobs in order for the occupational distribution of the two groups to be the same. The index of segregation is measured by taking the differences of the percentages of men and women in the labor force employed in occupation "i," summing across all the occupations, and multiplying by 0.5. ($D = 0$ if the distribution of men and women across occupations is identical; $D = 100$ if all occupations are either completely male or completely female.)

Vertical segregation can be somewhat more difficult to measure if occupation categories are highly disaggregated. A similar distinction can be made if we consider two racial or ethnic groups.

Occupational gender segregation is explained via supply-side and demand-side factors. These two groups of factors are difficult to disentangle as gender-based discrimination can affect supply-side factors indirectly by affecting people's tastes. These explanatory factors also contribute to the gender pay gap. Supply-side explanations refer to different tastes of employees for different types of work, their education, and their experience, as well as the size of the labor supply and the opportunity structure, which could also be affected by the division of labor. The latter could be a result of the fact that women are viewed as being more competent than men in certain areas, for example nurturing and caring, while men are viewed as being more competent in other areas, such as building and other manual tasks. Norms, culture, and preferences can also have an effect on supply-side factors. Women and men are idealized and seen as being good at different things, and consequently are pushed into gender-specific roles that dictate their behavior and aspirations. These norms contribute to the development of gendered preferences for work and education and subsequently lead to gendered occupational choices. Coincidently for women, they are primarily in occupations that are low-paid and lower in status. Human capital explanations for occupational gender segregation additionally posit that men are more likely than women to prefer work life over family life. However, Haveman and Beresford (2012) find that men and women engaged in a similar type of work have similar levels of commitment to work and display other similar preferences. Another supply-side mechanism referred to when explaining occupation segregation is self-selection. This argument suggests that women self-select out of certain types of jobs because they either take too much time out of domestic work, or they decide not to pursue certain occupations for the causes mentioned above or choose occupations with lower atrophy rates (Polachek 1981).

Demand-side explanations include employers' preferences for different types of workers, economic pressures, employer discrimination, and personnel practices. Educational differences could be another, although, over the past 40 years, women's educational attainment has outpaced men's. Women are still less likely to pursue hard sciences and are less present in STEM (science, technology, engineering, and mathematics) fields, as well as finance, which tend to be pipelines to higher-paying jobs. Women are clustered in education, services, and government jobs. Work experience differences could be another demand-side factor. The gap between men's and women's tenure rises with age, and female college graduates are more likely than males to interrupt their careers to raise children. The presence of women in female-dominated occupations that are lower status and lower paid may also be the result of their job search strategies and not a long-term choice made that maximizes pay and prestige. Women have networks with a smaller geographical reach than men, as often they prioritize proximity of paid employment due to their inter-household responsibilities when searching for a job.

SEE ALSO: Division of Labor, Gender; Employment Discrimination; Gender Wage Gap

REFERENCES

Duncan, Otis D., and Beverly Duncan. 1955. "A Methodological Analysis of Segregation Indexes." *American Sociological Review*, 20: 210–217.

Haveman, Heather A., and Lauren S. Beresford. 2012. "If You're So Smart, Why Aren't You the Boss? Explaining the Persistent Vertical Gender Gap in Management." *Annals of the American Academy of Political and Social Science*, 639: 114–130.

Polachek, Solomon W. 1981. "Occupational Self-Selection: A Human Capital Approach to Sex Differences in Occupational Structure." *Review of Economics and Statistics*, 63(1): 60–69.

FURTHER READING

Blau, Francine D., Anne E. Winkler, and Marianne A. Ferber. 2012. *The Economics of Women, Men and Work*. Upper Saddle River: Prentice Hall.

Queneau, Hervé. 2005. "Changes in Occupational Segregation by Race and Ethnicity in the USA." *Applied Economic Letters*, 12: 781–784.

Silber, Jacques. 2012. "Measuring Segregation: Basic Concepts and Extensions to Other Domains." In *Inequality, Mobility and Segregation: Essays in Honor of Jacques Silber*, edited by John A. Bishop and Rafael Salas. Bingley: Emerald Insight.

Occupy Movements

MANISSA M. MAHARAWAL
CUNY Graduate Center, USA

The Occupy movement began in September 2011 in New York City and rapidly became an international protest movement focused on issues of social and economic inequality. The first Occupy protest was the Occupy Wall Street (OWS) encampment in New York City's Zuccotti Park on September 17, 2011. By October 9, Occupy protests had appeared in 82 countries around the world. A popular slogan used during the Occupy movement was that of the "99% vs. the 1%," which invoked statistics on worldwide wealth inequality and also took the form of a popular chant: "*We are the 99%!*" Many movement participants, but not all, explicitly understood Occupy as an anti-capitalist movement. In the aftermath of

Occupy, the phrase "the 1%" became widely used as a stand-in for talking about class and the power of the super-rich. While the general focus of the Occupy movement was primarily centered on economic inequality, issues of gender and sexuality were of constant importance to the movement and often a central part of its everyday politics and practices.

Occupy was inspired by a variety of other protest movements and revolutions that occurred throughout the world in 2010–2011. Such international movements shared a focus on economic inequality and the demand for greater democratic practices. These included the Egyptian Revolution and occupation of Tahrir Square in January 2011 that led to the ousting of President Hosni Mubarak; the occupation of Syntagma Square in Greece in 2010–2012 to protest austerity measures enforced as a consequence of the Greek debt crisis; the Indignados movement in Spain and Portugal of 2011–2012, which was a response to continuing austerity measures enacted as a result of the European debt crisis; and the various events of the Arab Spring.

Worldwide, Occupy groups had differing foci based on their location and the particular local issues that affected them. A common concern of the international movement, however, was growing global economic inequity and the collusion between large financial institutions and governments, which many viewed as undermining structures of representative democracy. The movement was characterized by occupations and protest encampments of (mostly urban) public spaces and the use of direct democracy, popular assemblies, and consensus decision-making processes. It was also characterized by the proliferation of the term "Occupy" worldwide, which came to signify global affinities between varied struggles against injustice as well as a set of common political practices.

Operating as a decentralized movement, Occupy had no main organizing or decision-making body. Instead, each Occupy encampment or group organized autonomously. Many of the Occupy groups, such as Occupy Frankfurt in Germany, Occupy Central in Hong Kong, Occupy Wall Street in New York City, and Occupy London in the United Kingdom, focused on critiquing large banks and financial institutions for their role in the economic crash of 2008 and their culpability for creating and maintaining global wealth inequality. While such global economic issues most often became the material of slogans and the focus of media coverage, local issues and the practicalities of running a protest encampment were of central importance to the everyday politics of Occupy protests. Issues of student debt, austerity, hospital closures, immigration, local political corruption scandals, and a myriad of issues pertaining to gender justice and sexual politics (see below) were constitutive elements of Occupy's politics globally and locally.

Countries with active Occupy protests or groups included Armenia, Australia, Belgium, Brazil, Canada, Colombia, Czech Republic, Cyprus, Denmark, France, Germany, Hong Kong, Italy, Malaysia, Mexico, Mongolia, Nepal, Netherlands, New Zealand, Nigeria, Norway, Republic of Ireland, South Africa, South Korea, Spain, Switzerland, Taiwan, Turkey, and the United Kingdom. While common themes of global inequality, finance capitalism, and political corruption were shared across Occupy protests, such themes manifested and were articulated differently in each location. Activists often used social media and digital communication to coordinate protests and messaging translocally. When the Spanish group Plataforma ¡Democracia Real YA! called for a "global day of action" against economic inequality for October 15, 2011, the Occupy movement heeded the call and Occupy protesters in over 900 cities worldwide participated in the global protest event.

At the level of its international political profile, the Occupy movement was not explicitly focused on issues of gender and sexuality. However, within the movement, the politics of gender was a constant if complex presence. Issues of gender and sexuality were by turns foregrounded or marginalized at different times and spaces within the movement.

Issues of gender and sexuality were often excluded from the popular slogans and messaging of the movement, as many organizers believed that Occupy's message should remain clearly focused on the economic dimensions of "the 99% vs. the 1%." In contrast, others argued that in order for the movement to truly be about the "99%," issues of race, gender, and sexuality needed to be foregrounded as relations of power and inequality and not merely subsumed under a universalist rhetoric. Feminists in particular argued that economic inequality is fundamentally gendered and that a movement against it must also take on patriarchal relations throughout the world and their manifestation within the movement itself. This was a tension that continually played out throughout the course of Occupy's development and was never fully resolved. Within Occupy some understood feminist politics and the critique of patriarchy as fundamental to the revolutionary politics of the movement, while others viewed these issues as a distraction. Internal struggles over this issue often were viewed as emblematic of the success or failure of the movement as a whole.

An early example of this dynamic occurred in the struggle over the wording of the "Declaration of the Occupation of Wall Street." Originally the first line of the Declaration read: "As one people formerly divided by the color of our skin, gender, sexual orientation, religion, or lack thereof, political party and cultural background, we acknowledge the reality: that there is only one race, the human race." Here, feminist and anti-racist activists argued for this particular sentence to be changed from a populist and "universalist" language that elided differences and erased histories of racialized and gendered inequality. In order to do so at an early Occupy Wall Street General Assembly, feminist and anti-racist activists blocked the passage of the Declaration, arguing that this line dismissed and ignored the present reality of racialized and gendered oppression. These activists argued that ignoring and tokenizing such oppression is to be complicit in its reproduction. In response, the writers of the Declaration defended their position and tried to bypass and silence the dissenting voices. However, by "blocking" the General Assembly from coming to consensus about the document, these activists prevented the Declaration from becoming adopted by Occupy until the text was changed. After an extended conversation, these activists succeeded in changing the text of the Declaration. The final text now reads: "As one people united ... "

Many viewed the struggle over the language of the Declaration as emblematic of struggles over the centrality of issues of gender and sexuality as well as race and racism within Occupy. This struggle took place both within the movement's internal dynamics and in its outward focus and messaging. Although feminist and anti-racist activists prevailed in this instance and the specific line of the Declaration was changed, the incident spurred a wider discussion within Occupy Wall Street about how racialized and gendered inequalities were treated within and by the movement.

Issues of gender justice and activism about gender were present in the movement from the very beginning. The ways in which these issues were taken up at the various encampments and across the different spaces of the movement, of course, varied widely. Throughout Occupy encampments there was often the use of everyday tactics to address privilege, oppression, and gender inequity. This included the practice of "step up, step back" during meetings and General Assemblies. This is a practice in which people were asked to "step back" if they were speaking too much and to "step up" if they hadn't spoken very much, and the use of "progressive stack" in which "traditionally marginalized" voices, such as those of women and people of color, were privileged in the speaking order. Through these practices the movement attempted to take into account male privilege, white privilege, and dynamics in which such forms of power reproduce themselves in activist spaces.

The issue of a lack of women's participation in leadership roles in General Assemblies and domination of such spaces by male voices in these Assemblies was raised within the first weeks of New York City's occupation. In response, the "Speak Easy Caucus" was formed as a space for people affected by these issues to gather together. This group eventually became the Women's Caucus, and later the group "Women Occupying Wall Street" (WOW), a nationwide network of women's groups within Occupy that held weekly conference calls and organized coordinated events and actions.

The formation of "women's" groups at some Occupy encampments often spurred debates about inclusion and exclusion. The group "Women Occupy" was formed by CODEPINK to provide a safe space for women to organize and speak out for equality and economic justice; this group continued to exist into the second year of Occupy. While some people claimed that the creation of exclusionary groups based on identity went against Occupy's inclusive rhetoric, other debates focused on how to define "women" and whether the use of this term was inclusive enough for transgender people. This raised the issue of whether a "women's" caucus should be open to transgender women. The debate about the inclusion of trans women in New York City eventually prompted a self-identified group of "Trans Women Occupiers" to write a statement in which they identified themselves as feminists, pointed out the ways that transgender people had been integrally involved in Occupy from the outset, and wrote that fighting the systematic oppression, violence, and criminalization of trans women must be part of Occupy's goal. They wrote: "allowing any group or space to define gender by cis-centric standards is intrinsically at odds with gender liberation."

Other groups within Occupy that focused on issues of gender and sexuality included the Fem Direct Action Group and Feminist General Assemblies. Fem Direct Action was formed as a space for self-identified feminists to organize direct actions that would focus on women while also challenging masculinist versions of direct action. Feminist General Assemblies were organized at nationwide Occupy mobilizations in order to create public spaces to collaborate and address "patriarchy, violence, and hierarchical structures that harm everyone."

The occurrence of sexual violence at various Occupy encampments presented a grave challenge to the movement. At many encampments "Safer Spaces" groups were formed to address issues of sexual violence as well as broader issues of safety and mental health at the occupations. Such groups performed important functions at the occupations, including conflict mediation, dispute de-escalation, and survivor support in cases of sexual violence. In New York City, members of the Safer Spaces group responded to an incident of sexual assault at the occupation by providing survivor support that centered on the needs and wants of the survivor, and later issued a statement contesting the mainstream media's portrayal of sexual violence at Occupy. The Safer Spaces group also developed a community agreement for Occupy Wall Street that was eventually approved by the OWS spokescouncil on February 22, 2012, and included a commitment to anti-oppression and a statement about not assuming anyone's gender or sexuality based on a person's appearance. This statement put forward a code of ethics and practices that was formally adopted by the whole movement; this community agreement foregrounded a commitment to gender justice.

The Occupy movement also generated support from a variety of important feminist writers and thinkers. At the Occupy Wall Street encampment in New York City there were appearances and talks by Angela Davis, Judith Butler, Eve Ensler, Gayatri Spivak, Barbara Ehrenreich, Rebecca Solnit, and Naomi Klein.

In the United States, the protest encampments that characterized the Occupy movement were in place for approximately two months. Internationally, protest encampments lasted varying amounts of time, with some lasting over a year. In the United States, two of the most populous and highest-profile Occupy encampments in New York City and Oakland, California were forcibly removed by the police in mid-November 2011. In early February 2012 the two remaining large encampments in London and Washington, DC were also removed by the police. Deprived of its physical occupations in public space, the movement continued to organize protests and events, but by the fall of 2012 much of the popular support for Occupy had dissipated and the movement had transformed and splintered into a variety of smaller political projects, some of which continued to organize under the name of Occupy while others did not.

In the time following the original encampments there have been various manifestations of the Occupy movement. In New York City, after Hurricane Sandy damaged parts of the city in October 2012, the network of Occupy activists mobilized a massive disaster response drive and started Occupy Sandy, providing relief to storm-affected areas. In Hong Kong, Occupy Central lasted into late 2012 and then reemerged in 2014 as a protest for universal suffrage. In Turkey, Occupy Gezi began in May 2013 as a protest against the intersecting issues of freedom of the press, expression, and assembly, and development plans for Istanbul.

SEE ALSO: Anti-Poverty Activism; Arab Spring Movements; Capitalist Patriarchy; Community and Grassroots Activism; Feminist Activism; Feminist Economics; Feminist Organizations, Definition of; Transgender Movements in International Perspective

FURTHER READING

Blumenkranz, Carla, et al., eds. 2011. *Occupy! Scenes from Occupied America.* New York: Verso.

Khatib, Kate, Margaret Killjoy, and Mike McGuire, eds. 2012. *We Are Many: Reflections on Movement Strategy from Occupation to Liberation.* Oakland: AK Press.

Lang, Amy Schrager, and Daniel Lang/Levitsky, eds. 2012. *Dreaming in Public: Building the Occupy Movement.* Oxford: New Internationalist Publications.

Oedipal Conflict

KATE FOORD
Melbourne, Australia

In classical Freudian psychoanalysis, Oedipal conflict is the effect of the love and hatred a child experiences toward parents, with the resolution of this conflict leading to gendered and sexualized outcomes. Whilst the Oedipus complex is still commonly perceived as a central tenet of psychoanalysis, the applicability of Freud's Oedipus complex both within the psychoanalytic clinic and in social and cultural analysis has been widely contested to great effect from within and without psychoanalysis.

Sigmund Freud first linked the legend of Oedipus to childhood sexuality in *Interpretation of Dreams*, published in 1900, and he continued to develop his ideas regarding the Oedipus complex over the course of the next four decades. He cited the Oedipus legend to confirm what he had observed through long clinical experience: that most children have feelings of love and hatred toward parents and that these feelings are magnified in the case of "psychoneurotics" (Freud 1900, 261). According to Sophocles' tragedy *Oedipus the King*, in attempting to avert the fate predicted by the Delphic oracle that their son would murder his father and marry his mother, King Laius and Queen Jocasta arranged for him to be exposed on the mountainside. The child is rescued, and as a man he too travels to the oracle at Delphi and hears the prophecy that his parents had heard. He attempts to avert this fate by embarking on travels, and on his journey he kills a man without realizing that this man is his father. He then becomes husband to his own mother, and father and brother to his own children. When the horror that Oedipus has indeed acted according to the prediction of the oracle is revealed, Jocasta takes her own life and Oedipus blinds himself and forsakes his home.

For Freud, this legend's "universal" power derives from our sense that Oedipus' destiny could have been our own (1900, 262). Those same impulses – the development of sexual impulses toward the mother and the coloring of an original identification with the father with hatred and murderous wishes toward him (Freud 1900, 262; 1923, 32) – can still be found in us, although repressed (1900, 263).

Freud recognized that, even in the case of the boy, the Oedipus situation is made complex by its triangular nature and by the constitutive bisexuality of the human being, the latter producing both an active and a passive form. The active form is the boy's desire for the mother and the father as obstacle to its realization; the passive form is where the boy wants to take his mother's place in his father's affections (Freud 1925, 250). For the girl, Freud proposed for himself an additional difficulty: how to explain the process by which she abandons the mother as original object choice and instead takes the father as her object (1925, 251).

Freud took the boy child as the subject of his discussions of the Oedipus complex, and, whilst initially proposing a precise analogy between the Oedipus complex for the boy and the girl, he gave up this idea. In his paper on "The Dissolution of the Oedipus Complex" of 1924, Freud proposed that for both children dissolution comes about with the threat of castration (1924, 176). In the case of the boy, both active and passive Oedipal positions result in the loss of the penis, either through being punished for sexual relations with his mother or by taking the feminine position in which castration is a precondition (1924, 176).

For the boy, the resolution of the conflict between his narcissistic interest in his penis and the libidinal cathexis of his parents is a turning away from the latter and from the Oedipus complex. The wishes and impulses of the phallic phase (as Freud called the period of childhood between when the wishes arise and their repression) become desexualized and sublimated, and their aim is inhibited, ushering in the latency period in sexuality and the development of the superego (Freud 1924, 177).

The "normal" heterosexual resolution of the Oedipal conflict for the boy produces a more intense identification with his father, the retention of some of the affectionate relation to the mother, and a general consolidation of his masculinity (Freud 1923, 32). This outcome of the dissolution of the Oedipus complex, in which the child has a stable gender identification with the parent of the same sex, is one of three possible outcomes posited by Freud. The other two are homosexuality, and, for boys, fetishism and, for girls, frigidity. Freud acknowledged that the process for girls was more obscure, but also called it more simple: for her, the Oedipal conflict was resolved by the repression of two wishes: to have the penis that she has realized she lacks, and to have a child as a gift from her father (Freud 1924, 179).

Freud's posited universality of the Oedipal conflict is overturned within psychoanalysis by Jacques Lacan and Luce Irigaray. Lacan, whose reworking of Freud's ideas was a fundamental task of his life's work, criticized Freud for attempting to install a universal powerful father, when clinical material supported, rather, the existence of weak and fallible ones. For Lacan, this brought into question the status of the Oedipus complex in the clinic. Deleuze and Guattari critiqued Oedipus similarly, for installing a phallocentric frame – the theory of the Oedipus complex – through which the relation to the father is then interpreted. Luce Irigaray critiqued Freud for reducing feminine sexuality to the consequences of lacking a penis, proposing that Freud thereby rendered female sexuality invisible.

In anglophone feminist philosophy, Judith Butler argued that the incest taboo (of which Freud's Oedipus complex is an instance) produces heterosexuality as approved and homosexuality as subversive, neither of which exists prior to the prohibition. What these critiques from within and without psychoanalysis have in common is the identification of the blindspots that produced Freud's development of the ideas of the Oedipus complex, and an analysis of the consequences of those blindspots for knowledge.

In his critique of Freud's Oedipus complex, Lacan returned to an analysis of the discussion of Oedipus in the *Interpretation of Dreams*, a work that, Lacan notes, emerged from the death of Freud's own father (Freud 1990, xxvi) and which inaugurated Freud's pursuit of the question, what is a father? (Lacan 2006, 688). By the time of *The Other Side of Psychoanalysis*, Lacan was referring to Oedipus as Freud's dream, and arguing that it should be interpreted as having both manifest and latent content, as dreams are. The manifest contest, for Lacan, is the myth of Oedipus as Freud recounts it in *Interpretation of Dreams*. The latent content reveals the wish of the dream, which is, according to Lacan, Freud's desire to conceal the father's weakness and fallibility by installing an idealized, all-powerful father. Freud's Oedipus complex proposes the fear of castration as that of the child, thereby concealing, according to Lacan, the fact that it is the father who is castrated, from the origin.

For Lacan, Freud's belief in the universality of the Oedipus complex produced a refusal of the knowledge available to him from his female analysands: from Dora, Anna, and Emma. Their knowledge, argues Lacan, could have guided Freud in putting back into question essential aspects of truth and knowledge in psychoanalysis.

SEE ALSO: Compulsory Heterosexuality; Feminism and Psychoanalysis; Gender Development, Feminist Psychoanalytic Perspectives on; Heteronormativity and Homonormativity

REFERENCES

Freud, Sigmund. 1900. *Interpretation of Dreams.* In *The Standard Edition of the Complete*

Psychological Works of Sigmund Freud, trans. James Strachey, vols. 4 and 5, 1–610. London: Hogarth.

Freud, Sigmund. 1923. "The Ego and the Id." In *The Standard Edition of the Complete Psychological Works of Sigmund Freud*, trans. James Strachey, vol. 19, 3–68. London: Hogarth.

Freud, Sigmund. 1924. "The Dissolution of the Oedipus Complex." In *The Standard Edition of the Complete Psychological Works of Sigmund Freud*, trans. James Strachey, vol. 19, 173–182. London: Hogarth.

Freud, Sigmund. 1925. "Some Psychical Consequences of the Anatomical Distinction between the Sexes." In *The Standard Edition of the Complete Psychological Works of Sigmund Freud*, trans. James Strachey, vol. 19, 243–260. London: Hogarth.

Lacan, Jacques. 2006. *Écrits: The First Complete Edition in English*, trans. Bruce Fink. London: Norton.

FURTHER READING

Butler, Judith. 1990. *Gender Trouble: Feminism and the Subversion of Identity*. New York: Routledge.

Deleuze, Gilles, and Félix Guattari. 1977. *Anti-Oedipus: Capitalism and Schizophrenia*, trans. Robert Hurley, Mark Seem, and Helen R. Lane. New York: Viking Press.

Gallop, Jane. 1982. *The Daughter's Seduction*. Ithaca: Cornell University Press.

Grigg, Russell. 2006. "Beyond the Oedipus Complex." In *Jacques Lacan and the Other Side of Psychoanalysis*, edited by Justin Clemens and Russell Grigg, 50–68. Durham, NC: Duke University Press.

Irigaray, Luce. 1985. *This Sex Which is Not One*, trans. Catherine Porter. Ithaca: Cornell University Press.

Kofman, Sarah. 1985. *The Enigma of Woman: Woman in Freud's Writings*, trans. Catherine Porter. Ithaca: Cornell University Press.

Kristeva, Julia. 1984. *Revolution in Poetic Language*, trans. Margaret Waller. New York: Columbia University Press.

Lacan, Jacques. 1979. "The Neurotic's Individual Myth." *Psychoanalytic Quarterly*, 48: 404–425.

Lacan, Jacques. 2007. *The Other Side of Psychoanalysis: The Seminar of Jacques Lacan Book XVII*, trans. Russell Grigg. New York: Norton.

Lévi-Strauss, Claude. 1955. "The Structural Study of Myth." *Journal of American Folklore*, 78: 428–444.

Open and Affirming Religious Organizations

J. E. SUMERAU
University of Tampa, USA

Open and affirming religious organizations are religious collectivities characterized by the acceptance, affirmation, and/or conceptualization of lesbian, gay, bisexual, transgender, and queer (LGBTQ) people as natural, normal, and potentially moral social beings. Whereas many long-standing religious traditions define sexual minorities as deviants, sinners, and abominations in the eyes of their deity, these organizations reject such definitions and, at least in terms of official policy, welcome LGBTQ people into their religious practices, belief structures, and traditions. Although the existence of open and affirming religious organizations spans the entirety of religious traditions worldwide, they typically emerge in one of two forms: explicitly LGBTQ or predominantly heterosexual but LGBTQ-affirming religious groups.

Explicitly LGBTQ religious organizations are typically new forms of religious practice, experience, and organization constructed by groups of LGBTQ people that have either left or been exiled from mainstream religious organizations. While they may have existed beforehand, researchers have documented the proliferation of these open and affirming religious organizations at the end of the 1960s in response to the marginalization of LGBTQ people within mainstream religious traditions as well as the emergence of religious leaders denouncing LGBTQ experience following World War II (see Wilcox 2003,

2009). Further, researchers have found that these organizations may range from officially established congregations and denomination structures, such as the Metropolitan Community Churches, to informal Bible Studies, support groups, spiritually themed drag shows, and religious services conducted within and/or in conjunction with other LGBTQ organizations, such as gay bars, book clubs, and community centers (see Thumma and Gray 2005). In fact, researchers have noted the spread and growth of these organizations – especially in more politically progressive regions – internationally throughout the last six decades (Browne, Munt, and Yip 2010; Kane 2013). Rather than attempting to find a place for LGBTQ people within mainstream religious organizations, these open and affirming religious organizations have constructed specifically LGBTQ forms of religious practice and experience.

Alongside the efforts of explicitly LGBTQ religious organizations (and some scholars argue because of their success in drawing members from mainstream religions), recent years have witnessed the emergence of predominantly heterosexual but LGBTQ-affirming religious organizations. These open and affirming organizations maintain their more traditional (mostly heterosexual) populations while making room for sexual minorities within their traditions and belief structures. In so doing, they typically revise, denounce, or ignore long-standing condemnations of LGBTQ experience by conceptualizing these teachings as misguided human interpretations of the divine or outdated beliefs that do not adhere to today's social realities (see Moon 2004). Rather than establishing new forms of religious practice or revising the structural organization of their traditions, predominantly heterosexual but LGBTQ-affirming religious organizations create space for sexual minorities within the existing theological, institutional, and historical structures of the religious mainstream. Although the emergence of these organizations has facilitated confusion and (at times) outright scorn from other mainstream religious groups, they continue to emerge in a wide variety of religious and political contexts throughout the globe (Nynas, Akademi, and Yip 2012).

While the aforementioned types of open and affirming religious organizations may differ in many ways, researchers have found they often produce similar positive and negative results for LGBTQ people specifically as well as society at large. In terms of positive results, research shows they provide the social spaces, symbolic and structural resources, and moral affirmation many religious sexual minorities require to accomplish the identity-based, emotional, and ideological work necessary for integrating their – seemingly disparate – religious and sexual identities (Wolkomir 2006). Further, they may provide opportunities to challenge existing racial, classed, and gender inequalities embedded within more mainstream religions (Sumerau 2012a), and provide the foundation for faith-based partnerships between organizations fighting for sexual equality (Comstock 1996). On the other hand, research shows that open and affirming religious organizations often reproduce societal patterns of race, class, gender, and religious inequality despite making gains in terms of sexual rights and recognition (see, e.g., McQueeney 2009; Wilcox 2009; Sumerau 2012b). Further, they may inadvertently shift political debates from the pursuit of equality via anti-discrimination laws to more conservative issues like marriage and family (see McQueeney 2009) while enforcing very strict moral and emotional standards concerning what it means to be "respectably LGBTQ" (Moon 2004). In fact, the literature to date suggests that the overall impact of open and affirming religious organizations – for both LGBTQ people and other religious traditions – remains an open question in need of systematic empirical examination.

SEE ALSO: Religion and Homophobia; Religious Fundamentalism; Sexual Identity and Orientation

REFERENCES

Browne, Kath, Sally R. Munt, and Andrew Kam-Tuck Yip. 2010. *Queer Spiritual Spaces: Sexuality and Sacred Places.* London: Ashgate.
Comstock, Gary David. 1996. *Unrepentant, Self-Affirming, Practicing: Lesbian/Gay/Bisexual People Within Organized Religion.* New York: Continuum.
Kane, Melinda. 2013. "LGBT Religious Activism: Predicting State Variations in the Number of Metropolitan Community Churches 1974–2000." *Sociological Forum*, 28(1): 135–158.
McQueeney, Krista. 2009. "'We are God's children, y'all': Race, Gender, and Sexuality in Lesbian-and-Gay-Affirming Congregations." *Social Problems*, 56(1): 151–173.
Moon, Dawne. 2004. *God, Sex, and Politics: Homosexuality and Everyday Theologies.* Chicago: University of Chicago Press.
Nynas, Peter, Abo Akademi, and Andrew Kam-Tuck Yip. 2012. *Religion, Gender, and Sexuality in Everyday Life.* London: Ashgate.
Sumerau, J. E. 2012a. "Mobilizing Race, Class, and Gender Discourses in a Metropolitan Community Church." *Race, Gender, and Class*, 19(3–4): 93–112.
Sumerau, J. E. 2012b. "'That's what men are supposed to do': Compensatory Manhood Acts in an LGBT Christian Church." *Gender & Society*, 26: 461–487.
Thumma, Scott, and Edward R. Gray. 2005. *Gay Religion.* Walnut Creek: Alta Mira Press.
Wilcox, Melissa. 2003. *Coming Out in Christianity: Religion, Identity, and Community.* Bloomington: Indiana University Press.
Wilcox, Melissa M. 2009. *Queer Women and Religious Individualism.* Bloomington: Indiana University Press.
Wolkomir, Michelle. 2006. *Be Not Deceived: The Sacred and Sexual Struggles of Gay and Ex-Gay Christian Men.* New Brunswick: Rutgers University Press.

Oral Tradition

PAULINE GREENHILL
University of Winnipeg, Canada

Oral tradition, the verbal lore of spoken or sung texts communicated face to face, often transmitted across generations and geography, includes a variety of folktales and other narratives, folksongs, ballads, recitations, chants, and shorter forms like proverbs or sayings. Though oral tradition was once considered the sole subject matter for academic folklore studies, since the 1950s–1960s North American folkloristics has extended to include material culture and the structures/textures and contexts of communication. Further, the concept of oral tradition has broadened to embrace texts communicated via audio or audiovisual media, and its complex relation to written tradition brought to bear. These extensions have considerably nuanced oral tradition's implications in terms of sexes, genders, and sexualities.

Historically, folklorists usually looked at vernacular forms performed by non-professionals. However, foundational scholars of oral tradition, seeking the origin of Homeric epics, looked at the usually non-literate male bards, who extemporaneously performed lengthy sung rhyming epics over time periods from hours to days. Based on research by Milman Parry (1971), Albert Bates Lord (2000) posited the oral-formulaic theory that this feat was possible because the bards used mnemonic formulas – phrases that could be used in different contexts – rather than memorizing a text word for word. Later scholars found similar forms in other locations, including Jan Vansina (1985), who posited that formulas allowed the African keepers of oral testimonies accurately to recall and relate family and community histories and genealogies covering many generations. This work, like that of Julie Cruikshank (e.g., 2005), respects not only the wisdom but also the chronological accuracy of indigenous knowledges.

Indigenous knowledges were once wrongly presumed to be entirely confined to oral tradition. However, many First Peoples historically used (and continue to employ) sophisticated communication modes based on auditory and visual channels, including writing systems. Further, colonizers were often wrongly supposed to have societies and cultures based first and foremost in written traditions. Yet oral tradition remains significant to settler cultures – think of theater, film, university lectures, arguments in court, and a myriad other modes – as it does among First Peoples. Nevertheless, much key indigenous knowledge is based primarily in oral tradition, and First Peoples generally do not share settler cultures' disdain for that mode of communication as less sophisticated, more impermanent, and lacking in value. Crucial beliefs and ideas may be enshrined in oral tradition in indigenous knowledges, where settler cultures resort to and rely on written texts.

Anthropologists and historians have considered oral tradition. Some, including Ruth Finnegan (e.g., 2007) and Walter Ong (e.g., 1967), posit that oral structures are qualitatively different from written structures. These ideas have been extensively taken up and critiqued well beyond the discipline of anthropology. Much of this work ignores gender, too often focusing on male traditions and consulting primarily if not exclusively with male informants, and presuming them as representative of all humans, as critiqued by oral historians Sherna Berger Gluck and Daphne Patai (1991).

Indigenous studies scholars focus on oral tradition's meanings and uses more than on its forms and structures. They often analyze oral tradition's many uses as a site of resistance against colonialism. For example, settler cultures often imposed patriarchal structures and practices on indigenous societies that had historically been based on the need for reciprocal respect and the different but equally salient values of women and men and their social and cultural contributions. Indigenous knowledges also frequently challenge and contradict settler cultures' racism, classism, sexism, militarism, and economic hegemony, offering radical alternatives. Though oral tradition is not inherently revolutionary, the concept of using it to communicate alternatives to settler culture may be.

As in other areas of scholarship, until the 1960s oral tradition was studied primarily by male scholars, usually collecting from men. North American exceptions included folklorist-ethnographers Helen Creighton (e.g., 1957), Zora Neale Hurston (e.g., 1935), and Elsie Clews Parsons (e.g., 1929). But when women began entering the field of folklore in larger numbers they began looking at material communicated by and among and/or often associated with women and marginalized groups. Frequently these scholars took explicitly feminist perspectives, recognizing the sociocultural and performative context of patriarchy and its effects upon texts and structures. Susan Kalčik (1975) drew attention to a previously unidentified story type, examining the "kernel stories" (an abbreviated form focusing on the narrative's main point) used in women's consciousness-raising groups as touchstones for underlining common experiences and thus the idea that the personal is political. Similarly, hitherto understudied sung forms received due attention. Bess Lomax Hawes (1974) showed how lullabies with which women sing children to sleep were not simple, anodyne ditties but instead draw on a wide range of difficult subjects including adultery and could employ complex musical structures. Historical research uncovered women's participation in forms of oral tradition usually associated with men. For example, fairy tales linked to male collectors and anthologizers like the Brothers Grimm have been recognized as told to them mainly by female tellers.

Oral tradition continues to be significant in many different cultural contexts today. Feminist scholars also developed analytical tools specific to understanding the cultures of women and marginalized groups. Jo Radner elaborated upon the concept of coding, previously applied to African American spirituals and slave songs, to introduce the idea of feminist and queer coding. Radner (1993) posits that people socioculturally excluded from mainstream cultures and power structures, but who need nevertheless to function within them, must often (consciously or not) communicate via words, forms, and behaviors that allow multiple meanings. Their purposes may be playful and/or protective. The coded forms these folks use may be explicit, wherein only the covert message is comprehensible and the coding is thus obvious. Or coding may be complicit, when a group employs prearranged signals that may or may not seem odd to outsiders, with meanings known only to that group. Thus, the song "Follow the Drinking Gourd" instructed runaway slaves to seek the constellation of the Big Dipper, and the North Star, to get to freedom, but could pass as simply a song about drinking. In the case of implicit coding, even the fact of coding is questionable, but can be inferred from the context. For example, Irish women's loud keening and wailing at funerals could distract hearers from the content of their songs in which, for example, a widow might complain about the domestic violence she experienced from her late husband, while not wishing to draw direct attention to it. Similarly, the dismissal that a comment is just a joke often obscures serious underlying meaning and intent of criticism or anger.

Jokes are also a form of oral tradition notorious for displaying misogyny, sexism, homophobia, ableism, and racism. They show how powerful groups can use traditional texts to keep others in situations of psychological and social domination, while denying those serious consequences using the alibi of humor. But while tellers may get away with using such forms in face-to-face contexts, increasingly their use in broader, public, audio, and audiovisual media meets censure. When oral traditions move from more personal to more public contexts, their meanings may change. Sometimes this results from alteration of texts, such as when singers and storytellers may censor content they perceive as problematic for a wider audience, or that censorship may be applied retroactively by producers. For example, the Brothers Grimm and the Disney Corporation both removed heterosex from their written/filmed versions of fairy tales. Otherwise, changing context from face-to-face to mediated, and the resulting lack of control the performer has over the audience, may render a racist, sexist, or homophobic joke, for example, entirely inappropriate.

Ironically, many oral traditions become known outside very limited groups only when they are written and published. The relationship between oral tradition and written forms has long been fraught in scholarly discourse. Noting that oral texts become more widely available once they are transcribed/translated into written form, some folklorists nevertheless fear that the result is a fixed text which undermines its oral counterpart's flexibility and malleability for new audiences in different times and spaces. Others note a long-term productive relationship between oral and written traditions, in which each feeds the other.

SEE ALSO: Colonialism and Gender; Gender Bias in Research; Heterosexism and Homophobia; Immigration, Colonialism, and

Globalization; Popular Culture and Gender; Private/Public Spheres; Women as Cultural Markers/Bearers; Women as Producers of Culture

REFERENCES

Creighton, Helen. 1957. *Bluenose Ghosts*. Toronto: Ryerson Press.
Cruikshank, Julie. 2005. *Do Glaciers Listen? Local Knowledge, Colonial Encounters, and Social Imagination*. Vancouver: University of British Columbia Press.
Finnegan, Ruth. 2007. *The Oral and Beyond: Doing Things with Words in Africa*. Chicago: University of Chicago Press.
Gluck, Sherna Berger, and Daphne Patai. 1991. *Women's Words: The Feminist Practice of Oral History*. New York: Routledge.
Hawes, Beth Lomax. 1974. "Folksongs and Function: Some Thoughts on the American Lullaby." *Journal of American Folklore*, 87(344): 140–148.
Hurston, Zora Neale. 1935. *Mules and Men*. New York: J. B. Lippincott.
Kalčik, Susan. 1975. "'… Like Ann's Gynecologist or the Time I Was Almost Raped': Personal Narratives in Women's Rap Groups." *Journal of American Folklore*, 88(347): 3–11.
Lord, Albert Bates. 2000. *The Singer of Tales*. Cambridge, MA: Harvard University Press.
Ong, Walter. 1967. *The Presence of the Word: Some Prolegomena for Cultural and Religious History*. New Haven: Yale University Press.
Parry, Milman. 1971. *The Making of Homeric Verse: The Collected Papers of Milman Parry*, edited by Adam Parry. Oxford: Clarendon Press.
Parsons, Elsie Clews. 1929. *Kiowa Tales*. New York: American Folk-lore Society.
Radner, Joan Newlon, ed. 1993. *Feminist Messages: Coding in Women's Folk Culture*. Urbana: University of Illinois Press.
Vansina, Jan. 1985. *Oral Tradition as History*. Madison: University of Wisconsin Press.

FURTHER READING

Dei, George J. Sefa, Budd L. Hall, and Dorothy Goldin Rosenberg, eds. 2000. *Indigenous Knowledges in Global Contexts: Multiple Readings of Our World*. Toronto: University of Toronto Press.

Orientalism

BRONWYN WINTER
The University of Sydney, Australia

The term "orientalism" is believed to have been coined in France (the country most associated with its historical development) in the late eighteenth or early nineteenth century. At the time, the term characterized the development of scholarly knowledge and forms of artistic endeavor that reflected interest within Europe in things "Eastern" (both the Middle East and so-called "Far East"). It also, in colonial British India, characterized an administrative practice that conserved local Hindu and Muslim laws and customs to preserve social order. Whether scholarly, artistic, or administrative, orientalism was considered by its Western proponents to be either neutral or positive. Subsequently – and particularly since the publication of Edward Saïd's work *Orientalism* (Saïd 1978) – the Western/European gaze on the "Orient" came to be criticized as a process of racist Othering that stereotyped and belittled the cultures and peoples designated by the term. Some representations of Jewish people (such as the wide variety of retellings of the biblical story of Salomé) have also been considered orientalist. The gendered and feminizing aspects of orientalism have been foregrounded by both practitioners of orientalism and their critics. This entry focuses primarily on British, American, and French scholarly and artistic orientalism as it pertains to the Middle East and North Africa (MENA), but there are also Russian and German traditions of orientalist thought and writing, and orientalist scholarship and cultural production also exists in relation to Asian countries such as Japan and China in the east, India in the south and Afghanistan in the west.

A SHORT HISTORY

Political and cultural exchanges between Europe and MENA date back to the beginning of our era and indeed earlier. They have more often than not been characterized by political rivalry and military conquest (on both sides of the East/West divide), but also by cultural, literary, scientific, economic, and diplomatic exchange. These various interactions have found European literary expression since medieval times, most famously in the *Chanson de Roland* of the twelfth century, but it was during the Ottoman Empire that the European interest in "the Orient" started to develop in a concerted way. Renaissance Venice became a hub of East–West exchange and "oriental" influence on architecture and on themes of painting was apparent. In seventeenth century France, "chinoiseries" and "turqueries" were popular in fashion and décor and the court of Louis XIV established or re-established strong diplomatic ties with various countries under Ottoman reign. "Turkish style" was popularized in music by Lully and in theater by Molière, who used "the Turks" as a vehicle to mock the French in *Le Bourgeois Gentilhomme*. It was also at this that that the prestigious *Institut National des Langues et Civilisations Orientales* (INALCO) was founded. Its London "equivalent," the School of Oriental and African Studies (SOAS), was founded as the School of Oriental Studies in 1916. Both INALCO and SOAS remain key centers for Middle Eastern studies.

In the early eighteenth century, Lady Mary Montagu, accompanying her British ambassador husband to Constantinople (as Istanbul was then known), wrote positively of Turkish customs, including the freedoms enjoyed by Turkish women, in her extensive correspondence. But it was the publication, from 1704 to 1717, of Frenchman Antoine Galland's *The Thousand and One Nights* that symbolically marked the beginning of what would later become known as orientalism. Galland's sources were primarily Persian folk tales, themselves often derived from Arab-world folklore. Even though he embellished them in his own way, his work was considered authentic and a true scholarly contribution to the study of "oriental cultures." The work's best-known character, however, Scheherazade the storyteller, is a fictional creation of Galland's own, possibly inspired by European women he knew. Around the same time, philosopher Montesquieu's *Lettres Persanes* once more used "the orient" as a vehicle to satirize French society. From the outset, then, "scholarly" orientalism was a combination of actual first-hand knowledge, usually involving considerable time living and studying in the "Orient," and personal creativity.

It was in the nineteenth century that orientalism very much came into its own as a vehicle of artistic representation, concurrent with the development of colonialist ideology associated with positivism, "scientific" racism, and the "mission civilisatrice" (or White Man's Burden). Within this ideology, the "Orient" became increasingly feminized as a mysterious and mystical "world behind the veil" and locked into an essentializing narrative of backward Otherness. At the same time, orientalism became a vehicle for literary and artistic avant-gardes that rebelled against bourgeois scientism, including Romantic and post-Romantic poets such as Byron and Baudelaire and the French Symbolist and British Aesthetic movements of the late nineteenth century. Orientalism was also a vehicle for neoclassicist and romantic painters such as Ingres, Delacroix, and Gérôme (the last became one of the inaugural honorary presidents of the *Société des Peintres Orientalistes*, founded in 1893); and novelists such as Gustave Flaubert (*Salammbô*), Victor Hugo (*Les Orientales*), Théophile Gautier (*Le Roman de la Momie*) and the immensely popular orientalist writer Pierre Loti. Most notoriously, orientalism gave to a fashion in nude painting: the Odalisque (from the Turkish word *odalik*, chambermaid). The models for odalisques were invariably European women and personal friends of the painters, many of whom had never set foot in any MENA country. The odalisque remained a figure of avant-garde painting into the early twentieth century, for example, in the work of Matisse. The twentieth century saw the emergence of considerable "orientalist" scholarship, again notably in France and the United Kingdom (such as that of Maxime Rodinson, Jacques Berque, and Bernard Lewis), including a number of translations of the Koran (e.g., by Richard Bell, Régis Blachère, and Denise Masson). Also in the twentieth century, two new art forms were to rely heavily on orientalism as a vehicle: modern dance and cinema. The French Ballets Russes, with choreographies by Nijinsky and designs by Picasso and Bakst, used orientalist themes, and a number of female pioneers of modern dance, including Ruth St. Denis (US), Maud Allan (UK) and Loïe Fuller (France), incorporated orientalist styles and characters in their innovative approaches. In the cinema, orientalism quickly traveled to Hollywood, where it became packaged in epics, musicals, and animated films for a US adult and child audience hungry for the exotic.

CRITIQUES OF ORIENTALISM

The most well-known and exhaustively discussed critique of orientalism is that of Edward Saïd, to the extent that it is now difficult to discuss the concept without reference to Saïd's work, whether one agrees with it or not. His basic thesis is that the "Orient" is a fiction, a creation of Western narcissism, and that orientalism thus equates to Western colonialist, racist, and essentializing framings of the Arab Other. Drawing inspiration from the ideas of Foucault on discourse and the relationship between knowledge and power, and from Grasmci's analysis of hegemony, Saïd criticized scholars and artists alike. *Orientalism* has been much criticized, perhaps most famously by Princeton scholar Bernard Lewis (1993), one of the "orientalist" figures whom Saïd takes to task (see also Irwin 2006). Lewis himself then took Saïd to task for intellectual dishonesty and historical inaccuracies, and his caricatural and homogenizing representations of orientalist scholars. Feminist scholar Nikki Keddie argued that journalists, politicians, missionaries, and popular writers have had a much more decisive influence than scholars in creating and popularizing orientalist stereotypes (Keddie 2007, 58ff.). Moreover, many scholars, such as Albert Hourani, Anouar Abdel-Malek, and Mohamed Arkoun, were providing nuanced critiques of both orientalism and of the history of Islam and the Muslim world, and proposing different frameworks for contemporary MENA – West interactions, long before Saïd.

One thing that is missing from Saïd's work, and much other work on orientalism, whether it is "anti-orientalist" or not, is a serious discussion of orientalism and women. First, European and North American women were orientalist travelers, scholars, and creators, often very innovative ones (as in the case of modern dance). Second, feminist writers from MENA such as Assia Djebar and Leïla Sebbar have "written back" to orientalism in their work; more recently, Hanan Al-Shaykh (2013) has retold *One Thousand and One Nights* from a feminist perspective. The work was first performed on stage in 2011 in Arabic, French, and English. Third, feminist scholars have critiqued both orientalism and masculinist scholarship on it. Yegenoglu (1998) has challenged fantasies of the "veiled woman," and Lewis (2004) has looked at how women in the Ottoman Empire manipulated both orientalist and Ottoman cultural codes. Others such as Zayzafoon (2005) have argued that the "Muslim woman" is an invention in both Western orientalist and Arab nationalist or Islamic discourse.

SEE ALSO: Colonialism and Gender

REFERENCES

Al Shaykh, Hanan. 2013. *One Thousand and One Nights*. London: Bloomsbury.
Irwin, Robert. 2006. *For Lust of Knowing: the Orientalists and Their Enemies*. London: Allen Lane.
Keddie, Nikki. 2007. *Women in the Middle East: Past and Present*. Princeton: Princeton University Press.
Lewis, Bernard. 1993. *Islam and the West*. New York: Oxford University Press.
Lewis, Reina. 2004. *Rethinking Orientalism: Women, Travel and the Ottoman Harem*. New Brunswick: Rutgers University Press.
Saïd, Edward. 1978. *Orientalism*. London: Vintage Books.
Yegenoglu, Meyda. 1998. *Colonial Fantasies: Towards a Feminist Reading of Orientalism*. Cambridge: Cambridge University Press.
Zayzafoon, Lamia Ben Youssef. 2005. *The Production of the Muslim Woman: Negotiating Text, History and Ideology*. Lanham: Lexington Books.

FURTHER READING

Macfie, Alexander Lyon, ed. 2000. *Orientalism: a Reader*. New York: New York University Press.
Mackenzie, John M. 1995. *Orientalism: History, Theory and the Arts*. Manchester: Manchester University Press.

Outsider Within

RACHELLE S. GOLD
North Carolina Central University, USA

Sociologist Patricia Hill Collins was one of the first to use the term outsider within, but it was informed by Georg Simmel's (1969) work and by Nancy Hartsock's (1983) essay on feminism. It describes the phenomena whereby people who are oppressed due to their minority status have a keen knowledge of both themselves as outsiders and of the perspective of insiders. The term is also based on a theoretical framework of how individuals marginalized by institutional structures understand systems of exclusion and intersections of dominance and how they relate to insiders who, because of their positions of status, can suppress autonomy, job prospects, academic freedom, wages, access to homes and loans, or government services for outsiders.

The notion of "outsider within" is rooted in Simmel's essay about the sociological significance of the "stranger" who has greater objectivity than insiders to observe data and people based on his or her own perspective, yet the stranger is regarded with both a "concern and indifference" by the main "group" where the stranger lives (Simmel 1969). Due to their multiple and shifting perspectives of being both near to and far from societal power, they are more free from conventions that restrain those in the group; they are "less prejudiced [and] more objective ... [and] not confined in actions by custom, piety, or precedents" (Simmel 1969). As a paradigm for the complex position of any oppressed person or group is similar to W. E. B. Du Bois's (1903) idea of "double consciousness," the sociological dilemma of the person who is both American and African. This "peculiar sensation of ... two-ness" is a dual awareness of an identity as both an African and an American, but not acknowledged as fully one or the other. Du Bois writes of African Americans being gifted with a "second sight" that allows them to see themselves not truly as they are, but only through the eyes of others. Similarly, the concept of outsider within shares this DuBoisian "peculiar sensation," and Collins posits that this dilemma represents an ideological crisis for individuals who are disenfranchised by traditional power structures because they are caught between two worlds; yet, after they become aware of their marginality, they can neither be solely outsiders nor insiders.

Using examples of black women domestic workers and intellectuals, Collins explains that black women caretakers enjoyed demystifying white power by seeing it enacted daily, even though they knew that they could "never belong to their white 'families'," which resulted in a special and "curious outsider-within stance, a peculiar marginality" (Collins 1991). Similarly, men of color, lesbian, gay, bisexual, transgender people, women, and others who live on society's periphery, both benefit and suffer from their outsider status. For example, mainstream society perceived figures such as Ida B. Wells, Sojourner Truth, Betty Friedan, Rachel Carson, Harvey Milk, Bayard Rustin, Gloria Anzaldúa, Cesar Chavez, Gloria Steinem, and Wilma Mankiller as threatening even if they were later vindicated for their political, feminist, and ecological platforms. Writers such as Barbara Ehrenreich, Arlie Hochschild, Nicholas Kristof, Gloria Steinem, Studs Terkel, and Howard Zinn have exposed myths about war, gender, social class, history, poverty, and pay inequity to educate insiders and reveal hidden truths.

Dimensions of the topic revolve around inequities in intellectual communities, politics, history, the economy, immigration, banking, the legal system, healthcare, housing, education, human trafficking and the environment. Outsider within theory is relevant to gender and sexuality studies and the ways in which women, feminist men, gay and lesbian people, and people of color confront and decenter Eurocentric, male-centered views of government, public policies, and construction of knowledge in the academy. In the past, outsiders within connoted only those who were critical of masculine, heterosexist hierarchies and represented the views primarily of women desiring to subvert and challenge white male insider-ism, especially because their experiences had been excluded and their contributions erased. However, the purview has expanded to include the deconstruction of any power structure that reinforces domination through racism, sexism, ageism, classism, homophobia, and xenophobia, regardless of who controls it. By using their unique perspectives to transcend limitations, outsiders engage both their liminal and their insider statuses to expose contradictions in the dominant group's actions.

Over the last 35 years, the idea has extended to include any disenfranchised group, and how they choose to identify themselves. This standpoint frames the way powerful institutions perceive the locus of oppression that an outsider faces, thus shaping how they can advocate for any subjugated group or mobilize a course of liberating action once insiders are informed. For example, Ehrenreich's books have led to changes in wage policy, Hochschild's have created family leave laws, Kristof's have created NGOs dedicated to educating girls in Kenya and rescuing others from sexual slavery, and Zinn's have led to curricular changes in what public school children learn about hidden historical accounts.

Outsider allegiance interferes with choosing full insider status: they must remain outsiders within. Like Ellison's *Invisible Man*, they are "others": they never fully belong, yet they are essential because those at the margins clarify boundaries for insiders and emphasize the significance of belonging (Collins 1991). By critiquing the power of privilege that insiders are sometimes oblivious that they have, outsiders within empower minority voices and provide tools for social justice and coalition building. Importantly, outsiders within are not a homogeneous group, and they do not necessarily share identities and politics (Collins 1998).

The psychological costs of their status include isolation, anger, loneliness, and depression and physical costs can involve job loss, sexual violence, domestic abuse, poverty, malnourishment, illiteracy, and being deprived basic human dignities. The benefits include basic freedom from want, civil and human rights, solidarity, creative expression, political cooperation, and legislative and policy changes in the economy, education, and healthcare, among other realms. Possibilities for activism and advocacy exist within multiple structures of domination and offer hope for societal change in domestic and international situations, especially related to asylum seekers, who understand both the outsider view of the toll of a "foreign" war and the insider motive to protect a country's borders while at the same time considering humanitarian impulses.

Current emphases in the outsider within standpoint as an interpretive lens highlight epistemological "othering" in postcolonial studies, disability studies, the history of disenfranchised groups, sociological studies of people experiencing homelessness and veterans with post-traumatic stress disorder (PTSD), subaltern studies, and trauma studies. As outsiders, their difference sensitizes them to notice patterns, such as illegal, disparate treatment and institutional racism, which are difficult for insiders, who are often in positions to judge legal cases involving justice-seeking whistleblowers, to see. Outsiders who are ethnic minorities or culturally sensitive allies can teach insiders to become more aware of unintentional biases or unconscious stereotypes. For example, heterosexual men can be educated to be sensitive to women and LGBTQ people to avoid silencing them, or to reject their own entitlement by learning about what Peggy McIntosh calls "White Privilege: Unpacking the Invisible Knapsack."

Future directions in research include the fringe status of parents who adopt children transracially and the children they rear, the indigenous peoples of Australia as outsiders within the continent, modern Asian women writers carving out a place for themselves that defies submissive archetypes, women in science, technology, engineering, and math, transgender and intersex persons, and women researchers of color in the social sciences and humanities such as education, economics, literature, history, psychology, medicine, law, business, and technology.

SEE ALSO: Critical Race Theory; Feminist Standpoint Theory; Gender Oppression; Intersectionality; Subaltern

REFERENCES

Collins, Patricia Hill. 1991. *Black Feminist Thought: Knowledge, Consciousness, and the Politics of Empowerment*. New York: Routledge.

Collins, Patricia Hill. 1998. *Fighting Words: Black Women and the Search for Justice*. Minneapolis: University of Minnesota Press.

Du Bois, W. E. B. 1993. *The Souls of Black Folk*. New York: Knopf. First published 1903.

Hartsock, Nancy M. 1983. "The Feminist Standpoint: Developing the Ground for a Specifically Feminist Historical Materialism." In *Discovering Reality* edited by Sandra Harding and Marilyn Hintikka, 283–310. Boston: D. Reidel.

McIntosh, Peggy. 1988. "White Privilege and Male Privilege: A Personal Account of Coming to See Correspondences through Work in Women's Studies." Working Paper 189. Wellesley College Center for Research on Women.

Simmel, Georg. 1969. "The Sociological Significance of the 'Stranger'." *Introduction to the Science of Sociology*, edited by Robert E. Park and Ernest W. Burgess. Chicago: University of Chicago Press. First published 1921.

FURTHER READING

Anzaldúa, Gloria. 1987. *Borderlands/La Frontera: The New Mestiza*. San Francisco: Aunt Lute Books.

Collins, Patricia Hill. 1986. "Learning from the Outsider Within: The Sociological Significance of Black Feminist Thought." *Social Problems*, 33(6): 14–32.

Ehrenreich, Barbara. 2001. *Nickled and Dimed: On Getting By in America*. New York: Henry Holt.

Henwood, Karen, Christine Griffin, and Ann Phoenix, eds. 1998. *Standpoints and Differences: Essays in the Practice of Feminist Psychology.* London: Sage.

Hochschild, Arlie. 1989. *The Second Shift: Working Parents and the Revolution at Home.* New York: Viking Penguin.

hooks, bell. 1984. *From Margin to Center.* Boston: South End Press.

Kristof, Nicholas, and Sheryl WuDunn. 2009. *Half the Sky: Turning Oppression into Opportunity for Women Worldwide.* New York: Knopf.

Merton, Robert K. 1972. "Insiders and Outsiders: A Chapter in the Sociology of Knowledge." *American Journal of Sociology*, 78: 9–47.

Zinn, Howard. 1980. *A People's History of the United States: 1492–Present.* New York: Harper Collins.

P

Pacifism, Quakers, and Gender

ERIN BELL
University of Lincoln, UK

Quakerism, a Christian denomination, originated in the actions of a few radical preachers active throughout the British Isles but particularly in North West England and Bristol during the 1640s and 1650s, such as Barbara Blaugdone, possibly from Bristol (1609–1704), and George Fox from Leicestershire (1624–1691). "Friends," as members called themselves, were initially scorned by others, and the term "Quaker," although later used by the group themselves, was originally a form of abuse, mocking their physical shaking when divinely moved to speak. Most Quakers rejected the idea of paid ministry and traditional church hierarchies, favoring a more egalitarian structure based on spiritual maturity rather than social status, and the development of a series of testimonies, or guides to ethical living. One of the first was the peace testimony. Arising during a period of civil war in the British Isles, Quakerism was not, in the first instance, entirely pacifist: several members, including Fox, were part of the Parliamentarian army which rejected monarchy and sought a republic. Quakers spread radical new ideas, including the idea that everyone held "that of God" within them, developed from Luke 17:21. Such spiritual equality paralleled contemporary calls for political equality and was core to much early Quaker activity, but led to conflict with non-Quakers, particularly over gender and violence. Friends' support for women like Blaugdone had implications for external perceptions of both female and male Friends, leading to well-documented criticism of early Quaker men, by members of other denominations, as unable to control unruly Quaker women.

Despite this, as part of their creation of a distinct spiritual and political identity, the first generation of Quakers increasingly rejected physical violence, particularly that perpetuated by the military. In 1650, Fox had been offered his freedom from Derby Gaol, where he had been imprisoned for blasphemy after publicly rejecting mainstream Christian beliefs such as external baptism, in exchange for a captaincy in the army; he rejected the offer, claiming to fight with spiritual rather than material weapons. By 1660, shortly after his restoration to the throne, King Charles II received Fox and his unnamed co-authors' text, *A Declaration from the Harmless and Innocent People of God, called Quakers*, which explicitly announced their denial of all physical manifestations of violence. The early peace testimony, as represented by the *Declaration*, sought to emphasize

Friends' pious manliness in contrast to that of non-Quaker men who were often depicted as physically violent. Within the work, Fox and his co-authors explicitly contrasted the dishonorably violent – and therefore unmanly nature – of worldly men with the manly bravery of Quakers facing their assaults, depicted in the *Declaration* as Christ-like in their suffering, having peacefully resisted the violence of non-Quaker men. Passive and stoical endurance contrasted them to their oppressors for, as the work outlined, the Friends' war was to be spiritual and not carnal, a form of resistance to non-Quaker militarized masculinity. Alongside their refusal to serve in the armed forces, Friends refused to subsidize acts of war in any sense, moral or financial, including localized efforts to raise militia.

However, unlike the sometime shepherd and apprentice cobbler Fox, the military or maritime backgrounds of many of the first Quakers remained influential even for those who renounced violence and transferred their attention from a carnal to a spiritual plane. The experiences of men such as Thomas Lurting often influenced their representation of Quaker beliefs and their expectations of the world: "the Lamb's War" was fought by Friends for some decades after the Restoration, when they encountered wider society. Apocalyptic imagery of the Lamb and his followers at war with Satan was employed much as it had been during the civil war years. Although some scholars conclude that female Friends rejected such language, and certainly some male Friends did also, its use emphasizes how the ideals of Quaker manhood represented in Friends' autobiographical journals often related to willingness to undertake spiritual warfare. For example, Lurting converted in the early 1650s, influenced by Quakers on his ship who had previously endured his beatings. His account of life at sea in the 1650s and 1660s, *The Fighting Sailor Turn'd Peaceable Christian* (1711), demonstrates the nuances of Quaker masculinity and its relationship to pacifism in its earliest decades, maintained into the early eighteenth century, when the work was first published, and beyond. Certainly, as well as depicting physical suffering at the hands of non-Quakers, as the *Declaration* had done, Friends such as Lurting continued to wage spiritual warfare on those oppressing Friends. The autobiography additionally offers an account of a youthful Lurting's muscular form of Quakerism, describing how on one occasion in 1662 he undertook manual labor on-board ship and sweated profusely due to the toil, whilst the coxswain of a nearby man-of-war berated him for his pacifism. In another account, Lurting relates how, the following year (1663), he and his crew returned a number of Turks safely to their homeland albeit with, at one stage, a boat hook used by Lurting to strike the Turkish captain into submission. Life at sea, then, required a more varied interpretation of pacifism and therefore of Quaker masculinity than that suggested in the *Declaration*, which was increasingly recognized by later seventeenth- and eighteenth-century Friends.

Non-Quakers shared Quaker ambivalence in regard to violence: within later seventeenth- and early eighteenth-century British and North American society, men were expected to show self-control, and control of the passions thought to predominate in women, but displays of strength could earn men honor, and be used to maintain physical and patriarchal control over errant members of the household. If this was lost, a man could become the victim of social censure. As scholars of early modern violence concur, the right to use violence to correct wayward members of the household and wider community also united men in a shared responsibility to defend patriarchy. Friends left themselves open to criticism for their refusal to bear arms and apparent failure to control their women, for domestic violence was rejected by Friends as it was linked to disorder, particularly that of the alehouse. Quaker antipathy to alehouse culture can be identified in a number of Quaker journals. George Fox's archetypal *Journal* (1694) includes an account of his visit to a Wensleydale (Yorkshire) alehouse in which drunks threatened him for refusing to join them, while Cheshire-born Elizabeth Ashbridge's account of an occurrence in the early eighteenth century, when she had refused to dance in a Philadelphia tavern and faced the violence of her non-Quaker husband, paralleled Fox's account but specifically demonstrated a nexus perceived by many seventeenth- and eighteenth-century Quakers between alehouses, domestic violence, and disorder, leading to a desire, apparent in the records kept by Quaker meetings, to discipline those straying, literally and spiritually, into alehouses.

Friends' peace testimony was manifested in more proactive ways in their local communities than rejection of domestic violence. Some were well esteemed as local peacemakers, seeking to retain community peace through honest business practices, alongside other aspects of Quaker culture viewed positively by outsiders. Even if pacifism had to some degree been forced upon them by circumstances outside of their control at the end of a period of political and social turmoil, the nexus of masculinity and pacifism proved fruitful when developing an identifiably Quaker masculinity. Friends situated their pacifism within wider contemporary discourse about masculinity and were able to remain within wider notions of acceptable behavior by constructing their behavior as masculine self-control, restraint, and rationality.

Later Quakerism saw fresh challenges and offered new opportunities to expand and develop upon the *Declaration*. Friends' opposition to slavery, for example, which included recognition of the violence intrinsic to the capture and treatment of the enslaved, had roots in the late seventeenth century although progress to encourage all American Quakers to liberate their slaves was slow. By the 1750s, northern Quakers who owned slaves were no longer importing or purchasing further people and, with slow progress made towards the freeing of slaves, a small but distinctive group of black Quakers grew, many of whom, like David Mapps of Little Egg Harbor, New Jersey, rejected violence; during the 1812 war he refused to transport cannon balls in his schooner, although other freed slaves, and arguably men in particular, sought alternative solutions to the question of whether it was appropriate for those without power to embrace pacifism. Certainly, pacifism led many Friends in the early to mid-nineteenth century to oppose the activities of Quaker abolitionists such as Lucretia Mott, as they were seen as leading, potentially, to the stirring of violent revolutionary sentiments.

Twentieth-century Quakerism faced a number of challenges, not least two world wars, which specifically impacted on Friends. World War I (1914–1918) saw conscientious objectors (COs) imprisoned for their refusal to bear arms and defined as part of deviant masculinity, in contrast to martial manhood. Like Quakers in the seventeenth century, the language used to articulate their position was often militarized, drawing on gendered ideals of male heroic responses to oppression and in contrast to representations of COs, Quaker and otherwise, which depicted them as cowardly and effeminate, and for which they were often forced to wear white feathers. The practice spread to the United States from Britain and formed part of a campaign that, according to the *Boston Journal* in February 1917, included posters around the Harvard University campus alleging that those favoring American neutrality did so as it was "unladylike" to support involvement in the war. Quaker men were, in reality, sometimes members of bodies like the FAU, Friends' Ambulance Unit, funded initially by Quakers, which ran hospitals for the wounded in Britain, France, and Belgium as well as civilian relief work in France. Although "laid down" in 1919 after a year organizing relief work and repatriation in mainland Europe, the FAU was revived in September 1939 and involved a similar mix of male and female Friends from several nations.

World War II and the rise to power of the Nazi Party in Germany from 1933 saw Quaker activity in many additional areas including the *kindertransport* and medical assistance in liberated concentration camps, alongside other relief work for which they were, as a denomination, awarded the Nobel Peace Prize in 1947. Indeed, in both pre- and post-World War II responses to genocide and its threat, Quaker men and women were active. From 1933 the Birmingham Friend Bertha Bracey lobbied the British Parliament on behalf of the Germany Emergency Committee, set up in 1933, seeking assistance for Jewish and other refugees from mainland Europe. Her activities allowed Jewish children, as well as adults, to come to Britain as refugees, enabling the *kindertransport*, amongst other lifesaving work, to go ahead. Unnamed "Quaker ladies" are remembered by Holocaust survivors rescued from Czechoslovakia by the *kindertransport* in the late 1930s, whilst Mary Penman and Tessa Rowntree were active in saving Czech political refugees in the same period. German Quakers were, though, also victims of the regime and despite German officials' initially positive view of Quakers due to the "Quaker Speisung," a post-World War I relief effort in Germany, up to an eighth of German Friends were incarcerated, often dying in prisons or concentration camps for their pacifism and efforts to protect Jews. Towards the end of the conflict, the liberation of Bergen-Belsen involved Quaker relief teams of both male and female Friends, from April 1945, when Friends Relief Service, which had already been active in mainland Europe for a year working with displaced persons as part of a wider remit to relieve civilian distress, entered the camp.

Although the interwar period had seen a dip in American Quaker involvement with pacifism in particular, interest revived significantly during the Cold War. Quaker campaigns for nuclear disarmament into the twenty-first century have achieved some of the most significant support for Friends' pacifist activity, in which a pro-nuclear discourse which depicts weapons as linked to masculinity, strength and protection has been rejected, as Dutch Friends did in 1991, by linking sexism to militarism and specifically, by identifying that the choice to spend money on weapons and not social programs may be seen as part of violence against women. Therefore Quaker men, as well as Quaker women, they argued, should respond by practicing gender equality, and critiquing all social and organizational structures.

In the same decade, Friends responded to such calls by noting their concern for Iraqi civilians during the first Gulf War (1990–1991), drawing in part upon the peacebuilding work of QUNO, the Quaker United Nations Office, which from the 1950s has sought high-level international policy engagement and has supported dialogue amongst QUNO staff, UN diplomats, and NGOs for the maintenance of peace. The second Gulf War (2003–2011), with its origins in US President George Bush's declaration of a "War on Terror" in 2001, saw further Quaker involvement in anti-war activities, including a controversial mode of remembrance: American Friends' Service Committee's "Eyes Wide Open." In the initial version of the exhibit, from 2004, a pair of boots marked each US soldier killed in the second Gulf War although, as casualty numbers grew, it became necessary to represent individual states rather than US deaths as a whole. A field of shoes represented the unknown number of Iraqi deaths, leading to some criticism from commentators viewing the exhibition as unpatriotic, although the response of the soldiers' families was more nuanced. In a similar manner, the use of drones in warfare, especially in the Middle East, highlighted what some Quaker authors have identified since 2010 as a "PlayStation mentality" on the part of those responsible for the weapons, perceived as geographically, and therefore emotionally, distant from those targeted. Such comments led to criticism by pro-military commentators, but support from other pacifist groups such as the US-based women's organization CODEPINK. More controversially yet, the boycott of Israeli goods, which since 2011 has encouraged the specific rejection of items produced in occupied territories rather than the entire state, represents a twenty-first-century interpretation of the historically based Quaker ideal of removing obstacles to peace by refusing to engage with or support acts contravening international law. The boycott has been met with criticism by several commentators questioning the assertion that settlements are illegal, and at times aligning Friends' recommendations with wider anti-Semitism, although Quakers are not alone in seeking a middle path between complete boycott of goods and inaction.

The fine details of Quaker pacifism, and of how violence is defined, may then in some respects be open to debate and certainly to external criticism. However, pacifism remains core to Quaker identity and, because of the linking of violence and men in hegemonic masculinity, is central to the gendered experiences of both Quaker men and women.

SEE ALSO: Christianity, Gender and Sexuality; Masculinities; Pacifism, Peace Activism, and Gender

REFERENCES

Fox, George, et al. 1660. *A Declaration from the Harmless & Innocent People of God, called Quakers*. London.

Lurting, Thomas. 1711. *The Fighting Sailor Turn'd Peaceable Christian*. London: J. Sowle.

FURTHER READING

Cohen, Susan. 2010. "Winter in Prague: the Humanitarian Mission of Doreen Warriner." *Association of Jewish Refugees Journal*, August.

Fast, Vera K. 2011. *Children's Exodus: A History of the Kindertransport 1938–1948*. London: IB Tauris.

Haskins, Ekatarina V. 2011. "Ephemeral Visibility and the Art of Mourning: Eyes Wide Open Traveling Exhibit." In *Rhetoric, Remembrance, and Visual Form*, edited by Anne Teresa Demo and Bradford Vivian. London: Routledge.

Horton, James O., and Lois E. Horton. 1999. "Violence, Protest and Identity: Black Manhood in Antebellum America." In *A Question of Manhood: A Reader in U.S. Black Men's History and Masculinity*, edited by Darlene Clark Hine and Earnestine Jenkins. Bloomington: Indiana University Press.

Jones, Lee. 2008. "The Others: Gender and Conscientious Objection in the First World War." *NORMA: Nordic Journal For Masculinity Studies*, 3(2): 99–113.

Jones Lapsansky, Emma, and Anne A. Verplanck, eds. 2002. *Quaker Aesthetics*. Philadelphia: University of Pennsylvania Press.

Jordan, Ryan. 2007. "The Dilemma of Quaker Pacifism in a Slaveholding Republic, 1833–1865." *Civil War History*, 53(1).

Penn, William. 1693. *A Brief Account of the Rise and Progress of the People called Quakers*.

Penney, Norman, ed. 1924. *The Journal of George Fox*. London: J. M. Dent & Sons.

Schmitt, Hans A. 1997. *Quakers and Nazis: Inner Light in Outer Darkness*. Columbia: University of Missouri Press.

Smith, Allen. 1996. "The Renewal Movement: The Peace Testimony and Modern Quakerism." *Quaker History*, 85(2): 1–23.

Pacifism, Peace Activism, and Gender

KENNETH J. HEINEMAN
Angelo State University, USA

The revolutionary ferment of late eighteenth-century Europe spawned a number of transatlantic reform movements, including the abolition of slavery, women's rights, and peace activism. Women reformers sought to carve out a political sphere of their own, one in which they could influence such public policy issues as foreign relations, temperance, the abolition of slavery, equality under the law, and voting rights. Although many of their causes bore fruit, peace remained elusive as women reformers around the world continued through the twentieth and twenty-first centuries to oppose war as an instrument of foreign policy.

In the era of the American and French revolutions and the celebration of the rights of free men, the crusade against slavery awakened. British playwright and women's rights activist Hannah Moore (1745–1833) spoke out against the slave trade. She championed the parliamentary leader of the abolitionist movement, William Wilberforce (1759–1833). Their movement attracted new female activists, among them the English Quaker Anne Knight (1786–1862). As an abolitionist, pacifist, and supporter of women's rights, Knight reached across the Atlantic to build an international reform movement – one which largely succeeded in restricting the transatlantic slave trade in the early nineteenth century.

The transnational anti-slavery movement that Knight helped to build included such American allies as William Lloyd Garrison (1805–1879), the publisher of the influential abolitionist newspaper *The Liberator*. In 1840, Knight and Garrison helped organize the World Anti-Slavery Convention in London. Although British women were key in planning and hosting the convention, their male counterparts refused to seat female delegates from the United States. If British women were second-class citizens in their own country, American women were of even lower status as colonials.

As the abolitionist movement grew in Europe and the United States in the early nineteenth century, peace emerged as a kindred cause. In 1828, Harvard alumnus and New England scion William Ladd (1778–1841) founded the American Peace Society (APS). The APS quickly attracted an affluent membership of Quakers and evangelical Protestants, including William Lloyd Garrison and the abolitionist sisters Angelina Grimke (1805–1879) and Sarah Grimke (1792–1873), the daughters of a South Carolina planter.

For the Grimke sisters, opposing slavery, war, and alcohol were complementary causes; at root of each issue was male aggression and the subsequent subjugation of the vulnerable. Women, as exemplars of virtue, needed to enter the public sphere to tame men – whether by prohibiting alcohol or cooling martial ardor. So long as women did not have the vote, however, their influence would be limited – hence the Grimkes' championship of women's equality and voting rights at the 1848 Women's Rights Convention at Seneca Falls, New York.

Swedish novelist and women's rights activist Fredrika Bremer (1801–1865) founded the Women's Peace League in 1854 and recruited members across Europe and the United States. Hailing from an affluent, educated background, Bremer had the means to travel to the United States between 1849 and 1851 to study slavery. She made contacts with American abolitionist, peace, and women's rights activists. The period following the war with Mexico (1846–1848) and the 1850 Compromise over the admission of new territories as slave or free states could have given Bremer little hope that peace and abolition would go hand in hand.

In truth, there was an inevitable tension between rejecting violence and promoting the abolition of slavery. Although slavery did not exist in nineteenth-century Britain, the British military had used violence, the threat and its actual exercise, to achieve its suppression. Slave ships cowered under the threat of the Royal Navy's guns.

Given how extensive, and politically entrenched, slavery was in the American South, abolition could only be achieved by waging the bloodiest war in US history. Garrison set aside his pacifist principles to champion the Union cause in the Civil War. Susan B. Anthony (1820–1906), having been a part of both the Seneca Falls Convention and the APS, struggled to reconcile her opposition to violence with her conviction that the North's war was just. Early in the war, Anthony contended that if only US President Abraham Lincoln (1809–1865) armed African American males, the frightened South would immediately surrender.

Even as the United States tore itself apart, the Second German Empire emerged as a force of political destabilization in Europe. Built on the foundation of three wars (Denmark 1864, Austro-Hungary 1866, and France, 1870–1871), Germany fanned the flames of European militarism and nationalism. Alarmed, Austrian aristocrat Bertha von Suttner (1843–1914) helped establish a new peace organization, the International Council of Women (ICW). The ICW held its first peace conference in London in 1888, drawing delegates from throughout Europe and the United States. Among the Americans was former abolitionist and Seneca Falls veteran Elizabeth Cady Stanton (1815–1902).

Suttner wrote of the human suffering that came with war, framing militarism as the victimizer of women and children. As a friend and colleague of Fredrika Bremer, Suttner convinced Swedish industrialist Alfred Nobel (1833–1896) to honor her memory by establishing an international peace prize. Suttner herself became the first woman to win the Nobel Peace Prize in 1905.

Closer to home, Suttner found fewer allies. The Austro-Hungarian Empire tolerated Suttner's peace activism and did not interfere with her efforts to forge alliances across national borders. Germany, which exercised enormous influence over Austro-Hungary's foreign policy, proved less receptive. As a greatly militarized society that admired strong male figures, one in which socialist coal miners proudly displayed photographs of communist revolutionary Karl Marx (1818–1883) *and* Prussian chancellor Otto von Bismarck (1815–1898), Suttner's influence was destined to be limited.

Across the Atlantic, with slavery abolished, American women reformers focused on temperance and peace. In 1873, Frances Willard (1839–1898) helped found the Women's Christian Temperance Union (WCTU). Willard believed that alcohol consumption and militarism were linked. Although many WCTU members deemphasized women's voting rights – a stance which Willard rejected – the organization established a Department of Peace and Arbitration in 1887. Hannah Bailey (1836–1923), a Quaker and APS member, led the WCTU's efforts to persuade the public that alcohol heightened male aggression in the home and overseas.

Toward the end of the nineteenth century, a new generation of American women activists came of age. Frances "Fanny" Garrison Villard (1844–1928), the daughter of William Lloyd Garrison, carried on the family's reform tradition. With the moral and financial support of her railroad executive and publisher husband, Villard espoused the causes of racial and women's equality. Villard also became an indispensable ally of Quaker social worker and peace activist Jane Addams (1860–1935).

America's war with Spain in 1898 and the acquisition of Cuba, Puerto Rico, and the Philippines prompted the establishment of the Anti-Imperialist League. While Addams and Villard warned that the United States was in danger of becoming a soulless, expansionist colonial power like Britain, France, and Germany, others in the Anti-Imperialist League were not as high-minded in their criticism of American foreign policy. Former Union general and US Senator Carl Schurz, for example, warned that racially inferior non-whites from the Philippines could potentially claim American citizenship and voting rights. If that happened, America would lose its racial vitality and perish. Given the wide range of opinions and motivations among the critics of US foreign policy, American anti-war organizations in the early twentieth century were inevitably weak and faction ridden.

With the outbreak of World War I in Europe in 1914, women peace activists rallied to keep America out of the conflict. In 1915, Addams enlisted in the Women's Peace Party and then helped establish the Women's International League for Peace and Freedom (WILPF) – which was an extension of the ICW. Although a few of the 40,000 American women who joined Addams and Villard were pacifists, most were isolationists – less concerned about eradicating war than wishing to stay out of the European conflict as others killed.

To Addams's dismay, once the United States entered the war in 1917, many allies deserted her. The WCTU regarded military camps as excellent recruiting grounds for the temperance cause. In short order, the WCTU abandoned its pacifist principles. Other suffrage and anti-war activists rallied behind US President Woodrow Wilson (1856–1924), arguing that Addams, as a woman, would never see combat. Therefore, she had no right to condemn war since she could have no understanding of battle.

The harsh political realities Addams confronted in the United States as a peace activist could also be found in Europe. In 1915, Addams took part in an ICW initiative to forge a non-aggression pact across Europe. Scottish activist Chrystal Macmillan (1872–1937) and the Hungarian Rosika Schwimmer (1877–1948) convened an International Congress of Women for a Permanent Peace at The Hague in 1915. The Peace Congress drew 1,150 female delegates.

Both Macmillan and Schwimmer had, like their American counterparts, been active since the late nineteenth century promoting women's suffrage. Moreover, Schwimmer had collaborated with von Suttner in the ICW before World War I. Schwimmer's and Macmillan's chief obstacle, however, was that the electorally influential European socialist parties, which had for decades pledged not to support "capitalist wars," proved to be more militantly nationalist than pacifist. Ironically, the less politically significant American Socialist Party kept true to its antiwar principles – nearly dooming it to extinction after 1917.

While Macmillan and Schwimmer were destined to be frustrated in their efforts to end World War I, they enjoyed some measure of personal success after Germany surrendered. Macmillan became a rare female attorney and politician in Britain, while Schwimmer served as a diplomatic representative for the newly independent nation of Hungary. Schwimmer, however, found her life endangered by a postwar political reaction to defeat and fled to the United States in 1921. As for Addams, her postwar experiences were mixed. Although Addams received some measure of international recognition in 1931 when she received the Nobel Peace Prize, she never lacked for American detractors even after her death. In the classic 1967 *Star Trek* episode "The City on the Edge of Forever," a thinly disguised Addams appeared as a 1930s social worker and pacifist whose anti-war principles led to the military triumph of Nazi Germany in World War II and the destruction of civilization.

From the nineteenth century through the 1920s, European and American peace activists, whether male or female, were Protestant. After World War I, Europe did not produce influential Catholic peace activists – with the exception of Peter Maurin (1877–1949) who found the United States to be more accepting of Catholic pacifism than his native France. The birth of American Catholic pacifism may be attributed to female convert and journalist Dorothy Day (1897–1980). Although professionally successful, Day felt an emptiness in her life. Her romantic relationships fell short, with one suitor insisting that she have an abortion and another unwilling to be a father to their daughter. Day's conversion to Catholicism led her to found the Catholic Worker Movement in 1933. Committed to serving the poor, the Catholic Workers opened Houses of Hospitality to feed and educate the unemployed and helped priests and the laity to organize labor unions.

By 1940, Day's newspaper, *The Catholic Worker*, had a circulation of 190,000. Her admirers included Michigan governor (and later US Supreme Court Justice) Frank Murphy (1890–1949) and Father Charles Owen Rice (1908–2005), an adviser to Philip Murray (1886–1952), the president of the steel workers' union who became the leader of the Congress for Industrial Organizations (CIO) on the eve of World War II. Although Murphy, Rice, and Murray rejected Day's pacifism, they tried to live up to her moral example. Rice and Murray emphasized reconciliation between labor and management, not class confrontation, while as a Supreme Court Justice Murphy denounced the federal government's internment of Japanese immigrants and their American-born children as racist and unbecoming of a democracy (*Korematsu v. United States* 1944).

Day's opposition to conscription and military aid to Britain in 1940, and determination to oppose American entry into World War II following the Japanese attack on the US Pacific Fleet at Pearl Harbor, halved the ranks of the Catholic Worker Movement. She persisted, however, in criticizing American intervention in World War II, was alarmed at escalating tensions between the United States and the Soviet Union in the 1950s, and opposed the American war in Vietnam in the 1960s.

Since the United States had become the world's dominant economic and military power after 1945, it was inevitable that US and international peace activism focused on American foreign policy. It was also understandable that given America's outsize role in the world, and having a tradition of democratic dissent, domestic opposition to an assertive US foreign policy would loom large. The Vietnam War brought these political realities into focus.

As American anti-war and countercultural ranks swelled with opposition to the Vietnam War, Day and her followers stood apart. Day was skeptical of 1960s sexual liberation, believing that the only thing men became liberated from was responsibility to the children they may have been creating and abandoning. She always showed respect to the male Catholic Church hierarchy, believing that one could disagree without being disagreeable. Francis Cardinal Spellman (1889–1967), America's highest ranking member of the hierarchy and a stanch supporter of the Vietnam War, rebuffed conservatives who demanded Day's excommunication in the 1960s. Spellman believed that Day might be a saint and he was not about to be the one who burned her at the stake.

Day's commitment to civility, reconciliation, and sexual propriety in the 1960s became ever more pronounced as many American college campuses moved in the opposite direction. Greater numbers of women peace activists on the campus, even if they had never read *The Catholic Worker*, found themselves moving closer to Day's stance on rights and responsibilities. The female campus activists who joined the largest university-based anti-war organization of the 1960s, the Students for a Democratic Society (SDS), had considerable difficulty in being taken seriously by their male colleagues. Many male SDSers regarded women as servants, sex objects, or both. Some women activists chose to emulate the most aggressive males in the anti-war movement, joining the Weather Underground, an SDS splinter group, and battling police officers and planting bombs. Others joined women's consciousness groups and endeavored to counter the predatory, condescending activists within the anti-Vietnam War movement of the 1960s and 1970s.

In addition to student activism in the 1960s, there were significant efforts to build a pacifist movement off the campus. Women Strike for Peace (WSP), established in 1961, claimed 500,000 members by the end of the decade. Many of its female members were either white-collar professionals or married to white-collar professionals. WSP founder Dagmar Wilson (1916–2011), for example, was a children's book illustrator and resident of an upper-middle-class Georgetown neighborhood in Washington, DC. The WSP membership drew upon veterans of the WILPF and a 1930s campus peace organization, the American Student Union (ASU).

Quakers exercised enormous influence within the WSP, giving the organization a strong pacifist ideology. WSP members and leaders regarded the United States and the Soviet Union as immoral equivalents, spreading violence and exploitation around the world. Like their radical campus counterparts, however, the WSP believed that the United States was a greater danger to international peace than the Soviet Union, given America's vastly superior economic and military resources. In contrast to SDS, the WSP more readily merged women's rights and peace activism and continued its existence beyond the Vietnam War. The WSP also largely avoided the fracturing common among earlier American peace groups, particularly the APS, WILPF, the Catholic Worker Movement, and the ASU, holding fast to its pacifist principles.

Since the 1970s American pacifist and women's rights advocates have not been able to expand the demographics of their organizations – remaining ensconced in a middle-class, well-educated milieu. Their greatest success has been bringing their issues and influence to bear within the Democratic Party, though at the expense of losing influence within Republican circles.

American activism in the 1960s and 1970s inspired others across the Atlantic. Raised by a German mother and an American serviceman, Petra Kelly (1947–1992) had a foot in both Cold War Europe and the United States. While attending American University in Washington, DC, Kelly joined civil rights and peace organizations. Returning to West Germany, Kelly helped found the Green Party in 1979.

Regarding the German Socialist Party as too militaristic, the Greens believed that the United States kept relations with the Soviet Union so enflamed that German reunification was impossible. Elected to the West German parliament or Bundestag in 1983, Kelly condemned US president Ronald Reagan's (1911–2004) decision to place more nuclear weapons on her nation's soil pointed toward the Soviet Union. Kelly lived to see the reunification of Germany – though it was not achieved in the way the Greens had hoped. Anti-communist American and German politicians achieved reunification on their terms (fully armed) and with the economic collapse of the Soviet Union. Kelly died in 1992 at the hands of her boyfriend, who then killed himself.

While Petra Kelly challenged America's Cold War foreign policy in Europe, an Australian medical doctor, Helen Caldicott (1938–), came to the fore of the international peace movement. Although military defeat in World War II, followed by postwar economic dislocation, had ended France's status as a global colonial and military power, successive French governments refused to bow to reality. France performed atmospheric testing of atomic bombs in the Pacific even as the United States and the Soviet Union agreed to ban the practice in 1963 thanks in part to a WSP campaign.

Caldicott lobbied in Australia, New Zealand, Europe, and the United States to pressure France to stop spreading radiation across the Pacific. Caldicott and the Women's Action for Nuclear Disarmament also waged a political campaign to declare Australia and New Zealand "nuclear-free" zones. By 1982, her anti-nuclear efforts worked in New Zealand, severely limiting port calls from the Australian and United States navies.

Since Caldicott's New Zealand triumph, international women's peace activism has continued to advance. Leymah Gbowee (1972–), a Liberian social worker, found inspiration in the 1960s American civil rights movement, particularly its religious–pacifist component. Ending the Liberian civil war, which commenced in 1989, became Gbowee's passion. She served as the Liberian point person for Africa's Women in Peacebuilding Network and went into exile in Ghana.

Gbowee's activism and outreach helped end the bloody civil war in 2003 and led to a fellow Liberian peace activist, the Harvard-educated Ellen Johnson Sirleaf (1938–), becoming the first female president of an African nation in 2005. Like Petra Kelly and Sirleaf, Gbowee studied in the United States, taking graduate courses at Eastern Mennonite University in Virginia. Immersed in the values of one of America's traditional "peace faiths," Gbowee continued her work to build a non-violent society. In 2011, Gbowee, Sirleaf, and a female activist from Yemen shared the Nobel Peace Prize.

Prior to the blossoming of women's history in the late 1970s, peace organizations were often treated in isolated, episodic fashion. Moreover, there was little scholarly effort at demonstrating the ideological and cultural continuities across time of activists and their organizations. Integrating the women's rights struggle into the peace narrative was also rare. Little scholarly attention, at least from the American side, has been given to women's peace organizations outside the United States. Although scholars have largely remedied many of the methodological deficiencies, future researchers would do well to examine the ideological realignments of political parties across the globe since the 1960s within the context of gender and peace activism. There have been steps in this direction, but more scholarly analysis is needed. Further, more international context, especially outside Europe, is needed – along with an analysis of the interplay between American and non-American female activists. Clearly, since the 1960s, non-American activists have inspired and influenced Americans as much as Americans have influenced female peace activists globally.

SEE ALSO: Gender Violence; Militarism and Gender-Based Violence

FURTHER READING

BOOKS

Alonso, Harriet Hyman. 1993. *Peace as a Women's Issue: A History of the U.S. Movement for World Peace and Women's Rights.* Syracuse: Syracuse University Press.

Anderson, Bonnie S. 2000. *Joyous Greetings: The First International Women's Movement, 1830–1860.* New York: Oxford University Press.

Cortright, David. 2008. *Peace: A History of Movements and Ideas.* Cambridge: Cambridge University Press.

Drescher, Seymour. 2009. *Abolition: A History of Slavery and Antislavery.* Cambridge: Cambridge University Press.

Elshtain, Jean Bethke. 2002. *Jane Addams and the Dream of Democracy.* New York: Basic Books.

Evans, Sara. 1980. *Personal Politics: The Roots of Women's Liberation in the Civil Rights Movement and the New Left.* New York: Vintage Books.

Heineman, Kenneth J. 1993. *Campus Wars: The Peace Movement at American State Universities in the Vietnam Era.* New York: New York University Press.

Opdycke, Sandra. 2012. *Jane Addams and Her Vision for America.* Upper Saddle River: Prentice Hall.

Piehl, Mel. 1982. *Breaking Bread: The Catholic Worker and the Origin of Catholic Radicalism in America.* Philadelphia: Temple University Press.

Swerdlow, Amy. 1993. *Women Strike for Peace: Traditional Motherhood and Radical Politics in the 1960s.* Chicago: University of Chicago Press.

Taylor, Alice Felt. 1944. *Freedom's Ferment: Phases of American Social History from the Colonial Period to the Outbreak of Civil War.* New York: Harper and Row.

WEBSITES

Heinrich Böll Stiftung: The Green Political Foundation. 2015. Petra Kelly Archives. Accessed September 7, 2015, at www.boell.de/en.

Nobelprize.org. 2015. Leymah Gbowee. Accessed September 7, 2015, at www.nobelprize.org/.

Quakers in the World. 2015. Accessed September 7, 2015, at www.quakersintheworld.org.

Swarthmore College Peace Collection. 2015. Accessed September 7, 2015, at www.swarthmore.edu/library/peace.

Parental Leave in Comparative Perspective

MAUREEN BAKER
University of Auckland, New Zealand

For over a century, reform groups have fought for social programs to help reconcile childbearing with paid work. In the late nineteenth century, governments were lobbied to introduce unpaid leave for pregnant workers, including job protection during the latter stages of pregnancy, pregnancy-related sickness, childbirth, and recovery (Hantrais 2004). Paid leave for maternity, paternity, adoption, and paid parental leave were demanded and enacted much later, but advocates argue that these policies could encourage reproduction and promote fetal development, family well-being, workers' rights, employment equity, and job continuity for women. Although the fight for parental leave from employment initially began in Europe (Bock and Thane 1991), reform groups in many countries of the world have struggled for and gained the right to these social programs. Maternity/paternity leave may be unpaid or paid, their duration varies considerably cross-nationally, benefits can be funded in a variety of ways, and leave/benefits can be gender specific (maternity/paternity leave) or gender neutral (parental leave) (OECD 2007).

Cross-national comparisons of compensation during parental leave are difficult to calculate because leave may be long with low payments or short with high payments, and considerable variation is apparent among countries and jurisdictions. Maternity/parental benefits are usually financed through general revenue or from social insurance contributions. If they are financed from general revenue, wage compensation often approximates that of "welfare" payments, although benefits may be paid at a higher rate (as in Australia and New Zealand). If they are financed through social insurance, they vary with employment earnings, payments are more generous for employees with higher pre-leave earnings (often fathers and full-time workers), and fewer new parents qualify. Both employers and employees could be required to contribute to social insurance or only one of these groups, while governments may also contribute. The "replacement rate" for maternity benefits varies from 100 percent of previous earnings in some countries (including Algeria, Brazil, China, France, Germany, India, Indonesia, Norway, the Philippines, and Vietnam) to 60 percent in Japan, 55 percent in Canada, 50 percent in Nigeria, 25 percent in Botswana, to nothing in Papua New Guinea and most of the United States (OECD 2007; updated from Internet). Where wage replacement rates are low and other social benefits for caring are unavailable, parents often take less than the maximum leave entitlement because their full earnings are needed for economic survival.

In the early years of program development, policies in most countries focused on women and maternity. Maternity benefits for employed women were first established in Germany in the nineteenth century but, by World War I, several other European countries already had passed some form of national maternity insurance. The first and most influential international standard that recognized the needs of working mothers emerged from the 1919 International Labour Organization (ILO) Maternity Protection Convention (Baker 2006). This ILO agreement laid down basic principles such as women's right to maternity leave, nursing breaks, wage compensation, and job protection. In 1952, the ILO Convention was revised to include a 12-week minimum leave period, including six weeks after the birth. Additional leave was to be provided in cases of pregnancy-related illness, and medical benefits were to be provided by qualified midwives or medical practitioners. Employers could not give notice of dismissal during maternity leave and work breaks had to be given for breastfeeding. By the 1980s, paid leave at childbirth or adoption was extended to employed fathers in countries such as Sweden, the United Kingdom, and Canada, but for a shorter duration (Leira 2002). Typically, mothers were entitled to at least 14 weeks but fathers were given only one or two weeks of gender-specific leave at the time of their child's birth. In 2000, the ILO Convention was amended to include 14 weeks' leave and the European Union (EU) Social Charter also provides for a minimum of 14 weeks' paid leave or social security benefits. However, other countries (such as Papua New Guinea, Swaziland, and most of the United States) offer only unpaid leave for employees at childbirth.

Maternity leave is justified as gender specific because only women give birth and lactate, and such policies focus on the health and welfare of pregnant women, mothers, fetuses, and newborns. Allowing pregnant women to take job-protected leave recognizes potential health risks from overwork or exposure to work-related hazards, and permitting recovery time acknowledges that childbirth is physically and psychologically exhausting. Finally, maternity leave and benefits can be an inducement to reproduce by ensuring that employed women do not respond to the difficulties of combining work and childrearing by choosing to remain childless. Consequently, health and safety advocates, religious groups, and conservative women's groups have argued for gender-specific maternity leave from employment (Baker 2006).

Gender-specific maternity leave can also be used to secure and sustain the employment of women. If, after working for a designated period of time, women are guaranteed paid leave while their positions are held open, they are more likely to enter the workforce and to ensure that they have met eligibility qualifications before becoming pregnant. Leaving paid work for childbearing and childrearing and returning years later was only feasible for women when the labor market was expanding, technological change was slower, men were paid a family wage, and divorce rates were lower. Now, women experience more difficulty reentering the workforce after several years at home because of higher unemployment, more global competition, and rapid technological change. Furthermore, a smaller percentage of households can survive on one income and fewer mothers can depend on another earner, especially where separation and divorce rates are high. Consequently, feminist groups, "progressive" reform groups, and trade unions have fought for paid maternity leave, although there has been more debate about the wisdom of long-term leave for promoting gender equality in the home and workforce. Paternity leave is also gender specific but is granted simultaneous with maternity leave and has been advocated for similar reasons as parental leave (Baker 2006).

Parental and paternity leave incorporates some concerns about the biology of childbirth but emphasizes the gender-neutral processes of nurturing and bonding, and equal rights for men and women. The philosophy behind both parental and paternity leave is that fathers should be encouraged to be present during childbirth, to bond with their newborn infants, and to participate in their daily care. Parental benefits are justified by arguing that childbirth leave and benefits directed only to mothers could discourage employers from hiring women of childbearing age, discourage gender equality, and discriminate against men who want to care for their newborn infants. Some countries (such as Norway) require that fathers take a portion of parental leave or it must be forfeited by the couple, to promote paternal bonding and share care work. However, mothers typically take much more leave than fathers, although fathers take more leave where compensation rates are higher. Men who take full parental or paternity leave also tend to spend more time caring for their children, although they may be a self-selected group who are more interested in nurturing (OECD 2007).

The right to parental benefits has been fought on the principle of gender equality for men and equal rights for biological and adoptive fathers. Political pressure, especially from legal reformers and fathers' rights groups, has required many jurisdictions to ensure that both men and women are eligible for parental leave programs and that at least a portion of previous wages is replaced. Even when wages are fully replaced, fathers are far less likely than mothers to take parental leave especially for extended periods, as this could reduce the household income more (as husbands typically earn more than their wives), mothers need time off for childbirth recovery and breastfeeding, and men are often more concerned about the employment consequences of work absences. Despite changes in legislation, caring work continues to be gendered, partly through early socialization but also because policies have been implemented within a gendered labor market (Baker 2006). On average, women take more responsibility than men for "kin-keeping," childcare, and housework; they more often work part-time in low-paid jobs, even in Scandinavia. Feminists and progressive reformers agree that paid maternity/parental leave is essential in order to promote gender equity. In some countries, advocacy groups have successfully argued for cash benefits at the time of childbirth, regardless of parental work or caring status, to compensate for higher expenses at the time of childbirth.

Some governments continue to view pregnancy and childbirth as private or family matters, of little concern to either employers or the state, and argue that asking employers to share the expense of childbirth leave would be too costly and would encourage discrimination against female employees (OECD 2007). Employed women might also increase their fertility or work hours simply to take advantage of access to maternity benefits, causing extra expenses and disruptions for employers, although there is no research evidence to support this. If the state were to provide such benefits, those who opposed paid parental leave further argue that taxes would rise significantly. Such arguments have prevailed in countries such as the United States where, despite high levels of single-parent households, high fertility rates, and moderate female employment rates compared to other OECD countries, the federal government has created no national program for maternity or parental benefits. Instead, unpaid leave is provided by federal medical and family leave legislation, and individual states, employers, professional associations, and trade unions are left to decide whether or not to offer paid leave.

Reformers have found that initiating or expanding employment leave at childbirth or adoption requires effective lobbying and coalition building. Advocates for improvements to parental benefits are now arguing that statutory supports and services for parents who are balancing employment and family life are essential for poverty reduction, women's employment equity, and children's well-being. However, expanding social programs requires political commitment and the investment of public money, which is especially difficult with competing demands for smaller government and lower taxes (Baker 2006).

A number of controversies surround the development and expansion of maternity or parental benefits. First, critics argue that the underlying structure of legislation tends to assume that male work characteristics are the norm, as entitlement is sometimes based on a lengthy work record in standard employment even though many women work in temporary or part-time positions with fewer than the required hours to qualify. Second, the ideal duration of benefits remains contentious. Sweden offers 16 months of paid leave, but many other countries provide a relatively short period of parental benefits (about 14 weeks) with the option of longer unpaid leave or extended leave at a lower rate. Extended unpaid parental and childrearing leave can help reduce unemployment, share existing jobs, and create temporary positions for unemployed workers, but lone mothers and low-income parents can seldom afford to take unpaid leave or leave on half wages. However, a short leave that forces employees to return to work quickly after childbirth could discourage breastfeeding, encourage maternal or infant health problems, and lead to childcare difficulties.

Third, levels of compensation vary by jurisdiction, with some offering no benefits, others paying them at the poverty level, while other countries offer more generous benefits (such as 100 percent of previous earnings). When maternity/parental leave is unpaid or compensated at a low level, mothers are forced to return to work too soon, and fathers are unlikely to take leave. Fourth, these benefits have sometimes been added to existing social insurance programs, changing their original understandings. When they form part of unemployment insurance, the expectation that the unemployed worker is available for work is altered. Furthermore, because payments are based on previous work record and earnings, fewer women than men qualify and women receive lower average payments than men. Where they form part of disability or sickness benefits, childbirth and adoption are falsely portrayed as illnesses or disabilities. Providing gender-neutral programs that could be used by either males or females has sometimes dampened employer opposition, especially to contributory social insurance schemes.

Two international trends have been apparent in parental leave policies. First, gender-neutral terminology is increasingly used to equalize benefits for males/females and for biological/adoptive parents, and paid parental leave has replaced maternity or paternity leave in some jurisdictions and workplaces. A second trend is to extend *unpaid* parental leave for one to five years, which can help resolve the high cost and shortage of infant childcare without expanding public funding. In addition, extended leave allows mothers who choose to care for their own children and who can afford to forfeit their earnings to do so without relinquishing their jobs. Extended parental leave also reduces absenteeism by temporarily replacing parents of infants or young children with employees who have fewer domestic responsibilities. And finally, it can help reduce unemployment by offering short-term contracts as maternity replacements, providing job experience for otherwise unemployed or marginally employed people. Yet extended unpaid leave is only an option for higher-income and two-parent families, and could work against women's equality by solidifying traditional gender roles (Baker 2006).

In conclusion, maternity, paternity, and parental benefits can fulfill several different policy objectives. They can be perceived as an attempt to improve maternal and child health, a form of employment equity for women, an inducement to reproduction, and a citizenship right for every employee. They can also be seen as an expense and aggravation to employers or as a deterrent to hiring women. Which model is chosen by a jurisdiction depends mainly on the political ideology of the government in power and the strength of various advocacy groups. Political pressure may be national or it can originate from supranational organizations such as the ILO, which tries to encourage member states to develop minimum standards of employment benefits. However, the policies chosen by governments fit in with their priorities and the model of family they support, and certain policy choices suit some political interests more than others.

SEE ALSO: Division of Labor, Domestic; Division of Labor, Gender; Earner–Carer Model; Work–Family Balance

REFERENCES

Baker, Maureen. 2006. *Restructuring Family Policies: Convergence and Divergence.* Toronto: University of Toronto Press.

Bock, Gisela, and Pat Thane, eds. 1991. *Maternity and Gender Policies: Women and the Rise of European Welfare States 1880s–1950s.* New York: Routledge.

Hantrais, Linda. 2004. *Family Policy Matters: Responding to Family Change in Europe.* Bristol: The Policy Press.

Leira, Arnlaug. 2002. *Working Parents and the Welfare State: Family Change and Policy Reform in Scandinavia.* Cambridge: Cambridge University Press.

Organization for Economic Cooperation and Development (OECD). 2007. *Babies and Bosses: Reconciling Work and Family Life*, vol. 5. Paris: OECD Publications.

Parenting in Prison

BRITTNIE AIELLO
Merrimack College, USA

Parenting in prison is more common now than at any point in history. At least 25,000 children in Canada have a mother in prison. An estimated 160,000 children in the United Kingdom have a parent in prison. Across

Europe, nearly 1 million children have a parent in prison. In the United States, more than 1.5 million minor children have a parent in state or federal prison. Parental incarceration has followed the pattern of mass incarceration more generally. Largely attributed to the War on Drugs, prison population rates in the United States have doubled since 1991 (Schirmer, Nellis, and Mauer 2009). The effects of punitive drug policies are also reflected in increased prison populations in Latin America. Parental incarceration is a significant feature of many modern families.

The impact of parental incarceration is not shared equally across the population. In Canada, Aboriginal parents have a greater incidence of incarceration than whites. In Europe, Roma are highly likely to be incarcerated. In the United States, African American parents are disproportionately incarcerated. African American children are nine times more likely to experience parental incarceration than are white children (Pew Charitable Trusts 2008). Hispanic children are also more likely than white children to experience parental incarceration. These trends are in keeping with the rates of incarceration among the population in general, which are vastly disproportionate by race. Across the world, poor children are the most likely to have a parent in prison, as poverty is a key feature of incarcerated populations.

In the United States, men comprise 90 percent of the incarcerated population, and fathers are far more likely than mothers to become incarcerated. However, the remarkable increase in women's incarceration over the past 30 years has had a considerable effect on how children and families experience incarceration. Mothers' incarceration is more likely to result in a change of living situation for the children. Children of incarcerated mothers are also more likely to end up in foster care or to be cared for by kin than when fathers become incarcerated. This is because mothers are more likely to be primary caregivers of children prior to their arrest and incarceration. The children's mother in 86 percent of cases cares for the children of male inmates. However, only 26 percent of the children of female inmates rely on their father for caregiving (Women's Prison Association 2009).

Such trends are consistent across the globe. Incarcerated women are likely to come from precarious economic backgrounds that put them at risk for incarceration in the first place. Incarcerated mothers are more likely to be single parents and primary caregivers of children in Argentina, France, Germany, Hungary, Italy, Portugal, Spain, and the United Kingdom. Mothers' incarceration uproots children and puts further pressure on poor families to provide and give care for children. However, at least one study in the Netherlands found that children whose mothers go to prison are likely to live apart from their mothers prior to incarceration (Hissel, Bijleveld, and Kruttschnitt 2011).

Academic studies of the effects of parental incarceration have largely focused on the plight of children of incarcerated parents. Psychologists have found that the children of incarcerated parents experience higher levels of behavioral problems, trouble in school, and emotional distress than their peers with non-incarcerated parents. However, children cope well without their mothers when they have meaningful, consistent relationships with other adults. Sociologists have also found that the effects of parental incarceration on children's well-being are multifold. The economic loss to families is significant, both during incarceration when parents' income is lost, and after when they face greater challenges in employment due to a criminal record and time spent out of the labor force. Children whose parents have been incarcerated are more likely to go without basic necessities, experience residential instability, and be on public assistance than their peers whose parents have not been incarcerated. These economic disadvantages, in turn, can lead to adverse developmental outcomes, including behavior problems, poor verbal skills, and mental and physical health problems (Geller et al. 2009).

Social work scholarship has examined the effectiveness of programming for incarcerated parents. In particular, studies have focused on the utility of parenting classes and visitation for incarcerated parents and children. The results for parenting classes suggest that attitudes toward parenting, such as empathy and expectations for children, can improve with parenting classes, but little evidence is available regarding how these translate into better outcomes for parents and children. Studies of parent–child visitation suggest that regular visits are important for maintaining relationships and can reduce recidivism, but can also produce anxiety for inmates and their children.

Litigation regarding parenting during incarceration has often focused on parental rights balanced with the best interests of the child. Parental rights are not automatically terminated when a parent goes to jail, but physical separation is cause for the termination of parental rights under the Adoption and Safe Families Act (ASFA) of 1997. The law seeks to prevent children from languishing in foster care, and since its passage, the number of parental terminations related to incarceration has increased annually. More recently, legislation banning the widespread practice of shackling incarcerated women during labor has been gaining momentum. Thirteen states and the Federal Bureau of Prisons now ban the shackling of laboring women. Several other states have legislation pending.

There are a number of obstacles to parenting in prison. Beyond the mere fact of a parent's incarceration and separation from their children, inmates in the age of mass incarceration face additional challenges because of the sheer number of prisoners in the United States and the strategies that states have developed to manage them. Some states have outsourced prisoners to others with smaller inmate populations, sometimes placing inmates hundreds of miles away from their families, making visits strategically difficult and costly. In the case of inmates who are women, fewer facilities mean that mothers are likely to be imprisoned far away from their homes and families, even when incarcerated in their home state. The remote location of women's prisons is also a problem in Germany, Hungary, and Spain. These difficulties may be compounded by strained relationships with caregivers, as parents are usually reliant on their children's caregivers to provide transportation for visits. Communication is also costly, sometimes prohibitively so. A recent Federal Communications Commission (FCC) ruling capped rates for phone calls from prison at $.25 per minute or $3.75 for a 15-minute phone call, down from an average of $17 per minute. The global structure of the drug trade has led to an increased number of incarcerated migrants, making communication and visitation even more difficult.

Great distances and costs associated with visitation are serious disadvantages for incarcerated families because visitation is the primary way that parents and children maintain contact during incarceration. For small children in particular, being able to see and touch a parent is of primary importance. Visitation is advantageous for families because it can help alleviate anxiety due to separation, ease the transition back to parenting after incarceration, and, some argue, reduce recidivism. To these ends, many prisons have special visitation programs for parents and children. However, some parents report that the artificial environment, lack of privacy, and security procedures detract from the positive effects of visiting with their children.

Two recent trends mark a potential shift in how states deal with incarcerated mothers and their children: prison nurseries and residential facilities for incarcerated women and their children. In Portugal, children up to age 3 are permitted to reside with their parents in prison. In Argentina, children up to 4 can live with their mothers in designated facilities. Currently, there are nine prison nurseries in the United States. All but one of these facilities opened within the past 20 years (Women's Prison Association 2009). Prison nurseries enable women serving sentences for non-violent offenses to keep their babies with them for a designated period of time, thus reducing some of the negative effects of mother/child separation in the early period of infant development. Proponents of prison nurseries argue that mother/child bonding is crucial in early infancy. They point to a number of other advantages like reduced recidivism for mothers and developmental benefits for children. Such benefits have been realized through prison nursery programs in Britain, Germany, and France, but the supply of nursery programs is woefully inadequate in Italy, Hungary, and Spain. Critics of prison nurseries argue that prison is not an appropriate environment for infants.

Community-based residential programs (CBRP) divert women from traditional prisons to alternative-to-incarceration programs where they live during their pregnancy or with their young children. The length of time that children are permitted to live with their mothers varies by facility and the length of the mother's sentence, but most programs allow children to stay with their mothers until they reach school age. These residential programs are far more common than prison nurseries, and are usually based in the community. They are often entirely separate from the prison, and run by non-profit organizations in partnership with county and state governments. CBRPs are less costly than traditional prisons, and are thought to reduce recidivism by helping mothers maintain social ties and develop educational and vocational skills.

SEE ALSO: Criminal Justice System and Sexuality in the United States

REFERENCES

Geller, Amanda, Irwin Garfinkel, Carey E. Cooper, and Ronald B. Mincy. 2009. "Parental Incarceration and Child Wellbeing: Implications for Urban Families." *Social Science Quarterly*, 90(5): 1186–1202.

Hissel, Sanne C., Catrien Bijleveld, and Candace Kruttschnitt. 2011. "The Well-Being of Children of Incarcerated Mothers: An Exploratory Study for the Netherlands." *European Journal of Criminology*, 8: 346–360.

Pew Charitable Trusts. 2008. *One in 100: Behind Bars in America 2008*. Accessed July 1, 2015, at http://www.pewtrusts.org/en/research-and-analysis/reports/2008/02/28/one-in-100-behind-bars-in-america-2008.

Schirmer, Sarah, Ashley Nellis, and Marc Mauer. 2009. *Incarcerated Parents and Their Children: Trends 1991–2007*. Washington, DC: The Sentencing Project.

Women's Prison Association. 2009. *Mothers, Infants, and Imprisonment: A National Look at Prison Nurseries and Community-Based Alternatives*. Washington, DC: Women's Prison Association.

Passing

LINDA SCHLOSSBERG
Harvard University, USA

In its broadest sense, passing refers to the ability to convincingly appear as that which one is not, whether intentionally or accidentally. It is most commonly used in relation to race and sexuality (e.g., the ability of a light-skinned African American person to appear – or "pass as" – white, or a gay person's ability to pass as straight). It can also refer to an immigrant's ability to pass as a naturalized citizen, or a lower class person's ability to pass as upper class, and vice versa. The ease with which individuals often pass along multiple axes of identification calls into question the seeming fixity of social classifications.

The term's use has a rich history. Historically, the term has most commonly been used in relation to racial passing. Authors of the nineteenth century, such as Frances E. W. Harper (1893), William Wells Brown (1853), and Harriet Jacobs, frequently invoked the figure/literary trope of the "tragic mulatta" (a fair-skinned mixed-race woman) to highlight the cruel and arbitrary nature of racial classifications. Fictional accounts of female slaves – who appeared white, temporarily escaped their masters, and were eventually remanded back to slavery – were at once tragic and titillating, their very presence evidence of the sexual abuse of slaves that defenders of the "color line" fiercely denied.

More recently, the idea of passing has come to stand in for the instability of a range of social categories, including class, race, nationality, gender, religion, and sexuality. The intersection of racial and sexual passing is richly presented in Nella Larsen's Harlem Renaissance novel *Passing* (1929). On the surface a story of a light-skinned woman who passes for white, the novel has also been interpreted as a discussion of sexual passing, a coded depiction of lesbianism that passes as a story about race (McDowell 1986).

For gay and lesbian individuals, passing as straight can involve affecting traditionally gendered behaviors. For instance, a gay man whose natural behavior is read as feminine by his society's standards would affect more "masculine" behaviors or mannerisms in order to pass as straight. Gay men whose natural behavior is read as masculine by societal standards often pass as straight without any effort, even when they do not want to pass. The same applies to lesbians and "feminine" behavior. Passing can also involve getting into a relationship with a person of the opposite sex just to give others the impression of heterosexuality, with or without the full knowledge and consent of the other person in the relationship. The heterosexual individual in the relationship is colloquially known as the "beard" to the gay or lesbian individual attempting to pass as straight. In some instances, a lesbian and gay man will act as beards for each other, in order for them both to pass as heterosexual.

While many lesbian, gay, bisexual, and transgender (LGBT) individuals have found it necessary to pass as straight for reasons of physical safety or familial acceptance, the gay rights movement has encouraged and increasingly made it possible for the LGBT community to come out and make themselves visible. 1990s activist groups in the United States, most particularly Queer Nation, framed declaring one's sexual identity as a personally, morally, and politically crucial act, one that serves as a challenge to the presumptive and visible nature of heterosexual identity. More than simply a matter of personal choice, coming "out of the closet" was posited as a necessary precursor to the ultimate liberation of all sexual minorities. When and where one chooses not to pass, and to be out and visible, is still for many LGBT individuals a matter of physical safety, economic security, and emotional acceptance.

Passing has become a key issue in the theorization of transgender identity and experience. Some transgender people assigned male at birth wish to pass as female, and some transgender people assigned female at birth wish to pass as male. The ability to successfully pass after sex transitioning (from male to female, or female to male, with or without the assistance of hormones and/or surgical procedures) was long considered the ultimate sign of "success" – the goal that allows transgender individuals to live safely and comfortably. Sometimes this would involve a partial erasure or denial of one's past, such as one's childhood or adolescent life as the other sex. Many scholars (Stone 1996; Chase 1998), have questioned that formulation, suggesting that being vocal and transparent about one's gender history – telling the entire history of one's gender identity – is a more emotionally coherent, psychologically healthy, and politically engaged way of being in the world. The potential layers of reinvention and rewriting involved in narrating the transgender biography has called attention, for many theorists (Halberstam 2000), to the scripted and highly contingent nature of all stories of personal identity and self-revelation.

SEE ALSO: Coming Out; Gender Identities and Socialization; Gender Stereotypes; Sex Reassignment Surgery; Skin Lightening/Bleaching; Transsexuality

REFERENCES

Brown, William Wells. 1853. *Clotel; or, The President's Daughter*. London: Partridge and Oakey.
Chase, Cheryl. 1998. "Hermaphrodites with Attitude: Mapping the Emergence of Intersex Political Activism." *GLQ: A Journal of Lesbian and Gay Studies*, 4(2): 189–211.
Halberstam, Judith. 2000. "Brandon Teena, Billy Tipton, and Transgender Biography." *a/b: Auto/Biographical Studies*, 15(1): 62–81. DOI: 10.1080/08989575.2000.10815235.
Harper, Frances E.W. 1893. *Iola Leroy; or, Shadows Uplifted*. Philadelphia: Garrigues Brothers.
Larsen, Nella. 1929. *Passing*. New York: Knopf.
McDowell, Debora E. 1986. *Introduction to Passing and Quicksand*. Rutgers: Rutgers University Press.
Stone, Sandy. 1996. "The Empire Strikes Back: A Posttranssexual Manifesto." In *Body Guards: The Cultural Politics of Sexual Ambiguity*, edited by Kristina Straub and Julia Epstein, 280–304. New York: Routledge.

FURTHER READING

Bennet, Juda. 1996. *The Passing Figure: Racial Confusion in Modern American Literature*. New York: Peter Lang.
Butler, Judith. 1993. "Passing, Queering: Nella Larsen's Psychoanalytic Challenge." *Bodies That Matter: On the Discursive Limits of Sex*. New York: Routledge.
Fabi, M. Giulia. 2001. *Passing and the Rise of the African American Novel*. Urbana: University of Illinois Press.
Ginsberg, Elaine K., ed. 1996. *Passing and the Fictions of Identity*. Durham, NC: Duke University Press.
Hobbs, Allyson. 2014. *A Chosen Exile: A History of Racial Passing in American Life*. Cambridge, MA: Harvard University Press.
Roth, Phillip. 2000. *The Human Stain*. New York: Houghton Mifflin.
Sanchez, Maria C., and Linda Schlossberg, eds. 2001. *Passing: Identity and Interpretation in Sexuality, Race, and Religion*. New York: New York University Press.
Senna, Danzy. 1998. *Caucasia*. New York: Riverhead.
Sollors, Werner. 1997. *Neither Black Nor White Yet Both: Thematic Explorations of Interracial Literature*. New York: Oxford University Press.
Whitehead, Colson. 2000. *The Intuitionist*. New York: Anchor.

Patriarchy

DONALD P. LEVY
Siena College, New York, USA

Patriarchy is most commonly understood as a form of social organization in which cultural beliefs and institutional patterns accept, support, and reproduce the domination of women and younger men by older or more powerful men. Literally, the "rule of the father." Today, sociologists view as patriarchal any system that contributes to the social, cultural, and economic superiority or hegemony of men. Consequently, sociologists study the manner in which societies have become and continue to be patriarchal by investigating both social institutions and commonly held cultural beliefs. At the same time, scholars investigate the consequences of patriarchy (i.e., differential access to scarce societal resources including power, authority, and opportunity by gender).

Although some scholars simply use the word patriarchy to describe what they consider to be a natural or inevitable form of social organization, more recently scholars, stimulated by the work of early feminist writers (Bernard 1972; de Beauvoir 1972), have come to recognize patriarchy as a prevalent system of inequality similar in some ways to racism, or classism (Hartsock 1983). Prior to the critical work of feminist scholars, many considered patriarchy to be the natural result of biological difference or rather a truly complementary system based upon differential inclinations that served to address society's need for a division of labor (Durkheim 1933; Parsons 1956). A more critical analysis of the origins of patriarchy, however, looks to its cultural and social genesis as located within both beliefs and specific social institutions.

Scholars today explore the manner in which patriarchy, or male domination, is socially constructed, but has become institutionalized, that is, built into the major social systems including the family, religion, the economy, government, education, and the media. In so doing, the taken-for-grantedness of patriarchy is exposed, and analyzed (Smith 1987).

Many scholars have looked to the institution of the family in order to explain the origins and persistence of patriarchy. Engels (1970) described the patriarchal structure of the family but centered his analysis on its contribution to capitalism while Levi-Strauss (1967) observed and chronicled the cultural roots of patriarchy and highlighted a key implicit component, that of the objectification and devaluation of women by men.

Bernard (1972) demonstrated the differential structure of marriage and family by gender that deterministically reproduces patriarchy. The family, including the household division of labor (Hochschild and Machung 1997), divorce, child-rearing, as well as power and cultural perception (Smith 1993), have been and continue to be specific sites in which patriarchy is seen, analyzed, and in some cases resisted.

The family, as an institution, is at all times interacting with the economy or public sphere. Despite functionalist assertions of complementarity and balance, the women's movement and feminist scholars have continued to point to the multiple ways in which the economic sphere as well as the interaction between the family and the economy serve to reproduce and enforce patriarchy as a social system. Issues including initially access to economic opportunity, and more recently the gendering of occupations, the glass ceiling (Williams 1992), and sexual harassment, have concerned both activists and scholars. A Parsonian expression of balance between the public (economic) sphere and the private (family) sphere argues in favor of men being primarily active in the public and women in the private. Currently, feminist scholars and most sociologists dismiss this characterization as patriarchal and focus on the manner in which the institutions that perpetuate this unequal system are so structured.

Since the beginnings of feminism as a social movement in the nineteenth century, activists have sought equal legal rights for women. Theoretically, this movement demonstrated the irony of a social contract that disenfranchised half of its inferred signers (Pateman 1988). In other words, a democracy that promised equal representation to every citizen only so long as they were men represented a patriarchal system. Needless to say, other marginalized groups were also left unrepresented. Although first-wave feminists succeeded in obtaining women's suffrage, and despite a lull in the social movement subsequent to that victory, the struggle for full and practical legal rights and representation remained a focus of the feminist struggle against patriarchy in governmental institutions. Second-wave feminism rallied around abortion rights and the Equal Rights Amendment (ERA) as core issues in both the exposition of and struggle against patriarchy. Today, despite continuing successes in legal rights and apparent access in many areas, activists are once again involved in a dynamic public debate over abortion. Still, patriarchy is demonstrated in the continuing disproportionate power of men over women in government as noted in numbers of men and women in elected positions as well as in legal and judicial debates over issues including not only abortion, but also family leave, divorce, and sexual harassment.

Often, scholars as well as other social critics look to the education institution as a potential avenue of either conservative social reproduction or social change. Relative to patriarchy, education is discussed in both ways. Many now cite the successes of women in education in terms of the number of women obtaining college or postgraduate degrees. Still, critics note the gendering of credentials (i.e., women obtaining degrees in less highly valued fields; Kimmel 2000) as well as the "hidden curriculum" of education (Coleman 1961) in which the structure and beliefs of patriarchy are taught regardless of the gender of the recipient.

Patriarchy continues to be observed, reproduced, and resisted in other social institutions including the military, religion, and the media. Despite increasing participation in the military by women, the structure and culture of the institution remains patriarchal (Cohn 1993). Religion has long been seen by scholars, of course with extreme variation between traditions, as providing justification for patriarchy. Still, today many traditions are beginning to question and change their theologically mandated patriarchal structure while others remain virtually unchanged. The media, although more inclusive that either the military or religion, remains a domain in which examples of male domination often go unquestioned. One need only consider the centrality of male-dominated sport to see the manner in which the media participate in the perpetuation of patriarchy. Still, recent manifestations of popular culture sponsored by various media sources are beginning to place women in positions of power and centrality both of which may serve to lessen the seeming naturalness of patriarchy.

Given the ubiquity of patriarchy within individual societal institutions as well as the manner in which these institutions interact, it is no wonder that patriarchy continues to appear natural and necessary, that is, hegemonic (Gramsci 1971). Still, as feminist theory has pointed out, patriarchy is a political issue, for both groups and individuals. The "personal" is indeed "political." As such, patriarchy as a system of social organization, although deeply ingrained in both social institutions and consequently in the individuals that find themselves living within those institutions, is subject to both contestation and resistance. Gender relations as currently constituted in a patriarchal system are subject to change.

Feminist scholars today continue to struggle against patriarchy but have now broadened their focus to include multiple forms of privilege that serve to oppress not only women, but all women as well as other marginalized groups (Collins 1986; Johnson 2001). At the same time, scholars have begun to not only demonstrate how patriarchy is embedded in social institutions and ingrained in the manner in which we do gender (West and Zimmerman 1987), but also to call for undoing gender, that is, to remove gender and consequently patriarchy as a central organizing principle of social relations (Butler 2004; Lorber 2005).

Patriarchy is a system of social organization that recognizes, encourages, and reproduces the seeming natural and necessary domination of men over women. Despite the legal and social changes fought for and achieved by activists and supported by scholars over the last 150 years, patriarchy is indeed persistent. This persistence is due to the manner in which patriarchy has become deeply ingrained in each and every aspect of every significant societal institution and consequently into the manner in which individuals learn to practice gender. The deconstruction of patriarchy is therefore both an individual and institutional quest dependent on scholarly insight, exposition as well as individual courage, good will, and commitment to justice.

SEE ALSO: Division of Labor, Gender; Earner–Carer Model; Feminisms, First, Second, and Third Wave; Gender Wage Gap; Glass Ceiling and Glass Elevator

REFERENCES

Bernard, Jessie. 1972. *The Future of Marriage*. New York: World Publishing.
Butler, Judith. 2004. *Undoing Gender*. London: Routledge.
Cohn, C. 1993. "Wars, Wimps, and Women: Talking Gender and Thinking War." In *Gendering War Talk*, edited by Miriam G. Cooke and Angela Woollacott. Princeton: Princeton University Press.
Coleman, James. 1961. *The Adolescent Society*. New York: Harper and Row.
Collins, P.H. 1986."Learning from the Outsider Within: The Sociological Significance of Black Feminist Thought." *Social Problems*, 33(6): 14–32.
de Beauvoir, Simone. 1972. *The Second Sex*. Harmondsworth: Penguin.
Durkheim, Emile. 1933. *The Division of Labor in Society*. Glencoe, IL: Free Press.
Engels, Frederick. 1970. *The Origin of the Family, Private Property and the State*. Moscow: Progress Publishers.
Gramsci, Antonio. 1971. *Selections from the Prison Notebooks*. London: Lawrence and Wishart.
Hartsock, Nancy. 1983. *Sex and Power: Toward a Feminist Historical Materialism*. New York: Longman.
Hochschild, Arlie, and Anne Machung. 1997. *The Second Shift*. New York: Avon Books.
Johnson, Allan G. 2001. *Privilege, Power and Difference*. Boston: McGraw-Hill.
Kimmel, Michael S. 2000. *The Gendered Society*. New York: Oxford University Press.
Levi-Strauss, Claude. 1967. *Structural Anthropology*. New York: Basic Books.
Lorber, Judith. 2005. *Breaking the Bowls: Degendering and Feminist Change*. New York: Norton.
Parsons, Talcott. 1956. *Family Socialization and Interaction Process*. London: Routledge.
Pateman, Carole. 1988. *The Sexual Contract*. Stanford: Stanford University Press.
Smith, Dorothy E. 1987. *The Everyday World as Problematic: A Feminist Sociology*. Toronto: University of Toronto Press.
Smith, Dorothy E. 1993. "The Standard North American Family: SNAF as an Ideological Code." *Journal of Family Issues*, 14(1): 50–65.
West, C. and D.H. Zimmerman. 1987. "Doing Gender." *Gender and Society*, 1(2): 125–151.
Williams, C.L. 1992. "The Glass Escalator: Hidden Advantages for Men in the 'Female' Professions." *Social Problems*, 39(3): 253–267.

Performance Art

LOUIS VAN DEN HENGEL
Maastricht University, The Netherlands

Performance art, more specifically referred to as "body art" or "live art," is a contemporary art form that takes the materiality and temporality of the body – in its irreducible particularity – as the primary medium of creative expression. The term arose in the early 1960s primarily in Europe, North America, and Japan to describe the manifold actions of artists who sought to extend the boundaries of visual art into real time and space by offering the body as a vital site for the production and reception of aesthetic sensations, and as a vehicle for progressive personal, social, and political change. Challenging the conventional distinctions between artist, artwork, and audience, early performance artists not only effected a shift of visual art beyond its established representational or signifying functions, but also played a decisive role in negotiating new relationships between contemporary art and the cultural politics of gender, sexuality, race, ethnicity, and class.

Primarily an avant-garde form, performance often deploys a visceral aesthetics, engaging the spectator immediately at the embodied level of sensation and affect, either in the form of a live event or as an action to be experienced through representational media such as video, film, and photography. The aesthetic genealogy of performance can be traced to early twentieth-century modernist movements, from Futurism, Dada, and Surrealism to the various Russian avant-gardes and the development of Bauhaus in 1920s Germany. However, whereas performative actions in modern art were largely used to catalyze established forms into new directions, performance in the second half of the twentieth century became recognized as an artistic medium in its own right (Goldberg 2006; Warr 2006). In close correspondence to Conceptual Art and Minimalism, performance actively resisted the object status of visual art as it was privileged, and commodified, in the context of the art market and finance capitalism, by transforming the collectible "art object" into a temporal act or process. Further politicized by occasions such as the May 1968 events in France, the Vietnam War, and the rise of various feminist and civil rights movements, performance became an arena in which criticism – both social and artistic – was literally enacted through the creation of a new time- and body-based aesthetics.

Performance from the 1970s onwards has been pioneered by feminist artists such as Carolee Schneemann, VALIE EXPORT, Gina Pane, Ana Mendieta, and Karen Finley, whose staging of their own bodies and selves served to decode the female body as a site where sociocultural scripts of gender and sexuality are inscribed, and also to proclaim and affirm the creative agency of the body/subject displayed (Wark 2006). For example, EXPORT's *Tapp und Tastkino* (Tap and Touch Cinema), performed as a guerrilla street action across 10 European cities between 1968 and 1971, actively mobilized the artist's body to interrogate the workings of sexual objectification. In this work, EXPORT wore a cardboard "movie theatre" fronted by a small screen around her naked upper body, inviting people to reach inside and touch her breasts for 12 seconds. Anticipating the criticism of the male gaze developed in feminist film theory, EXPORT reversed the voyeuristic beholding of sexualized images of women in classical cinema, by offering a tactile – yet invisible – public encounter with herself as a subject, rather than object, of vision.

Male body artists such as Chris Burden, Vito Acconci, Paul McCarthy, and Bob Flanagan likewise sought the subversion of socially repressive norms of gender, sexuality, and able-bodiedness through focused acts of pain and vulnerability, often involving dangerous forms of self-violation. Similar performative tactics have been used by artists like Ron Athey and Franko B, whose work traces the interconnections between performance art, queer grassroots activism, and BDSM culture in the context of the conservative backlash of the early 1990s. Athey's *Four Scenes in a Harsh Life* (1994), for example, explored traumatic experience rooted in homophobia and religious fanaticism through ritualized acts of body piercing, blood-letting, and scarification. The performance was followed by media hysteria when the artist was (falsely) accused of exposing the audience to HIV-infected blood, which scandalized the religious right in the United States.

Art historians and cultural theorists have often considered performance art, especially in the earlier years, as the manifestation of an emergent postmodernist sensibility in Western culture. In this view, the challenges that performance posed to the structures and institutions of modern art imply a more fundamental dislocation of the Cartesian subject of modernism in a late capitalist and postcolonial context (Phelan 1993; Jones 1998). Nevertheless, the aesthetic and sensory experience of time-based art cannot be reduced to the deconstructive intent of many performance works. For example, the "durational" performances of artists such as Tehching Hsieh, Linda Montano, and Marina Abramović, which unfold over the course of months or years, implicate the artists and the audience in processes of physical, mental, and spiritual change that elude the scope of traditional hermeneutic and semiotic approaches to visual art. Moreover, the turn to performance is not confined to Western art traditions; the work of Latin American artists such as María Evelia Marmolejo and Artur Barrio, for example, played a vital, yet relatively under-recognized, role in the development of the genre. Since the late 1970s, performance has also made a significant impact on contemporary art in Asia, most notably post-Mao China, where Ma Liuming and Zhang Huan are two of the most prominent practitioners.

In the early twenty-first century, performance witnessed a remarkable resurgence in popularity, which has decisively moved the genre from the margins to the mainstream of contemporary art. This development has been sparked considerably by landmark exhibitions in major museums, most notably the performance retrospective *The Artist is Present* devoted to the work of Marina Abramović at the Museum of Modern Art in New York in 2010. As live art is moving into the institutions it once opposed, questions about the ontology of performance, and about the conservation of its aesthetic, art-historical, and activist legacy, are once again put firmly on the agenda of art scholars, cultural theorists, museum professionals, and artists or practitioners. At the same time, the performance avant-garde has become increasingly dispersed: its hubs and networks have moved beyond the traditional centers of the art world, spreading across a vibrant community of performance art festivals and biennials worldwide.

SEE ALSO: Body Politics; Feminist Art; Feminist Art Practice; Queer Performance; Visual Culture and Gender

REFERENCES

Goldberg, RoseLee. 2006. *Performance Art: From Futurism to the Present*. London: Thames and Hudson.

Jones, Amelia. 1998. *Body Art/Performing the Subject*. Minneapolis: University of Minnesota Press.

Phelan, Peggy. 1993. *Unmarked: The Politics of Performance*. London: Routledge.

Wark, Jayne. 2006. *Radical Gestures: Feminism and Performance Art in North America*. Montreal: McGill-Queen's University Press.

Warr, Tracey. 2006. *The Artist's Body*. London: Phaidon.

Personal is Political

THERESA MAN LING LEE
University of Guelph, Canada

The phrase "personal is political" is easily among the most widely known political slogans of our time. Historically, the phrase was associated with "radical feminism," which emerged in the late 1960s in the United States as some activists began to break ranks with existing feminist groups to form their own distinctive movement – the Women's Liberation Movement. The movement as shaped by these activists was radical because it maintained that neither the right-based approach adopted by liberal feminists at the time nor the class-based strategy advocated by the left could serve women as women appropriately and adequately. At the heart of radical feminism was the view that the so-called personal lives of women were in fact rife with power relations which consistently placed women in an inferior position to men, and even directly under their control. This was wrong and had to be redressed by society as a political issue that mattered to all rather than as a personal problem that individual women faced.

As a publicized political statement, the phrase had long been attributed to a short article published by Carol Hanisch in 1970 which uses these words as its title. Hanisch is an American feminist activist and a civil rights worker. The publication was *Notes from the Second Year: Women's Liberation*, which was "the first overground publication *by* radical feminists rather than *about* them" (Firestone and Koedt 1970, 2; emphases in original). Originally titled as "Some Thoughts in Response to Dottie's Thoughts on a Women's Liberation Movement," the essay sets out to defend "consciousness-raising" against feminists who were dismissive of its political seriousness. Coined by Kathie Sarachild, consciousness-raising involved women gathering together in small groups to talk about their personal lives, which at the time were typically confined to the household as wives and mothers. The aim was to identify shared experiences which would in turn shed light on common challenges that these women faced. But the aim of the sharing was not therapeutic. As Hanisch noted, this is because "therapy assumes that someone is sick and that there is a cure" (Hanisch 1970, 76). Rather, "one of the first things we discover in these groups is that personal problems are political problems. There are no personal solutions at this time. There is only collective action for a collective solution" (Hanisch 1970, 76).

In 2006, Hanisch noted on her website that it was in fact the editors, Shulamith Firestone (1945–2012) and Anne Koedt, who gave the piece its now well-known title. This historical detail is worth noting because it tells us how the central figures in the movement chose to represent its agenda. Indeed, Hanisch pointed out that the theory put forth was born out of the movement rather than from her alone. At stake was a new understanding of politics that aimed to account for power relations which fell outside the formal domain of politics and state governance. Not only did the new politics have new problems to address, it involved novice actors with improvised practices. It was, in short, a revolution.

The fact that the three words quickly caught on was indicative of the slogan's success in capturing the politics of the time. Betty Friedan's groundbreaking identification of the "problem that has no name," now named, had become a political cause that mobilized ordinary women who otherwise would not have considered themselves to be political actors capable of initiating and organizing change. Through consciousness-raising, its participants became aware that their problems were by no means unique nor specific to their individual circumstances. The so-called personal problems of women could only be resolved through political means by recognizing that patriarchy is pervasive and gender inequality is systemic. It was grassroots democracy at its best when ordinary women acted in concert in order to empower themselves not only as citizens, but as individuals whose agency had been denied by social practices and the values that supported them. As Hanisch pointed out, even feminist activists were not immune from the hubristic claim that they know better than "non-movement women" about what to do.

But even more important is the profound impact that "personal is political" has on Western liberal democracy. The politicization of women's personal lives means that their lives (and hence, men's) are not free of politics. The seemingly clear divide between the private and the public spheres is in question. While the distinction between the household (private) and the polis (public) is as old as the tradition of Western political thought, modern liberal thinkers make the divide central to the pursuit of individual freedom. The idea of a limited government is predicated on the assumption that it is both possible and desirable to keep politics out of the private sphere. Yet radical feminists challenged precisely the possibility and the desirability of that distinction on behalf of women, which for them was first and foremost a social identity. In other words, social identity has political bearing and, hence, it is the site for both political contestation and empowerment. Despite its multifaceted and varied configurations, identity politics is about making this connection. The fact that identity politics has become a major political dynamic, at least in the Western world, is testimony to how the politics of "personal is political" resonates beyond gender identity. Moreover, "personal is political" affirms that experience as it is lived can be a valid source of knowledge beyond the individual. As the first generation of feminist scholarship began to emerge in the 1970s, that insight was not lost to feminists who were concerned about the exclusion of women in the generation of knowledge – from knowing to being known. A body of distinctly feminist philosophical thought which has developed subsequently is standpoint epistemology. Nancy Hartsock (1944–2015), who was a pioneer in this field, argued that the standpoint of women puts them in an unparalleled position to understand power from the concrete experience of being the oppressed. That knowledge is no less valid than the knowledge generated by abstract philosophical reasoning. Understanding oppression was what "personal is political" had enabled.

SEE ALSO: Consciousness-Raising; Feminist Standpoint Theory; Identity Politics; Private/Public Spheres

REFERENCES

Firestone, Shulamith, and Anne Koedt. 1970. "Editorial." In *Notes from the Second Year: Women's Liberation*, edited by Shulamith Firestone and Anne Koedt, 2. New York: Radical Feminism.

Hanisch, Carol. 1970. "The Personal is Political." In *Notes from the Second Year: Women's Liberation*, edited by Shulamith Firestone and Anne Koedt, 76–78. New York: Radical Feminism.

Hanisch, Carol. 2006. "The Personal is Political: Introduction." Accessed August 20, 2015, at http://www.carolhanisch.org/CHwritings/PIP.html.

FURTHER READING

Crow, Barbara A., ed. 2000. *Radical Feminism: A Documentary Reader*. New York: New York University Press.

Lee, Theresa Man Ling. 2007. "Rethinking the Personal and the Political: Feminist Activism and Civic Engagement." *Hypatia*, 22: 163–179.

Phallocentrism and Phallogocentrism

RAMESH MARIO NITHIYENDRAN
University of New South Wales, Australia

Within a Western context, the implication of phallocentrism and phallogocentrism is a privileging of the hegemonic masculine and, by extension, the stabilizing of patriarchal, heteronormative, and misogynistic frameworks. A (gendered) schema of metaphysical oppositions is upheld in regards to this type of construction and cognition of meaning and social relations. Understanding these paradigms and their connections demands attention to their nomenclature and thus the compound nature in which both terms are formed. Phallocentrism, a noun formed through the combination of phallus and centric, connotes literal and symbolic centering upon the phallus. By extension, phallogocentrism is birthed through the conflation of phallocentrism and logocentrism. Logocentrism is derived from the term "logos." Within Western metaphysics, this implies rational, linguistic meaning derived from binary oppositions.

The central term, phallus, must be clarified in order to reveal the implications and workings of phallocentrism and phallogocentrism. Transculturally, a phallus can be perceived as an idealized, ideological, and symbolic archetype founded upon a particular (normative) image of the erect penis. Literally sacred in various historical and contemporary contexts (including various Hindu, ancient Egyptian, and Japanese cultures), the symbol has signified and continues to signify paradigms around fertility, race, gender relations, and dominance and submission. Yet, within Western patriarchal order, the phallus does not exist in physical form. Its closest approximation is a white, permanently hard, erect penis.

Western psychoanalysis has suggested symbolic functioning of the phallus extending beyond sexual symbolism into the foundations of language, meaning, and perception. Lacan's conception of the phallus as the *transcendental signifier* predicates the subject's very entrance into language upon negotiation of the phallus. With reference to this model, Western discourses are considered phallogocentric. Logocentric, as presence (as a subject), is constituted by rational, linguistic meaning, and phallocentric as these entry points into language are mediated through implicit and explicit reference(s) to the central, fixed symbol of the phallus. Consequently, the categorizations for what are considered determinate knowledge are constructed and reconstructed in relation to this central emblem. In this sense, while the phallus validates itself as the prime signifier and source of its own supremacy, its uniquely empowered position is maintained by a paradoxical presence. Elizabeth Stephens (2007) describes this standing as one of simultaneous ubiquity (through the distribution of phallicized and phallomorphic images) and invisibility (through its discursive centrality, yet intangible existence).

Lacan's seminal definition of the phallus (and, by extension, phallocentrism) has been scrutinized most famously by Jacques Derrida, who is privy to Lacan's bondage to phallogocentrism. In addition, much feminist scholarship has been dedicated to criticisms of this normative, Lacanian model. Particular focuses in this field of literature include the male constituted and dominated foundations of language and social reality, and the consequent oppression of and limitations imposed upon female subjectivities.

However, recent critical attention within masculinity studies is concerned with connections between lived, male corporeal experiences and phallocentric/phallogocentric hegemony. For example, Judith Butler, Lynne Segal, and Elizabeth Grosz impose feminist, poststructural lenses upon Lacan's paradigm to illuminate the gendered and phenomenological implications of his model in the context of male bodies. They argue that distinguishing the phallus (as transcendental signifier) from the physical penis ideologically detaches the biological penis and the entirety of its anatomical functions from the symbolic and signifying phallus.

As Stephens (2007) further argues, this polarization of synonyms (penis and phallus) stabilizes phallocentric discourse by a paradoxical process that privileges male corporeality, while negating penile specificity. Consequently, men are affected by phallocentric discourse as corporeality and phallocentric culture are merged. In other words, "nature" is modeled into a phallocentric vision of "culture" as the realities of male bodies are produced with fictionality relative to the idealized indexes of the phallus.

Yet it is crucial to consider ideas and definitions of phallocentrism and phallogocentrism outside Western constructions, for the mere use of these terms privileges whiteness as well as Eurocentric assumptions about meaning creation. For example, comparing Western definitions of phallocentrism and phallogocentrism within Hindu (Eastern) philosophies of phallus veneration reveals meaningful dialogue. In the context of Hinduism, the Shiva Lingam, an ithyphallic stone structure representing the phallus of Lord Shiva (the supreme being), is a central object of worship. It exists in intangible form (the Alingam) and tangible form as representation (the Lingam). This correlation between tangibility and intangibility, and by extension visibility and invisibility, clearly parallels Western constructions of the penis/phallus. Additionally, despite the dominant religious view that the entirety of the cosmos *is* Shiva Lingam, it embodies a paradigm of phallus-centeredness whereby the phallus does not justify its supremacy by reference to itself. This is because it is largely accepted that the Shiva Lingam (as phallus/*linga*) only "exists" in the situational context of its concave, vaginal base (the *yoni*). Proceeding from this symbolism and attached ideology, it can be argued that the union of (rather than mastery of or slavery to) what are deemed as gendered opposites is a defining index of its nature and significance, thus revealing a clear contrast to Western phallocentric and phallogocentric discourses which uphold gendered paradigms that allegorize dominance and submission in the context of meaning formation.

SEE ALSO: Discursive Theories of Gender; Feminism, Poststructural; Feminist Psychotherapy; Hegemonic Masculinity; Heteronormativity and Homonormativity; Masculinities; Patriarchy

REFERENCE

Stephens, Elizabeth. 2007. "The Spectacularised Penis: Contemporary Representations of the Phallic Male Body." *Men and Masculinities*, 10: 85–100.

FURTHER READING

Grosz, Elizabeth. 1990. *Jacques Lacan: A Feminist Introduction*. London: Routledge.

Lacan, Jacques. 1977. *Écrits: A Selection*, trans. Alan Sheridan. London: Routledge.

Lewis, Michael. 2008. *Derrida and Lacan: Another Writing*. Edinburgh: Edinburgh University Press.

Monick, Eugene. 1987. *Phallos: Sacred Image of the Masculine*. Toronto: Inner City Books.

Potts, Annie. 2000. "The Essence of the Hard On: Hegemonic Masculinity and the Cultural Construction of Erectile Dysfunction." *Men and Masculinities*, 3: 85–105.

Singh, N. K. 2004. *Siva Linga*. Delhi: Global Publishing House.

Waldby, Catherine. 1995. "Destruction: Boundary Erotics and Refigurations of the Heterosexual Male Body." In *Sexy Bodies: The Strange Carnalities of Feminism*, edited by Elizabeth Grosz, 266–277. London: Routledge.

Pink Triangle

RÜDIGER LAUTMANN
University of Bremen, Germany

The pink triangle – a small cloth badge on a prisoner's uniform – was used by the Nazis in concentration camps to designate a homosexual inmate. The emblem stands for one of the darkest periods of homophobia ever seen in a civilized state. One generation later, it was converted into a symbol of pride by the gay rights movement. The LGBT community needs to retain a clear memory of this persecution (Jensen 2005, 349).

In the camps, badges for different classes of inmates took the form of an isosceles triangle with sides 4–5 inches long, sewn on the jacket with the vertex pointing down. The color of the triangle varied with the prisoner's category: yellow for Jews, red for political prisoners, green for criminals, black for "asocials," brown for Romas/Sintis, purple for Jehovah's Witnesses, and pink for homosexuals. The seven colors were displayed on a chart prepared by the SS. The details were defined by the SS camp leader and varied somewhat over time and place. A unified marking system was introduced around 1937. Prior to that, other insignia were used (e.g., 175, the number of the law criminalizing male homosexual acts in the German penal code dating back to 1871).

Pink triangle inmates were interned in significant numbers only in concentration camps within Germany (Dachau, Buchenwald, Sachsenhausen, etc.), Austria, and other annexed regions. The pink triangle was not used at all in the extermination camps; thus it appeared in Auschwitz I but not in Auschwitz-Birkenau.

Our knowledge of pink triangle prisoners comes primarily from inmate rosters, most of which were destroyed before the camps were liberated. Only a small number of gay survivors have been interviewed. Homosexuals are occasionally mentioned in the memoirs of other survivors, mostly former political prisoners.

All documents report that homosexuals consistently occupied a very low position in the camp hierarchy and experienced the utmost contempt. The SS deliberately treated this group brutally, and other inmates looked down upon them. They were scorned and abused because the pink triangle marked them with a badge of shame. In this respect, the fate of homosexuals in concentration camps may be compared with that of Jews.

The living conditions of prisoners varied depending on their standing within the camp hierarchy and their ability to organize with others who shared the color of their triangle. In both regards, the cards were stacked against homosexuals. Nobody wanted to help them, and they were generally denied the indoor work assignments that might raise their chances of survival. Solidarity among gay prisoners was stifled in this situation of extreme repression. In contrast, most other groups, notably the political prisoners, did develop a strong sense of solidarity and organized themselves with the goal of survival.

A common refrain in survivors' memoirs and in their responses to inquiries about pink triangle prisoners is that although they did see homosexuals from time to time, they knew nothing about who they were or what happened with them. This extraordinary lack of visibility derives not just from the ostracism of homosexuals but from the speed of their death following camp internment.

The number of homosexual inmates in any particular concentration camp at any given moment varied. Immediately after the Nazi seizure of power, there was generally a total of several hundred homosexual concentration camp internees; later, the figure would rise to around 1,000. The absolute number of pink triangle prisoners remains uncertain, owing to the fragmentary state of documentation. The often cited estimate of "between 5,000 and 15,000" can be narrowed to roughly 8,000. Certainly not all gay inmates wore a triangle of pink color; some had a green triangle (for "criminal") or even a red triangle, both affording better survival chances. And there was the usual proportion of homosexuals in the racially defined victim groups, especially among the Jews and other "non-Aryans."

We have statistical data from a comparative study of three victim groups: homosexuals, political prisoners, and Jehovah's Witnesses (based on representative samples; see Lautmann 1981). These show that the death rate was much higher for homosexual prisoners (60%) than for political prisoners (41%) and Jehovah's Witnesses (35%). The reason for the high death rate is neither gayness per se nor biographical variables such as middle-class standing. Even marital status and number of children had only a small positive effect on the probability of survival. More than anything else, it was the social situation within the camps that determined survival or death.

Persecution started with police investigations based on raids of gay gathering places, interrogations by the Gestapo and criminal police, or denunciation of alleged homosexuals by informants. Those arrested were pressured to reveal further names. A judicial trial followed. The risk of arrest was unevenly distributed: members of the lower classes, especially poor and uneducated men, were more likely to seek contacts outdoors and be less able to dispute incrimination.

The Nazis directed their homophobic policy towards males, whereas female homosexuality, like all feminist issues, was deemed to be unimportant. That is why the pink triangle was initially meted out only to men, although there may have been some exceptions. Unlike Germany, Austria prosecuted lesbian acts, so after the annexation of Austria in 1938, the pink triangle may have been extended to some women. Lesbians were impacted in a more indirect way than gay men, largely because all same-sex love was condemned. All women were pushed back into old-fashioned family roles. If they refused, they risked ending up as "asocials" in a concentration camp.

Jewish homosexuals in the camps had to wear both yellow and pink triangles, the yellow posing the greater menace to their survival. Undoubtedly, far more lesbians and gay men died in the Holocaust than in the anti-homosexual persecution. A considerable number of such fates are documented in scattered biographical reports.

The pink triangle can be explained in terms of its societal background, the chief actor being SS leader Heinrich Himmler (Plant 1986, 71–104). Under the specific conditions of the Third Reich, the concentration camp served the same purposes and achieved the same goals as traditional incarceration and correctional procedures. The pink triangle can be seen as an instrument of macrosocial anti-homosexuality. Survivors seldom reported having received any aid from local residents. Compliance was rooted in traditional anti-homosexual prejudice. It became an element in widespread acquiescence to the Nazi regime, which seemed to be fulfilling its promise to create a new order. One should bear in mind that during the Weimar Republic (1919–1933), the homosexual emancipation process had developed with breathtaking speed to the highest level of any Western state. Even so, homosexuals had not yet shed their outsider status.

Following the collapse of the Third Reich, the former pink triangle prisoners continued to be ostracized. They were denied any rehabilitation, and their criminal status continued. Almost all attempts to get state compensation were fruitless. The closet endured for lesbians and gays. In 2000, the German government agreed to recognize gays as victims of the Third Reich, but in most cases the reparation, a small cash payment, came too late.

Today, the historical facts surrounding the pink triangle remain somewhat hidden. They are often obscured by the Holocaust, since the extermination of the European Jews was by far the greater atrocity. Both are macrocrimes, but they are dissimilar, in terms of numbers and structures, and they cannot be equated.

In the culture of remembrance, the pink triangle was neglected (Lautmann 2008). Gay movements that reemerged in the1950s were repressed by the German states in both West and East. The Prisoners' Committees and the development of a collective memory were dominated by survivors who had worn the red triangle. They agreed only reluctantly when other prisoner categories applied for recognition. For more than four decades, academic historical research omitted gays and lesbians.

The decades after Hitler were a staid, if not downcast, period. A rigorously anti-homosexual mood pervaded culture and control up to the mid-1960s. It seems fair to say that in this regard, the re-education measures of the camps had achieved their aim, at least in part.

The gay movement has transformed the insignia of abject horror into an increasingly recognized emblem of identity. This has sometimes been criticized as trivializing the suffering of historical victims and eliding the special situation of lesbians. Starting in the 1990s, the pink triangle began to lose its function as a symbol for the emancipation struggles. It was replaced by the rainbow flag, which includes lesbians in a historically more plausible way and tracks the shift away from thinking in terms of "gay identity" to the "queer" alliance of LGBT. Today, the pink triangle is a symbol of pride, and further, it has undergone a degree of commercialization, and "pink parties" afford subcultural socializing. Even more in the United States than in Europe, many gay men and women attribute their political consciousness to a collective memory of the Nazi persecution of homosexuals. This memory invokes a long historical pattern and may have the power to mobilize vigilance against contemporary oppression in many parts of the world.

SEE ALSO: Nazi Persecution of Homosexuals

REFERENCES

Jensen, Erik N. 2005. "Pink Triangle and Political Consciousness." In Dagmar Herzog, ed. *Sexuality and German Fascism*, 318–349. New York: Berghahn.

Lautmann, Rüdiger. 1981. "The Pink Triangle." *Journal of Homosexuality*, 6(1–2), 141–160. DOI: 10.1300/J082v06n01_13.

Lautmann, Rüdiger. 2008. "The Social Order of Commemoration." In *Beyond Camps and Forced Labour*, edited by Johannes-Dieter Steinert and Inge Weber-Newth, 850–864. Osnabrück: Secolo.

Plant, Richard. 1986 *The Pink Triangle*. New York: Henry Holt.

Plastic Sexuality

GRAHAM SCAMBLER
University of Surrey, UK

Although the concept might be said to have a long pedigree, the term "plastic sexuality" was introduced by Giddens (1992) as a companion to his notion of a "pure relationship." A pure relationship is one of sexual and emotional equality, and as such has explosive potential in the context of pre-existing forms of gender power. The modern concept of romantic love is, according to Giddens, the harbinger of the pure relationship but betrays a number of tensions. On the one hand it implied a radical, active engagement with the "maleness" of modern society, but on the other it confined women to "their place," to the home.

Plastic sexuality is critical for the emancipation implicit in the pure relationship, and also for women's claim to sexual pleasure. It denotes a "decentered sexuality," freed from the needs and demands of reproduction. It had its genesis, according to Giddens, in the late eighteenth century, a function of attempts to limit family size, but it spread rapidly as a result of modern contraception and the new reproductive technologies, and also of significant economic and social gains in the independence of women. By the end of the twentieth century, it was becoming a core component of the self. In principle, plastic sexuality promises to free sexuality from "the rule of the phallus." It provides a space that women might occupy.

However, gendered social structures run deep and, as the compulsive character of male sexuality is exposed, reactive male violence can set in. Writing in the early 1990s, Giddens argues that "an emotional abyss has opened up between the sexes, and one cannot say with any certainty how far it will be bridged." The potential exists for transforming intimacy towards a "transactional negotiation of personal ties by equals," but this would necessarily involve a wholesale democratizing of interpersonal relations. Such a transformation would call into question many of the other gendered and oppressive institutions in which love and sexuality remain embedded. This could "liberate" men as well as women. On the other hand, sexual "liberation" would not necessarily lead to a degendering of eroticism. The normalization of more and different forms of "malleable," commodified sexual pleasure will likely still be defined via the gazes of "the desiring and active man" (Hawkes 2007).

Plastic sexuality in this account implies enhanced flexibility in sexual relations and encounters and an increased premium on pleasure. It represents "autonomous" sexuality. A number of related issues surface. First, it is apparent that the longstanding biological and sociocultural binaries of male–female and man–woman, respectively, have been *subverted* in much of the developed world. The primacy of ("hierarchic") heterosexuality has yielded to a widespread acceptance of gay and transgender relations. Moreover, this shift is being ratified both in law and in convention: there is to some extent a coming together of Giddens's pure relationship and plastic sexuality. This is not to deny persistent antagonism and conflict, religious and sociocultural, in modern Western societies, and considerably more vigorously elsewhere (witness the debates around Putin's comments prior to the Winter Olympics in Russia and the tightening of religious and legal constraints found in many Middle Eastern and African countries).

Second, the emergence of plastic sexuality marks a renewed interrogation of the nuclear family. This does not imply the imminent demise of gendered relations or scripts, but does suggest that they might take different institutional forms in the future. Whether or not these will tend towards an extension of the pure relationship is open to debate The future of the family rests on many factors, economic, political, and sociocultural. What does seem clear is that spaces have opened up and a significant degendering of concept and practice in relations and sexuality is possible.

Third, "rival" partnerships are coming to the forefront, including non-familial relationships and households, extending from heterosexual cohabitation and non-cohabitation through homosexual variants of the same to serial monogamy or multiple or transitory liaisons on the one hand and celibacy on the other. These rival institutions are currently growing, especially in developed societies.

Fourth, new questions can be posed of age-old institutions such as prostitution. While prostitution was popularly cast as an "immoral" challenge to the "moral" family unit, how does it stand, redefined as *sex work*, in an era of plastic sexuality? Moreover, both women and men now purchase sexual services (and from women as well as from men), if as yet in small numbers. Do the emergence and social consolidation of plastic sexuality legitimize markets and commodification in sexuality, long subject to social and legal stigma?

Fifth, encounters such as speed dating and casual sex have increasingly switched to the Internet, facilitating novel and as yet under-researched worlds of cybersex. For some, virtual relationships and sexual experiences have succeeded or are a substitute for actual options. It has become possible to forge, belong, and live in accordance with virtual identities, to satisfy desire via social media and webcams.

Finally, the opening up of real and virtual spaces for change introduces unpredictability. Plastic sexuality has led over time to both negative and positive reactions. *Fundamentalist* campaigns have proliferated: homophobia has resurfaced; radical Islamacists have sought to reimpose constraints on female sexuality; radical feminists have formed alliances with evangelical Christians in projects to criminalize sex work; there is talk of censoring the Internet; and so on. In other words, innovations call to mind and reinvigorate not only the traditions and conventions they replace but no less imaginative oppositions.

Giddens's thesis has been critiqued by feminists who insist that the personal is social. Jamieson (1999) maintains that Giddens feeds into a therapeutic discourse that *individualizes* personal problems. Springer (1993) argues that we must "relocate the sexual not outside but at the intersection of a multiplicity of discourses by which bodies, pleasures and powers are circulated and exchanged. … We must also remember that in saying yes to sex we are not saying no to power." The concept of plastic sexuality, in short, can both close and open avenues of enquiry.

SEE ALSO: Cybersex; Heteronormativity and Homonormativity; Intimacy and Sexual Relationships; Monogamy, Sociological Perspectives on; Polyamory; Polygamy, Polygyny, and Polyandry

REFERENCES

Giddens, Anthony. 1992. *The Transformation of Intimacy: Sexuality, Love and Eroticism in Modern Societies*. Cambridge: Polity.

Hawkes, Gail. 2007. "Plastic Sexuality." In *The Blackwell Encyclopedia of Sociology*, edited by George Ritzer, vol. 7, 3411–3413. Oxford: Wiley Blackwell.

Jamieson, Lynn. 1999. "Intimacy Transformed? A Critical Look at the 'Pure Relationship'." *Sociology*, 33(3): 477–494.

Singer, Linda. 1993. *Erotic Welfare: Sexual Theory and Politics in the Age of Epidemics*. New York: Routledge.

FURTHER READING

Beck, Ulrich and Elisabeth Beck-Gernsheim. 1995. *Normal Chaos of Love*. Cambridge: Polity.

Beck, Ulrich and Elisabeth Beck-Gernsheim. 2013. *Distant Love*. Cambridge: Polity.

Jamieson, Lynn. 2013. "Personal Relationships, Intimacy and the Self in a Mediated Global Digital Age." In *Digital Sociology: Critical Perspectives*, edited by Kate Orton-Johnson and Nick Prior, 13–33. London: Macmillan.

Political Participation in Western Democracies

LENA WÄNGNERUD
University of Gothenburg, Sweden

In studies of political participation and political behavior, the notion of a gender gap is a recurrent theme. This term refers to a variety of phenomena, such as differences between women and men in turnout in general elections, political interest, support for different parties, and attitudes toward specific political issues. A useful distinction is to separate indicators of *political form*, which refers to engagement, and indicators of *political content*, which refers to attitudes and priorities. Both of these dimensions can be studied at the citizen level and at the level of elected representatives.

An important result from empirical research in Western democracies is that developments in political form and political content do not always work in tandem. When women become more equal to men in political participation and engagement, they will not necessarily behave the same way as men when it comes to political substance. Studies in Sweden show that today, women are almost on the same level as men when it comes to turnout in general elections, party membership, and self-reported political interest (turnout is higher among women than men). However, in the last general election, in 2010, there was a historically large gender gap in party choice: women voted less for the Conservative Party, and more for the Social Democratic Party, than men. Moreover, in that same election, there was a clear difference between women's and men's priority lists of important issues, with jobs as the number one issue among men, and social policy as the number one issue among women. In some policy areas, such as support for a 6-hour workday and for a ban on all forms of pornography, large differences in attitude remained.

The results from Sweden are interesting since, from an international perspective, Sweden is a forerunner in gender equality. Women's involvement in higher education and the labor market is strong. Men are increasingly using the opportunity, guaranteed by parental leave legislation, to stay home with small children for longer periods of time. Women are visible in top political positions: 45 percent of the members of the national parliament and 13 out of 23 cabinet ministers are women, although the prime minister and the influential minister of finance are men. Not even in situations where conditions seem favorable can one expect a linear process toward a uniform closure of the gender gap. What are the processes at work producing variation in gender gaps across time, countries, and different dimensions studied?

MODERNIZATION THEORIES

A major strand of research concerning women's political participation focuses on the role of modernization. One especially convincing study is presented in the book *Rising Tide: Gender Equality and Cultural Change around the World* by Inglehart and Norris (2003). Inglehart and Norris construct a gender equality scale from measurements of citizens' attitudes toward women as political leaders, women's professional and educational rights, and women's traditional role as mothers. Through extensive cross-country comparative research they show that egalitarian values are systematically related to higher levels of political participation among women. They conclude that modernization underpins cultural change, that is, attitudinal change from traditional to gender-equal values, and that these cultural changes create opportunities for upward mobility for women, resulting in, for example, higher numbers of women in top political positions.

ACTOR-ORIENTED THEORIES

Modernization involves slow developments, but research in the field shows that dramatic changes can occur over short periods of time. In the past two decades there has been a quota trend in which countries in Africa and Latin America have introduced a "fast track" to women's political participation (Dahlerup 2006). This has led to the revival of more actor-oriented theories emphasizing the role of political parties, but also of women activists working inside formal political institutions and/or in civil society. The influential theory of the politics of presence (Phillips 1995) portrays female politicians as a driving force behind changes, and numerous empirical studies show that female politicians all over the world tend to be more active than their male colleagues when it comes to placing gender equality policy on the political agenda (Wängnerud 2009). Women, both as politicians and as citizens, tend to be more supportive of liberalizing policies for lesbians and gay men.

A similar theme is to be found in exposure-based approaches. The fundamental concept in this strand of research is that individuals develop or change their understandings of women's place in society and their attitudes toward feminist issues when they encounter ideas and experiences that resonate with feminist ideals (Bolzendahl and Myers 2004). Thus, developments can come from above – from the political sphere – and from below – from individuals' encounters with feminist ideas and experiences in the family, educational settings, and workplaces.

INCREASED AWARENESS RESULTING IN LARGER GENDER GAPS?

The situation may be that increases in women's political participation (a closing gender gap in political form) result in higher levels of awareness among women of lingering gender inequalities, which, in turn, can create a ground for increasing differences in behavior such as party choice and attitudes toward political proposals with a bearing on self-determination for women (a widening gender gap in political content). However, there is always a need to take into account that general trends will look more complex if factors such as level of education, religiosity, and urbanization are introduced in the models. Studies in Western democracies show that developments in political form and political content do not always work in tandem, neither do developments in different subgroups of citizens. Future studies will show whether this conclusion holds for other parts of the world.

SEE ALSO: Femocrat; Gender Equality; Gender, Politics, and the State: Overview; Governance and Gender; Politics of Representation; Women's Political Representation

REFERENCES

Bolzendahl, Catherine I., and Daniel J. Myers. 2004. "Feminist Attitudes and Support for Gender Equality: Opinion Change in Women and Men, 1974–1998." *Social Forces*, 83: 759–789.

Dahlerup, Drude, ed. 2006. *Women, Quotas and Politics*. London: Routledge.

Inglehart, Ronald, and Pippa Norris. 2003. *Rising Tide: Gender Equality and Cultural Change around the World*. Cambridge: Cambridge University Press.

Phillips, Anne. 1995. *The Politics of Presence*. Oxford: Oxford University Press.

Wängnerud, Lena. 2009. "Women in Parliaments: Descriptive and Substantive Representation." *Annual Review of Political Science*, 12: 51–69.

FURTHER READING

Herek, Gregory M. 2002. "Gender Gaps in Public Opinion about Lesbians and Gay Men." *Public Opinion Quarterly*, 66: 40–66.

Politics of Representation

SANJUKTA T. GHOSH
Castleton State College, Vermont, USA

The politics of representation refers to the struggle in society over the meaning of images and depictions. It looks at the processes by which one mode of depiction or portrayal gains primacy over another. But it is much more that just that; it assigns a pivotal place to "culture" as a site of contestation about the way people think about their own identities, their world, and their place in it. The concept's theoretical underpinnings come from British cultural studies, the Frankfurt School, and audience studies.

Following the emphasis on the power of the "culture industry" put forward by Frankfurt School intellectuals Adorno and Horkheimer, most of the work in this area has focused on the study of media and, specifically, media "representations." Cultural studies theorists, such as Stuart Hall, have problematized the concept of "representation" to mean: to present, to image, to depict, to offer a depiction of something already there. They have shown that because the media *re-present* something that already exists, media *give meaning* to it. But these visual and oral languages, images, and portrayals on any platform have no fixed meaning; the meanings can change depending on the person encountering the message, the society where it is placed, and the historical period when it emerges. Therefore, cultural studies researchers engaged in textual analyses question the accuracy and truths of the meanings that are depicted in the media. For them, the issue is not whether images are "good" or "bad," but how they work and how they construct our identities. At the same time, audience studies researchers argue that there is no guarantee that a representational system will operate in the way one wants when it is created. Ien Ang (1991), Janice Radway (1991), David Morley (1992), and John Fiske (2010) are scholars who have studied the ways in which mass-produced culture is read and even subverted by different consumers. Yet, continually we see attempts to fix meaning and impose *one* essential or *true* meaning on representations. It is this struggle over meaning of visual and linguistic images that is called the "politics of representation."

It reveals the power relations and power structures in our society. It demonstrates that controlling the meaning of representations is an elemental part of how power structures work and how political power is maintained.

Because of the primacy given to the assumption that audiences are active producers of meaning and not mere passive consumers of popular culture, there are key questions for those studying the politics of representation. How are these images constructed? How are these images constructing what is being represented? Who constructs them? What motivates this representation? What does this image say about the producers of the image? What does it say about those being represented? And what does it say about the consumers of these representations? How do the representations attempt to speak for the consumers? What are the contradictions contained in the representation? How does it affect the lives of the people or situations being represented? To what extent does the representation produced challenge the status quo? How does it support the existing power structure? Answering these questions reveals the struggle and contestation over meaning and this is what animates those engaged in the politics of representation.

Representations of marginalized groups such as women and racial and sexual minorities have become significant arenas of such debates. Using Euro-communist Antonio Gramsci's notion of "hegemony," feminist, race, and queer theorists and activists have done much to expose how patriarchal ideologies are not "common sense," not "objective," and not "gender-neutral." From its inception, cultural studies has had a progressive impetus, linking theory to critical practice. It is not a politically neutral discipline; it is calibrated to encourage social change. Researchers in this field see their work as intentionally political – seeking to empower people by exposing the relationship between culture and various forms of power, changing the perceptions of the represented groups and expanding the very meanings of gender, racial, and sexual identities. In other words, despite the diversity of its subject matter, cultural studies always has a political dimension and the study of culture as forms is always embedded in a larger historical and sociopolitical inquiry. One's own political positioning and the question of social change are crucial to those concerned with representational politics. Thus, parsing the representations to examine whether they challenge or support the status quo is an important issue.

REPRESENTATIONS OF GENDER

The two main arenas where the politics of representation has played out are gender studies and sexuality studies. For more than a century, feminist activists and theorists have sought to reveal the power relations concealed in the definitions of what it means to be a "woman." Research on the concepts of "the cult of domesticity" and "true womanhood" have demonstrated that naturalizing certain virtues being as innately "feminine" or "masculine" simply succeeded in concealing the work of patriarchy. It naturalized the removal of women from paid labor force and made domestic work such as childrearing unpaid "tasks." It eliminated all educational opportunities for women and it also naturalized the idea that women's sphere of influence was less socially valuable. Works of Mary Wollstonecraft (1792), Betty Friedan (1963), Simone de Beauvoir (1971), and Judith Williamson (1978) are heralded as classic writings on this subject.

Other studies on the politics of gendered representations have pointed out that women are often trivialized or completely absent in certain media texts. Using the phrase "symbolic annihilation," Tuchman, Daniels, and Benet (1978) describe how US television effectively erases women's presence, or trivializes and mocks them. When women are shown, Tuchman et al. say, they are represented as "incompetents and inferiors." Drawing on Tuchman et al.'s important essay, researchers have remarked on the paucity of non-victim female representations in video games, in depictions of the workplace, and in portrayals of the business arena (Dyer 1990; Kilbourne 1999; Bordo 2008; Carter 2011). All these writings have two fundamental assumptions. First, that men and women are not biological entities but artifacts manufactured and shaped by what Italian scholar Teresa de Lauretis calls the "technologies of gender" – the church, the judiciary, mass media, and so on. Second, that the body is a site of social control and cultural rituals such as fashion and makeup are simply ways to discipline the female body and limit gender identity.

In 1975, an essay by Laura Mulvey revealed how cinematic techniques of Hollywood narrative cinema normalized both representations of women and certain ways of looking. Using psychoanalytical concepts of "voyeurism," "phallocentrism," and "narcissism" as a "political weapon," Mulvey showed that filmic codes and conventions, considered normative in the film industry, produced a "male gaze" that both fetishize the on-screen female body as well as produce the female viewer as a passive consumer. In subsequent revisions of her essay, Mulvey has said that to gain pleasure from classic Hollywood narrative cinema, women viewers have to move between male and female spectator positions, entering a metaphoric "tranvestism" in their viewing positions.

The politics of gender representation has been further problematized by transnational feminists who have foregrounded questions of colonialism, citizenship, and geopolitics. Indian-American scholar Chandra Talpade

Mohanty (1991), Malaysian anthropologist Aihwa Ong (1998), and Trinidadian feminist Jacqui Alexander (1997) have shown that mass-produced depictions, art, and even feminist discourses emanating from the Global North produce "the third world woman" as a unitary homogenous subject. Furthermore, these scholars argue that because her voiced is muffled and because she is never located in her own history, one "third world woman" becomes interchangeable with another. This lack of any information about her encourages the Western viewer/reader to code her as an "other" and as a victim – victimized by her own culture and her own men. It is this kind of subject-position that allows the trope of Western saviors to flourish, these theorists point out.

REPRESENTATIONS OF SEXUALITY

In addition to one's gender identity, representational politics also examines how men's control of women's sexuality has been deployed to maintain power relations. The emergence of queer theory in the late twentieth century became an important contribution to identity politics in three important ways. First, it sought to recoup the images of sexual minorities from dominant cultural narratives. Second, it opened up avenues for consumers to read against the grain of these narratives, thereby de-centering prevailing tropes. Third, and most importantly, it revealed the processes by which religious, state, medical, and media regulate acceptable sexual behaviors, creating a "normal" sexuality that is heterosexual (penetrative), monogamous, and procreative. The idealization of heterosexual marriage and the nuclear family by different cultural institutions are examples of this.

A key idea in queer studies is that not only does the category of woman as a "coherent and stable subject" not exist, neither do the binaries created between "woman" and "man" that ultimately create sexual identities. In her book *Gender Trouble*, Judith Butler draws on French philosopher Michel Foucault's ideas to argue that gender is constructed by mass-produced discourses. Furthermore, it is a performance, a certain kind of enactment of obligatory social norms to be one gender or the other. For her, gender is not something we have but something we do, something we reproduce from the dominant discourses. Because gender binaries are a construction, the reproduction of gender is always a negotiation with power. Therefore, by destabilizing these constructs, we can cause "gender trouble" and thus open up the possibility of a remaking of gendered reality along new lines. Furthermore, by dissolving the homosexuality/heterosexuality binary, all sexualities become merely points on a continuum of possibilities.

Here it is instructive to note that the Western category of the "homosexual" is a very recent creation, as recent as the nineteenth century. The word "heterosexual" was coined much later to act as a foil against the "deviant" homosexual. Furthermore, the meaning of "homosexual," like that of "woman," has never been fixed. The word "homosexual" initially was a descriptor of a sex act and only later did it change from a "behavior" to a "status" or a way of being. In terms of identity politics, the main issue facing queer activists has been the tension between accepting an essentialist (innately) homosexual identity for strategic reasons such as gaining visibility or decentering and destabilizing sexual identities to a degree where all subject positions are rendered fluid and forever changing. Some queer theorists and activists have embraced this "strategic essentialism" to make being homosexual a source of meaning. Other activists have insisted on seeing queer identity as layered; they have stressed the need to give equal importance to their sexual identities as well as their racial, class, gender, religious, and other identities. They see queer identity as a discourse that is shaped by cultural and social processes, network building, and lived experience in a heteropatriarchal society.

The notions of "symbolic annihilation," "male gaze," "technologies of gender," and "transvestism" in spectator/consumer space have all been used by queer theorists to question sexual identities represented in postindustrial mass culture. The works of Larry Gross, Richard Dyer, Teresa de Lauretis, and Judith Halberstam are all instrumental here. In general, Western representations of "the homosexual" in cinema, folklore, television, and the print media have undergone a number of turnovers in meanings: as villainous figures, as comedic foils for the protagonist, as bearers of illness, as poisonous influences in the fabric of heterosexual life, and as tragic figures. The onset of the HIV/AIDS crisis in the 1980s was a significant time that ushered in two contradictory developments: a rampant usage of the trope of the gay man as carrier of diseases, a resistance and ultimately a limited freedom from that connotation. Currently, homosexual identity is a contested terrain where battles against state strictures are fought on issues as varied as adoption, career paths, marriage, and self-presentation. Halberstam's work on drag and Dyer's work on queer readings have done much to unpack the term "queer" enlarging it from a sexual identity to non-sexual behaviors such as being effeminate or hypermasculine.

In many non-Western cultures, the appellation "homosexual" may not exist. But as scholars from the Global South have noted, this could be because of the non-stigmatization of a variety of sexual variations and not the non-recognition of same-sex acts or of the people engaging in these acts. In Hindu religious texts, gods such as Shiva contain within them both the masculine and the feminine. Contemporary Indian culture also recognizes a "third sex" that is neither man nor woman and not homosexual either. The *hijras* are a community of men whose penises and testicles have been surgically removed. Though they do not have a reconstructed vagina, they present themselves as women. In both Bangladesh and India, the *hijras* have attained a legal status as a "third gender." Similarly, the *mahus* of Polynesia, the "two-spirit" people of Native American nations, the *zaniths* in Islamic societies, and the *hito* in Japan all challenge Western conceptions of sexuality as well as sexual hierarchies in their own right.

SEE ALSO: Genderqueer; *Hijra/Hejira*; Queer Literary Criticism; Queer Theory

REFERENCES

Alexander, M. Jacqui, and Chandra Mohanty, eds. 1997. *Feminist Genealogies, Colonial Legacies, Democratic Futures*. New York: Routledge.

Ang, Ien. 1991. *Desperately Seeking the Audience*. New York: Routledge.

Bordo, Susan. 2008. "Anorexia Nervosa: Psychopathology as the Crystallization of Culture." In *Food and Culture*, edited by Carole Counihan and Penny Van Esterik, 162–186. New York: Routledge.

Carter, C. 2011. "Sex/Gender and the Media: From Sex Roles to Social Construction and Beyond." In *The Handbook of Gender, Sex and Media*, edited by Karen Ross. New York: Wiley Blackwell.

de Beauvoir, Simone. 1971. *The Second Sex*. New York: Knopf.

Dyer, Richard. 1990. *Now You See It: Historical Studies on Lesbian and Gay Film*. London: Routledge.

Fiske, John. 2010. *The John Fiske Collection: Reading the Popular*. New York: Routledge.

Friedan, Betty. 1963. *The Feminine Mystique*. New York: Norton.

Kilbourne, Jean. 1999. *Deadly Persuasion: Why Women and Girls Must Fight the Addictive Power of Advertising*. Boston: Free Press.

Mohanty, Chandra. 1991. "Under Western Eyes: Feminist Scholarship and Colonial Discourses."

In *Third World Women and the Politics of Feminism*, edited by C. Mohanty, A. Russo, and L. Torres, 51–80. Bloomington: Indiana University Press.
Morley, David. 1992. *Television, Audiences and Cultural Studies*. London: Routledge.
Ong, Aihwa. 1998. "Colonialism and Modernity: Feminist Re-presentations of Women in Non-Western Societies." *Inscriptions*, 3–4: 3–34.
Radway, Janice. 1991. *Reading the Romance*. Chapel Hill: University of North Carolina Press.
Tuchman, Gaye, Arlene Kaplan Daniels, and James Benet. 1978. *Hearth and Home: Images of Women in the Mass Media*. New York: Oxford University Press.
Williamson, Judith. 1978. *Decoding Advertisements: Ideology and Meaning in Advertising*. London: Boyars.
Wollstonecraft, Mary. 1792. *A Vindication of the Rights of Woman*. Accessed August 10, 2015, at http://www.bartleby.com/144/.

FURTHER READING

Bordo, Susan. 2004. *Unbearable Weight: Feminism, Western Culture, and the Body*, 10th ed. Berkeley: University of California Press.
Chen, Kuan-Hsing, and David Morley. 1996. *Stuart Hall: Critical Dialogues in Cultural Studies*. New York: Routledge.
Butler, Judith. 2006. *Gender Trouble: Feminism and the Subversion of Identity*. New York: Routledge.
Dyer, Richard. 2002. *The Culture of Queers*. New York: Routledge.
Gross, Larry, and James Woods. 1999. *The Columbia Reader on Lesbians and Gay Men in Media, Society and Politics*. New York: Columbia University Press.
Halberstam, Judith. 1998. *Female Masculinity*. Durham, NC: Duke University Press.
Halberstam, Judith, David Eng, and José Esteban Muñoz, eds. 2005. *What's Queer About Queer Studies Now?* Durham, NC: Duke University Press.
Mulvey, Laura. 2009. *Visual and Other Pleasures*. New York: Palgrave.
Nanda, Serena. 1990. *Neither Man Nor Woman: The Hijras of India*. Belmont: Wadsworth.
Vanita, Ruth. 2002. *Queering India: Same-Sex Love and Eroticism in Indian Culture and Society*. New York: Routledge.

Polyamory

NIKÓ ANTALFFY
Macquarie University, Australia
LOLA D. HOUSTON
University of Vermont, USA

Polyamory means the practice or desire of having multiple loving, romantic relationships at the same time with the full knowledge and consent of everyone involved. Defined literally, polyamory means *many loves* (*poly* from the Greek "many" or "multiple," *amor* from the Latin "love"). Together they denote "many loves." Polyamory is often abbreviated to poly. Persons who are polyamorous are sometimes referred to as *poly people* or *polyamorists*. From the perspective of the polyamorous individual, it is the full knowledge and consent of all involved that distinguishes polyamory from monogamous relationships in which one or both parties cheat without the knowledge of the other.

Although polyamory is often used to denote ethical, responsible non-monogamy, some who practice this approach to relationships also include other forms of non-monogamy such as swinging or what is sometimes called a *monogamish* relationship. In some cases, many discover polyamory through swinging or the gradual relaxation and renegotiation of the rules of an already existing monogamous relationship.

Biologists and sociologists distinguish between sexual and social monogamy. The former means sexual exclusivity of two individuals, while the latter addresses child-drearing and companionship. In most human societies today monogamy assumes both social and sexual exclusivity between two people, often formalized in the institution of marriage. Extramarital sexual encounters are fairly common, however, occurring in more than half of all long-term married couples.

As a culturally defined practice, polyamory is recently adopted in Western societies, with the biggest communities in the United States. In its current form, the practice dates to the 1990s, but ethical multiple relationships have a longer, albeit minor, history. In the West the most notable forebears are small intentional communities that practiced some form of open loving. These include the Oneida Christian commune in the mid-nineteenth century and San Francisco's Kerista commune of the 1970s.

There are no clear statistics on the numbers of persons engaged in a polyamorous structure. Since there is no clear legal status, none of the commonly found sources of such data exist at this time: medical forms, census data, health statistics or the like do not currently attempt to track this particular question. Thus, much of the data on the numbers of people practicing polyamory come from self-reporting sources. While there are many active and visible polyamorous communities in some Western liberal democracies, the number of polyamorists is impossible to estimate. Anecdotal evidence suggests that other sexual subcultures such as those who practice BDSM (bondage, discipline, sadism and masochism) or those who identify as bisexual have a markedly high percentage of persons who are also polyamorous.

It is important to distinguish the term from other, similar terms that describe relationship styles involving more than two persons at the same time. *Polygyny*, the practice of a male taking multiple wives at the same time, and *polyandry*, the practice of a female taking multiple husbands at the same time, are different in that the gender roles are explicitly defined in the context of the relationship. In polyamory, gender roles are not necessarily central to the nature of the relationship. All of these configurations can be understood as "polyamorous" in nature in that more than two individuals are intimately involved.

Anthropology has described an extensive variety of cultural practices in smaller societies that are variations on both monogamy and non-monogamy. Non-monogamous traditional societies outnumber monogamous ones. Polygyny is found in some African, Arabic, and Southeast Asian societies, and polyandry was known in parts of South Asia. Unlike other forms of multiply partnered relationships, polyamory is generally not imbued with any gendered aspect – any gender can partner with any other gender in any numbers or configuration that are desirable and manageable.

Polygamy is generally an institution associated with premodern traditions and religiosity, whereas polyamory is a modern secular phenomenon associated with progressive liberal thought. Consequently, while polygamy is the reserve of the traditional, religiously heterosexual (mostly Islamic faiths in various societies and minority Mormons in the West), many bisexual, gay, lesbian, and transgender persons are drawn to polyamory. Although occasionally the relationship structures of polygamy and polyamory bear some resemblance to each other (and the terms are frequently used interchangeably), the underlying values and philosophy differ greatly.

Polyamorous relationships can manifest in various structures. Loose networks are common in which most have more than one relationship and many know each other. There is no one structure that describes the practice concisely. Various relationship "configurations" exist. These include the "vee," which comprises three individuals, two of whom are in a relationship with the same (third) person without having a direct romantic connection between them (these two are called *metamours* of each other). There is also a "triad" (three individuals, all of whom are romantically involved with one another), while a "quad" is the same but with four people. Some practice non-hierarchical polyamory wherein everyone is considered to be an equal partner regardless of cohabitation and other patterns. Others maintain a hierarchy with primary, secondary, and tertiary relationships that may differ in strength, frequency of contact, cohabitation, finances, fluid bonding, and so on. Closed formations that restrict additional relationships are referred to as *polyfidelitous*.

There are a number of defining characteristics that most of those who advocate for or practice polyamory frequently hold to. One commonly agreed upon requirement is a commitment to honesty, openness, and communication. For many, this may mean that every individual who is part of a polyamorous relationship must be fully aware of all the other individuals similarly involved. This carries with it an implicit responsibility to communicate fully and honestly about many aspects of the relationship. One obvious example of this need appears with the sharing of sexual partner history and the willingness to divulge information about one's sexual health. The acquisition of a sexually transmitted infection is one obvious challenge to the success of the polyamorous complex. The extent to which information is shared depends on the underlying philosophy of the different participants, something that varies widely. On one end of the range are those who share information unconditionally, a "tell-all" style, while the opposite end may share information only minimally or not at all. In the middle are those who only share information that impacts physical and emotional safety. This highly variable approach is what often creates confusion for those who do not embrace polyamory, just as it signals a wide variation in actual, day-to-day practice. What's more, not all polyamorous relationships actually proceed in this manner. Violations of this implicitly understood protocol do occur, and this in turn may generate considerable "processing" that is well known amongst most polyamorous persons.

Most partners work out some form of rules or *agreements* that fit their relationship. These can be written down or spoken only, may contain definitive rules or more general intentions, values, and guidelines. Rules often refer to notification about other relationships, patterns and intentions of being away or at home, the nature of physical intimacy, degrees of emotional attachment, and so on. Some primary partners maintain a veto power on further relationships. Safety is often a primary topic, and covers things like safer sex, the limits of sexual contact, physical and emotional intimacy, and emotional safety. Safer sex is generally seen as a critical aspect of polyamorous relationships in that a violation of agreed-upon safer sex protocols may put others in physical danger, often without their knowledge or consent. An agreement around safer sex might include a frank discussion about *fluid bonding*, the practice of barrier-free sexual contact, as well as candid talk about STI (sexually transmitted infection) testing, the interval expected, the degree to which the bonded parties will disclose their own health status to others, and, often, a clear understanding of the extent to which members are permitted to have sexual contact with others not already in the structure.

Scheduling in polyamorous relationships is a recurring logistical issue that is commonly solved by the shared use of online calendars. The desire to spend time with all of one's other partners means that everyone in the group must be able to keep close track of who is spending time with who. One of the more common problems encountered in any close relationship is that of jealousy. Polyamory is not immune to this problem, and jealous partners are often a challenge. Polyamorists frequently approach jealousy through a mix of introspection, creative self-empowerment, and a lot of talking. Many profess not to experience jealousy while others talk of situational insecurity only, something that can sometimes be resolved by focusing on one's own needs and asking for help from others. For many, the willingness to forge agreements and the need for open communication can help make jealousy a manageable problem. Polyamorists often enjoy the flip side of jealousy: *compersion*, which refers to the state of happiness and joy experienced when a loved one experiences independent joy, especially with another partner or lover.

Economic issues figure into some polyamorous relationships by virtue of either cohabitation or the choice to share resources beyond the basics. Some partners are legally married, others are not. A polyamorous triad might, for example, elect to share housing. In the event that this entails purchase of a home, such a decision must involve a careful analysis of the financial state of the participants, as well as a clear set of agreements that not only establishes the extent of financial entanglement, but also meshes with the existing legal structure in a manner that makes dissolution possible.

There is no locale that, at present, sanctions polyamory in a legal sense from the standpoint of the partners themselves. Recent case law, although making allowances for more than two parents, does so *only* as a means of protecting children, and not for the purpose of sanctioning or expanding the legal rights of the adults in such a relationship. As such, polyamory remains an unrecognized legal status. While many of the social relationship structures found in various parts of the world informally tolerate multiple partners, they are not generally constructed to facilitate any legal resolution should the participants seek redress in a court over some aspect of the relationship. Children who are part of a polyamorous structure pose a significant challenge, since the conventional and commonly accepted understanding of a marriage involves recognition of parental responsibilities. A third (or other) partner involved in childrearing within a polyamorous structure may find that they have no legal standing at all should the recognized parents (either by way of biology or other means) elect to make choices that exclude that third person. Similarly, economic matters such as home or land ownership may be rendered moot for one or more members of a polyamorous structure in the event that those who hold legal title challenge such economic stakes. Notably, there are no legal protections against housing or employment discrimination for those identifying openly as polyamorous. While there is considerable interest in expanding the legal scope of relationships such as marriage to allow for multiple partners, any such changes might also be expected to come as part of a larger social and economic expansion.

Recent political debates around same-sex marriage have brought polyamory into the discussion in several Western countries. The "slippery slope" argument has been used by conservative opponents of same-sex marriage to argue that it would lead to an erosion of traditional marriage and result in plural marriage, bestiality, and marriage with inanimate objects. Polyamory advocates have rejected this and maintain that it is either best to keep plural marriage out of this particular debate, or that instead of a slippery slope it is more useful to talk about a deliberate and gradual societal process of progressively accepting new, ethical relationship forms.

As with gay and lesbian relationships there is a recurring moral panic about the status and well-being of children. Many studies clearly demonstrate that there is no disadvantage for children in gay and lesbian households. Emerging research is beginning to show the same for children in polyamorous households. Children may in fact benefit from multiple caring adults, extra resources, and abundant love, and grow up more emotionally resilient. Such studies may have a pivotal role in future custody cases relating to children in polyamorous families.

SEE ALSO: Cohabitation and *Ekageikama* in the Kandyan Kingdom (Sri Lanka); Kinship; Polygamy, Polygyny, and Polyandry; Same-Sex Marriage; Sexualities

FURTHER READING

Anapol, Deborah M. 1997. *Polyamory: The New Love Without Limits: Secrets of Sustainable Intimate Relationships*. San Rafael: IntiNet Resource Center.

Easton, Dossie, and Janet W. Hardy. 2009. *The Ethical Slut: A Roadmap for Relationship Pioneers*. Berkeley: Celestial Arts.

Taormino, Tristan. 2008. *Opening Up: A Guide to Creating and Sustaining Open Relationships*. San Francisco: Cleis Press.

Veaux, Franklin, and Eve Rickert. 2014. *More Than Two: A Practical Guide to Ethical Polyamory*. Portland: Thorntree Press.

Polygamy, Polygyny, and Polyandry

CASEY GOLOMSKI
University of Massachusetts Boston, USA

Polygamy refers to marriage between multiple individuals and is sometimes called plural marriage, while polygyny and polyandry denote different ratios of gendered individuals in a marriage. Polygynous marriages are between a single man and multiple women. Polyandrous marriages are between a single woman and multiple men. Historically Westernized nations have outlawed polygamy, with support from some feminist activists and scholars, in contrast to non-Western and or non-industrialized societies, which have long upheld forms of multiple marriage as an ideal kinship type. Some groups in North America and Europe increasingly challenge social and legal standards to make polygamy more acceptable, eroding a "West versus rest" perspective and renewing scholarly and popular attention to forms of multiple marriage and sexual-affective relations. Research has focused more on polygamous women, noting their ambiguous and diverse experiences, a similar finding in new work on polygamous men.

Polygamy has been a standard interest of evolutionary anthropology and behavioral ecology. They see polygamy in terms of cooperative breeding and investment in offspring for overall reproductive fitness. It is well known that women in polygynous marriages trend toward lower fertility, and studies showing poorer health outcomes for these women tend to shore up criticisms against polygyny. However, Mulder (2009) argues that these models bias against parental investment in offspring and obscure females' own reproductive strategies, arguing for her sample of Tanzanian Pimbwe horticulturalists that women benefit more than men from polygyny. Economic systems of subsistence, including horticulture, pastoralism, and foraging, influence the sexual division of labor in polygamous societies. For example, unlike African pastoralists where men control more resources, men in some indigenous South American groups spend more time clearing forests for gardens and suggestively attract fewer partners due to limited resource accumulation. Here, polygyny is more equally negotiated between genders (Winking et al. 2013).

For sociocultural anthropology, polygyny can be seen on a continuum whose range includes societies permitting women's autonomy in marital choice to societies invoking extreme, violent coercion and forced marriages. At this end patriarchal norms limit women's agency and reproductivity in public life, making them subordinate dependents on husbands and affines. Affluent polygyny reflects men's gains in prestige among male peers as they take more wives, and may include advantages for women as they marry up (hypergamy). Nwoye (2007) points out that some contemporary African writers do not denounce polygyny as an institution but rather criticize middle- and upper-class urban men who manipulate polygyny's ideal forms and obligations. For these writers, the focus should be on interventive polygyny where couples negotiate taking another spouse to help a struggling marriage. Here, polygyny is cast in a positive light to deal with problems of infertility, caregiving, and household economy.

Sororal polygyny, the marriage of women who are sisters to a single man, is one such intervention if equitably negotiated between husbands, wives, and their families. In Mardu and other Australian aboriginal societies, a wife may lobby her husband to marry her younger sister to help with domestic work. Both general and sororal polygyny can enable surrogate motherhood in cases where both wife and husband are infertile, which is often perceived as a malady in many societies. For example, in customary law in Swaziland women may decide or be compelled to "put [her own] child in the stomach" of her co-wife or sister, or bear a child on her co-wife's behalf if her co-wife cannot have a child of her own. Both women are seen as mothers of the child.

The few studies on polyandry also focus on plural marriage of collateral kin, but in its fraternal form where multiple brothers are married to a single woman. Goldstein's (1978) research on Tibetan and Nepalese societies showed that fraternal polyandry accommodates sociocultural goals within a unique mountainous ecosystem of limited farming and grazing land. Mulder (2009) and others have questioned why polyandry is supposedly so rare in human societies by rethinking the ways we conceptualize marriage. Focusing on women's strategies to achieve reproductive and social goals through multiple, sometimes concurrent and informal partnerships with men across the life course shows polyandry to be much more common.

Diverse religious traditions like Islam, Christianity, Judaism, and indigenous religions have justified plural marriage. Islam-inspired polygyny is common in Southeast Asia, West Africa, and the Middle East. Some Pukhtun men in Pakistan take second wives as a revenge tactic against their first wives. While the Qur'an condones polygyny, these local misogynistic norms do not tend to align with standard scriptural interpretations (Lindholm 2008). In Indonesia, both advocates and opponents of polygyny link to debates on democracy and religion: advocates argue that polygamy constitutes freedom of Islamic and local religious practice, while opponents cite polygamy as an assault on women as equal citizens (Brenner 2011). Christians worldwide have come to selectively shun polygyny. Mormon polygyny in the United States emerged in the 1830s and was promulgated by some as a moral, practical, and scientific imperative despite eventual mainstream social and legislative prohibitions.

Despite its affront to certain liberal perspectives, plural marriage continues worldwide, reflecting a conjuncture of gendered, structural inequalities and cultural or religious ideas about inabilities for social and sexual reproduction. Scholars must likewise consider how and why some might engage plural marriage for personal projects of gender and sexual identity formation.

SEE ALSO: Cohabitation and *Ekageikama* in the Kandyan Kingdom (Sri Lanka); Kinship; Polyamory; Religious Fundamentalism

REFERENCES

Brenner, Suzanne. 2011. "Private Moralities in the Public Sphere." *American Anthropologist*, 113(3): 478–490.

Goldstein, Melvyn. 1978. "Pahari and Tibetan Polyandry Revisited." *Ethnology*, 17(3): 325–337.

Lindholm, Charles. 2008. "Polygyny in Islamic Law and Pukhtun Practice." *Ethnology*, 47(2–3): 181–193.

Mulder, Monique Borgerhoff. 2009. "Serial Monogamy as Polygyny or Polyandry?" *Human Nature*, 20: 130–150.

Nwoye, Augustine. 2007. "The Practice of Interventive Polygyny in Two Regions of Africa." *Dialectical Anthropology*, 31: 383–421.

Winking, Jeffrey, Jonathan Stieglitz, Jenna Kurten, Hillard Kaplan, and Michael Gurven. 2013. "Polygyny Among the Tsimane of Bolivia: An Improved Method for Testing the Polygyny–Fertility Hypothesis." *Proceedings of the Royal Society B*, 280. DOI: 10.1098/rspb.2012.3078.

FURTHER READING

Clignet, Remi. 1970. *Many Wives, Many Powers.* Evanston: Northwestern University Press.

White, Douglas, and Michael Burton. 1988. "Causes of Polygyny: Ecology, Economy, Kinship and Warfare." *American Anthropologist*, 90(4): 871–887.

Popular Culture and Gender

DOMITILLA OLIVIERI
Utrecht University, The Netherlands

Gender and popular culture are deeply intertwined in multiple ways and their interrelation produces considerable and far-reaching effects in society. Popular culture is one of the major agents of socialization through which people learn norms and values. Therefore, it also plays an important role in the production and reproduction of gender norms and gendered subjects, as the socially constructed ideas of gender are reinforced by the dominant narratives in popular culture. Images, texts and sounds conveyed by a wide array of media and across cultural phenomena – such as television, film, music, performances, magazines, comics, novels, games, fashion, and advertising – all produce and represent the set of beliefs and values about masculinity and femininity dominant in a given culture at a given time. The pervasiveness of popular media and the shared understanding of the notions therein transmitted make it so that these ideas come to appear as the norm, as self-evident, and are taken for granted. However, a critical account of how gender is engaged in and by popular culture reveals a complexity of values and narratives, which have serious effects on society at large; namely, they contribute to the shaping of identities, behaviors and subjectivities, and also to the creation or strengthening of social, economic, and political power relations. Hence, reading popular culture in terms of how it affects and is affected by gender norms and behaviors means paying attention to how it is the product of, and also how it produces and reproduces, hegemonic (or potentially alternative) discourses about men and women, femininities and masculinities, and about other differences.

While there is a general understanding of what popular culture is, scholars have elaborated various definitions to pin down what this complex field of the "popular" is and does. Granted that it is a product of urbanization and industrialization, at least six ways to define popular culture have been identified: in terms of its quantitative dimension as being that brand of cultural production favored or liked by many people, or as being the product of a cultural hegemony (in a Gramscian sense), that is, a mean of the state or of otherwise dominant classes to impose indirectly norms and values on the people;

understanding it as the mass-produced, commercial result of the culture industries imposed on the masses, or as that culture that originates from the people; conceiving it as the culture that is "left over" after the canon of high culture has been established, or as an effect of the entanglement between commerce and culture which blurs the very distinction between high and low, elites and masses (Storey 2012, 1–13).

These criteria for definitions vary according to academic disciplinary (and interdisciplinary) discourses and also historical and geopolitical contexts and political values (for a history or a genealogy of the studies on popular culture see, for example, Jenkins, McPherson, and Shattuc 2002; Storey 2012). Nonetheless, many are the concepts shared by these approaches and theories, which have been developed in fields ranging from social sciences to gender studies, from cultural studies to psychology, from anthropology to media studies. Just to mention a few, ideology, hegemony, representation, discourse, identity, community, the everyday, and imagination are key notions when approaching the field of popular culture, in general and also from a perspective that focuses on gender.

When considering gender in relation to popular culture, what becomes crucial is not as much what popular culture is, but rather what it does and how it functions. In this regard, the role that power, discourse, and ideology play in the social construction of masculinities and femininities and of what it means to be men and women becomes central. Products of popular culture pervade our daily lives and, creating images and imaginaries, they influence the way we learn about and look at ourselves and others, at our society as well as at other cultures, at contemporary phenomena as well as at historical events. Popular culture also affects our daily experiences as gendered subjects by presenting norms and values about what kind of identities, ways of life, and modes of relations are acceptable or non-acceptable, e.g., in presenting some sexualities as normal and others as deviant, or in reproducing stereotypes about people of certain nationalities or ethnicities. Finally, popular culture also engages questions of gender in terms of who partakes in the production of popular texts and who does not, for example, how many men or women are involved in media production and how. These three facets of the relation between gender and popular culture could be summarized as pertaining, respectively, to the levels of representation, reception, and production (as presented in Milestone and Meyer 2012). Therefore, different tools and approaches are required in order to address these different aspects: textual analyses, where popular texts – in a broad understanding of the concept – are considered as systems of representation; studies on the broader context in which the texts are produced, for which political economic accounts become crucial; and audience reception studies, where surveys, interviews, and other methodologies from the social sciences prove to be necessary to map the effects of popular cultural products on people, viewer, users, and customers (Kellner 2002). These three domains, albeit requiring different methods of analysis, are always already intertwined.

Cultural studies scholars have shown that representational practices shape identities and affect experiences of the self (Hall 1997). Popular culture can be studied as a representational system wherein methods and concepts from poststructuralist theory, visual studies, semiotics, and feminist theory need to be employed in order to make sense of how these texts produce actual effects on how we inhabit the world and function in society. In dialogue with these conceptual frameworks, feminist scholars have focused specifically on gender as/and representation and on the mechanisms of its construction in visual media and popular culture. Teresa De Lauretis (1987) is one of the scholars who paved the way in thinking about gender as being constructed not only through implicit and explicit social rules such as policing of behaviors, laws, or education, but also through visual media.

Since the 1980s, many studies have analyzed how gender is represented across popular texts and phenomena, and how these representations in turn produce gender norms, gender stereotypes, and gendered behaviors. While some research on gender and popular culture focuses on the specificity of what kind of femininities and masculinities are created, other works address how these representations reproduce, maintain, and reinforce hegemonic, hierarchical, patriarchal, heteronormative, and all-in-all oppressive meanings and practices.

It should be remembered that these processes of production and reproduction of identities, and these practices of inclusion and exclusion, operate along lines of social and cultural differences that not only include gender, but also other differences in terms of, for example, ethnicity, sexuality, race, class, age, level of education, nationality, and body ability, among others. Therefore, in most contemporary research that focuses on popular culture in relation to gender, the latter is understood as always being entangled with other axes of difference. Moreover, gender becomes not only the object of analysis – i.e., how are gender identities constructed and how are masculinity and femininity represented? – but also a lens, one of the possible entry points, to observe and critically engage with the interconnections between power, representation, and differences. If one acknowledges that popular culture contributes to shaping experiences, imaginaries, and identities, then looking at how gender is constructed cannot but also entail looking at what other implicit values and assumptions reside therein. An intersectional approach is therefore almost always adopted when critically analyzing popular culture.

Additionally, the ways in which gender is engaged in popular culture and the mechanisms that structure this relation, at the level of production, representation, and reception, are strongly dependent upon the historical, economic, and geopolitical circumstances of the society or cultural contexts in question. Hence a critical stance that accounts for the situatedness and partiality of the analytical tools used to study gender and popular culture has to be wary of this variety of locations and specific dynamics. In other words, as in any other field of enquiry that takes into account gender, also when considering popular culture it becomes crucial not to assume universal or disembodied standpoints, but rather to pay attention to how the location of the viewer, listener, reader, or researcher plays a role in shaping the interpretation or perception of a given popular text. Accordingly, it becomes important to acknowledge that the kind of experience of, or way of interpreting, a film, or music video or any other cultural product is greatly dependent upon the specific location of the perceiver, in terms of, for example, their gender, race, sexual orientation, level of education or political convictions, to name just a few.

Another very important aspect to consider when thinking of gender and popular culture is the potential for resistance, reaction, and intervention that is inherent to these representations no matter how normative or widespread. As elaborated above, there are strong arguments that show how popular culture reproduces normative and oppressive power relations and hegemonic ideas of what normal femininities and masculinities should be like, thus affecting men and women. However, and also because of the malleability and fast-changing and intertextual nature of popular culture, various kinds of practices of resistance and reaction have been explored by viewers or users of popular media to react to, criticize, or appropriate the producers' intended meanings of, for example, TV series, comic books, and advertisements. These strategies are, for example, reappropriation, oppositional reading, and bricolage (i.e., taking mass-marketing products or images and reinterpreting them as creative or resistant responses to consumerism). One specific mention should go to fan fiction, a genre of textual or visual intervention which re-works the stories and characters of popular texts, with or without the direct aim of addressing the normative aspect of popular representation. Gender and sexuality are often the elements addressed or subverted in these reappropriations. Especially when the Internet is used as a medium to share and make visible these fan fictions, the impact of these practices is far reaching, to the extent that more and more TV producers, for example, are including suggestions or stories written by the fan back into the official TV series. Moreover, other subcultures or traditionally oppressed groups have now entered more predominantly in the field of the popular, with, for example, queer popular culture now being an actual field of enquiry (Peele 2011). Along these lines, popular culture has also been the field where subcultures or countercultures have found a source of inspiration or a space for critique and intervention. Communities organized around specific cultural trends, events, or political beliefs, and characterized by specific styles of clothing or behaviors, have been creating images, texts, sounds, performances and, more broadly, imaginaries alternative to what could be considered the dominant popular culture of the time. A good example of the complex phenomenon of countercultures is popular music (Whiteley and Sklower 2014): from some strands of punk to hip-hop, from the rising of what has been labeled as world music to various alternative rock styles – to mention but a few cases. The musical aspect of these genres is strongly intertwined, implicitly or explicitly so, with other elements of popular culture, as a critique or as a reworking of it: countercultures in popular music have thus produced not only new sounds, texts, and images, but also related communities and identities. Also in this context, gender and sexuality have been sites of direct contestation or otherwise intervention, both in counter- or subcultures and in popular music at large. Norms and ideas around femininities and masculinities are renegotiated or confirmed in and through popular music. Through music videos and song lyrics, in live performances and interviews, and also in the look and fashion of the musicians, gender is constantly defined and redefined, thus, once again, being an important lens to interpret the role that popular culture plays in the construction of subjectivities, groups and identities.

SEE ALSO: Discourse and Gender; Feminism and Postmodernism; Gender Belief System/Gender Ideology; Gender Stereotypes; Heterosexual Imaginary; Language and Gender; Social Identity; Visual Culture

REFERENCES

De Lauretis, Teresa. 1987. *Technologies of Gender. Essays on Theory, Film, and Fiction*. Bloomington: Indiana University Press.

Jenkins, Henry, Tara McPherson, and Jane Shattuc. 2002. *Hop on Pop: The Politics and Pleasures of Popular Culture*. Durham, NC: Duke University Press.

Kellner, Douglas. 2002. "Cultural Studies, Multiculturalism and Media Culture." In *Gender, Race and Class in Media: A Text-Reader*, edited by Gail Dines and Jean M. Humez, 9–20. Thousand Oaks: Sage.

Hall, Stuart. 1997. *Representation: Cultural Representations and Signifying Practices*. London: Sage.

Milestone, Katie, and Anneke Meyer. 2012. *Gender and Popular Culture*. Cambridge: Polity.

Peele, Thomas. 2011. *Queer Popular Culture. Literature, Media, Film, and Television*. New York: Palgrave Macmillan.
Storey, John. 2012. *Cultural Theory and Popular Culture*, 6th ed. Abingdon: Routledge.
Whiteley, Sheila, and Jedediah Sklower. 2014. *Countercultures and Popular Music*. Farnham: Ashgate.

FURTHER READING

Carter, Cynthia, Linda Steiner, and Lisa McLaughlin, eds. 2014. *The Routledge Companion to Media and Gender*. Abingdon: Routledge.
Cartwright, Lisa, and Marita Sturken. 2001. *Practices of Looking: An Introduction to Visual Culture*. Oxford: Oxford University Press.
Raymond, Diane. 2003. "Popular Culture and Queer Representation: A Critical Perspective." In *Gender, Race, and Class in Media: A Text-Reader*, edited by Gail Dines and Jean M. Humez, 98–110. Thousand Oaks: Sage.
Tasker, Yvonne, and Diane Negra. 2007. *Interrogating Postfeminism: Gender and the Politics of Popular Culture*. Durham, NC: Duke University Press.
Tasker, Yvonne, and Diane Negra. 2012. *Gendering the Recession: Media and Culture in an Age of Austerity*. Durham, NC: Duke University Press.
Trier-Bieniek, Adrienne, and Patricia Leavy. 2014. *Gender & Pop Culture. A Text-Reader*. Rotterdam: Sense Publishers.
Walton, David. 2012. *Doing Cultural Theory*. Thousand Oaks: Sage.
Whiteley, Sheila, ed. 1997. *Sexing the Groove: Popular Music and Gender*. London: Routledge.
Zeisler, Andi. 2008. *Feminism and Pop Culture*. Berkeley: Seal Press.

Population Control and Population Policy

ELIZABETH WIRTZ
Purdue University, USA

Population control is the practice of artificially altering the demographic composition of a given populace. Demographic composition refers to factors such as size, distribution, density, age, sex, ethnicity, and so on, that make up a particular population. Populations are frequently in flux due to natural causes such as birth and death rates and migration. However, population control is the intentional altering of a given group of people, typically achieved through population control policies enacted by national and international governing bodies. These policies focus on regulating fertility, emigration, and/or immigration to achieve the desired population size and demographics. Governing bodies are interested in attaining certain population demographics for varied purposes such as labor, taxation, political security, and ideology.

Throughout much of history, population demographics have been considered so fundamentally important to societies that diverse institutions including medical, religious, social, economic, and political, have subsumed the task of influencing population dynamics (Tobin 2004; Connelly 2010). Governments, for instance, implement such control through diverse laws, policies, and programs. Some of these are more direct such as China's one-child policy, or immigration laws restricting the number and national origin of immigrants, while others work more indirectly by encouraging or discouraging certain behavior. Examples of the latter include pro-natalist policies, such as government tax and labor benefits for citizens who have children, or immigrant employment programs that encourage laborers from foreign countries to cross national boarders in search of work (Tobin 2004; May 2012). Beyond national governments, international governmental organizations like the United Nations (particularly the United Nations Population Fund), World Bank, and World Health Organization, and various nongovernmental organizations throughout the world focus on issues of population control.

Within the last century, the term "population control" has referred more specifically to controlling the overall numerical population of the world. Those who support population control efforts claim that overpopulation is currently leading, or will eventually lead to a variety of problems, and therefore needs to be addressed through curtailing global population growth or reducing the current global population. Within the last century, there has been a drastic increase in the global population. The world reached its first billion people in the 1800s, second in the 1920s, third in the 1960s, fourth in the 1970s, fifth in the 1980s, and sixth in the 1990s. Today, there are more than 7 billion people in the world. While the rate of growth has decreased, the overall population continues to increase exponentially, with roughly 90% of this increase occurring in developing countries (Weisman 2013).

This rapid population growth is attributed to technological advancements made in the twentieth century, particularly medical and agricultural innovations, that decreased overall mortality and increased life expectancy (May 2012). More people are surviving, and for longer lifespans. Most consider these improvements beneficial for humanity. At the same time, such advancements resulted in a rapid and drastic increase in global population. Many scholars and activists argue that this spike in global population, and continued growth, is a major contributor to issues like environmental degradation, resource scarcity, poverty, disease, and so on (Friedman 2008; Weisman 2013). The rationale behind these connections was established prior to the recent global population increase. As far back as the 1700s, Thomas Malthus argued that unchecked population growth increases at a much faster rate than food production, causing food shortages (Mosher 2008; Rao 2004). Thus, he argued that the fertility of human populations needs to be controlled in order to avoid the negative impacts of overpopulation such as famine, disease, and political conflict (Tobin 2004).

Malthus based much of his theories on concepts of ecological carrying capacity. Carrying capacity is the maximum population that a given environment can sustain based on the balance between the resources available and the resources that are used. According to supporters of population control, humans have either already overpopulated beyond the carrying capacity of their global environment or are dangerously close to doing so. Neo-Malthusians argue that this overpopulation is the main source of resource scarcity, leading to crises such as poverty, famine, conflict, poor health, and environmental deterioration. In order to alleviate these crises, the earth's carrying capacity must be rebalanced by implementing measures to reduce the global population.

Because developing countries currently exhibit the highest birth rates, and therefore contribute the most to global population growth, most population control efforts have centered on lowering fertility rates in these areas (Hartmann 1995; Rao 2004). Efforts to reduce fertility in developing countries are intricately tied to larger development goals because of the perceived relationship between fertility and poverty. Many development schemes adhere to demographic transition theories that argue that societies undergo fertility shifts in progressive phases (Rao 2004). These theories argue that the first phase of high fertility rates and high mortality rates is characteristic of underdeveloped societies. As societies advance, they enter the second phase where mortality rates decline but fertility rates remain high. It is within this second stage that conditions foster dramatic population growth. Eventually, fertility levels fall to rebalance with lowered mortality rates. Finally, a fully developed society exhibits the third and final phase of low fertility rates and low mortality rates. These theories describe a teleological path that attributes progress, modernization, and development to demographic shifts in fertility and mortality. Demographic transition theories couple with Neo-Malthusianism to encourage opposition to population growth and support population control policies as a method to alleviate conflict over limited resources, improve global health indicators, spur economic growth, and reduce poverty.

Since the inception of population control theories, critics have argued against both the basic tenets of these theories and their implementations. These critics argue that there is not only a lack of data to substantiate the preceding claims, but that there also exists a plethora of data that contradict the claims. In addition, such fervent focus on reducing population growth detracts from the genuine causes of the aforementioned issues and can lead to human rights abuses.

First, critics argue that the primary cause of resource scarcity and environmental degradation is the distribution and usage of resources rather than overpopulation (Kasun 1999; Friedman 2008). Carrying capacity is not based on simply an overall number of maximum individuals in relation to resource availability, but rather how much of and in what way the resources are being used by individuals. Opponents argue that it is erroneous to target population growth in the poorest countries when it is the wealthiest individuals and societies who use a disproportionate amount of resources and contribute the most to pollution and resource use (Friedman 2008; Mosher 2008).

Another issue that has been raised with the logic behind population control is that many of the negative impacts listed such as environmental degradation and disease are due more to population distribution and density than overall population. Along with the technological advancements and industrialization that spurred much of the modern population growth, came massive urbanization. As large numbers of people move into urban areas, vast expanses of land are left un- or under-inhabited. In fact, many of the developing countries that are frequent targets of population control efforts are and historically have been under-populated in relation to potential resources.

Critics of population control also take issue with the supposed correlation between fertility, poverty, and development. Proponents of population control policies argue that reducing fertility, which is the key to reducing global population growth, will also alleviate poverty and increase development efforts, especially in developing countries where poverty levels remain high. While there may be a correlation between the aforementioned factors, there is little proof of any causative link (Kasun 1999; Rao 2004; Connelly 2010). A strong debate exists as to whether high fertility is a symptom or cause of poverty. The question remains as to whether people are poor because they have many children or whether people are having many children because they are poor. By linking fertility and development, larger structural and historical causes of poverty and inequality are ignored or given secondary importance, and a "blame the victim" mentality ensues in which poor people with high fertility are blamed for their poverty (Hartmann 1995; Kasun 1999; Connelly 2010).

Critics of population control have also raised issues with the practicality and feasibility of population control strategies. Most population control policies are geared toward reducing the fertility rates of people in developing countries, where the infant and child mortality rate remains high. Studies have established a strong relationship between high infant and child mortality rates and high fertility rates (Hartmann 1995; Kasun 1999). High fertility rates in this context ensures that an acceptable number of offspring reach reproductive maturity. According to the demographic transition theory, mortality rates lower prior to fertility rates and lowered mortality acts as a catalyst to lowered fertility. Thus, efforts to lower fertility, and thus population growth, in these areas are likely to fail until health and survival conditions improve.

Finally, important criticisms of population control have been raised over some of the methods employed to reduce population growth. Some proponents of population control use inflammatory and alarmist rhetoric to motivate governing bodies and others to take immediate and extreme action. This rhetoric instigates fear and panic, and in the resulting zeal to rapidly reduce fertility rates, many human rights abuses occur. These human rights abuses have ranged from slight coercion to outright exploitation and severe abuse. Examples include activities ranging from authorities withholding aid and services from individuals or communities who do not comply with family planning programs to forced sterilizations (Kasun 1999; Rao 2004; Tobin 2004; Mosher 2008; Connelly 2010).

A good example of the impacts of population control policies on local people's lives lies in the case of Puerto Rico (Hartmann 1995). Through a rigorous population control policy, one third of women in Puerto Rico were sterilized by 1986. Through national and international aid, sterilization was subsidized well over other forms of contraceptives, making sterilization the only form of family planning that many citizens could afford. In addition, women were given incentives such as longer hospital stays and better treatment if they agreed to be sterilized after giving birth. Many of the women were not aware that the procedure was permanent, nor of the side effects that could occur. As a result, many women found themselves unable to bear more children, resulting in marital tensions, domestic abuse, abandonment, and stigma.

Since the supposed "success" of the fertility reduction measures, Puerto Rico's economy has not markedly improved and environmental degradation continues unabated. The case of Puerto Rico prompts us to question the actual benefit of drastically and coercively curbing the population of the island.

Population control efforts have had a markedly gendered component, with the majority of population reduction programs geared toward women. This is partially because national fertility and birth rates are measured by number of births per *woman*. In addition, the realm of reproduction is largely considered a "woman's issue" because of women's greater involvement in reproductive capacities, namely gestation and breastfeeding. Thus, the majority of contraceptives have been developed for use by women rather than men (see Hartmann 1995, Chapter 10). Worldwide, it has been women who bear the brunt of these abuses since women are many times the primary targets of population control policies implemented through family planning programs.

While population control policies and pro- or anti-natalist rhetoric are directed at women in general, it is actually certain types of women who are the main focus of these efforts. Population control policies tend to target the "undesirables" of society, those considered unworthy of procreation: the poor, certain racial, ethnic, or religious groups, mentally or emotionally disabled, the infirm, and the criminal (Kasun 1999). Throughout the history of population control efforts, reducing human population and eugenics have, at times, become dangerously similar in theory and practice. In fact, many of the first arguments in favor of population control were couched under women's rights, rather under limiting the fertility of undesired populations. In reality, policies and programs that are intended to improve women's reproductive health and status many times actually end up hurting women and their families.

Furthermore, population control policies have resulted in a number of unintended consequences. First, strictly limiting fertility in societies that greatly value male children over female children results in severe gender imbalances within the population and gender-based violence such as abandonment of female children, female infanticide, and sex-selective abortion (Connelly 2010). In some countries, like Germany and Japan, population control policies have contributed to negative population growth and shifting demographics toward an "aging population," in which there are not enough youth to support the elderly (May 2012). These countries are in the process of reversing their population control measures by implementing alternative population policies such as encouraging high fertility and/or favorable immigration policies.

Given the complexities discussed above, it is not surprising that debates surrounding population control policies and the causes and effects of population growth continue today. Population demographics are essential to understanding larger global processes impacting resource use, environment, economics, development, and health. Most people agree that maintaining a sustainable global population, reducing negative impacts on the environment, balancing resource usage, and alleviating poverty are essential to the well-being of humanity. Questions for the future remain regarding how to define sustainable and how to reach the goal of sustainability while minimizing negative impacts and maximizing equality. In order to truly address the major issues we face as a global society, we must continue to explore and interrogate the complicated relationships between population, demographics, and development. We must also consider how best to balance the alleviation of pressing social, economic, and environmental problems with the protection of individual human rights.

SEE ALSO: Fertility Rates; Gender Development, Theories of; Gender Redistributive Policies; Life Expectancy

REFERENCES

Connelly, Matthew. 2010. *Fatal Misconception: The Struggle to Control World Population*. Cambridge, MA: Harvard University Press.

Friedman, Thomas. 2008. *Hot, Flat, and Crowded: Why We Need a Green Revolution – and How It Can Renew America*. New York: Farrar, Straus and Giroux.

Hartmann, Betsy. 1995. *Reproductive Rights and Wrongs: The Global Politics of Population Control*. Boston: South End Press.

Kasun, Jacqueline. 1999. *The War against Population: The Economics and Ideology of World Population Control*. San Francisco: Ignatius Press.

May, John. 2012. *World Population Policies: Their Origin, Evolution, and Impact*. Dordrecht: Springer.

Mosher, Steven. 2008. *Population Control: Real Costs, Illusory Benefits*. New Brunswick: Transaction Publishers.

Rao, Mohan. 2004. *From Population Control to Reproductive Health: Malthusian Arithmetic*. New Delhi: Sage.

Tobin, Kathleen. 2004. *Politics and Population Control: A Documentary History*. Westport: Greenwood Publishing Group.

Weisman, Alan. 2013. *Countdown: Our Last, Best Hope for a Future on Earth?* New York: Hachette Digital.

FURTHER READING

Birdsall, Nancy, Allen Kelley, and Steven Sinding, eds. 2001. *Population Matters: Demographic Change, Economic Growth, and Poverty in the Developing World*. New York: Oxford University Press.

Singh, Jyoti. 2009. *Creating a New Consensus on Population: The Politics of Reproductive Health, Reproductive Rights and Women's Empowerment*. London: Earthscan.

Pornography, Feminist Legal and Political Debates on

ANNA DODSON SAIKIN
Rice University, USA

The debate over the moral, social, and legal value of pornography, particularly in the United States, has divided feminist scholars and activists who seek to protect the autonomy and freedom of women's sexuality. Some claim that pornography fosters a culture of sexual violence against women, while others argue that pornography permits women greater sexual expression. This debate has focused on whether or not individuals who perform pornographic acts are harmed in the process, as well as the effects of viewing these acts as a consumer. While these debates have their origins in nineteenth- and twentieth-century anti-obscenity laws that were based on moral codes, contemporary debates consider whether pornography is an expression of free speech or if it constitutes sexual violence against women.

Feminist debates and legislation regarding pornography have largely occurred in the United States and Great Britain, but several other countries have passed anti-obscenity legislation and have been active participants in this debate. Many countries including the United States, Great Britain, Canada, and Australia have had difficulty establishing the legal definition of pornography, making attempts to legislate it more complicated. The feminist sex debates in the United States reached their height in the 1980s, when several anti-porn measures were put to national and state governments, leading to academic and public criticism regarding the distribution and consumption of pornography. The legal permissibility of pornography varies from country to country, though most countries regulate child pornography to some degree.

Many current feminist debates on pornography have their roots in anti-obscenity rulings from the nineteenth century and the first part of the twentieth century. The strict moral codes of Victorian England led to a series of court decisions that influenced future decisions in both England and the United States. Though obscene or pornographic literature had been subject to legal persecution in the eighteenth century, nineteenth-century courts attempted to further define what constituted obscene writings. The Obscene Publications Act of 1857 was the first to enforce prosecution of the distribution and consumption of lewd material. Lord Chief Justice John Campbell introduced the bill that would give police the right to search property where obscene publications were sold or on display and destroy objectionable material. After an outpouring of public support for the bill, it was adopted, though the definition of what constituted an "obscene" work was not set until 1868, when the Queen's Bench ordered that copies of Henry Scott's *The Confessional Unmasked* be destroyed because it depicted obscene moments in an Anglican confessional. The case, *Regina v. Hicklin*, prohibited works whose purpose was to deprave the minds of impressionable persons who came across them. The Hicklin decision focused on society rather than the individual and meant that these works were not permitted under freedom of expression and were to be strictly controlled. The Hicklin Test, used to determine what constituted an obscene publication, prevailed in English courts and influenced American courts for almost one hundred years.

Few obscenity prosecutions took place before the American Civil War. In 1873, Anthony Comstock, a United States Postal Inspector, founded the New York Society for the Suppression of Vice, an organization dedicated to preserving social morality. Comstock advocated for an expansion of the 1865 federal mail act to include the prohibition of the distribution of obscene materials through the mail. The Comstock Act of 1873 made Comstock a special agent of the Post Office and gave him significant authority to censor mail distribution as he saw fit. Comstock and his agents successfully drove the production of pornography underground until the 1950s.

Beginning in the 1930s, American courts further defined what constituted a work as obscene. In 1934, Judge John M. Wooley deemed that James Joyce's *Ulysses* was not obscene even though it contained offensive passages because the overall intent of the work was not pornographic (*United States v. One Book called Ulysses*). Though the Supreme Court had set a precedent for determining whether works were classified as obscene, it did not apply the First Amendment to such rulings until *Roth v. United States* (1957). Justice William J. Brennan, Jr. led the court in its decision that the First Amendment did not protect obscenity, and further ruled that obscenity was a narrower category than pornography more generally. According to the Roth standard, obscene works appealed to prurient interest in sex and contained no redeeming social or artistic value. The language used in the court was vague and did not attempt to set boundaries as to what constituted prurient interests or social merit. Similarly, in *Jacobellis v. Ohio* (1964), Justice Potter Steward used subjective and vague language to determine whether the French film *The Lovers/Les Amants* was obscene by claiming "I know it when I see it" (Rhode 1989).

The Roth standard was further redefined in *Memoirs v. Massachusetts* (1966). The Supreme Court attempted to apply the Roth standard to John Cleland's *Memoirs of a Woman of Pleasure* (1748), considered the first pornographic novel. Cleland and his publisher were arrested after its publication, but the novel continued to circulate underground until Putnam republished it in 1963, when it was immediately banned. According to the court's ruling, the Roth standard did not protect *Memoirs of a Woman of Pleasure* because it held only minimal social value, though publishers continued to reprint pornographic classics between 1967 and 1971, and lower courts failed to convict these books except in the most radical cases. The prosecution of one distributor led to *Miller v. California* (1973), which overturned *Memoirs v. Massachusetts* by emphasizing whether the text or film in question contained significant literary, artistic, political, or scientific value. The Miller Test provided states with greater authority to determine obscenity cases while not providing a definitive ruling on pornography per se.

Though most early obscenity cases dealt with novels and written material, pornographic films were made as early as 1908. Frenchmen Eugène Pirou and Albert Kirchner are credited as two of the earliest pornographic filmmakers, and pornographic features became widespread by the 1920s. Most of the time these movies, which were fairly expensive to produce, were shown in brothels and had limited distribution. The development of Super-8 mm film in 1965 made the production of pornography cheaper and more available for consumption. The number of pornographic films proliferated, and, as feminists who oppose pornography have argued, began to take on more violent characteristics. Critics of pornography argue that film is a medium that causes more harm than literature and other visual representations because women may be coerced into participating in pornographic films. In order to determine the relationship between sexual harm and pornography, President Lyndon Johnson formed the 1967 Commission on Obscenity and Pornography under congressional mandate, but many feminists were deeply critical of the inadequate attention the committee paid to women's exploitation and abuse. In the United Kingdom, the British Home Office created the Committee on Obscenity and Film Censorship, led by Bernard Williams, to address the increased volume of pornographic films being produced as well as the fragmented laws on obscenity. The Committee's Report (1980) found a lack of evidence that supported the argument that pornography causes violent crime, but nevertheless recommended that limits should be placed on the types of pornography that should be permitted by law, such as live sex shows and child pornography. By advocating a cautious approach toward the perception and reception of pornography, this committee in effect opened the door for further conversation on the topic of harm and pornography.

By the 1980s, debates regarding what constituted obscenity shifted to include the social and moral value of pornography more generally. During the debates that followed, Catharine MacKinnon and Andrea Dworkin emerged as two of the most outspoken critics of pornography. They argue that pornography is a violent act against women in that women are the victims of a system that seeks to place their bodies on display without granting them autonomy. In their view, pornography has no redemptive social value because it places women in the subordinate position from which they cannot achieve agency. According to MacKinnon, the argument that pornography represents a form of free speech does not apply because pornography silences women. Speech that limits female autonomy or devalues female speech is speech that should not be protected under the law. Dworkin's writings support MacKinnon's view while adding biological and social elements. For Dworkin, pornography represents a smaller-scale version of inequalities in a patriarchal system.

Feminist activists and scholars along these views formed the group Women Against Pornography in 1979. Feminist reactions against pornography became increasingly heightened after the publication of the book *Ordeal* (1980) by Linda Marciano (aka Linda Lovelace), in which she described the violent conditions under which she performed in *Deep Throat* (1972). In her book, Marciano claimed that she had been raped, beaten, and threatened until she performed in *Deep Throat*, even though the film made it appear that she performed of her own autonomy. Such testimony became an essential part of the movement to define and legislate the porn industry.

MacKinnon and Dworkin's writings and activism along with public outrage over Marciano's testimony led to the creation of the Attorney General's Commission on Obscenity and Pornography (1986), nicknamed the Meese Commission. The Meese Commission followed the example set by a previous committee on obscenity and pornography that had been appointed by President Richard Nixon in 1970 by taking testimony from survivors of abuse and examining both violent and non-violent materials. The Meese Commission's report controversially used anecdotal evidence to stereotype sex workers as fundamentally unable to give consent, and thereby in need of protection from the state through legal regulations. Though the committee was unable to arrive at a legal definition of pornography, it reaffirmed the precedents set by previous definitions of obscenity and recommended that the United States Congress investigate charges of civil rights abuses, particularly relating to trafficking and coercion. In spite of these recommendations, the production and distribution of pornography continue to proliferate.

Pornography tends to be economically profitable because it is a cheap medium; small production companies can make several films in rapid succession, and then sell them for an enormous profit. According to testimony in the Minneapolis Hearings, *Deep Throat* cost US$25,000 to produce and brought a return of US$50 million in the first few years (MacKinnon and Dworkin 1997). For this reason, there is a significant incentive for the porn industry to continue to create pornographic films, and according to its critics, this further encourages the culture of rape within the porn industry. While inequality and sexism pervade the porn industry, porn is made and distributed in a variety of ways, making obscenity laws increasingly hard to enforce. In addition, sexism and inequality pervade other forms of media, and online videos and sexually explicit content are difficult to police across national boundaries. The Internet has facilitated the distribution of pornographic films and has led to an increase in the number of subgenres and overall volume of porn being produced and consumed.

Researchers on human sexuality have yet to come to a consensus on whether an increased volume of sexually explicit content allows individuals to explore alternative sexualities or if it reinforces anti-social behavior. Some critics of Internet pornography argue that the increased amount of porn and limited amount of policing have led to its consumption by children and young adults who have not reached the age of consent, though the age of consent differs from country to country, typically ranging from 14 to 18 years of age. These critics point to what they see as the increased sexualization of childhood as a primary indicator for this phenomenon. Religious objectors to pornography similarly frame their criticism in moral terms, pointing to increased sexual promiscuity, increased risk of venereal disease, and the breakdown of the family as important factors to consider when debating its consumption. The relatively new practice of "sexting," or sending sexually explicit images via a mobile device, has led to prosecutions of teenagers for distributing child pornography. This remains an area of legal dispute, however, as those who send sexually explicit images often send images of themselves, leading to questions regarding the role of consent within this practice.

Questions of consent remain a topic of legal and ethical debate in the porn industry as a whole. The porn industry produces films using both scripted plots and non-scripted scenarios. One company that relies on non-scripted events, Girls Gone Wild, created by Joe Francis in 1997, typically features college-aged women who strip and have casual sexual encounters, but who usually do not have intercourse with men or women. For most of the series' history, the producers obtained consent from the women before filming them. However, several lawsuits were filed against the company from women who claimed they did not consent to being filmed. Many of these cases have been dismissed when the company was able to prove that the women signed letters of consent. Yet most of the actions are filmed while the women are inebriated, and critics have alleged that the producers provide the women with alcohol. The company filed for bankruptcy protection in 2013 due to loss of revenue.

In response to the anti-pornography feminist movement, some feminists have tried to balance competing perspectives on pornography with a sex-positive position that promotes sexual freedom as an essential part of women's liberation. Feminist critics such as Gayle Rubin, Ellen Willis, and Wendy McElroy have argued that sexual acts depicted in pornography are not essentially degrading to women and that sexual scenes should be taken in the context of the film to determine whether they constitute rape. Rubin maintains that the increased legal persecutions of obscene and pornographic works over the twentieth century are due in part to the belief that normative sexual behavior was being threatened by deviant sexualities, and that a hierarchy of sexual behaviors that favors heterosexuality has linked homosexual preference to social misbehavior. Willis suggests that pornography can only be defined insofar as it represents prurient attitudes about sex. She makes a distinction between pornography that harms women by portraying them in sexually violent ways and pornography that has the capacity to titillate women's sexual awareness. Responding to protests organized by Women Against Pornography, she argues that pornography should not be banned outright, nor should the viewing of it be restricted because it infringes on women's freedoms to enjoy sexual activity. Building on Willis's doubts regarding critiques against pornography, McElroy offers an explicit defense of pornography by arguing that pornography benefits women and that efforts to censor sexually explicit content have led to bans on feminist literature. McElroy claims that pornography presents women with a variety of sexual possibilities that may not be permissible or available in real life. She links this freedom to free speech, and argues that efforts to prohibit pornography amount to social policing of an individual's private life.

Members of the porn industry have responded to these supportive viewpoints by creating "feminist pornography" that is designed by and meant for female consumption. Though most of the consumers of porn tend to be male, a small but growing percentage of films is made for women. A number of porn and erotica photographers including Heather Corinna represent a growing trend toward sexual, racial, and gender inclusiveness in pornography while emphasizing safe-sex practices. Pornographic actresses such as Annie Sprinkle have used their position to educate the public on sexual awareness. The Feminist Porn Awards, which have been held in Toronto since 2006, are designed to showcase porn in which women had a significant part in developing it and that emphasize female pleasure.

Though pornography continues to be an area of social debate, the focus of these conversations has recently shifted to the safety of those working in the porn industry. Measures to promote safer working habits have been recently passed. During the 1980s, several porn actors contracted HIV, which led to the establishment of the Adult Industry Medical Health Care Foundation. California, the location of many porn production companies, proposed ballot initiatives to mandate condom use, but early efforts to regulate the industry proved ineffective until two notable HIV scares were revealed during routine screenings. A female actor became infected during her private life in the early twenty-first century, and more recently, Derrick Burts, who had worked in both straight and gay pornography, tested positive for the virus in 2010, causing the industry to temporarily cease production. As a result, California voters passed the Safer Sex in the Adult Film Industry Act in 2012 that requires producers of pornographic films to obtain a county public health permit and requires adult performers to use condoms while engaged in sex acts.

Feminist debates on pornography are likely to continue with renewed vigor with the launch in 2014 of the first peer-reviewed interdisciplinary academic journal devoted to the subject, *Porn Studies*. Upon its announcement, its editorial board was criticized for being overly weighted with scholars who support pornography, though the journal aims to publish articles that address pornography across historical periods and national contexts.

SEE ALSO: Body Politics; Gender-Based Violence; Militarism and Sex Industries

REFERENCES

MacKinnon, Catharine A., and Andrea Dworkin, eds. 1997. *In Harm's Way: The Pornography Civil Rights Hearings*. Cambridge, MA: Harvard University Press.

Rhode, Deborah L. 1989. *Justice and Gender: Sex Discrimination and the Law*. Cambridge, MA: Harvard University Press.

FURTHER READING

Assiter, Alison, and Avedon Carol, eds. 1993. *Bad Girls and Dirty Pictures: The Challenge to Reclaim Feminism*. London: Pluto Press.

Boyle, Karen, ed. 2010. *Everyday Pornography*. New York: Routledge.

Chancer, L. S. 2000. "From Pornography to Sadomasochism: Reconciling Feminist Differences." *Annals of the American Academy of Political and Social Science*, 571(1): 77–88.

Copp, David, and Susan Wendell, eds. 1983. *Pornography and Censorship*. New York: Prometheus Books.

Cornell, Drucilla, ed. 2000. *Feminism and Pornography*. Oxford: Oxford University Press.

Dines, Gail. 2010. *Pornland: How Porn Has Hijacked Our Sexuality*. Boston: Beacon Press.

Downs, Donald Alexander. 1989. *The New Politics of Pornography*. Chicago: University of Chicago Press.

Juffer, Jane. 1998. *At Home with Pornography: Women, Sex, and Everyday Life*. New York: NYU Press.

Langton, Rae. 2009. *Sexual Solipsism: Philosophical Essays on Pornography and Objectification*. Oxford: Oxford University Press.

Lederer, Laura. 1980. *Take Back the Night: Women on Pornography*. New York: Morrow.

Maschke, Karen J. 1997. *Pornography, Sex Work, and Hate Speech*. New York: Garland.

Positionality

DONGXIAO QIN

Western New England University, USA

One of the most influential elements about the research process is the concept of positionality. Positionality is about how people view the world from different embodied locations. The situatedness of knowledge means whether we are researchers or participants, we are differently situated by our social, intellectual, and spatial locations, by our intellectual history, and our lived experience, all of which shape our understandings of the world and the knowledge we produce. Positionality also refers to how we are positioned (by ourselves, by others, by particular discourses) in relation to multiple, relational social processes of difference (gender, class, race, ethnicity, age, sexuality, etc.), which also means we are differently positioned in hierarchies of power and privilege. Our positionality shapes our research and may inhibit or enable certain research insights (Moss 2001). Positionality has been further extended to include considering others' reactions to us as researchers. As researchers we are a visible, indeed embodied, and an integral part of the research process (rather than external, detached observers). So both our embodied presence as researchers and the participants' response to us mediate the information collected in the research encounter. All researchers are positioned. For qualitative and feminist researchers, writing about how we are positioned is part of reflexivity in the research process.

While reflexivity can make us more aware of power relations between researchers and participants in the research process, the concept of positionality reminds researchers that given attributes such as race, nationality, gender, and power are culturally ascribed. Such attributes require intentional disclosure when they affect the data and the researchers' interpretation of it. Positionality is also shaped by subjective-contextual factors such as personal life experiences as revealed in the reflexive account by the researcher. As has been suggested, researchers are always positioned but the disclosure of that positionality has not always found its way into the final research process. The qualitative research is perceived as a dialogical process in which the research situation is structured by both the researcher and the person being researched. Two issues flow from this point, the first is that the dialogical nature of a researcher increases the probability that the research may be transformed by the input of the researched. The second is that dialogism means that a researcher is a visible and an integral part of the research setting. Indeed, the research is never complete until it includes an understanding of the active role of the analyst's self which is exercised throughout the research process. In short, the researcher is an instrument in her/his research and despite some commonalities, researchers are not part of some universal monolith. Researchers are differently positioned subjects with different autobiographies and they are not abstracted or disembodied entities. This subjectivity does influence our research. As Carol Warren (1988) makes clear, the researcher is a person with particular gender, personality, or historical location, who would not objectively produce the same findings as any other person.

Another issue related to positionality is the "insider/outsider" debate. In line with positivist tradition, the outsider perspective was considered optimal for its "objective" and "accurate" account of the field, while insiders, who possessed deeper insights about the people, place, and events being studied, were believed to hold a biased position that complicated their ability to observe and interpret. However, scholars (Naples 1996; Banks 1998) have argued that the outsider–insider distinction is a false dichotomy since outsiders and insiders have to contend with similar methodological issues around positionality, a researcher's sense of self, and the situated knowledge she/he possesses as a result of her/his location in the social order. It is critical to articulate a researcher's positionality as an "insider" by looking at "others" (participants) similar to oneself. A researcher needs to be conscious of himself/herself as an intentional agent who researched and wrote about participants' lived experiences from an insider's point of view. As such, researchers experienced the seductiveness of similarities by seeking reflexivity into explicit and continuous account (Charmaz 2009). The reflexivity of researcher's positionality seeks to clarify the personal experiences that have shaped this research inquiry and to make transparent the reflexivity that informs the analyses and theorizing process. As a critical qualitative researcher one needs to be aware that he or she is a self-interpreting being that was multiply situated in many worlds as subjects. He or she needs to take on the process of conscious partiality (Mies 1983), that is, a connectedness and identification with the research participants that replaces the objectivist role of researcher in positivist social science research and, thereby, co-construct the knowledge presented herein. In the findings of the research, the researcher should discuss what he or she learned through this process and summarize the theorizing he or she did, drawing on the narratives of participants as they experienced and re-experienced themselves in diverse contexts. As Denzin (1989) pointed out, even though all interpretations are constructed, unfinished, and inconclusive, it is a worthy goal to attempt to make interpretations about the world of human experience, and, in turn, to make those interpretations available to others. As a result, the researcher is co-participant as she/he positions her/himself in relation to participants, and participants position themselves in relation to how a researcher is perceived. Ultimately, researchers as outsiders or insiders can be assured that their observations, interpretations, and representations are affected by their various identities or positionalities.

SEE ALSO: Postmodern Feminist Psychology; Reflexivity

REFERENCES

Banks, James A. 1998. "The Lives and Values of Researchers: Implications for Educating Citizens in a Multicultural Society." *Educational Researcher*, 7(7): 4–17.
Charmaz, Kathy. 2009. "Shifting the Grounds: Constructivist Grounded Theory Methods." In *Developing Grounded Theory*, edited by Janice M. Morse, et al. Walnut Creek: Left Coast Press.
Denzin, Norman. 1989. *The Research Act: A Theoretical Introduction to Sociological Methods*, 3rd ed. Englewood Cliffs: Prentice Hall.
Mies, Maria. 1983. "Towards a Methodology for Feminist Research." *Qualitative Sociology*, 19(1): 83–106.
Moss, Pamela. 2001. *Placing Autobiography in Geography*. Syracuse: Syracuse University Press.
Naples, Nancy A. 1996. "A Feminist Revisiting of the Insider/Outsider Debate: The 'Outsider Phenomenon' in Rural Iowa." *Qualitative Sociology*, 19(1): 83–106.
Warren, Carol. 1988. *Gender Issues in Field Research*. Newbury Park: Sage.

Post-Traumatic Stress Disorder

INGRID PALMARY
University of the Witwatersrand, South Africa

Post-traumatic stress disorder (PTSD) is a diagnostic category detailed in the *Diagnostic and Statistical Manual of Mental Disorders* (DSM) produced by the American Psychiatric Association (APA). PTSD is diagnosed primarily by psychiatrists and clinical psychologists to describe the reaction people have to experiencing, witnessing, or hearing of an event that is life threatening. In order for a diagnosis of PTSD to be given, a person must not only have experienced such an event, but must also have experienced intense fear, helplessness, or horror as a result. In order to be diagnosed with PTSD, a person must experience symptoms from each of four clusters of symptoms (although the number of symptoms required for a diagnosis of PTSD varies within each cluster). The first cluster is called *re-experiencing* and may include recollection of the event through dreams, images, and perceptions, reliving the feelings associated with the event, or an intense reaction to cues that symbolize or resemble the traumatic event. The second cluster of symptoms is called *avoidance* and includes avoiding feelings, memories, thoughts, or conversations about the event. The third category of symptoms is *negative cognitions and mood*, which may include outbursts of anger, blaming oneself for the traumatic event, diminished interest in activities, or estrangement from others. The fourth category of symptoms is *arousal*, which might include aggressive and self-destructive behavior, sleep disturbances, or hypervigilance. For a diagnosis of PTSD to be made, these symptoms must persist for more than one month and must cause clinically significant distress or impairment in social, occupational, and/or other functioning. PTSD can be chronic or acute (see APA 2013).

The emergence of PTSD as a way of understanding the impact of traumatic events lacks a clear historical trajectory. However, notions of trauma date back as far as the 1860s when John Erickson wrote on the effects of railway spine – a condition where victims of railway accidents showed evidence of lesions despite there being no sign of physical injury. Thus the idea that extreme fright could result in future symptomology has a long history. Charcot continued this work in his studies of hysteria leading up to World War I. However, during World War I, there was an increasing study of *traumatigenic shell shock* and this work is clearly a precursor to contemporary notions of PTSD. Until this time trauma had been seen as an affliction predominantly suffered by women, but during World War I there was increasing acceptance that men too might suffer consequences of experiencing traumatic or life-threatening events. In 1918, the first symptomology of war neuroses was published. During World War II, this process of classifying symptomology became even more established. Post-traumatic stress disorder was first given its name in 1980 with the publication of the DSM-III. This was, at least in part, a result of lobbying by Vietnam War veterans to have the distress that the war had caused them recognized. Classifying PTSD using the DSM represented a move away from earlier psychoanalytic accounts of trauma to a more biomedical system of diagnosis on the basis of symptoms (see Young 1995 for a detailed history). Since that time the DSM has been revised twice and the criteria for PTSD have changed somewhat. In particular the latest version, the DSM-5, is more specific about what constitutes a traumatic event and particularly mentions sexual assault.

There have been a number of critiques of PTSD in recent years. The first has been that, in spite of claims to represent a universal disorder, the symptoms described may well not be common to all people and are given different meanings in different contexts. Dreams of an event might be understood as PTSD or as an ancestral communication, for example. And so another related critique is that PTSD ignores the meaning people give to their distress and instead values the diagnosis given by a professional. Second, the medical model on which PTSD is based focuses on the symptoms experienced rather than the meaning of the event itself. For example, torture may have a different social significance to rape. Leading on from this, whether or not one experiences violence as traumatic is, critics claim, dependent on the social contexts in which the traumatic event occurs. A woman who is raped during a war may face stigma and shame from her family and community whereas a soldier who returns from the same war may be memorialized as a hero. This social meaning impacts on how people experience traumatic events – meaning that is not considered significant in the PTSD emphasis on symptoms. Furthermore, in the PTSD approach, some authors have argued that it implies that trauma is a one-off event and that, aside from the experience of a discrete traumatic event, the person lives an otherwise safe life. Thus the traumatic event is an anomaly. For many people in the world who live with ongoing violence, such as domestic violence or protracted conflicts, this is not the case. It also does not speak to the experiences of people who face broad social discrimination that is perpetual, such as sexism or racism. Finally, some writers have suggested that listing PTSD in the DSM pathologizes people's reactions to traumatic events and risks labeling them in prejudicial ways.

The notion of PTSD has been controversial among gender and sexuality studies scholars. Some feminists have used it to show the impact of the violence women suffer, particularly through domestic violence. This has led to the development of the notion of battered woman's syndrome. Other scholars have argued, however, that this labels women who experience domestic violence as pathological. In cases where women have killed an abusive partner, for example, these authors have argued that this should be seen as self-defense rather than as a result of a pathology on the part of the woman.

SEE ALSO: *Diagnostic and Statistical Manual of Mental Disorders* (DSM), Feminist Critiques of; Gender Stereotypes; Queer Theory; Sex Tourism; Taboo

REFERENCES

American Psychiatric Association (APA). 2013. *Diagnostic and Statistical Manual*, 5th ed. (DSM-5). Arlington, VA: American Psychiatric Association.

Young, Allan. 1995. *The Harmony of Illusions: Inventing Post Traumatic Stress Disorder*. Princeton: Princeton University Press.

FURTHER READING

Bracken, Patrick, and Celia Petty. 1998. *Rethinking the Trauma of War*. London: Free Association Books.

Eisenbruch, Maurice. 1991. "From Post-Traumatic Stress Disorder to Cultural Bereavement: Diagnosis of South East Asian Refugees." *Social Science and Medicine*, 33(6): 673–680.

Palmary, Ingrid. 2006. "(M)othering Women: Unpacking Refugee Women's Trauma and Trauma Service Delivery." *International Journal of Critical Psychology*, 17: 119–139.

Postcolonialism, Theoretical and Critical Perspectives on

MARIA CARBIN
Umeå University, Sweden

Postcolonialism is a heterogeneous field; therefore, it is not possible to describe it and present it in its entirety. This is particularly true because postcolonial scholars themselves are critical of seemingly neutral categorizations and illustrations of history, since these can be both ideological and problematic. Nevertheless, this entry aims to capture some traits and debates that form what one might call postcolonial theory and criticism. The term postcolonialism, like all terms, is contingent, and there has been much debate about how, or whether, to use it. The term has been applied to signal a historical condition, an *era*, and also, perhaps most commonly, to describe critical perspectives or *theories*.

Postcolonialism in its most basic definition means an era that comes after, and is a continuation of, colonialism. There have been many examples of colonialism throughout history, meaning the territorial occupation, building of settlements, and removal of resources by some peoples who claim power over others. Colonialism in this case, however, refers specifically to the European establishment, exploitation, and expansion of colonies and its "civilizing" mission from the sixteenth century up until the twentieth century, and how these histories of colonialism shape the world of today. The European colonial powers of Britain, France, Spain, Portugal, and the Netherlands (amongst others) established colonies in Asia, Africa, and the Americas, most of which were decolonized during the mid- to late twentieth century. The scope and magnitude of this colonization is unique in history since it also goes hand in hand with industrialization, modernization, and enlightenment, and a specific kind of rational knowledge (Sharp 2009). While the era of physical colonization is over, its effects are still visible and the decolonization of the cultural has proved to be difficult.

However, this basic understanding of the term has caused debate. The question is whether the era of the great European territorial empires is really over, and what it means to speak of "post" colonialism. Anne McClintock (1995) doubts whether Northern Ireland or Palestine, for example, can be regarded as *post*colonial. The term might further lead to the suggestion that history is singular and linear, an idea about which postcolonial scholars on other occasions have tended to be skeptical (McClintock 1995, 13). As Sara Ahmed has pointed out, the concept indicates a failed historicity, since the postcolonial can be reduced neither to a disruption of the past, nor to a simple continuation of it (2000, 10–11). It cannot really capture the fluidity and complexity of our contemporary global world, is the argument.

Back in the 1960s, other scholars, such as Marxists like Kwame Nkrumah from decolonized nations, instead used the concept of *neo*colonialism. This term has also been picked up by more recent scholars, who use it to refer to today's global condition, with the United States becoming the successor of the European colonial powers. Neocolonialism is a condition in which the great European colonial powers are losing ground to the United States, and the quest for power is not primarily territorial, but rather economic and cultural, as Gayatri Chakravorty Spivak (1991) argues. Today we can witness colonial power operating in more subtle forms. One form of sophisticated neocolonialism is the celebration of multiculturalism, in which "the Others" are seen as exotic and as positive assets, while still remaining different, a group for "us" to tolerate. There are different forms of neocolonialism, just as there were of colonialism: the mission of France in Algeria was not the same as the British approach to colonizing India. Another example where the term "post" colonialism does not really apply is the so-called war on terror waged by the Bush and Blair administrations (and later continued by President Obama), which can be regarded as colonialism in the more classical sense. The war on terror represents a way for the United States to police the world, and in that sense it resembles a civilizing mission, carried out like earlier imperial projects.

Nevertheless, the term postcolonialism still makes sense, and is used to signal a particular field of study. Postcolonialism can also be described as a field of critical *perspectives* or *theories*, which are engaged in careful descriptions of the structures that contribute to the production of knowledge about certain objects (Spivak 2006, 60). When postcolonialism signals a critical theory, or perspective, it has come to mean interrogations of the knowledge production of the West. At the center of the analysis is a critique of how the Western self has been constructed, and how Western institutions such as the media, literature, research, and governments have been producing knowledge about what they perceive to be other places, and other peoples, thereby constructing the center and the margins. The colonial history of the West, for example, has been described separately from the general history of the West. The exploitation of colonies is thus not described as being a part of the economic history or the industrial revolution of the West. Thus, while the general history of growth, modernization, and enlightenment is described as exclusively positive, colonialism, imperialism, and racism are set aside as part of a less glamorous past. Colonialism is thus constructed as being a matter of the past, whereas present political orders and processes are seen as legitimate and as having nothing to do with past mistakes. Postcolonial thinkers on the other hand have shown how these processes are intertwined and cannot be separated; indeed, racist ideas were part of the enlightenment and it was modernization and colonial processes that made (and still make) economic development possible. Colonization is an ongoing process of subjugation, both material and immaterial, that is displayed globally as well as in the very subject constitution of peoples.

The groundbreaking work *Orientalism* (1978) by literary theorist Edward Said has not only been described as one of the central works, but has even been characterized as *the* founding text of the postcolonial field. Drawing on the Foucauldian concept of discourse, Said explores how claims of knowledge about the "Orient" are political, and embedded in networks of power. The Western project of civilization, modernization, progress, and enlightenment is built upon the premise that there is some other that is seen as the opposite. The Orient is to be considered as a European invention that functions as the mirror image of the European self. Thus, the construction of Orientals as uncivilized, underdeveloped, stagnated, and unaware helps in presenting

Westerners as enlightened, civilized, and rational. The Orient stands for everything that is different, that Europe *is not*. The Orientals thereby become the others. By producing knowledge about whole regions as less developed and infantilizing them, that is, seeing the peoples inhabiting these areas as irrational children, unaware and naïve, it also became legitimate to "help" them or colonize them, even bomb them. This can be characterized as a hegemonic discourse that builds upon the idea that European culture and identity are superior to all others. These ideas gave the white man a specific position, a "white man's burden" in the words of the English author Rudyard Kipling, meaning that the colonial powers had a *duty* to civilize the barbaric non-European peoples. There is, according to Said, a pattern of relative strength between the Orient and the European, in which the Europeans will always have the upper hand. All this is not to say that the Orient is merely an idea with no corresponding reality. Instead, Said stresses that the Orient is not just a fantasy that would disappear if the "truth" about it were to come up; rather, it is a system of knowledge, a network of utterances with real consequences (Said 1978, 6).

Said's work opened up the field for interrogations of how the colonial powers had constructed knowledge about the colonies, and the colonized peoples, a kind of knowledge that served to legitimize the colonial project. His work has influenced scholars to revise and critically interrogate the meaning-making processes constructing, for example, "Africa" (Mudimbe 1988). Other central figures in the field are Frantz Fanon, Homi Bhabha, and Gayatri Chakravorty Spivak, but Chandra Mohanty, Ann Stoler, and Anne McClintock should also be mentioned here.

While Said's work on Orientalism provides the groundwork for postcolonial theory, it has also been criticized and developed by scholars such as Homi Bhabha, Anne McClintock, and Gayatri Chakravorty Spivak. McClintock points out that Said (and other male theorists) have missed the central position that gender has in colonial discourses and imperial projects (McClintock 1995, 14). In *Orientalism*, Said describes how the Others are depicted as inferior in terms of being constructed as uncivilized and barbaric, and how Europeans always remain in the dominant position. However, as Homi Bhabha (1994) points out, Orientals are also described in more positive terms – such as being beautiful, exotic, and friendly.

Homi Bhabha is known for his conceptualization of hybrid identity and does not want to fix the understanding of the relationship between the colonizer and the colonized in quite the same way as Said does. One could say that, if Said's analysis is structuralist, drawing on early Foucault and Gramsci, Homi Bhabha introduces deconstruction, psychoanalysis, and a poststructuralist approach to the question of Otherness. Inspired by the psychoanalyst Frantz Fanon, he explores the notion of ambivalence as being central to the racial stereotype and to the function of colonial discourse. Both Fanon and Bhabha describe how the dividing line between black (colonized) and white (colonizer) functions as a way to legitimize colonization. They argue that colonial discourse is dependent on the idea of the Other as being different (and inferior). However, Bhabha explores how, in the meeting between colonizer and colonized, the boundaries become blurred through a process he calls *mimicry*. Colonial mimicry is the desire for a changed, but still recognizable, Other; it is a subject that is *almost the same, but not quite* (Bhabha 1994). The colonized subject, for example the Indian bourgeoisie, speaking English and dressing like proper gentlemen, can "do Englishness" practically as well as any white, blue-eyed British man. If a brown man can act like that, what then is "real" Englishness? Mimicry is thus a form of resemblance that questions the very authority of colonial discourse, in this case the idea of Englishness. The desire for a recognizable other thus threatens to undermine the legitimacy of the colonial project. Thus, by introducing a discussion of gender and the position of the indigenous upper classes in colonial settings, the analysis is made more complex and intersecting identities are problematized.

The rethinking of questions of identity and nation is one of the major contributions of postcolonial theorizing, and is part of a general postmodern trend of destabilizing categories such as class, gender, and nation.

Spivak likewise, building on the work of *Orientalism*, problematizes intersecting identities, and refuses to fix identities or reduce them to easily recognizable categories. From a poststructuralist point of view, Western regimes of knowledge are employed in order to justify colonization, and thus to legitimize violence against other cultures. Using the concept of "epistemic violence," she addresses these issues and explores how the global division of labor (between North and South) makes it difficult to forge alliances or engage in solidarity work. The Western production of history has erased all other histories and, in Orientalist or neocolonial discourses, white researchers are often seen as agents of knowledge, whereas the others are not as easily seen as possessing knowledge, argues Spivak. She insists on intertwining the material and language, and constantly analyzes both utterances (literature) and material circumstances (global capitalism). Colonial discourse is not only language; rather, the economy and the episteme go hand in hand in her Marxist understanding.

With the concept of the "subaltern," Spivak adds yet another dimension, and area of contest, to the field of postcolonialism. Italian Marxist Antonio Gramsci initially deployed the subaltern in his famous book, *Prison Notebooks*, written during the 1930s from within an Italian prison. Gramsci's work concerned the history of the proletariat, how the subaltern classes were constituted, and how they could form resistance. Later, the Indian Marxist Subaltern Studies Group drew on the concept in their project to rewrite and explore Indian history from the perspective of the oppressed people. Being interested in the possibility of resisting colonial powers, Spivak has further developed the concept and criticized the Subaltern Studies Group for using a Western, Marxist model that does not fully capture the colonial situation. In her most famous, and yet also most criticized, work from 1988, she poses the rhetorical question, "Can the subaltern speak?" – and answers it negatively. The text provides a description of the structures that produce the subaltern through which she engages in an analysis of colonialism, capitalism, gender, class, and the global division of labor.

While being difficult to define, the concept "subaltern" is especially useful for Spivak's deconstructivist project since she wants to capture the very impossibility of finally fixing meaning, and the difficulties "we" have in understanding the resistance of subaltern groups. In her usage, the term subaltern signals a situation or a *position*, not an identity. If, for example, one talks about "workers" or "women," these are identity positions, around which identity politics has been built. The subaltern on the other hand is not an identity in that sense, it is a position that one can inhabit, but as soon as this position is recognized as an identity, the subalternity is lost. Despite this, Spivak uses identity-based examples to describe the subalterns, such as women in rural India. This is also intended to point out that subalterns do not resemble a shifting and fluid hegemonic identity, such as the hybrid identity that Homi Bhaba speaks of (Spivak 2006, 70). These are the people who are disconnected from available discourses; they have no connection with the hegemonic discourses of the colonizers, nor are the discourses of the resistance available to them. Subaltern resistance is by definition a resistance that cannot be recognized as such (Spivak 2006). Thus, when Spivak writes that the subaltern cannot speak, she means that the subalterns are positioned in the shadow of the Western episteme. The point is not to suggest that they are mute, but rather that, when they speak, no one listens. In a speech act, someone has to listen and engage in trying to talk *with* the subaltern. The Orientalist episteme of the Westerner, however, makes such speech difficult.

Another area of controversy in postcolonial studies concerns the relationship between Westerners and "the rest." It might seem that postcolonial theorists are arguing that it is impossible for Europeans and/or Westerners to speak and engage in a politics of solidarity across borders. In Said's work, for example, it seems as though Europeans will always remain the Orientalist explorers in relation to other places and people. Thus, this is yet another central and much-debated topic for postcolonial theory in general, and postcolonial feminism in particular. Postcolonial feminists have, for example, tried to develop ideas on how feminists could engage in a politics of solidarity, despite global capitalism, and how they could try to build alliances across divisions of place, identity, class, and so on (Trinh 1989; Mohanty 2003). Spivak writes about solidarity and the seeming impossibility of white Westerners speaking about the so-called third world, and urges educated white people to try to cultivate some kind of rage against the way in which history has been written, since the very construction of knowledge makes Westerners silenced (Spivak 1990, 62). She argues that it is crucial for Westerners to try to learn about the so-called third world, not only through studies of language and history, but also by constantly trying to scrutinize their own historical position as the investigating person. If you do this and try really hard, then you might be heard, and you achieve a position from which you can criticize, she argues (Spivak 1990, 62).

SEE ALSO: Black Feminist Thought; Colonialism and Gender; Colonialism and Sexuality; Discourse and Gender

REFERENCES

Ahmed, Sara. 2000. *Strange Encounters: Embodied Others in Post-Coloniality*. London: Routledge.

Bhabha, Homi. 1994. *The Location of Culture*. London: Routledge.

McClintock, Anne. 1995. *Imperial Leather: Race, Gender and Sexuality in the Colonial Contest*. New York: Routledge.

Mohanty, Chandra Talpade. 2003. *Feminism Without Borders: Decolonizing Theory, Practicing Solidarity*. Durham, NC: Duke University Press.

Mudimbe, Y. Valentin. 1988. *The Invention of Africa*. Bloomington: Indiana University Press.

Said, Edward. 1978. *Orientalism: Western Representations of the Orient*. London: Routledge and Kegan Paul.

Sharp, Joanne P. 2009. *Geographies of Postcolonialism*. London: Sage.

Spivak, Gayatri Chakravorty. 1988. "Can the Subaltern Speak?" In *Marxism and the Interpretation of Culture*, edited by C. Nelson and L. Grossberg, 271–313. Urbana: University of Illinois Press.

Spivak, Gayatri Chakravorty. 1990. "Questions of Multi-Culturalism." Interview by Sneja Gunew. In *The Post-Colonial Critic: Interviews, Strategies, Dialogues*. New York: Routledge.

Spivak, Gayatri Chakravorty. 1991. "Neocolonialism and the Secret Agent of Knowledge: An Interview with Robert J. C. Young." *Oxford Literary Review*, 13: 220–251.

Spivak, Gayatri Chakravorty. 2006. "Resistance that Cannot be Recognised as Such." In *Conversations with Gayatri Chakravorty Spivak: Conversations with Swapan Chakravorty, Suzana Milevska, and Tani E. Barlow*. New York: Seagull Books.

Trinh, T. Minh-ha. 1989. *Woman, Native, Other: Writing Postcoloniality and Feminism.* Bloomington: Indiana University Press.

FURTHER READING

Chakrabarty, Dipresh. 2007. *Provincializing Europe.* Princeton: Princeton University Press.

Childs, Peter, and Patrick R. J. Williams. 1997. *An Introduction to Post-Colonial Theory.* Upper Saddle River: Prentice Hall/Harvester Wheatsheaf.

Fanon, Frantz. 1967. *Black Skin, White Masks: The Experiences of a Black Man in a White World.* New York: Grove Press.

Morton, Stephen. 2003. *Gayatri Chakravorty Spivak.* New York: Routledge.

Young, Robert. 2003. *Postcolonialism: A Very Short Introduction.* New York: Oxford University Press.

Postfeminism

CAMILLE NURKA
Independent scholar

In its broadest sense, "postfeminism" means "after" or "beyond" feminism. The term simultaneously references feminism as a historical legacy and creates distance from that political identity. There are broadly three (sometimes overlapping) approaches to defining postfeminism in the scholarly literature. The first is that postfeminism is an anti-feminist backlash, as a politics which actively pushes back, or aggressively resists, feminism in periods where it has made the greatest gains (for example, see Faludi 1991). The concept of "backlash" implies a retrogressive movement backward, toward a prefeminist time. The second is that feminism is over or dead because it is assumed to have been successful in its aims, having passed into mainstream culture and politics, and is thus no longer needed. As Angela McRobbie puts it, "for feminism to be 'taken into account' it has to be understood as having already passed away" (2009, 12). This second approach is complex and should be distinguished from the simplified "backlash" position. This is because it depicts postfeminist discourse as accepting that female empowerment is of value, but promoting female agency on the condition that feminism "fades away."

The third approach positions postfeminism as signifying the evolution of feminism through the process of productive self-reflection – for instance, in its intersection with postmodernism (for example, see Brooks 1997). This approach also includes perspectives that associate postfeminism productively with third-wave feminism, to incorporate conservative *and* innovative tendencies (for example, see Genz and Brabon 2009). Although their emphasis is not strictly comparable, in the latter two approaches postfeminism is understood to be a contradictory politics that assumes familiarity with feminist concepts and refashions them in response to the demands of a changing social context where women are called upon to "do" gender politics and identify as female in strikingly new ways. The difference between theorists on this point is the extent to which this refashioning can be considered reactionary (where the "new" is a reformulation of the "old") or pragmatic (in the surprising alignments of competing discourses).

The prefix "post" also acts as a chronological marker that situates the "going beyond" of feminism in time. Susan Faludi suggests that in the US context, postfeminism emerged in response to the gains of first-wave feminism and that a postfeminist attitude was discernible in the reactionary responses to suffrage of the 1920s press (1991, 70). The term "postfeminism" is acknowledged to have become widely popularized in the 1980s (Faludi 1991, 14; Gamble 1998, 38; Brunsdon and Spigel 2008, 176) and commonplace in the 1990s (Tasker and Negra 2007, 8). The source of this more recent usage is usually attributed to a 1982 *New York Times* article written by Susan Bolotin, entitled "Voices from the Post-Feminist Generation" (Rosenfelt and Stacey 1987; Walters 1991; Dow 1996; Henry 2004; Genz and Brabon 2009), which sought to identify the reasons why feminism provoked a lack of interest and antipathy among young women. In the Bolotin article, postfeminism is represented as the historical product of generational change. Younger women display a tacit acknowledgment of gender inequality, while rejecting feminism as a political force for change; feminists are characterized as bitter and unhappy, and feminist politics is replaced with an individualist ethos of advancement. This particular article provides the context for more recent work that examines the ways in which the historical rise of postfeminism is imbricated in the rise of individualist "neoliberalism" as a dominant paradigm organizing social relations. Neoliberalist ideology holds that individuals are responsible for their conditions of existence and can therefore change those conditions through their own actions – there is no recognition, in this perspective, of shared experiences of oppression as a result of structural inequality. Much of the recent theoretical scholarship on postfeminism examines its currency in popular culture and highlights the way in which postfeminist narratives celebrate female autonomy through the rejection of a collectivist feminist identity in favor of an individualist mode of self-actualization. Moreover, the consumer culture embedded within late capitalist Western society is integral to significant changes in the way that gender is politicized and discursively represented. Postfeminist discourses can thus be situated as a feature of late capitalist society, where consumerism, rather than collectivist political movements like feminism, provides the primary means for identity construction and gender identification. Postfeminism, then, can be broadly defined in relation to its capacity as a marker of political identification in the current late capitalist era.

"Postfeminism" is a notoriously difficult term to define, although it has benefited greatly from feminist attempts at refinement over the past decade. Part of the problem of definition lies in disagreements over the nature of its relationship to feminism, with early feminist accounts of the term divided over whether postfeminist resistance to the feminist identity is radical or reactionary. Ann Brooks (1997) argues that while postfeminism in popular culture is crude, reactionary, and hostile to feminism, in the academy it signifies a shift in emphasis from equality to difference, a product of its engagement with the anti-foundationalist aims of postmodernism, poststructuralism, and postcolonialism. For Brooks, postfeminism's radical politics lies in its interrogation of the integrity of the stable categories of feminism (such as "oppression" and "woman") because they are implicated in maintaining "hegemonic" feminism and its unacknowledged hierarchies of class, race, and ethnicity among women (1997, 4–8). On the other hand, "difference" theory has been associated with postfeminism because it is seen to delegitimate feminist activism by turning away from feminist aims to achieve equality and erasing "woman" as the prioritized material category of feminist analysis (Walters 1995, 136; Murray 1997, 37–38; Walby 2011, 18, 20). Other arguments posit that postfeminism in the academy neutralizes feminism's political challenge to patriarchy through the appropriation of feminism – as well as femininity – by male-centered theory in an attempt to mitigate the threat of female empowerment (Modleski 1991; Jones 2003, 321–324).

Another problem of definition lies in postfeminism's relationship to third-wave feminism. It is difficult to determine whether postfeminism is synonymous with third-wave feminism, whether it is an offshoot of third-wave feminism, or whether it is a set of political claims that do not bear any association with the third wave at all. For instance, Amanda Lotz (2001), as well as Brooks, defines postfeminism as a progressive subset of the third wave, which productively diversifies and shifts central second-wave formations of identity and activism. But a counterview is that postfeminism is a conservative, oppositional politics that must be distinguished from the "third wave" (Heywood and Drake 1997, 1). For Heywood and Drake, "'postfeminist' characterizes a group of young, conservative feminists who explicitly define themselves against and criticize feminists of the second wave," while third-wave feminism is "neither incompatible [with] nor opposed" to the second wave (1997, 1). In this view, the waves model assumes continuity with, and identitarian commitment to, the second wave while also problematizing certain second-wave principles. The third wave is, for Heywood and Drake, a hybrid politics that draws on prior feminist critique of the power structures within which women are positioned, and also makes ironic use of those very same structures as a tool for female self-definition (1997, 3). For example, it allows for the seemingly contradictory pairing of "feminine" and "feminist" (Hollows 2000, 193). Similarly, Ednie Kaeh Garrison argues that the third wave should be distinguished from postfeminism because third-wave feminists still *identify* with feminism (2000, 149). However, Genz and Brabon argue that such attempts to separate "third-wave feminism" and "postfeminism" are faulty because they don't recognize the interrelatedness of the two terms, and tend to (wrongly) oversimplify the complex workings of postfeminism as anti-feminist backlash (2009, 156). Clearly, any attempt to outline the various theoretical approaches to postfeminism/third-wave feminism involves negotiating troubled, difficult, and contradictory terrain.

While some theorists position postfeminism as an expression of anti-feminist backlash (Faludi 1991; Modleski 1991; Walters 1995; Heywood and Drake 1997; Garrison 2000; Whelehan 2000; Jones 2003), other scholars prefer to define postfeminism as a contradictory movement between acknowledgment and disavowal (Rosenfelt and Stacey 1987; Stacey 1987; Rapp 1988; Dow 1996; Brunsdon 1997; Nurka 2002; Gill 2007; Tasker and Negra 2007; McRobbie 2009; Taylor 2012). This is best summarized by Judith Stacey as the "simultaneous incorporation, revision and depoliticization of many of the central goals of second wave feminism" (1987, 8) and is probably the definition that informs the key current definitions of postfeminism. Rosalind Gill argues that postfeminism is distinctive because it incorporates "feminist and anti-feminist ideas" (2007, 269), while McRobbie defines postfeminism as a "double entanglement," which refers to the way in which feminism becomes "commonsense" or mainstreamed, "while also fiercely repudiated, indeed almost hated" (2009, 12). Postfeminism thus represents both a presumption of feminist achievement and a dissociation from feminist politics. As Natasha Walter, author of the book *The New Feminism*, wrote, feminism now "works from the inside" (1998, 33), while Walter's ideological contemporary Rene Denfeld expressed, "we are feminists – in action, if not in name" (1995, 5).

According to McRobbie, a radical feminism that questions or critiques the social order, rather than one that can be aligned with female progress, is rejected as a site of identification for women (2009, 14–15). Yvonne Tasker and Diane Negra agree that postfeminism requires that as women assume feminist success in achieving equality, feminism is othered, constructed as "extreme, difficult, and unpleasurable" (2007, 4). According to Monica Dux and Zora Simic, millennial postfeminism "invites us to abandon feminism as a failure that has actually made women's lives worse" (2008, 21). Postfeminist discourse thus erects a "straw feminist" – usually the ubiquitous figure of the "hairy-legged lesbian" – who symbolizes "all that is wrong with feminism" (Dux and Simic 2008, 34). Second-wave feminism is charged with being puritanical, punitive, and too invested in female victimhood (Bulbeck 2010; Nurka 2002, 2003). Author of *DIY Feminism* Kathy Bail writes: "The word 'feminism' suggests a rigidity of style and behaviour and is still generally associated with a culture of complaint. Young women don't want to identify with something that sounds dowdy, asexual or shows them to be at a disadvantage. They don't want to be seen as victims" (1996, 4–5). Naomi Wolf's *Fire With Fire* (1993), Katie Roiphe's *The Morning After* (1993), and Rene Denfeld's *The New Victorians* (1995) are three US texts that are paradigmatic of the postfeminist critique of second-wave "victim feminism" (Genz and Brabon 2009). All three argue that contemporary women must be liberated from the sexual and ideological repression of second-wave values that emphasize danger over pleasure and disadvantage over empowerment.

A large part of the postfeminist resistance to feminism is based on a particular conception of a puritanical feminist view of heterosexual intercourse as a manifestation of patriarchal violence, a theory most notably espoused by US feminists Catharine McKinnon and Andrea Dworkin. Because postfeminist discourse can be identified via its positioning against a particular image of second-wave feminism (i.e., bra burning, man-hating lesbians), a central theme by which this differentiation is enacted is through an identification with a "pro-sex" narrative (Projansky 2001, 83), also called "do-me feminism" (Genz and Brabon 2009, ch. 4). Hence, one of the primary splits by which postfeminism can be identified is between the sexually repressive feminist mother and the sexually assertive and empowered postfeminist daughter (Nurka 2003; Henry 2004). Postfeminism has been articulated by Ariel Levy as "female chauvinism," an effect of what she terms "raunch culture," in which women are now the new male chauvinists making sex objects out of themselves, as well as other women (2005, 4). This is taking place as part of what is commonly dubbed "the sexualization of culture," which refers to the normalization of a pornographic aesthetic in "a hyper-culture of commercial sexuality" (McRobbie 2009, 18), where young women obtain a sense of sexual self-expression through mimicry of the visual codes found in heterosexual male-oriented pornography (Levy 2005; Gill 2007, 256–259).

In contemporary consumer culture, femininity is something to be improved upon through buying power, with its attainment a reflection of the value placed on the self. Therefore, the way in which women are hailed as sexual agents by advertisers is an important aspect of postfeminist culture. Where traditional sexist advertising says "buy this product and you will be irresistible to men!" postfeminist sexism says "this product gives you the choice to perform your own style of sexiness which is irresistible to men!" Choice, freedom, and individuality are essential concepts in defining the constitution of postfeminist sexual subjectivity. The concern for some feminists is that as Western culture becomes increasingly sexualized, there is less room for traditional feminist critique of the sexual objectification of women by men. For instance, Gill (2007) and McRobbie (2009) argue that "irony," as the ludic manipulation of culturally recognizable sexist imagery and discourse, justifies the sexism it represents through an implied historical separation between present and past audiences. The contemporary audience is invited to share an illicit enjoyment in sexist imagery through our distance to its content, which is presumed to render it harmless. It is this pretense of separation that works to legitimate sexism in the media because we "get the joke" (McRobbie 2009, 17).

In the postfeminist media context, feminist objections to the sexualization of women appear as a restriction of the pleasures of looking and being looked at. Yet, as Gill points out, young women are invited to inhabit sexual subjectivity on the condition that their bodies conform to a normative image of sexual attractiveness. Raunch culture constructs sexual desire in very precise ways: "only some women are constructed as active, desiring sexual subjects: women who desire sex with men (except when lesbian women 'perform' for men) and only young, slim and beautiful women" (Gill 2007, 259). Older or fat women, by contrast, are denied the pleasures of sexual subjecthood (Gill 2007, 259). The male gaze that second-wave feminism criticized for its dehumanizing, sexually objectifying effects on women is now internalized by women themselves as a "self-policing narcissistic gaze" through which an agentic feminine subject is constructed (Gill 2007, 258). On this basis, women are invited to express selfhood in the capacity for sexual empowerment, which is achieved through remaking the sexual body.

Attendant on these demands of sexualization is the intensification of body surveillance. As Gill argues, it is not a set of "feminine" characteristics that serve to define femininity today; rather, postfeminism prioritizes the accomplishment of the "sexy body" as the achievement of a feminine identity (2007, 255). For McRobbie, now that financially independent women are able to make choices that are not solely determined by their orientation to the marriage market, the Symbolic restores the balance upset by feminism through relocating female self-worth to the never-ending work of body maintenance required by the fashion–beauty complex. Hence, the feminist achievement of women's entrenchment in the workforce is undone by the symbolic imperatives of the fashion–beauty complex, which serves to restabilize gender relations under threat by female acquisition of independent economic capacity, or "female phallicism" (McRobbie 2009, 62–63). This restabilizing impulse reasserts traditional boundaries of gender and sexuality in that the freedoms gained by "the phallic girl" are enjoyed on the condition of a heterosexual gaze, thus reinforcing the repudiation of lesbian sexuality (McRobbie 2009, 86).

The association of feminism with lesbianism motivates the postfeminist assertion that feminism is at odds with the desires of an implicitly heterosexualized "feminine" subject, for whom it seeks to reaffirm and recuperate heterosexual romance. Anthea Taylor suggests that in the sexual sphere, feminism is blamed for robbing women of the pleasures of romance (in its critique of marriage, for example) and encapsulates a reaction against a feminism that is considered to be both an "unhappy" politics and the cause of contemporary women's unhappiness (2012, 26). One of the unhappiest heirs of feminism, according to postfeminist accounts, is "the single girl" (Dux and Simic 2008, 73; Taylor 2012), whose professional success is seen to come at the cost of personal failure. The postfeminist vision of the single woman is that she is a "lamentable product of the pervasive feminist rhetoric that encouraged women to pursue independence and autonomy at the cost of a husband and … a nuclear family" (Taylor 2012, 6). The most prominent fictional single women in recent decades – Bridget Jones in Helen Fielding's book *Bridget Jones's Diary*, Ally McBeal in David E. Kelley's TV series of the same name, and the women in *Sex and the City* – are characters who "endure as reference points for talking about women who are purported to be struggling to find a balance between their careers and their biological clocks" (Dux and Simic 2008, 75).

One of the defining characteristics of postfeminism is that it situates itself between public success and private failure (McRobbie 2009; Taylor 2012). According to Taylor, we find that in postfeminist rhetoric the deeply held "feminine" desire to be coupled is the undercurrent that upsets the valorization of single women as confident, financially autonomous, and sexually agentic. For Taylor, postfeminist narratives of feminism's failure to secure single women's happiness "work to manage the threat posed by the woman without a man" (2012, 14). This tension is typically expressed through the figure of the lonely, childless, single white professional. Figures such as Ally McBeal and Bridget Jones also share the qualities characteristic of the postfeminist assumption that feminism has wrested from young women the right to enjoy the "feminine" pleasures of romance and marriage (Gill 2007, 228; McRobbie 2009, 21; Taylor 2012, 26). Heterosexual romance is thus constructed as something which must be reclaimed from a perceived anti-male feminism. Postfeminism makes desirable for women a traditional organization of gender and sexuality (for example, heterosexual romance, sexual dependence on men, marriage, motherhood, family, and the home), presenting these highly structured gender relations as individual lifestyle options. McRobbie describes this as a "double entanglement," in which neoconservative (or new traditionalist) ideologies exist in tension with the liberal rhetoric of choice, in relation to gender, sexuality, and family (2009, 12).

McRobbie's companion concept of the "postfeminist masquerade" – which derives, via Butler, from Riviere's psychoanalytic account of the masquerade in which phallic women don the mask of "womanliness" to avert male retribution for their transgression – disavows feminism so that postfemininity, dressed in the garb of traditional desirable heterosexual femininity, can appear as freedom (of choice) and empowerment (2009, 64–66). The concept of freedom of choice in a postfeminist world no longer constrained by gender inequality allows for a return to traditional gender values, or what Elspeth Probyn (1990) calls the "new traditionalism." Probyn argues that postfeminist "new traditionalism" draws upon a false choice "posed as the possibility of choosing between the home or the career, the family or the successful job" (1990, 131) to reaffirm that the "natural" place for women is in the home. As Bonnie J. Dow notes, such a choice is constrained in more ways than one. It is a distinctly middle-class conundrum that is not available to women who don't have the option of returning home (Dow 1996, 99). Probyn explains that the ticking biological clock which is so present in popular media texts and which inspires such a sense of urgency among women is a powerful postfeminist trope that naturalizes women's place in the home. What makes this fantasy of a return to the home (and family) postfeminist is that it is articulated against feminism as the submerged or unspoken Other – a politics that is silenced because it has already passed on.

Negra extends this position to suggest that popular culture narratives which center on the professional urban woman's return to her hometown are symbolic of a "female retreatism," which works to recuperate the loss of the family represented by the dislocated femininity of feminism. The hometown fantasy is a response to "a set of social and economic conditions" increasingly defined by atomization, risk, and instability (Negra 2009, 15–16). The fantasy of home provided by postfeminism is a gendered expression of a nostalgic longing for stability as the answer to a restructured, itinerant, precarious, outsourced global marketplace in which workplace protections are being steadily chipped away. As traditional gender roles become dis-embedded through the changing requirements of global capital, postfeminism instates their symbolic redefinition alongside the "abandonment of critique of patriarchy" (McRobbie 2009, 57).

Postfeminism has thus emerged in a historical moment that marks a global shift to the right, increasing privatization in opposition to state regulation leading to a decrease in social welfare and an increase in economic inequality, "free market" ideology, and the rise of the individual alongside the dissolution of models of political solidarity (Tasker and Negra 2007, 6–7; McRobbie 2009, 18–19, 55; Gill and Scharff 2011, 5; Walby 2011, 11; Taylor 2012, 15). The work of Anthony Giddens (1991), Ulrich Beck (1992), Zygmunt Bauman (2000, 2001), and Nikolas Rose (1992) on individualization is influential to the current theorization of postfeminist neoliberalism as involving the construction of the individual freed from the ties of collective belonging, such as gender and class (Ringrose and Walkerdine 2008; McRobbie 2009, 18–19; Scharff 2012, 10–11); however, Beck and Giddens are criticized for failing to recognize that "individualization" can function as a regulatory force and does not *in actuality* entail the falling away of the constraints of gender, class, race, and sexuality, for example. It is, rather, "individualization" as an *ideology* – or a dominant mode of interpreting one's place in the world – that feminist theorists of postfeminism find most useful. In this respect, individualization is theorized as a mode of governmentality that "exerts power through techniques that autonomise and responsibilise subjects" (Scharff 2012, 11) in ways that "quite literally 'get inside us' to materialize or constitute our subjectivities" (Gill and Scharff 2011, 8).

Postindustrial capitalist consumer culture provides the overarching socioeconomic context for the articulation of postfeminist values, where the incorporation of feminism as a "lifestyle" is simultaneous to its commodification through the figure of the empowered female consumer (Tasker and Negra 2007, 2) free to take up sexual and economic opportunity, and free to choose between work and the home. Of course, such choice is, in reality, constrained by class and race: the housewife is a profoundly middle-class subject position available to privileged women who do not need an income to support themselves or their families, and the rewards of sexual subjectivity are not accorded evenly to women of color, who have historically been positioned by colonialism as the hypersexualized other of white femininity. As Tasker and Negra remind us, "postfeminism is white and middle class by default, anchored in consumption as a strategy (and leisure as a site) for the production of the self" (2007, 2). As neoliberal market ideology emphasizes the achievement of fiscal success through individual, rather than collective, means, so too does postfeminist discourse presume that middle-class women's wage-earning capacity be directed toward the improvement of the self, chiefly through beauty culture, in what McRobbie calls "the new sexual contract" (2009, 72).

Postfeminism ushers in a new era of intensified self-management for women, as the "makeover paradigm" gains ascendancy in popular media (Gill 2007, 262–264). Across all aspects of modern living, the makeover paradigm offers improvement as entertainment and draws ever more sharply distinctions of gender and class: for instance, television shows like *Extreme Makeover* present cosmetic surgery to women as a path to autonomy and happiness, while *Ladette to Lady* urges working-class women to conform to middle-class taste for self-betterment. Tasker and Negra suggest that one of the key contradictions of postfeminism is that female empowerment is dependent on the capacity to consume (2007, 8), thus requiring the exclusion of women who cannot meet these demands. Or, as Jessica Ringrose and Valerie Walkerdine put it, "this successful femininity is bourgeois, yet coded universal, normal and attainable for all" (2008, 228).

Women's economic capacity is encouraged at the same time as the changing global marketplace increasingly relies on the exploitation of women in the "third world" as women migrants take up poorly paid, unregulated domestic work and Western businesses secure cheap female labor offshore. The inevitable subject of capacity that is produced under these conditions is, therefore, white, Western, and middle class. Christina Scharff argues that in contemporary European societies, women's condition of freedom offered by postfeminism is in fact "intertwined with the construction of their cultural other, the 'oppressed Muslim woman,' who is portrayed as being a passive victim of patriarchal culture" (Scharff 2012, 1–2). Scharff found that the interviewees from her empirical research positioned themselves as liberated Western subjects beyond the need for feminism in contradistinction to Muslim women who were believed to be "powerless and subjugated" (Scharff 2012, 67).

In terms of television and film representation, African American women are still presented as the enduring other to white women's changing modalities of selfhood (Springer 2007, 249), which implies that they do not have the same access to "the individual" as a category of identity reserved for the white female subject whose self-construction depends upon a subordinated black female other. Another consequence of the commercializing thrust of postfeminist neoliberal discourse is that political difference (such as race) becomes commodified as a consumable brand identity (Banet-Weiser 2007).

Although the term "postfeminism" invites definitional ambiguity, in recent years scholars on the subject have done much to clarify its discursive constitution, particularly across the popular media. While initial attempts at definition saw fit to distinguish between postfeminism in the academy and in popular culture, it is to the latter manifestations that contemporary theorists are increasingly turning their critical attention. Theories postulating that postfeminist female disidentification with feminism constituted an anti-feminist "backlash" were crucial in providing chronology and context for a cultural moment in which feminism had been proclaimed dead; this approach has since been critically revised to account for the contradictory nature of postfeminism as a political position that simultaneously assumes and refuses feminist values. With the expansion of scholarship in this area, we now have a rich, albeit still developing, vocabulary with which to interrogate the complexities of postfeminism as one of the most fascinating cultural phenomena of the new millennium.

SEE ALSO: Backlash; Feminisms, First, Second, and Third Wave; Feminist Sex Wars; Individualism and Collectivism, Critical Feminist Perspectives on; Lesbian Stereotypes in the United States; Pornography, Feminist Legal and Political Debates on

REFERENCES

Bail, Kathy. 1996. *DIY Feminism*. St. Leonards: Allen and Unwin.

Banet-Weiser, Sarah. 2007. "What's Your Flava? Race and Postfeminism in Media Culture." In

Interrogating Postfeminism: Gender and the Politics of Popular Culture, edited by Yvonne Tasker and Diane Negra, 201–226. Durham, NC: Duke University Press.

Bauman, Zygmunt. 2000. *Liquid Modernity*. Cambridge: Polity.

Bauman, Zygmunt. 2001. *The Individualised Society*. Cambridge: Polity.

Beck, Ulrich. 1992. *Risk Society: Towards a New Modernity*. London: Sage.

Brooks, Ann. 1997. *Postfeminisms: Feminism, Cultural Theory and Cultural Forms*. London: Routledge.

Brunsdon, Charlotte. 1997. *Screen Tastes: Soap Opera to Satellite Dishes*. London: Routledge.

Brunsdon, Charlotte, and Lynn Spigel, eds. 2008. *Feminist Television Criticism: A Reader*, 2nd ed. Milton Keynes: Open University Press.

Bulbeck, Chilla. 2010. "Unpopularising Feminism: 'Blaming Feminism' in the Generation Debate and the Mother Wars." *Sociology Compass*, 4(1): 21–37. DOI: 10.1111/j.1751-9020.2009.00257.x.

Denfeld, Rene. 1995. *The New Victorians: A Young Woman's Challenge to the Old Feminist Order*. St. Leonards: Allen and Unwin.

Dow, Bonnie J. 1996. *Prime-Time Feminism: Television, Media Culture, and the Women's Movement since 1970*. Philadelphia: University of Pennsylvania Press.

Dux, Monica, and Zora Simic. 2008. *The Great Feminist Denial*. Carlton: Melbourne University Press.

Faludi, Susan. 1991. *Backlash: The Undeclared War against Women*. London: Vintage.

Gamble, Sarah. 1998. "Postfeminism." In The Routledge *Companion to Feminism and Postfeminism*, edited by Sarah Gamble, 36–45. London: Routledge.

Garrison, Ednie Kaeh. 2000. "US Feminism – Grrrl Style! Youth (Sub)cultures and the Technologies of the Third Wave." *Feminist Studies*, 26(1): 141–170.

Genz, Stephanie, and Benjamin A. Brabon. 2009. *Postfeminism: Cultural Texts and Theories*. Edinburgh: Edinburgh University Press.

Giddens, Anthony. 1991. *Modernity and Self-Identity*. Cambridge: Polity.

Gill, Rosalind. 2007. *Gender and the Media*. Cambridge: Polity.

Gill, Rosalind, and Christina Scharff. 2011. "Introduction." In *New Femininities: Postfeminism, Neoliberalism and Subjectivity*, edited by Rosalind Gill and Christina Scharff, 1–20. New York: Palgrave Macmillan.

Henry, Astrid. 2004. *Not My Mother's Sister: Generational Conflict and Third Wave Feminism*. Indiana: Indiana University Press.

Heywood, Leslie, and Jennifer Drake. 1997. "Introduction." In *Third Wave Agenda: Being Feminist, Doing Feminism*, edited by Leslie Heywood and Jennifer Drake, 1–24. Minneapolis: University of Minnesota Press.

Hollows, Joanne. 2000. *Feminism, Femininity and Popular Culture*. Manchester: Manchester University Press.

Jones, Amelia. 2003. "Feminism, Incorporated: Reading 'Postfeminism' in an Anti-Feminist Age." In *Feminism and Visual Culture Reader*, edited by Amelia Jones, 314–329. New York: Routledge.

Levy, Ariel. 2005. *Female Chauvinist Pigs: Women and the Rise of Raunch Culture*. Melbourne: Schwartz.

Lotz, Amanda D. 2001. "Postfeminist Television Criticism: Rehabilitating Critical Terms and Identifying Postfeminist Attributes." *Feminist Media Studies*, 1(1): 105–121. DOI: 10.1080/14680770120042891.

McRobbie, Angela. 2009. *The Aftermath of Feminism: Gender, Culture and Social Change*. London: Sage.

Modleski, Tania. 1991. *Feminism without Women: Culture and Criticism in a "Postfeminist" Age*. New York: Routledge.

Murray, Georgina. 1997. "Agonize, Don't Organize: A Critique of Postfeminism." *Current Sociology*, 45(2): 37–47. DOI: 10.1177/001139297045002004.

Negra, Diane. 2009. *What a Girl Wants? Fantasizing a Reclamation of Self in Postfeminism*. London: Routledge.

Nurka, Camille. 2002. "Postfeminist Autopsies". *Australian Feminist Studies*, 17(38): 177–189.

Nurka, Camille. 2003. *(Post)feminist Territories*. PhD diss., University of Sydney.

Probyn, Elspeth. 1990. "New Traditionalism and Post-Feminism: TV Does the Home." *Screen*, 31(2): 147–159. DOI: 10.1093/screen/31.2.147.

Projansky, Sarah. 2001. *Watching Rape: Film and Television in Postfeminist Culture*. New York: NYU Press.

Rapp, Rayna. 1988. "Is the Legacy of Second Wave Feminism Postfeminism?" *Socialist Review*, 18(1): 31–37.

Ringrose, Jessica, and Valerie Walkerdine. 2008. "Regulating the Abject: The TV Make-Over as a Site of Neo-Liberal Reinvention toward Bourgeois Femininity." *Feminist Media Studies*, 8(3): 227–246. DOI: 10.1080/14680770802217279.

Roiphe, Katie. 1993. *The Morning After: Sex, Fear and Feminism*. London: Hamish Hamilton.

Rose, Nikolas. 1992. "Governing the Enterprising Self." In *The Values of the Enterprise Culture: The Moral Debate*, edited by Paul Heelas and Paul Morris, 141–164. London: Routledge.

Rosenfelt, Deborah, and Judith Stacey. 1987. "Second Thoughts on the Second Wave" (review essay). *Feminist Studies*, 13(2): 341–361. DOI: 10.1057/fr.1987.37.

Scharff, Christina. 2012. *Repudiating Feminism: Young Women in a Neoliberal World*. Farnham: Ashgate.

Springer, Kimberly. 2007. "Divas, Evil Black Bitches, and Bitter Black Women: African American Women in Postfeminist and Post-Civil-Rights Popular Culture." In *Interrogating Postfeminism: Gender and the Politics of Popular Culture*, edited by Yvonne Tasker and Diane Negra, 249–276. Durham, NC: Duke University Press.

Stacey, Judith. 1987. "Sexism by a Subtler Name? Postindustrial Conditions and Postfeminist Consciousness in the Silicon Valley." *Socialist Review*, 17(6): 7–28.

Tasker, Yvonne, and Diane Negra. 2007. "Introduction: Feminist Politics and Postfeminist Culture." In *Interrogating Postfeminism: Gender and the Politics of Popular Culture*, edited by Yvonne Tasker and Diane Negra, 1–26. Durham, NC: Duke University Press.

Taylor, Anthea. 2012. *Single Women in Popular Culture: The Limits of Postfeminism*. New York: Palgrave Macmillan.

Walby, Sylvia. 2011. *The Future of Feminism*. Cambridge: Polity.

Walter, Natasha. 1998. *The New Feminism*. London: Virago.

Walters, Suzanna Danuta. 1991. "Premature Postmortems: 'Postfeminism' and Popular Culture." *New Politics*, 3(2): 103–112.

Walters, Suzanna Danuta. 1995. *Material Girls: Making Sense of Feminist Cultural Theory*. Berkeley: University of California Press.

Whelehan, Imelda. 2000. *Overloaded: Popular Culture and the Future of Feminism*. London: Women's Press.

Wolf, Naomi. 1993. *Fire With Fire: The New Female Power and How It Will Change the 21st Century*. London: Vintage Books.

FURTHER READING

Gamble, Sarah. 2000. *The Routledge Critical Dictionary of Feminism and Postfeminism*. New York: Routledge.

Munford, Rebecca, and Melanie Waters, eds. 2013. *Feminism and Popular Culture: Investigating the Postfeminist Mystique*. London: I. B. Tauris.

Phoca, Sophia, and Rebecca Wright. 1999. *Introducing Postfeminism*. New York: Totem Books.

Postmodern Feminist Psychology

LISA LAZARD, JEAN M. McAVOY and
ROSE CAPDEVILA
Open University, UK

Postmodern feminism brings together a number of feminist approaches which, broadly speaking, question the epistemological premises of realism and universal truth-finding that characterize the development of conventional psychology within the modernist epoch. It is against this backdrop that postmodern feminist approaches to psychology have been played out. Whilst the discipline of psychology has an indigenous critical and feminist tradition with roots in the late nineteenth century, postmodern approaches are not primarily indigenous to psychology, having developed from, as well as alongside, broader philosophical and theoretical critiques generated initially in other disciplines.

Modernist and postmodernist approaches to the study of gender in psychology raise crucial differences in the conceptualization of what it means to be a "woman" or a "man." Conventional (modernist) psychology, in its attempts to map and pin down the nature of sex/gender, has produced the characteristics of sex as a fixed and fundamental entity or "essence" of a person (laid down through either social or biological processes), and much research has been dedicated to identifying the differences between gendered groups. This stands in stark contrast to postmodern feminist ideas in that, far from being a foundational category, gender is construed as continuously (re)produced in and through social interactions and processes.

The focus of postmodern feminist work is on the construction of gender and the ways in which aspects of gender and gendered experience become understood as a truth. From this perspective, the construction of truth is inevitably situated, "based upon and inextricably intertwined with the contexts within which it was created" (Bohan 1993, 13). More precisely, postmodern feminist psychology seeks to unpack the situated discursive practices that create the grand narratives of mainstream psychological work. By rejecting the possibility of universal objective truths, postmodern feminist psychology can ask questions about the operation of gendered power relations and how these become played out in and through claims to knowledge.

A key tool for unpacking construction in postmodern feminist scholarship is deconstruction. This analytic tool focuses on breaking down dichotomies (e.g., man/woman, dominant/submissive, active/passive) to highlight the ways in which they are created and how they represent artificial categorizations that are embedded within power relationships and the accomplishment of privilege. This kind of analysis underscores the absence of universal truths as well as problematizing the notion of essential differences between men and women, and indeed the simplistic concept of binary sex (male or female).

Postmodern feminist psychology is closely related to feminist poststructuralism. The two are often conflated because of a shared basis for critique of the grand narratives and hegemony of positivist scientific knowledge as well as a focus on the constitutive aspects of language and representation. Whilst conflation is not necessarily a problem, it may skim over contentions between theoretical perspectives.

EPISTEMOLOGICAL CHALLENGES AND FEMINIST POLITICS

Feminist thought in general has offered a significant critique of the discipline of psychology, pointing to the ways in which women have been marginalized, ignored, or otherwise rendered invisible (see, for example, Weisstein 1968, 1993). Whilst postmodern feminist scholarship has undoubtedly contributed to the critique of psychology's treatment of women, it has also raised specific questions around the compatibility of the postmodern epistemological stances described above and feminist activism/theoretical challenge in psychology.

This question of compatibility is raised in debates around the divide between frameworks that either essentialize or focus on the construction of gender. Feminist psychologists working within the modernist tradition, in common mainstream psychology, adopt an essentialized view of gender. This involves a conceptualization of gender as a property of, and fixed within, the individual. For many feminists, working with an essentialized view of gender was crucial for reappropriating feminine traits that had been implicitly and explicitly denigrated in much mainstream psychological research (Gilligan 1982). In this feminist tradition, then, the emphasis was on celebrating women's difference from men by valuing those points of separation. Starting with the realist premise that gender has an objective material existence provided feminist scholars and activists with a potentially stable base on which to build solidarity and claim a legitimate voice around objectively shared experiences.

This essentialist view has come under heavy criticism from feminist psychologists drawing on postmodern theorizing. As Bohan (1993) points out, essentialist versions of feminism tend to homogenize women and so ignore important points of difference between them. It can also make specific kinds of collective action difficult because the problem of gender is rooted in the individual. Therefore change is centered at the level of the individual rather than in oppressive systems. Bohan goes on to argue that postmodern constructionist stances circumvent such problems. For example, by rejecting the idea of universality of womanhood, postmodern feminism is able to engage with women's diversity and acknowledge that women's identities and experiences are organized around many points of sameness and difference. Therefore it allows psychology to engage with the complexities framing gendered ways of being. In addition, the tenets of postmodernism allow for collective action based on the problematizing of oppressive social structures rather than individual change because gender is located, shaped, and reproduced within the social context rather than as a property of persons.

Postmodern feminism's emphasis on diversity and the specificity of context is not without problem. There is a danger of particularizing women to the point where there is no basis for commonality (Butler 1990, 1993; Bohan 1993). This highlights the key problem identified by some feminists in the field – the translation of postmodern thought to feminist action. The problems faced by feminists attempting to ground postmodern theorizing for the purposes of political action are summed up by Wilkinson and Kitzinger (1995):

- Postmodern emphasis on diversity makes it difficult to mobilize around a coherent single voice/identification.
- The emphasis on discursive diversity may mask power differentials in those diverse discourses.
- Stress on micro-politics in some close interactional discursive analyses may minimize the importance of macro/structural inequalities.
- The postmodern position of an absence of any unified truth gives rise to relativism, and "all versions being equal" displaces the grounding on which to make cogent political action.

This critique has been challenged by feminists taking a postmodern approach to psychology. For instance, Hepburn (2000) responds to the four points above as follows:

- Singularizing what people are "really" like is part of psychology's oppressive power. Postmodern emphasis on plural identities avoids replicating problems associated with homogeneity and related power dynamics that work to position all women as universally inferior.
- The emphasis on function of versions or accounts allows for an analysis of power.
- Micro-politics and macro/structural inequalities are inextricably interconnected. Macro/structural issues are constructed in and through micro practices.
- Relativism allows us to call into question traditional terms and categories. This allows for reflective and critical consideration of taken-for-granted discourses that may allow for political stances/aims to be honed, reimagined, or redefined. Instead of politics being grounded in appeals to a

prediscursive female identity, it becomes grounded in context.

For many feminists, postmodern thought provides a means to transcend questions of essentialism as well as reimagine the boundaries around sameness and difference that are threaded through debates on feminist identity politics (e.g., Fine and Addelston 1996).

CHANGES OVER TIME

This shifting from feminist essentialist positions, which broadly characterize feminist theory and debates in the 1970s, to consideration of what postmodernism could offer feminism occurred largely in the 1990s. The 1970s and 1980s saw an emerging and sustained critique of much feminist work as reflecting the perspectives and concerns of women who were enabled to take up spaces of power to voice their politics – those included the subject positions of Western, white, middle-class women. Postmodern feminism, with its emphasis on fragmented and shifting identities, contributed to this critique and seemed to resonate with a developing body of work on intersectionality. Originating in the voices of black women who drew attention to how their experience of subordination was not only gendered but raced, the concept of intersectionality questions the reduction of women's experiences of oppression to a primary or single identity category or point of difference (Crenshaw 1991). Thus, intersectionality has been used to highlight how women's lives are organized around multiple axes such as sexualities, race, (dis)ableism, age, and social class, to name but a few, and as such may experience intersecting points of oppression. Importantly, the move away from singular models of gendered power (such as patriarchy) in intersectional theories fitted with the fluid, dispersed tectonics of power envisioned by postmodern feminist theory.

In a similar vein, postmodern feminism's engagement with the complexities of the multiplex configurations of women's identities resonates with ideas emanating from queer theory, which uses sexualities as a central point of reference to question the fixity of identity. Queer theory has problematized identity categories, drawing attention to how identity labels regulate and reify categories. As Butler (1990, 5) notes, "Is the construction of the category of women as a coherent and stable subject an unwitting regulation and reification of gender relations?" Of particular importance is the critique offered by queer theory of the presumed naturalness of heterosexual identities and how this works to exclude other sexualities as well as (re)producing men and women with reference to heterosexualized relationships. This insight features in a body of postmodern feminist work that makes sense of the complexities of, for example, the operation of power in women's sexual relationships and sexual violence (e.g., Gavey 2005).

The recognition of multiplicity has undoubtedly opened up critical spaces to explore the complexities of fragmented, often contested identities and subjectivities that women become (re)produced by as well as negotiate. While this critical space can be attributed to the disavowal of an essential and prediscursive self, it has opened up a set of tensions around women's materiality. The appeal of moving away from locating political claims in the prediscursive is understandable given that feminism more generally has problematized the reduction of women to a biology that was rendered inferior to its so-called male counterpart. However, the lack of a prediscursive grounding has raised questions about the role of corporeality in postmodern feminist theorization when the body appears inextricably tied to women's experiences in general, and oppressions in particular. Engagement with the idea of embodiment – how one lives one's acculturated body – has been used to interrogate some of the tensions between bodily oppressions and postmodern thinking in the theoretical literature. Butler's troubling of the gendered body has been hugely influential in thinking through how we might conceptualize women's bodies in much of the scholarship in postmodern feminist psychology. Influenced by poststructuralist and psychoanalytic writers, Butler argues that the gendered body is "performatively" (re)produced through stylized repetitive acts – it is not simply the case that social meanings are written onto a passive body or that an individual chooses to perform; rather, the gendered body is produced in and through taken-for-granted regulatory everyday practices (see Butler 1993 for a more detailed examination of these issues). In keeping with the emphasis on multiplicity, it becomes possible to interrogate the many ways in which women's bodies become constituted.

RECENT DIRECTIONS

The 1990s onward have seen the opening up of critical dialogues between postmodern feminist approaches and "other" areas of scholarship attempting to theorize specific trajectories of marginalization. Postmodern feminist debates around embodiment, for example, have expanded with the interweaving of ideas with critical disability studies and health psychology. The interplay of ideas from across these areas of scholarship has opened up examination at the intersection of dis/abled and gender identities, the ways in which this becomes played out in different contexts across the lifespan, and the implications that this has for reading abilities of the gendered body. In a similar vein, conversations across postmodern feminisms and postcolonial psychology have allowed for developments in the unpacking of colonial and postcolonial discourses shaping the (re)production of gender identities.

SEE ALSO: Essentialism; Feminism and Postmodernism; Feminism, Poststructural; Feminisms, Postmodern; Gender Identity, Theories of; Intersectionality; Lesbian, Gay, Bisexual, and Transgender Psychologies; Masculinity and Femininity, Theories of; Psychological Theory, Research, Methodology, and Feminist Critiques; Queer Theory

REFERENCES

Bohan, Janis. 1993. "Regarding Gender: Essentialism, Constructionism and Feminist Psychology." *Psychology of Women Quarterly*, 17: 5–21.

Butler, Judith. 1990. *Gender Trouble: Feminism and the Subversion of Identity*. London: Routledge.

Butler, Judith. 1993. *Bodies that Matter: On the Discursive Limits of Sex*. London: Routledge.

Crenshaw, Kimberly W. 1991. "Mapping the Margins: Intersectionality, Identity Politics, and Violence against Women of Color." *Stanford Law Review*, 43(6): 1241–1299.

Fine, Michelle, and Judi Addelston. 1996. "Containing Questions of Gender and Power: The Discursive Limits of 'Sameness' and 'Difference'." In *Feminist Social Psychologies: International Perspectives*, edited by Sue Wilkinson, 66–86. Buckingham: Open University Press.

Gavey, Nicola. 2005. *Just Sex? The Cultural Scaffolding of Rape*. London: Routledge.

Gilligan, Carol. 1982. *In a Different Voice: Psychological Theory and Women's Development*. Cambridge, MA: Harvard University Press.

Hepburn, Alexa. 2000. "On the Alleged Incompatibility between Feminism and Relativism." *Feminism & Psychology*, 10(1): 91–106.

Weisstein, Naomi. 1968. *Kinder, Kuche, Kirche as Scientific Law: Psychology Constructs the Female*. Boston: New England Free Press.

Weisstein, Naomi. 1993. "Psychology Constructs the Female; or the Fantasy Life of the Male Psychologist (with Some Attention to the Fantasies of his Friends, the Male Biologist and the Male Anthropologist)." *Feminism & Psychology*, 3(2): 194–210. Revised and expanded version of Weisstein 1968.

Wilkinson, Sue, and Celia Kitzinger. 1995. *Feminism and Discourse*. London: Sage.

FURTHER READING

Burman, Erica, ed. 1998. *Deconstructing Feminist Psychology*. London: Sage.

Feminism & Psychology journal.

Feminist Theory journal.

Hare-Mustin, Rachel T., and Jeanne Marecek. 1988. "The Meaning of Difference: Gender Theory, Postmodernism, and Psychology." *American Psychologist*, 43(6): 455.

Magnusson, Eva, and Jeanne Marecek. 2012. *Gender and Culture in Psychology: Theories and Practices*. Cambridge: Cambridge University Press.

Psychology's feminist voices: http://www.feministvoices.com/

Poverty in Global Perspective

RHONDA VONSHAY SHARPE
Bucknell University, USA

KENDAL SWANSON
Duke University, USA

Poverty is defined as the pronounced deprivation in well-being. Well-being is complex, but is most simply defined as the command over commodities and resources. Well-being is measured by whether a household or individual has enough resources to meet needs. There are three common concepts of poverty – income poverty, human poverty, and capabilities deprivation.

Income poverty is defined as either absolute poverty (the set resources necessary to maintain a "minimum standard of living") or relative poverty (comparative well-being of an individual relative to the rest of society) (Mowafi 2015). Income poverty often considers household structure and characteristics – married/single, female/male, and presence of children – thereby potentially exposing social and economic inequality. The boundary for absolute poverty, after adjusting for inflation, may vary little over time. However, relative poverty might exhibit slow increases or jumps that correspond to changes in the overall standard of living. Examples of income poverty would include measures such as the World Bank's "$1/day" poverty line and the United Nation's $1.25-a-day standard.

Human poverty is measured using a composite index of three indicators: short life, lack of basic education, and lack of access to public and private resources (Mowafi 2015). Short life is intended to measure the vulnerability to death before age 40 for developing countries and before age 60 for industrialized countries. Lack of basic education is intended to measure a country's literacy rate. Overall standard of living is a composite of two percentages: the percentage of people with access to health services and safe water and the percentage of malnourished children under age 5. The human poverty measure is based on indicators of human welfare that provide insight into the changes in human development and poverty alleviation as a result of economic investments.

Capabilities deprivation is inadequate command over resources via markets, public provisions, or other non-market channels that result in the lack of basic capabilities – goods and services necessary to avoid preventable morbidity (Kakwani 2006). Kakwani stresses that there is a distinction between poverty and capability deprivation. Capability deprivation may have a myriad of causes, but poverty is concerned only with an inadequate command over resources necessary to generate basic capabilities as determined by society. Therefore, a rich person with a disability would experience capability deprivation but would not be considered impoverished. Human poverty and capabilities deprivation are reported as the overall incidence of poverty, not as a headcount.

While these definitions of poverty are gender neutral, poverty studies suggest that poverty has a 3-G dimension: geography, generation, and gender. Geography: rural residents have higher rates of poverty than non-rural residents. Generation: children born into poverty are more likely to live in poverty as adults than those not born into poverty. Gender: female-headed households tend to experience poverty at higher levels than male-headed households. Poverty operates on women in ways that increase the risk for women of domestic violence and sexual exploitation, and that erodes their equality of rights.

For example, cultural norms – laws about asset ownership, systematic anti-female bias, and patriarchal family structures – may prevent women from owning or inheriting assets, reduce control over fertility and increase child mortality, or lead to female feticide and/or underinvestment in/devaluing of girls. Cultural norms often produce labor market deficits, occupation segregation, informal work, and unequal pay and reduce a woman's fiscal independence, increasing the likelihood of remaining in an abusive partnership or the vulnerability to sexual exploitation. Cultural norms that promote intra-household inequalities devalue a "woman's worth" and deprive women of equal access to nutrition, healthcare, education, and employment – equal rights.

Given the influence of cultural norms on the vulnerability of poverty for women, poverty counts by head of household ignore that a woman may not have access to or authority over household resources, thereby undercounting the number of women in poverty. This is especially true for societies with patriarchal family structures. Although human poverty and capabilities deprivation can be reported by any identifiable group, "generally" reporting the incidence of poverty may hide social inequalities that impact women. This entry focuses on income poverty.

AUSTRALIA

Australia uses two measures, the Henderson Poverty Line (c. mid-1960s) and 50 percent of the median-income line, which is a more standard measure used by the Organisation for Economic Co-operation and Development (OECD). Under the latter measurement, poverty rates have remained relatively stagnant since 1990 except for a slight hike in the mid-2000s. As of 2010, the poverty rate stands at 12.8 percent. Disaggregated by gender, women bear slightly more of the burden of poverty at 13.5 percent compared to the 12.1 percent of men living below the poverty line. This disparity has been attributed to fewer employment opportunities and lower wages for women.

High school retention rates as well as university enrollment are higher now for women than for men, yet the wage gap persists at 19 percent. Poverty and related disparities exist at an even higher level for the Indigenous population of Australia. A 2006 study found that Indigenous Australians earn 65 percent less than other Australians and have three times the unemployment rate and that 45 percent of Indigenous Australians belong to the lowest income group.

CANADA

Canada has no official measure of poverty. Instead, Statistics Canada uses a measure of "low income" – earning less than half the median income. Using this measure, Statistics Canada reports that 14.9 percent of Canadians have "low income" or live in poverty. For women, 36 percent of Aboriginal women (First Nations, Métis, Inuit) live in poverty, followed by minority women, 35 percent; women with disabilities, 26 percent; single-parent mothers, 21 percent (7 percent of single-parent fathers are poor); and single senior women, 14 percent. The causes of low income for women in Canada are multifaceted: being a single parent, low skills, part-time and seasonal employment, physical and mental disability, and wage inequality.

EAST ASIA AND THE PACIFIC

Extreme poverty decreased from 56.2 percent in 1990 to 12.5 percent in 2010, making East and Southeast Asia the only region to already reach the Millennium Development Goal of the United Nations (UN) of halving extreme poverty by 2015. Except for Papua New Guinea, which has maintained a relatively fixed level of poverty since 1981, every country in the region has reported significant, if uneven, reductions in poverty during this time period.

However, while extreme poverty rates have fallen to 12.5 percent and continue to decrease in this region, an estimated 50 percent of women in the region are vulnerable to poverty and hunger. Precise estimations are difficult to calculate since data disaggregated by gender exist for only about 10 percent of countries in the region. According to UN reports, gender inequality and/or low social status of women is the cause of poverty for one tenth of poor women in the region (Watson Andaya 2015). Existing statutory and customary laws are also a contributing cause of women's poverty, particularly in East Asia, as such laws limit women's access to land and other types of property. Women in Southeast Asia face a slightly smaller gender equality gap, which can perhaps be explained by many factors, one of which is the fact that women there have traditionally played a strong role in the markets as well as in agriculture as laborers (Hughes 2009).

EUROPE

Poverty is defined in the European Union (EU) as household income that falls below 60 percent of the national median. Lone parents had risks of poverty that ranged from 28 percent in Nordic countries to 34 percent in northwestern countries. Plumb and Zimmer (2010) estimate that 17 percent of women in EU member states live in poverty. Given high rates of employment in the public services (healthcare, education, etc.), women were not initially impacted by the economic crises. However, austerity measures have hit women the hardest due to reductions in public services.

In 2008, elderly women had a risk of poverty of 22 percent compared to 16 percent for elderly men. On average and across the EU, working women are less likely than working men to live in households with poverty-level incomes. In-work-poverty risk is higher for women than men in the countries of Cyprus, Estonia, Germany, and Latvia. The in-work-poverty risk ranges from 2 percent in Malta and 3 percent in the Czech Republic and Denmark to 10 percent in Latvia and Poland and 12 percent in Greece. Although women are more likely than men to be employed in low-paid jobs and to work part-time, single women without children are on average less likely than men to have below-poverty-level incomes.

LATIN AMERICAN AND THE CARIBBEAN

In Latin America and the Caribbean (LAC) extreme poverty is defined as surviving on less than $2.50/day; the minimum needed to meet basic food requirements and moderate poverty is defined as $4/day. Of the 600 million people living in the LAC, about 80 million live in extreme poverty and reside in either Mexico or Brazil. The poverty rate for the LAC decreased from 26.3 percent in 1995 to 13.3 percent in 2011. The increase in labor force participation of women and the decline in the gender earnings gap in the LAC contributed greatly to the reduction of both extreme and moderate poverty.

In most LAC countries, men and women have similar poverty rates, the exceptions being Belize, the Dominican Republic, and Jamaica where the male–female poverty rate difference exceeds 3 percent. For most LAC countries the percentage of women living in poverty is between 50 and 54 percent; only Panama and Paraguay have lower rates. In Colombia, the Dominican Republic, Jamaica, Bolivia, and Venezuela, poverty rates are higher for female-headed households than for male-headed households. Poverty rates are higher for male-headed households in El Salvador, Guatemala, Honduras, Nicaragua, and Peru.

MIDDLE EAST AND NORTH AFRICA

Since 1908, the Middle East and North Africa region has lowered the headcount ratio of those living in extreme poverty to 2.4 percent (2010 estimate). In addition to decreasing the absolute number of people at or below $1.25 a day, the Middle East and North Africa region now has the lowest incidence of extreme poverty of any developing region in the world. These decreases are largely due to immense improvements in access to education and health services as well as food and energy subsidy programs.

Between 1960 and 2000, educational attainment for people aged 15 and up increased by 600 percent, with an even greater increase, 900 percent, for women aged 15 and up. The female literacy rate rose dramatically during that time as well, moving from less than 10 percent to 60 percent. In 1960, just 21.9 percent of the female labor force was participating in the formal sector. This rate has since risen to more than 32 percent as of 2000. It is difficult to accurately depict employment trends for women because many women, particularly those living in rural areas where most of the extremely impoverished population in this region is concentrated, are employed in the informal sector of the economy and thus are not captured by regional surveys.

SOUTH ASIA

With 51 percent of the population living below $1.25 in 1990, South Asia's robust and steady growth rate in recent years, stemming in large part from India, Bangladesh, and Pakistan, has lowered extreme poverty in the region to 30 percent as of 2010. The region contains more than 44 percent of the developing world's poor, with nearly half of all of Asia and the Pacific's extreme poor living in India alone (Hughes 2009). The majority of the poor in South Asia live in rural areas where female-headed households are typically found to be poorer than male-headed households. Faced with limited access to assets such as land and other property ownership, as well as with lower education levels, women in South Asia have far fewer opportunities to be employed than men. According to 2012 UN estimates, the employment-to-population ratio for women stood at 30 percent compared to a 78 percent ratio for men.

Additionally, Asia holds the second lowest percentage, a ranking held primarily because of South Asia, of married women taking part in intra-household decision-making. The existence of dowries and the practice of the bride moving from her parents' home to her husband's family home upon marriage help explain why such a gap in gender equality exists. Eight countries in the region have since pledged to increase the priority of women's rights. In India, women may now more freely participate in politics and even hold more elected positions.

SUB-SAHARAN AFRICA

The percentage of the population in sub-Saharan Africa living at or below $1.25 a day has decreased over the past few decades, from 57.6 percent in 1990 to 50.9 percent in 2005; however, the absolute number of people living in those conditions has increased during that time. Poverty levels vary widely across nations. In some countries, Togo and Côte d'Ivoire for instance, the incidence of poverty actually increased between 1990 and 2005, whereas only a handful of countries have reached or are on track to reach the Millennium Development Goal of halving extreme poverty by 2015.

While other developing regions have made significant progress toward the 2015 goal, sub-Saharan Africa has doubled its share of the world's extreme poor. However, accelerated, widespread economic growth beginning in the late 1990s may indicate the prospect of reducing poverty rates. The continent of Africa now ranks third in the world for number of national parliament seats held by women. Rights to land- and other property ownership, however, remain a challenge to gender equality in the region. Males still dominate intra-household decision-making power, with just 60 percent of married women able to exercise decision-making power over daily purchases and only 46 percent exercising power over major purchases.

UNITED STATES

Poverty in the United States is a function of family size and number of children under 18. In 1978, Dianna Pearce suggested that not only was the composition of the US poor female, but also that the intersection of gender and poor had caused a "feminization" of poverty (Pearce 1978). In the late 1970s when laws provided women with increased access to the labor market, women's earnings relative to men and the increasing number of female-headed households meant more women were economically disadvantaged and their households financially insecure.

In 2012, nearly 18 million women lived in poverty, with nearly 8 million of this group living in extreme poverty – income at or below 50 percent of the federal poverty level (Entmacher et al. 2013). Intersect the experience of women in general with race/ethnicity, and the poverty rate for all non-white women is appalling. The poverty rate for black and Hispanic women was 25 percent, Native American women 34 percent, and Asian women 11.5 percent compared to 10 percent for white women and 7.7 percent for white men (Entmacher et al. 2013). The poverty rates for female-headed households ranged from 33 percent for whites to 57 percent for Native Americans. The poverty rate for female-headed households was 3 to 6 times the poverty rate for married couples (9 percent) and 1.5 to 2.5 times the poverty rate for male-headed households. Labor market structural factors such as occupational segregation and wage inequality make it difficult for women to climb out of poverty. Despite increased labor force participation and educational attainment, women are still paid less than men: .77/$1.00 (Entmacher et al. 2013).

Although the great recession hit men harder than women, recovery has happened faster for men. The jobs gained by women have been in the 10 largest low-wage occupations: childcare, food service, and home healthcare.

SEE ALSO: Feminization of Labor; Gender Wage Gap; Occupational Segregation

Premenstrual Syndrome (PMS)

SUSAN MARKENS
Lehman College and The Graduate Center, City University of New York, USA

Originally medically recognized and labeled premenstrual tension (PMT) in 1931 by Dr. Arthur Frank, premenstrual syndrome (PMS) is the term coined in 1953 by Dr. Katrina Dalton to describe a wide range of symptoms women may experience in the days prior to the start of their menstrual cycle. The term PMS became well-known and firmly established in the public lexicon in the early 1980s when two British women used it as a mitigating factor for their defense in criminal murder trials. By the late 1980s, PMS was referred to clinically in the *Diagnostic and Statistical Manual* (DSM) of the American Psychiatric Association as late luteal phase dysphoric disorder (LLPDD) and subsequently as premenstrual dysphoric disorder (PMDD) in 2000. Currently, PMS and PMDD are used interchangeably; PMS is the term used more colloquially, while PMDD is considered a severe form of PMS.

There are 100–150 psychological and physical symptoms used to diagnose PMS. These symptoms range from anger, depression, anxiety, sadness, forgetfulness, difficulty concentrating, and irritability, to weight gain, bloating, acne, painful breasts, headache, backache, dizziness, lack of energy, and cravings. While less than 10 percent of women are clinically considered to have PMDD, there are estimates that upward of 75 percent of all women could be medically classified as suffering from PMS. Since so many women can potentially be diagnosed as having PMS, feminists have expressed concern that normal female physiological experiences have been pathologized and medicalized with its

REFERENCES

Entmacher, Joan, Gallagher Katherine Robbins, Julie Bogtman, and Lauren Frohlich. 2013. *Insecure & Unequal: Poverty Among Women and Families 2000–2012*. National Women's Law Center. Accessed August 15, 2015, at http://www.nwlc.org/resource/insecure-unequal-poverty-among-women-and-families-2000-2012.

Hughes, Barry. 2009. *Reducing Global Poverty*. Denver: Pardee Center of International Futures, University of Denver. Accessed August 15, 2015, at http://pardee.du.edu/sites/default/files/PPHP1_Full_Volume.pdf.

Kakwani, Nanak. 2006. "What is Poverty?" *International Poverty Centre*. Accessed November 21, 2012, at http://www.sarpn.org/documents/d0002176/IPC_Poverty_Sept2006.pdf.

Mowafi, Mona. 2015. "The Meaning and Measurement of Poverty: A Look into the Global Debate." Accessed August 15, 2015, at http://www.sas.upenn.edu/~dludden/Mowafi_Poverty_Measurement_Debate.pdf.

Pearce, Dianna. 1978. "The Feminization of Women, Work, and Welfare." *The Urban & Social Change Review*: 28–36.

Plumb, Rovana, and Gabriele Zimmer. 2010. *On the Face of Female Poverty in the European Union*. Committee on Women's Rights and Gender Inequality. Accessed August 15, 2015, at http://www.europarl.europa.eu/meetdocs/2009_2014/documents/femm/pr/837/837399/837399en.pdf.

Watson Andaya, Barbara. 2015. "Women in Southeast Asia." *Asia Society*. Accessed August 15, 2015, at http://asiasociety.org/women-southeast-asia.

FURTHER READING

Christopher, Karen, Paula England, Sara McLanahan, Katherine Ross, and Tim Smeeding. 2000. *Gender Inequality in Poverty in Affluent Nations: The Role of Single Motherhood and the State*. Center for Research on Child Wellbeing, Working Paper No. 00-12.

Iqbal, Farruk. 2006. "Sustaining Gains in Poverty Reduction and Human Development in the Middle East and North Africa." *World Bank*. Accessed November 15, 2013, at http://siteresources.worldbank.org/INTMENA/Resources/Poverty_complete_06_web.pdf.

inclusion in the official psychiatric diagnostic manual. PMS as a disease category is also criticized by feminists for reinforcing what is considered "normal" feminine behavior. For instance, the medical classification of PMS as a psychiatric disorder assumes that a "good," normal woman should be happy and caring, whereas a woman is "bad" and abnormal if she is angry.

The pathologization of women's reproductive bodies and assumptions of women's emotionality, particularly surrounding menstrual and hormonal changes, has long existed in Western culture from the myth of the traveling womb in Ancient Greece to women who were treated for "hysteria" in the nineteenth century. As with these previous conditions, PMS tends to label all or most women as potentially sick and in need of medical treatment. PMS as a medical diagnosis thus concerns feminists as it perpetuates the historical idea of women as emotional and the "weaker sex." For instance, the view of all premenstrual women as potentially erratic and unreliable has been criticized by feminists as a way to diminish and discourage women's role in the modern workplace as PMS ostensibly renders them less capable, competent, and manageable workers. Feminists are also critical of the inclusion of PMS/PMDD in the DSM as it reinforces women's greater likelihood of being labeled as "mad." Furthermore, a psychiatric diagnosis of PMS ascribes changes in women's moods primarily to biological causes as opposed to social factors. For instance, with a medical diagnosis of PMS, women's reports of premenstrual emotions such as anger, depression, and irritability are attributed to hormonal fluctuations instead of understandable emotional reactions to women's everyday life stresses and gendered norms and expectations. Given the history of overprescribing women mood-altering drugs, feminists remain alarmed that the biopsychiatric diagnosis of PMS leads women to be prescribed medications from hormones to selective serotonin reuptake inhibitors (SSRIs) to alleviate symptoms. Feminist scholars are specifically suspicious that the SSRI Prozac was repackaged as Sarafem to target women diagnosed with PMDD.

The influential role of family structure and gendered roles on the manifestation of PMS, rather than biology, is supported by research that finds that women who are mothers and who subscribe to a more traditional gender role ideology are more likely to complain about premenstrual distress. The heteronormative assumptions about appropriate and expected female behavior that impact women's experience of premenstrual symptoms is also supported by research that finds that women in heterosexual relationships are more likely than women in lesbian relationships to suffer from PMS symptoms. Additionally, PMS is viewed by its critics as a culture-bound syndrome because it is primarily reported in Western Europe, North America, and Australia. Women in non-Western countries, where different views of menstruation prevail, do not view changes experienced during the premenstrual period as significant or as a cause for medical intervention. Given the cultural variation in reports of premenstrual distress, as well as the numerous and vague ways in which PMS can be clinically diagnosed, feminists often argue that there is very little evidence that PMS is a widespread or scientifically substantiated "mental illness."

While critical of the biomedical classification of PMS as a psychiatric illness and the pharmaceutical response to women's premenstrual complaints, feminist scholars do not want to dismiss women's complaints as all in their heads and deny their experiences of premenstrual distress. By labeling PMS as a socially constructed disease, feminist researchers and activists bring to light the biosocial interactions that produce illness experience and responses to it, as well as the role gender has in normative assumptions about health, illness, and normality.

SEE ALSO: *Diagnostic and Statistical Manual of Mental Disorders* (DSM), Feminist Critiques of; Medicine and Medicalization; Menstrual Activism

FURTHER READING

Chrisler, Joan C., and Paula Caplan. 2002. "The Strange Case of Dr. Jekyll and Ms. Hyde: How PMS Became a Cultural Phenomenon and a Psychiatric Disorder." *Annual Review of Sex Research*, 13(1): 274–306.

Figert, Anne. 1996. *Women and the Ownership of PMS: The Structuring of a Psychiatric Disorder*. New York: Aline de Gruyter.

Markens, Susan. 1996. "The Problematic of 'Experience': A Political and Cultural Critique of PMS." *Gender & Society*, 10(1): 42–58.

Martin, Emily. 1987. *The Woman in the Body: A Cultural Analysis of Reproduction*. Boston: Beacon Press.

Rittenhouse, C. Amanda. 1991. "The Emergence of Premenstrual Syndrome as a Social Problem." *Social Problems*, 38(3): 412–425.

Ussher, Jane M. 2006. *Managing the Monstrous Feminine: Regulating the Reproductive Body*. New York: Routledge.

Ussher, Jane M. 2011. *The Madness of Women: Myth and Experience*. New York: Routledge.

Ussher, Jane M., and Janette Perz. 2013. "PMS as a Gendered Illness Linked to the Construction and Relational Experience of Hetero-Femininity." *Sex Roles*, 68: 132–150.

Private/Public Spheres

SUSAN B. BOYD
Professor Emerita, Allard School of Law, University of British Columbia, Canada

Dividing life into opposing spheres of private and public activities and responsibilities is central to Western knowledge and the liberal tradition. This marker is used to describe multiple distinctions between family and state; family and market; market and state; and community and state. Of particular relevance to women, domestic labor and domestic violence have been hidden in the private sphere of the household. Moreover, public space has been normatively constructed as male and heterosexual, whereas non-normative sexual identities are to be hidden within the private sphere of home or the closet.

The private/public divide has been critically analyzed, especially by feminists (e.g., Okin 1989; Pateman 1989). The divide is ideological, not real, with boundaries that shift and blur in different sociopolitical contexts. It most famously embodies an assumption that the social costs of reproduction and care labor will be borne by the privatized family rather than by society or state. It also embodies the notion that the family is a haven from the marketplace or state intervention. This deeply gendered division holds women responsible for children and family and constructs women as distinct from men. Women's private sphere responsibility supports men's ability to dominate and succeed in the public sphere and to have greater power in both spheres.

The public sphere is constructed as the legitimate realm of powerful groups and reflects the hegemony of heterosexuality. The consequences of being assigned to one sphere or the other are not neutral. In addition to relieving the state from responsibility and providing an unrecognized subsidy to society, privatizing domestic responsibilities generates disadvantages for those who assume the unpaid or underpaid tasks (Fineman 2004). These disadvantages transcend each sphere, affecting women's ability to compete in the public spheres of work and politics.

Factors such as gender, race, class, and sexual identity mediate the extent to which individuals or groups find haven in the private sphere and disrupt linear approaches to private/public. Poor women are less likely to be shielded in the private sphere and more likely to work in both spheres; family provided a haven against racism for African Americans during slavery; and African American and indigenous mothers are more likely to lose their children to the state.

Individuals with non-normative sexualities have a complex relationship with private and public spheres. Homosexuality is tolerated only if kept private. Histories of fields such as science and public health rarely record the presence of gay people despite the impact of "private" sexuality on public careers (Hansen 2002). Increasingly, lesbians and gay men leave the private sphere to "invade" public space through Pride Parades, for instance (Brickell 2010). For some heterosexuals, this "flaunting" of homosexuality invades their "private" space as well, due to the taken-for-grantedness of heternormativity (Elshtain 1982/1983). Yet the liberal ideal of privacy is differentially applied, often not protecting non-normative sex from prosecution. Even asserting a right to privacy against public "outings" problematically relegates homosexuality to the private sphere. The possibility of asserting "gay identity" is also culturally specific, generating problems for those negotiating public processes such as Western immigration that rely on an individual being "out."

Over recent decades, challenges have been mounted to the private/public divide, reflecting the rallying cry "the personal is political." Public policy no longer pretends to play no role in the private sphere. Technological developments blur the boundaries between private and public, with paid work entering the home and surveillance being enhanced. Social media diminish the ability to keep sexuality private.

Yet the private/public divide holds continuing resonance. Despite the increase in women's employment rate and pay equity initiatives, women with children are still less likely to be employed and women are paid less than men on average. Workplace structures fit poorly with private responsibilities. The gendered division of labor remains surprisingly intact in both private and public spheres and domestic violence continues at an alarming rate.

Neoliberalism has prompted a renegotiation of the appropriate division between private and public responsibilities. The relationship between neoliberalism and non-normative sexualities is ambivalent (Binnie 2010). The shrinking of the welfare state further privatizes responsibility for economic well-being and poverty becomes a personal responsibility. Women are expected to be both market workers and private sphere caregivers. If a single mother fails to take market opportunities, she is regarded as less than a full citizen. Even the increasing legal recognition of same-sex relationships reinforces "private welfare" within the family, as the state rolls back public responsibility. Responsible sexual citizens are expected to make the right personal choices, including about sex and safety risks (Gotell 2008). The consequences of this reconfiguring of private/public forms the subject of future study.

SEE ALSO: Division of Labor, Gender; Gendered Space; Personal is Political; Privatization

REFERENCES

Binnie, Jon. 2010. "Queer Theory, Neoliberalism and Urban Governance." In *Queer Theory, Law, Culture, Empire*, edited by Robert Leckey and Kim Brooks, 21–36. London: Routledge.

Brickell, Chris. 2010. "Heroes and Invaders: Gay and Lesbian Pride Parades and the Public/Private Distinction in New Zealand Media Accounts." *Gender, Place and Culture: A Journal of Feminist Geography*, 7(2): 163–178.

Elshtain, Jean Bethke. 1982/1983. "Homosexual Politics: The Paradox of Gay Liberation." *Salmagundi*, 58–59: 252–280.

Fineman, Martha Albertson. 2004. *The Autonomy Myth*. New York: The New Press.

Gotell, Lise. 2008. "Rethinking Affirmative Consent in Canadian Sexual Assault Law: Neoliberal Sexual Subjects and Risky Women." *Akron Law Review*, 41(4): 865–888.

Hansen, Bert. 2002. "Public Careers and Private Sexuality: Some Gay and Lesbian Lives in the History of Medicine and Public Health." *American Journal of Public Health*, 92(1): 36–44.

Okin, Susan Moller. 1989. *Justice, Gender, and the Family*. New York: Basic Books.

Pateman, Carole. 1989. *The Disorder of Women: Democracy, Feminism and Political Theory*. Stanford: Stanford University Press.

FURTHER READING

Ball, Carlos A. 2008. "Privacy, Property, and Public Sex." *Columbia Journal of Gender and Law*, 18(1): 1–60.

Boyd, Susan B., ed. 1997. *Challenging the Public/Private Divide: Feminism, Law, and Public Policy*. Toronto: University of Toronto Press.

O'Donovan, Katherine. 1985. *Sexual Divisions in Law*. London: Weidenfeld & Nicolson.

Thornton, Margaret, ed. 1995. *Public and Private: Feminist Legal Debates*. Melbourne: Oxford University Press.

Privatization

ROSE M. BREWER
University of Minnesota Twin Cities, USA

An analysis of privatization must begin with understanding the current logic of capitalism. This logic is rooted in neoliberalism. Neoliberalism is an approach to economy expressed in the idea that the market is the most efficient way to use and allocate resources (Starr 1988). In practice, this involves, among other actions, making prisons, schools, water, and so on, private. It entails "deregulation of industries, free trade agreements and structural adjustment programs" (Starr 1988). Resources are moved from the social sector to the private sector. In short, privatization as the primary political economic tool of neoliberal capitalism shifts the locus of the economy from public resources to private accumulation. When public enterprises owned and controlled by government are placed in the control and ownership of the private sector, the logic of privatization is expressed. The privatization process is broad, "from education to water, health care to public lands, contracting out and outsourcing" (*Monthly Review* 2003). Since the market is deemed the best guarantor of a robust economy for a profit-driven economy, private sector competition is privileged as the mechanism to achieve high profits.

Thus twenty-first-century privatization represents the increasing takeover of public goods by private corporations. Moreover, the logic of privatization is deeply ideological. It is expressed in the idea that the private sector can do economy best. Public ownership is painted as wasteful and inefficient. Government spending is treated as a drain on the economy and should be eliminated. The idea that competitiveness, individualism, and private ownership are foundational virtues are infused in the discourses centered on privatization. In sum, privatization expresses an ideological shift in the role of the state. It entails the explicit transfer of public assets to private ownership through sale or lease (Starr 1988), and it is a key ideological logic of advanced capitalism.

THE RISE OF NEOLIBERAL PRIVATIZATION

In the 1980s in the United Kingdom and the United States under the leadership of Margaret Thatcher and Ronald Reagan, the push for austerity-reduced public spending and privatization were the core policies of Thatcherism and Reaganism. Under Ronald

Reagan, a discourse of undeservedness was utilized to question welfare benefits to mothers (so-called welfare queens) with dependent children. The target was black mothers, so it was a racist/sexist narrative. The discourse centered on cutting AFDC (Aid to Families with Dependent Children) as a government program. Under Thatcherism, British markets were expanded into the public sector involving the selling of key industries and sectors to the private sector (*Monthly Review* 2003).

The World Trade Organization (WTO), established in 1995, is an international structure built to promote neoliberal free-market principles. Public goods were to be opened up to privatization and free trade. For example, in Senegal in West Africa, which was colonized by the French, structural adjustment was the policy required by transnational financial entities such as the International Monetary Fund (IMF) and World Bank for economic development. For a number of years under structural adjustment, resources in the Senegalese import sector were highly priced. Those goods in the export sector received little in terms of cash for goods. In other words, Senegal under the conditionalities of structural adjustment had to reduce its public sector spending and re-channel investments into the private sector. This concentrated resources into those industries that would benefit transnational corporations (Moody 1997).

Capital is organized. The transnational corporations are supranational entities with their own laws that transcend those of any particular nation state (Kloby 1999). In advanced economic societies and developing countries, neoliberal capitalism operating under the principle of privatization is a key feature of today's globalization. Agreements such as the North American Free Trade Agreement (NAFTA) and the General Agreement on Tariffs and Trade (GATT) and also other policies of international financial institutions create the conditions for this integration. For example, as Parenti (1995) pointed out, the WTO could by-pass the laws/regulations of any nation, i.e., environmental, social, labor laws, and so on. David Harvey calls the neoliberal process "accumulation by dispossession" (Harvey 2007). Prisons in the United States articulate neoliberal privatization in an advanced capitalist society.

THE PRIVATIZATION OF PRISONS IN THE UNITED STATES

In the United States, the privatization of prisons is strikingly indicative of this process of accumulation by dispossession. A disproportionate number of those incarcerated are black and brown men, although the incarceration rate for black and brown women is growing (Davis 2003). Money is made off the pain and suffering of the incarcerated. According to a recent study (Black Education for Liberation 2013), nearly 10 percent of US prisons and jails (meaning over 200,000 prisoners) have been privatized. The three largest firms in the prison-for-profit business are CCA, Wackenhut Corrections Corporation, and Cornell Corrections, Inc. "The federal government also contracts with these corporations to house a growing number of undocumented immigrants and resident aliens" asserts the researchers. Some of the companies also have facilities in countries outside the United States (Black Education for Liberation 2013). Corrections Corporation, for example, is "involved with the privatization of foreign services and systems" (Black Education for Liberation 2013).

The research findings of Black Prison USA cited by Talking Drum (2015) indicate that "in addition to the prison owners, profiteers also appear in the form of interest groups, all seeking economic opportunity." Architecture firms, construction companies, and investment banks provide the means to construct these private prisons, and a slew of other entities benefit (Talking Drum 2015).

In sum, placing public goods in the hands of private ownership is the signature feature of privatization. It works to the benefit of global corporations as transnational capitalism pushes to move all goods and services into the market for profit.

SEE ALSO: Informal Economy; Poverty in Global Perspective; Structural Adjustment

REFERENCES

Black Education for Liberation. 2013. Black Prison USA. Accessed October 28, 2014, at www.blackeducator.org/blackprisonusa.htm.
Davis, Angela. 2003. *Are Prisons Obsolete?* New York: Seven Stories Press.
Harvey, David. 2007. *A Brief History of Neoliberalism*. New York: Oxford University Press.
Kloby, J. 1999. *Inequality Power and Development*. New York: Humanity Books.
Monthly Review (2003) "Neoliberalism." *Monthly Review*, 54(8), January: 4–16.
Moody, Kim. 1997. *Workers in a Lean World: Unions in the International Economy*. London: Verso.
Parenti, Michael. 1995. *Against Empire*. San Francisco: City Lights Books.
Starr, Paul. 1988. "The Meaning of Privatization," *Yale Law and Policy Review*, 6: 6–20.
Talking Drum. 2015. The Prison Industrial Complex. Accessed September 5, 2015, at http://www.thetalkingdrum.com/prison.html.

FURTHER READING

Mansfield, Becky. 2004. "Rules of Privatization: Contradictions in Neoliberal Regulation of North Pacific Fisheries." *Annals of the Association of American Geographers*, 94(3): 565–584. Accessed August 23, 2013, at http://www.uky.edu/~tmute2/geography_methods/readingPDFs/mansfield_rules-privatiz.pdf.

Privilege

DAMIEN W. RIGGS
Flinders University of South Australia, Australia

The concept of privilege as used within both research and activism refers to the socially determined attribution of value to particular individuals on the basis of their group membership, and the unearned advantages that arise as a result of this attribution. The attribution of value – or what has been referred to as cultural capital – to particular groups results from the structuring of societies on the basis of particular social norms. Such norms are not necessarily the statistical norm, but rather are determined by the group that occupies a position of dominance through the historical assertion of power. In this sense, the accrual of privilege to particular groups of people is the product of historical factors (such as slavery, patriarchy, and colonization) that have served to legitimate certain groups of people as the norm against which all others are compared.

Importantly, the concept of privilege goes beyond simply stating that unearned advantages are accrued on the basis of group membership. Privilege is also something that individuals to whom it is accorded due to their social group membership are invested in maintaining. In other words, living in a world where particular groups of people are valued over others (and indeed at the expense of others) is only one part of how privilege works. The other part is how members of dominant social groups are willing to perpetuate historically unjust modes of distributing social, cultural, symbolic, and economic capital, primarily to their own benefit. Thus, whilst much of the academic and activist writing on privilege emphasizes the fact that those situated within a particular norm do not see the privilege they hold, such an assertion must be tempered by recognition of the investment that those within a given norm will differentially hold in maintaining their position of privilege in order to continue to benefit from the advantages that come with their group membership.

One way of understanding the operations of privilege involves the use of examples that highlight how privilege operates to make certain experiences commonplace or taken for granted by those positioned within a given norm. In terms of gender, examples of male privilege include:

- As a male I can be confident that the ordinary language of day-to-day existence will always include my sex, such as in sayings (e.g., "all men are created equal") and in categories (e.g., mailman, chairman).
- As a male I will never be expected to change my name upon marriage or questioned if I don't change my name.
- As a male, if I have children and a career, no one will think I'm selfish for not staying at home.
- As a male, I can most often walk alone at night without the fear of being raped or otherwise harmed.

These examples range from the mundane to the more explicitly violent, as is the case with most such lists exemplifying privilege. Importantly, these examples highlight that the privileges accorded to certain groups are unearned – there is nothing inherent to men as a category that should entitle them to feeling safe in public spaces. In terms of sexual orientation, examples of heterosexual privilege include:

- As a heterosexual student, I can be sure that curricula materials will present my sexual orientation positively.
- As a heterosexual parent, my children will not be taunted or bullied because of my sexual orientation.
- As a heterosexual person, the media can represent someone of my sexual orientation performing an act of intimacy such as kissing without this being considered remarkable.

More recently, recognition has been given to the privilege associated with being cisgendered, defined as inhabiting a gender identity that normatively accords with that expected of one's natally assigned sex (i.e., not being transgender). Examples of cisgender privilege include:

- As a cisgender person, if I am institutionalized I don't have to worry about being housed in the wrong section of a facility segregated by sex.
- As a cisgender person, it is highly unlikely that at my funeral my family would present me cross-dressed against my living wishes.
- As a cisgender person, I can be confident that people will not call me by a different name or use incorrect pronouns.

Importantly, none of these forms of privilege exist in isolation from one another. Rather, and as proponents of intersectionality theory have argued, identity categories should not be understood in isolation from one another, but instead as simultaneously occurring (and thus as simultaneously producing privilege and/or disadvantage). For example, a white middle-class cisgendered gay man might experience discrimination living in a heteronormative and homophobic society, but he will do so as someone who holds considerable privilege on the basis of living in a society where the majority of the identity categories he inhabits are privileged. Understanding privilege as the accumulation of benefits resulting from social norms thus allows for an understanding of how each individual lives in relation to a range of social norms that shape their experiences and accord either advantage or disadvantage.

As a concept, then, privilege both names a set of historical contingencies that are often left unnamed, and engenders the need for responsibility for privilege. In other words, the concept of privilege is typically used within research and by activists not simply to speak of privilege, but to question how it operates, what benefits it produces for those who occupy a place within a dominant social group, and to consider how it can be challenged. Importantly, this is not to claim that any given individual can necessarily step outside of their privileged location, but rather that they might reconsider what they do from that location, and how they can be better accountable for, and refuse to actively perpetuate, the privilege they hold.

SEE ALSO: Cisgender and Cissexual; Cisgenderism; Heterosexism and Homophobia; Intersectionality; Patriarchy; Sexism

FURTHER READING

Anderson, Sharon K., and Valeria A. Middleton, eds. 2010. *Explorations in Privilege, Oppression and Diversity*. Belmont: Brooks/Cole.

Crenshaw, Kimberlé M. 1991. "Mapping the Margins: Intersectionality, Identity Politics, and Violence Against Women of Color." *Stanford Law Review*, 43: 1241–1299.

Fish, Julie. 2006. *Heterosexism in Health and Social Care*. London: Palgrave Macmillan.

Kimmel, Michael S., and Abby L. Ferber, eds. 2003. *Privilege: A Reader*. Boulder: Westview Press.

Lamont, Michèle, and Annette Lareau. 1988. "Cultural Capital: Allusions, Gaps and Glissandos in Recent Theoretical Developments." *Sociological Theory*, 6: 153–168.

McIntosh, Peggy. 1999. "White Privilege: Unpacking the Invisible Knapsack." *Independent School*, 49: 31–36.

Nakamura, Lisa. 2012. "Queer Female of Color: The Highest Difficulty Setting There Is? Gaming Rhetoric as Gender Capital." *Ada: A Journal of Gender, New Media, and Technology*, 1. DOI: 10.7264/N37P8W9V.

Pro-Choice Movement in the United States

MALLARY ALLEN
Concordia College, USA

Contemporary pro-choice movements in the United States are built upon decades of evolving activism. The message of legislators and activists seeking to make abortion an option for women in medical crisis in the 1960s was quite different from the beliefs and protest slogans used to champion legal abortion on demand in the early 1970s. In turn, the sentiments of pro-choice Democrats, who today comprise a reproductive rights movement which has gone mainstream, are far removed from those of their second-wave feminist predecessors. On the other side of the abortion rights debate, the rhetorical tactics of a newly visible and angry anti-abortion movement in the 1980s and early 1990s are very different from the strategies of "street counselors" and prayerful activists holding vigils in front of clinics in the 2000s. In order to understand the meanings and strategies of contemporary pro-choice movements, we must understand the tactics of earlier activists as well as some of the history of their opponents in the pro-life movement.

Abortion has not always been a legal, nor even a medical, issue in the United States. Just as all issues concerning women's bodies and procreation were once private concerns to be managed by women, individually and communally and often with the aid of learned healers and midwives, methods of terminating viable pregnancies predate organized, male-centered medical practice. As medicine grew as a profession in the United States throughout the 1900s, physicians eager to elevate the status of their discipline sought authority over numerous bodily processes and conditions, childbirth perhaps chief among them. Displacing midwives and outlawing one of the most sought-after services they offered, abortion, was paramount to the gradual legal and social campaign which established the preeminence of professional medicine and led to the outlawing of abortion in all US states by 1900.

Women continued to seek and receive abortions in the succeeding decades through various means, some in safer settings and in more capable hands than others. Furthermore, debates surrounding abortion and the other means of birth control available prior to the 1960s differed greatly in comparison to those of subsequent decades. Early feminists varied in their orientations to birth control. Before suffrage became the unifying cause of turn-of-the-century feminists we today refer to as feminism's *first wave*, many educated and socially concerned women (as well as male reformers) drew attention to women's sexual rights within marriage – sexual abuse, the right to refuse sex, and the right to avoid pregnancy being chief issues of concern. Many of these early feminists did not advocate contraception, however, and believed that the use of even strategies like coitus interruptus would debase the status of married women; without the responsibilities accompanying procreative sex, many feared that a wife's social value would fall to that of a prostitute. As such, many feminists of this time advocated women's voluntary participation in marriage and in marital sexuality but endorsed strategic periods of abstinence as the solution to growing popular desires to control fertility.

Nonetheless, the turn of the twentieth century saw significant progress in contraceptive technology and its distribution, even as abortion remained one of the most reliable forms of birth control. Public indignation over women's use of illegal abortion did not fall evenly, however, as the fertility or infertility of some groups was seen as more problematic than others. These concerns were fueled by eugenics, or the then-popular "science of good breeding." While President Theodore Roosevelt, for instance, worried that the smaller families preferred by white middle-class women would threaten the genetic robustness of the US population as a whole (the term "race suicide" was widely used), concerns were reversed for poor, black, immigrant, and Native American women, whose families were deemed too big by social critics. Accordingly, Margaret Sanger's eventual success in opening the United States' first contraceptive clinic in a poor and largely immigrant neighborhood in New York City may be largely due to her claims that such clinics would reduce fertility among undesirable groups and to many of her supporters' fears of higher birth rates among non-whites. With regard to abortion, which was not openly advocated by eugenicists or feminists, it remained an important and reliable, albeit secretive and illegal, form of birth control well into the 1900s – some groups' use of it, as discussed above, more offensive to the larger culture than others'.

By the 1960s, the possibility of safe and legal abortions existed in many states, but doctors, and not their patients, were the sole determiners of when and in what situations an abortion was warranted. A social movement calling for *abortion reform* emerged in the 1960s as a moderate solution to inconsistencies which led to, for instance, women gaining access to abortion for nausea but being denied by the same doctors when pregnant due to rape or incest. Advocating for reform several years before the mobilization of the women's movement, these reformers did not necessarily call themselves feminists and counted among their ranks members of professional organizations and clergy members of liberal Jewish and Christian denominations.

Democratic and Republican women alike, many of them mothers, lobbied for a compromise which would allow women to terminate pregnancies in a range of circumstances. In fact, a regional children's television host, Sherri Finkbine, became a national symbol of the reform movement in 1962 when she was unable to procure an abortion in the United States after discovering that her prescription medication had likely caused serious complications for her pregnancy. Married mothers like Finkbine were the imagined beneficiaries of the reform movement, and tragic circumstances like hers provided inspiration for the movement's relatively moderate goals.

Reform forged ahead in many states and led to the establishment of review panels – groups of physicians and psychiatrists assembled to consider individual requests for abortions. By all accounts, reform made abortion much more accessible to women in some states. Foundational abortion movement scholar Kristen Luker cites a 2,000 percent increase in the number of recorded abortions performed in California just four years after the reform measures signed by then-governor Ronald Reagan took effect (1984, 94).

This moderate solution to reform, whereby doctors were situated as moral gatekeepers to procedures, was not satisfactory to everyone however. Adherents of feminism's newly visible second wave instead rallied in the late 1960s and early 1970s for safe medical terminations on demand and worked to situate the social consequences of motherhood, and not merely the physical health and safety of women and fetuses, as primary considerations surrounding abortion access. In 1973, the US Supreme Court ruled favorably for abortion on demand – the victory of the favorable three-part ruling (a separate and increasingly restrictive ruling for each trimester of pregnancy) tied closely to the efforts of second-wave feminists and their legal, journalistic, and activist efforts in the years leading to the case (and enduring thereafter).

For feminists of this era, abortion, like equal pay, was a civil rights issue – the ability to control one's fertility seen as an essential component of one's ability to participate in the economy on equal footing with men. At the same time, many middle-class women's desires to have fulfilling careers existed alongside the reality that the post-World War II ideal of the breadwinner–homemaker family, an arrangement achieved by a booming middle class in the 1950s but certainly not by all Americans, was becoming less attainable amid structural and economic change – even for white, middle-class women raised in the very suburbs that represented this fantasy for their parents' generation. A changing economy meant that society was increasingly unable, and perhaps culturally unwilling, to support women's omission from paid labor. (Consider, as Barbara Ehrenreich (1983) points out, the inception of *Playboy* magazine in 1953 and its contempt for the "parasitic housewife" – a sentiment that would continue to grow in popular culture throughout the 1960s alongside middle-class women's public sector ambitions.) Whether women desired occupations outside the home or held them out of necessity, the second wave drew attention to the social consequences of childbearing and demanded women's autonomy in making abortion decisions for whatever reason.

In addition to second-wave feminists' successful framing of abortion as a civil right much more than a medical issue, they also encouraged the public to imagine abortion contexts differently. While 1960s reformers highlighted stories of married mothers seeking abortion for medical reasons, the subsequent feminist message of the 1970s was one which applied abortion rights to single women as well, and those seeking abortion in a variety of circumstances. As the second wave was largely and visibly comprised of young, white, middle-class college-educated women, abortion became decoupled from earlier assumptions of abortion seekers as wives and mothers and shifted instead to images of young, single, liberated women perhaps encumbered by immediate educational goals and new careers; that is, abortion became associated with a new life stage – that of the teen and young adult rather than the married mother. This is not to say, however, that women necessarily began to access abortion differently; currently, and not much differently from decades past, mothers (at 60 percent of abortion patients) are a significant demographic, while poor women and women of color (and not middle-class college students) are overrepresented in official counts (Jones, Finer, and Singh 2010).

Thus, the years before and after Roe saw perhaps the broadest and most radical rhetoric with regard to abortion rights (whether single, white, middle-class advocates were representative of typical abortion seekers or not). This time period produced many recognizable and defiant slogans – "Keep your laws off my body" and "A woman's body, a woman's choice" – illustrate the general message. In addition to the verbal rhetoric prominent on signs and speeches associated with pro-choice demonstrations, the image of the coat hanger became a powerful symbol for the second wave and was used to symbolize the threat that illegal abortions (often performed with coat hangers and other sharp objects) posed to women's lives and safety without access to safe procedures. Amidst the dangers of such procedures, many feminist groups across the United States combined advocacy with efforts to connect women with safe abortion services. One such group, the Jane Collective in Chicago, provides a notable example as its members became trained in safe abortion techniques and then provided abortions to women directly, in spite of the illegality of abortion in Illinois at that time.

In addition to public activism and underground actions, the early 1970s also saw the institutionalization of several pro-choice social movement organizations. On the rhetorical front, in 1972, during its first year in operation, feminist magazine *Ms.* published a list of high-profile women who had had abortions. Several instrumental political and legal pro-choice organizations also took shape during these years, including the still-enduring National Abortion Federation and NARAL Pro-Choice America (originally The National Association to Repeal Abortion Laws). In 1972, the National Organization for Women (NOW) also made abortion rights one of its central, unifying causes.

Social movement organizations like these continue to mobilize resources to defend abortion rights against legal and political challenges. Meanwhile, the character and message of pro-choice movements, especially the activism most visible to the American public, has undergone significant change – more radical feminist messages gradually usurped by more moderate ones by the 1990s. The seeds of this moderating transition exist in the early movement for abortion on demand itself, as the pro-choice cause has received less vocal support from moderate advocates since the days of abortion reform.

In the first presidential nominating convention to follow *Roe v. Wade*, for instance, the Democratic platform is ambivalently supportive and states, "We fully recognize the religious and ethical nature of the concerns which many Americans have on the subject of abortion. We feel, however, that it is undesirable to attempt to amend the US Constitution to overturn the Supreme Court decision in this area" (Democratic National Committee 1976). More interestingly in light of its present-day pro-life character, the Republican Party did not take an explicit stance against abortion until 1980 and in its 1976 presidential platform acknowledged a party divided in its attitude towards abortion; without endorsing a position for or against, it merely observed, "The question of abortion is one of the most difficult and controversial of our time. It is undoubtedly a moral and personal issue but it also involves complex questions relating to medical science and criminal justice" (Republican National Committee 1976).

Throughout the 1980s, abortion remained ambiguous for both mainstream parties. Democrats, while upholding legal abortion in their 1980 national platform, recognized "religious and ethical concerns" (DNC 1980); Republicans likewise acknowledged a concern for "equality of rights under the law" but finally asserted support for "the right to life for unborn children" (RNC 1980). The most visible activism concerning the issue of abortion, then, remained the work of more unapologetic feminists into the 1980s, as well as an increasingly formidable rival – that of the angry and, at times, violent pro-life activist. Where pro-life efforts had previously been the terrain of US Catholics – often prayerful, sometimes verbally aggressive – it was during the 1980s that highly publicized violence against doctors and clinics, associated with a small and radical pro-life fringe, peaked and took center stage.

By the late 1980s, activism associated with both sides of the abortion rights debate changed significantly in terms of tactics and rhetoric. While violence against doctors and clinics continued throughout the 1990s and persists to this day, the late 1980s saw the dawn of the Christian Conservative and a growing emphasis on Evangelical Christianity in the Republican Party. Mainstream Republicans joined the enduring ranks of Catholics to comprise the most visible faction of the pro-life movement. Increasingly, activists shifted from shouting accusations of murder at women entering clinics and instead positioned themselves as "sidewalk counselors," shouting offers of help with medical care and infant supplies; others simply held quiet, prayerful vigils. Crisis pregnancy centers opened, and successful legal challenges to abortion access increased in the political arena.

By the 1990s, pro-choice activism was changing in response to the mainstream successes of pro-life rhetoric and politicians. During this time, pro-choice activists observed that many Americans' feelings about abortion were more in line with recent successful campaigns to limit abortion access than they were with 1970s demands for access to abortion no matter what. The watershed Supreme Court ruling in *Webster v. Reproductive Health Services* (1989), which prohibits the use of public funds, facilities, and personnel in elective abortion procedures and allows states to allocate resources to promote childbirth and adoption, is a case in point. Tonn (1996) suggests that major pro-choice figures thus scrambled in the early 1990s to appeal to a broader base which could encompass what they saw as an average American's gradualist views of fetal life and notions of sexual and personal responsibility.

Advocates began to uphold moral and emotional anguish as the undesirable – but inherent – features of abortion, emphasizing that all women strive to make a moral though arduous and painful decision when choosing abortion. Familiarly, the new rhetoric emphasized the pain and feelings of loss associated with abortion in cases of fetal abnormalities as well as the torment of pregnant women who were raped, abandoned, and/or seriously ill.

The mid-1990s saw what a new generation of feminists with a broad array of issues and orientations termed the *third wave*, many representatives of which would expand upon the rhetoric of abortion as a sad necessity.

Third-wave forerunner Naomi Wolf, for instance, called for a new pro-choice rhetoric in an influential essay published in *The New Republic* wherein she asserts the need to "fight to defend abortion rights within a moral framework that admits that the death of a fetus is a real death; that there are degrees of culpability, judgment and responsibility involved in the decision to abort a pregnancy" (1995, 26). Further, she calls for "an abortion-rights movement willing publicly to mourn the evil – necessary evil though it may be – that is abortion" (Wolf 1995, 28). Importantly, Wolf calls for a split with previous generations' pro-choice activism she characterizes as cold and out of touch. She says in summary, "Grief and respect are the proper tones for all discussions about choosing to endanger or destroy a manifestation of life" (Wolf 1995, 33).

The most visible pro-choice activism since the 1990s has been much more consistent with Wolf's conceptualization than with the defiant tone of the second-wave feminists whose efforts we so closely tie to the legalization of abortion on demand. With the more moderate, moral tone, mainstream and activist positions on abortion largely became one in the same. The conversations concerning abortion rights which were part of Bill Clinton's campaigns and presidency established the language of rarity and grief for the mainstream pro-choice movement during this time.

While Clinton's administration arguably secured abortion rights to a greater extent than was true in the years immediately following Webster, requisite patient anguish and increased scrutiny of the abortion decision by pro-choice advocates were cemented. Mirroring Wolf and other new feminist voices, Clinton famously proclaimed in his 1996 speech to the Democratic National Convention that, "Abortion should not only be safe and legal, it should be rare," ushering new language into his party's platform that would remain there in various wording until 2008.

Throughout the 1990s, major pro-choice campaign leaders spread the new movement's message of legal but less, necessary but sad. Slogans resonant in the 1970s like, "A woman's body, a woman's choice" existed alongside the more temperate refrain of "safe, legal, and rare." Hillary Rodham Clinton has exuded this moral gravity in regard to the abortion issue throughout her own political career, describing herself as personally opposed to abortion (i.e., asserting that she would not personally have an abortion) and describing the abortion decision as sad and even tragic for many women (Berns 2011).

Pro-choice movements have retained much of this moral emphasis throughout the 2000s and have seen new trajectories emerge as well. The early 2000s saw an elaboration of abortion's characterization by third-wave feminists as difficult and sad with the founding of Exhale, an organization with an online and telephone hotline presence which describes itself as offering an apolitical forum for women to discuss negative emotions following an abortion. While affirming abortion rights, the organization has also coined and applied to itself the label of *pro-voice*, rather than pro-choice. In line with the idea that abortion rights activism should promote difficult emotional and moral discussions seen as neglected by second-wave feminists, activist Jennifer Baumgardner launched a documentary, book, and *I Had an Abortion* t-shirt campaign to highlight the abortion stories of high-profile women. In her campaign, Baumgardner also advocates the reduction of later term abortions through contraceptive efforts and greater access to early procedures.

Media technologies, like the website and documentary cited above, have played a significant role in the pro-choice activism of the early 2000s. Other visible pro-choice activism during this time included the website

ImNotSorry.net, a forum displaying abortion experience stories contributed by hundreds of anonymous submitters. Interestingly, the site's irreverent moniker in particular and perhaps the upbeat tone of most of its content have drawn criticism from therapeutic and morally centered pro-choice campaigns like those spearheaded by Exhale and Baumgardner.

Social media has also played an important role in pro-choice activism throughout the 2000s, one notable example highlighting the roles of websites like Twitter and Facebook as well as the increasingly prominent place of pro-choice politicians – the latter a growing source of support amid spikes in legislative efforts to restrict abortion throughout the 2000s. In 2013, Democratic representative Wendy Davis held an 11-hour-long filibuster to block one such bill in the Texas House. Davis's filibuster was covered by C-SPAN and followed widely. During the filibuster, Davis read excerpts from abortion stories that women from across the country were sending her via social media in real time.

A commitment to protecting abortion rights was also a prominent feature of Barrack Obama's presidential campaigns. In 2008 and 2012, the Democratic National Convention featured speeches by Cecile Richards, president of Planned Parenthood – the nation's largest abortion provider and an important source of advocacy for the pro-choice movement. In 2008, the party's national platform also removed the language of "rare" abortion, affirming instead that the party "strongly and unequivocally supports *Roe v. Wade* and a woman's right to choose a safe and legal abortion, regardless of ability to pay" (DNC 2008).

In addition to the efforts of mainstream politicians and activists whose support has secured the Democratic Party as a major component of the contemporary mainstream pro-choice movement, the early 2000s heralded the beginnings of some new trajectories as well. In 2004, NARAL Pro-Life America, in partnership with other feminist and civil rights organizations including Black and Latina reproductive health advocacy groups, sponsored the March for Women's Lives in Washington DC. Attended by more than 1 million people, it was, by many accounts, the largest demonstration of its kind. Importantly, the march, whose purpose was mainly the support of abortion rights, chose its explicit emphasis on "Women's Lives" rather than "Choice" to reflect a larger reproductive rights message.

With multiracial and multiethnic leadership, the march drew attention to the emergent activist concept of reproductive justice, or support for women's rights to abortion as well as their rights to prenatal care, privacy, and autonomy during pregnancy, and the right to have and raise children in safe and healthy environments. Contemporary advocates for reproductive choice have observed that previous generations of pro-choice activism have ignored the experiences of women of color and poor women, who are overrepresented among abortion seekers and who also face significant barriers to having and raising children while endowed with the same rights and resources that wealthier and white families tend to enjoy. The March for Women's Lives was conceptualized by many of its organizers and participants as an effort to address these deficits in traditional pro-choice activism.

In the years since the march, advocacy groups like National Advocates for Pregnant Women, founded in 2001, have encountered successes, including interviews on National Public Radio, in drawing attention to the civil rights violations of pregnant women, including state laws allowing for the arrests of pregnant drug users, while also advocating for full abortion rights. Newly visible directions, like the emphasis on reproductive justice, as well as the persistence and elaboration of old themes like unapologetic abortion (harkening to the 1970s) or abortion advocacy with attention to emotion and morality (reminiscent of the 1990s) illustrate the ever-evolving nature of America's most visible pro-choice movements. The roles of new media and vocal Democratic politicians point to new forums into which activism may continue to expand.

SEE ALSO: Abortion and Religion; Birth Control, History and Politics of; Eugenics, Historical and Ethical Aspects of; Family Wage; Feminism, Liberal; Feminisms, First, Second, and Third Wave; Feminist Activism; Feminist Movements in Historical and Comparative Perspective; Feminist Organizations, Definition of; Pro-Life Movement in the United States; Reproductive Justice and Reproductive Rights in the United States

REFERENCES

Berns, Nancy. 2011. *Closure: The Rush to End Grief and What It Costs Us*. New York: Temple University Press.
Democratic National Committee (DNC). 1976. Democratic Party Platform of 1976. The American Presidency Project. Accessed September 15, 2012, at www.presidency.ucsb.edu/platforms.php.
Democratic National Committee. 1980. Democratic Party Platform of 1980. The American Presidency Project. Accessed September 15, 2012, at www.presidency.ucsb.edu/platforms.php.
Democratic National Committee. 2008. Democratic Party Platform of 2008. The American Presidency Project. Accessed September 15, 2012, at www.presidency.ucsb.edu/platforms.php.
Ehrenreich, Barbara. 1983. *The Hearts of Men: American Dreams and the Flight from Commitment*. New York: Anchor.
Jones, Rachel K., Lawrence B. Finer, and Susheela Singh. 2010. *Characteristics of US Abortion Patients, 2008*. New York: Guttmacher Institute.
Luker, Kristen. 1984. *Abortion and the Politics of Motherhood*. Berkeley: University of California Press.
Republican National Committee (RNC). 1976. Republican Party Platform of 1976. The American Presidency Project. Accessed September 15, 2012, at www.presidency.ucsb.edu/platforms.php.
Republican National Committee. 1980. Republican Party Platform of 1980. The American Presidency Project. Accessed September 15, 2012, at www.presidency.ucsb.edu/platforms.php.
Tonn, Mari Boor. 1996. "Donning Sackcloth and Ashes: *Webster v. Reproductive Health Services* and Moral Agony in Abortion Rights Rhetoric." *Communication Quarterly*, 44(3): 265–279.
Wolf, Naomi. 1995. "Our Bodies, Our Souls." *The New Republic*, October 16: 26–35.

FURTHER READING

Gordon, Linda. 1973. "Voluntary Motherhood: The Beginnings of Feminist Birth Control Ideas in the United States." *Feminist Studies*, 1(3–4): 5–22.
Roberts, Dorothy. 1997. *Killing the Black Body: Race, Reproduction, and the Meaning of Liberty*. New York: Vintage.

Pro-Life Movement in the United States

DANIEL K. WILLIAMS
University of West Georgia, USA

The pro-life movement is a grassroots campaign to restrict or prohibit abortion in public law and persuade women not to terminate their pregnancies. Pro-lifers argue that human life begins at conception, so the law should therefore protect prenatal life at every stage of development.

The pro-life movement has influenced abortion legislation throughout the world, but it is most active in the United States, where it began in the mid-twentieth century as a reaction against a movement to legalize abortion. It emerged as a national political force in the early 1970s, becoming especially visible after the United States Supreme Court required the legalization of abortion throughout the nation in the landmark case *Roe v. Wade* (1973). Though pro-lifers have not yet achieved their primary goal of securing full legal protection for fetal life, they have succeeded in restricting the availability of abortion in many parts of the United States and other countries and in reshaping the public debate over abortion.

THE PRO-LIFE MOVEMENT IN SCHOLARSHIP

Despite the pro-life movement's political significance, it is an understudied topic in academia. Scholars are only beginning to write about the movement, and many aspects of the topic have not been adequately covered in academic literature, in spite of the attempts of sociologists, historians, political scientists, legal scholars, and partisans on both sides of the abortion debate to apply the tools of their scholarly disciplines to the study of pro-life activism. While scholars such as David Garrow have produced detailed, sweeping histories of the pro-choice movement, no one has yet written a similarly comprehensive, 50-year history of the pro-life campaign.

The first sociological and historical monographs on the pro-life movement were not produced until the 1980s, but for two decades before that, legal scholars, physicians, philosophers, and advocates of abortion rights or pro-life ideology published numerous books and articles examining the legal and moral aspects of abortion. In the late 1960s and early 1970s pro-life Catholic professors such as Charles E. Rice and Germain Grisez published detailed philosophical defenses of the pro-life perspective that drew on natural law theory and biological science to argue that human personhood began at conception. These arguments still provide the framework for contemporary pro-life natural law philosophy, as seen in the work of current pro-life political theorists and philosophers such as Robert P. George, Christopher Tollefsen, and Francis Beckwith, who have applied some of Grisez's arguments to the question of embryonic stem-cell research and the continued debate over abortion.

When the first academic monographs on the pro-life movement appeared in the 1980s, much of the scholarship focused on the question of what motivated pro-life activists. This was a politically contentious question at the time, because pro-lifers claimed that they were motivated solely by a concern for unborn human life, while their opponents accused them of being anti-feminists who engaged in reproductive politics in order to restrict women's rights and control their sexuality. In 1984 sociologist Kristin Luker applied an academic perspective to this debate in her landmark study *Abortion and the Politics of Motherhood*. After conducting in-depth interviews with numerous pro-life and pro-choice women, Luker concluded that views of gender roles were the main determinant of whether a woman supported or opposed abortion rights. Women who viewed motherhood as a central facet of a woman's purpose and identity tended to be pro-life, while those who viewed motherhood as incidental to a woman's identity were more likely to be pro-choice. Because of its comprehensive coverage of the history, politics, and sociology of the abortion debate, Luker's study remained widely influential three decades after it was published, and its conclusions shaped the way that scholars viewed the pro-life movement.

Historians have also traced connections between the pro-life movement and the politics of gender, especially in regard to the politics of birth control. Studies of the history of birth control politics in the United States, such as those produced by Simone

Caron, Linda Gordon, and Leslie Reagan, have treated the abortion debate as part of this larger history, with the work of modern pro-life activists who oppose abortion portrayed as a direct descendant of Catholic campaigns against birth control in the early twentieth century.

Political scientists who have studied the pro-life movement have examined the effect that views of abortion have had on voter choices and partisan realignment, or the changes that have occurred in the pro-life movement's political strategy over time. Scholars also examined the relationship of the pro-life movement to the larger conservative cause, with some, such as Michele McKeegan, arguing that conservatives were divided on abortion, and that the pro-life movement occupied an uneasy place in the American conservative movement (McKeegan 1992).

Beginning in the late 1990s, several journalists and scholars published studies of anti-abortion violence. One of the most detailed of these studies, James Risen and Judy L. Thomas's *Wrath of Angels: The American Abortion War* (1998), traced the shift among a few activists in one wing of the pro-life movement from non-violent direct activism to violent attacks on abortion clinics and abortion doctors. Several other books on anti-abortion violence were published shortly thereafter, so today this remains one of the most widely covered aspects of the pro-life movement. Only a tiny percentage of pro-life activists have endorsed or participated in violent activities against abortionists, and the nation's largest pro-life organization, the National Right to Life Committee, has strongly condemned such violence, but this aspect of the pro-life movement has attracted attention from a number of scholars, serving as the focus of several monographs.

If the pro-life movement's activities in the United States have been under-studied, the international scope of the movement has received even less attention. Yet comparative international studies of abortion law may have the potential to provide insight into why abortion legalization became an issue of fervid political controversy in some countries – sparking a large pro-life backlash – while in other countries the subject was much less divisive. For instance, Mary Ann Glendon's *Abortion and Divorce in Western Law* (1987) argued that the process by which abortion was legalized in Western Europe, and the language in which the abortion laws were framed, ensured that abortion legalization in Europe was much less likely to be politically polarizing than it was in the United States.

Two new trends in the scholarship on the pro-life movement began to emerge in the twenty-first century: an interest in examining the history of the pro-life movement prior to *Roe v. Wade* and a greater interest in examining the religious and cultural dimensions of the pro-life movement. John McGreevy's *Catholicism and American Freedom: A History* (2003), which offered the first detailed study of the religious context of pro-life activism, argued that Catholic opposition to abortion legalization was directly related to a much longer history of Catholic ambivalence about conventional liberal views of individual autonomy. Sara Dubow's *Ourselves Unborn: A History of the Fetus in Modern America* (2011), which was a cultural history of American understandings of prenatal life, situated the modern abortion debate in the context of a much larger history of understandings of human personhood and human development, thus greatly enlarging upon the traditional historical narrative that examined pro-life activism primarily as a backlash against women's rights. McGreevy and Dubow's works acknowledged the presence of a vibrant pro-life movement prior to 1973, a phenomenon that scholars had long ignored. Linda Greenhouse and Reva Siegel's recent studies (2011) on abortion politics before *Roe* specifically focused on this early phase of the modern abortion debate and challenged traditional understandings of the movement by demonstrating that pro-life activism was not primarily a product of a popular backlash against a controversial Supreme Court decision, but was instead deeply rooted in religious, ethical, and political concerns that predated the Supreme Court's involvement in the issue.

Contemporary scholars who study the pro-life movement are still debating the central question that interested students of the movement in the 1980s – namely, the question of what motivates people to join the pro-life movement. Ziad Munson, who interviewed numerous pro-life activists as part of a sociological study that in some ways paralleled Luker's earlier work, has argued that many activists join the movement before their pro-life beliefs are fully formed, and that their decision to join the movement thus precedes their pro-life ideology (Munson 2008). While this theory has not yet had an effect on the way that most historians or those in other fields study the movement, it does offer an intriguing new perspective on an issue that continues to interest scholars in the field.

Up to this point, many scholars have framed their limited studies of pro-life activism largely in the language selected by the pro-choice movement – that is, language that focuses on reproductive rights and gender politics. But recent studies of the movement have suggested a variety of approaches that may produce a more complex picture of pro-life activism. By examining such issues as religious ideology, perceptions of the unborn, and diverse views of human freedom, a new generation of scholars is beginning to offer a picture of the pro-life movement that may challenge longstanding scholarly assumptions about the movement and offer new insight into the beliefs and behavior of a group of activists who have not yet received sufficient scholarly attention, despite their large numbers and growing political influence.

THE PRO-LIFE MOVEMENT IN POLITICS AND SOCIETY

Today the pro-life campaign is a large, religiously ecumenical political force, but when it first emerged in the United States in the mid-twentieth century, it was a small grassroots movement consisting mainly of devout Catholics. The movement emerged in reaction against an effort to overturn existing prohibitions on abortion in state laws in the United States, a campaign that began in the 1930s. These legal prohibitions against abortion had been in force in almost all states since the late nineteenth century, when a campaign by Protestant doctors had convinced state legislators to pass anti-abortion legislation in order to save fetal life and safeguard the standards of the medical profession. At the beginning of the twentieth century, the nation's leading newspapers, medical professionals, and clergy accepted these laws and expressed a general disapproval of abortion, but in the 1930s several Jewish and Protestant physicians and attorneys started calling for the legalization of "therapeutic" abortion in cases in which doctors believed the operation would benefit a pregnant woman's health or prevent the birth of a child with severe defects.

Although Protestant doctors and legislators created the late-nineteenth-century anti-abortion laws, Catholics became the staunchest opponents of abortion in the twentieth century, and Catholic physicians took the lead in opposing the first calls for abortion law liberalization. The Federation of Catholic Physicians' Guilds passed resolutions against abortion in 1937 and 1942. Despite their efforts, Catholic physicians were unable to stop a growing demand for the liberalization of state abortion laws. In 1959 the American Law Institute (ALI) advocated the legalization of abortion in cases of rape, incest, and suspected fetal deformity, as well as in cases in which abortion was necessary to protect a woman's health. This resolution sparked a campaign to liberalize state abortion laws, a campaign that accelerated in the early-to-mid 1960s as a result of increased public support for the legalization of abortion to prevent severe birth defects.

Catholics at first found themselves almost alone in their campaign to stop the legalization of "therapeutic" abortion, but nevertheless, they managed to block abortion law liberalization efforts for a few years. Catholic lawyers appealed to the scientific evidence of fetal development to argue that the law should continue to protect unborn human life from the moment of conception. They pointed out that the law treated fetuses as persons, since several state Supreme Court decisions had recognized the personhood of the fetus in tort cases involving prenatal injuries. The pro-life cause, they claimed, was based on the "due process" clause of the Fifth and Fourteenth Amendments, the "equal protection" clause of the Fourteenth Amendment, and the Declaration of Independence's proclamation of an inviolable "right to life" for all people.

The growing public sentiment in favor of abortion law liberalization – with more than three-quarters of the public favoring the legalization of abortion to protect a woman's health, according to a 1966 public opinion survey – allowed the proponents of abortion law liberalization to gain ground. In 1967, three states (Colorado, California, and North Carolina) legalized "therapeutic" abortion along the lines that ALI had suggested eight years earlier. Several more states followed suit shortly thereafter, so by the end of 1970, "therapeutic" abortion was legal in more than a dozen states.

The Catholic Church responded by encouraging the laity to organize a grassroots campaign against abortion, and pro-life Catholics made an effort to attract Protestant and Jewish allies to the cause. Cardinal James McIntyre, Archbishop of Los Angeles, helped Catholic lay professionals found the nation's first pro-life organization, the Right to Life League, in December 1966. In 1968, Fr. James McHugh, director of the US Catholic Conference's Family Life Bureau, created the National Right to Life Committee, which became the nation's largest pro-life organization.

At the end of the 1960s, pro-life women began moving into positions of leadership in the movement. From the beginning of the abortion debate, women were more likely than men to oppose abortion, but for most of the 1960s, male physicians, lawyers, and clergy had dominated the leadership ranks in organizations on both sides of the controversy. At the end of the 1960s, when women's rights advocates reframed the abortion legalization campaign as a battle for women's right to control their own bodies, women in the pro-life movement reacted by positing their own form of difference feminism – an ideology of gender that celebrated women's role as mothers – and taking the lead in speaking out on behalf of unborn life. Pro-life women such as Elizabeth Goodwin in California, Alice Hartle and Marjory Mecklenburg in Minnesota, Mildred Jefferson in Massachusetts, Gloria Klein in Michigan, and Carolyn Gerster in Arizona became leaders in their state pro-life organizations. In 1970 Mary Winter of Pittsburgh, Pennsylvania, founded Women Concerned for the Unborn Child to mobilize women for the cause. Most of these pro-life women, including Winter, were married, middle-class, white mothers, with Mildred Jefferson – a divorced African American Methodist doctor who had never had children – a rare exception to that profile.

Some pro-life women argued that abortion hurt the women who resorted to the procedure, and that it would be more compassionate to provide better prenatal care and social welfare assistance to women facing crisis pregnancies than to offer them abortion services. As the pro-life movement grew during this pre-*Roe* period, it became more politically diverse, with some members – especially college students – championing the causes of the Left, such as civil rights and opposition to the Vietnam War.

The pro-life movement suffered a few major defeats in 1970, when New York and three other states repealed almost all restrictions on abortion prior to the twentieth or twenty-fourth week of pregnancy, but after 1970, the movement blocked abortion legalization efforts in dozens of states. Between December 1970 and January 1973, only one state passed an abortion liberalization bill, and it did so only because of a court order. Although there were more than 500,000 legal abortions performed in the United States in 1972, the pro-life movement was successful in holding the line against additional legalization proposals in state legislatures.

The Supreme Court's ruling in *Roe v. Wade* (1973), which declared that women had a constitutional right to abortion during the first trimester of pregnancy and a mostly unrestricted right to abortion up to the point of viability, prompted the movement to change course once again. After *Roe*, the pro-life movement made passage of a Human Life Amendment (HLA), which would offer constitutional protection to human life from the moment of conception, its top priority. The National Right to Life Committee, which reconstituted itself in 1973 as an independent organization free of Catholic clerical control, led the movement into closer alliance with conservative Republican politicians as it looked for allies who would support the HLA. When the Republican Party adopted a platform endorsing an anti-abortion constitutional amendment in 1976, and when Ronald Reagan pledged his support for the HLA as a presidential candidate in 1980, pro-life leaders moved into the Republican Party – something they had not done in the 1960s or early 1970s.

As the pro-life movement in the United States continued to grow, the Catholic Church made pro-life work an international cause. Pope John Paul II's encyclical *Evangelium Vitae* (1985) denounced the legalization of abortion, and some heavily Catholic countries enacted prohibitions on the procedure. The Republic of Ireland instituted a constitutional ban on abortion in 1983. Human Life International, which Benedictine sociology professor Fr. Paul Marx founded in 1981, campaigned for greater restrictions on abortion throughout the world.

In the United States, the political mobilization of evangelicals in the late 1970s, which resulted in the formation of Christian Right organizations such as the Moral Majority, brought a new contingent of pro-lifers into the movement. The pro-life movement remained heavily Catholic, but after the early 1980s, many of the movement's staunchest supporters in Congress and among the voting public were evangelical Protestants. Yet while Catholics and evangelicals agreed on the need to oppose abortion, they sometimes disagreed about other priorities. In the 1980s many Catholics accepted Cardinal Joseph Bernardin's "seamless garment" life ethic, which combined opposition to abortion with opposition to the death penalty and nuclear arms build-up, treating all of these as "life" issues. A majority of evangelical Protestants, by contrast, supported capital punishment, and Christian Right leaders supported nuclear deterrence in order to fight communism.

For about five years after its founding in 1987, Randall Terry's Operation Rescue united thousands of Catholics and evangelical Protestants in a campaign of non-violent civil disobedience outside abortion clinics in order to shut the clinics down and "rescue" unborn children. The strategy attracted a lot of media attention and brought thousands of new volunteers into the pro-life movement. At least 40,000 pro-life activists went to jail for engaging in civil disobedience in front of abortion clinics. But the campaign probably did not produce many lasting benefits for the movement. Terry's confrontational tactics, though non-violent, were controversial; the National Right to Life Committee never approved of his strategy. When a few activists, especially those affiliated with the extremist anti-abortion organization Army of God, engaged in violence by bombing abortion clinics, and when five people in the 1990s murdered abortion doctors and their associates, there was a strong public backlash against the pro-life cause, even though most pro-life organizations, including the National Right to Life Committee, denounced the use of violence. A series of lawsuits against Operation Rescue, combined with the Freedom of Access to Clinic Entrances Act (1993), limited pro-lifers' protest activities and forced Operation Rescue to scale back its efforts.

Pro-lifers had more success in the courts and in Congress. In 1976 pro-lifers succeeded in cutting off most Medicaid funding for abortion through the Hyde Amendment, which the Supreme Court upheld in *Harris v. McRae* (1980). The Supreme Court upheld parental notification laws in *Planned Parenthood Inc. v. Ashcroft* (1983) and approved additional restrictions in *Webster v. Reproductive Health Services* (1989). In 2003, President George W. Bush signed into law the Partial Birth Abortion Ban Act, which was the first time that the Federal Government prohibited an abortion procedure. The Supreme Court upheld this law in *Gonzales v. Carhart* (2007). Though pro-choice Democratic presidential administrations rescinded a few anti-abortion policies, pro-lifers managed to maintain bans on federal funding for most abortions.

Yet pro-lifers were unable to get the Supreme Court to overturn *Roe v. Wade*. When the Supreme Court reexamined some of the fundamental tenets of *Roe v. Wade* in the 1992 case *Planned Parenthood v. Casey*, it decided, in a 5 to 4 decision, to leave *Roe*'s key provisions intact. More than two decades later, pro-lifers still lacked a majority on the Supreme Court. Nor did the pro-life movement succeed in passing a constitutional amendment banning abortion, despite repeated attempts to introduce such an amendment in Congress.

Deprived of a major victory, pro-lifers turned to an incremental strategy, choosing to lobby for more modest restrictions on abortion in state legislatures instead of holding out hope for an anti-abortion constitutional amendment or some other sweeping national measure. Between 1995 and 2014, states passed more than 800 restrictions on abortion, including ultrasound requirements, mandatory waiting periods, and bans on late-term abortions. Federal courts quickly struck down some of the restrictions that state governments adopted, but pro-life activists hope that the Supreme Court will uphold at least a few of these restrictions.

Pro-lifers have also made the public more uncomfortable with abortion, and the negative publicity – along with heavy regulations – that they have applied to abortion clinics has resulted in widespread clinic closures. In 1982 there were 2,900 abortion providers in the United States, but by 2008, fewer than 1,800 remained, and the number continued to fall during the next five years, with more than 50 abortion providers closing between 2010 and 2013. The abortion rate also decreased, though today US abortion doctors still perform more than 1 million legal abortions per year.

One of pro-lifers' greatest successes has been the establishment of crisis pregnancy centers that offer alternatives to abortion and use ultrasounds to persuade women facing unwanted pregnancies that their fetus is a human person and that it would be a mistake to abort it. Pro-lifers began offering crisis pregnancy counseling services in 1968, when Louise Summerhill founded Birthright, which quickly became a national organization. With more than 2,300 pro-life crisis pregnancy centers currently operating in the United States, the nation now has more crisis pregnancy centers than abortion clinics.

Beginning in the 1980s, pro-life organizations also began reaching out to women who had had abortions but who later regretted their decision. Numerous women who joined pro-life organizations in the late twentieth and early twenty-first centuries – including Norma McCorvey, the "Jane Roe" of *Roe v. Wade* – were former pro-choice advocates who decided that their earlier choices had been a mistake.

Today abortion remains one of the most divisive issues in US politics, and the pro-life movement continues to be a highly vocal political constituency. Pro-lifers have not yet won in the court of public opinion, but they believe that they are moving closer to that goal. Forty-eight percent of people in the United States consider themselves "pro-life," according to a 2013 Gallup poll, with 20 percent saying that abortion should not be legal under any circumstances. Although abortion remains legal in all 50 states and *Roe v. Wade* remains intact, pro-lifers continue to lobby for their cause, believing that their campaign will one day result in full legal protection for the unborn.

SEE ALSO: Abortion and Religion; Abortion, Legal Status in Global Perspective on; Pro-Choice Movement in the United States

REFERENCES

Dubow, Sara. 2011. *Ourselves Unborn: A History of the Fetus in Modern America*. New York: Oxford University Press.

Gallup. 2013. "Abortion." Accessed January 23, 2014, at http://www.gallup.com/poll/1576/abortion.aspx.

Greenhouse, Linda, and Reva B. Siegel. 2011. "Before (and after) *Roe v. Wade*: New Questions about Backlash." *Yale Law Journal*, 120: 2028–2087.

Luker, Kristin. 1984. *Abortion and the Politics of Motherhood*. Berkeley: University of California Press.

McGreevy, John T. 2003. *Catholicism and American Freedom: A History*. New York: Norton.

McKeegan, Michele. 1992. *Abortion Politics: Mutiny in the Ranks of the Right*. New York: Free Press.

Munson, Ziad W. 2008. *The Making of Pro-Life Activists: How Social Movement Mobilization Works*. Chicago: University of Chicago Press.

Risen, James, and Judy L. Thomas. 1998. *Wrath of Angels: The American Abortion War*. New York: Basic Books.

FURTHER READING

Basset, Laura. August 26, 2013. "Anti-Abortion Laws Take Dramatic Toll on Clinics Nationwide." Huffington Post. Accessed January 23, 2014, at http://www.huffingtonpost.com/2013/08/26/abortion-clinic-closures_n_3804529.html.

Beckwith, Francis J. 2007. *Defending Life: A Moral and Legal Case against Abortion Choice*. New York: Cambridge University Press.

Garrow, David J. 1994. *Liberty and Sexuality: The Right to Privacy and the Making of Roe v. Wade*. Berkeley: University of California Press.

Glendon, Mary Ann. 1987. *Abortion and Divorce in Western Law*. Cambridge, MA: Harvard University Press.

Guttmacher Institute. December 2013. "Facts on Induced Abortion in the United States." Accessed January 23, 2014, at http://www.guttmacher.org/pubs/fb_induced_abortion.html.

Karrer, Robert N. 2011. "The National Right to Life Committee: Its Founding, Its History, and the Emergence of the Pro-Life Movement Prior to *Roe V. Wade*." *Catholic Historical Review*, 97: 527–557.

Prostitution/Sex Work

LAURA CONNELLY and TEELA SANDERS
University of Leeds, UK

Sex work includes a wide range of directly and indirectly sexual activities, in which sexual services are negotiated and performed in exchange for some form of remuneration, usually, but not exclusively, money. Sex work is of course not an emergent feature of modernity but indeed has existed in diverse forms and been attributed diverse meanings throughout human history. In some regions and historical periods, sex work was closely associated with divinity and religion. For instance, Inanna, patron goddess of prostitutes, was considered by some to be one of the foremost deities of ancient Mesopotamia. Attitudes towards prostitution have, however, shifted historically, with feelings of intolerance becoming increasingly prominent from the sixteenth century onwards. In Western contexts, particularly in Great Britain and the United States, the Victorian era marked the emergence of harsher regulation of sex work, with a series of Contagious Diseases Acts that arrested, locked up, and marginalized women engaged in sex work, positioning such women as vectors for the spread of venereal disease and general licentiousness. Moral panics around "white slavery," or the coercion of white women into sex work, at this time functioned to construct women as devoid of agency and reinforce fear around the male, foreign "other" who presented a sexual threat to white womanhood. In contemporary societies, processes of globalization have enabled growth and diversification of sex industries, making the topic subject to international as well as local policy considerations. Some scholars suggest that policies of economic liberalization have created porous state borders, which, in conjunction with global regimes of economic inequality, creates a situation in which migration for the purpose of sex work can flourish.

So how can sex work/prostitution be defined? Sex work can encompass a vast range of sexual activities involving both physical contact or indirect sexual stimulation, for instance stripping, live sex shows, phone sex, erotic webcam performances, bondage, and domination. The term "prostitution" is itself less inclusive, typically used to refer only to the act of selling sex and often focused upon the street-based market. Sex work is therefore performed across many different sex markets, with the majority of activities occurring indoors rather than on the street. There has been an increase in the diversity and organization of sex work since the rise of the Internet and computer-mediated communication, with a significant amount of online sex work, particularly for advertising and negotiating business. Sex work is usually envisaged as a female occupation with male customers, ignoring the realities of male and transgender sex work (Smith and Laing 2012). It is the very diversity of the sex industry, in addition to its oft-clandestine nature, that has made it almost axiomatic for scholars to highlight the unreliability of attempts to measure its prevalence.

Research into sex work takes place within a highly politicized and contested terrain, in which academics and other stakeholders such as policymakers, NGOs, and campaign groups clash over the rights and wrongs of prostitution. The very morality of prostitution and sex work has historically dominated much of the discussions and theorizing on commercial sexual activities, and since the onset of "second-wave" feminism in Western contexts, considerations have largely shifted to the harms sex work enacts on women and the potential centrality of sex work to the reproduction of patriarchal gender relations. A notable ideological fragmentation therefore exists between the two major perspectives, leading to a polarized debate around conceptions of "choice" and "coercion." The first perspective, variously termed an abolitionist/anti-prostitution/radical feminist position, views prostitution as a fundamental violation of women's human rights and the epitome of violence against women. For scholars such as Kathleen Barry (1995) and Sheila Jeffreys (2009), prostitution is linked to sexual slavery and understood as a choice out of no choice. To this extent, they reject notions of voluntary prostitution and instead posit that no woman would chose to sell sex but rather, most enter the industry as trafficked women or girls. Prostitution is constructed as rape and abuse to which no woman can consent, and understood to fundamentally reduce women to sexual objects. The sex industry is therefore constructed as a patriarchal institution, one which strengthens male dominance and female subordination in society as a whole. From this perspective, prostitution is the foundation of all sexual exploitation against women and ultimately incompatible with the pursuit for gender equality. Broadly speaking, radical feminists tend to strive for the complete eradication of the sex industry through the criminalization of those profiting from the trade in women, whilst simultaneously constructing the prostitute as a victim in need of support to "exit" prostitution.

In stark contrast, a perspective that is referred to under the broad terms of liberal feminists/sex radicals/sex worker's rights regard the sale of sex as an understandable response to socioeconomic constraint and argue that most individuals partake in the industry voluntarily, exercising rational choice. For these theorists, sex work represents a viable and flexible labor option, particularly for migrant women and men seeking to escape poverty or pursue opportunities in the global North. Indeed, working in the sex industry, at least for many migrant sex workers, enables them to avoid the unrewarding and often more exploitative and physically dangerous conditions found in non-sexual jobs. Furthermore, with restrictive immigration policies preventing access to skilled employment, sex work offers a means in which migrants can uphold a dignified standard of living for both themselves and their families (Mai 2011). A fundamental tenet of this perspective, therefore, is that sex work should be understood in much the same way as any other mainstream business transaction and as such, sex workers should be considered legitimate workers rather than non-citizens. Constructing "sex as work," feminists within this scholarship argue that sex work itself is not inherently violent, rather that violence is the product of state prohibition, societal stigma, and a "discourse of disposability" (Lowman 2000) – that is, cultural attitudes in which sex workers are constructed as deplorable non-citizens and violence is condoned. With this in mind, they strive for sex workers to be accorded the same basic sociopolitical rights as other members of society.

Despite the omnipresence of this polarized "choice/coercion" binary in sex work scholarship, there is, however, growing awareness that it may be overly-simplistic in reality: one perspective is accused of denying women's agency, the other of over-endowing women's autonomy and claims that sex work can be empowering. To this extent, a growing body of scholars explore beyond the binary of choice and coercion to examine the heterogeneity of the sex industry and in so doing, offer a nuanced account of the complex intersection of power and resistance that defines the experience of sex workers. Intersectional accounts of sex work note that the extent to which workers are exploited, abused, and subject to violence is powerfully mediated by individual sex workers' structural position, particularly along national, class, and racial lines, with middle and upper class white women in particular being able to experience autonomy and high remuneration in the course of sex work, while trafficked women, non-citizens, poor women, and women of color being more routinely subject to coercion, dangerous working conditions, violence, and abuse (Bernstein 2007). Similarly, such scholarship also attends to the ways that inequality pervades sex industries, but that inequality and sexism are not necessarily endemic to such industries, but rather it is often gendered organizational structures – which systematically keep women in positions of subordination and dependence – working in conjunction with sexist ideologies – which shame and marginalize women engaged in sex work – that make women uniquely vulnerable to exploitation and abuse in sex industries (Price-Glynn 2010).

Most academic and policy attention globally has focused on the involvement of women in the sex industry. During the post-war years, inquiry was characterized by an academic focus on the functional aspects of prostitution to society (such as providing men with extra marital sex whilst not infringing upon marriage) alongside the location of prostitution within "deviancy" studies, with a preference for pathologizing the individual for their assumed wayward sexuality. Following this, the 1980s saw a shift to research which centered on the health aspects of commercial sexual interactions and sex workers assumed "risky" behaviors in the wake of HIV/AIDS outbreaks. At a similar time, concern over connections between intravenous drug use and prostitution also dominated the research, resulting in an overwhelming focus on street "vice" and female sex workers. Exiting strategies are thus often based upon addressing drug misuse issues, social exclusion, and inadequate housing.

Since the 1990s research has broadened out and the discipline of the "sociology of sex work" has begun to more rigorously investigate the heterogeneity of sex work, both in terms of how sex markets operate and who is involved in relation to age, sexuality, race, and socioeconomic status. Although the sale of sex for money is traditionally associated with the street sex market, most sex work does take place indoors often in unlicensed brothels, massage parlors, saunas, hotels, and private residences. One of the main reasons cited by sex workers as a benefit of working in a brothel is that the presence of a third-party improves security. Indeed, rates of violence against sex workers are high: in the United Kingdom sex workers are 12 times more likely to be victims of homicide compared to their non-sex worker peers. Comparatively, in the United States this is 18 times more likely. The everyday nature of sex workers experiencing violence is well documented, with studies on violence demonstrating between 50–100% of samples of street sex workers experiencing physical and sexual violence in the course of their work (see Salfati et al. 2008 for a review of literature on violence). Yet there are notable differences in levels of violence depending on the market, with the indoor markets tending to be safer (Sanders and Campbell 2007). A range of people perpetrate violence against sex workers, including organizers, clients, other sex workers, members of the community (vigilantes), and/or law enforcement personnel. Some scholars suggest that the violence experienced by sex workers is exacerbated by policies based upon an anti-prostitution agenda, which prevents women working in pairs, results in rushed engagement with clients, and leads to a breakdown in police–sex worker relations.

Less policy attention has, however, been directed at transgender and male sex workers. Unlike their female counterparts, male street-based sex workers tend to work in "cruising" areas within busy urban centers and rather than "kerb-crawling," their clients tend to approach on foot. Similar to the female indoor market, however, most male sex workers operate indoors, although premises tend to be less conspicuous. The majority of male sex work is organized via the Internet as well as occurring in more fluid ways through leisure spaces and social engagement in the gay community. While most clients of male sex workers are themselves male, heterosexual women may also purchase sex from men, often traveling to countries with high rates of poverty to buy sex from local men. Sex tourism is indeed a subdiscipline of its own with a significant amount of research carried out in Asia, the Caribbean, and South America that explores the overtly racialized and classist dynamic of wealthy white Western men purchasing sex from poor women of color in developing countries. The basics of sex tourism rests on the exoticization of women from these countries, perpetuating stereotypes about their sexuality and sexual identities.

Yet sex tourism is not only the domain of the wealthy white "gringo." Research into "sex tourism" – or "romance tourism" as it is more commonly termed when applied to women clients – has increased our knowledge in recent years. It indicates that affluent, typically white, females are increasingly utilizing their socioeconomic power to purchase sexual services from men in destinations such as Cuba, Goa, and the Caribbean. Yet the arrangement is not usually the straightforward purchase of sex for monetary remuneration; rather, gifts and meals are bought in exchange for a "boyfriend experience." Sánchez Taylor (2001) argues, however, that the construction of this as "romance," detracts from the exploitative reality of the situation. For her, the exchange ought to be viewed through the lens of racialized power imbalance. The international literature is also replete with concerns about the commercial sexual exploitation of children in major sex tourism destinations such as the Philippines and Thailand, with men from Western economically developed countries traveling to purchase sex in countries where child prostitution is legal or at least tolerated.

Men who purchase sex is one area where there has been least academic attention. Whilst the public imagination is focused on the image of the male kerb-crawler cruising the streets, this is again the least popular means of purchasing sex given the diversity and extent of the indoor market. There are no "types" of male customers as research suggests that men who buy sex come from all parts of society, across social categories of class, ethnicity, age, and educational and religious background. There are, however, different purchasing habits, with those who buy sex occasionally, compared to repeat customers who visit different sex workers or regular customers who visit the same sex workers over prolonged periods of time (Sanders 2008). Motivations for buying sex are vast: push factors stem from an individual's own life circumstances which encourage them to seek out physical sex and emotional intimacy. Research participants offer push factors such as being widowed, separated or divorced, or a lack of sex life within a conventional relationship, or with a partner who is ill or disabled. Equally there are "pull" factors that attract men to the sex industry, regardless of whether or not they are in a formal conventional relationship. For instance, the mainstreaming of the sex industries has been identified as a feature of the twenty-first century, whereby the availability, acceptability and sociability of purchasing sexual services has become embedded in leisure spaces and ordinary lifestyles. Assumptions exist regarding the type of engagements and relationships sex workers have with their clients. Yet we know that contemporary sex work can reflect more intimate and emotional exchanges as well as sexual exchange. Indeed, Bernstein (2007) writes of the "girlfriend experience" which has defined sex work for the middle classes in more recent times. This concept encapsulates the act of a client paying with cash for a relationship which goes beyond the provision of physical sex to involve the purchase of authentic emotional intimacy within the boundaries of the commercial financial relationship.

One other area that defines prostitution and sex work is how this discipline permeates the policy terrain as governments attempt to manage and control the industry and its workers. In light of the pervasiveness of the radical/liberal feminist debate (described earlier), it is therefore unsurprising that opinion is divided around the globe on the most appropriate model of regulation for controlling prostitution. Regulatory models crudely fall into three categories: legalization (where the state controls when and where sex work takes place); decriminalization (where sex work is taken out of the criminal justice system and regulated as ordinary work through employment law); and criminalization (where the majority of relationships are made illegal in an attempt to abolish the activity).

Many countries have adopted a criminalization approach which conveys a moral condemnation of sex work coupled with a commitment to prevent and deter exploitation and trafficking. The influence of a radical feminist/anti-prostitution standpoint is arguably best exemplified in the "Swedish model" introduced in 1998. This approach represented a shift away from an almost exclusive focus on the prostitute, to a new deviant: the client. To this extent, Sweden criminalized the purchase of sex and simultaneously positioned women as victims of male oppression. This shift towards focusing upon the "punter" has also been witnessed in the United States and the United Kingdom through punitive policing and re-education programs ("John schools"), albeit in a less radical form. This can be considered as a turn towards a neo-abolition mode of global regulation of sex work. At the same time, the sex workers rights movement across the world is fighting hard for human rights issues related to sex work to be taken seriously by the state, in particular the right to healthcare, the right to protection and to be safe, and the right to have self-determination over one's body and work.

Although evaluations of the Swedish model indicate that levels of street-based sex work initially decreased in response to the neo-abolitionist legislation, many scholars subsequently argue that it was likely to represent only a temporary movement of women into the indoor sex market, with the absence of any harm reduction causing greater inequality and danger for sex workers. Critics of this model argue that this form of regulation, which is frequently regarded as the radical feminist gold standard, over-emphasizes the impact of patriarchy and denies women's autonomy. Some therefore advocate for the recognition of sex work as a form of legitimate labor, an aim central to the rise of the sex workers' labor movement from the late 1960s onwards. Reflecting a more liberal feminist position, other states have adopted legislation which legalizes sex work under certain state-specified conditions, manifest in the legalized brothels of

Nevada in the United States and the "tipplezones" of the Netherlands. Others, such as New Zealand have introduced complete decriminalization – that is, the removal of all laws that criminalize the sale of sex. Indeed in 2003, New Zealand became the first country to employ this model of regulation and in so doing, sought to accord sex workers the same legal and employment rights as those found in other professions, a process termed by some scholars "the professionalization of prostitution." Research indicates that decriminalization has better enabled sex workers to negotiate safer sex practices, as well as preventing the involvement of, and offering protection to, vulnerable people engaged in the sex industry. That said, experiences of stigmatization remain among sex workers, largely as a product of prevailing negative social attitudes towards the sex industry (Abel et al. 2010).

The future directions of the discipline lie with continuing to explore the diversities of the sex industries, the sex workers, and how they intersect with cultural, economic, social, legal, and political dynamics. Further theoretical expansions are needed in relation to considering the role of commercial sex in perpetuating inequality beyond the stale choice/coercion dyad, developing more comprehensive intersectional perspectives on sex work and its place in a global economy. Methodologically, there is need to further extend innovative inquiry which utilizes participatory action research and visual methods to enable individual sex workers and sex worker communities and organizations to become peer researchers. Indeed, rather than academic inquiry perpetuating the passive subject–researcher relationship, there is great potential for participants to have more ownership over research. It is these methodological innovations that can particularly play a part in gauging the impact of policy and regulation, placing sex worker rights at the heart of any research rationale.

SEE ALSO: Internet Sex; Sex Tourism; Sex Trafficking; Sex Work and Sex Workers' Unionization

REFERENCES

Abel, Gillian, Lisa Fitzgerald, Catherine Healy, and Aline Taylor, eds. 2010. *Taking the Crime Out of Sex Work: New Zealand Sex Workers' Fight for Decriminalisation*. Bristol: Policy Press.

Barry, Kathleen. 1995. *The Prostitution of Sexuality*. New York: New York University Press.

Bernstein, Elizabeth. 2007. "Sex Work for the Middle Classes." *Sexualities*, 10: 473–488.

Jeffreys, Sheila. 2009. *The Industrial Vagina: The Political Economy of the Global Sex Trade*. London: Routledge.

Lowman, John. 2000 "Violence and the Outlaw Status of (Street) Prostitution in Canada." *Violence Against Women*, 6: 987–1011.

Mai, Nick. 2011. *In Whose Name? Migration and Trafficking in the UK Sex Industry: Delivering Social Interventions between Myths and Reality*. London: Economic and Social Research Council.

Price-Glynn, Kim. 2010. *Strip Club: Gender, Power, and Sex Work*. New York: New York University Press.

Salfati, C. Gabrielle, Alison James, and Lynn Ferguson. 2008. "Prostitute Homicides: A Descriptive Study." *Journal of Interpersonal Violence*, 23(4): 505–543.

Sánchez Taylor, Jacqueline . 2001. "Dollars are a Girl's Best Friend? Female Tourists' Sexual Behaviour in the Caribbean." *Sociology*, 35: 749–764.

Sanders, Teela. 2008 *Paying for Pleasure: Men who Buy Sex*. Cullompton: Willan.

Sanders, Teela, and Rosie Campbell. 2007. "Designing out Vulnerability, Building in Respect: Violence, Safety and Sex Work Policy." *The British Journal of Sociology*, 58: 1–19.

Smith, Nicola, and Mary Laing, eds. 2012. "Working Outside the (Hetero)Norm? Lesbian, Gay, Bisexual, Transgender and Queer Sex Work." *Sexualities*, 5: 5.

Psychological Theory, Research, Methodology, and Feminist Critiques

ROSE CAPDEVILA and JEAN M. McAVOY
Open University, UK

In conventional (Western) psychology the typical, normative subject has been conceptualized as the white heterosexual able-bodied male. Against this backdrop, psychological theory and practice have been subjected to sustained critiques from, amongst others, multiple feminisms. Traditionally, feminist critiques of psychological research and methods focused on three particular aspects: the invisibility of women, both as researchers and as participants; the ways in which men's experiences are taken as the norm against which women are judged; and the ways in which women are pathologized in psychology. More recently critiques have highlighted epistemological issues that focus on the very essence of psychology's attempts to constitute itself as a science.

BACKGROUND

Psychology has been a particularly successful discipline in the Euro-American context in the last half century. Psychologists work in many different locations and settings and it is unquestionably one of the most popular areas for undergraduate study. Over this period, the gender composition of psychology has changed dramatically. In what has been referred to as the "feminization" of psychology, the number of psychology PhDs awarded to women in the United States grew from 20 percent in 1970 to 72 percent by 2005 (Cynkar 2007).

There is no one unified approach to psychology that might be clearly understood to reflect a single conventional psychological theory. Psychology, almost since its inception, has entertained diverse and differently inspired approaches to understanding the human subject from psychophysics (the relationship between physical stimuli such as light or sound waves and perceptual and cognitive processes) to psychodynamics (the interaction of conscious and unconscious drives within a person). What has tended to be consistent across dominant approaches has been the understanding of the individual as a unitary, bounded subject. Resonant with this understanding, the dominant methodology has relied essentially on a hypothetico-deductive approach to knowledge creation. The proliferation of the "psy" disciplines, which conceive of the individual in this way, has become inextricably linked with the consolidation of neoliberal accounts of self and other.

Challenges to psychology's claim to "describe" and "explain" women have existed virtually from the beginning of its life as a discipline in the work, for example, of Mary Whiton Calkins and Leta Stetter Hollingworth. However, it was not until the 1960s that these critiques became formalized and institutionalized through, for instance, the formation of the Association for Women in Psychology in 1969. Latterly, psychology has come to encompass a number of perspectives that include biological, cognitive, phenomenological, psychodynamic, and constructionist/poststructuralist approaches. Feminisms have both critiqued and aligned themselves with each of these approaches.

TRADITIONAL CRITIQUES

In 1968, Naomi Weisstein stated that "psychology constructs the female" in that the "woman" that had been described and studied within the discipline reflected not "women's true nature" but rather the nature of psychology. In practice, Weisstein argued, conventional psychology knew very little about what it was like to be a woman. Indeed, she clearly stated in her original paper that "psychology has nothing to say about what women are really like, what they need and what they want, especially because psychology does not know" (1993, 197). The debates around this issue amongst others led to the establishment of a "psychology of women," which lent its name to numerous professional associations and journals, not least of which, in 1973, was the founding of the Division for the Psychology of Women of the American Psychological Association (APA) – the largest professional body of psychologists in the world.

Three intertwined critiques of conventional psychology were prominent up to this time. The first was the way in which women had been made invisible in psychology. As researchers, women were often not mentioned or listed as part of research teams, edited out of photographs, or credit was given primarily to their male partners. Much of the research conducted in conventional psychology experiments was carried out using only male participants, for instance Kohlberg's theory of moral development or Erikson's theory of identity development, which not only failed to describe female experience, but established criteria for assessment based on the incomplete data.

A second important feminist critique focused on the judging of women against a norm developed around men's experiences in psychology. Tavris, in discussing the mismeasure of women by psychology, has argued that "In any domain of life in which men set the standard of normalcy, women will be considered abnormal" (1993, 149). She provides as an example the description of psychological findings indicating that women have lower self-esteem than men, rather than that men are more conceited than women, or that women do not value their own efforts as much as men do, rather than that men overvalue their own work (1993, 152). Other examples abound, such as research on helping behavior which initially seemed to indicate that women were less helpful than men, until it was pointed out that this was an artifact of the way in which the term "help" has been defined in these studies.

The third critique, around the way in which women are pathologized, brings together the previous two. When psychological research is "womanless" and psychological norms are set in reference to men, women become pathologized as a result. Karen Horney, an early and prominent critic of Freudian psychoanalysis as androcentric, argued that insufficient attention was given to the sociocultural determinants of gender differences. She argued that penis envy, if it existed at all, was rooted, not in a wish to possess a penis but, rather, in a desire for the status and recognition afforded to men by the culture. Clinical judgments have similarly pathologized women in the differential diagnoses they are given in comparison to men reporting identical symptoms. Feminist researchers have further argued that diagnoses such as premenstrual syndrome (PMS) and postpartum depression pathologize women's everyday experience.

A number of feminist challenges to conventional psychology followed these critiques. The first, and possibly still the most dominant feminist approach, was the promotion of good scientific practice by removing research design bias. However, this approach risked reinforcing psychology's aspirations to be an objective "science" at the cost of other ways of developing legitimate knowledge. Another challenge to psychological claims to women's inferiority was to accept that women were indeed less successful; however, this was attributed not to their "inferiority" but to the internalization of oppression. This approach has many resonances with current popular media versions of feminist politics where women are encouraged to "lean in." However, many feminists see this strategy as victim blaming, arguing that its focus on the individual rather than social and political pathologies reinforces already existing biases of mainstream psychology.

Whilst feminist analyses have exposed biases in method and interpretation, they are themselves subject to feminist critique. For example, Carol Gilligan (1982) countered Lawrence Kohlberg's highly influential theory of moral development wherein women were held to be deficient in moral reasoning by postulating an ethic of care, identified through listening to women, as an alternative to the ethic of justice. A number of issues have been raised with this approach, primarily that it reinforces the idea that women "naturally" exist as a homogeneous and distinctive group, speaking with the same voice in spite of age, ethnicity, (dis)ability, class, sexuality, and other markers of difference. Similarly, Sandra Bem's (1974) work aimed to address the issues of women's "inferiority," displacing the question of sex differences by conceptualizing femininity, masculinity, and androgyny as traits. However, Bem's Sex Role Inventory was seen to underwrite the very notions of masculinity and femininity that it purported to challenge, as well as shifting focus away from questions of social structure and power differentials that might be seen to shape "appropriate" male and female behavior.

Some feminists further argued that it was psychology's "scientific" approach in itself that was problematic due to the insistence of the hypothetico-deductive approach on the stripping of context and the naïve positivist belief in a "value-free" science. This more essential feminist critique of psychological research methods was closely intertwined with that being produced through the crisis in social psychology. Its concern was not on correcting error within psychological research; rather, it was an attack on the experimental method itself. Feminists argued that because the experimental method looks at behavior rather than the person as "subject," it ignores the context – social, personal, cultural – in which this behavior takes place and is, as a result, blind to meaning. It lacks, thereby, any claim to environmental validity. Feminists and critical social psychologists argued together that the context was indeed meaningful and reproduced the existing disadvantages in society.

MORE RECENT CRITIQUES

The early critiques and challenges to conventional psychology were firmly rooted in positivism and relied on an essentialist epistemology. Consequently, conventional psychology was prepared to incorporate them into the dominant practices of the discipline. This allowed commentators from within and outwith conventional psychology to argue that feminism had made some impact on psychology within teaching and professional practice. But there were many different feminisms with varying approaches and epistemologies. The feminist psychology that was beginning to impact was primarily the "psychology of women," which had been championed institutionally. The concept and practice of a "psychology of women" was politically difficult for the conventional discipline to resist and, as Wilkinson (1997) noted, it was possible for feminist psychologists to make strategic use of the label "psychology of women" as a less politically contentious euphemism. The term was championed by Jean Baker Miller, who promoted a "relational" approach and critiqued the individualized approach psychology took. However, others, such as Mary Brown Parlee, were more skeptical of this designation, considering it to be a "conceptual monstrosity" (1975, 120). By the 1990s, the psychology of women, which had originally been used as a less politically charged euphemism for feminist psychology, had become so depoliticized that it was seen by many to be facilitating the perpetuation of conventional psychology.

A more fundamental critique gained leverage in the 1980s and 1990s as psychology encountered the postmodern turn to language that was developing across the social sciences. Feminism recognized the relationship between language, power, and the social construction of sex/gender (and other) differences. What is taken to be "true" and "real" is understood as a product of social practices. Sex/gender differences such as the biological categories of "men" and "women" are socially made and attempts to show that women are the "same as" or "different from" men are seen to reproduce those categories. Psychological perceptions of difference (such as measures of inferior capacity) are understood as principles of social organization, not inherent qualities of individuals.

Psychology is a particular target for this critique because of the way it has privileged the individualized subject, and both claimed and promoted the concept of objectivity and neutrality epitomized in its reliance on the experimental method. What psychology has been reluctant to take on are the intellectual and methodological resources made available by new theorizations of human subjectivity.

The postmodern reading of psychology has been simultaneously a powerful challenge to the authority claimed by its conventional psychological antecedents, and strongly resisted by some feminists because of several key features. The notion that deeply felt beliefs and emotions are neither "real" nor "natural" is for some an unintelligible and even anti-feminist refusal of "intuitive" knowledge and "commonsense" understandings of the world. Moreover, the theoretically sophisticated anti-realist stance can be difficult to translate into practical political action, either within psychology or beyond it in the wider social world. Nevertheless, this approach has impacted psychology in terms of epistemology and methodology, challenging concepts of empirical rigor and transparency. Qualitative and experiential approaches have become more common in feminist psychological research. These usually involve the use of reflexivity, which conceptualizes positioning and an inescapably situated perspective as a resource rather than a bias to be weaned out.

Despite, or possibly in response to, the postmodern challenge, biologically informed approaches to psychology are again becoming more dominant, due both to the increased popularity of evolutionary understandings of psychological development and to the technological advances in functional magnetic resonance imaging (fMRI) technology that allows us unprecedented access to brain activity. Advances in neuro-imaging techniques have posited technological developments as a route to an objective understanding of human behavior and experience. Whilst powerful, this research does not escape the issues inherent to the experimental method and feminists have pointed out that early interpretations of neural activity and implications for behavior have been heavily dependent on gendered stereotypes.

INTERSECTIONALITY AND TRANSNATIONALISM

A recognition of the multiplicity of feminisms that engage psychology has become a key component of the feminist narrative. Critiques that engage notions of intersectionality have developed to address issues around the dominance of a feminism, adopted by conventional psychology, that responds only to the interests of white, middle-class, educated (primarily Western) women. Attending to intersections of ethnicity, class, (dis)abilities, sexualities, age, and other forms of identification and subjectification challenges both conventional psychology and forms of feminism that homogenize women and elide consequential markers making oppressive practice possible. Postcolonial feminism (e.g., Mohanty 1984) has been one response that attempts to create a space not only for race and ethnicity in feminist thought, but a multiplicity of (post)colonial experience to be incorporated in understanding human subjectivity.

Feminist critique of conventional psychology has developed independently outside of, and often in relation to, the Anglo-American context – each location having its own history and specific characteristics (Rutherford et al. 2011). However, this critique has often been less visible for a number of reasons, including the dominance of US psychology in publishing as well as the enrollment of feminist activism into other political struggles such as those for democracy (e.g., South Africa) and liberation (e.g., Chile).

The relationship between psychology and feminism creates an inherent space for conflict and cooperation given that psychology is by definition the study of the individual and, in its conventional form, claims to be objective science, whilst feminism is explicitly concerned with social structures and institutionalized oppression and claims to be overtly political. This is a productive encounter. What feminism offers psychology is a critical appraisal of the scientific method, a different set of interpretive lenses, and it enables a "different voice" to be heard. Psychology has responded with a growing diversity in research methods and reinvigorated theories of subjectification, and offers a set of empirical research strategies to support critical, political, and practical interventions.

SEE ALSO: *Diagnostic and Statistical Manual of Mental Disorders* (DSM), Feminist Critiques of; Essentialism; Feminist Epistemology; Feminist Methodology; Gender Bias in Research; Intersectionality; Masculinity and Femininity, Theories of; Neuroscience, Brain Research, and Gender; Postmodern Feminist Psychology; Reflexivity

REFERENCES

Bem, Sandra. L. 1974. "The Measurement of Psychological Androgyny." *Journal of Consulting and Clinical Psychology*, 42(2): 155.

Cynkar, Amy. 2007. "The Changing Gender Composition of Psychology." *Monitor on Psychology*, 38(6): 46.

Gilligan, Carol. 1982. *In a Different Voice: Psychological Theory and Women's Development*. Boston: Harvard University Press.

Mohanty, Chandra Talpade. 1984. "Under Western Eyes: Feminist Scholarship and Colonial Discourses." *Boundary*, 2(12): 333–358.

Parlee, Mary Brown. 1975. "Psychology." *Signs*, 1(1): 119–138.

Rutherford, Alexandra, Rose Capdevila, Vindhya Undurti, and Ingrid Palmary, eds. 2011. *Handbook of International Feminisms*. New York: Springer.

Tavris, Carol. 1993. "The Mismeasure of Woman." *Feminism & Psychology*, 3(2): 149–168.

Weisstein, Naomi. 1993. "Psychology Constructs the Female; or The Fantasy Life of the Male Psychologist (with some attention to the fantasies of his friends, the male biologist and the male anthropologist)." *Feminism & Psychology*, 3(2): 194–210.

Wilkinson, Sue. 1997. "Feminist Psychology." In *Critical Psychology: An Introduction*, edited by Dennis R. Fox and Isaac Prilleltensky. London: Sage.

FURTHER READING

Magnusson, Eva, and Jeanne Marecek. 2012. *Gender and Culture in Psychology: Theories and Practices*. Cambridge: Cambridge University Press.

Psychology's Feminist Voices. http://www.feministvoices.com/.

Sherif, Carolyn W. 1998. "Bias in Psychology." *Feminism & Psychology*, 8: 58–75. First published 1979.

Unger, Rhoda K. 1998. *Resisting Gender: Twenty-Five Years of Feminist Psychology*. Thousand Oaks: Sage.

Psychology of Gender: History and Development of the Field

CLAIRE ETAUGH
Bradley University, USA

The purpose of this entry is to provide an overview of the history and development of the psychology of gender. This is a more complex endeavor than it may initially appear, since there are different lenses through which one can explore this topic. These include (1) women as psychological theorists and researchers, (2) women and gender as the topics of theory and research, and (3) organizations concerned with the psychology of women and gender (Unger 2001). We examine these three perspectives in the history and development of the psychology of gender.

GENDER AND SEX

Before embarking on a discussion of the psychology of gender, one needs to begin with a brief history of the usage of the terms "sex" and "gender" in psychology and other social sciences. There has been a long, ongoing debate about the use of these terms among psychologists and social scientists who do research in women's studies and gender studies. The distinction between the two terms was first made in the 1950s, when John Money and his colleagues, in their pioneering work on sex change and sex assignment, used the word "sex" to refer to individuals' physical and biological characteristics and the word "gender" to refer to their psychological characteristics and behavior.

Rhoda Unger argued that the word "sex" not only implied biological mechanisms and causes, but also promoted the essentialist view that differences between females and males were inherent and unchangeable (Unger 1979). She suggested use of the word "gender" to refer to characteristics culturally considered to be appropriate for females and females. Unger's article was influential in promoting a marked increase in the use of "gender" to refer to the meanings that societies give to female and male categories (Etaugh and Bridges 2013).

PSYCHOLOGY OF GENDER AND PSYCHOLOGY OF WOMEN

Most of the early textbooks (i.e., those published in the 1970s and 1980s) that dealt with gender issues had the words "Psychology" and "Women" somewhere in their title and many have continued to do so in recent editions. Examples of such titles include *Women's Lives: a Psychological Perspective* (Etaugh and Bridges 2013), *Half the Human Experience: the Psychology of Women* (Hyde 2007), *The Psychology of Women* (Matlin 2008), and *Our Voices: Psychology of Women* (Rider 2005). Why was the early focus on "women" instead of "gender"? Women had long been excluded from psychological research. Rachel Hare-Mustin and Jeanne Marecek call the early years of psychology "womanless," both because few psychologists were women and also because women's issues were not deemed important enough to study (Hare-Mustin and Marecek 1990). Thus, the early textbooks that considered gender issues aimed to redress this shortcoming by focusing on women and women's issues. In those days, when students in Psychology of Women courses would occasionally ask why there was no course on "Psychology of Men" in the Department, a standard (and accurate) response was that all the other psychology courses they were taking were essentially about the psychology of men.

In the mid-1990s, the first textbooks appeared that included the word "Gender" in their title, either along with or replacing the word "Women", for reasons that we shall examine shortly. Examples of the titles of more recent editions of such books are *Gender: Psychological Perspectives* (Brannon 2008), *Transformations: Women, Gender, and Psychology,* (Crawford 2006), *Psychology of Gender* (Helgeson 2005), and *Women and Gender: Transforming Psychology* (Yoder 2003). The similarities between textbooks labeled Psychology of Women and those titled Psychology of Gender are far greater than their differences. One approach to the study of gender is, in fact, the psychology of women approach. Gender theory and research draw heavily from research on the psychology of women. By the same token, psychology of women textbooks and courses, although they examine girls and women and issues unique to them, also include a great deal of information about boys and men, their interactions with girls and women, and the social contexts in which both females and males develop and function. It is artificial and arguably meaningless to examine the psychological journey of females through life without discussing the role played by males and the social constructions of both genders.

HISTORY OF THE PSYCHOLOGY OF GENDER

The history of the psychology of gender often is subdivided into three phases (Yoder 2003). In the early phase, critics began to raise questions about the male-centered nature of the field (the so-called "androcentric bias"). In this phase, for the most part, men were studied by male psychologists (even the rats used in animal research were male). Women and issues related to them simply were omitted or, at best, were marginalized during these early years of psychology. Women who wished to become psychologists faced enormous obstacles in obtaining credentials and academic positions. As one example of this androcentric bias, Janice Yoder cites a 1999 review of "A Century of Psychology," a multi-page special section that appeared in *Monitor on Psychology*, a monthly publication of the American Psychological Association. Yoder notes that the series begins with nine pages of tributes to great white men, followed by "ghettoized" coverage of women and men of color in the last two pages devoted to women and diversity.

Yoder (2003) refers to the second phase of the history of psychology of gender, which began in the late 1960s and early 1970s, as the "compensatory" phase. During this phase, women were "discovered" both as psychologists and as legitimate objects of research. Biographies of formerly unheralded women psychologists began to appear, spearheaded by the work of Agnes O'Connell and Nancy Russo (e.g., O'Connell and Russo 1980). The focus of inquiry began to shift from "women" to "gender."

The third phase, which is still in progress, is what Yoder calls the "transformational" phase. Women psychologists and research related to women and gender are no longer marginalized but are incorporated into psychology as a well-established and legitimate field of study. Early assumptions have been challenged, as feminist theorists and researchers develop new theoretical perspectives and methodological strategies, apply new insights to established topics in psychology, and explore previously neglected ones (Worell and Etaugh 1994).

These three phases in the history and development of the psychology of gender are now examined in greater detail.

PSYCHOLOGY OF GENDER: THE EARLY YEARS

In the early years of psychology, gender studies as such did not exist. Concepts in psychology were based on the male experience. For example, Sigmund Freud formulated his views of the Oedipus complex and penis envy from a male perspective, but applied them to both sexes The same was true of theories of life span development formulated by Erik Erikson and others (Etaugh and Bridges 2013).

In addition, early psychologists viewed women as different from and inferior to men. For example, G. Stanley Hall, considered the founder of child psychology, stated that it was impossible, without causing injury, to hold girls to the same standard of moral accountability and strenuous mental work required of boys (Hall 1904). Many eminent men in the field, including the noted historian of psychology Edwin G. Boring (1951), expressed the view that women were biologically and culturally unsuited for high-status careers, and that they naturally lacked the skills and drive needed to succeed in science. Women were excluded from both informal and formal professional networks. One influential group that explicitly banned women from its founding by Edward Titchener in 1904 until 1929 was The Experimentalists (later known as the Society of Experimental Psychology). One example will suffice to show the lengths to which researchers went to look for evidence of women's inferiority. In order to explain their premise that women are less intelligent than men, and thus unfit for higher education and/or scientific pursuits, male psychologists claimed that women's brains were smaller than those of men (Caplan and Caplan 2009).

This claim appeared to be discredited by the discovery that *relative* brain size – the weight of the brain relative to the weight of the body – is actually greater in women than in men. But stereotypes are not that easily dismissed. Scientists began to compare various areas of female and male brains in an effort to find the cause of women's supposedly inferior intellectual capabilities. No differences were found. Still, the search has continued even into the modern era. In 1982, the prestigious journal *Science* published a study (De LaCoste-Utamsing and Holloway 1982) which claimed that the corpus callosum (the connection between the two hemispheres of the brain) is larger in women than in men. According to the researchers, this difference might account for women's purportedly poorer spatial skills. The study was flawed in several ways, and the sample size was small – only nine male brains and five female brains. Ruth Bleier, a neuroanatomist, and her colleagues repeated the study, correcting the flaws and using a much larger sample of brains. No differences between men and women were found in the size of the corpus callosum. When Bleier and her colleagues submitted their findings to *Science*, the journal refused to publish them, stating that they were "too political" (Caplan and Caplan 2009).

EARLY WOMAN PSYCHOLOGISTS

The first women in psychology faced daunting obstacles, especially in establishing their credentials, since many universities in the late 1800s and early 1900s did not welcome women who wanted to pursue advanced degrees. If a woman married, she was no longer considered to be serious about her profession and was often turned down for academic positions. In spite of these obstacles, several women overcame the odds and became pioneers in the field In 1894, Margaret Floy Washburn became the first woman to receive a PhD in psychology in the United States. Another 40 years passed before doctoral degrees in psychology were awarded to African American women: Inez Beverly Prosser and Ruth Winifred Howard.

One year after the founding of the American Psychological Association (APA) in 1893, two of the 14 new members admitted were women: Mary Whiton Calkins and Christine Ladd-Franklin. Calkins later became the first woman president of the APA in 1905. Margaret Floy Washburn was elected the second woman president in 1921. It would be 51 years before APA chose its third woman president, Anne Anastasi.

The notion that women were inferior to men did not go unchallenged by women psychologists in the early 1900s. It is perhaps not a coincidence that during this period, the first wave of feminist activism in both the United States and the United Kingdom was demanding voting rights for women. Two women psychologists of the early twentieth century conducted studies that countered common assumptions of female inferiority and weakness. Helen Thompson Woolley found little difference in the intellectual skills of women and men. Leta Stetter Hollingworth's research challenged the then-popular assumption that women's menstrual cycles were debilitating, thus rendering women unfit to hold positions of leadership and responsibility. She found that women's intellectual and sensory-motor skills did not vary systematically across the menstrual cycle In addition, Karen Horney and Clara Thompson made important critiques of psychoanalytic theory during this period that stressed the social, cultural, and environmental factors in women's psychological development.

Unfortunately, many of these ideas languished, since few women were able to obtain academic positions that would allow them to study and do research on these subjects Those women who did have academic jobs were often employed at undergraduate women's colleges, where the focus was on teaching and relatively few resources were available to conduct research. Both Calkins and Washburn held faculty positions at such institutions. Women psychologists who married male academic psychologists faced the additional obstacle of nepotism rules. These policies, which were prevalent in many institutions of higher education at the time, did not allow married couples to hold faculty positions in the same department. Typically, the male member of the couple received the tenure track position, while the woman might be hired (or "allowed" to work for free) as a research associate in someone's laboratory. Clearly, this was a much less prestigious and more economically tenuous position, which often provided little opportunity to pursue their own research preferences.

Even after it became easier for women to obtain doctoral training and academic positions, the psychology of gender continued for many years to be viewed as a marginalized fringe area of study, and its specialized journals were considered to be of low quality. The career of Sandra Lipsitz Bem vividly illustrates the struggles faced by women who sought to carry out research on the psychology of gender. Bem, who received her PhD at the University of Michigan in 1968, entered the field two generations after Mary Whiton Calkins, Margaret Floy Washburn, and Christine Ladd-Franklin. The barriers that she faced in carrying out her feminist research remained formidable, however. A few years after receiving her PhD, Bem and her husband, Daryl, also a psychologist, were offered positions in Stanford University's highly ranked Psychology Department. Stanford was primarily interested in recruiting Daryl Bem, but knew that he would accept only if his wife also was offered a position. At Stanford, Sandra Bem developed a groundbreaking new instrument for measuring psychological femininity, masculinity, and androgyny, the Bem Sex Role Inventory (BSRI). For this work, she received a prestigious research grant from the National Institutes of Mental Health, an award from the APA for Distinguished Early Career Contributions to Psychology, and the Association of Women in Psychology's Distinguished Publication Award. Despite these accolades and her numerous publications, Sandra Bem was denied tenure at Stanford, apparently because her research was viewed as being out of the mainstream of psychology and thus not in keeping with Stanford's image. Sandra and Daryl Bem subsequently were hired as tenured associate (later full) professors at Cornell University, where they both went on to pursue highly successful careers.

In addition to the barriers faced by women in their quest to earn advanced degrees and academic positions, many of women's early contributions were overlooked and "lost" in psychology's written history. Even to this day, when the works of women psychologists are cited, they may be overlooked. Two related reasons may account for this apparent invisibility of many women psychologists. For one thing, the historical practice of citing references in scholarly psychological works is to refer to authors by using their last name and first initials only. Second, in the absence of information that identifies the sex of the author, people tend to assume that important scholarly contributions have been carried out by men (Etaugh and Bridges 2013). Although she is embarrassed to admit it, when the present author first learned about the Ladd-Franklin theory of color vision in her introductory psychology course, she assumed that two men named Ladd and Franklin had developed the theory. Only years later did she discover that it was the work of a woman, Christine Ladd-Franklin. Along the same lines, when asked who established the importance of touch in the development of attachment, most psychologists respond with the name "Harry Harlow." Many do not know that his wife, Margaret Kuenne Harlow, who also had a doctorate in psychology, was his research partner and co-developer of their influential theory. Margaret Kuenne Harlow was not alone in this dubious distinction. Other women psychologists who made notable contributions to the discipline – Helen Astin, Jeanne Block, Leta Hollingwoth, Carolyn Sherif, and Janet Spence – were married to eminent men in the field who often received the lion's share of the credit for their joint work.

MALE AS NORMATIVE

Another manifestation of the androcentric bias that characterized the early years of psychology is that research participants were almost always males. But they were not just any males: these males were young, white, middle class, able-bodied, and heterosexual. A major problem with such a restricted sample is that it can and did lead to unwarranted and inaccurate conclusions about the groups that are excluded. How, for example, could one draw conclusions about women's leadership styles by studying only male leaders (let alone learn how ethnic minority women lead by studying white male leaders)? Nonetheless, results from studies on male participants typically were generalized to female participants. Those few studies that involved only female participants were much more likely to be restricted to conclusions about females only. This practice suggests that males are considered normative, and results obtained from them considered generally applicable, whereas females are viewed as different. In other words, males are viewed as the standard against which others are measured (Etaugh and Bridges 2013).

Similarly, this "male as normative" bias often appeared when interpreting the results of research. One form of this bias is to interpret findings in ways that suggest female weakness or inferiority, yet another illustration of the robust nature of this assumption. For example, although girls earn higher grades in school than boys they tend to underestimate their grades, and also their overall intelligence and class standing, whereas boys tend to overestimate theirs. These results sometimes have been interpreted as illustrating girls' supposed lack of confidence. The equally likely possibility that boys are unrealistically overconfident is seldom offered as an explanation. Another example of the "female shortcoming" assumption is the interpretation of research which indicates that females are more likely than males to use speech sometimes referred to as "tentative." Such speech may contain tag questions (e.g., "It's hot in here, *don't you think*?"), uncertainty verbs (e.g., "She *seems* to be a strong candidate"), and hedges (e.g., "*I kind of feel* you shouldn't do that"). Some researchers (e.g., Lakoff 1990) have argued that this pattern of speech indicates females' lack of confidence, an interpretation that suggests a female deficit. Another equally plausible and more positive interpretation is that the language features used by females do not reflect tentativeness or lack of confidence, but instead result from women's more communal orientation, i.e., their desire to leave open the lines of communication and encourage participation of others. A further example of how a trait can be labeled to suggest female inferiority is the interpretation of gender differences that are found on the classic "field independence–field dependence" continuum. Men have been described as "field independent (i.e., not influenced by the surrounding context), which is considered a favorable attribute. Field *dependence*, on the other hand, has been viewed as a deficit that women allegedly have. Why not instead use the alternative label "field *sensitive*," which has a much more positive connotation? (Fiske 2010).

PSYCHOLOGY OF GENDER: THE COMPENSATORY YEARS

Several events in the 1960s ushered in the second wave of the feminist movement in the United States. Among these were the publication of Betty Friedan's 1963 groundbreaking book *The Feminine Mystique*, the passage of the Federal Equal Pay Act in 1963, and the formation of the National Organization for Women (NOW) in 1966. Each of these events turned the spotlight on the glaring social, political, and economic inequities that existed between women and men.

The influence of the women's movement during these years coincided with and no doubt helped to serve as a catalyst for the emergence of psychology of women as a separate, legitimate field of study within the discipline (Eagly et al. 2012). In 1969, the Association for Women in Psychology was founded outside the boundaries of mainstream psychology. This was followed in 1973 by the establishment within the APA of Division 35, the Division of (now Society for) the Psychology of Women. Several textbooks on the psychology of women for graduate and undergraduate courses were written, with the first ones appearing in 1971. Two major journals – *Psychology of Women Quarterly* and *Sex Roles* – were established in the mid-1970s, followed by the journal *Women and Therapy* in 1982. College courses on the topic began to appear, along with programs in women's studies (Etaugh and Bridges 2013). As important as the second wave of feminism was in serving as context and catalyst for these developments, one cannot overlook the important role played by organizational activism both within and outside the APA in creating both informal and formal networks of feminist women and men. These networks were instrumental in creating programs at professional conferences that highlighted ongoing research on women, women's issues and gender. In addition, Division 35 has been an influential contributor to the governance of its parent organization, the APA (Unger 2001).

One of the key activities of feminist researchers and theorists during the compensatory phase of the field's development was the demonstration of the sexist bias of much psychological theory, research, and practice. These scholars set about expanding knowledge about women and gender, and correcting erroneous misinformation from the past. One of the most influential essays from this period was Naomi Weisstein's "Kinder, Kuche, Kirche" as Scientific Law: Psychology Constructs the Female (Weisstein 1968). In it, she argued that the theories and assumptions about women promulgated by prominent psychologists and psychiatrists of the time, such as Sigmund Freud, Erik Erikson, and Bruno Bettelheim, were fatally flawed by the biases and fantasies of these male psychologists, often in the absence of empirical evidence. The widespread impact of Weisstein's critique on psychology and other disciplines is demonstrated by the fact that it was reprinted in more than 30 readers in a variety of academic fields. Weisstein and other feminist writers attributed existing sexist biases to a failure to examine the social and cultural contexts of the lives of girls and women. By focusing instead on what were assumed to be innate characteristics of females, they argued, many psychologists had concluded that women's lower status and gender-stereotypical characteristics were inborn and thus immutable.

As noted earlier, another corrective activity of this compensatory phase was a focus on the neglected "foremothers" of psychology. The recognition of the important women of the early days of psychology and their achievements was an important step in setting the historical record straight. However, as pointed out by Mary Crawford and Jeanne Marecek, a focus on exceptional women can be a double-edged sword, by possibly conveying the subtle message that only unusually gifted women were capable of becoming psychologists (Crawford and Marecek 1989). They cited the importance of publications by Agnes O'Connell, Nancy Russo, and others (e.g., O'Connell and Russo 1980) which demonstrated how social and structural obstacles had served to exclude or marginalize many early women psychologists. These barriers included the attitudes of male gatekeepers, lack of financial resources, and social norms concerning women's family roles and responsibilities. Efforts to document women's historical role in psychology continue to this day. A notable example is the creation in 2010 of Psychology's Feminist Voices, a digital multi-media archive project led by Alexandra Rutherford. The site includes oral history interviews, written profiles of past and current women psychologists, and a variety of other resources and pedagogical tools devoted to the history of women in psychology (MacArthur and Shields 2014).

Another activity that characterized the compensatory phase was labeled by Crawford and Marecek (1989) as "woman as problem or anomaly." In this approach, researchers emphasize explanations for women's supposed deficiencies or diminished achievements in terms of socially transmitted roles and expectations rather than inherent biological factors. Toward this end, some feminist researchers began to look at sexism in interpersonal attitudes and behavior. Another line of research investigated the effects of an individual's sex on how others evaluated their accomplishments. Early research on "fear of success" and "math anxiety" are additional examples of explorations into the social and cultural factors that shape women's behaviors and attitudes, as is the current exploration of reasons for the shortage of women pursuing careers in STEM (science, technology, engineering, and math).

A third characteristic of the compensatory phase, according to Crawford and Marecek (1989), was a shift in the focus of theory and research from women to gender. Importantly, gender was now conceptualized not just as an identifying category, but as a principle of social organization which structures the relationships between women and men. Thus, instead of looking at gender as an attribute that one has (i.e., using it as a noun), feminist psychologists proposed that gender should be viewed as a process (i.e., using it as a verb). This gave rise to the term "doing gender,", which is still used today. The shift in focus from women to gender during the compensatory phase accounts for the initial appearance at this time of psychology of gender textbooks and courses, as noted earlier.

Many of the studies on sex and gender that were carried out during this period were atheoretical and sometimes rather simplistic. Often, only one independent and one dependent variable were examined. Sample sizes sometimes were small and participants were usually quite homogeneous in their demographic characteristics (e.g., white, middle class, and probably mostly heterosexual, although questions about one's sexual orientation were almost never asked). Research frequently focused on looking for sex differences in an almost scattershot approach. These studies, and others that dealt with women's issues, were viewed by most established journals and by university tenure and promotion committees to be marginal and of low quality (Chrisler and McCreary 2010). (Stanford University's reaction to Sandra Bem's work, discussed earlier, is a case in point.)

Crawford and Marecek labeled the fourth trend of the compensatory phase "transformation." This trend was in its infancy at the time they wrote their article in 1989, and it remains very much in evidence today. In their view, the process of transformation involves a self-reflective challenging of the very assumptions, values, and practices of the field. Recall that Yoder (2013) similarly viewed transformation as characterizing the current stage of psychology of gender activity. We turn to this phase now.

PSYCHOLOGY OF GENDER: THE TRANSFORMATIONAL YEARS

Transformations in conceptualization, theory, and methodology in research on women and gender have been inextricably tied to the application of feminist perspectives and principles to psychological research. Judith Worell and Claire Etaugh described how the feminist perspective has transformed the way women and gender are studied:

> The lives of girls and women, submerged, undocumented, or distorted in the psychological literature, became the focus of research and inquiry. Established truths about women's lives were revisited with fresh views that entertained the validity of constructed realities. Feminist theories contributed to the discovery of problems that begged for solutions, to questions with no ready answers, and to hypotheses that framed new questions. (Worell and Etaugh 1994, 444)

These authors (Etaugh and Worell 2012; Worell and Etaugh 1994) enumerated a set of six feminist principles, beliefs, and values that have been, and continue to be, used to understand, interpret, and evaluate transformations in theory and research related to women and gender. In summary form (Etaugh and Worell 2012, 419–421), these principles are as follows:

Principle 1. Challenging the tenets of traditional scientific inquiry; recognizing that values enter into all scientific enterprises and that reality is, in part, created by the scientific process.

Principle 2. Focusing on the experience and lives of women; looking at women who differ from the majority group.

Principle 3. Viewing power relations as the basis of patriarchal political social arrangements; examining health concerns within the context of power arrangements.

Principle 4. Recognizing gender as an essential category of analysis; pointing out multiple conceptions of gender; emphasizing the situational context of gender and gendering as a process that structures social interactions.

Principle 5. Attention to the use of language and the power to name; reducing the polarity between private and public in women's lives, such as renaming women's work, concepts of family, and the appropriate place of these in private and public domains.

Principle 6. Promoting social activism toward the goal of societal change; creating a science that will benefit rather than oppress women and will correct as well as document prevalence of inequity, illness, violence, etc.

How far have we come in transforming the psychology of gender? The study of women and gender has now become an important focus of psychological science. The field is now well established, and research is guided both by strong theoretical constructs and by an impressive methodological and statistical toolkit. Since 1960, when little attention was paid to these topics, the last half century has witnessed a dramatic growth in the numbers of publications devoted to the psychology of women and gender. Partly as a corollary of this explosion in research, specialized journals in the field have become increasingly selective.

The transformation of the field of psychology of gender has recently been documented exhaustively by Alice Eagly and her colleagues (Eagly et al. 2012). Their painstaking analysis of 50 years of research on women and gender from 1960 to 2009 has made it an instant classic for scholars in the field, in much the same way that Eleanor Maccoby and Carol Nagy Jacklin's book *The Psychology of Sex Differences* (Maccoby and Jacklin 1974) became an overnight "must read" for gender researchers and scholars over 40 years ago. That book was the first not only to synthesize research findings on gender differences in development, but also to emphasize that few gender differences were well documented. In addition, the book made the important point that the differences within each gender were usually greater than those between the genders.

Eagly and her colleagues had the advantage of being able to undertake their monumental task with the assistance of tools unavailable to Maccoby and Jacklin, both statistical (e.g., meta-analysis) and technological. They used the PsycINFO database contained on the PsycNET platform of the APA. The database includes approximately 2,500 journals, of which about one-third are published in the United States.

The analyses of Eagly and co-workers revealed several important trends in the development of research on the psychology of gender. For one thing, a steep increase clearly was evident in the annual frequency of articles on the psychology of sex differences, gender, and women from 1960, when there were virtually no publications, to 2009, when the number exceeded 6,500. Clearly, psychology is no longer womanless!

Since part of the increase in research in gender and women reflects the growth in all published psychological research, Eagly and her colleagues then compared the number of articles on gender and women relative to the total of all articles in human psychology in a given year. The high point occurred in 1979, at the height of feminist activism in the United States. This was followed by a decline through the early 1980s, perhaps as a consequence of the defeat of the Equal Rights Amendment in 1982, and a resulting lessening of feminist activism. Another gradual climb ensued, peaking in the late 1990s and followed by another decline. Eagly and her colleagues believe that this relative decline resulted from a number of factors, including the addition to the database of neuroscience journals, which tend to have fewer articles on gender research. They also cite sociopolitical factors such as a slower pace of changes designed to promote gender equality, as well as backlash against such changes.

Eagly and co-workers found that articles on gender and women were most likely to appear in the subject area of social processes and social issues, followed by developmental psychology, personality psychology, social psychology, sport psychology, psychological and physical disorders, industrial and organizational psychology, and military psychology. Importantly, their analyses showed that articles on psychology of women and gender were not confined to journals that specialize in gender, but also were represented in psychology's core research journals.

During the third, most recent, wave of feminism, researchers have been urged to examine the heterogeneity of women's experiences by attending to the way in which gender intersects with other social identities such as race and ethnicity, nationality, social class, sexual orientation, ableness, marital status, parental status, and age. Eagly and colleagues, however, discovered that only a minority of articles through 2009 addressed such issues of intersectionality. Of these, race and ethnicity received the most research attention. Despite the rapid growth of the aging population, older women and men still tend to be largely invisible in psychological research. Even in textbooks on psychology of women and psychology of gender, information on women in middle and later life is surprisingly sparse (Etaugh and Bridges 2013).

Additionally, Eagly and colleagues examined the coverage of specific research topics over time. As might be expected, research about women and gender has been influenced by the intellectual, social, and political climate of the times. This context affects which questions and issues are viewed as compelling and worthy of study. It is not surprising that Eagly et al. noted a sharp rise in articles on gender stereotypes and sex-role attitudes during the late 1970s' peak of second-wave feminism. Research on gender and depression and on work–family attitudes, on the other hand, have shown a slower but steady increase since the late 1970s. Interest in the first of these has grown along with realization that gender differences in depression result from a complex interplay of internal affective, biological, and cognitive factors and negative life events. The increase in work–family research is no doubt influenced by women's increased participation in the labor force over the past several decades. Eagly et al. also looked at research topics related to feminism's activist efforts to empower women and improve their lives. Research on abortion has grown, peaking at the time of the 1973 Roe v. Wade Supreme Court decision. Articles on sexual harassment and intimate partner violence began to increase in the 1990s, and the latter remains an area of considerable research activity.

Finally, Eagly and colleagues explored the extent to which the psychology of gender and women is included in the most popular current introductory psychology textbooks. They found at least moderate coverage of various topics, unlike surveys of earlier introductory texts. Similarly, recent developmental psychology textbooks include greater coverage of gender and women than earlier ones (Etaugh and Bridges 2013).

It is clear that the psychology of gender has emerged since the 1960s as a vibrant discipline within psychological science. Feminist theorists and researchers have served as a driving force in the transformation of scholarship on gender. In recent years, the field has expanded to include a broad array of theoretical models, topics of study, and methodological and statistical tools. We review these briefly.

Many feminist scholars subscribe to the view that theoretical eclecticism is crucial both to the study of psychology of gender and the broader social goal of better understanding and improving the lives of women and men. One current variety of feminist theory called standpoint theory holds that women see the world from their own subjective perspective. This view has given rise to the feminist experiential research model discussed below. Another recent theoretical perspective is feminist social constructionism. A key tenet of this view is that "facts" are dependent on the forms of language and the language community that created them. Thus, social, cultural, and historical contexts influence what we know about the world. Another important new theoretical model is the biosocial constructionist theory of Alice Eagly and Wendy Wood. Instead of the traditional feminist separation of sex as nature and gender as nurture, their theory intertwines culture and biology in both distal evolutionary processes that shaped human psychology and proximal mechanisms that underlie similarities and differences in the behaviors of women and men (Eagly and Wood 2013).

Examples of recently emerging research topics of interest are the study of men and masculinity, body image, aggression and violence, homophobia and heterosexism, and more subtle forms of discrimination and stereotyping, and the examination of the complex interrelationships between mental and physical health issues, with a focus on how these relationships may differ in women and men. In addition, the greater focus on the diversity of women and men has produced an increasing body of multicultural and cross-cultural gender studies, including scholarship on indigenous, migrant, and bicultural women and men.

Within the realm of methodology, advances such as meta-analysis and the availability of electronic databases have already been mentioned. The development of more sophisticated qualitative analyses also bears mentioning. These include a variety of grounded theory, interview, discourse analytic, and ethnographic approaches. The field of feminist experiential research, noted earlier, relies on several of these qualitative methods.

Statistical advances also are having an important influence on the way in which researchers study the psychology of gender. For one thing, the increased use of moderating variable analyses has allowed researchers to progress from examining mean differences between females and males on a single variable to looking at the extent to which the associations between two or more variables differ as a function of gender or gender role. Moreover, the growing use of structural equation modeling has permitted researchers to incorporate multiple dependent, and also independent, variables into their gender research (Chrisler and McCreary 2010).

Thus, the field of psychology of gender continues to mirror and explore the transformations in the status of both women and men since the last third of the twentieth century.

Better understanding of the intersecting multiple identities within each gender remains a major task for future research.

SEE ALSO: Feminisms, First, Second, and Third Wave; Intersectionality

REFERENCES

Boring, Edwin G. 1951. "The Woman Problem." *American Psychologist*, 6, 679–682.

Brannon, Linda. 2007. *Gender: Psychological Perspectives*, 5th ed. Boston: Pearson.

Caplan, Paula J., and Jeremy B. Caplan. 2009. *Thinking Critically About Research on Sex and Gender*, 3rd ed. Boston: Pearson.

Chrisler, Joan C., and Donald R McCreary, eds. 2010. *Handbook of Gender Research in Psychology*, vols 1 and 2. New York: Springer.

Crawford, Mary E. 2006. *Transformations: Women, Gender, and Psychology*. New York: McGraw-Hill.

Crawford, Mary E., and Jeanne Marecek. 1989. "Psychology Reconstructs the Female: 1968–1988." *Psychology of Women Quarterly*, 13: 147–165. DOI: 10.1111/j.1471-6402.1989.tb00993.x.

De LaCoste-Utamsing, C. and R. L. Holloway. 1982. "Sexual Dimorphism in the Human Corpus Callosum." *Science*, 216: 1431–1432. DOI:10.1182/blood-2009-06-229658.

Eagly, Alice H., and Wendy Wood. 2013. "Feminism and Evolutionary Psychology: Moving Forward." *Sex Roles*, 69: 549–556.

Eagly, Alice H., Asia Eaton, Suzanna Rose, Stephanie Riger, and Maureen McHugh. 2012. "Feminism and Psychology: Analysis of a Half-Century of Research on Women and Gender." *American Psychologist*, 67: 211–230. DOI:10.1037/a0027260.

Etaugh, Claire A., and J.S. Bridges. 2013. *Women's Lives: a Psychological Exploration*, 3rd ed. Boston: Pearson.

Etaugh, Claire, and Judith Worell. 2012. "Contemporary Feminism for Gender Researchers: Not Just 'Our Bodies, Our Cells'." *Psychology of Women Quarterly*, 36: 419–422. DOI: 10.1177/0361684312461905.

Fiske, Susan T. 2010. "Venus and Mars or Down to Earth: Stereotypes and Realities of Gender Differences." *Perspectives on Psychological Science*, 5: 688–692.

Hall, G. Stanley. 1904. *Adolescence: Its Psychology and Its Relations to Physiology, Anthropology, Sociology, Sex, Crime, Religion, and Education*. New York: D. Appleton.

Hare-Mustin, Rachel T., and Jeanne Marecek. 1990 "On Making a Difference." In *Making a Difference: Psychology and the Construction of Gender*, edited by Rachel T. Hare-Mustin and Jeanne Marecek, 1–21. New Haven: Yale University Press.

Helgeson, Vicki S. 2005. *Psychology of Gender*, 2nd ed. Upper Saddle River: Pearson.

Hyde, Janet S. 2007. *Half the Human Experience: the Psychology of Women*, 7th ed. Boston: Houghton Mifflin.

Lakoff, Robin T. 1990. *Talking Power: the Politics of Language*. New York: Basic Books.

MacArthur, Heather J., and Stephanie A. Shields. 2014. "Psychology's Feminist Voices: a Critical Pedagogical Tool." *Sex Roles*, 70: 431–433. DOI: 10.1007/s11199-014-0349-9.

Maccoby, Eleanor E., and Carol Nagy Jacklin. 1974. *The Psychology of Sex Differences*. Stanford: Stanford University Press.

Matlin, Margaret W. 2008. *The Psychology of Women*, 6th ed. Belmont: Thomson.

O'Connell, Agnes N., and Nancy F. Russo. 1980. "Models for Achievement: Eminent Women in Psychology."*Psychology of Women Quarterly*, 5(Special Issue): 1–144. DOI: 10.1111/j.1471-6402.1980.tb01031.x.

Rider, Elizabeth A. 2005. *Our Voices: Psychology of Women*, 2nd ed. Hoboken: John Wiley & Sons.

Unger, Rhoda K. 1979. "Toward a Redefinition of Sex and Gender." *American Psychologist*, 34: 1085–1094. DOI:10.1037/0003-066X.34.11.1085.

Unger, Rhoda K., ed. 2001. *Handbook of the Psychology of Women and Gender*. New York: John Wiley & Sons.

Weisstein, Naomi. 1968. *"Kinder, Kuche, Kirche" as Scientific Law: Psychology Constructs the Female*. Boston: New England Free Press.

Worell, Judith, and Claire Etaugh. 1994. "Transforming Theory and Research with Women: Themes and Variations." *Psychology of Women Quarterly*, 18: 443–450. DOI: 10.1111/j.1471-6402.1994.tb01041.x.

Yoder, Janice D. 2003. *Women and Gender: Transforming Psychology*, 2nd ed. Upper Saddle River: Prentice Hall.

Psychology of Objectification

KASEY LYNN MORRIS and
JAMIE L. GOLDENBERG
University of South Florida, USA

Building on the intellectual foundation of decades of feminist scholarship (e.g., Nussbaum 1995), psychological research on the objectification of women was spearheaded by Fredrickson and Roberts's (1997) objectification theory. The theory suggests that objectification occurs when women are reduced to their physical appearance and their bodies are seen as capable of representing them. Women are routinely subject to objectifying experiences both in media depictions and in interpersonal interactions (Swim et al. 2001), and consequently come to adopt a third-person perspective, seeing themselves as an object to be looked at and evaluated. This is termed self-objectification, marked by heightened body surveillance and persistent monitoring of one's outward appearance. Objectification theory posits that heightened self-objectification increases body shame and anxiety, and disrupts cognitive functioning and the free flow of experience.

Several studies have examined causal links between self-objectification and its proposed consequences by experimentally manipulating the salience of self-objectification. In a formative study, researchers had participants try on either a swimsuit to heighten self-objectification, or a sweater in the control condition, and found that women (but not men) in the swimsuit condition reported higher levels of body shame and also restrained their consumption of a provided snack. Additionally, these women performed more poorly on a math exam (Fredrickson et al. 1998). A multitude of studies have replicated and followed these initial findings, demonstrating that heightened self-objectification (manipulated, or measured as an individual difference) is also linked with restrained movement (Harrison and Fredrickson 2003), a lack of intrinsic motivation (Gapinski, Brownell, and LaFrance 2003), and talking less in interpersonal interactions (Saguy et al. 2010). Further, the negative outcomes of heightened self-objectification have been replicated among racially and ethnically diverse samples (see Moradi and Huang 2008 for a review).

More recently, research in psychology has expanded from a focus on self-objectification to consideration of how women are perceived when they are objectified by others. These studies typically manipulate objectification with either explicit instruction to focus on a target's physical appearance or through sexualization (i.e., presenting the targets in a scantily clad manner). Objectified women are judged to be lacking "mind" and moral patiency (i.e., the ability to feel hunger, pain, desire; Loughnan et al. 2010), implicitly associated with objects (Rudman and Mescher 2012) and animals (Vaes, Paladino, and Puvia 2011), and cognitively perceived more similarly to objects (Bernard et al. 2012). Further, a heightened focus on appearance leads to perceptions of women, but not men, as being less competent, warm, and moral (Heflick et al. 2011), and also possessing fewer of the traits considered essential to human nature (Heflick and Goldenberg 2009). Taken together, this body of evidence is consistent with philosophical and feminist discourse on objectification (e.g., Nussbaum 1995) in which objectified women are quite literally depicted as objects rather than human beings (Gervais et al. 2013).

SEE ALSO: Animality and Women; Gender Identities and Socialization

REFERENCES

Bernard, Philippe, Sarah J. Gervais, Jill Allen, Sophie Campomizzi, and Olivier Klein. 2012. "Integrating Sexual Objectification with Object versus Person Recognition: The Sexualized Body-Inversion Hypothesis." *Psychological Science*, 23(5): 469–471.

Fredrickson, Barbara L., and Tomi-Ann Roberts. 1997. "Objectification Theory: Towards Understanding Women's Lived Experiences and Mental Health Risks." *Psychology of Women Quarterly*, 21: 173–206.

Fredrickson, Barbara L., Tomi-Ann Roberts, Stephanie M. Noll, Diane M. Quinn, and Jean M. Twenge. 1998. "That Swimsuit Becomes You: Sex Differences in Self-Objectification, Restrained Eating, and Math Performance." *Journal of Personality and Social Psychology*, 75: 269–284.

Gapinski, Kathrine D., Kelly D. Brownell, and Marianne LaFrance. 2003. "Body Objectification and 'Fat Talk': Effects on Emotion, Motivation, and Cognitive Performance." *Sex Roles*, 48: 377–388.

Gervais, Sarah J., Philippe Bernard, Olivier Klein, and Jill Allen. 2013. "Toward a Unified Theory of Objectification and Dehumanization." In *Objectification and (De)Humanization*, edited by Sarah J. Gervais, 1–23. New York: Springer.

Harrison, Kristen, and Barbara L. Fredrickson. 2003. "Women's Sports Media, Self-Objectification, and Mental Health in Black and White Adolescents." *Journal of Communication*, 53: 216–232.

Heflick, Nathan A., and Jamie L. Goldenberg. 2009. "Objectifying Sarah Palin: Evidence that Objectification Causes Women to be Perceived as Less Competent and Less Fully Human." *Journal of Experimental Social Psychology*, 45: 598–601.

Heflick, Nathan A., Jamie L. Goldenberg, Douglas Cooper, and Elisa Puvia. 2011. "From Women to Objects: Appearance Focus, Target Gender, and Perceptions of Warmth, Morality and Competence." *Journal of Experimental Social Psychology*, 47: 572–581.

Loughnan, Steve, et al. 2010. "Objectification Leads to Depersonalization: The Denial of Mind and Moral Concern to Objectified Others." *European Journal of Social Psychology*, 40: 709–717.

Moradi, Bonnie, and Yu-Ping Huang. 2008. "Objectification Theory and Psychology of Women: A Decade of Advances and Future Directions." *Psychology of Women Quarterly*, 32(4): 377–398.

Nussbaum, Martha. 1995. "Objectification." *Philosophy and Public Affairs*, 24(4): 249–291.

Rudman, Laurie A., and Kris Mescher. 2012. "Of Animals and Objects: Men's Implicit Dehumanization of Women and Male Sexual Aggression." *Personality and Social Psychology Bulletin*, 38: 734–746.

Saguy, Tamar, Diane M. Quinn, John F. Dovidio, and Felicia Pratto. 2010. "Interacting Like a Body: Objectification Can Lead Women to Narrow their Presence in Social Interactions." *Psychological Science*, 21: 178–182.

Swim, Janet, Lauri L. Hyers, Laurie L. Cohen, and Melissa J. Ferguson. 2001. "Everyday Sexism: Evidence for Its Incidence, Nature, and Psychological Impact from Three Daily Diary Studies." *Journal of Social Issues*, 57: 31–53. DOI: 10.1111/0022-4537.00200.

Vaes, Jeroen, Paola Paladino, and Elisa Puvia. 2011. "Are Sexualized Women Complete Human Beings? Why Men and Women Dehumanize Sexually Objectified Women." *European Journal of Social Psychology*, 41(6): 774–785.

FURTHER READING

Goldenberg, Jamie L. 2013. "Immortal Objects: The Objectification of Women as Terror Management." In *Objectification and (De)Humanization*, edited by Sarah J. Gervais, 73–95. New York: Springer.

Zurbriggen, Eileen L., and Tomi-Ann Roberts, eds. 2012. *The Sexualization of Girls and Girlhood: Causes, Consequences and Resistance*. New York: Oxford University Press.

Purity Versus Pollution

CASEY GOLOMSKI
University of Massachusetts Boston, USA

Purity and pollution can refer to things that are clean and dirty, but are used more widely to place different values on ideas and practices about gender, sexuality, the body, and society. They are metaphors that link and contrast phenomena in a symbolic web of meaning. Purity and pollution are powerful terms that often get mapped onto other dichotomies like good and evil, sacred and profane, normal and abnormal, man and woman, and life and death. Mary Douglas's *Purity and Danger* (1966) set the standard for understanding these concepts by arguing that cultures impose systems to classify certain objects or people as acceptable. Labeling things as pure or impure marks them as either a part of or beyond the social order. Society's taboos and laws work to lessen ambiguity and strengthen distinction between what is pure and what is polluting, namely who and what is allowed to belong or not.

The history and metaphorical language of purity and pollution texture other concepts like morality, justice, and difference. In classical Western philosophy, purity and pollution represent Aristotle's basic opposition, and ancient Greek notions point to a wide social domain that includes ritual impurities, dishonest behavior, and wrongdoings of piety, justice, and the law. With roots in antiquity, contemporary Western law still carries these moral connotations. Nussbaum (2006) argues that pollution or disgust often goes hand in hand with morality, as descriptions of disgusting things tend to get linked to condemning or prohibitive attitudes. She writes that disgusting things are actually more symbolically offensive to the senses than they are physically harmful, so notions of disgust should not form a basis for criminal law.

Psychological approaches see pollution or disgust as concerns about awareness and proximity. Unlike fear or hatred, where aversion avoids bodily harm, aversion to pollution puts it out of one's consciousness. Kristeva (1982) argues that in the formation of subjectivity, sexual drives and bodily elements become shut out to mark clean and proper bodies. One cannot totally get rid of these elements and feels abjection when one recognizes they are always present. Abjection entails self-reflection, and psychodynamic theories suggest that rejection of an Other, symbolized as a gross thing, involves partial rejection of oneself. In contrast, pollution or disgust can also simultaneously excite interest and arousal and be a source of indulgence and pleasure rather than horror.

Cross-culturally, values of purity symbolize order, hierarchy, virtue, and inclusiveness, and inform most local and world religious traditions: Judeo-Christian, South Asian, African, and Eastern. Purity norms usually appear to conscript gendered social interaction and bodies in these traditions. Recent scholarship rethinks the ways in which norms are understood, resisted, or remade as people forge gendered and sexual identities and communities.

Morality in Judeo-Christian religions is strengthened by purification rites, which enable holiness and godly encounters. Personal pollution has the capacity to affect wider communities, thus many prohibitions have religious justification. The biblical text of Leviticus places strict guidelines for men and women to live holy lives that center on purity in daily domestic practices, food consumption, sexual relations, and bodily hygiene, including the maintenance of menstruation and other discharges. Feminist biblical scholars have argued that menstruating women separated themselves *for* God, not *from* God, as an inspiring act of devotion, and that gendered prohibitions on sexual relations reflect historical logics of purity, rather than women's denigration. This revision focuses on gender complementarity and women's central roles in domestic and social reproduction as grounds for their stricter attention to purity norms.

For many South Asian Hindus, the body is an open network of channels, and one's bodily substances get easily attached to other people and things that one touches, whether in sharing items or casual and sexual contact. Social interaction is structured to avoid or permit the transfer of pure, *suddah*, or impure substances between genders and castes. For example, if a person wants to stay pure for ritual or social reasons, they might avoid touching heavily handled objects or exchange something by placing it on the ground for another person to pick up, rather than giving it directly hand to hand. Older women become more pure as they age because they no longer menstruate, give birth, or have sex. These reproductive changes symbolically make them more like men, who are seen as less polluting. Higher-caste people in contact with lower-caste people may bathe to get rid of impurities. Wives may eat husbands' food leftovers, but not vice versa. While women tend to conform to purity norms, they find ways to get around some norms to make everyday life more practical (Lamb 2000).

In southeastern Africa, indigenous religious rituals surrounding the life cycle and reproduction center on notions of dirtiness and cleanliness. Polluting darkness or dirtiness results from contaminating social and bodily processes. In Swaziland, mourners are sickened by death, and widows should stay in seclusion so as not to spread ill fortune to others. Indigenous and syncretic Christian healers can use herbal medicines to ward off this affliction. At the community level in KwaZulu-Natal, ritual specialists conduct periodic fertility rites to restore ecological balance of livelihoods and crops. Pollution can be understood in this ritual sense, as well as one of illness causation (Jewkes and Wood 1999). Regionally, the phenomenon of "dirty wombs" is couched in the symbolism of pollution, but also speaks to women's perception of sexual and reproductive health and the social valuation of disease. Comparatively, attention to language and culture shows how pollution and purity may multiply describe *and* explain how gendered bodies are healed.

SEE ALSO: Menstrual Activism; Menstrual Rituals; Taboo; Virginity

REFERENCES

Douglas, Mary. 1966. *Purity and Danger*. New York: Routledge.

Jewkes, Rachel, and Katharine Wood. 1999. "Problematizing Pollution: Dirty Wombs, Ritual Pollution, and Pathological Processes." *Medical Anthropology*, 18: 163–186.

Kristeva, Julia. 1982. *Powers of Horror*. New York: Columbia University Press.

Lamb, Sarah. 2000. *White Saris and Sweet Mangoes: Aging, Gender, and Body in North India*. Berkeley: University of California Press.

Nussbaum, Martha. 2006. *Hiding from Humanity: Disgust, Shame, and the Law*. Princeton: Princeton University Press.

Queer Anglophone Literature

JONATHON ZAPASNIK
Australian National University, Australia

While there has always been a recognizable body of literature characterized through the implicit or explicit reference to same-sex relations, sexual perversion, or gender variation, the emergence of "queer" literature is a recent phenomenon in the field of literary criticism, particularly in the anglophone world. Queer literature refers to writing, whether fiction or non-fiction, that concerns itself with the transgression of gendered and/or sexual norms. Historically, its emergence can be traced to the lesbian and gay liberation movement that is often symbolically associated with the 1969 Stonewall Riots and the AIDS crisis of the 1980s. Politically, it developed as a counter-discourse to normative understandings of sex, gender, and intimacy through an acknowledgment of diverse sexual cultures that existed prior to and in tension with the political milieu of the time. As Les Brookes (2009) notes, this antinormative resistance is largely reflected in the literary tradition that has emerged since Stonewall, and indeed, contributes toward the complexities associated with identifying the defining attributes of queer literature as a genre. Particularly within an Australian context, as Michael Hurley (1996) has observed, what is considered queer literature is quite often misunderstood and poorly received by its critics.

Queer literature is a product of the activist and scholarly setting of the 1970s and 1980s. In the United States, there was a renewal of radical activism demonstrated in groups such as ACT UP and Queer Nation in response to increasing pressures of the AIDS epidemic. The mainstream lesbian and gay movement was criticized for representing the values of white, middle class, gay men, rather than acknowledging the diversity of gendered and sexual experience. This challenge to established identity politics was incorporated into the academy under the influence of French poststructuralism, especially with the introduction of Michel Foucault's first volume to the *History of Sexuality* (1990). Foucault suggested that sexuality is a modern discourse that is sociocultural dependent. That is to say, it only makes sense to talk of gendered or sexual identities when there is a cultural understanding of what it means to act one way or another. Scholars, such as Eve Kosofsky Sedgwick (1990), elaborated on Foucault's premise and established how dominant culture is reliant on non-normative subjects to

The Wiley Blackwell Encyclopedia of Gender and Sexuality Studies, First Edition. Edited by Nancy A. Naples.
© 2016 John Wiley & Sons, Ltd. Published 2016 by John Wiley & Sons, Ltd.

sustain their privileged subject positions. The historicity of the notion of sexuality encouraged a new way of doing literary criticism. Indeed, queer literature gained visibility during this period with the inception of several specialist journals, including *GLQ: A Journal of Lesbian and Gay Studies*, as well as several academic manuscripts.

Despite growing visibility in the streets and in the academy, queer literature has proved to be a problematic category to define, namely because what exactly is meant by queer has been so heavily contested by its critics. In literary criticism, where queer can be used to signify anti-normative sexual experience or gendered identities more generally, it can also be used as a reference to what is being signified in the writing, who wrote it, or its intended readership. Queer, then, might include not only writing by gendered and sexual minorities – lesbian, gay, bisexual, or transgender – but also others who are considered outside of gender or sexual norms, extending the reach to heterosexual identifying subjects who might engage in "deviant" practices, such as cross-dressing, fetishism, or sadomasochism. There is also an appreciation that identities are intersected by multiple axes of oppression (e.g., class and race) and how these competing identities compliment and complicate each other. Therefore, queer serves as a convenient shorthand that conveys an awareness of the inherent contradictions and ambiguities of gendered and sexual identity categories. In some sense, this could be understood as reductive given the kind of writing that is produced, but queer is important for understanding how normative behavior might be interpreted differently by gendered or sexual outsiders, emphasizing the experiential quality of queer life, intimacy, and communities.

Opposing itself to the notion of a fixed and normative identity, queer emphasizes the idea that identity is something that is historically and relationally situated. It celebrates gender and sexual fluidity, implying how identity categories are restrictive, placing limitations on how a text can be read and assumes a literary canon that can be claimed by a certain readership. In other words, queer literature challenges the notion that a coherent narrative of sexual identity and experience forged through gender or sexual binaries can be read and recognized within a text. Homosexuality, for example, can be used to signify a constellation of meanings since what homosexual means is never a singular indicator, but rather a set of contradictory meanings. Meaning in queer literature is understood less through evident connotation presented by an author, but in conjunction to the discourses that allow sexuality to be articulated or interpreted according to specific cultural restraints. By leaving exposed outward-opening connections, a queer reading practice may foreground the visibility of other differences, some of them uneasily enclosed by the catch-all "gay" or "lesbian." Fiction is a valuable resource in this regard not because it answers such questions, but because it leaves them as problems for the reader.

Given its subversive nature, queer literature comes in multiple genres and mediums, including novels, short stories, poetry, and plays. Fiction, especially, has been important historically in developing self-understanding, a sense of identity, and a meaningful relationship to the past for both gendered and sexual minorities. In this regard, anthologies have always been an important genre for collecting and publishing queer writing, especially in places like Australia. It is also unsurprising that most queer literature is based on autobiographical experience. A good example of this is Scott Heim's *Mysterious Skin* (1995), an American novel. While published as fiction, much of the narrative is based on Heim's own coming out and experience with sexual violence (see Heim 1997). In this sense, queer literature often focuses on the writer's coming to terms with their sexuality, or in the case of transgender writing, their gendered difference, usually through coming out narratives.

As an emerging genre after Stonewall, coming out narratives were commonly published in student magazines and newspapers, various political leaflets, manifestos, and as submissions to government departments by groups such as CAMP and Gay Task Force. Coming out stories emphasize the construction of personal identity through the continual process of negotiating the boundaries of one's gender or sexuality. A good example of this is Patrick White's *Flaws in the Glass* (1981). As this autobiography suggests, there is an uncomfortable tension between self-acceptance, but also what it means to be a gay man and how to act accordingly. Closely related to this has been the role of family, whether it concerns the dissolution or the creation of new family units. Thus, the family is quite often represented in various, perhaps even conflicting ways. On the one hand, queer literature might signal the move away from the family unit since the family is often the source of abandonment or skepticism. On the other hand, literature produced around the AIDS epidemic, for example, has illustrated the possibility of conceiving alternative modes of family, as evident in Thomas Gunn's *The Man with Night Sweats* (1992). These writers make themselves available to a wide readership by framing their characters in such a way as to complicate their sexuality.

Ideological conflict – between assimilationist and liberationist politics – has been at the heart of much queer literature (Brookes 2009). Those who see the need for a revolution of heterosexist society and those who do not, often expressed through rhetoric of sameness or equality. Queer literature reproduces a mixture of these ideas, since it depends on how they are read or how they are interpreted. Notably Andrew Holleran's *Dancer from the Dance* (1979) and Larry Kramer's *Faggots* (1978) combine a unique sense of celebration mixed with distaste about post-Stonewall liberation and can be read as a precursor to the emergence of a distinct queer literary tradition. This irony between political ideologies has resulted in a multiplicity of stories rather than two distinct narrative trajectories. It not only demonstrates the same tensions as pre-Stonewall gay writing, but also the heightening of these pressures, particularly during the early 1980s, with the discovery of HIV/AIDS.

AIDS has played an important role in the formation and development of queer literature, whether directly or incidentally. Like the earlier coming out narratives, AIDS writing cuts across a range of mediums, incorporating fiction (poetry, memoirs, short stories, plays) and non-fiction (essay collections, autobiographies, journals) works. Fictions, especially in the form of short stories, have provided a space for those to exercise their voice in exploring the more intimate dimensions of the epidemic. While there was not much AIDS literature published in Australia during the early years of the epidemic, the first major publication by a person living with AIDS was Eric Michaels's *Unbecoming* (1990). Typically, through such representations AIDS is not viewed as the outcome of moral weakness, but rather it is seen as the consequence of intimacy, and thus resists the fulfillment of a tragic destiny commonly associated with an earlier period of lesbian and gay writing exemplified by Christopher Isherwood's *A Single Man* (1964). In the United States and the United Kingdom, as in Australia, the majority of writing produced about AIDS has focused on the Caucasian, middle-class experience of the epidemic.

An important element of queer literature has been its transgressive appeal to those considered gendered or sexual outsiders, inspired by sexual liberation and the realm of fantasy. While much lesbian and gay literature post-Stonewall has been about providing recognizable images of ordinary, often middle-class, gay men and lesbians, a queer sensibility has encouraged the push to bring eroticism to the foreground of identity expression. The protagonist in J. T. LeRoy's *The Heart Deceitful Above All Things* (2001), for example, is represented as a sexual outlaw – a young boy who develops an interest in sex with adult men and sadomasochism after suffering abuse at the hands of his mother and her various sexual flings – he becomes the living embodiment of transgression, especially to do with the norms associated with the representation of child sexuality. Likewise, Samuel R. Delany's pornographic fiction, *The Mad Man* (1994b) or *Hogg* (1994a) extends the transgressive metaphor though the incorporation of perverse pleasures into the fantasy of the novel. Scenes of sexual violence often complicate the ethical imperative of such inclusions. As Tim Dean (2011) notes, queer literature tests the limits not only of social norms but also of its most progressive readers. Literally representation has the potential to bring us into contact with matters that would typically remain, untouched, indeed, untouchable. Melissa Febos's memoir about being a dominatrix, *Whip Smart* (2010), reveals how transgressive literature that signifies extreme boundary violation actually signifies a source of its erotic power. Also, closely associated with transgression is the figure of the transgender subject.

Transgender, or trans more broadly, refers to individuals whose gender identity or expression does not conform to the social expectations for their assigned sex at birth (Love 2011). A highly contested term, much like queer, it also can be used to describe those who choose to live outside the gender binary, identifying as either male or female, both or neither. This work has seen an increased interest in memoirs, autobiographies, novels, and critical works dealing with trans themes in order to give trans-identifying people political agency and challenge the traditional frameworks though which they have been represented. Examples of this trend include Leslie Feinberg's *Stone Butch Blues* (1993) and Jamison Green's *Becoming a Visible Man* (2004). Feinberg in particular narrates a story of coming to terms with one's own gender set against the backdrop of gay and lesbian life. This story is embodied by the protagonist, Jess, who tries to make space in a world that will accommodate the complexity of her being. A more contemporary example dealing with gender variation is Jeffrey Eugenides's 2002 Pulitzer winning novel, *Middlesex*, which engages issues of intersexual embodiment. The interest in literature dealing with gender variation issues shows increased visibility and public tolerance toward narratives of difference.

SEE ALSO: Gay Male Literature; Identity Politics; Queer Theory; Representation

REFERENCES

Brookes, Les. 2009. *Gay Male Fiction Since Stonewall: Ideology, Conflict, and Aesthetics*. New York: Routledge.

Dean, Tim. 2011. "The Erotics of Transgression." In *The Cambridge Companion to Gay and Lesbian Writing*, edited by Hugh Stevens, 65–80. Cambridge: Cambridge University Press.

Delany, Samuel R. 1994a. *Hogg*. Normal: Black Ice Books.

Delany, Samuel R. 1994b. *The Man Men*. New York: Masquerade Books.

Eugenides, Jeffrey. 2002. *Middlesex*. New York: Farrar, Straus, and Giroux.

Febos, Melissa. 2010. *Whip Smart*. Sydney: Pan Macmillan.

Feinberg, Leslie. 1993. *Stone Butch Blues: A Novel*. Ithaca: Firebrand Books.

Foucault, Michel. 1990. *The History of Sexuality*, trans. Robert Hurley, vol. 1. New York: Vintage Books.

Green, Jamison. 2004. *Becoming a Visible Man*. Nashville: Vanderbilt University Press.
Gunn, Thom. 1992. *The Man with Night Sweats*. London: Faber and Faber.
Heim, Scott. 1995. *Mysterious Skin: A Novel*. New York: HarperCollins.
Heim, Scott. 1997. "Ant." In *Boys Like Us: Gay Writers Tell Their Coming out Stories*, edited by Patrick Merla, 275–283. London: Fourth Estate.
Holleran, Andrew. 1979. *Dancer from the Dance*. London: Bantam.
Hurley, Michael. 1996. *A Guide to Gay and Lesbian Writing in Australia*. St. Leonards: Allen and Unwin.
Isherwood, Christopher. 1964. *A Single Man*. London: Vintage.
Kramer, Larry. 1978. *Faggots*. New York: Random House.
LeRoy, J. T. 2001. *The Heart Is Deceitful above All Things*. London: Bloomsbury.
Love, Heather. 2011. "Transgender Fiction and Politics." In *The Cambridge Companion to Gay and Lesbian Writing*, edited by Hugh Stevens, 148–164. Cambridge: Cambridge University Press.
Michaels, Eric. 1990. *Unbecoming: An AIDS Diary*. Rose Bay: Empress.
Sedgwick, Eve Kosofsky. 1990. *Epistemology of the Closet*. Berkeley: University of California Press.
White, Patrick. 1981. *Flaws in the Glass: A Self-Portrait*. Harmondsworth: Penguin.

FURTHER READING

Stevens, Hugh, ed. 2011. *The Cambridge Companion to Gay and Lesbian Writing*. Cambridge: Cambridge University Press.
Woods, Gregory. 1998. *A History of Gay Literature: The Male Tradition*. New Haven: Yale University Press.

Queer Literary Criticism

TAMSIN SPARGO
Liverpool John Moores University, UK

Queer literary criticism is a term that can be used to label a diversity of approaches to literary and other texts that share a concern with sexual orientations, identities, relations, and politics. The term can be used specifically to describe work undertaken from a *queer* perspective, definitively anti-normative, but is also used more generally to encompass work by scholars whose concerns, or identifications are, lesbian, gay, bisexual, transgender, or intersex (LGBTI). Although those writing queer literary criticism may identify as LGBTI or queer, the practice is best understood as textual analysis and scholarship that adopts a non-normative stance in practice rather than being a reflection of its author's sexual identity. There is an overlap between those who would identify their literary scholarship as gay, or lesbian, or LGBTI, and queer, but the definition used here focuses on the latter, rather than on the myriad approaches that preceded and coexist with it. Queer, understood as either an adjective or as a verb, denotes a troubling or challenging of normal, and normative, definitions of sexuality, gender, sexual identities, and practices, and it is this, rather than any identification with currently understood identities, that defines queer literary criticism.

It is rare to find a queer textual study that limits its scope to the literary as traditionally understood. In common with other theoretically informed textual practices that emerged from poststructuralist critical theory in the postmodern era, queer cultural analysis tends to transgress disciplinary boundaries. It does so in order to prioritize and interrogate objects of study that might be excluded in traditional scholarship and, sometimes, to bring into question the assumptions of a given discipline about what it is proper to study. Queer criticism thus tends to encompass texts from popular culture and media and to consider literary texts within historical, social, and discursive formations and relations. Queer literary criticism uses the reading of texts within, and in order to develop, arguments about sexuality or sexual politics and can be seen as an interventionist approach to academic scholarship, sharing with feminist, LGBTI, and other political stances, a refusal of the illusion of disinterested critical enquiry.

The term queer, in its positive sense, derived from the political activism of the late 1980s when radical responses, by groups such as ACT-UP and Queer Nation, to the profound threats and deeply held prejudices of the AIDs era, helped to build a non-conformist and assertively different LGBTI coalition. This explicit political commitment to refusing the model of gay assimilation into a heterosexist society was combined with awareness of the power of intervention in language. A term that had been used to stigmatize and disempower those who did not fit norms of behavior, appearance, or identification was reappropriated as a positive label of refusal of those norms. Identity politics, which had been the dominant model for the assertion of gay rights in earlier decades, had proved limited in its effectiveness, notably for those people whose identifications and practices did not fit the oppositional identities available to them. Whereas gay or lesbian identities might be accommodated within a heternormative structure, albeit in subordinate or marginal positions, identification as queer resisted such assimilation. Queer politics also embraced a greater diversity of people, including cross-dressers and those identifying as intersex. Queer could be understood as whatever is at odds with the normal, or dominant understanding of proper gender and sexual identifications and practices, as a relation of difference, a critical stance, rather than an essential identity.

This political activism coincided with, informed, and was informed by, philosophical, anthropological, and theoretical work by figures such as Teresa de Lauretis, Gayle Rubin, and Judith Butler, who developed and extended feminist deconstruction of gender categorization. de Lauretis is credited with coining the phrase "queer theory" at a conference in 1990 and in a special issue of the journal *differences: A Journal of Feminist Cultural Studies* (de Lauretis 1991). Rubin's anthropological work, notably her studies of lesbian sadomasochism and gay male leather subculture, challenged normative associations and understandings of gender and sexuality. Butler's exploration of the performativity of gender suggested that gendered and sexual identities are not essential but produced through a form of scripted repetition. These subversive, politically engaged explorations brought some of the force of the social and cultural intervention of activists into the academy and, although there had been many scholars and literary critics working on LGBT issues, this "queering" moment marked a new emphasis, and broader recognition of, the exploration of non-normative sexualities in critical practice. Other theoretical influences on queer literary practice were, and are Michel Foucault's understanding of discursive structures and practices and power, Jacques Derrida's deconstruction of the binary structures of language as a social force, and the challenges to identity politics that stemmed from feminist, and other, psychoanalytic and philosophical traditions.

It is impossible to schematize queer literary criticism as it is not a formal school. Those who might define their literary criticism as queer have in common a commitment to uncover, deconstruct, and contest a pervasive but unstable heteronormativity rather than an agreed agenda or methodology. Some critics might focus on revealing the extent of heteronomative constructions of gender and sexuality within the literature of a given period, others might track changes to the literary representations of sexuality over time, most explore the tensions within such representations as they reflect, and contribute to, wider structures of meaning. Queer literary criticism is usually historicist, insisting on the specificity of a text's moment of production or circulation. Its methods often employ deconstructivist textual analysis that explores tensions and fissures in a literary work's production of meanings. Unlike some gay or lesbian literary critical approaches, queer literary criticism does not focus on recovering or championing neglected or marginalized writing by LGBT-identified authors, as this would seem, like traditional identity politics, to leave the binary oppositions structuring the field of knowledge in place. The inclusivity of the term queer has, however, encouraged the consideration of a wider range of texts produced by and about other marginalized groups. In this respect, queer literary criticism, like queer cultural theory, can be seen as addressing a revised field of study as well as a distinctive approach.

In this diverse range of studies, several figures have emerged as particularly influential, either in their writing or in their broader practice, including teaching or activism. Key figures include Lauren Berlant, Leo Bersani, Judith/Jack Halberstam, Michael Warner, and David Halperin, who co-founded *GLQ: A Journal of Lesbian and Gay Studies*, a key resource and context for gay critical studies that features the work of many critics cited here. Some of these are academics who specialize in literary studies, but the development of queer studies and of queer critical approaches has been consistently multidisciplinary. Although this is an overtly political academic practice, its practitioners have been notably successful in gaining recognition and in establishing research and pedagogic centers at universities, including Duke University.

The literary critic who is most strongly associated with the development and championing of queer criticism, mainly from her position at Duke, is Eve Kosofsky Sedgwick. Sedgwick's *Between Men: English Literature and Male Homosocial Desire* (1985), *Epistemology of the Closet* (1990), and *Tendencies* (1993), grew out of, and contributed to, the queer activism of their period and epitomize key features of queer literary criticism (Sedgwick 1985, 1990, 1993). *Between Men* analyzed the representation in, and participation of, literary texts in the complex relations between men in British culture from 1750 to 1850. Here, canonical texts from Restoration drama to Tennyson's poems were re-viewed as part of an exploration of homosocial bonding that oppressed women and depended on a refused homosexual identity. In *Epistemology of the Closet*, Sedgwick discussed, through analysis of canonical texts of English and North American literature, the apparent imperative to identify a person as either heterosexual or homosexual at the heart of twentieth-century forms of knowledge.

Sedgwick's studies locate literary texts within the interconnected structures and processes of knowledge production and circulation, and identity formation and power relations of specific historical moments. She also, as her collection of essays *Tendencies* demonstrates, wrote in a provocative, playful style that was as much part of her queer project as her argument. As the title of one of her best-known essays, "Jane Austen and the Masturbating Girl," demonstrates through harnessing an author frequently misread as conventionally romantic with an unexpected desiring subject, Sedgwick addressed and contested conventional assumptions and demarcations. The essay, which explored lesbian desire in *Sense and Sensibility*, challenged conventionally accepted knowledge about sexual practices, identities, and relations both as depicted in the literary text and in the ways in which literary texts are read and categorized. In addition to addressing the formation of sexual identities, Sedgwick explored sexual and erotic practices that transgressed gender and sexual-identity boundaries. This is another common feature of queer textual and cultural analysis, connecting with Butler's assertion of performativity, and contributing to an overarching challenge to traditional associations of certain practices with homosexual or heterosexual subjects. Although Sedgwick, who died in 2009, did not comment on her own sexuality, the fact that some people commented on the contrast between her queer literary practice and her marriage to a man has been taken as evidence of the pervasive social and cultural insistence on a gay/straight binary opposition that her work contests.

The reach, and impact, of heteronormative figures has been explored in the work of another key exponent of queer literary criticism. Lee Edelman's study *No Future: Queer Theory and the Death Drive* (Edelman 2004) explored the figure of the child as a representation of innocence within a politics of reproduction that positions the queer as antisocial, narcissistic, and future-negating. Edelman offered readings of novels and films that re-imagined them without their pivotal child figures in addition to offering a critique of normalizing acts such as gay marriage and parenting. This fusion of literary criticism, psychoanalysis, social critique, and polemic epitomized queer cultural praxis. Edelman's work connects with an emphasis in much queer literary criticism on identifying, and queering, negative associations in literature between homosexuality and death, brought into focus by homophobic representations during the AIDs crisis.

Some queer cultural criticism has focused on the literary representation of sexual practices, and their associated subcultures, such as sado-masochism, as foregrounding and perfomatively subverting conventional power relations; work in this area includes the study of queer and LGTBI fiction writers such as Pat Califia, and the intersections of pornographic, polemical, and performance texts. Work on subjects, and writers, who defy conventional gender and sexual classifications includes subcultural groups, such as South American *travesti*, and individual autobiographical writers who, like Kate Bornstein, both write and enact performative contestation of heteronormativity. A more overtly playful, but still politically charged, strand of queer critique, typified by the work of Moe Meyer, has focused on the ways in which drag, hyperbolic performance, and camp contest heteronormativity through parody. In such work, the analysis of dramatic or represented performance, in literary or popular culture, is approached as part of an exploration of the performativity of gendered and sexual identities.

Although some critics have suggested that it still privileges the white, middle-class male, there are multiple strands to queer literary and cultural criticism that explore the intersections and tensions between sexual, gendered, and racial subject positions. African American queer literary criticism ranges from re-evaluations of canonical texts such as those of James Baldwin, to explorations of the racial loading of sexual metaphor; key figures include Mae G. Henderson and E. Patrick Johnson. There is also a strong Latina/Latino tradition; influential figures include José Esteban Muñoz and Gloria Anzaldúa.

Although many of the earliest academic proponents of queer literary criticism were based in North American universities, it is best viewed as a trans-national phenomenon and explorations of culturally different identifications and practices have served to extend and modify its scope. In the United Kingdom, the term "sexual dissidence," taken from Rubin and championed at the University of Sussex, is used in addition to, or instead of, queer.

Criticisms of queer literary criticism and theory have been voiced from very different positions. In common with other forms of scholarship that share its transdisciplinary, overtly political approach, it has been accused by supporters of traditional literary criticism of making literary texts serve its ends rather than elucidating them. Some Marxist critics argue that, like poststructuralist and postmodern theory, it has been successful in gaining a strong foothold in the university system because its focus on the discursive limits its political challenge. Some LGTBI-identified critics of queer theory, and criticism, argue that its rejection of the idea of stable identities is easier to accept from a position of (academic) privilege and that its theoretical approach may exclude some people. Although there are an increasing number of literary critics who would identify their work as queer rather than LGTB or I, the ubiquity of the term, and its mainstream respectability, have led some writers who originally used the term, including de Lauretis, to stop using it to identify their work. New directions in the twenty-first century include links with postsecular theory, including the work of Marcella Althaus-Reid, and with queer ethics and phenomenology.

SEE ALSO: Heteronormativity and Homonormativity; Queer Theory

REFERENCES

de Lauretis, Teresa, ed. 1991. "Queer Theory: Lesbian and Gay Sexualities." *differences: A Journal of Feminist Cultural Studies*, 3(2): special issue.
Edelman, Lee. 2004. *No Future: Queer Theory and the Death Drive*. Durham, NC: Duke University Press.
Sedgwick, Eve Kosofsky. 1985. *Between Men: English Literature and Male Homosocial Desire*. New York: Columbia University Press.
Sedgwick, Eve Kosofsky. 1990. *Epistemology of the Closet*. Berkeley: University of California Press.
Sedgwick, Eve Kosofsky. 1993. *Tendencies*. Durham, NC: Duke University Press.

FURTHER READING

Althaus-Reid, Marcella. 2003. *The Queer God*. London: Routledge.
Anzaldúa, Gloria. 1987. *Borderlands/La Frontera: the New Mestiza*. San Francisco: Aunt Lute Books.
Bersani, Leo. 2009. *Is the Rectum a Grave? And Other Essays*. Chicago: University of Chicago Press.
Butler, Judith. 1990. *Gender Trouble: Feminism and the Subversion of Identity*. London: Routledge.
GLQ: A Journal of Gay and Lesbian Studies.
Halberstam, Judith. 1998. *Female Masculinity*. Durham, NC: Duke University Press.
Halperin, David. 1995. *Saint Foucault: Towards a Gay Hagiography*. New York: Oxford University Press.
Meyer, Moe. 2005. *The Politics and Poetics of Camp*. London: Routledge.
Muñoz, José Esteban. 1999. *Disidentifications: Queers of Color and the Performance of Politics*. Minneapolis: University of Minnesota Press.
Rubin, Gayle. 2012. *Deviations: a Gayle Rubin Reader*. Durham, NC: Duke University Press.

Queer Methods and Methodologies

KATH BROWNE
University of Brighton, UK

CATHERINE NASH
Brock University, Canada

Queer is a term associated with a theoretical or conceptual approach, a political perspective, and as a form of destabilized self-identification or self-understanding. Queer theory emerged in the 1990s and has moved through numerous phases, including discussions of heteronormativities and, since the turn of the century, homonormativities, with multiple relations to lesbian and gay studies (see the entry on queer theory for full details of the emergence of queer theory and its contemporary manifestations). As a conceptual approach or framework, it takes an anti-normative perspective as its main concern. In this context, its focus is on understanding how normative *sexual* and *gendered identities*, ordered along a *heterosexual/homosexual* binary, constitute social relations of exclusion and invisibility. By assuming that everyone is normatively gendered and that sexual interest is always opposite sex or heterosexual, queer ways of being and queer people are excluded or rendered invisible. In this way, "queer" approaches challenge our fundamental understanding of the nature of subjects and identities of our research projects and challenge normative understandings of our everyday lives, social relations, and social organization.

Queer research, then, works to destabilize these normative understandings and systems of meaning embedded within power relations, rendering visible and knowable that which was unseen and unknown. For example, as Lorena Muñoz (2010) argues, expectations that Latina street vendors in Los Angeles are heterosexual renders invisible the presence of queer women in these same places. Given this, queer methodologies constitute the relationship between queer's ontological and epistemological perspectives, that is, challenging normative understandings of social relations as well as the nature of the data generated within a research design. Queering research design, for example, might mean we reimagine both the "field" and the subjectivities of research participants as unstable and contested (rather than fixed), ensuring any knowledge that is created reflects this queered understanding of place and identity (Nash 2010). Whether queer methods and methodologies actually exist or what their characteristics might actually be is a highly contested and unstable area of inquiry (Browne and Nash 2010).

Queer approaches initially surfaced within philosophy, women's and lesbian studies, postmodern feminism, and gay and lesbian studies and owe a considerable debt to a number of scholars including Judith Butler, Eve Sedgwick, and Michel Foucault. Their formulation within distinctive disciplinary frameworks reflect disciplinary fixations and their processes of knowledge production (Corber and Valocchi 2003). Queer theory's applications and methodological approaches surfaced in both the humanities and social sciences in different ways and at different times. Their development and application have been largely in the Global North, and reflect their particular predilections. It is important to note that "queer methodologies" themselves have both a history and a geography (predominantly North America and the United Kingdom), and do not necessarily travel well to other locations where "queer" does not have the same historical or intellectual resonance. Broadly speaking, in the Global North, the humanities have largely taken up queer as method, often overlooking the epistemological and ontological implications. Conversely, the social sciences have engaged with queer as an epistemological position while frequently overlooking the methodological implications of using queer epistemologies to understand subjectivities, practices, desires, identities, and politics (Giffney and Hird 2008).

HUMANITIES: QUEER AS METHOD

In humanities, queer methodologies refer to how one addresses topics and issues using queer theoretical lenses. Queer as method poses questions regarding how queer theoretical work might be undertaken, that is, how does a research "get at" or "render visible" what is queer? Queer method explores the techniques of anti-normative analyses themselves. Core to this engagement with queer as method is the understanding that queer, as a contested and geographically contingent term, offers other possibilities in engaging in important debates (Boellstroff 2010).

Queer has become an important mode of analysis not only of gender and sexualities, but also of normativities more broadly, including in thinking through human/non-human divides (Giffney and Hird 2008). Queer, then, is the method one uses in approaching research design. It prompts the researcher to examine a range of questions grounded in explorations of normativities and how these might be addressed and critiqued. Often, however, "queer as method" often is presumed rather than discussed in terms of methodologies. Rather, there can be an implicit understanding that queer can be a method in terms of acting as a mode of engagement with cultural processes and products. In other words, it not only guides the types of questions asked and the methods of analysis used to get at normative frameworks underpinning social and political life, but also seeks to make visible those non-normative aspects often rendered invisible.

Practically, queer as method in the humanities has largely been engaged in discourse and forms of textual analysis that highlight normative systems of meaning engaged in knowledge production and the underlying power relations in play. Such an approach uses a wide range of "data," including "things," "novels ... visual phenomena to sounds and smells, from historical eras to the present" (Ambjörnsson, Laskar, and Steorn 2010, 10). Researchers are looking to tease out hidden queer moments submerged within the power relations regulating the normative frameworks guiding the creation of such texts.

Such an approach tends to focus on forms of cultural critique, which has been accused of being largely detached from everyday life experiences and offering little toward the development of a politic or forms of activism engaged with changing the inequalities of everyday life. While the critique of texts and other cultural products is useful to highlight the eradication of queer people in cultural and social knowledge, it does not provide much guidance on how to effect political and social change in the everyday life of queer people. Some of the engagements with queer anti-normativities have been heavily critiqued by activists and those who are the subjects of such queer methods. In particular, scholars and activists are critical of the way that (privileged, Global North, white, middle-class) theorists do not engage with the people who live (often painfully) in the transgressive/marginalized positionalities that form their queer analyses (Kulpa and Liinason 2009).

SOCIAL SCIENCE: QUEER EPISTEMOLOGIES AND SOCIAL SCIENCE METHODS

Queer methodologies are somewhat more complicated in their use in social sciences. Queer thinking, developed in the humanities, has meant that its incorporation into the social sciences has required some translation, particularly in its development and application. However, whilst some sociologists, for example, have explored the ways in which sociology can and cannot be queer/queered, in the main queer thinking is deployed and developed in the social sciences without much engagement with the issues of translation between humanities theorizing and social science methodologies (Seidman 1996). This is noticeable when one considers the traditions of social science methodologies and related and specific methods (for example, quantitative measures of social lives).

There can be little doubt that queer approaches are deeply engaged in questioning the existence and knowability of the social, including the nature of social subjects and their social relations. The entanglements of methods, lives, and research move beyond explaining the social to offer more complex engagements with how the social is constituted. This makes it clear that queer theorizing and social research fields are mutually constituted. In other words, the knowledge produced through queer methods and methodologies renders visible queer people and their lives, helping to transform understandings of social relations and social research.

Yet, the methodological deployment of queer theorizing can fundamentally undermine some of the key tenets of social science methods. For example, in terms of sampling processes, how can you sample around identities, if identities (and subjectivities) themselves are understood as unstable, fragmented, and fluid (Nash 2010)? Conversely, if the identity categories purportedly underpinning social relations are represented as problematic constructions that normalize and force coherence, how can you access participants who use (or indeed question) identities/labels? In these circumstances, data-gathering techniques such as interviews, surveys, and other social science research methods used in developing queer research and theorizing are brought into question, creating fundamental tensions between techniques and theories or methodologies and epistemologies (Browne 2008). Any analysis performed on such data, without addressing the dissonance between the theoretical frameworks/analysis and the modes of data collection, can create unacknowledged contradictions.

There have been a number of discussions of queer methodologies that argue that ethnography is indeed a "queer method," engaging as it does with complexities, fluidities, and interactions that constitute both the researcher and research fields (Boellstroff 2010). Engaging in queer methodologies requires understanding the destabilization of the researchers themselves, demonstrated through postmodern and feminist critiques of the "objective researcher" and the relational notion of truth in knowledge production. Queer research design must also grapple with the multiple, contingent, and unstable nature of the research subject, one that is historically and geographically specific. Ethnography is ideally placed to engage in questioning how subjectivities are created, as well as contesting notions of objective researchers due to its engagement with communities, groups, and people in in-depth and interactive ways that often define research design.

The "field" in queer research design is also a complicated and unstable place given the instability of both the researcher and the research subject. If we understand the field as thereby "queered," there exists a multitude of shifting and engaging subjectivities and identities being remade and reengaged with through and within research processes. Queer research recognizes how the field and social relations are remade, the messiness of engagement and narrative, and the queerness of communication, relational connections, and spatial connectivities (Nash 2010). This highlights the politics and social relations of knowledge production generated within this set of unstable and partial engagements. Similar to those debates raised in feminist methodological scholarship, these contingencies raise ethical and moral questions about the relations of the normalizing power relations that constitute the social relations of knowledge production.

Queer methodologies can undermine conventional social scientific measures of the veracity, reliability, and generalizability of social science research. This challenges core understandings of the "science" behind social science methods, questioning the idea that research can be reproduced exactly, instead queering normativities that structure these claims.

Discussions about the possibilities of "a queer method" have also been approached from the other angle, that is, the argument that there are methods that simply cannot be queered. For example, it might be argued that it is very difficult, if not impossible, to "queer" quantitative data (Browne 2008). Quantification relies on the delineation of fixed categories that can then both count and be counted. Such categorization is problematic for queer thinking, which can see categories and "boxes" as normative and normalizing in ways that render stable what is fluid and performative in the creation of identities, desires, and bodies. Supposedly mutually exclusive and binary categories, such as male/female or heterosexual/homosexual, neglect the ways that identities (and subjectivities) can be multiple and refuse the binaries imposed by boxes to be ticked. This is particularly problematic where categories are seen as mutually exclusive. For example, people can be both male and female, or neither male nor female. The inclusion of an "other" category in gender questions does not address the issue with quantification as it fails to come to grips with the complexities of how gender has been queered and queried.

The use of percentages and statistics can also homogenize groups, such as lesbian, gay, and bi, neglecting the ways in which these groupings are constructed and heterogeneous. However, just because a method is not queer or queerable does not mean that it is not useful within sexualities and gender research more broadly. Indeed, for instance, statistics have been shown to progress social change in terms of advocacy for mental health services for lesbian, gay, bisexual, and transgender (LGBT) people.

Conversely, the limitations of quantitative material can be explored using queer as method. The analytical tools offered by queer thinking can be used to expose the normalizing impulses of quantification and the ways in which statistics can be used to reiterate as well as contest hegemonies. In this way, queer as method developed in the humanities can be used to deconstruct social science tools and methodologies in order to destabilize particular hegemonies. This can also be used to address policies and other textual modes of normalizing relations, in ways that confuse the boundaries of social sciences/humanities.

Queer methodologies in the social sciences have also worked to overcome the critiques of humanities' reliance on discourse and textual analysis of both scholarly and popular texts. Discourse and textual analysis seeks to highlight how gender and sexualities and their normative systems of meaning are shaped through text. Arguably, an analysis of discourse and systems of meaning can overlook the material and institutional influences in the formulation of social life and social relations. Social science research, deploying queer methods and methodologies, not only examines the discursive constitution of sexual and gendered lives and everyday experiences but also works to uncover material inequalities and formulations. The focus is on how these are constituted within discourses and are implicated in the formulation and deployment of these very same systems of meaning (Liinason and Kulpa 2008).

In sum, queer methods and methodologies have been in the main differently deployed in the humanities and social sciences. In humanities queer as method has been used to examine normativities and hegemonies, exploring the boundaries of normal and seeking to queer and disrupt hegemonic norms. In the social sciences methods and methodologies have been related to methodologies, data collection, and data collection frameworks. Queer thinking in this context can be both deployed and contested through social science methods. Conversely, queer thinking can destabilize and question social science methodologies and data collection techniques.

SEE ALSO: Class, Caste, and Gender; Feminism and Postmodernism; Feminisms, Postmodern; Gender Difference Research; Heteronormativity and Homonormativity; Heterosexism and Homophobia; Privilege; Queer Theory; Sexualities

REFERENCES

Ambjörnsson, Fanny, Pia Laskar, and Patrik Steorn, eds. 2010. "Introduction." *Lambda Nordica*, 3–4: 9–14.

Boellstroff, Tom. 2010. "Queer Techne: Two Theses on Methodology and Queer Studies." In *Queer Methodologies and Methods: Intersecting Queer Theory and Social Science Research*, edited by Kath A. Browne and Catherine J. Nash, 215–230. Burlington: Ashgate.

Browne, Kath. 2008. "Selling My Queer Soul or Queerying Quantitative Research?" *Sociological Research Online*, 31(1). DOI: 10.5153/sro.1635.

Browne, Kath, and Catherine J. Nash, eds. 2010. *Queer Methodologies and Methods: Intersecting Queer Theory and Social Science Research*. Burlington: Ashgate.

Corber, Robert J., and Stephen Valocchi, eds. 2003. *Queer Studies: An Interdisciplinary Reader*. Oxford: Blackwell.

Giffney, Noreen, and M. Hird, eds. 2008. *Queering the Non/Human*. Aldershot: Ashgate.

Kulpa, Robert, and Mia Liinason, eds. 2009. "Queer Studies: Methodological Approaches, Follow up." *Graduate Journal of Social Science*, special issue, 6(1): 1–2.

Liinason, Mia, and Robert Kulpa, eds. 2008. "Queer Studies: Methodological Approaches." *Graduate Journal of Social Science*, special issue, 5(2): 1–4.

Muñoz, Lorena. 2010. "Brown, Queer and Gendered: Queering the Latina/o 'Street-Scapes' in Los Angeles." In *Queer Methodologies and Methods: Intersecting Queer Theory and Social Science Research*, edited by Kath A. Browne and Catherine J. Nash, 56–67. Burlington: Ashgate.

Nash, Catherine J. 2010. "Queer Conversation: Old-Time Lesbians, Transmen and the Politics of Queer Research." In *Queer Methodologies and Methods: Intersecting Queer Theory and Social Science Research*, edited by Kath A. Browne and Catherine J. Nash, 129–143. Burlington: Ashgate.

Seidman, Steven. 1996. *Queer Theory/Sociology*. Oxford: Blackwell.

Queer Performance

ELIAS KRELL
Vassar College, USA

Queer performance signals a wide array of artistic events, including musical theater, opera, performance art, dance, theater, film, and video, that stage lesbian, gay, bisexual, transgender, intersex, asexual, queer and questioning (LGBTIAQQ) lives. As it is used most commonly, queer performance refers to artistic representation of gay and lesbian, less commonly bisexual, transgender, or intersex identities.

Like queer politics, queer performance has a paradoxical relationship to gay liberationist and lesbian feminist models, at times drawing and at other times departing from their claims. Some artists define their performance art as "queer" rather than gay and/or lesbian, in order to mark the transphobia, transmisogyny, and racism they have experienced therein. The individual terms "queer" and "performance" have shifted considerably in the transnational scholarly, artistic, and social discourses of the last 30 years. As a verb, "queering" can connote a bending of or oblique intervention into cultural norms, rather than their outright rejection (Jagose 1996). For example, the late performance scholar José E. Muñoz theorized "disidentification" as a strategy of resistance in which queers of color creatively manipulate hegemonic cultural norms through performance (Muñoz 1999). "Queer" has also been defined as a politics of difference whose primary constitutive aspect is the investigation of its aims and presumed constituents (Davis 2013). The term "performance" traditionally refers to staged performances, but recent interventions in performance studies have extended the term to include performances of everyday life, identity, ritual, activism, and any other act done for an audience, even if that audience is only self (Schechner 2006; Madison 2010). In fact, there is significant overlap in the development of the terms "queer" and "performance," for example, in the writings of philosopher and cultural critic Judith Butler. Butler writes that gender is *performative*. But we do not perform gender by choice; rather, we are enculturated and coerced to embody and replicate gender via various political, economic, and cultural institutions. For more on the convergences and divergences of performativity and performance, see Madison and Hamera (2006).

Queer performance can refer to a staged event that presents LGBTIAQQ life and/or an aesthetic that is odd, uncategorizable, or invokes almost any variety of cultural taboo. It can refer to a presentation of self, for example, a clothing or movement style that flouts societal expectations, especially those related to gender and sexuality. Queer performance has been nominated "the art of failure," where the failure to approximate various social, economic, and political norms becomes a site for (dis)identification, community, and resistance (Halberstam 2011). Stefan Brecht's *Queer Theater* provides a reference point for New York's avant-garde performance circuit in the 1960s and 1970s. He transcribes various performances and suggests that queer performance is an affect or feeling that can be campy, gleeful, lecherous, depraved, evil, ridiculous, or beautiful (Brecht 1978). Like queer theory, what "counts" as a queer aesthetic is a contentious topic. Queer feminist performance, for example, might also characterize itself as womanist, mestiza, boring, mystical, butch, ugly, trans, asexual, femme, and/or disabled.

The translation of "queer" into non-English languages and across different cultural frames is also highly contested (Kulick 1998; Pelúcio 2012; Viteri 2014); this does not mean, however, that identities and practices that fall outside Western heteronormativity have not existed long before, during, and after European colonialism and in and outside Anglo-American contexts (Feinberg 1996; Weismantel 2012). For example, Sor Juana Inés de la Cruz was a seventeenth-century nun and poet in colonial Mexico; she penned some of the earliest surviving feminist writings and erotic poems. This work was saved from burning by the Inquisition by her long-time confidant, the Spanish vicereine, with whom she was rumored to have a relationship (Lucero 1999). Modern queer of color performance troupe Mangos with Chili, based in Oakland, California, cite Sor Juana, Chavela Vargas, and Frida Kahlo as some of their queer elders. The contemporary Argentinean punk artists Sentime Dominga and Suzy Shock consider themes of indigeneity, colonialism, and queerness in Argentina, while Mexican-born performance artist Guillermo Gomez-Peña directs La Pocha Nostra, a company that performs internationally in Spanish, English, and Spanglish on queer themes. Since the 1980s, the Philippines has hosted a beauty pageant that celebrates *Bakla*, variously translated into English as queer or "third gender." Titica, the new face of Angola's *kuduro* music genre, has become a key figure in both "transsexual" and "gay" visibility in the central African country. As a final example, the Indian film *Fire* (1996), written and directed by Deepa Mehta, depicts a central love affair between the female protagonists, both of whom are married to men; the film was met with confusion by American critics unaccustomed to seeing queerness represented in the Global South and outside the Anglo narratives of "coming out" (Gopinath 2005).

Soon after the rise of "queer theory" in the 1990s in the United States, critiques arose of its institutionalization in the academy (deLauretis 1991; Halperin 2003), and of its cleavage from feminism (Gopinath 2005), anti-racism (Johnson and Henderson 2005), and anti-ableism (McCruer 2006). Performers such as Vaginal Crème Davis, Kelly Moe, and others artists of the "post-soul era" explored in recent work by Francesca Royster (2013), exploit the ways in which their bodies are read as multiply gendered, raced, *and* classed on stage. Dark Matter, Heels on Wheels, Ignacio Rivera, Angelica Ross, Misty deBerry, Sharon Bridgforth, and Willy Wilkinson are a few queer of color artists advancing queer performance in the United States at present, while Sean Dorsey and Sins Invalid have placed transgender dance and disabled of color performance art, respectively, on the map.

Elin Diamond (1996) observes that staged performances can open a crucial space of critique by re-presenting society to itself. Queer performance thus aims to shift societal structures that confer sexual "rights" to some over others by amplifying the linkages between quotidian realities and larger structures that organize queer lives. Future directions might include further exploration of queer anti-colonial and indigenous movements, queer asexuality, transspecies identities, and alternative sex practices.

SEE ALSO: Queer Literary Criticism; Visual Culture

REFERENCES

Brecht, Stefan. 1978. *Queer Theatre: The Original Theatre of the City of New York*. Frankfurt am Main: Suhrkamp.

Cohen, Cathy. 2005. "Punks, Bulldaggers, and Welfare Queens: The Radical Potential of Queer Politics?" In *Black Queer Studies: A Critical Anthology*, edited by E. Patrick Johnson and Mae G. Henderson, 21–51. Durham, NC: Duke University Press.

Davis, Nick (2013). *The Desiring-Image: Gilles Deleuze and Contemporary Queer Cinema*. New York: Oxford University Press.

de Lauretis, Tereas, ed. 1991. "Queer Theory: Lesbian and Gay Sexualities" [Special Issue]. *Differences*, 3(2).

Diamond, Elin. 1996. *Performance and Cultural Politics*. New York: Routledge.

Feinberg, Leslie. 1996. *Transgender Warriors: Making History from Joan of Arc to Dennis Rodman*. Boston: Beacon Press.

Gopinath, Gayatri. 2005. *Impossible Desires Queer Diasporas and South Asian Public Cultures*. Durham, NC: Duke University Press.

Halberstam, Judith. 2011. *The Queer Art of Failure*. Durham, NC: Duke University Press.

Halperin, David. 2003. "The Normalization of Queer Theory." *Journal of Homosexuality*, 45(2–4): 339–343.

Jagose, Annamarie. 1996. *Queer Theory: An Introduction*. New York: New York University Press.

Johnson, E. Patrick. 2005. "'Quare' Studies, or (Almost) Everything I Know About Queer Studies I Learned from My Grandmother." In *Black Queer Studies: A Critical Anthology*, edited by E. Patrick Johnson and Mae G. Henderson, 124–160. Durham, NC: Duke University Press.

Johnson, E. Patrick, and Mae Henderson. 2005. "Queering Black Studies/'Quaring' Queer Studies." In *Black Queer Studies: A Critical Anthology*, edited by E. Patrick Johnson and Mae G. Henderson, 1–17. Durham, NC: Duke University Press.

Kulick, Don. 1998. *Travesti: Sex, Gender, and Culture Among Brazilian Transgendered Prostitutes*. Chicago: University of Chicago Press.

Lucero, Carla. 1999. *Juana*. Co-librettists Carla Lucero and Alicia Gaspar de Alba. Albuquerque: University of Mexico Press.

Madison, D. Soyini. 2010. *Acts of Activism: Human Rights as Radical Performance. Theatre and Performance Theory*. New York: Cambridge University Press.

Madison, D. Soyini, and Judith Hamera. 2006. "Introduction: Performance Studies at the Intersections." *The Sage Handbook of Performance Studies*, xi–xxv. Thousand Oaks: Sage.

McRuer, Robert. 2006. *Crip Theory: Cultural Signs of Queerness and Disability*. New York: New York University Press.

Muñoz, José. 1999. *Disidentifications: Queers of Color and the Performance of Politics*. Minneapolis: University of Minnesota Press.

Pelúcio, Larissa. 2012. "Subalterno Quem, Cara Pálida? Apontamentos às Margens sobre Póscolonialismos, Feminismos e Estudos Queer." *Contemporanea: Revista de Sociologica de Ufscar*, 2(2): 395–418.

Royster, Francesca T. 2013. *Sounding Like a No-No: Queer Sounds and Eccentric Acts in the Post-Soul Era*. Ann Arbor: University of Michigan Press.

Sandahl, Carrie, and Philip Auslander. 2005. *Bodies in Commotion: Disability & Performance, Corporealities*. Ann Arbor: University of Michigan Press.

Schechner, Richard. 2006. *Performance Studies. An Introduction*. New York: New York University Press.

Viteri, María-Amelia. 2014. *Desbordes: Translating Racial, Ethnic, Sexual, and Gender Identities Across the Americas*. Albany: SUNY Press.

Weismantel, Mary. 2012. "Towards a Transgender Archaeology: A Queer Rampage Through Prehistory." In *The Transgender Studies Reader*, edited by Susan Stryker and Aren Aizura, vol. 2, 319–334. New York: Routledge.

Queer Space

JASON ALLEY
University of California, Santa Cruz, USA

Queer space pricked the intellectual imagination of many scholars in the 1990s. The political and cultural energies unleashed by "queer" as a keyword – designating a kind of theory, activism, and identity all at once – produced vibrant counterpublics (Warner 2005) that harkened back to the anti-establishment ethos of gay liberation and lesbian feminism in the 1970s and 1980s. A revamped interest in space simultaneously took hold in many quarters of cultural analysis, building off work taking place in the 1980s. While place as community, milieu, and country had long been the terrain of geographers, historians, and anthropologists, the "spatial turn" in social theory helped usher in newfound interests and intellectual itineraries. Chief amongst these was a revisiting of earlier philosophic and phenomenological treatments while exploring the peculiar predicaments of a postmodernity that imagined space as inaugurating new forms of power, capitalist rule, and geographic apartheid. Michel Foucault's dissections of the violences of modernity often relied on spatial images and turns of phrase, but it was a 1986 English translation of a piece entitled "Of Other Spaces," a talk originally delivered in 1967, that suggested an important interest the author had in the kinds of spatial logics then associated with an ascendant postmodernity (Foucault 1986). Postmodern spatial imaginaries nonetheless did not receive universal endorsement as critics countered with forms of negative critique or wondered pointedly about the gendered exclusions that scholars of space and place trafficked in. Explorations of sexuality, queerness, and space throughout the 1990s brought a postmodern inflected theoretical eclecticism to the table while offering up situated historical, ethnographic, and geographic mappings.

As the 1990s gave way to the 2000s, globalization gained ascendancy as the preferred analytic frame for exploring the politics of place and culture. Queer tourism came under scrutiny as problematic spatial practice while ethnographic work reminded scholars that "local" and "global" imaginaries shaped the desires of ordinary queer subjects as much as they did those of tourists. Recent work around queer space has creatively looked at histories of urban encounters and place-making in addition to critiquing trajectories that figure cities as ultimate locations of and for queer authenticity. Queer unpackings of the nation continue to be important interventions in the work of feminists of color, reminding scholars that other spatial terms of analysis – including home, diaspora, reservation, nation, borderlands – are needed. Renewed attention to the politics of immigration and occupation in queer social worlds echo these arguments. Future directions point towards continuing work exploring the queer histories of specific locales alongside investigations of displacements – from prisons to settler colonialisms to gentrifications – and their queer discontents.

SEE ALSO: Feminist Epistemology; Gendered Space; Private/Public Spheres; Queer Methods and Methodologies; Queer Theory; Tearoom Trade

REFERENCES

Foucault, Michel. 1986 [1967]. "Of Other Spaces." *Diacritics* 16(1): 22–27.
Warner, Michael. 2005. *Publics and Counterpublics*. New York: Zone Books.

FURTHER READING

Abraham, Julie. 2009. *Metropolitan Lovers: The Homosexuality of Cities*. Minneapolis: University of Minnesota Press.
Anzaldúa, Gloria. 1987. *Borderlands/La Frontera: The New Mestiza*. San Francisco: Aunt Lute books.
Bell, David, and Gill Valentine, eds. 1995. *Mapping Desire: Geographies of Sexualities*. London: Routledge.
Betsky, Aaron. 1997. *Queer Space: Architecture and Same-Sex Desire*. New York: William Morrow.
El-Tayeb, Fatima. 2011. *European Others: Queering Ethnicity in Postnational Europe*. Minneapolis: University of Minnesota Press.
Hanhardt, Christina B. 2013. *Safe Space: Gay Neighborhood History and the Politics of Violence*. Durham, NC: Duke University Press.
Herring, Scott. 2010. *Another Country: Queer Anti-Urbanism*. New York: New York University Press.
Ingram, Gordon Brent, Anne-Marie Bouthillette, and Yolanda Retter, eds. 1997. *Queers in Space: Communities, Public Places, Sites of Resistance*. Seattle: Bay Press.
Kuntsman, Adi. 2009. *Figurations of Violence and Belonging: Queerness, Migranthood and Nationalism in Cyberspace and Beyond*. Oxford: Peter Lang.
Leap, William L., ed. 1999. *Public Sex/Gay Space*. New York: Columbia University Press.
Manalansan, Martin F. 2003. *Global Divas: Filipino Gay Men in the Diaspora*. Durham, NC: Duke University Press.
Rubin, Gayle S. 1997. "Elegy for the Valley of Kings: AIDS and the Leather Community in San Francisco, 1981–1996." In *In Changing Times: Gay Men and Lesbians Encounter HIV/AIDS*, edited by Martin P. Levine, Peter M. Nardi, and John H. Gagnon. Chicago: University of Chicago Press.
Tongson, Karen. 2011. *Relocations: Queer Suburban Imaginaries*. New York: NYU Press.

Queer Theory

NOHA FIKRY and J. MICHAEL RYAN
The American University in Cairo, Egypt

To attempt to construct a coherent definition of queer theory would be to run counter to the ethos of the theory itself. One of queer theory's main aims is to problematize and question clear-cut boundaries, and thus defining it would be to defy it. This account, therefore, should not be regarded as a formal, extensive definition of queer theory but rather as an attempt to trace its main ideas, hallmarks, and key contributors.

The main contention of queer theory is that identities are never fixed or stable but rather are historically and socially situated and constructed. For queer theory, it is not possible to group people into holistic categories such as "black transsexuals" because the group itself includes numerous varieties that cannot be condensed under one label. Members are not seen as a homogeneous group but rather are diverse and vary widely in terms of income, country of origin, age, and education, for example. In other words, categorizing groups on the basis of limited characteristics is seen as simultaneously ignoring others. Queer theorists would argue, therefore, that it is neither useful nor legitimate to homogenize a group's heterogeneity. Accordingly, queer theory aims to question the legitimacy of fixed identities and opts instead for a more inclusive identity paradigm, one in which all differences are accepted without any attempt to obviate varieties or group them.

Linguistically, the term *queer* has come to take on different meanings in various contexts. For some people, it is a derogatory word for those with a same-sex desire. For others, including many queer theorists, however, it means broad varieties of identities or arguably a kind of anti-identity or non-identity altogether.

As mentioned before, to define queer theory would go against the very ethos of the theory itself. That said, we can outline some critical contributions of the theory and standpoints from which those working within it tend to operate. Arlene Stein and Ken Plummer (1994) have suggested four such "hallmarks" of queer theory.

First, queer theory holds that understanding sexuality is always associated with relations of sexual power that are to be found in multiple arenas of daily life, including those spheres that are not customarily thought to be sexual. For example, for some queer theorists, sexuality can be understood by analyzing popular culture, education, or economics even though these spheres are not always automatically thought to denote sexuality. Further, queer theory suggests that relations of power within these various spheres are maintained through reenactment, reproduction, and policing the boundaries between sexual categories. For example, by normalizing one form of identity and criticizing or rejecting other forms altogether, these spheres emphasize the fixed boundaries between different categories. These boundaries are problematic not only because they are fixed but also because by virtue of normalizing, one form of identity is seen as "right" while another is seen as deviant.

Second, queer theory attempts to problematize the coherence and uniformity of the boundaries that are constructed and maintained between different categories. Thus, for example, both heterosexuality and homosexuality are made units of analysis and discursively produced as subjects for research. In other words, identities are viewed as ways of "doing" rather than ways of "being." Identity is viewed as an elusive category that rests on ever-shifting and unknowable bases.

Third, queer theory rejects strategies, such as identity politics, that favor the totalizing of one identity category at the expense of others. The claim is that these strategies only legitimate the very power structure they are fighting against by advocating for rights based on minority identities. Queer theory, on the other hand, holds a more deconstructive and decentering reading of identities in all shapes and forms.

Fourth, sexuality is seen to operate in almost every sphere of conduct. Thus, queer theorists can analyze sexuality as portrayed, or used, in media, music festivals, popular culture, literature, or social movements. In other words, no area is immune from being influenced by sexuality; all texts and spheres of social life can be interpreted through a lens of sexuality.

These abovementioned hallmarks are only a brief discussion of one of the suggested frameworks of queer theory and can thus be contested, expanded, or contracted. Generally, the first two hallmarks can be understood to belong to radical deconstruction that welcomes fluidity and rejects solidity of identities whereas the last two hallmarks belong more to subversive sexual politics.

It is important to note that queer theory is not synonymous with gay and lesbian studies. Gay and lesbian studies put sexuality as the center of their project whereas queer theory is centered on the contestation of a knowable identity. Queer theory nonetheless is still interested in the homosexual/heterosexual divide but more in the vein of Foucauldian genealogy. Queer theory looks at the knowledge–power relationship in this assumed binary and attempts to deconstruct it. For this reason, queer theory sees homosexuality and heterosexuality not as natural binary identities but rather as mutually constituted in historic and culturally specific ways. In other words, the main idea of queer theory is challenging fixed notions of identity and forms of knowing more broadly. This is taken to an extent that some people believe that queer theory is not a body of institutional knowledge but rather a broader deconstructive process.

The origins of queer theory are highly contested and ambiguous. Some trace its formal beginnings in academic circles to Teresa de Lauretis's lecture at a conference at the University of California at Santa Cruz in 1989. Others, however, point to key works such as Eve Kosofsky Sedgwick's *Between Men* (1985) and *Epistemology of the Closet* (1990). Still others trace the formal beginnings of queer theory to Judith Butler's key publication *Gender Trouble* (1999/1990) or as far back as Michel Foucault's work on *The History of Sexuality*, volume 1 (1978). Regardless of its exact moment of origin, queer theory began to flourish as a subject of inquiry in the late 1980s and early 1990s. Queer theory is generally believed to be interdisciplinary because its academic roots and key publications fall under many fields, including feminist studies, gay and lesbian studies, sociology, and literary theory.

Queer theory no doubt finds much of its origin in the work of Michel Foucault, especially his work on sexuality. One of Foucault's main ideas, and one that was pivotal to queer theory, is the genealogy of power (Foucault 1969). The genealogy of power is a method of intellectual history which looks at the linkages between knowledge and power, tracing the different trajectories that historical processes follow to reach a specific point. This method aims at uncovering the multiplicity of ways through which historical processes take shape. Thus, a genealogy of power seeks to understand how people and society are regulated through the production and control of knowledge. Another of Foucault's ideas that was adopted by queer theory is the archaeology of knowledge, which involves searching for the underlying laws that govern what can be said in any discourse at a given moment. The goal of this idea is to historicize the present forms of discourse, especially what is capable of being contributed to that discourse.

Another scholar whose work was seminal in pioneering queer theory is Eve Kosofsky Sedgwick. Her *Epistemology of the Closet* (1990) explores "the closet" and its relation to "coming out"; people hide their identities in closets, which become now metaphorical objects. Thus, in this paradigm, coming out includes the revelation of these hidden identities to others. Similar to Foucault's ideas of the confession, coming out is embedded in a knowledge–power relationship. The closet, for example, creates possibilities for some people to gain power over others by using the knowledge they possess about people's sexuality against them.

Judith Butler's work has also made contributions to queer theory. Arguing that both gender and sexuality are performances based on repetitive stylizations, her book *Gender Trouble* has been influential to many working in queer theory (Butler 1999/1990). For Butler, labels such as "naturalness" or "normalcy" have their power and dominance due to their constant repetition, even by those who are considered to fall outside of these categories. Whether individuals are aware of their performances is not the issue; rather, what is at stake is that these performances are continually repeated. She identifies what she calls "repetitive disruption," which is a way of consciously acting to undermine dominant paradigms through repetition. Butler (2004, 27) has also argued that it is possible to question and undo existing hegemonic gender constructions, "to disrupt what has become settled knowledge and knowable reality and to use ... one's unreality to make an otherwise impossible or illegible claim."

More generally, the rise of queer theory can also be traced to a rise in the institutionalization of poststructuralism as a form of academic inquiry. One of the main contentions of poststructuralist thought is that there is no grand Truth (but rather multiple "truths"), and an emphasis on the importance of asking questions rather than seeking answers per se. Queer theory adopted these deconstructionist notions from poststructuralism with a similar joy in the asking of questions rather than the "discovery" of answers.

Queer theory has also been influential outside the academic sphere. For example, the beginnings of the acquired immunodeficiency syndrome (AIDS) epidemic (originally called GRID – gay-related immunodeficiency) sparked a wave of grassroots activism of which Queer Nation and ACT UP were but two prominent examples. This wave of activism was seeking, among other things, to disrupt the dominance of the heterosexual paradigm. Similarly, queer politics has contributed to critiques of many gay and lesbian political rights organizations by means of questioning the hierarchies of privilege and oppression existing within homosexual communities.

Despite its major contributions in academia and political scenes, queer theory still has a number of criticisms. One of these criticisms is that rejecting single modes of identity such as class or sex undermines political action, which consequently ignores the materiality of the everyday experience of some groups. Thus, if one views identity as a playground to be parodied, it is difficult to form coherent political action.

Another criticism of queer theory is that the more it is accepted and incorporated into academic discourse, the farther it gets removed from its revolutionary potential, or the less "queer" it becomes (Halperlin 1995). In this way the institutionalization of that which seeks to question institutions is a means of undoing its disruptive potential.

Others critique queer theory on the basis that much of its produced knowledge is not made available, financially or intellectually, to those for whom it ideally could hold the most benefit. As much of the work that is done in the field tends to be written in highly abstract academic jargon, it is out of the intellectual reach of many.

Max Kirsch (2000, 7) has suggested that a potential compromise to many of the critiques leveled at queer theory is to regard identity as a "mode of affiliation rather than strictly a category of personal definition." This suggestion attempts to hold queer theory's critical and questioning stance while at the same time keeping identity as a powerful tool for collective social action. Another possible suggestion, proposed by Adam Isaiah Green (2002), is to move toward a more post-queer study of sexuality by focusing on a more empirical basis for queer theory. Green explains that queer theory can be divided into two strands: *radical deconstructionism*, which suggests a postmodernist understanding of sexuality while ignoring the institutionalization of sexuality, and *radical subversion*, which imposes political marginality onto homosexual individuals, thus simplifying the historical complexity of the development of sexual identification. Both strands, according to Green, do not adequately prioritize the everyday materiality and institutionalized nature of the actors' situation.

Regardless of its criticisms, queer theory still holds a number of strengths. Among other things, it advocates inclusion and acceptance and emphasizes the importance of questioning the center. Further, queer theory focuses on sexuality, a topic long silenced in academia. It also seeks to disrupt dominant myths and hierarchies related to identity. It is important to note that queer theory is only a few decades old and has already made significant contributions to a number of academic disciplines.

SEE ALSO: Feminism, Poststructural; Feminisms, Postmodern; Identity Politics; Queer Methods and Methodologies

REFERENCES

Butler, Judith. 1999. *Gender Trouble: Feminism and the Subversion of Identity*. New York: Routledge. First published 1990.

Butler, Judith. 2004. *Undoing Gender*. New York: Routledge.

Foucault, Michel. 1969. *The Archeology of Knowledge*. New York: Routledge.

Foucault, Michel. 1978. *The History of Sexuality*, vol. 1. New York: Vintage.

Green, Adam Isaiah. 2002. "Gay but Not Queer: Toward a Post-Queer Study of Sexuality." *Theory and Society*, 31(4): 521–545.

Halperlin, David M. 1995. *Saint Foucault: Towards a Gay Hagiography*. New York: Routledge.

Kirsch, Max H. 2000. *Queer Theory and Social Change*. New York: Routledge.

Sedgwick, Eve Kosofsky. 1985. *Between Men: English Literature and Male Homosocial Desire*. New York: Columbia University Press.

Sedgwick, Eve Kosofsky. 1990. *Epistemology of the Closet*. Berkeley: University of California Press.

Stein, Arlene, and Ken Plummer. 1994. "'I Can't Even Think Straight': 'Queer' Theory and the Missing Sexual Revolution in Sociology." *Sociological Theory*, 12(2): 178–187.

Radical Lesbianism

BRONWYN WINTER
The University of Sydney, Australia

Radical lesbianism as a theoretical and political position is most famously associated with France and with Monique Wittig, and by extension with Québec. There were, however, some groups and individuals that identified as "radical lesbian," but without the same theorization of the position as in Wittig's work, in the early years of the so-called "second wave" of feminism in the United States in the late 1960s. Most importantly, Radicalesbians authored in 1970 an article titled "The Woman Identified Woman," which they distributed during the "Lavender Menace" protest at the Second Congress to Unite Women in New York. Among its most famous authors was Rita Mae Brown, and the article provided a political definition of lesbianism: "a lesbian is the rage of all women condensed to the point of explosion." Radicalesbians argued that lesbians were at the forefront of women's liberation because they refused to define themselves in relation to men, hence the title "The Woman Identified Woman." In the United States and the rest of the Western English-speaking world, radical lesbian thought became closely identified with separatist feminism. In the United Kingdom, it took on expression as political lesbianism: a political withdrawal from heterosexuality.

FRENCH RADICAL LESBIANISM AND THE SPLIT WITH RADICAL FEMINISM

French radical lesbians took this idea further. Associated with a group that was for short time known as the *Front des Lesbiennes Radicales* (formed in 1981), the defining moment of radical lesbianism is a split in 1980 within the group of materialist feminist intellectuals (the early French equivalent to radical feminism) that published the journal *Questions Féministes* (*QF*), of which the editor-in-chief was Simone de Beauvoir. That materialist feminist group included Christine Delphy, who is now the editor-in-chief of the journal's later incarnation, *Nouvelles Questions Féministes*. The split within the *QF* group occurred over a fundamental disagreement concerning analysis of heterosexuality as a political system and political choices that must ensue, and was centered on experimental novelist and essayist Monique Wittig's now famous essay "La Pensée Straight" ("The Straight Mind"), published in the journal in 1980 (Wittig 1992). Using Simone de Beauvoir's analysis that one is not born woman but becomes woman, Wittig argued that as "woman" was a construct within heterosexuality, itself a fundamental structuring principle in male supremacist ideology, lesbians, in refusing this construct, were not "women." Prior to Wittig's article, feminism, including radical or materialist feminism, had not seriously questioned the conceptual categories of "man" and "woman" as defined one in relation to the other. French radical lesbians argued that lesbians challenged that conceptual order and the political system of domination that was dependent on its continuation, and as such could not align themselves with feminism.

Among the others in the radical lesbian group within QF were anthropologist Nicole-Claude Mathieu and sociologist Colette Guillaumin. The split was very public and very acrimonious, and included a court battle commenced by the radical lesbians over the naming and continuation of QF. The QF collective was dissolved in 1980 and Delphy and her group won the court battle, launching *Nouvelles Questions Féministes* in 1981, still with Beauvoir as the editor-in-chief but with Delphy the managing editor in reality. *Nouvelles Questions Féministes* has been published continuously since that time with Delphy at its helm, and is now published in Lausanne.

Across the Atlantic, in Montreal, a radical lesbian group inspired by the ideas of the French radical lesbians set up in 1982 the magazine *Amazones d'Hier, Lesbiennes d'Aujourd'hui* (Yesterday's Amazons, Today's Lesbians). The publishing collective included Louise Turcotte and Danielle Charest, the latter of whom subsequently moved to France and became very active in both the feminist and lesbian movements, with a particular focus on issues of international solidarity. Charest, like many other radical lesbians, was openly hostile to queer theory and politics. In France, Suzette Robichon and Michèle Causse set up *Vlasta: Revue des Fictions et Utopies Amazoniennes* (1983–1985).

LEGACY

Radical lesbian theories became well known in the English-speaking world both through translations and through the fact that in 1976, Wittig, then aged 41, moved to the United States, where she worked in women's studies in universities in California and Arizona. Her work and that of other radical lesbian theorists continue to have a political and intellectual impact today, and there has perhaps been renewed attention to it in recent years, following Wittig's death in 2003, followed by that of Danielle Charest in 2012 and of Nicole-Claude Mathieu in 2014. Among the new generation is Natacha Chetcuti, who with "first-generation" radical lesbian Claire Michard co-edited *Lesbianisme et Féminisme: Histoires Politiques* (Chetcuti and Michard 2003). The anthology, which has a number of radical lesbian contributors, offers historical perspectives on the radical feminism–radical lesbianism debate, and the editors argue that the political content of lesbianism as theorized by Wittig is constantly pushed aside, in favor of, among other things, queer politics.

Yet Wittig's work continues to be celebrated, as much for its literary innovation in developing a new lesbian literary language as for its theoretical impact, such as in the anthology *On Monique Wittig: Theoretical, Political and Literary Essays* (Shaktini 2005), the first book on Wittig to be published after her death in 2003, or the anthology *Lire Monique Wittig Aujourd'hui* (Auclerc and Chevalier 2012), both of which include contributions by Wittig specialist Dominique Bourque. The latter anthology includes contributions by both men and women and by both radical lesbians such as Bourque and queer-identified lesbians such as Marie-Hélène Bourcier. Ironically, in fact, some of those theorists most famously connected with queer theory, such as Judith Butler

(1990), have drawn on Wittig's work on the construction of the category of "woman" and lesbian refusal of it, although Wittig herself disagreed with queer theory. Butler does not identify as radical lesbian, situating her work more explicitly in the lineage of poststructuralism.

A further irony, which also perhaps demonstrates the political lineage and ongoing close relationship between radical feminism and radical lesbianism, is that when US poet and essayist Adrienne Rich (d. 2012) published her essay "Compulsory Heterosexuality and Lesbian Existence" (Rich 1980), in which she analyzes heterosexuality as a violent system of oppression (a position more in line with radical lesbian analysis), both radical feminists and radical lesbians claimed her analysis as close to their own. This irony is brought home by the fact that at the height of the French split, the first issue of *Nouvelles Questions Féministes* – the radical feminist "side" – published a French translation of the essay.

SEE ALSO: Feminism, Lesbian; Feminism, Radical; Lesbian and Womyn's Separatism; Sexual Coercion

REFERENCES

Auclerc, Benoît, and Yannick Chevalier, eds. 2012. *Lire Monique Wittig aujourd'hui*. Lyon: Presses Universitaires de Lyon.
Butler, Judith. 1990. *Gender Trouble: Feminism and the Subversion of Sexuality*. New York: Routledge.
Chetcuti, Natacha, and Claire Michard, eds. 2003. *Lesbianisme et féminisme. Histoires politiques*. Paris: L'Harmattan.
Rich, Adrienne. 1980. "Compulsory Heterosexuality and Lesbian Existence." *Signs: Journal of Women in Culture and Society*, 5(4): 631–660.
Shaktini, Namascar. 2005. *On Monique Wittig: Theoretical, Political and Literary Essays*. Champaign: University of Illinois Press.
Wittig, Monique. 1992. *The Straight Mind and Other Essays*. Boston: Beacon Press.

FURTHER READING

Leeds Revolutionary Feminist Group. 1981. *Love Your Enemy?: Debate Between Heterosexual Feminism and Political Lesbianism*. London: Onlywomen Press.
Guillaumin, Colette. 1995. *Racism, Sexism, Power and Ideology*. London: Routledge.
Mathieu, Nicole-Claude. 1991. *L'Anatomie politique. Catégorisations et idéologies du sexe*. Paris: côté-femmes.

Rape Culture

ANN BURNETT
North Dakota State University, USA

Rape culture exists when rape, or sexual assault, is a normalized expectation. The definition of rape culture originated in the 1970s, coinciding with the second wave of the feminist movement. Dianne Herman (1984), the first scholar to articulate the definition, posited that rape will continue to be pervasive as long as sexual violence and male dominance are glamorized. Buchwald, Fletcher, and Roth (1993) defined rape culture as one in which rape is a fact of life, like death or taxes. Rape culture does not only pertain to women – men, and gay, lesbian, bisexual, and transgender individuals are raped (Stotzer 2009; Ridgway 2014). Disabled people are raped at a high rate (80 percent) as well (Madden 2014). As a result, rape culture is an intersectional phenomenon that crosses gender, race, ability, ethnicity, sexuality, and so forth.

Rape is prevalent around the world. In the United States, the Rape, Abuse and Incest National Network (RAINN) reports that a rape occurs every 107 seconds; 68 percent of those assaults are not reported, and two thirds of them are committed by someone the victim knows (RAINN, 2015). In the United Kingdom, more than 85,000 women are raped and 400,000 are assaulted each year (Bates 2014). Men in nine countries in Asia and the South Pacific reported committing single- and multiple-perpetrator rape, with over 50 percent having raped as young teenagers (Jewkes et al. 2013). In India, after the gang rape of the student on the bus in New Delhi, activists began to shed light on the widespread problem in that country (Udas 2013). Other countries known for a high incidence of rape include Lesotho, Sweden, South Africa, St. Vincent and the Grenadines, New Zealand, and Belgium (Iaccino 2014). Thus, rape and the culture that normalizes it is a worldwide problem.

This culture reinforces itself in a number of ways: through hegemonic masculinity, the media, language, politics, and rape myths. Regardless of where one lives, a culture exists in which men are taught to be dominant, sexually aggressive, and powerful (Kivel 2012). This is the most acceptable way for boys and men to behave, and if they stray from this behavior, they are teased, beaten, or made to conform to the man box; such pressure creates an environment that fosters the idea that rape is part of being a man.

The media, reinforcing the notion of hegemonic masculinity, depict men as aggressive, and rape as a common occurrence. For example, the teen drama, *Reign*, created controversy in late 2014 when it showed a violent rape scene (Davies 2014); *Law and Order: Special Victims Unit* is supposed to educate its audience about rape culture, but instead it often portrays the victims as being at fault (Madden 2014). Movies such as *Say Anything, Crazy Stupid Love, The Fast and the Furious, Neighbors, American Pie, Hitch, The Notebook,* and even the Disney movie, *Beauty and the Beast* demonstrate that assault is a normal part of any story (Maxwell 2014). Further, when the media objectify the human body, especially that of black women, in television, movies, and magazines, the message is that bodies are "things" that can be violated (Maxwell 2014). Beyond fictional drama, media perpetuate rape culture by referring to "rape" as "sex," or sympathizing with the rapists rather than the victims, as evidenced by a CNN reporter's coverage of the Steubenville rape case (Madden 2014).

Popular music and social media reinforce rape culture. Lyrics from the 2013 Robin Thicke song, "Blurred Lines" intone, "I know you want it" (Ridgway 2014); Rick Ross, in his 2013 song, U.O.E.N.O., rapped, "Put molly all in her champagne, she ain't even know it. I took her home and I enjoyed that, she ain't even know it." Twitter feeds in 2014 degraded the victim and promoted the aggressor in both the United Kingdom and United States (Bates 2014; Ridgway 2014).

Not only do media play an influential role in fostering rape culture, so does misogynistic language (Najumi 2013; Madden 2014). For example, "rape" is used to describe success ("I raped that test," "We raped that team."). The normalcy of assault is reflected in language on contemporary t-shirts ("I've got a dick and a knife. At least one of them is going inside you tonight," "You say no? Challenge accepted").

Rape culture has not escaped politics, either. In representative Todd Akin's campaign for Missouri Senate, he claimed that women's bodies shut down if they are being legitimately raped (Kacmarek and Geffre 2013). In a Senate debate, Richard Mourdock argued that even in cases of rape, God must have intended it if the woman got pregnant (Kacmarek and Geffre 2013). These false statements demonstrate that even in public dialogue, rape culture is perpetuated.

Rape myths continue to dominate the dialogue about sexual assault, and they also tend to place blame on those who have been victimized. According to a research study on the role of communication in perpetuating rape culture, Burnett et al. (2009) provide a number of examples of rape myths. For instance, if a woman says "no," she really means "yes"; women are strong enough to resist rape; women who get raped are promiscuous; and women tend to falsely report rapes. Further, rape culture is created when victims are challenged about what they were wearing at the time of the incident, what/how much they were drinking, and with whom they chose to spend their time. Victim blaming, then, emphasizes the victim's supposed role in the rape and places responsibility on her/him.

Rape culture may be found in any number of contexts. Often it is used to describe a college or university campus in the United States in which it is not unusual for rape to occur. In fact, one in four women will be raped in college (RAINN). Rape cultures on college campuses remain intact for the reasons described above. Additionally, college men's athletics fosters rape culture because of the inherent aggressive nature of sport. The nature of some sports fosters a culture in which male athletes who are lauded as perfect physical specimens, celebrated as heroes, and allowed privileges that other students do not enjoy, expect women to provide for their sexual needs. In fact, the promise of a number of beautiful, willing women can sometimes be a not-so-subtle recruiting strategy.

Likewise, fraternities on campus foster a party atmosphere in which women and sexuality play a significant role. Although the epic movie, "Animal House," was released in 1978, the sex and party scenes depicted might only be a slight exaggeration from today's reality. One might find several fraternity parties during the course of a weekend (and some parties in between) in which alcohol is readily available, and first-year female students are targeted for sexual exploits because their alcohol tolerance levels are low, and they are naïve.

In fact, fraternity men and sorority women are more likely than independent men and women to use alcohol before having sex, which may contribute further to the perpetuation of rape culture on college campuses. With the ease of obtaining alcohol illegally in the United States, and the idea that one cannot have fun without it, alcohol contributes a great deal to rape culture. The combination of alcohol, college fraternity/sorority students, and sex creates a culture in which rape is normalized – it is part of everyday life. As a result, reporting rates of rape on college campuses is low, which protects the perpetrators and creates a sense of tolerance, thereby reinforcing the rape culture.

In countries outside the United States, rape culture may come about due to reasons described above, as well as poverty, alcohol abuse, and childhood abuse (Jewkes et al. 2013). Many individuals in these countries do not report rape because of fear of retaliation or because it is a taboo topic (Udas, 2013; Iaccino 2014). Most of the perpetrators are not punished (Jewkes et al. 2013). In particular, rape in wartime occurs as a way to intimidate and dislocate civilians, especially women and children (United Nations Human Rights 2015).

In the post-2010 era, rape culture has become more widely discussed and debated in the US and other countries such as India. The Obama Administration, in 2011, began to use Title IX as a way to compel colleges to take sexual assault seriously on campus, threatening to withhold funding to those campuses that failed to address the problem. In 2014, 55 campuses were placed under federal scrutiny for not effectively handling sexual assault and rape. In India, there is now wider discussion of sexual assault and rape culture, especially among young men and women (Udas 2013).

President Obama also created a task force to address sexual assault on college campuses. This task force, The White House Council on Women and Girls, prepared a report, "Rape and Sexual Assault: A Renewed Call to Action," that was released in early 2014. The report noted, "sexual assault is pervasive because our *culture* still allows it to persist" (author's emphasis, p. 5); it called for society to view rape as a crime and not a private matter, and it promoted bystander training.

Concurrent with the Obama Administration's actions, *Time Magazine* (Gray 2014; see also Goldberg 2014) headlined a story about "the crisis in higher education." The story centered on the number of rapes at the University of Montana, but argued that Montana was not the exception, but the rule, suggesting that rape culture was the rule on many college campuses. The story created an uproar in which some experts (Sommers 2014; Kitchens 2014) and the Rape, Abuse, and Incest National Network (RAINN) either denied the existence of rape culture or argued that sexual assaults on campus should not be attributed to it. Other experts (Maxwell 2014; Dockterman 2014) refuted these claims, providing evidence from scholarly research to support the existence of rape culture. It remains to be seen whether or not the increased attention to the subject will result in any change of rape culture, especially on the college campus.

Rape culture is complex and vast; therefore, solutions are complicated. Education must begin early on male role socialization and media literacy; attempts must be made to alleviate root causes of rape, including poverty and childhood sexual abuse (Jewkes et al. 2013). Individuals can work to interrupt rape culture by pointing out that rape jokes are not funny, emailing complaints to artists and advertisers, refusing to buy certain products, and talking about/naming rape culture with family and friends (Najumi 2013). Burnett et al. (2009) suggest that such "talking about" be about rape before it occurs, during the rape itself, and after the rape. In fact, they conclude that communication is muted about rape in all three areas. Before rape occurs, the definition of rape is ambiguous and peer pressure about drinking alcohol and having sex is confusing. During the attack, how to go about articulating consent or non-consent is not clear. After the rape occurs, the victim may doubt what occurred, or be encouraged not to report. Although there is no simple solution to rape culture, there may be small efforts to chip away at it.

The encouraging news is that people the world over are talking about and defining "rape culture." Despite the individuals who have benefited from the culture and who will argue that it does not exist, there is more possibility today than ever before to make a change. If any culture is to change, talking about it may be the first step.

SEE ALSO: Gender-Based Violence; Sexual Assault/Sexual Violence; Victimization

REFERENCES

Bates, L. 2014. "This Is Rape Culture – and Look at the Damage It Does." *The Guardian*, February 14. Accessed August 1, at http://www.theguardian.com/lifeandstyle/womens-blog/2014/feb/14/rape-culture-damage-it-does-everyday-sexism.

Buchwald, Emilie, Pamela R. Fletcher, and Martha Roth. 1993. *Transforming a Rape Culture*. Minneapolis: Milkweed Editions.

Burnett, Ann, et al. 2009. "Communicating/Muting Date Rape: A Co-Cultural Theoretical Analysis of Communication Factors Related to Rape Culture on a College Campus." *Journal of Applied Communication Research*, 37(4): 465–485. DOI: 10.1080/00909880903233150.

Davies, M. 2014. CW's Royal Teen Drama *Reign* Showed a Graphic Rape Scene. Jezebel, December 5. Accessed August 1, 2015, at http://jezebel.com/cws-royal-teen-drama-reign-showed-a-graphic-rape-scene-1667460775.

Dockterman, Eliana. 2014. "There's a Reason There's So Much Rape on Your Favorite TV Shows." *Time Magazine*, April 10. Accessed August 1, 2015, at http://time.com/50328/

theres-a-reason-theres-so-much-rape-on-your-favorite-tv-shows/.
Goldberg, Michelle. 2014. Why the Campus Rape Crisis Confounds Colleges. *The Nation*, June 24. Accessed August 1, 2015, at http://www.thenation.com/article/180114/why-campus-rape-crisis-confounds-colleges#.
Gray, Eliza. 2014. "The Sexual Assault Crisis on American Campuses." *Time Magazine*, May 25. Accessed August 1, 2015, at http://time.com/100542/the-sexual-assault-crisis-on-american-campuses/.
Herman, Dianne F. 1984. "The Rape Culture." In *Women: A Feminist Perspective*, edited by Jo Freeman, 3rd ed., 45–53. Mountain View: Mayfield.
Iaccino, L. 2014. "Top 5 Countries with the Highest Rates of Rape." *International Business Times*, January 29. Accessed August 1, 2015, at http://www.ibtimes.co.uk/top-5-countries-highest-rates-rape-1434355.
Jewkes, R., E. Fulu, T. Roselli, and C. Garcia-Moreno. 2013. "Prevalence of and Factors Associated with Non-Partner Rape Perpetration: Findings from the UN Multi-Country Cross-Sectional Study on Men and Violence in Asia and the Pacific." *The Lancet: Global Health*, 1(4): e208–e218.
Kacmarek, J., and E. Geffre. 2013. "Rape Culture Is: Know It when You See It." *Huffington Post*, June 11. Accessed August 1, 2015, at http://www.huffingtonpost.com/julia-kacmarek/rape-culture-is_b_3368577.html.
Kivel, P. 2012. "The Act-Like-a-Man Box." In *Men's Lives*, edited by M. Kimmel and M. Messner, 9th ed., 14–16. Boston: Pearson Education.
Madden, K. 2014. "Rape Culture: The Media's Role in Normalizing Assault." *Campus Time*, May 16. Accessed August 1, 2015, at http://laverne.edu/campus-times/2014/05/rape-culture-the-medias-role-in-normalizing-assault/.
Maxwell, Z. 2014. Rape Culture is Everywhere Our Children Can See – Watch Your Favorite Movies Prove It, July 30. http://mic.com/articles/94844/rape-culture-is-everywhere-our-children-can-see-watch-your-favorite-movies-prove-it.
Najumi, M. 2013. We Live in a Rape Culture, June 9. Accessed August 1, 2015, at http://thefeministwire.com/2013/06/we-live-in-a-rape-culture/.
Rape, Abuse, and Incent National Network (RAINN). 2015. Statistics. Accessed July 15, 2015, at www.rainn.org/statistics.
Ridgway, S. 2014. 25 Everyday Examples of Rape Culture, March 10. Accessed August 1, 2015, at http://everydayfeminism.com/2014/03/examples-of-rape-culture/.
Stotzer, R. L. 2009. "Violence Against Transgender People: A Review of United States Data." *Aggression and Violent Behavior*, 14, 170–179. DOI: 10.1016/j.avb.2009.01.006.
Udas, S. 2013. Covering the Rape Case that Changed India. CNN.com, December, 15. http://www.cnn.com/2013/12/04/world/asia/india-rape-problem-udas/
United Nations Human Rights, Office of the High Commission for Human Rights. 2015. Rape: Weapon of War. Accessed August 1, 2015, at http://www.ohchr.org/en/newsevents/pages/rapeweaponwar.aspx.
White House Council on Women and Girls and Office of the Vice President. 2014. Rape and Sexual Assault: A Renewed Call to Action. Accessed August 1, 2015, at http://www.whitehouse.gov/sites/default/files/docs/sexual_assault_report_1-21-14.pdf.

FURTHER READING

Sanday, Peggy Reeves. 2007. *Fraternity Gang Rape: Sex, Brotherhood, and Privilege on Campus*, 2nd ed. New York: NYU Press.

Rape Law

JENNIFER MCMAHON-HOWARD
Kennesaw State University, USA

A rape law is a criminal statute that prohibits and punishes certain forced and/or nonconsensual sex acts (i.e., oral, anal, and/or vaginal penetration). While the crime of rape is prohibited under almost all penal codes, the specific elements of these rape laws have varied across jurisdictions and over time.[1] For statutory rape laws, which criminalize sexual acts committed with a person who has not reached the age of consent, the actual age of consent has varied over time and across jurisdictions. For forcible rape laws, both the purpose of the laws and the definition of rape have varied over time and across jurisdictions. Originally, most forcible rape laws defined rape as the carnal knowledge of a female, not a spouse, forcibly and against her will. Such rape laws limited the crime of rape to an act in which a man used force to engage in nonconsensual, penile-vaginal penetration of a woman who was not his spouse. While some jurisdictions still retain this limited definition of rape, other jurisdictions have reformed their rape laws to broaden the scope of the law. In many jurisdictions, such rape law reforms included the creation of gender neutral statutes that recognize both male and female offenders and victims, the elimination of the spousal exemption, and an expanded definition of rape that includes other sex acts (oral, anal, or vaginal penetration by a penis or object) that are committed by force, threat of force, *or* without the victim's consent.

PURPOSE OF ORIGINAL RAPE LAWS

Since most rape laws can be traced back to ancient Babylonian and Mosaic laws, the crime of rape was constructed originally as a crime against public morality and/or as a property crime, not a violent crime. Thus, the laws were designed to enforce moral standards and protect men's property. Since a woman was considered to be the property of either her father or her husband, these rape laws primarily focused on extramarital vaginal intercourse. For an unmarried woman, her chastity determined her value for her father in terms of her bride price. Thus, if a man raped an unmarried woman, this damaged her father's property. For a married woman, her exclusive sexual relationship with her husband was important for determining the rightful inheritance of his property. Thus, if a man raped a married woman, this threatened the legitimacy of her husband's offspring and interfered with the ability to determine the proper inheritance of her husband's property. In some jurisdictions, the rape of a married woman was punished more severely than the rape of an unmarried woman, primarily because the "harm" in raping an unmarried woman (the devaluing of the man's property) could be resolved by having the rapist marry the victim (Brownmiller 1975).

LIMITATIONS OF ORIGINAL RAPE LAWS

Given the narrow focus of the original rape laws, there were a number of limitations to these laws. First, since the concern was with the chastity of an unmarried woman or the sexual exclusivity of a married woman, the narrow focus on extramarital vaginal intercourse limited the crime to forced penile-vaginal penetration only; other forced sexual activities (i.e., oral/anal sodomy) were not included under the original rape laws. Also, these laws were gender-specific in that only a man could be an offender and only a woman could be a victim. Furthermore, since a man's wife was considered to be his property, there were no laws that criminalized spousal rape; since a man could do whatever he wanted with his own property, he was permitted to force his wife to have sex.

In addition to the limitations in the legal definition of rape, many jurisdictions

---

[1] In the few countries that do not have a specific rape law, the crime of rape is treated as a form of adultery in which the extramarital element of the sex act takes precedence over the nonconsensual element of the act.

included special evidentiary laws/requirements that were unique to rape prosecutions. For example, rape laws that were based upon the English Common Law included a chastity requirement in the case of the rape of an unmarried woman. Such a chastity requirement can be seen in the laws pertaining to the admissibility of evidence of the victim's past sexual history. Here, evidence that the victim was unchaste prior to the rape was permissible on the grounds that it could demonstrate that the woman was already "damaged" property prior to the rape; that is, with evidence that the victim was not a virgin at the time of the rape, the rapist could claim that he did not damage the man's property since his daughter (the victim) had already been devalued prior to the rape. Evidence of a woman's past sexual history also could be used to cast doubt about her lack of consent and to question her credibility.

Since it was assumed that a woman who was caught voluntarily engaging in extramarital sex would have a strong motivation to lie and claim that she was raped, some jurisdictions also included a resistance requirement, a corroboration requirement, and/or cautionary jury instructions for rape cases. For example, under the original rape laws in the United States, in order to prove that the rape was committed by force there had to be evidence that the victim resisted the offender to the "utmost of her ability." Also, concerned with false allegations of rape, some jurisdictions prohibited rape prosecutions that relied solely on the testimony of the victim; instead, there either had to be evidence to corroborate each element of the crime (i.e., physical injury, torn clothing, etc.) or the judge could read the cautionary jury instruction. Using the cautionary jury instruction, judges would read a statement to the jury prior to deliberation to caution them that it is easy to accuse someone of rape, it is very hard to defend against a rape accusation, and that they should carefully scrutinize the testimony of the victim (Anderson 2002).

RAPE LAW REFORMS

Throughout the mid-to-late twentieth century, a wave of rape law reforms emerged throughout the globe. During this time, the focus on individual human rights contributed to a reclassification of the crime of rape in many countries. That is, in countries that reformed their rape laws, the purpose of rape laws shifted from protecting morality and/or men's property to protecting an individual's right to have control over his/her body. As a result, instead of being classified as a property crime or a crime against public morality, the rape laws in many, but not all, jurisdictions were redefined as a violent crime against the person/victim (Frank, Hardinge, and Wosick-Correa 2009).

In many countries, the rape law reform movement was a part of the larger women's rights movement. For example, in the United States, women's rights organizations, such as the National Organization for Women (NOW), heavily criticized the traditional rape laws and initiated the rape law reform movement. Since women were no longer considered men's property, these feminist activists argued that the current rape laws were based on outdated, sexist and patriarchal views and, therefore, needed to be changed. They also argued that the rape laws did not provide equal protection for all victims; the rape laws failed to protect male victims, same-sex victims, spousal victims, and "unchaste" victims from unwanted sexual penetration. Furthermore, the activists claimed that the special evidentiary rules (i.e., the resistance requirement, corroboration requirement, and cautionary jury instructions), which were not required in prosecutions for other serious violent crimes, resulted in low rates of reporting, arrest, and conviction for rape (Spohn and Horney 1992).

While the scope of the rape law reform effort varied from country to country, most reform efforts focused on the following changes to the rape laws: (1) to redefine rape in gender-neutral terms so that both men and women could be both victims and offenders, (2) to expand the crime of rape to include other forms of sexual penetration (oral, anal, and vaginal penetration by a penis or an object), and (3) to eliminate the spousal exemption. In countries whose laws were derived from English Common Law, such as Canada and the United States, the rape law reform activists also sought to eliminate the special evidentiary requirements and to pass "rape shield laws" that prohibited or limited the admissibility of information about a victim's past sexual history in court (Spohn and Horney 1992).

Looking at the outcomes of the rape law reform movement, it is clear that there has been significant variation in the success of these reforms. For example, in the United States, the majority of states have created gender-neutral statutes, expanded the crime of rape to include other forms of sexual penetration, eliminated the resistance requirement, and passed rape shield laws (McMahon-Howard 2011); however, only about half of the states have completely eliminated the spousal exemption (McMahon-Howard, Clay-Warner, and Renzulli 2009). Similarly, at the global level, research indicates that approximately 75 countries have expanded the scope of their rape laws (Frank, Hardinge, and Wosick-Correa 2009); however, according to the United Nations' 2011 Progress of the World's Women report, 127 countries have not criminalized spousal rape (UN Women 2011).

While research indicates that the passage of rape law reforms is associated with an increase in reporting rapes to the police (Clay-Warner and Burt 2005; Frank, Hardinge, and Wosick-Correa 2009), it is important to note that rape still remains one of the most underreported violent crimes. Also, even when victims do report a rape to the police, the majority of cases do not proceed to prosecution (Daly and Bouhours 2010). Thus, despite the advances in the rape laws, the majority of rape cases do not result in a conviction.

SEE ALSO: Age of Consent in Historical and International Perspective; Battered Women; Chastity; Domestic Violence in the United States; Dowry and Bride-Price; Intimate Partner Abuse; Sexual Assault/Sexual Violence

REFERENCES

Anderson, Michelle J. 2002. "From Chastity Requirement to Sexuality License: Sexual Consent and a New Rape Shield Law." *George Washington Law Review*, 70: 51.

Brownmiller, Susan. 1975. *Against Our Will: Men, Women, and Rape*. New York: Ballantine Publishing Group.

Clay-Warner, Jody, and Callie Burt. 2005. "Rape Reporting After Reforms: Have Times Really Changed?" *Violence Against Women*, 11: 150–176. DOI: 10.1177/1077801204271566.

Daly, Kathleen, and Brigitte Bouhours. 2010. "Rape and Attrition in the Legal Process: A Comparative Analysis of Five Countries." *Crime and Justice*, 39: 565–649.

Frank, John D., Tara Hardinge, and Kassia Wosick-Correa. 2009. "The Global Dimensions of Rape-law Reform: A Cross-National Study of Policy Outcomes." *American Sociological Review*, 74: 272–290. DOI: 10.1177/000312240907400206.

McMahon-Howard, Jennifer. 2011. "Does the Controversy Matter? Comparing the Causal Determinants of Controversial and Non-Controversial Rape Law Reforms." *Law & Society Review*, 45: 401–432. DOI: 10.1111/j.1540-5893.2011.00438.x.

McMahon-Howard, Jennifer, Jody Clay-Warner, and Linda Renzulli. 2009. "Criminalizing Spousal Rape: The Diffusion of Legal Reforms." *Sociological Perspectives*, 52: 505–531.

Spohn, Cassia, and Julie Horney. 1992. *Rape Law Reform: A Grassroots Revolution and Its Impact*. New York: Plenum Press.

UN Women. 2011. *Progress of the World's Women: In Pursuit of Justice*. New York: UN Women. Accessed January 15, 2014, at http://www.unwomen.org/~/media/headquarters/attachments/sections/library/publications/2011/progressoftheworldswomen-2011-en.pdf.

Rape and Re-Victimization, Treatment of

TERRI L. MESSMAN-MOORE and JULIA KAPLINSKA
Miami University, USA

Approximately two out of three women with a history of rape report multiple experiences of rape or sexual assault in their lifetime (Classen, Palesh, and Aggarwal 2005). Similarly, women with a history of child sexual abuse (CSA) are between 2 and 11 times more likely to experience rape in adulthood (Messman-Moore and Long 2003). Survivors of child abuse (typically sexual abuse, but also physical and psychological abuse) are more likely to experience sexual, physical, and psychological victimization in adolescence and adulthood, a phenomenon called re-victimization (Cloitre and Rosenberg 2006). Patterns of re-victimization have been documented among college students, community women, inpatients, female inmates, and military veterans. Re-victimization also affects diverse populations, including Latina, African American, and Asian American women, bisexual women and gay men, and low-income, urban women.

Re-victimization appears to have a cumulative effect, compounding and even amplifying the negative impact of earlier childhood abuse experiences, resulting in increased levels of distress. Compared with individuals only abused in childhood or adulthood, or those with a single incident of victimization, re-victimized individuals typically present with significantly greater psychological distress, including post-traumatic stress disorder (PTSD), fear, avoidance, and other anxiety disorders; depression and suicidality; dissociation; alcohol abuse or dependence and substance use disorders; binge eating and other eating disorders; risky sexual behavior; and interpersonal difficulties (Classen, Palesh, and Aggarwal 2005). Negative outcomes associated with child abuse and re-victimization increase the likelihood of additional episodes of re-victimization, as perpetrators of interpersonal violence often target vulnerable individuals, including those with psychological and interpersonal impairment (Messman-Moore and Long 2003). Thus, intervention is critical not only to reduce psychological distress and improve functioning among re-victimized individuals, but also to reduce the likelihood of additional episodes of re-victimization.

Child abuse can interfere with the attainment of key developmental milestones in relation to development of the self, affect regulation, and interpersonal relationships (Cloitre and Rosenberg 2006). Given this developmental context, re-victimized individuals often present with a complex array of symptoms in addition to PTSD and depression, including alexithymia, impaired affect regulation and related difficulties (e.g., self-injurious behavior, disordered eating, substance use), clinically significant dissociation (e.g., depersonalization, amnesia), and attachment disruption and impaired interpersonal functioning (e.g., difficulties expressing assertiveness and maintaining boundaries, problems with sexual intimacy), particularly in intimate relationships.

Correlates of child abuse such as risky sexual behavior and problematic substance use not only predict re-victimization, but appear to reflect underlying difficulties in affect regulation and dysfunctional coping strategies. Because such risky behavior increases vulnerability and the likelihood of future re-victimization (Messman-Moore and Long 2003), these difficulties are critical targets for intervention.

PHASE-BASED APPROACH

Because the clinical presentation of re-victimized individuals is more complex, intervention often must address a broader array of emotional, behavioral, and social impairment and a more severe symptom presentation. Intervention for re-victimized individuals typically focuses on addressing traumatic sequelae represented by a variety of diagnoses, including chronic PTSD, dissociative disorders, mood disorders, and pervasive negative interpersonal patterns, as well as concomitant risky and maladaptive coping behavior, including substance use, risky sex, and self-injurious behavior. This complex presentation requires an approach that considers the developmental context of difficulties (e.g., affect dysregulation, dysfunctional interpersonal patterns) in addition to chronic PTSD and related problems. Given this, intervention for revictimization typically involves a sequential, phase-based approach, focusing on (1) stabilization and establishing safety, (2) trauma processing, and (3) functional reintegration (Ford et al. 2005).

Stabilization and safety

The initial phase of therapy focuses on safety as well as skills building (i.e., adaptive coping strategies) and psychoeducation. Establishment of safety includes improving the client's ability to cope with intense negative affect, self-destructive behavior (e.g., risky behavior such as sex with strangers), and reducing suicidal ideation and other aspects of self-harm (e.g., self-injurious behavior, disordered eating). Safety planning and conjunctive pharmacological intervention should be included if indicated. Psychoeducation involves information pertaining to the emotional, physical, and social symptoms and behaviors involved in post-traumatic syndromes, teaching adaptive coping skills, and information regarding the process of therapy. Stabilization and safety (as well as subsequent stages) must take place within an empathic and consistent therapeutic relationship which is essential to help the client resolve long-standing feelings of mistrust, to model adaptive interpersonal relationships, and to function as a supportive setting in which to "contain" rather than avoid intense emotions and impulses (Ford et al. 2005).

Trauma processing

The second phase of treatment involves an emphasis on client recall of traumatic memories, emotions, and perceptions, in a manner that is manageable and safe (Ford et al. 2005). In this stage, continued use and development of affect regulation skills and therapist co-regulation are a central aspect of the successful resolution of traumatic memories and related beliefs (e.g., shame, self-blame) that impact client functioning. Although there are not yet evidence-based guidelines for therapeutic trauma memory work, there is emerging evidence that repetitive exposure to trauma memories may not be required, as other approaches with limited exposure and an increased emphasis on challenging maladaptive trauma-related beliefs are effective (e.g., Resick et al. 2002). Once PTSD symptoms decrease to manageable levels, issues such as traumatic grief, shame, and rage may emerge and become the focus of the second phase of treatment.

Functional reintegration

The final phase of treatment involves an emphasis on focusing on reconnection, establishment or deepening of relationships, and "normal life" (Ford et al. 2005, 440). This phase focuses on the client's quality of life in interpersonal, vocational, recreational, and spiritual domains, and involves a refinement of self-regulation skills taught in the first phase of treatment. Across all phases, this approach focuses on enhancing the recognition of post-traumatic self-dysregulation in order to promote adaptive self-regulation.

TRAUMA-FOCUSED INTERVENTION

Cognitive-behavioral treatments for PTSD such as cognitive processing therapy (CPT; Resick et al. 2002) can be used to address sequelae of re-victimization. CPT alone is sufficient to address complex PTSD, but has been successfully combined with other approaches to address compulsive, self-injurious behavior in addition to chronic PTSD and depression. Furthermore, different variants of CPT (CPT versus CPT-C [cognitive therapy only]) may be tailored to presenting problems, given that individuals with high levels of depersonalization dissociation respond better to the full protocol of CPT rather than CPT-C. However, different forms of CPT are equally likely to reduce PTSD and depressive symptoms, which subsequently reduce risk for future intimate partner violence re-victimization (Iverson et al. 2011).

Another cognitive-behavioral treatment approach, Skills Training in Affect and Interpersonal Regulation with Modified Prolonged Exposure (STAIR-MPE; Cloitre et al. 2002), was designed specifically to improve emotion regulation skills and address interpersonal dysfunction associated with chronic PTSD and re-victimization. The STAIR-MPE method involves a focused, sequential approach which aims to (1) improve emotion regulation capacity via psychoeducation and behavioral intervention; (2) address chronic PTSD through cognitive-behavioral narrative exposure; and (3) improve interpersonal relationships and assertiveness via cognitive intervention focused on maladaptive interpersonal schemas (Cloitre et al. 2002). STAIR-MPE has demonstrated significant improvement in affect regulation problems, interpersonal skills deficits, and PTSD symptoms among adults with histories of childhood sexual and physical abuse (Cloitre et al. 2002).

Present-centered therapy (PCT; McDonagh-Coyle et al. 2005) and present-focused group therapy (PFGT; Spiegel et al. 2004) are two promising new approaches based upon interpersonal therapy, which are designed to reduce PTSD and improve self-regulation skills. These approaches focus on improving social problem-solving skills, and an awareness of the connection between risky behavior or problematic relational patterns and PTSD symptoms. PCT leads to decreases in PTSD and affect dysregulation, with improvements comparable to CBT-based approaches (McDonagh-Coyle et al. 2005). PFGT has been shown to reduce PTSD symptoms, risky sexual or substance use, and sexual re-victimization, as well as improve interpersonal functioning (Spiegel et al. 2004).

Ancillary approaches

If significant emotion dysregulation is present, clinicians may incorporate aspects of empirically supported approaches such as dialectical behavior therapy (Linehan 1993). In addition, Seeking Safety (Najavits 2002) may be a useful precursor to PTSD-focused treatments (e.g., STAIR, CPT, or PCT) for re-victimized individuals who struggle with substance (or other behavioral) addiction (e.g., unsafe sex practices, sex with strangers).

Seeking Safety does not directly focus on processing traumatic memories, but is designed to enhance safe coping skills as well as challenge maladaptive beliefs related to traumatic experiences and substance use, and appears to reduce PTSD symptom severity and co-occurring substance use disorders, as well as decrease levels of anxiety, depression, hostility, suicidality, and interpersonal problems (Najavits 2002).

SUMMARY

Sexual re-victimization affects a significant number of women who experience sexual violence. In addition, other forms of re-victimization may occur, impacting levels of post-assault distress. For example, re-victimization may occur in the form of victim-blaming reactions from recipients of disclosure (including friends, family, or the police) which contribute to levels of distress beyond the initial experience of sexual violence (Mason et al. 2009). In addition, negative experiences involved in the medical, criminal, or legal system may constitute another type of re-victimization (Maier 2008). Supportive responses to abuse disclosure are paramount in order to protect victims of sexual violence and to mitigate negative psychological effects. Moreover, disclosure may actually facilitate the curtailment of ongoing abuse, thus effective responses are potentially critical in decreasing risk for subsequent re-victimization. Such findings indicate that immediate and supportive intervention to stop ongoing sexual victimization and to provide treatment for victimization sequelae is of upmost importance in stopping the cycle of abuse that is re-victimization.

SEE ALSO: Child Sexual Abuse and Trauma; Drug and Alcohol Abuse; Eating Disorders and Disordered Eating; Post-Traumatic Stress Disorder; Recovered Memories; Self-Esteem; Sexual Assault/Sexual Violence

REFERENCES

Classen, Catherine C., Oxana G. Palesh, and Rashi Aggarwal. 2005. "Sexual Revictimization: A Review of the Empirical Literature." *Trauma, Violence, & Abuse*, 6(2): 103–129. DOI: 10.1177/1524838005275087.

Cloitre, Marylene, Karestan C. Koenen, Lisa R. Cohen, and Hymee Han. 2002. "Skills Training in Affective and Interpersonal Regulation Followed by Exposure: A Phase-Based Treatment for PTSD Related to Childhood Abuse." *Journal of Consulting and Clinical Psychology*, 70(5): 1067–1074. DOI: 10.1037/0022-006X.70.5.1067.

Cloitre, Marylene, and Anna Rosenberg. 2006. "Sexual Revictimization: Risk Factors and Prevention." In *Cognitive-Behavioral Therapies for Trauma*, edited by Victoria M. Follette and Joseph I. Ruzek, 321–361. New York: Guilford Press.

Ford, Julian D., Christine A. Courtois, Kathy Steele, Onno van der Hart, and Ellert R. S. Nijenhuis. 2005. "Treatment of Complex Post-Traumatic Dysregulation." *Journal of Traumatic Stress*, 18(5): 437–447. DOI: 10.1002/jts.20051.

Iverson, Katherine M., Jaimie L. Gradus, Patricia A. Resick, Michael K. Suvak, Kamala F. Smith, and Candice M. Monson. 2011. "Cognitive-Behavioral Therapy for PTSD and Depression Symptoms Reduces Risk for Future Intimate Partner Violence among Interpersonal Trauma Survivors." *Journal of Consulting and Clinical Psychology*, 79(2): 193–202. DOI: 10.1037/a0022512.

Linehan, Marsha M. 1993. *Cognitive-Behavioral Treatment of Borderline Personality Disorder*. New York: Guilford Press.

Maier, Shana L. 2008. "'I have heard horrible stories …' Rape Victim Advocates' Perceptions of the Revictimization of Rape Victims by the Police and Medical System." *Violence Against Women*, 14(7): 786–808. DOI: 10.1177/1077801208320245.

Mason, Gillan E., Sarah Ullman, Susan E. Long, LaDonna Long, L., and Laura Sarzynski. 2009. "Social Support and Risk of Sexual

Assault Revictimization." *Journal of Community Psychology*, 37(10): 58–72. DOI: 10.1002/jcop.20270.

McDonagh-Coyle, Annmarie, Matthew Friedman, Gregory McHugo, Julian Ford, Anjana Sengupta, Kim Mueser, et al. 2005. "Psychometric Outcomes of a Randomized Clinical Trial of Psychotherapies for PTSD-SA." *Journal of Consulting and Clinical Psychology*, 73: 515–524.

Messman-Moore, Terri L., and Patricia J. Long. 2003. "The Role of Childhood Sexual Abuse Sequelae in Sexual Revictimization: An Empirical Review and Theoretical Reformulation." *Clinical Psychology Review*, 23(4): 537–571. DOI: 10.1016/S0272-7358(02)00203-9.

Najavits, Lisa M. 2002. *Seeking Safety: A Treatment Manual for PTSD and Substance Abuse*. New York: Guilford Press.

Resick, Patricia A., Pallavi Nishith, Terri L. Weaver, Millie C. Astin, and Catherine A. Feuer. 2002. "A Comparison of Cognitive-Processing Therapy with Prolonged Exposure and a Waiting Condition for the Treatment of Chronic Posttraumatic Stress Disorder in Female Rape Victims." *Journal of Consulting and Clinical Psychology*, 70(4): 867–879. DOI: 10.1037/0022-006X.70.4.867.

Spiegel, David, Catherine Classen, Elisabeth Thurston, and Lisa Butler. 2004. "Trauma-Focused versus Present-Focused Models of Group Therapy for Women Sexually Abused in Childhood." In *From child sexual abuse to adult sexual risk: Trauma, revictimization, and intervention*, edited by Linda J. Koenig, Lynda S. Doll, Ann O'Leary, and Willo Pequegnat, 251–268. Washington, DC: American Psychological Association.

FURTHER READING

Cloitre, Marylene, Lisa R. Cohen, and Karestan C. Koenen. 2006. *Treating Survivors of Childhood Abuse: Psychotherapy for the Interrupted Life*. New York: Guilford Press.

Courtois, Christine A., and Julian D. Ford. 2013. *Treatment of Complex Trauma: A Sequenced, Relationship-Based Approach*. New York: Guilford Press.

Resick, Patricia A., and Monica K. Schnicke. 1993. *Cognitive Processing Therapy for Rape Victims: A Treatment Manual*. Thousand Oaks: Sage.

Recovered Memories

STEVEN JAY LYNN and JESSICA BALTMAN
Binghamton University, USA

The topic of recovered memories has been marked by controversy (Lynn et al. 2014). The concept of recovered memories originated with Freud (1896/1966), who argued that psychological symptoms could be caused by repressed memories of trauma. Today, some trauma theorists have asserted that memories of traumatic events are not simply forgotten like ordinary memories, but instead are repressed from consciousness as a means of protecting against confronting painful experiences. Nevertheless, although unconscious, such memories are believed to engender psychological symptoms (anxiety, depression, somatization) and necessitate efforts in psychotherapy to bring them into awareness to achieve insight and symptom relief.

In the early 1990s, in response to highly publicized criminal court cases, memory researchers began to critically evaluate the concept of memory repression. Because recovered memories in some court cases were determined to be inaccurate, misleading eyewitness testimony resulted in false convictions for serious crimes (e.g., murder, child abuse). In some court and civil cases, patients "recovered" memories for traumatic events during psychotherapy undertaken with the initial goal of treating common psychological symptoms such as anxiety, depression, and bulimia.

Over the past 30 years, research has vigorously challenged the concept of recovered memories. Studies of basic memory processes have demonstrated that, rather than forgetting, people typically recall more detailed and vivid memories of traumatic or highly emotional events, compared with memories of ordinary events (Kensinger

2007). Moreover, contrary to the repressed memory hypothesis, adults diagnosed with post-traumatic stress disorder (PTSD), originating from documented childhood sexual abuse, for example, experience intrusive memories for trauma-related events (McNally 1998).

Research indicates that recovered memories may be inaccurate. Memories, whether recovered or not, are not exact replicas of past events (i.e., memories are reconstructive) and are affected by expectancies, beliefs about what occurred in the past, decay of memory over time, and implicit and explicit suggestions. Approximately 20 to 30 percent of people tested in laboratory settings develop false memories in response to misleading questions and other suggestive procedures (Loftus 2005). False memories, often believed-in with confidence, have been documented for many events, ranging from mundane (e.g., getting lost in the mall), to improbable and bizarre (e.g., participation in satanic rituals, abduction by aliens). Common memory recovery procedures used in psychotherapy (e.g., repeated questioning about early experiences, guided imagery, hypnosis, age regression, dream interpretation) are often suggestive and risk creating false memories.

Despite the lack of evidence for repression, surveys show that the belief in the repression of traumatic memories is common. In a recent survey (Patihis et al. 2014), 19.4 percent of clinical psychology researchers in US research universities, 60.3 percent of board-certified clinical psychology practitioners, and 83.9 percent of adults from the general population indicated at least some agreement with the statement, "Traumatic memories are often repressed." Moreover, 16.1 percent of the research-oriented clinical psychologists, 43.1 percent of the clinical practitioners, and 77.7 percent of adults from the general population indicated at least some agreement with the statement "Repressed memories can be retrieved in therapy accurately." These statistics are consistent with previous surveys of psychologist and adults from the general population (see Lynn et al. 2015).

Although memories "recovered" during psychotherapy may be inaccurate, this outcome is not necessarily the case. Normal forgetting, rather than repression, may explain why people forget traumatic events long after they occur (McNally and Geraerts 2009). All memories tend to weaken with the passage of time or may not be salient in the present. A person might "recover" memories of abuse simply because he or she encounters a trigger for the memory. Alternatively, some individuals who recover memories for childhood sexual abuse, for example, may not have experienced the events as particularly traumatic during childhood. Yet during psychotherapy, the person might recognize for the first time that the event meets criteria for abuse and then become distressed with this knowledge (McNally and Geraerts 2009).

Traumatic events can have serious long-term consequences and require attention in psychotherapy. Still, interventions that emphasize memory recovery are no more effective, and may be less effective and risk false memory formation, compared with present-oriented therapies (e.g., cognitive-behavioral, acceptance-based approaches), which enjoy an extensive foundation of empirical support (Lynn et al. 2015).

SEE ALSO: Child Sexual Abuse and Trauma; Post-Traumatic Stress Disorder

REFERENCES

Freud, Sigmund. 1966. "Further Remarks on the Neuro-Psychoses of Defence." In *Standard Edition*, vol. 3. London: Hogarth Press. First published 1896.

Kensinger, Elizabeth A. 2007. "Negative Emotion Enhances Memory Accuracy: Behavioral and Neuroimaging Evidence." *Current Directions in Psychological Science*, 16(4): 213–218. DOI: 10.1111/j.1467-8721.2007.00506.x.

Loftus, Elizabeth F. 2005. "Planting Misinformation in the Human Mind: A 30-Year Investigation of the Malleability of Memory." *Learning & Memory*, 12(4): 361–366. DOI: 10.1101/lm.94705.

Lynn, Steven Jay, Elisa Krackow, Elizabeth F. Loftus, Timothy G. Locke, and Scott O. Lilienfeld. 2015. "Constructing the Past: Problematic Memory Recovery Techniques in Psychotherapy." In *Science and Pseudoscience in Clinical Psychology*, 2nd ed., edited by Scott O. Lilienfeld, Steven Jay Lynn, and Jeffrey M. Lohr. New York: Guilford Press.

Lynn, Steven Jay, et al. 2014. "The Trauma Model of Dissociation: Inconvenient Truths and Stubborn Fictions: Comment on Dalenberg et al." (2012) *Psychological Bulletin*, 140(3): 896–910. DOI: 10.1037/a0035570.

McNally, Richard J. 1998. "Experimental Approaches to Cognitive Abnormality in Post-traumatic Stress Disorder." *Clinical Psychology Review*, 18(8): 971–982. DOI: 10.1016/s0272-7358(98)00036-1.

McNally, Richard J., and Elke Geraerts. 2009. "A New Solution to the Recovered Memory Debate." *Perspectives on Psychological Science*, 4(2): 126–134. DOI: 10.1111/j.1745-6924.2009.01112.x.

Patihis, Lawrence, Lavina Y. Ho, Ian W. Tingen, Scott O. Lilienfeld, and Elizabeth F. Loftus. 2014. "Are the 'Memory Wars' Over? A Scientist-Practitioner Gap in Beliefs about Repressed Memory." *Psychological Science*, 25(2): 519–530. DOI: 10.1177/0956797613510718.

FURTHER READING

Dalenberg, Constance J., et al. 2012. "Evaluation of the Evidence for the Trauma and Fantasy Models of Dissociation." *Psychological Bulletin*, 138(3): 550. DOI: 10.1037/a0027447.

Loftus, Elizabeth F. 1993. "The Reality of Repressed Memories." *American Psychologist*, 48(5): 518–537. DOI: 10.1037/0003-066x.48.5.518.

McNally, Richard J. 2005. *Remembering Trauma*. Cambridge, MA: Harvard University Press.

Reflexivity

PATTI GIUFFRE and APRIL HUDSON
Texas State University, USA

Reflexivity refers to researchers seeing themselves as part of the research process beyond collecting and analyzing data. It presumes that researchers' biases, feelings, and interactions are a part of the data, not extraneous to them. According to Guillemin and Gillam (2004), reflexivity encompasses how researchers' construction of knowledge influences preparing, conducting, analyzing, and writing findings from their research. Reflexivity presumes that true neutrality within a traditional researcher role (a researcher who has no thoughts or emotions about meeting respondents, etc.) is false, not possible, and in fact, not desirable.

Reflexive researchers carefully consider how their various social locations and statuses influence the respondents, the setting, and their own interpretations of the data. Depending on the topic of study, researchers consider the fact that they are male, female, cisgender, transgender, are of particular social classes, their race and ethnicity, religion, sexual orientation, physical abilities, citizenship, and their place in the globalizing world, among others. How does the intersectionality of the researchers, in concert with the context of the study, alter the research process and the relationships with respondents?

Kristin Esterberg (2002) offers several guiding questions that can encourage reflexivity: Who is the researcher in relation to the respondents or the site? What kinds of connections does she or he already have to the group of respondents or setting? Does she or he have stereotypes about the group and setting? Is the researcher an insider or outsider to the group and culture in the study? Although all researchers are reflexive to some degree, many have been trained to attempt to adhere to the traditional researcher role, which involves collecting data and then never interacting with respondents again. This traditional role assumes a strict separation between the researcher and respondent that is not applicable for qualitative studies. Qualitative researchers are more likely than quantitative researchers to discuss their place in the research process because they are more closely and intimately involved with their participants and the setting. In contrast to surveys and experimental studies, qualitative research requires interaction with the respondents in their everyday settings. Ethnographies and in-depth interview studies (with individuals and in focus groups) involve finding informants, gaining access, conducting interviews, making observations, and leaving the field. An ethnographer who spends a few months to several years with a group of people becomes a part of the research process beyond data collection.

Reflexivity involves a careful consideration of whether we are insiders or outsiders, and how our insider or outsider status influences our interpretations of the data, access to the setting, our interactions with respondents, and how to enter and leave the field. Debates remain whether being an insider or outsider offers researchers a more accurate insight into the group under study. In the past, some researchers have argued that insiders ask better questions, get more complete access, collect more accurate data, and offer more accurate interpretations of the findings because they are already a part of the group under study. They maintained that insiders are familiar with the context, nomenclature, values, and norms of the group. Other researchers have questioned whether insiders will be able to critique the group of which they are already a part. An outsider might be more likely to ask additional or different types of questions because they know little about the norms and values of the group other than what they have learned from previous literature. Currently, researchers argue that the advantages of being an insider or outsider are context dependent. For example, Reuben Buford May (2014) is an African American sociologist who has studied college student experiences. He describes how he is both an insider and an outsider when interviewing white college students. He is an insider to the particular college and region in which he interviewed students, and an outsider in terms of race. May experienced "insider moments" in which rapport was enhanced at different times during the interviews based on his insider and outsider statuses.

Researchers' emotions during the research process can include fear, anger, exhilaration, and sadness. Reflexive researchers negotiate and write about these feelings toward their respondents, topics, and the contexts in which they complete their research. Several sociologists have published reflexive pieces about their place in the research process, particularly about their biases and emotional responses to their respondents. For example, Kathleen Blee (1998) wrote about her lack of empathy and neutrality toward the racist hate group members she interviewed, her fear during interviews, and the respondents' use of fear. Her emotional responses to this group became an integral part of the study as these were just as significant as the findings from the interviews. Discussing emotions and biases can be considered a limitation to being "truly objective"; however, reflexive researchers argue that it is better to account for one's personal vulnerabilities than pretend to be value-neutral.

Researchers can create more reflexivity by either "bracketing" or/and writing a research journal that tracks issues, thoughts, biases, and emotions through the research process. Bracketing involves writing memos throughout the research process as a check for unintentional biases. Writing a journal can initiate a deeper understanding of the qualitative research process, as well as what it means to become a qualitative researcher. In her study of gay and lesbian teachers, Catherine Connell (2015) kept a journal about her emotional responses to her respondents and the context of her interviews (including her mood and concerns about some of the respondents' comments, which she perceived as socially offensive). Connell argues that journaling in this way made her research more analytical and critical.

Reflexivity is necessary because it aids the researchers' understanding of the social phenomenon under study. Reflecting on previous knowledge and thoughts creates a milieu for continuously improving methodological skill and rigor. Engaging in reflexivity can contribute to greater accuracy about the research process. According to Gloria González-López (2011), it also permits researchers to treat their respondents in the most ethical way possible. For reflexive researchers, the benefits of reflexivity far outweigh potential criticisms that reflexivity detracts from objectivity.

SEE ALSO: Feminist Ethnography; Intersectionality

REFERENCES

Blee, Kathleen M. 1998. "White-Knuckle Research: Emotional Dynamics in Fieldwork with Racist Activists." *Qualitative Sociology*, 21(4): 381–400.

Connell, Catherine. 2015. *School's Out: Gay and Lesbian Teachers in the Classroom*. Berkeley: University of California Press.

Esterberg, Kristin. 2002. *Qualitative Methods in Social Research*. Boston: McGraw-Hill.

González-López, Gloria. 2011. "Mindful Ethics: Comments on Informant-Centered Practices in Sociological Research." *Qualitative Sociology*, 34: 447–461.

Guillemin, Marilys, and Lynn Gillam. 2004. "Ethics, Reflexivity, and 'Ethically Important Moments' in Research." *Qualitative Inquiry*, 10(2): 261–280.

May, Reuben A. Buford. 2014. "When the Methodological Shoe is on the Other Foot: African American Interviewer and White Interviewees." *Qualitative Sociology*, 37(1): 117–136.

FURTHER READING

Brown-Saracino, Japonica. 2014. "From Methodological Stumbles to Substantive Insights: Gaining Ethnographic Access to Queer Communities." *Qualitative Sociology*, 37(1): 43–68.

Finlay, Linda. 2002. "Negotiating the Swamp: The Opportunity and Challenge of Reflexivity in Research Practice." *Qualitative Research*, 2(2): 209–230.

Tufford, Lea, and Peter Newman. 2010. "Bracketing in Qualitative Research." *Qualitative Social Work*, 11(1): 80–96.

Refugee Women and Violence Against Women

RIA E. BAKER
Houston Graduate School of Theology, USA

Refugee women make up over half of all persons displaced by war, natural disasters, civil unrest, violence, religious or political persecution, and sexual and gender-based violence (SGBV). SGBV pervades virtually all societies, causing women to flee their homes, communities, or countries to seek protection. When women flee, they are vulnerable to various forms of abuse prior to, during, and after migration and displacement, which have social, psychological, and economic implications. The United Nations High Commissioner for Refugees (UNHCR) has defined refugee status and advocates for displaced persons across the globe.

SGBV affects women internationally, regardless of their age, educational background, ethnicity, socioeconomic status, and spiritual or religious orientation. SGBV consists of violent actions against women and girls, such as trafficking for sexual and labor exploitation, forced marriage, forced sterilization, female genital mutilation, the threat of honor crimes, sexual violence, and rape (UNHCR 2014a). Women who are subject to SGBV flee their homes and countries to seek asylum.

The Geneva Convention (1951) defined a refugee as someone who, due to a well-founded fear of being persecuted for reasons of race, religion, nationality, membership of a particular social group or political opinion, is outside the country of his or her nationality, and is unable to, or due to such fear, is unwilling to avail himself or herself of the protection of that country. Over half of the adult refugee population is female. As a result of the use of weapons of mass destruction, the scale of displacement is unique in the history of refugees and has reached unprecedented levels in the twenty-first century (UNHCR 2014b).

When women and their families are uprooted by civil unrest or violence, they are driven from their homes and are displaced within their own countries (i.e., internally displaced; Martin 2004) or across borders (Cole, Espin, and Rothblum 1992). Involuntary migration takes place on almost every continent. Asia has been reported to be the largest producer of refugees and Africa the second largest. In Africa, for example, millions have been displaced internally, many have faced displacement several times in their lifetime, and many are confined to refugee camps for numerous years. Reports indicate that refugees in Africa are housed in warehouses, sometimes for up to 20 years. Thousands have been killed, disabled, and left homeless, and millions of women and children have been uprooted from their homes by the loss of their extended families or their homes. These people, scarred by the trauma of war, detention, sexual assault, long-term settlement in poverty-stricken and violent refugee camps, the loss of children along the way, and the brutal murder of their family members, await relocation by the UNHCR. The office of the UNHCR, established after World War II by the United Nations General Assembly on December 14, 1950, is an agency that leads and coordinates international action to protect and advocate for the rights and well-being of refugees. The UNHCR provides shelter, registration for asylum, water and food, and other health and wellness resources for those who have been displaced globally (UNHCR 2014b). Additionally, the UNHCR facilitates global consultations to seek and implement durable strategies for the international protection of refugee women in gender-related persecution, legal issues, and violence (Global Consultations 2002).

Studies on the experiences of refugee women from Asia, Europe, Central and South America, and the Middle East, reveal that many are the victims of sexual abuse and assault. Sexual assault or rape is used as a weapon of war by the enemy. As they are displaced, women lose control over their basic conditions because of the impermanence of communities and the lack of reliable resources (Cole, Espin, and Rothblum 1992). Refugee camps, which consist mostly of women and children, do not necessarily provide a safe haven for women, as they are often subject to sexual exploitation by humanitarian workers or male refugees and often lack adequate reproductive healthcare (Buscher 2010). Women and girls sometimes turn to prostitution to secure relief items for their family. They may also be subject to sex trafficking and, in male-dominated societies, treated as possessions rather than individuals with rights. These migration experiences make great demands on their coping skills, starting first as they are confronted with the fear and dangers of fleeing and their desire not to leave home or family (Gong-Guy et al. 1991). Fleeing can be life-threatening. The migration experience can entail escaping the violence of war, experiencing loss of family members, dealing with the aftermath of sexual assault (e.g., contraction of HIV/AIDS or unwanted pregnancies) or torture, living in poor and squalid refugee camp conditions, and experiencing famine (Gong-Guy et al. 1991; Cole, Espin, and Rothblum 1992; Mayotte 1992; Buscher 2010).

Asylum seekers experience grueling times as they await decisions about their future place of residence. The isolation, alienation, or racism they may experience while seeking refuge can seriously affect their mental health. Migration and refugee camp confinement cause a great deal of psychological strain which can result in mental disorders. Many refugee women suffer from mental health problems such as depression, schizophrenia, post-traumatic stress disorder (PTSD), suicide, and psychosis (Beiser 2005). Long-term refugee camp confinement contributes greatly towards the development of mental health problems and feelings of helplessness, humiliation, frustration, and insecurity. Many women seeking asylum are apprehended by immigration law enforcement agents and find themselves in detention centers for months or years. Often mixed in with criminals, they are vulnerable and traumatized, and lack adequate healthcare (Brané and Wang 2013).

When women and their families are finally resettled in a receiving country by the UN refugee program and resettlement agencies, or are granted asylum, they arrive with limited resources and often fall into a cycle of poverty. As a result of language and cultural barriers, they often have to resort to unskilled labor and women who typically stayed at home to care for their children may need to seek outside employment when husbands are unemployed or underemployed. Loneliness, traumatic memories, depression, and anxiety are also commonly experienced (Mollica and Son 1989). Unanticipated social and economic barriers contribute to stress, family conflict, and partner violence (Guruge, Roche, and Catallo 2012). The identity of a woman, wife, and/or mother and gender roles change almost instantaneously when the refugee is displaced (Mayotte 1992). As refugees lose their families and communities, they often also lose access to their traditional healing and coping sources.

Despite the innumerable advances that the UNHCR has made in 20 years (1990–2010) in the arena of policy development for the protection of refugee women, achievement in practice lags behind. New issues that are gaining attention by the humanitarian community are: (1) providing economic empowerment opportunities (Martin 2004) for refugee women for the protection of the health and well-being of their families and for the eventual eradication of sexual exploitation of these women; and (2) programming towards the achievement of gender equality by educating men of the benefits to them and their children that women's equality can bring (Buscher 2010).

SEE ALSO: Gender Violence; Refugees and Refugee Camps; Violence Against Women in Global Perspective; Violence Against Women, Movements Against

REFERENCES

Beiser, M. 2005. *The Health of Immigrants and Refugees in Canada*. Ottawa: Canadian Institutes of Health Research.

Brané, Michelle, and Wang, Lee. 2013. *Women: The Invisible Detainees*. Accessed May 16, 2015, at www.aclu.org/sexual-abuse-immigration-detention.

Buscher, Dale. 2010. "Refugee Women: Twenty Years On." *Refugee Survey Quarterly*, 29(2): 4–20.

Cole, Ellen, Oliva Espin, and Esther Rothblum, eds. 1992. *Refugee Women and Their Mental Health:*

Shattered Societies, Shattered Lives. Binghamton: Haworth.

Geneva Convention. 1951. "Convention and Protocol Relating to the Status of Refugees." Accessed August 4, 2015, at http://www.unhcr.org/3b66c2aa10.html.

Global Consultations. 2002. "The Search for Protection-based Solutions and Protection of Refugee Women and Refugee Children." *Refugee Survey Quarterly*, 22(2/3): 276–283.

Gong-Guy, E., R. Cravens, and T. Patterson. 1991. "Clinical Issues in Mental Health Service Delivery to Refugees." *American Psychologist*, 46: 642–648.

Guruge, Sepali, Brenda Roche, and Cristina Catallo. 2012. "Violence against Women: An Exploration of the physical and Mental Health Trends among Immigrant and Refugee Women in Canada." *Nursing Research and Practice*, 2012: 1–15. DOI: 10.1155/2012/434592.

Martin, Susan F. 2004. *Refugee Women*. Lanham: Lexington Books.

Mayotte, Judy A. 1992. *Disposable People: The Plight of Refugees*. New York: Orbis Books.

Mollica, Richard L., and I. Son. 1989. "Cultural Dimensions in the Evaluation and Treatment of Sexual Trauma." *Treatment of Victims of Sexual Abuse*, 12: 363–379.

United Nations High Commissioner for Refugees. 2014a. "UNHCR Welcomes Council of Europe Convention on Combating Violence Against Women." Accessed August 4, 2015, at http://www.unhcr.org/53da56749.html.

United Nations High Commissioner for Refugees. 2014b. "War's Human Cost: UNHCR Global Trends 2013." Accessed August 4, 2015, at http://www.unhcr.org/5399a14f9.html.

FURTHER READING

Hammoury, M.S., M. Khawaja, Z. Mahfoud, R.A. Afifi, and H. Mad. 2009. "Domestic Violence against Women during Pregnancy: The Case of Palestinian Refugees Attending an Antenatal Clinic in Lebanon." *Journal of Women's Health*, 18: 337–345. DOI: 10.1089/jwh.2007.0740

Koss, Mary P. and Jacqueline W. White. 2008. "National and Global Agendas on Violence Against Women: Historical Perspective and Consensus." *American Journal of Orthopsychiatry*, 78: 386–393. DOI: 10.1037/a0014347.

Martin, Susan F. 2012. "Refugee Women." In *Refugees Worldwide*, edited by Uma A. Segal and Doreen Elliott, 207–233. Santa Barbara: Praeger.

Price, M.E. 2009. *Rethinking Asylum: History, Purpose, and Limits*. Cambridge: Cambridge University Press.

Refugees and Refugee Camps

LINDA BARTOLOMEI
University of New South Wales, Australia

Regardless of whether refugees are men, women, boys, or girls, they face uncertain futures, precarious existences and ongoing human rights abuses. For some the risks are extreme: political activists may be targeted across international borders; refugees with disabilities, unaccompanied minor children, and elderly people often face heightened risk; others may face discrimination and persecution on grounds of their sexual orientation or gender identity. Gender cuts across these groups with women and girls facing compounded and intersecting risks based on social and cultural constructions of gender roles and norms, combined with their lack of citizenship as refugees. Although common gender-related barriers and abuses are faced by refugees across a range of settings, in the context of refugee camps, issues of gender, power and lack of citizenship intersect in particular ways to marginalize and increase risks for women and girls. While not all refugees live in camps, in 2013 approximately half of the 15.4 million refugees did (UNHCR 2013).

Refugee camps vary in size and structure with some informal camps accommodating only several hundred refugees, while other more established camps, such as those in Kenya, Pakistan, and Bangladesh have hosted thousands of refugees for several decades (Milner and Loescher 2011). In spite of the protracted nature of many refugee situations and the many years spent in camps, the camps remain temporary structures which keep refugee populations in legal limbo without work rights, freedom of movement, or access to effective justice. The negative and decapacitating impacts of encampment have been well documented in the works of Barbara Harrell-Bond and others who have compared refugee camps to warehouses in which the capacities of refugee communities are wasted and denied (Crisp 2000; Harrell-Bond 2002; Hyndman 2000). With the exception of some limited access to economic, social, and cultural rights in the form of food rations, education and vocational training, refugees continue to be denied the vast majority of their rights in the camp setting including their civil and political rights to freedom of movement, autonomy, and self-determination.

Common issues compounding the risks in the camps include:

- overcrowded and inadequate shelters
- insufficient water and poor sanitation
- latrines and bathing facilities lacking privacy
- family groups having to live in close proximity
- poor lighting, exacerbating safety concerns
- lack of access to justice
- inadequate opportunities for work and further training
- unsafe and overcrowded schools
- women and girls being forced to walk long distances to collect water and firewood.

Though refugee camps are located in diverse locations around the world, a common set of gendered human rights abuses and intersecting risks has been documented.

The isolation, confinement, lack of autonomy and self-determination, and economic disempowerment faced by the refugee communities fosters and contributes to high levels of gendered violence including:

- domestic violence
- sexual exploitation
- rape in the camp setting
- forced and early marriage
- survival sex and trafficking.

While refugee boys and men also face risks of rape and sexual violence, for women and girls the risks pervade all aspects of their lives both in public and in private (Akram 2013; UNHCR 2011).

A significant body of academic literature has developed to explore refugee camps as gendered spaces (Fiddian-Qasmiyeh 2014; Freedman 2010; Hyndman 2000; Indra 1998). This critical body of work addresses the historic gender "blindness" of law and policy frameworks which guide refugee protection, masking the gendered nature of displacement and the particular problems of women and girls. Much of this literature explores the way in which experiences of conflict, displacement and encampment transform social relationships, disrupting traditional gender roles and norms which can exert a negative impact on both men and women.

Women and girls face particular human rights abuses due to their gender roles and position in society. In situations of displacement and protracted encampment, abuses of women's rights and gender discrimination increase. Changed gender roles, including men's loss of status and breadwinner role, compounded by stress and lack of family income leads to increased conflict between husbands and wives, which has been documented as contributing to increased domestic violence and intergenerational conflict in refugee settings. For some women and girls, camps may provide opportunities for education and empowerment that were not available at home; however, for many, camp life is characterized by heightened risks of gender-related violence and discrimination.

The lack of citizenship rights including lack of freedom of movement, denial of the right to work and a lack of access to justice intersect with women's unequal social status to compound the risks and abuses that women and girls face. The status of a refugee and the denial of the rights of citizenship, in effect compound and increase the negative impact of pre-existing social and cultural norms which deny women equal status with men. In the context of a refugee camp, economic deprivation often increases the risks women and girls face of being forced into marriage, into engaging in survival sex or of being trafficked. A lack of access to education further increases women's vulnerability through low self-esteem and a lack of awareness of their rights. Women's vulnerability also increases when they do not have the skills or opportunities to earn their own money heightening their dependence on men and the risks of sexual exploitation (Bartolomei, Pittaway, and Pittaway 2003; Martin 2011).

In situations of armed conflict, rape and sexual violence are widespread phenomena, with women and adolescent girls often the targets, as a means of demoralizing families and communities and emasculating husbands and fathers who are unable to protect them. The impact of rape and sexual violence in conflict is often compounded when refugee women and girls move into the refugee camps. A previous experience of rape increases the risk of further experience of rape, sexual abuse, and exploitation, with the refugee woman or girl often facing stigmatization and social exclusion, which may lead to domestic violence, family fragmentation, and force women and girls into prostitution or "survival sex" in order to meet their own and their children's basic needs (UNHCR 2011).

Sexual and gender-based violence in refugee camp settings is endemic and pervasive, compounded by the denial of other human rights and the lack of gender equality in camps. In the camp setting, the loss of family and community and an erosion of the protections generally associated with citizenship, including access to justice and economic opportunities, intersect to heighten all refugees' vulnerabilities to multiple forms of abuse and exploitation. Women and girls' vulnerabilities are tied to their socially ascribed gender roles. In the public sphere, women are raped while collecting firewood or water, or while travelling to the market. Young girls and boys may be sexually assaulted or raped in schools or forced to exchange sex for grades or scholastic materials (UNHCR 2011). Girls who are pregnant or have given birth to babies of rape are denied access to education. Abusers include men in the local community, authority figures including police, security officers, teachers, NGO and UN staff, and other refugees. Unaccompanied minor girls are also vulnerable to rape or sexual abuse by carers in informal and unsupervised foster arrangements. This can lead to early and unwanted pregnancies. Other groups of women and girls who face heightened risks of sexual abuse include women and girls with a disability and lesbian women, who report high levels of discrimination and risks of "corrective" rape (UNHCR 2011).

Education facilities in camps are limited; class sizes are large with often poorly qualified teachers trying to manage classes of over 100 students. Female students face particular problems in accessing education in camps, often experiencing interrupted schooling due to the gendered distribution of household labor and the pressure to assist with household chores. Limited water points in camps and competition for often-limited supplies of firewood mean that girls and women waste many hours queuing for water and walking long distances to and from the camp to collect firewood. This not only leads to many days of missed schooling but also puts them at heightened risk of rape and sexual abuse. Limited access to sanitary materials in many camps also forces girls to routinely miss one week of school each month during their menstrual period (UNHCR 2011).

A lack of effective justice systems in camps contributes to a climate of impunity for acts of sexual and other forms of violence perpetrated within and against the refugee communities. This includes insufficient or corrupt police and government officials, and gender-blind and discriminatory traditional justice systems which also increase risks for women. Traditional justice systems often free rapists following payment of a bribe to the victim's family or force young women to marry their rapists. In some settings, women have been detained and accused of adultery (Harrell-Bond 2002). Domestic violence is frequently not punished which contributes to normalizing violence against women and children. In such a climate of permissiveness, when authorities fail to take action, women will often stop reporting, which further contributes to a culture of impunity. A lack of gender-sensitive mechanisms also discourages women from reporting (Ho and Pavlish 2011).

Women are often marginalized by powerful men in their communities and are routinely excluded from meaningful positions in camp committees and justice systems. In addition to cultural obstacles, practical considerations including access to childcare, compensation for lost income, access to training and transportation often prevent or inhibit women's active participation. Women and girls' low socioeconomic status, lack of development opportunities, and lack of participation in camp committees contributes to their lack of social power in the camp and ability to have their voices heard. Their lack of involvement in leadership often means that the particular needs of women and girls are not adequately acknowledged or addressed, which impacts negatively not only on women and girls, but on their families and communities (Freedman 2010; UNHCR 2011).

Contemporary studies continue to demonstrate that in spite of extensive guidelines and policies designed to improve camp conditions, protection and accountability, refugee camps often remain sites of risk, terror, and abuse for many of the refugees who live there. This research highlights the way in which human rights violations ranging from a lack of women's participation in leadership, education, and livelihoods as well as the lack of effective legal systems, intersect to increase women and girls' risks of rape and sexual exploitation (Ho and Pavlish 2011; UNHCR 2011). A lack of commitment to gender equality as well as the absence of active and ongoing involvement of refugee women are highlighted as significant causes of ongoing problems. In seeking to understand the multiple barriers that exclude refugee women from leadership roles in camps and increase their vulnerability to abuse, significant contributions have been made by feminist academics. A number of scholars have explored the tendency of many refugee and development agencies to characterize refugee women as victims without agency and capacity, while at the same time characterizing humanitarian actors as experts in solving refugee problems (Hajdukowski-Ahmed 2009; Hyndman 2000). Such representations of refugee women's identities legitimize practices and programs that exclude women from participating in decision-making and planning roles. In this regard, refugee women and girls are impacted not only by unequal power relations with men in their communities, but also in their relationships with UNHCR and NGOs.

The negative impacts of refugee women's exclusion from decision-making are often further compounded by perceptions of violence against women, in particular domestic violence and forced and early marriage, as solely negative cultural practices found in refugee-producing countries across the global south. As Freedman (2010) argues one of the key consequences is that violence and persecution is "attributed to immutable social and cultural characteristics which inhibit an effective analysis of the real dynamics of gender inequality underlying all types of gender-related violence whether 'here' or 'there'" (p. 602). Instead, more nuanced and context-specific analyses are required, which allow an understanding of the ways in which conflict and displacement might intersect with harmful traditional practices. It is commonly agreed that developing more accurate gendered understandings of the experience of refugee women, and indeed men, will only come about through far greater active engagement of refugees in identifying and defining problems. Through such approaches, refugee women and men are engaged not solely as the subjects of abuses but as rights holders and active participants, struggling for access to and enjoyment of their entitlements. In this way the particular risks faced by refugee women and girls as well as those faced by men and boys in all their diversities can be better addressed.

SEE ALSO: Domestic Violence in the United States; Feminism, Postcolonial; Gender Blind; Gender Violence; Refugee Women and Violence Against Women

REFERENCES

Akram, Susan M. 2013. "Millennium Development Goals and the Protection of Displaced and Refugee Women and Girls." *Laws*, 2: 283–313. DOI: 10.3390/laws2030283.

Bartolomei, Linda, Eileen Pittaway, and Emma Pittaway. 2003. "Who Am I? Identity and Citizenship in Kakuma Refugee Camp in Northern Kenya." *Development*, 46(3): 87–93. DOI: 10.1177/10116370030463014.

Crisp, Jeff. 2000, "A State of Insecurity: The Political Economy of Violence in Kenya's Refugee Camps." *African Affairs*, 99: 601–632. DOI: 10.1093/afraf/99.397.601.

Freedman, Jane. 2010. "Mainstreaming Gender in Refugee Protection." *Cambridge Review of International Affairs*, 23(4): 589–605. DOI: 10.1080/09557571.2010.523820.

Harrell-Bond, Barbara. 2002. "Can Humanitarian Work With Refugees Be Humane?" *Human Rights Quarterly*, 24: 51–85.

Ho, Anita, and Carol Pavlish. 2011. "Indivisibility of Accountability and Empowerment in Tackling Gender-Based Violence: Lessons from a Refugee Camp in Rwanda." *Journal of Refugee Studies*, 24(1): 88–109. DOI: 10.1093/jrs/feq052.

Hyndman, Jennifer. 2000. *Managing Displacement: Refugees and the Politics of Humanitarianism*. Minneapolis: University of Minnesota Press.

Indra, Doreen, ed. 1998. *Engendering Forced Migration: Theory and Practice*. New York: Berghahn Books.

Martin, Susan F. 2011. "Refugee and Displaced Women: 60 Years of Progress and Setbacks." *Amsterdam Law Forum*, 3(2): 72–91.

Milner, James, and Gil Loescher. 2011. "Responding to Protracted Refugee Situations. Lessons from a Decade of Discussion." Refugees Studies Centre, Forced Migration Policy Briefing 6. Accessed August 17, 2015, at http://www.rsc.ox.ac.uk/files/publications/policy-briefing-series/pb6-responding-protracted-refugee-situations-2011.pdf.

UNHCR. 2011. "Survivors, Protectors, Providers: Refugee Women Speak Out." Summary Report, November 2011. Accessed December 12, 2013, at http://www.unhcr.org/4ec5337d9.html.

UNHCR. 2013. "New UNHCR Report Says Global Forced Displacement at 18-year High." News Stories, June 19, 2013. Accessed January 15, 2014, at http://www.unhcr.org/51c071816.html.

FURTHER READING

Freedman, Jane. 2007. *Gendering the International Asylum and Refugee Debate*. Basingstoke: Palgrave Macmillan.

Regulation of Queer Sexualities

GARY KINSMAN
Laurentian University, Canada

INTRODUCTION

The regulation of queer sexualities addresses the regulation of diverse groups engaging in erotic and gender experiences that rupture with institutionalized heterosexuality (including in contexts where this is still in formation) and the imposition of a two-gender (male/female) way of doing gender. This regulation, originally articulated within the framework of nation-states, is increasingly global in character.

Critical researchers use the term social regulation rather than social control. Social control has a monolithic character, cannot adequately address history and change, and suggests there is little basis for resistance. Social regulation provides more space for agency, recognizing that people conform to regulations when they feel the consequences of resistance are too great, while resisting more overtly when this is possible.

Central to current oppressive forms of sexual regulation are heterosexism, sexism, and anti-trans oppression. These social practices play a key part in the regulation of queer sexualities – the diverse experiences named as gay, lesbian, bisexual, trans, two-spirit, many other indigenous expressions, and all those participating in sexual and gender practices that rupture with the two-gender binary system.

While some researchers argue that gender determines sexuality and others argue that sexual and gender regulation are separate (Rubin 1984), in a more dialectical sense the regulations addressing sexuality are both autonomous from the regulation of gender and mutually constructed (or mediated) through the regulation of gender and other relations. Sexual regulation has a moment of autonomy, but in a concrete historical sense is always made in and through gender and other relations. This requires the development of a relational and mediational social analysis (Bannerji 1995).

Queer is a broader term than homosexual, lesbian, or gay and attempts to capture diverse erotic and gendered experiences. Queer is used first to reclaim it from being a term of abuse; as Chauncey points out in *Gay New York* (1994), it was originally adopted by some queer people in the early twentieth century. This acts to neutralize it as a weapon that can be used against queer people. Second, it is used as a broader term that can potentially include the experiences of all those who live in rupture with institutionalized heterosexuality and the two-gender binary system. Exactly what is included within "queer" remains contested. The naming of queer has unfortunately been able to be used to marginalize lesbians and it also does not always include trans experiences.

Third, queer is used to denormalize hegemonic relations. This creates a social standpoint from which to queer social relations, as in queering the nation or the family. Others do not use it to displace class and class struggle, as has often taken place in poststructuralist-oriented queer theory. Instead it can be used in a more queer historical materialist sense to queer Marxism and to use Marxism to queer the disappearance of class struggle from much queer theory (Kinsman 1996; Hennessy 2000; Kinsman and Gentile 2010).

Questions remain as to whether queer includes the experiences of people in the Global South. Researchers are asking whether queer works to learn from and include these experiences, or whether a broader term is needed. At the same time, queer carries with it a more critical perspective than the expression SOGI (sexual orientation, gender identity), which is being increasingly used in United Nations-related organizing. Sexual orientation, which developed as a Western human rights category, is rooted in an essentialist theory of different sexual orientations (especially homosexuality and heterosexuality) and is combined with gender identity, which attempts to cover trans experiences but limits this with Western notions of "identity."

Eroticism or sexuality cannot simply be seen as biologically determined (Fausto-Sterling 2000). Instead eroticism and sexualities are socially made, building on physiological potentials. There is a major historical and cross-cultural diversity in how sexualities and genders are organized. There is no essential sexuality, including no transhistorical heterosexuality or homosexuality. An analogy with language can be useful. Most people (but not all) are born with the physiological capacities for speech. But this does not mean that people will learn a language since this is a social process that builds on physiological potentials. The physiological capacity for speech does not in any way determine what language people will speak or how good they will be at speaking it. In a similar fashion, most people are born with the physiological potentialities to derive erotic pleasure from their bodies and their interactions with the bodies of others. But this does not determine what form this eroticism will take or how it will be understood as a sexuality. The formation of people's capacities for language and their capacities for eroticism and sexual practices occurs in an embodied social fashion. This leads to a diversity of experiences, needs, and social identifications.

It is against this diversity of experiences that oppressive sexual and gender regulation works. These regulatory regimes try to fit these diverse social experiences into their classifications of sexual "norms" and "deviances." There is nothing natural about the two-gender system and institutionalized heterosexuality. These have their own social and historical conditions of existence and are tied up with relations of social power.

SEXUAL REGULATION

Sexual regulation is the complex web of relations that regulate people's erotic lives. Sexual regulation in some form exists in all societies. All societies have to make collective and ethical decisions regarding eroticism. The question is how to move away from oppressive and toward non-oppressive forms of regulation.

These practices of oppressive regulation range from legal, police, and national security practices (including administrative law; Spade 2011), to social and family policies, schooling, the mass media, popular cultures and what are sometimes referred to as "cultural practices," churches and religious practices, sexual advice literatures, the medical and psychiatric professions, peer group pressures, and others. There are also new strategies of regulation that have emerged with the development of "sexual citizenship" claims out of rights-based struggles in the Global North which now also have impact in parts of the Global South. These lead to some queer people being regulated through strategies of respectability and responsibility as "patriotic" and "loyal" citizens within the nation-state, or as married, as spouses, as families, and as members of the military. This consolidation of queer integration into still heterosexual-dominated relations and neoliberalism has been characterized as "homonormativity" by Lisa Duggan (2003). This leads to some queers becoming integrated into global capitalist relations (Hennessy 2000).

There is often a consumer basis to this "sexual citizenship" based on queer people's ability to purchase commodities and perform certain "lifestyles" that include some white and middle-class queer people but also simultaneously exclude lesbians, poorer queer people, young queers, trans people, working-class queer people, queers of color, and many people in the Global South. These become practices of inclusion *and* exclusion, leading some queer people to being excluded from mainstream queer community formation, with very differential abilities to participate in these relations.

These practices of regulation have shifted from being based in local community and church (even as the context for this changes) regulations in the West in the eighteenth and nineteenth centuries to more translocal forms of organization, first through the nation-state (including criminal codes and social and family policies) as well as professional psychiatric, psychological, and sexological discourses, then through colonialism, and now through broader global social relations.

Global sexual regulation is now bound up with capitalist globalization. While capitalist social relations have always had a global character, since the mid-1970s there have been new waves of capitalist globalization (McNally 2002) that have expanded the terrains of sexual and gender regulation. As Foucault (1980) pointed out, within capitalist social relations sexual classifications (heterosexual/homosexual) in the West become the truth of our beings and the character of our sexualities and genders becomes the basis for alliance systems within the new ruling classes before they get exported to the working class and then to the "outcast" poor. These sexual classifications are now being exported around the world and into the Global South. There is an uneven and combined process of opening up and closing down of social spaces, resistance to sexual policing, and oppressive regulations and sexual regulation in terms of the imposition of the hetero/homo binary around the world with a clear relation to the imposition of the two-gender system.

This has had an impact on indigenous practices in many societies, which had a great deal of acceptance for same-sex/gender eroticism without linking it to sexual identities and also for third and fourth gender groupings. Indigenous forms of different- and same-sex/gender eroticisms have been displaced and colonized by classifications of heterosexuality and homosexuality. In some societies in the Global South there now exist these indigenous gender/erotic practices combined with an imposed hetero/homo polarity, and therefore an uneven emergence of lesbian/gay and even queer identifications as ways of articulating social experience in these new social contexts.

There are several different social responses to this. Joseph Massad (2007) makes crucial critiques of the imposition of Western notions of the heterosexual/homosexual polarity on Arab worlds, including by some Western gay and lesbian rights activists. However, despite these insights, he is not able to see that the social basis has also been created for some to take up gay/lesbian and even queer identifications in these societies. A more complex approach is required. This requires defending indigenous erotic and gender practices from attack and resisting the imposition of the hetero/homo polarity in these cultures while at the same time defending those who now identify as being gay/lesbian or queer.

This exporting of heterosexuality/homosexuality has also provoked various "fundamentalist" responses to queer sexualities, ranging from Christian fundamentalism, which has had an impact not only in the Global North but also in efforts to criminalize same-gender eroticism in Uganda and other places, to various forms of Islamic fundamentalism, Hindu fundamentalism, and others that define "their" cultures as excluding queer sexualities. All fundamentalist approaches that construct an essential sexuality outside of history are anti-queer. Queer liberationist approaches are anti-fundamentalist but at the same time need to oppose the imposition of Western-derived sexual identifications as the "truth" of people's beings.

REGULATORY STRATEGIES

Various regulatory strategies addressing queer sexualities have been developed. The first strategy developed in the West was that of total criminalization, often informed by moral conservative approaches that identified male-dominated monogamous heterosexuality as necessary for "civilization." In the Global South this was often bound up with colonialism. This strategy can take many different forms, including in the Global South the position that homosexuality is a Western imposition despite often widespread indigenous same-sex/gender erotic practices, and that the criminalization of homosexual practices was itself a result of Western colonialism.

There were different impacts of colonialism on sexualities and genders. Britain is used as an example. The one common feature of the British Empire and then the Commonwealth is the history of British imperialism, including the imposition of legal and social regimes regarding the criminalization of homosexuality, and gender and sexual regulation more generally. This is experienced unevenly and differentially, depending on the historical period and the character of colonization, the strength of indigenous gender and sexual practices, and the imposition of capitalist relations of "underdevelopment" and "development." Specific investigations are required, including regarding gender and sexual regulation and of the movements that have developed in response to them.

Criminal code provisions in Britain were imposed on other countries as part of colonial rule and impacted directly on legal and social regulation following the official ending of colonial rule. Since then there have been uneven struggles for decriminalization. In 2013, the Indian Supreme Court overturned a lower court ruling and recriminalized homosexual practices under a colonially imposed law. This was a reassertion of the British-imposed criminalization approach in response to decriminalization efforts.

Other regulatory strategies have been developed in response to social transformations. In England and Wales the Wolfenden Committee on Homosexual Offences and Prostitution (1957), tasked to develop new conceptual practices to regulate both street prostitution and male homosexuality, articulated a liberal strategy that revolved around public/private and adult/youth distinctions (Kinsman 2013). This led to homosexual acts in "private" (behind bedroom doors) being partially decriminalized between two consenting adults aged 21 and over in England and Wales in 1967 and in Canada in 1969. Outside this context criminalization continued, as this was an attempt to contain homosexual sex within a limited private realm. The Wolfenden approach became an active text (Smith 1990) informing public/private sexual law reform efforts in many English-speaking countries around the world, including countries in the Global South.

This contradictory approach led both to growing public visibility of queer sexualities as queer people seized more social space and to escalating sexual policing against these "public" expressions of queer sex. Combined with gay and lesbian organizing, human rights initiatives, and the development of sexual citizenship and consumer rights, these efforts led to the expansion of queer communities and to new strategies of "respectability" and "responsibility" as new queer middle-class elites emerged. This lays the basis not only for homonormativity, but also for what Puar (2007) describes as "homonationalism" based on queer identifications with their nation-state as defending gay rights and as being more "advanced" on these questions than more "backward" countries in the Global South.

RESISTANCE

There are diverse forms of struggle against these oppressive regulations, including struggles in defense of indigenous erotic and gender practices, struggles for gay and lesbian liberation and against police repression (the 1969 Stonewall riots and the Toronto resistance to the bath raids in 1981), for human rights, for trans needs and rights (including the Compton's Cafeteria riots in 1966 and struggles against the administrative legal construction of gender; Spade 2011), and more generally for sexual rights and for people to have control over their gender and erotic bodies and lives. These forms of resistance are not always articulated in relation to lesbian, gay, or queer rights, given the different social conditions people face, and can be put forward as a broader sexual and gender politics. At the same time, there are some common features such as establishing more control for people over their own bodies and lives.

CONTINUING QUESTIONS

Remaining questions include the possibilities for a non-oppressive sexual regulation arising out of these struggles, and what this might look like. This moves far beyond not only strategies of criminalization and moral conservatism, but also liberal regulatory strategies of public/private and adult/youth as well as human rights-based and "responsibility" and "respectability" regulatory strategies. The development of non-oppressive regulation requires the removal of social power, sexism, heterosexism, and trans oppression from social regulation. It would be informed by what Jeffrey Weeks (1985) once described as "radical pluralism," but would move past the liberal pluralism that still informs this approach. This approach is based on sexual and gender difference not being the problem, and that there can be numerous consensual sexual alternatives. Regulation is based not on "deviance" or "normality" but on expanding choice, consent, pleasure, and uprooting real violence and social power relations. Material social transformations to bring these social changes about are required. This includes uprooting heterosexual hegemony and the two-gender binary system. The objective is not simply a tolerance of minority sexualities, but instead a radical transformation of sexual and gender relations that moves far beyond limited legal rights and sexual-minority politics.

SEE ALSO: Colonialism and Sexuality; Cross-Cultural Gender Roles; Fundamentalism and Public Policy; Heteronormativity and Homonormativity; Heterosexism and Homophobia; Queer Theory; Sexual Regulation and Social Control; Third Genders

REFERENCES

Bannerji, Himani. 1995. *Thinking Through: Essays in Feminism, Marxism, and Anti-Racism*. Toronto: Women's Press.

Chauncey, George. 1994. *Gay New York: Gender, Urban Culture, and the Making of the Gay Male World, 1890–1940*. New York: Basic Books.

Committee on Homosexual Offences and Prostitution (The Wolfenden Report). 1957. *Report of* the *Committee of Homosexual Offences and Prostitution*. London: HMSO.

Duggan, Lisa. 2003. *The Twilight of Equality? Neoliberalism, Cultural Politics and the Attack on Democracy*. Boston: Beacon Press.

Fausto-Sterling, Anne. 2000. *Sexing the Body: Gender Politics and the Construction of Sexuality*. New York: Basic Books.

Foucault, Michel. 1980. *The History of Sexuality. Volume 1: An Introduction*. New York: Vintage Books.

Hennessy, Rosemary. 2000. *Profit and Pleasure: Sexual Identities in Late Capitalism*. New York: Routledge.

Kinsman, Gary. 1996. *The Regulation of Desire: Homo and Hetero Sexualities*. Montreal: Black Rose.

Kinsman, Gary. 2013. "Wolfenden in Canada: Within and Beyond Official Discourse in Law Reform Struggles." In *Human Rights, Sexual Orientation and Gender Identity in the Commonwealth: Struggles for Decriminalization and Change*, edited by Corinne Lennox and Matthew Waites, 183–205. London: Institute of Commonwealth Studies/Human Rights Consortium.

Kinsman, Gary, and Patrizia Gentile. 2010. *The Canadian War on Queers: National Security as Sexual Regulation*. Vancouver: University of British Columbia Press.

Massad, Joseph. 2007. *Desiring Arabs*. Chicago: University of Chicago Press.

McNally, David. 2002. *Another World is Possible: Globalization and Anti-Capitalism*. Winnipeg: Arbeiter Ring Publishing.

Puar, Jasbir K. 2007. *Terrorist Assemblages: Homonationalism in Queer Times*. Durham, NC: Duke University Press.

Rubin, Gayle. 1984. "Thinking Sex: Notes for a Radical Theory of the Politics of Sexuality." In *Pleasure and Danger: Exploring Female Sexuality*, edited by Carole Vance, 267–319. London: Routledge and Kegan Paul.

Smith, Dorothy. 1990. "The Active Text." In *Texts, Facts and Femininity: Exploring the Relations of Ruling*. New York: Routledge.

Spade, Dean. 2011. *Normal Life, Administrative Violence, Critical Trans Politics, and the Limits of Law*. New York: South End Press.

Weeks, Jeffrey. 1985. *Sexuality and Its Discontents*. London: Routledge and Kegan Paul.

Relations of Ruling

ALISON I. GRIFFITH
York University, Toronto, Canada

The relations of ruling are complexes of institutionally located practices. Institutions are understood to be interconnected organizations of governance, and ruling relations are the coordinated activities through which governance is done. Ruling relations are not objects in themselves. They are processes that transform the actual and particular experiences of individual lives into objectified accounts through which the social world can be managed. Subjects are subordinated to the objective, rational, and (apparently) neutral texts of ruling. The complexities of individual lives are obscured as the ruling text stands in for individual particularity.

Ruling relations are textually mediated relations. Texts have particular characteristics. They are replicable. They appear as the same text regardless of who is reading or working with them. They are located outside the temporal confines of time and space. As Foucault noted, texts are written in conversation with other texts. However, texts cannot speak or act. Someone, somewhere, must activate them at the actual intersection where the text and reader meet. Textually mediated ruling relations enable institutions to act.

Ruling relations are sequences of institutional action in which people select from actualities to build textual representations fitting an authoritative or "boss" text (law, policy, managerial objectives, frames of discourse, and so on). As people take up the texts of their everyday work, an institutional course of action follows, shaping and coordinating what happens next. People are actively at work in these circuits, transforming their everyday activities into institutionally actionable texts.

Gender and sexuality, while experienced individually, are coordinated by a range of historical ruling relations. Their accomplishment and resistance involve people active in different ways within an institutional complex. Women's access to birth control and abortion is an ongoing historical struggle involving physicians, nurses, community activists, police, the criminal court, and politicians. Similarly, sexuality is constrained under law. George Smith (1988; reprinted in Turner and Smith 2014), in his analysis of the policing of gay men, describes the processes through which sexual activities by gay men in Toronto bathhouses were transformed by ordinary police work into offenses that could be prosecuted in the criminal justice system.

The institutional origins of the ruling relations of gender and sexuality are often occluded. Many of our ordinary ways of speaking have been generated institutionally. For example, the concept "a single-parent family" is a commonly used descriptor of a family form – one parent (typically the mother) caring for at least one underage child. The concept originates in our marriage and divorce and birth registration laws. Even when the concept has been normalized, its use still speaks back to institutional ruling relations, and speaks forward to continuing notions of social difference.

Ruling relations are trans-local processes. They link people whose everyday activities are coordinated within the standardized practices of governing. Ruling relations may be developed to manage local, national, or international institutions or to coordinate ruling relations between institutions. The institutional complexity of a globalizing world has increased the necessary coordination across institutions. For example, national educational achievement databases (in which gender is one variable) are often linked to the Program for Institutional Student Assessment rankings developed by the Organisation of Economic Co-operation and Development. This synchronization is not seamless, but it is coordinated – a record generated by a government agency shows up as a ranking by a globalized non-government agency. Ruling relations are also hierarchically organized. One text may be a regulatory or "boss" text, which coordinates a whole range of other texts within an institutional complex. For example, in schools some courses, such as home economics or mathematics, are seen to be more appropriate for one gender or the other. This is not simply an individual matter of choice. Rather, course choices are made based on social notions of a gendered student as portrayed in policy manuals, textbooks, course outlines, enrolment histories, and enacted by the gendered responses of educators and students in the local context of the school.

Ruling relations are not static, nor are they deterministic. Their appearance of ontological permanence is both real and imaginary. It is real in the capacity of texts to coordinate action objectively, without apparent agency, such as a job description. It is imaginary in that ruling relations are not objects. They are the products of someone(s) work at a particular time and place – work that disappears into the constructed objectivity of the text, for example, the data showing the effect of single parenting on school achievement.

All ruling relations are empirically available as a research topic. The ruling relations of gender and sexuality are no exception. There have been a few research studies that focused explicitly on the ruling relations of gender and sexuality (e.g., Smith 1987). More often, the complexity of the topic means that gender and sexuality are integral, but not the focus of the analysis (e.g., Ng 2007). The research problematic is found in the disjuncture between lived experience and objectively organized ruling relations.

SEE ALSO: Governance and Gender; Sexualities

REFERENCES

Ng, Roxana. 2007. "Garment Production in Canada: Social and Political Implications." *Studies in Political Economy*, 79(Spring): 193–211.

Smith, Dorothy E. 1987. *The Everyday World as Problematic*. Boston: Northeastern University Press.

Turner, Susan, and Dorothy E. Smith, eds. 2014. *Incorporating Texts into Institutional Ethnographies*. Toronto: University of Toronto Press.

FURTHER READING

Campbell, Marie L., and Frances M. Gregor. 2002. *Mapping Social Relations: A Primer in Doing Institutional Ethnography*. Walnut Creek: AltaMira Press.

DeVault, Marjorie, ed. 2008. *People at Work: Life, Power, and Social Inclusion in the New Economy*. New York: NYU Press.

Eastwood, Lauren E. 2005. *The Social Organization of Policy: An Institutional Ethnography of UN Forest Deliberations*. New York: Routledge.

Griffith, Alison, and Dorothy E. Smith, eds. 2014. *Under New Public Management: Institutional Ethnographies of Changing Front Line Work*. Toronto: University of Toronto Press.

Nichols, Naomi. 2014. *Youth Work: An Institutional Ethnography of Youth Homelessness*. Toronto: University of Toronto Press.

Smith, Dorothy E. 2005. *Institutional Ethnography: A Sociology for People*. Lanham: AltaMira Press.

Religion and Homophobia

JAMES D. WILETS
Nova Southeastern University, USA

Although religion frequently appears to, and sometimes does, exercise a direct impact on the attitudes of certain individuals towards sexual minorities, the connections between religion and homophobia are frequently much less direct, and cannot be analyzed without reference to cultural norms regarding gender and race.

As is conceded by the great majority of social scientists, religion is as much a product of preexisting socioeconomic and sociocultural conditions as it is a factor in the creation of those sociocultural attitudes themselves. In this respect, religion operates as a kind of proxy for preexisting cultural norms, and can be an instrument in reinforcing those cultural norms.

Therefore, although there often may be a relationship between religion and homophobia, religion alone is not always the primary agent of creation of homophobic attitudes, and sometimes does not contribute to homophobic attitudes at all. Indeed, in some cases religion may in fact reinforce or sanction existing positive attitudes towards homosexuality.

A first observation about the relationship between religion and homophobia is that being "religious" is not synonymous with being homophobic. This runs counter to the assertions of some theologians who would argue in defense of the universalism and essentialism of their theological position.

A wide array of anthropological and historical evidence demonstrates that societies throughout history have demonstrated a highly varied view of homosexuality and varied gender identities. As just one example, in 1951, in a seminal anthropological study, *Patterns of Sexual Behavior*, Yale Professors Clellan S. Ford and Frank A. Beach found that "[i]n 49 (64 percent) of the 76 societies other than our own for which information is available, homosexual activities of one sort or another are considered normal and socially acceptable for certain members of the community" (Ford and Beach 1951, 130).

Same-sex unions and transgender unions have existed in many societies, including nineteenth-century Nigerian society, pre-Columbian Native American societies, nineteenth-century Zuni society, ancient Egyptian, Greek, Roman, and Mesopotamian societies, the African societies of Azande, Siwah, el Garah, Basotho, Venda, Meru, Phalaborwa, Nuer, Bantu, and Lovedu, the Asian societies of Paleo-Siberia, China, Vietnam, India, Japan, Burma (Myanmar), Korea, and Nepal, and in the society in what is now New Zealand and the Cook Islands (Eskridge 1993).

Homosexual relationships have been documented in other ancient societies. Societally sanctioned homosexual relationships existed in ancient Mesopotamian (e.g., Hittite, Assyrian, Babylonian), Chinese, Mayan, Incan, Aztec, Egyptian, Etruscan, Indian, Greek, and Roman cultures. Ford and Beach, Greenberg, and other scholars have also documented widespread recognition of same-sex relationships among Native American peoples in North, Central, and South America. The existence of socially accepted transgender individuals and same-gender sexual relationships in Polynesia has also been documented (Besnier 1994).

It would appear that the existence of such socially sanctioned same-gender relationships could only exist if the theological beliefs of those societies would permit it. It would therefore appear that being "religious" is not synonymous with being homophobic, as some theologians would argue, when arguing that their anti-LGBT position is both universal and essential in nature.

The greater acceptance of homosexuality in Western antiquity came to an end with the spread of ascetic philosophies such as the Judeo-Christian-Islamic faiths (Greenberg 1988; Human Rights Watch 2008). This was especially true in the context of Catholicism, which traditionally prohibited all sex outside of procreation. It should be noted, however, that even this phenomenon was not absolute; Yale historian Boswell documented church-sanctioned same-sex union in medieval Christian Europe until the twelfth century (Boswell 1980, 1994).

Second, despite the existence, and even acceptance, of same-sex relationships in most societies in history, those relationships would not necessarily correspond to our contemporary understanding of the term "same-sex relationship" or "gay relationship." Two considerations must be kept in mind when thinking about gender roles both historically and cross-culturally. The first is that a society's conception of gender may not always consist of the rigid, bipolar "male" and "female" construct prevalent in modern Western society. For instance, the Native American berdaches and Indian hijras appear to a Western observer to be transsexuals, when really their identity and "gender" are more complex, consisting of more than four separate gender identities (Valdes 1995). The second consideration to keep in mind is the role that power relationships have in determining a society's definition of gender (Greenberg 1988). For example, a persistent theme in anthropologic evidence regarding same-gender sexual unions is that many cultures and/or religions have treated class, age, and power differentials as analogous to gender differentiation.

Thus, past religious, cultural, and "legal" recognition of same-sex unions has generally, although not always, occurred within relatively narrow gender constructs that mimicked the dominant–passive construct of "traditional" heterosexual relationships (Eskridge 1993). Thus, those societies that recognized same-sex unions did so only when gender roles were not threatened. Conversely, such acceptance was not generally present when same-sex relationships occurred outside accepted gender constructs.

Therefore, to the extent that societal cultures and religions have been uncomfortable with homosexuality, it is usually because such activity has been perceived as crossing gender rather than sexual boundaries. The historical and anthropological evidence also reveals a strong connection between intolerance of same-sex relationships and oppression of women. Regulating women's place in society has certainly been a significant component of numerous religions, historically and cross-culturally. The Hawaii Supreme Court recognized this correlation when it applied strict scrutiny to the Hawaii marriage law prohibiting same-sex marriage in *Baehr v. Lewin*, 852 P.2d 44 68 (Haw. 1993). The majority held that Hawaii's marriage law constituted sex discrimination because it created a classification prohibiting women from doing something (marrying a woman) that men were entitled to do, and vice versa. Thus, how a society views gender roles often determines how it treats sexual minorities.

Third, related to the observation above, religion may simply be a reflection of, and response to, preexisting socioeconomic and cultural realities that are not religious in nature, and may in fact operate in a manner that completely transforms a religion into the antithesis of its original tenets. This has been particularly true where racism, ethnic conflict, and colonialism created a religious opposition to homophobia to support the racist, colonial, or ethnic struggles existing independently of religion. A salient example of this phenomenon can be seen in the United States, India, Africa, and the Caribbean.

The United States is often recognized as an exception among Western industrialized nations because of the presence of uniquely American religions with strong tenets of racism, sexism, and homophobia. The reason for this phenomenon is not related to any essential nature of the religions themselves. Indeed, the original religions of the United States, such as Puritanism, evolved from a very theologically harsh religion into moderate mainstream forms of Protestantism with generally progressive views on matters of gender and sexuality. Even the Baptist faith was, in its original incarnation on the North American continent, a relatively tolerant faith. However, the Southern Baptist Convention, currently the largest protestant denomination in the United States, was created through a split between southern and northern Baptists over the issue of slavery, and later over segregation. In 1845, the Southern Baptists split with the national Baptist denomination when the national denomination refused to allow slaveholders to be Baptist missionaries. The Southern Baptist Convention shares a history with the South African Dutch Reformed Church of using religion to justify the legal separation of the races. The correlation of states with a majority of adherents of the Southern Baptist Convention and former US slave states is almost perfect, with the exception of the newly Catholic regions of Florida and Texas. In other words, a religion without an inordinately hierarchical view of social relations of a racial or gender nature diverged in diametrically opposite directions depending on whether the different Baptist denominations predominated in slave or non-slave states. Although not in the South, a similar phenomenon may be observed with another American denomination in the western United States, Mormonism. The predominant branch of Mormonism has historically been characterized by discriminatory policies based on race, gender, and sexual orientation. As late as 1978, persons of African descent were forbidden to participate as priests in the Mormon religion. It is no coincidence that both the Southern Baptist Convention and the Mormon religion endorse strictly defined gender roles, eschew gender equality, and exhibit strong animus towards sexual minorities. There are many theories as to why sexism, racism, and homophobia are so strongly correlated, but the overwhelming empirical evidence is that they are. It is beyond the scope of this entry to explore in detail the *reasons* for the correlation among gender, racial, and sexual orientation discrimination, but it is reasonable to suppose that they share certain hierarchical assumptions that transcend specific categories.

Many historians now recognize that much of the contemporary hostility towards sexual minorities in non-Western nations is a direct result of Western – particularly British – colonialism (Human Rights Watch 2008), Judeo–Christian–Islamic homophobia, and anti-sexuality in general, none of which is rooted in indigenous tradition. For example, Tielman and Hammelburg (1993, 251) argue that:

> From a historical perspective, the English legislation against homosexuality has had (and unfortunately still has) appalling consequences for the legal position of homosexual men, and, to a lesser extent, lesbians in the former British colonies. The effects of the former French, Dutch, Spanish, and Portuguese colonial legislation against homosexuality are less severe. In general, nevertheless, Christian-based homophobia has damaged many cultures in which sexual contacts and relationships between men and between women used to be tolerated or even accepted.

The generally anti-sexual attitude of these Western-derived ideologies, and their tendency to view genitally based sexual classifications as the principal determinant of sexual boundaries, seems to be at odds with the manner in which most societies have tended to construct sexuality.

The anti-sexual minority effects of colonialism are most pronounced in British colonies (Kirby 2007). In fact, as of December 2008, over half of the countries in the world with sodomy laws were former British colonies, and all of those countries' sodomy laws were imposed by the British. India, a former British colony now populated by over 1 billion people, only recently eliminated vestiges of its British-imposed sodomy law when the Delhi High Court invalidated Section 377, which had been introduced by the British in 1860 in response to what they deemed the excessive tolerance of traditional Indian culture. However, the decriminalization did not last long. In 2014, India's Supreme Court struck down that 2009 ruling; sodomy in India is once again illegal. Despite these progressive developments, the British colonial legacy remains particularly potent in Africa and the Caribbean, where most former British colonies continue to retain their colonial-era sodomy laws. In recent years, at least some of this anti-gay animus in Africa and elsewhere in the world has been fueled by Western anti-gay groups (Gettleman 2010). Indeed, a lawsuit against one such anti-gay group in Massachusetts led by Scott Lively, alleging the group's commission of crimes against humanity because of its anti-gay work in Africa, survived a motion for summary judgment in a District Federal Court. These effects suggest that a new kind of Western religious colonialism has emerged with a distinctly homophobic focus.

SEE ALSO: Heterosexism and Homophobia; Open and Affirming Religious Organizations; Same-Sex Marriage

REFERENCES

Besnier, Niko. 1994. "Polynesian Gender Liminality Through Time and Space." In *Third Sex, Third Gender: Beyond Sexual Dimorphism in Culture and History*, edited by Gilbert Herdt, 285–328. New York: Zone Books.

Boswell, John. 1980. *Christianity, Social Tolerance, and Homosexuality: Gay People in Western Europe from the Beginning of the Christian Era to the Fourteenth Century*. Chicago: University of Chicago Press.

Boswell, John. 1994. *Same-Sex Unions in Premodern Europe*. New York: Vintage Books.

Eskridge, William N. 1993. *A History of Same-Sex Marriage*. New Haven: Yale Law School Legal Scholarship Repository.

Ford, Clellan, and Frank Beach. 1951. *Patterns of Sexual Behavior*. New York: Harper and Brothers.

Gettleman, Jeffrey. 2010. "Americans' Role Seen in Uganda Anti-Gay Push." *New York Times*, January 3, 2010. Accessed June 13, 2015, at http://www.nytimes.com/2010/01/04/world/africa/04uganda.html.

Greenberg, David. 1988. *The Construction of Homosexuality*. Chicago: University of Chicago Press.

Human Rights Watch. 2008. *This Alien Legacy*. New York: Human Rights Watch.

Kirby, Michael. 2007. "Homosexuality: a Commonwealth Blind Spot on Human Rights." *Commonwealth Human Rights Initiative Newsletter*, 14(4): 1. Accessed June 13, 2015, at http://www.humanrightsinitiative.org/publications/nl/newsletter_winter_2007/article4.htm.

Tielman, Rob, and Hans Hammelburg. 1993. "World Survey on the Social and Legal Position of Gays and Lesbians." In *The Third Pink Book*, edited by Aart Hendriks, Rob Tielman, and Evert van der Veen, 249–251. Buffalo: Prometheus Books

Valdes, Francisco. 1995. "Queers, Sissies, Dykes, and Tomboys: Deconstructing the Conflation of 'Sex,' 'Gender,' and 'Sexual Orientation'." *Euro-American Law and Society*, 83(1): 237.

FURTHER READING

Amnesty International. 2015. *LGBT Legal Status Around the World*. Accessed June 13, 2015, at http://www.amnestyusa.org/lgbt-human-rights/country-information/page.do?id=1106576.

Klein, Herbert S. and Ben Vinson, III. 2007. *African Slavery in Latin America and the Caribbean*, 2nd ed. New York: Oxford University Press.

Polgreen, Lydia, and Laurie Goodstein. 2006. "At Axis of Episcopal Split, an Anti-Gay Nigerian."*New York Times*, December 25, 2006.

Reddock, Rhoda. 1998. "History of the Women's Movement in the Caribbean (Part I)." Address to the HIVOS/UNIFEM Meeting of Women's Organizations. Accessed June 13, 2015, at http://www.cafra.org/spip.php?article681.

Religious Fundamentalism

BONITA ALEAZ
University of Calcutta, India

Close readings of historical developments unravel the myths associated with religious fundamentalism and also establish, despite its discursive journey across religions, the very specific relationship it has with gender and sexuality. Fundamentalism is projected as a *Weltanschauung*, or worldview, that seeks to establish its own order, which is believed to be divinely ordained. It seeks to segregate its own ideologues from the rest of humanity in their efforts at remaking the world, so in this process it becomes both exclusive and inclusive. The reordering of the world does not remain a mere religious reformative endeavor but is very much a political exercise. The true fundamentalist, according to Bassam Tibi, "is basically a political man, with a political outlook"; he is not a religionist (Tibi 1998, xv). The fall of the Berlin Wall and the collapse of the Soviet Union were perceived as having brought an end to the Cold War, but religious fundamentalism has taken over the vacuum in the political divide. In its contemporary manifestation, it steps in as the prime motivator and challenge to the capitalist West, replacing Marxism-Leninism, nationalism-socialism, or even colonialism.

Even though its fruition occurred in the 1980s and 1990s, the term fundamentalism originated in early twentieth-century American Protestant Christianity as a self-designation by certain sects whose leaders hoped to fend off secular forces of a modernizing world through the restoration of fundamental "beliefs and practices" derived from an inerrant Bible. An initial response was made in 1910 by two devout Christian brothers, Milton and Lyman Stewart, who embarked upon a five-year program of sponsorship of pamphlets that was meant to reacquaint American society with the fundamentals of the Christian faith: the infallibility of the Bible, the virgin birth, and the crucifixion. This work, entitled *The Fundamentals, a Testimony of Truth*, was written by a number of leading conservative American and British theologians and was meant to stop the erosion of the Christian faith. Subsequently, it became a theoretical concept applied to all religious groups who defined themselves as defenders of orthodoxy. As the vanguards of a "return" to an idealized tradition, their identity continues to be constructed in important ways in confrontation with an external other. The "otherness" has been less a perception of difference and more a recognition of threat, fanning the flames of militant response.

Fundamentalism, like other words, did not remain static but projected a life and energy of its own, so the applications or meanings attached to words cannot be confined to the particular contexts in which they originated. At its broadest it may be described as a religious way of being that manifests itself in a strategy by which beleaguered believers attempt to preserve their distinctive identities as individuals or groups in the act of modernity and secularization. Fundamentalism and modernity are crucially linked together, hence the word goes beyond the original Protestant matrix; it is, rather, a multifocal phenomenon precisely because the Enlightenment project and the ensuing modernist hegemony originating in some parts of the West were not limited to Protestant Christianity. Rather, they influenced Jews and Muslims in the nineteenth and twentieth centuries. One may add to this Hinduism, which has responded in like manner under the impact of colonialism.

The rapid growth of urbanization, industrialization, and above all the large-scale influx of migrants introduced contextual changes that impelled perceptions of immense insecurity in the lives of early settlers in the United States of America. Urban growth meant the emergence of a pluralistic society with innumerable groups mixing freely in institutions of primary socialization such as schools. The new ideas not only contested and challenged the existence of a free and fair society, but the alternative belief systems were couched in a scientific and revisionist tone that threatened the hitherto held infallibility of the Bible, its translation, and even its sanctity. Such developments forced fundamentalists to put classroom teaching under surveillance, and the question of whether the evolution of species should be taught in the light of Darwinist or biblical narratives gained significance.

Religious fundamentalism has exhibited varied forms, yet it is possible to talk in terms of two categories: first-wave fundamentalism with its exclusivist principles, and a second, more culturally integrative wave. In the contemporary period it is also possible to classify fundamentalists as traditionalists, who hold views in isolation from mainstream communities. Their views on abortion, for instance, do not hamper the support of abortion by others since their efforts do not prevent its use by others. These may be referred to as "quaint" groups. Distinct from them are the politically motivated groups who deliberately project their views on others, with a vigor akin to the notion of the "Christian man's burden." The second wave of fundamentalism has appropriated hybrid forms and need not be wholly exclusivist. It uses popular media, modern music, and psychological and even political trends to proselytize. Significantly, these trends have led ethnographers to label second-wave fundamentalists as "new religious movements" rather than as direct descendants of the first wave.

In the contemporary period, a landmark US Supreme Court decision in 1961 extended to secular humanists the legal protection accorded to followers of religious faiths. Ironically, this judgment was issued by fundamentalists to proclaim that secular humanism is also a religion, and should be curbed by the state. Religious fundamentalists in the United States do not have their own political party as such, but try to operate from within the Republican Party. The inclusion of daily prayers in public schools has been fraught with controversy; legislation in Alabama sought to include periods of silent meditation, but this was eventually struck down on the grounds of not having sufficient secular purpose. In public schools in some other states, equal time must be given for the teaching of evolution and creationism. The 1973 (*Roe v. Wade*) judgment by the Supreme Court on abortion remains one of the most controversial issues that instigated the religious right. It had repealed a state law that banned abortions. It was held that the decision amounted to legalizing the murder of human life with flimsy constitutional justifications.

While there are basic similarities in the emergence of fundamentalism in other religions, the language in which it was couched was different. In Islam, for instance, the term was coined by H. R. Gibb in his book *Mohammedanism* (1949), later titled *Islam*. It was used with reference to the activities of two Islamists, Jamal al-Din al-Afghani, a pan-Islamic reformer and political activist, and King Abd al-Aziz Ibn Saud of Jeddah, who was labeled a strong "fundamentalist" due to his condemnation of women who mix with men under the cloak of progress. Both the movements headed by Saud and al-Afghani exhibited some of the "family resemblances" referred to by Wittgenstein. Both involved a radical, in some cases armed, defense of a religious tradition that felt challenged by modernity. In both cases the modernity in question was complicated by the interventions of international politics. Their intention was to return to the seventh-century scriptural roots of Islam, imagined as pristine, without taking into consideration the accumulated customs, traditions, or doctrines of the intervening period.

In India, on the other hand, in the period preceding independence, the Hindu revivalists encountering colonialism were unable to depend on any kind of media to disseminate their message. They used the instrument of language, since it was far simpler to develop Hindi as a medium of modern education. The Hindi-speaking elites of northern India sought to establish their hold over the evolving state apparatus of the nascent republic by projecting a strong case for Hindi as the national language, thereby outmaneuvering the Westernized elites; they transformed Hindi from a spoken language to an important dialect of social and political communication also as a means to disseminate Hindu cultural values.

The modes of operation and the impact created by religious fundamentalists reveal that, of the many areas in which they seek alterations, they have been most successful in those of faith, family, and the state. The first provides the ideological impulse establishing the desire to communicate; the state is the arena of protest that has to absorb the demands of faith and be reconstituted by it; the family constitutes the microcosm of the divine order through which continuity and further strengthening of the godly society can be maintained. It is in this manner that fundamentalism establishes its discourse with gender and sexuality. While the state provides the whipping tools and faith the necessary instruction, it is the family, revolving around the nurturing female, that epitomizes the purity of beliefs and tradition. In an era of rapid socioeconomic and political change it is this core, and the values intrinsic to it, that is perceived as being violently threatened. Cutting across religions, sex – or, more specifically, female sexuality and the controls to be exercised over it – looms large in the repertoire of fundamentalists.

Highly dramatic language has been used to link the public expression of female sexuality to the harsh effects of Darwinism. For instance, in the 1920s, the American fundamentalist John R. Stratton explicitly linked it to "animalism." Similar pronouncements have been made by revolutionary Islamist groups such as the Fedayan-i-Islami while denouncing the effects of unveiled women on society, and on young men in particular. The Islamic Republic of Iran introduced a law in 1981 to codify Qur'anic prescriptions; in this legislation, 107 of the 195 articles were concerned with sexual activities, ranging from the prosecution of adultery and homosexuality to preventing unrelated persons of the same sex lying naked under a blanket. Similarities have been observed by the sociologist Martin Reisebrodt in the original American religious fundamentalism of the 1920s and the Shi'i version expressed by the Iranian government since it came to power in 1979. The strict surveillance of the female could be referred to as an aspect of the patriarchal protest and its obsession with sexuality, commonly visible as a reaction to broader anxieties resulting from rural displacement and economic change. Fundamentalism then becomes a common protest against the assault on patriarchal principles in the family, economy, and politics.

Even though the symptoms of patriarchal decline manifest themselves primarily in the spheres of the family and sexual morality, the underlying causes point toward socioeconomic factors: the erosion of small-scale, family-owned businesses, the displacement of males from rural to urban production centers, and formal and codified relationships at the expense of intimate patriarchal relations between employers and employees. In resisting such aspects of what Max Weber referred to as the disenchantment of the world, fundamentalists may appear to be anti-modern. What they cannot prevent in the way of structural transformation, according to Reisebrodt, they attempt to impose symbolically. Under contemporary conditions, when women are supposed to add to family incomes by venturing into the public space, segregation is sought by imposing dress codes or sartorial coding.

Fundamentalists attempt to recreate the traditional image of the ideal family in which the male and the female are complementary to each other, but they are neither interchangeable nor equatable. So the model relationship is hierarchical, where authority rests with the male and the female positions herself as the assistant to the God-given power of the male, first by submitting herself, and then by socializing her children to do the same. There are certain other equally crucial associated views related to the perfect wife and mother. These include abjuring paid employment outside; rather than pursuing independent intellectual and political activity, the woman should be constantly available to the family. These become the symbolic rendering of gender encompassing a variety of issues related to privacy, domesticity, patriarchy, and sexuality. Perceptions about these emanate from the growing power of feminism and the threats of homosexuality and legalization of abortion. A corollary to these beliefs is the stigma attached to non-reproductive sex of any kind, and the belief that children are the gift of God, born of divine grace, through the will of the male, and women have to submit to this process. Radical fundamentalisms have resorted to varying degrees of violence to enforce these norms, their methods ranging from the retrieval of corporal punishment, as resorted to by Ayatollah Khomeini, to genital mutilation in such forms as infibulation and clitoridectomy. The intention is to control female sexuality not only by making heterosexual intercourse painful, but also by preventing orgasm.

Fundamentalism has been a serious engagement in Jewish societies as well. The reason for this is the definition of fundamentalism itself; like other fundamentalisms, it also refers to a kind of return to a former "golden age." The sexual component is made clear in much of Jewish anti-liberalization, anti-feminist rhetoric, particularly that which focuses on women's modesty. Women who participate in women's prayer groups, for example, are accused of making themselves part of the "licentiousness" of feminism; transgressions of women's traditional roles are read as if they were sexual transgressions, and women rabbis and other Jewish women leaders are spoken of as "brazen." Even women who speak publicly at their own family gatherings are discouraged, since they are presumed to be breaching the law.

A very significant alternative exposition rests on the question of why women, across religious traditions, submit to fundamentalist norms. There are various ethnographic studies of the reasons why women yield to the precepts advocated by the community when these creeds visibly subject them to self-denying servitude. Findings also detail the methods they adopt while countenancing, refurbishing, and rechanneling fundamentalist dictates. In the enactment of such methods, subtle subterfuge may also be visible that actually aids in their empowerment.

Studies of the reactions of women across communities reveal most women share with men the same perceptions of threat, alienation, deprivation, and marginalization as a result of urbanization and its effect of displacement. Change in any form is equated with loss of identity and status. Women are attracted to the message of fundamentalism, which invokes the language of kinship, and in which religion itself substitutes the family. Such a notion provides desired security, so despite the presentiment of being caged in, women respond in like measure to men to overcome the ill effects of dislocation and disempowerment. A response from women is also elicited since alignment with fundamentalism is interpreted as the highest form of morality and uprightness. Such evocations strike the right chord among females. In certain postcolonial contexts such as India, the impact of Western education and culture, the growth of plural ideologies in the context of democracy, and a sense of their negative impact on the family helped the validation of the Hindutva ideology. Women of the Rashtriya Swayam Sevika Sangh, the prime advocate of the ideology, willingly support stringent rules governing their conduct. The rules assign life and meaning to the *sevikas*, or servers, as women devotees are termed. The Sanskritic orthopraxy not only serves as a cultural marker clearly delineating between "us" and "them," but also specifies women's and men's role in building a Hindu India. Going far beyond the cultural training that is imparted to them, both the female and her male counterpart become highly specialized agents of a political project. A nationalist interpretation is built into the notion of service; both render service to *Bharat Mata* or the nation–mother. In many contexts, fear of reprisal for non-compliance or disobedience plays upon both sexes. For women this may include seclusion and restriction, withdrawal of economic support, battery, separation of the children, and divorce. Fear of divine reprimand is perhaps even more acute in the case of nonconformity, propelled by the fear of ostracism and spiritual banishment to "outer darkness."

Confusion prevails regarding the categorization of fundamentalism. Can a person be labeled a fundamentalist by wishing for purity in the reading and interpretation of the Qur'an or Bible? This does not, however, disclose the person as a militant or a pacifist. On the other hand, critics of the term say it is just a dirty 14-letter word used abusively by liberals who denounce the challenges posed by anti-Enlightenment attitudes. Another school may be identified which holds that it is a caricature or mirror-image of the post-Enlightenment outlook it professes to oppose, adopting "the same rational style of argument used by the secular enemy, repressing the multifaceted, polysemic ways in which myth and religions appeal to all aspects of the human psyche," not just to the rational mind (Sister Maria Anicia 2002, 17).

Recent developments such as the influence of the media and the corporatization of religion, along with the prerequisites of governance, have brought about differential impacts on fundamentalisms. On the one hand, widespread dissemination of views shaped by the media have aided deregularization of the normative categories of gender and sexuality beyond the controls of religious institutions. On the other, corporatization of religion produces sharp disjunctions between the fundamentalist tenets of the religious imperative to regulate morality, the "normalization" of gender roles, and "proper" use of sexual activity and the requirements of governance, such as control of disease and political empowerment of hitherto marginalized groups. In late modernity, religious fundamentalism has entered a new phase of confrontations with modernity.

SEE ALSO: Christianity and Homosexuality; Fundamentalism and Public Policy; Hinduism; Islam and Homosexuality; Judaism and Sexuality

REFERENCES

Anicia, Sister Maria, 2002. "Some Perspectives on Fundamentalism and Its Impact on Youth." In *Youth in Asia: Challenges of Fundamentalism and Relativism*, edited by Father Vimal Tirimanna, 3–42. Quezon City: New Day Publications.

Tibi, Bassam. 1998. *The Challenge of Fundamentalisms: Political Islam and the New World Order*. Berkeley: University of California Press.

FURTHER READING

Brink, Judy, and Joan Mencher, eds. 1997. *Mixed Blessing: Gender and Religious Fundamentalism Cross Culturally*. New York: Routledge.

Hardacre, Helen. 1991. "The Impact of Fundamentalisms on Women, the Family, and Interpersonal Relations." In *Fundamentalisms and Society: Reclaiming the Sciences, the Family and Education*, edited by Marin E. Marty and R. Scott Appleby, 129–150. Chicago: University of Chicago Press.

Lawrence, Bruce. 1989. *The Defenders of God*. San Francisco: Harper and Row.

Marty, Marin E., and R. Scott Appleby, eds. 1991. *Fundamentalisms and Society: Reclaiming the Sciences, the Family and Education*. Chicago: University of Chicago Press.

Ruthven, Malise. 2007. *Fundamentalism: A Very Short Introduction*. New York: Oxford University Press.

Sharma, Arvind, and Katherine K. Young, eds. 2007. *Fundamentalism and Women in World Religions*. New York: T&T Clark.

Representation

HELENE MEYERS
Southwestern University, USA

Representation can refer to the characterization of a group, or to the act of standing in for a group's or individual's beliefs or interests.

The diverse meanings and conceptualizations of "representation" in gender studies demonstrate the interdisciplinary and transdisciplinary nature of the field. Some of these conceptualizations include linguistic/literary representation, the intersectional complexities of representing the interests of marginalized groups, limited or objectifying representation of women, feminism's representation of women, representation of feminism, and political representation, each of which will be discussed in this entry. The field of gender studies has historically been interested in issues of representation because language and images not only reflect the world but also shape it. Representation also gets to the central political issue of who speaks for whom and with what authority.

The attention to non-sexist language that was a hallmark of second-wave feminism in general and linguists/literary critics in particular is fundamentally an issue of representation. Referring to humanity as "mankind" promotes the invisibility of women and the assumption that men are historical agents while women have been passive objects or spectators. Similarly, referring to God or authors with masculine pronouns codifies the connection between masculinity and authority. In literary studies, feminist critics such as Sandra Gilbert and Susan Gubar (1979) traced the impact that such images have upon the psyche and consciousness of women writers as well as upon the literary canon. The development of female literary traditions forced the question of whether male and female writers have fundamentally different modes of representing gender and, if they do, the extent to which those differences are the result of culturally and historically specific norms and standards.

Both academic and popular critiques of feminist discourse often focus on the cultural effects of representing women as victims. Some argue that, by emphasizing sexual violence, feminism unwittingly embodies and reproduces patriarchal, misogynist thought. Thus the representation of feminism itself in both academic and popular discourses has become an important area of inquiry. Susan Faludi (1991) popularized the idea that negative portrayals of feminism are a form of "backlash." Postfeminist thought is also centrally concerned with the representation of feminism; whether postfeminism repudiates or assimilates feminism is a debate that began in the 1920s and has resurfaced in the contemporary period, especially within media studies.

In a related vein, feminist theorists across disciplines question whether or not the term "woman" adequately represents the diversity of human beings included in that category. The recognition that women's – and men's – experiences are informed by gender in relation to race, ethnicity, class, sexuality, and nationality led to the development of intersectional analysis and considerably complicated the idea that gender identity can be represented in any universal ways. Black abolitionist Sojourner Truth's famous question, "Ain't I a woman?" eloquently summarizes the conundrum of representing gender.

Cultural representation is another area of contention. Scholarly debates about pornography and feminist discourse provide a case study for understanding issues of representation and their complex cultural effects. While some argue that pornographic imagery ranging from magazines such as *Hustler* to art films to advertisements contributes to violence against real women, others insist that a one-to-one correspondence cannot be assumed between images and reality, even and especially when sexual fantasies are involved. Psychoanalytic questions of identification, subject position, and the working through of ambivalence through fantasy challenge the idea that cultural representations convey a clear, unambiguous narrative about the world.

Political scientists remind us that questions about representation are central to electoral politics and the possibilities of democratic process. When female elected officials constitute only a small proportion of governmental bodies, the question of whether or not women are truly represented arises. Discussions about female representation in government that is not proportional to the percentage of females in a population focus on factors that might discourage women from becoming candidates as well as gendered double standards that impact perceptions, and thus the electability, of women. The effects that gender imbalance might have on political culture is also a concern. Although statistical analysis of the number of women serving in supposedly representative governmental bodies functions as one measure of gender equity, feminist political theorists, aware of the dangers of essentialism, remain skeptical about assuming that gender is the master key to political ideology. Female political leaders such as the former British prime minister Margaret Thatcher and US vice presidential candidate Sarah Palin usefully remind us that women do not necessarily represent feminist political agendas.

The ethics of representation are complex. As Linda Alcoff (1991–1992) has argued, those who have cultural power have a responsibility to speak for those who are not empowered to speak for themselves and must also strive not to appropriate the voices of others. While self-representation is always preferred, it is not always possible.

Representation has multiple meanings in gender studies; however, across the field, questions about representation expose and revise disciplinary, ethical, and cultural assumptions about gender, feminism, and inclusion.

SEE ALSO: Backlash; Essentialism; Intersectionality; Politics of Representation; Postfeminism

REFERENCES

Alcoff, Linda. 1991–1992. "The Problem of Speaking for Others." *Cultural Critique*, 20: 5–32.
Faludi, Susan. 1991. *Backlash: The Undeclared War Against American Women*. New York: Crown.
Gilbert, Sandra M., and Susan Gubar. 1979. *The Madwoman in the Attic: The Woman Writer and the Nineteenth-Century Literary Imagination*. New Haven: Yale University Press.

FURTHER READING

Gill, Rosalind. 2007. "Postfeminist Media Culture: Elements of a Sensibility." *European Journal of Cultural Studies*, 10(2): 147–166. DOI: 10.1177/1367549407075898.
Meyers, Helene. 2001. *Femicidal Fears: Narratives of the Female Gothic Experience*. Albany: SUNY Press.
Young, Iris Marion. 2012. *Inclusion and Democracy*. New York: Oxford University Press.

Reproductive Choice

DANIELLE GRIFFITHS and JOHN HARRIS
University of Manchester, UK

The notion of reproductive choice captures both the freedom to decide whether or not to have children as well as the liberty to control one's reproductive capacity. The question of whether such liberty is compromised when individuals are restricted in their ability to reproduce due to infertility, or reproduce in ways of their own choosing, raises debate over how far they should be allowed access (or have such access facilitated) to artificial reproductive technologies (ARTs) to overcome such infertility or restriction on choice.

One of the greatest of contemporary legal theorists, Ronald Dworkin, has defended a strong right to "procreative autonomy" which he characterized as: "a right [of people] to control their own role in procreation unless the state has a compelling reason for denying them that control" (1993, 148). Dworkin (1993, 160) strongly believed the Constitution of the United States (First and Fourteenth Amendments) "also guarantee the right of procreative autonomy."

Artificial reproductive technologies (ARTs) such as donor conception, surrogacy, and pre-implantation genetic diagnosis (PGD) challenge traditional models of the family and parenthood and extend the "normal" reproductive capabilities of particular human bodies. This raises ethical questions about the scope of reproductive autonomy, in particular, if there is a right to access ARTs or should they be strictly regulated, controlled, and, perhaps, denied to certain groups (Sparrow 2008). Liberal democracies have to justify limitations on freedom. Purported restrictions cannot simply invoke unease about unnaturalness or transgression of certain traditional boundaries, rather there must be evidence and adequate argument to show that they point to serious and real dangers to others and/or society. Lacking such evidence and argument there is scant justification to constrain procreative liberty in this area (Harris 2005).

QUESTIONS OF "CHOICE"

While the advent of the contraceptive pill in the 1960s made reproduction a real choice for many for the first time in human history, ARTs have also made many of the actual features of reproduction a choice. From the development of IVF in the 1970s, techniques such as surrogacy, PGD, and donor conception have flourished and helped many infertile and same-sex couples and individuals to gestate their own (often genetically related) children and allowed more choice and control over reproductive matters. Choice ranges from avoidance of pregnancy by using a surrogate, choosing from different modalities of conception, choosing who one wants to reproduce with, one's same-sex partner, a known or unknown gamete donor, or potentially oneself (Palacios-González, Harris, and Testa 2014), to choosing to use PGD to prevent the transmission of certain disabilities and diseases.

Forms of ARTs are multiplying and the take up is significant. Globally, substantially in excess of 5 million babies have been born using IVF (ScienceDaily 2012). While other techniques such as surrogacy have been around for some time, rising rates of infertility and legislation which extended who can enter into these arrangements have meant rates of surrogacy have risen sharply. Since the introduction of regulation and monitoring of donor conception in 1991, over 35,000 children have been born in the United Kingdom as a result of donated gametes and many more donor-conceived people have been born as a result of sperm donation outside of licensed clinics or through overseas clinics (Nuffield Council on Bioethics 2013).

Future technologies on the horizon of reproductive science promise further choice and control in reproductive matters. Experiments have shown that ectogenesis (involving IVF with gestation for 9 months in an artificial uterine environment) is possible and it is predicted that human artificial wombs are likely to become a reality within the next couple of decades if not sooner (Alghrani 2008). Experimental evidence also shows that it is possible to implant an embryo into tissue in the abdominal cavity of a man such that a placenta would form and fetal development commence to the point where a baby could be delivered by cesarean section. Uterine transplants show even more potential for making male pregnancy possible as well as offering a treatment option for women with uterine factor infertility. The advent of somatic cell reprogramming, with the possibility to derive human induced pluripotent stem cells from any individual, could enable the first in-human use of in vitro generated gametes with far-reaching implications for reproductive choice including allowing single people to reproduce without a partner and without a gamete donor, allowing both members of same-sex couples to engage in genetic parenting and in allowing more than two persons to engage simultaneously in genetic parenting (Palacios-González, Harris, and Testa 2014). Finally, mitochondria replacement techniques, currently subject to a government consultation in the United Kingdom and very close to being used in clinical practice, will allow women carrying severe forms of the disease, to have genetically related children with no risk of passing on the disease to their children.

QUESTIONS OF HARM AND CHOICE

The role of ARTs in facilitating reproductive choice for all, coupled with the strong demand, suggests there may be powerful reasons to support an obligation to provide equitable access to them. Such obligation has to recognize potential harms. Existing, new, and future ARTs challenge the ways in which we think of concepts such as the family and parenting and the way we see the "normal" reproductive body which for many is ethically controversial. ARTs and increasing knowledge of genetics have undermined the belief that parenthood is a matter of genetics. It can also be based on social, intentional, and/or gestational ties. The two-parent heterosexual nuclear family and the genetic ties on which it is based is just one family form among many. Claims alleging harmful effects to children born as a result of ARTs and growing up in the "new" families have largely been refuted (Jadva and Imrie 2013). There has also been well-known opposition to certain procedures including surrogacy, sex selection, selecting against or for disability, and the creation of "three parent babies" through techniques of mitochondria replacement on the basis that they are potentially harmful and exploitative (Baylis 2013). On the other side of the debate are arguments that eschew any irrelevant reference to the unnaturalness of ARTs and which instead offer well-reasoned argument and evidence which points to the value of such procedures (Harris 2005).

Reproduction is one of the most consequential choices humans can make and it is also often highly intimate and personal. It is perhaps for these reasons that it is also the most controversial. But liberty cannot be protected without both effort and cost, and as we have suggested, the costs have been greatly exaggerated when compared to the benefits. Reproductive liberty involves taking responsibility for the creation and usually also for the sustaining of new life. The happiness and the future survival of the human race depend upon how this freedom is exercised. For this reason the present authors firmly believe that reproductive choices are safest when left to those most concerned, those willing to take responsibility for the future of what is possibly the only intelligent and self-conscious lifeform in the universe (Harris 1985).

SEE ALSO: Birth Control, History and Politics of; Ethics, Moral Development, and Gender; Fertility Rates; Same-Sex Families

REFERENCES

Alghrani, Amel. 2008. "Regulating the Reproductive Revolution: Ectogenesis – A Regulatory Minefield." In *Law and Bioethics: Current Legal Issues*, edited by Michael Freeman. Oxford: Oxford University Press.

Baylis, Françoise. 2013. "The Ethics of Creating Children with Three Genetic Parents." *Reproductive Biomedicine Online*, 26.

Dworkin, Ronald. 1993. *Life's Dominion*. London: HarperCollins.

Harris, John. 1985. *The Value of Life*. London: Routledge.
Harris, John. 2005. "Reproductive Liberty, Disease and Disability." *Reproductive Medicine Online*, 10(Supp. 1): 13–16.
Jadva, Vashanti, and Susan Imrie. 2013. "Children of Surrogate Mothers: Psychological Well-Being, Family Relationships and Experiences of Surrogacy." *Human Reproduction*, 29(1): 90–96.
Nuffield Council on Bioethics. 2013. *Donor Conception: Ethical Aspects of Information Sharing*. London: Nuffield Council of Bioethics.
Palacios-González, César, John Harris, and Giuseppe Testa. 2014. "Multiplex Parenting: IVG and the Generations to Come." *Journal of Medical Ethics*, 40(11): 752–758.
ScienceDaily. 2012. World's Number of IVF and ICSI Babies Has Now Reached a Calculated Total of 5 Million. Accessed July 16, 2014, at http://www.sciencedaily.com/releases/2012/07/120702134746.htm.
Sparrow, Robert. 2008. "Is It 'Every Man's Right to Have Children if He Wants Them'? Male Pregnancy and the Limits of Reproductive Liberty." *Kennedy Institute of Ethics Journal*, 18(3): 275–299.

FURTHER READING

Robertson, John. 1994. *Children of Choice: Freedom and the New Reproductive Technologies*. Princeton: Princeton University Press.
Wilkinson, Stephen. 2009. *Choosing Tomorrow's Children: The Ethics of Selective Reproduction*. Oxford: Oxford University Press.

Reproductive Health

ELIZABETH WIRTZ
Purdue University, USA

Reproductive health, as defined by the 4th International Conference on Population and Development, is "a state of complete physical, mental, and social well-being, and not merely the absence of disease or infirmity, in all matters relating to the reproductive system and to its functions and processes" (Glasier et al. 2006). This definition situates reproductive health as a human right and argues that all individuals should enjoy safe and satisfying sexual activity, have access to reproductive health services, and have the freedom to determine if, when, and in what manner to procreate. It also recognizes that reproductive health is as much a social process as it is a physical one. Most scholars and practitioners focusing on reproductive health take a holistic approach and define reproductive health broadly to include variant topics, including but not limited to: conception, pregnancy, parturition (birthing), lactation and breastfeeding, puberty, menstruation, abortion, reproductive cancers, sexual dysfunctions, birth control, fertility and infertility, and sexually transmitted illnesses. Reproductive health is many times examined in conjunction with sexual health, sexuality, and sexual practices because of the intimate connection between sex and reproduction (Baer, Singer, and Susser 2004; Inhorn 2006). Thus, reproductive health refers to a wide variety of topics that relate to reproductive functioning and span the entire life cycle.

The past 50 years have seen a growing international focus on issues of reproductive health. An immense amount of research has shown that good reproductive health is essential to good overall health and well-being of individuals and societies at large (Baer, Singer, and Susser 2004; Farmer 2005). Unfortunately, much of the world's population experiences poor reproductive health that leads to a large proportion of global morbidity and mortality. Every day, approximately 800 women die from pregnancy-related complications that are preventable, and 99 percent of these cases occur in developing countries (World Health Organization 2014). Each year, roughly 873,700 women die of cervical, ovarian, or breast cancer (Jemal et al. 2011), and more than 1 million people contract a sexually transmitted infection every day (World Health Organization 2013). Most of these cases occur in developing countries and among the world's poorest populations. Many of these reproductive morbidities and mortalities are preventable and/or treatable, yet are not addressed – partially because of a lack of access to quality healthcare. Poor reproductive health not only leads to poor overall health but also has far-reaching impacts on individuals and communities. Given the pressing need to improve reproductive health, a proliferation of international campaigns centered on reproductive health issues has been implemented with varying levels of success.

National and international projects focusing on reproductive health are formed in a variety of ways depending on the background and purpose of the institution. Medical and public health practitioners tend to view reproductive health as a biological system, and good reproductive health constitutes the absence of disease or dysfunction (Inhorn 2006). With the global growth of biomedicine, reproduction has become increasingly standardized and medicalized. Standardization refers to the process of creating a set of rules or parameters for what constitutes normal or acceptable, while medicalization involves a process of redefining or pathologizing human conditions and experiences into medical conditions that need to be monitored, diagnosed, prevented, or treated by medical professionals within medical establishments.

The standardization and medicalization of reproductive health issues has been beneficial in many ways. First, these processes have helped to frame pressing reproductive health problems and needs through the study and documentation of disease and illness. By being able to track things like the spread of sexually transmitted infections and rates of maternal mortality, we can better understand causes of poor reproductive health and better implement solutions. Second, medical and technological advancements have been instrumental in improving reproductive health worldwide (Baer, Singer, and Susser 2004). Improved access to quality medical care reduces maternal and infant mortality and complications due to sexually transmitted infections and reproductive cancers (Glasier et al. 2006). In some cases, new advancements in reproductive technology have given individuals – who otherwise may not have been able to – the opportunity to produce children through fertility treatments and surrogacy. Third, biomedical approaches to reproductive health have improved understandings of the interconnection between various reproductive processes (Ellison 2001). For example, sexually transmitted infections lead to other reproductive issues such as reproductive cancers, infertility, and pregnancy complications. Finally, biomedical knowledge demonstrates the ways in which other health issues affect reproductive health, such as the impact of nutrition on pregnancy, breastfeeding, menstruation, infertility, and sexual dysfunctions (Ellison 2001).

Despite the positive impacts of biomedical advancements on reproductive health, this standardization and medicalization have had negative impacts as well. First, the need to standardize biological functions ignores variations in human populations and individual bodies. Many reproductive functions that fall outside of medical standards are then considered not "normal" and, therefore, not healthy by medical establishments. One area in which this has been debated is within the field of obstetrics (Morgan 1998). Various medical and public health studies have contributed to the development of normative guidelines and measurements for a proper birthing process. Women are expected to exhibit cervical dilation progress according to these standards, even though many women take longer than the expected or recommended time to dilate. Longer cervical dilation time does not necessarily indicate problems or complications in birthing. Nonetheless, these medical standards surrounding cervical dilation have contributed to sometimes unnecessary administration of manual cervical manipulation, the use of cervical dilation drugs to induce birth, and cesarean operations that have harmed women.

Second, the medicalization of reproductive health can sometimes be counterproductive to the health needs of individuals and abusive toward them. A prime example of this is in the medicalization of pregnancy in which pregnancy and birthing are transformed from a natural process to a medical condition or illness that requires medical attention and management. While pregnancies with complications may require medical technology and expertise, the vast majority of births do not. In addition, medical facilities frequently employ practices that can be unnecessary and harmful depending on the situation, such as forcing the woman to remain in the lithotomy position, the removal of pubic hair, amniocentesis, and episiotomies (Davis-Floyd 1987). In many parts of the world, medical facilities are overcrowded, underfunded, and understaffed, and therefore women do not receive the type of personal and attentive care that is required during the birthing process. Alternatively, traditional birth attendants, midwives, and doulas offer different forms of maternity care that are many times more personal, compassionate, and flexible than those found in biomedical institutions. In many parts of the world, where medical facilities are not widely available, women primarily use traditional birth attendants for reproductive health needs, especially pregnancy and birthing. However, with the growth of biomedical advancements, alternative birthing practices are discouraged, leaving women with fewer pregnancy and birthing options.

Most scholars and activists agree that access to affordable quality health services is essential to achieving and maintaining good reproductive health. However, good reproductive health requires much more than access to medical care. Social scientists have worked to frame reproductive health as more than simply a biological process, but rather situate it within social, economic, ideological, and political power dynamics (Ginsburg and Rapp 1991; Browner and Sargent 2011; Morgan and Roberts 2012). Understanding these power dynamics calls attention to the structural factors that shape reproductive health. Reproduction itself is an intensely contested process as it involves culturally informed beliefs such as sexuality, kinship, fertility, morality, and identity (Browner 2000; Baer, Singer, and Susser 2004). Cultural belief systems determine what is acceptable and possible within a field of social action, thus rendering some reproductive and sexual behaviors possible, and others not. This can be seen through global debates on contraceptives and abortion in which some cultural or religious belief systems allow for their use while others prohibit them.

A view of reproduction as a process that is deeply embedded within belief systems and structural conditions reveals the ways in which reproductive health issues arise and are addressed. Social beliefs and political agendas frame the very concept and definition of reproductive health, which issues are focused on (and conversely, which ones are not), and how these issues are approached (Ginsburg and Rapp 1991; Browner 2000; Morgan and Roberts 2012). Some of the most pressing reproductive health issues for women in developing countries, such as obstetric fistulas, miscarriages, difficulty in breastfeeding, and infant mortality, receive little attention compared to other issues such as family planning, which are prioritized in international reproductive health agendas (Inhorn 2006). This holds particularly true for developing countries where women have relatively little influence on international and national policies addressing their reproductive health.

Of particular importance is the way in which reproductive health has been framed as a "woman's issue." The vast majority of reproductive health initiatives across the globe have focused primarily on women. Women are essentialized for their reproductive capacities while men's roles are downplayed. Part of this focus stems from the fact that women perform more biological reproductive duties than men. Women have the unique capacity to gestate, give birth, and breastfeed, so there are more areas of concern for women's reproductive health than men's. However, this biological fact has translated to an unequal focus on women, even in cases where it is not biologically correlated (Glasier et al. 2006). Failures of reproduction such as infertility, miscarriage, the spread of sexually transmitted infections, and infant death are frequently blamed on women. Medical technologies and procedures are disproportionately focused on women, as evidenced by the abundance of family planning methods targeted at women, and lack thereof at men (Glasier et al. 2006). Worldwide, population control policies, sexually transmitted infection initiatives, and fertility treatments disproportionately target women as the beneficiaries of these programs to the exclusion of men. Women are seen as more responsible for and involved in matters of reproduction and are therefore often the primary targets of reproductive health campaigns. In fact, one of the only topics in which men seem to get equal or greater attention than women is that of sexual dysfunction. Male sexual dysfunction such as premature ejaculation and erectile dysfunction garner far more attention than female sexual dysfunction. These unequal focuses are exemplary of social beliefs that view women as reproducers and men as sexual beings. However, there have been recent efforts to increase the focus on men's reproductive health. There is more research conducted and more policies and programs targeting men's issues such as prostate cancer, infertility, and the impacts of sexually transmitted disease (Maternowska, Withers, and Brindis 2014). In addition, there is a greater focus on men's roles and behavior in impacting women's reproductive health.

One of the most important concepts that a social view of reproductive health has highlighted is the ways in which poverty and inequalities, drawn along lines of gender, race, religion, ethnicity, class, and sexuality, impact reproductive health. Disadvantaged and marginalized groups typically exhibit worse overall health indicators than more advantaged groups, many times based on one or more of the aforementioned characteristics (Farmer 2005; Inhorn 2006; Browner and Sargent 2011). These disadvantages are compounded so that an ethnic minority woman is likely to experience more reproductive problems than an ethnic majority man or ethnic majority woman. As noted earlier, the vast majority of reproductive morbidities and mortalities occur in developing countries and among the poorest populations in developed countries. Levels of reproductive morbidity and mortality remain high in much of the world not from lack of ability to solve these problems or deficient resources, but rather through unequal access to resources. Poverty remains one of the primary factors contributing to poor health worldwide and leads to unequal access to healthcare services and knowledge about reproductive health (Farmer 2005). Reproductive health related morbidity and mortality cannot be alleviated without addressing economic and social inequalities. Poverty and inequality not only contribute to poor reproductive health, but poor reproductive health perpetuates poverty and inequality, thereby creating a complex and repeating cycle (Farmer 2005). As long as developing countries experience high levels of maternal mortality and sexually transmitted infections, particularly HIV/AIDS, they will not achieve economic improvement.

International and national organizations addressing reproductive health issues have recently embraced the understanding that reproductive health is deeply embedded in and reliant on economic and social factors. To this end, reproductive health policies and programs have expanded to include education and livelihood initiatives. Policies and programs have also become more locally relevant by targeting conditions unique to a particular area such as using mobile technology to disseminate reproductive health information in areas lacking adequate infrastructure. Reproductive health initiatives have also become more culturally sensitive with the realization of the influence of cultural beliefs and practices on behavior. For instance, programs and policies will work to eradicate cultural practices that are harmful to reproductive health such as domestic abuse, female genital cutting, circumcising an age-group of males with the same unsanitized knife, and unequal access to food between males and females within households.

In the past few years, reproductive health has increasingly come to be understood as a basic human right that is essential to the overall health, well-being, and success of individuals, and their families and communities. A relatively new class of lawyers, activists, and scholars have emerged specifically targeting reproductive rights in order to improve and safeguard reproductive health. Within reproductive justice frameworks, individual bodily autonomy and control over personal reproductive functions are imperative to achieving good reproductive health (Morgan and Roberts 2012). Individuals must be able to have access to knowledge about their body and control over what happens to it, in order to make global reproductive health goals a reality.

Many of the current debates surrounding reproductive health issues center on questions of what constitutes good or bad reproductive health, what should be done to improve it, and who is responsible for ensuring good reproductive health and reproductive health rights. Reproductive health initiatives focusing on both the medical/biological aspect of health and the social/economic ones have drastically improved many aspects of reproductive health over the last few decades. Globally, maternal mortality rates have declined by almost 50 percent since 1990 (World Health Organization 2014), drugs and vaccinations have been developed to prevent and treat sexually transmitted diseases and sexual dysfunctions, reproductive technologies are now available to mitigate infertility, and new methods are being developed to detect and treat reproductive cancers. Notwithstanding, there remains much work to do to improve global reproductive health. Aside from reducing poverty and inequality, there is an urgent need to develop innovative ways to deliver reproductive health services to underserved and underprivileged populations.

SEE ALSO: Abortion, Legal Status in Global Perspective on; Birth Control, History and Politics of; Fertility Rates; Poverty in Global Perspective; Reproductive Justice and Reproductive Rights in the United States; Stratified Reproduction

REFERENCES

Baer, Hans A., Merrill Singer, and Ida Susser. 2004. *Medical Anthropology and the World System: Critical Perspective*. Westport: Bergin & Garvey.

Browner, Carole H. 2000. "Situating Women's Reproductive Activities." *American Anthropologist*, 102(4): 773–788.

Browner, Carole H., and Carolyn F. Sargent. 2011. "Toward Global Anthropological Studies of Reproduction: Concepts, Methods, Theoretical Approaches." In *Reproduction, Globalization, and the State: New Theoretical and Ethnographic Perspectives*, edited by Carol H. Browner and Carolyn F. Sargent, 1–18. Durham, NC: Duke University Press.

Davis-Floyd, Robbie. 1987. "The Technological Model of Birth." *Journal of American Folklore*, 100(398): 479–495.

Ellison, Peter T. 2001. *On Fertile Ground: A Natural History of Human Reproduction*. Cambridge, MA: Harvard University Press.

Farmer, Paul. 2005. *Pathologies of Power: Health, Human Rights, and the New War on the Poor*. Los Angeles: University of California Press.

Ginsburg, Faye, and Rayna Rapp. 1991. "The Politics of Reproduction." *Annual Review of Anthropology*, 20: 311–343.

Glasier, Anna, A. Mentin Gulmezoglu, George P. Schmid, Claudia Garcia Moreno, and Paul F.A. Van Look. 2006. "Sexual and Reproductive Health: A Matter of Life and Death." *Lancet*, 368: 1595–1607.

Inhorn, Marcia C. 2006. "Defining Women's Health: A Dozen Messages from More than 150 Ethnographies." *Medical Anthropology Quarterly*, 20(3): 345–378.

Jemal, Ahmedin, Freddie Bray, Melissa M. Center, Jacques Ferlay, Elizabeth Ward, and David Forman. 2011. "Global Cancer Statistics." *CA: A Cancer Journal for Clinicians*, 6(2): 69–90.

Maternowska, Catherine, Mellissa Withers, and Claire Brindis. 2014. "Gender, Masculinity and Migration: Mexican Men and Reproductive Health in the Californian Context." *Culture, Health & Sexuality: An International Journal for Research, Intervention and Care*, 16(8): 989–1002.

Morgan, Kathryn. 1998. "Contested Bodies, Contested Knowledges: Women, Health, and the Politics of Medicalization." In *The Politics of Women's Health: Exploring Agency and Autonomy*, edited by Susan Sherwin, 83–121. Philadelphia: Temple University Press.

Morgan, Lynn M., and Elizabeth F. S. Roberts. 2012. "Reproductive Governance in Latin America." *Anthropology and Medicine*, 19(2): 241–254.

World Health Organization. 2013. Sexually Transmitted Infections Fact Sheet. Accessed November 2, 2014, at http://www.who.int/mediacentre/factsheets/fs110/en/.

World Health Organization. 2014. Maternal Mortality Fact Sheet. Accessed November 9, 2014, at http://www.who.int/mediacentre/factsheets/fs348/en/.

FURTHER READING

Haberland, Nicola, and Diana Measham. 2002. *Responding to Cairo: Case Studies of Changing Practice in Reproductive Health and Family Planning*. New York: Population Council.

Jenkins, Gwynne L., and Marcia C. Inhorn. 2003. "Editorial: Reproduction Gone Awry: Medical Anthropological Perspectives." *Social Science and Medicine*, 56: 1831–1836.

Reproductive Justice and Reproductive Rights in the United States

ZAKIYA LUNA
University of California, Santa Barbara, USA

OVERVIEW

A myriad of social and economic institutions, legal structures, and identities both enable and constrain reproductive experiences. Reproductive health, reproductive rights, and reproductive justice are related concepts that together describe the range of sites, forms of struggle, and goals within the broader reproductive movements. The terms point to how reproductive politics has been engaged in the United States and, to some degree, globally. Reproductive politics was a phrase coined by feminist activists to describe how reproduction is a site of political meaning and struggle (Solinger 2005).

In the United States, the reproductive health approach has focused on education and access to reproductive healthcare, the reproductive rights approach has focused on abortion (and contraception) and maintaining legal protection through courts, and the reproductive justice approach has focused on community-based, local advocacy around a range of reproductive issues that encompass the right to have children and the right to parents (Asian Communities for Reproductive Justice 2005).

Reproduction is a controversial issue in many countries as it is a nexus for the relationship between gender regimes, sexuality, and national identity. Thus, reproduction is regulated and controlled through various policies and laws that affect how people, in particular, but not exclusively, women, control their bodies and family formation (Luna and Luker 2013). Reproductive policy most obviously intersects with family policy, but other areas such as work are also important. Further, differing roles of religion and morality are critical for understanding the different ways in which reproductive health, rights, and justice have been important in different societies.

THE LEGAL STORY

A typical reproductive history of the United States focuses on two landmark legal rulings, *Griswold v. Connecticut* (1965), which legalized contraception for married couples, and *Roe v. Wade* (1973), which legalized abortion. However, a deeper look reveals the panoply of reproductive histories and concerns that have been influenced by race, class, nationality, and other statuses. In particular, they highlight the differences between birth control, how individuals seek control over their bodies and reproduction, and population control, the various practices that authorities have exercised over particular groups to control their reproduction. This deeper look also demonstrates the importance of attention to how different groups have collectively organized both against and for varying forms of reproductive controls.

In the United States, different labor arrangements had a large influence on reproduction. In the early colonial period, ensuring that the correct man was identified as the father of a child was important due to legal obligations. Later, slave women were legally considered property and thus so were the children they birthed (Roberts 1997). It is important to keep in mind that non-slave women were still considered under the care of the men in their lives and had few, if any, legal rights. Women of different social groupings had different ways of controlling their fertility, such as through the use of medicinal herbs purported to prevent pregnancy or terminate one. Post-slavery, for differing reasons, social reformers and public health advocates increasingly sought ways for women to control their own fertility.

Starting in the early twentieth century, the United States saw the rise of government-supported programs that forced sterilization of people deemed unfit due to mental "inferiority," criminal conviction, suspected promiscuity, and other behaviors deemed a threat to the progress of society. The number of total sterilizations is unclear owing to limited record keeping, but approximately 30 states had laws permitting sterilization (Stern 2005). Again, the specific programs varied in their exact motivation and mechanism, but they all involved judgment by an authority – medical, legal, or other – that a specific person or groups of people should not be allowed the potential to reproduce or to continue reproducing. In *Buck v. Bell* (1927), an unmarried young, poor woman who had been interned in a mental institution after giving birth to a child challenged the practice. In his comments on the ruling, which upheld the legality of forced sterilization, Supreme Court Justice Holmes argued that sterilization was beneficial to society.

Sterilization continued for decades with poorer and minority communities disproportionately affected. Native American women were coerced into accepting sterilization in exchange for welfare benefits through Indian Health Services in the 1970s (Carpio 2004). There were many reported cases of doctors requiring women in labor to sign consent forms, performing the sterilization on an unknowing woman after she gave birth, claiming the procedure was routine. In the *Madrigal v. Quilligan* case (1978), a group of Mexican women who had been forcibly sterilized sued a county hospital for its consistent discriminatory practice of coerced sterilization (Gutiérrez 2008). However, while sterilization was commonly recommended – or forced – poorer and minority women and middle-class white women had difficulty obtaining sterilizations because doctors did not trust that they would not want children later. They had to go through an extensive approval process that in part determined eligibility based on the rule of 120, which was the minimum their age times the number of children they already had could equal (Kluchin 2011). Various mainstream women's organizations of the time advocated against creating sterilization guidelines. Many racial minority women organized against these abuses including working with politically radical white social feminists who infused their analysis of reproductive rights with attention to class and race differences. Perhaps the best known group was CESA, the Committee to End Sterilization Abuse and a later iteration, CARASA, the Committee Against Rape and Sterilization Abuse. Ultimately, membership in different social groups has produced different experiences of reproduction.

The oral contraceptive methods commonly used and debated over today such as "the Pill" were introduced in 1960. The landmark *Connecticut v. Griswold* (1965) legalized contraception for married heterosexual couples using a privacy argument. Before *Griswold*, contraceptives had to be obtained illegally or upon prescription for a different use. It was not until *Eisenstadt v. Baird* (1972) that unmarried women could legally obtain contraceptives. Reproductive health advocates have focused on the benefits of wider availability, reproductive rights advocates have focused on opposing back any legal challenges to this availability, and reproductive justice advocates have focused on how the histories of contraception point to different cultural ideas about whose reproduction is valued. For example, oral contraceptives were tested on Puerto Rican women with little attention to research protocols (Marks 2001): while this testing eventually made contraception more widely available, it came at a cost that many argue was too high. Further, different types of contraception have been recommended – or forced – at different rates for different groups of women.

The second landmark case is *Roe v. Wade* (1973), which decriminalized abortion at the federal level. Although exact data on prevalence are difficult to obtain owing to the varying legal statuses of abortion in different states, abortion occurred regularly and became illegal in part through efforts of doctors (see Luker 1984 and Halfmann 2011 for a more detailed discussion). Around legalization, the idea of the "back-alley butchers" – unscrupulous people who would provide abortions in unsanitary conditions at times leading to death – was also raised by advocates seeking widespread legalization. Some historians question the utility of this imagery (Solinger 2001), but it was and continues to be invoked by advocates on both sides of the abortion debate. A few states such as New York offered legal abortion, where women who could secure the funds obtained abortions in large numbers. Others traveled abroad. Since the ruling, it has been one of the key issues focused upon in the women's movement and, some would argue, to the detriment of attention to many other issues that women face regarding reproduction and other aspects of their lives. For example, the Hyde Amendment that prohibited federal funding for abortion was introduced shortly after the *Roe* ruling, and upheld in *Harris v. McRae* (1980). Critics contend that reproductive rights-focused organizations did little to challenge the ban, which primarily affects poor women on Medicare, because reproductive rights organizations generally focus on socioeconomically privileged white women.

Sociologists have explored how the *Roe* decision helped mobilize previously diffuse anti-abortion leaning people into a powerful movement (Luker 1984). Reproduction has played an increasing role in formal politics as a point of contention in electoral politics. Even though there was activism occurring in support of legalization of abortion, abortion only slowly became an issue around which political parties needed to address (Halfmann 2011). Since then, multiple organizations have focused on electing "pro-choice" leaders who support abortion rights and create voter guides that are focused solely on the position of candidates regarding abortion. Some researchers argue that if legalization of abortion had continued to occur through state-based legislation rather than federal ruling, it would have been less politically divisive (Halfmann 2011). But it was and remains a controversial issue around which many organizations devote their time.

REPRODUCTIVE JUSTICE

The phrase "reproductive justice" was coined in 1994 by a group of black women who were attending a pro-choice conference. The ideas connect reproductive rights and social justice (Ross 2006). Many of these women had been part of the reproductive rights movement but felt they had difficulty getting their perspectives on issues heard.

Reproductive justice organizing is also heavily influenced by the theoretical contributions of feminist theorists, particularly those hailing from critical race theory approaches such as Kimberle Crenshaw (1989) and Dorothy Roberts (1997). Crenshaw's work has been influential in general as it gave the name "intersectionality" to the idea that multiple identities affect our experiences, not just our gender, race, or age, for example. Rather than any one identity fully determining our experience, they all determine our experience. One identity may be more salient in a particular setting, but they are all there at once. Therefore, the category of "women" is complicated when we ask questions such as: What is the race of the different women? Their class? Their age? All of this matters for how, for example, an individual woman will be treated by a doctor, or if she goes to court, or in the workplace. Historically, it also matters in regard to how women and their communities understand the nuanced ways particular social issues are important and why.

CONTEMPORARY REPRODUCTIVE JUSTICE

Again, the differences between individual access to control fertility and forced population control often lie at the heart of reproductive justice. Individuals may indeed want to be sterilized, but having doctors coerce consent does not respect autonomy. Further, another difference is how activists mobilize around the issues.

Another area of contention, as with many social justice-connected efforts, is the difference between theory and practice. For various reproductive justice advocates, reproductive justice is not just a consideration of a different/broader set of issues but also a way of deciding what issues are important and proceeding from there (Luna and Luker 2013). Reproductive justice advocates would argue that part of what makes something reproductive justice is not the topic but the approach in taking action around the issue. For example, advocacy around abortion is *not* reproductive justice, per se. Rather, what would make it reproductive justice is consideration of how the issue affected marginal groups, working with marginal groups to develop ideas of how to address the issue.

To be clear, these issues are not by any means settled. For example, concerns about forced sterilization came into the public eye when in 2013 Justice Now, a prisoner advocacy organization, while conducting a participatory research project with its own members, present and former inmates, and their families, revealed various cases of forced sterilization. Further investigation resulted in a comprehensive report, legislative hearings, and, eventually, a proposed total ban on sterilization of California prisoners (Johnson 2013). The sterilization issue reemerged at the federal level in 2014 when the Medicaid regulations were being debated.

New issues continue to emerge in all of these arenas and movements, such as the addressing of the different ways men factor into the reproductive experience (Alemling and Waggoner 2013; Barnes 2014) and how transgender health issues push our understanding of reproduction and advocacy (Nixon 2013). Ultimately, these three approaches and movements are interconnected but distinct, based on their emphasis on where and why to focus their efforts in particular ways (medical arena, legal advocacy, and constituency), and always political.

SEE ALSO: Abortion, Legal Status in Global Perspective on; Abortion and Religion; Assisted Reproduction; Reproductive Choice; Reproductive Health; Women's Health Movement in the United States

REFERENCES

Almeling, Rene, and Miranda R. Waggoner. 2013. "More and Less than Equal: How Men Factor in the Reproductive Equation." *Gender & Society*, 27(6): 821–842.

Asian Communities for Reproductive Justice. 2005. *A New Vision for Advancing Our Movement for Reproductive Health, Reproductive Rights and Reproductive Justice*. Accessed June 22, 2015, at www.strongfamiliesmovement.org/assets/docs/ACRJ-A-New-Vision.pdf.

Barnes, Liberty Walther. 2014. *Conceiving Masculinity: Male Infertility, Medicine, and Identity*. Philadelphia: Temple University Press.

Carpio, Myla Vicenti. 2004. "The Lost Generation: American Indian Women and Sterilization Abuse." *Social Justice*, 31(4): 40–53.

Crenshaw, Kimberle. 1989. "Demarginalizing the Intersection of Race and Sex: A Black Feminist Critique of Antidiscrimination Doctrine, Feminist Theory and Antiracist Politics." *University of Chicago Legal Forum*, 140: 139–167.

Gold, Susan D. 2005. *Roe v. Wade: A Woman's Choice? Supreme Court Milestones*. Tarrytown: Benchmark.

Gutiérrez, Elena R. 2008. *Fertile Matters: The Politics of Mexican Origin Women's Reproduction*. Austin: University of Texas Press.

Halfmann, Drew. 2011. *Doctors and Demonstrators: How Political Institutions Shape Abortion Law in the United States, Britain, and Canada*. Chicago: University of Chicago Press.

Johnson, Corey G. 2013. *Female Inmates Sterilized in California Prisons Without Approval*. Sacramento: Center for Investigative Reporting. Accessed 10 August 2015 at http://cironline.org/reports/female-inmates-sterilized-california-prisons-without-approval-4917.

Kluchin, Rebecca M. 2011. *Fit to Be Tied: Sterilization and Reproductive Rights in America, 1950-1980*. New Brunswick: Rutgers University Press.

Luker, Kristin. 1984. *Abortion and the Politics of Motherhood*. Berkeley: University of California Press.

Luna, Zakiya, and Kristin Luker. 2013. "Reproductive Justice." *Annual Review of Law and Social Science*, 9(1): 327–352.

Marks, Lara. 2001. *Sexual Chemistry: A History of the Contraceptive Pill*. New Haven: Yale University Press.

Nixon, Laura. 2013. "The Right to (Trans) Parent: A Reproductive Justice Approach to Reproductive Rights, Fertility, and Family-Building Issues Facing Transgender People." *William & Mary Journal of Women and the Law*, 20(1): 73.

Roberts, Dorothy E. 1997. *Killing the Black Body: Race, Reproduction, and the Meaning of Liberty*. New York: Pantheon Books.

Ross, Loretta. 2006. "Understanding Reproductive Justice." SisterSong Women of Color Reproductive Justice Collective. Accessed June 22, 2015, at http://www.trustblackwomen.org/our-work/what-is-reproductive-justice.

Solinger, Rickie. 2005. *Pregnancy and Power: A Short History of Reproductive Politics in America*. New York: NYU Press.

Stern, Alexandra Minna. 2005. *Eugenic Nation: Faults and Frontiers of Better Breeding in Modern America*. Berkeley: University of California Press.

Right-Wing Women's Movements

SOLANGE SIMÕES
Eastern Michigan University, USA

Right-wing women's movements (RWWM) encompass a variety of past and current, social and political movements and groups, organized across the world, autonomously, or as women's sections of larger organizations (such as political parties or issue-oriented groups), whose composition is solely or mostly made up of women informed by a variety of right-wing ideologies and active participants in right-wing action. RWWM have been organized around not only one but often a combined number of right-wing issues, including active support of fascist and authoritarian regimes, anti-communism, racism, and conservative religious values, Christian, Hindu, or Islamic. In the last decades, right-wing women's organizations have rallied around social conservative issues (such as against abortion rights), but also engaged in the promotion of neoliberal, pro-market, and anti-state roles in the economy and social policies. These right-wing segments of the women's movement and organizations have promoted traditional gender roles and ideology, and have been, most often but not always, anti-feminist.

RWWM have been an understudied field, but one growing in the last three decades. The study of RWWM has been conducted mostly by feminist historians intrigued by the lack of scholarly attention to this sector of the women's movement. The English language scholarly literature has produced work focused on women in Europe and the Americas, but in the last decade has also sought to include research on right-wing women in Africa, the Middle East, and Asia. Publications on RWWM have included case studies on a variety of causes, geographic locations, and historical periods:

- Women's participation in fascist parties in Europe, especially in Germany (Koonz 1987), Italy, and Britain, but also covering a wide number of other central and European countries (Passmore 2003).
- Women's movements invested in "popular support" to legitimize authoritarian regimes in Latin America, such as in the 1964 military coup in Brazil (Simões 1985), and the 1973 military overthrow of Allende in Chile (Power 2002).

- Women's groups in the American Ku Klux Klan and other hate movements (Blee 2002).
- Indian women in the Hindu right (Sarkar and Butalia 1996).
- Anti-suffrage (Marshall 1997), and current anti-feminism and conservative women in America (Schreiber 2008).
- International comparative perspectives on RWWM and collaboration across borders (Bacchetta and Power 2002; Blee and Deutsch 2012).

Researchers in this relatively new field started by tackling core questions in the very definition of their object of study: What are the varieties of RWWM? What are the similarities and divergences among RWWM? Who are those women? What motivates them to join right-wing movements? How do they reconcile their gender identities with support for movements opposing gender equality? Why do women participate in RWWM?

Answers to these questions have been informed by sometimes competing theoretical frameworks such as Marxist feminism, emphasizing gender and class interests and structural and political factors; theories viewing women's participation in right-wing movements as determined by patriarchal structures; and gender theory on women's agency and subjective identity formation allowing interpretations in which women are partly instrumentalized by patriarchal ideology and men, while participating by choice.

Researchers have contextualized RWWM asking "when" and "how" women participated in order to help understand "why." In some cases researchers also sought to see local factors as shaped by global processes (from fascism and anti-communism to globalized neoliberalism).

Studies disclosed a number of similarities and divergences, as well as complexities and tensions within RWWM. Standing out are the centrality of traditional gender roles and anti-feminism versus women's rights; the divide between a private sphere for women and a public sphere for men; controversies on women's agency versus instrumentalization; competing views on gender identity versus class, race, ethnic, nationality, and sexuality differences among right-wing women. In order to understand the developments in the study of RWWM, it is important to address these key complexities and tensions within and across women's right-wing movements.

POLITICS OF MOTHERHOOD AND ANTI-FEMINISM VERSUS THE PROMOTION OF WOMEN'S RIGHTS

A common feature of RWWM has been the appeal to women's traditional roles as mothers and wives in recruitment and the promotion of activism in right-wing organizations and movements. In the past, this was true for anti-suffrage movements, and those in support of fascism and authoritarian regimes. More recently, right-wing women's organizations have backed conservative views about preserving a culture based on women's social and biological differences from men. Prominent among them have been the American STOP ERA (Stop the Equal Rights Amendment) and, currently, Concerned Women For America (CWA), and the Independent Women's Forum (IWF).

However, it is noteworthy that appeals to a traditional "feminine consciousness" have fostered women's public action in right as well as left ideological directions. Women also joined left-wing movements as mothers seeking to improve their families' living conditions, and early feminist movements appealed to women's family roles to elevate their position in society, and to recruit women to the suffrage movement.

The centrality of such appeals reached new levels and meanings in right-leaning women's movements.

Men in right-wing organizations "discovered" in the women a new political actor bringing new appeal for mass mobilization: at home, mothers took care of the family; the militant mother should look after the citizens and the "big family," the nation. As mothers and housewives, women were seen as an ideal political actor, able to help create strategic "popular support" that could legitimize overthrowing democratic governments, or the ideology and social policies of fascist regimes. In that context, women transferred to the public sphere their private role as family guardians. Self-identifying with the "motherland," women treated the country as the bigger family they had to save from the "communist threat," or from "inferior" racial and ethnic groups. "Biological bearers" in the private sphere, they transformed themselves into "ideological reproducers" in the public sphere.

It is noteworthy that the idealization of motherhood sometimes – as in the case of Nazism – was applied to Aryan women, whereas sterilization was promoted for non-Aryan women, who were regarded as not fit to reproduce. Moreover, in spite of a "maternalist" ideology, women in fascist movements were sometimes present in scenes of violence and bloodshed. In Chile, "most rightist women applauded the establishment of the brutal Pinochet dictatorship, and subsequently rallied around it as it arrested, tortured and killed tens of thousands of their compatriots for over seventeen years" (Power 2002). Similarly to RWWM in Europe and the Americas, Indian nationalist women in the Hindu right constructed maternalist frames that valorized women, but also marched in support of widow immolation.

The political mobilization of women as mothers and wives can be illustrated with examples from European fascist parties and Latin American authoritarian movements. In the 1960s, Brazilian women were recruited as "mothers and housewives" by military and businessmen leaders needing to mobilize strategic popular support for a military coup against a social reformist government. Women were placed at the forefront – with their rosaries and crucifixes – organizing and leading the then largest street demonstrations in the history of the country, the Marches of the Family with God for Freedom, demanding, and later in support of, military intervention. Similarly, and inspired by Brazilian women, right-wing Chilean women had a key role creating anti-Allende sentiments, enabling the military coup that overthrew his socialist government in 1973.

Nazism mobilized women as guardians of German family, culture, and values, as important players in the defense of the nation's integrity, domestically as well as in disputed territories. In its turn, the Italian fascists called mothers to offer their sons to the fatherland. Symbolic public acts, such as giving away their wedding rings to support the war, served to confirm them in traditional roles as wives and mothers.

Given RWWM's promotion of traditional gender roles, researchers have asked why women joined movements that often were anti-women's rights. Women's motivations have ranged from ideology (especially anti-communism and religious conservatism) to material interests (possibilities for positions of power or influence in women's groups), indoctrination (through the educational system), to class interests and racist and nativists sentiments. Moreover, anti-feminism has also been a major factor drawing women to RWWM. In the United States, for instance, anti-feminist rhetoric had a central role in the anti-suffragists cause. In recent decades, the CWA, which espouses a social conservative agenda, has opposed issues ranging from legal abortion and stem cell research, same-sex marriage and other rights for gays and lesbians to international causes, such as funding the United Nations, and the ratification of the Convention on the Elimination of All Forms of Discrimination against Women (CEDAW), dubbed women's international Bill of Rights. The IWF, which subscribes to a conservative economic agenda, has also opposed the ratification of CEDAW, but supported the war in Iraq; opposed Title IX and affirmative action while supporting the mobilization of women on campuses to challenge feminist professors, and arguing for attention to biological differences between men and women in research. Consistent with its neoliberal economic agenda, the IWF supported privatizing Social Security, and argued against federal funding of childcare.

Nevertheless, right-wing movements have been able to recruit a wide range of women, feminist and non-feminist, by trying to appropriate feminist issues while simultaneously appealing to conservative women. CWA, despite its anti-feminist agenda, has opposed sex trafficking in women, and supported laws regulating child pornography; IWF has promoted workplace flex-time.

Nazism presented itself as a modern movement open to women, and attempted to repress its anti-woman image by postulating that equal rights for women were to be protected in a Nazi state. Despite the fact that feminists might have joined, and fascist parties sometimes tried to address women's rights, some argue that the dominant tendency in fascism was explicitly anti-feminist. Fascism or racist organizations such as the American Ku Klux Klan were certainly not defending universalism – seen as essential to feminism – as they incorporated the rights of "some" women, while excluding, segregating, or physically exterminating women of the "wrong" race or ethnic group. Beyond the extreme right, women who join RWWM often abandon solidarity with women on the basis of their class, race, religion, or sexuality. In this line of reasoning, right-wing movements ultimately undermine feminism.

BLURRING THE DIVIDE BETWEEN THE PRIVATE AND PUBLIC SPHERES

Another question revolves around the issue of RWWM's impact on the traditional division of gender roles, in which men dominate the public sphere and women are relegated to the household. An important theoretical implication from the scholarly research on RWWM was to point out the blurring of boundaries between private and public spheres, when RWWM often politicize and publicize the private sphere. When women have taken to the streets as idealized mothers and wives, they have extended the private into the public. It was through those attributes that they frequently saw themselves as qualified for militant action and with moral authority to act in the public sphere.

GENDER IDENTITY VERSUS CLASS INTERESTS AND RACIST MOTIVATIONS

Besides anti-communism and conservative religious values, factors motivating women to join RWWM have included interests related to class position, racial/ethnic background, and national origin, among other differences within right-wing women. RWWM across history and across countries have often been initiated and led by middle and upper-middle class women, although in some cases membership was extended to poorer women and women of color. It has been argued that women have often joined RWWM as members of their class rather than of their gender. Most often they have neither questioned nor challenged male domination and patriarchal oppression; they have actually fought to maintain traditional gender relations, since motherhood and family have been central components of their identities. Some scholars claim that anti-suffrage women organized to protect gendered class interests. Anti-suffragists leaders often were wealthy, educated women who exercised political influence through their family ties to men, as well as by their own positions as leaders of their organizations.

Brazilian women's groups – such as the Women's Campaign for Democracy – were led by the wives, sisters, and daughters of the businessmen and military elites that planned the 1964 military coup. In order to build mass support for the military intervention, however, they had to bring a wider range of women into the streets. This was achieved through recruitment in churches, as well as in the businesses and factories owned by their families and allies. Similarly, in Chile, the elite women in the leadership of Poder Femenino sent their maids into the poor neighborhoods with messages and concealed fliers promoting their movement.

The class composition of the Italian Fasci Femminili was predominantly middle or upper class, recruited to engage mostly in welfare work. In doing so they came into contact with poorer women, who were eventually recruited into the party. Female teachers and other public employees also joined in since they could not be employed without proof of party membership.

WOMEN'S AGENCY VERSUS WOMEN'S INSTRUMENTALIZATION

Another controversy concerns diverging views about right-wing women's agency and autonomy versus dependency, instrumentalization, and false-consciousness. The instrumentalization perspective highlights women's subordinate and segregated positions in organizations, while the agency approach contends that women in right-wing movements were not completely without power.

The instrumentalization view emphasizes the subordination of Nazi women's groups to male leaders, who even chose their leaders. In Brazil, RWWM had male business and military leaders, usually husbands and brothers, as advisors and counselors. In Chile, after overthrowing Allende with the help of Poder Femenino, the military dissolved it and reoriented the movement, which had been semi-autonomous, into volunteer organizations they controlled. In Italy, fascist women had power only over other women, the poorer women who were recipients of the party welfare.

Historians of RWWM have called for further research on women's agency, and have contended that women, ultimately, emerged as active political subjects. They claim that, even when recruited as mothers and not as citizens, women unleashed a great potential for political action, and became active partners in political agendas they came to share. They exercised political influence through their family ties to men as well as by their own positions as leaders of RWWM.

In that fashion, while engaging in the Italian fascist party's welfare activities, upper and middle-class women were creating new opportunities for themselves. Men relegated them to welfare, a "woman's job," but welfare became increasingly important with the world economic depression, and this empowered women. In Spain, women's sections were created in the Falange because of women's pressure. Some authors claim that women used the Nazi idealization of motherhood to empower themselves, and also suggest that women were able to use the notion of domesticity as a basis for intervention in society and even for formulating demands for equality. In a similar fashion, Hindu nationalists portray "Mother India" as "mother of the universe," symbolically transferring power and agency from men to women.

Anti-suffrage women have also been regarded not as mere pawns of liquor businesses and patriarchal interests, but rather as influential political strategists. Interestingly, in order to present a rationale for their opposition to women's suffrage, they established a distinction between two sub-dimensions of the concept of "public life": "political" and "civic" participation. Accordingly, anti-suffragists opposed women in politics but not women's participation in community work.

Brazilian women's groups did not "spontaneously" organize and take to the streets; they were recruited and "advised" by their husbands, military and business leaders. Nevertheless, they were – at least in part – knowingly and willingly active participants. Instrumentalized as gender through appeals to patriarchal and religious ideology, they were ultimately active subjects serving their own class interests. A similar analysis applies to elite Chilean women's movements against Allende.

Despite those instances of women carving out new spaces for themselves, feminist critiques of the ways RWWM empowered themselves have contended that those women promoted individual empowerment or empowerment of their own class and racial communities, rather than women's collective empowerment.

NEW DEVELOPING AREAS OF RESEARCH ON RWWM

Scholars have raised the need for further research on women's agency in RWWM. Another issue to be properly investigated is the political trajectory of women in right-wing movements. Some work has been carried out on the antecedents of women's involvement with totalitarian and authoritarian regimes, but the question of what other trajectories in public life right-wing women might have engaged in following their participation in RWWM is still to be investigated. Whether women who joined public action as mothers subsequently participated in other capacities deserves investigation. A couple of English language edited books have tried to include RWWM beyond the Americas and Europe, but much more needs to be known about RWWM in Africa, the Middle East, and Asia. Moreover, RWWM's often nationalistic ideology did not prevent international connections, which need to be further investigated. Finally, it is noteworthy that the majority of studies about RWWM have been conducted by feminist historians trying to fill in a gap in the historiography of women's movements. More involvement of social scientists and interdisciplinary approaches should help address the gap in the scholarly literature addressing more recent and ongoing RWWM.

SEE ALSO: Gender, Politics, and the State: Overview; Pro-Choice Movement in the United States; Suffrage; Xenophobia and Gender

REFERENCES

Bacchetta, Paola, and Margaret Power, eds. 2002. *Right-Wing Women: From Conservatives to Extremists Around the World*. New York: Routledge.

Blee, Kathleen M. 2002. *Inside Organized Racism: Women in the Hate Movement*. Berkeley: University of California Press.

Blee, Kathleen M., and Sandra McGee Deutsch, eds. 2012. *Women of the Right: Comparisons and Interplay Across Borders*. University Park: Pennsylvania State University Press.

Koonz, Claudia. 1987. *Mothers in the Fatherland: Women, the Family, and Nazi Politics*. New York: St. Martin's Press.

Marshall, Susan E. 1997. *Splintered Sisterhood: Gender and Class in the Campaign Against Woman Suffrage*. Madison: University of Wisconsin Press.

Passmore, Kevin. 2003. *Women, Gender and Fascism in Europe, 1919–45*. New Brunswick: Rutgers University Press.

Power, Margaret. 2002. *Right-Wing Women in Chile: Feminine Power and the Struggle Against Allende, 1964–1973*. University Park: Pennsylvania State University Press.

Sarkar, Tanika, and Urvashi Butalia, eds. 1996. *Women and the Hindu Right: A Collection of Essays*. Delhi: Kali for Women.

Schreiber, Ronnee. 2008. *Righting Feminism: Conservative Women and American Politics*. New York: Oxford University Press.

Simões, Solange de Deus. 1985. *Pátria e Família: As Mulheres no Golpe de 1964*. Petrópolis, Brazil: Vozes.

Riot grrrl

MALAENA TAYLOR
University of Connecticut, USA

Riot grrrl is a feminist movement that emerged from the punk/indie rock subcultures of Olympia, Washington and Washington, DC in the early 1990s. The youth-based movement revolved around DIY (do-it-yourself) politics, music, and zines (homemade, photocopied magazines about music and politics). The term "riot grrrl" was first used in 1991; by 1993 dozens of riot grrrl chapters had sprung up across the country, but riot grrrl as a movement in the United States was considered "dead" by the mid-1990s. Original riot grrrl bands include Bikini Kill, Bratmobile, Heavens to Betsy, and the United Kingdom's Huggy Bear.

The term "grrrl" was coined by Tobi Vail, creator of the zine *Jigsaw* and drummer for the band Bikini Kill. Vail, partly mocking the second-wave feminist spelling of women as "womyn," adjusted the word "girl" by adding the growling triple-r in order to convey the anger she and her contemporaries felt at patriarchy, especially as it manifested in the punk and indie rock subcultures. The "riot grrrl" moniker was a collaborative effort inspired by Vail and Jen Smith, a friend of the band Bratmobile. Smith wrote of a "girl riot" in a letter to Allison Wolfe, Bratmobile's singer, regarding Bratmobile and Bikini Kill's plans to spend the summer of 1991 in Smith's hometown of Washington, DC (Marcus 2010). That summer, Smith and others created the zine *Riot Grrrl*, and a movement was born.

Riot grrrl music featured the stripped-down sound aesthetic of punk rock, along with raw, sometimes monotone and often screaming vocals. Riot grrrl bands were usually comprised of guitar, bass, and drums, though at least one notable band related to riot grrrl, Sleater Kinney, featured two guitarists and no bass player. Riot grrrl as a genre of music focused less on musical talent and more on the empowerment of female artists. Forming a band was a way for young women to claim space within the male-dominated punk subculture. The early founders of the movement encouraged grrrls to form their own bands, regardless of whether band members had any prior experience playing an instrument.

Queercore – sometimes referred to as homocore (e.g., Giminelli and Knox 2005) – is also intertwined with riot grrrl as a musical genre and a subculture, with Team Dresch, Tribe 8, and Pansy Division being some of the most notable queercore bands. Many queercore and riot grrrl bands had interchanging members. Heavens to Betsy, Excuse 17, Sleater Kinney, Cadallaca, The Haggard, and The Lookers, for example, each had at least one band member in common.

More important than the music, however, was the politics. Riot grrrl chapters, inspired by the Olympia and DC scenes and informed by zine and pen pal networks, began popping up as early as 1991. Made up mostly of teenaged feminists, these riot grrrls held regular consciousness-raising meetings at punk collectives, members' homes, and apartment complex laundry rooms. Kathleen Hanna, Bikini Kill's singer, made the promotional flyer for the very first riot grrrl meeting in 1991, which described it as "an all girl meeting to discuss the status of punk rock and revolution" and listed its planned activities as: "talking about ways to encourage higher female scene input and ways to help each other learn to play instruments and get stuff done" (reprinted in Marcus 2010, 88). Many meetings served as "safe spaces" for young women to share their experiences of sexual violence with a supportive and empowering community of peers. Riot grrrl chapters continued to remain active in Europe through the first decade of the twenty-first century.

Riot grrrl conventions began in 1992, and various chapters hosted conventions every year or so. Spinoffs of riot grrrl conventions, Ladyfest and CLITfest, began in the early 2000s and have continued through the 2010s in various locations across North America and Europe. Conventions tend to be 3-day events featuring performances by female-fronted bands, group discussions on sexual violence, and workshops on various topics such as self-defense, DIY music recording, automotive maintenance, and bike repairs.

Aggressive media attention followed the first riot grrrl convention, and the fallout had both negative and positive consequences for the movement. While media attention spread word of the movement to isolated young women in suburban and rural patches of the United States and United Kingdom, original founders of the movement grew frustrated with the generalizations and misrepresentations perpetuated by the mainstream press. Frustrated by the lack of control mainstream media allowed them, and angry at the media's attempts to make riot grrrl another item of consumption for trend-obsessed teens, the founders of the movement called for a media blackout in 1992. While their refusal to speak to journalists gave them the control they wanted, it may have led to the so-called death of the movement.

Today, the word "grrrl" continues to be used as an identity marker – one that is indirectly linked to politics. The term has been co-opted by diverse young feminist groups, especially those involved in forms of DIY art. A variety of documentaries related to riot grrrl have been made, including: *It Changed My Life: Bikini Kill in the UK* (1993), *She's Real (Worse than Queer)* (1997), *C.L.I.T.fest 2004: The Documentary* (2006), *Don't Need You: Herstory of Riot Grrrl* (2006), *Grrrl Love and Revolution: Riot Grrrl NYC* (2011), and 2013's *The Punk Singer: A Documentary*, which focuses on a year in the life of Kathleen Hanna. In 2013, The Fullbright Company released a narrative computer game, *Gone Home*, which is set in 1995 and features a teenage girl discovering riot grrrl music; its soundtrack includes Bratmobile and Heavens to Betsy songs. An impressive array of riot grrrl zines and other artifacts is archived at NYU's Fales Library and Special Collections.

SEE ALSO: Alternative Media; Consciousness-Raising; Feminist Art Practice; Identity Politics

REFERENCES

Giminelli, David, and Ken Knox. 2005. *Homocore: The Loud and Raucous Rise of Queer Rock*. Los Angeles: Alyson Books.

Marcus, Sara. 2010. *Girls to the Front: The True Story of the Riot Grrrl Revolution*. New York: Harper Perennial.

FURTHER READING

Leblanc, Lauraine. 1999. *Pretty in Punk: Girls' Gender Resistance in a Boys' Subculture*. New Brunswick: Rutgers University Press.

Raha, Maria. 2005. *Cinderella's Big Score: Women of the Punk and Indie Underground*. Emeryville: Seal Press.

Raphael, Amy. 1995. *Grrrls: Viva Rock Divas*. New York: St. Martin's Griffin.

Romantic Friendship

MARYLYNNE DIGGS
Clark College, USA

The term "romantic friendship" is used in historical and literary research to denote intimate relationships between same-sex partners during eras when such relationships were viewed as socially acceptable for men or women.

Many historians believe that in Anglo-European culture, prior to the twentieth century, intimate, exclusive, and often erotic relations between women were perceived as normal, expected, and compatible with heterosexuality. In the United States, these relationships were sometimes called "Boston marriages." Men also engaged openly in intimate relationships characterized by love letters and physical intimacy without social disapproval, especially in the United States, where sodomy laws and scientific discourses defining homosexuality as a medical condition were less prevalent.

Scholars have debated the degree to which these relationships were sexual. While many historical documents representing romantic friendship lack explicit sexual references, the same is true of most traditional marriages. Indeed, while allusions to sex were plentiful in the Victorian era, particularly in scientific and religious writing, explicit references to sexual activity were fairly rare in diaries, letters, and literature regardless of sexual orientation. Thus, it is likely that sex was a component in many romantic friendships as well, and that standards of privacy simply masked the sexual aspects, but not the romantic ones.

The idea of romantic friendship became prominent in lesbian-feminist scholarship during the 1970s and persisted as a frequent topic of research and debate into the 1990s. The two most influential works on the subject were Carroll Smith-Rosenberg's article "The Female World of Love and Ritual" (1975) and Lillian Faderman's book *Surpassing the Love of Men: Romantic Friendship and Love between Women from the Renaissance to the Present* (1981). In a subsequent study, *Odd Girls and Twilight Lovers* (1991), Faderman claimed that "women's intimate relationships were universally encouraged in centuries outside of our own" (1).

Despite the evidence in Faderman's two well-received books, historians and literary scholars debated the implications of the concept. While the "woman-identified-women" of the 1970s and early 1980s celebrated the notion of romantic friendship, and gay and lesbian studies scholars of the 1980s and early 1990s complicated the analysis of it, queer theorists, emboldened by the "sex wars," saw it as a censored interpretation of both queer and anti-queer sentiment in society. As a result, literary critics and historians began to challenge the hypothesis. In 1992, the Lesbian Issue of the journal *Feminist Studies* included articles by Martha Vicinus, who historicized the romantic friendship hypothesis within particular aspects of 1980s lesbian feminist thought, and Lisa Moore, who argued that the model had created a "prohibition against reading sex between women in history" (499). In a later issue of *Feminist Studies*, Marylynne Diggs (1995) argued that historians had overstated the social acceptance prior to World War I, and that as early as 1850 American literature revealed a subtext of both medical pathology and social resistance.

Although the phrase was used less frequently in scholarship about men's relationships, the concept itself – socially accepted intimate and exclusive relationships between men – was part of American literary scholarship by the middle of the twentieth century. The most influential early work on this theme is Leslie Fiedler's *Love and Death in the American Novel* (1960), a comprehensive study of American characters' rejection of marriage in favor of same-sex bonds and freedom in the woods, on the frontiers, and on the battlefield. Historian Jonathan Katz covered similar ground in *Gay American History* (1976), but provided exhaustive documentary evidence and tied it more tightly to contemporary gay identity. A decade later, Robert K. Martin (1986, 1989) surveyed the representation of romantic friendship among men in nineteenth-century American literature. While the scholarship on men's romantic friendships did not escape the assumptions underlying lesbian-feminist work on the concept, the emerging field of queer theory tended to ignore the issue rather than critique it directly.

Ironically, the concept of "romantic friendship" both emerged from and went out of fashion as a result of poststructuralist approaches to history and literature. Whereas early gay and lesbian scholarship focused on uncovering a "hidden history," later work historicized queer identities by placing them in the context of their own cultural moments. Informed by the Frankfurt School, deconstruction, and the new historicism, queer theorists emphasized the social construction of cultural norms, their influence on experiences of identity, and their redeployment in transgressive cultural performance. This theoretical shift produced a more radical production of meaning and identity, deepening our understanding and forcing scholars to distinguish historical subjects from contemporary articulations of them.

Romantic friendship remains a contested category. While the concept is still used in literary and historical research, it has found new life in the contemporary asexual community, where it poses an implicit challenge to both early romantic friendship scholarship and its sex-positive queer theory detractors. The asexual community has embraced a romantic, non-sexual denotation of the phrase, indicating how integral culture is to the definition of identity as well as the appropriation of the language of the past for new uses in the present. Given the socially constructed nature of sexual identity, any history of same-sex relationships must wrestle with the complexity of examining historical subjects through the historian's own contemporary moment. Regardless of the meaning of intimate and erotic relationships between women and between men prior to the emergence of modern sexual identities, the romantic friendship concept deepened our understanding of history and became a lasting part of the idiom of queerness.

SEE ALSO: Feminism, Lesbian; Feminism, Poststructural; Feminist Sex Wars; Queer Theory

REFERENCES

Diggs, Marylynne. 1995. "Romantic Friends or a 'Different Race of Creatures'? The Representation of Lesbian Pathology in Nineteenth-Century America." *Feminist Studies*, 21(2): 317–340.

Faderman, Lillian. 1981. *Surpassing the Love of Men: Romantic Friendship and Love between Women from the Renaissance to the Present.* New York: William and Morrow.

Faderman, Lillian. 1991. *Odd Girls and Twilight Lovers: A History of Lesbian Life in Twentieth-Century America.* New York: Columbia University Press.

Fiedler, Leslie. 1960. *Love and Death in the American Novel.* New York: Criterion.

Katz, Jonathan. 1976. *Gay American History: Lesbians and Gay Men in the U.S.A.* New York: Avon.

Martin, Robert K. 1986. *Hero, Captain, Stranger: Male Friendship, Social Critique, and Literary Form in the Sea Novels of Herman Melville.* Chapel Hill: University of North Carolina Press.

Martin, Robert K. 1989. "Knights Errant and Gothic Seducers: The Representation of Romantic Friendship in Nineteenth-Century America." In *Hidden from History: Reclaiming the Gay and*

Lesbian Past, edited by Martin Bauml Duberman, Martha Vicinus, and George Chauncey, Jr. New York: NAL.

Moore, Lisa. 1992. "'Something More Tender Still than Friendship': Romantic Friendship in Early Nineteenth-Century England." Feminist Studies, 18: 499–520.

Smith-Rosenberg, Carroll. 1975. "The Female World of Love and Ritual: Relations between Women in Nineteenth-Century America." Signs, 1: 1–29.

Vicinus, Martha. 1992. "'They Wonder to Which Sex I Belong': The Historical Roots of the Modern Lesbian Identity." Feminist Studies, 18: 467–497.

FURTHER READING

Abelove, Henry, Michele Aina Barale, and David M. Halperin, eds. 1993. The Lesbian and Gay Studies Reader. New York: Routledge.